SECOND EDITION

EXCEPTIONAL LIVES

Special Education in Today's Schools

ANN TURNBULL
The University of Kansas

RUD TURNBULL
The University of Kansas

MARILYN SHANK
University of South Alabama

DOROTHY LEAL
Ohio University

MERRILL
an imprint of Prentice Hall
Upper Saddle River, New Jersey • Columbus, Ohio

Library of Congress Cataloging-in-Publication Data

Exceptional lives: special education in today's schools / Ann P.
  Turnbull . . . [et al.]. — 2nd ed.
      p.   cm.
    Includes bibliographical references and index.
    ISBN 0-13-079993-9 (pbk.)
      1. Handicapped children—Education—United States—Case studies.
    2. Special education—United States—Case studies.   3. Inclusive
    education—United States—Case studies.   I. Turnbull, Ann P.
    LC4031.E87   1999   98-11874
    371.9'0973—dc21   CIP

Editor: Ann Castel Davis
Developmental Editor: Linda Ashe Montgomery
Production Editor: Sheryl Glicker Langner
Photo Coordinator: Nancy Ritz
Design Coordinator: Karrie M. Converse / Tracey B. Ward
Text Designer: StellarvIsions / Rebecca Bobb
Cover Designer: Karrie M. Converse
Production Manager: Laura Messerly
Director of Marketing: Kevin Flanagan
Marketing Manager: Suzanne Stanton
Advertising/Marketing Coordinator: Krista Groshong

This book was set in Garamond Book by the Clarinda Company and was printed and bound by
R.R. Donnelley & Sons Company. The cover was printed by R.R. Donnelley & Sons Company.

©1999, 1995 by Prentice-Hall, Inc.
Simon & Schuster/A. Viacom Company
Upper Saddle River, New Jersey 07458

Printed in the United States of America

10 9 8 7 6 5 4 3 2 1

ISBN: 0-13-079993-9

Prentice-Hall International (UK) Limited, *London*
Prentice-Hall of Australia Pty. Limited, *Sydney*
Prentice-Hall of Canada, Inc., *Toronto*
Prentice-Hall Hispanoamericana, S.A., *Mexico*
Prentice-Hall of India Private Limited, *New Delhi*
Prentice-Hall of Japan, Inc., *Tokyo*
Simon & Schuster Asia Pte. Ltd., *Singapore*
Editora Prentice-Hall do Brasil, Ltda., *Rio de Janeiro*

A vision of special education! That is what this book is all about. That vision derives from our many years as parents, special and general education teachers, teachers of teachers, advocates, and researchers. The vision is simply this: When principles and values guide teaching techniques and the techniques are at a state-of-the-art level, no challenge that confronts students, families, schools, or policies is too daunting.

A Value-Based Book

Having said this much, we owe it to our readers to put our values up front. We do that in Chapter 1, where we define the six values that guide us as professionals and as authors in the field of special education. In a nutshell, those values are: *envisioning the great expectations* students with exceptionalities can reach; *enhancing the positive contributions* students with exceptionalities can make; *building on the inherent strengths* students with exceptionalities have; enabling students with exceptionalities to *act on the choices* they should and can make; encouraging students with exceptionalities to *expand their relationships;* and honoring the rights of students with exceptionalities, *ensuring their rights for full citizenship.* Promoting these values is the initiative that drives this book.

Features of the Text

Real People, Real Schools

There is no fiction in this book. Every student in each chapter's opening vignette is a real person. For confidentiality's sake, we have used pseudonyms in Chapter 5 (Jennifer Shulman) and in Chapter 13 (Jimmy Eagle McVay). Each depiction of these students' families, the teachers and professionals they work with, and the communities in which they live is real and serves didactic purposes. Through their own lives and voices, these individuals describe how special education benefits them in a multitude of ways. They show what can happen when special education, based on principles and state-of-the-art techniques, is practiced effectively.

Emphasis on Today's Schools

We emphasize special education in today's and tomorrow's schools. Although we recognize the roots of special education, we concentrate on its most recent history, not the history of the field over several hundred years. Yes, a historical perspective is necessary, but we believe the immediacy of today's challenges should be the captivating focus of our book.

Inclusion

While acknowledging the challenges of inclusion, we advocate to include students with exceptionalities in all aspects of America's schools, but with effective, individualized support. The great majority of students with disabilities can receive an appropriate education in general education programs if programs and classrooms are designed to individualize instruction and if supplementary supports and services are available. Sadly, many general and special educators are not prepared for inclusive education. Our job is to help prepare them.

So, we (1) write about the reality of special and general education and the placement of students with disabilities into the general curriculum and into separate special educational settings, (2) present a wide range of perspectives about the benefits and problems associated with general education placements for students with exceptionalities, and (3) emphasize access to the general curriculum because that is what the law requires, what benefits students with and without disabilities, and what shapes America's future—a future in which everyone is valued, whether or not they have particular challenges or gifts.

Collaboration

We also advocate for all kinds of collaboration. By collaborating with each other, students, their families, teachers and other professionals, and communities can ensure that students will have an appropriate education in an inclusive school and thus, over time, the opportunity to live effectively in inclusive communities. Briefly, collaboration involves:

- *Students*—who are the principal beneficiaries of special education and who need maximum opportunities for participation and decision making in order to be self-determining adults.

- *Families*—who are the nucleus of social organization and support and the next beneficiaries of special education.

- *Teachers and other professionals*—who make the principles, laws and policies, practices, procedures, and curricula come alive to benefit students and their families.

- *Community and its citizens*—whose shared strengths, interests, and visions create effective education and hospitable contexts for students, families, and educators alike.

TEXT ORGANIZATION

Three introductory chapters lay a foundation for the rest of our book and give an historical perspective to today's schools. These foundational chapters describe the *Individuals with Disabilities Education Act (IDEA)*, the process of nondiscriminatory evaluation, and core guidelines for inclusion and collaboration. The introductory chapters are followed by thirteen chapters, each of which describes a category of exceptionality and includes a chapter on students who are gifted and talented and a new chapter on those with attention deficit/hyperactivity disorder.

Chapter Features

We have organized each chapter from 4 through 16 alike. This structure enabled us to do two things: First, we could introduce real people whose lives are often governed by the characteristics that they share with others who have the same or similar exceptionalities. This approach allowed us to present special education services as they are now organized, relate this information categorically as most professors report they prefer to teach, and provide the information in a way that is most easily understood.

Second, this organization gave us an opportunity to describe real people whose exceptional lives are touched, influenced, and changed by individuals, family members, teachers, administrators, and people in community services who are determined to make a difference. Each categorical chapter is therefore ordered in the following way:

- *Vignettes.* Each chapter begins with a vignette; each introduces real children and adolescents with real needs and expectations. Each vignette describes how, through a collaborative effort in their schools and communities, individuals with exceptionalities find their real strengths, make real choices, and develop real relationships. Notably, students in these vignettes represent a wide range of cultural, linguistic, and socioeconomic groups, and live in a wide variety of geographic locations.

- *Categorical Information.* Then we define the exceptionality, describe its characteristics, and identify its prevalence and causes so you get a sharp picture of the exceptionality, framed in its most basic dimensions.

- *Evaluation Procedures.* Next, a section in each chapter takes you into teachers' working environments, explaining how and why evaluations are conducted and

Vignettes feature real people in real-life situations, and allow readers to apply chapter information about nondiscriminatory evaluation, curriculum and methods, inclusion, and collaboration opportunities.

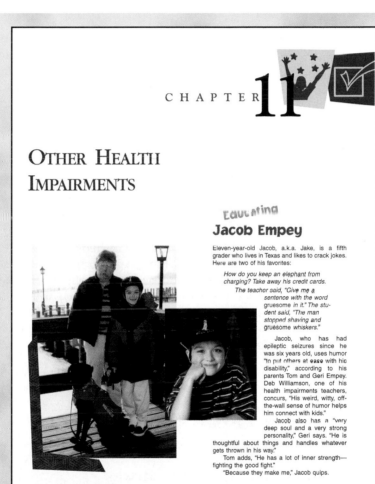

CHAPTER **11**

OTHER HEALTH IMPAIRMENTS

Educating
Jacob Empey

Eleven-year-old Jacob, a.k.a. Jake, is a fifth grader who lives in Texas and likes to crack jokes. Here are two of his favorites:

How do you keep an elephant from charging? Take away his credit cards.

The teacher said, "Give me a sentence with the word gruesome in it." The student said, "The man stopped shaving and gruesome whiskers."

Jacob, who has had epileptic seizures since he was six years old, uses humor "to put others at ease with his disability," according to his parents Tom and Geri Empey. Deb Williamson, one of his health impairments teachers, concurs, "His weird, witty, off-the-wall sense of humor helps him connect with kids."

Jacob also has a "very deep soul and a very strong personality," Geri says. "He is thoughtful about things and handles whatever gets thrown in his way."

Tom adds, "He has a lot of inner strength—fighting the good fight."

"Because they make me," Jacob quips.

prehensive and extensive atten- d students so that both are able n attendant (usually a person of ch self-care matters as feeding, n, and operating assistive tech- provides students with a list of interviewing, training, and dis- ates and payment procedures.

gram arranges for students to r-made recreational programs. s, ranging from intramural bas- ee jumping.

assists students with registra- nent. It offers advocacy services various local, state, and federal f a student's disability, how it made related to the effects of essors to discuss those accom- gies necessary for studying, test C. Jay, September 1, 1993).

rs, lab assistants, and mobility , field trips, reports, and home- o choose which aide will assist

dents develop job experience part-time, summer, and volun- rs specialized consultation for n, job restructuring, and assis- r 1, 1993).

A Vision for the Future projects how, in the immediate future, the featured vignette students realize some of their potentials when they benefit from best practice and related services.

A VISION FOR THE FUTURE

Rommel Nanasca and his family have to adjust their vision as his physical disabilities change over time. There is practically nothing constant about his disabilities. Inexorably, they compel new visions and elicit new responses.

There are, however, constants in their life: Rommel's indominatable spirit; his razor-sharp mind; Lorna and Romy's unending and loving commitment to Rommel, Ariel, and Melanie; the support of Rommel's grandparents and uncles and aunts; and the loyalty and competence of an extraordinary team of professionals.

Who would have thought that a boy with so many and such extensive physical challenges would have been able to attend school with students who do not have disabilities?

What Would You Recommend . . .

1. To ensure, through specific action steps, that Rommel's family and the school-based team continue to have positive collaboration?

2. To provide Rommel with interaction with his classmates should he have to receive a good deal of his education at home?

3. To enable Rommel to increasingly use the assistance of the school nurse or other aides as he attends classes and takes tests?

how and why special education and related services are provided. We highlight one evaluation procedure for determining whether an exceptionality exists and another evaluation procedure for determining the nature and extent of needed special education. We emphasize different evaluation procedures in each chapter so that readers will have a more in-depth knowledge of procedures such as curriculum-based assessment, authentic assessment, and functional assessment. Many of these assessments, however, can be used with students across various categories of exceptionalities.

• *Issues for Professionals.* Moving the reader's focus from environments to teaching issues, each chapter deals with two critical topics: curriculum and methods. We describe best practices and provide many examples from students, families, and teachers.

• *Participation in Schools.* To illustrate how schools now include students with disabilities in the general curriculum, we describe how students with exceptionalities are educated and how they can be more effectively included in the general curriculum. Then we describe how teachers, administrators, parents/family members, and students can collaborate with each other to increase the participation of students with exceptionalities in the typical activities and rhythms of today's schools. Finally, we describe the types of careers available for professionals working with students with exceptionalities.

• *Program Options.* To portray special education across students' school careers, we tell what educators do when effectively working with students of different ages, namely early intervention and preschool years, elementary years, middle and secondary years, and transition and postsecondary years.

• *A Vision for the Future.* We conclude the body of each chapter with "A Vision for the Future." These visions return to the student featured in the chapter's opening vignette. In that vision, we examine the differences that special and general education educators can make if best practices are put into place and if students, families, professionals, and community citizens collaborate for inclusion. In the chapter's conclusion, we ask readers to consider the concepts developed in the chapter and make recommendations for their application.

• *Summaries and Resources.* Finally, we include a chapter summary and an extensive list of resources. Books, journals, organizations, media, and on-line data specific to each disability provide additional direction and guidance to general and special education teachers.

Special Chapter Features

The following special features highlight the triumphs, challenges, and disappointments of people who have exceptionalities and those who work to improve their lives.

ABCNews Videos. Integrated into this text are video selections from recent ABC news programs. These video segments illustrate people living exceptional lives and the issues they face. The videos will promote reflective classroom discussions and a better understanding of what it is like to live with an exceptionality.

BILL COSBY'S DYSLEXIA CRUSADE

"If you don't know about dyslexia, you think that the person has something wrong or is dumb, not as bright," Bill Cosby says. Cosby is determined to change that misunderstanding. His son Ennis loved learning, but dyslexia cut him off from learning, according to Carolyn Olivier, who is currently the Education Director of the Hello Friend Ennis William Cosby Foundation. And yet, students with dyslexia "are often really gifted in the area of dealing with ideas and visual thinking and understanding," she comments.

In this ABC video, young people share what it is like to live with dyslexia. Bill Cosby also discusses Ennis's dyslexia and how his son reached out to another family member he suspected might have the condition.

What do you think? Ennis Cosby learned the importance of self-advocacy in dealing with dyslexia. How will you help your students learn to be self-advocates?

What opportunities can you create in your classroom for students with dyslexia to use their strengths in dealing with ideas and visual thinking?

How does this video relate to our earlier discussion of the causes of dyslexia?

ABC Video Reflections describe people whose exceptional lives or exceptional issues have paved the way for others and thus illustrate the values that undergird this text, including: envisioning of great expectations, recognizing positive contributions, building on natural strengths, acting on choices, expanding relationships, and ensuring full citizenship.

- *Feature Boxes.* Throughout each chapter are personal accounts of persons with exceptionalities or those who assist them. These accounts are featured in boxes which describe best instructional practice. "My Voice" boxes provide first-person descriptions of the unique joys, challenges, and triumphs associated with special education. "Making a Difference" boxes focus on teachers, administrators, students, families, and community citizens who have made significant and sustainable contributions to special and general education. "Into Practice" boxes exemplify best practices in teaching and highlight programs that support students in general and special education.

- *Inclusion and Collaboration Tips.* Most popular and practical from our first edition are feature boxes entitled "Inclusion Tips." These appear within each categorical chapter and present strategies that facilitate successful interaction between exceptional students and their classrooms peers. New to this edition are "Collaboration Tips." These describe a wide variety of ways students, parents, teachers, administrators, and general classroom and special education teachers can work together to support the inclusion of students with exceptionalities in classrooms and communities. Each "Collaboration Tips" box identifies a specific collaborative event and goal conducive to including students with exceptionalities into classroom, after-school, and community activities.

- *Tables and Figures.* Each chapter has tables and figures illustrating the narrative content. In every categorical chapter, an assessment table synthesizes practices of screening, identification, evaluation, and special education programming. A comprehensive table (Table 2-2) identifies all of the assessment measures that are described in the text.

- *Margin Notes.* Each chapter has margin notes that define boldfaced terms, highlight important concepts, pose reflective questions, supplement additional information, or cross-reference other portions of the book.

Supplements

Several ancillaries supplement this text:

- *Videos.* In choosing video selections to accompany this text, we have identified *ABCNews* video segments that allow the viewer to observe students and individuals who are making a difference in special education. These videos provide ideas and strategies to support inclusion and collaboration.

• *Student Study Guide.* A Student Study Guide helps students understand, analyze, and evaluate the chapter concepts and prepare for in-class lectures and presentations. Each chapter in the Guide sets out instructional objectives, key issues and focus questions, answers to margin notes as applicable, and a guided review of the chapter content. Self-check quizzes and expected answers are also included. Ideas for completing individual or group projects are located in a separate section of the guide to provide opportunities for more authentic, concrete learning experiences.

• *Transparencies.* The transparencies compare and contrast information from the text. These transparencies also help explain certain statistics and information in figures and tables that appear in the text.

Feature Boxes supplement the main text with "people-first" accounts. They focus on three areas. "My Voice" boxes relate unique insights, told by persons who know firsthand the highs and lows of special education. "Making a Difference" boxes showcase individuals whose special contributions make a difference in the lives of exceptional people. "Into Practice" boxes spotlight the best practices in a wide variety of learning environments.

280 Chapter 7

BOX 7-2 — MY VOICE

WEDGE CREE

People say I'm gifted. I also have AD/HD. I'm fourteen years old now, and I manage to get all As and Bs without even trying. That sometimes alienates people because I always use big words and have actually read the dictionary and the whole encyclopedia. I got into a special gifted class in first grade. I was one of two kids in the entire school district. I was working with kids in sixth grade on a similar level of understanding. Sometimes it's weird knowing more about a particular subject than the teacher and most of my peers. History is my favorite. Twentieth century wars are a small hobby of mine.

AD/HD? I was diagnosed about two years ago. Actually, I'm the one who got my parents thinking about AD/HD. I was visiting my uncle and was reading an article in *Time* magazine when I saw an article about AD/HD. As I read through it I came to a column about signs of AD/HD. I thought, "Hey, I fit a lot of these," and brought it my parents' attention. My parents took me to a specialist in AD/HD. I went to her once every few weeks and began to learn more about it and my problems. We also began trying me out on various medicines to help me. Not all of them were successful. Finally we got to Ritalin, With Ritalin, I've been able to calm down and focus. My social life has improved big time, and kids are actually willing to stay within twenty feet of me. I even joined the school wrestling team as a reserve. I wasn't so good, but I was finally on a team.

What's it like being gifted and AD/HD? Having AD/HD and being gifted is really hard to put into terms. Before we knew I had AD/HD, it was like having the worst part of adolescence before you're even a teen-ager. I had very few friends. I began to spend all my time at the school library. Often people would see me walking around on the playground with a book six inches from my face. While this

Now, I still know everything but I'm bored by everything that doesn't challenge me. It feels like you have a capacity to be the smartest guy in the world but whenever you walk forward, someone sticks their foot out and you trip over it. It's so frustrating. I have the capacity [...] yet I'm only minimally using it. If I wer[...] more, I could probably skip grades, g[...] years early, or anything. But because I[...] much ahead of the average fourteen-y[...]

Some advice I'd give teachers is to [...] lenged. I find when teachers give me [...] just worksheets, but creative things tha[...] really put my heart into it. Do stuff that[...] I'm using both sides of my brain to actu[...] in, whether it's aircraft design, WWII,[...] whatever. Try to find ways to relate proj[...] interest. It always works for me. Get ti[...] monotonous. Don't have the capacity [...] times and memorize facts. Get them [...] step further. Have them really go into [...] themselves. If the kid won't do anythin[...] anything. My best advice is get the kid[...] appealing to their creative side with [...] Learn what it's like for the kids. If you [...] be in their shoes, that's a very valuable[...] with them. Earn their trust. Make them [...] and have fun working with you.

I don't know many gifted kids with [...] Those that are generally are outcasts. [...] them special attention in front of oth[...] them make friends. Be willing to answe[...] I was blessed with teachers who we[...] answer my questions about how to dea[...] others who were always willing to len[...] me up. It's the help they'll need to suc[...]

Learning Disabi[...]

BOX 4-7 — INTO PRACTICE

DEVELOPING YOUR OWN LEARNING STRATEGY

1. Specify the type of task that the strategy is designed to facilitate. . . . As a rough guideline, a task should be described so that the student would be able to complete the task at least 15 to 20 times during an instructional period. In this way, you may obtain a sensitive performance measure. . . .
2. Describe the task in such a way that students can see a *sequential order* in the specific aspects of the task. . . .
3. Write a brief statement that *summarizes* each step. Make sure that the directions for each step are precise and concise, so that students can easily memorize the instructions.

4. *Limit* the strategy to particular tasks[...] dents to discriminate between tas[...] strategy is appropriate and other ta[...]
5. Develop a *mnemonic* to help stude[...] steps; acronyms seem to be a use[...] this. . . . Print the strategy on a ca[...] refer to during instruction.

One teacher designed a multiple choic[...]

R	Read	Read the question c[...]
E	Examine	Examine each answ[...]
A	Accent	Accent important w[...] lem and the answe[...] them.
D	Decide	Decide on the corr[...]

Note: From "Teachers Create Learning Strategies: Guidelines for Classroom Creation" by J. W. Marks, J. Van Laeys, W. N. Bender, & K. S. Scott. Teaching Exceptional Children, Summer 1996, pp. 34-39. Copyright 1996 by The Council for Exceptional Children. Reprinted with permission.

In Box 4-7, "Into Practice," you can learn how to write your own learning strategies. After you design a strategy, you will want to (a) pretest the students on the skill, (b) enlist

BOX 4-9 — MAKING A DIFFERENCE

ENNIS WILLIAM COSBY

"The happiest day of my life occurred when I found out I was dyslexic," Ennis William Cosby wrote. "I believe that life is finding solutions, and the worst feeling in the world to me is confusion" (Cosby, 1993—Hello Friend Ennis William Cosby Foundation).

Ennis must have experienced considerable confusion. He struggled academically in a home with two parents who have doctorates in education. His father, Bill Cosby, modeled his TV son Theo Huxtable after Ennis, mirroring his birth son's humor, intelligence, and struggles in school.

When Ennis was a freshman at Morehouse College in Atlanta, his mother's friend suggested that he be tested at a specialized college for people with dyslexia. The findings not only led him to answers about his academic difficulties, but also to a career. Ennis attended an intense summer program and received comprehensive tutoring to address his dyslexia. When he returned to Morehouse in the fall, his grades leaped from a 2.3 average to more than a 3.5 average. He made the dean's list.

Ennis determined to dedicate his life to helping others who struggled with learning. "A true test for a healer is to heal people who need it most," he said (Cosby, 1993—Hello Friend Ennis William Cosby Foundation).

During Ennis' years at Morehouse, he student taught a class of third graders in Atlanta. Ennis' supervising teacher pointed out to him that the African American males in Ennis' class who did not have male role models in their homes performed better when Ennis worked with them. "That is what convinced me that I was needed in the academic field," he wrote. "It amazed me that academic performance by children could be altered by a simple motivational factor like a direct role model" (Cosby, 1993—Hello Friend Ennis William Cosby Foundation). Ennis decided he could be most effective as a role model to African American males with dyslexia.

I got so involved with the elementary school that I began to go to the special education classes and offered my services to the teacher. I really bonded with the kids in the special education class. I was 'teaching from the

heart,' and the kids' biggest need seemed to be a teacher who cared about them and their individual needs. (Cosby, 1993—Hello Friend Ennis William Cosby Foundation)

In 1995, Ennis earned a master's degree in special education at Columbia University and was enrolled in the doctoral program there at the time of his death. He tutored students with dyslexia and language-based learning differences in New York City during this time. His work led him to rethink the terms commonly used to describe individuals who are having trouble learning. "I prefer to refer to students who are classified as having learning disabilities as children who learn differently" (Cosby, 1996—Hello Friend Ennis William Cosby Foundation)

One of his pupils said about his tutoring experience with Ennis: "It was the best time of my life. Before I met him, I felt college would be too hard, but he taught me that if I could overcome the same problem I had, I could go to college, too" (cited in Castro, 1997).

"He was my hero," Bill Cosby said about his son. He was certainly a hero to the students he taught. Ennis's legacy lives on in the Hello Friend, Ennis William Cosby Foundation, which benefits students with learning differences, and in those who, inspired by his story, decide to follow his path. Ennis wrote, "I believe that if more teachers are aware of the signs of dyslexia and learning differences, . . . then fewer students like me will slip through the cracks" (Cosby, 1993—Hello Friend Ennis William Cosby Foundation).

Note: Quotes from Ennis Cosby's work are reprinted with permission of the Hello Friend, Ennis William Cosby Foundation.

- *Instructor's Manual.* An Instructor's Manual provides a guide for professors to introduce and present the key issues for each chapter. This Manual includes brief chapter overviews, introductory information about the vignette students, instructional objectives, and Chapter At-a-Glance charts that align the focus questions with the content. Each chapter also has a presentation outline with directives for using transparencies to visually highlight core information. Additionally, the Manual includes answers to the margin notes and quizzes. To allow for more flexibility in instructional strategies and provide opportunities for authentic learning and assessment, the Instructor's Manual lists individual and group projects, videos, and children's literature suggestions.

- *Test Bank.* Research indicates that students learn better when they are held accountable for what they have learned. To consistently analyze, synthesize, and evaluate the information we study is an inherent part of our growth as human beings. That is why we have developed a bank of test questions that match the issues, questions, and projects assigned and discussed.

- *Companion Website.* The companion website is both a student and professor resource. It provides access to helpful features from the text, interactive self-tests, chat, message boards, and other valuable resources. In addition to the student portion of the site, professors also have access to syllabus builder. This feature allows instructors to customize and create syllabi online and gives them access to all of the transparencies and transparency masters referenced in the Instructor's Manual.

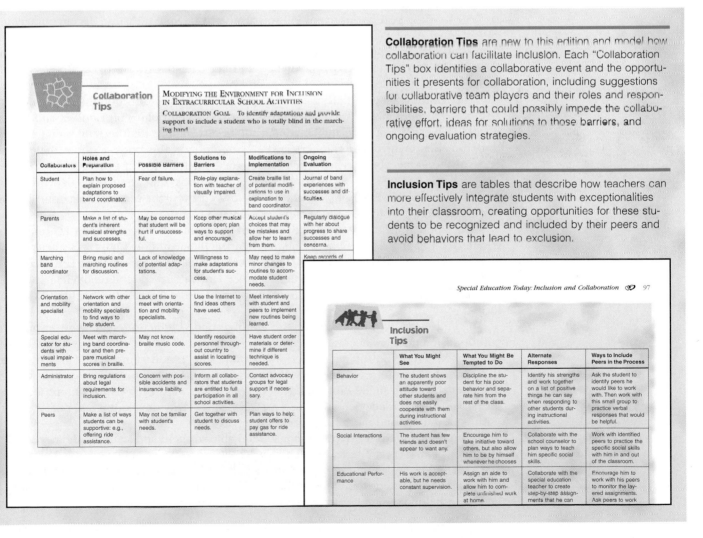

Collaboration Tips are new to this edition and model how collaboration can facilitate inclusion. Each "Collaboration Tips" box identifies a collaborative event and the opportunities it presents for collaboration, including suggestions for collaborative team players and their roles and responsibilities, barriers that could possibly impede the collaborative effort, ideas for solutions to those barriers, and ongoing evaluation strategies.

Inclusion Tips are tables that describe how teachers can more effectively integrate students with exceptionalities into their classroom, creating opportunities for these students to be recognized and included by their peers and avoid behaviors that lead to exclusion.

Special Education Today: Inclusion and Collaboration ❧ 97

ACKNOWLEDGMENTS

This book is collaborative in more than one sense. It focuses on collaboration in schools and models that very trait. It is collaborative in the sense that people with disabilities, their families, and many professionals opened their lives to us, allowing us to bring them to the center stage of each chapter, where, as actors in a play or as indispensable behind-the-scenes contributors, they inspire, inform, and personalize our concepts, lessons, and approaches. We wish to thank those people who inspired and encouraged our writing.

There is one person who, beyond all others, has inspired the Turnbulls and the Beach Center team. Unable to write a single word of text, he nonetheless is an indispensable source of our knowledge, our greatest teacher, and the focal point of all of our work: "JT." Thank you, Jay Turnbull.

Because Amy and Kate Turnbull, JT's younger sisters, have taught us so much about the possibilities of inclusion, the reality about and hope for families, and the myriad ways of bringing this book's six principles to life on an everyday basis, we also honor them with this text and our gratitude.

Marilyn Shank expresses appreciation to her father Joe Shank, who provided a listening ear, wisdom, and encouragement. She also acknowledges her deceased mother Lenah Shank, who encouraged her to write, love learning, and value all people; her brother Tom Shank and his wife, Kathy, who support her writing endeavors; and her niece, Jennifer, and nephew Matthew, who are a source of joy, especially during the challenging times that are a natural part of the writing process. Finally, Dr. Shank acknowledges all her students who over the years have taught her more than she could ever have hoped to teach them.

For Dorothy Leal, her husband Bill was a support beyond measure. His encouragement and wisdom, as well as computer expertise, kept her going in her various role as special education novice, general education spokesperson, and author. Her children, Jonathan and Jenny, were also an appreciative audience; and her friends Dow and Lois Robinson were mentors who provided inspiration, focus, and perspective.

The author team gratefully acknowledges the invaluable contributions that our former and present colleagues at The University of Kansas' Beach Center on Families and Disability and Department of Special Education made in researching, drafting, and seeing through to completion many of the chapters in the first edition of this book. Without their knowledge of the issues about which they wrote, their forbearance of our rethinking and redirecting the content, style, and approach of this book, and their diligence in making numerous revisions, this book would not have seen the light of day. Their contributions endure in large part in this, the second, edition.

Dan Boudah, who also was affiliated with the Center for Research on Learning, contributed to Chapter 4 (learning disabilities); Martha Blue-Banning, Chapter 8 (mental retardation); Mary Morningstar, Chapter 9 (severe and multiple disabilities); Ilene Lee, Chapter 11 (other health impairments); Mike Ruef, Chapter 12 (physical disabilities); Vicki Turbiville, Chapter 14 (speech and language disabilities); and Marnie Campbell, Chapter 15 (hearing loss).

Behind every writing team are the editorial and production staff, who ensure that authors' references are accurate, their words grammatical, their spelling correct, their permissions secured, and their manuscripts fit to go into production. At the Beach Center, Ben Furnish is our intrepid Sherlock Holmes of references and permissions, a sleuth who does not tolerate a single omission. He converted awkward phrases into more facile language, and shepherded a large manuscript through its many developmental phases, always with good humor and more than a bit of tolerance.

With their superb senses of humor, indomitable strength and stamina, and never-failing tolerance of authors' multiple, frequently repetitive, and overlapping demands, Lois Weldon and Opal Folks, a daughter-mother team, aided in the preparation of seemingly endless drafts of chapters, kept our work product and even our offices and lives organized, and, in Lois' case, helped design illustrative features that appear throughout.

At Merrill, we have had the benefit of an effective, tolerant, and loyal team. When we were delinquent, they were forgiving; when we were plain late, they were insistent; and when we went astray of our goals and concepts, they were redirecting. In all matters, they were consummate professionals. They are Ann Davis, acquisitions editor; Linda Montgomery, developmental editor; Jeff Johnston, editor-in-chief; Nancy Ritz, photographic researcher; Pat Grogg, editorial assistant; and Sheryl Langner, production editor. We benefited immeasurably from the judicious editing that Luanne Dreyer-Elliott brought to our sense of style; more than that, she assured consistency of presentation and organization throughout a large book, thereby making the book more didactically effective and reader-friendly. If this book is as attractive as it is informative, they deserve much of the credit.

We especially appreciate Ann Davis, who initially conceived the idea of a focus on the real lives of today's students; Ann's extensive and informed perspective about publishing and about special education helped shape the first edition's content, tone, and design—in a word, she made this book possible by soliciting us to write it and by helping us make it more readable and durable in the marketplace. Her contributions survive into this edition, of course.

We also are especially grateful to Linda Montgomery; it was she who, when chaos threatened to seize the writing and production, brought order to our work; it was she who, with steadfast good judgment and a ready chuckle, mediated between the sometimes sorely tested authors; it was she who diligently sought out and brought into our book some of the people featured in the vignettes and in other elements of the text; and it was she who, with consummate attention to detail and collaborative skill, orchestrated the Merrill team and the authors to be an effective whole.

Our colleagues at other universities have contributed mightily. Sandy Lewis at Florida State University has the gift of writing a nearly flawless first draft; her knowledge of visual impairments appears in chapter 16, as it did in the first edition. Two others are new to this edition. Joyce McNeill of The University of South Alabama (home of Marilyn Shank, one of the book's four co-authors) contributed her knowledge of communication impairments (Chapter 14) and Barbara Schirmer at Kent State University did likewise but with respect to hearing impairments (Chapter 15). To Sandy, Joyce, and Barbara, the simple phrase, "we are greatly indebted," seems hardly enough but we hope it suffices; their knowledge is powerful, and so too is their ability to model one of this book's features, namely, the power of collaboration.

Others played their important roles. The families, students, and professionals in each vignette were unfailingly generous. They helped us bridge the geographical gaps between us; we know a few of them, face to face, but we do not know many of the others in the same way. Yet, each has become an indispensable part of the whole. It is as though each of them, sensing that they will make a difference to you, the reader, tacitly agreed to become members of a larger, extended community—the community of families affected by disability and the community of families who, though so affected, nonetheless persevere and teach us all. Their lessons are encapsulated in the six values that permeate the book.

Similarly, many professionals have contributed. For their considerate reviews, we thank Andrew Beigel, SUNY, New Paltz; Robert A. Berner, Slippery Rock University (PA); Nancy Brawner-Jones, Portland State University; Linda J. Bufkin, Saint Louis University; Greg Conderman, University of Wisconsin at Eau Claire; Beverly Brown Dupre, Southern University at New Orleans; Nancy B. Hertzog, University of Illinois; Pauline P. Hook, University of Science & Arts of Oklahoma; Judith J. Ivarie, Eastern Illinois University; Douglas Knowlton, University of North Dakota; Linda Ladmer, University of Tennessee at Chattanooga; Mickie Y. Mathes, Brenau University (GA); Joyce H. McNeill, University of South Alabama; Susan W. Meslang, Old Dominion University (VA); Robert E. Owens, Jr., State University of New York at Geneseo; Holly A. Reiling, Phillips University (OK); Barbara R. Schirmer, Lewis & Clark College (OR); Janna Siegel, Eastern New Mexico University; and Eleanor B. Wright, University of North Carolina at Wilmington.

CONTENTS

11
OTHER HEALTH IMPAIRMENTS 442

12
PHYSICAL DISABILITIES 494

13
TRAUMATIC BRAIN INJURY 540

PRELUDES, LAWS, STUDENTS, AND STAFF

Laying the Foundation for
Danny Ramirez

Imagine what it would be like to have a mental disability. What kinds of limitations would you experience? What could you not do that you can do now? Where would you go to school, and what would you be taught there and by whom?

Imagine, too, that you were born into a family that came to the United States from Mexico, one that is bilingual but that has its cultural roots in a non-Anglo culture. Imagine further that you and your family experience prejudice on account of your ethnic traits and national origins. How would that kind of bias affect your education?

For Danny Ramirez and his family and, indeed, for many students in special education, these circumstances are real and immediate, so immediate that the memory of them is painful to his mother, Carmen, and his father, Alfredo.

Just after he was born in 1983, Danny was diagnosed as having a disability. He was, in the doctor's words, a "Mongoloid," and for that reason alone, the head nurse in the newborn nursery even suggested to Carmen and Alfredo that they put Danny into a bassinet in the back corner of the nursery where no one else could see him.

"That's when I knew we were in for a long battle," recalls Carmen.

"We learned in Danny's first week of life what a fight we'd have to wage to have him treated like any other kid," adds Alfredo. To be treated like all other youngsters meant that Carmen and Alfredo would commit to having Danny included in typical programs. That commitment was not easy to achieve.

When Danny entered a preschool early intervention program operated by the local mental health/retardation center for infants and toddlers from birth to three years of age, the staff thought he was quite capable, but the director wrote in Danny's file: "Danny's not going to make any progress or learn anything."

Upon his graduation from the early intervention program and admission to an early childhood special education program for children ages three through five, the El Paso public schools (which operated the program) simply accepted the early intervention program's evaluation of Danny and automatically classified him as "educably mentally retarded." Acting on that label, the school district put him into a separate special education program—one where he would have no contacts at all with typically developing students. The school's position was that Danny not only did not belong in the academic program, but he also should not even eat lunch with students who do not have disabilities unless accompanied by his mother.

These "placement" decisions were disconcerting to the Ramirezes, who understood that isolating Danny did not allow him to learn how to connect socially and emotionally to others. As all parents do, Carmen and Alfredo wanted Danny to be treated with the respect and regard guaranteed to other children

simply because they are a part of the school community.

This difference in perception of human need triggered a long and heated dispute between the Ramirezes and the schools, with Carmen and Alfredo exercising their legal rights to have a court review the school's decision. The court's judgment recognized that Danny and other students with disabilities have the right to be included in general education programs, if inclusion would benefit them. In a nutshell, the Ramirezes and the court said yes to appropriate education in the least restrictive, most typical programs.

Danny now receives all of his special education (specially designed instruction) in general education programs. So do many other students with disabilities. Others do not have all, or even most, of their special education with students who do not have disabilities.

What explains the difference? One explanation lies in the nature of special education. For many educators

and students, "special" means separate. Sometimes, that is not appropriate; other times, it is. Another explanation lies in the nature of the Ramirez family.

"Persistence is the key," says Carmen. "We've been through hell as parents of a child with a disability, especially as minority parents. We know what it takes to achieve our dreams. Who would have thought we could sue a huge school district and gain Danny's inclusion? So much is possible because we have the law on our side."

The law is only one foundation for what happens in today's schools. But the law needs to be implemented by educators. So today's educators have to apply curriculum and methodologies that promote appropriate education of students—those with disabilities and those who are extraordinarily gifted and talented. They also have to include all students in their programs; to do this, schools have to be places where parents and a wide array of educators and other professionals collaborate with each other. This book focuses on today's schools. It shows how current law affects all that happens in today's schools. It describes how curriculum, methodologies, inclusion, and collaboration occur. It looks less to the past than to the future. To understand today's schools, however, you need to understand their predecessors. That is why this chapter not only describes the students who are in special education in today's schools but also briefly reviews the history of special education in the last fifty years of this century.

What Do You Think?

1. Who are the students who, like Danny, are in special education, who are the professionals who serve them, and what are the outcomes of special education?

2. What and who are the sources of the rights that Danny and other students with disabilities now enjoy?

3. What are the legal principles that shape special education and make it effective for students like Danny?

Profile of Special Education Students and Personnel in Today's Schools

Almost certainly you have heard

. . . never send to know for whom the bell tolls. It tolls for thee.
(John Donne, 1624, *Devotions upon Emergent Occasions,* no. 17)

Disability tolls for nearly 15 percent of all students; it eventually falls on nearly all of us as we age. For you, then, the disability bell could toll at least twice: once as you teach, and once as you age. For some of you, it peals more frequently because you have a family member or close friend with a disability, or perhaps have special needs yourself.

When the bell tolls, it tolls not only for people with the disability but also for their families, friends, teachers, administrators, and communities. We know that to be the case from our own lives. It is why we profile for you stories about real families with real children who have disabilities.

As we profile students in special education for you, you will see our commitment to challenge the real and authentic issues of exceptionality that affect people's lives on a daily basis. These challenges often go against the sometimes arid scholarship of traditional special education textbooks. We seek to close the gap between the human dimensions of exceptionality and the distance that people and professional literature sometimes take from those dimensions. Accordingly, we merge the up-front and personal portrayal of real students and their families with extensive reviews of the most current and relevant theory, research, and best practice.

We think that best practice is best accomplished when certain values guide teaching behaviors and strategies. Figure 1–1 identifies these values. You will see throughout this book why and how these values form the foundation for special education. We hope you will adopt these values and act and educate all students committed to them. We believe that when values guide teaching techniques and when the techniques are as state-of-the-art as the ones you will learn about in this text, no challenge that students, families, schools, or policies pose will be too daunting. We are confident that balancing your heart and your head, seeing reality and visions, and implementing best practice with academic inquiry will all increase the likelihood of providing an appropriate and successful education for all students.

We have found that disabilities are more disabling than they need to be because people who do not experience exceptionalities firsthand often see and set greater limitations than the person who has the disability.

To what extent would you like for the values shown in Figure 1–1 to apply to your own education? What benefits and drawbacks can you see for applying these values to the education of students with exceptionalities?

FIGURE 1–1 *Values to guide teaching*

Envisioning Great Expectations. Students have many capabilities that have not been tapped. We can develop new visions of what is possible. These visions can become realities. We need new perspectives of what life can be as well as support for fulfilling these dreams.

Enhancing Positive Contributions. Students contribute positively to their families, schools, friends, and communities. We need to develop greater opportunities for these contributions.

Building on Strengths. Students and families have many natural capacities. They need opportunities for educational programs to identify, highlight, and build upon their strengths.

Acting on Choices. Students and families can direct their own lives. Enabling them to act on their own preferences promotes their self-determination.

Expanding Relationships. Connections are crucial to quality of life. Students and families need to connect with each other, educators, and friends in the community.

Ensuring Full Citizenship. *Less able* does not mean less worthy. All students, including those with exceptionalities, and their families are entitled to full participation in American life.

Who Are the Students?

To answer the question "Who are the students in special education?", we describe next (a) the total number of students with disabilities, (b) the age groups of these students, (c) provision of gifted education, (d) the categories of disabilities, (e) issues about labels and language, and (f) the socioeconomic, racial, and ethnic profiles of students with disabilities.

Total Number of Students Served.   In the 1994–1995 school year, nearly 5.5 million students, ages three to twenty-one, received some form of special education (U.S. Department of Education, 1996). Stated differently, 12 percent of all of America's students were in special education that year, a huge 44 percent increase since 1975, when Congress enacted the federal special education law that governs today's schools.

Age Groups of Students Served.   Figure 1–2 depicts the percentage of students served in the 1994–1995 school year, according to four age groups (3 to 5, 6 to 11, 12 to 17, and 18 to 21). Almost 90 percent of the students are in elementary and secondary schools, and approximately twice as many preschool students, ages three to five, are receiving special education services as are students who are eighteen to twenty-one years of age.

Provision of Gifted Education.   Students who have disabilities are only one group of students in special education. The other group consists of students who have unusual gifts and talents. Unlike students with disabilities, they are not served under the federal special education law for students with disabilities. Instead, forty-three states have policies related to initial screening to identify students who are gifted, and 60 percent of states require adapted instructional programs for students who are gifted (Coleman, Gallagher, & Foster, 1994). So, the demographic profile that we just presented does not include students in gifted education.

Disability Categories.   Until 1997, the U.S. Department of Education required states to count students with disabilities according to their type or category of disability. The corresponding numbers and percentages of students associated with each category are set out in Table 1–1.

   Nearly three-fourths of all students with disabilities are classified into two categories: specific learning disabilities (51.1 percent) and speech or language impairments (20.8 percent). These two categories, when combined with the categories of mental retardation (11.6 percent) and emotional disturbance (8.7 percent), account for almost 95 percent of all students with disabilities. Beginning in Chapter 4, you will be introduced to students who have disabilities linked to each of these categories, just as you have been introduced to Danny in this and the next two chapters. You will read about their characteristics and

Under the 1997 amendments to the federal law, a state may now count its students with disabilities according to the federal categories. If a state wants not to use categorical head counts, it may do so, adopting a "noncategorical" approach.

FIGURE 1–2   *Percentage of students served by age groups (in the 1993–1995 school year)*

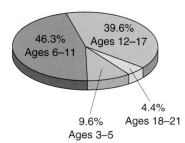

Note: From *To Assure the Free Appropriate Public Education of All Children With Disabilities: Eighteenth Annual Report to Congress in the Implementation of the Individuals With Disabilities Education Act* by U.S. Department of Education, 1996, Washington, DC: U.S. Department of Education.

Disability	IDEA, Part B	
	Number	**Percent**
Specific learning disabilities	2,513,977	51.1
Speech or language impairments	1,023,655	20.8
Mental retardation	570,855	11.6
Serious emotional disturbance[a]	428,168	8.7
Multiple disabilities	89,646	1.8
Hearing impairments	65,568	1.3
Orthopedic impairments	60,604	1.2
Other health impairments	106,509	2.1
Visual impairments	24,877	0.5
Deaf-blindness	1,331	0.0002
Autism	22,780	0.4
Traumatic brain injury	7,188	0.0014
All disabilities	4,915,168	100.0

TABLE 1–1 🐾 *Categories of disabilities and coresponding numbers and percentages of students ages six to twenty-one served in the 1994–1995 school year*

[a]IDEA now also calls this category "emotional disturbance," dropping "serious" in some but not all of its provisions.

Note: From *To Assure the Free Appropriate Public Education of All Children With Disabilities: Eighteenth Annual Report to Congress in the Implementation of the Individuals With Disabilities Education Act* (p. 7) by U.S. Department of Education, 1996, Washington, DC. U.S. Department of Education.

the education they receive. But before you read about "categories" and "characteristics," a word of caution is in order.

Labels and Language.   First, we want to caution you about labels. How would you have reacted if you were Carmen and Alfredo and a physician told you that your son was a "Mongoloid"? How would you feel if you were known only by your disability and not according to your abilities? The chances are that you, like Carmen and Alfredo, would feel devalued. Indeed, that is precisely how many families and special educators respond when people with disabilities are classified or labeled as a "disabled person," first and foremost.

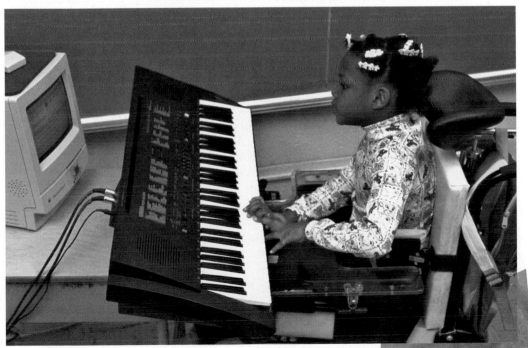

🐾 *Like this student who, in spite of her disability, uses a computer, other students with disabilities have many strengths. Their disabilities are only a part of who they are. That is why as a general rule we refer to them as "students with disabilities" rather than as "disabled students."*

TABLE 1–2 ❧ *Terms reflecting social changes*

Areas of Disability	Past	Present
Mental retardation	Idiots, feebleminded, cretin, mentally deficient, educably retarded or trainably retarded, morons, high level or low level	Mild, moderate, severe retardation and intermittent, pervasive, extensive, and limited retardation
Learning disabilities	Dyslexia, minimal cerebral dysfunction, specific learning disabilities, learning disabilities	Learning disabilities
Emotional disturbance	Unsocialized, dementia, emotionally disturbed, acting out, withdrawn	Emotional/behavioral disorders (E/BD)
Attention deficit disorder (with or without hyperactivity)	Hyperactivity, specific learning disabilities	ADD (Attention Deficit Disorder without hyperactivity) or ADHD (with hyperactivity) and combined
Head injuries	Strephosymbolia, brain crippled children, brain injured, closed head injury	Traumatic brain injury
Deafness	Deaf and dumb, deaf mute	Severely/profoundly hearing impaired
Persons with orthopedic disabilities	Crippled children, physically handicapped	Physical disabilities
Learning disability in reading	Dyslexia, minimal cerebral dysfunction, specific learning disabilities	Dyslexia
Autism	Childhood schizophrenia, children with refrigerator parents, Kanner's syndrome, autoid	Autism (high functioning or low functioning)

Note: From "The Ins and Outs of Special Education Terminology" by G. A. Vergason and M. L. Anderegg, 1997, *Teaching Exceptional Children, 29*(5), p. 36. Copyright 1997 by the Council for Exceptional Children. Reprinted with permission.

In Table 1–2, you will find examples of how the terms that educators have used have changed over the years.

Some scholars have argued that research on the harmful effects of labels is not definitive. For some students, the benefits of identifying them to receive services and additional instructional support truly does outweigh the harm of the label (MacMillan & Meyers, 1979). Not only does classifying and labeling students identify them so that they may qualify for special education, but as you will read in the chapters on hearing and visual impairments (Chapters 15 and 16), some people with disabilities welcome the labels.

On the other hand, classifying and labeling can segregate students with disabilities from their classmates without disabilities (Adelman & Taylor, 1984; Kliewer & Biklin, 1996; Lipsky & Gartner, 1989). Labeling also can attribute pathology to a trait of the individual (Adelman, 1992; Hobbs, 1975; Reschly, 1996). Finally, labeling does not necessarily lead to specific educational curriculum and methods (Adelman, 1996; Reynolds, 1991; Reynolds, Wang, & Walberg, 1987). Also, there are serious multicultural concerns about labeling:

> *Only when formal education came to the Indian Nations were labels supplied to the differences between children. Public Law 94-142, the Education for All Handicapped Children Act (1975), was a two-edged sword for Indian people. On*

BOX 1-1   **MY VOICE**

LABELING

I became a self-advocate ten years ago. Being a self-advocate is very important to me because my self-advocacy skills taught me how to see myself as a person because of all the labels placed on me. People used to make fun of me all the time.

It is real hard for me not to be upset by being called retarded or dummy, names like that. They would really hurt my feelings. It is real hard for me to deal with my feelings now. I have learned that getting mad does not do any good. I have learned to talk to people about how that makes me feel.

—*Nancy Ward*

Note: From *Self-Determination* by N. Ward, 1989, January. Paper presented at the National Conference on Self-determination, Arlington, VA.

the one hand, it provided educational opportunities for severely disabled children who were once institutionalized off the reservation by the Bureau of Indian Affairs, but on the other hand, it caused multitudes of children to be labeled mentally retarded or learning disabled who up until that time were not considered handicapped in their cultures. (Locust, 1988, p. 326)

Rather than continue the debate over the relative benefits and drawbacks of labels, some special educators are developing new classification systems. These emphasize students' instructional needs so teachers can provide them with appropriate education.

The interest of many is in replacing current categories with a system that identifies special individual needs (1) only as such needs become relevant to providing an appropriate education and (2) through a process and terminology that have direct relevance to intervention and that minimize negative consequences. (Adelman, 1996, p. 99)

So, caution is warranted when categories and labels are used. Accordingly, we gently offer a word of advice. If you must use labels, we hope you will avoid demeaning labels and use instead esteeming ones. In Box 1-1, "My Voice," Nancy Ward tells her perspective about labels. Given how strongly people with disabilities feel about the effect of labels, it is safe to say that she speaks for many people.

Demeaning labels can be dangerous. For example, if you knew only that Danny Ramirez has mental retardation as a result of having Down syndrome, what kind of education would you expect him to receive, and where would you expect him to receive it? Would you expect him to participate in the general education program? A demeaning label almost always contributes to separation and devaluation (Goffman, 1963). Stigma—the negative connotation that accompanies a demeaning label—can limit one's perspectives about another person and in turn that person's opportunities in school and life. Nancy Ward (1989) provides examples of demeaning labels in Box 1-1—"retarded" and "dummy." On the other hand, after reading about Nancy, what are some esteeming labels that you might use to describe her? Perhaps, insightful, good communicator, assertive. Figure 1-3 illustrates some effects of those kinds of labels.

Because labels can affect great expectations, we hope that you will learn to look at each of your students with an eye to seeing what they can do rather than what they can't—expecting Danny and other students with disabilities to have or develop inherent strengths and make positive contributions to others and to their communities, typically by being in the same schools and programs as their peers without disabilities. One way to esteem people is to be careful about the language we use. That is why many educators use

FIGURE 1–3 *The impact of labels*

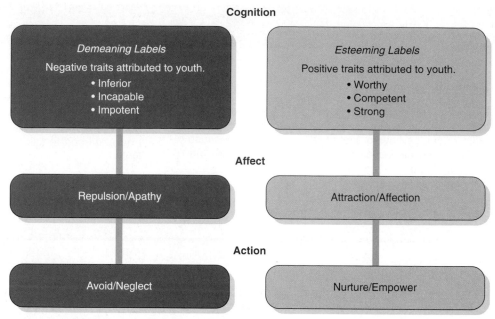

Note: From *Reclaiming Youth at Risk: Our Hope for the Future* (pp. 15–16) by L. K. Brendtro, M. Brokenleg, and S. Van Bockern, 1990, Bloomington, IN: National Educational Services. Copyright 1990 by National Educational Services. Reprinted with permission.

"people-first" language. For example, instead of using phrases such as "the retarded" or "retarded children," most prefer "students with mental retardation."

We do not use people-first language because it seems politically correct, is expected by the U.S. Department of Education (U.S. Department of Education, Office of Civil Rights, 1993), or is widely accepted among journalists and the public (President's Committee on Employment of People With Disabilities, 1992). Nor do we use people-first language in this book to shy away from or deny disability. Rather, we use it to emphasize that disability does not supersede every other characteristic that a person might have.

> Alternatively, the National Federation of the Blind strongly rejects terms such as "people with blindness" or "visually challenged," as you will read in Chapter 16.

Socioeconomic, Racial, and Ethnic Profile. Students' exceptionalities and how professionals refer to them are only some of students' characteristics. As a teacher, you will encounter others that affect the students you teach and how you will work with them. Among those aspects are those related to the students' socioeconomic status (SES). SES refers to a family's income, the level of family members' education, and the social status associated with the occupations of the family's wage earners. The greatest number of special education students come from low-income families who live in urban areas (47 percent); then in rural areas (34 percent); and, last, in suburban areas (19 percent) (U.S. Department of Education, 1996).

> Statistically, poverty and disability go hand-in-hand—they have a positive correlation with each other.

To call the interaction of urban living, poverty, and disability distressing is understated. For example, researchers have reported that in 165 urban schools serving 140,000 students, more than 80 percent of the entire population lives in poverty (Gottlieb, Alter, Gottlieb, & Wishner, 1994). Within the school population, approximately one-third of the children in the general education program were able to read at or above grade level. The researchers indicted a belief that the "vast majority of children who are classified as learning disabled and placed in special education in many urban school districts are not disabled in the sense demanded by legislation and regulation. Instead, they are children who suffer the many ravages of poverty, not the least of which is its effect on academic performance" (Gottlieb et al., 1994, p. 456). Another report confirmed a similar interaction: More than 66 percent of high school students with disabilities live in families with an annual household income below $25,000, whereas 55 percent of high school students in

❧ *Nearly half of all students in special education are from low-income families in urban areas.*

general education live in families with annual incomes below $25,000 (U.S. Department of Education, 1992).

Likewise, disability and a family's education level are related. Twenty-three percent of the heads of households that have high school students who have disabilities have completed some college course work, but 35 percent of heads of households that have students in general education have completed college work (U.S. Department of Education, 1992). Higher education seems to reduce the chance of disability.

Differences in a family's and a student's language sometimes account for the identification of students with limited English proficiency as qualifying for special education. Students with limited English proficiency increased by 27 percent in the 1980s (U.S. Department of Commerce, 1980–1990, p. 85, cited in U.S. Department of Education, 1996). Indeed, the limited-English proficient population is the fastest growing in the country. This growth occurs in many parts of the United States, although the majority of these students live in three states—California, Texas, and New York—usually in urban areas. Four percent of all high school students with disabilities who attend urban schools speak another language at home, as contrasted to 2 percent of those in nonurban areas (Valdés, Williamson, & Wagner, 1990, p. 85).

Socioeconomic status and limited English proficiency are not, alone, an entirely accurate gauge of the student population in special education. Race also enters the picture. As Congress noted when it amended the Individuals with Disabilities Education Act (IDEA) (Public Law [PL] 105-17) in 1997, the racial profile in our country is changing rapidly. Between 1980 and 1990, the rate of increase in the population for white Americans was 6 percent, while the rate of increase for culturally and linguistically diverse individuals was much higher: 53 percent for Hispanics, 13.2 percent for African Americans, and 107.8 percent for Asians. Indeed, by the year 2000, nearly one of every three individuals in this country will be either African American, Hispanic, Asian American, or Native American.

These data have profound implications for special education: They signify that, based on current demographics, representation of culturally and linguistically diverse students in special education, now already large, is apt to grow larger. Already, and taken as a group, these students comprise an ever larger percentage of the public school population, with some large cities having few white students.

Table 1-3 highlights the representation of students in five racial/ethnic groups in the total school population (top row) and their representation in programs for students with giftedness, mild and moderate mental retardation, serious emotional disturbance, and learning disabilities. As you compare and contrast the representation of each of these

As of 1993, culturally and linguistically diverse students comprised 89 percent of Chicago, 88 percent of Los Angeles, and 84 percent of Miami public school enrollment.

TABLE 1–3 *Representation of students in special education as opposed to representation in the total school population*

	Native American (%)	Asian (%)	Hispanic (%)	African American (%)	Caucasian (%)
Representation in total population	1	3	12	16	68
Percent labeled gifted and talented	1	6	6	8	79
Percent labeled educable mentally retarded	1	1	8	35	56
Percent labeled trainable mentally retarded	1	2	20	32	46
Percent labeled seriously emotionally disturbed	1	1	6	22	71
Percent labeled specific learning disability	1	1	11	17	70

Note: From *1990 Elementary and Secondary School Civil Rights Survey Adjusted National Estimated Data* (February 1993) by U.S. Department of Education, Office for Civil Rights, 1993, Washington, DC: U.S. Department of Education.

In Chapter 8, you will read more about poverty's impact and about Project Eagle, a comprehensive early intervention program that benefits people affected by both poverty and the risk of disability.

groups in the total population with their identification as having a disability, what trends do you detect? You will see that the greatest extent of disproportionality is in the placement of African American students. These students are twice as likely to be enrolled in programs for students with mental retardation and only half as likely to be enrolled in programs for students who are gifted and talented. By contrast, Asian American students are overrepresented in the gifted category. White students are consistently overrepresented in the categories of giftedness and learning disability.

What accounts for the overrepresentation of African American students in special education? A careful analysis of the disproportionate representation of culturally and linguistically diverse students in special education found that they are overrepresented even in disability categories that typically rely on objective, nonbiased criteria, such as deaf/blindness, visual impairments, physical disabilities, and other health impairments (Wagner, 1995).

More likely, poverty itself and its collateral and devastating effects on human development substantially account for the overrepresentation of African Americans (Wagner, 1995). Indeed, the U.S. Department of Education (1996) recently concluded that "The disproportionate representation of African Americans in special education is a function of relatively low income and the disabilities associated with poverty" (p. 86).

With this profile of the students in mind, you are ready to learn about their teachers and other professionals involved in their education.

Who Are Special Education Personnel?

Cross-categorical classes are those in which students with various kinds of disabilities are educated together. For example, students with mild mental retardation and learning disabilities may be in the same class, thus making it cross-categorical (the students cut across both categories).

Teachers of students with specific learning disabilities and those who teach students in **cross-categorical classes** comprise the two largest groups of special educators.

If you are considering a career in special education, your job prospects are quite good. According to the most recent data from the U.S. Department of Education (1996), approximately 330,000 special education teachers were employed in 1993–94 to teach students ages six through twenty-one—up by 6.5 percent over the number of teachers in the previous academic year.

Approximately 93 percent of all teachers are fully certified, but 6 percent are not. One percent of the teacher positions are vacant, the largest number being in the areas of speech or language impairment (30 percent of all vacant positions), specific learning disabilities (21 percent), and cross-categorical (15 percent). Vacancies for special education teachers are particularly prevalent in inner-city areas and in districts that serve culturally and linguistically diverse students.

Not all special education professionals are teachers. Some provide related services such as speech therapy, physical or occupational therapy, psychological services, and social work services (see Figure 1-6, which defines related services). The number of related services personnel is almost identical to the number of special education teachers—approximately 331,000. This represents a 3 percent rate of growth between the 1992–1993 and 1993–1994 school years. Teacher aides account for about 60 percent of these positions. About one-third of the related services vacancies are in the areas of occupational therapy, physical therapy, and psychology.

You now have a profile of the professionals, but you might also ask this question: Just how effective are the schools and these professionals in educating their students? That is a legitimate question, but the answer is a combination of good and not-so-good news.

As you read all of the chapters of this book, we encourage you to reflect very carefully on your own interests in careers related to providing special education and related services to students with exceptionalities.

WHAT ARE THE RESULTS FOR STUDENTS WITH DISABILITIES?

Between 1985 and 1990, the National Longitudinal Transition Study of Special Education Students (NLTS) collected data on students with disabilities, determining their postsecondary education participation, employment, residential arrangements, and community participation. This study concluded that students with disabilities face rather dismal prospects after leaving school. A summary of the data is in Table 1–4.

Furthermore, Blackorby and Wagner (1996) report the following:

- The competitive employment of students with disabilities lagged significantly behind the employment rate for peers in the general population at two years and at three to five years after completing school.

- High school graduates with disabilities were significantly more likely to be employed than were peers with disabilities who had dropped out of school.

- Only 14 percent of youth with disabilities who had been out of school for two years had attended some type of postsecondary school, as contrasted to 53 percent for youth in the general population.

- Only 13 percent of youth with disabilities lived independently less than two years after completing secondary school, as contrasted to one-third of youth in the general population.

- Three to five years after completing school, the proportion of youth with disabilities earning more than $6.00 per hour increased fourfold, from 9 percent to nearly 40 percent.

- Women with disabilities were less likely to be employed and more likely to live independently as compared to men with disabilities.

- White youth with disabilities had higher rates and received higher wages than their counterparts who were African American and Hispanic.

Until the last several years, the major criterion for progress in special education was simply numerical—how many more students were being served annually since 1975, when the federal special education law (now IDEA) was enacted. Instead of focusing on the number of students being served, however, policy makers and educators are now concerned with the adult-life results of students who receive special education services. The fundamental challenge facing special education today is to improve results. Indeed, Congress in the federal special education law and other laws has established these results:

- *Independence.* Persons with disabilities will assert control and choice over their own lives. This goal is also known in the federal special education law as *independent living.*

- *Productivity.* Persons with disabilities will have income-producing work, or their work will contribute to a household or community. This goal is also called *employment* in the federal special education law.

TABLE 1–4 ✐ *Postschool results for youth with disabilities up to three years out of secondary school*

	All Conditions[a]	Specific Learning Disability	Serious Emotional Disturbance	Speech or Language Impairments	Mental Retardation	Visual Impairments	Hard of Hearing	Deaf	Orthopedic Impairments	Other Health Impairments	Multiple Disabilities
Percentage enrolled in post-secondary academic program since high school	16.5 (2.1)	18.7 (3.3)	15.3 (4.7)	37.0 (6.6)	2.5 (1.6)	53.9 (4.9)	35.0 (4.8)	28.3 (4.3)	30.9 (5.5)	35.1 (7.4)	8.0 (4.0)
Percentage enrolled in post-secondary vocational program since high school	14.7 (2.0)	17.8 (3.2)	13.3 (4.4)	17.9 (5.3)	5.7 (2.4)	14.9 (3.5)	20.0 (4.1)	19.9 (3.8)	13.4 (4.0)	23.5 (6.5)	4.0 (2.9)
Percentage currently competitively employed	55.0 (2.8)	63.1 (4.1)	52.0 (6.5)	58.5 (6.7)	40.8 (5.0)	30.3 (4.5)	43.6 (5.0)	24.8 (4.0)	26.4 (5.2)	47.5 (7.6)	15.8 (5.2)
Average annual total compensation (dollars, all youth)	5,524 (429)	6,932 (724)	5,310 (926)	4,389 (829)	3,078 (490)	2,027 (448)	2,773 (489)	1,689 (387)	1,636 (467)	4,388 (954)	778 (332)
Average annual total compensation (dollars, workers)	10,840 (557)	11,671 (808)	11,267 (1,023)	8,145 (1,087)	8,274 (701)	7,303 (.)	7,596 (811)	8,897 (906)	7,586 (.)	9,723 (.)	—
Percentage living independently	27.8 (2.5)	33.9 (4.0)	21.1 (5.1)	36.4 (6.3)	14.8 (3.5)	39.3 (4.7)	25.9 (4.4)	32.3 (4.3)	16.6 (4.3)	17.2 (5.7)	8.0 (3.9)
n	1,763	265	119	115	188	235	211	253	161	101	100

[a]All conditions includes youth in each of the 11 Federal special education disability categories. Percentages are reported separately only for categories with at least 25 youth. Schools were those attended by youth with disabilities in the 1985–1986 or 1986–1987 school years; special and regular schools are included.

Note: From *The National Longitudinal Transition Study of Special Education Students. Statistical Almanac, Vol. 1: Overview* by K. A. Valdéz, C. L. Williamson, and M. Wagner, 1990, Menlo Park, CA: SRI International. Copyright 1990 by SRI International. Reprinted with permission.

⁓ *Productivity (income-producing work) and inclusion in the community are two important results Congress has sought through IDEA.*

• *Integration.* Persons with disabilities will use the same community resources and participate in the same community activities as persons who do not have disabilities, they will have regular contact with those citizens, and they will reside in homes or in home like settings near community resources. This goal is also known as **inclusion,** which is the term educators use.

Inclusion means integrating students with disabilities into the same classrooms, community activities and resources, and home settings as students without disabilities.

To answer the challenge about the results of special education, and, indeed, to be able to appreciate special education as it exists in today's schools, it is helpful to learn about special education in yesterday's schools.

THREE LEADERS WHO CHANGED SPECIAL EDUCATION: A HISTORY OF REFORM

Special education today is not what it was in the 1960s or even in the 1970s. What changed it? Or, more to the point, who changed it? Among the many correct answers is this one: Three pioneers envisioned a different profession. By showing new ways to serve children with disabilities, they helped all educators abandon the old ones.

Lloyd Dunn: Questioning the Efficacy of Special Education Placement

As early as 1968, Lloyd Dunn, a special education professor at Peabody College (now Vanderbilt University) and a former president of the Council for Exceptional Children, had sufficient insight and stature to question the efficacy of placing students with mild disabilities into special classes.

In the late 1960s, people-first language was not encouraged. At that time using the term *the retarded* was not considered pejorative; whereas, today many people consider it highly insensitive. This is a good example of how favored terminology changes over time. What do you think future terminology changes will be?

Reflect on your experiences in elementary and secondary school. Do you recall instances when students with disabilities were called names associated with their labels? Does a student's label influence *great expectations* and *social relationships*? Does it convey *strengths* and *positive contributions*? Does it promote *full citizenship* and *choice*?

In 1994, an entire issue of *The Journal of Special Education,* entitled "Theory and Practice of Special Education: Taking Stock a Quarter Century after Deno and Dunn," reviewed and critiqued recent practices that have resulted from Dunn and Deno's influences.

The number of special day classes for the retarded has been increasing by leaps and bounds. The most recent 1967–1968 statistics compiled by the US Office of Education now indicate that there are approximately 32,000 teachers of the retarded employed by local school systems—over one-third of all special educators in the nation. In my best judgment, about 60 to 80 percent of the people taught by these teachers are children from low status backgrounds—including Afro-Americans, American Indians, Mexican, and Puerto Rican Americans; those from nonstandard-English-speaking, broken, disorganized, and inadequate homes; and children from other nonmiddle class environments. This expensive proliferation of self-contained special schools and classes raises serious educational and civil rights issues which must be squarely faced. It is my thesis that we must stop labeling these deprived children as mentally retarded. Furthermore we must stop segregating them by placing them into our allegedly special programs. (Dunn, 1968, p. 8)

Dunn argued that special educators should assume fundamentally new roles. They should provide resources and consultation to general education teachers; if they were to do so, many more students could remain in general education and avoid separate placements. While advocating for general class placement for students with mild disabilities, Dunn also emphasized the importance of special education placement for students with more severe disabilities. Had Danny been in school when Dunn was writing—and it is not by any means certain that Danny would have been included in any school program at all, since many students with disabilities were excluded from school altogether in the late 1960s—Danny most likely would have been in the separate programs that Dunn was trying to reform.

Dunn extended his criticism beyond placement issues, questioning the utility of disability labeling: "None of these labels are badges of distinction" (Dunn, 1968, p. 11). Instead, he recommended using labels that describe the nature of the education the students would receive. In place of labels that describe the nature of a disability, "we would thus talk of students who need special instruction in language or cognitive development, in sensory training, in personality development, in vocational training, and other areas" (Dunn, 1968, p. 17).

Like a cannon shot heard around the special education world, Dunn's article heralded imminent change. It caused educators to be more aware of the needs for nondiscriminatory assessment and for placement in general education settings. As you will soon learn, its echoes reverberate, even today, in the federal laws that govern today's special education.

Evelyn Deno: Proposing a Cascade of Services

In 1970, only two years later, Evelyn Deno published her own benchmark article. Having been a preschool and elementary teacher of children from a broad range of ethnic and socioeconomic backgrounds, and with a research base as professor at the University of Minnesota, she was committed to making schools more responsive to diversity among children (Deno, 1994). Accordingly, she argued that the special education system should serve as "developmental capital" (Deno, 1970, p. 62) to improve the effectiveness of public school education for all students.

Special education should conceive of itself primarily as an instrument for facilitation of educational change and development of better means of meeting the learning needs of children who are different; and . . . it (should) organize itself to do that kind of educational services job rather than organize itself as primarily a curriculum and instruction resource for clientele defined as pathologically different by categorical criteria. (Deno, 1970, p. 60)

To reshape school systems in 1970, Deno proposed the concept of a cascade of services, depicted in Figure 1–4. She commented:

The cascade system is designed to make available whatever different-from-the-mainstream kind of setting is required to control the learning variables deemed critical for the individual case. It is a system which facilitates tailoring of treat-

FIGURE 1–4 *Cascade of services*

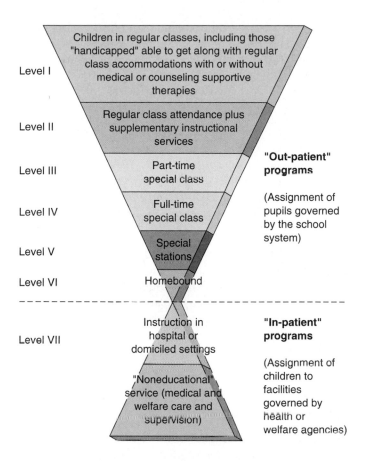

Level I — Children in regular classes, including those "handicapped" able to get along with regular class accommodations with or without medical or counseling supportive therapies

Level II — Regular class attendance plus supplementary instructional services

Level III — Part-time special class

Level IV — Full-time special class

Level V — Special stations

Level VI — Homebound

"Out-patient" programs

(Assignment of pupils governed by the school system)

Level VII — Instruction in hospital or domiciled settings

"Noneducational" service (medical and welfare care and supervision)

"In-patient" programs

(Assignment of children to facilities governed by health or welfare agencies)

The cascade system of special education service. The tapered design indicates the considerable difference in the numbers involved at the different levels and calls attention to the fact that the system serves as a diagnostic filter. The most specialized facilities are likely to be needed by the fewest children on a long term basis. This organizational model can be applied to development of special education services for all types of disability.

Note: From "Special Education as Developmental Capital" by E. Deno, 1970, *Exceptional Children, 37,* p. 235. Copyright 1970 by the Council for Exceptional Children. Reprinted with permission.

ment to individual needs rather than a system for sorting out children so they will fit conditions designed according to group standards not necessarily suitable for the particular case. (Deno, 1970, pp. 66–67)

Deno's major argument was in favor of individualized, student-centered education and against system-centered sorting. The concept of a cascade of services became the second cannon shot heard around the special education world. It was the blueprint for the continuum of placement options that is an integral part of federal and state special education law and practice. You will learn just how fundamental the Deno cascade is when you read in Chapters 2 and 3 about the school placements that Danny Ramirez and other students with disabilities are offered.

Deno's "cascade" can promote relationships between students who have disabilities and those who do not. But it can also justify separation, which in turn can inhibit friendships from developing between those students.

James Gallagher: Advocating for a Special Education Contract

In 1972, four years after Dunn's critique of labeling and segregation and two years after Deno's proposal of a cascade of services, James Gallagher, director of the Frank Porter Graham Child Development Center at the University of North Carolina at Chapel Hill, fired

Gallagher's proposal for an individualized education contract has many benefits. Among others, it helps educators emphasize students' strengths and positive contributions. Like Gallagher, and like Dunn and Deno before him, you too might make a difference in the lives of students in special education.

the last of the three cannons. Concerned that students with mild disabilities were being retained in special education though their needs for special education may have expired, Gallagher advocated for a special education contract that would safeguard against incorrect and permanent placements:

> *Placement of primary school-age mildly retarded or disturbed or learning disabled children in a special education unit would require a contract signed between parents and educators, with specific goals and a clear time limit. This contract should be for a* maximum of 2 years *and would be nonrenewable, or renewable only under a quasi-judicial type of hearing, with parents represented by legal or child advocate counsel. The contract, composed after a careful educational diagnosis, would commit the special educational personnel to measurable objectives that would be upgraded on a 6-month interval. (Gallagher, 1972, pp. 151–152)*

At that time, there were very few ways for families of special education students to hold educators accountable for the students' progress. Three short years later, Gallagher's ideas, modified to some extent, found their way into federal law in the form of an individualized education program (IEP) and a due process hearing. Indeed, Gallagher's idea is the basis for Danny's education—his IEP—and for his parents' direct and regular involvement in the process whereby Danny's schools decide not just where to "place" him but also what he will learn and with whom he will learn and socialize, in and out of school.

JUDICIAL PRELUDES TO FEDERAL SPECIAL EDUCATION LAW: A HISTORY OF DISCRIMINATION

Dunn, Deno, and Gallagher made a difference on several levels: They articulated fundamental problems in special education; they proposed solutions; and they added fuel to a revolution that had been brewing for a few short years. These three professors were only part of the special education revolution of the 1970s. Others were involved in that revolution; among them were civil rights activists, families, educators, organizations representing families and special educators, and their lawyers.

Two Types of Discrimination

Had he been born before federal law gave him the right to a free appropriate public education, Danny might have been one of the students who was excluded altogether or who, having been enrolled, received no benefit from being in school. As it was, Danny's very early identification as a person with Down syndrome negatively affected his opportunities in school.

For a long time, schools had practiced two kinds of discrimination related to students with disabilities. First, they completely excluded many students with disabilities (House Committee Report on the Education for All Handicapped Children Act, 1975; Lippman & Goldberg, 1973; Weintraub, Abeson, & Braddock, 1971). Or, having admitted students with disabilities, schools did not always provide them with an effective or appropriate education.

Second, schools often classified students as having disabilities when they in fact did not have disabilities. Frequently, these students, like Danny, were members of culturally and linguistically diverse groups. In addition, schools sometimes labeled students with one kind of disability when the students really had other kinds of disabilities (Hobbs, 1975; Kirp, 1973; Sarason & Doris, 1979; Senate Committee Report on the Education of All Handicapped Children Act, 1975; Sorgen, 1976). Clearly, Dunn, Deno, and Gallagher sought to solve the twin problems of exclusion and misclassification. Fortunately, they were not alone.

While arguing his case in *Brown v. Board of Education,* one lawyer tried to persuade the U.S. Supreme Court not to order racial integration in the schools by predicting that, if the Court were to order racial integration, it would eventually have to order the integration of students with disabilities into programs with students who do not have disabilities. How prophetic he was!

Beginning in the early 1970s, advocates for students with disabilities—primarily, their families, parent advocacy organizations, and civil-rights lawyers—began to sue state and local school officials, claiming that exclusion and misclassification violated the students' rights to an equal education opportunity under the U.S. Constitution. Relying on the Supreme Court's decision in the school race-desegregation case (*Brown v. Board of Education,* 1954), they argued that, because *Brown* held that schools may not segregate by race, schools also may not segregate or otherwise discriminate by ability and disability. Students are students regardless of their race or disability.

Two Revolutionary Judicial Decisions

The advocates' arguments proved to be very successful. In 1972, federal courts ordered the Commonwealth of Pennsylvania and the District of Columbia to (a) provide a free appropriate public education to all students with disabilities, (b) educate students with disabilities in the same schools and basically the same programs as students without disabilities, and (c) put into place certain procedural safeguards so that students with disabilities can challenge schools that do not live up to the courts' orders (*Pennsylvania Association for Retarded Citizens [PARC] v. Commonwealth of Pennsylvania*, 1972; *Mills v. Washington, DC, Board of Education*, 1972). Box 1–2, "My Voice," contains an excerpt from testimony given at the Pennsylvania trial by the father of a daughter with mental retardation.

Within a very short time, families began advocating in Congress for a federal law and federal money that would guarantee students' rights to an education and help states pay for special education. They were armed with these court orders and were supported by professionals, organized as the Council for Exceptional Children, and by governors and state legislators. And they were immensely successful, as you are about to learn.

INDIVIDUALS WITH DISABILITIES EDUCATION ACT: INTRODUCTION AND ELIGIBILITY

The advocates' success culminated in Congress's enactment of the IDEA. We begin by giving a general introduction to that law. Then we discuss eligibility for special education and its six principles. Finally, we address some of the concerns about the law.

Introduction to IDEA: Progress but Problems

In 1975, Congress enacted the federal special education law that governs how students with disabilities are educated in today's schools. The 1975 law was named Education of All Handicapped Students Act and was known as Public Law (PL) 94-142. Since then, Congress has amended the law several times, most recently in 1997.

In enacting the federal law in 1975, Congress found as a matter of fact that "more than half of the children with disabilities in the United States do not receive appropriate educational services" and that one million of them were "excluded entirely from the public school system." In light of these findings, Congress asserted that "it is the national interest that the Federal government assist State and local efforts to provide programs to meet the educational needs of children with disabilities in order to assure equal protection of the law" (IDEA, 20 U.S.C. § 1400 (c)).

When Congress reauthorized IDEA in 1997 (PL 105-17), it found that, despite the law's success in ensuring that students with disabilities have access to a free appropriate public education and in improving the educational results for them, IDEA's implementation has been impeded by (a) low expectations concerning students with disabilities and special education programs and (b) an insufficient focus on applying research-based proven methods of teaching and learning for those students. These congressional findings were only a summary of the findings made by the **National Council on Disability** (1995) as a result of testimony it took from parents and educators all across America.

In its 1995 report, the National Council on Disability concluded that IDEA's basic principles and features are still valid but that the law's implementation needed to be improved:

- Not all school buildings were accessible to students with physical disabilities.

- Too many students were being removed from school because of behavior related to their disabilities, whereas they should be kept in school so their behaviors can be improved.

- Students were evaluated more for the purpose of classifying them than determining what educational services they need.

❧ When Congress amended the Act in 1990, it renamed it. The federal law is now named Individuals with Disabilities Education Act (IDEA). Not a bad "idea" to use people-first language in a federal law, is it? That kind of language conveys images of strengths, positive contributions, full citizenship, and choices.

The **National Council on Disability** is an independent federal agency responsible for making recommendations on policy matters to Congress and the President.

BOX 1-2   MY VOICE

A FATHER'S VOICE IN *PARC V. COMMONWEALTH OF PENNSYLVANIA*

I would just like to call to the Court's attention [to] what the realities of that situation are, and I think I can speak with some authority because for the last nine years, my fifteen-year-old daughter has been denied access to public education without due process, but consistently denied, and as a result of which we have had her in private schools for the last nine years.

Now in those nine years, not counting the present year which started last summer, we have spent approximately forty thousand dollars on her private schooling, shall I say. At the present time we have her in a private school, a residential school where we pay a tuition of twelve thousand dollars a year, and I want to say to the Court that . . . our situation is paralleled by many other situations of many other children, and their parents.

Now if a public facility were established that comes anywhere near striking distance of appropriateness for my child,

Your Honors can rest assured that I will welcome that public facility with open arms. The financial burden of giving my child private education is very considerable. There is no pride or status symbol involved in having a child in private school such as the private schools to which my child and others in the same situation would go. In other words, it isn't out of any feeling of status that I am undertaking this heavy financial burden. It is simply because there is no public facility.

Now the moment a public facility is indicated, even just on the drawing board or on brochures, or papers of any kind which will look reasonably appropriate, I will assure Your Honors that ninety-five per cent or more of all parents will rush to get their children in there because every one of the parents is laboring under a backbreaking financial burden. We're not talking about wealthy people here. We are talking about ordinary people, and I know a great many of them who send their children to the same school where I send mine, and I have had my child in one other school before this, and I have had her with a private tutor for a year.

Note: From *PARC v. Commonwealth of Pennsylvania*, 343 F. Supp. 279, 287 (1972).

- Services were not sufficiently individualized, with the result that some students were not benefiting from school.

- Too many students were placed out of the general education curriculum and too few, who could benefit from being placed into it, were in fact educated in the regular program.

- Special education has become a place to which students are sent who pose challenges to their teachers or the school district, but it should become a service that makes it possible for many more students to stay in the general education program.

- Parents were not real partners with educators in making decisions about their children's education.

- School reform in general education was not taking special education into account but should.

Congress also found that research and experience have demonstrated that special education can be made more effective by

- Having higher expectations for the students

- Ensuring students' access to the general curriculum

- Strengthening parents' roles and opportunities to participate in their children's education

- Coordinating special education with other school improvement efforts so that special education will become a service, not a place where students with disabilities are sent

☙ *In the 1970s, advocates seeking equal rights for children with disabilities to pursue education brought cases all the way to the U.S. Supreme Court, shown here. Although the Court's stone letters say "Equal Justice Under Law," many public buildings are inaccessible to people with physical disabilities.*

- Providing special education, with related services, aids, and supports in the regular classroom, whenever appropriate

- Supporting teacher preparation and in-service education

- Reducing the need to label students as having a disability in order to address their learning needs

- Focusing resources on teaching and learning while reducing paperwork requirements that do not assist in improving educational results

Given the history of exclusion and misclassification that underlay the 1975 law, the problems that the National Council on Disability identified in 1995, and the barriers and solutions that Congress specified in the 1997 reauthorization of IDEA, you may be tempted to think that special education and its governing law are in bad shape. That would be the wrong conclusion. As you will learn from all of the other chapters in this book, special education is a powerful and beneficial force in America's schools.

IDEA is such a comprehensive law that Congress has divided it into several parts. In your work in the schools, you will hear your colleagues speak about IDEA's Part A, Part B, and Part C. What do they mean? Quite simply, Part A sets out the findings of fact on which Congress justifies the rest of IDEA; it also describes the purposes and policies that Congress intends to implement by enacting IDEA. Part B and Part C declare the rights that students have under IDEA, but with this one important distinction: Part B benefits students who are between the ages of 3 and 21 (starting when the students turn 3 and continuing until they turn 21). You may want to think of Part B as including students in early education (ages 3 through 5) and elementary, middle, and secondary school (ages 6 through 21). By contrast, Part C benefits infants and toddlers (starting at birth and continuing through age 2). Sometimes, you will hear your colleagues talk about Part C as a "birth through two" law, and sometimes they will call it the "zero to three" law. It doesn't really matter what they call it, so long as you know that it benefits infants and toddlers. Sometimes, out of habit, they may also call it "Part H," but that is a big mistake. Before IDEA was reauthorized in 1997, the infants and toddlers were covered by Part H, but, with the reauthorization, they are now covered by Part C (i.e., Part H has been retitled Part C).

Eligibility for Special Education: Need and Age Groups

Eligibility: Need. IDEA defines special education as specially designed instruction, including instruction in physical education, to meet the unique needs of a student with a disability. Individualized decision making—the sort of education that Dunn, Deno, and Gallagher advocated—is now the law of the land. The instruction is free, provided in various settings (reflecting Deno's "cascade of services") and includes related services. The places where special education is delivered are classrooms, homes, hospitals and institutions, and other settings.

A student is eligible for special education services if the student has a disability and, because of the disability, needs special education and related services. Note the two-part standard for eligibility: (a) first, there is a categorical element—the student must have a disability; and second (b) there is a functional element—the disability must cause the student to need specially designed instruction.

Eligibility for Special Education: Age Groups. When IDEA was first enacted in 1975, the major problems that Congress addressed were exclusion and misclassification of students who were of school age, that is, between six and eighteen. As IDEA was implemented and schools became more accessible to and appropriate for those students and as the benefits of early education for very young children with disabilities were established, Congress became willing to include more children under IDEA's protection. Thus, in 1983 and again in 1986, Congress amended the law to provide for early childhood special education for children between the ages of three and five. Also, although IDEA clearly helped students while they were in school, it seemed that it could help them more in the transition from school to the world of adulthood; accordingly, Congress amended the law in 1983 and again in 1986 so that students ages sixteen and older would have an education that is specifically geared to helping them become independent, productive, and included in the mainstream of American life. All provisions for students ages three through twenty-one are set out in Part B of IDEA.

In keeping with its history of gradually expanding IDEA's benefits, Congress in 1986 amended IDEA to provide for early intervention for children ages birth through two (or zero to three). The law that affects these children is set out in Part C of IDEA.

Ages Three to Twenty-One and Part B. Remembering that Part B benefits students ages three through twenty-one and that a student does not qualify for IDEA benefits unless the student has a disability that adversely affects the student's ability to learn in the general education program, you now need to know that Part B still relies on a categorical approach to disabilities.

The IDEA categories are the following (you will learn about these categories in Chapters 4 to 16):

- For children aged six through twenty-one:

    Specific learning disabilities

    Emotional disturbance (IDEA has just changed this term from *serious emotional disturbance* to *emotional disturbance*)

    Mental retardation, including severe and multiple disabilities

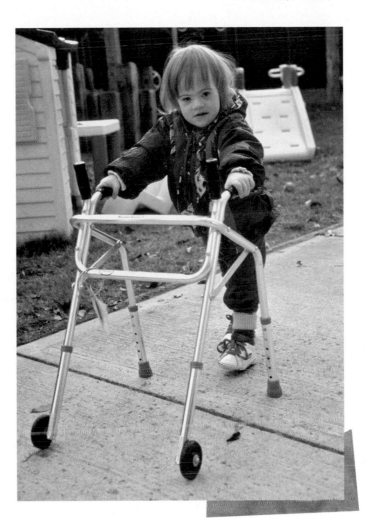

IDEA now grants educational rights to children with disabilities from birth through age two (Part C) as well as from ages three through twenty-one (Part B).

Autism

Other health impairments

Orthopedic impairments (physical disabilities)

Traumatic brain injury

Speech or language impairments

Hearing impairments, including deafness

Visual impairments, including blindness

- For children aged three to nine (early childhood special education), these same categories apply, but each state, in its own discretion, may include children who

  Are experiencing developmental delays in one or more of the following areas: physical development, cognitive development, communication development, social or emotional development, or adaptive development

  Because of these delays, need special education and related services

Ages Birth Through Two and Part C.   Part C (infants and toddlers) benefits any child under age three who needs (a) early intervention services because of developmental delays (as measured by appropriate diagnostic instruments or procedures) in one or more of the areas of cognitive development, physical development, social or emotional development, or adaptive development, or (b) has a diagnosed physical or mental condition that has a high probability of resulting in a developmental delay. Each state has the option of serving at-risk infants and toddlers: those who would be at risk of experiencing a substantial developmental delay if they did not receive early intervention services. Early intervention services

- Must be provided by qualified personnel

- Must be provided in natural environments to the maximum extent appropriate for the infant or toddler (i.e., in the same environments the infant/toddler would participate in if he or she did not have a disability)

- Must be provided in conformity with an Individualized Family Service Plan

- Include the services listed in Figure 1-6, later in this chapter.

IDEA: SIX PRINCIPLES

It is not enough for IDEA to simply identify those students who are entitled to its benefits and to specify the nature of the services they get. It is also necessary for IDEA to specify what those benefits are. In very clear terms, IDEA does just that, setting out six principles for the education of students with disabilities. These principles are set out in Figure 1-5. They follow a logical sequence, describing in order what schools do for students with disabilities.

The sequence of the six principles and schools' actions is straightforward. First, schools enroll the students. This is the principle of zero reject. Second, the schools determine what each student's disability is and how it relates to the student's education. This is the principle of nondiscriminatory evaluation. Third, the schools provide an individualized program for the students, appropriate to their educational strengths and needs. This is the principle of appropriate education. Fourth, the schools provide this education in the general curriculum, to the maximum extent appropriate for each student. This is the principle of the least restrictive environment. Fifth, the schools and parents have opportunities to resolve any differences they have with each other. This is the principle of procedural due process. Finally, the parents have opportunities to participate with the schools in making decisions about the education of their child. This is the principle of parent participation.

The first four principles are essentially inputs into the student's education; they describe what the schools contribute to the student. The last two principles are essential

FIGURE 1–5 *Six principles governing the education of students with disabilities*

- **Zero reject:** A rule against excluding any student.

- **Nondiscriminatory evaluation:** A rule requiring schools to evaluate students fairly to determine if they have a disability and, if so, what kind and how extensive.

- **Appropriate education:** A rule requiring schools to provide individually tailored education for each student based on the evaluation and augmented by related services and supplementary aids and services.

- **Least restrictive environment:** A rule requiring schools to educate students with disabilities with students without disabilities to the maximum extent appropriate for the students with disabilities.

- **Procedural due process:** A rule providing safeguards for students against schools' actions, including a right to sue in court.

- **Parental and student participation:** A rule requiring schools to collaborate with parents and adolescent students in designing and carrying out special education programs.

outputs to the student's education; they are checks and balances that ensure that the result (output) of the education is what it is meant to be. Having briefly described each of the six principles, we now discuss each in more detail.

Zero Reject

The zero-reject principle prohibits schools from excluding any student with a disability from a free appropriate public education. The purpose of the zero-reject principle is to ensure that all children and youth (ages three to twenty-one), no matter how severe their disabilities, have an appropriate education provided free (at public expense). To carry out this purpose, the zero-reject rule applies to the state, each school district, private schools, and state-operated programs such as schools for students with visual or hearing impairments, psychiatric hospitals, and institutions for people with other disabilities. Related services are not available to a student unless the student requires them in order to benefit from special education. Figure 1–6 lists the 1997 IDEA-related services and defines them.

> The zero-reject principle responds directly to the history of people with disabilities, a history in which the schools excluded many of these people from any education whatsoever.

Educability. To carry out the zero-reject rule, courts have ordered state and local education agencies to provide services to children who traditionally have been regarded as ineducable (not able to learn) because of the profound extent of their disabilities. The leading case is *Timothy W. v. Rochester School District* (1988). There, a New Hampshire school district refused to serve a thirteen-year-old boy who was blind and deaf, had cerebral palsy, was subject to frequent seizures, was profoundly retarded, and had no communication skills. He had acquired some ability to respond to light and noise but had made no progress in about a year. The court held that Congress intended for no child to be excluded from an opportunity to learn and that Timothy W.'s school district must make every effort to help him acquire even the most rudimentary skills (You will learn about the education of students with severe and multiple disabilities in Chapter 9.)

Expulsion. Courts also have ordered schools not to expel or suspend students whose behavior is caused by their disabilities. In the leading case, *Honig v. Doe* (1988), a California school district had expelled students who had learning disabilities and mental retardation for spiking the punch at a school dance. The U.S. Supreme Court held that, if a student's behavior arises out of the student's disability, IDEA prohibits the district from excluding him or her from school. So, if there is a manifestation of the disability in the student's conduct, the student may not be excluded entirely from school. (You will learn more about discipline and IDEA in Chapter 5.)

Contagious Diseases. The courts also have ordered schools not to exclude children who have contagious diseases (e.g., tuberculosis, herpes, acquired immune deficiency syndrome [AIDS]) from education with other students unless there is a high risk that the contagious students will infect other students. Even if they may not be educated with other students, they still must be educated at home or in a hospital. A panel of medical experts determines the degree to which a student endangers other students or faculty or is endangered by them. The placement determination must be made on a student-by-student basis. A practice of relying on expert judgments and making individualized decisions balances the student's educational rights against the public health and safety interests of others in the school. (You will learn about the education of children with health impairments, including contagious diseases, in Chapter 11.)

> The zero-reject principle reflects the full citizenship value. It assures students with disabilities that they, like students who do not have disabilities, are fully entitled to attend school, which is a right of citizenship.

In essence, the zero-reject rule means what it says: No student may be excluded from an appropriate education because of a disability. Danny will never have to worry about whether he may attend school through the age of twenty-one. It's his right.

FIGURE 1–6 *Definitions of related services in IDEA*

- **Audiology:** Determining the range, nature, and degree of hearing loss and operating programs for treatment and prevention of hearing loss

- **Counseling services:** Counseling by social workers, psychologists, guidance counselors, and rehabilitation specialists

- **Early identification:** Identifying a disability as early as possible in a child's life

- **Family training, counseling, and home visits:** Assisting families to enhance their child's development (Part C only)

- **Health services:** Enabling a child to benefit from other early intervention services (Part C only)

- **Medical services:** Determining a child's medically related disability that results in the child's need for special education and related services

- **Nursing services:** Assessing health status, preventing health problems, and administering medications, treatments, and regimens prescribed by a licensed physician (Part C only)

- **Nutrition services:** Conducting individual assessments to address the nutritional needs of children (Part C only)

- **Occupational therapy:** Improving, developing, or restoring functions impaired or lost through illness, injury, or deprivation

- **Orientation and mobility services:** Assisting a student to get around within various environments

- **Parent counseling and training:** Providing parents with information about child development

- **Physical therapy:** Screening, referral, and service provision for therapy regarding bone and muscle capacity

- **Psychological services:** Administering and interpreting psychological and educational tests and other assessment procedures and managing a program of psychological services, including psychological counseling for children and parents

- **Recreation and therapeutic recreation:** Assessing leisure function, recreation programs in schools and community agencies, and leisure education

- **Rehabilitative counseling services:** Planning for career development, employment preparation, achieving independence, and integration in the workplace and community

- **School health services:** Attending to educationally related health needs through services provided by a school nurse

- **Service coordination services:** Assistance and services by a service coordinator to a child and family (Part C only)

- **Social work services in schools:** Preparing a social or developmental history on a child, group and individual counseling, and mobilizing school and community resources

- **Speech pathology and speech-language pathology:** Diagnosing specific speech or language impairments and giving guidance regarding speech and language impairments

- **Transportation and related costs:** Providing travel to and from services and schools, travel in and around school buildings, and specialized equipment (e.g., special or adapted buses, lifts, and ramps)

- **Assistive technology and services:** Acquiring and using devices and services to restore lost capacities or improve impaired capacities

Nondiscriminatory Evaluation

The effect of the zero-reject rule is to guarantee all students with a disability access to school. So, students who obviously have a disability may attend school; Danny Ramirez has an obvious disability and benefits from the zero-reject rule. The same is true of students who develop a disability after they have been enrolled in school; for example, one student may acquire a head injury in an automobile accident, and another may acquire AIDS as a result of a blood transfusion. Both of them are entitled to stay in school, and both are entitled to an unbiased evaluation of their educational strengths and newly acquired needs.

Two Purposes.   Nondiscriminatory evaluation has two purposes. The first is to determine whether a student has a disability. If the student does not have a disability, then he or she does not receive special education or any further evaluation related to special education. By contrast, if the evaluation reveals that the student has a disability, the evaluation process continues.

The second purpose has two subparts: (1) to determine that because of the disability, the student needs special education and related services; and (2) to begin to define what kind of special education and related services the student will receive. This information is necessary to plan an appropriate education for the student.

Through the principle of nondiscriminatory evaluation, IDEA ensures unbiased, multi-faceted, multidisciplinary, and professionally sound evaluation. Chapter 2 describes in more detail the elements of a nondiscriminatory evaluation and how the evaluation process works.

Evaluation to Eliminate Bias.   You may well ask, why is nonbiased evaluation such a concern? The answer lies in part in the concerns that Lloyd Dunn expressed. You will recall that he was concerned about labeling and the overclassification of students from culturally and linguistically diverse backgrounds. For the twenty-plus years since IDEA was first enacted, Congress, too, has been continually concerned about problems of misclassification, as you have read. Yet the misclassification of students from culturally and linguistically diverse backgrounds persists, as you learned earlier in this chapter. There has been another concern about bias in schools, one that early on captured the close attention of the federal courts.

The issue was whether standardized tests necessarily discriminate against culturally and linguistically diverse students. The issue wound its way into the courts early in the 1970s. In an early and still controversial decision, a federal judge in California ruled that the state education agency may not use standardized IQ tests (the Stanford-Binet, Wechsler, and Leiter IQ tests). His rationale was that the tests were validated on white students and discriminated against African American students in three ways (*Larry P. v. Riles,* 1984):

- First, the tests measure achievement, not ability. Because African American students traditionally have been denied equal educational opportunities as a result of school segregation based on race, many will have lower achievement scores and thus be discriminated against in testing.

- Second, the tests rest on a defensible but not-yet-proved assumption that intelligence is distributed across the entire population in conformation with a normal statistical curve (a bell-shaped curve) and thus the tests are man-made techniques to rank individuals.

- Third, the tests necessarily lead to the placement of more African American students than white students in classes for students with mild-to-moderate mental retardation (see Chapter 8, on mental retardation).

The decision in *Larry P. v. Riles* was provocative, to say the least. Some educators and advocates applauded it because they believed the decision would not only strike down

For students who come from homes where English is one of several languages or is not the preferred language, the evaluation must take their language and should take their family's culture into account.

the tests but also help keep students from culturally and linguistically diverse backgrounds from being labeled as having mild mental retardation. Others condemned it because they felt it would prevent them from determining whether a student had a disability and from responding to that student's legitimate educational needs (Reschly, 1988). For a while, indeed, the status of testing and the legality of using the intelligence tests that *Larry P. v. Riles* condemned was up in the air.

This uncertainty finally was resolved by two developments. First, Congress enacted IDEA and provided students with nondiscriminatory evaluation safeguards (see Chapter 2). Second, another challenge to the tests was brought in another court but failed. In that case, *Parents in Action in Special Education [PASE] v. Hannon* (1980), a federal judge in Illinois upheld the same three tests. The judge found that only 9 of 488 test questions in the three different tests were or might be racially biased and that the tests on the whole were not discriminatory.

Equally important, the judge found that the tests were not the sole basis for special education classification. The judge observed that clinical judgment plays a large role in interpreting the IQ tests results. An evaluator who knows the child's social, economic, cultural, and linguistic background can correct for any test-question bias by asking the questions and interpreting the answers in a culturally sensitive way. If the student's answer is substantially correct, even though it may not be precisely the answer the test seeks, the test permits the examiner to give the student credit for a correct answer. Thus, the possibility that a few biased items on the tests would cause a student to be misclassified is "practically nonexistent" according to the court. The decision in *PASE v. Hannon* basically resolved the controversy about the use of intelligence tests. It gave a green light to educators to use the intelligence tests so long as they also complied with all other IDEA evaluation procedural safeguards.

Appropriate Education

Simply enrolling students (zero reject) and evaluating their strengths and needs (nondiscriminatory evaluation) do not ensure that their education will be appropriate and beneficial. That is why Congress has given each student in special education the right to an appropriate education and related services. (Figure 1-6 lists the related services.) An appropriate education consists of specially designed instruction (at no cost to parents or

VIDEO
REFLECTIONS

COMMON MIRACLES: THE NEW AMERICAN REVOLUTION IN LEARNING, PART I

In Chapter 1, we discuss how IDEA guarantees a free and appropriate education for all children and adolescents. The assumption of this law is that no matter what the type or severity of disability, each child and adolescent can profit from attending school. Is this assumption true? In *Common Miracles*, ABC correspondent Bill Blakemore says, "The human mind turns out to be far more flexible and capable in all of us than we ever thought. Scientists believe now that whenever you learn something, you literally grow brain. . . . The fact that we grow brain helps explain why anyone can learn."

All students can learn and change. This truth is the foundation underlying great expectations for students with exceptionalities. In this video, you will discover how you can encourage these common miracles for your students.

What do you think? What factors contribute to a person "growing brain"?
Why is flow important to encourage learning?
What are some ways you can encourage flow for students with exceptionalities in general classrooms?
We have mentioned how *Common Miracles* reflects great expectations for students. What examples of positive contributions, inherent strengths, choices, relationships, and full citizenship did you see in this video?

guardians) that may be conducted in general and/or special education classrooms, in the student's home, in a hospital or institution, and in other settings.

Planning for Individual Needs.

The key to an appropriate special education is individualization. That was the point Gallagher (1972) was making when he advocated for a special education contract for each student. IDEA provides for two major types of individualized plans. The plan for students aged three through twenty-one is called an **individualized education program (IEP)**. The plan for students from birth through two (also called "zero to three") is called an **individualized family services plan (IFSP)**. You will learn about both of these plans in Chapter 2, but at this point, you will learn about that meaning of appropriate education. Curiously, the meaning was set by judges, not educators. Because the interpretations of IDEA by the U.S. Supreme Court are binding throughout the country, the first IDEA case before the Court drew a great deal of attention. That case involved Amy Rowley, a student who is deaf.

An **individualized education program (IEP)** is a written plan for serving students with disabilities ages three to twenty-one.

An **individualized family services plan (IFSP)** is a written plan for serving infants and toddlers, ages zero to three, and their families.

Interpreting "Appropriate."

Amy's case posed an interesting question: What does the appropriate education principle mean? Amy was a first grader who had passed kindergarten easily. She was an excellent lip reader. Her teachers had taken a course in sign-language instruction. In the beginning of her first-grade year, she was scheduled to receive a hearing aid so she could hear her teachers and classmates better. She also was to have a tutor for one hour a day and a speech therapist for three hours a week, all at the school's expense.

Amy's parents, however, wanted her to have still another service—an interpreter in school, hired and paid for by the school. They argued that Amy was entitled to an interpreter as a related service that is necessary in order for her to benefit from her education, but the school refused to provide the interpreter. Ultimately, the U.S. Supreme Court agreed with the school; Amy and her parents lost their case.

The Benefit Rule. The Supreme Court noted that Amy was achieving academically, educationally, and socially without an interpreter. She was passing her schoolwork without an interpreter, and, indeed, her education was clearly benefiting her. The Court interpreted IDEA as giving students a right to an *appropriate education,* but *not* to the *best education possible.* The proof that Amy was receiving an appropriate education was her progress from kindergarten to first grade without an interpreter. Thus, concluded the Court, an appropriate education is one that benefits the student.

Other courts have interpreted this definition of an appropriate education—sometimes called the **benefit standard**—to mean that an appropriate education does not exist if the student is regressing or making only trivial progress. There must be real progress and thus real benefit. The 1997 amendments to IDEA strengthen the "benefit" standard, as you will learn in Chapter 2.

Benefit standard refers to a U.S. Supreme Court interpretation of "appropriate education" requiring the education to benefit the student.

The Process Rule. In addition, the Supreme Court observed the truth of an old legal maxim: Fair procedures produce fair results. IDEA establishes elaborate procedures that, if followed, will help ensure that a student will get an appropriate education. IDEA's process is zero reject, nondiscriminatory evaluation, and IEP development. Thus, an appropriate education follows the IDEA process. This is the **process definition,** and you will learn about it in detail in Chapter 2.

Process definition refers to a U.S. Supreme Court interpretation of "appropriate education" as one that effectively implements IDEA's six principles.

Least Restrictive Environment

Once the schools have enrolled a student (the zero-reject principle), fairly evaluated the student (the nondiscriminatory evaluation principle), and provided an IEP (the appropriate education principle), they must provide one more input into the student's education. That provision is education with students who do not have disabilities: the least restrictive environment (LRE) principle, also known as the mainstreaming, integration, or inclusion principle.

The value of relationships is reflected in the LRE principle. When students with disabilities are educated with students who do not have disabilities, there is an opportunity for them to develop mutually beneficial relationships.

Reasons for the Rule. There are many reasons why IDEA has adopted the LRE rule.

- The Supreme Court created the principle as a matter of constitutional (fundamental) law.

- There is a long history of segregating students with disabilities from students who do not have disabilities.

- Students with disabilities will be more likely to achieve the national policy results of independence, productivity, and interpretation if they have meaningful access to the general curriculum.

- Students with disabilities should have the opportunity to associate with students without disabilities so that each can develop relationships with the other.

- It is unnecessarily expensive to operate two education systems (special and general education).

- Any kind of segregation in education simply runs against the grain of the U.S. Constitution, which requires equal treatment of all people who are in equal or highly similar circumstances.

The Rule: A Presumption in Favor of Inclusion. Accordingly, IDEA creates a presumption in favor of educating students with disabilities with those who do not have disabilities. IDEA's rule is that (a) a school system must educate a student with a disability with students who do not have disabilities to the maximum extent appropriate for the student and that (b) the school may not remove the student from general education unless he or she cannot be educated there successfully (appropriately, in the sense that the student will benefit), even after the school provides **supplementary aids and support services** for the student.

Setting Aside the Presumption. The presumption in favor of inclusion can be set aside (rebutted) only if the student cannot benefit from being educated with students who do not have disabilities and only after the school has provided the student with supplementary aids and services. In that event, the student may be placed in a less typical, more specialized, less inclusive program. These programs are part of a continuum of services, modeled on Evelyn Deno's concept of a cascade of services (see Figure 1-3).

The Continuum of Services. Schools must offer a continuum or range of services from more to less typical and inclusive: that is, from less to more restrictive or separate. The most typical and inclusive setting is general education, followed by resource rooms, special classes, special schools, homebound services, and hospitals and institutions (also called residential or long-term care facilities).

Nonacademic Inclusion. Schools also have to ensure that students with disabilities may participate in extracurricular and in other general education activities. These include meals, recess periods, and other services such as counseling, athletics, transportation, health services, recreational activities, special interest groups or clubs, and referrals to agencies that assist in employment and other aspects of life outside of school. When providing these services to students who do not have disabilities, schools must include students with disabilities to the maximum extent appropriate.

Courts and LRE. Over the twenty-two years since IDEA was enacted, many courts have interpreted the LRE principle. One of the most important decisions involved Danny Ramirez. In *Daniel R.R. v. State Board of Education* (1989), a federal court of appeals held that students with disabilities have the right, to the maximum extent appropriate for each of them, to be included in both the academic and the extracurricular and other programs of general education. The court's decision was important because it recognized that Danny

Supplementary aids and support services are those that are provided in general education classes or other education settings so that students with disabilities will be educated with students who do not have disabilities to the maximum extent appropriate for the students with disabilities.

may have some academic inclusion along with inclusion in the other activities of his school. It also was important because it laid the foundation for the most recent and comprehensive decision on LRE.

In the case *Board of Education, Sacramento City Unified School District v. Holland* (1994), the court held that the following factors must be taken into account in determining whether a student will receive an appropriate education in the LRE:

1. The educational benefits of an integrated setting compared to those of the segregated setting

2. The nonacademic benefits of the student's interaction with peers who do not have disabilities

3. The effect of the student's presence in the general education program on the teacher and other students

4. The costs of supplementary services that are required to maintain the student in the integrated program

Thus, a student is entitled to an appropriate education (the benefits test, or factor 1) and to social benefits (factor 2). The key, of course, is the word *benefit*. If inclusion with students who do not have disabilities would not benefit a student academically or in any other way, then including the student is not appropriate, and the school may place the student in a less typical, less inclusive program or setting. That's all the LRE rule is. There is no absolute right to be included; if inclusion will benefit the student, fine but, if not, then inclusion is not appropriate and not required.

Moreover, the interests of other students and faculty come into play (factors 3 and 4). Inclusion is not an absolute right that "trumps" the rights or interests of other students to receive their own appropriate education. Indeed, the last factor safeguards against the costs of one student's education becoming so expensive that few funds are left over for educating other students. (As you will learn in Chapter 3, the 1997 amendments to IDEA substantially strengthen the LRE rule.)

> Due process reorganizes the full citizenship rights of students with disabilities. Like every other student, they have a right to be treated fairly.

Procedural Due Process

Schools sometimes do not always carry out IDEA's first four principles: zero reject, nondiscriminatory evaluation, appropriate education, and LRE. What's a parent to do? Or what if a school wants one type of special education but a parent disagrees, perhaps to the detriment of the child? The answer lies in the due process principle, which basically seeks to make the schools and parents accountable to each other for carrying out the student's IDEA rights.

When parents and state or local educational agencies disagree, IDEA provides each with an opportunity to engage in a process of **mediation** and, if that is unsuccessful in resolving the dispute, to have a **due process hearing.** Although mediation is not required, it is strongly encouraged; indeed, if a parent decides to reject mediation, the parent must receive counseling about the benefits of mediation. Only after receiving the counseling may a parent go to a due process hearing.

> **Mediation** is the process whereby both parties to a dispute agree to discuss and try to resolve their differences with the help of an independent third party. A *due process* hearing is like a trial, an adversarial process held before an impartial person called a *hearing officer.* The hearing is conducted like a trial, and the hearing officer is like a judge.

Due Process Hearing. A hearing is similar to a minitrial and is conducted before a disinterested person, called **a due process hearing officer.** At the hearing, the parents and schools are entitled to have lawyers, present evidence, and cross-examine each other's witnesses. Whoever loses the due process hearing may appeal to the state education agency; and whoever loses at the state-level hearing may appeal to and get a new hearing in a federal or state court.

Appeal to Court. The due process procedures are ones that the Ramirez, Rowley, and Holland families followed. Each set of parents exercised their rights to a due process hearing. Then, having not won at the hearing, they took their case to court, with the

FIGURE 1–7 *Notice requirements of IDEA*

Notice: Parents have the right to be notified whenever their child's school proposes or refuses to change the student's identification, evaluation, or placement, or the provision of free appropriate public education.

Form of notice: Each notice must be written in the parents' native language (unless it is clearly not feasible to do so), must be written in an easily understandable manner, and must fully explain all procedural safeguards available to the parents and child.

Content of notice, generally: All notices to parents must:

- Describe what the school wants to do or refuses to do.

- Explain why the school reached that decision.

- Describe any other options that the school considered and why the school rejected them.

- Describe each evaluation procedure, test, record, or report that the school used in order to reach its decision.

- Describe any other factors relevant to the school's decision.

- Inform the parents that they have a right to go to a due process hearing.

- List the sources the parents may contact to obtain assistance in understanding Part B (student and parent rights).

Procedural safeguards notice: A local education agency must also give the parents a special notice, called the "Procedural Safeguards Notice," on at least these three occasions:

- Whenever a school proposes an initial referral

- Whenever the school notifies the parents that there will be an IEP meeting and whenever it reevaluates the student

- Whenever the school receives from a parent a complaint that triggers the mediation or due process hearing process

Content of procedural safeguards notice: The notice must describe the parents' and students' rights to due process.

Rowleys going even as far as the Supreme Court. The entire legal process is very time-consuming, emotionally exhausting, and expensive (Martin, 1991).

Notice to Parents. Parents are always entitled to be notified concerning the school's decisions about their children. Figure 1-7 sets out the notice requirements.

Although due process hearings and other procedural safeguards can provide a system of checks and balances between schools and families, IDEA also offers another, less adversarial accountability technique: the parent-student participation principle.

Parent–Student Participation

The parent-student participation principle is a mechanism for shared decision making. Although the nondiscriminatory evaluation and the development of an IEP are two points at which families can share in the educational decision-making process, they are not the only ones. IDEA also gives parents other extensive rights, set out in Figure 1-8.

FEDERAL FUNDING OF INDIVIDUALS WITH DISABILITIES EDUCATION ACT

IDEA and its six principles benefit students by clearly setting out their rights to have access to school and to have certain inputs and checks and balances once they are enrolled. As important as the six principles are, however, they would amount to nothing

Parents and, when they attain the age of majority, students themselves have these rights:

- To have their own experts conduct nondiscriminatory evaluations and to require the schools to consider those evaluations (sometimes, those evaluations are at school expense)

- To be reimbursed for any tuition or other expenses they pay to secure a free appropriate education and related services, provided the school has failed to provide these benefits

- To be notified whenever a school plans to conduct a nondiscriminatory evaluation and to give or withhold consent to all evaluations (if they withhold consent, the school may not do an evaluation unless a due process hearing officer or court so orders)

- To receive a copy of the evaluation report and documentation of the student's eligibility for special education

- To have their concerns about the student considered by the professionals on the IFSP and IEP teams

- To receive notice (as often as parents of students without disabilities receive notice, but at least once a year) concerning the student's progress toward achieving the goals of the IFSP and IEP

- Have access to the student's school records

- Prevent those records from being disclosed to anyone not directly involved in the student's education

- Receive notice, attend, and participate at hearings about the state and local educational agencies' plans for system-wide special education programs

- Be appointed by the governor of their state to a state special education advisory panel

FIGURE 1–8 *Shared decision-making rights*

but rights on paper unless Congress put money behind them. After all, rights run with revenues. Accordingly, Congress grants federal money to state and local educational agencies (school districts) to assist them in educating students ages birth to twenty-one. The state and local agencies, however, must agree to comply with IDEA's principles, or else they will not receive the federal money.

IDEA as Grant-in-Aid for States

IDEA is a typical grant-in-aid law: The federal government grants financial aid to the states on the condition that the states comply with federal law . . . a sort of carrot-and-stick approach. As a general rule, the state and local agencies may not simply substitute the federal money for the funds that they themselves receive and spend for special education. The federal money generally supplements (not supplants) state and local contributions. There is nothing inherently wrong in this approach; and, not surprisingly, all states have agreed to accept the IDEA money and to follow IDEA's regulations. Indeed, governors and state legislators wanted the federal aid and worked hard to persuade Congress to enact IDEA in 1975 (Turnbull & Turnbull, 1996).

Cost Pressures.   As a rule, state and local education agencies have put the money to good use in today's schools, although there are serious concerns about the costs of special education. These relate to several factors. The population in special education has been growing much faster than the population in general education. Also, the per pupil expenditures in special education have been growing at a faster rate than those in general education. As states seek to make education more efficient, will they sacrifice effectiveness? Will cost cutting be undertaken at the expense of good services? And how can schools be made more accountable for producing the results that Congress wants—inde-

When Congress authorizes money, it basically agrees that it may spend that amount and no more. When it appropriates money, it commits the money and budgets for it. IDEA authorization always has been higher than the appropriation.

pendence, productivity, and integration—in light of the fact that the demand for services may be larger than the resources available to meet the demand (Parrish, O'Reilly, Dueñas, & Wolman, 1997)?

Excess Costs Issues.   Moreover, some critics of IDEA and Congress have pointed to the "overpromise but underperformance" problems associated with IDEA. Simply put, states have been entitled to receive from the federal government a good deal more money than Congress has in fact sent to them. Congress has authorized expenditures at one (higher) level but appropriated money at another (lower) level.

Looked at one way, there is a shortfall in what Congress said it could do; that is the underperformance problem. Looked at another way, however, each state has taken upon itself, usually in its constitution, the obligation to educate all children, including those with disabilities. Thus, IDEA assists the states to do what they would have to do in any event—educate all children with disabilities. IDEA supplements state and local school budgets. To criticize IDEA on the basis of overpromise/underperformance, then, seems unwarranted.

Costs and Schools' Expanded Functions.   Finally, special education consists of services that mental health, public health, social service, and corrections agencies would have to provide to students who would be in their programs if they were not in special education. The costs of maintaining students with disabilities in state institutions (psychiatric hospitals, long-term health-care facilities, or other institutions) is huge and far exceeds the costs of community-based special education (Braddock, Hemp, Fujiura, Bachelder, & Mitchell, 1990). In a very real sense, many of these costs have been transferred to the schools. So, there is a valid answer to the criticism that special education costs too much and benefits too few.

OTHER FEDERAL LAWS: ENTITLEMENTS AND ANTIDISCRIMINATION

You have just read about the six IDEA principles that govern the education of students with disabilities in today's schools, and you should now have a general understanding of these principles. In Chapter 2, you will learn even more about how IDEA's requirements benefit Danny and other students with disabilities. As important as IDEA is, other federal laws affect special education and students in those programs. There are two types of those laws: (a) Some create an entitlement for students or authorize services for them, and (b) others prohibit them from being discriminated against because of their disabilities.

Entitlements and Other Services

Supported employment means the employment of a person with a disability for at least the minimum wage, working alongside other employees who do not have disabilities. The person is assisted by a job coach, a person who teaches the job and helps perform some of it.

"Rehabilitation" Act.   The Rehabilitation Act, originally enacted to help wounded veterans of World War I secure therapy so they could return to work, now opens employment doors for students who have disabilities. If a person has a severe disability but, with rehabilitation, is able to work, despite the disability, the person is entitled to two types of vocational rehabilitation services. First, when they are sixteen years old, these individuals can receive from their state vocational rehabilitation agencies work evaluations, financial aid so they can pursue job training, and job locator services. Second, some of them can receive another service, called **supported employment.**

A **job coach** is a person who supports an individual with a severe disability to be successful in supported employment by teaching the individual job skills and helping him or her perform the job.

Under the supported employment program, persons with severe disabilities work with the assistance of a **job coach.** The coach's duties include teaching the supported worker (the person with a disability) how to do a job and then helping him or her do it independently; in some situations, the coach and the supported worker job-share. The sup-

〰 *Many students with disabilities qualify for supported employment services under the Rehabilitation Act when they turn sixteen. Here, a job coach works with students participating in the community-based training program at North Shelby School, Shelby, North Carolina.*

ported worker must be paid at least the minimum wage, work at least twenty hours a week in a typical work setting, and be able, after eighteen months of supported employment, to do the job alone, without support.

Tech Act.   The Technology-Related Assistance to Individuals with Disabilities Act of 1988, often called the *tech act,* authorizes federal funds to be granted to the states to help create statewide systems for delivering assistive technology and technology services to people with disabilities, including students. The services include consultation, education, and assistance in acquiring and using the devices. In Chapter 12, you will learn about a wide variety of assistive technologies—adapted equipment, computers, medical devices, and communication aids.

It is best to think of IDEA and the Rehabilitation Act as creating personal entitlements; they provide direct services to eligible people. It is best to think of the tech act as creating a statewide capacity to serve people with disabilities; instead of directly benefiting the people themselves, these laws help states meet the people's needs.

Prohibition of Discrimination

Education and rehabilitation are, of course, necessary to ameliorate the effect of the student's disability. But, though they are necessary, they are not sufficient, by themselves, to overcome the effect of the disability. IDEA, for example, does not prohibit public or private agencies from discriminating against the student on the basis of the student's disability. Yes, a student may receive special education, but that service might not create opportunities for the student to use the skills he or she has acquired through special education. Prejudice against people with disabilities may still foreclose opportunities for the student to show that, although he or she has a disability, he is nonetheless still able.

How can society attack the prejudice? One answer is to use antidiscrimination laws— laws like those that prohibit discrimination based on race or gender. The first such law, enacted in 1975 as an amendment to the Rehabilitation Act, is known as Section 504; the second, enacted in 1990, is called the Americans with Disabilities Act (ADA) (42 U.S.C. §§ 12101–12213). These are fundamentally similar laws.

Persons Protected.   Section 504 of the Rehabilitation Act and ADA both provide that no otherwise qualified individual with a disability shall, solely by reason of his or her disability, be discriminated against in certain realms of American life. Figure 1–9 sets out the meaning of "person with a disability" under Section 504 and ADA. Both laws use basically the same definition.

Section 504 and ADA Coverage.   Section 504 applies to any program or activity receiving federal financial assistance. Because state and local education agencies receive federal funds, they may not discriminate against students or other persons with disabilities on account of their disabilities. Clearly, Section 504 is limited in scope. What if an individual seeks employment from a company that does not receive any federal funds? or wants to participate in state and local government programs that are not federally aided? or wants to have access to telecommunications systems, such as closed captioning for people with hearing impairments? In none of those domains of life will the person receive any protection from Section 504. Instead, ADA comes to the rescue.

ADA extends its civil rights/nondiscrimination protection to the following sectors of American life: private sector employment, transportation, state and local government activities and programs, privately operated businesses that are open to the public ("public accommodations"), and telecommunications.

IDEA, Section 504, and ADA: Overlapping Purposes.   Basically, IDEA and the Rehabilitation Act deal respectively with education and training for employment, while Section 504 and ADA make sure that the students can put their education and training to use (Turnbull, Bateman, & Turnbull, 1993) through the IEP and its transition provisions, as you will learn in Chapter 2. In short, the transition components of the IEP anticipate outcomes that are largely consistent with those that any student—whether one with a disability or not—typically will want: work, education, and opportunities to participate in the community. Those results cannot be achieved as long as there are barriers erected on the foundation of discrimination. These barriers—the deeply rooted discrimination— are the targets of Section 504 and ADA.

The "Insiders" and Their Role.   You may be interested to know the story behind the story about ADA and why and how the insiders in Congress acted as they did. One of its early sponsors was U.S. Senator Lowell Weicker, whose son has mental retardation. When Senator Weicker left the Congress before his version of ADA was enacted, the antidiscrimination battle standard passed to yet another senator who, like Senator Weicker, knew about disability from a family perspective. Senator Tom Harkin, Democrat of Iowa,

FIGURE 1–9 *Definition of "person with a disability" in the Rehabilitation Act*

Section 504 of the Rehabilitation Act and ADA define a person with a disability as one who

- Has a physical or mental impairment that substantially limits one or more of the major life activities of such individual (e.g., traumatic brain injury)

- Has a record of such an impairment (history of cancer that is now in remission)

- Is regarded as having such an impairment (a person who is "wonkish" or especially creative may be regarded as having some emotional disturbances)

Note: A student who has HIV but is not so impaired that he or she needs special education is protected under Section 504 and ADA because the person meets the last two criteria: the person has a history of a disability, and others regard that person as having a disability. The same is true of a person who has attention deficit/hyperactivity disorder. See Chapters 11 and 6, respectively, for discussions of those conditions and the students' rights under IDEA, Section 504, and ADA.

MY VOICE

SENATOR TOM HARKIN SPEAKS OUT IN FAVOR OF ADA

Senator Tom Harkin (D. Iowa), sponsor of ADA, said that the law's promise is that every person with a disability will have a chance to "maximize his or her own potential to live proud, productive, and prosperous lives in the mainstream of our society" and he added, noting that his brother is profoundly deaf, that ADA's spirit is one of welcoming people with disabilities and their families into all of America's communities (Congressional Record, Vol. 136, P. S9689, 13 July 1990).

was the principal sponsor of the bill that eventually was enacted as ADA. Significantly, his brother was born with severe hearing loss, and Senator Harkin grew up understanding, firsthand, the impact of disability on his brother and the entire Harkin family. That is why his comments about ADA, made just before the Senate took its final vote to enact ADA, are so important. They state not just what ADA intends to do, but also its anticipated effects. Senator Harkin's remarks are set out in Box 1-3, "My Voice."

A VISION FOR THE FUTURE

From the day he was born, Danny Ramirez had rights, rights that were the legacies of progressive educators and a civil rights movement. It is one thing to have rights; it is another altogether to benefit from them. Students will benefit if schools develop and carry out policies, procedures, and practices that implement the laws, if they employ professionals who are willing and able to deliver state-of-the-art services, if the professionals use curriculum and methodologies that advance inclusion, and if they collaborate with each other and with parents. How, then, do today's schools and professionals deliver state-of-the-art services? For an answer to that question, let's turn to Chapters 2 and 3.

ᏯᎠ *Senator Tom Harkin sponsored the Americans with Disabilities Act. Here, he says "I love you" in sign language to the ADA's supporters.*

What Do You Think?

- From what you know about Danny and his education, to what extent are IDEA's six principles being reflected in his educational program?

- What would have happened to Danny if his parents had not had the right to due process hearings and appeals in the courts?

- How would Danny "get a life" if he did not have a right to be free of disability discrimination?

- To what extent do you believe inclusion is an appropriate educational arrangement for Danny?

SUMMARY

PROFILE OF SPECIAL EDUCATION STUDENTS AND PERSONNEL

- Nearly 5.5 million students with disabilities were served in America's schools in the 1994–1995 school year.

- Special education also serves gifted and talented students.

- Infants and toddlers in special education are between the ages of birth and three.

- Children and youth in special education are between the ages of three and twenty-one.

- There are ten categories of disabilities under IDEA.

- People-first language is preferred, and labels can be demeaning.

- Minority students are overrepresented in special education.

- Special education personnel include teachers, related service providers, administrators, paraprofessionals, and others.

WHAT ARE THE RESULTS FOR STUDENTS WITH DISABILITIES?

- Students with disabilities face rather dismal prospects after leaving school.

- The dismal results are independence, productivity, and integration.

THREE LEADERS WHO CHANGED SPECIAL EDUCATION

- Lloyd Dunn questioned the efficacy of special education.

- Evelyn Deno proposed a cascade of services.

- James Gallagher proposed individualized contracts between educators and students.

JUDICIAL PRELUDES TO SPECIAL EDUCATION LAW

- Schools practiced two kinds of discrimination, namely, exclusion and misclassification.

- In the early 1970s, federal courts ruled those practices unconstitutional and established students' rights to a free appropriate public education.

IDEA: INTRODUCTION AND ELIGIBILITY

- Passed in 1975 and amended most recently in 1997, IDEA contains three parts: Part A lists findings that show the need for the law, while Part B (for students ages three through twenty-one) and Part C (for students ages birth through two) specify the educational rights of students with disabilities.

- A student must have a disability and need special education and related services to be eligible for rights under IDEA, and age factors further determine those rights.

IDEA: SIX PRINCIPLES

- IDEA has six principles that govern the entire special education enterprise.

- IDEA's six principles are zero reject (a rule against exclusion), nondiscriminatory evaluation (a rule of fair assessment), appropriate education (a rule of individualized benefit), LRE (a presumption in favor of placement in typical programs), procedural due process (a rule of fair dealing and accountability), and parent participation (a rule of shared decision making).

IDEA: FEDERAL FUNDING AND CRITICISMS

- Rights run with revenues, so Congress grants money to states to help them pay for special education services.

- The states get the federal funds only if they agree to comply with the six principles of IDEA.

- As the number of special education students has increased (in absolute terms and relative to the increase in the number of students in general education), the cost of special education also has risen (in absolute and relative terms).

- Schools now perform many of the services that other agencies formerly performed, such as paying for some of the cost of health, mental health, social service, and institutional/hospital services for students with disabilities.

OTHER FEDERAL LAWS: ENTITLEMENTS AND ANTIDISCRIMINATION

- Entitlements are services that students may receive if they meet certain qualification and eligibility standards.

- Two entitlements that students with disabilities have are vocational rehabilitation services and access to assistive technology.

- Federal law prohibits discrimination based solely on a person's disability, so long as a person is able, with reasonable accommodations, to participate in a service or program in spite of the disability.

- Section 504 of the Rehabilitation Act prohibits disability discrimination by recipients of federal funds; ADA prohibits it in nearly every other sector of American life.

RESOURCES

BOOKS

Dictionary of Special Education and Rehabilitation (4th Ed.). (1997). By Glenn A. Vergason & M. L. Anderegg. Denver, CO: Love. This dictionary clearly defines over 2,000 terms in special education and rehabilitation.

Directory of Programs for Preparing Individuals for Careers in Special Education. (1997). By The Council for Exceptional Children. Reston, VA: Author. This book with searchable diskette lists contact and other information for over 600 college and university programs in special education.

Families, Professionals, and Exceptionality: A Special Partnership. (1997). By Ann P. Turnbull & H. Rutherford Turnbull, III. Upper Saddle River, NJ: Merrill/Prentice Hall. This text provides an overview of family systems theory and its application in developing empowering and collaborative relationships with families based on their individual preferences and needs.

Free Appropriate Public Education: The Law and Children with Disabilities (5th Ed.). (1998). By H. Rutherford Turnbull, Ann P. Turnbull, Amy Buchele-Ash, & Kate Rainbolt. Denver, CO: Love. This text includes up-to-date information on case law and statutory techniques, due process, and more regarding the Americans with Disabilities Act and the amended Individuals with Disabilities Education Act.

Negotiating the Special Education Maze: A Guide for Parents and Teachers (3rd Ed.). (1997). By Winifred Anderson, Stephen Chitwood, & Deidre Hayden. Bethesda, MD: Woodbine House. This book guides readers step-by-step in developing a special education program for their child or student.

New Solutions: Reducing Disproportionate Representation of Culturally Diverse Students and Gifted Education. (in press). Edited by Alfredo Artiles & Grace Zamora Durán. Reston, VA: The Council for Exceptional Children. This book offers perspectives on how to address the disproportionate representation of culturally diverse students in special education.

JOURNALS AND MAGAZINES

Exceptional Children. Council for Exceptional Children, 1920 Association Drive, Reston, VA 22091-9810. Articles cover a wide range of research and best-practice issues within the field of special education from infancy through transition to adulthood.

Exceptional Parent. P.O. Box 3000, Department EP, Denville, NJ 07834. A monthly magazine for parents of students with exceptionalities, including current information aimed toward immediate application. It covers issues related to all exceptionalities. The November/December issue each year lists numerous technology resources helpful for parents and professionals.

MULTIMEDIA

The following videos are available at local rental and retail stores:

Born on the 4th of July. (1989, R, U.S., 145 minutes). A veteran becomes a disability activist.

Philadelphia. (1994, PG-13, U.S., 125 minutes). A young lawyer uses the Americans with Disabilities Act to build a case of discrimination after he is fired from his job for having AIDS.

Boyz N the Hood. (1991, R, U.S., color, 107 minutes). A moving account by writer–director John Singleton of the temptations faced by young African American males to join gangs.

Criss Cross. (1992, R, U.S., color, 100 minutes). Goldie Hawn is a single mother trying to bring up a rebellious young son.

Lean on Me. (1989, PG-13, U.S., color, 104 minutes). Morgan Freeman stars as an inner-city principal who brings order to a New Jersey high school.

To Sir, With Love. (1967, not rated, U.K., color, 105 minutes). Sidney Poitier teaches inner-city youth in London how to function in everyday life.

ON-LINE INFORMATION, USEFUL DATABASES, AND SOFTWARE

Disability-Related Sites on the World Wide Web. Internet address: www.thearc.org/misc/dislnkin.html. Sources and links on parenting information and support, directories, disability organizations, assistive technology, commercial disability sites, university-based programs, disability service providers and legislation.

Disability Resources on the Internet. Internet address: disability.com/links/cool.shtml. Offers information on many topics, including careers, government resources and medicine.

MAINSTREAM Online. Internet address: www.mainstream-mag.com. An on-line magazine with leading news, advocacy, and lifestyle information for people with disabilities.

National Information Center for Children and Youth With Disabilities. Internet address: www.nichcy.org. Information and referral center that provides information on disabilities and disability-related issues for families, educators, and other professionals. A focus on children and youth (birth to age twenty-two).

Solutions @ disability.com. Internet address: disability.com/index.html. Links to resources, products, and services that promote active, healthy independent living.

ORGANIZATIONS

Council for Exceptional Children. 1920 Association Drive, Reston, VA 22091-9801. Internet address: www.cec.sped.org/home.htm. The largest professional organization in the field of special education. It provides a wide range of journals, conferences, and printed information.

U.S. Disability Law. Internet address: www.law.cornell.edu/topics/disability.html. Information about laws affecting people with disabilities.

IMPLEMENTING IDEA's PRINCIPLES

Educating
Danny Ramirez

Danny Ramirez declared, at the age of ten, that he wanted to be "a dog doctor, a Dallas Cowboy, or a cop." Four years later, having modified his goals, Danny declared to all who would hear that he wanted to be a dog trainer. He had put football aside; it's enough to play sports with his friends from school. And his inclination toward policing seems to have dropped by the wayside, too. But training animals or being a vet's assistant, or both, are hardly out of reach for this remarkable young man and his equally remarkable family. Why is that so? There are three reasons.

First, the law requires Danny's schools to evaluate his strengths and needs, and to do so in a way that does not discriminate against him. As a member of the Latino community and an individual with a disability, Danny has often faced prejudices and discrimination. Despite the law's safeguards and the fact that, as Carmen puts it, the entire family "swims in the mainstream" and is truly bicultural and bilingual, the Ramirez family has to be on guard against both cultural and economic discrimination.

Because the Ramirezes live in a part of El Paso that is largely populated by culturally and linguistically diverse and low-income citizens, Carmen perceives that their socioeconomic status makes a difference in how Danny and other students are treated in the schools themselves. She therefore, suspects that Danny's mental abilities are not the only barrier he must overcome. "Many of our teachers appear to have low expectations of Mexican American students. The area we live in is regarded as no good, so the kids and parents are regarded that way, too! It's a self-fulfilling prophecy." But the law is on Danny's side. Schools must develop the strengths inherent in *all* students.

The second reason Danny can look forward with confidence to being a dog trainer or a vet's assistant is because school practices have changed. The change reflects the fact that the law entitles him to an appropriate education. An appropriate education is one that benefits him by building on his strengths, responding to his needs, acknowledging his preferences, and providing an education that helps him achieve his preferred outcomes. To do all that, his school has to individualize his education. An education that is custom tailored to Danny takes into account that Danny may need accommodations in his curriculum and specialized services. The combination of a modified general education curriculum, on the one hand, and high expectations for Danny to be employed and to live independently, on the other, are what the law requires. It also is what good educators deliver.

Finally, Danny and his family are justified in expecting that he will attain his goals because of the kind of people they are. They have great expectations for him and they participate actively in his education. Carmen points to the fact that the school

psychologist most in charge of evaluating Danny is, herself, Hispanic American. Carmen was reassured when this psychologist spent a great deal of time taking information from Alfredo, Danny, and herself concerning Danny's social skills, his physical strengths and needs, and his out-of-school activities. So much depends, Carmen notes, on who carries out the law and the degree of sensitivity they bring to their work with students and families.

Yet change comes too slowly for them, and it seems that every change for the better is one that Carmen and Alfredo have to initiate and must lead. The good thing is that the law makes them full-fledged members of the team that has to evaluate Danny and then develop his individualized program on the basis of the evaluation. In this chapter, you will read how parents and schools jointly conduct nondiscriminatory evaluations and develop individualized approaches to teaching Danny and other students with disabilities.

What Do You Think?

1. What is the process initially for deciding whether Danny should receive a formal nondiscriminatory evaluation?

2. What are the purposes of a nondiscriminatory evaluation of students such as Danny, what is the evaluation process, and what standards do educators use in evaluating Danny and other students?

3. What is the meaning of the term *appropriate education* for students with disabilities such as Danny, and what are the student outcomes that an appropriate education should help achieve?

FRAMEWORK FOR IMPLEMENTING IDEA

Chapter 1 introduced you to the values that guide special educators and to the six principles of the Individuals with Disabilities Education Act (IDEA). By way of refreshing your memory, the six values (in Figure 1–1) are

- Envisioning great expectations
- Enhancing positive contributions
- Building on strengths
- Acting on choices
- Expanding relationships
- Ensuring full citizenship

And the six IDEA principles are

- Zero reject (no exclusion)
- Nondiscriminatory evaluation (fair, unbiased evaluation)
- Appropriate education (individualized and accompanied by related services)
- Least restrictive environment (access to general education)
- Procedural due process (checks and balances)
- Parent and student participation (shared decision making)

In this chapter, we focus on IDEA's principles of nondiscriminatory evaluation and appropriate education. As we discuss these two principles, we also connect them to the six values, usually by notes in the margin. Figure 2-1 is a framework showing how the six principles relate to each other. We will refer to this framework throughout this chapter and in other chapters as well. It contains your major guidelines for implementing IDEA.

The legend in Figure 2-1 explains the meaning of the shapes within the figure. The six ovals represent IDEA's six principles: zero reject, nondiscriminatory evaluation, appropriate education, least restrictive placement, due process, and parent and student participation. The oval for zero reject is at the top of Figure 2-1. The next similar oval is for nondiscriminatory evaluation, and so on. Attached by a dotted line to the *right* of each oval/major principle is a hexagon that states the principle's purpose(s). For example, the hexagon attached to the oval for nondiscriminatory evaluation says that there are two purposes for evaluating a student. We will review these purposes in the earliest part of our discussion of each principle, following. Attached by a solid line to the *left* of each oval/major principle is a rectangle that sets out the components of each major principle. We will discuss each of these components after we state the purposes of the principle;

FIGURE 2–1   *The relationships among the six principles of IDEA*

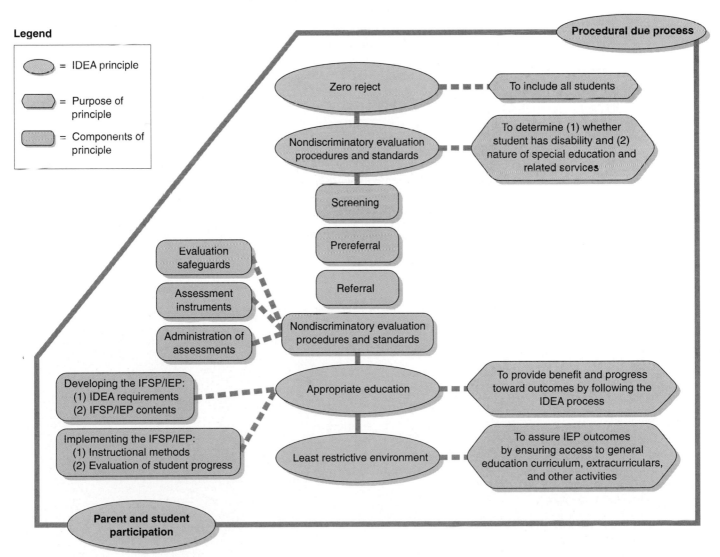

Screening is a routine test that helps school staff identify which students might need further testing to determine whether they qualify for special education.

each component thus becomes the topic of a subsection of the discussion of the principle. In this chapter, we describe how educators implement the two principles of nondiscriminatory evaluation and appropriate education.

NONDISCRIMINATORY EVALUATION: SCREENING, PREREFERRAL, AND REFERRAL

As we point out later, the two purposes of nondiscriminatory evaluation are to (a) determine whether a student has a disability and (b) decide the nature of the special education and related services the student needs. To accomplish these very important purposes, educators typically follow a careful four-step process. Figure 2–2 lists those steps as components of the nondiscriminatory evaluation principle: **screening, prereferral, referral,** and **nondiscriminatory evaluation** procedures and standards. The first three of these four steps are not required by IDEA but are put into place by educators as a matter of good practice or state or local policy. Picture these four steps as a funnel (see Figure 2–2).

Prereferral occurs when a student's general education teacher asks others (educators and families) to help problem solve in order to identify instructional strategies to adequately address learning and behavioral challenges.

The first step, screening, involves all students; it is universal. After screening, the prereferral process involves fewer students, selecting some for further evaluation. Referral and formal nondiscriminatory evaluation involve fewer and fewer students (are more and more selective) as the process moves toward making the most informed decisions about which students have a disability and therefore need special education and related services.

You may ask, "Who does all these procedures? Who makes these decisions?" The answer is that typically a special team in each school coordinates the overall process and identifies the appropriate staff to participate in the process. IDEA specifies the membership on the team that does the formal nondiscriminatory evaluation, but it does not specify who will be involved before the full nondiscriminatory evaluation occurs.

Referral occurs when an educator or a parent submits a formal request for the student to be considered for a full and formal nondiscriminatory evaluation.

Screening

All students enrolled in school routinely receive screening tests. These tests help school staff identify which students might need further testing to determine whether they qualify for special education. Screening tests include group intelligence and achievement tests that can be administered simultaneously to more than one student. Generally, these tests can also be quickly scored, but they can only begin to identify a student's ability and needs. The vision and hearing tests that school nurses routinely administer to students also are screening tests. These tests are not as sensitive or informative as those given by an optometrist or audiologist.

Nondiscriminatory evaluation is a rule requiring schools to evaluate students fairly to determine if they have a disability and, if so, what kind and how extensive a disability they have.

FIGURE 2–2 *Nondiscriminatory evaluation: A funneling process*

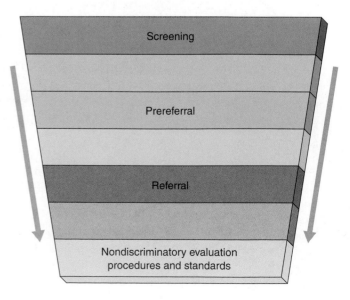

The teams may be called by different names, such as special education committees, multidisciplinary staffing teams, or student study committees. IDEA uses the term *evaluation team* to describe the group that performs the full nondiscriminatory evaluation. We use that term or *nondiscriminatory evaluation team.*

 This student is taking a routine vision test, one form of screening that helps school staff to identify disabilities that can affect children's educational performance.

Babies with significant and usually obvious disabilities are often identified at birth or shortly afterward. If they participate in infant-toddler programs, they are provided nondiscriminatory evaluations and appropriate services. Also, students who have disabilities identifiable at birth, such as Down syndrome (Danny's condition), often do not undergo screening. Because their disabilities are obvious, they are immediately referred for the formal nondiscriminatory evaluation. Finally, many students do not appear to need special education or less intensive accommodations until they enter the second and third or later grades. That is when they begin to struggle academically or socially and when screening can be particularly helpful to them. Screening helps school staff identify whether a student is having difficulties because of some mild or "invisible" impairments, whether a student so identified may benefit from still further evaluation, and whether there may be other causes for their difficulties.

 In Danny's situation, his disability—mental retardation—was diagnosed at birth. He has received numerous evaluations since then.

Prereferral

Prereferral is the second step in the process. It has two purposes: (a) providing immediate and necessary help to teachers who are experiencing challenges in teaching students and (b) guarding against misidentifying students as having disabilities, because misidentification can have serious consequences. Let's focus now on the first purpose: helping teachers and perhaps avoiding referral for the formal nondiscriminatory evaluation.

Prereferral begins when teachers in a general education classroom determine that a particular student is having learning difficulties. Teachers typically explore ways in which

BOX 2-1   INTO PRACTICE

MURRAY ELEMENTARY SCHOOL

Murray Elementary School, located in Albemarle County, Virginia, has a unique approach to problem solving that helps account for its success in addressing the learning needs of all students, as well as the staff development needs of its faculty. Characteristics of Murray's approach include an extremely flexible schedule determined by the teachers; parent, student and staff involvement; and issue-driven meeting agendas.

A central feature of Murray's approach is the school's participatory problem-solving process, known as the CARE Committee. When a student is having difficulty (i.e., reading problems, behavior problems, counseling needs, resource needs, etc.), a teacher will bring the student's problem to the attention of the CARE Committee for discussion by all interested parties, including the parent(s), teachers, principal, and the student when appropriate. The committee reviews areas of concern, interventions tried by the teacher, student strengths and weaknesses, and then develops

assistance strategies. The strategies focus on teacher and parent needs as well as the needs of the student. Tasks are then delegated for implementation of the strategies. The CARE Committee periodically reconvenes to review the student's progress or for further problem solving.

Weekly staff meetings are designed by teachers to meet teacher and student needs. The agendas are based on student/staff issues rather than administrative concerns. The meetings, organized by grade level or across grade level (depending on the issues), provide teachers with opportunities for research, sharing information, training and problem solving.

According to Murray's principal, "We create more solutions to the problems of our kids when we don't view them or treat them as members of a particular special needs category." All of these characteristics add up to creating a school environment focused on the individual needs of all students and teachers—a formula for success when it comes to implementing inclusion.

Note: From *Winning Ways: Creating Inclusive Schools, Classrooms, and Communities* (p. 21) by V. Roach, J. Ascroft, and A. Stamp, 1995, Alexandria, VA: National Association of State Boards of Education. Copyright 1995 by National Association of State Boards of Education.

the student might overcome the learning problems if additional services are provided within the general education classroom.

Teachers' explorations often begin the prereferral process. They do not actually refer a student for a formal nondiscriminatory evaluation. Instead, they call upon their colleagues for assistance. The colleagues from whom they seek help often are members of the school's evaluation team: special educators, school psychologists, guidance counselors, school nurses, or related services providers. Often, the colleagues themselves form a teacher assistance team whose members are selected on the basis of their special ability to help a particular teacher work with a particular student (Fuchs, Fuchs, & Bahr, 1990; Strickland & Turnbull, 1990). One or more of these colleagues may then observe a teacher while he or she works with the student. They may suggest how the teacher can change the curriculum in small ways or how the teacher can deliver it more effectively for that particular student. Through this kind of problem solving, the team may avoid a formal nondiscriminatory evaluation.

Prereferral generally follows the problem-solving process by identifying the nature of the problem, generating a range of alternatives and analyzing each, developing a plan, taking action, and evaluating the action. When schools follow a systematic process that includes these four steps, it is likely that classroom teachers will be able to provide appropriate supplementary aids and services for many students who encounter learning challenges (Fuchs, Fuchs, Bahr, Ferstrom, & Strecker, 1990). In Box 2-1, "Into Practice", you will read about Murray Elementary School in Virginia, which uses participatory problem solving to address the learning needs of all students.

If you were a first-year teacher at Murray Elementary School, what difference do you think the CARE Committee would make in your own ability to provide supplementary aids and services for students with learning and behavioral challenges?

We said earlier that prereferral has two purposes. One, which we just reviewed, is to provide assistance to teachers and students and thereby prevent referral for the nondiscriminatory evaluation. The other is to safeguard against misclassification. This purpose relates to some disturbing facts about the consequences of classification. Referred students are almost always identified as having exceptionalities (Galagan, 1985; Ysseldyke, Reynolds, & Weinburg, 1984). Moreover, once students are identified, about 98 percent are likely to retain the disability label and remain in special education for their entire academic career (Bartoli, 1989). Finally, as you learned in Chapter 1 and as you will understand more fully after you read Chapter 8, students with cultural and linguistic differences are disproportionately identified as having a disability.

For that reason, if for no other, it is extremely important during prereferral to distinguish between cultural and language differences that are inherent in a student's background and learning problems that are not. Figure 2–3 identifies multicultural issues the prereferral process should take into account. When students from culturally and linguistically diverse backgrounds are involved in the prereferral process, bilingual and English-as-a-second-language teachers should be part of the evaluation team (Baca & Almanza, 1991). Indeed, the 1997 amendments to IDEA prohibit schools from classifying into special education any students who have experienced a lack of instruction in reading or math or who have limited English proficiency. Because of this restriction, it is all the more important for the prereferral process to determine whether students' challenges arise from a disability or from cultural or linguistic differences.

Referral

Sometimes, prereferral is sufficient to assist teachers and students in overcoming any learning challenges that the teacher and colleagues have identified and addressed. Sometimes, however, it is not. In that case, the teacher (or another member of the prereferral team) usually moves to the third step in the process by submitting a formal written request for a student to receive a full and formal nondiscriminatory evaluation. Typically, the evaluation is carried out at the school building level by the evaluation team. The team usually sets the criteria that teachers must follow in making referrals to it and oversees the entire referral and evaluation process. It carries out these two duties by using a referral form that typically asks for specific and comprehensive information about the student, including

- Basic screening information

- Areas of educational concerns that prompted the prereferral intervention

- The nature of the prereferral intervention and the results that were achieved

- Any concerns expressed by the student or the student's family (e.g., loneliness, self-esteem)

The referral form may require more information than is covered by these four categories, especially since, as you will soon learn, the 1997 amendments to IDEA now require the student's evaluation to be far more comprehensive than in the past.

NONDISCRIMINATORY EVALUATION

As we have pointed out earlier, students are formally referred for a nondiscriminatory evaluation to answer two key questions:

1. Does the student have a disability?

2. If so, what is the nature of the specially designed instruction and related services that the student needs?

Experiential Background

- Are there any factors in the student's school history that may be related to the current difficulty?
  - Attendance/mobility
  - Opportunities to learn
  - Program placement(s)
  - Quality of prior instruction

- Are there any variables related to family history that may have affected school performance?
  - Lifestyle
  - Length of residence in the U.S.
  - Stress (e.g., poverty, lack of emotional support)

- Are there any variables related to the student's medical history that may have affected school performance?
  - Vision
  - Nutrition
  - Illness
  - Hearing
  - Trauma or injury

Culture

- How is the student's cultural background different from the culture of the school and larger society? (Mattes & Omark, 1984; Saville-Troike, 1978)
  - Family (family size and structure, roles, responsibilities, expectations)
  - Aspirations (success, goals)
  - Language and communication (rules for adult, adult–child, child–child communication, language use at home, nonverbal communication)
  - Religion (dietary restrictions, role expectations)
  - Traditions and history (contact with homeland, reason for immigration)
  - Decorum and discipline (standards for acceptable behavior)

- To what extent are the student's characteristics representative of the larger group?
  - Continuum of culture (traditional, dualistic, atraditional [Ramírez & Castañeda, 1974])

- Is the student able to function successfully in more than one cultural setting?

- Is the student's behavior culturally appropriate?

Language Proficiency

- Which is the student's dominant language? Which is the preferred?
  - Settings (school, playground, home, church, etc.)
  - Topics (academic subjects, day-to-day interactions)
  - Speakers (parents, teachers, siblings, peers, etc.)
  - Aspects of each language (syntax, vocabulary, phonology, use)
  - Expressive versus receptive

- What is the student's level of proficiency in the primary language and in English? (Cummins, 1984)
  - Interpersonal communication skills

- Cognitive/academic literacy-related skills
- Are the styles of verbal interaction used in the primary language different from those most valued at school, in English? (Heath, 1986)
  - Label quests (e.g., What's this? Who?)
  - Meaning quests (adult infers for child, interprets or asks for explanation)
  - Accounts (generated by teller, information new to listener; e.g., show and tell, creative writing)
  - Eventcasts (running narrative on events as they unfold, or forecast of events in preparation)
  - Stories
- If so, has the student been exposed to those that are unfamiliar?
- What is the extent and nature of exposure to each language?
  - What language(s) do the parents speak to each other?
  - What language(s) do the parents speak to the child?
  - What language(s) do the children use with each other?
  - What television programs are seen in each language?
  - Are stories read to the child? In what language(s)?
- Are student behaviors characteristic of second language acquisition?
- What types of language intervention has the student received?
  - Bilingual versus monolingual instruction
  - Language development, enrichment, remediation
  - Additive versus subtractive bilingualism (transition versus maintenance)

Learning Style

- Does the student's learning style require curricular/instructional accommodation?
  - Perceptual style differences (e.g., visual versus auditory learner)
  - Cognitive style differences (e.g., inductive versus deductive thinking)
  - Preferred style of participation (e.g., teacher versus student directed, small versus large group)
- If so, were these characteristics accommodated, or were alternative styles taught?

Motivational Influences

- Is the student's self-concept enhanced by school experiences?
  - School environment communicates respect for culture and language
  - Student experiences academic and social success
- Is schooling perceived as relevant and necessary for success in the student's family and community?
  - Aspirations
  - Realistic expectations based on community experience
  - Culturally different criteria for success
  - Education perceived by the community as a tool for assimilation

Note: From "Preventing Inappropriate Referrals of Language Minority Students to Special Education" by S. Garcia and A. Ortiz, 1988, *New Focus, 5,* p. 7. Copyright 1988 by The National Clearinghouse for Bilingual Education. Reprinted with permission.

Under IDEA, nondiscriminatory evaluation is full and formal. It is full in the sense that it consists of many different procedures, and it is formal in the sense that it must conform to certain standards.

There is a great deal of complexity surrounding IDEA's nondiscriminatory evaluation requirements. For one thing, the procedures and standards that professionals must follow are highly detailed and specific. They deserve your careful attention because, if you or your colleagues do not comply with them, you may put a student into or out of special education who should not be so classified. You may also classify a student as having one type of exceptionality when in fact the student has another. IDEA mandates procedures and standards that are safeguards against misclassification.

Still another matter adds to the complexity of nondiscriminatory evaluation. The very nature of testing and what it can and cannot tell educators is controversial.

FIGURE 2–4 *Nondiscriminatory evaluation safeguards*

The nondiscriminatory evaluation procedures and standards include the following:

Breadth of the Assessment

• Include more than one test, since no single procedure may be used as the sole basis of evaluation.

• Use a variety of assessment tools and strategies to gather relevant functional and developmental information for determining whether the student has a disability and the content of the IEP, including how the student can be involved in and progress in the general curriculum.

• Assess the relative contribution of cognitive, behavioral, physical, or developmental factors.

• Assess in all areas related to the suspected disability, including health, vision, hearing, social and emotional status, general intelligence, academic performance, communicative status, and motor abilities.

• Assess specific areas of the student's educational need, and do not rely on a single IQ score.

Administration of the Assessment Procedures

• Are selected and administered so as not to be discriminatory on a racial or cultural basis.

• Are validated for the specific purposes for which they are used (later in this chapter, you will be introduced to issues related to validation).

• Are selected and administered so as to best ensure that, when administered to a student with sensory, manual, or speaking impairments, the results accurately reflect the student's aptitude or achievement level or whatever factors they purport to measure; must not reflect the student's sensory, manual, or speaking impairments unless the test or procedures themselves purport to measure skills in those areas.

• Are administered in the student's native language or other mode of communication (e.g., Braille or signing for students with visual or hearing impairments).

• Are administered by trained personnel in conformance with instructions by the producer of the tests or material.

• Are accompanied by a review of existing evaluation data, including evaluations and information provided by parents, current classroom-based assessments and observations, and observations from teachers and related services providers.

• Identify what additional data are needed to determine

  Whether the student has a disability or, in case of a reevaluation, whether the student continues to have such a disability

To sort out these matters, we discuss (a) nondiscriminatory evaluation procedures and standards, (b) assessment instruments, and (c) administration of nondiscriminatory assessments. Figure 2–1 highlights these topics in the rectangles attached to the left of the nondiscriminatory evaluation oval.

Nondiscriminatory Evaluation Procedures and Standards

Because evaluation has such a significant impact on students and their families, IDEA surrounds the evaluation process with procedural safeguards, described in Figure 2–4. Because the **evaluation team** must reflect certain types of expertise in order to ensure that the evaluation is correctly performed and interpreted, IDEA also specifies who must be on the team. As you will note, these individuals individually and collectively represent

Evaluation team is the IDEA term referring to the team responsible for administering a nondiscriminatory evaluation to determine if the student qualifies for special education.

The student's present levels of performance and educational needs

Whether the student needs special education and related services, or in the case of a reevaluation, whether the student continues to need special education and related services

Whether any additions or modifications to special education and related services are needed so the student can meet IEP annual goals and participate in the general curriculum

Timing of the Assessment

- Nondiscriminatory evaluation occurs before initial placement into or out of special education.

- Reevaluation occurs every three years or more frequently if conditions warrant or if requested by the student's parent or teacher.

Parental Notice and Consent

- Parents must be fully informed and provide written consent before each evaluation and reevaluation.

- Before any reevaluation, consent is required unless the school can demonstrate that it has taken reasonable measures to obtain consent and parents have failed to respond.

- Parents must receive a full explanation of all due process rights, a description of what the school proposes or refuses to do, each evaluation procedure that was used, and any other factors that influenced the decisions.

- Parent consent for evaluation is not parent consent for placement into or out of a special education program; separate consent is required for placement.

Interpretation of Assessment Information

- Draw upon and carefully consider a wide variety of information sources, including aptitude and achievement tests, teacher recommendations, physical status, social or cultural background, and adaptive behavior.

- The interpretation must be made by a group of persons consisting of educators and parents.

- Refuse to determine that the student has a disability if the determining factor is the student's lack of instruction in reading or math or limited English proficiency.

a wide range of competencies and thus are another important safeguard. Under the 1997 amendments to IDEA, the evaluation team must consist of

- The student's parents

- At least one general education teacher of the student, if the student is or may be participating in the general education environment

- At least one special education teacher or (where appropriate) a provider of special education to the student

- A representative of the school district who is (a) qualified to provide or supervise specially designed instruction to meet the unique needs of students with disabilities, (b) knowledgeable about general curriculum, and (c) knowledgeable about the availability of local educational resources

- An individual who can interpret the instructional implications of evaluation results (who may already be a member of the team)

- At the parents' or school's discretion, other individuals who have knowledge or special expertise (including related services personnel), and the student (when appropriate)

Assessment Instruments

The terminology related to the nondiscriminatory evaluation process can be confusing. **Assessment** refers to the specific instruments used to gather information and usually includes standardized and nonstandardized tests; the student's cumulative records and work products; and teacher and other observations of the student in the classroom, other school environments, and even outside the school (Overton, 1992). **Evaluation** refers to the interpretation of information secured through assessment.

There are many different kinds of tests. The types of tests the evaluation team decides to administer depend on the student's suspected exceptionality. In later chapters, you will learn about many different kinds of tests. Two types of frequently used tests are **norm-referenced tests** and **criterion-referenced tests.** These tests have different purposes and characteristics.

Norm-Referenced Tests.
Norm-referenced tests compare a student with his or her age- or grade-level peers and have two purposes: to help to determine whether a student has a disability and to assess various skills. These tests are standardized, which means they are administered, scored, and interpreted the same way each time they are given. The tester compares the student's score on a specific test to scores made by a sample of peers—called the *normative sample,* or *norm group.* The normative sample is a group of students chosen randomly to represent the entire population to decide if the student's score is at, above, or below the performance of students who are the same age or grade.

All norm-referenced tests have two criteria: **reliability** and **validity.** *Reliability* refers to how consistently a test yields similar results across time and among raters. If a particular test is given at several different times to different students and is administered and scored by different people and if the test questions do not change, the test is reliable if the raters basically agree on the scores of the test takers.

Validity refers to how well the test measures what it says it measures. A test is valid when it accurately measures one or more of a student's skills or needs, such as the capacity to see, hear, talk, reason, remember, or conform to certain standards of behavior.

Evaluators frequently administer norm-referenced intelligence, achievement, developmental, motor, adaptive behavior, creativity, and behavior tests. Classifying a student as having an exceptionality shall not be made on the sole basis of an IQ score (see Figure 2–4). There must be more than one procedure, and the assessment must be broad-based. Because intelligence tests are given to nearly every student who is being evaluated for

Assessment refers to the specific instruments used to gather information and usually includes standardized and nonstandardized tests; the student's cumulative records and work products; and teacher and other observations of the student in the classroom, other school environments, and even outside the school.

Evaluation refers to the interpretation of information secured through assessment.

Norm-referenced tests compare a student with his or her age- or grade-level peers and have two purposes: to help to determine whether a student has an exceptionality and to assess various skills.

Criterion-referenced tests determine whether a student has mastered a particular skill; thus, these tests compare a student to a standard of mastery.

Reliability refers to how consistently a test yields similar results across time and among raters.

Validity refers to how well the test measures what it says it measures.

special education purposes, we introduce you to those tests at this point of the book. Throughout Chapters 4 to 16, you will learn about other norm-referenced tests.

Intelligence Tests.   Often—indeed, almost always—a nondiscriminatory evaluation uses a norm-referenced test to measure intelligence. You learned in Chapter 1 that students from culturally and linguistically diverse backgrounds are disproportionately classified as having exceptionalities and that legal claims of racial and cultural bias have been raised. These issues highlight questions about the nature of testing and intelligence (you may recall that you read about these matters in connection with the *Larry P. v. Riles* (1984) and *PASE v. Hannon* (1980) cases in Chapter 1).

What do IQ tests really measure? Intelligence tests generally measure a sample of a student's performance on tasks related to reasoning, memory, learning, comprehension, and a student's ability to learn academic skills (Day & Borkowski, 1987). Based on the student's performance, the evaluation team typically *infers* from the test responses the student's intellectual capacity.

Intelligence tests yield an intelligence quotient (IQ) that is a ratio of the student's mental age to his or her chronological age. IQ = MA (mental age) ÷ CA (chronological age) × 100. If a student has a mental age of twelve years as measured on an IQ test and a chronological age of ten years, then the student's IQ would compute as 12 ÷ 10 × 100, or 120.

The **bell-shaped curve** in Figure 2–5 shows below-average, average, and above-average ranges of intelligence on the Wechsler Intelligence Scale for Children—III (Wechsler, 1991). Note that 50 percent of students at any particular age average an IQ below 100 and 50 percent average an IQ at or above 100. Most states identify students with IQ at or above 130 as gifted (see Chapter 7), and those who have IQs below 70 as having mental retardation if they also meet other criteria (see Chapters 8 and 9).

A student's performance sample on an IQ test is influenced by the child's cultural experiences. Testing experts explain:

> . . . *we could ask a child to identify the seasons of the year. The experiences available in children's environments are reflected in the way they respond to this item. Children from central Illinois, who experience four discernibly different climatic conditions, may well respond, "summer, fall, winter, and spring." Children from central Pennsylvania, who also experience four discernibly different climatic conditions but who live in an environment where hunting is prevalent, often respond, "Buck season, doe season, rabbit season, and squirrel season." Response differences are a function of experiential differences. Within specific cultures, both responses are logical and appropriate; only one is scored as correct. (Salvia & Ysseldyke, 1985, p. 148)*

A **bell-shaped curve** depicts the normal distribution of a characteristic (e.g., intelligence) in the general population.

What answer do you think Pacific Islanders might give to the question about seasons? What about Native Alaskans?

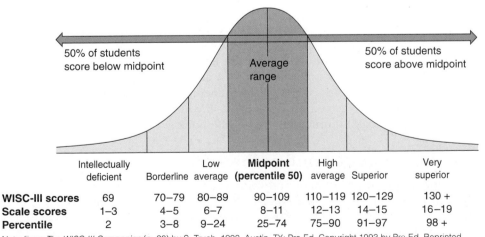

FIGURE 2–5 *Ranges of intelligence*

	Intellectually deficient	Borderline	Low average	Midpoint (percentile 50)	High average	Superior	Very superior
WISC-III scores	69	70–79	80–89	90–109	110–119	120–129	130 +
Scale scores	1–3	4–5	6–7	8–11	12–13	14–15	16–19
Percentile	2	3–8	9–24	25–74	75–90	91–97	98 +

Note: From *The WISC-III Companion* (p. 30) by S. Truch, 1993, Austin, TX: Pro-Ed. Copyright 1993 by Pro-Ed. Reprinted with permission.

In addition to cultural influences, a number of problems arise when administering intelligence tests to students with exceptionalities, including

- The normative sample on whom the test scoring is based often does not include students with disabilities (Sigafoos, Cole, & McQuarter, 1987).

- Some students are unable to respond to test items because of specific impairments (Salvia & Ysseldyke, 1995).

- Some items require academic knowledge that the students have not yet been taught (Evans, 1991).

- Students are given a test version for younger students, with the result that the test norms do not apply.

- Students lack the attention span to focus on what they are being asked to do.

- A gap exists between the sample of performance that the test provides and the instructional decision making that the evaluators and other professionals have to make about how to provide the student with an appropriate education (Day & Hall, 1987).

Although, as we have noted, IQ tests are typically given for the purpose of identifying whether or not a student has an exceptionality, some teachers and parents often complain that IQ tests give very limited information on the second purpose, which is to determine the nature of special education and related services that the student needs. That is why IDEA requires additional testing and why Carmen and Alfredo Ramirez are justified in their opinion:

All of the formal instruments and assessments of IQ are just . . . well, they're just not all that useful. They haven't translated easily into strategies for teaching him or into modifications of the general education curriculum. They only identify how "retarded" he is, and we already know that.

Criterion-Referenced Tests.   Criterion-referenced tests determine whether a student has mastered a particular skill. They compare a student to a standard of mastery. Unlike norm-referenced tests, criterion-referenced tests do not assess how a student performs in comparison to his or her peers. Instead, they assess how well a student performs on a test of a particular skill. Thus, they typically are more helpful than norm-referenced tests for determining a student's educational needs and special education programming and placement. Table 2–1 lists some of the differences between norm-referenced and criterion-referenced tests.

Summary of Tests   Having learned that there are norm-referenced and criterion-referenced tests, you will continue to add to your knowledge about many specific tests that fall under these two categories. You will also learn about some methods of assessment that cannot be classified as either a norm-referenced or a criterion-referenced test. Table 2–2 introduces you to the various assessment instruments that will be described in Chapters 4 to 16. As you will note as you review Table 2–2, your knowledge of assessment instruments will greatly expand throughout each of the book's chapters.

Administration of Nondiscriminatory Assessments

In this section, you will learn about three aspects of nondiscriminatory evaluation that are involved in the administration of tests, namely, (a) the alleged cultural and linguistic bias of some tests, (b) parental input on the evaluation team, and (c) the completion of assessment data and the process of making evaluation decisions.

Dimension	NRT	CRT
Average number of students who get an item right	50%	80%
Compares a student's performance to	The performance of other students.	Standards indicative of mastery.
Breadth of content sampled	Broad, covers many objectives.	Narrow, covers a few objectives
Comprehensiveness of content sampled	Shallow, usually one or two items per objective.	Comprehensive, usually three or more items per objective.
Variability	Since the meaningfulness of a norm-referenced score basically depends on the relative position of the score in comparison with other scores, the more variability or spread of scores, the better.	The meaning of the score does not depend on comparison with other scores: It flows directly from the connection between the items and the criterion. Thus, variability may be minimal.
Item construction	Items are chosen to promote variance or spread. Items that are "too easy" or "too hard" are avoided. One aim is to produce good "distractor options."	Items are chosen to reflect the criterion behavior. Emphasis is placed upon identifying the domain of relevant responses.
Reporting and interpreting considerations	Percentile rank and standard scores used (relative rankings)	Number succeeding or failing or range of acceptable performance used (e.g., 90% proficiency achieved, or 80% of class reached 90% proficiency).

Note: From *Educational Testing and Measurement: Classroom Application and Practice* (5th ed., p. 33) by Tom Kubiszyn and Gary Borich, 1996, New York: HarperCollins. Copyright 1996 by HarperCollins College Publishers. Reprinted with permission of Addison Wesley Educational Publishers, Inc.

Cultural and Linguistic Bias. Special education leaders from culturally and linguistically diverse backgrounds have argued that students from those same backgrounds are at an unfair disadvantage because bias and differential treatment may occur in the evaluation process (Artiles & Trent, 1994; Harry, 1992; Harry, Grenot-Scheyer, et al., 1995). They encourage using assessment procedures of a broader scope than those that have traditionally been used in special education. For example, Harry, Allen, and McLaughlin (1995) encourage educators to (a) replace long-term predictions of achievement with short-term predictions, (b) stop relying on knowledge previously accumulated about the student from potentially biased evaluations, (c) begin focusing on observed learning and problem solving, and (d) tie assessment to curriculum goals and objectives.

To comply with IDEA and address concerns about cultural and linguistic bias, the evaluation team must consider formal assessments as well as informal information, such as the student's educational history, the student's cultural base, the teacher's instructional style, the student's preferences, the student's classroom environment, and information on how the student compares to other students in the same grade or class (Strickland & Turnbull, 1990). One technique for taking such a broad view of the student and mitigating some of the bias that may occur in standardized tests and the way they are administered and scored is to conduct a **portfolio assessment.** For example, Danny's portfolio assessment

Portfolio assessment is a technique for assembling exemplars of a student's work, such as homework, in-class tests, artwork, journal, and other evidence of the student's strengths and needs.

TABLE 2–2 ❧ *Highlighted assessment instruments commonly used for students with exceptionalities*

Chapter	Assessment Tools	Description	Uses
4: Learning Disabilities	a. individualized achievement tests b. curriculum-based assessment	a. standardized tests that evaluate current skills in one or more academic areas b. formal or informal tests that evaluate student progress in a particular curriculum	a. frequently used during nondiscriminatory evaluation for students who are gifted or have disabilities; useful for determining discrepancy between ability and achievement for students with learning disabilities b. useful for on-going evaluation of students who have giftedness or a disability in their current academic, behavioral, social, or functional curricula
5: Emotional or Behavioral Disorders	a. behavior rating scales b. direct observation c. applied behavior analysis	a. formal or informal measures that require someone familiar with the student to rate to what degree particular behaviors are displayed b. a method of recording specific behaviors that occur during observation c. graphs occurrences of specific behaviors	a. essential for identification of students with emotional or behavioral disorders; useful for determining behavior problems in students with other exceptionalities as well b. essential for identification of students with all exceptionalities; useful also for planning interventions for students with emotional or behavioral disorders c. allows professionals to graph student progress toward specific academic, behavioral, social, or functional goals
6: Attention-Deficit/ Hyperactivity Disorder	a. attention-deficit/hyperactivity disorder scales b. Wechsler Intelligence Scale for Children (WISC III) c. continuous performance tests	a. rating scales specifically designed to measure AD/HD b. includes a Freedom from Distractibility Scale that may suggest AD/HD c. students indicate when they see particular patterns of numbers or figures on the computer	a. useful for identifying specific subtypes of AD/HD the student has and for targeting behaviors for intervention b. the WISC III is the most commonly used intelligence test for identifying students with various exceptionalities c. can determine difficulties with attention and/or memory
7: Giftedness	a. creativity tests b. product evaluation c. process or reflective evaluation	a. measure original thinking b. includes standardized teacher-made pretests and posttests to measure knowledge of content c. includes portfolio assessment—gathering student work products for a specified period of time and holding conferences with the student to discuss progress	a. important for identifying a specific type of giftedness and for identifying an inherent strength for some students with disabilities b. essential to evaluate the progress of students with all exceptionalities who must master academic content c. beneficial for writing and establishing progress toward specific objectives for students with various exceptionalities

Chapter	Assessment Tools	Description	Uses
8: Mental Retardation	a. adaptive behavior scales b. self-determination scales	a. ratings scales completed by someone knowledgeable about the student; raters rank the student on functional skills such as language development, independent functioning, and prevocational skills b. determines extent to which student demonstrates skills in four domains of self-determination	a. essential for establishing that a person has mental retardation; also useful for planning functional curricular needs b. essential for determining instructional level in a self-determination curriculum
9: Severe and Multiple Disabilities	a. APGAR scales b. developmental assessment c. ecological assessment d. behavior states assessment e. action plan assessment	a. screens children at birth on a scale that may indicate risk for disabilities b. compares student progress toward developmental skills achieved at specific ages by young children without disabilities c. evaluates which conditions in the student's environment encourage or limit the likelihood of skill development d. identifies specific times students with severe disabilities are most aware and responsive e. group consensus of student strengths, preferences, and needs	a. infant may be at risk for mild or severe and multiple disabilities b. may be especially useful in early intervention programs for students with exceptionalities c. important to obtain for student with any exceptionality for whom environmental factors might be affecting progress toward objectives d. essential for finding periods when students with severe disabilities might be most accessible for stimulation and learning e. useful for establishing a support network and for setting long-range goals for students with various exceptionalities
10: Autism	a. autism-specific scales b. functional assessment	a. rating scales that allow person knowledgeable of the student to rank student on behaviors associated with autism b. determining what contributing conditions occur before, during, and after a targeted behavior	a. useful for identifying presence of autism and for selecting behaviors to target for intervention b. important for improving the likelihood that specific behaviors will or will not occur for students with various exceptionalities
11: Health Impairments	a. medical evaluation b. medical history	a. physician assesses student to identify condition and determine specific limitations and needs b. information collected into one report during the assessment process; includes anecdotal information from parents and information from previous school records and physician evaluations	a. essential for all students with health impairments, physical disabilities, and any other exceptionalities that may have a medical component b. essential for establishing appropriate accommodations and objectives for students with any exceptionality that may have a medical component
12: Physical Disabilities	mobility assessment	generally assessed by occupational and/or physical therapists; determines limitations and needs in movement	may also be essential for some students with severe and multiple disabilities

continued

TABLE 2–2   *continued*

Chapter	Assessment Tools	Description	Uses
13: Brain Injury	a. coma scales b. neurological examination c. scanning instruments d. cognitive processing tests	a. provide some information about probable outcome of disability b. neurologist determines extent of disability and possible outcome c. technology, such as EEGs, MRIs, CAT scans, etc., reveal extent of brain injury d. assesses memory, attention, information-processing and problem-solving skills	a. essential for students who experience coma b. essential for students with brain injury; may be useful for students with other types of physical or health-related disabilities c. essential for students with brain injury; may be useful for students with other types of physical or health-related disabilities d. essential for ongoing assessment of students with brain injury; may yield useful information for students with AD/HD or learning disabilities
14: Communication Disorders	a. speech and language tests b. oral-muscular functioning	a. standardized tests that evaluate student skills and limitations in articulation/phonology, language samples, receptive language, and expressive language b. determines physical limitations that might interfere with speech production	a. essential for students with various disabilities that might contribute to impairments in speech and/or language; essential for planning intervention for students who qualify b. essential to determine if medical or physical therapy intervention is needed
15: Hearing Loss	a. audiological assessment b. aural habilitation	a. an audiogram reveals what levels of frequency and intensity of sounds the student can and cannot identify b. identification of residual hearing	a. essential for identification of students with suspected hearing loss b. essential to establish curriculum, including communication training, that makes effective use of residual hearing
16: Blindness and Low Vision	a. ophthomological assessment b. functional vision evaluation c. orientation and mobility evaluation d. learning media assessment	a. ophthomologist conducts tests to determine vision limitations b. determines how student uses residual vision in task performance c. ascertains how student is able to orient in the environment and travel to desired locations d. determines appropriate reading media for student use	a. essential for identifying students as having blindness or low vision b. essential for planning appropriate curriculum and orientation training c. needed for determining goals and objectives d. needed to determine students' approaches, tactual or visual, to new situations or environments, the nature and stability of eye condition, and students' visual stamina and motivation

assembles his homework, in-class tests, and other tangible evidence of his strengths and needs. Taken together, these types of documents can give a profile of Danny on a day-to-day, week-to-week basis and in the context of his school and home life. Carmen and Alfredo like this approach: "It's a good way to get germane information, information that can really help Danny. It shows what he does most of the time and how well he does it. That's useful."

Parental Input on the Evaluation Team.   As we have already pointed out, IDEA requires the evaluation team to consist of professionals, parents, and even students, especially when they reach the age of majority. IDEA also provides that parents have the right to submit and require the evaluation team to consider evaluation and information that they themselves initiate or provide. Parents provide invaluable information about the student's strengths and needs and help clarify test results, possibly avoiding cultural bias and inappropriate conclusions. In particular, parents may contribute to an education by

- Sharing their family story

- Stating their own and their child's preferences, great expectations, strengths, and needs

- Helping to administer nonstandardized assessment

- Collecting samples of student's work in a folder

- Sharing their own and the student's priorities, resources, and concerns (Turnbull & Turnbull, 1997)

Compiling Assessment Data and Making Evaluation Decisions.   Typically, professionals on the evaluation team who administer assessment instruments compile a written report describing the tests and their results or findings. All team members (including parents) also review and document their consideration of anecdotal records, work products, and findings from direct observations of the student in the classroom or other school settings and in places outside of school. At the team meeting, each member reports what the test, other data, or observations revealed about the student.

Danny, for example, has been evaluated many times. His most recent evaluation in 1995 was the three-year reevaluation required by IDEA, and it was a fairly standard evaluation. The team administered an intelligence test and two achievement tests to Danny. He also underwent an assessment of his **adaptive behavior**—his ability to behave in the same way as peers his age who do not have disabilities.

After considering all the information secured in the evaluation process, the team responds to the first purpose of nondiscriminatory evaluation: It decides whether the student has a disability and is therefore eligible for special education and related services (see Figure 2-1).

If the student does not have a disability and is ineligible for special education for students with disabilities, the team must give the parents the required notice of ineligibility (see Figure 1-7 for the contents of that notice). A determination of ineligibility means that the student remains in the general education classroom without special education services.

If the team answers the first question of nondiscriminatory evaluation (Does the student have a disability?) in the affirmative, it then proceeds to the second question (If so, what is the nature of the specially designed instruction and related services that the student needs?).

To answer the second question, the evaluation team uses the information to determine what kind of special education and related services the student should receive. This step of the decision-making process focuses on the student's specific educational needs and connects the evaluation process to the schools' duty to provide an appropriate education and access to the general curriculum. Figure 2-1 depicts this connection. You will see this second purpose of nondiscriminatory evaluation illustrated in Figure 2-1 in the hexagon on the right of the oval for nondiscriminatory evaluation procedures and standards.

One of the most challenging times for many families is the initial diagnosis of their child as having a disability (Turnbull & Turnbull, 1997). Parents are often unfamiliar with special education terminology, do not know about community resources, and worry about the implications for the future. An extremely helpful resource, to which you can refer parents, is the Parent to Parent program. Currently, nearly 20,000 families receive services from approximately 400 Parent to Parent programs (Santelli, Turnbull, Marquis, & Lerner,

Parents also can tell professionals whether they have great expectations for their children (professionals should encourage those expectations), and then professionals can connect the evaluation to the expectations. Remember that IDEA declares that high expectations are among the solutions to disappointing outcomes for students with disabilities.

Adaptive behavior represents skill areas that are central to successful life functioning, such as communication, self-care, home living, and social skills.

In each of the chapters that follow, you will learn about the criteria used to determine whether the student has a particular exceptionality (disability or special gifts and talents) and, if so, how extensive the exceptionality is.

MY VOICE

Speaking out on Parent to Parent

"Parent to Parent has been my lifeline. When I first heard the diagnosis, I was devastated. . . . It was only when I finally connected with another parent through the Parent to Parent program that I could begin to hope for a future for us all. My veteran parent was gently there for me whenever I needed her."

* * *

"Even though I have received lots of information about autism from many different professionals, until I connected with Parent to Parent, I had not had an opportunity to talk to another parent who shared my experiences, my frustrations, and, yes, my special joys. I felt very alone with my feeling."

* * *

"For us, the scariest part of being a family for Mark is that there are so many unknowns—for him and for us. Will he be able to make himself understood by using a communication board? Will he have friends who accept him as he is? Will a quality educational program be available for him in our community? How much will our insurance pay for his upcoming surgery'? Who can we talk to when we are 'down'? Will Mark ever be able to live and work on his own? Who will look after him when we can no longer do so?"

* * *

"Being directly involved with a veteran parent has given me desired and necessary information on how to best plan for my child's emotional and educational development, and how to facilitate all facets (medical, educational, and emotional) of her development. Without this contact, I would be lost in a confused model of misinformation! I highly recommend this experience to all parents for the emotional and informational support for their child."

* * *

"Ours is an informal program, and the phone is used a lot to discuss problems or to relay good information between families. I think one of the most important things is to be there either physically or by phone when parents need someone to talk to. Listening is very important! Offering optimism is equally important."

1993). Parent to Parent programs are developed and run by volunteer parents. They match a veteran parent, who has successfully faced challenges associated with disability, with a new parent, who is just beginning to deal with various challenges. These challenges may be associated with the initial identification of a child as having a disability; however, Parent to Parent matches are made on the basis of other challenges, such as being part of an inclusion program, learning to use a motorized wheelchair, and/or graduating from high school and needing to find employment. The matching usually occurs soon after the child is identified as having a disability. The program offers someone to provide emotional support, information about disabilities and community resources, and assistance with referrals. "My Voice," Box 2-2, highlights what parents say about the kinds of supports they have received through Parent to Parent. In the resource list at the end of the chapter, you will find information on how you can obtain a catalog that provides a national listing of programs. We encourage you, as a teacher, to contact the program near you and refer parents to this helpful resource.

In each of the chapters that focus on a particular exceptionality (Chapters 4 to 16), you will learn about an assessment procedure that is particularly appropriate for determining that the student has a disability and another assessment procedure for determining the nature of special education and related services. By highlighting in each chapter one example of each type of assessment, we introduce you to a broad range of assessment procedures. As you will learn, many assessment procedures are appropriate for more than one exceptionality. For example, in Chapter 10 you will learn about functional assessment as an appropriate procedure for determining the nature of special education and related services appropriate for a student with autism. Functional assessment is also appropriate to use with students with any other type of disability.

Once the evaluation team has determined that a student has a disability (or is especially gifted), and once it has also determined what kind of special education and related services the student needs, IDEA requires educators to provide the student with that kind of education and those services. In short, the nondiscriminatory evaluation leads to and is the very foundation of the student's appropriate education. In the next section, you will learn how the evaluation guides educators in developing individualized (appropriate education) plans.

APPROPRIATE EDUCATION

Enrolling Danny in school (zero reject) and evaluating his strengths and needs (nondiscriminatory evaluation) do not ensure that his education will provide benefit and progress toward the outcomes of independence, productivity, and inclusion in society. That is why IDEA gives Danny and every other student in special education the right to an individually appropriate education, as set out in each student's individualized educational plan. We encourage you to look back at Figure 2-1. Locate the oval on appropriate education, note its location as an outcome of nondiscriminatory evaluation, and scan the two rectangles on the left of the oval. These state the components that will be highlighted in this chapter: developing the individualized family services plan (IFSP) and individualized education program (IEP) and implementing the IFSP/IEP.

Developing the IFSP/IEP

IDEA Requirements. To guide you through the IDEA appropriate education requirements, we will discuss (a) age-specific provisions, (b) the participants who develop the IFSP/IEP, (c) the contents of IFSP/IEPs, and (d) timelines.

Age-Specific Provisions. *Infants and toddlers.* As you read in Chapter 1, Part C of IDEA authorizes federally funded services for infants and toddlers (ages birth through two), and their families. These children and their families are entitled to an IFSP.

Students ages three to twenty-one. You also learned in Chapter 1 that Part B of IDEA authorizes federally funded programs for children and youth and beginning at the age of three and continuing until they are twenty-one or leave school, whichever occurs first. Students in this age group receive an IEP.

Students ages fourteen to twenty-one. There is one last age-specific rule, and it concerns adolescents who are in "transition" from school to postschool activities. These students have the same basic rights as students ages three to twenty-one, but they have explicit, outcome-oriented rights when they turn fourteen (see Figure 2-8). One transition component must be added when the student reaches the age of fourteen. Another transition component must be added at least when the student reaches the age of sixteen, and a third one must be added one year before the student reaches the age of majority.

Participants Who Develop the IFSP/IEP. Because the nondiscriminatory evaluation lays the foundation for the student's individualized plan (IFSP or IEP), the members of the IFSP/IEP teams must be the same people who were on the evaluation team, now called the IEP team because its function differs.

The 1997 amendments increased the number of individuals who must be part of the IFSP/IEP team, adding parents and general educators to that team. In the past, their membership and participation was optional; now, it is mandatory. Other people may be included in the IFSP or IEP conference. For example, a parent might wish to bring a friend—an advocate—who is knowledgeable about the special education process (Shank & Turnbull, 1993). In addition, some of the student's friends can provide suggestions and support for inclusion (Vandercook, Fleetham, Sinclair, & Tetlie, 1988; Villa & Thousand, 1992). So, the team must consist of those individuals listed in Figure 2-6 but may include others.

Advocates protect the interests of other people. **Self-advocates** protect their own interests.

Contents of IFSP/IEP. In this section, you will learn about the content of the IFSP and the IEP and the role of parent consent related to the content of these individualized plans.

FIGURE 2–6   *IFSP/IEP team members*

The members of a student's IEP team include those who are on the evaluation team. It consists of

- The student's parents

- The student, when appropriate before the age of majority and almost always after that age

- At least one general education teacher of the student, if the student is or may be participating in the general education environment

- At least one special education teacher or (where appropriate) a provider of special education to the student

- A representative of the local agency who is qualified to provide or supervise specially designed instruction to meet the unique needs of students with disabilities and is knowledgeable about general curriculum and the availability of local agency resources

- An individual who can interpret the instructional implications of evaluation results (who may already be a member of the team)

- At the parents' or agency's discretion, other individuals who have knowledge or special expertise (including related services personnel), and the student (when appropriate)

- The family's service coordinator when the IFSP for an infant/toddler and the family is being developed

The IFSP. The IFSP describes the services that both the infant–toddler and the family will receive. Like the IEP, the IFSP is based on the child's development and needs; it specifies outcomes for the child. Unlike the IEP, however, the IFSP also provides the option for a family-directed assessment and for the provision of supports and services for families. Figure 2–7 sets out the contents of the IFSP.

The IEP. The IEP is based on the student's evaluation, is developed by the same people who evaluated the student, and is outcome-oriented. IDEA specifies the content of each IEP, as shown in Figure 2–8. Taken as a whole, the IEP's content is the foundation for

IFSP and IEP teams such as this one must include the student's parents, at least one general educator, one special educator, one school district representative, one individual qualified to interpret evaluation results, and, optionally, others such as related services personnel, parent advocates, and, if appropriate, the student.

The IFSP is a written statement for each infant or toddler, ages birth to two. Whenever it is developed and/or revised, it must contain the following content:

- The infant or toddler's present levels of cognitive, physical, communication, social or emotional, and adaptive development, based on objective criteria

- The family's resources, priorities, and concerns related to enhancing their child's development

- The major outcomes for the infant or toddler and family and criteria, procedures, and timelines for determining whether the outcomes are achieved and whether modifications of the outcomes or early intervention services are necessary

- The early intervention services to be provided to the infant or toddler and family, and their frequency, intensity, and method of delivery

- The natural environments in which they will be provided and why they will not be provided in those environments if the plan so provides

- The dates for starting the services and how long they will last

- The family's service coordinator

- The infant or toddler's transition plan (leaving early intervention and entering preschool or other appropriate services)

FIGURE 2–7 *Required content of an IFSP*

COMMON MIRACLES: THE NEW AMERICAN REVOLUTION IN LEARNING, PART II

One of the more dangerous components of assessment occurs during interpretation. Reports written by evaluation teams may emphasize student deficits, causing teachers to assume their primary purpose on the IEP is to write goals and objectives that address those deficits.

In Chapter 1, we discussed how the video *Common Miracles* justifies why all children and adolescents can benefit from education and exemplifies the six values for individuals with disabilities. One of those values is inherent strengths. When assessing students, it is important to identify strengths as well as needs in order to plan an educational program that encourages motivation, increases learning, and helps students compensate for their disabilities. Not only must we believe in students' capacity, we must also understand "how to bring it alive," ABC anchor Peter Jennings comments. *Common Miracles* illustrates how teachers accomplish this feat by identifying types of intellectual skills, encouraging original thinking, incorporating computer technology, providing opportunities for cooperative learning, and increasing metacognition. You will learn more about these strategies throughout this textbook.

What do you think? Think for a moment about the subject that was most difficult for you in school. Now imagine having a teacher who decided the most effective way to instruct you was to have you spend all day every school day working on that subject. What would happen to your motivation?
What teachers motivated you? What strategies did they use?
How will you find the inherent strengths of students in your classroom?
What will you do if you receive an evaluation that only describes student deficits?
How will you get your students actively involved in their own learning?

FIGURE 2–8 *Required contents on an IEP*

The IEP is a written statement for each student, ages three to twenty-one. Whenever it is developed and/or revised, it must contain the following:

- The student's present levels of educational performance, including
  - How the disability of a student (ages six through 21) affects his or her involvement and progress in the general curriculum, or
  - How the disability of a preschooler (ages three through five) affects his or her participation in appropriate activities

- Measurable annual goals, including "benchmarks" or short-term objectives, related to
  - Meeting needs resulting from the disability, in order to enable the student to be involved in and progress in the general curriculum
  - Meeting each of the student's other disability-related needs

- The special education and related services and supplementary aids and services that will be provided to the student or on the student's behalf, and the program modifications or supports for school personnel that will be provided so that the student
  - Can advance appropriately toward attaining the annual goals
  - Be involved and progress in the general curriculum and participate in extracurricular and other nonacademic activities
  - Be educated and participate with other students with disabilities and with students who do not have disabilities in general education

- The extent, if any, to which the student will not participate with students who do not have disabilities in general education classes and in extracurricular and other nonacademic activities of the general curriculum

- Any individual modifications in the administration of state or district-wide assessments of student achievement, so that the student can participate in those assessments; moreover, if the IEP determines that the student will not participate in a particular state or district-wide assessment or any part of an assessment, why that assessment is not appropriate for the student and how the student will be assessed

- The projected date for beginning the services and program modifications and the anticipated frequency, location, and duration of each

- Transition plans, including
  - Beginning at age fourteen and each year thereafter, a statement of the student's needs that are related to transition services, including those that focus on the student's courses of study (e.g., the student's participation in advanced-placement courses or in a vocational education program)
  - Beginning at age sixteen (or sooner, if the IEP team decides it is appropriate), a statement of needed transition services, including when appropriate a statement of the interagency responsibilities or any other needed linkages
  - Beginning at least one year before the student reaches the age of majority under state law (usually, at age eighteen), a statement that the student has been informed of those rights under IDEA that will transfer to the student from the parents when the student becomes of age

- How the student's progress toward annual goals will be measured and how the student's parents will be informed—at least as often as parents of students who do not have disabilities are informed—of the student's progress toward annual goals and the extent to which the progress is sufficient to enable the student to achieve the goals by the end of the school year

the student's appropriate education; it is the ensurance that the student will benefit from special education and have real opportunities for the outcomes of independence, productivity, and inclusion.

In addition to the required content, IDEA also requires the IEP team, when developing each IEP, from the student's very first one to the very last one, to consider the following factors:

- The student's strengths

- The parents' concerns

- The results of all evaluations

- Special factors, namely

> For students whose behavior impedes their own or others' learning, appropriate strategies, including positive behavioral interventions, strategies, and supports, to address that behavior

> For students with limited English proficiency, their language needs

> For students who are blind or visually impaired, the use of Braille or other appropriate reading and writing media

> For all students, their communication needs and, for students who are deaf or hard of hearing, their language and communication needs, opportunities for direct communications with peers and professionals in their own language and communication mode, academic level, and full range of needs

> For all students, whether assistive technology devices and services are appropriate

As Figure 2–8 (IEP content) shows, the IEPs for students who are in transition from school to postschool activities must describe the "needed transition services" the student will get, beginning at age sixteen (or sooner). Transition services promote movement from school to these seven specific adult outcomes:

- Postsecondary education (e.g., college or university)

- Vocational training (e.g., junior college or technical institute)

- Employment (including supported employment) in a setting where there are workers without disabilities (called *integrated employment* because the person with a disability is included in the workforce with people without disabilities)

- Continuing and adult education (e.g., formal or informal courses)

- Adult services (for people with disabilities)

- Independent living (living alone, with or without assistance)

- Community participation (use of public and private services available in the community to people without disabilities)

Since Danny wants to be a dog trainer or a vet's assistant and since he is now fourteen, it is entirely appropriate for his IEP to reflect these goals because it must include a statement of his needs related to transition services. Moreover, since Danny also wants to live on his own or with his brother, Freddy, it is also appropriate for his IEP to address his independent living skills.

Parent consent to IFSP/IEP content. If a parent does not want to participate in the IEP meeting, the school staff still must meet to develop an IEP because schools may not serve a student who does not have an IEP. IDEA does not require schools to obtain parental consent to the content of their child's IEP. If parents do consent, fine; if they do

---

When an IEP focuses on a student's social skills, it enhances the value of relationships, enables the student to make positive contributions to others, and may even expand the great expectations— IDEA calls them "high expectations"—that family, teachers, and even the student may have.

Special education, particularly the transition provisions, make it possible for a student to participate in a society in which, under Section 504 and the Americans with Disabilities Act (ADA), discrimination based on disability is prohibited.

Conscientious collaboration to develop an IEP/IFSP will acknowledge a student's strengths and abilities to make a positive contribution to others. That is what the new IDEA (PL 105-17) intends.

In its transition provisions, IDEA provides that a result of special education should be access to higher education. Here, a student who was in special education takes advantage of IDEA and other laws—the antidiscrimination provisions of Section 504 of the Rehabilitation Act and ADA—to go to college.

not, the schools may still implement the IEP but the parent may challenge the IEP in a due process hearing. Remember, however, that IDEA does require notice to and consent from parents for every evaluation. IDEA also prohibits a school from placing a student into special education without first having an evaluation and IEP. Furthermore, IDEA provides that the school may not place the student out of special education (if the student has already been placed into special education) without a nondiscriminatory evaluation. Finally, a parent may challenge all placement decisions in a due process hearing.

Carmen and Alfredo have been very much involved in developing Danny's IEP, attending all of the IEP meetings and meeting frequently with Danny's teachers to make sure that Danny's education benefits him. When they disagreed with his school's plan for him many years ago, they used the due process safeguards to contest the plan, and they prevailed.

Timelines. IDEA requires an IFSP to be developed within a reasonable time after the infant receives a multidisciplinary assessment. It must be reviewed with the family at six-month intervals or more often if a more frequent review is warranted. Then on an annual basis, the infant or toddler's progress toward meeting the outcomes must be evaluated.

IDEA requires an IEP to be developed for all students, ages three through twenty-one, and to be in effect at the beginning of each school year. The requirement that the IEP must be in effect when school starts is a new (1997) requirement; no longer may schools wait until the beginning of a school year to develop an IEP. Another timing rule requires the team to review and, if appropriate, revise the student's IEP at least once a year and more often if conditions warrant or if the student's parents or teacher request a review.

IFSP/IEP Conferences. Ideally, IFSP/IEP conferences will be conducted in such a manner that they help ensure collaborative decision making by all team members. Certainly, the 1997 amendments facilitate that result by requiring the parents to be members of both the nondiscriminatory evaluation and IEP teams. Research on the IFSP/IEP, however, has generally reported that the traditional process has been more of a legal compliance–paperwork process than a problem-solving, dynamic process (Harry, Allen, & McLaughlin, 1995; Smith, 1990; Turnbull & Turnbull, 1997). To make the conference more collaborative, we recommend that you follow these eight components of the conference:

1. Prepare in advance.

2. Connect and get started.

3. Share visions and great expectations.

4. Review evaluation information and current levels of performance.

5. Share resources, priorities, and concerns.

6. Develop goals and objectives related to outcomes.

7. Determine placement, related services, and supplementary aids and services.

8. Conclude the conference. (Turnbull & Turnbull, 1997)

Box 2-3, "Into Practice," includes specific suggestions for enhancing collaboration with parents and other participants for each of these components in the IFSP/IEP conference.

Mandatory review conferences have one principal reason: to determine whether the student's annual goals are being achieved. Accordingly, the IEP team must revise the IEP (as appropriate) to address five separate matters:

- Any lack of progress toward the student's annual goals and any lack of progress in the general curriculum

- The results of any reevaluations

- Information about the student provided to or by the parents

- The student's anticipated needs

- Other matters (e.g., increasing inclusion in extracurricular activities)

If the team identifies any of these five matters during the review conference, it may want to reevaluate the student, revise the IEP, reconsider the student's placement, or carry out all three of these actions.

Now that you have learned about appropriate education—IDEA requirements and the IFSP/IEP conference—you may wonder how parents of children with disabilities, who do not have the benefit of formal course work, learn all of this information to prepare them to be collaborative partners in the process. After all, IDEA empowers parents to be collaborative educational decision makers; that is why IDEA also provides a training resource for them. Pursuant to IDEA, Congress funds 71 Parent Training and Information Centers. There is at least one in each state. Most centers are directed and staffed by parents of children with a disability; and, under IDEA, the majority of board members must be parents of individuals with disabilities. The centers' mission is to provide information to parents to enable them to be effective educational decision makers as schools and they together implement the six IDEA principles. The "Making a Difference" box (see Box 2-4) provides the perspective of a parent who learned about the IEP process through one of the workshops of the Kansas Parent Training and Information Center and then became a parent trainer herself.

BOX 2-3   INTO PRACTICE

BEST PRACTICES FOR IFSP/IEP CONFERENCES

Preconference Preparation

- Appoint a service coordinator to organize all aspects of the IEP conference.
- Solicit information from the family about their preferences and needs regarding the conference.
- Discuss the meeting with the student and consider his or her preferences concerning the conference.
- Decide who should attend the conference and include the student, if appropriate.
- Arrange a convenient time and location for the meeting.
- Assist families with logistical needs such as transportation and child care.
- Without educational jargon, inform the family verbally and/or in writing of the following:
  - Explain the purpose of the meeting.
  - State the time and location of the conference.
  - Give the names of participants.
- Share information the family wants before the conference.
- Encourage the student, family members, and their advocates to visit the proposed placements for the student before the conference.
- Encourage families to share information and discuss concerns with participants before the conference.
- Gather needed information from school personnel.
- Prepare an agenda to cover the remaining components of the IEP conference.

Initial Conference Proceedings

- Greet the students, family, and their advocates.
- Provide a list of all participants or use name tags.
- Introduce each participant with a brief description of his or her role in the conference.
- State the purpose of the meeting. Review the agenda, and ask for additional issues to be covered.

- Determine the amount of time participants have available for the conference, and offer the option of rescheduling if needed to complete the agenda.
- Ask if family members desire clarification of their legal rights.

Review of Formal Evaluation and Current Levels of Performance

- Provide family members with a written copy of evaluation results if desired.
- Avoid educational jargon as much as possible, and clarify diagnostic terminology throughout the conference.
- If a separate evaluation conference has not been scheduled, ask diagnostic personnel to report the following:
  - What tests were administered?
  - What were the results of each?
  - What are the options based on the evaluation?
  - Summarize the findings, including strengths, gifts, abilities, and needs.
- Identify implications of test results for involvement and progress in the general curriculum and extracurricular activities.
- Ask all participants for areas of agreement and disagreement with corresponding reasons.
- Proceed with the IEP only when consensus is reached about the student's exceptionality and current levels of performance.

Development of Annual Goals and Objectives

- Encourage the student, family members, and advocates to share their expectations for the student's participation in the home, school (including general curriculum), and community.
- Collaboratively generate appropriate annual goals and objectives for all subject areas requiring special instruction consistent with expectations.
- Discuss annual goals and objectives for future educational and vocational options based on great expectations for the student.

Implementing the IFSP/IEP

Once the IFSP/IEP is developed, the next step is implementation. Implementation involves placing the student in the least restrictive environment and providing supplementary aids and services to ensure that the student will benefit from that placement. It also means providing the necessary related services so that the student will benefit from

- Identify objectives to expand the positive contributions the student can make to family, friends, and community.
- Prioritize all annual goals and objectives in light of student preferences and needs.
- Discuss and specify transition plans at age fourteen (needs statement), sixteen (needed transition services; inter-agency responsibilities); and at least one year before age of majority (student rights for decision making when student becomes of age).
- Clarify the manner in which the responsibility for teaching the objectives will be shared among the student's teachers.
- Ask family members and advocates if they would like to share in the responsibility for teaching some of the objectives at home or in the community.
- Determine evaluation procedures and schedules for identified annual goals and objectives and how the student's parents will be informed at least as often as parents of students without disabilities are informed.
- Discuss and specify any individual modifications in the administration of state or district assessments of student achievement; if the committee determines the student will not participate in the assessment, state the rationale.
- Explain to family members and advocates that the IEP is not a guarantee that the student will attain the goals; rather, it represents a good-faith effort on the part of school personnel that they will teach these goals and objectives.

Determination of Placement and Related Services

- Discuss the benefits and drawbacks of viable placement options.

- Select a placement option that allows the student to be involved with peers without exceptionalities as much as possible.
- Agree on a tentative placement until the student and family can visit and confirm its appropriateness.
- Discuss and specify the supplementary aids and services that will be provided to enable the student to be successful in the general education curriculum, extracurricular activities, and nonacademic activities.
- Specify the extent the student will *not* be participating in general education curriculum, extracurricular activities, and nonacademic activities.
- Discuss the benefits and drawbacks of modes of delivery for related services the student needs.
- Specify the dates for initiating related services and anticipated duration, frequency, and location of each.
- Share with family members and advocates the names and qualifications of all personnel who will provide services.

Concluding the Conference

- Assign follow-up responsibility for any tasks requiring attention.
- Summarize orally and on paper the major decisions and follow-up responsibilities of all participants.
- Set a tentative date for reviewing the IFSP/IEP document.
- Identify strategies for ongoing communication among participants.
- Express appreciation to all participants for their help in the decision-making process.

Note: From *Families, Professionals, and Exceptionality: A Special Partnership* (3rd ed., pp. 234–235) by A. P. Turnbull and H. R. Turnbull, 1997, Upper Saddle River, NJ: Merrill/Prentice Hall. Copyright © 1997. Reprinted with permission of Prentice Hall, Inc., Upper Saddle River, NJ.

the specially designed instruction. Two issues to be addressed in implementation include the selection of appropriate instructional methods and strategies for evaluating student progress. At this point, we encourage you to locate on Figure 2-1 the rectangle entitled "Implementing the IFSP/IEP." That is the point in the process to which we have come in our discussion.

BOX 2-4   MAKING A DIFFERENCE

PARENT TRAINING AND INFORMATION IN KANSAS

The Kansas Parent Training and Information Center is aptly named "Families Together." The name is appropriate because it describes how families from all across the state teach and learn from each other not only what IDEA provides but how to collaborate with Kansas educators in implementing IDEA.

Once each year, Families Together holds its statewide conference, offering, among other training events, an overview of IDEA. The trainers, who are parents of students with disabilities, begin with the zero-reject principle and continue through nondiscriminatory evaluation, appropriate education, least restrictive placement, due process, and parent and student participation. They also distribute materials about IDEA and state and national sources of further information, and they answer questions.

This overview is a prelude to later in-depth training about the appropriate education principle. At those regional training sessions, each of IDEA's appropriate education provisions is reviewed in detail. Trainers emphasize how parents have a right to participate in education decision making and on the skills they need to be effective collaborators.

Denise Poston got her first introduction to IDEA and special education when, just after A.J. (her son with autism, to whom you will be introduced in Chapter 10) entered school,

she attended a Families Together workshop. Knowing how much she learned at the workshop and building on her training in adult education and her nearly twenty years of experience as a trainer in the U.S. Army, she volunteered to become a trainer for other parents. Before she qualified, however, she herself had to receive still more intensive training by Families Together trainers. Now, as a trainer, parent of A.J., and special education doctoral student at the University of Kansas, Denise hopes to give to other parents what she received from Families Together.

"I benefited in three ways," Denise notes. "First, I simply acquired information. If knowledge is power, then I started becoming powerful because of Families Together."

But although knowledge is necessary, it is not sufficient, Denise says. "At Families Together, we also impart skills, the how-to techniques are the ways for using what we know to participate in our children's education. It is amazing how much parents have learned about negotiating the special education system. And all that accumulated savvy is available at Families Together."

There is still one other benefit from being involved in Families Together. "Like many other parents, I am much more confident when I work with A.J.'s teachers. I can draw on information about IDEA and on collaboration skills that other parents have tested and found useful. Together, we families do a lot for each other, our children, and even the schools."

Instructional Methods: Cooperative Learning.

All instructional practices fall at some point on a continuum where one end represents competition and the other end represents cooperation. Most schools in the United States emphasize competition and encourage students to try to do better than their classmates (D. W. Johnson & Johnson, 1991).

Cooperative learning is an alternative to the competitive approach. This model provides a structure for students to work together toward mutual goals and emphasizes the importance of having all members in the group work together to achieve their individual and collective goals (Stainback & Stainback, 1996; Thousand, Villa, & Nevin, 1994). Cooperative learning consists of five basic components (R. T. Johnson & Johnson, 1994):

In the "competitive model," students learn that success means surpassing others. In a cooperative model, students learn that, through their relationships with each other, they can enhance each others' abilities and strengths.

- *Positive interdependence.* Group members establish mutual goals, divide the prerequisite tasks, share materials and resources, assume shared roles, and give joint rewards

- *Face-to-face interaction.* Group members encourage and facilitate each others' efforts to complete tasks through direct communication.

- *Individual accountability/personal responsibility.* Individual performance is assessed, and results are reported back to the individual and the group. The group holds each member responsible for completing his or her fair share of responsibility.

 Cooperative learning, in which students work together as a group rather than competing against each other, can be useful in any subject area. Here, students collaborate in a middle school science class.

- *Interpersonal and small-group skills.* Students are responsible for getting to know and trust each other, communicating accurately and clearly, accepting and supporting each other, and resolving conflicts in a constructive manner.

- *Group processing.* Group reflection includes describing which contributions of members are helpful or unhelpful in making decisions and which group actions should be continued or changed.

The value of heterogeneous (diverse) or homogeneous (similar) groups largely depends upon the support that students receive for developing genuine cooperation. Because some students who are gifted can become frustrated by working in heterogeneous groups with students who need a lot of support and who do not catch on nearly as quickly as they do, some people have asserted that cooperative learning may have questionable value for students who are gifted (Matthews, 1992). An alternative view is that one of the most important skills for students who are gifted is to know how to interact with others who are not as cognitively capable. Because all students will encounter demands to respond to cognitive differences in others, cooperative learning can teach social skills and peer interaction.

Some of the benefits for students who have been instructed through cooperative learning (as compared to individualistic and competitive instructional strategies) include the following (D. W. Johnson & Johnson, 1989):

- Higher achievement

- More advanced reasoning, increased generation of new ideas, and greater transfer of what is learned in the classroom to other situations

- Greater liking of fellow classmates and teachers

- Greater interest in helping classmates who have disabilities

- Greater ability to take the perspectives of others

- Enhanced creativity

- Higher levels of self-esteem

Cooperative learning can be used in any subject area. The following examples focus on teaching geography and language skills:

In Mrs. G.'s second grade class students are working on maps of South America. S., a student with multiple intellectual, motoric, and sensory disabilities, is a member of a cooperative group. While other students draw and label countries on maps at the table, her partner does the work on her slanted tray table. Periodically, he pauses and shines a bright flashlight on the tray, moving slowly to outline his work. S. tracks and scans the colorful map drawing.

Mrs. P.'s first grade class is working on sight words using a lotto game. A student with mild disabilities works on his IEP objective for reading by calling out the words from index cards at the front of the class while classmates put raisins on their cards. M., a student with severe intellectual and motor disabilities, uses a picture-based communication to point with his eyes to the correct "word." His teacher sits behind him to whisper guidance while a peer checks his work, puts a raisin on his card for him, and calls out "Bingo" when M. wins. (Salisbury, Palombaro, & Hollowood, 1993)

Evaluation of Student Progress. Among other things, the IFSP/IEP must contain a statement concerning how the student's outcomes or progress will be evaluated. The same evaluation procedures that help determine special education programming and placement also help evaluate a student's ongoing progress.

A key issue in monitoring student progress is grading. The majority of schools have some kind of district policy on grading. Of those schools with a policy, slightly more than half have a specific policy for students with disabilities (Polloway et al., 1994). Grading modifications usually are incorporated into the part of the IEP related to progress-monitoring procedures. These grading modifications are particularly essential given research indicating that students with disabilities are passing general education classes but doing so in many cases with low grade-point averages (GPAs) (Donahue & Zigmond, 1990; Valdés, Williamson, & Wagner, 1990).

While grading modifications may not guarantee higher GPAs, they may contribute to that outcome. Most school district policies rely on letter and number grades. They typically base these grades on homework, tests, and quizzes. A national survey of elementary and secondary general education teachers reported that general education teachers typically prefer pass–fail and checklist-type grades as more helpful than letter and number grades for reporting the progress of students with disabilities. The authors of the national survey point out the importance of (a) providing skill development to students in taking tests and organizing assignments, (b) ensuring that homework and tests are appropriately adapted, and (c) training general education teachers in the development of valid classroom tests (Bursuck et al., 1996).

A VISION FOR THE FUTURE

Imagine Danny at the age of thirty. He has been out of school for nine years and now works as an assistant to a veterinarian who tends to large and small animals. Gathered in his own apartment are Danny, his mother Carmen, and his father Alfredo. Looking back on his last seven years in school (the years covered by the 1997 amendments to IDEA,

namely, the 1997–1998 school year through 2001–2002), they have a happier memory of those last years than of his schooling from preschool through the 1996–1997 school year.

Yes, they concede, Danny's right to attend school had not been in doubt; the zero-reject principle had seen to that. What had been doubtful, they say, was whether educators would connect what they knew about him with the education they provided him. Their fear that the connection would not be made proved to be groundless. Beginning in 1997, what educators knew about Danny derived from many sources: a battery of tests and assessment instruments, data from other sources, and the collective expertise of a host of professionals and his family.

Those tests and assessments took into account his strengths, needs, and preference to be a vet's assistant; they determined what skills he needed to perform the job he holds now, they were focused on that outcome, and they measured his abilities to secure that result. The bottom line, as Danny moved into his transition years, was that nondiscriminatory evaluation yielded much more robust and outcome-oriented information.

As a consequence, Danny, Carmen, and Alfredo believe that Danny's education was appropriate in several important ways. It built on the evaluation data, was tailored to his preferences and needs, and was delivered in the least restrictive environment, with support.

Just as they are about to tell you more about Danny's education under the 1997 IDEA, Danny's pager buzzes. It's a call from the vet for whom he has worked for the last five years; an emergency has arisen at the clinic, and Danny is needed immediately. End of the conversation: Danny has a job to do, and reflection can wait because the job and the animals can't.

What made the difference in Danny's life? For Danny while he was in school and for students who benefit from the 1997 IDEA, these questions are relevant:

What Do You Think?

- What are the purposes of and distinctions among screening, prereferral, referral, and full and formal nondiscriminatory evaluation? Which one of these did Danny receive, and how useful are those activities?

- What are the two purposes of nondiscriminatory evaluation for Danny and other students with a disability, and how does an evaluation connect to their appropriate education requirement?

- What are the contents of an IFSP and IEP, how does the IEP lead to the outcomes that IDEA specifies, and what should Danny's IEP contain, given his goal of being a veterinarian's assistant?

SUMMARY

NONDISCRIMINATORY EVALUATION: SCREENING, PREREFERRAL, AND REFERRAL

- Screening involves routine tests that help school staff identify which students might need further testing to determine whether they qualify for special education.

- Prereferral occurs when a student's general education teacher asks others to identify instructional strategies to address learning and behavioral challenges.

- Referral occurs when an educator or a parent submits a formal request for a full and formal nondiscriminatory evaluation.

NONDISCRIMINATORY EVALUATION PROCEDURES AND STANDARDS

- Nondiscriminatory evaluation is a fair, unbiased evaluation of the student to determine whether the student has a disability and, if so, what the student's special education and related services needs are.

- IDEA contains detailed procedural safeguards to ensure that evaluation is free of cultural and linguistic bias.

- There is a strong link between evaluation and a student's successful participation in the general education curriculum.

- Procedural safeguards relate to the breadth of the assessment, administration of the assessment procedures, timing of the assessment, parent notice and consent, and interpretation of assessment information.

- Two categories of tests include norm-referenced tests and criterion-referenced tests.

- Norm-referenced tests (e.g., intelligence tests) are standardized and compare a student with his or her age- or grade-level peers.

- Criterion-referenced tests determine whether a student has mastered a particular skill; they compare a student to a standard of mastery.

APPROPRIATE EDUCATION

- The age-specific provisions of IDEA require that infants and toddlers have an IFSP, students ages three to twenty-one have an IEP, and students ages fourteen to twenty-one have transition components within their IEP.

- The IFSP/IEP teams must comprise the same people as the evaluation team.

- The IFSP must be developed within a reasonable time after the infant or toddler receives an assessment, and it must be reviewed with the family at six-month intervals or more often if necessary.

- The IFSP must include
The infant or toddler's present levels of development
The family's resources, priorities, and concerns
Major outcomes for the infant or toddler and family and criteria, procedures, and time lines for determining whether the outcomes are achieved
Early intervention services to be provided and their frequency, intensity, and method of delivery
Natural environments in which services will be provided and rationale for not providing any services in natural environments
Dates for starting the services and how long they will last
The family's service coordinator
A transition plan when leaving early intervention and entering preschool or other appropriate services

- The IEP must contain
The student's present levels of educational performance
Measurable annual goals and short-term objectives
Special education and related services and supplementary aids and services that will be provided to the student
The extent to which the student will *not* participate with students who do not have disabilities in general education classes and in extracurricular/nonacademic activities
Individual modifications in the administration of state or district-wide assessments of student achievement and a rationale for the student's nonparticipation
The projected date for beginning the services and modifications and the anticipated frequency, location, and duration of each
Transition activities beginning at age fourteen, sixteen, and again at least one year before the student reaches the age of majority
How the student's progress toward annual goals will be measured and how the student's parents will be informed of the student's progress

- Eight components of the IFSP/IEP conference include
Preparing in advance
Connecting and getting started
Sharing visions and great expectations
Reviewing evaluation information and current levels of performance
Sharing resources, priorities, and concerns
Developing goals and objectives related to outcomes
Determining placement, related services, and supplementary aids and services
Concluding the conference

- Cooperative learning is a shared learning experience consisting of positive interdependence, face-to-face interactions, individual accountability, personal responsibility, interpersonal and small-group skills, and group processing.

- Evaluating student progress is an important component of the IFSP/IEP and often includes grading modifications.

RESOURCES

BOOKS

Addressing Cultural and Linguistic Diversity in Special Education: Issues and Trends. (1994). Edited by Shernaz B. Garcia. Reston, VA: The Council for Exceptional Children. This collection of articles focuses on education reform, evaluation of instruction, and student assessment for ethnically and linguistically diverse students.

Controversial Issues Confronting Special Education: Divergent Perspectives. (1996). By William Stainback & Susan Stainback. Boston: Allyn & Bacon. Twelve controversial issues are discussed, most of which have both point and counterpoint perspectives. Examples of issues are classification and labeling, assessment, and classroom management.

Creating Schools for All of Our Students: What 12 Schools Have to Say. (1994). By the Working Forum on Inclusive Schools. Reston, VA: The Council for Exceptional Children. This resource features teachers, principals, classroom aides, parents, and other school staff and their observations about what makes inclusion the preferred setting for serving all students.

Developing Cross-Cultural Competence: A Guide for Working With Young Children and Their Families. (1992). Edited by Eleanor W. Lynch & Marci J. Hanson. Baltimore, MD: Brookes. Offering both a cross-cultural view and a specific cultural analysis, this book provides valuable information in promoting cultural competence. Eight core chapters, each focusing on a particular culture, are written by a professional from the culture.

Nobody's Perfect: Living and Growing With Children Who Have Special Needs. (1994). Edited by Nancy B. Miller. Baltimore, MD: Brookes. Writing a family perspective, this book offers specific tips for how families can be successful in raising children with disabilities. The perspectives of four mothers who have children with disabilities are included throughout the book in providing a particularly candid perspective of daily life.

Resourcing: Handbook for Special Education Resource Teachers. (1992). By Mary Yeomans Jackson. Reston, VA: The Council for Exceptional Children. This book shows special education teachers how to belong to and offer leadership for school-based teams.

The Special Education Sourcebook: A Teacher's Guide to Programs, Materials, and Information Sources. (1994). By Michael S. Rosenberg & Irene Edmond-Rosenberg. Bethesda, MD: Woodbine House. This resource guide serves special educators from early intervention through high school.

JOURNALS AND MAGAZINES

Educational Leadership. Association for Supervision and Curriculum Development, 1250 North Pitt Street, Alexandria, VA 22314-1453. Monthly journals for leaders in elementary, middle, and secondary education with interests in curriculum, instruction, supervision, and leadership.

Journal of Early Intervention. Division for Early Childhood, Council for Exceptional Children, 1920 Association Drive, Reston, VA 22091. Published quarterly with an emphasis on current research and best practice related to educating infants, toddlers, and preschool children.

Journal of Vocational Rehabilitation. Elsevier Science, P.O. Box 945, New York, NY 10159-0945. Published quarterly with a focus on current research and cutting-edge issues related to the preparation of people with disabilities for employment and community contribution as adults.

The Journal of Special Education. Pro-Ed Journals, Inc., 8700 Shoal Creek Boulevard, Austin, TX 78757-6897. This quarterly professional journal publishes research articles in all subspecialties of special education.

Teaching Exceptional Children. The Council for Exceptional Children, 1920 Association Drive, Reston, VA 22091. This classroom-oriented magazine features articles that blend theory and practice.

MULTIMEDIA

A Child Is Waiting. (1962, U.S., 102 minutes). A boy with mental retardation is placed in a residential school for children with disabilities.

Amy. (1981, G, U.S., 100 minutes). A teacher instructs children with disabilities in the early 1900s.

Crisis at Central High. (1981, not rated, U.S., 125 minutes). Portrays events that occurred at Central High School in Little Rock, Arkansas, when integration was mandated after *Brown v. Board of Education.*

Separate But Equal. (1991, not rated, U.S., 200 minutes). Details *Brown v. Board of Education.*

ON-LINE INFORMATION AND USEFUL DATABASES

The Federal Resource Center for Special Education. Internet address: www.dssc.org/frc/frcl.htm. Provides special education technical assistance information and general information about and news pertaining to special education.

OSERS IDEA Home Page. Internet address: www.ed.gov/offices/OSERS/IDEA. Explanation of IDEA.

Pitsco's Launch to special education resources. Internet address: www.pitsco.com/pitsco/specialed.html. Links to many useful special education and disability related sites.

Special Education Resources on the Internet. Internet address: www.hood.edu/seri/serihome.htm. A collection of internet-accessible information resources of interest to those involved in the fields related to special education.

CHAPTER 3

SPECIAL EDUCATION TODAY: INCLUSION AND COLLABORATION

Collaborating for
Danny Ramirez

Reflecting on the first few moments after Danny's birth, Carmen and Alfredo promised themselves right then and there, that "Danny was going to be part of everybody's life; he was not going to be separated from anybody."

Undertaking such a commitment has not been easy. In the past, isolation of people with disabilities from the mainstream of society and in schools has been more the rule than the exception. However, Carmen and Alfredo have fought for inclusion. Many families, students, and professionals favor inclusion; others object. Even people with different perspectives nevertheless have the same objective: to provide students with disabilities an appropriate education. Their dispute is about the means to reach that end.

For Danny and other students with disabilities, being part of other students' lives and being part of the schools means being in the same programs as the students who do not have disabilities. For example, when Danny was ten years old, he was a school crossing-guard; he performed the same duties as students who did not have disabilities. Now that

he is fourteen, being part of the school means that he takes the general education curriculum, is involved in cooperative learning activities, dances folkloria (Mexican folklore), and plays basketball with his peers.

His friends and teachers describe him as "nice, well-mannered, and sociable." Others, however, need some encouragement to be involved with him; they derive it from Danny's circle of friends. It is made up of Danny, his parents, his teachers, and his peers (guided by Carmen), to support Danny's inclusion in general education programs.

Through the circle, Danny has come to meet two of his best friends, Jason, an African American student, and Yolanda, a Mexican American student. Both are just a year younger than Danny, but they are important to him. Jason has appointed himself to be Danny's "bodyguard" when other students tease Danny or take advantage of his slight build during pickup games. Jason has taken such a liking to Danny that he has arranged to have the same class schedule as Danny; often, Jason hangs out with Danny during lunch recess. Yolanda also blunts the effect of some students' teasing, comforting Danny when he needs it. Equally importantly, she assists him when he needs extra help in his classwork.

Despite Danny's progress in school and his support systems, Carmen and Alfredo are wary about the future. They sense that not everyone believes that Danny should or always will experience so much inclusion. In their opinion, some administrators still are leery of the inclusion movement; they refuse to release teachers to attend workshops on effectively adapting instruction. Also, some teachers still do not believe inclusion can work. They believe that "disabled" equates to "unable" and so are skeptical about Danny's ability to learn. Still other professionals are "too busy" to collaborate with Danny's team so that instructional adaptations made just for him can be carried out consistently across all of his classes.

It is not, Carmen and Alfredo believe, that the "skeptical" professionals have anything against Danny; they

are not ill-spirited. Instead, those professionals believe that Danny will benefit less from inclusion than from a combination of inclusion and separation. And they believe that their time and expertise can be better used—for Danny's sake and for the sake of other students, too—if they focus more on students whose achievement is "at or above grade level." Professionals who hold these beliefs are numerous. Danny's school is typical in that it includes teachers who favor, as well as those who disfavor, inclusion.

And so, in Danny's school in El Paso as in all of America's schools, inclusion and collaboration pose

challenges: Modifying the general education curriculum so Danny can participate in it; using such techniques as cooperative learning; providing such related services as speech and language therapy; and organizing a circle of friends so Danny can, in the slang of the day, "Get a Life!"—these make Danny's inclusion possible, but collaboration is the key. Not Danny alone, not even Carmen and Alfredo alone can ensure inclusion. They need reliable allies—people willing to collaborate with them. Not everyone, however, is willing or knows how. Yet schools are changing. Reform is in the air. Inclusion and collaboration do not seem to be fads.

In light of the reform movements, the issues that most new teachers—and a good number of experienced ones, too—will need to address relate to the impact of school reform on all students, the ways in which students with disabilities will have access to the general curriculum, and the ways that parents and professionals can best collaborate.

What Do You Think?

1. What are educators and others doing to improve America's schools for Danny, and how does school reform influence the inclusion of students with disabilities?

2. What is the meaning of inclusion, and what can educators do to foster Danny's inclusion and simultaneously ensure the benefits of an appropriate special education?

3. How can educators and parents like Carmen and Alfredo collaborate to ensure appropriate and inclusive education?

SCHOOL REFORM

Educators are influenced by whole movements—megatrends—within the field of education. Within the megatrend known as school reform, two important laws are Goals 2000 and IDEA.

School Reform via Goals 2000

Special education reform takes place within a broader context, namely, the need to reform general education. In 1993, Congress enacted Goals 2000: Educate America Act. Under that law, federal funds became available to states that created plans to achieve, by the year 2000, eight national educational goals (see Figure 3-1).

What does all this have to do with children and youth with disabilities? The Senate committee that recommended the Goals 2000 law noted in 1993 that this law should "serve as a vehicle for making the promise of . . . IDEA a reality for all students with disabilities." Students with disabilities, therefore, must be "an integral part of all aspects of

FIGURE 3–1 *National education goals*

Ready to Learn

By the year 2000, all children in the United States will start school ready to learn.

School Completion

By the year 2000, the high school graduation rate will increase to at least 90 percent.

Student Achievement and Citizenship

By the year 2000, all students will leave grades 4, 8, and 12 having demonstrated competency in challenging subject matter including English, mathematics, science, foreign languages, civics and government, economics, arts, history, and geography; and every school in the United States will ensure that all students learn to use their minds well, so they may be prepared for responsible citizenship, further learning, and productive employment in our nation's modern economy.

Mathematics and Science

By the year 2000, U.S. students will be the first in the world in mathematics and science achievement.

Adult Literacy and Lifelong Learning

By the year 2000, every adult American will be literate and will possess the knowledge and skills necessary to compete in a global economy and exercise the rights and responsibilities of citizenship.

Safe, Disciplined, and Drug-Free Schools

By the year 2000, every school in the United States will be free of drugs, violence, and the unauthorized presence of firearms and alcohol and will offer a disciplined environment conducive to learning.

Teacher Education and Professional Development

By the year 2000, members of the nation's teaching force will have access to programs for the continued improvement of their skills and the opportunity to acquire the knowledge and skills needed to instruct and prepare all American students for the next century.

Parental Participation

By the year 2000, every school will promote partnerships that will increase parental involvement and participation in promoting the social, emotional, and academic growth of children.

education reform," entitled to the "same high expectations, treatment, and leadership offered to their nondisabled peers" (Senate Report 103-85, 103d Congress, 1st Session).

The school reform effort of Goals 2000 seeks to raise the standards and expectations for *all* students, teachers, and families (Lewis, 1989; McDonnell, McLaughlin, & Morison; 1997; Paul & Rosselli, 1995). To that end, schools need to redesign their

- Curriculum (Bell, 1993; Cuban, 1989)

- Structure (Cook, Weintraub, & Morse, 1995; Sailor & Skrtic, 1995)

- Services (Doktor & Poertner, 1996; Kagan & Neville, 1993; U.S. Department of Education and American Educational Research Association, 1995)

The values of great expectations and full citizenship are embedded in school reform. That is why Congress uses the phrases *high expectations* and *same treatment* when referring to students with disabilities and those who do not have disabilities.

The National Academy of Sciences convened an expert committee to study the implications of the Goals 2000 standards-based reforms on the education of students with disabilities (McDonnell et al., 1997). This committee was established through the Goals 2000 legislation to ensure that Goals 2000 would not just apply to students in general education but to students being served by special education as well. The Committee's recommendations were based on these two key principles:

- All students should have access to challenging standards.

- Policy makers and educators should be held publicly accountable for every student's performance. (McDonnell et al., 1997, p. 9)

One of the major future changes that will occur for students with disabilities is much greater emphasis on the extent to which they meet challenging standards associated with their school's curriculum.

School Reform via the Individuals with Disabilities Education Act

When Congress reauthorized the Individuals with Disabilities Education Act (IDEA) in 1997 (Public Law [PL] 105-17) it put even greater weight behind Goals 2000 and its expectation that schools would be held accountable for the standards-based outcomes of students with disabilities. IDEA now also uses an outcome-based approach to special education. It seeks to improve services to students by

- Identifying the outcomes you read about in Chapter 1, namely independence and independent living, productivity and employment, and integration and inclusion

- Enumerating barriers (low expectations and failure to apply research and state-of-the-art programs)

- Declaring solutions (having high expectations, improving teaching)

- Including students in state and local assessments

- Clarifying that students must benefit from coordinated systems of special education and other service-agency operations and funding

These provisions of the new IDEA (PL 105-17) set performance goals and standards not only for students with disabilities and their teachers but also for state and local school systems themselves.

In addition, IDEA also connects state and local special education agencies to school reform by requiring them to

- Use their funds to build a stronger state-local capacity (e.g., personnel preparation, teacher certification standards, reporting of discipline decisions)

- Coordinate services through interagency agreements

- Carry out school improvement plans that are linked to general education school improvement activities

- Fund school improvements by earmarking money for poor states and districts and by allowing schools to use federal special education money even though that use might create an "indirect benefit" for students without disabilities

There are two related themes of school reform in special education. The first theme, inclusion, builds on the IDEA doctrine of the least restrictive environment and seeks to ensure a place for students with disabilities in the general education curriculum, to the maximum extent appropriate for each student. The inclusion efforts have not been limited to general academic programs; efforts at inclusion also have been directed at extracurricular and other school activities (e.g., transportation, recess, and social events).

The second theme, collaboration, is a strategy that advances inclusion and enhances the likelihood of its success. Collaboration consists of special and general educators,

❧ *This general education classroom includes a student who has a hearing impairment. Through collaboration with other professionals, his teacher succeeds in meeting his educational needs while at the same time introducing other students to sign as a language.*

administrators, families, students, related service providers, school staff (e.g., secretaries, custodians, bus drivers), and community citizens working in teams to educate all students as much as possible in the general curriculum.

In the sections that follow, you will learn about inclusion and collaboration. We draw your attention to the research literature that is more and less favorable to inclusion; and, when we discuss collaboration, we also discuss its benefits and its barriers.

INCLUSION

Special education reform for inclusion has occurred and is currently occurring in four consecutive phases:

- Mainstreaming
- The Regular Education Initiative
- First-generation inclusion
- Second-generation inclusion

An entire issue of the *Journal of Special Education, 27* (4), published in 1994 (Hallahan & Kauffman, 1994), reviews research on the implementation of the principle of the least restrictive environment. It provides a comprehensive overview of programs throughout the nation—their successes, failures, and needs for improvement.

Mainstreaming

When IDEA first was implemented in the 1977–1978 school year and until sometime in the mid-1980s, the term that described the education of students with disabilities with those who did not have disabilities was *mainstreaming,* defined as "the educational arrangement of placing handicapped students in regular classes with their nonhandicapped peers to the maximum extent appropriate" (Turnbull & Schulz, 1979, p. 52).

Typically, mainstreaming was implemented by having students with disabilities participate in the nonacademic portions of the general education program, such as art, music, and physical education. Most of those students were, however, still enrolled in self-contained special education classes; they "visited" general education classes for a relatively small portion of time. No matter how receptive general educators may have been to stu-

❧ Notice the use of the term *handicapped students.* As you learned in Chapter 1, it was common during the mid-1970s to mid-1980s to use this term rather than today's preferred term, *students with a disability.* Remember, this change in terminology reflects a change in values, from a needs to a strengths perspective.

dents with disabilities in their classes (and not all general educators wanted mainstreaming), most clearly were unprepared to implement the concept (Grosenick & Reynolds, 1978). There were, as well, other problems associated with mainstreaming.

The Regular Education Initiative

For many educators and parents, mainstreaming provided far too little and came much too late for the students. Sometime in the mid-1980s, their impatience became evident in another movement: the Regular Education Initiative.

Madeleine Will and Special Education Reform.   The Regular Education Initiative debate officially began in 1986 when Madeleine Will, Assistant Secretary of the Office of Special Education and Rehabilitative Services of the U.S. Department of Education, criticized special education services for

- Excluding many students who need special educational support

- Stigmatizing students placed in special education by segregating them from their peers and general school activities

- Withholding special programs until the student fails rather than making specially designed instruction available earlier to prevent failure

> Although the Regular Education Initiative is a phenomenon of the mid-1980s, Lloyd Dunn's call for placement in general education occurred approximately seventeen years earlier. Change happens slowly, but why do students like Danny Ramirez have to wait so long to have the right and a genuine opportunity to develop relationships with their peers?

Madeleine Will, shown here with her son Jon, who has Down syndrome, was the sponsor of the Regular Education Initiative when she served as Assistant Secretary of the U.S. Department of Education. Jon and her hopes for him inspired much of her work and greatly influenced public policy.

BOX 3-1 **MY VOICE**

MADELEINE WILL

With a little reflection, I decided that what I really wanted for Jon was for him to dream big dreams, his own dreams. I wanted him to be his own man, a man with a disability who could and would define himself. Most importantly, I wanted him to become an adult who would know himself well enough to understand his own needs and assume responsibility to the greatest extent possible for his own happiness. . . .

In my imaginary world of care and education for people with disabilities, the emphasis on making and maintaining friends would grow more pronounced in the adolescent years, especially as nondisabled friends went off to college or became preoccupied with job responsibilities. A job, an apartment or a house, and various material goods do not constitute a fulfilled existence for any of us. What matters most to people are their families and loved ones and the quality of those relationships. This fundamental human need should be reflected throughout every phase of education.

Note: Reprinted from *Journal of Vocational Rehabilitation, 3*(2), M. C. Will, "The Question of Personal Autonomy," pp. 9–10, 1993, with kind permission from Elsevier Science Ireland Ltd., Bay 15K, Shannon Industrial Estate, Co. Clare. Ireland.

- Not promoting cooperative, supported partnerships between educators and parents

- Using pull-out programs to serve students with disabilities rather than adapting the general education program to accommodate their needs (Will, 1986)

Madeleine Will is the mother of a young man, Jon, who has mental retardation. Jon has long since graduated from high school; he now works full-time in suburban Washington, DC, is an avid fan of the Baltimore Orioles, and is an experienced traveler on the DC Metro system. As Box 3-1 makes clear, Madeleine Will approached the Regular Education Initiative with Jon in mind and with a vision that adult independence and a network of friends should and could be the outcomes of special education

Controversy Over the Regular Education Initiative.

Special education leaders varied in their support for the Regular Education Initiative. Some leaders' opinions can be described as polarized; and among other leaders there were many shades of gray. The different perspectives are outlined in Figure 3-2. A trenchant critique of the debate is that the Regular Education Initiative was "a wedding in which we, as special educators, have forgotten to invite the bride [general educators]" (Lieberman, 1985). Special educators were calling on general educators to assume more responsibility; predictably, general educators viewed the Regular Education Initiative as an outsiders' attempt to direct them into undesired roles.

Even more than the polarization between special and general education leaders, there appeared to be a dichotomy of opinion between different groups within the special education field. There were the "abolitionists," who wanted to eliminate the continuum of services and implement the Regular Education Initiative; and there were the "conservationists," who wanted to maintain the continuum and go very slowly in the direction that the Regular Education Initiative took (Fuchs & Fuchs, 1992). The abolitionists typically advocated for students with severe disabilities; the conservationists focused more on students with mild disabilities. Although this language—abolitionists and conservationists—appeared in the professional literature of the time, it is important for you to know that many special and general educators were able to see some of the benefits and drawbacks of both positions.

What became of the Regular Education Initiative? Madeleine Will's efforts ultimately caused significant changes not just in the terms of the debate but also in the entire approach to special education. A new term, inclusion, and a new technique, collaboration, evolved from the Regular Education Initiative.

Whose argument, that of the supporters or that of the opponents of the Regular Education Initiative, is more likely to give Danny an appropriate education in the least restrictive placement?

FIGURE 3–2 *Perspectives on the Regular Education Initiative*

The questions that the Regular Education Initiative raised were significant and challenging. At their core, they focused as much on the way students are taught as on the structure and organization of special education and its relatives up to general education. Among other questions raised by the Regular Education Initiative (REI) were these:

- Which existing efficacy studies demonstrate that special education is effective, and for whom and to what extent? (Biklen & Zollers, 1986; Carlberg & Kavale, 1980; Hallahan, Keller, McKinney, Lloyd, & Bryan 1988; Keogh, 1988a; Lipsky & Gartner, 1991; Madden & Slavin, 1983).

- To what extent is the classification of children reliable/valid or relevant to instruction? Which classification systems lead to stigma? (Ysseldyke & Algozzine, 1990; Ysseldyke, Algozzine, & Epps, 1983; Reynolds, 1991)

- To what extent are students identified as mildly handicapped, especially learning disabled, who in fact may not have disabilities and need of special education? (Bryan, Bay, & Donahue, 1988; Kauffman, Gerber, & Semmel, 1988; Keogh, 1988a; Ysseldyke & Algozzine, 1990)

- To what extent can students' failures be attributed to systemic problems, e.g., the shortcomings of teachers? (Biklen & Zollers, 1986; Kauffman, Gerber, & Semmel, 1988)

- Is the REI a "gross oversimplification of a complex problem . . . of significant differences that exist between the organizational structures, curricula, and other features of elementary and secondary schools?" (Schumaker & Deshler, 1988, p. 36)

- How effective is the Adaptive Learning Environments Model, the empirical model associated with the REI, in educating disabled students in mainstream classes, and how valid and reliable are the data to support its claims of effectiveness? (Bryan & Bryan, 1988; Fuchs & Fuchs, 1988; Hallahan, Keller, McKinney, Lloyd, & Bryan, 1988; Kauffman, Gerber, & Semmel, 1988)

- How capable is general education of serving all students effectively? (Bryan, Bay, & Donahue, 1988; Kauffman, Gerber, & Semmel, 1988; Keogh, 1988a, 1988b; McKinney & Hocutt, 1988; Walker & Bullis, 1991; Wang & Birch, 1984; Wang, Peverly, & Randolph, 1984)

- To what degree is the existence of parallel systems of education, that is, general and special education, a defensible use of limited fiscal and personnel resources? (Reynolds, 1991; Reynolds & Wang, 1983)

Note: From "Moving Beyond the Regular Education Initiative: National Reform in Special Education," by A. Hocutt and J. D. McKinney in *Integrating School Restructuring and Special Education Reform* (pp. 45–46), edited by James L. Paul, Hilda Rosselli, and Donnie Evans, 1995, Fort Worth, TX: Harcourt Brace College Publishers. Copyright 1995 by Harcourt Brace & Company. Reprinted with permission of the publisher.

FIRST-GENERATION INCLUSION

To introduce the first generation of the inclusion movement, we describe (a) the evolution toward inclusion, (b) the ways the continuum has "caught" students and kept them out of the general education curriculum, and (c) how first-generation inclusion tried to revise the continuum concept.

The Evolution Toward Inclusion

❉ Advocates were seeking to eliminate two options on IDEA's continuum of services: residential schools and special schools. Those options, they argued, inhibited relationships with peers and community members and choices about the place students would be educated.

During the mid-to-late 1980s, many advocates for students with severe and multiple disabilities began to argue for moving those students from special schools to special classes within neighborhood schools (Biklen, 1985; Snell, 1988; S. Stainback & Stainback, 1984). They were fortunate in the timing of their arguments. The Regular Education Initiative debate had concentrated so much on students with mild rather than severe and multiple disabilities that there was limited philosophical opposition to placing students with severe and multiple disabilities in typical schools.

Philosophy may have been a relative nonissue, but there were other issues. The opposition to inclusion was financial and logistical in nature. It arose at local and state levels when school administrators had to redirect fiscal resources from separate schools to more inclusive programs and to find space in regular school buildings for students who previously had been placed in their own separate schools and programs.

Over time and in spite of the opposition, proponents of inclusion began to challenge the very nature of schools: the separation of general and special education. Instead of trying to persuade school authorities to close special schools and create special classes for students with severe and multiple disabilities within general education schools, inclusion advocates—people like Carmen and Alfredo Ramirez—called on school officials to eliminate the continuum of services altogether. These advocates supported placing students with disabilities, from the very start of their education, into general classrooms, with supplementary aids and services (Lipsky & Gartner, 1989; Taylor, 1988).

"Caught in the Continuum"

Taylor (1988) asserted that students with disabilities were "caught in the *continuum.*" Often, accommodating those students in the general education classroom through supplementary aids and services was not even considered a viable option. Unfortunately, once students were slotted, they became caught, since traditionally few students placed in a more restrictive setting were returned to a general education classroom setting.

Essentially, the inclusion advocates abandoned the Regular Education Initiative's emphasis on improving the academic achievement of students with mild and moderate disabilities. They focused instead on enhancing social relationships (Snell, 1991; W. Stainback & Stainback, 1990) and preparing students with severe and multiple disabilities for adult living (P. M. Ferguson, Ferguson, & Jones, 1988; Gartner & Lipsky, 1987).

Continuum is the concept that services for students with disabilities begin with the most typical and extend to the least typical, most segregated, as the students' disabilities become more and more severe.

Like every other large institution for people with disabilities, Winfield State Hospital and Training School, in Kansas, segregated people with disabilities from the community, kept them out of school, and deprived them of their opportunities for growth and development. With the enactment of IDEA in 1975 and the establishment of right-to-treatment laws in the early 1970s, school-aged people began to leave the institutions and attend schools. That was a slow process, with Winfield being converted from a hospital to a prison as late as 1998.

Revising the Concept of the Continuum

The inclusive schools movement has been built on the same basic philosophy as the Regular Education Initiative: a new partnership between special and general education. Unlike the Regular Education Initiative, however, the inclusive schools movement has generated a significant amount of literature on how to individualize instruction and reorganize the delivery of special education services and supports (Bauwens & Hourcade, 1995; Falvey, 1995; Giangreco, Cloninger, & Iverson, 1993; Peck, Odom, & Bricker, 1993; Pugach & Johnson, 1995; W. Stainback & Stainback, 1996; Thousand, Villa, & Nevin, 1994; Villa, Thousand, Stainback, & Stainback, 1992; Zionts, 1997). The fundamental issue is to provide individualized instruction in general education classrooms that has typically been ascribed to special classrooms and special schools. Thus, proponents of inclusion call for a revision in the continuum concept, believing that it is not necessary for students to be pulled out of the general education classroom in order to get individualized and appropriate instruction.

Many inclusion advocates draw important differences between mainstreaming, the Regular Education Initiative, and the initial inclusion concept (which we call first-generation inclusion). They argue that mainstreaming primarily sought opportunities for students with disabilities to visit general classrooms. They also argue that the Regular Education Initiative sought merely to create more individualization within general education so that it could better accommodate the needs of students with mild disabilities. Inclusion advocates say that inclusion begins with the premise that general education classrooms should be structured so that all students belong from the very outset and so that student diversity is celebrated. As Carmen Ramirez believes, "Schools are for everyone." A leading special educator explains it this way:

> *Inclusion . . . is a value that is manifested in the way we plan, promote, and conceptualize the education and development of young children. . . . In inclusive programs, the diverse needs of all children are accommodated to the maximum extent possible within the general education curriculum. . . . Driven by a vision of schools as a place where all children learn well what we want them to learn, schools become creative and successful environments for adults and the children they serve. (Salisbury, 1991)*

Extent of Implementation

To what extent is inclusion currently being implemented? The question is difficult to answer. Data reveal the percentage of students with exceptionalities who spend a majority of their day in a general education classroom. They do not, however, indicate the quality of implementation.

Figure 3–3 sets forth the definitions that the U.S. Department of Education has used to report students' placements. Based on these definitions, Figure 3–4 illustrates the percentage of students with disabilities, ages three through twenty-one, who were served in different educational environments as of October 1995.

A larger percentage of elementary students than high school students are in general education. Among preschoolers, ages three-to-five, almost half are served in general education classrooms, but an additional 9 percent are served in resource rooms, and 31 percent are educated in separate classes. Among infants and toddlers with disabilities, almost half receive services in their families' home, but another one-third are in early intervention programs for infants and toddlers (birth to three), and 17 percent are in outpatient facilities (U.S. Department of Education, 1996).

Three Key Components

Inclusion refers to students with exceptionalities being authentic members of general education programs. The following are three key components of first-generation inclusion (Sailor, 1991):

Regular class includes students who receive the majority of their education program in a regular classroom and receive special education and related services outside the regular classroom for less than 21 percent of the school day.

Resource room includes students who receive special education and related services outside of the regular classroom for at least 21 percent but no more than 60 percent of the school day.

Separate class includes students who receive special education and related services outside the regular class for more than 60 percent of the school day.

Separate school includes students who receive special education and related services in a public or private separate day school for students with disabilities, at public expense, for more than 50 percent of the school day.

Residential facility includes students who receive special education in a public or private residential facility, at public expense, for more than 50 percent of the school day.

Homebound/hospital environment includes students placed in and receiving special education in a hospital or homebound program.

Note: From *To Assure the Free Appropriate Public Education of All Children With Disabilities: Eighteenth Annual Report to Congress on the Implementation of the Individuals With Disabilities Education Act,* by U.S. Department of Education, 1996, Washington, DC: U.S. Department of Education.

FIGURE 3–3 *Definitions of educational environments for students with disabilities*

- All students receive education in the school they would attend if they had no disability.
- School and general education placements are age- and grade-appropriate.
- Special education supports exist within the general education classes.

Three different terms are used in the literature: (a) *full inclusion* (Jakupcak, 1993); (b) *inclusion* (Putnam, 1993; Salisbury, Palombaro, & Hollowood, 1993); and (c) *inclusive education* (Giangreco et al., 1993; Sailor & Skrtic, 1995).

Home-School Placement. The first component of inclusion is home-school placement. Mixed opinions exist on the principle that students should attend their home schools. Some school administrators believe that they can provide more effective specialized services to a larger number of students by having all special education teachers and related services providers at the same school. This is the "critical mass" approach: A large

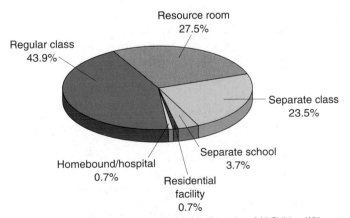

FIGURE 3–4 *Educational placement of students with disabilities*

Note: From *To Assure the Free Appropriate Public Education of All Children With Disabilities: Eighteenth Annual Report to Congress on the Implementation of the Individuals With Disabilities Education Act,* by U.S. Department of Education, 1996, Washington, DC: U.S. Department of Education.

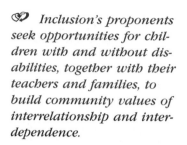
❧ *Inclusion's proponents seek opportunities for children with and without disabilities, together with their teachers and families, to build community values of interrelationship and interdependence.*

and concentrated number of students with disabilities at a single site promotes their appropriate education and makes it less costly, more efficient, and more effective to deliver related services and curricular benefits to them. That is one reason some school districts and administrators (a) operate special schools for students with severe or multiple disabilities, visual impairment, and hearing impairment; (b) group all students with a given exceptionality at one school; or (c) combine these approaches.

Inclusion proponents object to this kind of separation, seeking, instead, home-school placement. They contend that students should attend the same school that they would attend if they did not have a disability. A major purpose of inclusion, achieved through the presence of all students in their home school, is to develop a sense of community (S. Stainback & Stainback, 1992). As Carmen Ramirez observes, "Most people are social beings. Their sense of self and ability to function in an increasingly complex and mobile society depends in a surprisingly large part on interdependence and relationships."

There are three options to achieve the home-school principle: (a) the neighborhood school, (b) a transportation school, or (c) a school of choice (Sailor, Gerry, & Wilson, 1987). The neighborhood school often can provide greater opportunities for social inclusion in school and neighborhood activities. It enables schools to "take care of their own" by having an open-door policy for all students within the school's jurisdiction. Consistent with his parents' advocacy for inclusion, Danny Ramirez attends his neighborhood school. In the first part of this chapter, you read about Danny's school activities and how one result of neighborhood schooling is that Danny has friends in his own community.

Two other home-school strategies exist. Some school systems have established transportation schools in order to obtain specific racial or ethnic balances among the entire school population. A transportation school is one to which students are bused or otherwise transported for certain purposes, including racial balance. Some transportation schools are not the neighborhood schools for some of the students who attend them.

Other school systems use schools of choice, allowing families to choose the school that is most appropriate for meeting their child's needs. Schools of choice can include magnet schools, specialized schools operated by many school districts whereby the school curriculum is focused in math and science, performing arts, vocational/technical, or humanities. Attendance at a magnet school may be decided by lottery or parental choice. Admission may be competitive.

Charter schools offer a new choice. In charter schools, teachers and parents basically create a school, under charter or authority of the state, that reflects their values and approaches to educating students. Unfortunately, school-choice policy and magnet and charter schools seem to pay only limited attention to the needs of students identified as having exceptionalities (Ysseldyke, Thurlow, Algozzine, & Nathan, 1993).

Age- and Grade-Appropriate Placements.

The second component of first-generation inclusion favors educating all students in age- and grade-appropriate placements. Three major issues are at the heart of the inclusion debate: (a) eliminating the continuum of services; (b) increasing the amount of time students spend in the general education classroom; and (c) defining *all students.*

Eliminating the Continuum of Services. As you have learned, the inclusion movement opposes IDEA's continuum concept. Critics of the continuum (S. Stainback, Stainback, & Ayres, 1996; Taylor, 1988) challenge the traditional view that intensive services can be provided only in specialized settings where a critical mass of students have similar disabilities. The same critics accordingly seek to intensify special education services in the general education classroom. Their purpose is to ensure that students with special needs attain the supplementary aids and services that they need to benefit from being in school.

Not everyone agrees with eliminating the continuum (Manset & Semmel, 1997; Zigmond et al., 1995; Zigmond & Baker, 1995). Indeed, there is a wide range of perspectives about the benefits and drawbacks of the continuum of services. The Council for Exceptional Children's executive director, Nancy Safer (Council for Exceptional Children, 1997), endorses the individualized benefit of the continuum:

> *To meet individual needs, it is essential that schools provide a range of educational options and services for their students. We are glad to see so many schools providing those options while working to find new, innovative ways to include students with exceptionalities in the general classroom and neighborhood school. (p. 4)*

We encourage you to note this quote's dual emphasis on providing a *range* of options and services, while simultaneously creating new inclusion models. This is a good example of the differences in the field concerning the continuum.

Extent of General Classroom Placement. Educators favoring inclusion endorse placing all students with disabilities into general education classrooms; however, they also point out that there is a difference between being "based-in" and "confined to" general education classrooms:

> *"Based-in" refers to "being a member of a real class," "where and with whom you start the school day," "you may not spend all of your time with your class, but it is still your group and everyone knows it." . . . "Confined to" refers to spending 100% of each school day in regular education classes, leaving only, if, when, and under the same circumstances as nondisabled classmates. (Brown et al., 1991)*

Inclusion proponents generally agree that placement in general education classrooms does not mean that the student never leaves those classrooms for special services. The key is that the student is truly "a member of the class." At one point in his education, Danny took all but one course in general education; he went to a different program for language arts. Yet he continued to "hang out" with his typical peers at recess and lunch and to have a study group with them. Yes, he left the general education program, albeit briefly; but he was still a "member of the class."

Thus, first-generation inclusion allows students to leave the general education setting or program in order to receive instruction in resource rooms or in inclusive community settings. Leaving the classroom is especially nonstigmatizing when instruction in general classrooms is individualized to the degree that most, if not all, students receive special help in smaller groups in other school settings, including labs, the library, cafeteria, auditorium, other classrooms, and community learning environments.

The Council for Exceptional Children (CEC) is the oldest and largest professional association in the field of special education.

General and special educators can individualize instruction to such an extent that most students, with and without disabilities, receive help as individuals or as members of small groups within a class or in resource rooms, labs, and other settings.

The Meaning of All.   Many inclusion advocates ascribe great importance to having all children fully included in general classrooms: "An *inclusive school* [emphasis added] or classroom educates all students in the mainstream. . . . In these schools, no students, including those with disabilities, are relegated to the fringes of the school by placement in segregated wings, trailers, or special classes" (S. Stainback & Stainback, 1992).

Critics of including all students in general education classes have pointed out that the vast majority of advocates for inclusion are from The Association for Persons with Severe Handicaps (TASH) and represent the needs of students with severe and multiple disabilities. These critics question whether *one* constituency (professionals and families from the field of severe and multiple disabilities) has sufficient knowledge and accountability to speak for *all* other constituencies. In fact, many special education professionals whose work focuses on students with mild and moderate disabilities disagree with inclusion proponents who represent students with severe and multiple disabilities.

Clearly, educators and families vary in their opinions about inclusion.

> *For years, we've been impressed by arguments for the inclusion of children with severe intellectual disabilities in regular schools and classrooms. Fix your attention on these children and permit the parents and professional advocates of children with severe behavior problems, hearing impairments, learning disabilities, and etc., to speak on behalf of the children they know best. . . . Recognize that you are probably at the apex of your power. Use it to build bridges. Choose compromise over principles. By doing this, you will transform adversaries into allies willing to help you secure the full inclusion, not of all children, but of those who are the touchstone of your work and dreams.* (D. Fuchs & Fuchs, 1994)

The core issue of the debate is whether the *dominant* theme in educational decision making for students with exceptionalities is and should be placement (inclusion) or should be individualized and appropriate instruction related to priority educational outcomes. Some people believe it must be either-or; others, especially inclusion proponents, believe both goals—inclusion and appropriate education—can be accomplished. They contend

FIGURE 3–5 *Various organizational positions on inclusion*

Council for Exceptional Children

CEC believes that a continuum of services must be available for all children, youth, and young adults. CEC also believes that the concept of inclusion is a meaningful goal to be pursued in our schools and communities. In addition, CEC believes children, youth, and young adults with disabilities should be served whenever possible in general education classrooms in inclusive neighborhood schools and community settings. Such settings should be strengthened and supported by an infusion of especially trained personnel and other appropriate supportive practices according to the individual needs of the child. (CEC, 1993)

Council for Learning Disabilities

The Board of Trustees of the Council for Learning Disabilities (CLD) *supports* school reform efforts that enhance the education of all students, including those with learning disabilities (LD). The Council *supports* the education of students with LD in general education classrooms when deemed appropriate by the Individual Education Program (IEP) team. Such inclusion efforts require the provision of needed support services in order to be successful. One policy that the Council *cannot support* is the indiscriminate full-time placement of *all* students with LD in the regular education classroom, a policy often referred to as "full inclusion." CLD has grave concerns about any placement policy that ignores a critical component of special education service delivery: Program placement of each student should be based on an evaluation of that student's individual needs. The Council *cannot support* any policy that minimizes or eliminates service options designed to enhance the education of students with LD that are guaranteed by the Individuals with Disabilities Education Act. (Council for Learning Disabilities, 1993)

Council for Children with Behavioral Disorders (Subdivision of the Council for Exceptional Children)

Consistent with IDEA, CCBD supports a full continuum of mental health and special education services for children and youth with emotional and behavioral disorders. Educational decisions depend on individual student needs. Consequently, in contrast to those individuals in groups who advocate for full inclusion, CCBD does not support the notion that all special education students, including those students with emotional and behavioral disorders, are always best served in general education classrooms. . . .

CCBD supports the concept of inclusive schools whereby public schools serve all children, and whereby all personnel demonstrate ownership of all children in their school. (*CCBD Newsletter,* 1993)

Division for Early Childhood (Subdivision of the Council for Exceptional Children)

Inclusion, as a value, supports the right of all children, regardless of the diverse abilities, to participate actively in natural settings within their communities. A natural setting is one in which the child would spend time had he or she not had a disability. Such settings include but are not limited to home and family, play groups, child care, nursery schools, Head Start programs, kindergartens, and neighborhood school classrooms.

DEC believes in and supports full and successful access to health, social service, education, and other supports and services for young children and their families that promote full participation in community life. DEC values the diversity of families and supports a family-guided process for determining services that are based on the needs and preferences of individual families and children. (Division for Early Childhood, 1993)

continued

93

FIGURE 3–5   *continued*

The American Council of the Blind and Seven Additional Organizations in the Area of Blindness in the United States and Canada

"Full Inclusion," a philosophical concept currently advanced by a number of educators, is not a federal requirement of special education law. Proponents of "Full Inclusion" take the position that all students with disabilities must receive their total instruction in the general public school classroom regardless of individual needs. Unfortunately "full inclusion" would eliminate all special placements, including "pull out" services, resource rooms and specialized schools. Such an arrangement would be seriously detrimental to the educational development of many students with disabilities.

- Educational decisions must be made on a case-by-case basis consistent with the Individuals with Disabilities Education Act.

- Extreme caution must be exercised so that full inclusion does not result in "full submersion," social isolation, lowered self-esteem, poor performance, or a setting in which services are unavailable.

- The mandate in IDEA that states "To the maximum extent appropriate, children with disabilities [should be] educated with children who are nondisabled," does not intend that blind children avoid interaction with each other. ("Full Inclusion," 1993)

The Association for Persons with Severe Handicaps (TASH)

Resolution
WHEREAS the democratic ideals of American society can be best served and protected when diversity is highly valued and seen as the norm in all schools; when *all* students are viewed as active, fully participating members of the school community; and when the reciprocal benefits of full inclusion for all students is understood and celebrated;

BE IT RESOLVED that TASH reaffirms a definition of inclusion that begins with the educational and moral imperatives that students with disabilities belong in general education classrooms and that they receive the supports and services necessary to benefit from their education in the general education setting. Inclusion proceeds to and is fully defined by a new way of thinking based upon current understandings about how *all* children and young people are educated—a new way of thinking that embraces a sociology of acceptance of *all* children into the school community as active, fully participating members; that views diversity as the norm and maintains a high quality education for each student by assuring effective teaching powerful pedagogues and necessary supports to each child in the general education setting.

BE IT FURTHER RESOLVED that TASH calls upon local, state, provincial, regional and federal governments, as well as all related organizations, to stand accountable for the development and maintenance of educational opportunities for *all* students that are fully inclusive and ultimately effective; and that the United States Government be urged to vigorously enforce, at all levels, legislation *already enacted* that assures such accountability, development, and maintenance. (TASH, 1993)

American Federation of Teachers, AFL-CIO

Full inclusion poses a number of problems. First, there is no one-size-fits-all placement for disabled students. Different students have different needs, and the continuum of placements was designed to provide for them. Second, many districts adopting full inclusion are not providing regular classroom teachers with the training, equipment, qualified aides, and other supports they need to teach disabled children effectively. Finally, some disabled children are so violent and disruptive that their presence in the regular classroom virtually brings education to a halt for all of the students there. Existing laws make it difficult to remove such students from the classroom and place them in alternative settings.

The American Federation of Teachers has called for a moratorium on full inclusion and supports a review of federal, state, and local laws and regulations governing special education. The AFT believes that placements should be determined by the needs and abilities of the child and that when disabled students are appropriately "included" in regular classes, teachers be given adequate training and support services. (American Federation of Teachers, 1996)

American Speech-Language-Hearing Association (ASHA)

ASHA recognizes that the provision of speech, language, and hearing services in educational settings is moving toward service-delivery models that integrate intervention with general educational programming, often termed inclusion. Inclusion has numerous strengths, including natural opportunities for peer interaction, and available research suggests cautious optimism regarding its effectiveness in promoting communication abilities and skills in related developmental domains. ASHA believes that the shift toward inclusion will not be optimal when implemented in absolute terms. Rather, the unique and specific needs of each child and family must always be considered.

The broad goal of inclusive service delivery should be compatible with continued recognition of the individual's unique needs and concerns. Inclusive practices are recommended as a guide in the development of intervention programming for children and youths with communication disorders. (Asha, Suppl. 16, 1996, Spring, p. 35)

Council of Administrators of Special Education, Inc. (CASE) (Subdivision of the CEC)

CASE believes in and supports the evolving practice of inclusion for all students as an appropriate goal of our educational community. CASE believes that the decisions about an appropriate education for students must be made on an individual student basis. While there are those exceptions where full inclusion is not appropriate, we believe strongly in the goal of including ALL children with disabilities into their own school and community. This necessitates a shift in the focus of IEP teams *from* the place for a student *to* the intensity and scope of services that a student needs to be appropriately educated. (Council of Administrators of Special Education, 1994)

that students with exceptionalities can be authentic members of general education classes and *simultaneously* receive individualized and appropriate instruction and services.

Various professional organizations, as well as various family organizations, have taken positions about inclusion. Not unexpectedly, these positions differ, and yet all organizations are committed to providing an appropriate education to the students they represent (see Figure 3-5, pp. 91-93).

Special Education Supports Exist Within General Education Classes.

Tremendous variability exists in how special education supports are provided within general education classrooms. In fact, it is this component that we believe most distinguishes first- and second-generation inclusion. Typically, first-generation inclusion models have *added* teaching procedures and resources to general education classes. Some of the teaching procedures include adapted instruction, curriculum modification, and additional resources. Paraprofessionals are major resources in general education classrooms. Although in many cases paraprofessionals have added appropriate and meaningful support for students with disabilities as well as their classmates, often the *add-on* paraprofessional model has resulted in the following description:

During the years of our research, my colleagues and I saw students walking through hallways with clipboard-bearing adults "attached" to them or sitting apart in classrooms with an adult hovering over them showing them how to use books and papers unlike any others in the class. Often these "Velcroed" adults were easily identifiable as "special education" teachers because the students called them by their first names while using the more formal Ms. or Mr. to

✿ *Paraprofessionals like the woman standing in the center of this photo often support students with disabilities to be fully included in general education classrooms. Today, general educators, special educators, and paraprofessionals collaborate for inclusion.*

refer to the general education teacher. The included students seemed in, but not of the class. Indeed, we observed teachers who referred to particular students as "my inclusion student." It seemed to us that these students were caught inside a bubble that teachers didn't seem to notice but that nonetheless succeeded in keeping other students and teachers at a distance. . . .

- *These "inclusion" students are "irregular," even though they are in "regular" classrooms.*

- *They need "special" stuff that the "regular" teacher is neither competent nor approved to provide.*

- *The "special" educator is the officially designated provider of these "special" things.*

In trying to change everything, inclusion all too often seems to be leaving everything the same. But in a new place. (D. L. Ferguson, 1995, p. 284)

Second-generation inclusion, on the other hand, is characterized by *systemic* change in which the strengths and expertise of general and special education are merged to create new ways of delivering services to all students—those with and without exceptionalities. It goes far beyond simply adding adapted instructional strategies, modified curriculum, and additional resources. We will discuss second-generation inclusion later in the chapter. For now, the important point for you to understand is that there are many different ways for special education supports to exist within general education classes. Often, the way those supports are combined with general education can determine the success or failure of inclusion.

Throughout this book, we suggest how you can ensure that students with disabilities will be included in their schools' general curriculum. We do this in each of the following chapters in a section called "How Is Participation Encouraged?" In that section, you will find a box called "Inclusion Tips," which gives you brief tips on how to include students with disabilities. The box describes what you might see in the student: the behaviors, social interactions, educational performance, and classroom attitudes. Then, the box describes what you might be tempted to do—the wrong response. Next, it describes what you should do—the better response. Finally, it shows you how to include the student's peers in the inclusion process. See the accompanying box describing general inclusion tips.

Inclusion Tips

	What You Might See	What You Might Be Tempted to Do	Alternate Responses	Ways to Include Peers in the Process
Behavior	The student shows an apparently poor attitude toward other students and does not easily cooperate with them during instructional activities.	Discipline the student for his poor behavior and separate him from the rest of the class.	Identify his strengths and work together on a list of positive things he can say when responding to other students during instructional activities.	Ask the student to identify peers he would like to work with. Then work with this small group to practice verbal responses that would be helpful.
Social Interactions	The student has few friends and doesn't appear to want any.	Encourage him to take initiative toward others, but also allow him to be by himself whenever he chooses	Collaborate with the school counselor to plan ways to teach him specific social skills.	Work with identified peers to practice the specific social skills with him in and out of the classroom.
Educational Performance	His work is acceptable, but he needs constant supervision.	Assign an aide to work with him and allow him to complete unfinished work at home.	Collaborate with the special education teacher to create step-by-step assignments that he can do on his own. Set up a reward system for each layer successfully completed without supervision.	Encourage him to work with his peers to monitor the layered assignments. Ask peers to work with him to construct a tracking system for class assignments.
Classroom Attitudes	The student never volunteers answers and is reluctant to participate in class activities.	Carefully choose activities that allow him to work alone.	Together with the special education teacher, work with him ahead of time on content to be covered, and plan specific things for him to contribute.	Plan with peers positive contributions that each can make to upcoming class activities.

Challenges Encountered in First-Generation Inclusion

Many educators are concerned about the tremendous challenges of implementing inclusion. They fear that it dilutes what students need, which is *intense instruction* (Fuchs & Fuchs, 1995; Zigmond et al., 1995). They are not alone in this concern. Some parents also have expressed concerns about inclusion, but, paradoxically, the parents who are most positive about inclusion are those of children with more severe disabilities (Erwin & Soodak, 1995; Ryndak, Downing, Jacqueline, & Morrison, 1995).

You will recall that Carmen Ramirez values inclusion as the most significant aspect of the law and school programs. She has great expectations that one day the focus will be on enhancing the quality of mainstreaming rather than debating its merits.

With the types of problems that (my son) has, he needs one-on-one instruction. He needs someone to closely follow that he's comprehending what he's being taught. If he had the self-esteem and the motivation to learn, then he could be in the regular classroom (Green & Shinn, 1994, p. 274).

According to various researchers, general education teachers typically teach to the entire group of students in their classes and make few instructional adaptations to accommodate a particular student or small group of students (Baker & Zigmond, 1995; McIntosh, Vaughn, Schumm, Haager, & Lee, 1993). Based on extensive observation of five inclusion programs across the United States, researchers drew this conclusion:

Regardless of how well prepared a general educator is, the focus of general education practice is on the group: managing instruction for a large group of students, managing behavior within a large group of students, designing assessment suitable for a large group, and so forth. The special educator's focus has always been, and should continue to be on the individual, providing unique and response-contingent instruction, teaching socially appropriate behavior, designing tailored assessments that are both diagnostic and summative, and so forth. (Zigmond & Baker, 1995, p. 249)

Teachers identify class size as one of the major obstacles to inclusion. Smaller class size alone, however, is not enough to make inclusion effective. Approximately two-thirds of the 170 urban teachers who said that smaller is better could not identify resources they would need to successfully teach special education students in the general education classroom (Gottlieb, Alter, Gottlieb, & Wishner, 1994). Only 10 percent of them could identify any curriculum adaptations that they had made, and only 16 percent believed they could develop the necessary skills to effectively teach the children in their own classes.

Moreover, many teachers report that instructional adaptations for students with disabilities are not feasible in general education programs as a whole, especially for students beyond elementary school (Houck & Rogers, 1994; Pearman, Huang, & Mellblom, 1997; Schumm & Vaughn, 1991; Ysseldyke, Thurlow, Wotruba, & Nania, 1990). The lack of individualization in general education may explain why many general educators still endorse resource or pullout programs (Marston, 1996; Semmel, Abernathy, Butera, & Lesar, 1991). Finally, teachers consistently report that special education resources have not been infused into general education so as to ensure effective teaching in inclusive classes (Minke, Bear, Deemer, & Griffin, 1996; Vaughn & Schumm, 1995; Werts, Wolery, Snyder, & Caldwell, 1996).

Three recent studies have comprehensively reviewed inclusion literature. The first analyzed twenty-eight studies, conducted from 1958 to 1995, and summarized their implications for inclusion with respect to time, training, personnel, materials, class size, and severity of disability (Scruggs & Mastropieri, 1996). These findings are highlighted in Figure 3–6. These implications indicate teachers' perspectives that significantly more resources are needed in order to make inclusion successful.

The second review compared eight different inclusion models for elementary students with mild disabilities (Manset & Semmel, 1997). Results indicated that students in two of the models (Madden, Slavin, Karweit, Dolan, & Wasik, 1993; Jenkins, Jewell, Leicester, O'Connor, Jenkins, & Troutner, 1994) made significantly greater gains than students in resource programs in the subject areas of reading and language arts; students in one model (Schulte, Osborne, & McKinney, 1990) made significantly greater gains in reading, writing, and math. The authors concluded:

The evidence presented does suggest that inclusive programming for some students with mild disabilities can be an effective means of providing services, but the evidence clearly indicates that a model of wholesale inclusive programming that is superior to more traditional special education service delivery models does not exist at present. In addition, the data from these studies do not consti-

FIGURE 3–6 *Implications from Scruggs and Mastropieri's (1996) research synthesis*

- *Time*—Teachers report a need for one hour or more per day to plan for students with disabilities.

- *Training*—Teachers need systematic, intensive training, either as part of their certification programs, as intensive and well-planned in-services, or as an ongoing process with consultants.

- *Personnel resources*—Teachers report a need for additional personnel assistance to carry out mainstreaming objectives. This could include a half-time paraprofessional and daily contact with special education teachers.

- *Materials resources*—Teachers need adequate curriculum materials and other classroom equipment appropriate to the needs of students with disabilities.

- *Class size*—Teachers agree that their class size should be reduced, to fewer than twenty students, if students with disabilities are included.

- *Consideration of severity of disability*—Teachers are more willing to include students with mild disabilities than students with more severe disabilities, apparently because of teachers' perceived ability to carry on their teaching mission for the entire classroom. By implications, the more severe the disabilities represented in the inclusive setting, the more the previously mentioned sources of support would be needed.

Note: From "Teacher Perceptions of Mainstreaming/Inclusion, 1958–1995: A Research Synthesis," by Thomas E. Scruggs and Mary A. Mastropieri, *Exceptional Children, 63,* 1996, p. 74. Copyright 1996 by The Council For Exceptional Children. Reprinted with permission.

> *tute support for the dismantling of special education. In fact, collectively these studies highlight the importance of maintaining the opportunity for direct services by a specialist. If anything, results suggest that specialized programming should be expanded to maintain opportunities for intensive, individualized instruction that may prove beneficial to students with special needs, particularly on basic skills. (Manset & Semmel, 1997, pp. 177–178)*

The third review focused on students with severe disabilities. As you have learned, leaders in the field of severe and multiple disabilities have been the primary advocates for inclusive education (Falvey, 1995; W. Stainback & Stainback, 1996; Thousand, Villa, & Nevin, 1994). A comprehensive analysis and synthesis of nineteen research studies on the inclusion of students with severe disabilities in general education classes identified a number of successful inclusion outcomes (Hunt & Goetz, 1997). The review also identified six major themes of successful inclusion:

1. Active collaboration with parents is essential (Erwin & Soodak, 1995; Ryndak et al., 1995).

2. Students with severe disabilities successfully learn new skills in general education classrooms (Giangreco, Dennis, Cloninger, Edelman, & Schattman, 1993; Hunt, Staub, Alwell, & Goetz, 1994).

3. Students with severe disabilities have successful friendships in inclusive settings and often have more friendships in general education settings than they do in separate settings (Hunt, Farron-Davis, Beckstead, Curtis, & Goetz, 1994; Hunt, Alwell, Farron-Davis, & Goetz, 1996; Staub, Schwartz, Galluci, & Peck, 1994).

4. Classmates without disabilities experience positive outcomes when students with severe disabilities are included in their classes (Giangreco, Edelman, Dennis, & Cloninger, 1993; Hollowood, Salisbury, Rainforth, & Palombaro, 1994; Sharpe, York, & Knight, 1994).

5. Successful inclusion requires collaboration among professionals and parents at classroom, building, and system levels (Salisbury, Palombaro, & Hollowood, 1993; York-Barr, Schultz, Doyle, Kronberg, & Crossett, 1996).

6. Successful inclusion requires curriculum adaptation (Giangreco, Dennis, Cloninger, Edelman, & Schattman, 1993; Hunt, Alwell, Farron-Davis, & Goetz, 1996).

What is it about efforts in the area of severe and multiple disabilities that have led to more successful inclusion outcomes? There are a host of factors, but a significant one is that the severe and multiple disabilities literature clearly emphasizes *systemic* changes rather than *add-on* instructional adaptations, curriculum modifications, and resources. This brings us to the crossroads of first- and second-generation inclusion.

SECOND-GENERATION INCLUSION

Now that you have an understanding of first-generation inclusion, you will learn more about (a) the crossroads between first- and second-generation inclusion, (b) the expectations that special education leaders have for this next phase of inclusion, and (c) key issues associated with second-generation inclusion.

Crossroads: From First- to Second-Generation Inclusion

It is clear that the forces of school reform from Goals 2000 and IDEA and the special education field's history and, indeed, frustration with first-generation inclusion have brought special education to a crossroads. During the twenty-two years between IDEA's first enactment (1975) and its most recent reauthorization (1997), which strengthened its inclusion provisions, legitimate concerns have emerged. Some educators, parents, and researchers have expressed concerns about the ways in which inclusion has been implemented and even about whether inclusion itself is a desirable approach. During those twenty-two years, however, some extraordinary progress has also been made toward including students with disabilities in schools and in the general curriculum. Many teachers and parents found ways to implement the least restrictive environment principle and to move from mere mainstreaming to authentic inclusion. Researchers have also documented the effectiveness of these initiatives.

Not only are researchers of severe disabilities calling for *systems* change, but researchers of mild disabilities have similar perspectives.

> *Special educators must be part of the ongoing dialogue in general education that will lead to reform of curriculum, school organization, and professional development. We must be part of the team that* recreates *[emphasis added] schools so that all children and youth, among those with disabilities, might succeed. (Zigmond & Baker, 1995, p. 248)*

If special education indeed is at a crossroads, what are the next steps? Will special education take the path that parallels the past or the path that pursues second-generation inclusion, as appropriate and as consistent with the 1997 version of IDEA?

The answers to these questions depend on many factors. As we said in Chapters 1 and 2 and in this chapter, IDEA points educators down the path less traveled, the second-generation inclusion path. And as we pointed out earlier in this chapter, the entire school reform movement (in both general and special education) makes it possible for schools to restructure themselves *systemically* to be more inclusive. Chapters 4 to 16 show how educators participate in the restructuring effort.

At the core of the matter is a conceptual problem. First-generation inclusion has basically *added* new approaches to existing school practices. As a leading theorist has observed, such terms as *modification* and *adaptation* have characterized past inclusion efforts. Thus, the techniques of special education have been *added onto,* and thus have merely modified or adapted, the approaches used in general education (Pugach, 1995). An additive approach has been fundamentally limiting. That is so because it has taken, as a constant or unchangeable factor, the present organization of schools, especially the present relationship between general and special education. That relationship is one of "cousins"—general and special educators are kin to each other but not members of the same immediate family.

By contrast, future efforts on behalf of inclusion—what we call second-generation inclusion—require a marital rather than a cousin relationship. For that to happen, the education enterprise needs to be redesigned at the systems level.

D. L. Ferguson (1995), a researcher in severe disabilities, described the shift from first- to second generation inclusion as follows:

> *the lesson to be learned from special education's inclusion initiative is that the real challenge is a lot harder and more complicated than we thought. Neither special nor general education alone has either the capacity or the vision to challenge and change the deep-rooted assumptions that separate and track children and youths according to presumptions about ability, achievement, and eventual social contribution. Meaningful change will require nothing less than a joint effort to reinvent [emphasis added] schools to be more accommodating to all dimensions of human diversity. (D. L. Ferguson, 1995, p. 285)*

Key Issues for Second-Generation Inclusion

Schools that have adopted second-generation inclusion are placing students with exceptionalities in general education classes and restructuring their schools for the benefit of all students (Falvey, 1995; Pugach, 1995; Villa & Thousand, 1995). The "Making a Difference" box (Box 3–2) highlights key points from a panel discussion at the National School Boards Association annual conference in which school superintendents addressed the necessity of *systems change.*

As stated by Stuart Berger, superintendent of the Baltimore County, MD, school system, "inclusion is not a policy change, it is a culture change. . . ."

A school *culture* change can turn teaching for diversity into the norm rather than teaching for the group. How might general and special education classrooms be organized if teaching for diversity is the norm? One successful approach is cooperative teaching, which provides special education within general education classroom environments. Typically, cooperative teaching involves two or more educators sharing the responsibility for planning, delivering, and evaluating instruction for students (Bauwens & Hourcade, 1995; Thousand, Villa, & Nevin, 1994). Cooperative teaching benefits students with exceptionalities by reducing the need for pullout programs and by making individualization more effective in general education classrooms. It benefits students without exceptionalities because they, too, have increased access to individualization. The accompanying "Into Practice" profile (Box 3–3) describes a cooperative teaching team consisting of two classroom teachers and one teacher with expertise in learning disabilities.

What benefits and drawbacks might Danny derive from the cooperative teaching approach described in "Into Practice," Box 3–2?

One of the leading second-generation inclusion reformers is Marlene Pugach. Figure 3–7 describes her expectations for second-generation inclusion.

Research is only now beginning to report on the perspectives of teachers and administrators about second-generation inclusion. In the most comprehensive study to date, the majority of almost 700 general and special education teachers and administrators from five states and one Canadian province viewed that kind of schooling favorably:

- *General and special educators share responsibility for meeting the needs of all children.*

- *General and special educators are able to work together as coequal partners.*

BOX 3-2   MAKING A DIFFERENCE

"THE ROAD TO INCLUSION CAN BE SMOOTH OR HELLISH"

The following article, reprinted from School Board News, *covered a panel discussion at the National School Boards Association Annual Conference that reinforced the importance of careful planning and communication when a district begins its move to inclusion.*

"Inclusion is not a policy change, it is a culture change," said Stuart Berger, superintendent of the Baltimore County, MD, school system. . . . Berger joined Mike Izquierdo, board president of the Ysleta Independent School District in El Paso, Texas, and Waldemar Rojas, superintendent of the San Francisco school district, in a panel discussion about the best way to include special education students in the regular classroom. Each stressed the importance of staff and parent training.

When Baltimore County moved from educating all special education students in separate facilities to allowing parents to choose between a special school or a comprehensive school, the district experienced unexpected opposition from parents, Berger says. Those whose special education children had negative experiences in "regular" education programs did not want their children moved. Other parents feared the "top" special education students would be removed from special schools, thus eliminating role models for other students, he adds. Middle class parents of "regular" students felt special education students would water down the curriculum in the comprehensive schools. When

several groups, including the teachers' union, sued the district and talk radio got involved, the district had a crisis on its hands. "It was pure, non-stop hell," he says.

But in San Francisco, Rojas reports, inclusion was implemented "without a peep" because the district worked for two years before the changeover to prepare teachers, administrators, and parents. He says the district first asked the question, "Is the community ready philosophically, emotionally, academically, and politically?"

When the Ysleta school district moved to an inclusion plan two years ago, the watch-words were "educate and communicate," says Izquierdo. The district spent "lots of money" on teacher training, he says.

What educators, parents, and school boards need to understand, says Berger, is the fundamental difference between mainstreaming and inclusion. Mainstreaming starts with the premise that children will be isolated until they demonstrate that they can do more, he says. Inclusion, on the other hand, assumes that the child is going to start out in the regular classroom. Inclusion is a civil rights issue, Berger adds. Every child ought to be given the opportunity to learn and students must be exposed to the differences they are going to find in the world, he says.

School boards also must understand that preparing staff and parents for a change to inclusion is a "process without a destination," says Rojas. Making people comfortable with a new program takes a long time. "You can't expect people to become zealots just because you say, 'this is the policy.'"

Note: From "The Road to Inclusion Can Be Smooth or Hellish," 1995, April 2, *School Board News/Conference Edition*, p. 5, courtesy of the National Schools Boards Association.

• *The achievement level of students with disabilities does not decrease in general education classrooms.*

• *Team teaching by general and special educators results in enhanced feelings of competency for both general and special educators. (Villa, Thousand, Meyers, & Nevin, 1996, p. 40)*

This research is backed by practices that you will learn about in Chapters 4 to 16. A key practice is collaboration, which we discuss in the next section of this chapter.

In our view, IDEA, as reauthorized in 1997, demands and probably will accomplish a significant transformation of the schools. That kind of pervasive change will not, however, come easily; as you have just read, there have been imposing barriers to mainstreaming, the Regular Education Initiative, and first-generation inclusion. Now, however, IDEA strengthens the evolution toward second-generation inclusion and the means to accomplish it, as you are about to learn.

BOX 3-3   INTO PRACTICE

COOPERATIVE TEACHING IN FIFTH-GRADE CLASSES

The teaching team was made up of two fifth-grade classroom teachers and one teacher of students with learning disabilities. Classes were in an elementary school that served approximately 580 students, of whom about 40% were minorities and 60% were Caucasian. The two fifth-grade classrooms were located next to each and the former classroom for students with learning disabilities was adjacent to one of these classrooms. There were also some small study rooms located across the hall that were used for small group work.

All students were assigned to one of the two fifth-grade classroom teachers; both of the teachers taught reading and math, with one teaching science and the other teaching social studies. The special education teacher moved back and forth between classes offering assistance to individual students as appropriate. As the year progressed, the special education teacher began to teach some of the curriculum subjects and also to do more whole-class instruction. The three teachers met as a small group, in which all had equal status. They met each day for about forty-five minutes for joint planning and had frequent informal discussions throughout the day. A formal team meeting, held one day each week, enabled them to give close attention to how things were going and ways they needed to improve.

Interviews with nine students with learning disabilities, nine students without disabilities, and the three teachers focused on (a) classroom social climate, (b) instructional effects, and (c) teacher roles and tasks.

Concerning classroom climate, half of the students used the word "fun" to describe school. They reported that they thought they were doing better academically than they had done in other classroom arrangements and that they liked school more than in past years. They emphasized the importance of working together in getting and receiving help. Since they considered all three teachers available to them, they felt that help was always close by. All students were expected to help each other including those with learning disabilities. One of the special education students commented: "Last year I'd get up all grumpy and mean and never wanted to go to school, but now I always go. Sometimes I don't want to go, but I get up and I just know that I'm going to have a great day. So I'll just get up and go with a smile on my face."

Concerning instructional effects, students discussed "varied instruction" and small-group assistance. Varied instruction meant that there was flexibility in grouping so that no group was viewed as permanently deficient in skills and always requiring remedial assistance. A couple of the students with learning disabilities commented about how hard it had been in previous years to be pulled out of the general classroom and then to come back and to not be clear about what they had missed. Although different groups of students were sometimes pulled aside for special instruction, there was not a continuous pull out at a regular time that always resulted in students missing a certain part of the classroom activities. No student with learning disabilities was labeled as such by any of the general education students that were interviewed.

The third theme was teachers' roles and tasks. All of the students emphasized that it was helpful to have the "helping teacher" who assisted them in understanding things that were difficult. In only one instance did one of the students identify the special education teacher as a teacher for children with learning disabilities: "I think she's more of an aide . . . [for] kids with disabilities, to learn and stuff. [S]he takes them in her room and shows them how to do it in an easier way . . . and faster." The same student also went on to say, "When the teacher starts getting headaches or getting strained out, [she] can take over and help the other teacher out." Many of the students used the term "taking turns" to describe how the three teachers shared roles. They emphasized the fact that the special education teacher's role was to help with small-group work. They tended to see the special education teacher as attending to individual needs and the classroom teachers as delivering content.

The teachers reported that they felt more capable of meeting the needs of high achieving students with this arrangement because it was easier to provide small-group assistance. "Teachers reported that their combined classes received the majority of awards at the annual end-of-year ceremony in the areas of citizenship, sportsmanship, and academics and that teams from their classrooms also won citywide and mathematics competition."

Expectation 1: School-wide reform includes inclusion. "A school would not have an inclusion program alone as evidence of reform. The move toward inclusion would be part of a dynamic effort to rethink what it means to educate all children, an effort rich with coordinated curriculum and instructional and social reform. Our observers 10 years hence would need to look how the full context for reform supports inclusion."

Expectation 2: Teacher renewal is an acknowledged and prominent goal of the partnerships formed between special and general education teachers. "Through collaborative action research projects, special and general education teachers could work together as equal partners toward implementing curricular and instructional change (Pugach & Johnson, 1990). . . . A coordinated agenda would drive the partnership with students *and* teacher growth both as focal points of their work. More than anything, such teachers would be interested in new frameworks for teaching and learning, so that when promising approaches they cannot yet imagine are developed, they are eager to try them out. At the same time, they would be wary of each successive bandwagon, measuring new approaches against their philosophical orientation to teaching."

Expectation 3: Intensive student needs are important. "But in the next generation of inclusive classrooms, a flexible approach to grouping that enables teachers to meet with students who need remediation as well as those who need enrichment needs to be in place (Pugach & Wesson, 1995). . . . Group membership would depend upon the project assignment or task, and as part of their regular planning, teachers would reflect on whether they are flexible in the expectations they hold for their students. . . . By monitoring their own attitudes, teachers can push the limits of what they expect from their students."

Expectation 4: What counts as "special" may not always stand out. These classrooms offer something special, then, because "they provide a context in which students are given a real opportunity to discard their labels of disability and teachers are given the opportunity to create classrooms where such labels do not drive practice. They exemplify new sets of beliefs about who does and does not belong and incorporate sound methodologies to enact those beliefs."

Note. From "On the Failure of Imagination in Inclusive Schools," by M. C. Pugach, 1995, *Journal of Special Education, 29,* pp. 219–229. Copyright 1995 by Pro-Ed. Reprinted with permission.

THE INCLUSION REQUIREMENTS OF IDEA: THE LEAST RESTRICTIVE ENVIRONMENT

The Basic Rule: Rebuttable Presumption

As you read in Chapter 1, IDEA creates a rebuttable presumption in favor of inclusion: To the maximum extent appropriate for each of them, students with disabilities must be educated with students who are not disabled. Separate classes, separate schooling, or other removal from the general educational environment may occur only when the nature or severity of their disability is such that education in general education classes with the use of supplementary aids and services cannot be achieved satisfactorily.

Provisions Advancing Inclusion

IDEA sets out additional provisions that advance the doctrine of the least restrictive environment and second-generation inclusion. You should be familiar with these from reading Chapters 1 and 2. As you may recall, IDEA creates a seamless approach to a student's appropriate education in inclusive settings, beginning with a definition of special education, then addressing evaluation standards, and finally specifying eight different inclusion-related requirements within the individualized education program (IEP) process.

- *Definition of special education*—IDEA lists, in order of preference, the environments where services will occur, starting with typical settings such as classrooms and moving toward the less typical, namely, homes, hospitals and institutions, and other settings.

• *Nondiscriminatory evaluation*—IDEA requires a general educator to be a member of the evaluation team, assigns specific duties to that person, requires the school district representative on the team to know about the general curriculum, and requires the team to evaluate the student for any potential to participate in the general curriculum.

• *Individualized education program*—IDEA requires the IEP team to (a) identify how a student can participate in the general curriculum and what educators will do to increase that participation; (b) enumerate the related services and supplementary aids and services that will be provided so the student can participate in the general curriculum; (c) describe the modifications in the general curriculum that will be made for the student and how general educators will be supported to accommodate the student; (d) describe the extent to which the student will not be included in the general curriculum (i.e., the student starts in general education, not in special education); (e) state how the student will participate in state and district assessments; (f) state how infants and toddlers will participate in natural environments.

In summary, the revised IDEA (1997) is far more proinclusion than IDEA ever was. Yes, a rebuttable presumption still exists, and placement in the general curriculum can be set aside under limited conditions. But, there are now so many new provisions—largely related to the nondiscriminatory evaluation and the individualized family services plan (IFSP)/IEP process—that the schools will be hard-pressed to simply assume that any student should not participate in some general education settings and programs. Instead, schools carry the responsibility and accountability of proving that a student should be kept out of the general curriculum. The rule is that a student begins in the general curriculum and is removed from it only for cause.

COLLABORATION AS A PREREQUISITE FOR INCLUSION

Given the school reform initiatives in general education (Goals 2000) and that IDEA has strong proinclusion provisions, it is fair to say that IDEA supports and fosters a redesigned school system that fully and meaningfully incorporates special education personnel and resources into all general education programs and settings. To redesign a school and accomplish that merger, collaboration between a host of people will be necessary. So, let's consider what collaboration means and how it can work. In this section, we (a) define collaboration, (b) give a rationale for it, and (c) discuss the roles of potential collaborators.

Definition

Collaboration is "an interactive process which enables people with diverse expertise to generate creative solutions to mutually defined problems" (Idol, Paolucci-Whitcomb, & Nevin, 1986). Collaboration builds on the expertise, interests, and strengths of everyone involved in the educational process: students, families, teachers, related service providers, paraprofessionals, school staff, administrators, and community members. Because collaboration acknowledges that each of these people can participate in creative problem solving, it tries to create opportunities for them to solve problems jointly. It seeks to apply the adage that "all of us are smarter than one of us." As a professional, you will be able to play four roles in school-wide collaboration:

• **Supportive role**—Caring and being there for your colleagues to share in times of need and in times of joy

• **Facilitative role**—Helping your colleagues develop a capacity to solve problems, engage in tasks, or deal independently with professional challenges

• **Information-giving role**—Providing direct assistance to your colleagues so they are better equipped to deal with problems on an ongoing basis

As IDEA says, special education is a service, not a place to which students with disabilities are sent.

The **supportive role** means caring and being there for your colleagues to share in times of need and in times of joy.

The **facilitative role** means helping your colleagues develop a capacity to solve problems, engage in tasks, or deal independently with professional challenges.

The **information-giving role** means providing direct assistance to your colleagues so they are better equipped to deal with problems on an ongoing basis.

IDEA's least restrictive environment doctrine of access to the general curriculum means access not just to the academics but also to the extracurriculars. When students team up with each other, they can make that kind of access a reality.

The **prescriptive role** means prescribing a path of action to your colleagues.

• **Prescriptive role**—Prescribing a path of action to your colleagues (Pugach & Johnson, 1995, pp. 38–42)

Rationale for Collaboration

In general and special education, each professional historically has had an explicit job description and has been expected to fit into a certain niche and to perform duties in an independent manner. Because education is typically administered as a bureaucracy, educators have functioned as bureaucrats (Skrtic, 1987), with general and special education teachers often working in isolation from each other. Because teachers typically spend 80 to 90 percent of their work day in direct student contact and use planning periods, recesses, or lunch breaks to provide extra attention to students or to communicate with parents (Hoerr, 1996), they cannot capitalize upon each other's potentially valuable contributions.

An alternative approach, associated with school restructuring, is collaboration that responds specifically to school-based, student-focused needs (Skrtic, 1991). Collaborative organization can enable diverse problem-solving teams to work on mutual challenges and to devise innovative solutions. Research soundly documents collaboration's benefits (Thousand, Villa, & Nevin, 1996):

Preschool and School-Age Outcomes

• Action plans generated by a team of general and special educators to resolve instructional problems in an elementary school resulted in fewer and more appropriate referrals for special education placement (Saver & Downes, 1991).

• After thirteen California special educators collaborated to implement specialized reading and behavior instructions to students in elementary school resource rooms (special education classrooms) and general education classes, a substantial number of students were able to leave the special education program and be included in general education (Givens-Ogle, Christ, & Idol, 1991).

BOX 3-4	**MAKING A DIFFERENCE**

SYSTEM-WIDE COLLABORATION OUTCOMES

Vermont leads the nation in including students with disabilities in general education, with 83 percent of those children being educated in general education classes, as distinguished from 36 percent nationwide. That impressive figure is the result of state law, Vermont Act 230, which declared a state policy that each local school shall collaborate with parents to create a local, comprehensive system of education that will ensure that, to the maximum extent possible, all students—repeat: all—will succeed in general education classrooms.

To implement this statement of purpose, the Vermont legislature committed 1 percent of the state's total special education budget to training teachers and administrators in strategies for effectively collaborating to support special education students in general education programs and community settings. Each local school established a collaboration team, called an Instructional Support Team, to help all of its staff avoid referring students to special education; the Team provided each teacher with advice and additional classroom support.

As a result of the policy, budget, and implementation plans, the number of students identified for special education decreased in Vermont by over 17 percent from 1990–1994; student performance, behavior, and social engagement has not diminished in general education; each school now uses an Instructional Support Team approach; many schools have restructured themselves to integrate special education and other remedial services into general education programs; and every school uses state funds to expand professional development opportunities for all of its staff in such areas as collaboration, technology, integrated curriculum, discipline, and crisis prevention.

Note: From "Collaboration," by J. Thousand, R. A. Villa, and A. Nevin, in *Improving the Implementation of the Individuals With Disabilities Education Act: Making Schools Work for All of America's Children* (pp. 565–602) edited by the National Council on Disability, 1996, Washington, DC: National Council on Disability.

- Two factors are associated with positive outcomes after students leave school: employment training and collaboration with parents and among agencies (Kohler, 1993).

Professional Outcomes

- Approximately three-fourths of the general education staff from an Arizona elementary school district used district-wide collaboration to help them meet the instructional needs of students with exceptionalities (Lutkemier, 1991).

- Forty-three percent of the general and special education staff in a K–12 Vermont school district reported that collaboration had increased their competence to teach students with disabilities in general education classes (Cross & Villa, 1992).

- Collaboration skills enabled special educators and related-service providers to reduce their risk of burnout and job attrition (Cooley & Yovanoff, 1996).

System-Wide Outcomes

- Students' academic and social gains and enhanced positive responses from teachers, parents, and administrators resulted from staff development focused on collaboration techniques (Chapple, 1994).

- Vermont schools that established collaborative teams achieved the success reported in Box 3-4.

Collaboration is such an important matter that in the section of each of the following chapters entitled "How Is Participation Encouraged?" you will find a box called "Collaboration Tips" (see the accompanying box), which shows how educators, students, and families can collaborate. We list the people who are the collaborators, their roles, the barriers that they may face in collaborating with each other, the solutions to those barriers, the

Collaboration Tips

PLANNING FOR SECOND GENERATION INCLUSION

COLLABORATION GOAL   To plan second-generation inclusion by merging the expertise and resources of general and special education teachers in order to meet the individual needs of all students in their neighborhood school.

Collaborators	Roles and Preparation	Possible Barriers	Solutions to Barriers	Modifications to Implementation	Ongoing Evaluation
Students with disabilities	Students share perspectives on what would be personally most helpful for them.	Fear that their ideas will not be accepted or valued.	Make a list of their needs and possible solutions to meet those needs.	Meet with parents and peers to explain and extend the list of solutions to make inclusion work.	Turn the list into a working document in which newly recognized needs can be added and new ideas tried.
Parents	Participate as full team members; advocate for stronger family–professional partnerships.	Fear of losing special education expertise in working with child; knowledge of curriculum.	Arrange a panel presentation of parents who have been successful with second-generation inclusion.	Ensure that district and building long-range plan addresses ongoing training and support of parents.	Monitor extent to which parents overcome fears and actively collaborate with educators.
General Educator(s)	Share expertise in typical development; create supplementary aids and services.	Letting go of autonomy of teaching in a separate classroom; recognize roles shift in working more with adults.	Work with teacher mentors who have been involved in successful second-generation inclusion programs.	Build on each teacher's strengths and preferences in developing building capacity.	Monitor rate and extent of student progress; monitor expanding expertise of teachers.
Special Educator(s)	Share expertise in atypical development; create supplementary aids and services.	Letting go of autonomy of teaching in a separate classroom; recognize roles shift in working more with adults.	Work with teacher mentors who have been involved in successful second-generation inclusion programs.	Build on each teacher's strengths and preferences in developing building capacity.	Monitor rate and extent of student progress; monitor expanding expertise of teachers.

ways to implement their collaboration, and the ways to evaluate whether their collaboration has been effective.

Roles of Potential Collaborators

Students, families, teachers, related-service providers, paraprofessionals, translators/interpreters, and administrators can be collaborators, as indeed can anyone who can help solve problems facing schools and students.

Collaborators	Roles and Preparation	Possible Barriers	Solutions to Barriers	Modifications to Implementation	Ongoing Evaluation
Related Service Providers	Integrate related services in inclusive settings.	Time requirements to travel between schools; knowledge of related services integration	Reduce case loads; work with mentors who have been involved in successful second-generation inclusion.	Increase time consulting with general and special education teachers to integrate related services activities in their work with students.	Monitor rate and extent of student progress; monitor expanding expertise of teachers.
Administrative Personnel	Establish district- and building-level planning teams. Develop a shared mission statement and core values.	Limited experience and knowledge; rigid district policies	Work with administrative mentors who have successful second-generation inclusion programs.	Incorporate successful strategies learned from mentors; work with team on long-term planning.	Specify indicators of success for each of the major tasks on the long-term plan.
Students without disabilities	Student council representatives share perspectives on creating inclusive opportunities.	Being credible to adults; having an adequate attention span for planning meetings	Prioritize topics on which students with special needs have the most to contribute.	Create a student council forum to brainstorm creative ideas to make inclusion work.	Students help to track the success of solutions tried.
All	Write out the strengths of each collaborator.	Personal agendas	Voice strengths; develop goals tied to contract of awards and consequences.	Meet together to celebrate milestones and plan new ones.	Plan goals and strategies for future success; share successes with others.

Students.   Students themselves can be valuable members of collaboration teams. Danny Ramirez is a member of two collaboration teams; in fact, he is the reason the teams exist. One team consists of the students who practice cooperative learning; the other consists of the teachers, family members, and friends who form Danny's circle of friends. As important as these teams are for Danny, his family, his teachers, and his peers, Danny still has a way to go before reaching his full potential as a collaborator. For one thing, he does not yet participate in developing his own IEP, though Carmen and Alfredo do.

❧   When collaboration involves students and families, as well as professionals, it builds on everyone's strengths—their abilities to contribute. It also recognizes that, to a degree, students should have choices about their education and that they can make positive contributions to decision making.

Students as Collaborators: Self-Determination.   Special education values student **self-determination** (Sands & Wehmeyer, 1996); however, fostering student autonomy in educational decision making is not prized in some cultures. Consider the perspective of a Taiwanese mother of a high school student enrolled in a gifted program. She describes how emphasis on student autonomy runs contrary to her cultural values:

> *When my daughter, Jean, was in junior high school, the gifted education counselor . . . never asked me [what I wanted for my daughter] and then . . . never gave me eye contact. During the meeting she only asked my daughter what she wanted to do in the next year, and she didn't ask me. After she asked my daughter, then she'd give me the papers and say, "Okay, sign your name." That was really frustrating. (Turnbull & Turnbull, 1997, p. 237)*

Successful collaboration with students, as well as with other team members, must always be culturally sensitive. Thus, we encourage you to always adapt your approaches to the cultural values of the student and family with whom you are working.

The majority of students in special education are, like Danny, not participating in the development of their IEPs. Although there are many reasons for this, a common one is that teachers and parents are unsure of the most supportive ways to enable students to participate in collaborative decision making.

Strategies for Self-Determination.   There are, however, strategies for preparing students and their parents for meaningful student involvement (Martin & Marshall, 1996; Van Reusen & Bos, 1994). In addition to IEP involvement, students can work with each other through peer tutoring, serve on school committees, advocate for classmates with special needs, resolve conflicts through mediation, and provide assistance in making friends (Thousand, Villa, & Nevin 1994).

> *In a high school, the accountability committee and the student council cosponsored a forum for interested students to talk about the school, how it was doing, how it could be improved, and to explore student opinions on issues that students faced. In addition, each student council member called several students who had dropped out in order to collect feedback from them. The school collected a large bank of suggestions for improvement. As a result of the usefulness of this activity, several students, including two students with disabilities, were invited to become members of the school and district accountability committees. (Buswell, 1993)*

Parents.   As you learned in Chapters 1 and 2, IDEA gives parents extensive rights to participate in decisions related to their children's evaluation, programs, and placement. Teachers tend to view parents as more capable of participating in decision making when they have more frequent interactions with them and when the focus students are younger (Michael, Arnold, Magliocca, & Miller, 1992); educators are less likely to seek parental involvement as the child ages.

Power Relationships.   Too frequently, parents believe that professional educators have "expert power" and that they can contribute little to educational decision making. A "we–they" posture is particularly problematic, especially for parents who have low incomes or who are from a different culture than that of the educators (DeGangi, Wietlisbach, Poisson, Stein, & Royeen, 1994; Harry, Allen, & McLaughlin, 1995).

Benefits of Power Sharing.   Nevertheless, successful collaboration and the new IDEA provisions require professionals and parents to have more contacts with each other, enabling parents to share their important insights and goals. An important lesson from the Ramirezes' experiences—a lesson that IDEA does not want to be repeated—is that schools that refuse to take parents' perspectives into account may well be providing an inappropriate education. They may overlook the students' strengths, not know what the student can do outside of school, not learn how to involve parents in following through on what

ABC NEWS

VIDEO REFLECTIONS

COMMON MIRACLES: THE NEW AMERICAN REVOLUTION IN LEARNING, PART III

"We have found some entire communities where learning has become a common miracle—that is to say, everyone participates," ABC anchor Peter Jennings comments in Part II of *Common Miracles.* The sound of successful school reform results when communities ask a critical question: What kinds of people must schools produce? According to ABC correspondent Bill Blakemore, when communities commit to answering this question and making changes based on the results, "new links between the different cells and communities seem to make the schools come alive again." These different cells may include "schools, parent groups, businesses, counselors, career planners, the police, the ethnic and neighborhood organizations, government, museums, service clubs, theaters, colleges." The most important link, however, is parents. "Parents are gold," Blakemore adds. In this video, you will learn about some strategies schools use to increase collaboration with parents and extend the invitation to collaborate throughout our communities.

What do you think? How would you answer the question, What kinds of people must schools produce? Blakemore comments, "the successful people we found were not only looking for the answer, but looking to create the answer." What will you need to do in your classroom to create the answer?

How can you incorporate parent power in your classroom? How would you use apprenticeships if you were a third-grade teacher? A tenth-grade science teacher? A special educator in a resource or inclusionary setting?

the student is taught, and ignore the parents' preferences for certain types of teaching (e.g., total communication vs. signing, in the case of a child who is hard of hearing). After all, the lawsuits that families like the Ramirezes brought might be avoided if the schools respond to parents' judgments, knowledge, and preferences. This is not to say that all parents always have a full and accurate picture of their children's educational strengths or needs, or that their preferences are always educationally defensible. But many parents do have a great deal to contribute to the decision-making process, and IDEA wants their children and teachers to benefit from parents' knowledge and perspectives.

Teachers. Many people mistakenly think special education necessarily requires instruction by a special education teacher in a special education classroom. On the contrary, all teachers can be responsible for teaching students with and without exceptionalities, and under IDEA, almost all, if not all, will have to be.

> *Local schools have within them a natural and oftentimes untapped pool of "experts." These "experts" are the grade level teachers, school nurses, language arts and math teachers, guidance counselors, resource room teachers, vocational educators, physical education teachers, home economic teachers, and sign language teachers who make up the instructional staff of the school and who have expertise not only in their assigned teaching areas but in a wide range of other areas. Each teacher's unique skills and interest may be of value to another and a broader range of students than the subset of students assigned to his or her class. (Thousand et al., 1986)*

Barriers to Collaboration. Nonetheless, a national survey of elementary-school teachers of students with learning disabilities and general education teachers revealed only a modest level of collaboration. These teachers note that, ideally, collaboration would be far more extensive than it has been. The lack of scheduled opportunities during the school day, after school, or away from direct instructional responsibilities are major barriers to collaboration.

Solution: Reconceptualize Roles. Because school restructuring makes new demands on curriculum, curriculum reform is a major priority for elementary and secondary schools (Pugach & Warger, 1996). Often, however, general classroom teachers have been regarded as the curriculum experts, whereas special education teachers have been thought to have more expertise in remedial instructional strategies. So it often has been assumed that, when collaboration takes place, special education teachers have expertise at adapting lessons and instructional activities and general classroom teachers do not. This approach clearly is outdated and disavowed by IDEA.

> *Perhaps the most important potential outcome for refocusing collaboration on curriculum is that this approach provides a more level playing field for both special and general education teachers. Because the curriculum itself—and the instructional methods to support new curriculum philosophies and content—is undergoing such major reform, the likelihood is great that both special and general education teachers will need to learn how to conceptualize and implement new curricula. Because both participants in curriculum-centered collaboration are likely to be learners in curriculum reform, past problems with achieving parity are diminished from the outset (Warger & Pugach, 1993).*

Related-Service Providers. Related-service personnel are important members of collaboration teams because they provide instruction and other services for students with exceptionalities. In Chapter 1, you learned the definitions of related services (see Figure 1.5) and that there are almost as many related-service personnel as there are special education teachers.

Research on a variety of early education programs (Head Start, public school prekindergarten, and community preschool/child care) dictated that the inclusive programs employ more related-service providers than those that are less inclusive (Wolery et al., 1994). This is surprising because other research has concluded that the lack of related services is a barrier to inclusion in early childhood programs (Odom & McEvoy, 1990). Various organizations of related services providers endorse collaboration. Table 3–1 includes excerpts from the guidelines of three of these organizations.

Paraprofessionals. More **paraprofessionals** work in special education than any other area of education. In typical urban school districts, 80 percent of all paraprofessionals are likely to work in special education and related services (Blalock, 1991). The benefits of paraprofessionals are numerous (Jones & Bender, 1993):

A paraprofessional is a person who may have as much training as a teacher (although usually less) and who functions essentially like a teacher and works under a teacher's supervision.

- Ninety-one percent of teachers working with students with moderate disabilities indicated that they have more time to respond to students' individual needs when paraprofessionals are available.

- Seventy percent of the teachers indicated that they believed students made more academic gains because of help from paraprofessionals.

- Eighty-seven percent of administrators were pleased with the use of paraprofessionals.

- Ninety-eight percent of the paraprofessionals believed that their participation enabled teachers to spend more time responding to students' individual needs.

Although a vast number of paraprofessionals work in special education, issues about their certification, training, role descriptions, and career advancement are unresolved (Frith & Lindsey, 1982; Frith & Mims, 1985; Pickett, 1986; Salzberg & Morgan, 1995), as are strategies for reducing the time and effort that teachers spend in supervising them (Boomer, 1994).

Language Translators and Interpreters. Translators concentrate on written material, whereas interpreters concentrate on oral communication. These roles are increasingly important, given that approximately one-quarter million to 1 million students with

Sources	Major Provisions in Support of Collaborative Teamwork
American Physical Therapy Association. (1990). *Physical therapy practice in educational environments.* Alexandria, VA: Author.	Physical therapy traditionally has been considered something that occurs in a specially equipped and private room during a scheduled block of time. The LRE requirement means that physical therapists need to: (a) emphasize intervention strategies rather than places and (b) make every effort to identify strategies that team members can use in the course of the child's daily routines, when postural control, mobility, and sensory processing are really required. When related services focus first on the natural opportunities for children to develop and practice motor competence in routine activities in integrated environments, there is greater assurance that the related services will fulfill their mandated purpose to assist a handicapped child to benefit from special education.
American Speech-Language-Hearing Association. (1996). Inclusive practices for children and youths with communication disorders. *ASHA, 38,* 35–44.	There are a variety of models through which inclusive practices can be provided, including direct (pullout) programs, in classroom-based service delivery, community-based models, and consultative interventions. "These models should be seen as flexible options that may change depending on students' needs. The speech-language pathologist—in collaboration with parents, the student, teachers, support personnel, and others—will be in the best position to determine the model or combination of models that best meets a student's needs in early intervention through secondary school programs."
American Occupational Therapy Association, School System/Early Intervention Guidelines Revision Task Force. (1997). *Occupational therapy services for children and youth under the Individuals with Disabilities Education Act.* Bethesda, MD: Author.	Occupational therapists and certified occupational therapy assistants provide essential services to infants, toddlers, children, and youth with disabilities and their families. These professionals bring special perspectives to early childhood and educational teams, particularly in situations where a child's development and occupational performance are disrupted by disabilities or vulnerabilities in activities of daily living, in work and production activities, and in play or leisure. Occupational therapy practitioners provide individualized, contextualized, culturally relevant services by building effective partnerships with children, family members, and other providers from a broad range of educational, medical, and social services disciplines.

TABLE 3–1 🐦
Excerpts from professional policies and guidelines on the provision of related services

disabilities have limited English proficiency (Baca & Cervantes, 1989, cited in U.S. Department of Education, 1993). In a study of 59 Chinese families, 58 of whom used Chinese as their primary language, 60 percent of the families reported that none of the professionals involved in the diagnosis of their child spoke Chinese: "It was hard for us to understand because we were confused. We did not know how to start or who to turn to. We felt alone and helpless" (Smith & Ryan, 1987, pp. 347–348).

Because many schools have not added translators and interpreters to their collaboration teams, they sometimes ask the children or family friends to interpret for their parents. Both of these options are inappropriate, given the complexity of the information that needs to be shared and issues associated with confidentiality and privacy. Moreover, having friends or family members interpret may result in confidential information being shared with people who normally would not have that information. And having children interpret for their parents places them in a "power" role that can be extremely awkward for everyone.

Translating and interpreting are complex skills that require trained and experienced personnel.

Simply speaking Spanish does not mean that one is able to read or write Spanish, nor that one is a skilled interpreter. High quality interpretation is a learned skill comprising knowledge of the English and Spanish languages, knowledge of

❧ Professional language interpreters play a key role in overcoming barriers in serving families who do not speak English. Given the complexity of information and importance of preserving family privacy, the interpreter's role should not be left to the child or family friend.

. . . terminology, skill in asking for clarification, avoiding "improving" or changing what has been said, and the ability to elicit valid and accurate responses from both parties. (Smart & Smart, 1992, p. 35)

Administrators.   Principals, superintendents, and directors of special education are indispensable collaborators because they have a great deal of power to arrange teaching schedules and in-service education so that teachers can collaborate for inclusion. Administrators can promote collaboration when they assign duties to teachers and other staff, foster family–teacher partnerships, allocate money, and set the tone and direction of schools and entire school districts. The school reform movement has substantially increased administrators' influence within the school, across the school district, and within the community at large. IDEA, with its emphasis on local school improvement, will increase it even more, building on states' own initiatives to reform schools by giving local administrators substantial power to carry out site-based reform.

In California . . . passage of a school-based coordination act (AD777) by the state legislature has enhanced efforts by school principals to gain greater access to funds and resources needed to better plan for meeting the diverse needs of a wide range of students at the school, including those with special education needs. Under models of this type, site administrators often utilize resource management teams at the school site, made up of parents as well as school staff (certificated and non-certificated), to formulate resource plans that include attention to all of the specialized needs to students in categorical programs at the school. The resource plan for the school is then used as a basis for negotiating with the district office for resources under the various categorical programs to implement the plan. (Sailor et al., 1987)

   As we indicated earlier, one of the key challenges in implementing collaboration is arranging schedules and finding time for team members to have frequent, face-to-face interactions for the purpose of creative problem solving. In Chapter 2, you read about the collaboration process that is often used during prereferral and at other times. Administrators have a key role in creating opportunities for that kind of collaboration by making teachers' schedules compatible so that they can collaborate.

Administrative support at the state level is another key to successful collaboration. You've already read in Box 3–3 about the role of state-level leadership in Vermont. This leadership has enabled Vermont to lead the nation in the percentage of students with disabilities who are educated in general education classrooms.

Not only are state policies critical, but so too is local innovation, facilitated by flexible and progressive state policy. In Chapter 8, you will read about a local school (Morristown Elementary) in Vermont that has benefited from both state and local leadership.

A VISION FOR THE FUTURE

If Danny Ramirez had been born just ten years earlier, in 1973 instead of 1983, his life would have been much different. In 1973, Congress had not yet enacted IDEA; it did that in 1975. In 1973, federal courts in Pennsylvania and the District of Columbia had just ruled that students with disabilities had a right to go to school; but there was no similar decision in Texas, where Danny was born. And in 1973, bias in evaluation was widespread and likely to result in less-than-effective education for students with disabilities, especially those from families from diverse cultural and linguistic backgrounds. In short, Danny would have been one of those students about whom Lloyd Dunn, Evelyn Deno, and Jim Gallagher were concerned.

In today's schools, however, not only is the law much different, but so are the practices and trends. IDEA grants rights; Section 504 of the Rehabilitation Act and the Americans with Disabilities Act (ADA) prohibit discrimination. The six IDEA principles of zero reject, nondiscriminatory evaluation, individualized and beneficial education, least restrictive placements, procedural due process, and parent/student participation are now in their third decade and, under the 1997 amendments, are substantially more outcome-oriented and proinclusion than ever before. Professionals' practices are far more effective in assuring students that they will benefit from their years in school. Inclusion and collaboration are no longer trends or ideas whose time is yet to come; they are best practices and they are the mandates and expectations of the new IDEA. And their potential effect is awesome: restructuring America's schools so they will be truly inclusive.

What difference does all of this make? For one thing, it assures students like Danny that the outcomes of special education will be more positive. It is no longer a fantasy that Danny will be able to work full-time in competitive employment for at least the minimum wage in a job that suits his choices. There is a legitimate great expectation that he will be a dog trainer or a vet's assistant. His strengths and abilities to make a positive contribution in his school and community are now well recognized and welcome. His relationships with his peers are unlimited by his separation from them in school. He is enjoying the rights of full citizenship.

Danny is not the only student who benefits from IDEA and other laws, from established and developing best practices of inclusion and collaboration, and from a new set of values. In each of the chapters that follow, you will be introduced to other students—many with disabilities, some with extraordinary gifts. They, too, have the benefit of today's schools, and some are even fortunate enough to be in schools that have already crossed the threshold of today (first-generation inclusion) and have entered the domain of tomorrow (second-generation inclusion)—the domain in which we hope you will practice your valued profession as an educator for all of America's students.

What Do You Think?

1. What are the major barriers still facing Danny and other students with disabilities in today's schools and communities?

2. How do you answer someone who says, "Kids like Danny take too much time and attention away from the kids who want to go to college."

3. What single major difference do you want to make for Danny or any other student who has a disability or is gifted?

SUMMARY

SCHOOL REFORM

- School reform in special education takes place within the broader context of school reform in general education.

- In general education, school reform is guided by Goals 2000 and its eight national goals: readiness to learn, student achievement and citizenship, mathematics and science achievement, adult literacy and lifelong learning, safe schools, teacher and professional development, and parental participation.

- In special education, IDEA requires state and local school agencies to connect their reforms to those they are undertaking in general education.

- Two themes permeate special education reform: inclusion and collaboration.

INCLUSION

- There have been four phases of school reform in the area of inclusion.

- The first phase is called *mainstreaming*. The second was characterized by the Regular Education Initiative. The third is known as *first-generation* inclusion. The current phase is *second-generation* inclusion.

FIRST-GENERATION INCLUSION

- First-generation inclusion began when advocates for students with severe and multiple disabilities sought to move them from special classes and schools into general education settings.

- These advocates recognized the students were "caught in the continuum" and wanted to revise the concept of a continuum.

- Three key components of first-generation inclusion are home-school placement, age- and grade-appropriate placement, and special education support within general education classes.

- First-generation inclusion encountered challenges related to time, training, personnel resources, materials resources, class size, and the severity of students' disabilities.

- First-generation inclusion, however, also proved to be effective when these challenges were met.

SECOND-GENERATION INCLUSION

- Whereas first-generation inclusion was additive (in the sense that resources and students with disabilities were added to the general curriculum), second-generation inclusion is generative in the sense that it requires the overhaul of the entire educational enterprise.

- The extent of this reform calls for all educators to teach to the diversity that now occurs in schools, rather than teaching to a homogenized group of relatively similar students.

- Second-generation inclusion expects school-wide reform, teacher renewal, intensive support for students, and a retreat from education based on labels.

THE INCLUSION REQUIREMENTS OF IDEA

- IDEA creates a presumption in favor of inclusion by redefining special education, requiring nondiscriminatory evaluation that is linked to including a student in the general curriculum, and an individualized program that is delivered in the general curriculum.

- The rule now is that, because special education is a service, not a place to which students are sent, the student begins in the general curriculum and is gradually removed from it only when support makes it impossible for the student to benefit from being educated there.

COLLABORATION

- Collaboration is an interactive process that builds on the expertise, interests, and strengths of everyone involved in the educational process.

- Educators play four roles in collaboration: supportive, facilitative, information-giving, and prescriptive.

- Collaboration is justified on the basis of the schools' need to become "adhocracies" and on the basis of research on student outcomes, professional outcomes, and system wide outcomes.

- The roles that collaborators play are varied and depend on who they are, but, for students with disabilities, self-determination is an important part of their curriculum and leads to them being effective collaborators in their own education.

- For parents, collaboration is best done through power sharing; teachers' power over parents discourages collaboration.

- For teachers, collaboration requires special and regular educators to reconceptualize their roles, and for related-service providers, paraprofessionals, and administrators, it includes being essential parts of a collaboration team.

RESOURCES

BOOKS

Collaborative Practitioners, Collaborative Schools. (1995). By Marleen C. Pugach & Lawrence J. Johnson. Denver, CO. Love. This book covers specific classroom problem solving, team teaching, school–university and school–family collaboration, group work communication skills, and conflict resolution.

Cooperative Teaching: Rebuilding the Schoolhouse for All Students. (1995). By Jeanne Bauwens & Jack J. Hourcade. Reston, VA: The Council for Exceptional Children. This practical guide shows educators how to plan, implement, and self-evaluate their cooperative teaching efforts.

Creativity and Collaborative Learning: A Practical Guide to Empowering Students and Teachers. (1994). Edited by Jacqueline S. Thousand, Richard A. Villa, & Ann I. Nevin. Baltimore: Paul H. Brookes. This book shows how professionals can creatively respond to behavioral and academic challenges at preschool through college levels.

Inclusion: A Guide for Educators. (1996). Edited by Susan Stainback & William Stainback. Baltimore: Paul H. Brookes. This book provides educators with tools and techniques to make inclusion work.

Inclusion and School Reform: Transforming America's Classrooms. (1997). By Dorothy Kerzner Lipsky & Alan Gartner. Baltimore: Paul H. Brookes. This book offers a sound understanding of inclusion and the processes of school reform and restructuring.

Multiple Voices for Ethnically Diverse Exceptional Learners. (1995). Edited by Bridgie Alexis Ford. Reston, VA: The Council for Exceptional Children. This collection of articles offers information and activities for working with students from diverse cultural and linguistical backgrounds.

Strategies for Teacher Collaboration. (1991). By Loviah E. Aldinger, Cynthia L. Warger, & Paul W. Eavy. Reston, VA: The Council for Exceptional Children. The eighteen in-service activities in this resource help school-based teams to practice the kind of collaborative teaching that is essential to inclusive school settings.

Rethinking Pull-Out Services in Early Intervention: A Professional Resource. (1996). Edited by R. A. McWilliam. Baltimore, MD: Brookes. Building on research and state-of-the-art practice, this book identifies the advantages and barriers to inclusive verses specialized services during early intervention years. These services are provided by professionals from the broad range of disciplines that work with children with disabilities during the early years.

JOURNALS AND MAGAZINES

The Elementary School Journal. University of Chicago Press, Journals Division, 5720 South Woodlawn Avenue, Chicago, IL 60637. Published five times a year; includes original research, reviews of research, and conceptual papers for researchers and practitioners interested in elementary education.

Exceptional Child Education Resources. Council for Exceptional Children. 1920 Association Drive, Reston, VA 22091. This quarterly abstract journal surveys book, nonprint media, and journal literature in special and gifted education.

NASSP Bulletin. National Association of Secondary School Principals, 1904 Association Drive, Reston, VA 22091. Research and best-practice articles address contemporary issues of leadership in secondary schools.

MULTIMEDIA

A Collaborative Approach to Social Skills Instruction. (1996). By Cynthia L. Warger & Robert Rutherford, Jr. Available from The Council for Exceptional Children, 1920 Association Drive, Reston, VA 20191. This training package, in loose-leaf notebook with video, features teachers using collaborative approaches in elementary classrooms and is especially designed to help educators work in team or partnership situations.

Educating Peter. (1991). Available from Program Development Associates, 5620 Business Avenue, Suite B, Cicero, NY 13039. This thirty-minute documentary video, which won an Academy Award, tells the story of a boy with Down syndrome and his third-grade classmates testing the limits of inclusion.

Just Friends. (1997). Available from Program Development Associates, 5620 Business Avenue, Suite B, Cicero, NY 13039. This twenty-two minute video illustrates the mutual value of being in a friendship with an individual who has a disability.

Last One Picked . . . First One Picked On! (1996). Available from Program Development Associates, 5620 Business Avenue, Suite B, Cicero, NY 13039. This video, available in separate versions for parents and teachers, gives examples on how to help children with learning disabilities succeed in situations outside the classroom.

The Power of Two: Making a Difference Through Co-Teaching. (1996). By Marilyn Friend. Available from The Council for Exceptional Children, 1920 Association Drive, Reston, VA 20191. This forty-two-minute video (with thirty-five-page facilitator's manual) leads the viewer through six different co-teaching situations.

People in Motion. (1996). Available from Program Development Associates, 5620 Business Avenue, Suite B, Cicero, NY 13039. This series of sixty-minute videos features compelling stories of how technology is transforming the lives of—and societal attitudes toward—people with disabilities.

Regular Lives! (1987). Available from Program Development Associates, 5620 Business Avenue, Suite B, Cicero, NY 13039. This thirty-minute video narrated by Martin Sheen demonstrates successful mainstreaming in schools, jobs, and the community.

Small Differences. (1995). Available from Program Development Associates, 5620 Business Avenue, Suite B, Cicero, NY 13039. This twenty-minute, professionally edited video was produced by elementary and middle school children with and without disabilities.

Warriors of Virtue. (1997, PG, U.S., 108 minutes). A young man with a disability wants to be included on his peers' football team. During an initiation activity, he ends up in the land of Tao, where he learns valuable lessons.

ON-LINE INFORMATION AND USEFUL DATABASES

Friends of Inclusion Resource Page. Internet address: inclusion.com/resource.html. Links to various disability-related sites with an emphasis on inclusion.

Just Because We Have A Disability Doesn't Mean We BYTE! Internet address: library.advanced.org/11799. A web site developed by children with disabilities focusing on accepting differences.

The Inclusion Series. Internet address: www.comforty.com/inclusionseries.htm. Encourages inclusion of people with disabilities into school and community life.

Training Resource Network, Inc. Internet address: http://www.oldcity.com/trn. Offers resources on the full inclusion of persons with disabilities in their communities.

ORGANIZATIONS

Inclusion Press/Centre for Integrated Education and Community, 24 Thome Crescent, Toronto, Ontario M6H 2S5, Canada. Publishes books, videos, newsletter on inclusion; offers seminars and workshops.

Institute on Community Integration, University of Minnesota, 109 Pattee Hall, 150 Pillsbury Drive, S. E., Minneapolis, MN 55455. Facilitates independence and social inclusion of people with disabilities.

National Association of State Boards of Education (NASBE), 1012 Cameron Street, Alexandria, VA 22314. Promotes joint research and policy efforts among state board of education members.

CHAPTER **4**

LEARNING
DISABILITIES

Educating
Raquel Osorto

Raquel (pronounced *Rachel*) sifts through the set of Disney books her Tío (Uncle) Lio bought her recently. She pulls out *Pocahontas,* one of her favorites, and begins to read. The fifth grader hesitates on only a few words and sounds out some words that would challenge many children her age. It's hard to believe that Raquel was virtually a nonreader a year previously.

Raquel has a type of learning disability in reading that is often referred to as *dyslexia.* She is benefiting from recent research on the brain that opened a new understanding of the cause of dyslexia and resulted in pioneering approaches for remediation. Raquel's resource teacher, Debbie Navarro, began using those approaches last year. The results for students like Raquel have often been dramatic.

Raquel's Tía (Aunt) Belinda comments that the entire family was thrilled when they realized Raquel's reading skills were improving: "Raquel's grandmother got excited when Raquel was able to read signs when we were riding in the car. She couldn't do that before." Belinda

Alvarez says that Raquel couldn't read at all when she was going into the second grade.

In Raquel's Hispanic culture, immediate and extended family members support and take responsibility for each other. So Raquel's mother—Belinda's sister—sent Raquel to Honduras for more than a year, hoping that it would be easier for Raquel to learn to read in Spanish. Raquel still struggled.

Debbie says that she does not consider Raquel's problems in reading to be the result of her being bilingual: "She doesn't roll her *r's,* and she can make an /n/ sound. Her problem is much more complex than that. Raquel has difficulty with hearing the different sounds in words. That's why learning to read has been hard for her."

When Raquel returned from Honduras, she lived with her mother again. The school system evaluated Raquel and discovered that she had a significant discrepancy between her academic achievement in some areas, including reading, and what she would be expected to achieve based on her IQ. Therefore, the evaluation team concluded that she has specific learning disabilities.

Because Raquel didn't seem to be making much progress while living at home, her mother made a difficult decision. She allowed Raquel to move from Louisiana to Alabama to live with her uncle, aunt, and cousins Erica and John. "My sister doesn't limit Raquel," Belinda says. "She was willing to have Raquel move in with us because that was what Raquel needed."

Raquel seems to enjoy living with her aunt and uncle. However, according to Belinda, Raquel is sometimes concerned about her place in the family and feels pulled to be with absent family members. "I would like to go back to Honduras sometime," Raquel says. "My nanny has a husband now. One time I went, and we got to ride a horse with my grandfather. My tía had a parrot that could talk. She says her name. I would just like it if all my family could live in one city."

When Raquel moved in with her aunt and uncle, she started attending school in Baldwin County along the Gulf Coast of Alabama. When she first came to the school, Debbie, her teacher, says Raquel was like a sea anemone. "If you came near her with a book, she would close up."

"Her number one problem related to school work is concentration and attention,"

Belinda comments. "She finds getting things in order a challenge—keeping up with what she has to do and getting started; she spends so much time getting her supplies out."

Although school has presented some challenges, Raquel has many strengths. Belinda says that she asks a lot of questions and is very curious. "She also helps me a lot by making the bed, straightening the bathroom, and helping in the kitchen. If you have the patience and the time to teach her, there's no limit to what she can do."

Raquel's cousin Erica adds, "She's active, really active and likes to play a lot. She makes friends easily."

Debbie agrees, "Socially, Raquel gets along with everyone. She is personable and sweet—a doll really, and very outgoing."

Raquel enjoys a diversity of activities. At school she likes computer time, physical education, reading, and art. She also enjoys speech because she gets to do plays with puppets. At home, she likes to skate with her Roller Blades®, ride her bike, draw, create crafts, and play Barbies® with her best friend, Brianna.

Raquel has good role models for learning to read in her aunt and uncle. They both work with tutors from the Gulf Coast Literacy Council to improve their reading skills. Belinda comments:

I know with overcrowding that it's hard to see the child. But if teachers see the child, they will be able to see what the child can bring to the class. When I was a child, no one noticed that my father was a chronic alcoholic, that I couldn't read, or how intelligent I was. No one ever saw. There's so much involved when a child doesn't participate. Teachers need to sit the child down privately and ask them to read. No one found out my secret until I went to the Literacy Council. I could read to get through things, but not to read what I wanted to read.

When I went to the Literacy Council, they told me, "You could keep going and going with reading." No one ever told me that before.

The enthusiasm of Raquel's aunt and uncle for learning to read is contagious. Raquel is hopeful about her continued academic improvement: "Mrs. Navarro calls our reading group the Skeedaddle Group. She says we are going to skeedaddle out of there!"

Although Raquel's reading has improved dramatically, Belinda still worries about her self-esteem. She is concerned that Raquel will fall into the wrong crowd as she enters adolescence. You will learn more about social issues for students with learning disabilities in this chapter.

What Do You Think?

1. Why did Raquel's evaluation team use the word *specific* when referring to her learning disabilities?

2. Do students like Raquel share common characteristics other than academic discrepancy?

3. What brain research has contributed to a better understanding of dyslexia?

4. What specific techniques were used to teach Raquel how to read?

WHAT ARE LEARNING DISABILITIES?

Kristina Kops remembers learning to read in first grade:

> *Sitting in the front of my classroom, I began to read out loud slowly and steadily, "The boy looked down at his God."*
> *"Dog," corrected my teacher.*
> *"No, my book says God," I said in my defense.*
> *"No, it says dog," insisted my teacher.*
> *Finally, when I looked at it for the fourth time, I realized it said dog. (Tuttle & Tuttle, 1995, p. 67)*

Kristina's experience illustrates the confusion students with learning disabilities often experience. This confusion can lead to frustration and ultimately, *learned helplessness* (Seligman, 1990). When students reach the point of learned helplessness, they refuse to risk failure, a safeguard for their fragile self-esteem. Eric, a bright student with learning disabilities, describes this process:

> *I was so sick of hearing that I could do better if I'd just try. . . . Every time I got a paper back, I could hardly see what I had written because of all my mistakes. I started making excuses for the work I wasn't doing, then basically stopped working. When I started to get into drugs, that's when I saw I had a problem. (Olivier & Bowler, 1996, p. 143)*

Learned helplessness results in lowered self-esteem, which in turn contributes to even lower achievement. It will be important for you to know how to help students with learning disabilities out of this downward spiral that leads to discouragement and sometimes despair. The first two steps are understanding the definition of learning disabilities and recognizing which of your students have the condition.

Defining Learning Disabilities

Since Sam Kirk coined the term **learning disabilities** in 1963, legislators, parents, and professionals have debated the best way to define the condition (Coutinho, 1995; Shaw, Cullen, & Brinckerhoff, 1995). Despite this ongoing controversy, students who qualify for special education services because they have a learning disability must meet specific criteria outlined in the Individuals with Disabilities Education Act (IDEA) and also by the state and local school district in which they live.

IDEA currently uses a definition with only slight modifications from the definition that was originally used when Public Law (PL) 94-142 was first enacted in 1977:

> *IN GENERAL: The term "specific learning disability" means a disorder in one or more of the **basic psychological processes** involved in understanding or in using language, spoken or written, which disorder may manifest itself in imperfect ability to listen, think, speak, read, write, spell, or do mathematical calculations.*
> *DISORDERS INCLUDED: Such term includes such conditions as perceptual disabilities, brain injury, minimal brain dysfunction, dyslexia and developmental aphasia.*
> *DISORDERS NOT INCLUDED: Such term does not include a learning problem that is primarily the result of visual, hearing, or motor disabilities, of mental retardation, of emotional disturbance, or of environmental, cultural, or economic disadvantage. (IDEA, 20 U.S.C., §§ 1400 et seq., 1997).*

Many professionals express concern that the wording in this definition can lead to misinterpretation (National Joint Committee on Learning Disabilities, 1994). For example, some of the terms used in "disorders included" are seldom mentioned in current literature. *Brain*

Learning disabilities include disorders involved in understanding or in using spoken or written language that result in substantial difficulties in listening, speaking, reading, written expression, or mathematics. Other conditions such as emotional disturbance or sensory impairments may occur along with a learning disability but are not the cause of the learning disability.

"Over time, various individuals, groups, and organizations have acted like Humpty Dumpty in insisting that LD was to mean what they chose it to mean" (Kavale, Forness, & Lorsbach, 1991).

Basic psychological processes are the ability to interpret information received through auditory (oral), visual (sight), kinesthetic (motor) and tactile (touch) channels and to communicate information through those channels.

injury is served under a separate definition of IDEA (see Chapter 13). Also, the "disorders not included" section may imply to some people that students cannot be identified with learning disabilities if they have another condition. A dual diagnosis is appropriate for some students.

Professionals often prefer a definition adopted in 1988 by the National Joint Committee on Learning Disabilities (NJCLD), a coalition of professional and parent organizations concerned with learning disabilities:

> Learning disabilities *is a general term that refers to a heterogenous group of disorders manifested by significant difficulties in the acquisition and use of listening, speaking, reading, writing, reasoning, or mathematical abilities. These disorders are intrinsic to the individual and presumed to be due to central nervous system dysfunction, and may appear across the life span. Problems in self-regulatory behaviors, social perception, and social interaction may exist with learning disabilities but do not themselves constitute a learning disability. Although learning disabilities may occur concomitantly with other handicapping conditions (for example, sensory impairment, mental retardation, serious emotional disturbance) or with extrinsic influences (such as cultural differences, insufficient or inappropriate instruction), they are not the result of those conditions or influences. (National Committee on Learning Disabilities, 1994)*

This definition mentions several important criteria. First, the condition is *heterogenous,* or varied. If you observed twenty students with learning disabilities, you would find twenty different ways the condition manifests itself. That is why learning disabilities are referred to as *specific* learning disabilities in the IDEA definition. As both the IDEA and NJCLD definitions mention, a student with learning disabilities may have difficulty with only one or many academic areas. The NJCLD definition also emphasizes that students with learning disabilities *may* have associated social and behavioral difficulties, but they cannot qualify for services on the basis of these issues alone. They must also have significant academic difficulty. In Figure 4–1, we provide an example of this academic difficulty manifested in the written expression of a nine-year-old girl with dyslexia.

Learning disabilities occur *across the life span,* according to the NJCLD definition. Although this statement probably sounds like common sense to you, in the pioneering days of the field, preschool and postsecondary students with learning disabilities did not receive much attention. By adding this phrase, the NJCLD emphasized the needs of these two groups and the necessity of providing them with appropriate services.

Although the IDEA definition does not specifically mention etiology, the NJCLD definition assumes the cause to be *intrinsic,* or inside the student, and most likely the result of **central nervous system dysfunction.** *Extrinsic* causes for academic problems such as poor instruction and cultural differences can exist **concomitantly** with learning disabilities, but if they are the only cause, the student does not qualify as having learning disabilities.

The NJCLD definition further states that learning disabilities can occur concomitantly with other disabilities or extrinsic factors. However, the student does not qualify as having learning disabilities if the academic problems occur as a direct result of another disability.

Raquel is an example of concomitance. Her cultural difference from the majority of students in the United States enriches her with the ability to be bilingual. However, if her English language skills are poor, that could cause academic deficiencies. It was imperative that her evaluation team determine whether using English as a second language contributed significantly to her academic difficulties or whether her academic difficulties resulted from specific learning disabilities. After thorough assessment, the team concluded that Raquel has learning disabilities.

Classification Criteria.

Consistent with the IDEA and NJCLD definitions, most states and local districts require students to meet three criteria to receive the learning disabilities classification (Mercer, Jordan, Allsopp, & Mercer, 1996):

What do you think might happen if students could qualify as having learning disabilities solely on the basis of poor social skills?

Central nervous system dysfunction is a disorder in the messaging system of the brain and/or spinal cord.

Concomitance means occurring at the same time without causal relationship.

The definition of learning disabilities includes what learning disabilities are *not,* as much as what they are.

FIGURE 4–1 *Writing sample by a child with dyslexia, a disorder defined as a "specific learning disability," by IDEA*

> when I krt reed
> peopally fink I have
> a bag of penuts for a
> bran and fink i am
> plient TrAcy 9 yes old

When I can't read people think I have a bag of peanuts for a brain and think I am blind.

Tracy, 9 years old

- *Inclusionary criterion:* The student demonstrates a **severe discrepancy** between perceived potential and actual achievement, as measured by individually administered standardized intelligence and achievement tests. A case in point would be a student in your class who scores high on the verbal section of an intelligence test, but low on reading. You would expect such a student to master reading easily. We explain discrepancy in more detail when we discuss assessment issues, later in this chapter.

- *Exclusionary criterion:* The learning disability is not the result of other factors such as sensory impairment, mental retardation, serious emotional disturbance, or cultural differences. Some states include specific extrinsic factors such as stress, lack of opportunity, curriculum change, and inadequate instruction.

- *Need criterion:* The student manifests a demonstrated need for special education services.

Raquel meets all these criteria. She meets the inclusionary criterion because her intelligence is average, but she is performing significantly below her expected achievement in several academic areas. We have already mentioned that her cultural difference is not the cause of her academic difficulties. Therefore, she does meet the exclusionary criterion, which would prevent her from qualifying. She also needs and benefits from special education and speech, a related service.

Distinguishing students with learning disabilities from students who are low achievers for other reasons is sometimes challenging. Research indicates, however, that a distinction does exist (Gresham, MacMillan, & Bocian, 1996; Kavale, Fuchs, & Scruggs, 1994). Students with learning disabilities generally perform better on cognitive tests than low achievers. The low achievers, on the other hand, tend to score higher on achievement tests than those with learning disabilities.

> In this context, a **severe discrepancy** is a statistically significant difference between ability and achievement as measured by standardized tests. Interpretation of *severe discrepancy* varies widely among states. A student may qualify as having learning disabilities in one state, but when she moves across the state line, she may no longer qualify (McLeskey & Waldron, 1991). This lack of consistency in state definitions is a major concern for the field.

> Students with learning disabilities are often the lowest of the low achievers (Deshler, Schumaker, Alley, Warner, & Clark, 1982).

BOX 4-1   MY VOICE

JILL, A COLLEGE FRESHMAN

I think that when I was born, I was put in a rocket ship and taken to another planet—Earth. I never felt like I was like anyone else here. From the time I was five, I can recall feeling like an outsider. I first remember feeling like an alien when I tried to communicate. People would raise their eyebrows and make other facial expressions of confusion when I tried to express myself. I was aware of starting a sentence in my head, but only the last half came out of my mouth. I know how E. T. must have felt. It was like I was speaking another language and thinking on another wavelength. Constant rejection created feelings of isolation, isolation created anger, and anger created self-defeat. I could not judge time and was anxious about being late. I never got a joke (no matter how simple) because it was abstract, and I could never get myself or my work in order because of my sequencing problems. [Writing] was murder because of my perceptual problems, and my spacing was the worst. I could never remember anything but the first part of a direction, and the noise level of the then-popular "open classroom" drove me crazy. I always wondered why everyone got everything the leader said but me. Definitely [the] wrong planet! . . .

High school was a turning point. I started noticing things. Dr. Silver, a psychiatrist who really understands how to explain learning disabilities, made me aware of ways to compensate for my shortcomings. I began to read people from their faces and body language. If their faces looked confused, I would say, "Did I say something wrong?" Or I would make a joke. Sometimes I would just start over. . . .

At college, there is a wonderful learning disability program, [and] the term LD has come to mean *learning desirable* for me. I have found my planet! People like me do exist, and they are not crazy. We even joke about being LD. It's like a private club, and it's not unpopular. At dinner, if someone forgets their silverware, there is a chorus of "LD, LD, LD," and a knowing smile of acceptance. Once, four of us got lost driving to a dance, and my friend the driver said, "Oh, no! Four LDs, and no one has a pencil." She quickly assigned one part of the directions to each of us. "You remember the first part, you the second, and you the third." We all laughed at ourselves. . . .

I have recently begun to feel better about myself and to like myself. I am having success. I will be LD forever. It will never go away, but each day I learn to handle another thing or work something out, and things get better for me. How many people can say that?

Note: From *The Misunderstood Child: A Guide for Parents of Children With Learning Disabilities* (2nd ed., pp 46–48), by L. B. Silver, 1992, Blue Ridge Summit, PA: TAB Books. Copyright 1992 by McGraw-Hill. Reprinted with permission.

Describing the Characteristics

There is no such thing as a typical profile of students with learning disabilities. Although they share a severe discrepancy, how that discrepancy occurs varies widely. For example, one student exhibits strengths in math and nonverbal reasoning and weaknesses in receptive and expressive language skills. Another student may be strong in motor skills, reading, and receptive language but weak in math and expressive language.

No matter what characteristics manifest, however, students with learning disabilities often face challenges related to *learning, behavior,* and *social skills.* Box 4–1 describes some of the challenges facing Jill, a college student with a learning disability.

Learning Characteristics.   Individuals with learning disabilities, such as Raquel, commonly have average or above-average intelligence. Did you realize that students can have learning disabilities and be gifted? Professionals in this field often speculate that highly gifted people such as Albert Einstein, Thomas Edison, and Amadeus Mozart, among many others, had learning disabilities (Roeper, 1996). Identifying these students is difficult because they may be achieving at an average level, or their learning disabilities may mask their giftedness in other ways. When you teach, look for creativity, task commitment, and exceptional problem-solving ability to identify them (Tallent-Runnels & Sigler, 1995).

Students with learning disabilities also have strengths that manifest in a myriad of ways. Raquel's strengths, for example, include good social skills, artistic talent, and willingness to help others and cooperate. Despite their strengths, however, the most fundamen-

Raquel's inherent strengths provide skills that can help her overcome her learning disabilities.

tal characteristic of students with learning disabilities is their lack of academic achievement in one or more areas. Raquel has had to work hard to overcome her challenges with reading and written language. The Council for Learning Disabilities (CLD) (1997) groups the learning characteristics of these students into five categories: reading, written language, mathematics, memory, and **metacognition.**

Metacognition is the ability to think about one's thinking or organize one's thoughts in a meaningful way.

Reading. Students in your class who have learning disabilities in reading (called reading disabilities) may exhibit word recognition errors (CLD, 1997). When you ask them to read orally, they may omit, insert, substitute, and/or reverse words. They may have difficulty comprehending what they have read because they have limited ability in recalling or discerning basic facts, sequence, and/or theme. Reading can also be frustrating to them because they may lose their place while reading or read in a choppy, halting manner (CLD, 1997).

A word often used in conjunction with reading disabilities is **dyslexia.** Dyslexic characteristics are a subgroup of reading disability characteristics and represent a developmental language impairment (CLD, 1997). During the preschool years, the impairment is revealed by difficulties in learning spoken language and, during the school years, in acquiring word recognition and spelling skills. Reading comprehension problems result.

Dyslexia is a disorder in recognizing and comprehending written words as a result of a developmental language impairment.

Recent research seems to suggest that dyslexia stems from an underlying difficulty in **phonological awareness** (CLD, 1997). Students who lack skills in phonological awareness cannot recognize sound segments in spoken words (*push* has three sound segments or *phonemes:* /p/ /u/ /sh/). When they cannot recognize these sounds, the relationship of letter–sound identification to reading doesn't make sense. In Box 4–2, "My Voice," Debbie Navarro, Raquel's special education teacher, shares her thoughts on reading disabilities.

Phonological awareness is a foundational reading skill in which a student recognizes sound segments in words presented orally.

Written Language. "I couldn't draw well, but most of all, I couldn't write," says Russell, a student with learning disabilities. "That made me feel double dumb" (Olivier & Bowler, 1996). A learning disability in handwriting is referred to as dysgraphia. For some students, their only learning disability is dysgraphia.

Difficulties associated with poor written language performance usually occur in the areas of handwriting, spelling, productivity, text structure, sentence structure, word usage, and composition (Scott, 1991). Students may have difficulties in any one of these areas or in a combination of them. In addition, students with difficulties in one area, such as composition, may have strengths in other areas, such as handwriting, spelling, and other written language mechanics (CLD, 1997).

Many students with learning disabilities have difficulties in both reading and writing. This fact is not surprising, because both can result from lack of phonological awareness.

Mathematics. Your students with learning disabilities in math, dyscalculia, will not all make the same types of errors. Difficulties associated with poor math performance may include any of the following (CLD, 1997):

- Visual perception (differentiating numbers or copying shapes)

- Memory (recalling math facts)

- Motor functions (writing numbers legibly or in small spaces)

- Language (relating arithmetic terms to meaning or using math vocabulary)

- Abstract reasoning (solving word problems and making comparisons)

- Metacognition (identifying, using, and monitoring the use of strategies to solve problems)

A major concern about students with learning disabilities in mathematics and other areas is that many of them find **generalization** difficult (Riviera, 1996). For example, you

Generalization is the ability to apply what is learned in one setting to another.

BOX 4-2

MY VOICE

DEBBIE NAVARRO: THOUGHTS ON TEACHING STUDENTS TO READ

I had surgery for primary lateral sclerosis, which made the bottom half of my body spastic. I probably never should have been able to walk; I walked on my toes. After the surgery reduced the spasms, I've had to learn to walk all over again. I had to do a task analysis (breaking a skill into sequential steps) for walking. It's given me an appreciation for what these children go through when they are learning to read. When I go to therapy, my physical therapist takes each tiny little muscle and will feel it. "This is what we need to work on now," she will say.

We have to see that learning to read is a series of small steps. With kids who are having trouble, we have to go back to Step 1. That's what phonological awareness makes us do—go back to Step 1 in reading.

I didn't realize all the muscles involved in walking. If one's not working properly, I'm not going to be able to walk properly.

It's the same with reading. It's a whole lot easier to learn to walk or read right the first time. If we start teaching reading right in kindergarten, kids might not have all these problems when they get in fifth or sixth grade.

If we just let it go when students mispronounce words, we're just reinforcing bad habits. I walked, but not as I should have. When we let students' reading problems slide, we will cause more problems later.

—Debbie Navarro

BOX 4-3 — MY VOICE

SELF-PORTRAIT

To show you who I am
I crawled inside a tree, became its roots, bark and
leaves,
listened to its whispers in the wind.
When fall came and painted the leaves red and
gold
I wanted to shake them across your lawn
to transform the grass into a quilt, a gift spread at
your feet,
but their numbers eluded me,
so I turned a piece of paper into my soul
to send to you so that you might see
how easily it can be crumpled and flattened out
again.
I wanted you to see my resilience,
but I wasn't sure how to arrange the numbers in
your address,

so I danced with the Indians in the forest
and collected the feathers that fell from the
eagle's wings,
each one a wish for my future,
but I lost track of their numbers, gathered too
many,
and was unable to carry them home
so I reaped the wind with my hair,
relived its journey though my senses, and
felt its whispered loneliness, like lakes in winter,
but it was too far and you could not follow me.

Now I've written out their shadows
like the wind collects its secrets
to whisper into receptive ears, and I
will leave them at your doorstep,
a reminder of what others cannot see,
a reminder of what I can and cannot be.

—*Samantha Abeel*

Note: From *What Once Was White: Reach for the Moon*, by S. Abeel, 1994, Duluth, MN: Pfeifer-Hamitton. Copyright 1994 by Pfeifer-Hamilton. Reprinted with permission.

might teach them to add two numbers at school, but when they go to the store, they may not understand that that skill applies to adding two items costing twenty-five cents and fifty cents. In Box 4-3, "My Voice," Samantha Abeel shares what it is like to be a teenager with math learning disabilities.

Memory. Someday, you might tutor one of your students with learning disabilities to prepare him for a test. You and the student work hard, and you both believe the student knows the material before the session ends. The next day, the student fails the test. Some teachers would accuse the student of not trying. What actually happened? The student experiences difficulty with long-term memory. Memory difficulties may include the following (CLD, 1997): (a) poor short-term memory, which is related to problems in comparing, organizing, processing, and coding information, and (b) poor long-term memory for timely and organized searches for information. Remember the problems Jill and her college friends had with remembering directions (in Box 4-1)?

These difficulties with memory suggest that students' performance may be erratic. Many teachers reward their students only for exceptional performance. If students with learning disabilities seldom receive praise, discouragement can lead them to give up. How do you remedy this situation? If you choose to reward character instead of outcome, all your students have the opportunity to receive encouragement. For example, what would you say to the student who failed your test? Instead of scolding or blaming for the outcome, you could say, "I know you are disappointed in your grade. But I want you to know that I'm proud of you for your effort. We'll find a way for you to master the information. What's most important, though, is that you are sticking with it. That's an important characteristic to have when you get a job. Some people for whom learning is easy never develop perseverance."

Metacognition.   When you study for a test on this chapter, how will you do so? You might review chapter headings, definitions, and summaries; reorganize your notes; use flashcards, and/or memory devices such as acronyms for lists. You have probably found an approach to studying that works best for you. Students with learning disabilities, however, have difficulty approaching tasks that require metacognition, the awareness of how one thinks and the monitoring of one's thinking. Research suggests that many individuals with learning disabilities have deficits in the following areas of metacognition (CLD, 1997):

• Knowing a large number of strategies for acquiring, storing, and processing information

• Understanding when, where, and why these strategies are important

• Selecting and monitoring the use of these strategies wisely and reflectively

Later in this chapter, we share two techniques for helping students with metacognitive deficits: learning strategies and graphic organizers.

Behavioral and Social Characteristics.   Imagine not being able to interpret gestures, facial expressions, and voice inflections. How might the lack of these skills affect you socially and behaviorally? The processing problems that many students with learning disabilities experience can create difficulty in understanding social cues and how to behave in socially acceptable ways. Add to this the frustration of not being able to learn commensurate with their ability level and of dealing with people who do not understand this poor performance, and you have students at risk for behavioral and social problems.

Forness (1996) identified groups of students with learning disabilities based on their processing difficulties and the resulting behavioral and social characteristics. Forness also identified a subtype with a non-learning disabilities pattern that might be mistakenly identified as having learning disabilities. These characteristics are described in Table 4-1. In Chapters 5 and 6, you will learn more about severe emotional disturbance and attention-deficit/hyperactivity disorder. As you can see, students with learning disabilities are at risk for these conditions.

TABLE 4–1 ❧ *Subtypes of learning disabilities, classified by their underlying cognitive processing disorders.*

Type	Problems	Percent of Learning Disabilities
1. Nonverbal organization disorders	• Visual-spatial-motor deficits • Possible social misperception/withdrawal	11%–15%
2. Verbal organization disorders	• Poor understanding/use of language • Possible aggression/acting out	14%–17%
3. Global disorders	• Multiple deficits in processing • Possible problems in all coping skills	8%–10%
4. Production deficits	• Inefficient cognitive strategies • Possible inattention/hyperactivity	22%–30%
5. Non-learning disability pattern	• Discrepancy from grade but not IQ • Possible frustration, absences	25%–38%

Note: From "Social and Emotional Dimensions of Learning Disabilities," by S. Forness in *Learning Disabilities: Contemporary Viewpoints* (p. 76), edited by B. J. Cratty and R. L. Goldman, 1996, Amsterdam: Harwood Academic. Copyright 1996 by Harwood Academic. Reprinted by permission.

BOX 4-4

TEN TIPS FOR MAKING AND KEEPING FRIENDS

When you encounter students who need assistance with socializing, you might find it helpful to share the following tips from *The Survival Guide for Kids with LD:*

1. Watch other kids in class and on the playground. See if you can find some who play without teasing or fighting. They would probably make good friends.
2. Take part in games on the playground where kids line up to play and take turns.
3. Watch to see what the other kids like. Find out as much as you can about what they like. Then you can talk with them about the things they like.
4. Do not try to make other kids be your friends, especially the most popular ones. You might find good friends in students who are not part of the "in crowd." Is there someone who seems shy? Maybe that person is waiting for you to act friendly first.
5. Do not wander around the playground by yourself and hope someone will ask you to play. Instead, choose a game and ask someone to join you.
6. When you play with others, say nice things to them, take your turn, and be a good sport.
7. Do not show off or get into trouble to get noticed.
8. Most people like to talk about themselves. Ask other kids questions about what they like to do. Or, ask them about their favorite TV shows, sports, or games.
9. Be friendly, share things, and do not tease. Treat other kids the way you want them to treat you. (That's right: This is the Golden Rule!)
10. Like yourself. Kids like other kids who like themselves.

Note: Excerpted from *The Survival Guide for Kids With LD,* (*Learning Differences), by Gary Fisher, Ph.D., and Rhoda Cummings, Ed.D. 1990. Used with permission from Free Spirit Publishing, Minneapolis, MN; 1-800-735-7323. ALL RIGHTS RESERVED.

Raquel is sociable and friendly, but even for children with an outgoing personality, learning disabilities can make them apprehensive around others. "Sometimes I don't like to tell people I have learning disabilities, because they might make fun of me," she says. Her Aunt Belinda comments that learning disabilities sometimes limit her in new situations, "When she went to church, she was afraid they would call on her to read."

Helping children with learning disabilities to advocate for themselves is crucial for their social development. To do so, they need to understand about their learning disability and how to respond to others. The *Survival Guide for Kids With LD* (Fisher & Cummings, 1990) is available in book form or audiotape and teaches important self-advocacy skills. In "Into Practice," Box 4-4, we share a list from that book for making friends.

The diverse learning and behavioral characteristics of students with learning disabilities have led some researchers to conclude that **subtyping** might be beneficial for research and instructional purposes. In Table 4-1, we list one way these students have been subtyped. Many others have been proposed. The challenge is finding the appropriate method for subtyping all students. Students with learning disabilities are so heterogenous that it would be difficult to find groups that they would all neatly fit.

> **Subtyping** is the practice of dividing students into smaller groups based on common characteristics.

Identifying the Causes of Learning Disabilities

Both the IDEA and NJCLD definitions presume that there is an underlying neurological problem in individuals with learning disabilities. Since the first edition of this textbook, researchers have come closer to identifying the etiology of learning disabilities. This medical and educational research promises potential for early screening and improved treatment. Currently, students who lag developmentally behind their age mates or who are underachievers as the result of inadequate educational opportunities, socioeconomic factors, or lack of motivation are at risk for misidentification as learning disabled. In the future, learning disabilities might be diagnosed through neurological and blood tests, eliminating this misidentification. As you read about the postulated neurological and genetic causes, keep Raquel in mind. How do you think these causes apply to her?

Neurological Causes.   Throughout the history of the learning disabilities field, most researchers and educators have presumed that learning disabilities result from a central nervous system dysfunction: that is, from an underlying neurological problem (Hammill, 1993; Wiederholt, 1974). The earliest research in learning disabilities can be traced back to studies of the learning processes of soldiers with brain injuries. Much of this early research confirmed that specific parts of the brain were responsible for specific learning behaviors and that neurological impairments or injuries to certain parts of the brain resulted in learning problems.

Researchers soon recognized that similar learning problems could be identified in people who had never had a brain injury. In 1895, James Hinshelwood identified a condition called "word blindness," which he suspected to be the result of central nervous system dysfunction (Hammill, 1993; Wiederholt, 1974). His work laid the foundation for the field of learning disabilities.

The concept of *information processing* may help clarify the notion of central nervous system dysfunction. Information processing—how people acquire, retain, and interpret information received through the senses—differs for each person. Personal strengths in information processing are called *learning styles*. Try this experiment to understand your learning style: New neighbors ask you for directions to the closest airport. Think about what you would tell them for a moment before you continue to read.

Did you think about the directions in words? Did you visualize them? Perhaps you felt yourself getting in the car and driving to the airport. Maybe you did more than one of these. Your response to this may indicate your preferred learning style: auditory, visual, kinesthetic, or a combination.

Students differ in their learning style, with strengths and preferences in learning auditorily, visually, sequentially, in pieces or chunks, through physical movements, and/or at

If you would like to understand how to teach students more effectively based on their learning style differences, we strongly suggest the paperback book *Learning to Learn* (Olivier & Bowler, 1996).

❧ *Teachers need to consider learning style during instruction. This teacher provides auditory, visual, and kinesthetic opportunities to help some of her students learn to tell time.*

certain speeds (Olivier & Bowler, 1996). Students with learning disabilities often do not have the ability to process information as effectively and efficiently as others of their same chronological age, suggesting a central nervous system dysfunction. It is especially important that teachers instruct these students based on their learning style.

> *Anna, a student with learning disabilities, comments: Students who learn differently do not get the kind of attention and instruction they need. If someone had figured out that I was truly capable of learning something but marched to a different drummer, maybe I would not have had so many problems in school and then later in my relationships with people. (Olivier & Bowler, 1996)*

Researchers are trying to understand the differences experienced by Anna and others with learning disabilities. As a case in point, recent research indicates that some students with learning disabilities may have visual-spatial difficulties (Eden, Stein, & Wood, 1995). The findings suggest that letters and numbers they see in one eye fixation may blur into the next. Students may also experience difficulties with eye movements necessary for reading and calculation.

New technologies such as *brain mapping* attempt to pinpoint deficiencies that may cause learning disabilities (Duffy & McAnulty, 1985; A. A. Silver & Hagin, 1990). While a person tackles different cognitive tasks, the brain-mapping equipment marks the flow of blood and specific brain-activating chemicals through the parts of the brain known to be responsible for specific learning processes (Pechura & Martin, 1991). Figure 4-2 is a photograph of brain scans showing brain activity during different cognitive tasks involving language.

An exciting finding from brain-mapping research is that a relationship exists between learning disabilities and subtle abnormalities in the parts of the brain that process language (Dawes, 1996; Manis, 1996). Three types of problems can result: (a) word-finding problems, (b) difficulty temporarily storing words and phrases in short-term memory for analysis of meaning, and (c) being able to identify the forty sound segments or phonemes in spoken words (Manis, 1996). Through coordinated efforts between neurologists, pedia-

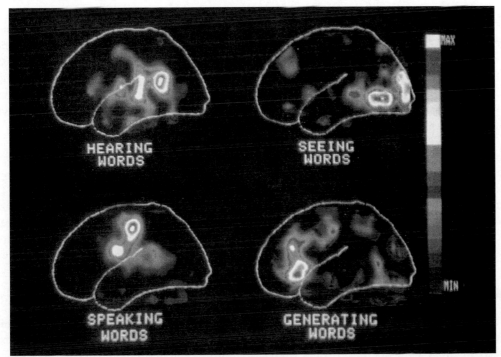

FIGURE 4–2 *Brain scan maps*

Note: From Pechura, C. M., & Martin, J. B. (Eds.). (1991). *Mapping the brain and its functions: Integrating enabling technologies into neuroscience research.* Washington, DC: National Academy Press. Image courtesy of Marcus Raichle, Washington University, St. Louis, MO.

tricians, speech and language therapists, and educators, these findings have resulted in reading programs, such as the one Raquel uses, that emphasize developing phonological awareness to remediate the language processing deficit.

"Uncovering the gene or genes related to learning disabilities could help us identify children who are at increased risk for learning disabilities, which could enable them to begin intervention programs before they have trouble in school"—Wendy Raskind, MD (Dawes, 1996).

Genetic Causes. As early as 1905, T. C. Thomas correlated a strong family history with "word blindness" (Light & Defries, 1995). After researching the family history of 101 students with learning disabilities, one group of researchers agreed that learning disabilities seem to "run in the family" (Oliver, Cole, & Hollingsworth, 1991). Other research, especially twin studies, verifies that almost 50 percent of reading disabilities are caused by genetic factors; family history also plays an important role in mathematics disabilities (Light & Defries, 1995). In fact, researchers appear to be closing in on the gene for dyslexia and its relationship with the processing difficulties we mentioned earlier. Scientists are focusing on chromosome 6 (Sherman, 1995).

Raquel's aunt mentioned the struggles Raquel has experienced with reading, suggesting that genetics might play a role in Raquel's learning disability. It is likely that parents of children with learning disabilities may confide to you that they have struggled with the same academic subjects as their children. You may want to recommend that they join a local chapter of the Learning Disabilities Association, which has a strong family orientation, to provide them with self-knowledge and support.

For years, people with learning disabilities have experienced anguish from others who have blamed the victim, "You are just not trying hard enough." One adult with learning disabilities explains the devastating result: "Unfortunately some children and parents believe this criticism, accept the laziness excuse, and give up on finding a way to help the child learn" (Lee & Jackson, 1992).

Research is providing a new perspective on what causes learning disabilities. We hope that, as more people become aware of this research, people with learning disabilities will find more acceptance and understanding of the very real challenges they face.

Identifying the Prevalence of Learning Disabilities

Students with learning disabilities (ages six to twenty-one) constitute the largest percentage of students served in special education: close to 50 percent. Between 1977 and 1995, the percentage of students identified as having learning disabilities increased from 1.8 percent (796,000) to 5.8 percent of the total public K–12 (2,508,000) enrollment (U.S. Department of Education, 1997). So it is probable that at least two students in every class of thirty students (with and without disabilities) have been identified as having a learning disability. Clearly, all educators need to know about these students because they will very likely address the needs of one or more of them in classes they teach or in other services they provide.

Figure 4–3 illustrates how the prevalence of learning disabilities has increased relative to the two other largest disability groups: speech or language impairments and mental retardation. This dramatic increase alarms some professionals who fear that students are being overidentified with learning disabilities; others believe the increased prevalence is reasonable, considering the newness of the field (Artiles & Trent, 1994; Hallahan, 1992; Mercer, 1997). Those who express concern cite causes in increase ranging from the social acceptability of the label *learning disabilities* compared with mental retardation or emotional or behavioral disorders to the variance in state eligibility requirements.

WHAT ARE EVALUATION PROCEDURES?

In Chapter 2, you learned about the nondiscriminatory evaluation procedures mandated by IDEA. Earlier in this chapter, we mentioned the inclusionary criterion that is emphasized in most state definitions of learning disabilities: The student must have a demonstrated discrepancy between perceived ability and actual achievement. This discrepancy is

Children from birth to age twenty-one who were served by federally supported programs for students with disabilities, by type of disability: School years ending 1977–1995

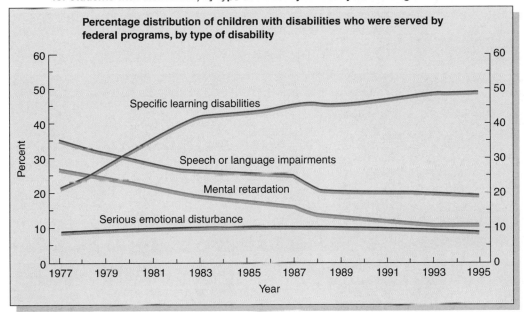

FIGURE 4–3 *Prevalence growth*

Note: This analysis includes students who were served under Chapter 1 of the Education Consolidation and Improvement Act (ECIA) and Part B of the Individuals with Disabilities Education Act (IDEA). Data for 1995 are for children aged three to twenty-one.

Note: From U.S. Department of Education, Office of Special Education and Rehabilitative Services, *Eighteenth Annual Report to Congress on the Implementation of the Individuals with Disabilities Education Act;* and National Center for Education Statistics, *Digest of Education Statistics,* 1996.

determined through nondiscriminatory evaluation. In addition, for a student to be eligible for services under IDEA, the evaluation must demonstrate that a student has an educational need that is not, and presumably cannot be, met without special educational services.

Determining the Presence of a Learning Disability

Figure 4-4 shows the nondiscriminatory evaluation procedures for students with learning disabilities. Generally, a student is referred for evaluation because, even after prereferral suggestions, the student seems to have more ability than his academic performance indicates in one or more subject areas.

An important aspect of nondiscriminatory evaluation for students with learning disabilities is establishing a discrepancy between ability, as measured by an IQ test, and achievement, as measured by a standardized achievement test. Due to the critical decisions that result from nondiscriminatory evaluation, the tests used must have solid reliability and validity. In the field of learning disabilities, the most commonly used test to measure a student's cognitive abilities or intelligence is the Wechsler Intelligence Scale for Children-III (WISC-III) (Wechsler, 1993). This test has two scales: performance (measures skills that relate closely to mathematics achievement) and verbal (measures skills that relate closely to reading and written expression). Performance and verbal scores are combined to yield a full-scale IQ score.

Student achievement is often measured using the Wechsler Individualized Achievement Test (WIAT) (The Psychological Corporation, 1992). This test reveals the student's academic skills in reading, written language, and mathematics. One benefit of using these two tests concurrently is that the same group of students (called a norm group) took the tests initially to develop standard scores. Both tests have a *mean* or average score of 100 and a *standard deviation* (a way to determine how much a particular score differs from

FIGURE 4–4 *Evaluating whether a student has a learning disability*

Nondiscriminatory Evaluation	

Observation	
Teacher and parents observe	Student appears frustrated with academic tasks and may have stopped trying.

Screening	
Assessment measures	**Findings that indicate need for further evaluation**
Classroom work products	Work is inconsistent or generally poor. Teacher feels that student is capable of doing better.
Group intelligence tests	Usually the tests indicate average or above average intelligence. However, tests may not reveal true ability because of reading requirements.
Group achievement tests	Student performs below peers in one or more areas or scores lower than would be expected according to group intelligence tests. Performance may not be a true reflection of achievement because of reading requirements.
Vision and hearing screening	Results do not explain academic difficulties.

Prereferral	
Teacher implements suggestions from school-based team.	The student still experiences frustration and/or academic difficulty despite interventions. Ineffective instruction is eliminated as the cause for academic difficulty.

Referral	

Protection in evaluation procedures	
Assessment measures	**Findings that suggest a learning disability**
Individualized intelligence test	Student has average or above average intelligence, so mental retardation is ruled out. Student may also have peaks and valleys in subtests. The multidisciplinary team makes sure that the test used is culturally fair for the student.
Individualized achievement test	A significant discrepancy (difference) exists between what the student is capable of learning (as measured by intelligence test) and what the student has actually learned (as measured by the achievement test). The difference exists in one or more of the following areas: listening, thinking, reading, written language, mathematics. The team makes sure the test used is culturally fair for the student.
Behavior rating scale	The student's learning problems cannot be explained by the presence of emotional or behavioral problems.
Anecdotal records	The student's academic problems are not of short duration but have been apparent throughout time in school.
Curriculum-based assessment	The student is experiencing difficulty in one or more areas of the curriculum used by the local school district.
Direct observation	The student is experiencing difficulty and/or frustration in the classroom.
Ecological assessment	The student's environment does not cause the learning difficulty.
Portfolio assessment	The student's work is inconsistent and/or poor in specific subjects.

Multidisciplinary Team determines that student has a learning disability and needs special education and related services.

Appropriate Education

the mean) of 15 points. Therefore, comparing a student's IQ and achievement scores is simplified.

Woodcock (1990) has described three types of discrepancies:

- *Aptitude–achievement* (also called ability–achievement): the discrepancy between different abilities and areas of achievement

- *Intracognitive:* the discrepancy between different abilities (i.e., performance and verbal scores)

- *Intra-achievement:* the discrepancy between different areas of academic achievement

When schools determine a severe discrepancy, they nearly always look at the first type: aptitude–achievement (Frankenberger & Fronzaglio, 1991). We have mentioned that states have different criteria for what constitutes a severe discrepancy. Your state might use 1 standard deviation (15 points), 1.5 standard deviations (22 or 23 points), or 2 standard deviations (30 points). Some states change the discrepancy requirement based on age, and others use a complicated regression formula to determine discrepancy.

We will try to clarify severe discrepancy with the hypothetical scores of a student named Joe (see Figure 4–5). You notice that Joe has peaks and valleys in his scores, suggesting the possibility of a severe discrepancy. (Students with mental retardation typically have flat profiles.) The first obvious discrepancy is intracognitive. He has a difference of 36 points (more than 2 standard deviations) between his verbal and performance IQ. Some states would allow him to qualify for services based on this criterion alone. An intra-achievement discrepancy of 2 standard deviations exists between his reading and mathematics scores.

Joe also has an aptitude–achievement discrepancy between his full-scale IQ and reading and written expression. However, he would not qualify for services in mathematics based on his full-scale IQ. If the state compares verbal with reading and written expression, the student might qualify for services in reading but not written expression. However, now Joe could qualify for mathematics when that score is compared to his performance IQ. You are probably beginning to understand the need for more consistency in state definitions! The CLD suggests that the use of discrepancy formulae should be phased out (CLD, 1986b).

We do not want to reveal Raquel's exact test scores, but we can share some generalities. She has a severe discrepancy in her state between full-scale IQ compared with reading and written expression scores. Although she did not have a severe discrepancy between her full-scale IQ and mathematics achievement, when her team compared her performance IQ and mathematics achievement, the discrepancy qualified for resource room support in math.

FIGURE 4–5 *Joe's nondiscriminatory evaluation scores*

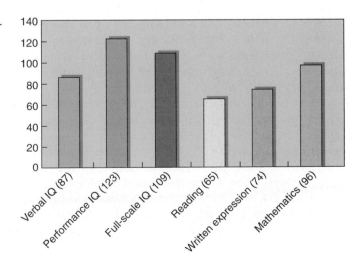

Students like Raquel who are bilingual need special precautions during their evaluation to ascertain that any severe discrepancy is the result of a learning disability and not because of cultural difference. Some safeguards include use of (a) a bilingual evaluator, (b) an interpreter, and (c) performance scales or nonverbal IQ tests. The severe discrepancy should occur in the student's primary language (Ochoa, Rivera, & Powell, 1997).

Debbie Navarro, Raquel's resource teacher, says that Raquel is due for her three-year reevaluation soon: "She will be given an IQ test, a standardized achievement test, and curriculum-based assessment in language arts and math to see how well she knows basic skills."

As Debbie mentioned, it is important that the evaluation team consider more than discrepancy on standardized tests when evaluating students. As you can see in Figure 4–4, the team typically reviews (a) observation information, (b) a behavior rating scale (to rule out severe emotional disturbance as the primary cause of the discrepancy), (c) ecological assessment (see Chapter 8), (d) portfolio assessment (see Chapter 7), and (e) curriculum-based assessment, which we describe in the next section, to assist with decision making. Figure 4–6 is a chart that explains the decision-making process for identifying learning disabilities in students.

Determining the Nature and Extent of Special Education and Related Services

A major concern about typical standardized assessment measures used during nondiscriminatory evaluation is that the test items generally do not represent the exact content of the school's curriculum. That is why these tests, while useful for identification purposes, have limited use for developing individualized education programs (IEPs) (Ysseldyke, Algozzine, & Thurlow, 1994). It is inappropriate, for example, to assume that because a student receives a grade equivalent of 4–2 (fourth grade, second month) in reading on a standardized achievement test, that she should be placed in the fourth-grade reader used in your school. Your reading series might have a higher or lower readability than the same grade-level items on the standardized achievement test.

Curriculum-based assessment is a test whose items reflect the content of the student's curriculum; the test may be norm-referenced or criterion-referenced.

Curriculum-Based Assessment.   **Curriculum-based assessment** can be used for nondiscriminatory evaluation, developing IEPs, determining instructional effectiveness, and monitoring ongoing student progress (Meltzer & Reid, 1994). Some curriculum-based assessment instruments are norm-referenced (referred to as curriculum-based measurement). School districts standardize the tests, which are pulled from items in the curriculum used at each grade. A representative group of students from the district take the test to help establish standard scores that can be used to compare performance of all students in the district. Fluency is emphasized along with accuracy (the student's reading score might be based on the number of words read correctly in two minutes). The tests are generally quick to administer and easily scored (Ysseldyke, Algozzine, & Thurlow, 1994).

Most curriculum-based assessment is criterion-referenced; however, tests are based on specific objectives from the students' curriculum. Students must receive a certain score for mastery (a 70 percent or better is a "C," perhaps). The tests can be administered often, and student progress can be graphed. Sometimes curriculum-based assessment is included with the curriculum. Most math textbooks include chapter tests in the teacher's manual. Often, though, teachers must develop their own curriculum-based assessment instruments. When developing curriculum-based assessment, you will want to make sure that (a) the test items directly reflect the objectives emphasized in the curriculum, (b) the items are clearly stated, and (c) the time limit and level of mastery are reasonable.

FIGURE 4–6   *Decision-making steps for identification of learning disabilities*

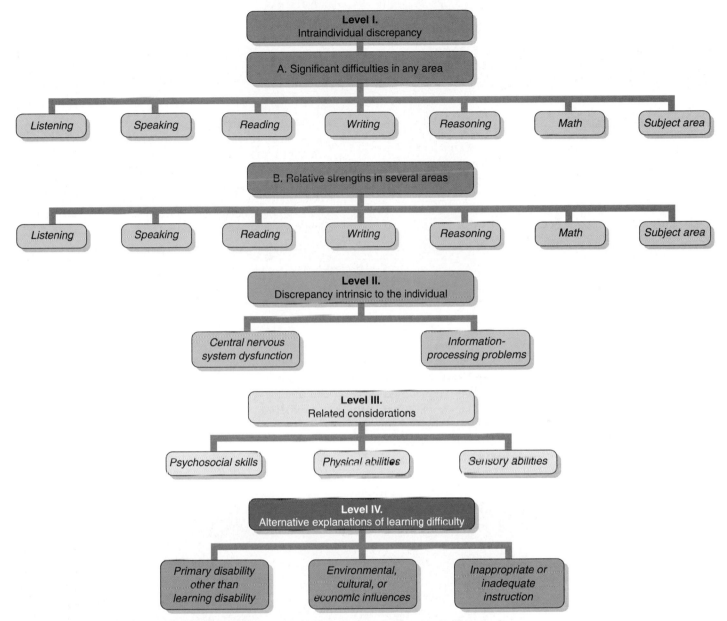

Note: From "An Operational Definition of Learning Disabilities Across the Age Span," in *Promoting Postsecondary Education for Students With Learning Disabilities: A Handbook for Practitioners* (pp. 74–75), by L. Brinckerhoff, S. Shaw, and J. McGuire, 1993, Austin, TX: PRO-ED. Copyright 1993 by PRO-ED. Adapted with permission.

Later in this chapter, we discuss the use of curriculum-based assessment for academic clubs.

Developing the IEP.   Raquel transferred from another school in a different state. How do schools manage compliance with IEP regulations when that happens? Debbie Navarro says that when Raquel first came to their school, "she obviously needed help. We got her records and set up an IEP meeting for the first day. We placed her with a temporary IEP. We had two IEP meetings before all her test results came back."

BOX 4-5   INTO PRACTICE

EFFECTIVE IEPs

- Incorporate the parents' best hopes for the child
- Point toward a future of full involvement in the community
- Embody high expectations for accomplishment
- Recognize the need for individualization and accommodation
- Emphasize functional skills

- Use people friendly language
- Represent realistic assessment of what can be done in the course of a school year
- Are workable, usable documents that will govern classroom activities every day
- Are written as a team at the IEP meeting
- Are flexible documents that can change as the child changes

Note: From "IEPs Made in Heaven," *LDA Newsbriefs,* 1996, March/April, p. 13. Copyright 1996 by PLUK. Reprinted with permission.

As you have learned from your reading so far, *learning disability* is a difficult concept to grasp, even for professionals. Imagine being a family member who has no background about the condition. Debbie says that during the first IEP meeting, Raquel's aunt and cousins "were concerned that she had mental retardation. The other children, the cousins, are good students. This was their first experience with one of the children having academic difficulty." Making sure that the student and family understand learning disabilities is an important component of the IEP process. In Box 4-5, we list some conditions for effective IEPs.

Curriculum-based assessment is essential for determining IEP objectives and planning instruction. A teacher analyzes the errors a student makes while reading.

WHAT AND HOW DO PROFESSIONALS TEACH?

Historical Approaches

Contemporary approaches to curriculum and methods for students with learning disabilities differ significantly from the approaches used in the 1960s and 1970s. As early as the 1930s and 1940s, pioneers such as Kurt Goldstein, Grace Fernald, Helmer Myklebust, and Samuel Kirk sought to translate medical research and hypotheses into workable solutions for teaching students with learning disabilities (Hammill, 1993; Wiederholt, 1974). Researchers had speculated that students had learning disabilities because of difficulty processing information through auditory, visual, and/or kinesthetic channels. Therefore, the logical solution for remediation seemed to be to teach the students to process the information more efficiently. Assessment instruments, including the most widely used—the *Illinois Test of Psycholinguistic Abilities* (J. J. McCarthy & Kirk, 1961)—measured student ability to distinguish and remember sounds and visual stimuli as well as to respond to motor tasks.

Assessing cerebral dominance also gained popularity during this period. The examiner might have handed the student a paper towel tube and asked the student to look through it. Then the examiner told the student to step up on a stool. If the student took the tube with the right hand, looked through it with the left eye, and stepped on the stool with the left foot, the examiner recorded that the student had mixed dominance, which was thought to contribute to dyslexia. However, this assessment approach fell out of favor when researchers discovered that effective readers, as well as those with dyslexia, sometimes showed signs of mixed dominance.

After testing students for processing difficulties, the classroom teacher might require a student who scored poorly in discriminating sounds to listen to a tape and distinguish a fire engine siren from a train whistle. A student with visual discrimination difficulty might work on copying a pattern onto a geoboard. If a student demonstrated motor limitations during testing, the teacher might have her practice walking on a balance beam.

This approach, referred to as *psycholinguistic* or *perceptual motor training,* seemed based on a reasonable premise, but unfortunately, research in the 1970s revealed that the students with learning disabilities did not *generalize* (apply to other areas) their processing training (Hammill & Larsen, 1974). Students who received the training did not significantly improve their ability to deal with academic material, although they improved their skills on processing tests.

After the learning disabilities field recovered from the shock of this revelation, teachers began to search for new methods and curricula. The field moved away from the processing model to a skill-based model based on research findings about effective teaching strategies for students with learning disabilities.

Teachers who use a skill-based model determine specific academic, behavioral, or social skills the student needs to learn through preassessment. They develop a behavioral objective based on a skill the student needs, and then they create lessons to teach the student the skill in a sequential, sometimes standardized manner. After teaching a specific skill, they administer a post-test to make sure the student has achieved mastery of the objective. This style of teaching is called *direct instruction* and is foundational in many curricula being used today for students with learning disabilities.

Curriculum

Often, students with learning disabilities in the general classroom must contend with a curriculum that is too advanced for their ability level or moves too quickly. When you have students in that predicament, you might find it helpful to analyze the materials according to this checklist (Lenz, Marrs, Schumaker, & Deshler, 1993):

- Is the content too abstract? If so, how can it be made more concrete?

- Is the information poorly organized? If so, how can it be reorganized and clarified?

- Is the content relevant? If not, how can a teacher justify having students learn it?

- Is the content interesting? If not, how can it be made less boring?

- Do students have adequate prior knowledge to learn this content? If not, how can a teacher compensate for poor background knowledge?

- Is the information complex? If so, how can it be simplified?

- Is there too much information presented at one time? If so, how can a teacher promote recall of the information?

In this section, we will share how you can teach reading, written language, mathematics, and general content areas more effectively.

Reading.   The Clearinghouse on Disabilities and Education (ERIC, 1995) makes the following recommendations for you to help students achieve phonological awareness. Start with demonstrating relationships of parts to wholes by asking students to identify how many words are in short sentences and use chips or another manipulative to represent the number. Then move to the word level and help them to learn to identify how many syllables are in a word presented orally. Finally, move to the phoneme stage. Model a specific sound and have students produce the sound in isolation and in words and syllables.

Specific examples of tasks include phoneme deletion ("What word is left if /b/ is taken from bat?"), word-to-word matching ("Do *sat* and *pat* begin with the same sound?"), rhyming ("What words sound the same as *dog*?"), blending ("What word does /m/ /a/ /n/ make?"), phoneme counting ("How many sounds are in *fast*?"), and phoneme segmentation ("What sounds are in *pet*?") (ERIC, 1995). In the section entitled "Elementary Years," in "What Are Program Options?" we describe Raquel's reading program, which emphasizes phonological awareness.

Even after developing phonological awareness, some students have difficulty reading. In "Into Practice," Box 4–6, Spear-Swerling and Sternberg (1994) identify four types of reading disabilities (nonalphabetic, compensatory, nonautomatic, and delayed readers) along with appropriate interventions for each.

Written Language.   A *process approach* to written language helps students with learning disabilities overcome their fear of the blank page. You can model each stage for your students by completing the assignment and sharing your thoughts on your own writing as the process progresses (Hallenbeck, 1996). The first stage is *prewriting.* During this stage, your students plan (identify purpose for writing and intended audience) and organize (combine brainstormed ideas into groups or categories through the use of a "think-sheet") what they will write (Hallenbeck, 1996). You can list structured questions on the think-sheet to help students categorize their thoughts, or you can help the student use webbing, which we describe later, in "Methods."

In the second stage, *drafting,* your students create a rough draft from their think-sheet or web. You might need to emphasize that their primary concern is content rather than writing conventions to encourage free-flow of thoughts. They will deal with grammar and spelling during editing.

During the third stage, *editing,* students rate their own papers and receive suggestions from peer editors. By providing the student and peers with edit think-sheets, you can (a) guide specific skills for review emphasis, (b) make sure the editing is constructive, and (c) encourage positive feedback.

The fourth stage, *revising,* allows your students to compile suggestions provided from the editing stage and decide which ones they will use to improve their writing. Emphasizing that authors and editors work together until the final product is produced will encourage ongoing collaboration with peer editors. The use of this process can dramatically improve the writing skills of elementary and secondary students with learning disabilities (Hallenbeck, 1996).

BOX 4-6   INTO PRACTICE

TYPES OF READING DISABILITIES AND INTERVENTIONS

Type of Reading Disability	Characteristics	Instructional Methods
Nonalphabetic readers	Go astray at level of visual-cue word recognition; inability to use phonetic skills in recognizing words—especially lacking in phonological awareness; have not yet experienced "alphabetic insight" to understand how to use phonetic skills in word recognition	Benefit from activities to promote phonological awareness, letter–sound knowledge, and understanding of alphabetic principle (that letters have sounds associated with them)
Compensatory readers	Go astray at phonetic-cue word recognition; can make partial use of rudimentary skills; tend to use other skills such as sight-word reading or context cues to understand what they are trying to read; may experience early success, but eventually impaired comprehension as reading demands become greater	Benefit from direct instruction in decoding skills and encouragement in applying skills when reading in context, rather than guessing
Nonautomatic readers	Go astray at controlled word recognition; can fully decode words but only with effort; rely on sentence context to speed word recognition but at cost to comprehension; may have rapid naming difficulty due to a variety of phonological deficiencies	Benefit from increased practice with motivational reading materials; choices in reading materials, and encouragement of independent reading
Delayed readers	Finally, with much effort, do acquire automatic word recognition skills but lag far behind peers in doing so; not ready for comprehension instruction at time it was delivered; therefore, never achieve strategic reading comprehension	Benefit from direct instruction in reading instruction and higher level comprehension skills

Note. From "The Road Not Taken: An Integrative Theoretical Model of Reading Disability," by L. Spear-Swerling and R. Sternberg, 1994, *Journal of Learning Disabilities, 27*, pp. 91–103. Copyright 1994 by PRO-ED. Adapted with permission.

Mathematics.   The goal of the National Council of Teachers of Mathematics is to help students become active learners who use math to solve meaningful problems and evaluate their own performance in mathematics (National Council of Teachers of Mathematics, 1993).

What can you do to encourage discouraged students with learning disabilities to become active learners? Salend and Hofstetter (1996) provide the following suggestions:

1. *Teach the language of mathematics and encourage its everyday use.* For example, have them look for two-dimensional geometric shapes in the newspaper.

✉ *A student uses manipulatives to learn a new math concept. Students with math disabilities often need to use manipulatives several times before working with pictures and numbers.*

2. *Use visual presentations:* Draw pictures and diagrams to illustrate key concepts and aspects of problems. Also, encourage students to draw pictures when they work problems.

3. *Use manipulatives and concrete teaching aids:* Students need to use items such as counters, dice, fraction circles, Popsicle sticks, geoblocks, and geoboards when learning new skills in mathematics, even on the secondary level. Raquel's teacher Debbie says she uses Touch Math with Raquel (a curriculum in which students touch numerals according to their value: a 2 is touched two times, at the beginning and end of the formed numeral), and with this method, Raquel understood multiplication. She told Debbie that nobody had ever taught her multiplication before. "I know they did," Debbie says. "The difference was in the way she was taught."

4. *Use peer-mediated instruction.* Let students help each other. (The value of peer tutoring is discussed further under "Collaboration," later in the chapter.)

5. *Provide models, cues, and prompts.* You might give students a correct-format model on a note card to use while completing their problems or draw an answer-box model that places squares where they need to write digits.

6. *Teach self-management techniques and learning strategies.* Try giving students a sheet with a list of steps they need to perform, and have them check them off as they work.

7. *Allow students to use calculators.* These tools help students focus on problem-solving components and improve their attitude toward mathematics.

8. *Involve students in the assessment process.* Students need to set goals, choose appropriate assessment techniques, and identify instructional strategies and materials that they believe will help them achieve those goals.

Academic Clubs. How can you make sure that students achieve the content in their general education classes? Smith (1995) noticed that children are motivated by club membership. She decided to capitalize on that factor to help her students with learning disabilities master content skills. Academic clubs, like the whole language approach, teach students skills in a variety of areas around a central theme (see Chapter 7 for further discussion of whole language). Appropriate for general education classes from preschool through high school, academic clubs make sure that students of all ability levels and needs conquer age-appropriate learning tasks. The clubs foster self-esteem by providing students with a sense of mastery and belonging.

The first question to ask when developing an academic club is *What do students need to know?* Marco, a new seventh-grade general education teacher, begins by reading the grade level objectives from the **scope and sequence chart** in the curriculum course guide. As he and Sandi, his inclusion specialist, review the course objectives for the seventh grade, they look for themes. Because Marco teaches social studies, they peruse seventh-grade social studies objectives first and discover that their students need to study people from a culture different from their own, taking into account concepts and facts related to history, geography, sociology, and anthropology. Other objectives for seventh grade focus on the solar system in science, observing patterns and problem solving in math, and process writing in English. While thinking this over, Marco suggests to Sandi that they consider a unit on early people who lived in North America so students can compare and contrast historical and cultural differences from their personal lifestyle.

As Marco and Sandi discuss some thematic connections they can make, Marco becomes excited. He remembers that the advanced culture of the Mayan Indians used tools that tracked planetary orbits as a time-measuring tool. By studying the Mayan culture, students can focus on essential social studies objectives and still learn some rudimentary science objectives about planetary orbits as well as other astronomical concepts. Marco and Sandi begin to plan a unit on the Mayan Civilization that will also introduce some math and English objectives.

In developing content objectives for this unit, Marco and Sandi know they will need to take into consideration individual needs of their students. Sandi checks the IEP objectives of the students with exceptionalities in Marco's class. Some students will require enrichment activities, including one student with learning disabilities who is also gifted. A couple of students will need to concentrate only on the most critical content objectives. The IEPs contain some supplemental academic and behavioral objectives that they can easily incorporate in their academic club for specific students. Once their objectives are in place, Marco and Sandi align the assessment tools they will use, including a pretest and posttest to determine the learning needs of each student and to make sure students master the objectives.

The second question to ask when developing ideas for an academic club is *What motivational framework can convey what I want to teach?* Marco and Sandi decide to motivate students by taking them back into time throughout the year via a time machine, with their first stop being the Mayan Civilization. They decide to call the academic club "The Time Travelers," believing that the title is both age-appropriate and motivational. They plan to show a movie based on H. G. Wells's *The Time Machine* to generate discussion about time travel, including places students would visit if they had such a machine. Students will help decide the rules and infringement policies for the club. They will rotate serving on a Time Monitors Council to help resolve discipline issues that might occur.

Marco and Sandi plan to convert the classroom door into the entrance of a time machine. Students must use a password (vocabulary word and definition) from the previous day to enter the class. Several students who have artistic talent, including one with learning disabilities, will be asked to create the machine. All students will be asked to share ideas for and help with decorating the classroom according to the Mayan culture.

After setting students up with a synopsis of where the time machine will land, Marco and Sandi plan to provide each cooperative learning team with different Time Continuum Glitches: lists of challenging questions about the Mayans. Toward the end of the Mayan Unit, the students will plan a Mayan festival. Each team will present the information they have learned for a grade in any manner they choose—art, music, drama, or writing—during the festival. Each team member actively participates in the presentation.

Marco and Sandi prepared to assist students in their search for information. They have chosen books from the library with lots of good visuals and appropriate reading levels for both independent and instructional reading. Sandi has requested some books on tape about the Mayans from the library, and she asked a student who is gifted to record the information from the seventh-grade textbooks on Central America and the solar system.

A **scope and sequence chart** lists objectives in grade-level sequence that are used in a particular curriculum.

By bringing in objectives from other subjects, Marco and Sandi teach their students that all learning is integrated. This concept is not automatically grasped by many students with learning disabilities who have problems with generalization.

Students with learning disabilities need to have choices.

Students who are poorer readers can then follow along and listen to this information as they gather facts related to their study. Students will also be encouraged to use the Internet, which is available on classroom computers, and videos for references.

Marco has some ideas for integrating some software programs and web sites for club use. He plans to show the entire class two videos that he feels will help the students grasp essential information. Plans have also been made for a field trip to either the planetarium or an anthropological site, depending on the direction of the discoveries students make and the intrinsic student interest the unit may uncover.

Through their preplanning, Marco and Sandi are confident that the academic club will promote meaningful learning, student motivation, and success in relating information to present-day living for all students, including those with learning and other disabilities. Even though their preplanning was a lot of work, Marco and Sandi are excited about teaching the club and know that next year's planning for the club will be much easier.

Methods

Some of the specialized curricula and methods for educating students with learning disabilities employ intensive instructional procedures and materials. These methods and materials often cut across subject areas (e.g., math, science, and language) and age and grade levels.

In this section, you will learn about several types of instructional methods: learning strategies, graphic organizers, techniques for overcoming learned helplessness, and computer technology. As students shift from the skills emphasis of elementary grades to the content emphasis of secondary grades, they face new demands. For students who may not have acquired some of the important academic skills, the task of applying an incomplete set of tools to the content is often fraught with failure. For example, when Raquel enters middle school, in her inclusive general classes she will be expected to work independently, take notes on new information from lectures, and express understanding in written compositions and objective tests. These methods will be important to ensure her success.

Learning Strategies.   Based on the principle that students with learning disabilities lack metacognitive skills, learning strategies help students learn how to learn more effectively and efficiently. Students master sequential steps for attacking a specific task. A **mnemonic,** generally an acronym, helps students remember the steps. For example, *RAP* (**R**ead a paragraph. **A**sk questions about the main idea and details. **P**ut the paragraph information into your own words.) is a strategy for paraphrasing. Learning strategies are designed to complement the general classroom curriculum and instruction by emphasizing learner independence, mastery of cognitive strategy use, and student motivation in all classrooms (Schumaker & Deshler, 1992).

The primary research and development of learning strategies have come from researchers at the University of Kansas Center for Research on Learning. They have developed a curriculum of strategies for three academic tasks:

1. *Acquisition of information:* Available strategies include, among many, word identification, paraphrasing, solving math word problems, and using maps.

2. *Storage or remembering of information:* Strategies to help students remember what they learn include first-letter mnemonic strategy, a listening strategy, and a note-taking strategy.

3. *Expression and demonstration of understanding:* Examples include a sentence-writing strategy, an error-monitoring strategy, a test-taking strategy, and even one for participating actively in IEP meetings.

Students practice learning strategies in small groups until they reach mastery, typically in a resource room through short, intensive lessons over several weeks. They practice the strategy on content materials consistent with their ability levels. Finally, they use it successfully with course materials from general classes.

A **mnemonic** is a device such as a rhyme, formula, or acronym that is used to aid memory.

Developing Your Own Learning Strategy

1. Specify the type of task that the strategy is designed to facilitate. . . . As a rough guideline, a task should be described so that the student would be able to complete the task at least 15 to 20 times during an instructional period. In this way, you may obtain a sensitive performance measure. . . .
2. Describe the task in such a way that students can see a *sequential order* in the specific aspects of the task. . . .
3. Write a brief statement that *summarizes* each step. Make sure that the directions for each step are precise and concise, so that students can easily memorize the instructions.

4. *Limit* the strategy to particular tasks. . . . Teach students to discriminate between tasks for which the strategy is appropriate and other tasks.
5. Develop a *mnemonic* to help students memorize the steps; acronyms seem to be a useful technique for this. . . . Print the strategy on a card for students to refer to during instruction.

One teacher designed a multiple choice acronymn as

R	Read	Read the question carefully.
E	Examine	Examine each answer choice.
A	Accent	Accent important words in the problem and the answer by underlining them.
D	Decide	Decide on the correct answer.

Note: From "Teachers Create Learning Strategies: Guidelines for Classroom Creation" by J. W. Marks, J. Van Laeys, W. N. Bender, & K. S. Scott, *Teaching Exceptional Children*, Summer 1996, pp. 34–38. Copyright 1996 by The Council for Exceptional Children. Reprinted with permission.

In Box 4-7, "Into Practice," you can learn how to write your own learning strategies. After you design a strategy, you will want to (a) pretest the students on the skill, (b) enlist their desire to learn the strategy by providing motivation for doing so, (c) model how to use the strategy, (d) drill the strategy, (e) provide daily performance checks until the students achieve mastery, and (f) periodically review the strategy and make sure the students continue to use it in their classes (Marks, Van Laeys, Bender, & Scott, 1996).

Graphic Organizers. Sometimes referred to as webs, maps, or concept diagrams, graphic organizers are another metacognitive device for helping students organize and remember information. Graphic organizers facilitate learning skills in a variety of subjects by students of all ages. Graphic organizers assist students in (a) identifying key concepts and subconcepts, (b) comparing and contrasting information, and (c) relating cause to effect (Brigham, & Scruggs, 1995; Lovitt & Horton, 1994; Kolstad, Wilkinson, & Briggs, 1997; Levy, 1996; Woodard, 1997). By visualizing information in an organized fashion, graphic organizers help students who have difficulty mastering material from reading or listening to lectures grasp key information. The styles of graphic organizers vary, depending on concepts being taught and the maturity of the student. Generally, teachers and students brainstorm together to determine an effective model.

One effective way to begin a graphic organizer is to write the concept in the middle of the chalkboard. Then ask students to share what they remember about the concept. As they do so, ask them whether their comment is a major point or a subpoint of another point. (You will probably want to do this on the chalkboard or a large piece of paper. This type of webbing sometimes requires a lot of space during the generation stage.) Draw lines branching out from the concept to major points and list subpoints underneath. In Figure 4-7, we provide a graphic organizer that Marco and Sandi developed on the Mayan civilization for their academic club.

FIGURE 4–7 *A graphic organizer for the Time Travelers academic club*

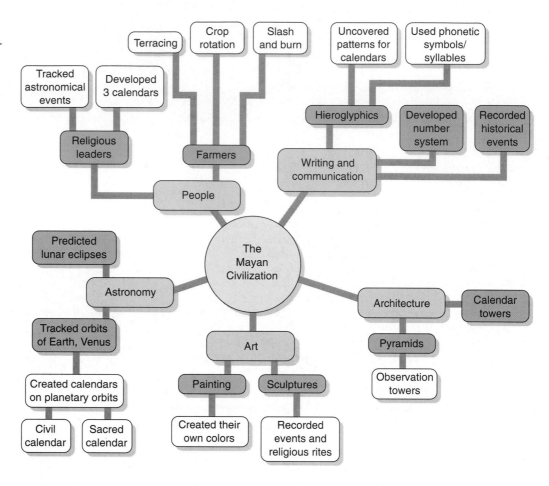

We highly recommend the paperback book *Learned Optimism* (Seligman, 1990a) and the audiotape *The Optimistic Child* (Seligman, 1990b). Seligman, who originated the term *learned helplessness,* explains how teachers and students can become optimistic by altering the way they view good and bad events in their life.

Three instructional levels for a student—frustrational, instructional, and independent—can be determined through assessment.

Overcoming Learned Helplessness.

We mentioned at the beginning of this chapter the vicious downward spiral that students can fall into once they experience learned helplessness. Raquel struggled with learned helplessness. You might recall how her teacher Debbie described her as a sea anemone who withdrew when presented with a book. Raquel became afraid to try to read. Her withdrawal indicated her sense of helplessness. Because the downward spiral results from lowered achievement and self-esteem, the key to helping students work their way up out of that spiral is to encourage achievement and self-esteem.

In the next chapter, we discuss in more detail the four components of self-esteem: significance, power, competence, and virtue (Coopersmith, 1967). By providing students with opportunities to experience these four components, they will be less likely to slide into learned helplessness. Students with learning disabilities need to feel that they (a) are important to you and others, (b) have power through the choices they make, (c) are capable of learning, and (d) contribute to the well-being of people, animals, and the environment. (The "Middle and Secondary Years" section of "What Are Program Options?" describes Service Learning, an excellent program that encourages these four components.)

Research suggests that competence is the most lacking and desired component of self-esteem in students with learning disabilities (Deci, Hodges, Pierson, & Tomassone, 1992). To help these students feel competent, you can use appropriate curricular materials and adaptations. One mistake that some teachers make is to assess students and start with materials at their instructional level. However, when students experience learned helplessness, it is important to guarantee success initially by starting instruction at their independent level. Then, you can gradually provide more challenging material.

To prevent students from feeling they are doing "baby work," the curriculum and instructional materials must be age-appropriate. Jane Fell Greene's *Language!* program—which Raquel uses and we highlight in the "Elementary Years" section in "What Are Program Options?"—begins with simple concepts, but the materials feature older students engaged in adolescent-appropriate activities, making them relevant for students in upper-elementary through high school. Some publishers (Globe Fearon, Weisner, and Wright are listed in the "Resources" section at the end of the chapter) list high-interest/low-readability textbooks, workbooks, and independent reading materials in their catalogs. Other adaptations, such as longer time on tests, reduced homework requirements, and allowing students to copy another student's notes, might help encourage a student, especially in inclusionary settings.

In Chapter 6, we provide an extensive list of adaptations for students with attention-deficit/hyperactivity disorder, many of which are also appropriate for students with learning disabilities.

Computer Technology.   Raquel says that using computers is one of her favorite activities at school. The use of technology, particularly computers, benefits students with learning disabilities in a number of ways (Anderson-Inman, Knox-Quinn, & Horney, 1996; Behrmann, 1994; Fitzgerald & Koury, 1996). For example, computers can be used to make individualized drill and practice more enjoyable and to provide immediate feedback to prevent students from practicing errors. Software games such as Davidson's *Math Blaster* series and The Learning Company's *Reader Rabbit* series reinforce basic math and reading skills for elementary students. Secondary students benefit from programs such as Encore's *Middle School Advantage* and Piranha™ Interactive Publishing's *The Academic Edge.*

Students can also compensate for deficient skills in writing through software that reads orally what they write and checks spelling and grammar. Some software programs (IBM's Simply Speaking and Kurzweil's Voice Pad) even allow them to dictate through a

"We are embarking upon an educational era in which it will become increasingly important to envision the teacher and the microcomputer as partners in constructing . . . learning environments for students" (Behrmann, 1996).

💕   *Raquel, like many students with learning disabilities, finds computer technology helpful for motivation and skill mastery.*

microphone while the computer types what they speak. For those who have difficulty reading, multimedia books and encyclopedias encourage motivation through added pictures, videos, and sound bytes. Some programs read the entire text to the students or give them an opportunity to highlight words they cannot identify and the computer reads those orally. In addition, student textbooks and workbooks can be scanned into the computer to be read orally to students.

Computer software can help teach problem solving and social skills through the use of simulation experiences. *The Oregon Trail II* (from Softkey Multimedia, Inc.), for example, can be completed by a small group of students, each one taking a specific role. The group must work together to survive until they reach Oregon.

For students to be able to benefit from computer usage, they must have access. The value of technology increases greatly when educators can readily align it with existing curricula in useful and creative ways (Edyburn, 1992). If students use computers only when the teacher wishes to reward them for good behavior or when the teacher needs to complete some paperwork, students view computers as toys rather than effective and enjoyable tools for lifelong learning.

HOW IS PARTICIPATION ENCOURAGED?

Inclusion

Thirty years ago, most students with learning disabilities were not being served in special education programs or even recognized as having a disability. The field of learning disabilities was still in its infancy, and if the school did have a specialized class, the students were often labeled as having minimal brain dysfunction. A few were mislabeled as having mental retardation or emotional and behavioral disorders.

The field has come a long way in a relatively short period of time. We've mentioned how prevalence has increased, along with awareness and understanding of learning disabilities. Students are protected under IDEA and guaranteed the right to education in the least restrictive environment. In Figure 4–8 a pie chart is a visualization of the placements of these students in 1995.

As you can see, the resource room is the most common placement for students with learning disabilities (U.S. Department of Education, 1997). Students in resource placement spend part or most of their day in the general classroom. They also attend the resource room for one or more classes, usually on a regularly scheduled basis, to receive more individualized instruction from a special education teacher. The efficacy of resource rooms for

FIGURE 4–8 *Percentage of students with specific learning disabilities in educational placements*

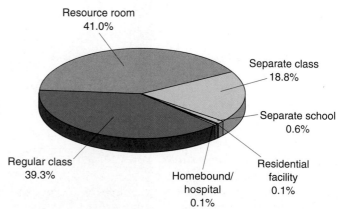

Note: From U.S. Department of Education (1995). *To Assure the Free Appropriate Public Education of All Children With Disabilities: Seventeenth Annual Report to Congress on the Implementation of the Individuals with Disabilities Education Act.* Washington, DC: Author.

students with learning disabilities is contested in research. Some studies seem to indicate more academic and social gain if the student attends the resource room; other research favors full-time general education placement (Albinger, 1995; Howard-Rose & Rose, 1994; Madge et al., 1990; Vaughn & Schumm, 1995). Perhaps what all this research really suggests is that different students function better in resource rooms while others function better in general classrooms.

This premise is at the heart of the debate over the efficacy of inclusion for students with learning disabilities. Some researchers emphasize *place* over *student* (Vaughn & Schumm, 1995; Vaughn, Elbaum, & Schumm, 1996), contending that "[general] education is not only where the responsibility lies, but also where those with learning disabilities deserve to be educated" (Taylor, 1994). Others, including some parents, emphasize resource placement, asserting that student needs have been unrecognized or not addressed appropriately in general classrooms.

Most professionals in the field have moved toward a more balanced position. "The goal of special education," say Mercer and Lane (1994), "should be to provide the knowledge and skills that students with learning disabilities need to lead full and independent lives." Responsible inclusion for these students, then, is the *most enabling environment*. For some, this implies full inclusion, for others, part-time or full-time special education classes. In Box 4–8, "Into Practice," one researcher shares the difference between responsible and irresponsible inclusion for students with learning disabilities.

A result of the responsible inclusion movement has been a shift in focus: IEP teams have been more inclined to ask *why* the general education classroom is not the appropriate placement, rather than *if* it is the appropriate placement. Now IDEA requires educators to justify any placement outside the general classroom, presuming that the student begins in general education and is moved away from it incrementally, only as necessary to provide appropriate education. This approach is the one that works well if it is implemented properly, with these components in place: cooperative learning to reinforce skills; peer and cross-age tutoring; assistance from special services staff and paraprofessionals; technology, including audiotapes and computer software; curriculum-based measurement; and learning strategies taught in the general classroom (Bracker, 1994). Tips for inclusion are shown in the box on page 154.

Collaboration

Collaboration With Professionals.
Students with learning disabilities need their teachers to work together on their behalf. How do busy general educators and special educators, whether serving in resource or inclusionary settings, find the time to talk to each other? To work together effectively, teachers must have time to cooperatively plan, share information, and evaluate their instruction. Project CLASP (Voltz, Elliott, & Harris, 1995) required participating schools to provide two thirty-minute periods per week for teachers to meet. During these periods, teachers solved problems using the CLASP acronym:

C = Clarify the problem. Teachers share information about students and determine areas of student difficulty.

L = Look at influencing factors. What happens before, during, and after the student exhibits the problem?

A = Actively brainstorm interventions. Teachers generate a list of options along with identifying collaborative roles to facilitate success.

S = Select an intervention. The list is evaluated according to "probability of success, ease of implementation, possible side effects, and resources required." The teachers decide which intervention should be tried first.

P = Plan for success. Teachers plan roles in implementation and decide how they will evaluate the plan's success. (Voltz et al., 1995)

❧ Many students with learning disabilities who are in general education part-time are benefiting from the inclusion movement, which emphasizes co-teaching, such as Marco and Sandi did for their academic club. Prior to this movement, these students had no support from a special educator while in general education.

❧ What skills do you have that will make you effective as a collaborator for students with learning disabilities? What skills do you still need to work on, and how can you improve them?

BOX 4-8   INTO PRACTICE

RESPONSIBLE INCLUSION FOR STUDENTS WITH LEARNING DISABILITIES

Responsible Inclusion	Irresponsible Inclusion
Student first The first priority is the extent to which the student with disabilities is making academic and/or social progress in the general education classroom. Ongoing assessment, monitoring, and placement consideration is critical to success.	**Place first** Students' academic and social progress is second to the location in which their education occurs. If the student is in the general education classroom, there is little else to consider because place is the foremost consideration.
Teachers choose to participate in inclusive classrooms Teachers are provided opportunities to participate in inclusive classrooms and self-select their involvement.	**Teachers are mandated to participate in inclusive classrooms** Teachers are mandated to participate and feel no opportunity to provide feedback about the extent to which their skills will allow them to be successful in general education classrooms.
Adequate resources are considered and provided for inclusive classrooms Personnel understand that for inclusion to be successful, considerable resources, related to both personnel and material, are required to develop and maintain effective inclusive classrooms.	**Resources are not considered prior to the establishment of inclusive classrooms** The inclusion model does not initially consider that additional resources are needed, and inclusive classrooms are established with little consideration of the personnel and physical resources required.
Models are developed and implemented at the school-based level School-site personnel develop inclusive models that are implemented and evaluated to meet the needs of students and families in their community.	**School district, state, and/or federal directives provide the guidelines for inclusion** School-based models are mandated at the district and/or state level, and key personnel in the school and community are rarely engaged in the development of the model.
A continuum of services is maintained A range of education programs are available to meet the needs of students with learning disabilities. It is not expected that the needs of all students will be met with full-time placement in the general education classroom.	**Full inclusion is the only service delivery model** All students are placed in general education classrooms full time, regardless of their needs or their successes.

To keep collaboration effective, general and special educators need to celebrate, reevaluate, create, and self-monitor (Driver, 1996). Many teachers neglect the important task of celebrating their accomplishments. Two teams at one elementary school met together for lunch once a month for the specific purpose of sharing successes. The positive focus of these meetings increased motivation and encouraged ideas.

Teams also need to take time periodically to reevaluate their goals and make sure that responsibilities are divided equitably (Driver, 1996). Can you imagine how disheartening it would be for a special educator to be treated as an aide in an inclusionary setting?

Two factors ensure continuous improvement in general/special educator teams: promoting innovation and creativity and constructive feedback (Driver, 1996). The temptation

Responsible Inclusion	Irresponsible Inclusion
Service delivery model is evaluated on an ongoing basis The success of the service delivery model is considered and fine-tuned in light of the nature of the students with learning disabilities and with consideration for the extent to which it meets their academic and social needs.	**Service delivery model is established and implemented** If problems occur, personnel are blamed rather than the model being evaluated to determine its effectiveness.
Ongoing professional development Personnel realize that for teachers and others to be effective at inclusion, ongoing professional development at the school-site level is required.	**Professional development not part of the model** Teachers and other individuals are not provided adequate time or opportunity to improve their skills and/or increase their knowledge about effectively meeting the needs of students with learning disabilities.
Teachers and other key personnel discuss and develop their own philosophy on inclusion This philosophy on inclusion guides practice at the school and sets a tone of acceptance for all students.	**A school philosophy on inclusion is not developed** Several teachers in the school may participate and understand inclusion, but it is not part of the school philosophy as a whole.
Curricula and instruction that meet the needs of all students are developed and refined Successful inclusion provides for curricula and instructional practices that meet the needs of all students.	**Curricula and instruction that meet the needs of all students are not considered** The success of average- and high-achieving students is of little interest as long as students with disabilities are included in general education classrooms. Specialized curricula and instruction for students with [learning disabilities] are not considered.

Note: From "Responsible Inclusion for Students With Learning Disabilities," by S. Vaughn and J. S. Schumm, 1995, *Journal of Learning Disabilities, 28*(5), pp. 264–271. Copyright 1995 by the PRO-ED, Inc. Reprinted with permission.

to use the same lesson plans and interventions year after year is great, but the result is stagnation. Brainstorming must occur for lesson plans as well as for problem solving.

Feedback is crucial for team success. A third party who observes team interactions occasionally can bring new insights. The team also needs to self-evaluate. Driver (1996) recommends responding to the following with a five-point scale (always, often, sometimes, rarely, never):

To what extent have we . . .

• Scheduled time to recognize accomplishments?

• Reevaluated our goals regularly?

Inclusion Tips

	What You Might See	What You Might Be Tempted to Do	Alternate Responses	Ways to Include Peers in the Process
Behavior	The student continually disrupts other students when she needs to be working independently on assignments.	Move the student away from peers or put out of the class.	Check to be sure he understands and is able to do assignments. Develop a behavior management plan to reinforce on-task behavior.	Match him with a peer tutor when working on class assignments. Discuss with peers how to help him within the behavior management plan.
Social Interactions	The student misinterprets social cues. The student misinterprets facial gestures and/or verbal inflections.	Point out the misinterpretation and tell her how to do it "right."	Collaborate with the school counselor or resource teacher to plan ways to teach her needed social skills.	Establish a peer-partnership where the peer can practice specific social cues with her.
Educational Performance	His work is inconsistent or generally poor.	Grade him down for poor or incomplete work.	Collaborate with special educators to teach him learning strategies. Provide extra time to complete.	Use age-appropriate materials with peer tutoring for reading assignments.
Classroom Attitudes	The student easily gives up in areas of weakness to get out of work.	Excuse her from some assignments or reprimand her for unwillingness to try.	Promote success with appropriate learning tasks that can be accomplished, and then provide a strong reward system.	Give the student opportunities to tutor others (peers or younger students) in areas of success.

• Ensured equitable teaming practices by sharing leadership?

• Strived for continuous improvement?

Peer tutoring is the instruction of one student by another for the purposes of instructional and social support.

Collaboration With Peers.   Raquel enjoys working with other students. **Peer tutoring** is an effective strategy for helping students like Raquel to master skills, increase socialization, and gain confidence (Greenwood & Delquadri, 1995; King-Sears & Bradley, 1995; Maag & Weber, 1995). In one model, the student with learning disabilities is tutored on a specific skill by another student; in a second model, the student teaches another student in the same grade in an area of strength; in a third, the student tutors a younger student (cross-age tutoring).

During *classwide peer tutoring* (a model developed by Charles Greenwood and associates at Juniper Gardens Children's Project in Kansas), all students have opportunities to serve as tutors and tutees, according to their relative strengths (Greenwood, 1991; Greenwood & Delquadri, 1995). Teachers who use classwide peer tutoring cite several benefits: (a) increased student enthusiasm for learning, (b) encouragement of both student-to-student and student-to-teacher interaction, (c) increased student self-esteem, (d) improvement in resolving differences without teacher intervention, and (e) increased positive and cooperative treatment of each other (Phillips, Fuchs, & Fuchs, 1994). Even when not in peer tutoring situations, students tend to be more inclined to help each other and use questioning or explanations rather than providing correct answers. Peer tutors also tend to use more age-appropriate vocabulary and examples than a teacher does, identify with the frustration of learning the material, and to be more direct and supportive than adults (Good & Brophy, 1990).

Phillips et al. (1994) developed a classwide peer tutoring model in which each student served as tutor (coach) for at least two of six weeks. When not coaching, the student was a player. Each session lasted for thirty minutes and occurred at least twice a week and was divided into coaching and practice components. Students practiced twelve instances of the targeted skill.

Coaches asked a series of questions to guide and prompt the player in math problem solving. Each time the student wrote a digit correctly, the coach circled it and praised the player. If the player answered incorrectly, the coach shared an explanation or strategy. After the first row, the player completed the other problems independently, as long as the preceding problem was completed correctly without explanation. When the coaching session finished, the player and coach completed a worksheet containing similar problems as well as some easier problems using skills the player had already mastered. Afterward, coach and player exchanged papers and scored each others' work.

Peer tutoring is used with success at both elementary and secondary levels. The key is finding a model that works for you in your setting. Collaboration tips for peer tutoring are shown on pages 156–157.

Collaboration With Family. Raquel's resource teacher Debbie Navarro says that she is fortunate to work with the family. "They want only the best for her. They're from the old school. The teacher knows best." This devotion to Raquel's progress comes through in their willingness to work with her on homework, despite the fact that her uncle and aunt both work and have extremely busy schedules. Homework is especially challenging for Raquel because of her difficulty with getting and staying on task. Her teacher Debbie is committed to keeping the family informed about what Raquel needs to do and helping them accomplish it. "Every Thursday," she says, "we confer about what Raquel has finished and what still needs to be completed."

As Raquel's family situation suggests, research indicates that families who have a child with learning disabilities are generally well-functioning and healthy (Dyson, 1996; Stoddard, Valcante, Roemer, & O'Shea, 1994). However, they do tend to experience more stress, and homework can contribute to that stress.

A typical high schooler may have two to three hours of homework per night (Polloway, Epstein, Bursuck, Hayanthi, & Cumblad, 1994). Imagine how much longer a student with learning disabilities must spend to complete the same amount of homework. In addition, students with learning disabilities may have more homework to begin with, because the majority of assigned work is uncompleted classwork (Palloway et al., 1994).

How can you make homework easier for students with learning disabilities and their families (Shank, 1997)? First, ask yourself *your purpose* in assigning homework. Is it to build character? To reinforce skills? To provide enrichment? After you decide, then you can evaluate whether your assignments match your purpose. Can you assign less homework and still meet your goals?

You also need to make sure homework is *meaningful to students*. Do they understand how the homework will benefit them? Have you clarified in class how the skill they are learning is relevant for something other than a grade?

Homework needs to *match student learning styles*. Some students with learning disabilities might benefit from presenting a skit on a book they read rather than writing a report on it. Another student might want to illustrate the book and add captions. Allow students freedom to be creative in assignments.

How would you use classwide peer tutoring in a high school history class?

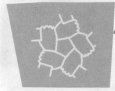

Collaboration Tips

DEVELOPING A PLAN TO INITIATE PEER TUTORING

COLLABORATION GOAL   To initiate peer tutoring to help a student with learning disabilities master basic skills and increase socialization.

Collaborators	Roles and Preparation	Possible Barriers	Solutions to Barriers	Modifications to Implementation	Ongoing Evaluation
Student	Open to working with other students.	May feel embarrassed by lack of skills.	Allow student to tutor others in areas of strengths or to tutor younger students.	Create a safe classroom environment in which everyone, including yourself, is comfortable sharing strengths and needs.	Ask student to complete a short questionnaire, orally or in writing, about peer tutoring progress.
Peers	Open to working with students with disabilities.	May come across as bossy or condescending. May have a negative attitude toward students with learning disabilities.	Check your own attitude. Students tend to reflect attitudes of their role models. Provide training. Avoid using a student as a tutor until attitude is positive.	Ask students to share what they've liked and disliked about teachers (no names, of course). Ask students to evaluate the kind of teacher they want to be when tutoring. Role play.	Ask student to complete a short questionnaire, orally or in writing, about peer tutoring progress.
General Educator(s)	Need to decide how peer tutoring can be incorporated in lessons.	May not know how to implement peer tutoring.	Discuss with special educator; find another general educator who is using peer tutoring and ask to observe; attend in-service.	Start slow. Begin with a few students during a few lessons. Add more opportunities as confidence grows.	Consider feedback from questionnaires; monitor student learning.
Special Educator(s)	Need to provide suggestions and monitor tutoring.	May believe it is more efficient to teach themselves.	Recognize the solialization value and the increase of self-esteem when student serves as tutor.	During the IEP meeting, decide how peer tutoring can be incorporated.	Keep portfolio of student work and questionnaires.

Collaborators	Roles and Preparation	Possible Barriers	Solutions to Barriers	Modifications to Implementation	Ongoing Evaluation
Parents of students with disabilities	Provide opportunities at home for student to socialize with children/teens without learning disabilities.	May fear that student will not learn as well or will learn misinformation from peers.	Share how you train students to serve as peer tutors and how you provide them with guidelines for what to teach.	Pretest to make sure student has necessary skills. Have a plan for training tutors, and always provide a list of skills the tutor should cover.	Ask parents for feedback on peer tutoring progress at conferences.
Parents of peers	Encourage openness toward people with learning disabilities.	May believe their child is wasting time tutoring others.	Emphasize how tutoring builds self-esteem, helps the tutor learn the information in more depth, and provides motivation.	Encourage parents to observe your class during peer tutoring sessions.	Ask for feedback on peer tutoring during conferences.
Administrator	Encourage teachers to use peer tutoring; provide in-service training.	May believe that the teacher should be teaching instead of the students teaching.	Invite administrator to observe peer tutoring; share documentation of student learning gains.	Prepare a plan for an in-service on peer tutoring yourself and share your ideas; busy administrators often appreciate suggestions.	When administrator observes your classroom, ask for specific feedback on peer tutoring.
School counselor	Help student develop social skills for participation.	May be used to seeing student in isolation; is unable to identify social needs.	Invite counselor to classroom to observe peer interactions during classwide peer tutoring.	Ask counselor for suggestions about the way to make peer tutoring effective for the student.	With student's permission, share feedback about student performance with counselor.

Making homework meaningful and limited is important for the parent as well as the child with learning disabilities.

Accommodate students' learning disabilities. If a student takes longer to complete a math assignment, can he do half the problems only and still demonstrate mastery? Also, parents should not be expected to teach a skill. If you have not been able to teach the skill when you are trained as a teacher, the student probably is not ready to learn it. Homework should be for reinforcement or enrichment only.

Add fun into homework. Why not have a "make and take" night when students and parents come to school and work together on a project (see Stoddard et al., 1994)? To practice multiplication in math class, you might have students generate ideas for determining how many beans are in a jar. Offer a prize to the person who comes closest and to the one who generates the most ideas for solving the puzzle. And to give students a chance to be kids, campaign for occasional *no-homework weekends* at your school.

Careers

Resource teachers may be called learning specialists, learning consultants, learning center teachers, or something different, depending on the school district.

Resource teachers provide instruction and encouragement to students with learning disabilities. Their primary responsibility is to support students with learning disabilities in one or more school settings.

Because most students with learning disabilities are educated for part of the school day in a resource room setting and part of the day in general classes, resource teachers also spend part of their day in each setting. Their responsibilities entail assessment, developing IEPs, collaborating with general classroom teachers, meeting with parents, and more. Because inclusion is becoming more common, their role is changing to co-teacher in many districts. In Box 4-9, "Making a Difference," we share a portrait of Ennis Cosby, who devoted his life to teaching students with learning disabilities.

WHAT ARE PROGRAM OPTIONS?

Over 40 percent of students with learning disabilities do not complete high school compared to 25 percent of the general school population (Barga, 1996). Moreover, students with learning disabilities are more likely to drop out of school than students with other types of disabilities. Research also suggests that students with learning disabilities who

BOX 4-9 **MAKING A DIFFERENCE**

ENNIS WILLIAM COSBY

"The happiest day of my life occurred when I found out I was dyslexic," Ennis William Cosby wrote. "I believe that life is finding solutions, and the worst feeling in the world to me is confusion" (Cosby, 1993—Hello Friend Ennis William Cosby Foundation).

Ennis must have experienced considerable confusion. He struggled academically in a home with two parents who have doctorates in education. His father, Bill Cosby, modeled his TV son Theo Huxtable after Ennis, mirroring his birth son's humor, intelligence, and struggles in school.

When Ennis was a freshman at Morehouse College in Atlanta, his mother's friend suggested that he be tested at a specialized college for people with dyslexia. The findings not only led him to answers about his academic difficulties, but also to a career. Ennis attended an intense summer program and received comprehensive tutoring to address his dyslexia. When he returned to Morehouse in the fall, his grades leaped from a 2.3 average to more than a 3.5 average. He made the dean's list.

Ennis determined to dedicate his life to helping others who struggled with learning. "A true test for a healer is to heal people who need it most," he said (Cosby, 1993—Hello Friend Ennis William Cosby Foundation).

During Ennis' years at Morehouse, he student taught a class of third graders in Atlanta. Ennis' supervising teacher pointed out to him that the African American males in Ennis' class who did not have male role models in their homes performed better when Ennis worked with them. "That is what convinced me that I was needed in the academic field," he wrote. "It amazed me that academic performance by children could be altered by a simple motivational factor like a direct role model" (Cosby, 1993—Hello Friend Ennis William Cosby Foundation). Ennis decided he could be most effective as a role model to African American males with dyslexia:

I got so involved with the elementary school that I began to go to the special education classes and offered my services to the teacher. I really bonded with the kids in the special education class. I was 'teaching from the

heart,' and the kids' biggest need seemed to be a teacher who cared about them and their individual needs. (Cosby, 1993—Hello Friend Ennis William Cosby Foundation)

In 1995, Ennis earned a master's degree in special education at Columbia University and was enrolled in the doctoral program there at the time of his death. He tutored students with dyslexia and language-based learning differences in New York City during this time. His work led him to rethink the terms commonly used to describe individuals who are having trouble learning. "I prefer to refer to students who are classified as having learning disabilities as children who learn differently" (Cosby, 1996—Hello Friend Ennis William Cosby Foundation)

One of his pupils said about his tutoring experience with Ennis: "It was the best time of my life. Before I met him, I felt college would be too hard, but he taught me that if he could overcome the same problem I had, I could go to college, too" (cited in Castro, 1997).

"He was my hero," Bill Cosby said about his son. He was certainly a hero to the students he taught. Ennis's legacy lives on in the Hello Friend, Ennis William Cosby Foundation, which benefits students with learning differences, and in those who, inspired by his story, decide to follow his path. Ennis wrote, "I believe that if more teachers are aware of the signs of dyslexia and learning differences, . . . then fewer students like me will slip through the cracks" (Cosby, 1993—Hello Friend Ennis William Cosby Foundation).

Note: Quotes from Ennis Cosby's work are reprinted with permission of the Hello Friend Ennis William Cosby Foundation.

have dropped out of school are the young people with the greatest risk of having "lifelong economic and social difficulties" (Barga, 1996).

These distressing statistics emphasize the importance of creating effective programs for students with learning disabilities, beginning during the preschool years. Many such programs exist.

Early Intervention and Preschool Years

Determining which preschoolers have or are at risk for learning disabilities is an arduous task. We discussed earlier that many states use a significant discrepancy between ability and achievement to diagnose a learning disability. How is this discrepancy possible when a child is too young to have been exposed to academic tasks? Yet, serving these children before they confront academic tasks is imperative to avoid failure experiences. Furthermore, IDEA mandates that preschoolers with disabilities, including those with learning disabilities, receive a free and appropriate public education.

J. M. McCarthy, Harris, and Reeves (1997) surveyed how states identified preschoolers at risk for learning disabilities. Over half the states used a noncategorical approach to identifying preschoolers with disabilities. These states allowed children to qualify as "at-risk" or "developmentally young" rather than as having learning disabilities, mental retardation, or another category-specific term. Recognizing that children develop at different rates, these states are avoiding stigmatizing labels that may later prove inappropriate. Those states that choose to use the learning disabilities category for preschoolers often modify the federal definition to include young children. They qualify children on the basis of the definitional components that can be measured in young children: listening, thinking, and speaking.

These three areas—listening, thinking, and speaking—relate to the language difficulties that seem to be the foundation of many learning disabilities, including problems with phonological awareness. By remediating language during the preschool years, schools may be able to prevent or at least lessen the severity of future academic problems. The Language Acquisition Preschool (Bunce, 1995; Rice & Wilcox, 1995) operated by the Department of Speech, Language, and Hearing at the University of Kansas, helps children develop language skills in an enjoyable, inclusionary setting.

The Language Acquisition Preschool serves thirty-six children from the ages of three to five: eighteen in the morning and eighteen in the afternoon. One-third of these children have clear language delays. Another third speak English as a second language. And the other third have no language problems at all. Because the Language Acquisition Preschool focuses on language facilitation, it provides each of these children with many opportunities to listen and to use language within the classroom setting. The many emergent literacy activities also provide a foundation for future literacy development (Watkins & Bunce, 1996). The program may thereby prevent later discrepancies that may result in children being classified as having a learning disability.

The Language Acquisition Preschool is a concentrated normative model (Rice, 1995), meaning that it provides activities emphasizing commonalities among children and allowing for language intervention in a natural setting. Normative models of language acquisition emphasize the importance of children's language use at home and encourage collaboration with families in their children's language intervention programs. The concentrated normative model also includes a curriculum that focuses on the development of language skills through daily activities and embeds occasions to highlight specific language skills.

The Language Acquisition Preschool includes both child-centered and teacher-directed activities (see Bunce, 1995, for a description of the curriculum and lesson plans). During the child-centered activities, each child chooses what to do from among the school's many centers, such as dramatic play, art, and quiet or manipulative areas. During center time, the children are free to participate in an activity for whatever length of time

The Learning Disabilities Association provides an Early Childhood Fact Sheet that lists characteristics suggesting a child is at risk for developing learning disabilities. You can access the fact sheet online at www.ldanatl.org/factsheets/Early Childhood.html.

they choose and can move freely from activity to activity. This makes learning a natural consequence of willed activity. During the teacher-directed activities such as story, sharing, or group time, the children learn to listen and are taught new concepts.

All activities seek to enrich the child's language. For example, during sharing time, the children are prompted by staff to ask each other questions so they can learn to listen and answer. Likewise, the staff invite especially shy or retiring children into interactions with staff members and with other children so that dialogue occurs spontaneously in pleasurable activities. The staff help the children develop appropriate social skills so they will feel more comfortable talking with other children. (See Rice, Sell, & Hadley, 1990, for a description of the social interaction coding system used in the Language Acquisition Preschool.)

Almost all of this work is carried out in an inclusive setting with no pull-out for individual language therapy. There is really no way for an uninformed observer to detect which of the children have language delays and which do not.

The director, the lead teacher, the family services coordinator and school-district liaison, the assistant teacher, the speech-language therapists, and the student teachers develop IEPs for the children with language delays as well as individual programs (not formal IEPs) for the other children, thus ensuring that all instruction for all children is individualized.

The family services coordinator encourages home–school communication and collaboration in the following ways:

- Publish a weekly newsletter.

- Frequently contact the families by telephone and in person.

- Explain a video on how to facilitate children's language.

- Make suggestions for families on how to increase their children's use of language.

- Advocate for the families and children in IEP conferences.

- Schedule regular and as-needed conferences.

- Provide various kinds of family support, including baby-sitters, admission to other preschools, transition into elementary school, and related services such as transportation and occupational therapy.

What difference does all this make for the dozen children who are identified as having language delays? Follow-up data from the Language Acquisition Preschool indicate that, of the preschoolers who received speech-language therapy at the preschool, approximately one-third did not receive additional speech or language therapy in elementary school. The Language Acquisition Preschool's follow-up data also indicate that 61 percent had followed the educational progression typically expected through the primary grades. Thirty-eight percent altered normal education by completing an alternate sequence, including **developmental first grade,** delay of kindergarten entry, or grade retention (Sergeant, 1995).

Developmental first grade provides a transition year between kindergarten and first grade for children who are not ready for first grade.

Would these children have had learning disability classification without concentrated language intervention? It's hard to say for certain, but early childhood programs like the Language Acquisition Preschool work at school and with families to give children the language skills to beat the odds.

Elementary Years

Most children with learning disabilities are first identified in the elementary grades and begin at that point to benefit from some of the instructional methods you have read about. The methods used in elementary and middle school often overlap, and middle school and high school assistance may overlap as well. You will find this to be true about the program model we share in this section.

Along with *Language!,* two other programs you have learned about in this chapter, strategy training and direct instruction, benefit students with learning disabilities who are deductive learners.

We've mentioned that Raquel learned to read this past year through the program adopted by her school district in Alabama. *Language!*—a curriculum for at-risk students and students learning English as a second language in grades 2 through 12—teaches writing, spelling, reading, grammar, and vocabulary (see the "Resources" section for ordering information). "It was much, much more than learning to recognize sounds, which Raquel could do," Raquel's teacher Debbie comments. "The program was exactly what Raquel needed."

Jane Fell Greene (1995–1996), the author of the *Language!* program, seeks to remediate the phonological awareness difficulties that you've read about throughout this chapter. Jane distinguishes between *inductive learners,* who learn best by assimilating the whole and analyzing its parts, and *deductive learners,* who learn best from parts to the whole. Most inductive learners find little difficulty learning to read with the traditional basal reader approach, but deductive learners need to learn language in an organized, structured, and mechanistic manner, according to Jane. Reading difficulties, then, are due more to learning style differences than lack of ability.

Whereas traditional approaches often emphasize sight vocabulary, the Structured Language Program, on which *Language!* is based, constructs vocabulary from phonetically regular words, enabling students to grasp meaning-based, grammar-based, and knowledge-based patterns. To succeed in this task, students learn symbol–sound (grapheme–phoneme) correspondence code.

When a student first enters the program, the teacher administers a code-based placement test, and students are placed according to their level of mastery. To promote phonological awareness, nonreaders begin with learning to isolate and blend phonemes in words. Thus, they assimilate that *cat* has three phonemes: /k/ /a/t/. Students are rewarded for individual gain. Besides learning code-based, phonetically regular words, students are systematically taught nonphonetic words and review them regularly for mastery. Students master meanings of roots, prefixes, and suffixes to increase their vocabulary. They also learn grammar throughout the program, even at the earliest stages. Masterpiece Plots, a five-stage process, is a format used to teach reading comprehension skills. Although we mention the Masterpiece Plots program here, in the "Elementary Years" section, the content of the stories and accompanying pictures makes it age-appropriate for secondary learners as well. In Figure 4-9, we provide samples from the nine student texts used in *Language!*

BILL COSBY'S DYSLEXIA CRUSADE

"If you don't know about dyslexia, you think that the person has something wrong or is dumb, not as bright," Bill Cosby says. Cosby is determined to change that misunderstanding. His son Ennis loved learning, but dyslexia cut him off from learning, according to Carolyn Olivier, who is currently the Education Director of the Hello Friend Ennis William Cosby Foundation. And yet, students with dyslexia "are often really gifted in the area of dealing with ideas and visual thinking and understanding," she comments.

In this ABC video, young people share what it is like to live with dyslexia. Bill Cosby also discusses Ennis's dyslexia and how his son reached out to another family member he suspected might have the condition.

What do you think? Ennis Cosby learned the importance of self-advocacy in dealing with dyslexia. How will you help your students learn to be self-advocates?

What opportunities can you create in your classroom for students with dyslexia to use their strengths in dealing with ideas and visual thinking?

How does this video relate to our earlier discussion of the causes of dyslexia?

FIGURE 4–9 *Samples from the student texts used in* Language!

UNIT 4

Phonemic concepts
- A single unit of sound is a phoneme
  - Consonant phonemes are closed sounds
  - Consonant sound-symbol relationship
    - **w**
- Vowel phoneme concept: Every word has a vowel phoneme
  - Vowel phonemes are open sounds
  - Vowel sound-symbol: Short /i/
- Spoken words are made of phonemes

Orthographic concepts
- English words are written with 26 letters (graphemes)
  - This group of 26 letters is called the **alphabet**
- The alphabet is a code. In the code of English, letters (graphemes) represent sounds (phonemes)
  - Each of the 26 letters may be formed in upper- or lower-case
    - *Examples*
      - I i   W w
  - Each of the 26 letters may be formed in print or in script
    - *Examples*
      - I i   W w
- Some English words are nonphonetic
  - A nonphonetic word is not spelled (encoded) the way that it sounds
  - The nonphonetic words in unit four are **have** and **I**

Grammatic concepts
- Nouns: A noun may be concrete or abstract
  - Concrete nouns name a person, place, or thing that you can see or touch
    - *Examples*
      - **table, car**
  - Abstract nouns name an idea or a thought that you cannot see
    - *Examples*
      - **love, happiness**
- A noun may be used as the subject of a sentence
  - The subject names the person, place, thing, or idea that the sentence describes

Reading and spelling vocabulary

in	did	big	mit	*have*
Mac	is	kid	rig	*I*
hit	pig	sit	tin	
bit	rim	him		
lid	his	wit		
rip	it	win		

Reading assignment
J & J Language Readers, Unit 4, book 1: *A Big Mac;* Book 2: *I Am the Kid;* Book 3: *Al at the Nr.*

Task 2: Phoneme segmentation

	Student mastery score	Minimum mastery score	Maximum mastery score
		35	44

80% or more correct, progress to next task.

(A) Copy each word in the blank beside it. As you print each letter, say the sound it represents.

1. in ___	2. sit ___	3. lid ___	4. pig ___
5. hit ___	6. did ___	7. his ___	8. him ___
9. kid ___	10. him ___	11. sit ___	12. rim ___
13. big ___	14. wit ___	15. big ___	16. wit ___
17. it ___	18. kid ___	19. it ___	20. his ___
21. mit ___	22. win ___	23. sit ___	24. tin ___
25. big ___	26. wit ___	27. rig ___	28. mit ___
29. rig ___	30. tin ___	31. it ___	32. win ___

(B) Listen to each word that your instructor reads aloud. You will write **part of** each word. I will tell you which sound of the word to **omit**.

33. ___	34. ___	35. ___	36. ___
37. ___	38. ___	39. ___	40. ___
41. ___	42. ___	43. ___	44. ___

Task 3: Hearing different sounds in similar words

	Student mastery score	Minimum mastery score	Maximum mastery score
		5	6

80% or more correct, progress to next task.

Listen to the words that your instructor reads aloud. After you hear the word pairs, print them in the following blanks.

1. ___	2. ___	3. ___
4. ___	5. ___	6. ___

Language! Book A

Unit 4

Note: From *Language! A Curriculum for At-Risk and ESL Students at Grades 2–12* (pp. 21, 23), by ... F. Greene 1995–1996, Longmont, CO: Sopris West. Copyright 1995–1996 by Sopris West. Reprinted with permission.

Middle and Secondary Years

Imagine students turning the tables—giving service to others instead of always being on the receiving end of services.

Imagine students learning in a school without walls—except the walls and corridors and gardens of community-based sites where elderly people live or little children play.

Imagine students with disabilities getting excited about possible careers and polishing their "people skills" in the process.

Imagine kids using math and English and social studies in the "real world."
(Yoder, Retish, & Wade, 1996)

At the beginning of one school year, a resource teacher and English as a second language (ESL) teacher teamed up to turn imagination into reality (Yoder et al., 1996). Their program, Service Learning, provided opportunities for their seventh and eighth graders to practice communication and social skills across ages and in natural settings. Twenty-four students participated: six with learning disabilities, six for whom English is a second language, and twelve without disabilities who were enrolled in general education classes. Two university students assisted.

An elementary school and retirement center in close proximity to the school agreed to participate. Students visited both the schools and the center and chose which site they preferred for their service-learning experiences. Three twenty-minute training sessions before school started in the morning prepared students for their roles. Taught by the resource teacher, English-as-a-second-language teacher, university practicum students, and site staff, the sessions informed students about signing in and out at school and site as well as the necessity of promptness, courtesy, appropriate language, and carrying out assigned tasks.

Students completed their assignments during study hall or selected classes that met twice a week. A project teacher or practicum student walked with students to their sites. At the retirement home, students chose from various tasks, including writing letters, talking, and playing games with the residents. Those who participated at the elementary school completed tasks requested by the teacher and then read to younger students, played educational games with them, answered questions about junior high, and tutored in math.

Periodic debriefing sessions gave students an opportunity to reflect on their experiences. They wrote in journals, shared experiences, and problem solved. The teachers who conducted this program found that their students increased in self-esteem; self-knowledge; and communication, problem solving, and social skills. Some of the participating students' comments follow:

David, whose learning disabilities caused him to hesitate to work with "little kids," said after the program that he found out he "could read."

Kari commented, "It's really fun and makes you feel a little bit better about yourself."

When asked what she had learned during her experiences, Diane said, "that something so easy can make somebody happy" (Yoder et al., 1996).

Transition and Postsecondary Years

For students with learning disabilities, the rule for transition services is the earlier the better. Even in elementary school, teachers need to begin discovering and encouraging student strengths (Learning Disabilities Association, 1993). Teachers can talk to students about what they would like to be when they grow up and what must happen for them to achieve their goals. Arranging for students to have mentors who share career interests and/or are successful adults with learning disabilities can help them see that they, too, can lead happy and productive lives.

Despite the best efforts of some elementary and secondary programs, however, some students with learning disabilities flounder in college settings. Landmark College was designed especially for them.

Nestled in Putney, Vermont, Landmark College—the only fully accredited college in the country designed exclusively for students with dyslexia, attention-deficit/hyperactivity disorder, or specific learning disabilities—has a student-to-faculty ratio of 3:1 (Landmark College, 1997). The typical class consists of seven students. The school serves students who need career exploration or college services. More than 80 percent of alumni pursue their education after leaving Landmark, and the school has sent students on to more than 500 colleges, graduate programs, and professional schools.

Although some students come directly from high schools, others come from colleges and professional schools. Many have experienced "disappointing grades, frustration, overwork or avoidance, diminished dreams, or lowered self-esteem" (Landmark College, 1997).

Each student receives an advisor and a tutor. The advisor reviews diagnostic information from testing and interviews and meets with student and tutor to develop a plan to address the student's specific needs. As the student works with the tutor, also a member of the faculty, on language and study skills four times a week, the advisor monitors progress. "The student/teacher/advisor relationship is the single most important feature of Landmark's individualized approach to education" (Landmark College, 1997).

Because the purpose of the tutoring sessions is not to support specific course content, the student learns skills and topics that are personally challenging. The tutors help students understand their own learning style and how to use strengths to address needs.

Students can attend a Skills-Development Summer Session, or take credit courses throughout the school year to achieve an Associate of Arts Degree. "The goal is to develop lifelong learners" (Olivier & Bowler, 1996).

Dan Munley, a law student comments:

> *For the first time I learned how to plan and organize my time and materials. My tutor has worked with me to develop three-day plans. I know how to select and highlight the points that are critical to an argument. I've learned grammatical skills, so that there is no longer a stone wall between my ideas and writing.*
>
> *After I finished at Landmark, I headed back to the University of Tulsa to resume my legal studies. But I did not leave empty-handed. The skills I learned have enabled me to have my best semester in law school. I even won the American Jurisprudence Award for excellence in Trial Advocacy. (Olivier & Bowler, 1996)*

A VISION FOR THE FUTURE

Although Raquel has improved her academic skills and seems to have adjusted well to school, her uncle and aunt are still concerned about her future.

"The most important thing to our family is making sure our children finish school," Belinda says.

Lio comments that his biggest concern for the future is the family's health. "How can we go ahead if the family isn't healthy?" he asks.

Both these concerns are born from the challenges Lio and Belinda have faced. They've had to work long, hard hours cleaning and repairing houses.

Belinda says, "We've always wanted to have a better life. My husband and I work so hard because we don't have a high school diploma. I know how important that is, and I want Raquel to finish her education. I hope she gets out of special education and gets a regular diploma someday."

Adults with learning disabilities who have successful lives and careers share their stories in *Succeeding Against the Odds* (Smith, 1991) and *Exceeding Expectations: Successful Adults With Learning Disabilities* (Reiff, Gerber, & Ginsberg, 1997).

"Remember to respect people for what they are, for what they can become, and for the struggle it takes to make that change," Jim Olivier, Founding President, Landmark College (Olivier & Bowler, 1996).

Raquel wants to grow up and be rich, have a high school diploma, and go to college. "My tio and tia and Erica say that they want me to grow up and be smart."

Lio and Belinda's vision is that Raquel will finish school, be healthy, and be happy with herself. Belinda says for that to happen, "She's going to need help with her education and knowing that she's loved so she feels secure."

What Would You Recommend . . .

1. To help Raquel overcome learned helplessness when faced with challenging academic tasks?

2. To provide encouragement to Raquel's family?

3. As transition services for Raquel to prepare her for middle school?

4. To increase the likelihood that Raquel will complete high school?

SUMMARY

WHAT ARE LEARNING DISABILITIES?

- The definition of learning disabilities has been debated since the inception of the field. The IDEA and NJCLD definitions are commonly used.

- Each state has criteria for identifying these students, which usually includes three parts: a severe discrepancy between demonstrated ability and actual achievement, exclusion of other factors, and substantiated need for special services.

- Students with learning disabilities are a heterogenous population with varied learning, behavioral, and social characteristics.

- Approximately 50 percent of all students with disabilities have learning disabilities. In 1995, 5.8 percent of all public school students had learning disabilities.

- Research suggests that learning disabilities may be caused by central nervous system dysfunction that results in deficits in visual-spatial processing and phonological awareness.

WHAT ARE EVALUATION PROCEDURES?

- Nondiscriminatory evaluation includes the use of standardized intelligence and achievement tests to determine discrepancy. Students may have intracognitive, intra-achievement, and/or ability–achievement discrepancies.

- Curriculum-based assessment can be norm-referenced or criterion-referenced.

- The IEP process should include careful explanation of the term *learning disabilities* to the student and family.

WHAT AND HOW DO PROFESSIONALS TEACH?

- Specific curricular approaches in reading (phonological awareness), written expression (process approach), and mathematics (creating active learners) benefit students with learning disabilities.

- Academic clubs can encourage motivation, generalization, and age-appropriate content skills in general classrooms.

- Effective methods include learning strategies, graphic organizers, overcoming learned helplessness, and computer technology.

HOW IS PARTICIPATION ENCOURAGED?

• The least restrictive environment must focus on the student rather than the place in order to be the most enabling environment. Most students with learning disabilities are educated in a combination of resource room and general class settings.

WHAT ARE PROGRAM OPTIONS?

• Many service issues cut across the years of schooling.

• Programs such as the Language Acquisition Preschool address the language processing deficits of young children at risk for learning disabilities.

• *Language!* is a structured curriculum that teaches phonological awareness along with reading comprehension, grammar, writing, and spelling.

• Effective collaboration methods include CLASP for general and special educators and peer tutoring for students.

• Homework should be meaningful and accommodating for students with learning disabilities.

• Service learning can increase motivation and self-esteem for students with learning disabilities.

• Landmark College teaches learning strategies, organizational skills, and self-advocacy to students with learning disabilities.

RESOURCES

BOOKS

Language! (1995-1996). By J. F. Greene. Longmont, CO: Sopris West. Instructor's manual and student texts for the program described under "Elementary Years." Contact (303) 651-2829 or www.sopriswest.com for more information.

No Easy Answers: The Learning Disabled Child at Home and at School (rev. ed.). (1995). By S. L. Smith. This easy-to-understand paperback provides an overview of learning disabilities and suggestions for curriculum and instruction.

Students with Learning Disabilities (5th ed.). (1997). By C. D. Mercer. Upper Saddle River, NJ: Merrill/Prentice Hall. An extensive overview of issues, topics, and trends in learning disabilities. Major sections include foundations of learning disabilities, assessment and services, and specific learning disorders.

JOURNALS, MAGAZINES, AND CATALOGS

Adults and Children with Learning and Developmental Disabilities. 265 Post Avenue, Westbury, NY 11590. (516) 334-4210. A parent and professional membership organization offering information, advocacy, and a network of home, community, and educational services to children and adults with learning and developmental disabilities.

Exclusively LD. 3100 4th Ave., East Moline, IL 61244-9700. (800) 776-4332. Lists teaching aids specifically designed for students with learning disabilities.

Globe Fearon Educational Publisher Catalog. 4350 Equity Dr., P.O. Box 2649, Columbus, OH 43216. (800) 848-9500. High interest/low reading level textbooks in a variety of subjects.

LDA Newsbriefs. Learning Disabilities Association, 4156 Library Road, Pittsburgh, PA 15234. Published six times per year, with articles regarding legislative and education news and issues.

Learning Disabilities Association. 4156 Library Road, Pittsburgh, PA 15234. (412) 341-1515. From *LDA Newsbriefs:* "A nonprofit organization whose purpose is to advance the education and general welfare of children of normal or potentially normal intelligence who have learning disabilities of a perceptual, conceptual, or coordinative nature." Devoted to families and children with learning disabilities. Provides advocacy and resources, which are also available through local and state chapters.

Learning Disabilities Forum. Council for Learning Disabilities, P.O. Box 40303, Overland Park, KS 66204. Published quarterly, with articles for parents, professionals, and practitioners on topics such as assessment; behavior management collaboration; early childhood, elementary, and secondary education issues; technology; and transition.

Learning Disabilities Research & Practice. Lawrence Erlbaum Associates, 365 Broadway, Hillsdale, NJ 07642-1487. A publication of the Division for Learning Disabilities, Council for Exceptional Children. Published quarterly, with articles on current, data-based research reports and descriptions of validated practices in identification, assessment, placement, teacher education, and service delivery.

Remedial and Special Education. Pro-Ed, 8700 Shoal Creek Boulevard, Austin, TX 78575. Published six times a year for professionals and educators, with articles to bridge the gap between research and practice in areas such as assessment and methods.

MULTIMEDIA

Helping Students Master Social Skills. Edge Enterprises, P.O. Box 1304, Lawrence, KS 66044. (913) 749-1473. Developed for teachers to illustrate the step-by-step instructional process for custom-designing and teaching social skills to adolescents with learning disabilities.

Keys to Success in Learning Strategy Instruction. Edge Enterprises, P.O. Box 1304, Lawrence, KS 66044. (913) 749-1473. Enables teachers to learn the eight basic procedures necessary for effective learning strategy instruction, which helps students with learning disabilities become successful learners.

Recordings for the Blind and Dyslexic. Anne T. MacDonald Center, 20 Roszel Road, Princeton, NJ 08540. (609) 452-0606. Audiotapes of many books for children and young adults. (Tapes may also be available through Library of Congress services at local public libraries.)

The Wright Group. 19201 120th Ave. NE, Bothell, WA 98011. (800) 523-2371. Provides books in English and Spanish for integrated language arts programs.

Weiser Educational, Inc. 3085 Comercio Dept. 97, Rancho Santa Margarita, CA 92688. (800) 880-4433. Describes high-interest materials for middle school through adult levels.

We Can Learn. National Center for Learning Disabilities, 99 Park Avenue, New York, NY 10016. (212) 687-7211. A video with accompanying resource guide for parents, teachers, and other professionals.

The following videos are available at local retail and rental stores:

The Loneliness of the Long-Distance Runner. (1962, not rated, U.K., B & W, 103 minutes). A young man with learning difficulties robs a bakery and is sent to a reform school where he discovers he has athletic ability.

Stanley and Iris. (1990, PG-13, U.S., color, 104 minutes). Stanley (Robert De Niro), who is illiterate and in his forties, is taught to read by Iris (Jane Fonda).

ON-LINE INFORMATION AND USEFUL DATABASES

Children's Literature and Disability. Internet address: http://www.kidsource.com/NICHCY/literature.html. Lists children's literature for and about students with disabilities, including those with learning disabilities.

Edmark. P.O. Box 3218, Redmond, WA 98073-3218. (800) 362-2890. Company catalog contains a variety of software for students with learning disabilities.

Franklin Education Catalog. 122 Burrs Road, Mount Holly, NJ 08060. (800) 525-9673. Catalog lists hand-held Speaking Language Master LM-6000, a device that pronounces words aloud and contains a dictionary, thesaurus, and grammar check.

Learning Disabilities. Internet address: http://openseason.com/annex/library/cic/X0054_leardis.txt.hbig. The National Institute of Mental Health provides fact sheets on a variety of topics related to learning disabilities.

Soundproof It. Humanware, 6245 King Road, Loomis, CA 95650. (916) 652-7296. Designed specifically for people of all ages with learning disabilities, this software allows users to hear words spoken by a speech synthesizer as they are simultaneously highlighted on a computer screen.

Special Times. Cambridge Development Laboratory, 86 West Street, Waltham, MA 02154. (800) 637-0047. Special education catalog offering software for elementary and secondary students.

Sunburst. 101 Castleton Street, P.O. Box 100, Pleasantville, NY 10570-0100. Company catalog offers support software for teaching a variety of subjects to students with learning disabilities.

Taming the Dragons. Internet address: http://members.aol.com/susans29/book.html. Excerpts from the book by the same title; provides practical suggestions for helping students with learning disabilities at home and school.

Teacher Support Software. 1035 Northwest 57th Street, Gainesville, FL 32605-4486. Special education catalog offers software for elementary and secondary students.

ORGANIZATIONS

Orton Dyslexia Society. 724 York Road, Baltimore, MD 21204. (301) 296-0232. A professional and parent organization providing leadership related to language programs, research, and publication of information about dyslexia.

National Center for Learning Disabilities. 99 Park Avenue, New York, NY 10016. (212) 687-7211. A professional and parent organization promoting public awareness, resources, referrals, grant making, and legislative advocacy for families with children who have learning disabilities.

CHAPTER 5

EMOTIONAL OR BEHAVIORAL DISORDERS*

Educating
Jennifer Shulman

After Jennifer Shulman had her thirteenth birthday, she declared, "I'm turning over a new leaf." Why did she make this decision? "I didn't like the way some of the other kids in my class acted. It was irritating. I realized I had acted the same way. I guess I thought it was stupid and decided to change."

For Jen, after years of discouragement and anger, this decision reflects renewed commitment and hope—hope that she can indeed make different choices about her behavior. How does a student with emotional or behavior disorders regain this hope? As you will see, Jen's hope emerged because a dedicated group of professionals and her family wrapped great expectations, acceptance, understanding, consistent interventions, and encouragement around her.

Jen's challenging behaviors began in infancy. "Jennifer came into the world fighting," Mary Shulman, Jen's mother, comments. "She ran everywhere. She never had any fear. You couldn't blink but she was running. She didn't even know where she was going."

*With continuing gratitude to Patty M. Barbetta, Florida International University, for her contributions to this chapter.

When Jen was older, "she had fits of rage; she would bang her head and make holes in the wall. She had holes all over her bedroom. I would take my son and myself into my room and lock the door."

When Jen was eight, she began attending Highlands Elementary School. Due to curriculum differences between Jen's previous school and Highlands Elementary, Jen repeated second grade. Jen and those who work closely with her say this set the stage for her loss of hope and feelings of being different and unaccepted, which impelled her to act out at school.

Jen tried to show how tough she was by intimidating her classmates and teacher, threatening to use and sometimes using physical force, and "thrashing out" when she was angry. Her peers feared her, and some teachers seemed afraid as well. Jen refused to complete assignments or homework and often left the classroom without permission. On one occasion, she left the school grounds, crossed the busy street by her school, and went home. The school tried many interventions—numerous trips to the principal's office, parent conferences, out-of-school suspensions, and after-school detentions—to no avail. Even providing a one-on-one aide did not change Jennifer's behavior. Despite all Jen's difficulties, however, she did not yet receive special education services.

Sometimes it takes a crisis to jumpstart change in a person's life. After Jen's psychiatrist prescribed Tegretol, Jen took an overdose and was hospitalized. A mental health service network referred the family to the LaGrange Area Department of Special Education (LADSE) Emotional and Behavioral Disabilities (EBD) Network in Chicago. Involvement with this program was a turning point in Jen's life.

Jen's family now receives support from LADSE's wraparound network, which assists the Shulman family in their home, at Jen's schools, and in any other area in which the family needs support. Jen's wraparound team members, including Jen and her family meet weekly to talk about Jen's progress and communicate informally each day to ensure that they all have the same information and are working with Jen toward the same goals.

LADSE provided a family service facilitator to coordinate services for Jen and her family.

The family service facilitator is the liaison between the family, community, and school. Through observations in the home and other settings, she observed challenges in the family's interactions and took the family's focus off Jen as the "one who needed to be fixed." She also helped the family develop rules for Jen, her brother, and her sister around issues such as homework and telephone time.

Jen's mother, Mary, appreciates this ongoing support. "I talk to her like I talk to one of my friends," Mary

says. "I can say, 'Look, this is what she's done and this is what I did. What did I do wrong?' She will be brutally honest. She's pretty in tune with Jen, too." With the family service facilitator, Mary has reexamined how she interacts with Jen. Mary now conducts family meetings and consistently sticks to family rules.

After leaving the hospital, Jen began her day in a special class at Park Junior High, and ended her day at Highlands Middle School, her neighborhood school. The family services facilitator and team teacher collaborated closely with Jen's two schools. At Park, Jen joined a self-contained class for students with emotional or behavioral disorders. Gradually, Jen returned to Highlands full-time as part of her personal goals for change.

Jen is learning the skills she needs to meet her goals in her self-contained classroom at Park. Her special education teacher recognized that the first step to helping Jen was to establish a relationship with her. The special education teacher focused on Jen's many strengths, including her intelligence, her honesty, and her love of art, music, sports, and animals. The two of them even strengthened their bond through attending an exhibit on frogs—Jen's favorite animal—together.

The special education teacher also helps Jen meet the challenge of her disability by helping her learn why she behaves in certain ways and teaching her alternative responses. For example, in the past, when discussions at meetings revolved around Jen's inappropriate behavior, Jen would storm out of the room. Now Jen has learned to anticipate the content of these discussions and to role play how she plans to handle them. Through this technique, Jen can now participate in meetings.

For Jen to be successful in her home school, Highlands teachers and staff needed to change their perspective of her. The wraparound team helped them do so by making specific recommendations. Currently, they have accepted that Jen *does* have a disability, changed their attitudes about her, and committed to include her in their building.

Jen has already changed in many ways. Two crucial changes include her willingness to take responsibility for herself and accept the help that LADSE and the school offered her. One wraparound team member says Jen's changes result from "feeling more accepted in all her environments."*

What Do You Think?

1. What considerations might an evaluation team take into account in deciding that students such as Jen have emotional or behavioral disorders?

2. What strategies can teachers incorporate to encourage change in students like Jen?

3. What is the wraparound process, and how can this approach be incorporated into a student's program?

4. How can students such as Jen develop a productive self-concept?

*The name Jennifer Shulman is being used in this chapter as a pseudonym to respect the privacy of the actual vignette family, Merrill Education thanks Bridget Lenahan, a sixth grader at Dublin Middle School, Dublin, Ohio for portraying "Jennifer."

WHAT ARE EMOTIONAL OR BEHAVIORAL DISORDERS?

Torey Hayden describes her first day in class with a six-year-old with emotional and behavioral disorders:

> *Sheila and I sat in icy silence. . . . I did not have the endurance to stare her down, nor did I feel the need to do so. After a few moments I rose from my chair and went to collect the math papers from the correction basket.*
>
> *"You can't make me talk," she said.*
>
> *I continued shuffling through the papers trying to find the marking pen. Three-fourths of being a good teacher is timing.*
>
> *"I said you can't make me talk. There don't be no way you can do that."*
>
> *I looked over at her.*
>
> *"You can't make me."*
>
> *"No, I can't," I smiled. "But you will. That's part of your job here."*
>
> *"I don't like you."*
>
> *"You don't have to."*
>
> *"I hate you."*
>
> *I did not respond. That was one of those statements that I find is often best left unanswered. So I continued my search for the pen, wondering who had walked off with it this time.*
>
> *"You can't make me do nothing in here. You can't make me talk."*
>
> *"Maybe not." I dropped the papers back into the basket and came over to her. "Shall we go to lunch?" I extended a hand to her. Some of the anger had dissipated to be replaced by a less readable emotion. Then without further urging, she got off the chair and came with me, careful not to touch me. (Hayden, 1980, pp. 24–25)*

You can read more about Torey Hayden and Sheila in *One Child* (1980) and *The Tiger's Child* (1995).

When Sheila stood up from her chair and walked of her own volition with her teacher, she was taking her first tiny steps toward hope and trust. In this chapter, you will learn about the challenges and rewards of working with students like Jen and Sheila who have emotional or behavioral disorders. Someday, by incorporating appropriate interventions in the classroom, you might be the professional who encourages commitment and hope in some of these students, just as the wraparound team did for Jen and Torey Hayden did for Sheila.

Defining Emotional or Behavioral Disorders

Why should students like Jen be identified as having an emotional or behavioral disorder? At one time or another, doesn't every student have conflicts with teachers, parents, or friends? The difference is that Jen and Sheila's behavior and adjustment problems are chronic and severe enough to interfere with their learning and seriously compromise them in other ways. The Individuals with Disabilities Education Act (IDEA) definition refers to *emotionally disturbed* (IDEA does not add behavioral disorders to the term) in the following way:

> *(i) The term means a condition exhibiting one or more of the following characteristics over a long time and to a marked degree that adversely affects a student's educational performance:*
>
> - *An inability to learn that cannot be explained by intellectual, sensory, or other health factors*
>
> - *An inability to build or maintain satisfactory interpersonal relationships with peers and teachers*
>
> - *Inappropriate types of behavior or feelings under normal circumstances*
>
> - *A general pervasive mood of unhappiness or depression*
>
> - *A tendency to develop physical symptoms or fears associated with personal or school problems*

BOX 5-1   INTO PRACTICE

IDEA AND DISCIPLINE

IDEA limits what schools may do by way of disciplining students with disabilities. The first general rule is that no school may completely terminate a student's right to a free appropriate public education; this is a rule against cessation of services.

The second major rule deals with the "manifestation determination." That phrase refers to the relationship between the student's disability and the student's behavior. If the student's disability causes or is related to the student's behavior, that is, if the student's behavior is a manifestation of the student's disability, then the school is limited to what it may do. But, first, who determines whether there is a "manifestation"?

The student's IEP team makes the "manifestation determination" and may add "other qualified personnel" to the team to help make that determination. Of course, the team includes the student's parent(s), as you learned in Chapter 2.

The team must consider all information relevant to the student's disability and behavior, including evaluations, information supplied by the parent(s), observations by others, and the student's present IEP and placement.

After considering this information, the team must find that the student's behavior was *not* a manifestation of disability if

1. The student's IEP and placement were appropriate and the school provided all the services the IEP called for.
2. The disability did not impair the student's ability to understand the impact and consequences of the behavior.

3. The disability did not impair the student's ability to control the behavior.

The first standard—that the school satisfied its IDEA duties to the student—allows the student to shift blame for the behavior to the school. If the school did not discharge its duties to the student, the school may not hold the student responsible for the behavior it should have targeted for remediation.

The second and third standards allow the student to escape discipline because of cognitive incapacity or behavioral incapacity: The student did not know (cognitive) and could not control (behavioral).

What happens if the IEP team determines that the student's behavior is a manifestation of disability?

1. The school may suspend the student, place the student in a different setting, or place the student in "an interim alternative educational setting" (IAES) for up to ten days. If the school uses this ten-day "safety valve," the student must remain in his or her present placement even if the student's parent(s) challenge the school's action in a due process hearing. In other words, the student "stays put" in and returns to the present placement, but the school may still use the ten-day discipline. For example, a student in a fully inclusive program will stay in that program and not be subject to a change of placement (out of that program) simply because the school uses the ten-day discipline. But, at the same time, the school may discipline the student for ten days.

2. The school may place a student in an "interim alternative educational setting" for up to forty-five days if the student carries a weapon to school or illegally possesses or sells certain drugs. This is the weapons/ drugs provision. In these situations, the stay-put rule is not available to the student. Thus,

(ii) The term includes schizophrenia. The term does not apply to children who are socially maladjusted, unless it is determined that they have an emotional disturbance. (IDEA, 1997)

Along with defining emotional disturbance, IDEA specifies discipline consequences for students with this condition who engage in dangerous behaviors. These regulations are found in Box 5-1 and are important for teachers and administrators to understand.

In Chapter 4, you learned how the National Joint Committee on Learning Disabilities (NJCLD) developed a definition that is often preferred by professionals and families over the Federal definition. Likewise, twenty-one professional, parent, and advocacy groups for

the student in a fully inclusive setting may not return to that setting after the weapons/drugs discipline unless the school allows it.

3. The school may place a student in an interim alternative educational setting for up to forty-five days if maintaining the student's present placement is substantially likely to result in injury to the student or others. This is the "dangerousness" provision. In these situations, the stay-put rule also does not apply. Thus, the student in a fully inclusive program may not return to it after the discipline unless the school allows it.

IDEA imposes strict rules that schools and due process hearing officers must follow when they make manifestation determinations.

1. Parents are entitled to special notices when a school wants to impose discipline (see Chapter 2).

2. No discipline may be applied to a student with a disability unless it may also be applied to a student who does not have a disability.

3. A hearing before a due process hearing officer on a discipline matter related to the "dangerousness" provision must be expedited (put onto a fast-track).

4. Each IAES must meet standards prescribed by IDEA.

5. The hearing officer may not authorize placement into an IAES unless (a) the school proves that maintaining the student's present placement is substantially likely to result in injury to the student or others, (b) the officer considers the appropriateness of the student's present placement, (c) the officer considers whether the school made reasonable efforts to minimize the risk of harm in the student's present placement, and (d) the IAES allows the student to participate in the general curriculum.

6. If the school has not yet conducted a functional behavior assessment and implemented a behavioral intervention plan before it disciplines the student, it must convene the IEP to address the behavior; if it has already conducted such an assessment and has such a plan in place, the school must convene the IEP team to review and modify the plan, if necessary, to address the behavior.

Another IDEA provision is related to the requirement about functional assessment and behavioral intervention. It applies to any student (whether or not the student has been subjected to discipline) whose behavior impedes his or her learning or that of others. For that student, the IEP team must consider, when appropriate, strategies, including positive behavioral intervention strategies and supports, to address that behavior. In developing the student's IEP, a regular educator must be a member of the IEP team and participate by determining appropriate positive support interventions and strategies. The rule does not require the school to use functional assessments and positive behavioral supports; it does require it to consider using them.

7. Finally, the school may report to any appropriate authority (e.g., police, prosecutors, or other law enforcement agencies) any crime committed by a student. If it reports the crime, the school must send the student's special education records to the law enforcement authority. If required to do so by state law or regulation, a school must include in the student's file a statement of current or previous disciplinary action and transmit that information to the same extent it transmits information about students who do not have disabilities; the information may include anything relevant to the safety of the student or others.

students with emotional or behavioral disorders formed the Mental Health and Special Education Coalition (MHSEC). This organization developed the following definition for the students we describe in this chapter:

(A) *The term **emotional or behavioral disorder** means a disability that is . . .*
   (i) *characterized by behavioral or emotional responses in school programs so different from appropriate age, cultural, or ethnic norms that the responses adversely affect educational performance, including academic, social, vocational or personal skills;*

Emotional or behavioral disorder is a chronic condition that is characterized by behavioral or emotional responses that differ from age, cultural, or ethnic norms to such a degree that educational performance is adversely affected.

> *(ii) more than a temporary, expected response to stressful events in the environment;*
>
> *(iii) consistently exhibited in two different settings, at least one of which is school-related; and*
>
> *(iv) unresponsive to direct intervention applied in general education, or the condition of a child such that general education interventions would be insufficient.*
>
> *(B) The term includes such a disability that co-exists with other disabilities.*
>
> *(C) The term includes a schizophrenic disorder, affective disorder, anxiety disorder, or other sustained disorder of conduct or adjustment, affecting a child if the disorder affects educational performance as described in paragraph (i). (quoted in McIntyre & Forness, 1996, p. 5)*

Social maladjustment is an adaptive response to environmental conditions resulting in socialized aggression (e.g., gang-related behavior or juvenile delinquency).

Although the definitions differ in several important ways, perhaps the most striking difference in the two definitions is that the IDEA definition excludes students with **social maladjustment,** while the MHSEC definition does not. For a number of years, professionals have hotly contested whether students with social maladjustment should receive special education and related services. Some express concern that including these students will "overburden" this category of special education. They suggest that the behavior of the students with social maladjustment is somehow intentional, while the behavior of those with emotional or behavioral disorders is not (McIntyre & Forness, 1996).

Others take the opposite view, stating that the second criterion of the IDEA definition ("inability to build or maintain satisfactory relationships with peers and teachers") describes students with social maladjustment (Forness & Knitzer, 1992). They emphasize that the original intent of Congress was only to exclude juvenile delinquency, although the term *social maladjustment* currently excludes many more students. Furthermore, many students, in their opinion, may be masking depression or other behavioral disorders by their social maladjustment (Forness & Knitzer, 1992). The Council on Children with Behavioral Disorders (CCBD) recommends the inclusion of these students under the IDEA category of emotional disorders (McIntyre & Forness, 1996).

States vary in the terminology used to describe these students. States and local school districts also vary widely in their interpretation of the definition and their qualifying criteria (McIntyre & Forness, 1996). Therefore, students may qualify as having emotional or behavioral disorders in one school district but not in another.

⚮ *Professionals debate whether students with social maladjustment that results in juvenile delinquency should receive special education services. What is your opinion?*

Describing the Characteristics

Before we describe the characteristics that can lead these students to be identified as having emotional or behavioral disorders, we want to emphasize that they also possess many positive characteristics. If you think about the positive behaviors of these children and the difficulties many of them must overcome, you can probably develop a list of potential strengths. You might include words such as *authentic, creative, sense of humor, helpful, smart, brave, resourceful, energetic,* and *resilient.* In addition, the inappropriate behaviors leading to their identification can improve with consistent interventions, allowing their strengths to shine more clearly. Jen's intelligence, honesty, and her love of art, music, sports, and animals became more apparent to others as she improved her behavior.

As you continue to read this section, it is important to remember that these students are *heterogenous:* each one possesses unique strengths and needs. Also, some students with these characteristics may not be identified under IDEA, because their characteristics do not interfere with their educational progress. A student with a phobia of heights, for instance, may not need to be identified. But a student who has a phobia of attending school would probably need services under IDEA. In Box 5–2, "My Voice," Nathan Bennett shares how important it is for professionals to recognize his strengths.

> 🐾 As Jen learned how to let her strengths shine, Jen's wraparound team also helped to facilitate Jen's friendship with other students.

Emotional Characteristics. Several categories of emotional disorders included in the *Diagnostic and Statistical Manual of Mental Disorders* (fourth edition) (DSM-IV) (American Psychiatric Association, 1994) apply to children and adolescents. These conditions can contribute to their identification as having emotional or behavioral disorders. A few of the most common follow (National Mental Health Services Knowledge Exchange Network, 1996c):

Anxiety disorder, the most common childhood disorder, affects approximately 8 to 10 percent of young people (National Mental Health Services Knowledge Exchange Network, 1996). Characterized by excessive fear, worry, or uneasiness, these disorders include (a) *phobia* (unrealistic, overwhelming fear of an object or situation), (b) *generalized anxiety disorder* (excessive, overwhelming worry not caused by any recent experience), (c) *panic disorder* (overwhelming panic attacks that result in rapid heartbeat, dizziness, and/or other physical symptoms), (d) *obsessive-compulsive disorder* (obsessions manifest as repetitive, persistent, and intrusive impulses, images, or thoughts, such as repetitive thoughts about death or illness; compulsions manifest as repetitive, stereotypical behaviors such as handwashing or counting), and (e) *post-traumatic stress disorder* (flashbacks and other symptoms of "a psychologically distressing event such as physical or sexual abuse, being a victim or witness of violence, or exposure to some other traumatic event such as a bombing or hurricane," National Mental Health Services Knowledge Exchange Network, 1996). Anxiety disorders can seriously interfere with a student's school functioning (Rapaport, 1989):

> *Laura was seven when she began to exhibit OCD [obsessive-compulsive disorder]. Her first symptom was hand washing. Within months this soon changed to a compulsion to fill in with a pencil the space in every letter. . . . The most time-consuming ritual of all for Laura was having to count up to fifty in between reading or writing each word. The silent counting had never stopped. Understandably, this made her extraordinarily slow, particularly when she began second grade. (p. 139)*

> **Anxiety disorder** is characterized by overwhelming fear, worry, and/or uneasiness. The condition includes phobia, generalized anxiety disorder, panic disorder, obsessive-compulsive disorder, and post-traumatic stress disorder.

Major depression can occur at any age, including childhood. An estimated 6 percent of children and adolescents experience major depression at some point in their lives (National Mental Health Services Knowledge Exchange Network, 1996). The student with major depression may experience changes in (a) emotion (feels sad and worthless, cries often or looks tearful), (b) motivation (loses interest in play, friends, and schoolwork, resulting in a decline in grades), (c) physical well-being (eats or sleeps too much or too

> **Major depression** is characterized by excessive perceptions of sadness and worthlessness, with changes in emotion, motivation, physical well-being, and thoughts.

BOX 5-2   MY VOICE

SOMETHING TO SAY

I hope
this poem
catches your
attention
I have
something
to get across
to you
I know
you probably
expected this poem
to be offensive

I hate
to let
you down by
proving you wrong
I'm not
as bad
as you think I've
always been
I've got
my good side
too.

Nathan Bennett, age sixteen
Douglasville, GA

little, disregards hygiene, makes vague physical complaints), and (d) thoughts (believes he or she is ugly and unable to do anything right and that life or the world is hopeless). Ten-year-old Nicholas who has childhood depression once sat in a closet and held a toy gun to his head, screaming that he wished it were real. Fortunately, he received treatment, including counseling and medication. He describes this dark period in his life:

> *I felt really scared about telling people how I felt. . . . I was sad and upset and angry the whole time. . . . I used that gun to make a point that I needed help. (Baskervill, 1996)*

Sometimes depression goes unrecognized in children and adolescents because they do not respond as expected. Depression is sometimes referred to as anger turned inward, but that anger can also overflow onto others as the sadness becomes overwhelming (Kerns & Lieberman, 1993). Jen, for example, exhibited more acting-out and risk-taking behaviors before her suicide attempt.

How do you tell, then, if a student is depressed? As we've mentioned, one of the key factors in recognizing depression is change. If you find yourself saying, "What's gotten into this kid?" the answer might be depression. And often this change can be tied to loss. The loss could involve separation from a significant person or pet caused by moving, divorce, death, or the breakup of a relationship. The loss of home or even a beloved object can trigger depression. Other factors that can cause depression are having family members with emotional disorders, any significant family change, chronic stress in the family, and child abuse (Wright-Strawderman, Lindsey, Bavarette, & Flippo, 1996). Because of their lack of life experience, children and adolescents are more likely to view their circumstances as hopeless, especially if they already have emotional or behavioral disorders. An important strategy for preventing or helping students overcome depression is to restore their sense of hope, which we discuss more under "Methods."

Tragically, depression sometimes leads to suicide. In 1990, 30 percent of all students surveyed reported thinking about suicide, and an estimated one million attempted suicide

(McCoy, 1994). Since the 1950s, the number of young men between fifteen and twenty-four who have committed suicide has tripled, and suicide is the third leading cause of death in this age group (U.S. Department of Health and Human Services, 1995). Females are more likely to attempt suicide, but males are more likely to die because they are more likely than females to use potentially fatal methods (National Center for Injury Prevention and Control, 1997). Research also suggests that female adolescents with emotional and behavioral disorders are more likely to experience suicidal thoughts and attempt suicide than males with emotional or behavioral disorders and those without the condition (Miller, 1994).

Hopelessness is the most frequent reason cited by adolescents for considering suicide (Miller, 1994). It is important to help students see that suicide is a permanent solution to a temporary problem. In "Into Practice," Box 5-3, we list suggestions that may help you prevent a suicide someday.

> The risk of suicide among students becomes significantly higher when they know another adult or student who has committed suicide.

Bipolar disorder, also referred to as *manic-depressive illness,* occurs in children and adolescents as well as adults (National Mental Health Services Knowledge Exchange Network, 1996). In fact, adults with bipolar disorder often report that their symptoms first occurred in adolescence. The condition is characterized by exaggerated mood swings. At times, the student may experience the features of depression we have already described. At other times, the student experiences manic or excited phases and may "talk nonstop, need very little sleep, and show unusually poor judgment."

> **Bipolar disorder** is characterized by extreme mood swings from depressive to manic phases.

Oppositional-defiant disorder causes a pattern of negativistic, hostile, disobedient, and defiant behaviors. These occur without the serious violations of the rights of others resulting from conduct disorders ("Fact Sheet," n.d.). Symptoms include loss of temper, arguing with and defying adults, irritability, vindictiveness, swearing and using obscenities, blaming others for mistakes and misbehavior, and low self-esteem. The student may abuse drugs and alcohol. This condition does not result from willful defiance but is probably inherited and may result from neurological causes, including chemical imbalances. Because these students need special responses from adults to establish rapport, we provide suggestions for working with them in "Into Practice," Box 5-4. "Our efforts to 'turn these students around' so they can benefit from more positive and interpersonally rewarding relationships will pay big dividends for these children and potentially even for our society at large" (Knowlton, 1995, p. 10).

> **Oppositional-defiant disorder** is characterized by negativistic, disobedient, hostile, and defiant behaviors without serious violations of the rights of others.

Conduct disorder results in students' acting out their feelings or impulses toward others destructively (National Mental Health Services Knowledge Exchange Network, 1996). Oppositional-defiant disorder is often a predecessor of a conduct disorder, emphasizing the need to provide interventions for students with oppositional-defiant disorder (National Mental Health Services Knowledge Exchange Network, 1996). Students with conduct disorder repeatedly violate other's rights and disregard society's rules. Their offenses tend to become more severe with age and may include "lying, theft, aggression, truancy, firesetting, and vandalism." As many as 4 to 10 percent of children and adolescents may have conduct disorders (National Mental Health Services Knowledge Exchange Network, 1996). Students are more likely to develop conduct disorders when they experience "(a) inconsistent rules and harsh discipline, (b) lack of enough supervision or guidance, (c) frequent change in caregivers, (d) poverty, (e) neglect or abuse, and (f) a delinquent peer group" (National Mental Health Services Knowledge Exchange Network, 1996). Students with this condition may not receive services, because professionals misperceive that they have social maladjustment rather than an emotional disorder.

> **Conduct disorder** is characterized by acting out destructive feelings or impulses, which results in serious and repeated violations of society's rules and the rights of others.

Eating disorders take two forms (National Mental Health Services Knowledge Exchange Network, 1996). *Anorexia nervosa* occurs when the student cannot be persuaded to maintain normal body weight because of a fear of gaining weight. *Bulimia nervosa* causes the student to binge and eat huge amounts of food at one time and then purge the food through vomiting, abuse of laxatives or enemas, and/or exercising to excess. As many as 1 to 3 percent of students may have this condition. A counselor explained eating disorders to a group of clients this way:

> **Eating disorders** are inappropriate eating behaviors resulting in eating too little (anorexia nervosa) or too much at one time and purging (bulimia nervosa).

BOX 5-3   INTO PRACTICE

SUICIDE PREVENTION

Warning signs (Kerns & Lieberman, 1993, p. 143)

1. Personality change: a gregarious child becomes withdrawn or a shy child becomes extremely outgoing.
2. Disregard for appearance: an adolescent who is normally scrupulous about how he looks suddenly begins to neglect his grooming, hygiene, and clothing.
3. Social withdrawal.
4. Giving away treasured possessions and putting affairs in order.
5. Preoccupation with death or morbid themes, including rock music, drawings, poems, and essays.
6. Overt or veiled suicide threats: "I won't be around much longer." "They'd be better off without me." "I wish I were dead."
7. Prior suicide attempts.
8. Acquisition of a means (ropes, guns, hoses).
9. Substance abuse.
10. School failure.
11. Sudden elevation of mood in a depressed child. This may mean the depressed child has found a "solution"—suicide.
12. Increased accidents or multiple physical complaints with no medical basis.

When a student has any of these symptoms, ask the following (McCoy, 1994)

- "It looks like you're feeling unhappy. Are you?"
- "Do you ever get the feeling that life isn't worth living?"
- "Do you sometimes feel like you don't want to live anymore?"
- "What have you thought about doing to end your life?"

If the student is not suicidal, you can say that you are glad because you care about her. You will not give her ideas. If the student is suicidal, she will probably be relieved that you cared enough to ask. If the student has a plan, do not leave her alone and immediately seek help.

What not to do (Oster & Montgomery, 1995)

- Do not be sworn to secrecy.
- Never leave a suicidal person alone.
- Do not appear shocked or alarmed.
- Do not try to be a therapist; just listen to concerns nonjudgmentally.
- Do not debate the morality of suicide; this can increase feelings of guilt and sadness.
- Do not point out that others have worse troubles; this leads to feelings of incompetence and being misunderstood.

Other strategies (McCoy, 1994)

- *Take student's comments seriously.* "Take *all* symptoms of depression, *all* comments about death, *all* suicide threats or attempts seriously." Avoid dismissing these words or actions as manipulative or attention getting.
- *Show that you care.* Ask the student to share his feelings and listen supportively without judging or feeling a need to give easy advice. Help the student problem solve alternative solutions. "What else could you do? How would that work?" Encourage the student to sign a contract that he will not hurt himself intentionally or by accident.
- *Help the student regain a glimmer of hope.* Emphasize that even serious depression is a temporary feeling, and if he will hang on, he will probably feel better in a week or so. Remind him that you will continue to be there for him.
- *Find skilled help.* The student may need crisis intervention and long-term counseling.

Self-destruction is not intentional. When parents and friends ask you, "Why are you doing this to yourself? Why are you risking your health?" they need to understand—and we need to understand—that eating disorders are a way we try to feel better about ourselves, a way we help ourselves function in a world that threatens or upsets us. It's hard for parents to see that, when all they see on the outside is an anorectic girl who's eating only 300 or 400 calories a day and whose weight seems to drop every week, or a bulimic girl who's emptying the pantry shelves and maybe stealing money from Mom's purse. . . . But we all

BOX 5-4 **INTO PRACTICE**

ENCOURAGING COMPLIANCE FROM STUDENTS WITH OPPOSITIONAL-DEFIANT DISORDER

- **Avoid direct positive reinforcement.** Use of this technique can backfire with these students. Because they feel compelled to do the opposite of your request, especially in front of peers, when you praise them directly, publicly, and obviously, they may retaliate with the unwanted response (e.g., tearing up a paper you had praised).
- **Use indirect reinforcement.** To avoid public praise but still encourage the student for desired responses, the following techniques may be useful:

  Whisper. Brief whispered encouragement without sustained eye contact allows a positive response. Comment on the product rather than your feelings about it.

  Leave notes. Leave a brief message in a note on students' desks, mail it to them, or hand it to them as they leave the room.

  Provide rewards. Concrete reinforcements can be used as long as you place stickers or marks on a chart without verbal comment. Give rewards without fanfare by simply placing them in their desks or give them a note that tells them what they have earned. Avoid using response cost, a method that involves subtracting points or taking away rewards. This can backfire because students with this condition may view this as proof that they are not complying with what you want.

- *Avoid arguing.* Arguing can reinforce their oppositional position. Enforce the consequence and let it go.
- *Defer control.* Relabel who or what is in control. For instance, say, "The clock says it's time to go" rather than "It's time to go."
- *Provide choices.* By giving the students limited choices, the student retains a sense of control. If the student refuses to make a choice, you will need to make sure the consequence is clear.
- *Anticipate problems.* Prepare the student for difficult times or activities. By saying that you know this might be difficult, students can be placed in a double bind. This paradoxical approach may encourage them to prove it will not be difficult.
- *Allow them to release anger.* Physical activity can help these students dispel anger in a manageable way. Sports, working with clay, or even punching a pillow or tearing up an old magazine can be acceptable ways to release anger. Avoid emphasizing involvement in competitive sports until students have adequate control of their anger.
- *Outline consequences.* Having oppositional-defiant disorders does not excuse these students from taking responsibility for their behaviors. Provide students with a specific list of behaviors and consequences and enforce them consistently.
- *Offer therapy or counseling.* Make sure that the therapist or counselor you recommend is familiar with the needs of these students.

Note: From "Managing Children With Oppositional Behavior," by D. Knowlton, 1995, *Beyond Behavior, 6*(3), pp. 5–10. Copyright 1995 by the Council for Children with Behavior Disorders. Adapted with permission.

have to understand that this destructiveness—and it is taking a tremendous destructive toll, emotionally and physically—is a by-product of our problem. (Jablow, 1992, pp. 18–19)

Schizophrenia causes students to have psychotic periods that result in *hallucinations* (sensing things that do not exist), withdrawal, *delusions* (grandiose or paranoid thoughts), inability to experience pleasure, and loss of contact with reality (National Mental Health Services Knowledge Exchange Network, 1996). The condition probably affects 3 of every 1,000 adolescents and is even more rare in children under twelve (National Mental Health Services Knowledge Exchange Network, 1996).

Schizophrenia is characterized by psychotic periods resulting in hallucinations, delusions, inability to experience pleasure, and loss of contact with reality.

ALMOST HOME

Tens of thousands of adolescents each year begin to experience the delusions and hallucinations associated with schizophrenia. Therapists used to blame parents for the condition, but now researchers have determined a physiological cause.

In this ABC video, Diane Sawyer talks to Lori Schiller, who has schizophrenia, as well as to her parents. Fortunately for some individuals, the medication Clozapine works to reduce symptoms, giving them an opportunity to enjoy life again. "Almost Home" chronicles the dramatic change this medication made for Lori.

What do you think? Schizophrenia is no longer blamed on parents. What conditions continue to be blamed on parents in current society? Do you believe that blame is justified? Why or why not?

The decision to use medication that can have serious side effects is often difficult for families. What criteria would you use to make that decision for your child? How would you provide support to families who are faced with this decision?

Behavioral Characteristics.

A generally accepted classification system describes two broad categories of behavior disorders: externalizing and internalizing (Achenbach & Edelbrock, 1981). The emotional disorders we have described, as well as others, can result in externalizing and/or internalizing behavior disorders. Figure 5–1 is a checklist of internalizing and externalizing behaviors.

Externalizing behaviors are behavior disorders comprising aggressive, acting-out, and noncompliant behaviors.

Externalizing behaviors—persistent aggressive, acting out, noncompliant behaviors—often characterize conduct and oppositional-defiant disorders (H. M. Walker & Bullis, 1991). However, students with depression, schizophrenia, and other conditions also may exhibit externalizing behaviors from time to time. Jen exhibited many externalizing behaviors, including temper outbursts, banging her head on the wall, and threatening peers and adults. Commonly heard teacher concerns that suggest externalizing behaviors include the following:

- "He gets frustrated so easily."

- "When he gets angry, he can be so verbally abusive."

- "Some days she's an angel. Other days she won't follow a simple direction."

- "He just won't sit still."

Internalizing behaviors are behavior disorders comprising social withdrawal, depression, anxiety, obsessions, and compulsions.

Internalizing behaviors are most often associated with social withdrawal, depression, and anxiety. A smaller group of children and youth also engages in obsessions and compulsions (Milby & Weber, 1991). Teachers may make statements like the following about students with internalizing behaviors:

- "She always seems so depressed."

- "At recess, he rarely talks with anyone or joins in a game."

- "It's embarrassing to admit, but sometimes I completely forget she's here."

Typically, students with externalizing and internalizing behavior have problems in two areas of school: teacher-related adjustment and peer-related adjustment (H. M. Walker & Bullis, 1991). Teacher-related adjustment refers to meeting the behavioral demands and expectations of teachers: for example, following classroom rules, attending to tasks, and completing assignments. Peer-related adjustment refers to those skills needed to interact successfully with peers, particularly during free time. Students with externalizing behavior problems typically experience serious difficulty adjusting to the behavioral expectations and performance requirements of their teachers (H. M. Walker & Bullis, 1991).

Internalizing

- ❏ Exhibits sad affect, depression, and feelings of worthlessness
- ❏ Has auditory or visual hallucinations
- ❏ Cannot keep mind off certain thoughts, ideas, or situations
- ❏ Cannot keep self from engaging in repetitive and/or useless actions
- ❏ Suddenly cries, cries frequently, or displays totally unexpected and atypical affect for the situation
- ❏ Complains of severe headaches or other somatic problems (stomachaches, nausea, dizziness, vomiting) as a result of fear or anxiety
- ❏ Talks of killing self—reports suicidal thoughts and/or is preoccupied with death
- ❏ Shows decreased interest in activities which were previously of interest
- ❏ Is excessively teased, verbally or physically abused, neglected and/or avoided by peers
- ❏ Has severely restricted activity levels
- ❏ Shows signs of physical, emotional, and/or sexual abuse
- ❏ Exhibits other specific behaviors such as: withdrawal, avoidance of social interactions, and/or lack of personal care to an extent which prevents the development or maintenance of satisfactory personal relationships

Externalizing

- ❏ Displays recurring pattern of aggression toward objects or persons
- ❏ Argues excessively
- ❏ Forces the submission of others through physical and/or verbal means
- ❏ Is noncompliant with reasonable requests
- ❏ Exhibits persistent pattern of tantrums
- ❏ Exhibits persistent patterns of lying, and/or stealing
- ❏ Frequently exhibits lack of self-control and acting out behaviors
- ❏ Exhibits other specific behavior(s) that intrude(s) upon other people, staff, self, or the physical environment to an extent which prevents the development or maintenance of satisfactory interpersonal relationships

FIGURE 5–1 *Internalizing and externalizing behaviors*

Note: From the University of Kentucky, Department of Special Education and Rehabilitation Counseling, 1997, *Behavior Home Page* [On-line]. Available: http://www.state.ky.us/agencies/behave/beexaman.html. Reprinted with permission.

The peer-related adjustments of students with externalizing behaviors are variable. Some of these students are rated favorably by their peers (H. M. Walker & Bullis, 1991), while others receive unfavorable ratings (Reid & Patterson, 1991). These students may also demonstrate more subtle behaviors that interfere with the development of friendships, such as lower levels of empathic responding (Schonert-Reichl, 1993) and limited ability to associate affect with facial expressions (D. W. Walker & Leister, 1994).

Internalizing behaviors (which sometimes seem like a lack of behavior) typically do not place students in conflict with teachers. On the contrary, many of these students tend to have high levels of appropriate classroom behavior, reducing their chances of being identified and of receiving needed special services (Kerr & Nelson, 1989). With peers, these students generally have low social status and participate infrequently in peer-controlled activities. They often seem to lack the specific social skills needed for making and keeping friends.

Behavioral earthquakes are high-intensity, low-frequency behaviors that can be externalizing or internalizing.

Behavioral earthquakes are high-intensity but low-frequency externalizing and internalizing behaviors (H. M. Walker & Severson, 1990). Some examples include fire setting, sleep disturbances, self-abuse, and depression (Gresham, MacMillan, & Bocian, 1996). Behavioral earthquakes seem to be good predictors of which students will need to be evaluated for emotional or behavioral disorders.

Academic Characteristics.

Most students identified as having emotional or behavioral disorders also have academic problems (Richards, Symons, Greene, & Szuszkiewicz, 1995). Although they generally have IQs in the low average range, some have mental retardation, and others are gifted. A classroom profile of a student with emotional or behavioral disorders might include these behaviors: frequently off task, poor academic work-related skills, splinter skills in basic academics, underachievement, and poor language skills (Colvin, Greenberg, & Sherman, 1993; Foley & Epstein, 1992; Warr-Leeper, Wright, & Mack, 1994). Students with externalizing behaviors seem especially at risk for learning difficulties (Richards et al., 1995). In addition, their academic performance often deteriorates as they proceed from elementary to secondary school (Colvin et al., 1993).

One study found the most effective tool for increasing homework productivity of students with emotional or behavioral disorders was to have parents sign a homework journal indicating the homework completed and the amount of time spent (Epstein et al., 1995).

Students with emotional or behavioral disorders also experience more difficulty with completing homework than their peers (Epstein, Foley, & Polloway, 1995). Jen is very bright, but completing homework and in-class assignments was a challenge for her. She would fall behind, which caused conflict with her teachers and family. Jen responded to the conflicts with aggressive outbursts. The wraparound team made a rule that Jen could not do homework at home because of these conflicts. As you discovered in the techniques for oppositional defiant disorder, this put Jen in a paradoxical position. Her response? She started secretly doing her homework at home without telling her family or the teachers. Then, when her special education teacher asked her if she needed time to complete her homework at school, Jen told her it was done. Jen has moved beyond this point now. Recently, she started falling behind in one of her classes and took the initiative to talk to her teacher and ask for extra help.

Research also suggests that approximately 30 to 40 percent of students with emotional or behavioral problems also have learning disabilities (see Chapter 4) (Fessler, Rosenberg, & Rosenberg, 1991). Compared to a 71 percent graduation rate for students without disabilities and a 54 percent rate for students with disabilities, the graduation rate for students with

✑ *Students with emotional or behavioral disorders may also experience difficulty with academics.*

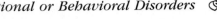

emotional or behavioral disorders is 36 percent (Koyanagi & Gaines, 1993). Keep in mind, however, that all of these students do not experience academic problems; one-third function at or above grade level (Epstein, Kinder, & Bursuck, 1989; Steinberg & Knitzer, 1992).

Identifying the Causes of Emotional or Behavioral Disorders

Seldom can professionals determine with absolute confidence why these children and youth behave as they do, and rarely can professionals find one determining factor (Kauffman, 1993). As you read about biological and environmental causes, keep in mind three important points:

- There is probably a range of factors that contributes interactively to emotional or behavior disorders.

- How people view the causes is probably influenced by their views on the causes of all human behavior (both desirable and undesirable) and also is influenced by their professional discipline and personal experiences.

- Finding a contributing cause of emotional or behavioral disorders is helpful *only* to the extent that it leads to the development of effective interventions and preventions.

Biological Causes. "We know that children don't just develop psychiatric disorders as a result of outside stimuli," Koplewicz (1996, p. 47), a child psychiatrist says. "They're born with them, or at least a vulnerability to them. It's a function of the brain." It is important, therefore, to understand biological components of personality and behavior.

Genetics. The role of genes in the development of many emotional and behavioral disorders should not be overlooked. Hallowell (1996) comments:

> Bedwetting . . . is a condition that for years had been attributed to psychological conflict but that we know now is, in most instances, genetically transmitted. Scientists are hot on the trail of the gene, or combination of genes, behind numerous other conditions. All behavior and all personality are in some way genetically influenced, and to a greater degree than most of us take into account. (p. 62)

Biological Insults. Difficult births, traumatic brain injuries, and childhood illnesses are biological insults that may contribute to the development of emotional or behavioral disorders (H. C. Johnson & Friesen, 1993). For example, recent studies suggest that a strep infection might lead to obsessive-compulsive and other disorders in some students (Talan, 1996). In several studies, children who received a placebo showed no improvement in obsessive-compulsive symptoms or tics, but those who received treatment to flush the strep antibodies showed significant decrease in their behaviors. "Throat cultures could supply the answer" for some students (Swedo cited in Talan, 1996).

Research involving men with a predisposition toward violence revealed that many of them might have experienced damage to the prefrontal portion of the brain. Birth complications, traumatic brain injuries, and lead ingestion may factor into this type of damage (Friend, 1994). "Better prenatal care may very likely be one answer to reducing violence" (Buka & Raine cited in Friend, 1994).

Jen's mother, Mary, believes that some of her daughter's behaviors might be the result of being in the hospital for the first two weeks of her life. Jen had a high white blood cell count and required a spinal tap and intravenous lines. Mary was not allowed to hold her; she says Jen seemed to come out of this experience fighting.

Medications. Because of the neurological aspects of many emotional and behavioral disorders, some of your students might take medications. Medications are often used, for example, to treat students who have anxiety disorders, depression, eating disorders, bipolar disorder, or psychosis. The American Academy of Child and Adolescent Psychiatry

> "The genes provide the base from which all human qualities derive, but experience, free will, chance, and the grace of God create the ultimate shape" (Hallowell, 1996, p. 64).

(1996b) contends, "When prescribed appropriately by an experienced physician, medication may help children and adolescents with psychiatric disorders feel restored to their normal selves." A psychiatrist (Hallowell, 1996) describes the improvement in a child with bipolar disorder: "After Tyrone started taking Tegretol, his tantrums abated. Mom and Dad were no longer worn out, and Tyrone no longer felt like an unpredictable volcano" (p. 67). The following categories of medications are dispensed to children and adolescents:

- *Stimulant medications* such as Dexedrine or methylphenidate (Ritalin). These are useful as part of the treatment of attention-deficit/hyperactivity disorder (see Chapter 6).

- *Antidepressants* are used in the treatment of serious depression, school phobias, some other serious anxiety disorders, bedwetting, some bulimic-type eating disorders, and attention-deficit/hyperactivity disorder.

- *Antipsychotic medication* such as Haldol, Stelazine, or Thorazine. These agents usually give more inner control to a student with psychotic symptoms; stop or at least take the panic out of irrational beliefs and hallucinations.

- *Lithium and carbamazepine* (Tegretol) are very helpful in treating manic-depressive episodes.

- *Antianxiety medications* are prescribed for short-term use for certain conditions associated with high anxiety (American Academy of Child and Adolescent Psychiatry, 1996b, p. 2).

The effectiveness of medication for children and adolescents has not been adequately researched, because conducting controlled studies with young people presents serious ethical and legal problems (Perlman, 1996). Furthermore, medication is only one aspect of appropriate interventions, which often include ongoing evaluation, counseling, and support services, such as the wraparound processes provided for Jen and her family. Along with their beneficial effects, medications can cause side effects "ranging from just annoying to very serious" (American Academy of Child and Adolescent Psychiatry, 1996b). For that reason, it will be important for you to ask the parents to provide the following information about the student's medication:

- *The name of the medication and what it is supposed to do*

- *When [the student is supposed] to take it and when to stop taking it*

- *What foods, drinks, other medications, or activities should be avoided while taking the prescribed medication*

- *What are the [possible] side effects, and what should be done if they occur*

- *If any written information is available [for you to read] about the medication (Perlman, 1996, p. A05)*

Perspective on Families.   "We must learn to recognize the signs of [emotional or behavioral disorders] so that we don't treat them simply as diseases of the will, moral failings on our children's part, or parental failings," Hallowell (1996, p. 59) comments. As research closes in on neurological causes for emotional or behavioral disorders, the loving and supportive parents of many of these students will, hopefully, experience fewer stigmas from society. Norm Linder, who has an adolescent with emotional and behavioral disorders, is one of these parents. He and his wife Ellen raised three healthy children, but with their oldest son Marcus, "they were fighting something beyond their control" (Hadley, 1995). Linder says,

> *If my son had cancer or a brain tumor, would you still . . . tell the world that I am irresponsible? You must understand that mentally ill and emotionally disturbed children are just as sick. They have an invisible disease just as debilitating and potentially just as deadly. (Linder quoted in Hadley, 1995, p. B-1)*

Placing blame does nothing to improve the lives of these students. Sometimes professionals may be tempted to do so to alleviate some of their own responsibility in dealing with a particular student. Jennifer Shulman's parents suggest that professionals need to look at students like their daughter and the student's families individually instead of stereotyping. A collaborative, proactive, problem-solving approach is more likely to benefit both student and family. Figure 5-2 shows the philosophy statement of the Federation of Families for Children's Mental Health.

Environmental Factors. Stresses can act as "a kind of poison in the delicate balance of brain chemicals" (Soulsman, 1994). "If a person's body chemistry is genetically linked to depression, it may take relatively little to trigger a depressive episode" (Research and Training Center on Family Support and Children's Mental Health, 1990).

We have already mentioned how a significant loss in a student's life can trigger depression. Two other categories of environmental stresses—living conditions and child abuse—increase the likelihood that a student may develop emotional or behavioral disorders (H. C. Johnson & Friesen, 1993).

Living Conditions. Although many families who live in poverty are emotionally healthy, the risk of a student developing emotional or behavioral disorders is more likely in these circumstances. Alcohol or drug abuse within the family system can also create an undependable, highly stressful environment (H. C. Johnson & Friesen, 1993).

Another factor that fuels emotional or behavioral disorders is exposure to violence. "Many kids in this country are living in a war zone," one college professor says. "On my way to observe a graduate student at one school, I saw drugs being sold within a block of the school. When I told the student about it, she said that the children in her class had to get down on the floor at times because of drive-by shootings. How could we expect these children not to develop post-traumatic stress disorder?"

Child Abuse. An insidious type of violence inflicted by adults on children and adolescents is child abuse. While child abuse and neglect can be an uncomfortable topic, anyone planning to work with children needs to be familiar with what constitutes child abuse and neglect and what to do if you suspect that a child is being neglected or abused. In Figure 5-3, we provide a list of questions and answers about child abuse.

Students who have experienced abuse may display (a) a poor self-image; (b) inability to depend on and trust others; (c) aggressive and destructive—sometimes illegal—behavior; (d) passive and withdrawn behavior, with fear of entering into new relationships or activities; (e) school failure; and (f) serious drug and alcohol abuse (American Academy of Child and Adolescent Psychiatry, 1996a). Some may conceal the abuse so well that they are popular, straight-A students. In Figure 5-4, we provide a chart for documenting suspected child abuse.

By the preschool years, different behaviors appear to be associated with different types of abuse (Lowenthal, 1996). Students who experience abuse and neglect and have not had

> "When [parents] first brought their children to see me, virtually all of them thought . . . that what was wrong with their children was their fault. Those worried, guilt-ridden parents couldn't be more wrong. What's troubling their children is *nobody's fault*" (Koplewicz, 1996, p. 4).

> Professionals who use sarcasm and react in anger can emotionally abuse students. "It is as painful as physical assault," Vachss (1994) says. "It leaves no visible marks, but it scars the heart and damages the soul." Can you remember incidents of emotional abuse from your childhood?

FIGURE 5–2 *Philosophy statement*

Children and adolescents who have serious emotional, behavioral, or mental disorders come from a broad array of families who have a variety of strengths and needs.

- Inflexible policies and practices of the different systems that serve this population must become flexible in order to meet the families' range of needs and resources.

- Inflexible policies and practices create unnecessary stress and overwhelming responsibilities for the families of children and adolescents who have serious emotional, behavioral, or mental disorders. *It is not the children per se who create the stress.*

- Families are often perceived as being dysfunctional when they are experiencing normal reactions to the serious lack of appropriate, accessible, and affordable services and supports available to them.

- The term "dysfunctional families" is blaming and unnecessary and *must not be used in written or spoken language.*

Note: From *Philosophy Statement,* by the Federation of Families for Children's Mental Health, 1990, February, Alexandia, VA: Federation of Families for Children's Mental Health. Copyright 1990 by the Federation of Families for Children's Mental Health. Reprinted with permission.

FIGURE 5–3 *Questions and answers about child abuse*

What is child abuse?   Child abuse and neglect include acts or failures to act that result in an imminent risk of serious harm, death, serious physical or emotional harm, sexual abuse, or exploitation by a parent or caretaker who is responsible for the child's welfare. This generally applies to a person under the age of eighteen.

How common is it?   The National Clearinghouse on Child Abuse and Neglect reported that over one million children were victims of child abuse and neglect in 1995. Children who have disabilities are at a 1.7 times higher risk of abuse and neglect by their caregivers (families and professionals) than children without disabilities.

How do I know if it is occurring?   Physical indicators may include skin or bone injuries, evidence of neglect such as malnutrition, failure to meet medical needs, or lack of warm clothing in cold weather. Behavioral indicators may include a demonstration of sexual knowledge that is not developmentally or age appropriate.

What do I do about it if I think a child is being abused? Is this really my business?   It is your business. The lasting effects of child abuse and neglect create barriers to learning. School professionals are in a unique position to identify when a child is being abused or neglected because they have contact with the child each day.

If you suspect that a child is being abused or neglected, it is your responsibility to report it to your state's child protection agency. Each state has an agency responsible for child protection, and every state legally mandates that educators report suspected child abuse or neglect. Most states have penalties for mandated reporters who fail to report suspected abuse or neglect. On the other side, all states provide immunity from civil or criminal penalty for mandated reporters who were acting in good faith. Many school systems have their own policies concerning child abuse and neglect. These policies usually state their support for state reporting laws by requiring educators to report child abuse and neglect. They also may provide administrative penalties for not complying with the policies.

An easy way to find out your state's hotline number is to call 1-800-4-A-CHILD. They will direct you to your state's agency.

While it is your responsibility to report suspected abuse, it is not your responsibility to conduct your own investigation to determine if a child is being abused. Your child protection agency is trained to do that. No state requires that the person reporting has proof—only that the person suspects, has an uncomfortable feeling, or a reasonable cause to believe that abuse is occurring.

What kind of information will they want when I make a report?   If you find that you need to make a child abuse or neglect report, you will want to have as much of the following information ready when you make the call: The child's name, age, address, and telephone number, the parent's name, address, and telephone number, the reason for your call.

What should I do when a student confides in me about abuse?

- Avoid promising the student you will not tell. You can say that you will inform the student about who you may need to tell and why.

- Encourage the student to talk freely, and avoid judgmental comments.

- Take the student seriously. Psychiatrists have found that students who are listened to and understood at this time fare much better in therapy than those who are not (American Academy of Child and Adolescent Psychiatry, 1996c).

- Emphasize that the student did the right thing by telling.

- Tell the student that she or he is not at fault, but avoid making derogatory comments about the abuser. The abuser may be someone the student cares for deeply, and such comments might cause the student to retract what was said.

- Promise that you will continue to be there for the student and will take steps to see that the abuse stops.

FIGURE 5-4 Abuse checklist

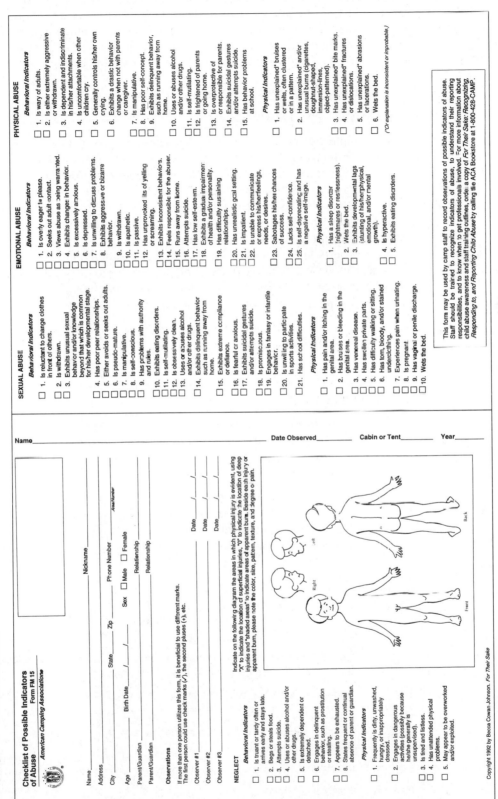

Checklist of Possible Indicators of Abuse
Form FM 15
American Camping Association®

Name_____ Nickname_____

Address_____

City_____ State_____ Zip_____ Phone Number_____ Area/Number

Age_____ Birth Date___/___/___ Sex □ Male □ Female

Parent/Guardian_____ Relationship_____

Parent/Guardian_____ Relationship_____

Observations

If more than one person utilizes this form, it is beneficial to use different marks. The first person could use check marks (✓), the second person plusses (+), etc.

Observer #1_____ Date___/___/___

Observer #2_____ Date___/___/___

Observer #3_____ Date___/___/___

NEGLECT

Behavioral Indicators

1. Is truant or tardy often or arrives early and stays late.
2. Begs or steals food.
3. Attempts suicide.
4. Uses or abuses alcohol and/or other drugs.
5. Is extremely dependent or detached.
6. Engages in delinquent behavior, such as prostitution or stealing.
7. Appears to be exhausted.
8. States frequent or continual absence of parent or guardian.

Physical Indicators

1. Frequently is dirty, unwashed, hungry, or inappropriately dressed.
2. Engages in dangerous activities (possibly because he/she generally is unsupervised).
3. Is tired and listless.
4. Has unattended physical problems.
5. May appear to be overworked and/or exploited.

Indicate on the following diagram the areas in which physical injury is evident, using "X" to indicate the location of superficial injuries, "0" to indicate the location of deep injuries and "shaded areas" to indicate areas of apparent burn. Beside each injury or apparent burn, please note the color, size, pattern, texture, and degree of pain.

Right   Left   Front   Back

SEXUAL ABUSE

Behavioral Indicators

1. Is reluctant to change clothes in front of others.
2. Is withdrawn.
3. Exhibits unusual sexual behavior and/or knowledge beyond that which is common for his/her developmental stage.
4. Has poor peer relationships.
5. Either avoids or seeks out adults.
6. Is pseudo-mature.
7. Is manipulative.
8. Is self-conscious.
9. Has problems with authority and rules.
10. Exhibits eating disorders.
11. Is self-mutilating.
12. Is obsessively clean.
13. Uses or abuses alcohol and/or other drugs.
14. Exhibits delinquent behavior such as running away from home.
15. Exhibits extreme compliance or defiance.
16. Is fearful or anxious.
17. Exhibits suicidal gestures and/or attempts suicide.
18. Is promiscuous.
19. Engages in fantasy or infantile behavior.
20. Is unwilling to participate in sports activities.
21. Has school difficulties.

Physical Indicators

1. Has pain and/or itching in the genital area.
2. Has bruises or bleeding in the genital area.
3. Has venereal disease.
4. Has swollen private parts.
5. Has difficulty walking or sitting.
6. Has torn, bloody, and/or stained underclothing.
7. Experiences pain when urinating.
8. Is pregnant.
9. Has vaginal or penile discharge.
10. Wets the bed.

EMOTIONAL ABUSE

Behavioral Indicators

1. Is overly eager to please.
2. Seeks out adult contact.
3. Views abuse as being warranted.
4. Exhibits changes in behavior.
5. Is excessively anxious.
6. Is depressed.
7. Is unwilling to discuss problems.
8. Exhibits aggressive or bizarre behavior.
9. Is withdrawn.
10. Is apathetic.
11. Is passive.
12. Has unprovoked fits of yelling or screaming.
13. Exhibits inconsistent behaviors.
14. Feels responsible for the abuser.
15. Runs away from home.
16. Attempts suicide.
17. Exhibits a gradual impairment of health and/or personality.
18. Exhibits delinquent behavior such as running away from home.
19. Has difficulty sustaining relationships.
20. Has unrealistic goal setting.
21. Is impatient.
22. Is unable to communicate or express his/her feelings, needs, or desires.
23. Sabotages his/her chances of success.
24. Lacks self-confidence.
25. Is self-deprecating, and has a negative self-image.

Physical Indicators

1. Has a sleep disorder (nightmares or restlessness).
2. Wets the bed.
3. Exhibits developmental lags (stunting of his/her physical, emotional, and/or mental growth).
4. Is hyperactive.
5. Exhibits eating disorders.

PHYSICAL ABUSE

Behavioral Indicators

1. Is wary of adults.
2. Is either extremely aggressive or withdrawn.
3. Is dependent and indiscriminate in his/her attachments.
4. Is uncomfortable when other children cry.
5. Generally controls his/her own crying.
6. Exhibits a drastic behavior change when not with parents or caregiver.
7. Has poor self-concept.
8. Has poor self-concept.
9. Exhibits delinquent behavior, such as running away from home.
10. Uses or abuses alcohol and/or other drugs.
11. Is self-mutilating.
12. Is frightened of parents or going home.
13. Is overprotective of or responsible for parents.
14. Exhibits suicidal gestures and/or attempts suicide.
15. Has behavior problems at school.

Physical Indicators

1. Has unexplained* bruises or welts, often clustered or in a pattern.
2. Has unexplained* and/or unusual burns (cigarettes, doughnut-shaped, immersion-lines, object-patterned).
3. Has unexplained* bite marks.
4. Has unexplained* fractures or dislocations.
5. Has unexplained* abrasions or lacerations.
6. Wets the bed.

(*Or explanation is inconsistent or improbable.)

This form may be used by camp staff to record observations of possible indicators of abuse. Staff should be trained to recognize indicators of abuse, to understand their reporting responsibilities, and to know when to get professionals involved. For more information about child abuse awareness and staff training outlines, order a copy of *For Their Sake: Recognizing, Responding to, and Reporting Child Abuse* by calling the ACA Bookstore at 1-800-428-CAMP.

Copyright 1992 by Becca Cowan Johnson. *For Their Sake*

Note: From Becca Cowan Johnson. (1992). *For their sake: Recognizing, responding to, and reporting child abuse.* Reproduced by permission from publisher, American Camping Association, 5000 State Road 67 North, Martinsville, IN 46151-7902. For permission to reprint beyond limited personal use or limited internal use please contact the publisher at (765) 342-8456.

Attachment disorder is characterized by behavior disorders and difficulty empathizing with others, caused by a lack of bonding to a primary caregiver during early childhood.

the opportunity to bond with a significant adult in infancy can develop an **attachment disorder,** making it difficult for them to learn empathy for others (Mansfield & Waldmann, 1994). We know that the brains of young children need compassionate human touch and stimulation to develop normally. The serious consequences of attachment disorder point to the need for babies and young children to have consistent, caring adults in their life.

Identifying the Prevalence of Emotional or Behavioral Disorders

Given the subjective criteria, it is not surprising that prevalence estimates vary considerably for this population. A review of major studies suggests that 3 to 5 percent of children and adolescents have emotional or behavioral disorders (Koyanagi & Gaines, 1993). The number of these students between ages six and twenty-one who were served under IDEA during the 1993–1994 school year was 413,000—8.5 percent of the special education population or .95 of all school-age students, making this the fourth-largest category of students receiving special education services.

Many experts in the field contend that these students are seriously underidentified and underserved (Burns & Friedman, 1990; Duchnowski & Friedman, 1990; U.S. Department of Education, 1990). The gap between students who need and those who receive services is shown by three different national reports (Koyanagi & Gaines, 1993):

- Department of Education, 1993 Report to Congress: 0.89 percent are receiving special education and related services.

- Unclaimed Children, Children's Defense Fund: 1.7 percent are not receiving any services; "two thirds are not getting the services they need; countless others get inappropriate care."

- Office of Technology Assessment: Less than 1 percent receive treatment in hospitals or residential treatment centers, and only 5 percent receive mental health treatment in outpatient settings. "From 70–80 percent of children in need may not be getting appropriate mental health services."

Although there is an underidentification of students overall, young African American males are overrepresented in this category (U.S. Department of Education, 1992). Figure 5-5 summarizes some of the possible reasons why schools are failing to meet the needs of all students with emotional or behavioral disorders.

Girls, perhaps because many of them exhibit internalizing behaviors, seem to be seriously underrepresented among emotional or behavioral disorders, even when they have been served in psychiatric settings (Caseau, Luckasson, & Kroth, 1994). The book *Reviving Ophelia* (Pipher, 1994) discusses strategies for "saving the lives of adolescent girls."

FIGURE 5–5 *Possible reasons for the underidentification of students with emotional or behavioral problems*

> Reason 1: reluctance to serve those students who have aversive conduct disorders. The view is that these students are willful troublemakers rather than students disabled by behavior.
>
> Reason 2: federal constraints about disciplinary practices permitted for special education students. (Note: Districts are not permitted to expel students who are served by IDEA.)
>
> Reason 3: significant costs associated with the education and treatment of these children and youth (residential programs, psychiatric services, and hospitalization).
>
> Reason 4: insensitivity to disorders such as depression, anxiety, peer neglect and rejection, and affective disturbances.
>
> Reason 5: the subjectivity involved in identification of emotional or behavioral disorders.
>
> Reason 6: the label as stigma.

Note: From "Behavior Disorders and the Social Context of Regular Class Integration: A Conceptual Dilemma?" by H. M. Walker and M. Bullis, in *The Regular Education Initiative: Alternative Perspectives on Concepts, Issues, and Models* (pp. 78–79), edited by J. W. Lloyd, N. N. Singh, and A. C. Repp, 1991, Pacific Grove, CA: Brooks/Cole Publishing Co. Copyright © 1991 by Brooks/Cole Publishing Co. Adapted with permission of Wadsworth Publishing Co., Belmont, CA.

WHAT ARE EVALUATION PROCEDURES?

Determining the Presence of Emotional or Behavioral Disorders

Because students with emotional or behavioral disorders are seriously underidentified and underserved, it is important that general educators know which students to refer for nondiscriminatory evaluation. Although teachers might be more likely to refer students with acting-out behaviors, those who are depressed and withdrawn (but cause no problems in the classroom) may need services as much or more.

How do you decide which of your students to select for prereferral or referral? The checklist of internalizing and externalizing behaviors we provided in Figure 5-1 can help. If a student has exhibited these behaviors consistently in your class and the behaviors are interfering with the student's educational progress, initiating the prereferral process—or the referral process if the behaviors make the student a danger to self or others—is important. You might want to keep a copy of this checklist with your plan book to help you to remember to look for these behaviors.

During the nondiscriminatory evaluation process (Figure 5-6), the student generally receives a standardized intelligence test. The psychologist might also administer **projective tests** that require students to fill in incomplete sentences or tell a story about a picture. Sometimes the psychologist asks the student to complete a personality, social skills, or self-concept inventory.

A psychometrist administers an achievement test to determine if and how the emotional or behavioral disorder has affected the student's educational progress. Moreover, at least one member of the evaluation team will observe the student in the classroom and in other settings and record information about the student's behavior.

Another important component of the nondiscriminatory process is the use of behavior checklists or rating scales. Many of these instruments can help a multidisciplinary team decide if a student's behaviors significantly differ from peers'. Behavior checklists are lists of behaviors gathered from record reviews and teachers' reports that have been standardized on groups of students. Most checklists include only inappropriate or negative behaviors (e.g., steals, has tantrums, exhibits painful shyness). Some also include appropriate behaviors (e.g., follows classroom rules, complies with teacher requests, initiates appropriate interactions with peers). A rater, who might be a student's teacher, parent, peer, or even the student, checks the items on the list that describe the student who is being rated.

Rating scales are similar to behavior checklists in that they comprise a list of behaviors to which the rater responds. Instead of simply indicating the occurrence or nonoccurrence of the behavior, however, the rater estimates the student's performance on the listed behavior along some continuum (e.g., always, sometimes, seldom, never) (Heron & Harris, 1993).

When the evaluation team meets, they will interpret the information from the screening process and the nondiscriminatory evaluation. They will also investigate anecdotal records, interview information, and work samples. The team will decide from this information if the student has a condition that qualifies as an emotional or behavioral disorder and if the condition has an adverse effect on the student's education (Smith, Wood, & Grimes, 1988). If both criteria are met, the student is eligible for services under IDEA. The team will also decide if related services such as counseling are warranted.

A **projective test** is a psychological test in which a student's responses to unstructured stimuli, such as pictures or incomplete sentences, are analyzed for underlying personality traits, feelings, or attitudes.

Determining the Nature and Extent of Special Education and Related Services

In previous chapters, you learned about writing goals and objectives for individualized education programs (IEPs). We mentioned the use of curriculum-based assessment for determining academic objectives, an assessment tool that is also useful for students with

FIGURE 5–6 *Evaluation of students with emotional and behavioral disorders*

Nondiscriminatory Evaluation

Observation

Teacher and parents observe	Student has difficulty with appropriate social adjustments; may be unable to build and maintain satisfactory interpersonal relationships; may engage in aggressive behaviors; may have pervasive mood of unhappiness or depression. The student acts out or withdraws during classroom instruction and independent activities. Problematic behavior occurs in more than one setting.

Screening

Assessment measures	Findings that indicate need for further evaluation
Classroom work products	Student may require one-to-one assistance to stay on task. The student has difficulty following basic classroom behavioral expectations during instruction or assignments, resulting in incomplete or unsatisfactory work products.
Group intelligence tests	Most students perform in the low average to slow learner range. Performance may not accurately reflect ability because the emotional/behavioral disorder can prevent the student from staying on task.
Group achievement tests	Student performs below peers or scores lower than would be expected according to group intelligence tests. Performance may not be a true reflection of achievement because the student has difficulty staying on task as a result of the emotional/behavioral disorder.
Vision and hearing screening	Results do not explain behavior.

Prereferral

Teacher implements suggestions from school-based team.	The student is not responsive to reasonable adaptations of the curriculum and behavior management techniques.

Referral

Protection in evaluation procedures

Assessment measures	Findings that suggest emotional and behavioral disorders
Individualized intelligence test	Intelligence is usually, but not always, in the low average to slow learner range. The multidisciplinary team makes sure that the results do not reflect cultural difference rather than ability. The evaluator can sometimes detect emotional and behavioral disorders by performance on subtests of the intelligence measure and the student's behavior while taking the test.
Individualized achievement test	Usually, but not always, the student scores below average across academic areas in comparison to peers. The evaluator may notice acting-out or withdrawal behaviors that affect results.
Behavior rating scale	The student scores in the significant range on specific behavioral excesses or deficiencies when compared with others of the same culture and developmental stage.
Assessment measures of social skills, self-esteem, personality, and/or adjustment	Student's performance indicates significant difficulties in one or more areas according to the criteria established by test developers and in comparison with others of the same culture and developmental stage.
Anecdotal records	The student's challenging behaviors are not of short duration but have been apparent throughout time in school. Also, records indicate that behaviors have been observed in more than one setting and are adversely affecting educational progress.
Curriculum-based assessment	The student often is experiencing difficulty in one or more areas of the curriculum used by the local school district.
Direct observation	The student is experiencing difficulty relating to peers or adults and in adjusting to school or classroom structure or routine.

Evaluation Team determines that student has emotional and behavioral disorders and needs special education and related services.

Appropriate Education

emotional or behavioral disorders. How, though, do you write objectives for behavior? The first step is to target what behaviors need to change.

Direct observation is an effective method for obtaining specific information regarding a student's behavior. Direct observation involves watching and recording the behavior of a single student or a group of students for a specified time while students are engaging in a specific task, working on an assignment, playing during recess, or interacting with peers. Such observation is much more than simply looking at the student (Morgan & Jenson, 1988). Direct observation makes use of structured recording sheets to collect data and a set of codes for target behaviors (those that the IEP participants want to strengthen or diminish). The target behaviors must be observable (meaning that the teacher can see the behaviors) and measurable (meaning that the behaviors can be tallied on some dimension). Observable and measurable dimensions of behavior include the following:

- *Frequency:* how often it occurs

- *Duration:* how long it lasts

- *Latency:* how long it takes for the behavior to begin once there is an opportunity

- *Topography:* the shape of the response

- *Magnitude:* the intensity of the response

How will you decide which dimension to measure? It depends on your concern. For example, if you are interested in how many times Jen interacts with her peers, you might collect frequency data. If you are interested in the time it takes Jen to begin her work, latency recording is appropriate. Regardless of the direct observation approach used, repeated measures of the target behavior are taken (perhaps daily) so that patterns and trends can be observed.

Applied behavior analysis is a structured technique that allows professionals to monitor student progress toward specific behavioral objectives. After direct observation of a third grader named Jim, his teacher, Betty Martin, decides Jim's most immediate need is to stop making undesirable comments under his breath during math class, his most difficult subject. The first thing Betty does is to collect frequency data; she records for three days how many times Jim makes these comments during math class. She does not tell Jim she's doing this. Betty graphs this information, and at the end of the three days, she draws

Direct observation is used to obtain specific information on a student's behavior through watching and recording to what degree, how often, or for what length of time a behavior does or does not occur.

Applied behavior analysis is the systematic collection and graphing of data to ascertain a student's progress toward a specific objective.

Difficult tasks are associated with more frequent off-task and disruptive behaviors by students with emotional or behavioral disorders (DePaepe, Shores, Jack, & Denny, 1996).

 An observer collects duration information. She measures the length of time the student in the black shirt remains on task. This information will be used to plan an intervention to increase the student's on-task behavior.

A **contingency contract** is a signed agreement between student and teacher that if the student performs in a certain way, the teacher will provide the student with a desired reinforcer.

Have you ever tried to change a behavior that had become habitual? Maybe you've tried to lose weight or stop smoking. Change is not easy for anyone.

a dotted vertical line on the graph. These three days represent a *baseline*. Betty determines that the behavior occurred an average of ten times during the three days. Then she sets up a conference with Jim to develop a **contingency contract** (see Figure 5-7).

During the conference with Jim, Betty explains, "Jim, I know you dislike math. When you make comments about it under your breath, you don't hear the instructions and it makes math even harder and more frustrating. I've got an idea that might help." Betty's purpose is to help him see that it is to his benefit to change the behavior. For contingency contracting to work, the student must be invested in change.

Betty shows the graph to Jim and tells him that she knows it's hard to change. "For the last three days, you've muttered under your breath about ten times each math class. What do you think about us aiming for five or fewer times each class?" Jim agrees. Then the two of them decide what reward Jim will receive for his progress. Jim chooses to spend twenty minutes at the art center painting. Figure 5-7, shows the contract Betty and Jim wrote. Betty graphs Jim's progress, and within two weeks, he earns time at the art center. Betty and Jim meet to revise the contract periodically until the behavior seldom occurs.

Applied behavior analysis is only one intervention that Betty uses. She also guarantees that Jim achieves success in math by giving him easy tasks until his confidence builds. Betty also incorporates more manipulatives in math for Jim. The contingency contract, however, helps Jim focus on exactly what behavior needs to change and how. This structure helps many of these students and allows teachers to document their progress.

FIGURE 5–7 *Applied behavior analysis and contingency contract for Jim*

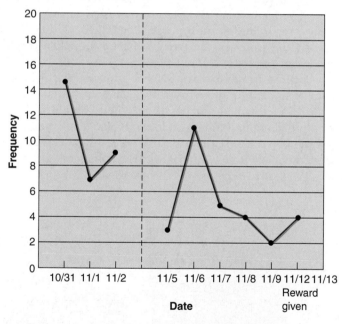

Contract

I ___Betty Martin___ agree that if Jim mutters under his breath five times or less, I will let him put a star on his chart. When he has five stars, he can paint at the craft center for 20 minutes.

Signed *Betty Martin*

I ___Jim___ agree that I will not mutter under my breath more than five times during math class.

Signed *Jim*

11/5 ★	11/6	11/7 ★	11/8 ★	11/9 ★	11/12 ★		

WHAT AND HOW DO PROFESSIONALS TEACH?

Curriculum

Research indicates that incorporating personal interests into curriculum assignments improves the conduct and engagement of students with emotional or behavioral disorders (Clarke et al., 1995). The challenge for educators, therefore, is to frame needed academic and social skills into activities that build on those interests. Jen says that she believes it is important for teachers to make subjects interesting. Her special education teacher developed curriculum activities related to Jen's interest in animals. Hetfield (1994) motivated her students by having them create a school newspaper.

McWhiter and Bloom (1994) taught a math curriculum based on a student-operated business to students with emotional or behavioral disorders. Students decorated wooden baskets filled with candy and sold them through an open house, a school store, and word of mouth. The students made the decisions about what they would make, how they would make it, how they would sell it, and so on. They operated the business in the afternoon. They also completed math tasks—based on their IEP objectives—that were related to the business. Instead of doing addition worksheets, for instance, they added numbers on their time cards or business receipts. Multiplication tasks might involve calculating their pay based on the number of hours they worked.

McWhiter and Bloom (1994) discovered several benefits: (a) on-task behavior increased, (b) grades improved, and (c) students had opportunities to learn and practice real-life social skills, such as making telephone contacts, selling products, and working together to produce a product. A point system was in effect throughout the school year, but the improvement in behavior during the time the business was incorporated led

❤ *Making instruction and learning activities relevant and enjoyable increases on-task behavior of students with emotional or behavioral disorders.*

McWhiter and Bloom to conclude, "on-task behavior appeared to be more dependent on the type of instruction than on the externally imposed point system."

Students with emotional or behavioral disorders will also need to receive direct instruction in appropriate behaviors and social skills. The PATHS (Providing Alternative Thinking Strategies) curriculum is an example of an effective program that emphasizes respect and responsibility (Greenberg, 1997). Designed for elementary children, the curriculum teaches three major skills. The first phase teaches children *emotional recognition and communication.* "Knowing and being able to express one's feelings is [sic] not only a step in self-awareness, but often the best solution in difficult, conflictual situations," Greenberg says. Students receive and personalize forty different Feeling Faces, in developmental order, moving from basic to more complex emotions as their skills increase. Throughout the day, students are asked to evaluate how they feel and show the appropriate face(s).

The second phase emphasizes *self-control.* Students learn to use a Control Signals Poster. The red light signals "Stop—Calm Down," the yellow light "Go Slow—Think," and the green light "Go—Try My Plan." At the bottom, the sign says "Evaluate—How Did My Plan Work?" After learning to use this chart, DeShawn's teacher put a red dot on his desk. She told him to put his thumb on the spot when he felt angry, take a deep breath, and let the anger flow into the spot. "He learned he did not have to react to other kids when he got angry. . . . He was learning a way to gain better control" (Greenberg, 1997).

In the third phase, the students practice using the previous skills and add the more advanced problem-solving skills of generating alternatives, thinking of consequences, choosing a solution, and making a plan (Greenberg, 1997). Students learn to apply the skills in class meetings in which they discuss more complicated adolescent issues as they mature. Studies show that students in general education significantly benefit in emotional understanding and problem solving through this curriculum, while students with emotional and behavioral disorders also decrease internalizing and externalizing behaviors.

Methods

In this section, we highlight a few of the many effective strategies for working with students who have emotional or behavioral disorders. By restoring hope, encouraging a productive self-concept, setting limits, and taking care of yourself, you might make a difference someday for many of these students.

Restoring Hope.   "People with hope chase rainbows, and sometimes catch them" Curwin (1992) says. "Those without hope see little reason to try. They do not believe that rainbows can be caught, and that even if a rainbow could be caught, it would be nothing more than colored mist."

We have described the hopelessness experienced by many students with emotional or behavioral disorders. People tend to reflect the feelings of those around them. Therefore, when a student despairs, a teacher might begin to reflect that despair and believe the student cannot change. Sister Mary Rose McGeady is President and CEO of Covenant House International. She works with homeless and displaced young people, many of whom have emotional or behavioral disorders. She comments:

> *I have discovered that even in the most desperate child, there is hope. It may be only the very smallest of sparks—impossible to see at first. Finding it often takes time and patience, requiring us to carefully scrape away the layers of scars, pain, hurt, rejection, and suffering to find the hope abiding in every human heart. The child may not even know it is there. But it is. And [it is our responsibility to] shelter this tiny spark, feed it, nurture it. When you read between the lines, you will find in their stories something beautiful. (McGeady, 1997, p. 32)*

Mathews (1996) emphasizes the importance of communicating hope when we first encounter students with emotional or behavioral disorders. We need to ask ourselves:

Write-on or preprinted response cards (cards, signs, or items, such as the Feeling Faces, held up by each student in response to a question during a group lesson) allow all students to participate in class, even those with internalizing behaviors who fear speaking aloud.

"Hope is the driving force of change" (Curwin, 1992).

Through my example, what is the invitation I am extending to this youth? Will it bring him or her toward me, toward what I have to offer, toward hope and a belief that changing his or her life circumstances is possible? What is reflected in my own life, in my own values, attitudes, and beliefs, that would help heal, inspire, and give support to this young person" (p. 52)?

Hope leads to resilience. Students who become successful, caring adults despite seemingly insurmountable odds often trace their success to having one adult who believed in, encouraged, and supported them. Referred to as mentors or polestars, these adults formed a hope-giving, trusting, often long-lasting, relationship with the students (Guetzloe, 1991). A teacher often played that role.

Your expression of hope must be sincere. Jen's special education teacher emphasizes that you must like and accept these students to work well with them. "These kids are perceptive, and if you are not sincere, they'll know it," she says.

Setting Limits.   We have stressed the importance of compassion in this chapter. One result of compassion is setting limits. Yes, these students need choices and a sense of personal power. But they also need to experience the natural consequences of their choices and not be protected from them. Torey Hayden (1980), who taught Sheila, the little girl introduced in the opening of this chapter, comments about the great expectations she has for students:

I had always felt strongly about setting expectations for my kids. . . . None of them was frail. Much to the contrary. The fact that they had survived enough to be where they were after what most of them had been through was a testimony to their strength. However, . . . I did not feel it was my right to add to the chaos [already present in their lives] by leaving them to guess what I expected. I found establishing a structure a useful and productive method with all the children. . . . Obviously, they had already shown they could not handle their own limits without help. . . . As soon as the time came that they could, I began the process of transferring the power to them. (p. 24)

Empowerment—through increasing self-esteem, giving students choices, and teaching them to self-advocate and monitor their own behavior—helps students take responsibility for their own behavior (Henley, 1997). One way to do this is to allow students to generate

   Compassion differs from pity. Compassion says, "I care about what's happening to you and believe in your ability to make good *choices* and change." Pity says, "You are a victim, and I must rescue you because you are helpless."

   When students know the behavioral limits in a classroom, they are more likely to behave responsibly, even in stressful situations.

BOX 5–5   INTO PRACTICE

THE SIX P'S OF STRATEGIC INTERACTION

PREPARE

Be aware of the dynamics of interactions and power struggles. Ask yourself: What buttons do I have that students can push easily? What kinds of looks and attitudes annoy me? What are the student's hooks and buttons that I might be tempted to push? How do I know when I am in a negative interaction (e.g., tight stomach, anger, frustration, dread).

PREDICT

Make an educated guess about how the interaction might proceed. How will the student react to this situation? How will she or he invite me to play the losing game?

PLAN

Decide what steps you need to take. What will I say or do instead of what I normally say or do? What is my game plan for staying out of the power struggle? Which of the following phrases will I memorize and use?

- Wow!
- "I never thought of it that way before."
- "I'm not sure I understand. Could you tell me more about it?"
- "It seems that I've made you angry. What was it that I did?"
- "I know you're going to be [mad, disappointed, etc.], but the consequence of breaking the rule is. . . ."
- "That's interesting."
- "Come to me with an alternative plan."
- "I'm sorry."

- "What do you think about it?"
- "What do you think should happen?"
- "I'm going to have to think about that for a while."
- "I can see why you'd be [mad, upset, sad, frustrated, etc.]"
- "I wish things could be better between us. Let me know if you have any ideas about how we can do that."
- "We seem to be at a standstill. Let's meet to talk about this again [some definite time in the future]."

PRACTICE

Try out your plan with a spouse or friend. Afterwards, ask if the partner (a) perceived him- or herself as less able to argue, (b) felt at a loss as to how to continue the argument, and (c) felt heard and respected or manipulated and overpowered. Did you feel in control of the situation, even if you did not feel in control of your partner?

PAT (PRAISE, APPRECIATE, THANK) THE STUDENT

Look for ways to create positive, warm, respectful interactions. Thank the student for compliance, and enforce consequences in a warm, caring way. "I wish this didn't have to happen. Let me know if there's anything we can do together to prevent this from happening again."

PATIENCE

Changing how one interacts is not easy. In some cases, results will be immediate. In others, it may take more time before the student stops engaging in power struggles. Over time, the interactions become increasingly positive and productive.

Note: From "Control the Interaction, Not the Child!" by J. Raser, 1997, *Reaching Today's Youth, 1*(3), pp. 44–49. Copyright 1997 by National Education Service. Adapted with permission.

rules and consequences for infringement at the beginning of the year. When they feel ownership in the rules, rather than that the rules are being imposed by an adult, they are more likely to abide by them. Your classroom rules will be more meaningful if they (a) are clear and specific, (b) indicate if and when the rule is broken or followed, (c) make sense to the people who enforce and receive it, (d) state what is allowed as well as what is not allowed, and (e) are simply stated and demonstrated in a way that all students understand (Mendler, 1992). Students are more likely to comply with rules that are positively rather than negatively stated. "Keep your hands and feet to yourself" is more effective than "Don't bother others."

Consistent enforcement is critical. What do you do when conflict occurs? "Control the interaction, not the child," Raser (1997) says. In "Into Practice," Box 5–5, we list Raser's Six P's of Strategic Interaction to use with students. After you read these, review Torey Hayden's interaction with Sheila at the beginning of this chapter to see how she incorporated these techniques. Faber and Mazlish (1996) describe effective, positive ways to improve interactions and reduce conflicts with students. We highly recommend *How to Talk so Kids Can Learn.*

It is also important to recognize positive behaviors. The adage "catch students being good" has merit. *Point* and *level systems* (students achieve various privileges based on what level they have earned for complying with rules) can help provide needed structure. Compliments need to focus on character traits rather than outcomes, which are difficult to control: "You really worked hard on that test!" rather than "You made a 'B'!"

Encouraging a Productive Self-Concept.

A balance between setting limits and creating an environment that promotes positive rather than negative behavior is essential (Henley, 1997). The ultimate goal is that students achieve appropriate behavior because of the way they view themselves and others rather than as a result of the limits others initiate. How does this happen? As we mentioned in Chapter 4, Coopersmith—in his classic book, *The Antecedents of Self Esteem* (1967)—identified four components of self-esteem: significance, power, virtue, and competence.

When teachers provide students with opportunities to experience the four components of self-esteem, students will be less likely to misbehave. The reason for this can be seen in Table 5–1. Dreikurs (1998) specified four mistaken goals of behavior. As you can see in Table 5–1, the components and goals appear to be conversely related. Dreikurs stresses that usually the correct response to misbehavior is the opposite of your initial inclination. For that reason, you might ignore student attempts to get your attention but look for ways to help them feel significant and important to you at other times. When a student tries to engage you in a power struggle, instead of trying to prove your own power, the best response, in most cases, is to refuse to play, while still emphasizing that the choice to behave or misbehave has consequences. You may be tempted to reflect a student's feelings and give up on him when he exhibits inadequacy. Instead, you will want to assure the student that you believe in his ability and will help him find a way to learn the skill, whether academic or behavioral.

When students try to hurt you to achieve revenge, instead of retaliating, as you will probably feel like doing, Dreikurs suggests telling the students that you care about them no matter what they say or do. And part of the way that you will show that caring is to

> We cannot (nor should we feel the responsibility to) control the behavior of another person. We can only control our own actions and responses.

> Using effective listening skills and providing encouragement help students feel significant. Two books that can help you strengthen these skills are *How to Talk so Kids Will Listen and Listen so Kids Will Talk* (Faber & Mazlish, 1980) and *The Magic of Encouragement* (Marston, 1990).

Coopersmith's Components of Self-esteem (1967)	Dreikurs's Mistaken Goals of Misbehavior (1998)
Significance—Student feels important to and noticed by valued people	**Attention**—Student perceives a need to misbehave for others to notice him or her
Power—Student perceives opportunities to make choices and provide input	**Power**—Student engages in power contests because she or he feels powerless
Virtue—Student perceives himself or herself as capable of demonstrating positive character traits and participating in the betterment of the environment, other people, and animals	**Revenge**—The student perceives a need to "get back at" others for past injustices
Competence—Student feels capable and skillful in school and personal endeavors	**Inadequacy**—The student feels hopeless and gives up

TABLE 5–1 *Components of self-esteem and mistaken goals of behavior*

A **natural or logical consequence** is a consequence for behavior that relates directly to the offense.

The book *Reclaiming Youth at Risk: Our Hope for the Future* (Brendtro, Brokenleg, & Van Bockern, 1990) describes a program that incorporates the four components within the context of Native American culture.

"We cannot take another person past where we are in our own lives because we do not possess a map for the journey" (Mathews, 1996, p. 52).

enforce consequences for their actions. Dreikurs also emphasizes the need for **natural or logical consequences.** When students write on a desk, for example, a natural consequence is to have them sand the desk. Natural consequences help teach students that life will also give them consequences, and they are more likely to learn from the experience than if they receive detention or lose points or a level.

Many effective programs use the four components of self-esteem in their work with students who have emotional or behavioral disorders. It is especially important to give students opportunities for virtue and altruism. We have mentioned Jen's love of animals. A number of programs are finding that these students benefit from caring for and even training animals (see Kaufmann, 1997; Murry, 1996; Siegel, Murdock, & Colley, 1997). Because Jen functioned at a higher academic level than the rest of her self-contained class, she enjoyed tutoring some of the other students. Box 5-6, "My Voice," describes how one teacher made a difference in a student's life by providing him with altruistic opportunities.

Personal Wellness.   Working with students who have emotional or behavioral disorders can be rewarding, but it is also stressful at times. Making sure that you take care of yourself will be essential if you are to have the needed energy to work effectively with these students. Curwin (1992) suggests the following strategies:

- Remember why you wanted to be a teacher. Keep those reasons in mind every day you teach.

- Understand what you love to teach and what you do not. Teach more of what you love, and find ways to energize yourself for what you don't by using techniques and methods you enjoy, or by teaching it in a way that the kids enjoy.

- Do at least one activity you love at least once a day, or once a period for secondary teachers. The special activity might only take five minutes of class time. Focus on how much you are looking forward to teaching it on your way to school.

- Ignore cynical teachers or administrators. Do not let them diminish your love of teaching.

- Strive to be a great teacher every day. Take pride in your profession and your ability to do it well. Think of yourself as the Bruce Springsteen, Barbra Streisand, Frank Sinatra, or Joe Montana of teaching.

- Do not be afraid to show off. Let yourself go, and be a ham every now and then for your students.

- Let your students know why you love teaching, and why you love what you teach. Do this with energy and commitment, not preaching.

- Do the unexpected; surprise your students and surprise yourself. Make your classroom an event. Look forward to being there, and do things that get your students to think, "I wonder what will happen next?" rather than, "I wonder if I can make it through another class?"

HOW IS PARTICIPATION ENCOURAGED?

Inclusion

Jen temporarily spent half of her school day in a self-contained classroom and the other half in her home school. She wanted desperately to be fully included in her home school and worked hard to make that happen. Inclusion of students with emotional or behavioral disorders is controversial. The Council for Children with Behavior Disorders (CCBD) adopted the following position:

BOX 5-6 MY VOICE

DAVID L. FURR

Mrs. Eldridge came screaming down the hall, "Dr. Furr, HELP!" I ran out of my classroom to meet our school secretary and other female office workers. . . . They yelled that Mrs. Davis had just called over the intercom. There was a big fight in her room and she needed help. We all ran up the stairs to the middle school section of our building. . . . When I entered her classroom, I saw Cory. I'm six feet tall and weigh 230 pounds; Cory outweighed me but was a foot shorter. He was holding a much smaller boy against the wall.

With the deepest voice I could muster, I said, "LET HIM GO!" Cory looked at me and let the smaller boy go, who promptly ran to a counselor standing at the door. I said to Cory, "Please talk to me." I didn't know Cory, but I thought it would be best to let everyone, the adults too, calm down.

We walked to the stairwell and sat on the steps. I asked him what the problem was. Very calmly, he explained that this boy had been saying nasty things about his mom. He told me it made him really mad because his mom had died two years ago. We talked some more and I escorted him to the office. As we walked there, he thanked me for breaking up the fight and talking to him! I was amazed!

When we reached the office, the principal said to Cory, "Not you again! What did you do now?" I went back to class. . . . [I found out later that] his mother had died of a drug overdose when he was in fifth grade, and it had all been downhill from there. He had never met his father and was being raised by his grandmother. He was in fights almost daily. . . . He had missed 52 days [of school] and it was only midyear. . . .

I just could not get it out of my head how he had thanked me for talking to him. Having a background in psychology and special education really did not give me much of any idea how to help him. [I attended some workshops and read some books about how children like Cory were "disconnected" and needed to belong] and that sometimes you could get them hooked on helping others. . . . I felt very strongly about the need for respect and dignity for children, even in the toughest situations.

I called Cory at home because he had not been to school all week. When I told him who I was, he said, "I know you, you're the nice big guy, right?" I told him that I needed some help with the second-grade class I worked with, that I had heard how smart he was, and was just calling to see if he was interested. I could almost feel the excitement in his voice. He wanted to know if he should come to school right then. It was 3:30 in the afternoon. I told him to come in the morning.

The next day Cory arrived and stuck out his hand. I shook it and told him to step outside. We talked about what he would do, and I told him that he had to follow a couple of rules. He was not to fight anywhere in the school and could not miss another day of school. He agreed!

I asked him why he missed so many days and had been in so much trouble. He said . . . that at least sometimes, he didn't come to school because the bus did not pick him up. I told Cory that was baloney and that if he was going to lie to me, we would just end this deal now. . . . One week later [I learned], about a certain bus not picking up kids two or three times a week. . . . I had called Cory a liar and he was not. . . . [When I apologized], he said, "That's okay. . . . You know, I sometimes fight, but I really don't ever lie. It's something my mom taught me." . . .

Cory loved coming to Mrs. Dimling's class. I asked him why and he told me that he liked coming "because everyone likes and respects me here." He was a master with the second graders. He spoke their language, and they loved him. He lived in the pit of poverty, yet he always bought the second graders candy to reward their efforts.

One day, he asked me why Ryan was such a problem. Ryan was always in trouble of one sort or another. I told him I didn't know, and he said, "How about if I talk to him in the hall and find out what he likes? Then we can make up some work for him to do based on that." I almost fell on the floor. Hey, I knew that! Why had I not done it? He spoke to Ryan for almost an hour, and not only came up with a plan for school but also found out about some serious problems Ryan was having at home. I said, "Cory, you're a genius!" Cory replied, "No, he's just like me, that's all."

Note: From "Now I Understand the Rage," by D. L. Furr, 1996, *Reaching Today's Youth*, 1(1), pp. 9–12. Copyright 1996 by National Education Service. Reprinted with permission.

CCBD supports a full continuum of mental health and special education services for children and youth with emotional or behavioral disorders. We believe that educational decisions depend on individual student needs. Consequently, in contrast to those individuals and groups who advocate full inclusion, CCBD does not support the notion that all special education students, including those students with emotional or behavioral disorders, are always best served in general education classrooms. (Council for Children with Behavioral Disorders, 1993)

How do you feel about the inclusion of students with emotional or behavioral disorders? Would your viewpoint be the same or different if you were a parent of a child with emotional or behavioral disorders?

As you can see in Figure 5-8, the largest percentage of these students (35.3 percent) is educated in self-contained special education classrooms, with as many as 13.4 percent educated in separate schools. Even though students identified as having emotional or behavioral disorders represent only 8 to 9 percent of students in special education, they represent more than 50 percent of all students served in residential facilities. Once placed in segregated educational environments, they are the least likely to be included in the general education classroom (Braaten et al., 1988).

IDEA's presumption is that students with disabilities, including those with emotional or behavioral disorders, will be included in general classrooms. The evaluation/IEP team must justify why a student is placed in a more restrictive environment.

Long (1994) states that the following five criteria could "ensure that [students with emotional or behavioral disorders] have a level playing field and . . . an opportunity to be successful in their [general education] classrooms":

• The school staff must meet and agree to participate in the Inclusion Movement. This means a willingness to participate in any ongoing training in this area.

• A[student with emotional disorders] should not be administratively assigned to a classroom teacher. A mutual process should take place to find the best fit between the teacher and the student. The receiving classroom teacher also must be willing to serve as this student's advocate.

• The support staff, including the principal, must agree to participate in advanced crisis-intervention training in order to have the skills to support the classroom teacher and the student during times of conflict.

• The classroom group must be open to accepting new students, or at least not scapegoat or reject them.

• The emotionally disturbed student must function no more than two years below the academic norm of the classroom, be motivated to keep up with the daily academic assignments, use the support staff, and make a personal commitment to this placement. (Long, 1994, pp. 22, 23)

General education teachers are successfully teaching students with emotional or behavioral disorders in their classrooms everyday. You may find the accompanying box, "Inclusion Tips," useful when you include these students in general classrooms.

FIGURE 5–8 *Percentage of students with serious emotional disturbance in educational placements*

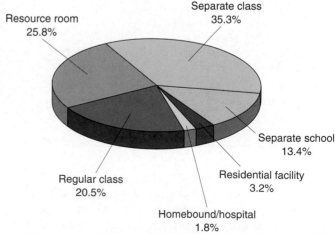

Resource room
25.8%

Separate class
35.3%

Separate school
13.4%

Residential facility
3.2%

Homebound/hospital
1.8%

Regular class
20.5%

Note: From U.S. Department of Education (1995). *To assure the free appropriate public education of all children with disabilities: Seventeenth annual Report to Congress on the implementation of the Individuals with Disabilities Education Act.* Washington, DC: Author

Inclusion Tips

	What You Might See	What You Might Be Tempted to Do	Alternate Responses	Ways to Include Peers in the Process
Behavior	The student refuses to follow directions and uses inappropriate language.	Respond in anger and send her out of the classroom. Place her in "time-out" for extended periods of time.	Building on her strengths and interests, try an approach based on catching her being good. Also try contingency contracting.	Use peer mediation and/or a classroom court as well as group contingencies.
Social Interactions	He fights with other students and is always on the defensive.	Separate him from other students to prevent fights.	Give him time to calm down. Then teach appropriate social skills using modeling, videos, and social skills programs.	Pair him with different students who can model and help him practice social skills and responses.
Educational Performance	The student is rarely on-task and appears to have an inability to learn.	Give poor grades and require her to remain until all work is done.	Develop a curriculum based on student interests and a motivational reward system for completed tasks.	Use peer tutoring and also find a "buddy" (see "The Buddy Program") willing to be a friend and helpful tutor.
Classroom Attitudes	He is depressed or sad all the time and does not speak or interact with others.	Discipline him for nonparticipation, and instruct him to "cheer up."	Recognize the warning signs. Refer him for help. Collaborate with the school counselor.	Have different students daily write something good about him, and then verbally present it to him.

Improved and increased collaboration among various professionals and families is also likely to increase inclusion opportunities and improve inclusion efforts. In Box 5–7, Jim Cain, a school superintendent whose son David has emotional or behavioral disorders, shares advice with administrators about ways they can help increase inclusive options for students with emotional or behavioral disorders.

Collaboration

Many students require services that involve multiple disciplines, such as education, mental health, social services, public welfare, public health, and the juvenile justice system. Several unique efforts exist to help families and professionals better coordinate educational and mental health services.

Professional Collaboration. The type and degree of mental health services available for students vary. Most mental health services are optional (unlike education, which is mandated), and some students receive no direct, specialized mental health

BOX 5-7

MY VOICE

ADVICE TO ADMINISTRATORS FOR INCREASING INCLUSIVE OPTIONS

1. It's much more economical to educate students in their neighborhood schools than it is to pay for expensive out-of-home and out-of-district programs. We need funding streams to be redirected from institutional programs and into our school districts. It's entirely possible to create the support that students with the most severe emotional or behavioral challenges need in order to succeed in their own schools.
2. Treat all students as individuals, because no two students are ever the same. Evaluate their strengths and weaknesses, help make their strengths stronger, and certainly help them find ways to overcome their weaknesses. It doesn't make a difference if the weakness is academic or behavioral. All of us have areas where we need to improve.
3. As administrators, we're responsible for finding the right combinations for all students to be successful. If they're not successful, it means we have not yet successfully found the combination they need.
4. We must believe that all children and youth can learn and behave appropriately. I'm talking about more than lip service.
5. We need to ask students directly what we can do to make their education work for them. We need to be able to give them the power they need and even bend our rules if necessary. We need to show them that we want them to succeed and be willing to meet them halfway. We have to stop forcing students with emotional or behavioral disorders into a corner where they have no choices and we have all the control in our hands.
6. We must find ways for these students to get involved in extracurricular activities and to recognize that having friends is an important part of school. Many students act out because they feel alienated from their peers and on the fringe of school life. An appropriate education has to extend beyond the classroom and academic instruction.
7. A frequent barrier to successful inclusion is to wait until a student has a crisis to provide more individualized and personalized support. Administrators, teachers, and families must respond immediately to the first inkling that a problem is brewing. We must gather as collaborative teams and come up with creative approaches to prevent little problems from escalating into major crises, which, in turn, too often lead to long-term restrictive placements.

Jim Cain
Superintendent; Williamsburg, Kansas

---

services. Box 5-8, "Into Practice," describes several innovative approaches for linking educational and mental health services.

Jen's wraparound team includes a community mental health professional, a family services facilitator, a team teacher who supports the classroom teacher, the classroom teacher, the school principal, the parents, Jen's aunt, a family friend, and Jen herself. Jen's wraparound team members credit the Highlands building principal for his decisive role in providing the kinds of support and facilitation that made Jen's full-time return to general education possible,

Family Collaboration. Communicating with families is a critical part of working with students (Friesen, 1989; Friesen & Huff, 1990; Friesen & Koroloff, 1990). The wraparound team's support not only made a difference in Jen's life, but in her family's as well. They enjoy the relationship they have with the LADSE family service facilitator. This trust helps them to accept suggestions from her and ask her questions. The family and other team members share insights freely.

Another effective program that emphasizes family collaboration is Kaleidoscope, which is located in Chicago. This model family support program empowers families of children and youth at risk for institutionalization. Its mission is to design individualized services, building on the strengths of children and families in inclusive community settings. Services include the following (Kaleidoscope, 1992):

- Therapeutic foster family homes for children and adolescent parents and their babies, including those born with acquired immune deficiency syndrome (AIDS)

- Youth development programs to encourage youth who have grown up in foster care or in institutional settings to become independent

- Satellite family outreach to reunite children in residential care with their families by providing whatever resources are necessary to achieve success

BOX 5-8   INTO PRACTICE

INNOVATIVE APPROACHES LINKING EDUCATIONAL AND MENTAL HEALTH SERVICES

1. A program in Ventura County, California, places mental health workers in classrooms for students with emotional or behavioral disorders. The mental health worker provides services to the students and teachers and also makes home visits.
2. The public school program in Montgomery County, Pennsylvania, organizes daily classroom meeting groups attended by teachers to discuss the emotional/behavioral concerns of their students. Teachers meet four days a week, and one day a week they are joined by a consulting mental health professional (a psychiatrist or a psychologist) to provide suggestions or guidance regarding specific concerns.
3. A program called ELMO (Elementary Mental Health Overlay) located in Pinellas County, Florida, provides

an assigned counselor to ten or twelve children. The counselor (who is paid by the Juvenile Welfare Board) provides individual or group counseling, runs parent groups, and visits homes.
4. The Rockland Children's Psychiatric Center, in cooperation with Orange County Board of Cooperative Educational Services, provides therapeutic services in nineteen different school districts in seven counties in New York. Services include school-based mental health clinics in forty schools, twenty-seven school-based day treatment programs, and a ninety-day day treatment class as an alternative to hospitalization. The center has also organized and implemented Project CATCH (Community Alternatives to Treatment of Children in Hospitals). Project CATCH requires the day treatment supervisors to make rounds on the inpatient ward in various hospitals to help plan for an expeditious discharge of children and youth and to coordinate school-based follow-up support services.

Note. From *At the Schoolhouse Door: An Examination of Programs and Policies for Children With Behavioral and Emotional Problems* by J. Knitzer, Z. Steinberg, and B. Fleisch, 1990, New York: Bank Street College of Education. Copyright 1990 by Bank Street College of Education. Adapted with permission.

Since 1980, the number of family groups that focus on the needs of students with emotional or behavioral disorders has increased dramatically (Johnson, 1993). Most of these groups emphasize the importance of legal and legislative action on behalf of the children. In addition, these groups provide support for individual families. The Federation of Families for Children's Mental Health is one highly successful national organization, cofounded by Barbara Huff, a mother, and Naomi Karp, a former special educator and current "advocrat" for the U.S. Department of Education.

The federation is dedicated to improving training, services, and policies that pertain to children with emotional, behavioral, or mental disorders (Karp, 1991). It refuses to regard families as dysfunctional and instead sees them as "experiencing normal reactions to the serious lack of appropriate, affordable, and accessible community-based services and supports available to them" (Karp, 1991). It emphasizes family strengths as the foundation upon which new supports can be provided. This support is family defined, comprehensive, and flexible. The organization has three goals for families: (a) to secure an appropriate education for their children in the community, (b) to secure mental health services for their children in the community, and (c) to secure supports for themselves in the community.

Jim Cain is quick to highlight that one of the factors that sustained him during the dark days of David's hospitalization was Keys for Networking, the Kansas state affiliate of the federation, and the support of Barbara Huff, its cofounder and charter executive director: "The most profound difference is that Barbara gave us hope. Until we found Barbara, we really didn't have hope. Almost all the professionals who ever worked with David had

"We make a difference on a one-on-one basis," reflects Barbara Huff. "The power of one should not be ignored."

BOX 5-9   INTO PRACTICE

HOW PARENTS AND PROFESSIONALS CAN WORK TOGETHER AS ADVOCATES

Advice for Professionals

- Work as partners with parents in advocacy efforts.
- Listen carefully to what parents tell you, and be open to new perspectives.
- Be candid about barriers to change.
- Be a resource to parents.
- Invest in the development of parents as advocates.
- Insist on family participation within your organization and in all meetings and task forces you attend.

Advice for Parents

- Recognize that professionals need support too.
- Acknowledge the constraints that professionals may face as advocates, especially those who work within the system.
- Be a resource for professionals.
- Foster a collaborative attitude within your organization. Do not engage in "professional bashing" without initiating positive action.

Note: From Friesen, B. J., & Huff, B. (1990). Parents and professionals as advocacy partners. *Preventing School Failure* *34*(3) 31–35. Reprinted with permission of the Helen Dwight Reid Educational Foundation. Published by Heldref Publications, 1319 Eighteenth Street NW, Washington, DC 20036-1802. © 1990.

given up on him. When we had our tough times, we would always go to Barbara and she would say, 'You can do it.'" Useful suggestions for encouraging professional–family collaboration and shared decision making are included in Box 5-9, "Into Practice."

Community Collaboration. As the concepts of community-based, comprehensive, individualized services become more prevalent throughout the United States, more students are living in their homes or returning from institutional care to live in their communities, many times with their own families (Burchard & Clarke, 1990). In Figure 5-9, Knoff (1990) offers ten guidelines for encouraging community involvement in the education and treatment of these children and youth.

Many practical ideas have grown from these guidelines. For example, some communities have developed late-night basketball programs as a strategy to keep youth off the streets. Other communities have centers that provide services such as latchkey programs and substance-abuse counseling.

Peer Collaboration. Students influence each other both positively and negatively with respect to academic achievement, values and attitudes, and social skills (Berndt, 1989). Unfortunately, the inappropriate social behaviors of many students with emotional or behavioral disorders often limit their positive peer interactions. In these cases, students often are placed in more restrictive settings; and those placements may, in turn, further restrict opportunities for them to learn and practice appropriate interpersonal skills (Knitzer, Steinberg, & Fleisch, 1990).

Fortunately, there are many ways to facilitate positive interactions, including peer tutoring, group meetings (Hobbs, 1982), counseling by resilient adolescents (Stuart, 1994), peer confrontation (Arllen, Gable, & Hendrickson, 1996), and group-oriented contingencies (e.g., everyone earns a party when the total number of points all student earn reaches a certain amount) (Barbetta, 1990). Other interventions emphasize both skill development

FIGURE 5–9 *Ten guide-lines for enhancing community involvement*

1. Respond to what people want for their children by understanding the conditions of family and community life.

2. Adopt an ecological perspective; that is, see the child in the context of the family and the family in the context of its social network and community environment.

3. Identify and capitalize on the strengths of children, families, and the community.

4. Promote a sense of community by fostering mutual aid, affiliation, and involvement in community life.

5. Promote empowerment by creating community processes that foster competence, control, and involvement.

6. Provide flexibility and diversity in programming as needed to adapt to community environments.

7. Coordinate with other groups and services to enhance the quality and continuity of programming.

8. Facilitate clients' [children's] access to other services.

9. Identify how institutions can adapt to provide optimal support to children and families.

10. Provide ongoing evaluation to identify and document the intended and unintended impacts on the child, family, social network, and community environment.

Note: From "Summarizing the Important Elements of Early Childhood Primary Prevention Programs for Emotional or Behavioral Problems," by H. M. Knoff, 1990, December, *Communiqué.* Copyright 1990 by the National Association of School Psychologists. Reprinted by permission of the publisher.

and the creation of environments in which students feel empowered (Rappaport, 1981) and in which they have opportunities for healthy psychosocial interactions (Zins, Conyne, & Ponti, 1988).

One such approach is called *peer mediation* (Schrumpf, 1994). Peer mediation involves the voluntary solving of differences among peers and takes place in the presence of trained peer mediators (Colucci, 1993). The process is summarized in Figure 5–10. Peer mediation can be initiated on a school-wide basis or within a single classroom (Schrumpf, 1994). Between six and twelve hours are needed for students to learn and practice the basic skills of mediation, and training materials for students in grades four through twelve are available (Sadalla, Holmberg, & Halligan, 1990; Schrumpf, Crawford, & Usadel, 1991). At some schools, all students are trained in conflict-resolution skills (D. Johnson, Johnson, Dudley, & Burnett, 1992), while at other schools, students volunteer or are nominated by teachers (Colucci, 1993). Mediators are taught the following (Schrumpf, 1994):

• To understand conflict, the goal of mediation, and the role of mediators

• To communicate effectively

• To understand the mediation process

Peer mediation reduces dropout rates (Millhause, 1989), suspensions (McDonald & Moriarty, 1990), and student assaults (Meek, 1992). Project SMART (Student Mediation and Resolution Teams) is a peer-mediation program in an urban Rhode Island junior high school (Colucci, 1993). In Project SMART, eleven of twenty-four mediators were English-as-a-second-language students, and eighteen were able to understand and speak another language. This was important due to the high percentage of English-as-a-second-language (35 percent) and bilingual (45 percent) students in the school's population. Preliminary evaluations indicate that Project SMART was successful on several levels, including a significant improvement in student perceptions of teacher treatment and opportunities for autonomy and a significant decrease in endorsing avoidance as a mediation tactic

Once students understand the process, peer mediation can occur informally to resolve disputes without adult intervention.

(Colucci, 1993). The accompanying box, "Collaboration Tips," (pages 210–211) describes strategies for making peer mediation work.

Careers

If you are interested in working with students who have emotional or behavioral disorders, you have many career options, including positions as a classroom teacher, counselor, therapist, behavior specialist, social worker, psychologist, or psychiatrist. There is a higher vacancy rate for teachers of students with emotional or behavioral disorders than for any other area of exceptionality (U.S. Department of Education, 1992). Alan Amtzis, a special educator, has worked for ten years in a program for adolescents and young adults with drug and alcohol problems. Many of his students have been identified as having emotional or behavioral disorders. He shares some of his experiences in Box 5-10, "My Voice" (page 212).

WHAT ARE PROGRAM OPTIONS?

Early Intervention and Preschool Years

The old adage, "It takes a whole village to raise a child," really needs to be changed, says Robin Hazel, director of the Lawrence, Kansas, school district's Parents as Teachers program.

"It takes a whole community to raise parents and parents to raise a child," is the way Robin puts it (crediting Chuck Smith, a professor at Kansas State University).

Step 1: OPEN THE SESSION

• Make introductions.

• State the ground rules.
  1. Mediators remain neutral.
  2. Everything said is confidential.
  3. No interruptions.
  4. Agree to solve the conflict.

• Get a commitment to the ground rules.

Step 2: GATHER INFORMATION

• Ask each person, "Please tell me what happened." (Listen and summarize.)

• Ask each person, "Do you want to add anything?" (Listen, summarize, and clarify with questions.)

• Repeat until the problem is understood. (Summarize.)

Step 3: FOCUS ON INTERESTS

• Determine interests; ask each person:
  "What do you really want?"
  "What might happen if you don't reach agreement?"
  "What do each of you have in common?" (Listen, summarize, and question.)

• Summarize shared interests:
  State what disputants have in common.

Step 4: CREATE OPTIONS

• Brainstorm a solution; ask disputants:
  "What could be done to resolve the problem?"

Step 5: EVALUATE OPTIONS—DECIDE ON A SOLUTION

• Choose a solution; ask each person:
  "Which of these options are you willing to do?"

• Restate: "You both agree to. . . ."

Step 6: WRITE AGREEMENT AND CLOSE

• Write the agreement and sign it.

• Shake hands.

FIGURE 5–10 *Peer mediation process summary*

Note: From "The Role of Students in Resolving Conflicts in Schools," by F. Schrumpf, in *Creativity and Collaborative Learning: A Practical Guide to Empowering Students and Teachers,* edited by J. S. Thousand, R. A. Villa, and A. I. Nevin, 1994, Baltimore, MD: Brookes. Copyright 1994 by Paul H. Brookes Publishing Company. Reprinted by permission of Paul H. Brookes Publishing Company, P.O. Box 10624, Baltimore, MD 21285-0624.

In Parents as Teachers, the whole village consists of the public schools, the local health, mental health agencies, child protective services, Even Start (family literacy), preschool, Part C/Interagency Coordinating Council (for infants and toddlers with disabilities), Head Start, and Women-Infants-Children (WIC) program. The parents are those who are as well off as the American dream can make them and those who are challenged economically and by their own disabilities or sheer youth. As Kim Wilson-Young, an early childhood specialist who is one of the teachers explains, "We are a non-targeted program." And the child is any baby or child under the age of three.

To Molly Day, a social worker and early educator in the program, "to raise a child" means to take powerfully preventive measures so the baby will not acquire a disability or experience anything that might exacerbate an existing disability.

Does your community provide early intervention services such as these for children at risk for emotional or behavioral disorders?

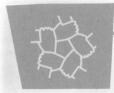

Collaboration Tips

INCORPORATING PEER MEDIATION

COLLABORATION GOAL   To team peers who can help the student with an emotional and behavioral disorder learn appropriate tools for problem solving and conflict resolution and the use of natural consequences for one's actions.

Collaborators	Roles and Preparation	Possible Barriers	Solutions to Barriers	Modifications to Implementation	Ongoing Evaluation
Student	Willingness to accept what peers suggest.	May not want peers involved in the dispute.	Give student a choice of presenting offense before a panel of peers or a panel of faculty.	Make sure all students have a chance to recommend peers who will serve. Voting form should include questions such as "Who do you trust?", "Who would you like to confide to about a problem?", and "Who do you admire?"	Follow up to determine effectiveness of peer mediation in changing the student's behavior or attitude.
Parents	Willingness to accept the decision of the peer mediators for their child.	May believe that peers should not be allowed to make these decisions for their child.	At the beginning of the year, parents need to be educated about the benefits of peer mediation for students.	Plans should be made for providing easy-to-read brochures or flyers about peer mediation to parents. Parent-teacher meetings and conferences also provide opportunities for educating parents.	Ask parents for feedback on peer mediation process during conferences.
General Educator(s)	Need to help students understand the peer mediation process.	May not want to take class time to provide this instruction.	Administrator or special educator needs to clarify how this process could improve behavior, resulting in more instructional time; have a school-wide assembly rather than asking teachers to explain the process individually.	Ask participants from another school to share the benefits of peer mediation at a faculty meeting.	At the end of the year, general educators should complete an evaluation form about the peer mediation process.

Collaborators	Roles and Preparation	Possible Barriers	Solutions to Barriers	Modifications to Implementation	Ongoing Evaluation
Special educator(s)	Willingness to help train peer mediators about IDEA discipline regulations.	Peers might misinterpret this training as suggesting that they should "go easy" on students with disabilities.	Explicitly state that students with disabilities should not receive lesser consequences, but that they, like each student, need to have an appropriate consequence that considers all information.	Special educator also needs to explain the peer mediation process to students in special education classes at the beginning of the school year.	Special educator needs to keep records of peer mediation sessions of students with disabilities as well as their effectiveness for behavior change.
Administrator	Need to value the peer mediation process and be willing to help organize the process.	May believe that it is more efficient and effective for administration and faculty to handle offenses.	Special educator and/or counselor need(s) to provide administrator with research on the effectiveness of peer mediation.	Ask an administrator from another school that is using peer mediation effectively to talk to the administrator.	Ask the administrators to complete an evaluation form on the effectiveness of peer mediation and suggestions for improving the process.
School counselor	Provide training to peer mediators.	May not have adequate background in peer mediation.	Encourage the school district to pay for the counselor's training.	Encourage a well-respected student with leadership ability to attend the training with the counselor, if possible.	Counselor needs to coordinate evaluation of the effectiveness of peer mediation.
Peers	Openness to working with other on the panel to determine a reasonable consequence for a behavior.	May not know how to determine a "reasonable" consequence.	Train peer mediators in problem solving, conflict resolution, and use of natural consequences; make sure role playing is part of the training.	Provide this training to all students, not just peer mediators, to help prevent misbehavior by students.	Have peer mediators complete an evaluation form periodicaly that asks what they think about the process and if they have benefited from participating.

BOX 5-10   MY VOICE

ALAN AMTZIS

As a teacher, Alan Amtzis finds that making learning as relevant as possible to his students is a real key to helping them reconnect to the world.

"Let's begin by answering six basic questions: who, what, when, where, why, and how." As I have used this format on so many occasions with my students, so will I use it to tell you about my career as a special education teacher.

Who? I'm Alan Amtzis. I'm forty-two, and I've been teaching for ten years. I came to teaching a little later than most professionals. I began substitute teaching in inner-city high schools in New York City, mostly to supplement my income while trying to make it in the business (show business, that is). I never expected to like teaching, much less make a career of it. Nevertheless, I found myself wanting to work with the most "impossible" students.

What? Now I'm a certified special education teacher. I returned to school and got a master's degree.

Where? I work in a residential, therapeutic, drug-treatment community, more commonly known as a TC. Our TC is a highly structured, peer-managed environment. Our residents participate in a rigorous program of introspection, self-disclosure, and accountability. The program has graduated levels of responsibility and privileges. Successful movement through treatment levels helps the residents discover, understand, and change the issues and behaviors underlying their flight into addiction. Treatment lasts anywhere from eight months to two years.

My primary role at the TC is as a teacher of the basic skills classes for residents who need remedial work. I also

work very closely with other members of our multidisciplinary team to increase the likelihood of my students' conquering their drug and alcohol problems.

When? The program is in operation twelve months a year—all day, every day, or "24–7–365" (24 hours a day, 7 days a week, 365 days a year) as my students would say in the jargon that has become a codified part of the TC experience. The jargon is referred to as "data." Want to learn more? A "belly" is an instinctual reaction; "run a wire" means to divulge confidential information; and "drop guilt" means to confess to a wrongdoing. I have heard entire students' conversations that no outsider could reasonably be expected to understand. To my benefit, however, this esoteric dialect makes it rather easy to teach poetry, as my students already possess a built-in understanding of figurative language.

Why? Because I love it. Because I can. As teachers, we all try to find a place where we can make the most difference—a place where who we are matters most: that is, has a maximum effect. In a surprising way, what makes it easier to work in a TC with students who are chemically dependent instead of in many schools is that the motivation to learn is here and the drugs aren't. My students aren't high. This way I work with my students, not the drugs. Of course, a critical part of our program is providing them with the skills needed to stay away from drugs when they return to their communities.

How? This is the trickiest part of my job. When you teach eighteen-year-old students who once had $300-a-day cocaine habits, your approach needs to be a bit different. My students bring with them a sense of urgency—not an urgency to obtain knowledge but an urgency to learn information that can apply to their real-life situations. It's important for them to see how they fit into the big picture. For example, they need to see how the revolution of the Earth impacts them by making it warm in the summer and cold in the winter; to see that history is not just a list of dates but a river of human drama that flowed before them, flows around them, and will certainly flow after them.

I've been relatively successful with this approach. Perhaps it works because it hooks directly into one of the underlying roots of substance abuse: the absence of a strong connection between self and environment. Kids on drugs disconnect from their environments. In many cases, their environments become very small: just themselves and their drugs. I believe they want to reconnect; they just don't know how. I want them to see how they are a part of the big picture, a very important part.

Alan Amtzis
Teacher, Daytop Village Secondary School,
Rhinebeck, New York
Contributed by Patricia M. Barbetta, Florida
International University

With nearly 100 families being served in just one term of an academic year and another 100 waiting for services, Parents as Teachers is a valued addition to this university town. All parents benefit from home visits; it's the best way to observe them and their babies together, to brainstorm about problems in child raising, and to let them have research-based information about child development. Those parents who are still in high school and those who have their own disabilities can expect a visit every month; other parents get a visit every six to eight weeks. But all get the same curriculum on child development, the same passed-on tips from other parents about raising babies, the same information and referral to other agencies for specialized services, and the same philosophy . . . one of "empowerment."

Empowerment means that Parents as Teachers simply helps the parents use the skills they already had. "We don't do for them but with them," says Robin. Molly explains empowerment this way: "We help them uncover the answers to their questions." To Molly, empowerment adopts a strengths perspective. Kim explains, "We try to motivate them and give them information and skills," says Kim, "but so often we don't have to do anything except reinforce what they already are doing. Sometimes, we have to do more, but we try to be subtle about it."

It's not always possible to motivate and provide skills, subtly or otherwise. Sometimes, parents simply neglect their babies, putting them at risk for physical or emotional damage. That's when Parents as Teachers has to move from positive prevention—information, motivation, referrals—to an intervention posture, one that usually is "very painful," Robin points out.

Sometimes, Robin acknowledges, reality flies in the face of the program's philosophy. "We believe that all parents want to be good parents. We hold that they are the experts on their babies. We are just the generalists about child development. We regard ourselves as parents' partners. We don't do for them, but with them. The parents are a baby's first and foremost teachers. But at-risk situations can occur in any family—those with two working parents and those with a single mom."

When program staff have to report parents, it is heartbreakingly hard. But the program philosophy never never yields. Why? In part because of the data on the effectiveness of Parents as Teachers. Robin is quick to point out that those parents who have been in the program are more likely to stay active in their child's schooling and the child is more likely to be successful in school.

And sometimes, says Molly, it is absolutely maddening. What with the local school budget being cut, the long waiting list, and the agency's nontargeting policy, some babies and their families will simply go without. "There is a perception," says Molly, "that social programs should help only the desperately needy." That is shortsighted for, as Robin, Kim, and Molly can attest, risks can occur in any family.

Elementary Years

Providing students with emotional or behavioral disorders and their families with services should not end with the IFSP provided during the preschool years. These families need ongoing support. Here's what one parent says about the changes she's seen in her child after the family received services:

> My son faced long-term residential placement following two years of psychiatric hospitalization. Now I watch him from my door as he boards a bus every morning for a day school. We are now working on plans to integrate him into our neighborhood school. (La Grange Area Department of Special Education, 1993)

These encouraging words came from the mother of a child involved in a school-based wraparound project in La Grange, Illinois. The goal of a wraparound approach is to keep children included in their homes, schools, and communities by creating an individualized network of support around the child and family in their natural environments (Eber, Nelson, & Miles, 1997, 1993).

The types of services that are wrapped around each child and his or her family depend on the child's strengths and needs. They may include behavior-management planning, in-home counseling, case management, parent-advocacy training, or other services needed by student and family. Money for clubs, sports, special lessons, or basic family needs is available through interagency networking. Wraparound programs use funds already allocated to education, social services, and mental health agencies and redirect these existing funds to meet individual needs rather than to place children into program slots.

The LADSE EBD Network began as a grant-funded project that initiated partnerships with parents and mental health and social service agencies. This wraparound project (1991–1996) organized a WRAP coordinating council consisting of key policymakers and service providers from state and local agencies as well as parents and private providers. The council grew into a Local Area Network (LAN), which continues to work on changing policy and funding and coordinating interagency wraparound plans.

> The essence of the wraparound process is collaboration: The team looks comprehensively at all aspects of the family's needs and at school needs, all as part of addressing the needs of students such as Jen.

School-Based Wraparound Teams.

Beginning in 1993, LADSE restructured their K–8 EBD program to the current EBD Network, which applies wraparound approaches to all students identified with EBD who need special education. This has increased the number of LADSE students with EBD who are successfully included in general education classrooms (Eber, 1996; Eber, Nelson, & Miles, 1997).

Support services may include classroom-based support such as team teaching as well as behavioral interventions, crisis intervention support, in-school respite services, integration of mental health services at school sites, and peer support programs. Special education teachers function as wraparound facilitators, consultants, and co-teachers to help successfully include these students in general education classroom.

Parent Partners.

Parents of children and youth with emotional or behavioral disorders are hired and trained to provide support and guidance to other parents dealing with similar challenges. Support is available when parents are having a difficult time with their child or when they need guidance in working more successfully with service providers. This program has led to lasting support networks and friendships among parents.

The Buddy Program.

Buddies are people ages seventeen to thirty who are recruited to be friends and provide social and recreational opportunities for designated children. They include young adults without disabilities as well as at-risk students and students with emotional or behavioral disorders. Buddies are trained to provide support through social activities, academic assistance, or one-on-one relationships. Not only are buddies tremendously important to children and youth, they are a strong support for parents.

John Thompson, a young man who is currently studying to be a special educator, was a buddy in LADSE's program. He comments:

> *I quickly learned that becoming a buddy was easy, but that at times being a buddy could be a challenge. . . . Marcus and I both got a lot out of the buddy program. He learned how to channel some of his energy positively. . . . And I really enjoyed watching his progress. The most important thing that we both got out of the program was a new friend.*

Middle and Secondary Years

Is it possible to educate students with very serious emotional or behavioral disorders in an inclusive secondary setting? For students in a rural southeast Kansas school district, the answer is "yes." The reasons why inclusion is possible are not mysterious. For one thing, the superintendent, Jim Cain, is the adoptive father of such a student; he has imbued the district's faculty with a fervor for inclusion and collaboration. In addition, many people who worked with Jim's son, David, learned that, in the words of the anthropologist Margaret Mead, the world can indeed be changed through the efforts of a small group of committed people.

🖤 *Having a buddy can make a difference in the life of a student with emotional or behavioral disorders.*

After many unsuccessful school and hospital placements, David entered his freshman year faced with a bleak future. More than anything, he wanted to play varsity football at Williamsburg High School. Jim saw David's desire as the key to inclusion—if only the school faculty and others would collaborate with each other and David.

David began to transition out of a state hospital in August, spending every other night at home and starting football practice on his home-visitation evenings. As part of his transition and a community-support plan, the local mental health center hired a special education paraprofessional, Bart, to support David in football practice and games. Bart was regarded by everyone as an assistant coach, so his support for David did not set him apart. If David started getting out of control or showing any signs that were not appropriate, Bart would say, "David, you need to come with me. We're going to work on some blocking drills."

During David's first week in school, he had to leave eight times during each practice; by the fourth week of practice, he had to leave practice only once. By the end of the season, David never had to leave. Making the team was David's ticket to self-esteem. Starting football in August also meant that he had friends by the time school started, and David had never had friends before. Bart spent about fifteen hours a week with David, which cost the mental health center about $100 a week. As Jim had said so often, "Give me just half of what hospitalization costs, and we can do twice as well."

At an in-service training for all the high school faculty, which was conducted by hospital staff, Jim explained that the best thing that teachers can do to help David is to be nonconfrontational. For example, imagine that David is in class and begins to cause a disruption. The best thing to say is "David, you're not allowed to talk, and you have two options. You can stop talking in class; or if you need to, you can leave the class and go to the counselor's office and talk to him." Teachers need to give options, and each option has to help David make constructive choices. Power is important to him, and allowing him to make a choice gives him power. As Jim observes, power is important to all people.

As soon as David walked into school in the morning, the school counselor, Stan Lantis, checked with him to determine his mood. He might decide that everything seems to be moving in a positive direction and that David needs very little support. He might, however, immediately contact Bart and suggest that he stick close to David during the first several periods and then make a decision about the rest of the day. Bart then stayed in David's classroom, but he tried to not draw too much attention to David or himself.

David's class schedule was applied math, English, basic biology, vocational agriculture, health, and woodworking. At the Williamsburg High School, three staff members who were special education teachers worked in a single room and shared it with a skills lab that had a teacher and a paraprofessional. These five people worked with whoever walked in the door. The district was not interested in labeling students, only in improving individualized support for them. David could get help on the days he needed it; so could other students. Flexibility is the key in responding to him as well as to everyone else.

There was also an itinerant resource teacher specializing in emotional or behavioral disorders who worked with three different schools. Her role was not to be David's teacher but to serve as a resource in helping his teachers and parents devise strategies to handle challenging situations.

In addition, David had a companion, Darnell Johnson (paid for by the mental health agency), to support him several afternoons a week. Darnell had been a basketball player in college, and he and David had many similar interests. Because of David's respect for him, Darnell could get David to do things when no one else could. Darnell did lots of therapy while they played basketball, bowled, or just cruised around town in Darnell's sports car. "What these kids with emotional or behavioral disorders need is a friend who becomes a source of help, connecting them to friends and places in their community so that they feel good about themselves," explained Jim.

The high school faculty involved with David, Bart, Darnell, and Jim met on a fairly regular basis to say what was going well, what was not going well, and where they needed to make changes. Usually there was a group of about ten. The key is to act promptly when there is a problem: assess it, figure out how to handle it, and take care of it.

Although David is no longer in school, the program he inspired still exists. The school board has promoted an experienced principal to be an assistant superintendent and given her two basic jobs: to work with the fifteen or so students with severe emotional disabilities so that they have individualized wraparound services in inclusive settings, such as David had; and to mentor new teachers so that they will be effective participants in the Cain program.

As Jim Cain looks back on what he and David started, he admits it was novel, even radical. Four years later, however, it has become the "normal way of educating students, so routine that it is not at all out of the ordinary." Tomorrow, however, may be more problematic. Budget crunches threaten such a labor-intensive program, and a backlash against students with disabilities seems to be underway among some members of the community. "What people don't understand," Jim laments, "is that today's investment in these students can pay long-term dividends for everyone."

Transitional and Postsecondary Years

If you were to look at the data describing the relatively dismal outcomes of special education for students with emotional disabilities, you would become discouraged. More students with emotional disabilities drop out, do not go to college or technical school, and experience unemployment or (if employed) experience frequent job turnover and menial and lower paying jobs than other students with disabilities (Bullis & Paris, 1996).

Many of them are like Sarah (Bullis & Paris, 1996). At the age of seventeen, Sarah was in special education, classified as having serious emotional disabilities. She tested at a full-scale IQ of 80, had neurological deficits and seizure disorders, took two different medicines for the seizure disorder, and engaged in mild forms of self-abuse (picking at her skin). While she was fifteen and sixteen, she had lived in a group home and had cycled in and out of various part-time jobs. What was Sarah's future; what is the future of people with similar needs? The data alone would lead you to conclude that her future is dim. That would not be an entirely correct conclusion. Underlying the data are hope and help in concrete form.

Recognizing that public schools are the "last concentrated service delivery effort" but that the schools alone cannot secure the desired outcomes of independence, productivity, and integration, Jobs Design, a nonprofit agency in western Oregon, has adopted a philosophy that is explicitly based on self-determination (Bullis & Paris, 1996). Sarah and others with disabilities are centrally involved in planning their own service program by identifying their strengths and interest, being responsible to the maximum extent possible for securing work and social services, and making decisions about their lives after they leave Jobs Design. Given that Sarah had bounced from one job to another and then to yet another, it was important for her to declare that she wanted to work in a restaurant and for Jobs Design to act on that preference.

Beyond philosophy, Jobs Design helps through systematic action. To get to know about Sarah and others, its service coordination specialists assemble a comprehensive set of information. This profile includes the student's emotional and behavioral characteristics, vocational and life goals and interests, and current agency and family assistance. There is only one purpose to the information: to secure appropriate work and necessary supports at and outside of the job.

With this information, Sarah, assisted by her family and friends and Jobs Design's service coordinator, then plans what support she needs. Like many other students with her disability, the support includes services from vocational, postsecondary, recreational, medical, mental health, and housing agencies. Sarah, again assisted by her informal support network and her service coordinator, then is responsible for securing these services. Learning to interact effectively with other adults and with service providers helps Sarah learn the skills she needs to adjust to life after school. There is no mystery about the key to a successful coordinated service network. It is a positive personal relationship with individuals in the service agencies. Knowing how to develop those kinds of relationships is, in every respect, a survival skill for students.

Because most people with disabilities locate, keep, and advance in their jobs through help from a network of family and friends, and because most of them get and stay in those jobs when they are doing the kind of work they want, Sarah's networks and her preferences become the points of her entry into the workplace.

Networks and preferences are important, but so too are skills. Like other students, Sarah needs training to do the job, and she needs on-the-job support. So, the service coordination specialists become her teachers (before Sarah gets her job) and her mentors (once she has it). They help her solve such problems as Sarah's inattention to personal hygiene and her candid and sometimes inappropriate discussions with co-workers and restaurant customers about her mental and physical health. The amount of time and the issues around which the specialists are teachers and mentors depends entirely on what Sarah and other Jobs Design clients need and on what the employer needs.

Did Jobs Design benefit Sarah, as it has benefitted other students? The answer is "yes." Having entered the Jobs Design program at the age of seventeen, she obtained a job in a pizza restaurant, held it for two years, and graduated from high school at the age of twenty. So far, one would have evaluated her and Jobs Design as successful. But, that's only to the point of graduation.

Upon graduation, however, Sarah gradually reverted to her preemployment behaviors. She feigned seizures, fought with her family, missed appointments at the local mental health agency, threatened suicide, and finally was admitted to a psychiatric hospital for evaluation and treatment. Within about three months, she left the hospital for a group home and two part-time paid jobs.

With support from Jobs Design, Sarah holds those jobs successfully, has a stronger system of interagency support than during her last year in high school, and is beginning to make friends in her community. For her, self-determination, coupled with a system of personal supports on the job and in the community, have been the antidotes to the dismal data on postschool outcomes for students with emotional disabilities. Hope and help. It sounds simple enough, but help has to be provided over a long period of time: in Sarah's case, a three-year period, interrupted but not totally derailed by a recurrence of crises related to her disability and the necessary hospitalization.

A VISION FOR THE FUTURE

Jen's life has changed for the better. Her future is much more hopeful than it was before her involvement with LADSE. For example, Jen has rebuilt relationships with the faculty and staff at Highlands Middle School. She has learned to "bite her tongue" and listen instead of argue. She is taking responsibility for complying with rules, handling anger appropriately, keeping up with school assignments, and taking the initiative to ask for extra help after school when she needs it.

Jen was able to return to Highlands by the beginning of the next semester. She was even up for the challenge of leaving her special education teachers and returning to Highlands School, knowing that she would always be able to count on the support of such wraparound team members.

Jen's wraparound team has great expectations for Jen. They see Jen as organized, artistic, and creative and envision the day when Jen will no longer need LADSE's support. Jen's parents hope that Jen will become involved in the arts because she has a lot of talent in that area, but want her to do whatever will make her happy. They demonstrate confidence that Jen can reach whatever goals she sets for herself, saying, "If she's focused in a certain direction, she's going to go all the way," graduating and then going to college. This vision for Jen's future is certainly possible.

We close this chapter with our vision for you—that you will find the hope, the good, the potential in all your future students with emotional or behavioral disorders. We need to "wage peace" in the lives of our students (Lantieri & Patti, 1996). Robert Kennedy (quoted in Lantieri & Patti, 1996, p. 46) said:

> *Each time one stands up for an ideal, or acts to improve the lot of the rest, or strikes out against injustice, one sends forth a ripple of hope, and crossing each other from a million different centers of energy and daring, those ripples build a current that can sweep down the mightiest walls of oppression and resistance.*

What Would You Recommend?

1. To help Jen make the transition to full-time placement at Highlands School? If you were her general educator, how would you facilitate her inclusion in your classroom?

2. To help Jen begin thinking about a vocation that matches her strengths?

3. To "send forth ripples of hope" to students like Jen with emotional or behavioral disorders?

SUMMARY

WHAT ARE EMOTIONAL OR BEHAVIORAL DISORDERS?

• Students with emotional or behavioral disorders are those whose behavior and adjustment problems are chronic and severe and adversely affect their lives.

• Numerous definitions of emotional or behavioral disorders have been proposed over the years, but no single definition is universally embraced.

• Students may exhibit emotional disorders, including, but not limited to, anxiety disorder, major depression, bipolar disorder, oppositional-defiant disorder, conduct disorder, eating disorders, or schizophrenia.

• There are two broad categories of emotional or behavioral disorders: externalizing (aggressive, acting-out, anti-social behaviors) and internalizing (withdrawn, fearful, anxious, depressed, or lacking in social competence). Many children identified as having emotional or behavioral disorders do not exclusively fall into one of these two categories.

• Most students with emotional or behavioral disorders have academic problems.

• Given the subjective nature of what constitutes emotional or behavioral disorders, prevalence estimates vary considerably from 3 to 5 percent. However, only about 1 percent are identified. Emotional or behavioral disorders is the fourth largest category in special education.

• We can seldom determine with absolute confidence why these students behave as they do, and rarely can we find one determining factor.

• Biological causes include genetics and biological insults. Medications can play an important role in their treatment.

• Parents need to realize that emotional or behavioral disorders are generally nobody's fault.

• Environmental causes include living conditions and child abuse.

WHAT ARE EVALUATION PROCEDURES?

• A checklist of internalizing and externalizing behaviors can be useful for teachers to use to decide which students in their classes might need to be evaluated for emotional or behavioral disorders.

• Direct observations of student behavior (systemically watching and recording student behavior using structured recording sheets) allows professionals to obtain specific information regarding a student's behavior.

• Applied behavior analysis allows professionals to monitor student performance toward achieving specific objectives.

WHAT AND HOW DO PROFESSIONALS TEACH?

• Curriculum needs to reflect the interests of students and guarantee success initially.

• The PATHS curriculum teaches students respect and responsibility through three phases: emotional recognition and communication, self-control, and social problem solving.

• Restoring hope, encouraging a productive self-concept, setting limits, listening, and taking care of yourself are important methods for helping students change.

HOW IS PARTICIPATION ENCOURAGED?

• Differing perspectives exist on the most appropriate place to educate these students.

• Once identified as having emotional or behavioral disorders, most students are educated in self-contained special education classrooms.

• Many students with emotional or behavior disorders require multiple services that involve several disciplines, including education, mental health, public welfare, and the juvenile justice system.

- Working with families is a critical part of work with students who have emotional or behavioral disorders.

- Peer mediation involves the voluntary resolution of differences between peers in the presence of trained peer mediators.

- There are many career options for working with students with emotional or behavioral disorders, including positions as classroom teacher, counselor, therapist, behavior specialist, social worker, psychologist, or psychiatrist.

WHAT ARE PROGRAM OPTIONS?

- The Parents as Teachers program helps the parents use the skills they already had by providing support and helping them uncover the answers to their questions.

- LASDE's wraparound process is an innovative inclusion approach for students with emotional or behavioral disorders and their families. The goal of a wraparound approach is to keep students in their community schools and keep their families together by "wrapping" needed services around them.

- The creative and flexible use of available personnel has been effective in meeting the needs of students with serious behavior problems in inclusive secondary settings.

- Jobs Design helps young adults through a systematic action approach to meeting individuals needs.

RESOURCES

BOOKS

Characteristics of Emotional and Behavioral Disorders of Children and Youth. (1993). By J. M. Kauffman. New York: Macmillan. In-depth information about students with emotional or behavioral disorders.

How to Achieve Discipline With Dignity in the Schools. (1992). By A. N. Mendler. Bloomington, IN: National Education Service. Provides methods for discipline and conflict resolution.

Reclaiming Youth at Risk: Our Hope for the Future. (1990). By L. K. Brendtro, M. Brokenleg, and S. Van Bockern. Bloomington, IN: National Education Service. How to encourage a productive self-concept in students.

Teaching Self-Control: A Curriculum for Responsible Behavior. (1997). By M. Henley. Bloomington, IN: National Education Service. Sequential skills needed by students to help them control impulses, follow school routines, manage group situations, manage stress, and solve social problems.

Working With Behavioral Disorders: Mini Library. (1991). Reston, VA: Council for Exceptional Children. A set of nine booklets designed to help practitioners understand the problems of children with emotional or behavioral disorders.

JOURNALS, MAGAZINES, AND CATALOGS

Behavioral Disorders. Council for Children with Behavior Disorders (CCBD), Council for Exceptional Children, 1920 Association Drive, Reston, VA 22091-1589. Quarterly journal for professionals in the field of emotional or behavioral disorders. Sent to all CCBD members.

Beyond Behavior. Council for Children with Behavior Disorders (CCBD), Council for Exceptional Children, 1920 Association Drive, Reston, VA 22091-1589. Follows an easy-to-read magazine format that includes editorials, in-depth feature articles, and reviews. Sent to all CCBD members.

Claiming Children. Federation of Families for Children's Mental Health, National Mental Health Association, 1021 Prince Street, Alexandria, VA 22314-2971. Newsletter provides parents and professionals with up-to-date information relating to the education and treatment of children with emotional, behavioral, or mental disorders and their families.

Journal of Emotional and Behavioral Disorders. Pro-Ed, 8700 Shoal Creek Boulevard, Austin, TX 78757-6897. This multidisciplinary journal publishes quarterly articles on research, practice, and theory.

Reaching Today's Youth: The Community Circle of Caring Journal. 1252 Loesch Road, P.O. Box 8. Bloomington, IN 47402-0008. Thematic journal based on a philosophy of hope and caring.

MULTIMEDIA

Dealing with Anger: A Violence Prevention Program for African American Youth. Research Press Books and Video Programs, Dept. G., Box 9177, Champaign, IL 61826. (217) 352-3273. A unique video-based training program designed to reduce the number of African-American youths who become victims or perpetrators of violence.

Discipline Diagnostician. Exceptional Innovations, P.O. Box 6085, Ann Arbor, MI 48106. (419) 536-8560. Provides suggestions for helping students overcome specific behavior problems.

Kids Talk to Kids About Drugs. Films for Humanities and Sciences, P.O. Box 2053, Princeton, NJ 08543. (800) 257-5126. Inner-city kids describe their experiences living in an urban drug culture. They talk about how to say no in the face of overwhelming pressure.

Language Experience Recorder. Teacher Support Software, 1035 Northwest Fifty-seventh Street, Gainesville, FL 32605-4486. Helps students tell and write stories.

Learning to Cope With Pressure. Sunburst Communications, 39 Washington Avenue, Pleasantville, NY 10570. Biofeedback program for stress management.

Obsessive-Compulsive Disorder: The Boy Who Couldn't Stop Washing. Films for Humanities and Sciences, P.O. Box 2053, Princeton, NJ 08543. (800) 257-5126. An expert examines obsessive-compulsive behavior, symptoms, diagnosis, and treatments.

Parent Perspectives: Raising Children With Emotional Disorders. PACER Center, 4826 Chicago Avenue South, Minneapolis, MN 55417. (612) 827-2966. Several parents discuss their views of what they and their children need from professionals.

SHERI. Performance Monitoring Systems, P.O. Box 148, Cambridge, MN 55008. (612) 690-2688. Monitors student behavior or academic performance.

Teenage Depression. Films for Humanities and Sciences, P.O. Box 2053, Princeton, NJ 08543. (800) 257-5126. A nineteen-minute film that examines the common symptoms of depression and the threat of suicide. Evidence for probable causes are presented, including biological and environmental factors.

Teenage Suicide. Films for Humanities and Sciences, P.O. Box 2053, Princeton, NJ 08543. (800) 257-5126. A nineteen-minute film that examines the reasons for why teens commit suicide and reasons for recent increases in adolescent suicide rates. Describes behavior patterns that are warning signals for families and friends.

Tom Snyder Productions. 80 Coolidge Hill Road, Watertown, MA 02172-2817. (800) 342-0236. Catalog contains software that emphasizes student communication on topics such as making choices, conflict resolution, media ethics, prejudice, and substance abuse.

What Parents Want From Professionals. University of Connecticut, School of Social Work, 1798 Asylum Avenue, West Hartford, CT 06117. (203) 241-4776. Two fifty-minute segments. In the first one, the parent of a young person with schizophrenia talks about the experiences of his family and instructs professionals about the way to help persons with mental illness and their families.

The following videos are available at local rental and retail stores:

The Best Little Girl in the World. (1981, not rated, U.S., color, 100 minutes). An adolescent copes with anorexia nervosa.

David and Lisa. (1963, not rated, U.S., B & W, 94 minutes). Chronicles the life and treatment of two teenagers with emotional and behavioral disorders.

Dead Poet's Society. (1989, PG, U.S., color, 128 minutes). An outstanding student at a prep school has conflict with his father, struggles with depression, and eventually commits suicide.

I Never Promised You a Rose Garden. (1977, R, U.S., 96 minutes). A teenager struggles with schizophrenia.

Ordinary People. (1980, R, U.S., color, 123 minutes). An adolescent who becomes suicidal after his brother drowns is counselled by an excellent therapist. Family and peer interactions are insightfully portrayed.

ON-LINE INFORMATION AND USEFUL DATABASES

Children's Mental Health. Internet address: http://www.mentalhealth.org./INDEX.HTM. Provides description of various conditions and related matters.

Facts for Families. Internet address: http://www.aacap.org/factsfam/. Psychiatric and health information.

ORGANIZATIONS

Council for Children with Behavioral Disorders. c/o Council for Exceptional Children, 1920 Association Drive, Reston, VA 22091-1589. Organization of professionals dedicated to the education and treatment of children and youth with emotional or behavioral disorders.

Federation of Families for Children's Mental Health. c/o National Mental Health Association, 1021 Prince Street, Alexandria, VA 22314-2971. A national parent-run organization focused on the needs of children and youth with emotional, behavioral, or mental disorders and their families.

National Association of Mental Health. 1800 North Kent Street, Rosslyn Station, Arlington, VA 22209. The national office refers individuals to local affiliations, directs research programs and a public information program, and acts as a liaison with governmental and private organizations. Also a source of information on both public and private mental health facilities.

ATTENTION-DEFICIT/ HYPERACTIVITY DISORDER

Educating
Taylor Wiggand

Two parents, nine kids, two dogs, one rabbit, eight cats, and a donkey—that's the Wiggand household! Ten-year-old Taylor, a fifth grader at a rural elementary school in Ohio, is sandwiched in the middle of this contemporary Brady Bunch. The good news about having so many people in the family, say his parents, Wayne and Suellyn, is that the whole family works together to help Taylor learn how to handle his hyperactive behavior and inability to concentrate on one activity very long.

Wayne and Sue recognized early on that Taylor's behavior differed from the typical behavior of their other birth children. Initially, they tried to attribute his hyperactive behavior to being an unusually active child who wanted to know how everything worked. However, Wayne and Sue couldn't ignore the gnawing feeling that Taylor shared characteristics with a few of the 100 foster children they had cared for over the last 27 years—those who had attention-deficit/hyperactivity disorder (AD/HD).

Their suspicions were confirmed when Taylor started school. His first-grade teacher expressed concern to the Wiggands that Taylor had difficulty

completing his work and paying attention. Although she assigned Taylor a tutor who helped him learn to read, many of Taylor's skills still lagged behind those of his peers. His teacher recommended that Taylor be retained in first grade because of his immaturity (a common characteristic in children with AD/HD).

Although Taylor was young for his class, Wayne and Suellyn didn't want him retained, because "he's a good-size boy and very bright." Instead, they proposed hiring a tutor during the summer and reevaluating the retention issue before school started in the fall.

The school agreed, and Linda Montgomery tutored him. "I became confident that Taylor was well within the range of competence in reading and math for his grade level," Linda says. "However, I also observed that Taylor's attention span was limited to about five minutes." Because she, too, suspected that Taylor might have AD/HD, she recommended having Taylor's pediatrician, Dr. David Dowdy, evaluate him. Suellyn described Taylor's characteristics to him:

> *It's sort of like Taylor's in another world sometimes, like he's not paying attention to you. He has some friends, but he goes off by himself a lot where it's quiet. He is impatient, however, and his hyperactivity sometimes comes out in anger. He just wants to do so much.*

After a series of tests and parent conferences, Taylor's pediatrician confirmed the diagnosis of AD/HD. He began to work with Taylor to find an appropriate medication and dosage to treat the condition. When the school learned the results of the tutoring and pediatrician's evaluation, they moved Taylor on to second grade.

Becky Swickard, Taylor's second-grade teacher, worked diligently with Taylor that year:

> *At the beginning of the year, Taylor had real difficulty focusing in on anything I presented to the entire group. When I finished teaching a new concept, I took Taylor back to the table to work with him one-on-one. I had to list the steps in a very specific way for him to understand. If I did that, he could learn the information.*

When Taylor was put on Ritalin, it wasn't a miracle, but he could get things easier from whole group instruction. I still needed to teach him one-on-one sometimes, but not nearly as often. After he began the medication, Taylor could get his work down on paper.

Taylor is now in the fifth grade and, with the polish of accommodated instruction as well as the benefits of medication, his strengths now shine brightly. His teacher, Beverly Thompson, says:

Taylor is very friendly and enjoys helping other people. He's also very observant and creative. One time I asked him if he had finished an experiment already. He said yes because he had figured out a different way to do it. It was very exciting. Taylor had thought of a way to do the experiment that I had not even thought of!

Beverly adds, "Taylor has such a positive attitude. Somebody might say to him, 'You can't do something.' But he will say, 'Yes, I can!'"

Beverly is not the only one who regards Taylor as especially insightful. Suellyn relishes his strengths:

He's so deep; such a thinker. He picks things apart and comes up with ideas others don't seem to recognize or think about. Once when my microwave quit working, Taylor suggested unplugging it and plugging it back in again to see if it would recalibrate itself. Wayne and I were ready to buy a new microwave, but Taylor's idea worked!

Wayne notes:

He's just an outstanding little kid to me. Taylor is caring for other people and especially for animals. He's real pleasant to be around most of the time, unless he's a little short on medicine!

And Taylor thinks of himself in rather typical ways: Swimming, playing football and basketball or having skating parties with his family, helping at church, reading, and playing with animals are his favorite pastimes.

What will the future hold for Taylor? Clearly, monitoring his medication is part of it. Suellyn puts it well: "I'm glad the school is accommodating his needs for now. I wonder if we hadn't known about the existence of AD/HD if Taylor would have fallen between the cracks. I still worry about what the future holds when he goes to junior high and high school."

What Do You Think?

1. How does the controversy over attention-deficit/hyperactivity disorder (AD/HD) affect students like Taylor?

2. Is there more than one type of AD/HD? If so, what type does Taylor have?

3. How is the use of medication warranted for students like Taylor?

4. How can you provide accommodations for students like Taylor so they receive an appropriate education in your classroom?

What Is Attention-Deficit/Hyperactivity Disorder?

Attention-deficit/hyperactivity disorder (AD/HD), "continues to gain ground as the label *du jour* in American education," writes Armstrong (1996, p. 428). "It's time to take stock of this 'disorder' and decide whether it really exists or is instead more of a manifestation of society's need to have such a disorder."

The controversy over AD/HD, the most commonly diagnosed childhood psychiatric disorder (Lang, 1996), is rampant in professional journals and the popular press alike. Critics cite concerns over the dramatic increase in identification of individuals with AD/HD as well as the use of **psychotropic medication** such as Ritalin to treat the condition.

For example, Machan (1996) calls AD/HD "an agreeable affliction" that results in diagnosed children being "fed Ritalin," a stimulant that "can produce a powerful euphoric rush. . . . But that's only petty cash," continues Machan. "The bankable perks come when it's time for college. . . . The teen can qualify for an extended or untimed Scholastic Assessment Test in a private, distraction-free room."

"AD/HD has the allure of a label of forgiveness," Reid (quoted in Wallis, Bloch, Cole, & Willmerth, 1994) adds. "The kid's problems are not his parents' fault, not the teacher's fault, not the kid's fault. It's better to say this kid has AD/HD than to say this kid drives everybody up the wall."

Those who acknowledge AD/HD as a viable disability argue that the condition has a long history of identification under a variety of labels, including *moral deficit, minimal brain dysfunction, hyperkinesis, hyperactivity, attention deficit disorder,* and to the current standard, *attention-deficit/hyperactivity disorder.* They posit that research suggests a biological basis for the condition as well as the potential benefits of multimodal treatment, which often includes medication for affected individuals.

In 1902, George Still, a London physician, identified a new class of "sick" children with average or higher intelligence who suffered from "an abnormal deficit of moral control" (cited in Lang, 1996). When considering these twenty children, who seemed not to be able to obey adults or delay gratification, Still turned to the works of William James, the American psychologist, for guidance.

Attention-deficit/hyperactivity disorder (AD/HD) is characterized by symptoms of inattention, hyperactivity, and/or impulsivity that are developmentally inappropriate and are not the result of other conditions. Symptoms must have occurred before age seven and exist in two or more settings. Students may be classified with one of three types: predominantly inattentive, predominantly hyperactive-impulsive, or combined.

Psychotropic medication is medication that alters perception, feelings, and/or behavior.

  AD/HD is not a new phenomenon. As early as 1902, George Still identified students who had characteristics of AD/HD.

James stated that the essential phenomenon of will is "the effort of attention." Still concluded, therefore, that these children lacked the power to choose their actions and had "a quite abnormal incapacity for sustained attention" (Lang, 1996). He believed the cause of the attention problems was a subtle brain injury.

After a 1917–1918 epidemic of viral encephalitis, doctors noted that the disease left some of the affected children with impaired attention, memory, and impulse control, similar to the symptoms of Still's patients. Still's theory of subtle brain injury gained credence (Wallis et al., 1994). A Rhode Island pediatrician discovered in 1937 that giving stimulants called amphetamines to children with the symptoms identified by Still had a surprisingly calming effect.

Russell Barkley is often considered the father of AD/HD because of his extensive research and prolific writing on this condition. Barkley (1995b), like Still, continues to receive inspiration from William James's theory about the will:

> *The developmental-neurological nature of AD/HD directly contradicts our strongly held beliefs that self-control and free will are totally determined by the person and his or her upbringing. I believe that this contradiction is what underlies much of society's resistance to admitting this disorder into the class of developmental disabilities for which we have great empathy and on behalf of which we make special allowances and rights. Society has struggled before with scientific advances that contradict the common wisdom of the time, and it has changed to accommodate them. It is my hope that society will come to do the same for AD/HD.*

What are your preconceptions about AD/HD?

AD/HD is only beginning to be recognized and diagnosed appropriately, according to researchers who advocate for the viability of the condition. "In the meantime, the media circus surrounding AD/HD and Ritalin, they say, is hurting kids . . . who need medication" (Leutwyter, 1996).

Defining Attention-Deficit/Hyperactivity Disorder

Each of the other categorical chapters in this textbook presents one of the general subdivisions of disability specified by the Individuals with Disabilities Education Act (IDEA). This chapter is different. Students with AD/HD who need special education and related services are served as other health impaired under IDEA (see Chapter 11). Other health impairments cause limitations in strength, vitality, or alertness, due to chronic or acute health problems. AD/HD is considered a chronic health problem that causes limitations in alertness.

We have decided to dedicate an entire chapter to AD/HD because of the relatively large prevalence of the condition. In addition, most of these students are served in general classrooms in which they will need to have special accommodations.

If you refer a student for another disability, be sure to let the evaluation team members know whether they also need to assess for AD/HD as well.

Deciding how to classify students with AD/HD under IDEA was not easy (Council for Exceptional Children's Task Force on Children with AD/HD, 1992). One reason is that the condition is frequently associated with learning disabilities and serious emotional disturbance. Between 10 and 26 percent of children with AD/HD also have a learning disability (Barkley, 1990; Reeve, 1990). In addition, approximately 33 percent of students with learning disabilities also have AD/HD (often the inattentive type), and between 30 and 65 percent have concurrent emotional or serious emotional disturbance. Frequent concomitant serious emotional disturbance includes oppositional/defiant disorder, conduct disorder, anxiety and mood disorders, and personality disorders (Brown, 1994; Reeve, 1990; Stanford & Hynd, 1994). The overlap with emotional disturbances is seen mainly in children who have hyperactivity-impulsivity (Barkley, 1990).

Some students with AD/HD may be eligible to receive a dual diagnosis and be served for learning disabilities or serious emotional disturbance as well as for AD/HD. Many young children with AD/HD (approximately 50 percent) also have speech and language disorders (Goldstein, 1991). Furthermore, some students with mental retardation or autism have symptoms of AD/HD. To receive the additional diagnosis of AD/HD, however, the student must have symptoms that are excessive for his or her mental age rather than chronological age (American Psychiatric Association, 1994). Also, some students with AD/HD are gifted (see Chapter 7 for a discussion of AD/HD and giftedness).

Because IDEA does not define AD/HD, we are using the definition provided by the American Psychiatric Association (1994) in its *Diagnostic and Statistical Manual of Mental Disorders* (fourth edition) (DSM-IV). Physicians, psychologists, and psychometrists generally use this definition for identifying AD/HD:

> *The essential feature of Attention-Deficit/Hyperactivity Disorder is a persistent pattern of inattention and/or hyperactivity-impulsivity that is more frequent and severe than is typically observed in individuals at a comparable level of development (Criterion A). Some hyperactive-impulsive or inattentive symptoms that cause impairment must have been present before age 7 years, although many individuals are diagnosed after the symptoms have been present for a number of years (Criterion B). Some impairment from the symptoms must be present in at least two settings (e.g., at home and at school or work) (Criterion C). There must be clear evidence of interference with developmentally appropriate social, academic, or occupational functioning (Criterion D). The disturbance does not occur exclusively during the course of a Pervasive Developmental Disorder, Schizophrenia, or other Psychotic Disorder and is not better accounted for by another mental disorder (e.g., a Mood Disorder, Anxiety Disorder, Dissociative Disorder, or Personality Disorder) (Criterion E).* *

As you continue to read about AD/HD, you might recognize some of these characteristics in yourself. Remember the criteria of frequency and severity. Everyone is forgetful and absentminded at times, especially during periods of stress. Also, some people are simply more or less energetic than others. For people with AD/HD, however, the characteristics are chronic, severe, and consistently interfere with their ability to function in everyday life. In Box 6–1, "My Voice," is a poem written by a twenty-two-year-old with AD/HD portraying the severity and chronic nature of AD/HD.

Hallowell and Ratey (1995) refer to **pseudo-ADD**, or culturally induced attention-deficit disorder. Our high-tech society, according to these authors, with its sound bites and emphasis on instant gratification, is an "ADD-ogenic society." How do you tell if a person has AD/HD or pseudo-ADD? "If you take an individual with pseudo-ADD and put him on a farm in Vermont," Hallowell and Ratey comment, "in a few months his symptoms will have subsided. If, on the other hand, you take a person with true [AD/HD] and put him on that same farm, in a few months the farm will really be hopping."

Types of Attention-Deficit/Hyperactivity Disorder.
Students with AD/HD differ significantly from peers in their ability to concentrate and control impulses. However, not all students with AD/HD are hyperactive. In fact, some are hypoactive, which means they move and respond too slowly.

Figure 6–1 shows the diagnostic criteria of AD/HD listed in DSM-IV. The American Psychiatric Association has identified three subtypes of AD/HD: predominately inattentive type, predominately hyperactive-impulsive type, and combined type.

Inattentive Type. The first type of AD/HD, **predominantly inattentive type,** describes students who have trouble paying attention in class and are forgetful and easily distracted. Hallowell and Ratey (1994) describe these students:

> *These are the daydreamers. These are the kids—often girls—who sit in the back of the class and twirl their hair through their fingers while staring out the win-*

*Reprinted with permission from the *Diagnostic and Statistical Manual of Mental Disorders*, Fourth Edition. Copyright 1994 American Psychiatric Association.

In Chapter 4, you read about Raquel Osorto, who has learning disabilities. Her aunt and uncle plan to have her evaluated this year for AD/HD. If the evaluation team discovers that Raquel has AD/HD, they will list learning disabilities as her primary diagnosis and other health impairments as her secondary diagnosis.

The *Diagnostic and Statistical Manual of Mental Disorders* (fourth edition) is commonly referred to as DSM-IV.

Pseudo-ADD is a condition with characteristics of AD/HD resulting from living in a fast-paced society that emphasizes self-gratification.

"Sometimes I get all scribbly," three-year-old Brian—who had undiagnosed AD/HD—told his mother. "This side of my brain makes me be good and this side makes me be bad. My brain is all mixed up like it's opposite day" (Neuville, 1991).

The **predominantly inattentive type of AD/HD** is characterized by daydreaming, careless work, inability to follow through, organizational difficulties, losing things, distractibility, hypoactivity, lethargy, and/or forgetfulness.

BOX 6-1 MY VOICE

MICHAEL JOHN TUMINELLO

A Life of ADHD

Born with a gift of creativity as an alibi,
I am an uneven flow of personality.

Flooded with thought containing a little of everything,
never harnessing this energy to purity.

My true ability trapped deep inside,
diluted when others try to measure.

So much to see but no map to decide direction.

In a world where you must go through the necessary
        process
to build a future, it stimulates my beginning
but leaves me without completion.

Labeled as an underachiever, I am the only one
who has met their person behind the wall of ice.

Elements of frustration fill my parachute,
delaying my desires.

I am without a diver's mask to find the
penny at the bottom of this clouded pool.

The faucet is only running in absolute emergency or
        tragedy.

I am somewhere amongst the clutter,
sealed tight in a box like a seed waiting
under a dark blanket of earth for the rain.

*Michael John Tuminello, a twenty-two-year-old with
attention-deficit/hyperactivity disorder*

dow and thinking long, long thoughts. These are the adults who drift off during conversations or in the midst of reading a page. These are the people, often highly imaginative, who are building stairways to heaven in the midst of conversations, or writing plays in their minds while not finishing the day's work, or nodding agreeably and politely while not hearing what is being said at all. They steal away silently, without the noisemaking of their hyperactive brethren, but they steal away just the same.

Students with the inattentive type often appear lethargic, apathetic, or hypoactive. They tend to be internally rather than externally focused. Their minds may be hyperactive—thinking simultaneous thoughts, often with creative outcomes—although their bodies may seem to move in slow motion.

Although these students are not as likely to be actively rejected as are those with hyperactivity/impulsivity, they are often socially neglected because of their withdrawal (Lahey & Carlson, 1991). Academically, students with the inattentive type are usually underachievers. In fact, they tend to have more learning difficulties than students with hyperactivity/impulsivity have (Council for Exceptional Children's Task Force on Children with AD/HD, 1992). Barkley (1990) summarized some of the characteristics of the inattentive type:

• Often daydreams or is "lost in a fog"

• Is frequently spacey or internally preoccupied

• Is often confused or lost in thought

• Often appears apathetic or unmotivated

• Frequently is sluggish or slow-moving

• Often stares

In the literature, you may see the inattentive type called ADD, ADD-WOH (without hyperactivity), ADHD-NOS (not otherwise specified), or AD/HD-I. The hyperactive/impulsive type may be referred to as ADHD, ADD-H, or AD/HD-HI. Some denote the combined type as AD/HD-C. The general category is sometimes identified as ADD and ADHD at other times. Confusing, we know. We will avoid this awkwardness by referring to the types by name and using the acronym AD/HD only when we include students of all types.

A. Either (1) or (2):

(1) Six (or more) of the following symptoms of **inattention** have persisted for at least six months to a degree that is maladaptive and inconsistent with developmental level:

Inattention:

(a) Often fails to give close attention to details or makes careless mistakes in schoolwork, work, or other activities.

(b) Often has difficulty sustaining attention in tasks or play activities.

(c) Often does not seem to listen when spoken to directly.

(d) Often does not follow through on instructions and fails to finish schoolwork, chores, or duties in the workplace (not due to oppositional behavior or failure to understand instructions).

(e) Often has difficulty organizing tasks and activities.

(f) Often avoids, dislikes, or is reluctant to engage in tasks that require sustained mental effort (such as schoolwork or homework).

(g) Often loses things necessary for tasks or activities (e.g., toys, school assignments, pencils, books, or tools).

(h) Is often easily distracted by extraneous stimuli.

(i) Is often forgetful in daily activities.

(2) Six (or more) of the following symptoms of **hyperactivity-impulsivity** have persisted for at least six months to a degree that is maladaptive and inconsistent with developmental level:

Hyperactivity:

(a) Often fidgets with hands or feet or squirms in seat.

(b) Often leaves seat in classroom or in other situations in which remaining seated is expected.

(c) Often runs about or climbs excessively in situations in which it is inappropriate (in adolescents or adults, may be limited to subjective feelings of restlessness).

(d) Often has difficulty playing or engaging in leisure activities quietly.

(e) Is often "on the go" or often acts as if "driven by a motor."

(f) Often talks excessively.

Impulsivity

(g) Often blurts out answers before questions have been completed.

(h) Often has difficulty awaiting turn.

(i) Often interrupts or intrudes on others (e.g., butts into conversations or games).

B. Some hyperactive-impulsive or inattentive symptoms that caused impairment were present before age 7 years.

C. Some impairment from the symptoms is present in two or more settings (e.g., at school [or work] and at home).

D. There must be clear evidence of clinically significant impairment in social, academic, or occupational functioning.

E. The symptoms do not occur exclusively during the course of a Pervasive Developmental Disorder, Schizophrenia, or other Psychotic Disorder, and are not better accounted for by another mental disorder (e.g., Mood Disorder, Anxiety Disorder, Dissociative Disorder, or a Personality Disorder).

Code based on type:

314.01 Attention-deficit/Hyperactivity Disorder, Combined type: if both Criteria A1 and A2 are met for the past six months.

314.00 Attention-deficit/Hyperactivity Disorder, Predominantly Inattentive Type: if Criterion A1 is met but Criterion A2 is not met for the past six months.

314.01 Attention-deficit/Hyperactivity Disorder, Predominantly Hyperactive-Impulsive Type: if Criterion A2 is met but Criterion A1 is not met for the past six months.

FIGURE 6–1 *Diagnostic Criteria for AD/HD*

Note: Reprinted with permission from the *Diagnostic and Statistical Manual of Mental Disorders* (4th ed.), by the American Psychiatric Association, 1994, Washington, DC: American Psychiatric Association. Copyright 1994 by the American Psychiatric Association.

≀ *Students with the inattentive type of AD/HD may daydream frequently.*

Moreover, students with the inattentive type tend to be more anxious and depressed than students with hyperactivity-impulsivity are (Lahey & Carlson, 1991). Because these children are not as disruptive as students with hyperactivity/impulsivity, it is easy for teachers to overlook their problems in the classroom. Without a specific diagnosis and the helpful interventions that can follow, this group of children is at increased risk for long-term academic, social, and emotional difficulties (Epstein, Shaywitz, Shaywitz, & Woolston, 1991).

Hyperactive-Impulsive Type. The second type of AD/HD, **predominantly hyperactive-impulsive type,** includes students who cannot seem to sit still, often talk excessively, and find playing quietly difficult. Children with hyperactivity-impulsivity often challenge parents' child-rearing skills (Aust, 1994). These children evidence more difficulty with bedwetting, sleep problems, stubbornness, and temper tantrums than children with the inattentive type or those without AD/HD. They also tend to be more accident-prone, seriously injured, or accidentally poisoned than other children.

McBurnett (1995) states that the hyperactive-impulsive type is seen more in young children who have not attended school. As they progress through school, many also develop problems with inattention. Those who do not develop those features seem to have less severe problems than those with the combined type.

Relatively few adolescents and adults with AD/HD fall into this type (Hynd, 1995). Most also have features of the inattentive type. However, those who have the hyperactive-impulsive type can become workaholics who require limited rest. Despite being productive in their chosen occupations, they can frustrate those around them because of their tendency to be brutally frank, blurt out impulsive comments, and interrupt conversations. Table 6–1 lists differences between the inattentive and hyperactive-impulsive types.

Combined Type. The third AD/HD classification—**combined type**—describes students who have features of inattention and hyperactivity/impulsivity. Taylor has the combined type. He manifests characteristics of inattention as well as hyperactivity and impulsivity. Suellyn described Taylor as inattentive and "in another world sometimes." Yet she and Taylor both emphasize his problems with hyperactivity and impulsivity. As Taylor explains, "Sometimes I don't think before I do stuff. If someone bothers me, I go off on them. It's very easy for them to get me angry if I haven't taken my pill. It's hard to keep me back from fighting other people. It's hard to tell them you don't want to fight."

The **predominantly hyperactive-impulsive type of AD/HD** is characterized by fidgeting, restlessness, difficulty engaging in quiet activities, excessive talking, driven personality, blurting out inappropriate comments, and/or the tendency to interrupt or intrude.

Individuals with the **combined type of AD/HD** manifest characteristics of both the inattentive type and hyperactive-impulsive type of AD/HD.

Trait	Hyperactive-Impulsive Type	Inattentive Type
Decision making	Impulsive	Sluggish
Boundaries	Intrusive, rebellious	Honors boundaries, polite, obedient
Assertion	Bossy, irritating	Underassertive, overly polite, docile
Attention seeking	Shows off, egotistical, best at worst	Modest, shy, socially withdrawn
Popularity	Attracts new friends but doesn't bond	Bonds but doesn't attract
Most common diagnosis	Oppositional defiant, conduct disorder	Depression, energy focused in

TABLE 6–1 🙠 *Differences between inattentive and hyperactive-impulsive types*

Note: Reprinted with permission from John F. Taylor, Ph.D., Salem, OR. For more information, see his book *Helping Your Hyperactive ADD Child*. (1997). Rockin, CA: Prima.

Barkley (1996) considers the inattentive type of AD/HD to be significantly different from the hyperactive-impulsive and combined types. His research suggests that those with the inattentive type may have a core problem in focused or selective attention. The hyperactive-impulsive and combined types appear to have core problems with poor goal-directed persistence and interference control (inhibiting distraction). This difference suggests that if you have a student with the inattentive type and you assign seatwork, that student will have difficulty getting started on the task and setting priorities for completing the assignment. Your student with the combined type, on the other hand, will find completing the task difficult because he is distracted by everything that is happening around him.

To receive the diagnosis of AD/HD, DSM-IV emphasizes that the student must manifest the symptoms of one of these types before the age of seven and for at least six months. Children and teenagers who are depressed or who are going through stressful periods may exhibit features of AD/HD. Thus, these two criteria are essential in making an accurate diagnosis.

After reading Table 6–1 and Figure 6–1, review Taylor's story to see what characteristics of each type you can identify.

Describing the Characteristics of AD/HD

In "A Life of ADHD" (see Box 6–1, "My Voice"), Tuminello (1996) illuminates the internal struggle of living in a world in which his piece of the puzzle does not fit. By providing students who have AD/HD with support and accommodations instead of condemnation, teachers and other professionals may prevent some of the high-risk outcomes associated with the condition, including low self-esteem, conduct disorders, delinquency, poor grades, dropping-out, employment problems, and interpersonal difficulties (Barkley cited in Ch.A.D.D., 1996b). In Box 6–2, "My Voice," is a story written by Bob Seay, who has AD/HD, about what might happen when a child with AD/HD is misunderstood.

You will find it easier to be supportive of students with AD/HD when you understand their characteristics. We will discuss some common internal characteristics of AD/HD in this section. In later sections, we will describe some of the external social, academic, and behavioral results of these characteristics.

Barkley (1995a) promotes a new theory of AD/HD that is grounded in medical and educational research. He contends that AD/HD is the result of a **developmental delay of inhibition.** You will remember that Taylor's first-grade teacher expressed concern about his immaturity. The four characteristics of this delay in inhibition—difficulties (a) in separating facts from feelings, (b) in having a sense of past and future, (c) in using self-directed

Developmental delay of inhibition is a feature of AD/HD that results in immature responses and difficulties in separating facts from feelings, in having a sense of past and future, in using self-directed speech, and in breaking apart and recombining information.

BOX 6-2   MY VOICE

BOB SEAY

The Story of "D"

Once upon a time, not so long ago, a beautiful child was born. There was nothing exceptional about this birth, except the same things that make every birth exceptional. Her parents loved her very much, and gave her a name which reflected how they felt about their beautiful, perfect daughter.

Like all beautiful, perfect newborns, this child could not say her name. As she grew from infant to toddler, the name was still difficult for her to pronounce. This was OK—none of her little toddler friends could pronounce it either. In fact, they mutilated the name in all kinds of creative ways. Her parents, reasoning that the child should have a name by which her friends could call her, decided to call her by her initial. So, at age two and a half, this beautiful, perfect child with a name so aptly chosen at birth was essentially renamed for the convenience of those around her.

Her new name was simply "D."

D grew and was soon ready to go to school. Her parents hugged her, told her that they loved her, and put her on the bus.

Once at school, her teacher asked her what her name was. The little girl, assuming that her teacher was probably no more articulate than her little friends, simply said "My name is D", and she smiled, remembering the name her parents had told her the D stood for and how special it was.

The teacher didn't ask why she smiled, or what the D stood for, or what the girl would preferred to be called. She simply repeated, parrot-like, the single letter given by the child—D—and thought nothing more about the possible background of this unusual name.

After just a few days of being compared to all the other children in first grade, and all the children in last year's first grade, and all the children in the 20 or so years of first graders in this teacher's career, D was found to be unique. She didn't color in the lines as she should. She didn't behave as she should. Though she seemed to be bright enough, very bright in fact, she seldom gave the expected, and therefore the "right" responses.

Her teacher decided that the D must have stood for "Different." And so, rather than thinking of the girl in a way that showed love, as her parents had intended when they named their beautiful, perfect daughter, the teacher began to treat her according to the name she had chosen for the girl: Different.

By the end of first grade, D suspected that she had somehow been "renamed," although she certainly couldn't verbalize such a concept and she certainly would not have chosen the same D word for herself that her teacher had. In fact, by this time, her parents and even the little girl herself had begun to forget what the initial D had stood for in the first place. So, when she went to second grade and the teacher asked her name, the little girl, without smiling or remembering anything more than just the information required to answer the immediate question, simply said

---

"The power to wait is not a passive act. Inhibition takes effort" (Barkley, 1994).

speech, and (d) in breaking apart and recombining information—can cause students in your class to act younger than they are.

Separating Facts From Feelings. Because students with AD/HD may not be able to inhibit their reactions to a situation, they respond on the basis of their feelings instead of facts. Emotional outbursts can occur. Taylor mentioned his difficulty with "going off on people." His medication and support from family, teachers, and friends help him control his temper. The positive attribute associated with this characteristic for students like Taylor is a passion for whatever interests them.

Having a Sense of Past and Future. Research by Barkley and his associates (cited in Ch.A.D.D., 1996b) uncovered an important finding about students with AD/HD: They tend to overestimate time intervals and underproduce, "which tells us they are perceiv-

"My name is D."

"Ahhhh . . ." the teacher thought. "This is D. This is 'Different.'" And she treated the girl accordingly.

After a few weeks, this new teacher had her own interpretation of the initial. Dummy. Of course, in the calls to the child's parents, or in the conferences with the school psychologists, she still referred to the little girl as D, but she began to treat D in a manner that was consistent with this new, unspoken, name. Dummy.

And so it went . . . year after year, teacher after teacher, each renaming the child according to their own expectations . . .

Different, Dummy, Distracted, Distant. . . .

Finally, one teacher looked into the eyes of this child and saw an even deeper meaning of the single letter name.

He had no idea of the original meaning; he saw only what it had come to mean.

Destroyed.

Parents were called in. Psychologists were summoned. Forms were filled out, signed and implemented.

Nothing changed.

There were more meetings . . . more plans . . . more frustration . . .

more nothing.

All of the educational professionals agreed. All of the psych people agreed. The Department of Social Services agreed. This child was obviously the victim of emotional abuse. "Bad Parents" the professionals said, as if they were scolding a puppy for soiling the rug. (Although, to their credit, they never said those hurtful words out loud, just as they had never used any of the hurtful names for D out loud.) "Bad Parents" they said silently, a loud deafening silent name calling. When they finally did speak out loud, they began to "explore" this abuse.

"The girl doesn't even have a decent name. No wonder her self esteem is so low."

Then, as if they hadn't already decided, each in their own mind, exactly what the D stood for—Different, Dummy, Distracted, Distant, Damaged, Disappointment, Depressed, Defeated . . . Destroyed—they asked the parents what kind of name was "D" for a little girl.

D's parents looked at the floor. They looked at each other. Together, silently, they remembered the birth of their beautiful, perfect little girl—the little girl they had loved, the daughter they had named, and the child they had apparently failed. Her Dad wiped away a tear and spoke.

"Her name is Delightful."

Bob Seay, 1996

ing time as moving more slowly than it really does." Because of this time confusion, students with AD/HD may be late often, because they think they have more time than they do. It would not be surprising if your students with AD/HD do not meet deadlines and find waiting intolerable because the time period seems to last much longer than it actually does.

This inaccurate perception of time also contributes to procrastination. The students function from crisis to crisis; a task grabs their attention only when a deadline is impending. This characteristic may cause them to seem unreliable to others. However, what this characteristic actually suggests is that these students need to have tasks broken down for them so that the deadlines are more frequent and each deadline requires less work.

Once the crisis orientation occurs or a task grabs their attention because of novelty or interest, students with AD/HD often have the ability to hyperfocus (Hallowell & Ratey, 1994): They attend to that task while completely oblivious to everything else that is going

How would you break down a term paper into smaller assignments for a high school student with AD/HD?

This self-portrait by a 7½-year-old student with AD/HD portrays the tension and frustration these students can experience when their needs are not appropriately addressed.

Nussbaum, N., & Bigler, E. (1990) *Identification and treatment of attention deficit disorder.* Austin, TX: Pro-Ed.

People with AD/HD are more at risk for health problems than the general public. Besides ignoring diet and exercise, they tend to be more prone to drug and alcohol abuse. They also have a higher percentage of car accidents and unprotected sex (Ch.A.D.D., 1996b; Wilens & Lineham, 1995).

on around them. This ability to hyperfocus allows some students and adults with AD/HD to appear highly successful. That success, however, may come at the cost of family, friends, and personal health.

Using Self-Directed Speech.

We generally use self-talk to help us control our behavior. This "rule-governed behavior" (Barkley, 1995b) allows us to set goals, plan for the future, and behave in such a way that we attain those goals. Because students with AD/HD are frequently controlled by "momentary events and immediate consequences," you may need to guide them in problem solving. They need you to help them think about what they want to do in the future and how to achieve it.

Several other characteristics of AD/HD may be related to difficulties in self-directed speech. Students with the hyperactive-impulsive and combined types of AD/HD may talk more than others do because their speech is "less internalized and private" (Barkley, 1995b). Students may seem more immature because of their inability to use rules at a developmentally appropriate level. More than likely, your students with AD/HD will also be influenced more by what seems to be rewarding at the moment, rather than by what may be more rewarding in the long-term. For example, students with AD/HD may be more tempted to go to a party the night before your test than other students.

Breaking Apart and Recombining Information.

Research suggests that students with AD/HD find analyzing and synthesizing information challenging. Being able to take apart messages we receive and recombine them into different patterns allows us to choose ways of responding that are most successful and adaptive for a particular situation, a process called *reconstitution* (Barkley, 1995b). Research with children who have AD/HD reveals that they have more difficulty generating a variety of solutions to a problem than children without AD/HD. Furthermore, during play, children with AD/HD do not seem to evaluate and explore objects as well as students without AD/HD. These findings suggest they may have difficulty with reconstitution.

"Shame and humiliation burn away the fabric of self-esteem like acid" according to Hallowell and Ratey (1994). Because a developmental delay in inhibition can cause frustration in significant adults who do not understand, students with AD/HD tend to receive many reprimands (Lang, 1996). Low self-esteem is a frequent characteristic of this population.

Positive Traits Associated with Attention-Deficit/Hyperactivity Disorder.   Along with the types and general characteristics of AD/HD, it is important for you to be aware of the strengths that frequently accompany the disability. People with AD/HD, according to Hallowell (1996),

> *are highly imaginative and intuitive. They have a "feel" for things, a way of seeing right to the heart of matters while others have to reason their way along methodically. This is the child who can't explain how he thought of the solution, or where the idea for the story came from, or why suddenly he produced a painting, or how he knew the shortcut to the answer, but all he can say is, he just knew it, he could feel it. This is the man or woman who makes million-dollar deals . . . and pulls them off the next day. This is the child, who, having been reprimanded for blurting something out, is then praised for having blurted out something brilliant. These are the children who learn and know and do and go by touch and feel.*

Because connections are made randomly in the brain of someone with AD/HD, he or she might be able to find a novel solution to a problem. The answer may seem so obvious at that point that others wonder why they hadn't thought of it.

Another positive trait associated with many people who have AD/HD is a sense of humor and the ability to laugh at themselves. See the web site called "Humorous ADDults Intriguing Themselves" (H.A.D.D. IT) (Curtiss, Whitman, Rea, & Smith Ruetz, 1996). To read examples of their humor, see www.busprod.com/scurtiss/homepg.html.

Identifying the Causes of Attention-Deficit/Hyperactivity Disorder

Before we talk about what causes AD/HD, it might be helpful for you to learn what does *not* cause AD/HD. The myths are unmitigated in the media. For example, in the last couple of decades, many people believed that sugar caused hyperactivity. Parents referred to their children as being "sugar sensitive."

Hoover and Milich (1994) studied thirty-five children ages five to seven whose mothers said they were sugar sensitive. They divided the children into two groups. All children received a placebo, but the researchers told the mothers of one group that their child received a large dose of sugar. Mothers who thought their child received sugar rated the child as more hyperactive, interacted with and criticized the child more, and exercised more control over their child than the other mothers.

These findings suggest that myths perpetuated by society can influence how we treat children. Research indicates the following are also myths about the cause of AD/HD: too little sugar, aspartame, food sensitivity, food additives/coloring, lack of vitamins, television, video games, yeast, lightening, fluorescent lighting, and allergies (Baren, 1994; Barkley, 1995b).

So what does cause AD/HD? We will look at two categories of probable causes: environmental and biological explanations.

Environmental Explanations.   Research has discounted many proposed environmental explanations, including poor parenting. Have you ever heard somebody say, "Why doesn't that parent just get control of that kid?" Taylor's AD/HD is not the result of living within a busy, sometimes chaotic environment that is typical of a large family. If that were true, Taylor's siblings would also have AD/HD. One study of parenting as a contributor to

---

Students who have AD/HD often demonstrate inherent strengths, including creativity, as a direct result of their condition.

Did you want to defend any of these myths? Think about the experiences you've had that contribute to your desire to justify these theories.

 Research reveals that both identical twins are twice as likely to receive a diagnosis of AD/HD as both fraternal twins.

AD/HD revealed that "the negative behavior of mothers [toward their child with AD/HD] seemed to be in response to the difficult behavior of these children and not the cause of it" (Barkley, 1995b).

Stress in a family or environment sometimes does cause symptoms of AD/HD. Have you ever stayed up all night to study for a test? If so, what was the next day like for you? The combination of stress and lack of sleep may have made you temporarily hyperactive. You were agitated, and when you tried to rest after the test, you couldn't. But these symptoms were temporary. Stress can create the symptoms of AD/HD, but it does not create AD/HD.

Biological Explanations.   Recent improvements in medical technology pull us closer to discovering biological explanations for AD/HD. Three biological explanations have moved to the forefront: genetics; pre-, peri-, and postnatal trauma; and brain differences.

Genetics.   Heredity explains 50 to 92 percent of hyperactive-impulsive behavior; other factors explain only 1 to 10 percent (Barkley, 1995b). At least 30 to 40 percent of children and adolescents with AD/HD have relatives with the condition (Baren, 1994).

Studies of monozygotic (identical) twins and dizygotic (fraternal) twins revealed that monozygotic twins have twice the concordance rate (both twins receiving the diagnosis) of AD/HD compared with dizygotic twins. This is the expected result for an inherited condition (Todd cited in Ch.A.D.D., 1996a).

As genetic research improves, however, the likelihood of finding the gene for AD/HD increases. With that discovery, early identification and treatment of AD/HD could make life better for people who have the condition.

A genetic link suggests that AD/HD is not a pathological condition but is, instead, a human trait. As a trait, AD/HD exists on a continuum, and society determines where the line for "abnormal" is drawn, just as it does with issues of "height, weight, or reading ability" (Barkley, 1995b). All of us have some characteristics of AD/HD, but those who receive the diagnosis represent the extreme on the continuum.

Pre-, Peri-, and Postnatal Trauma.   A child is more likely to develop AD/HD if the mother had complications before or during birth. Barkley (1995b) points out, though, that those complications may result because the mother has AD/HD and does not properly care for herself and her unborn child. Heredity may be a stronger factor than the complications.

In Chapter 9 ("Severe and Multiple Disabilities"), you will learn about **teratogens,** substances that block the normal development of a fetus. Research indicates that certain teratogens increase the likelihood that a child will develop AD/HD (Baren, 1994). Prenatal (before birth) teratogens include maternal smoking and alcohol or drug abuse, poor maternal nutrition, and the mother's exposure to chemical poisons. If the mother has AD/HD, she is more likely to expose the fetus to these teratogens. Peri- and postnatal trauma (during and after birth) such as brain injuries, infections, iron deficiency anemia, and exposure to chemical poisons also affect the likelihood that a child will develop AD/HD (Baren, 1994).

Brain Differences.   For almost 100 years, researchers have studied the brain, trying to learn the secrets of AD/HD. Similar to what is happening in the field of learning disabilities, recent research is beginning to uncover some of the answers.

Historically, research has primarily centered around the orbital-frontal region of the brain. When people sustain injuries to this area of the brain, they develop difficulties with inhibiting behavior, employing self-control, maintaining attention, and planning for the future (Barkley, 1995b). Figure 6–2 is a diagram of the brain showing specific areas that might be associated with AD/HD. Although early researchers could only speculate, current research is vindicating their efforts.

Studies in the United States and Denmark using positron emission therapy (PET) scans on adults and children with and without AD/HD show that the blood flow and activity in the frontal areas of the brain differ in those with AD/HD (Lou, Henriksen, & Bruhn cited in Barkley, 1995b; Riccio, Hynd, Cohen, & Gonzalez, 1993). This difference is especially pronounced in the area that connects to the limbic system, which is responsible for memory, motivation, and attention. When children in these studies received stimulant medication, their blood flow became more similar to the blood flow of children without AD/HD.

A study by Schweitzer (cited in Hendrick, 1995) revealed that men with AD/HD had more difficulty processing mathematical problems presented aloud. Their brains, as measured by their blood flow in the visual association cortex region, worked harder, however. The men with AD/HD needed to visualize instructions. They could not add 2 plus 3, for

Teratogens are substances that can interfere with normal fetal development.

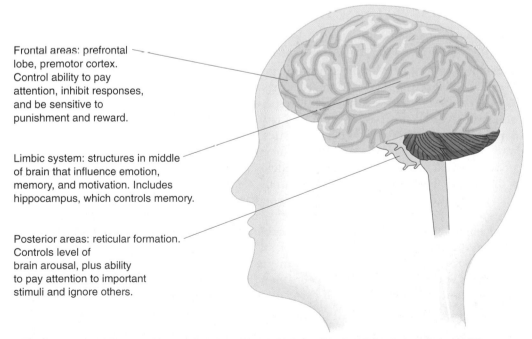

FIGURE 6–2 *Areas of the brain and attention-deficit/ hyperactivity disorder*

Frontal areas: prefrontal lobe, premotor cortex. Control ability to pay attention, inhibit responses, and be sensitive to punishment and reward.

Limbic system: structures in middle of brain that influence emotion, memory, and motivation. Includes hippocampus, which controls memory.

Posterior areas: reticular formation. Controls level of brain arousal, plus ability to pay attention to important stimuli and ignore others.

Note: From "The Human Brain," in *Teenagers With ADD: A Parent's Guide* (p. 12), by C. A. Z. Dendy, 1995, Bethesda, MD: Woodbine House. Copyright 1995 by Woodbine House. Reprinted with permission.

example, until they had visualized the numbers in their head. When the men took Ritalin, their blood flow became more normal. The need to visualize suggests that your students may profit from jotting notes on paper before answering orally.

Crawford and Barabasz (1996) found through electroencephalogram (EEG) studies that girls and boys with all types of AD/HD have greater right than left hemisphere activity in the frontal lobe. These researchers conclude that the frontocentrotemporal region of the brain is not as cognitively activated as the left hemisphere. EEG research by Buchsbaum and Wender (cited in Barkley, 1995b) demonstrated that children with AD/HD may have a less mature pattern of electrical brain activity than those without AD/HD. Stimulant medication seems to reduce those differences.

Neurochemical imbalances may also play a role in AD/HD. You probably remember studying neurons (nerve cells) in biology. The point at which a signal from one nerve jumps to another is called a *synapse.* Chemicals, called *neurotransmitters,* are required for the signal jump or firing to occur. If those signals fire erratically, too quickly, or not at all, a student may exhibit symptoms of AD/HD.

Two neurotransmitters (dopamine and norepinephrine), which are critical for vigilance and attention, appear to be present at significantly lower levels in students with AD/HD (Barabasz & Barabasz, 1996). Furthermore, stimulant drugs and antidepressants that affect neurotransmitters often improve the behavior and concentration of students with specific types of AD/HD (Barkley, 1995b; Hallowell & Ratey, 1994).

The results of all these studies indicate that brain differences are, more than likely, doors to future solutions to the challenges of AD/HD. These differences may result from heredity or pre-, peri-, or postnatal causes. Furthermore, the variety of brain differences discovered through research suggests that more than one cause of AD/HD is probable (Hynd, Voeller, Hern, & Marshall, 1991).

This new understanding of the biological causes for AD/HD leads researchers to conclude that the student with AD/HD "has a genetic, biological imbalance and usually can't help the way he behaves" (Comings, 1992). Rather than blaming the student, professionals need to teach the student how to manage AD/HD, just as they would for any other physical condition.

Identifying the Prevalence of Attention-Deficit/Hyperactivity Disorder

Children and Adults with Attention Deficit Disorders (Ch.A.D.D.)—the largest organization for individuals with AD/HD—provides advocacy, education, and support. This group estimates that 3 to 5 percent of the school-age population (approximately 2 million children) have AD/HD. Probably every general classroom has at least one or two children with AD/HD (Barkley, 1995b). Estimates of the ratio of boys to girls has changed in recent years. Some articles from the 1980s specify the ratio as nine boys to one girl. Today, as professionals become more aware of characteristics of the inattentive type, they are identifying more girls. Most now report the ratio as three to one or three to two.

"In our zeal to identify and help individuals with [AD/HD], have we become too quick to diagnosis?" Ingersoll (1995) asks. Reasons for the increase in prevalence, Ingersoll believes, result from several factors: heightened awareness, improved diagnostic practices, and societal changes that require more structure and concentration. Despite these improvements, Ch.A.D.D. (1995a) estimates that 50 percent of children with AD/HD never receive a diagnosis.

AD/HD seems to occur more often in the United States than other countries. Some researchers speculate that AD/HD occurs more in this country because of our genetic history. The founding parents left their own country, family, and security to start a new life in an unknown land:

> *Certain qualities are often associated with the American temperament. Our violent, rough-and-tumble society, our bottom-line pragmatism, our impatience, our*

intolerance of class distinctions, our love of intense stimulation—these qualities, which are sometimes explained by our youth as a country, may in part arise from the heavy load of [AD/HD] in our gene pool. (Hallowell & Ratey, 1994)

Yet others warn that overdiagnosis of AD/HD also occurs. There are reasons why "some over-diagnosis of [AD/HD] is inevitable, perhaps just as inevitable as under-diagnosis," Gordon (1995) warns. These reasons include (a) lack of consistent and complete diagnostic practices for identification, (b) difficulty separating behaviors associated with AD/HD from those exhibited by people without disabilities or those caused by other problems, (c) clinical judgment required to decide how severe is severe and what constitutes underachievement, and (d) changes in societal demands that cause children to look like they have AD/HD when they do not.

How does prevalence relate to the three subtypes of AD/HD? The DSM-IV field trials (McBurnett, 1995) studied 380 children referred to clinics; 276 received a diagnosis of AD/HD. Of these 276, 152 (55 percent), were diagnosed with the combined type; 74 (27 percent) had the inattentive type, and 50 (18 percent) had the hyperactive-impulsive type. Younger children (4 to 6 years) comprised most of the hyperactive-impulsive group (76 percent). The inattentive group contained the largest percentage of girls (27 percent); the hyperactive-impulsive group contained 20 percent girls; and the combined type contained 12 percent girls.

The increase of AD/HD in recent years does not alarm many psychiatrists and psychologists who believe identification is just now beginning to catch up with the true prevalence.

WHAT ARE EVALUATION PROCEDURES?

Determining the Presence of Attention-Deficit/Hyperactivity Disorder

Initial diagnosis of AD/HD often involves a pediatrician, psychologist, or psychiatrist outside the school system. In fact, the student may receive a diagnosis of AD/HD before starting school. Taylor received the diagnosis of AD/HD from his pediatrician, although the diagnosis did not occur until he had completed first grade.

If a practitioner has already diagnosed a student's AD/HD, the evaluation team's efforts will center on determining how the condition affects the student's school performance. Because AD/HD can affect so many areas, the team may also need to assess intellectual, academic, emotional, behavioral, and social functioning. The team conducts interviews with child and parent to establish whether a history of the condition is present. If initial diagnosis comes from the evaluation team, the student should also receive an evaluation by a pediatrician or psychiatrist to determine if medication is warranted. Figure 6–3 describes the evaluation process for identifying students who have AD/HD.

If you suspect that a student in your class has AD/HD, you will want to keep a record of characteristics (following the DSM-IV criteria) that you notice in the classroom. Your input is crucial for diagnosis. Once you refer the student, you may be interviewed and asked to provide a judgment based on your observations about the student's performance in the classroom. You may also be asked to complete an attention-deficit or behavior rating scale to help with the evaluation process.

Assessment Instruments for Attention-Deficit/Hyperactivity Disorder. You read about behavioral rating scales in Chapter 5, "Emotional or Behavioral Disorders." A number of these scales assess AD/HD as well as other conditions. Some behavior rating scales, such as the Attention Deficit Disorders Evaluation Scale (McCarney, 1989), are specifically designed to identify AD/HD. Teachers rate statements such as "rushes through assignments with little or no regard to accuracy or work" and "attends more successfully

If you want to learn more about girls and women with AD/HD, we recommend the following: *Attention!* (1996, spring, volume 2, issue 4), the trade paperback *Women With Attention Deficit,* and *ADDvance,* a magazine devoted to women with AD/HD (see the resources section for more information).

"Much like intelligence, AD/HD is viewed as being on a continuum. . . . Eligibility criteria may vary, based on the diagnostic system being applied. Perhaps it would be more appropriate to move away from the concept of sorting and labeling children to defining and evaluating needs that support the family and improve the child's education" (Burcham & DeMers, 1995).

FIGURE 6–3 *Evaluating if a student has attention-deficit/hyperactivity disorder*

Nondiscriminatory Evaluation

Observation

Teacher and parents observe	*Predominantly inattentive type*: Student makes careless mistakes, has difficulty sustaining attention, doesn't seem to be listening, fails to follow through on tasks, has difficulty organizing, often loses things, is easily distracted, or is forgetful. *Predominantly hyperactive-impulsive type*: Student is fidgety, leaves seat when expected to be seated, runs or climbs excessively or inappropriately, has difficulty playing quietly, talks excessively, blurts out answers or comments, has difficulty taking turns, or acts as if always on the go. *Combined type*: Characteristics of both are observed.

Screening

Assessment measures	Findings that indicate need for further evaluation
Classroom work products	Work is consistently or generally poor. Student has difficulty staying on task, so work may be incomplete or completed haphazardly.
Group intelligence tests	Tests may not reveal true ability because student has difficulty staying on task.
Group achievement tests	Performance may not be a true reflection of achievement because student has difficulty staying on task.
Medical screening	Physician or psychiatrist does not find physical condition that could cause inattention or hyperactivity-impulsivity. Medication may be prescribed.
Vision and hearing screening	Results do not explain academic difficulties.

Prereferral

Teacher implements suggestions from school-based team	The student still experiences frustration, inattention, or hyperactivity despite reasonable curricular and behavioral modifications.

Referral

Protection in evaluation procedures

Assessment measures	Findings that suggest AD/HD
Psychological evaluation	Psychiatrist or psychologist determines that student meets DSM-IV criteria for AD/HD.
Individualized intelligence tests	Student's intelligence may range from below average to gifted.
Individualized achievement tests	Performance on achievement tests may suggest that student's educational performance has been adversely affected by the condition.
Behavior rating scales or AD/HD-specific scales	The student scores in the significant range on measures of inattention or hyperactivity-impulsivity.
Teacher observation	The student's educational performance has been adversely affected by the condition. The behaviors have been present in more than one setting, were first observed before age seven, and have lasted for more than six months.
Curriculum-based assessment	The student may be experiencing difficulty in one or more areas of the curriculum used by the local school district because the behaviors have caused the student to miss important skills.
Direct observation	The student exhibits inattention or hyperactivity-impulsivity during the observation.

Evaluation Team determines that student has attention-deficit/hyperactivity disorder and needs special education and related services.

Appropriate Education

when close to the source of sound (e.g., when seated close to the teacher)" on a scale of 0 ("does not engage in the behavior") to 4 ("one to several times per hour") (McCarney, 1989). Three subscales—inattention, hyperactivity, and impulsivity—compose the test. Home and school versions are available, and computerized scoring includes suggested behavioral goals and objectives that teachers can consider for individualized education programs (IEPs).

AD/HD seems to diminish IQ "to a small degree" because of its effects on "prolongation/ working memory, internalization of speech, separation and self-regulation of affect, and analysis/synthesis or reconsitution" (Barkley, 1995a). The Wechsler Intelligence Scale for Children (WISC-III) includes a Freedom from Distractibility scale. Students who score poorly on this scale in relation to other scales may have AD/HD, and further assessment is warranted. Nevertheless, students who do not score significantly lower on this section may still have AD/HD (Anastapoulos, Spisto, & Maher, 1994). This finding points to the importance of more than one assessment measure for determining the presence of AD/HD.

Continuous performance tests (CPTs) were first used to detect lapses of attention in people with brain damage (Stein, Szumowski, & Halperin, 1994). Currently, some psychologists and psychiatrists use continuous performance tests to assess students for AD/HD. In the Intermediate Visual and Auditory Continuous Performance Test (Sandford & Turner, n.d.), students click a mouse only if they see or hear a "1" and do not click when they see or hear a "2." Sandford and Turner state that the Intermediate Visual and Auditory Continuous Performance Test "correctly identified clinician diagnosed AD/HD children 92.3% of the time and had a low false positive rate of 10%."

Although continuous performance tests reliably and objectively measure traits associated with AD/HD, some students with AD/HD perform well on these tests, and others without AD/HD perform poorly. Many factors besides AD/HD affect performance, including age, IQ, motivation, co-morbid symptoms, time and situational factors, depression, misunderstanding directions, visual deficits, and absence seizures (Stein et al., 1994). "At present," Stein et al. emphasize, continuous performance tests "are best thought of as a tool to augment the diagnostic skills of the clinician and not as a clinical test."

Cultural Issues in Diagnosis. "Cultural, ethnic, and economic factors may result in either over-diagnosis or under-diagnosis" of AD/HD (Williams, Lerner, Wigal, & Swanson, 1995). Limited access to medical services may prevent some students from being identified. Overdiagnosis can occur because some students have activity levels that are culturally appropriate but differ significantly from the majority culture of same-age peers.

Research to develop an AD/HD assessment instrument for Puerto Rican children (Bauermeister, 1995) revealed that one-fourth of their teachers rated them as having symptoms of AD/HD. Hispanic students, especially those from Puerto Rico, according to Bauermeister, often manifest more body movements, gestures, and facial expressions than Anglo students do. These traits can cause teachers who are not familiar with the culture to think a student is hyperactive. Furthermore, Hispanic culture tends to organize activities "in circular fashion, doing many things in one unit of time (polychronic), whereas the Anglo culture organizes activities linearly, sequentially, doing one thing at a time (monochronic)." This finding suggests that students who are Hispanic might be more inclined to talk at the same time they are doing seatwork. To an unknowledgeable teacher, this behavior might inaccurately point to the student having AD/HD.

Barbarin and Soler (1993) report that some adolescent African American males may suffer from **stress-induced agitation syndrome** caused by living in poverty and potentially violent situations. Because they have characteristics similar to AD/HD, the students risk misdiagnosis. "Symptoms of agitation could be the thread that ties together disturbances of mood and underachievement in school," Barbarin and Soler comment. "The inability to concentrate could be attributable to worry and concern about personal safety or peril to loved ones rather than" to AD/HD.

Although certain behaviors occur more frequently because of culture, it is important to remember that people vary widely within cultural groups, just as people with a partic-

Continuous performance tests are machines or computer software that measure sustained attention or vigilance, reaction time, distractibility, and impulsivity.

Stress-induced agitation syndrome consists of characteristics of AD/HD resulting from the stress of living in poverty and potentially violent situations.

ular disability vary widely. Assessment must consider cultural issues; however, the student's individuality and the existence of subcultures must also be recognized. Most adolescent African American males, for example, do not have agitation syndrome. To compare them with those who do when assessing for AD/HD would be inappropriate.

The use of behavioral rating instruments—because they rely on subjective opinions of raters—create problems in identification when the rater's cultural group varies from the student's (Reid, 1995). "It is important that educators be wary of the seductive quality of this pseudo-objectivity," Reid warns.

Instruments such as the Child Behavior Checklist—Direct Observation Form (Auchenbach, 1986) that allow the evaluator to compare a student to control peers from the same cultural group and observed in the same setting improve the likelihood of appropriate diagnosis. When assessing a student for AD/HD, it is important to make sure that at least one member of the team is a member of or has expertise in evaluating the student's cultural group (Council for Exceptional Children, 1992).

Determining the Nature and Extent of Special Education and Related Services

The evaluation team decides if AD/HD is present, the type of AD/HD the student has, and the severity of the condition and its effect on educational progress. They also determine from that information whether special education and related services are warranted. This issue is especially challenging when the student has AD/HD.

As we have previously stated, students with AD/HD who need special education and related services are served as other health impaired under IDEA. For them to be served under IDEA, the condition must significantly and negatively affect their educational progress. Some students with AD/HD have concomitant conditions such as learning disabilities and serious emotional disturbance. They may be served as having a dual diagnosis under IDEA. Thus, a student's primary disability may be learning disabilities, while the secondary disability may be other health impairments (AD/HD).

Students whose only disability is a health impairment, including AD/HD, may be served in any environment that provides them an appropriate education and is the least restrictive for the student. This means that a student whose only disability is AD/HD might be served in a resource room with students who have learning disabilities or receive services from a special education collaborative teacher in a general classroom.

Many students with AD/HD, especially when they begin a treatment regimen that includes medication, can function well in a general classroom—with accommodations. These accommodations might include extra time for tests or taking tests orally, a behavior modification plan, a peer note taker, and/or a set time to leave the classroom for medication.

Taylor Wiggand is one of those students. He makes above average and average grades, consistent with his ability—when he takes his medication and receives accommodations. He does not need to be served under IDEA, but he needs appropriate accommodations in the general classroom. Wayne Wiggand, Taylor's father, says, "An outline of what the kids are dealing with is the biggest help. It lets everybody understand." An IEP does that for a child who needs special education and related services. What can be used in place of that document for students like Taylor?

Besides IDEA, two other laws, Section 504 of the Rehabilitation Act and the Americans with Disabilities Act (ADA), provide protection against discrimination for Taylor and other students with disabilities (see Chapter 1). These two laws protect people with disabilities that "substantially limit a major life activity" (Roberts & Mather, 1995). Section 504 and ADA offer other options than those found in IDEA for AD/HD (Ch.A.D.D., 1995b). Section 504 states that people with disabilities in federally assisted programs and activities shall not be discriminated against solely on the basis of their disabilities and shall receive "reasonable accommodations." ADA requires all educational and other institutions (except those operated by religious organizations) to meet the needs of students with disabilities, including AD/HD.

Sometimes teachers express concern that giving accommodations to students with exceptionalities is not fair to the rest of class. *Fair* is providing students with what they need, not treating them all the same.

 Taylor, like many students with AD/HD, does not need special education or related services. He is served more appropriately by a 504 Plan rather than an IEP.

To comply with these laws, states offer 504 or ADA plans (terminology differs). A team from the school, which may include the student's teacher, the principal or principal's designee, and someone who is knowledgeable about the disability, decides what accommodations are necessary, based on limitations resulting from the disability (Fossey, Hosie, & Zirkel, 1995). Parent and student participation is not mandated but is usually advisable. The team writes the accommodations into the plan.

These accommodations may be temporary or permanent. In some cases, the student may need some accommodations only when learning needed skills, such as organizing. However, the student may always need to take tests in a quiet room because of being easily distracted.

Generally, one person in a school monitors 504 or ADA plans to make sure the students receive the appropriate accommodations. If the student is not performing as expected with one of these plans, however, the team needs to reconvene and reevaluate if the student needs special education and related services to receive an appropriate education. In Box 6-3, "Into Practice," you will find a list of possible accommodations to include for students with AD/HD on 504 or ADA plans. This list is not exhaustive, however. As you read, think of others you could add for a student with AD/HD.

When addressing behavioral issues of a student with AD/HD on the IEP or 504/ADA Plan, Maag and Reid (1994) recommend identifying the student's specific skill deficit. Generally, the factors that contribute to a student's behavior stem from four types of deficits: (a) behavioral skill deficit—not knowing how to perform the appropriate behavior; (b) problem-solving deficit—not being able to generate feasible options and/or choose an appropriate solution; (c) cognitive distortion—misinterpreting the situation or results; and (d) self-control deficit—not thinking before acting. A student with AD/HD who doesn't have needed materials for your class could be experiencing any of these deficits: The student may not have (a) remembered what materials are needed, (b) known how to organize her locker so she could find the materials in the limited time between classes,

BOX 6-3   INTO PRACTICE

ACCOMMODATIONS FOR ATTENTION-DEFICIT/HYPERACTIVITY DISORDER

Inattention

- Seat student in quiet area.
- Seat student near good role model.
- Seat student near "study buddy."
- Increase distance between desks.
- Allow extra time to complete assigned work.
- Shorten assignments or work periods to coincide with span of attention; use timer.
- Break long assignments into smaller parts so student can see end to work.
- Assist student in setting short-term goals.
- Give assignments one at a time to avoid work overload.
- Require fewer correct responses for grade.
- Reduce amount of homework.
- Instruct student in self-monitoring using cueing.
- Pair written instructions with oral instructions.
- Provide peer assistance in note taking.
- Give clear, concise instructions.
- Seek to involve student in lesson presentation.
- Cue student to stay on task, i.e. private signal.

Impulsiveness

- Ignore minor, inappropriate behavior.
- Increase immediacy of rewards and consequences.
- Use time-out procedure for misbehavior.
- Supervise closely during transition times.
- Use "prudent" reprimands for misbehavior (i.e., avoid lecturing or criticism).
- Attend to positive behavior with compliments etc.
- Acknowledge positive behavior of nearby students.
- Seat student near role model or near teacher.
- Set up behavior contract.
- Instruct student in self-monitoring of behavior, i.e., hand raising, calling out.
- Call on only when hand is raised in appropriate manner.
- Praise when hand raised to answer question.

Motor Activity

- Allow student to stand at times while working.
- Provide opportunity for "seat breaks" i.e., run errands, etc.
- Provide short break between assignments.
- Supervise closely during transition times.
- Remind student to check over work product if performance is rushed and careless.
- Give extra time to complete tasks (especially for students with slow motor tempo).

Mood

- Provide reassurance and encouragement.
- Frequently compliment positive behavior and work product.
- Speak softly in nonthreatening manner if student shows nervousness.
- Review instructions when giving new assignments to make sure student comprehends directions.
- Look for opportunities for student to display leadership role in class.
- Conference frequently with parents to learn about student's interests and achievements outside of school.
- Send positive notes home.
- Make time to talk alone with student.
- Encourage social interactions with classmates if student is withdrawn or excessively shy.
- Reinforce frequently when signs of frustration are noticed.
- Look for signs of stress build up and provide encouragement or reduced work load to alleviate pressure and avoid temper outburst.
- Spend more time talking to students who seem pent up or display anger easily.
- Provide brief training in anger control: encourage student to walk away; use calming strategies; tell nearby adult if getting angry.

Academic Skills

- If reading is weak: provide additional reading time; use "previewing" strategies; select text with less on a page; shorten amount of required reading; avoid oral reading.
- If oral expression is weak: accept all oral responses; substitute display for oral report; encourage student to tell about new ideas or experiences; pick topics easy for student to talk about
- If written language is weak: accept nonwritten forms for reports (i.e., displays, oral, projects); accept use of typewriter, word processor, tape recorder; do not assign large quantity of written work; test with multiple-choice or fill-in questions.
- If math is weak: allow use of calculator; use graph paper to space numbers; provide additional math time; provide immediate correctness feedback and instruction via modeling of the correct computational procedure.

Organization Planning

- Ask for parental help in encouraging organization, provide organization rules.
- Encourage student to have notebook with dividers and folders for work.
- Provide student with homework assignment book.
- Supervise writing down of homework assignments.
- Send daily/weekly progress reports home.
- Regularly check desk and notebook for neatness, encourage neatness rather than penalize sloppiness.
- Allow student to have extra set of books at home.
- Give assignments one at a time.
- Assist student in setting short-term goals.
- Do not penalize for poor handwriting if visual-motor defects are present.
- Encourage learning of keyboarding skills.
- Allow student to tape record assignments or homework.

Compliance

- Praise compliant behavior.
- Provide immediate feedback.
- Ignore minor misbehavior.
- Use teacher attention to reinforce positive behavior.
- Use "prudent" reprimands for misbehavior (i.e., avoid lecturing or criticism).
- Acknowledge positive behavior of nearby student.
- Supervise student closely during transition times.
- Seat student near teacher.
- Set up behavior contract.
- Implement classroom behavior management system.
- Instruct student in self-monitoring of behavior.

Socialization

- Praise appropriate behavior.
- Monitor social interactions.
- Set up social behavior goals with student, and implement a reward program.
- Prompt appropriate social behavior either verbally or with private signal.
- Encourage cooperative learning tasks with other students.
- Provide small group social skills training.
- Praise student frequently.
- Assign special responsibilities to student in presence of peer group so others observe student in a positive light.

Note: From "Adapt: Accommodations Help Students With Attention Deficit Disorders," by H. C. Parker, 1996, *ADD Warehouse Articles on ADD* [On-line]. Available: http://www.addwarehouse.com.

(c) understood what the consequences of not having the materials would be, or (d) thought about how visiting with her friends between classes would prevent her from having time to go to her locker. As you can see, creating effective behavioral objectives, remediation strategies, and accommodations depends on knowledge of the specific skill the student is lacking.

WHAT AND HOW DO PROFESSIONALS TEACH?

Curriculum

For many students with AD/HD, the standard general education curriculum is appropriate. What will differ for them will be how those materials are used. A student may need to listen to a textbook on tape, for example, while reading silently to stay focused on the content. Another student might need extra time to complete assignments. The accommodations must match the student's particular needs (refer back to Box 6-3). An important accommodation for Taylor is taking his spelling tests orally. His mother says, "At first he could not get his spelling right at school. He would get them right at home because we did them verbally. He couldn't get them right when he had to write them."

Not only are accommodations important for students with AD/HD, but the way in which the curriculum is presented also makes a difference. When you are presenting curriculum to these students, you will be more likely to sustain their attention if you remember five key words: *relevance, novelty, variety, choices,* and *activity* (Shank, in preparation). Think of your own learning experiences. Is it easier for you to learn when a professor helps you to see the relevance of the information? If you believe that the information in this class can make you a better teacher, one of your life goals, you are more likely to focus your attention in class and while reading this chapter.

You are also more likely to focus attention when the information is novel for you. How many times have you said to yourself, "This is boring; I've heard it ten times already"? Material must be repeated for mastery, however. Professors who use variety in their presentation style of familiar material probably hold your attention more than those who use the same style—lecture, perhaps—all the time. Varying the mode of student response, for example, debates, role playing, projects, keeping a journal, and so on, can also encourage your attention.

You might be thinking, "I would enjoy debates, but I'd hate to keep a journal." That is why, as much as possible, you need to give your students choices about how they learn and respond to the curriculum. Contracting for grades allows choices and can benefit all of your students, not just those with AD/HD.

At the beginning of each quarter, provide students with a three-page contract. The first page specifies what they will need to do to get a grade of A, B, C, or D in your class. List percentages needed on tests and quizzes and the number of projects they will need to do for each grade, as well as the dates each will be due. List possible projects on the second page, making sure the projects address varied learning styles. Inform students that you will also consider their ideas for projects. Students return the third page to you. This page has lines for (a) the contracted grade, (b) the chosen projects and when they will be submitted, and (c) student and parent signatures. Grade contracts allow students with AD/HD and their parents to know what is expected at the beginning of the quarter. This approach also accommodates workload according to ability. You can mail a copy of the contract home in the middle of the quarter, give a copy to students in class, and review it at parent conferences. This allows parents and students to be reminded of their commitment, which is necessary when AD/HD is involved.

Many students with AD/HD benefit from activity involving multisensory learning (a combination of auditory [oral], visual [sight], kinesthetic [motor], and tactile [touch] approaches). Active involvement engages these students. Taylor says that he learns most effectively from activity: "It's fun doing all the projects, and it's fun to see what happens.

Have you ever had a professor who lectured each class but still held your attention? Sense of humor, enthusiasm, emphasizing and using examples for key points, and telling human-interest anecdotes add variety and facilitate student attention during lectures.

Many students with AD/HD benefit from computer-assisted instruction. A game format tends to increase novelty, variety, activity, and choices. The Internet can be AD/HD paradise. Students can link to another site for similar information in a novel format when their attention wavers.

❤ *Multisensory activities engage students with AD/HD in their learning.*

Every time you experiment, you learn that science can tell you what will happen before and after the experiment."

Methods

Multimodal treatment is generally more effective for individuals with AD/HD than any single intervention. Students may benefit from some or all of the following:

Medical Management.   Medication is not a panacea for AD/HD. Some students experience unmanageable side effects or do not seem to benefit from medication. Others with milder symptoms may be able to manage the condition without medication. On the other hand, one parent succinctly points out what many parents of children and adolescents with AD/HD experience: "Our son's life began when he started taking medication."

Medical management, which often involves placing students on a stimulant medication (popular brand names include Ritalin, Dexedrine, or Cylert), may need to occur before the other methods or curriculum can benefit the student. As many as 60 to 80 percent of students with hyperactivity/impulsivity respond favorably to treatment by stimulants (Reeve, 1990). In smaller doses, stimulant medication also has potential effectiveness for many individuals with the inattentive type (Lahey & Carlson, 1991). Other students with the inattentive type respond better to antidepressants, which stimulate neurotransmitters differently, or to a combination of stimulants and antidepressants.

School personnel and parents need to work closely with the student's physician or psychiatrist to make sure that a particular medication and dosage provide optimal benefits with the fewest side effects (see Table 6–2 for side effects of common stimulants and antidepressants). The more common side effects often subside as the student continues to take the medication. It is important to communicate with parents and/or the physician to determine potential side effects for a student's particular medication.

Multimodal treatment is the use of concurrent treatment approaches. For those with AD/HD, treatment may include as many as six components: medical management, education, coaching, counseling, organizational training, and behavior modification.

Prior to diagnosis and treatment, many adolescents and adults with AD/HD have tried to self-medicate unproductively through caffeine, smoking, alcohol, or drug use.

Forms for monitoring effects of medication during school are available from Southeastern Psychological Institute, P.O. Box 12389, Atlanta, GA 30305-2389.

TABLE 6–2 ␝ *Possible side effects of medications for treating attention-deficit/hyperactivity disorder*

Type	Stimulants	Antidepressants (Novel)
Common side effects	Insomnia Decreased appetite Gastrointestinal pain Irritability Increased heart rate (clinically insignificant) Paradoxical worsening of symptoms	Gastrointestinal (Nausea, diarrhea, dyspepsia) Decreased appetite Weight loss Nervousness Insomnia Excess sweating Sedation Dream intensification Motor restlessness Dry mouth Sexual dysfunction
Uncommon side effects	Psychosis Sadness/isolation Major depressive episodes Cognitive impairment Growth retardation Tic disorders (e.g., Tourette's syndrome) Increased heart rate (clinically significant) Impaired liver functioning (Cylert only) Increased blood pressure Dizziness, lethargy, fatigue Nausea, constipation Rash/hives Acute sense of hearing Skin sensation, sensitivity to touch	Subjective sensation of exitation Hypomania/mania Rash/allergic reactions Seizure Hair loss

Note: From "An Update on Pharmacologic Medication: What Teachers, Clinicians, and Parents Need to Know," by D. P. Sweeney, S. R. Forness, K. A. Kavale, and J. G. Levitt, 1997, *Intervention, 33*(1), pp. 4–21. Copyright 1997 by PRO-ED, Inc. Adapted and reprinted with permission.

Most physicians now recognize that the biological nature of AD/HD suggests that the student needs the medication at home as well as at school. Physicians may recommend trial periods without medication to determine if dosages need to be adjusted or eliminated as the student matures physically; however, the formerly common practice of "drug holidays" is not as widely accepted as it used to be (Copps, n.d.).

One major concern about drug treatment is that sometimes parents, teachers, and students have unrealistic expectations about the effects of stimulant medication (Copps, n.d.). Use of medication may increase tolerance, sustained attention, and solitary play. It also tends to decrease impulsivity, task-irrelevant physical activity, and boredom. The student's handwriting, academic performance, peer relations, extracurricular activities, and family interactions generally improve (Copps, n.d.). The student will probably not experience long-term improvement in academic achievement or reduction of antisocial behavior. Koplewicz (1996) comments, "Ritalin lets a kid pay attention more. It doesn't force kids to do their homework, it doesn't teach social skills, it doesn't make them smart, it just makes them more accessible to perform in these areas."

Taylor benefits from taking Ritalin. His mother comments about the improvement medication has made:

Since he's been on medication, he's been so much better with his school work. He used to make D's and F's. Now he makes B's and C's and sometimes an A.

ABCNEWS
VIDEO
REFLECTIONS

TEACHER'S LITTLE HELPER: SCHOOLCHILDREN AND DRUGS

"Today, a conflict has evolved over controlling the minds and emotions of children," Tom Jarrell says. "At issue, experts say, is a drug with proven benefits being pushed to extremes to control troublesome kids. The drug is Ritalin."

In "Teacher's Little Helper," some parents share how they felt pressured to have their child put on Ritalin by teachers. Others express concern that their children were placed on Ritalin without a thorough evaluation. While emphasizing that medication is an effective component of intervention for many students who actually have AD/HD, this video warns of the detrimental effects medication can have for students who truly do not need it.

What do you think? "Spontaneity and self-control—children are born with one, but must learn the other," Tom Jarrell commented in the video. Do you agree with this statement? Why or why not?

When you suspect that a student in your class might have AD/HD, what will you say to the parents? What will you not say?

You suspect that a student who has been in your class for two months was misdiagnosed with AD/HD during the previous school year, due to lack of a thorough evaluation. How will you handle the situation?

And he can do two or three things at a time now. I used to tell him one thing to do, and he would forget what I had asked. His temper has improved even more since he's been on a time-release medication.

Beverly Thompson, Taylor's teacher, shares the difference between Taylor and a boy with AD/HD in her class who is not on medication:

At the beginning of the year, they adjusted Taylor's medication, and I could see a marked, good difference for him. I have another boy in my class with AD/HD, and he doesn't take medication. It's hard. He's up and around the room all the time. Taylor can concentrate and do his work.

Although medication can improve a student's functioning, it is important not to equate behavior with medication. Saying to a student who is misbehaving, "Did you take your medicine today?" can cause the student to believe that she is not responsible for her behavior.

Students may resent taking medication because they feel different from their peers. Taylor experienced these feelings, and his parents agreed to let him have a trial period without it. His mother describes the results:

Taylor was getting so he wouldn't take the medication. He wanted me to try stopping the Ritalin at the beginning of the year. We let him be weaned off. His grades went down a lot. He just didn't have the attention, focusing. He can become very impulsive. Taylor saw the importance of the medication for himself. He asked to be put back on it after a month and has been taking it everyday since.

Education. Students with AD/HD need to understand their condition (Hallowell & Ratey, 1994). Labels of stupid, lazy, and dumb have haunted them. You will want to make sure that students understand both what the condition is, and what it is not. Two other important aspects of educating students are teaching them to respond to comments from others and helping them learn how to ask others for needed accommodations.

Coaching. Students with AD/HD need someone in their corner. A coach does not have to be a teacher or a family member. A coach can be a peer, a neighbor, or someone specially trained to perform that type of service, such as a professional organizer or someone who has taken training in coaching people with AD/HD. For Taylor, that someone is Linda

Ritalin is being abused by teenagers as "the poor man's cocaine." Schools need to carefully monitor a student's use of Ritalin. Students with AD/HD who sell Ritalin illegally are subject to discipline under IDEA, as are the buyers. Time-release medication may help eliminate the need for a school dosage for many students.

Contact Professional and Personal Coaches Association at (415) 522-8789 to find a coach in your area.

Montgomery, his neighbor and tutor. "Linda has helped a lot," Wayne Wiggand says. "She's trying to encourage Taylor more that he's not that different. She tells him that in some areas he's more advanced than other people."

Counselors sometimes serve in this capacity. The crucial factor is the relationship the student builds with his coach. If the student perceives the coach as intrusive rather than supportive, another coach must be found. Hallowell and Ratey (1994) use the acronym HOPE to specify the questions a coach asks a student with AD/HD on a regular basis:

Help: What help do you need?

Obligations: What's coming up and what are you doing to prepare?

Plans: What are your goals?

Encouragement: You are making progress!

Counseling. Counseling does not usually result in identifiable changes in the student's behavior in the classroom (Klein, 1992). It can, however, be beneficial in helping to improve the student's understanding of the condition as well as increase self-esteem. Students can improve social skills through a peer support group directed by a counselor. Family counseling can help members solve problems and improve relationships.

Organizational Training. For people with AD/HD, organization is a bed of hot coals they must cross to be able to function in life. They need a guide to teach them how. Telling a student with AD/HD to get her notebook organized is like telling someone with two broken legs to walk. The student must be shown exactly how to organize the notebook. Professional organizers often know how to teach these skills. In Box 6-4, "Making a Difference," Lee R. Donald, a professional organizer, tells about her work. In Figure 6-4, she explains developmental tasks for organization that professionals can teach students at various ages.

Ed Koch, a former mayor of New York City, is famous for asking people "How am I doing?" Students with AD/HD also need frequent feedback on their performance (Hallowell, 1996).

Behavior Management. Many students with AD/HD benefit from the structure they receive from behavior management. Breaking tasks into manageable subtasks and rewarding a student for completion of each is a useful approach. Students also benefit from a token economy, an approach that applies frequent tangible reinforcers for desired behaviors.

Behavior management techniques seem to be especially beneficial when combined with cognitive training that allows the student to monitor and be responsible for personal behavior (Ajibola & Clement, 1995; Nussbaum & Bigler, 1990). Ajibola and Clement (1995) found that students with AD/HD who were taking medication and participated in a self-reinforcement program made more improvement in completing reading questions than students who took medication only or participated in self-reinforcement only. For self-reinforcement, the students clicked a counter on their wrist each time they completed a reading question. They received a stamp in a payment book each day they met or exceeded their goal. When they received a specified number of stamps, they cashed in their payment books for a reward.

HOW IS PARTICIPATION ENCOURAGED?

Inclusion

"I'm glad Taylor has been able to stay in regular classrooms," Taylor's mother, Suellyn, comments. The majority of students with AD/HD are served appropriately in general classrooms.

Rural schools like Taylor's face unique challenges in practicing inclusion. Taylor's school only has one class per grade, and access to specialists for support services is limited. Becky

Because students with AD/HD are identified as health impaired but are frequently more like students with learning disabilities or behavior disorder, serving them can be challenging. Lang (1996) comments, "In the education bureaucracy, AD/HD wanders like a lost child."

BOX 6-4   MAKING A DIFFERENCE

LEE R. DONALD

Lee R. Donald, who founded Organizing Associates in Mobile, Alabama, understands the value of people with AD/HD. "Think of all the people in society who were geniuses and had AD/HD," she says. "These are the people who have given us some of the most innovative ideas and products that have ever been. Think about Beethoven's music, Michelangelo's Sistine Chapel, Ford's first car, Edison's light bulb, Einstein's theory of relativity. Many researchers believe that these inventors probably had AD/HD."

Lee's sensitivity toward people with AD/HD and belief in what they can accomplish helps her make a difference in the lives of her clients:

Since I began working with people who have AD/HD, I have learned that they are a population unto themselves. They're creative, imaginative, and eager to learn new things. I have yet to meet a client with AD/HD who I didn't feel honored to have as a friend—child or adult.

I believe that the use of organizational skills for this population will enhance their lives beyond measure. Their needs are quite different from those who do not have AD/HD. The clients with AD/HD have shorter attention spans, need to have things repeated frequently and need to repeat things back to me that I've said to them. Also, a great deal of creativity has to be used in setting up "a system" for them because they do not think sequentially as other clients might.

One of the best aids to me has been my membership in the National Association of Professional Organizers (NAPO). This organization is made up of people throughout the United States, Canada, and Europe who are interested in the profession of organizing. They have many different levels of expertise and interest areas, including a subspecialty of people who work with AD/HD.

There is no one solution for children with AD/HD. For example, to be able to get out the door with the things they need for that day, some of the children we work with need to have everything they need for the day in one place. They shouldn't have to remember a sequence of things in the morning.

However, a child who is artistic and visually oriented may need to have her clothes laid out in her room, her shoes outside the bedroom door, and the backpack in the kitchen on the floor by the refrigerator. She will take her lunch out of the refrigerator, put it in her backpack, and go out the back door. We need to get creative in her organization so she will not get bored with it and stop doing it. It also helps a child like this to keep moving through her morning routine.

When you are dealing with children with AD/HD, please remember to have lots of patience, use your creative energy, and be flexible. Celebrate their differences!

If you want to find a professional organizer in your area, call the national office in Austin, Texas. We have listed their phone number, e-mail, web page, and address in the "Resources" section at the end of this chapter.

Note: From manuscript in preparation by Lee R. Donald. Copyright 1997 by L. Donald. Reprinted with permission.

Swickard, Taylor's second-grade teacher, says that increased class size also creates challenges for inclusion: "Our classes are getting larger. I started off with 19 students 8 years ago. This year I have 32. You can only do so much with your day when your classes get that large."

Beverly Thompson, Taylor's current teacher, comments about the importance of teacher preparation for inclusion:

> *I encourage everyone who wants to be an elementary, junior high, or high school teacher to take as many classes as possible about special needs kids. We are moving to a place where inclusion is happening. That was unheard of when I went to college. I graduated in 1980, and I felt helpless at first. I've had to go back and take classes and attend seminars and in-services.*

Taylor's school, despite the challenges, is making inclusion work through flexibility and creativity. Beverly Thompson explains:

> *Every child is different. What works for one might not work for another. I have another child with AD/HD in my class. What works for Taylor doesn't always work for the other boy. We have to be open to suggestions and to different ways of getting to the same ending. These children may not learn the same way other children do, and we have to vary our teaching to suit the needs of the child.*

FIGURE 6–4 *Developmental organization skills*

K–4 and K–5

Begin teaching the concept of time by marking off each day of the week on a large calendar as it passes. Remember to mark off Saturday and Sunday each week.

Stickers may be used on the calendar to denote special occasions such as birthdays and holidays. Let each student locate the day of the month on which his or her birthday falls and place a sticker on that date.

K–5

Have students create individual calendars each month and decorate them with seasonal pictures. Let them place stickers to denote special dates for themselves, their friends, and their families.

Encourage parents to keep a large calendar at home. Use stickers to mark holidays, days for weekly music lessons, after school activities, games, etc.

Grades 1 and 2

Teach students to write homework assignments in a simple notebook used only for that purpose. It should be standard size and therefore hard to lose. Or, teach students to write homework assignments on a colored index card and use that card to mark the page of the textbook they will need to take home to complete the assignment. At the end of the day, the books with cards in them go home and the others don't. Students may choose to put books with cards directly into their backpack as the cards are completed. This makes it even harder to get home without the needed books. Use the same color for all student homework assignments. Yellow is hard to miss. Consider having parents sign each card daily and use the card to communicate with teachers concerning difficulties a student may have had with a particular assignment. It beats playing phone tag.

Grades 3, 4, and 5

Begin the use of a simple personal daily planner to record homework assignments, tests, quizzes, holidays, field trips, and even a weekly reminder on Fridays to take home PE clothes.

Teach students to color code their notebooks, spiral notebooks, or binders to match their texts. Or, have them choose a color for each subject notebook and use the same color from year to year, i.e., language—blue, science—green, math—red, etc.

Note. From manuscript in preparation, by Lee R. Donald. Copyright 1997 by Lee R. Donald. Reprinted with permission.

Taylor's school also makes creative use of local resources. "In Taylor's school," Suellyn comments, "the teachers have mothers come in and work with the kids in the classroom when they need it." The support Taylor has received from these mothers has helped improve his academic functioning. See the accompanying "Inclusion Tips" box for students with AD/HD.

Collaboration

As a result of collaboration between his parents and teachers, Taylor has received appropriate accommodations. Students with AD/HD need to sense that all the important people in their life are working together for them.

Collaboration With Other Professionals.

Every professional and paraprofessional involved with the student who has AD/HD needs to understand and agree to follow guidelines for accommodations and behavior management specified in the 504/ADA plan or IEP. Teachers and others who work closely with the student will also need to monitor how the student responds to any changes in medication. The team leader should design an easy-to-

If you want to contact the student's physician, psychologist, or psychiatrist, make sure you have written permission from the parents first. Ask the parents to provide the professional with a release to talk to you as well.

An often overlooked organizational item is the book bag or backpack. There are many good ones available that help the student by providing specific spaces for everything from books to pencils, planners, calculators, and keys. A place for everything, and everything in its place!

By fifth grade, students should know simple filing methods. Consider having them take turns filing nonconfidential papers in a classroom file cabinet on a rotating basis.

Encourage parents to have them color code and file their papers in their room at home rather than stacking them on a table or shoving them in a drawer. Remember to use the same colors for folders at home that are used for notebooks at school.

Grades 6–12

Planners become an essential tool. They may be the small electronic type, which operate with batteries and fit in the pocket, or the zipper type, which has different sections for a calendar, address book, projects, etc. The needs of the student will determine the actual section labels. Whatever type of planner is used, it needs to be present with the student throughout the school day so that all necessary information is included.

Students in these grades need the help of locker organizers. Many types are available. Some have adjustable plastic shelves, some have tension shelves, and others are metal. Using these not only helps keep books and notebooks together and in order for the daily class schedule but also keeps lunches from being crushed before they are eaten. There are magnetic pen/pencil holders for the inside of locker doors. Some are hard plastic with mirrors, and some are soft plastic and have rows of pockets for everything from calculators and tissues to water bottles.

Of course, by now the student is consistently color coding and organizing the papers he needs to keep by subject as well as by grade level. They should be labeled and stored in corrugated boxes with handles or in plastic crates. Then, when a teacher asks the student to write a paper on a certain subject and he has already completed a similar one, he can draw from that paper to write the new one.

One last essential organizing tool is the Rolodex. Students need to learn to use this tool while in middle school and high school because when they go to college, it will become invaluable. Friends will move from place to place, changing addresses and phone numbers frequently. E-mail addresses will need to be recorded, and part-time employers will have office numbers students will need to remember, and when a professor assigns an impossible task, the student will have her favorite high school teacher's phone number for assistance.

use form that everyone can use to track the student's behavior and energy level. The parents should give the completed form to the physician at regular intervals.

Professionals will need to help students with AD/HD advocate for themselves. These students face challenges with adults on the school bus, on the playground, and in their communities who do not know about their condition; no professionals are available to explain. Wayne Wiggand expresses concern about Taylor's involvement in basketball and baseball. "He's not taught by teachers, and the coaches don't always understand. Taylor might get yelled at a lot more than the other kids because of that." It is important that professionals working with Taylor teach him to explain to these adults about his AD/HD and the accommodations he will need. See the accompanying box, "Collaboration Tips" to help a student develop self-advocacy skills.

Collaboration With Family.　Parenting a child with AD/HD is often challenging. Parents can experience doubt and depression about their parenting skills (Dendy, 1995). One parent commented to a therapist, as her child jumped on the sofa: "I've tried everything and nothing works. It's easier just to let him have his way than to correct him" (Flick, 1996). Siblings are often affected, too (Goldstein, 1996).

Inclusion Tips

	What You Might See	What You Might Be Tempted to Do	Alternate Responses	Ways to Include Peers in the Process
Behavior	*Inattentive Type:* Student is inattentive, withdrawn, forgetful, a daydreamer, and/or lethargic. *Hyperactive/Impulsive Type:* Student is restless, talkative, impulsive, and/or easily distracted. *Combined Type:* Features of both.	*Inattentive Type:* Overlook the student. *Hyperactive/Impulsive and Combined Types:* Be critical and punitive.	*Inattentive Type:* Recognize the student's presence daily in a positive way. *Hyperactive/Impulsive and Combined Types:* Catch the student being good. Look for opportunities to praise. Work with parents on consistent behavior management plan.	Model acceptance and appreciation for the student. Then peers are more likely to do the same.
Social interactions	*Inattentive Type:* Student withdraws from social situations. *Hyperactive/Impulsive and Combined Types:* Student bursts into social situations and may be socially gregarious or inappropriate and annoying.	*Inattentive Type:* Call attention to child's isolation in front of other students; try to force student to play. *Hyperactive/Impulsive and Combined Types:* Pull student out of social situation for inappropriate behavior.	Role play friendship skills. Help students discover their strengths, and encourage group participation in those activities. Start with small groups. Encourage membership in a support group for students with AD/HD.	For projects, pair student with another student who has similar interests and tends to be accepting. The initial goal is achieving one close friend.
Educational performance	Work is incomplete and/or sloppy. Homework is lost or forgotten. Materials are disorganized. Student may experience success in areas of strength and interest.	Make punitive or sarcastic comments.	Teach students how to organize their materials. Help them find a coach. Break assignments into manageable parts.	Use peer tutors with the student.
Classroom attitudes	Student motivation is inconsistent or lacking.	Give up on the student.	Use the principles of relevance, novelty, variety, choices, and activity in your teaching.	Use cooperative learning activities that are based on the five principles.

You will want to be sensitive to the stressors these families face and offer support. Taylor's second-grade teacher, Becky Swickard, shares this advice about supporting parents who might be frustrated or angry because of the stress:

> *Remember we work for the kids and the parents. When you have your first conference, you need to let parents know how much you care about them and their child. I have had a parent come to the conference angry. When that happens, if you try to get through to them that what you do is because you care, then they will be in your court. They need to see that you have the child's best interest at heart.*

Beverly Thompson, Taylor's teacher, concurs: "I meet with parents at least twice a year, many more times if needed. I see Mrs. Wiggand throughout the year. I'm always looking for suggestions from parents." This type of openness with parents is important when working with families who have a child or adolescent with AD/HD. It is prudent to remember that parents have probably tried a number of interventions already and may know what is most effective for their child. They can often give you helpful advice.

It is also important to help parents identify sources of support to cope with stress. Wayne and Suellyn Wiggand have identified several. Suellyn comments, "I go to church and rely a lot on the Lord. I've prayed a lot about Taylor. Our pediatrician is very knowledgeable and has been a lot of help. Our families—my husband's and mine—have also been very supportive." You might also want to help parents contact Ch.A.D.D. to find a local support group.

Hallowell and Ratey (1994) refer to the "Big Struggle" that can happen in families. A downward spiral may occur when the child with AD/HD is noncompliant with parental expectations. The parents attempt to enforce stringent penalties and restrictions, which lead to *more* stringent penalties and limitations. The child becomes defiant and alienated, causing the parents to "feel more exasperated with what increasingly appears to be an attitude problem, under voluntary control, rather than the neurological problem" of AD/HD.

For this reason, helping parents know how to respond "can be one of the most important and effective interventions for a child" with AD/HD (Ch.A.D.D., 1996c). Edwards (1995) recommends a useful strategy that you can teach parents; you will also find it beneficial in your classroom. By applying the approach at home and school, the child experiences consistency. You can provide parents with the following chart as you explain the strategy:

Positive Strategies	*Negative Strategies*
Praise	Ignoring
Rewards	Penalties
Special time	Time-Out

Help them identify three levels of behaviors they want to help the child change: (a) minor misbehaviors, (b) noncompliance with requests, and (c) violations of major household rules. Suggest that parents *ignore* minor misbehaviors that are probably not under the child's control (e.g., fidgeting, talking too much, bouncing around) and *praise* often for appropriate behaviors (catch them being good).

Rewards and penalties are reserved for compliance or noncompliance. Using poker chips for a token economy, a child earns or loses chips based on whether she complies with a parent's request. The poker chips are cashed in for privileges, money, or a price under specified conditions. A specific request is tied to a specific *reward* or *penalty.* For example, if you clean your room, you can go to the mall. If you don't clean your room, you will have to stay home.

Time-out, removal from access to privileges or attention for a short period of time, is reserved for the most severe rule violations. By reserving it for these behaviors, time-out is "a far more potent negative consequence" (Edwards, 1995). Parents also need to designate

Two books you might want to recommend to parents are *Power Parenting for Children with ADD/ADHD* (G. Flick, 1996, West Nyack, NY: The Center for Applied Research in Education) and *Teenagers with ADD: A Parent's Guide* (C. A. Zeigler Dendy, 1995, Bethesda, MD: Woodbine House).

Collaboration Tips

TEACHING SELF-ADVOCACY SKILLS

COLLABORATION GOAL To develop skills for the student with Attention-deficit/Hyperactivity Disorder that enable the student to eliminate learned helplessness and enhance self-esteem.

Collaborators	Roles and Preparation	Possible Barriers	Solutions to Barriers	Modifications to Implementation	Ongoing Evaluation
Student	List concerns about and ideas for self-advocacy.	May refuse to learn self-advocacy skills due to previous experiences, low self-esteem, and/or learned helplessness.	Work with therapist to overcome fears; encourage participation in a support group for students with AD/HD.	Make sure student has ownership of goals. Have the student role play self-advocacy in a safe environment before trying it in the real world.	Monitor student progress on specific skills. Have students determine how they will reward themselves when they achieve a goal.
Parents	List ideas for encouraging self-advocacy at home.	May feel need to protect and advocate for student.	Encourage parents to share their vision for the child's future and consider what self-advocacy skills the student will need to achieve that vision.	Encourage parents to develop a plan for family meetings in which the student is encouraged to voice opinions and share ideas.	Have a conference with parents periodically to determine progress. Remember that parents need positive reinforcement, too.
General Educator(s)	List what would be helpful for students with AD/HD to tell them.	May not want students to advocate because teacher does not see need to accommodate.	May not recognize that providing accommodations can make instruction easier. Educate about law and how to provide appropriate and easily-implemented accommodations.	Plan in-services for teachers about accommodating for students with AD/HD.	Ask teachers to share examples of when students self-advocate in their classes. Encourage teachers and students for desired responses.

ten to fifteen minutes a day as a *special time* with the child (Ch.A.D.D., 1996d). During this time, the child receives the parent's undivided attention. The special time should not be contingent on the child's behavior.

How can you create special times with students in your classroom?

Taylor's special time is just after dinner. Taylor loves to have this opportunity to share what's happened to him during the day. Sue and Wayne are attentive as Taylor tells his sometimes lengthy stories. They affirm him by their listening and positively commenting about how clever he is to have noticed or learned something new.

Collaboration With Peers. Many students with AD/HD have seriously impaired social relationships (Barkley, 1995b). Problems with social relationships can lead to low self-esteem, depression, antisocial behavior, and loneliness (Ch.A.D.D., 1996d). Whereas students with the hyperactive-impulsive and combined types have more difficulty with aggressive behaviors that annoy peers, students with the inattentive type are more likely to withdraw and be overlooked by peers.

Collaborators	Roles and Preparation	Possible Barriers	Solutions to Barriers	Modifications to Implementation	Ongoing Evaluation
Special Educator(s)	Collect lists, identify skills needed for self-advocacy, generate goals with student.	May want to protect and advocate for students, especially younger ones.	Remember that the ultimate goal of special educators is to bring their students to the point of not needing them.	Look for ways teachers might be encouraging dependency in their students and determine a plan for change.	Have students share their self-advocacy skills with younger students with AD/HD.
Student's physician	List what student needs to know and tell others about medication.	May not have time to generate list.	Ask administrator to write a brief letter explaining importance of physician being on the student's school team.	Provide the physician with an easy-to-complete checklist of self-help skills related to use of medication and a self-addressed stamped envelope.	Check mastery of skills in a second column on the physician's self-help checklist.
Counselor/ Psychologist/ Psychiatrist	Identify personality traits that may inhibit or encourage self-advocacy.	May not want to reveal this information.	Make sure parents and student understand and agree to how the information will be shared and sign a release.	Encourage counselor participation in reducing student anxiety about self-advocacy.	Ask counselor periodically for suggestions for other team members to assist student in improving self-advocacy skills.

Ch.A.D.D. (1996d) recommends the following steps to improve peer relationships: (a) observe the student to determine effective, poor, and absent social behaviors; (b) focus on one or two behaviors for change; (c) directly coach, model, and role play important behaviors; and (d) praise and reward the student for appropriate behaviors.

Two behaviors seem to be especially important for students with AD/HD to learn in order to be accepted by their peers: group awareness and self-acceptance. Popular children take the time to find out what is going on in a group and match their behavior to the group (Roan, 1994). Furthermore, students are more likely to be accepted when they can laugh at themselves and do not try to hide who they are.

Teachers can facilitate self-acceptance. "Fred likes bats," one mother comments (cited in Roan, 1994). "His teacher has made a point about allowing him to show his knowledge about bats to his class. So he had a chance to impress the other kids. Things like that really help."

"A lonely child, a child who feels bad for whatever reason, will simply not concentrate on the task at hand" (Roan, 1994).

Students with AD/HD do not need a large number of friends to feel good about themselves. Often, one close friend will do. Taylor doesn't have a lot of friends. In fact, he doesn't get invited to spend the night with anyone because the parents find his behavior "exhausting" at times. However, Taylor's best friend is Aaron. "Aaron lives right near me," Taylor says. "We like to ride bikes down our road. And we go up to his room and play Parchesi and Monopoly and jump on his trampoline."

"The close friends Taylor has are devoted to him," Suellyn Wiggand says. "When Taylor goes out at recess, his friend Aaron will tell the others, 'Let Taylor play the game.'"

Careers

Because many students with AD/HD do not require special education and related services, their attitude toward school and their perception of themselves as learners are often solely in the hands of general educators. Taylor remembers with fondness and gratitude the general educators who have enhanced his learning through a motivational curriculum and made sure he received the accommodations he needed. What a difference you can make in the lives of your students as a general educator!

Besides being a general educator, several other careers that we have mentioned can directly affect the lives of students with AD/HD. You might want to consider being a school psychologist or therapist who specializes in working with students who have AD/HD. Perhaps you will want to start your own business, as Lee R. Donald has, and become a professional organizer. Whatever field you enter, you will probably encounter people with AD/HD. Being understanding of their condition is another way you can make a difference.

WHAT ARE PROGRAM OPTIONS?

Professionals once believed that students with AD/HD outgrew the condition in adolescence. Current research suggests that most continue to face challenges as a result of the condition even into adulthood. A child who receives a diagnosis and program during the preschool years will have weapons to win the self-esteem, academic, social, and vocational battles that people with AD/HD usually face throughout life.

Early Intervention and Preschool Years

Somewhere between 5 and 10 percent of all infants exhibit "difficult temperament" (Goldstein, 1991). Obviously, all these children do not develop AD/HD, but research suggests that 70 percent will develop problems with learning, behavior, and socialization; therefore, they can be regarded as at risk.

Determining whether a preschool child has AD/HD is challenging. When you have observed typical three-year-olds, you probably noticed their boundless energy and curiosity. They have extremely short attention spans, and their responses to stimulation are "frequently unrestrained, enthusiastic, and exuberant" (Goldstein, 1991). Parental responses to (and ability to tolerate this normal behavior) differ, which contributes to whether the behavior escalates into misbehavior.

Research suggests that at least "70% to 80% of children later identified as AD/HD could have been identified from parental history by four years of age" (Goldstein, 1991). Goldstein recommends that by reviewing infant behavior such as crying, activity level, sleep difficulties, and feeding problems along with preschool behaviors ("language, activity level, attention span, mood, parent behavior, etc."), children who are high risk for AD/HD can be identified. Physicians need to screen for infants with difficult temperaments and provide parents with resources to prevent other behavior problems that can result from lack of attachment.

 Identifying preschool children is challenging because symptoms of AD/HD may result from developmental immaturity.

Many preschool programs include children with AD/HD. What makes an effective preschool program for these students? Szumowski (1996) recommends the following: (a) a half-day schedule; (b) small class size; (c) low teacher–student ratio; (d) trained teachers who enjoy their work and who emphasize encouragement and "positively toned discipline"; (e) a structured environment, which includes predictable routines, clear, consistently reinforced rules, limited down time, and exposure to some school-type activities that require sitting quietly and listening; (f) freedom for the child to choose from several activities that involve quiet and active play as well as freedom to use materials creatively; and (g) emphasis on the development of socialization and appropriate behavioral skills. Programs designed from these criteria can help children with AD/HD to enjoy school and attain the skills needed to become effective students.

"Peer rejection is a serious outcome of AD/HD because children who are rejected early in life tend to be at high risk for many adult adjustment difficulties, including job terminations, bad conduct discharge from the military, negative contact with police, and psychiatric hospitalization" (Landau & McAnich, 1993).

Elementary Years

The academics and structure of a classroom spotlight many previously undiagnosed children with AD/HD. Taylor experienced such difficulty that his kindergarten and first-grade teachers wanted to retain him. Thirty to fifty percent of children with AD/HD are retained a year or more. Retention contributes to poor self-esteem and generally does not improve the academic status of children with AD/HD (Barkley, 1995b). Finding alternatives, such as the following program, is important:

Mary-Jane Beach is a family therapist and consultant who also has AD/HD. She has collaborated with educators, artists, and specialists, including her husband John, an educational psychologist and learning disabilities specialist, to develop a unique multisensory curriculum called KanDoo™ (the logo is a kangaroo) to teach personal management skills to children with AD/HD and their families (Beach, 1997). The goals of her company, Bridges Associates, Inc., include helping students gain satisfaction, achievement, and enjoyment from life and relationships. The program also helps them achieve full membership and benefit from inclusionary classrooms.

Students savor learning songs, holding a plastic toy such as a ball to remind them to "get the ball rolling," and looking at picture cards that they also learn to associate with specific skills. The program, which is available for adolescents and adults as well, incorporates storytelling, puppets, and dramatic play for elementary-age children. Students also develop KanDoo Goals, use KanDoo Cards for Affirmation, and receive KanDid™ Awards for asking for help and achieving goals.

In addition, the program emphasizes having a coach. KanDoo Kangaroo Coaching Materials enable coaches to encourage skill learning for students with a variety of learning styles and preferences. Coaches learn to instruct students with AD/HD through these stages: (1) care and KanDoo attitude, (2) FOCUS on learning and attention, (3) get started, (4) develop confidence, (5) set goals, (6) build structure, (7) balance life, and (8) juggle life and maintain skills.

Middle and Secondary Years

Current findings show that 80 percent of students with AD/HD continue to experience AD/HD into adolescence (Ch.A.D.D., 1995a). Middle school and secondary students with AD/HD face new challenges: Classes change each hour, and each class has a different teacher. They have to remember locker combinations and which supplies to take to which classes. The schools are larger and often more impersonal. Furthermore, even though these students generally have poor social skills, having friends can become the most important aspect of life. It is not surprising that 35 percent of students with AD/HD drop out, and over 25 percent are expelled from high school as a result of misconduct (Barkley, 1995b).

Therefore, communication among secondary teachers about a student with AD/HD that they share is also critical. Lehigh University-Consulting Center for Adolescents with Attention Deficit Disorders (LU-CCADD) developed a grant to help middle school teachers work more effectively with their students who have AD/HD (Shapiro, DuPaul, Bradley, & Bailey, 1996). The program has three components: inservice training, on-site consultation, and advanced knowledge dissemination and follow-up consultation.

Lehigh's first step was to provide school representatives with basic information about AD/HD through a two-day in-service training. Attendees learned five important tasks for assisting students with AD/HD: (a) school-based self-management strategies, (b) school-based behavior management skills for teachers, (c) home-based behavior management for parents, (d) medication monitoring and pharmacological interventions, and (e) social skills and problem-solving training.

After the teachers were trained, a staff member from LU-CCADD worked with each participating school. The staff member held an action plan meeting with the primary team who had attended the in-service training. That team provided in-service training for the entire middle school faculty. Teachers from this meeting volunteered to serve as grade-level teams to coordinate services for the students.

The team targeted specific students who experienced difficulties stemming from their AD/HD. One student, for example, had difficulty following directions, disturbed classmates, and was frequently off-task. The team decided to implement one of the self-management programs they had learned about during the in-service training. They helped the student systematically judge his behavior against the behavior teachers expected of him. This intervention was coordinated with all his teachers by the team.

Parents received information during the program to help them understand policies that the district had developed. They also had their child's rights under IDEA and Section 504 explained, and they were told how to contact the local Ch.A.D.D. organization.

After the program was implemented, LU-CCADD staff turned the program over to the school. LU-CCADD continued to provide consultation services as needed, however.

Programs like this one offer a feasible way to keep secondary students with AD/HD from getting lost in these larger settings. Schools must make sure that all faculty under-

If you are interested in the Kan-Doo materials, write to Bridges Associates, Inc., 712 Main Street, Hyannis, MA 02601, or send an e-mail to Bridges@cape.com.

"This is what it is like to be a person with AD/HD. We try, delay, try again, procrastinate, and finally get it right. We are in a constant fight with the universe, but somehow we manage." (Mike Ginsberg, an adolescent with AD/HD; Ginsberg & Sartain, 1996).

stand AD/HD and how to provide accommodations. Coordination of services for the students with AD/HD must also occur.

Transitional and Postsecondary Years

Often, people have the misconception that individuals with AD/HD outgrow the disorder in adolescence. Certainly, some do. As many as 30 to 70 percent of children with AD/HD, however, continue to have symptoms of inattention, impulsivity, and/or hyperactivity as adults (Murphy, 1992). This condition, sometimes referred to as attention-deficit/hyperactivity disorder, residual state (AD/HD, RS), must have been present in childhood for the person to receive the diagnosis (Shekim, 1992).

Some adults with AD/HD predominantly inattentive type will continue to experience the lethargy, daydreaming, and withdrawal that was characteristic of their childhood. They "are mentally hyperactive but the noise they experience is internal" (Ratey, 1992). Ratey suggests that some of these people grow up to be the prototype of the absent-minded professor. Those with the hyperactive/impulsive or combined types may bounce from job to job and relationship to relationship.

Without the multimodal interventions we described earlier, adults with AD/HD are more likely to be less successful than their contemporaries (Cowley & Ramo, 1993). In addition, adults with AD/HD have a higher risk for alcoholism, personality disorders, and episodes of heightened stress than their peers (Ratey, 1992). On the other hand, many of these individuals, despite their AD/HD, are highly successful in their chosen occupations. Along with their success, however, they have a common feature—"their feeling of drivenness"—and describe themselves as "puppets at the mercy of some inner force" (Ratey, 1992).

Because of these characteristics, most postsecondary programs recognize that students with AD/HD often need accommodations to allow them to achieve their potential. Although special programs for those with AD/HD are uncommon, college campuses are required by the Americans with Disabilities Act to provide support services, such as alternative test-taking strategies, to help students with AD/HD succeed.

Vassar College long has been noted for its high academic standards, both in admissions decisions and in classroom expectations. Nonetheless, Vassar admitted Andrew Batshaw, despite the fact that he has a learning disability and has been diagnosed as having AD/HD. And Andrew has done well there.

Being accepted by a college or university that complies with the Americans with Disabilities Act, as Vassar does, does not guarantee success for the student. Support services alone will not be enough to cause a postsecondary student with AD/HD to meet the academic challenges. The student needs to be a self-advocate, helping others understand the support services he or she needs. Andrew learned self-advocacy skills early in his school career. In elementary school, Andrew began taking medication for AD/HD, along with receiving support from teachers, tutoring from his mother, and inspiration from his physician father, a specialist in children with disabilities. Through their encouragement, Andrew learned he could do whatever he chose as long as he worked hard. "I became comfortable with who I was," Andrew says. Being able to say those words is the foundation for self-advocacy.

By middle school, Andrew readily shared his disability with others. In a school report, he wrote, "I have found that while a disability inherently leaves you with a weakness, adapting to that disability can provide rewards. I feel that from coping with my disability, I have gained pride, determination, and a strength that will be with me all my life."

Another important component of postsecondary success is for students to choose a career that matches their strengths. Although flattered when asked by a professor to major in English (the curriculum with which he struggled until he was a tenth grader), Andrew chose computer science. The technology of that science itself facilitates his talents at problem solving. "Like some other people, I just think a certain way," the way that makes him so masterful of that field.

The fall 1996 issue of *Attention!* (see the "Resources" section for information) highlights transition issues for postsecondary students with AD/HD. Articles include "Using Strategies and Services for Success in College," "Key Steps to Selecting a College," and "Planning for the Future: Alternatives to College."

Self-knowledge, work, and memory . . . these three traits combine in Andrew to make him an exemplar of great expectations.

Now a successful junior at Vassar, Andrew, when asked what he would tell a room full of high schoolers with AD/HD, paused, thought for a moment, and then responded:

> *Don't limit yourselves. If you apply yourselves and really want something, you will find you can do it. Look where you've come from, at what you've already succeeded in doing.*

His answer to a similar question about tips to teachers?

> *Don't limit your students. Understand that they have disabilities. Accommodate to them. But purge the word* can't. *It's enough simply to say that the student has trouble doing something. Don't limit their will to try everything.*

Capitalizing on personal strengths, diligence, self-confidence, and self-knowledge—a history of discovering, knowing, and being comfortable with oneself—are critical traits that help Andrew and others with AD/HD succeed in their chosen fields.

A VISION FOR THE FUTURE

Taylor's parents have the same dreams for Taylor that they have for all their children. The Wiggands believe their children should take responsibility for decisions about their future. Suellyn shares her thoughts:

> *We want all our children to serve God. We want them to get an education and be what they want to be—their choice—and pursue their dreams and goals with us guiding them. I want Taylor to graduate from high school. And then I want him to pursue his dreams. I just want Taylor to be happy. Wayne emphasizes Taylor's need for a good education: The biggest thing overall is to see that they get as good an education as possible. Taylor needs to put forth as much effort as he can. Better trained people get better jobs. He will need good work habits and to be dependable, even if he works for himself like I do. He will still need to get in that groove.*

Wayne and Suellyn also recognize that Taylor will face challenges. According to Suellyn:

> *He'll probably always be on medication, and he'll have to make it on his own without his supportive family. We try to prepare Taylor and not shelter him. Besides, Taylor doesn't want to be treated differently.*
> *At school, they're trying to prepare Taylor for junior high. That scares me. They just don't give an inch in junior high and high school.*

Taylor already has big plans for his future. He says:

> *I'd like to be a zoologist because I like animals. I like working with animals and going to the zoo to see them. My favorite animal has to be the mountain gorilla. I'd also like to do carpetting because my dad, he owns a carpet business.*

Are these realistic dreams for a ten-year-old with AD/HD? Suellyn thinks so:

> *He can be a zoologist if he wants to. We have a vet up the road from us, and I think he might be able to start working some with him as he gets older. For him to be successful, he'll just have to make the decisions it takes. He'll need to be prepared to make the conscious decision to pursue what he wants to do.*

Wayne agrees, "If he gets a job in a field he likes, he will be an outstanding employee. I look for him to have a very bright future. He has the potential to do anything."

"I know with his positive attitude that he can do anything he wants to do," Suellyn adds. "He's not a quitter!"

Suellyn sums up the vision that everyone who knows Taylor has for him: "I hope he jumps right in there and gets it!"

What Would You Recommend . . .

1. To help Taylor adjust to junior high?

2. To prepare Taylor for a vocation?

3. To teach Taylor to advocate for himself at school and as an adult?

SUMMARY

WHAT IS ATTENTION-DEFICIT/HYPERACTIVITY DISORDER?

- AD/HD is defined by criteria in the *Diagnostic and Statistical Manual of the American Psychiatric Association* (4th edition) (DSM-IV).

- Under IDEA, students with AD/HD are served under the other health impairments category.

- There are three types of AD/HD: (1) predominately inattentive type, (2) predominately hyperactive-impulsive type, and (3) combined type.

- Students with AD/HD appear to experience a developmental delay of inhibition, which affects their ability to separate facts from feelings, use self-directed speech, and break apart and recombine information.

- Students with AD/HD often experience associated positive characteristics, including creativity and a sense of humor.

- Prevalence estimates of AD/HD are 3 to 5 percent of the general population.

- Many myths about causes of AD/HD exist. Probable causes are more likely biological than environmental, and it is likely that more than one cause is responsible.

WHAT ARE EVALUATION PROCEDURES?

- Diagnosis of AD/HD by a psychologist, psychiatrist, or physician often occurs outside the school system. The person who makes the diagnosis becomes part of the evaluation team.

- Behavior rating scales designed specifically for AD/HD and continuous performance tests are often used during evaluation.

- Some students may falsely appear to have AD/HD to evaluators outside their culture.

- Students who have AD/HD that adversely affects their educational progress may receive an IEP as other health impaired if they need special education and related services. If the AD/HD does not adversely affect educational performance, the student receives a 504/ADA plan. Appropriate accommodations for skill deficits are included in each plan.

HOW IS PARTICIPATION ENCOURAGED?

- For most students with AD/HD, the general classroom is the appropriate placement.

- Collaboration among professionals is important to provide the student with consistency and to monitor the effects of medication.

- Families sometimes get caught in the big struggle, a downward spiral of escalating discipline and negative behavior. It's important to provide support and resources to families who have a child with AD/HD. They need to learn to use positive and negative strategies based on the level of the student's behavior.

- Sometimes having one close friend can make a positive difference for a student with AD/HD.

WHAT AND HOW DO PROFESSIONALS TEACH?

- A multimodal approach to remediation, which may include medication, behavior management, coaching, education, counseling, and/or organizational training, is essential for students with AD/HD.

- Students with AD/HD benefit from a curriculum that incorporates relevance, novelty, variety, and activity.

WHAT ARE PROGRAM OPTIONS?

- Retention generally does not benefit students with AD/HD.

- Early intervention programs need to concentrate on family involvement.

- Elementary students can benefit from a multisensory, motivational program such as KanDoo.™

- Effective middle and secondary programs, such as those at Lehigh, concentrate on coordination of efforts for students with AD/HD across all teachers involved.

- Career options include professional coach or professional organizer to provide support services for students with AD/HD.

- Many adults have never been appropriately assessed with AD/HD. They continue to need a multimodal approach to remediation. Coaches benefit this population as well as children and adolescents.

RESOURCES

BOOKS

Driven to Distraction. (1994). By E. M. Hallowell and J. J. Ratey. New York: Simon & Schuster. Describes types of AD/HD and methods for remediation through a case study format. (See also *Answers to Distraction* (1995) by the same authors and publisher.)

How to Reach and Teach ADD/ADHD Children. (1994). By S. Rief. Upper Saddle River, NJ: Prentice Hall. Includes classroom-tested techniques, strategies, and interventions.

BOOKS FOR CHILDREN AND ADOLESCENTS

Active Andy: An elementary school child's guide to understanding AD/HD. (1993). By K. Bauer. Wauwatusa: IMDW Publications. Tips for children with AD/HD.

Learning to slow down and pay attention (2nd ed.). (1993). By K. Nadeau and E. Dixon. Ammandale, Chesapeake Psychological Publications. Tips for children and adolescents with AD/HD.

JOURNALS, MAGAZINES, AND CATALOGS

A.D.D. Warehouse. 300 Northwest Seventieth Avenue, Suite 102, Plantation, FL 33317. (800) 233-9273. Free catalog of resources for helping students with AD/HD. Internet address: http://www.addwarehouse.com.

Women with Attention Deficit Disorder (1995). By S. Solden. Grass Valley: Underwood Books. Discusses girls and women with the inattentive type of AD/HD.

Making the grade. (1994). By R. Parker Plantation, FL: Specialty Press. An adolescent's struggle with ADD.

Otto learns about his medicine. (1988). By M. Galum. New York: Imagination Press. A child learns about Ritalin.

Slam Dunk. (1995). By R. Parker. Plantation, FL: Specialty Press. Young people's guide to understanding ADD.

ADDvance. A magazine devoted to women with AD/HD. Call (888) 238-2588 to subscribe.

Attention! The journal of the organization Ch.A.D.D. Call (954) 587-3700 to subscribe.

MULTIMEDIA

AD/HD-Inclusive Instruction and Collaborative Practices (video). By S. F. Rief. Plantation, FL: A.D.D. Warehouse. Describes suggestions for including students with AD/HD in general classrooms.

AD/HD—What Can We Do? (video). By R. A. Barkley, Plantation, FL: A.D.D. Warehouse. Effective ways to manage AD/HD at home and school. Companion versions include *AD/HD—What Do We Know?* and special versions for parents.

AD/HD in the Classroom—Strategies for Teachers (video). By R. A. Barkley. Plantation, FL: A.D.D. Warehouse. Effective methods for accommodating students with AD/HD.

Answers to A.D.D.—The School Success Tool Kit (video). By J. F. Taylor. Plantation, FL: A.D.D. Warehouse. Features teachers and parents using many practical techniques.

ON-LINE INFORMATION AND USEFUL DATABASES

Attention Deficit Disorder. Internet address: http://comp.uark.edu/%7Ejwiggins/add/index/html. Information and fact sheets as well as poems and stories by people with attention deficit hyperactivity disorder.

Attention Deficit Disorder: Bob Seay's Mining Company. Internet address: http://add.miningco.com/. The author of "The Story of D" has many useful articles on AD/HD.

Brakes. Internet address: www.bmpub.com. An on-line newsletter for children and adolescents with AD/HD.

Glen Danforth's Humor Factory. Internet address: http://www.cris.com/~nd1irish/index.htm. Includes comments about AD/HD.

One A.D.D. Place. Internet address: http://www.iquest.net/great-connect/oneaddplace/. Consolidates resources on AD/HD in one place.

Shari Lander's Attention Deficit Disorder Site. Internet address: http://www.cogsci.princeton.edu/~shari/add.html. Links to on-line support groups, information on colleges and secondary schools, and links for children and adults with AD/HD.

Welcome to H.A.D.D. IT! (Humorous ADDults Intriguing Themselves). Internet address: http://www.busprod.com/scurtiss/homepg.html. Enjoy the unabridged version of the ADD Dictionary, a Miss ADD contest, and more.

ORGANIZATIONS

Children and Adults with Attention Deficit Disorder (Ch.A.D.D.). 1859 North Pine Island Road, Suite 185, Plantation, FL 33322. (954) 587-3700. Internet address: http://www.chadd.org/. Offers supports to people with attention deficit disorder and their families; journals available.

National Attention Deficit Disorder Association. 9930 Johnnycake Ridge Road, Suite 3E, Mentor, OH 44060. (800) 487-2282. Internet address: http://www.add.org

National Association of Professional Organizers (NAPO). 1033 LaPosada Dr., Suite 220, Austin, TX 78752-3880. (512) 454-8626, fax (512) 454-3036. Internet address: http://www.ccsi.com/~asmi/GROUPS/NAPO/napo.html. Find a professional organizer in your area.

CHAPTER 7

GIFTEDNESS

Educating
Nadine Cambridge

Nadine Cambridge is a ten-year-old fifth grader at Morrison Elementary School in Athens, Ohio. Nadine's parents are from Guyana, South America, but Nadine and her four-year-old brother, Nigel, were born here in the United States. Nadine's life is like most other ten-year-olds in that she daily attends a regular fifth-grade class and participates in everyday class instruction and activities. As typical of many middle grade students, she has different teachers for different subject areas. She spends most of her time in the classroom of Ms. Van Dyke, where she studies math and language arts. She learns science with Ms. Lunsford and social studies with Ms. Conroy. Every day except for Tuesday, Nadine works, and sometimes struggles, to complete all of the assignments required. She admits she has a problem with neatness. She says, "It's because they don't give enough time to get all my ideas down." In this setting, Nadine doesn't appear to be a risk-taking student who is gifted.

Then, on Tuesday, Nadine takes on another role as a gifted and talented young girl in a pullout

talented and gifted program sponsored by the Athens City Schools. On Tuesday, all fifth-grade students identified as gifted in the city of Athens attend Ms. Korn's challenging learning environment at East Elementary School. Nadine loves Tuesdays. On Tuesday, Nadine becomes a risk taker, willing to ask and answer provocative questions, willing to work at and solve difficult problems.

Students like Nadine are often an enigma to their teachers. In her general class setting Nadine has many subjects to cover with little time for creativity or individualized attention. On the other hand, in the gifted class setting, she focuses on completely different learning material. Nadine says she would "love the learning to be more integrated," but it is hard for general and gifted education teachers to find time to integrate learning topics on behalf of each of their students.

Nadine does her best to handle the two different worlds. She wants to fit in and to please her regular classroom teacher, Ms. Van Dyke, so she asks procedural questions to be sure she is on the right track. She also wants to learn and benefit from her time with Ms. Korn. The learning environment that Ms. Korn has created is more conducive to meet the needs of students who are gifted like Nadine. A typical day in the talented and gifted program includes many creative opportunities for students who are gifted to collaborate on their learning with one another. For example, each ten weeks, students in Nadine's talented and gifted class cover two different units on such diverse subjects as criminal and civil law, media criticism, or math logic. Ms. Korn tries to help her students broaden and develop their own understanding in these areas.

For instance, one afternoon as part of a media criticism unit, Nadine and her classmates walked up town and, as pairs, interviewed Ohio University students about their television viewing. The class had previously worked together to develop the interview, and now, after data collecting, they were going to tally and compare their findings. Ms. Korn has plans to expand this particular research study to survey university students in other cities and thus provide her students an opportunity

to submit their findings for publication to an education journal. It is in this type of educational setting Nadine flourishes. She has more ideas than she has time to explore. Often Nadine and her friend Jessica spend time together outside of their talented and gifted class to work on other creative projects, like writing poems together. Nadine points out that they do this "not for grades, but just for fun!"

Nadine's mom and dad have seen this side of Nadine from an early age. At two, Nadine was sounding out words without any parental instructions. On her own, she read and enjoyed books by Dr. Souss and Bridwoll, who wrote the Clifford books.

Pat Cambridge, Nadine's mother, describes her daughter as analytical. "She sees problems and then goes below the surface to understand them." Nadine was four years old at the time of the Gulf War. Because of her intense interest in countries around the world, she watched news and documentaries with her parents. She asked her mother, "Why is it that Egypt is in Africa, but they make it sound as if the people are from the Middle East?" At age four, Nadine recognized the discrepancy. Today Nadine describes herself as someone who thinks deeply about things. "It's like I think of all the possible answers to a problem, evaluate each one and then choose the best one."

Parental support has always been a high priority in Nadine's family. Nadine's mom and dad are both profes-sors at Ohio University and have heavy demands on their time. But their first priority is family, and they make a point of eating meals together and taking vacations together. Last year, when Nadine's mom had a teaching assign-ment in Malaysia, the whole family accompanied her. It was the chance of a lifetime for Nadine. She can talk for hours about all she learned, showing examples of artifacts and souvenirs and explaining their cultural relevance.

It's clear that Nadine loves to learn and that her par-ents have great expectations for her. It's also clear that not all her daily experiences provide the environment most conducive to reaching those expectations. These are typical challenges faced by students who are gifted and talented. Solutions are best found through collabo-ration by all involved with the student's schooling.

What Do You Think?

1. How could Nadine's teachers and parents help Nadine understand the charac-teristics of her giftedness to overcome her insecurities and encourage her to work in areas that are not as interesting or easy for her?

2. How could Nadine's teachers and parents find and utilize all the people and resources, methods, and curriculum necessary to the success of gifted and talented students like Nadine?

3. How could you collaborate with all of Nadine's teachers to encourage them to build on Nadine's inherent strengths in the regular education classroom?

What Is Giftedness?

Defining Giftedness

Gifted people have high perfor-mance capability in areas such as intellectual, creative, artistic, lead-ership, physical or intuitive/intrapersonal ability, or in specific academic fields.

Think for a minute about someone you consider **gifted.** Did you choose an adult or child you know personally? Is that person in any way like Nadine? Or is your choice a histori-cal figure, perhaps Mozart, Madame Curie, Einstein, or Martin Luther King, Jr.? In making your selection, you used certain criteria as a basis for your decision.

If you chose an adult, your criteria reflected prodigious accomplishments in a specific field of work, such as Mozart's musical works. If you chose a child, you may have relied on several criteria. She may do well in school, have high scores on standardized tests, be mature for her age, or have exceptional talent in art or dance. These characteristics may qualify her for service under some of the current definitions of giftedness.

From the example of Nadine, as well as from the individual you selected, you can see the great diversity of characteristics in people who are gifted. It is not always an easy task to identify and plan effective learning experiences for students who are gifted. In this chapter you will learn about various types of giftedness and how to understand and work effectively with individuals who are gifted.

Historical Overview. Historically, giftedness has been defined in a multitude of ways, each according to its relevance in culture. Currently, forty-seven states have enacted definitions of giftedness to guide their schools' programs and obtain federal funds. The definitions vary, but many are based on the federal definition. This definition of individuals who are gifted was a part of the 1994 reauthorization of the Jacob K. Javits Gifted and Talented Students Education Act of 1988:

> *The term "gifted and talented" when used in respect to students, children or youth means students, children or youth who give evidence of high performance capability in areas such as intellectual, creative, artistic, or leadership ability, or in specific academic fields, and who require service or activities not ordinarily provided by the school in order to fully develop such capabilities. (Public Law 103-382—Title XIV, 1988, p. 388)*

This definition acknowledges that giftedness is worthy of federal attention, states that these students require services, describes areas and characteristics of giftedness, and establishes a standard for distributing funds.

Paradoxically, the definition and accompanying legislation do not require states to establish programs for students who are gifted and talented. This means that students who are talented and gifted are *not* guaranteed special education by federal legislation or laws. The choice to provide service or not belongs to state or local education agencies. Their right to choose is one substantial difference between gifted education and special education for students with disabilities (see Chapter 1). Fifteen states and Puerto Rico require nondiscriminatory evaluations, similar to those used in special education programs for students with disabilities, before they serve a student in special education programs tailored for giftedness (Jenkins-Friedman & Nielsen, 1990). All but six states have legislation that either mandates or encourages specialized services for gifted learners (Council for Exceptional Children, 1995). While some states require an individualized education program (IEP) for placement in the gifted program, Ohio, Nadine's state, allows students to be placed into existing gifted education programs with less standardized procedures or without planning the individual services to be provided.

Although the federal definition now guides many education agencies, it was by no means the first attempt to identify students of high ability. Lewis Terman laid the groundwork for this definition when in 1922 he began to study individuals with high IQs. In his research for *Genetic Studies of Genius,* he collected data on 1,500 youngsters with IQs over 140 (Terman, 1926; Terman & Oden, 1959). This work was especially important because it was the initial effort to collect extensive data and report on the health of individuals with high IQs, and it helped dispel the mythical tie between extraordinary ability and neuroticism.

On the other hand, Terman's work created two misconceptions. He developed an IQ test to assess aptitude for performing cognitive tasks and then equated **genius** with IQ, thus ruling out giftedness in the arts, leadership, or other fields. He also connected genius with genetics, leading to the false implication that intelligence was an inherited commodity that didn't change. While intelligence and giftedness do in part depend on genetic patterns, the two traits also vary according to psychosocial factors and therefore may be influenced and even changed by various opportunities throughout life.

Nadine's state, Ohio, has increased its support for teaching students who are gifted and talented by funding over 200 new positions for the 1996–1997 school year. What funding or support does your state provide for students who are gifted?

Genius is a term reserved for persons or works that are not only expert and creative but also assume a universal, or quasiuniversal, significance.

Previously, it was erroneously thought that people who were highly intelligent were also high strung and neurotic. Historically, geniuses have been equated with madmen (Tannenbaum, 1983).

Recent Perspectives. Today, a shift in the understanding of the nature of giftedness is reflected by a controversy about what to call these students. The federal report *National Excellence: A Case for Developing America's Talent* (U.S. Department of Education, 1993) has deleted the word *gifted* and has substituted the words *outstandingly talented* and *exceptionally talented.* While many researchers support the use of the concept of *talent,* still others believe that the descriptor *gifted* more accurately reflects the broad range of abilities demonstrated by these individuals.

As the disagreement over terminology reflects, there have been definite changes in how educators define students who are gifted. Feldman (1992) provides a concise overview of these changes (see Table 7–1).

In Table 7–1, note the complexity of change in our understanding of how to identify and effectively educate individuals who are gifted. One of the key changes centers on the need to include more than one category to define what giftedness is. This is important because *how you define students who are gifted will help determine how you identify and teach them.*

Two Conceptual Models. Some researchers have proposed conceptual models that explain the different factors involved in giftedness. For example, according to Renzulli (1978), *gifted* should be defined to include three factors essential for high-quality, creative productivity in any type of activity or endeavor. As shown in Figure 7–1, he proposed that an individual who produced new, original contributions in a field would possess the following characteristics: (a) above-average ability, (b) **creativity,** and (c) task commitment. Such clarifications in definition have helped direct changes in how students such as Nadine are served in today's educational world.

Sternberg and Zhang (1995) have also proposed a conceptual theory, termed the *pentagonal implicit theory,* whose model encompasses five necessary criteria that a person must meet in order to be judged gifted: the excellence criterion, the rarity criterion, the productivity criterion, the demonstrability criterion, and the value criterion. Table 7–2 defines the five criteria and how they are determined. The goal of this theory is to decide "what we value as gifted before embarking on a program of identification" (Sternberg & Zhang, 1995, p. 88) and to encourage us to "capture and systematize people's intuitions about what makes an individual gifted" (p. 89).

Two Domain-Specific Models. A definition that regards intelligence as multidimensional within different domains of giftedness and not unidimensional (based on scores alone), is referred to as ***domain-specific giftedness,*** an approach that has broad support (Blythe & Gardner, 1990; Csikszentmihalyi & Robinson, 1986; Gardner, 1983; Gardner, 1993b). Domain-specific giftedness does not imply that giftedness operates in isolation.

Creativity is reserved for unusual or unique expressions within a domain. Students who are creative may be more adventurous, independent, curious, spontaneous, flexible, sensitive, intuitive, and insightful than their peers. They also have more original ideas and may have a zany sense of humor.

Domain-specific giftedness refers to giftedness that occurs in a specific area such as math, art, leadership, or athletics. This does not imply that giftedness operates in isolation but rather that some children have specific abilities that are not revealed by test scores alone. Researchers agree that within each domain or category, there are varying degrees of giftedness, ranging from gifted and talented to the rare genius.

TABLE 7–1 ❧ *Differences in emphasis between the traditional and the emerging paradigms for gifted education*

Traditional Paradigm	Emerging Paradigm
Giftedness = High IQ	Multiple forms
Trait theory: stable, unchangeable	Trait theory: developmental, process-oriented
Identification based on tests	Identification based on performance
Elitist in orientation	Excellence a focus
Giftedness expresses itself without special intervention	Context is crucial
Authoritarian, top-down	Collaborative at all levels
School-oriented	Field-oriented
Ethnocentric	Diversity central to mission

Note: From "Has There Been a Paradigm Shift in Gifted Education?" by D. H. Feldman, in *Talent Development: Proceedings from the 1991 Henry B. and Jocelyn Wallace National Research Symposium on Talent Development* (p. 93), edited by N. Coangelo, S. G. Assouline, and D. L. Ambroson, 1992, New York: Trillium. Copyright 1992 by Trillium. Reprinted with permission.

FIGURE 7–1 *Renzulli's graphic three-ring definition of giftedness*

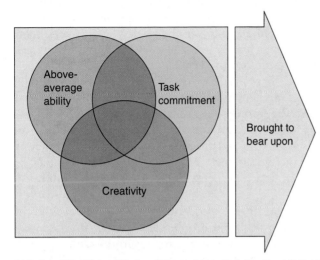

General performance areas

Mathematics • Visual Arts • Physical Sciences • Philosophy • Social Sciences • Law • Religion • Language Arts • Music • Life Sciences • Movement Arts

Specific performance areas

Cartooning • Astronomy • Public Opinion Polling • Jewelry Design • Map Making • Choreography • Biography • Film Making • Statistics • Local History • Electronics • Musical Composition • Landscape Architecture • Chemistry • Demography • Microphotography • City Planning • Pollution Control • Poetry • Fashion Design • Weaving • Play Writing • Advertising • Costume Design • Meteorology • Puppetry • Marketing • Game Design • Journalism • Electronic Music • Child Care • Consumer Protection • Cooking • Ornithology • Furniture Design • Navigation • Genealogy • Sculpture • Wildlife Management • Set Design • Agricultural Research • Animal Learning • Film Criticism • etc.

Note: From "What Makes Giftedness? Reexamining a Definition," by J. S. Renzulli, 1978, *Phi Delta Kappan, 60,* p. 184. Copyright 1978 by J. S. Renzulli. Reprinted with permission.

TABLE 7–2 ✍ *Pentagonal implicit theory: an adaptation of Sternberg and Zhang's Five Criteria (1995)*

Criterion	Definition	How Determined	Example: Eight-year-old piano player
Excellence	Superior in some dimension or set of dimensions relative to peers.	Determined by an abundance in the dimension "relative to peers." The designation of excellence depends upon the skills of those against whom one is judged.	Plays the piano much better than other eight-year-olds with similar training.
Rarity	High level of an attribute that is rare relative to peers.	Determined by an abundance of an attribute only when an evaluation of that attribute is judged to be rare "relative to peers."	Playing is not only superior but rare compared to peers.
Productivity	The dimension(s) along which the individual is evaluated as superior must lead to or potentially lead to productivity.	For children, productivity is more often determined by potential products rather than actual products. But to earn the label *gifted* without qualification, a person must accomplish something.	Not only plays but writes music recognized as excellent by other musicians.
Demonstrability	The superiority of the individual on the dimension(s) that determine giftedness must be demonstrable through one or more tests that are valid assessments.	Determined by an assessment instrument that must have been validated.	Wins adult performing artists contest governed by official standards.
Value	Superior performance in a dimension that is valued for that person by his or her society.	Determined by what is valuable in a specific culture, time and/or place.	Is recognized by culture for superior performance—appears on television talk shows.

Note: Copyrighted material from Gifted Child Quarterly (GCQ) Vol. 39, No. 2, *What Do We Mean by "Giftedness"? A Pentagonal Implicit Theory,* by Robert J. Sternberg and Li-fang Zhang. Reprinted with permission from the National Association for Gifted Children, Washington, DC.

Even as early as 1940, one researcher maintained that giftedness belongs to those "whose performance is consistently remarkable in any potentially valuable area" (Witty, 1940, p. 516).

Certainly, a gifted mathematician may also be equally gifted in art, leadership, and athletics. In fact, some people exhibit more than one area of giftedness, while others excel in one area only. While Nadine is an example of students in the general intellectual category, she is also uniquely creative. For example, Nadine and her friend Jessica have created their own newspaper called *Cool News*. It's a paper just for girls. They not only write the articles and features but also use a computer to design the layout.

Although most definitions of giftedness reflect the federal definition, some researchers include additional categories in their definition. Clark (1997) theorizes that gifted students learn differently because they process information differently. Her definition of giftedness focuses on the four major functions of the brain: cognitive, affective, physical, and intuitive. These functions are expressed through different abilities, such as intellectual, leadership, artistic, and predictive abilities. When an individual has one or more of these abilities, he or she is gifted and may need additional services to develop capabilities more fully.

Like Clark (1997), Gardner (1983, 1993a, 1993b) also proposes a definition different from the federal definition by including physical and intuitive/intrapersonal giftedness. Gardner now describes eight specific intelligences found across cultures and societies. These **multiple intelligences** are musical, bodily-kinesthetic, linguistic, logical-mathematical, spatial, interpersonal, intrapersonal and naturalistic. Table 7–3 gives a general overview of how Clark's and Gardner's categories line up with the federal definition.

Consistent with the domain-specific perspective, Table 7–4 sets out Gardner's eight areas of potential giftedness and lists the typical characteristics and distinctive features parents and educators might see in gifted students. Interestingly, recent research on the

Multiple intelligences describe different kinds of giftedness that are found across cultures and societies.

How would you describe Michael Jordan: gifted, prodigious, or genius? Can you project the kinds of difficulties he might have had in school?

Federal Category	Clark's (1997) Category	Gardner's (1983, 1993a, 1993b, in press) Category
Performing/visual arts	Physical: sensing	Musical
	Physical: movement	Bodily-kinesthetic
Leadership	Affective: social and emotional	Interpersonal
Creative	Cognitive: spatial	Spatial
Intellectual/academic	Cognitive: linear	Linguistic
Intellectual/academic	Cognitive: linear	Logical-mathematical
	Intuitive/predictive	Intrapersonal
		Naturalist

TABLE 7–3 🐦 *Contrasting perspectives on definitions of giftedness*

brain also indicates that there are windows of opportunity for developing these different areas because circuits in different regions of the brain mature at different times (Begley, 1996).

Researchers agree that within each domain or category, there are varying degrees of giftedness, ranging from gifted and talented to the rare genius. Gardner's work (1993b, in press) offers definitions that can better help explain the spectrum for children who are gifted and talented within any area of intelligence. According to Gardner, "*giftedness* is a sign of precocious biopsychological potential in whichever domains exist in a culture," whereas "*prodigiousness* is an extreme form of giftedness in a domain" (1993b, p. 51). In other words, a gifted individual shows unusual promise in a specific task or domain, but a **prodigy** goes beyond unusual promise to being unmistakably extraordinary.

A student who has shown unusual promise in linguistic, logical/mathematical, spatial, and interpersonal abilities is Michael Kearney. Michael, unmistakably extraordinary with an IQ over 200, graduated from college at the age of ten with a B.A. in anthropology and is now at age thirteen completing a master's degree in chemistry. Few students fall into the same category as Michael, who is prodigiously gifted. Box 7-1 describes what it was like for Michael to be a child prodigy.

Individuals who display a particular domain of giftedness, says Gardner (1993b), often will show both **expertise** and creativity within that domain. Expertise pertains to the technical mastery of skills and lore within a domain. In contrast, creativity is reserved for unusual or unique expressions within a domain. For example, Michael demonstrated unusual ability to create and solve algebraic equations at the age of three.

Finally, Gardner proposes that the term *genius* be reserved for "those persons or works that are not only expert and creative but that also assume a universal, or quasi-universal significance" (1993b, p. 52). While it is clear that Michael already has a high degree of intelligence, only time will reveal whether he will demonstrate the expertise and creativity to contribute significant work to meet Gardner's definition of a genius.

Another recent perspective on giftedness that has received increased attention is that of emotional intelligence (Goleman, 1995). Brain and behavioral researcher Daniel Goleman has described the factors at work when people of high IQ struggle to succeed while those of average IQ flourish. According to Goleman's theory, intelligence is not fixed at birth, and the qualities of self-awareness, impulse control, persistence, self-motivation, empathy, and social deftness can be nurtured and strengthened in any individual. Goleman explains that these factors contribute to a different way of being smart—one he terms *emotional intelligence.* Having high cognitive intelligence does not imply skills in any other area of life, and in fact, such a person may be very low in terms of emotional intelligence. This theory of intelligence, similar to Gardner's interpersonal and intrapersonal domains of giftedness, provides a broader explanation for how giftedness can be demonstrated.

A **prodigy** is a gifted individual who shows extraordinary promise in a specific task or domain.

Expertise pertains to the technical mastery of skills and lore within a domain.

TABLE 7–4 ❧ *Potential areas of giftedness: An adaptation of Howard Gardner's seven areas of intelligence*

Area	Gifted Person	Possible Characteristics of Giftedness	Early Indicators of Giftedness
Musical	Ella Fitzgerald Itzhak Perlman	Unusual awareness and sensitivity to pitch, rhythm, and timbre Ability may be apparent without musical training Uses music as a way of capturing feelings	Ability to sing or play instrument at an early age Ability to match and mimic segments of song Fascination with sounds
Bodily-kinesthetic	Michael Jordan Nadia Comenici	Ability can be seen before formal training Remarkable control of bodily movement Control, craft, poise	Skilled use of body Good sense of timing
Logical-mathematical	Albert Einstein Stephen Hawking	Loves dealing with abstraction Problem solving is remarkably rapid Solutions can be formulated before articulated: Aha! Ability to skillfully handle long chains of reasoning	Doesn't need hands-on methods to understand concepts Fascinated by and capable of making patterns Ability to figure things out without paper Loves to order and reorder objects
Linguistic	Virginia Woolf Maya Angelou	Remarkable ability to use words Prolific in linguistic output, even at a young age	Unusual ability in mimicking adult speech style and register Rapidity and skill of language mastery Unusual kinds of words first uttered
Spatial	Picasso Frank Lloyd Wright	Ability to conjure up mental imagery and then transform it Ability to recognize instances of the same element Ability to make transformations of one element into another	Intuitive knowledge of layout Able to see many perspectives Notices fine details, makes mental maps
Interpersonal	Martin Luther King, Jr. Madeleine Albright	Great capacity to notice and make distinctions among people: contrasts in moods, temperaments, motivations, and intentions Ability to read intention and desire of others in social interactions: not dependent on language	Able to pretend or "play act" different roles of adults Easily senses the moods of others; often able to motivate, encourage, and help others
Intrapersonal	Sigmund Freud Ruth Westheimer ("Dr. Ruth")	Extensive knowledge of the internal aspects of a person Increased access to one's own feelings and emotions Mature sense of self	Sensitivity to feeling (sometimes overly sensitive) Unusual maturity in understanding of self
Naturalist	Margaret Mead John Audubon	Relates to the world around them In tune with the environment	Recognizes and differentiates many types of an environmental item such as different makes of cars Recognizes many different rocks, minerals, trees

BOX 7-1   **MY VOICE**

MICHAEL KEARNEY

Thinking back on my years of college, I can see that I've dealt with many issues such as the difficulty of development discrepancies, problems of conformity, and the general lack of understanding and support from the majority of people. I am constantly trying to maintain my emotional balance as I confront disbelieving educators and students. At the same time I am trying to be myself—a child, who has the ability to learn and the desire to be educated.

Don't believe the myths about children like myself that we will not become an achieving and well-adjusted adult. On the contrary, research shows that acceleration is beneficial, both academically and socially. Given appropriate education and personal support, children like myself will make a major contribution to the future.

To understand what life is like for someone like me, I must go back to the day I received my IQ results. Being told that I am not just somewhat different, but dramatically different, was both thrilling and terrifying. The thrill was being told that I am extremely bright, but the terror was knowing that society could never learn to put a square peg in a round hole.

Growing up, I have dealt with teachers who have never knowingly met, much less taught someone like me. I had to deal with principals who doubted my test results, who disliked the word *gifted,* who were reluctant to make special accommodations for my needs, and who if encouraged by law or policy, did so at a snail's pace.

In addition to struggles around decision making about school, I faced a general lack of understanding and support when it came time to attend my first day in college. I remember going through the hallways, looking at the faces of these students, and listening to them refer to me as "Doogie Howser." I thought to myself, I don't look anything like him, and I could never be a doctor. I hate the sight of blood and hospitals. Later, I came to realize that the general public is only aware of children like me through television. Well, any type of awareness is better than none.

Another issue that I had to deal with while attending college was the chatter of my classmates. They felt that my parents had pushed me; I beg to differ. My parents have done their best to see that I am a well-adjusted and a loving human being. For example, when I decided I wanted to go to college, they had to deal with the unexpected financial costs of early college attendance. They have been behind me 100 percent.

I started out at the age of six, as a child who thrived on learning and craved for a stimulating educational system that would enhance my academic spirit. At the University of South Alabama, I was allowed the freedom to think, act independently, and to pursue my educational excellence even though I was only eight. These educators believed that children like myself have the potential to excel in an appropriate education.

After I graduate, I plan to travel and then work on a graduate degree in biochemistry to gain whatever knowledge is out there for me to grasp. My life captures the essence of the pursuit of excellence as a personal journey to overcome creative barriers imposed by the necessities of everyday college life. To be passionately in love with my work in college provides meaning for my existence.

A life of quiet desperation awaits those who will not strive for excellence. My journey is not over, but I have come a long way. My life experiences are quite different from most, and the wisdom I can share at this moment is that individual differences do exist in society and we must learn to accept and encourage those with such differences.

Michael Kearney at age nine

"Giftedness is something we invent, not something we discover. It is what one society or another wants it to be" (Sternberg & Davidson, 1986, p. 3).

Multicultural Perspectives.   If giftedness and genius include all types of human intelligences, how might the definition vary by culture? In some cultures, a cultural definition may include a gifted healer. The Hopi Indians, for instance, value each individual as a part of the whole and help prepare each one to be a candidate for a valued role such as a tribal healer (Coady, 1989). When there is a need for a new tribal healer, the community selects the person who best demonstrates both expertise and creativity necessary for a gifted healer.

Other cultures may focus on completely different areas of giftedness. For example, people from Polynesia recognize and highly prize sports, art, song, and dance more than Western-type academic and technological pursuits (Reid, 1989). As a teacher you will need to recognize the construct of cultural giftedness, because children from cultures different from your own may demonstrate giftedness in domains outside your knowledge or experience.

Describing the Characteristics

You can see that identifying the characteristics of all people who are gifted is complicated. Yet all special abilities often provide clues to parents and educators. Parents and general educators are the ones who most often identify students with exceptional abilities (Scott, Peron, Urbano, Hogan, & Gold, 1992; Webb, Meckstroth, & Tolan, 1982; Winner, 1996). But what exactly do they see? How early can giftedness be recognized? Nadine's parents recognized her exceptional abilities when she began reading on her own at age two.

Expected Characteristics.   Although the great diversity in giftedness means there is no typical gifted student, most who are gifted have some common traits. Building on the federal categories for giftedness, let's first examine characteristics common to individuals who are gifted:

- General intellect

- Specific academic ability

- Creative productive thinking

- Leadership ability

- Visual and performing artisticness

Do you think a child who shows concern with values, ethics, or justice may be giving clues that reveal intrapersonal giftedness? What other categories of giftedness might these characteristics fit into?

General Intellect.   Students who demonstrate high general intellect are able to grasp concepts, generalize, analyze, or synthesize new ideas or products far more easily than other students their age (Bloom, 1956; Clark, 1997). In addition, such students may indicate concern for issues or events relating to values, ethics, or justice at a young age. Do you remember Nadine's questioning the accuracy of television reports that made it sound like the people of Egypt were from the Middle East? Even at age four, she had an internal sense of what was right and that it was being wrongly represented by TV coverage.

Many students who are gifted have excellent memories and ask many questions. In preschool-age children, advanced vocabulary and extended periods of concentration are often typical. It is not unusual for children who are gifted to process information both faster and more efficiently than other children. Nadine, for example, assimilates information quickly and then lets her mind drift to other topics while in her regular classroom. For Nadine and others like her, this can pose problems. It is probably at the root of her difficulty in being more successful in certain subjects in her regular classroom.

Specific Academic Aptitude.   Students with exceptional ability may have an unusual aptitude in specific scholastic areas such as verbal or mathematical reasoning. Some, like Nadine, read much earlier than the average student. Many read independently and avidly. You may recall that at a very early age Nadine also showed an ability and interest in geography and the social sciences. She even took her atlas to preschool to share her excitement about the world with her friends. She didn't understand that they couldn't read and had different interests.

 Nadine enjoys the challenges and joys of being part of a prize winning Geography Olympiad team.

Nadine's interest and ability in geography continues. Recently, she obtained the highest score in the Geography Olympiad at her school. Her team then went on to place first in the state and in the top ten schools in the nation in the National Geography Olympiad. She was also among the top ten students for the language arts and science categories.

In contrast, high-ability students with language, hearing, visual, or physical disabilities may have a notable difficulty in one area but nonetheless show specific academic aptitude in another area. These students may earn good grades or have high achievement scores on standardized tests in one or more areas of curriculum. Jason Lowe is this type of student. Jason is a ten-year-old academically gifted student who also has cerebral palsy. He has demonstrated a remarkable ability to create unusual layout designs for letters and notes using sophisticated computer software. He also uses the computer as a tool for drawing army pictures. Jason enjoys spending time working diligently to get his pictures just right before printing them out. Other students, however, such as those learning English as a second language or students with physical or attention problems, may not perform well on tests and therefore will not reveal their true abilities on those tests.

Creative Productive Thinking. Students who are creative show many distinct characteristics. In comparison to their peers, they may be more adventurous, independent, curious, spontaneous, flexible, sensitive, intuitive, and insightful. They may have little tolerance for boredom and may take risks more readily. They may also have a zany sense of humor and have more original ideas (Clark, 1997). You may remember the *class clown* in one of your classes and the difficulties that he or she had in a traditional classroom. When you consider these characteristics carefully, you may understand why some schools do not always necessarily encourage creativity. Yet such creativity is linked with giftedness throughout history. It is impossible to think of Einstein's creation of the theory of relativity without seeing characteristics of creativity: independence, risk taking, originality, and intuitiveness surely were all part of the process (Gardner, 1993b).

Leadership Ability. Students classified in the leadership category typically display well-developed social skills, empathy, ability to motivate others, ability to keep others united or on task, and communication skills. National political leaders, like Mahatma Gandhi, fit in this category. Interestingly, Gandhi was not a good student (Gardner, 1993b).

Consider how you might address Nadine's ability to process information quickly. How might you help alleviate some of her reluctance or worry about classroom performances?

❧ *Physical challenges do not keep ten-year-old Jason Lowe from using his keen mind and exercising an unusual ability to use computers creatively.*

❧ What inherent strengths demonstrate the potential of students with high giftedness to make many positive contributions to families, schools, friends, and communities?

Yet with his peers, he took the role of peacemaker and became a moral arbiter. Years later, he displayed genius in his ability to lead.

Visual and Performing Arts. In the visual and performing arts, students show many of the same traits associated with creativity, general intellect, and specific academic aptitude, including rapidity in mastering subject matter. In addition, they may have highly developed nonverbal communication skills, physical coordination, exceptional awareness of where they are in relationship to other things and people, or specific skills in music, dance, mime, storytelling, drawing, or painting. Although Stravinsky was immersed in music as a child, he was not a musical prodigy (Gardner, 1993b). He had, however, a keen sense of sound and was interested in improvisation and creating his own tunes and variations. He persisted even when others belittled his attempts.

Unexpected Characteristics of Giftedness. Some characteristics of giftedness are easy to recognize. Parents and general education teachers recognize the obvious hallmarks, and the student's identification is fairly easily confirmed. Some students, however, are overlooked because their parents or teachers have the misconception that *gifted* students always present themselves in particular ways. That is not the case at all. For instance, some students who are gifted behave well and some poorly, just like their classmates, and girls can be overlooked entirely.

Unexpected Behavioral Characteristics. Some unexpected characteristics involve student behavior. For instance, children who are gifted may have a strong sense of humor or unquenchable curiosity that can sometimes be a distraction in class. Other similar behavioral characteristics that may not be associated with giftedness are shown in Figure 7–2 as *unexpected characteristics.*

There is growing concern over the number of students who are being misdiagnosed as learning disabled or having attention-deficit/hyperactivity disorder (AD/HD) when actually they are gifted (Dorry, 1994; Runnels & Sigler, 1994). By one estimate, there may be between 120,000 and 180,000 gifted and learning disabled students in American schools (Winner, 1996). Since many of the characteristics of giftedness are also characteristics associated with learning disabilities, or AD/HD, it is not always easy to recognize their giftedness. While these students can be easily distracted by external stimuli, perfectionistic, and/or unable to maintain attention or control their impulses, they also have a positive view of others, sensitivity, a forgiving nature, and the ability to produce work of significant quality when motivated (Dorry, 1994; Lovecky, 1994). Box 7–2 is Wedge Cree's personal account of his struggles with being both gifted and diagnosed as having AD/HD.

- Exhibit high sensitivity
- Have excessive amounts of energy
- Bore easily and may appear to have short attention spans
- Require emotionally stable and secure adults around them
- Resist authority if it is not democratically oriented
- Have preferred ways of learning, particularly in reading and mathematics
- Become easily frustrated because they have big ideas but lack the resources or people to assist in carrying these tasks to fruition
- Learn from explorations and resist rote memory or just being a listener
- Cannot sit still unless absorbed in something highly interesting
- Are very compassionate and have many fears, such as fears of death and loss of loved ones
- May give up and develop permanent learning blocks if they experience failure early

FIGURE 7–2 *Unexpected characteristics of gifted and creative children*

Note: From Characteristics of Gifted/Creative Children, by M. Friedel, 1993, Warwick, RI: National Foundation for Gifted and Creative Children. Copyright 1993 by the National Foundation for Gifted and Creative Children. Reprinted with permission.

Leal, Kearney, and Kearney (1995) identified four unusual characteristics of giftedness that may also be associated with AD/HD. One of these, the tendency to try out scientific or conceptual world theories in unique or socially unacceptable ways, is the one most likely to cause misdiagnosis. Webb and Latimer (1993) found a key indicator to determine AD/HD and/or giftedness is to ask, "Where are the problems occurring?" In a child with AD/HD, problematic behaviors tend to surface in all settings, both at home and at school. In contrast, a gifted student with AD/HD may exhibit AD/HD behavior in one class but not in another. In Table 7–5, you can see the differences between behaviors often identified as characteristics of both giftedness and AD/HD (Webb & Latimer, 1993).

Unexpected Gender-Related Characteristics. Another population that faces special difficulties, particularly at the secondary level, is girls who are gifted or talented. For them, probably more than for any other group or age, *gifted* is a label to be shunned. They may find their talents unappreciated or unrewarded and therefore lack motivation to

TABLE 7–5 〰 *Distinguishing between AD/HD and giftedness*

Behaviors Associated With AD/HD (Barkley, 1990)	Behaviors Associated With Giftedness (Webb, 1993)
Poorly sustained attention in almost all situations	Poor attention, boredom, daydreaming in specific situations
Diminished persistence on tasks not having immediate consequences	Low tolerance for persistence on tasks that seem irrelevant
Impulsivity, poor delay of gratification	Judgment lags behind development of intellect
Impaired adherence to commands to regulate or inhibit behavior in social contexts	Intensity may lead to power struggles with authorities
More active, restless than normal children	High activity level; may need less sleep
Difficulty adhering to rules and regulations	Questions rules, customs, and traditions

Note: From ADHD and Children Who Are Gifted (ERIC Digest No. EDO-EC-93-5), by J. T. Webb and D. Latimer, 1993, Reston, VA: Council for Exceptional Children, ERIC Clearinghouse on Disabilities and Gifted Education.

BOX 7-2   MY VOICE

WEDGE CREE

People say I'm gifted. I also have AD/HD. I'm fourteen years old now, and I manage to get all As and Bs without even trying. That sometimes alienates people because I always use big words and have actually read the dictionary and the whole encyclopedia. I got into a special gifted class in first grade. I was one of two kids in the entire school district. I was working with kids in sixth grade on a similar level of understanding. Sometimes it's weird knowing more about a particular subject than the teacher and most of my peers. History is my favorite. Twentieth century wars are a small hobby of mine.

AD/HD? I was diagnosed about two years ago. Actually, I'm the one who got my parents thinking about AD/HD. I was visiting my uncle and was reading an article in *Time* magazine when I saw an article about AD/HD. As I read through it I came to a column about signs of AD/HD. I thought, "Hey, I fit a lot of these," and brought it my parents' attention. My parents took me to a specialist in AD/HD. I went to her once every few weeks and began to learn more about it and my problems. We also began trying me out on various medicines to help me. Not all of them were successful. Finally we got to Ritalin. With Ritalin, I've been able to calm down and focus. My social life has improved big time, and kids are actually willing to stay within twenty feet of me. I even joined the school wrestling team as a reserve. I wasn't so good, but I was finally on a team.

What's it like being gifted and AD/HD? Having AD/HD and being gifted is really hard to put into terms. Before we knew I had AD/HD, it was like having the worst part of adolescence before you're even a teen-ager. I had very few friends. I began to spend all my time at the school library. Often people would see me walking around on the playground with a book six inches from my face. While this helped me learn quite a bit and did wonders for my imagination, it didn't make me many friends. Things got worse. One time I had to go home from an overnight camp because I burst into tears and went crazy. The kids weren't even that mean or anything. I was going insane at home and getting ultra depressed. It's like a couple steps down from beginning to contemplate suicide.

Now, I still know everything but I'm bored by everything that doesn't challenge me. It feels like you have a capacity to be the smartest guy in the world but whenever you walk forward, someone sticks their foot out and you trip over it. It's so frustrating. I have the capacity to be so much, and yet I'm only minimally using it. If I were using my capacity more, I could probably skip grades, go to college a few years early, or anything. But because I don't use it, I'm not much ahead of the average fourteen-year-old kid.

Some advice I'd give teachers is to make kids feel challenged. I find when teachers give me special projects, not just worksheets, but creative things that make me feel like I'm using both sides of my brain to actually do something, I really put my heart into it. Do stuff that the kid is interested in, whether it's aircraft design, WWII, city government, or whatever. Try to find ways to relate projects to their areas of interest. It always works for me. Get things to be fun, not monotonous. Don't have the kids recite things a thousand times and memorize facts. Get them beyond that—go a step further. Have them really go into it so they will push themselves. If the kid won't do anything then you can't do anything. My best advice is get the kid to want to do it by appealing to their creative side without feeling forced. Learn what it's like for the kids. If you know what it's like to be in their shoes, that's a very valuable asset. Sympathize with them. Earn their trust. Make them want to come to you and have fun working with you.

I don't know many gifted kids with AD/HD besides me. Those that are generally are outcasts. So please don't give them special attention in front of other kids. Try to help them make friends. Be willing to answer all their questions. I was blessed with teachers who were always willing to answer my questions about how to deal with kids as well as parents who were always willing to lend a hand and back me up. It's the help they'll need to succeed with other kids. Help kids see the good sides of themselves and make good impressions. Try not to get actively involved in their social life, but indirectly. The best thing you can do is to help them learn how to handle themselves and then sit back and let them sail on—once they've constructed their own sail with your help.

pursue academic excellence (Gallagher & Gallagher, 1994). Unfortunately, girls who are gifted have often gone undetected or had to fight their way through successive levels of adverse circumstances (Callahan, Cornell, & Loyd, 1992; Goldsmith, 1987). This may even happen in their own families. For example, Golda Meir, future Prime Minister of Israel, left her parents' house and moved into her aunt's home at the age of fourteen in order to continue her education beyond grammar school (Noble, 1972). Her actions defied her parents' wishes because they believed that too much education was unnecessary for women, even bad, and that marriage was the only option for girls.

Beyond familial attitudes, some cultures and communities also deem it socially unacceptable for girls to act "too intelligent" (Davis & Rimm, 1998, pp. 308–341; Silverman, 1994/1995). Females as a group still face sex discrimination, and all girls must deal with that issue. However, girls who are gifted are extraordinarily capable and exceptionally sensitive to the fact that they are still treated differently because they are girls.

In addition, girls who are gifted often deal with minimal support or open antagonism from their peers (Lovecky, 1994/1995). For instance, Nadine has been labeled a brat and stuck up because she would rather read than socialize. She has a passion to learn about the world when most of her friends would rather talk about boys or what was on television last night.

Women who are gifted may face the conflicting demands of creating and sustaining a home and family and of pursuing successful careers (Kerr, 1992). There is also "a growing body of research that indicates that school is not a nurturing environment for gifted girls" (Smutney & Blockson, 1990, p. 43). This research indicates that girls receive less attention than boys throughout their education (Kerr, 1991), which is shown by the fact that boys are called on more frequently and are more often rewarded for calling out answers. Girls, in contrast, are reprimanded for this behavior. This differential instruction does not nurture the intellectual curiosity of girls who are gifted (Allen, 1995).

Identifying Causes of Giftedness

Most researchers today attribute giftedness to a combination of nature (genetic factors) and nurture (psychosocial factors), but they also disagree about the proportions between the two factors. One perspective is that "giftedness is a biologically rooted concept that serves as a label for a high level of intelligence and indicates an advanced and accelerated development of functions within the brain" (Clark, 1997, p. 26). This explanation represents a genetically based cause of giftedness.

A contrasting perspective claims that while heredity does play a considerable role in genius, psychosocial factors are also significant (Clark, 1992, p. 72). Some of these environmental factors are

- Excellent early opportunities with encouragement from family and friends

- Superior, early, and continuing guidance and instruction

- Frequent and continuous opportunity to practice and extend their special abilities and to progress as they are able

- Close association with others of similar ability

- Opportunities for real accomplishment within their capabilities, but with increasing challenge

- Provision for strong success experiences and recognition of successes

When you read Chapter 8, you may want to consider how this information compares to psychosocial causes of mental retardation.

Today, there are proponents for both genetic and environmental causes. For example, if you believe that environment has the greatest influence on intellect, you may read environmental authors such as Doman to try to create a superbaby (1984). In his book, *How to Multiply Your Baby's Intelligence,* he tells parents to present stimulating learning activities from birth in order to produce superior intelligence in their children. On the other hand, if you listen to authors such as Elkind (1981, 1987, 1988), you will be more cautious. Elkind points out the dangers of *hurried children*—those who are pressured to learn too much too soon.

Identifying the Prevalence of Giftedness

As you have already read, finding and identifying students who are gifted is not always an easy task. Not only are their characteristics often misleading, but there is also controversy over what giftedness really is and thus a controversy over how many gifted students there are.

As we previously noted, giftedness was traditionally defined by IQ alone. This chapter indicates that giftedness is not defined by IQ alone. According to the federal definition, an IQ score should not be the only determining factor for creative, visual, or performing arts abilities. Other evaluations are appropriate, such as for independence or artistic talent.

When IQ test scores are equated with giftedness, the top 2 or 3 percent of the general population is considered gifted (Webb et al., 1982). Most schools use an IQ score of 125 to 130 as a beginning score for identifying these students. IQ tests often record scores as high as 160, but scores of 180 to 200 have been estimated by other methods (Webb et al., 1982).

These scores mean that the IQ of people in the gifted population ranges from 125 to 200 and that those at one end of the *gifted* spectrum may be very different from those at the other. Most researchers today, however, distinguish only two levels of giftedness—gifted and highly gifted, or genius. Table 7-6 shows how IQ levels and their approximate occurrences vary within a population (Tannenbaum, 1983).

A contrasting opinion—one that explicitly does not rely on IQ alone to determine giftedness—is that there is a talent pool that includes the top 15 to 20 percent of students in general ability or specific performance areas (Renzulli & Reis, 1986). An IQ of 115 is the lowest acceptable score for inclusion in this talent pool. A talent pool allows more students to participate in gifted programs.

The best way to estimate the current prevalence of giftedness in schools is to examine how many students receive gifted services. One study showed that 4.5 percent of the nation's student population receives services through a gifted and talented program (Reis, 1989). Using this 4.5 percent figure, an elementary school of 350 students would serve about 16 students, or approximately 1 per classroom. Under the more inclusive talent pool approach, about 20 percent, or 70 students, would be served, with four or five students per classroom.

The *1994 State of the States Gifted and Talented Education Report* (Council of States Directors of Programs for the Gifted 1994) revealed that greater numbers of states are mandating either identification of or services for students who are gifted. Between 1990 and 1993, states mandating services rose from twenty-six to thirty-three states. With increasing numbers of states mandating services for students who are gifted and talented, numbers served may increase. However, not all states with a mandate for services provide state funding to support those services. Nadine is fortunate to live in Ohio, where many new positions for teachers and coordinators of gifted and talented students have been recently funded.

TABLE 7–6 ℞

Expected occurrence of IQ scores

IQ	Approximate Expected Occurrence		
100	50	out of	100
107	31	out of	100
115	16	out of	100
122	7	out of	100
130	2	out of	100
137	7	out of	1,000
145	1	out of	1,000
152	2.3	out of	10,000
160	3	out of	100,000
167	3	out of	1,000,000
175	3	out of	10,000,000
190	1	out of	1,000,000,000

Note: From *Gifted Children: Psychological and Educational Perspectives*, by A. J. Tannenbaum, 1983, Upper Saddle River, NJ: Merrill/Prentice Hall. Copyright © 1983 by Abraham J. Tannenbaum. Reprinted with permission of Prentice-Hall, Inc., Upper Saddle River, NJ.

This 1994 report also revealed at what grade level services must be provided. Of thirty-one states responding to the question, five states begin at the prekindergarten level, eighteen begin in kindergarten, and three begin in first grade. Five states provide other alternatives. For instance, South Carolina mandates its program for grades 3–12 while Mississippi only requires services for grades 2–6.

WHAT ARE EVALUATION PROCEDURES?

To identify and serve students who are gifted, educators undertake a thorough two-step diagnostic evaluation, similar to the Individuals with Disabilities Education Act (IDEA) approach to nondiscriminatory evaluation for students with disabilities. First, they determine the presence of giftedness. Then, they determine the nature and extent of special education needed to challenge individuals and develop their talents.

Determining the Presence of Giftedness

Educators typically rely on formal means for identifying giftedness. Three specific benefits result from formal assessment:

- Schools will obtain data to validate a student's placement.

- There is an increased likelihood of an appropriate education for a student.

- Criteria will be met to ensure federal funding when available.

There are, however, problems associated with testing for giftedness. Standardized tests have been criticized for demonstrating bias against minority populations, low socioeconomic groups, and students learning English as a second language (Maker, 1996; Reyes, Fletcher, & Paez, 1996; Shore, Dewey, Robinson, & Ward, 1991). Because educators rely so heavily on test scores, discrimination has been a continuing problem. Many populations are still vastly underrepresented in current gifted programs (Hunsaker, 1994). Figures published by the U.S. Department of Education's Office of Civil Rights reveal that students from minority groups such as African Americans and Latinos are underrepresented by thirty to seventy percent in gifted programs throughout the nation as well as overrepresented by forty to fifty percent in special education programs for students with disabilities (see Chapter 1) (U.S. Department of Education, Office of Civil Rights, 1993). Although some tests now claim to be culture-fair or multicultural, and to be designed to help correct such biases, they clearly have not yet solved the problem.

> What factors do you think influence the underrepresentation of minority groups in gifted programs? How can their full participation in gifted programs be encouraged?

To ensure that assessments do not discriminate against students from minority populations, researchers advocate using several types of measurement for determining the presence of giftedness (Baldwin, 1987; Clark, 1997; Naidu & Presley, 1995). They favor balancing IQ and creativity test results with a combination of other selection criteria, such as behavior rating scales, samples of artwork or creative writing, photographs of a previous science project, a videotape of an oral presentation, or other material from parents or teachers. These additional measures are called *documentation* and should be appropriate for the type of program to be provided. Nadine's school district is culturally quite diverse and uses a variety of measures to determine a child's level of giftedness. Nadine was identified as gifted by parents and friends when she was very young. Her preschool teachers noted her exceptional abilities as well. However, she was not formally identified for the gifted program until third grade. In Nadine's school district, students are referred by their third-grade teachers for the talented and gifted program. Ms. Hoch, her third-grade teacher, filled out a teacher nomination form for Nadine, which evaluated twenty different characteristics. This nomination along with test results from the Hawthorne Gifted Evaluation Scale (McCarney, 1987) were then submitted to consider Nadine's candidacy for the gifted program. The results from both of these evaluations revealed that Nadine was exceptionally creative and had strong academic aptitude. Her

Documentation describes types of measurement used to determine giftedness.

ℙ *Many teachers, like Nadine's teacher Ms. Conroy, are collaborators who contribute to the success of students who are gifted.*

referral nomination was then placed with other students' applications, and Nadine was then selected to join the talented and gifted program beginning in fourth grade.

Figure 7–3 shows the types of evaluation tools used and includes some typical findings in the progression from the first observations of unusual characteristics to a nondiscriminatory evaluation.

Because we have already discussed intelligence testing in Chapter 2, we will focus in this chapter on two additional forms of assessment. First, we will look at a new alternative assessment developed to identify giftedness among minorities based on multiple domains of intelligence. Then we will examine creativity assessment as a means for determining whether a student is gifted or talented and what kind of special education is appropriate.

Multiple Intelligences DISCOVER Assessment. Maker, Nielson, and Rogers (1994) developed the DISCOVER (Discovering Intellectual Strengths and Capabilities through Observation while allowing for Varied Ethnic Responses) assessment as an alternative assessment for identifying giftedness among minorities. The rationale is that if minorities typically score low on standardized IQ tests then an instrument is needed that taps into minority students' abilities in a more valid way (Maker, 1993).

The DISCOVER assessment is a performance-based instrument, presenting the student with tasks requiring problem-solving behaviors in six of Gardner's different domains of intelligence: spatial, logical-mathematical, linguistic, bodily-kinesthetic, interpersonal, and intrapersonal, with musical and naturalistic intelligences not presently covered. The tasks increase in complexity and openness as the assessment progresses. During the assessment process, highly trained evaluators use a checklist to record specific behaviors.

The instrument draws on Maker's definition of giftedness as "the ability to solve the most complex problems in the most efficient, effective, or economical ways" (1993, p. 71). At present, eighty-two behaviors and sixty-eight characteristics of products (Maker, 1996) help assess which of six intelligences are strongest in each child.

The actual evaluation process is as follows (Seraphim, 1997, p. 88): Students work in small groups while trained observers use standard observation sheets, pictures, and video to note the students' problem-solving processes and products. Over a two- and one-half-hour period, observers accept all products, give helpful clues when asked, adopt a nonjudgmental attitude, and rotate regularly to minimize observer bias.

FIGURE 7-3 *Assessing if a student or child is gifted*

Nondiscriminatory Evaluation

Observation

Teacher and parents observe	Student may be bored with school or intensely interested in academic pursuits, has high vocabulary or specialized talents and interests, shows curiosity and frequently asks questions (especially *how* and *why*), is insightful, has novel ideas and approaches to tasks.

Screening

Assessment measures	Findings that indicate need for further evaluation
Classroom work products	Work is consistently superior in one or more academic areas or, in case of underachieving gifted, products are inconsistent, with only work of special interest being superior.
Group intelligence tests	Tests often indicate exceptional intelligence.
Group achievement tests	Student usually performs above average in one or more areas of achievement (cutoff for screening purposes is an IQ of 115).

Prereferral

Generally, prereferral is not used for students who are potentially gifted.

Referral

Protection in evaluation procedures

Assessment measures	Findings that suggest giftedness
Individualized Intelligence test	Student scores in the upper 2 to 3 percent of the population (most states have cutoff scores of 130 or 132 depending on test). Because of cultural biases of standardized IQ tests, students from minority backgrounds are considered if their IQs do not meet the cutoff but other indicators suggest giftedness.
Individualized achievement test	The student scores in the upper 2 to 3 percent in one or more areas of achievement.
Creativity assessment	The student demonstrates unusual creativity in work products as judged by experts or performs exceptionally on tests designed to assess creativity. The student does not have to be academically gifted to qualify.
Checklists of gifted characteristics	These checklists are often completed by teachers, parents, peers, or others who know the student well. The student scores in the range that suggests giftedness as established by checklist developers.
Anecdotal records	The student's records suggest high ability in one or more areas.
Curriculum-based assessment	The student is performing at a level beyond peers in one or more areas of the curriculum used by the local school district.
Direct observation	The student may be a model student or could have behavior problems as a result of being bored with classwork. If the student is perfectionistic, anxiety might be observed. Observations should occur in other settings besides the school.
Visual and performing arts assessment	The student's performance in visual or performing arts is judged by individuals with expertise in the specific area. The student does not have to be academically gifted to qualify.
Leadership assessment	Peer nomination, parent nomination, and teacher nomination are generally used. However, self-nomination can also be a good predictor of leadership. Leadership in extracurricular activities is often an effective indicator. The student does not have to be academically gifted to qualify.
Case-study approach	Determination of student's giftedness is based on looking at all areas of assessment described above without adding special weight to one factor.

**Evaluation Team determines that student is gifted
and needs special education and related services.**

Appropriate Education

Afterward, the observers collaborate to rate the students' strengths on a scale of 1 to 5, from *no strength observed* to a *definite strength observed*. A student with *definite* ratings in two or more activities is considered a superior problem-solver and referred for placement into a program for gifted students or for further testing.

The following description for assessing the spatial intelligence (Seraphim, 1997) will help you visualize what kinds of tasks children are called on to perform. The material for this spatial activity (Pablo) in grades K–8 consists of colored cardboard pieces of different shapes, designs and sizes. The tasks differ from one grade level to the next. For example, in kindergarten, the observer holds a big square-shaped piece, and children are requested to find a piece that is shaped like it. Then the observer holds a picture of a rainbow, and again the children are told to find pieces that look like a rainbow. This is followed by constructions of mountains, animals, and anything the child would like to make. In more advanced grades, students are asked to make more complex constructions, such as "something that moves" (grades 3–5) or a container (grades 6–9). Observers note the complexity of the construction, the extent to which it resembles the design the child is attempting to make, symmetry or asymmetry, the number of constructions, their uniqueness, and whether they are two or three-dimensional. In grades 9–12, other materials are used, such as art supplies and Capsela (a mechanical construction kit) (Seraphim, 1997, pp. 91–92).

Several descriptive, distinctive features of the DISCOVER assessment make it an excellent choice for multicultural competency. First, all instructions are given in the dominant language of the child. Second, the assessment tasks are designed for children from kindergarten through twelfth grades. Third, the assessment allows more than one way of solving problems with multiple possible correct answers. In addition, the assessment is not the end product but the basis for how the curriculum is used with students.

Creativity Assessment.   Most tests of creativity measure its intellectual aspects only. The level of creativity of performers and artists is difficult to evaluate, and such individuals are regarded as gifted primarily through consensus of knowledgeable evaluators.

Fortunately, some tests, such as the Torrance Tests of Creative Thinking (Torrance, 1966a, 1966b), measure more than one domain-specific area of giftedness. These tests are frequently used to evaluate students' creativity. Some researchers object to Torrance's creativity tests, saying that there is no evidence that they assess human creativity (Borland, 1989; Tannenbaum, 1983), yet many educators find them useful in identifying students who are gifted.

Torrance's tests assess two aspects of creativity. Thinking Creatively With Words (1966b) focuses on the verbal, linguistic side of creativity. This test may be used in fourth grade through graduate school. Thinking Creatively With Pictures (1966a) evaluates a student's figural and spatial creativity and may be used from kindergarten through graduate school. Both tests may be administered individually or in groups, and students are allowed to work at their own speed.

Thinking Creatively With Words is an assessment measure that asks students to complete seven verbal activities. The first three activities focus on a simple picture, such as two boys being chased off a baseball field.

- Activity 1 asks the student to write out all the questions he or she can conceive about the picture.

- Activity 2 requires the student to list possible causes for the action shown in the picture.

- Activity 3 asks the student to list all the possible consequences of the action in the picture.

- Activity 4 changes the focus and examines a student's ability at product improvement by introducing another picture, such as a drawing of a stuffed animal. It then asks the student to list the cleverest, most interesting, and most unusual ways to change this toy to have more fun playing with it.

On which tests would you do well? Think about that as you read about the contents of these tests.

For Nadine, who loves words, this type of creativity assessment would be fun. Her only problem would be choosing the best selections from a multitude of ideas and words to use.

- Activity 5 examines a student's ideas about unusual uses of an ordinary object such as buttons.

- Activity 6 asks the student to think of as many questions as possible about the ordinary object in order to lead to a variety of different answers and arouse interest and curiosity in others concerning the object.

- Activity 7 requires the student to accept an improbable situation such as imagining that people suddenly become invisible. It then asks the student to predict what would happen as a result of this situation. This activity focuses on the student's ability to predict outcomes and consequences.

Thinking Creatively With Pictures is an assessment measure that determines a student's spatial abilities using pictures.

- Activity 1 presents a dark curved shape. The test then asks the student to think of a picture or an object to draw incorporating this shape. The student is also encouraged to expand on the picture and to title it.

- Activity 2 asks the student to complete a number of pictures by adding lines to incomplete figures. The instructions ask the student to make things no one else will think of and to sequence and title the pictures to make an interesting story.

- Activity 3 gives the student ten minutes to see how many objects or pictures can be made from a series of identical shapes, such as squares or triangles. The instructions again ask the student to sequence and title the objects or pictures.

When the tests have been completed, scoring may be done by the teacher or a specialist. The tests are evaluated using several criteria. For example, the verbal creativity tests are scored for fluency, originality, and flexibility according to the scoring guide that accompanies the test. Very specific guidelines with examples are given for evaluating student answers. Scores are then summarized, interpreted, and reported.

Determining the Nature and Extent of Special Education and Related Services

Once educators have identified a student as gifted, they implement educational planning and regular evaluations based on IEP goals. In the case of gifted students, authentic assessment, which you read about in Chapter 2, takes on new dimensions. In most educational settings, the teacher evaluates a student's performance. With students who are gifted, the potential for placing some of the evaluation responsibility on the students themselves adds new possibilities to the evaluation process. Student responsibility for assessment can be integrated into the IEP goals and is appropriate for two areas of assessment: product measures and process measures.

Product Evaluation. Academic assessment for students in both gifted and general education classrooms is commonly based on a written test of the product of the student's learning. Tests to evaluate student learning are normally given after the lessons have been studied. The test results are used so that a teacher can track grades and learning, and they have the following characteristics (Leal, 1990):

- Teacher (not student) ownership of process and goals

- Focus on final grade rather than on learning

- Time dependent

- Predetermined information

- Single measure

- Backward looking, assessing what is remembered

❧ *What positive contributions might this person give to others? What great expectations do you think his teachers ascribed for him that continue to contribute to his success?*

These characteristics are restrictive because they do not provide the teachers or students with tools for understanding the process of the learning. Good teachers, however, have always used product measures not just for grades but also for students' benefit. When teachers return tests, they are using them to review the material and help students understand what they still need to learn. These teachers may also have students who are gifted record their own progress on these measures and compete with themselves rather than with classmates. In addition, good teachers use product measures to assess the thoroughness of their own teaching, looking for areas that need further or different instruction.

Process Evaluation.   Educators should also evaluate the student's learning *process* (Johnston, 1986; Leal, 1990). This type of evaluation happens when a teacher attempts to watch and learn from student comments or work that demonstrates their unfolding understanding of the task or learning situation. Teachers formalize "kid watching" when they take notes on the strengths and weaknesses students demonstrate during problem-solving and learning activities. These notes are good resources during parent–teacher conferences.

Yet another type of evaluation is similar, but not identical to process evaluation. This is *reflective assessment or evaluation* (Leal, 1990). This type of assessment involves teaching students to become aware of the process of their own learning. Hansen has stated that:

> *Good learners not only know what they can do now, but they have plans for what to learn next. . . . In order for them to tell us what they need, they must be aware of what options lie ahead. Our task is to find out what their plans are and help them generate options along the way. They must learn to monitor their journey. (Hansen, 1987, pp. 97, 100)*

Reflective assessment results in students being able to actively monitor their own learning. Table 7–7 shows how four areas of assessment work together on the student's behalf.

Reflective assessment—teaching students how to monitor their own learning—results in "the fulfillment of one's own purposes, not as one's placement relative to others" (Winograd & Niquette, 1988, p. 52). In addition, such a process provides a creative way for teachers to help students learn to monitor the accomplishment of IEP goals. This process can also be a good indicator of the success of the gifted education program being used. Box 7–3, "Into Practice," suggests potential areas for a student to record in a portfolio of reflective assessment.

Process assessment also includes the development and assessment of a portfolio of representative examples of the student's work. Teachers then review these portfolios with parents as well as students.

When your professor returns an exam, how likely are your classmates to ask you, "What do you still need to learn?" rather than "What grade did you get?"

BOX 7-3

INTO PRACTICE

SUGGESTED CONTENTS FOR A REFLECTIVE LEARNING PORTFOLIO

- Written reflective evaluations in which students monitor their learning goals with lists and self-evaluations such as "things I can do well, things I'm working on, and things I plan to learn."
- Written evaluations of content area learning. For instance, in handwriting, teach students to use appropriate criteria for handwriting and then have them evaluate their own writing based on the learned criteria. Teachers could grade the evaluations rather than the writing itself.
- Written evaluations that include students' reflections about their thinking processes and text purposes: questions such as "Does this make sense? What is not clear here? What does this text really mean? What does the teacher mean? How good is this argument or explanation? What did I do to figure out what was coming? Where can I apply these ideas? What will I do with what I learn here?"
- Lists of books, magazines, and other materials reflectively evaluated by the student.
- Lists of topics and authors in subject areas that interest the student, including evaluative recommendations for peers.

- Charts, audio, and video recordings that the student keeps on his own learning. These may include retellings or free recall of both narrative and expository information or texts.
- Records of strategies used in different content areas and why they were or were not effective. A strategy such as the "know, want to know, learn" strategy (Ogle, 1989) is used to help students trace how their learning changes over the course of a unit of study.
- Interviews that focus on reflective evaluation. These interviews with teachers, peers, parents, or community members would be a record of the student's understanding of a topic in relation to the one interviewed.
- Reflective evaluations of compositions, speeches, debates, discussions, or other demonstrations of learning in domain-specific areas, with changes traced over time.
- Written records of prior knowledge on topics to be learned; tracing how this knowledge changes.
- List of wonderings, including self-questioning records for each content area.
- Regular evaluations of this reflective learning portfolio and IEP goals.

Note: From Leal, D. (1990). *The power of reflective assessment.* Unpublished manuscript.

TABLE 7-7 ❧ *Focus points for assessment*

	Product	**Process**
Teacher Uses	*Written Tests/Projects*	*Kid watching: Teacher Portfolios*
	• Teacher's grade book • Report card • How student compares to other students	• Teacher's understanding of student • Teacher's instructional planning • Parent conferences
Student Uses	*Written Tests/Projects*	*Reflective Evaluation; Student Portfolios*
	• Student understanding of what still needs to be learned • Review of material • How student compares to peers in the class	• Active participation and responsibility in the assessment process • Development of self-monitoring strategies that use higher order thinking skills

Note: From Leal, D. (1990). *The power of reflective assessment.* Unpublished manuscript.

What and How Do Professionals Teach?

There are many curricula and methods for teaching students identified as gifted. These options vary by age level and area of ability. However, there are also difficulties in selecting and developing appropriate curriculum and methods. Understanding students' individual needs is pivotal to effective planning.

Curriculum

The Council for Exceptional Children (CEC) has described standards for curriculum as follows: "Students (shall) develop critical and creative thinking skills through instruction and experiences rooted in the content areas" (Council for Exceptional Children, 1989, p. 15). Within any content area, the curriculum should also include the acquisition of specific skills. Thus, you may find students learning research skills, independent study habits, or questioning strategies in addition to covering standard content areas such as math or science.

Teachers may use any number of curricula to instill critical and creative thinking. However, research shows that three types particularly benefit students who are gifted and talented (Parke, 1989; VanTassel-Baska, 1989): curriculum that is modified according to the interests of the student, curriculum that modifies the pace of the learning, and curriculum that modifies the depth of content coverage. The following examples incorporate curriculum modifications to challenge students and help them develop higher order thinking skills as well as self-monitoring strategies.

To accommodate curriculum modification for students in the broadest possible manner, Maker, Nielson, and Rogers (1994) have emphasized that curriculum must also consider students' areas of giftedness, including differences in specific areas of intelligence, culture, or language. To address these concerns, the DISCOVER project was developed. Consistent with the DISCOVER assessment, the goals of the DISCOVER curriculum focus on Gardner's (1983, 1993a, 1993b) theory of multiple forms of intelligences, integration of cultural and linguistic components of the community, and problem solving. The following guidelines cover the overall DISCOVER plan for helping students become engaged learners:

- *Present content that is related to the interdisciplinary themes, returning to these themes as students grow and change. (content)*

- *Develop problem-solving skills in different intelligences. (process)*

- *Develop products using self-selected formats that are relevant in a particular cultural context. (product)*

- *Provide exploratory learning centers or stations in which the tools of each intelligence are readily available. (learning environment). (Maker & Nielson, 1996, p. 275).*

Featured in Box 7-4 are examples of social studies activities on the theme of *change* for each of the eight areas of intelligence for students in grades 3-5.

Higher Level Thinking Curricula   A focus on higher level thinking curricula coincided with the emergence of Bloom's (1956) taxonomy of higher level thinking skills (see Table 7-8). This type of curriculum focus, which modifies the depth of content coverage, has helped move cognitive learning theory forward. This focus can be integrated into any curriculum or study.

Whole Language Interdisciplinary Curricula.   Other curricula build on a whole language interdisciplinary approach (Maker & Nielson, 1996; Pappas, Kiefer, & Levstik, 1995). Building on the interests of the student, this approach integrates various content-area subjects such as reading, math, and science into the study of one particular topic.

Looking at these different ideas, can you think of a spatial activity that would be appropriate for the topic of *patterns?*

☙ In what ways can the use of higher level thinking skills increase and validate the great expectations teachers have for students who are gifted and talented?

BOX 7–4

SAMPLE CURRICULAR ACTIVITIES FOR DIFFERENT INTELLIGENCES ON THE TOPIC OF *CHANGE*

Types of Intelligences	Sample Activities
Bodily Kinesthetic	Show with your body how a caterpillar changes into a butterfly
Interpersonal	Compare your pictures or drawings of how you have changed with the pictures or drawings of others in your class.
Intrapersonal	Make a collection of pictures or drawings showing how you have changed since you were born.
Linguistic	Tell about the life of a piece of paper. Tell how it was made, where it came from, what it was used for, where it went.
Logical-think Mathematical	Observe an insect, an animal, or a plant, and show or tell how it changes. Tell why you these changes have happened.
Musical	Listen to a familiar piece of music and one that is unfamiliar. What are some ways they change? Using an instrument, play the parts that change.
Spatial	Choose two objects, and make a series of drawings showing how one changes into the other.
Naturalistic/ Connections	Ask someone older than you to tell you some stories about how the world has changed since they were your age.

Note: From *Curriculum Development and Teaching Strategies for Gifted Learners* (p. 289), by C. J. Maker and A. B. Nielson, 1996, Austin, TX: Pro-Ed. Copyright 1996 by Pro-Ed. Reprinted with permission.

TABLE 7–8 *Two applications of Bloom's taxonomy*

Knowledge	Comprehension	Application	Analysis	Synthesis	Evaluation
Memorize a list of spelling words	Give a definition in your own words	Correctly use a word in a sentence	Break words into families, identify prefixes and suffixes	Use word parts to create imaginary words	Choose most appropriate or effective word to convey meaning in new situation
Name the notes of a musical scale	Explain that notes symbolize higher or lower sounds	Play music from a written score	Recognize different movements in a symphony or parts of a song	Compose a symphony or a song	Compare style and quality of two sonatas

Thematic interdiscipli-
nary studies build on students'
inherent strengths while giving
them choices to direct their own
learning.

Interdisciplinary studies are appropriate in a pullout program that seeks to overlap subject matter with the general education classroom curriculum. Within the general education classroom, it has an added benefit: Students who are gifted can broaden their interests in areas that would not ordinarily be studied.

For example, an extended study by a student interested in the Civil War might include research on the history of weapons, math as it relates to the lifestyles or economics of the North and South, literature through the writers from that era, and geography that examines the impact of the war on various regions of the United States. Such interdisciplinary studies require students to use their abilities to see the larger picture. This type of curriculum also modifies the pace of the learning by providing more time for content coverage.

The Syntopicon, which was developed by Adler and Hutchin (Feldhusen & Robinson, 1986), lists curricular areas of study that represent many ideas from Western culture and topics that can be used in an interdisciplinary study for students who are gifted (see Figure 7-4). Science and math are standard curricula, but some areas may seem unusual to you. While these topics can be used with all students, those who are gifted might find it easier to develop an interest in learning about beauty, justice, or wisdom. Students with higher level thinking skills are interested in and capable of handling such abstract subject matter.

The Syntopicon list can also be adapted for use with students from diverse ethnic backgrounds. For example, if the list were revised for the Hopi people, spirituality might be an included topic. If the list were revised for the Polynesians, who highly value music, sports, dance, and art, then the topics included might reflect those priorities.

Differentiated Reading Curricula.   One researcher's concern for students who are gifted and who receive all or most of their education within the regular classrooms led to the development of The Critical Reading Guide (Dooley, 1993), a differentiated reading program for the academic growth of highly capable readers. This program modifies the depth of coverage by compacting the curriculum and eliminating study of concepts already mastered (Renzulli, 1977). It modifies the lesson by providing a different process that gives students opportunities to read and think about selections in greater depth.

The Critical Reading Guide accelerates the introduction of advanced research skills while also building on reflective evaluation by students. Students learn to read, ask questions, think, and evaluate before, during, and after reading complex material. For example, when reading historical fiction, students are asked to distinguish relevant from irrelevant information and to examine assumptions that the author and characters make. After reading, students are asked to evaluate the characters' actions and to reflect on their own developing perspectives. This type of strategy challenges students who are gifted and may be used within the regular classroom as well as in a pullout program.

Methods

A variety of methods are appropriate for teaching students who are gifted. Educators might use one of these methods alone or in combination with other methods. Each builds on the premise that students who are gifted need both acceleration and enrichment in various forms.

Acceleration.   Acceleration means moving faster through the grades or through mastery of a particular subject area. Debate over whether acceleration or enrichment is best for gifted students continues (Benbow, 1991; Davis & Rimm, 1994; Feldhusen, Van Winkle, & Ehle, 1996). General educators typically do not favor acceleration but instead prefer to keep children together by age and grade (Tannenbaum, 1986). Teachers often dislike acceleration because of its social impact on students who are placed with older classmates. While they may easily be able to keep up with these new peers academically, the struggles of fitting in socially can be detrimental to their learning process.

1. Angel	35. Honor	69. Poetry
2. Animal	36. Hypothesis	70. Principle
3. Aristocracy	37. Idea	71. Progress
4. Art	38. Immortality	72. Prophecy
5. Astronomy	39. Induction	73. Prudence
6. Beauty	40. Infinity	74. Punishment
7. Being	41. Judgment	75. Quality
8. Cause	42. Justice	76. Quantity
9. Chance	43. Knowledge	77. Reasoning
10. Change	44. Labor	78. Relation
11. Citizen	45. Language	79. Religion
12. Constitution	46. Law	80. Revolution
13. Courage	47. Liberty	81. Rhetoric
14. Custom and convention	48. Life and death	82. Same and other
15. Definition	49. Logic	83. Science
16. Democracy	50. Love	84. Sense
17. Desire	51. Man	85. Sign and symbol
18. Dialectic	52. Mathematics	86. Sin
19. Duty	53. Matter	87. Slavery
20. Education	54. Mechanics	88. Soul
21. Element	55. Medicine	89. Space
22. Emotion	56. Memory and imagination	90. State
23. Eternity	57. Metaphysics	91. Temperance
24. Evolution	58. Mind	92. Theology
25. Experience	59. Monarchy	93. Time
26. Family	60. Nature	94. Truth
27. Fate	61. Necessity and contingency	95. Tyranny
28. Form	62. Oligarchy	96. Universal and particular
29. God	63. One and many	97. Virtue and vice
30. Good and evil	64. Opinion	98. War and peace
31. Government	65. Opposition	99. Wealth
32. Habit	66. Philosophy	100. Will
33. Happiness	67. Physics	101. Wisdom
34. History	68. Pleasure and pain	102. World

FIGURE 7–4 *The Syntopicon: Suggested curricular areas of study for the gifted*

Note: From "The Purdue Secondary Model for Gifted and Talented Youth," by J. Feldhusen and A. Robinson, in *Systems and Models for Developing Programs for the Gifted and Talented*, edited by J. S. Renzulli, 1986, Mansfield Center, CT: Creative Learning Press. Copyright 1986 by Creative Learning Press. Reprinted with permission.

You will not find acceleration used frequently except in secondary schools where advanced placement classes are available. Yet Feldhusen, et al. (1996) point out that "each child has the right to learn new material commensurate with his or her ability and knowledge, even if other students who are ready for that material are 3 years older" (p. 50) and suggest that perhaps part of the solution is to find a more accurate term to describe what students need. Benbow (1991) has suggested the terms *curricular flexibility, flexible pacing,* and *developmental placement.* Read on, and see what you think is a plausible solution to this methodology debate.

Another type of acceleration is possible without advancing a student one or more grades. Compacting, or telescoping, the standard curriculum areas is accomplished by compressing standard material into less time than is normally required (Renzulli & Smith, 1978). This method may give students time for individual research or challenging projects that may not be appropriate for all students.

Content Enrichment and Pullout Programs.

What you may find more often than acceleration is the use of enrichment programs to meet the needs of students with exceptional ability. Schools always provide instruction in standard curricular topics, but enrichment studies that broaden students' understanding are particularly helpful for high-ability students.

Typically, students in enrichment programs are part of a pullout program that allows them to work in a resource room for a few hours a day or perhaps for one full day each week. The pullout model is the most common approach because it is the easiest or least costly to implement and because it is effective in providing for student needs. One research study showed that pullout, content-enrichment programs can produce significant learning in a positive environment (Vaughn et al., 1991). For Nadine, her pullout class is a welcome challenge. Here she is presented with reading material at a much higher reading level and is given real problem-solving situations. Reading and studying laws regarding felonies such as burglary, with all the fine print, is no simple task. Organizing the step-by-step plan of investigation and planning for the trial is time-consuming and requires a great deal of synthesis of difficult material. Yet students in Nadine's talented and gifted class readily engage the material.

How many connections can you see between the revolving door model and this textbook's focus on great expectations?

Another type of enrichment method, the revolving door model (Renzulli, 1986), builds on the broader understanding of giftedness as a talent pool. In most school situations, students are considered either gifted or not gifted. Some schools, however, adopt a model that is not an *all or nothing* approach. The revolving door model includes the top fifteen to twenty percent of the school population as chosen by test scores. This model assumes that anyone in that part of the population may exhibit gifted behaviors at some time or

---

ABCNEWS VIDEO REFLECTIONS

Gee Whiz, Whiz Kids

What is normal for a child who is profoundly gifted? In "Gee Whiz, Whiz Kids", Michael Kearney's father says that normal was sending his six-year-old son to college, because normal for his cognitive level meant receiving the same instruction as young adults.

But there is more to being a human being who is profoundly gifted than having an extremely high IQ. Does the child become lost in a mind that operates like that of an adult's? Several children who are profoundly gifted and their families share their thoughts in this video.

What do you think?

If you were the parent of a child who was highly or profoundly gifted, how would you decide whether to keep your child with age peers or to accelerate their education?

What do children who are profoundly gifted need in terms of affective education, which deals with their emotional needs? Do you believe the children in this video were receiving such an education? Why or why not?

Can an inclusive classroom be an appropriate placement for a child who is profoundly gifted? If so, how would their needs be met?

other and allows students access to a resource room or enrichment studies when they are ready to do a special project or attempt some creative endeavor.

Imagine a student such as Nadine becoming involved in research on a species of insects, particularly on identifying a beetle that she cannot find in any standard beetle guide. In a revolving door program, she would be able to take time away from traditional studies to contact experts or university professors and do research into other sources. If she then found an existing identification, she would revolve back into the general education class, enriched by the experience. But imagine the thrill if she had discovered a new type of beetle and then presented her findings to a scholarly audience at a national convention (Friedman, 1990).

The revolving door model, with its flexible placement, has the advantage of permitting educators to serve a larger population of students. A student can try out the gifted program and decide to stay or not, without a costly investment by the school or teacher. A facilitator can observe new or borderline student performances in the program and assess the fit between the student's talents and the opportunities in the revolving door program. This is especially useful when a student makes an exceptional contribution.

Magnet Schools.   A final type of enrichment focus that is becoming increasingly popular is the magnet school. Magnet, or special, schools are not new, but today their focus often goes beyond academic talent alone. In addition, they are available to students in preschool through high school (Piirto, 1994). A **magnet school** is a school that educates gifted and talented students by placing a strong instructional emphasis on one or two specific domains of talent. Some possible areas of talent could include math, foreign languages, performing arts, or technology.

Extensive instruction is provided in these domains and often integrated into standard curricular areas as well. For example, a magnet school that is for students gifted in the performing arts will encourage and strengthen all areas of learning through the medium of the performing arts. Magnet schools are popular, and entrance into magnet schools is typically competitive.

A **magnet school** is a school that educates gifted and talented students by placing a strong instructional emphasis on one or two specific domains of talent.

Magnet schools build on inherent strengths of students who are gifted, providing many opportunities for growth and challenge in a specific domain of talent.

HOW IS PARTICIPATION ENCOURAGED?

Participation and belonging are critical for all students, including children who are gifted. However, social and emotional factors often become obstacles for them. Students who are gifted may have interests or ways of thinking that differ from that of their peers. Typical problems experienced by gifted students include anxiety, heightened sensitivity, divergent thinking, excitability, perfectionism, and feelings of isolation (Coleman, 1996; Lovecky, 1992). Students who are "highly motivated, single-minded in the pursuit of their own goals, and very strong-willed" (Lovecky, 1992, p. 24) may appear rebellious and stubborn. As a result, these students may feel different, alone, or isolated. These feelings may cause an inability to focus, and even manifest themselves in physical symptoms. It is important that these students recognize, accept, and value their individuality and special abilities, as well as find acceptance and a place or role among peers.

Educators must recognize the needs of students who are gifted to be included and must help these students discuss and explore their feelings and frustrations. When students see themselves as assets rather than albatrosses (Del Prete, 1996), everyone benefits. Recognizing these needs will help you understand the role of inclusion and **collaboration** on behalf of gifted students in your classroom.

> **Collaboration** is "an interactive process" that "enables people with diverse expertise to generate creative solutions to mutually defined problems" (Idol, Paolucci-Whitcomb, & Nevin, 1986).

Inclusion

Most gifted programs involve some kind of pullout program. This means that students who are gifted typically are included only part-time in general education classrooms for academic instruction. However, this is not the inclusion that is being encouraged by education reformers. Consider the issues at stake as educators struggle to find the balance.

Inclusion for gifted students in regular classrooms is an area receiving more and more attention. There are strong feelings on both sides (Delisle, 1994; Goree, 1996). Most agree with the ideal that students like Nadine and her peers of varying abilities should work on an assortment of engaging tasks at their own points of interest, talent, and readiness (Renzulli, 1996; Tomlinson, 1994/1995). How to meet those ideals is another matter.

Many advocates of gifted education worry about the move toward inclusion. Teachers of gifted students fear that inclusion will result in the dissolution of a quality education for students who are gifted and that these students will not get the help necessary to develop their strengths (Sapon-Shevin, 1994/1995). Inclusion, meaning no pullout time and no full-time gifted programs, would mean more work for the general education teacher. If the teacher wants to encourage the gifted student's identified strengths, there will be a need for "differentiated" activities rather than just "more" activities (McKay, 1993).

Another concern with inclusion is that some general teachers may not feel comfortable working with gifted students in math, science, or other subject areas. Sometimes gifted students may know more than the teacher, which can present difficulties for both teacher and student, as illustrated by the following example:

> *A gifted nine-year-old once explained to one of his favorite teachers that, contrary to what she had just said, a mile had to be longer than a kilometer because the map said that 805 kilometers equal 500 miles. She was not convinced and told him that no matter what the map said, a kilometer was longer than a mile. Later, when he shared this story with his aunt, she asked him what he told his teacher. He shrugged his shoulders and said quite calmly, "Nothing. I figured she could be just as ignorant as she wanted to be."*

> What do you think schools with inclusion need to do differently to better serve students like Nadine?

Because you may be in a position to identify and work with students who are gifted, you need to learn some ways to identify and help students who are gifted or talented in the classroom. (See the accompanying "Inclusion Tips" box.) You may conclude that you should avoid being too quick to judge some student behaviors and that when you have hunches about giftedness, you will discuss them with a gifted education specialist.

Inclusion Tips

	What You Might See	What You Might Be Tempted to Do	Alternate Responses	Ways to Include Peers in the Process
Behavior	The student might be the perfect student; or you might see the "know-it-all," the "put-down artist"; or he may ask so many questions that there is time for nothing else.	Tell the student to be quiet and pay attention to his work.	Begin a dialogue journal. Ask him to write down his questions, using either paper, computer, or a tape recorder. Then together research and discuss the answers.	Have an all-class "Challenge Box," where students can write questions they think are difficult. Then allow the students who are gifted to work on these in small groups with their peers.
Social Interactions	The student might be a leader who gets along well with everyone, or she might look like an "instigator" or a "manipulator" who cannot see another's point.	Keep the student separated from other students to avoid potential problems.	Build on her leadership by using "Reciprocal Teaching," giving her responsibility for leading a class discussion of major concepts.	Have the student work with small groups, teaching the other students to be the leaders in the "Reciprocal Teaching" activity.
Educational Performance	You might see academic aptitude in any area, or you might see the "dreamy doodler" or the student who can't change from one subject to another.	Discipline the student for inattentiveness or give additional work to reinforce the lesson.	Ask the dreamer to design a better way to teach the content being covered.	Pair him with another student during these lessons, and allow them to take notes together on the topic being covered.
Classroom Attitudes	You might see attentive curiosity and creativity, or you might see the student who's into everything, the "stubborn mule," the "cut-up," and the one who can't leave anything alone.	Discipline her for her poor attitude. If it continues, you might be tempted to refer him for AD/HD testing.	Try giving this student the opportunity to use the learning in areas of his own interest, working on individual projects with the teacher.	Continue the projects by allowing other students to join the group and test out his ideas.

The difficulties of inclusion, however, are not insurmountable. In fact, there may be more benefits than drawbacks (Delisle, 1994). For instance, one positive outcome is the mounting evidence that we have defined giftedness too narrowly and that we need a more inclusive view of who would benefit from ability development (Council for Exceptional Children, 1995). Those advocating inclusion believe that our stance should be to encourage talent development as the primary focus, rather than dwelling on talent identification. Renzulli clarified this issue when he stated that "We need to move our orientation toward developing giftedness rather than certifying it" (quoted in Kirschenbaum, 1995, p. 7). If this is the case, then teachers need to know how this can be accomplished.

One advocate of students who are gifted in the general classroom is Susan Winebrenner. She considers it her mission to "reach as many kids as possible" (Winebrenner, 1994, p. 54). Consequently, she has developed strategies and techniques that every teacher can use to meet the needs of gifted and talented students (Winebrenner, 1992). Teachers can learn to use these differentiated assignments on a daily basis. Such differentiation takes into account several factors: learning style, ability level, and student interests. Differentiation addresses the pace and the breadth of learning. Box 7–5 shows Winebrenner's Tic-Tac-Toe Menu for Differentiated Learning. These options provide a great variety of ways for students to continue and deepen their understanding in all areas of learning. These resources can help with both subject and time problems for the teacher while providing stimulating and appropriate learning materials for the gifted learner.

For inclusion and strategies such as differentiated curriculum to be successful, a strong in-service program is necessary. Discussion about ways to implement strategies and promote reform during faculty meetings could be very useful (McKay, 1993; Schack, 1996). Research indicates the impact that staff development can have on teachers' abilities to modify curriculum (Hansen & Feldhusen, 1994; Reis & Westburg, 1994). One study compared trained with untrained regular education teachers of gifted students and found that trained teachers used more concept-based approaches to subjects and fostered more in-depth study of topics than untrained teachers. Untrained teachers were more fact oriented and used more whole group instruction, focusing on children who were slower in their learning (Hansen & Feldhusen, 1994).

Collaboration

Issues that affect individuals who are gifted also affect their families, communities, and the professionals who serve them. The collaboration of all these participants in students' lives can add new dimensions in the balance and thoroughness of students' preparation. A team effort helps serve students more effectively so they can reach their full potential. Understanding the role and contribution of each participant is vitally important in preparing students to become productive members of their own families and communities. For instance, you can see in the accompanying "Collaboration Tips" box many ways different collaborators could help to adapt the general classroom environment for an unproductive gifted student.

Professional Collaboration   Professional collaboration is beneficial at all levels. It may seem quite obvious that having general educators and gifted education teachers collaborate benefits students who are gifted. In practice, one area of special benefit is curriculum planning. When general educators and gifted specialists work together on short-term and long-term curricular goals, then everyone benefits, teachers and students alike.

By contrast, in some situations, a student who attends the gifted program for a period of time must then return to the regular classroom and make up all work that has been missed. If the work covers new material that the student has not yet learned, then the makeup work is appropriate. But often the return merely means that the student has to complete worksheets or assignments that are more busywork than an educational tool for developing the student's strengths.

A key person who can help in the implementation of inclusion in such situations is the gifted education specialist. This person can be the bridge between the general classroom setting and the resources needed for serving students who are gifted. Joan Peterson, a high school gifted specialist, is one such innovative teacher who is developing strategies for dealing with some of these issues (Peterson, 1993). She has learned to successfully use collaboration on behalf of gifted students.

INTO PRACTICE

TIC-TAC-TOE MENU

Collect	**Teach**	**Compare**
facts or ideas which are important to you.	a lesson about your topic to our class. Include at least one visual aid.	two things from your study. Look for ways they are alike and ways they are different.
Photograph,	**Graph**	**Demonstrate**
videotape, or film part of your presentation.	some part of your study to show how many or how few.	something to show what you have learned.
Survey	**Dramatize**	**Forecast**
others to learn their opinions and feelings about some fact, idea, or feature of your study.	something to show what you have learned.	how your topic will change in the next 10 years.

Directions: Choose activities in a tic-tac-toe design. When you have completed the activities in a row—horizontally, vertically, or diagonally—you may decide to be finished. Or you may decide to keep going and complete more activities.

I choose activities #_____, #_____, #_____, #_____

Do you have ideas for alternate activities you'd like to do instead? Talk them over with your teacher.

I prefer to do the following alternate activities:_____

_____

Student's signature _____ Date_____

Collaboration Tips

ADAPT THE GENERAL CLASSROOM ENVIRONMENT FOR THE UNPRODUCTIVE STUDENT

COLLABORATION GOALS: To identify and plan strategies to engage a student who is gifted but appears lazy or unproductive in the general education classroom.

Collaborators	Roles and Preparation	Possible Barriers	Solutions to Barriers	Modifications to Implementation	Ongoing Evaluation
Student	Write out personal goals and strengths.	Expected failure; feels hopeless or discouraged.	Relate goals and strengths to class goals and activities.	Develop projects to do with peers built on goals and class activities.	Develop assessment for projects and goals.
Parents	Share things that parent does at home that are effective.	Overconcern with student's low performance or attitude.	Reinforce student's awards and consequences at home.	Readjust awards and consequences as needed.	Honor student for positive accomplishments.
General Educator(s)	Bring record of activities and positive expectations.	Disappointment with student, feelings of own inadequacy.	Tie inherent strengths to class goals and work.	Broaden and challenge him with new goals.	Recognize wise choices that meet goals.
Talented and Gifted Educator(s)	Make list of accomplishments and strengths.	Lack of time to observe and help student in general classroom setting.	Dialogue with journal entries among home, class, and talented and gifted program.	Exchange an afternoon with general education teacher to broaden ideas.	Focus on additional projects tied to classwork.
Administrator	Talk with each person involved to gather perspectives before meeting.	Many pressing responsibilities for students in greater trouble.	Support all collaborators: contribute rewards.	Visit and observe both settings, and record positive accomplishments.	Recognize student for classroom contribution.
School Psychologist	Bring test records and list of goals/possibilities.	Lack of first-hand knowledge of student classroom performance.	Reassess tests to highlight new potential strengths student has.	Gather ideas/tests for teachers to use in both settings.	Retest and direct student to new challenges.

 Which of this textbook's six values (see Figure 1–1) can you see highly operative in Joan Peterson's gifted program?

Understanding the characteristics of her successful program can help you when you work with students who are gifted. First, her program had as little pullout time as possible, thus respecting the importance of class attendance. Instead, she sought to develop programs and activities that would entice students to come before and after school, as well as during lunch periods. Second, she published a monthly newsletter for the regular faculty. Her newsletters and program emphasized the challenges of high capability. She also focused on students who are underachieving as a key to her program. While she affirmed student accomplishments, she also focused on their needs. In addition, her newsletter recognized teachers who were contributing to the program.

For inclusion to be most effective for these students, it takes the support and collaboration of all involved. Peterson's low-key program made her more available as a resource for students, parents, and teachers alike. These key factors, coupled with her effective public relations, helped the program generate respect and support and a great deal of success.

Resource consultation is an alternative model that is based on a collaborative problem-solving process (Ward & Landrum, 1994). In this consultation model, shared responsibility among school personnel is encouraged at three levels. At level 1, activities primarily involve regular classroom teachers, with team preparation and teaching of shared gifted students. Level 2 involves the gifted education specialist in shared responsibility to provide the most appropriate education for the gifted. At level 3, the collaboration and consultation reaches to the instructional staff, counselors, school psychologists, administrators and/or other support personnel. In this model, each participant comes to realize the demands upon and abilities of others. Through school staff training and consultation, both teachers and students benefit.

It is also beneficial for a guidance counselor to be involved in the collaboration for students who are gifted. Helping build professional collaboration and understanding of students who are gifted is a key factor in their success; this can be a guidance counselor's major contribution. An important definition of the term *giftedness* that encompasses the need for special guidance states: "Giftedness is a greater awareness, a greater sensitivity, and a greater ability to understand and transform perceptions into intellectual and emotional experiences" (Roeper, 1992). Understanding this side of giftedness and appreciating the sensitivities and intensities of students who are gifted is important for all involved in their education (Lovecky, 1990, 1992).

In discussing a model of counseling, Silverman (1993) shows that, in addition to helping students with course selection and testing them for special programs, "the focus of counseling is on growth toward high ideals" (Silverman, 1993, p. 74). She encourages the following ideals:

• Moral courage	• Authenticity
• Compassion	• Altruism
• Reflective judgment	• Strong sense of self-efficacy
• Responsibility	• Self-actualization
• Commitment to goals	• Contribution to society
• Sense of wonder	• Global awareness
• Integrity	• Devotion to high ideals
• Ethical behavior	• High state of moral development
• Creativity	• Advanced emotional development
• Autonomy	• Wisdom

Family Collaboration.   Now, as they did long ago, parents typically come to identify their exceptionally able child through the day-to-day process of caregiving, relying on their observations of their child's needs and the informal teaching associated with parenting. How families respond to their child's perceived needs varies. Family members who share special interests in some subject with their child may act as teachers or mentors. Families with financial resources may hire tutors, coaches, and special teachers, or may provide tuition to special schools.

Kevin Kearney, father of two children who are gifted, believes gifted students need all the support their families can offer and that "children like ours are thirty-two-bit children in an eight-bit world." He also recognizes that these children may well be our next great philosophers, an Aristotle or a Plato. His insights and advice for how to support and structure the environment for children who are gifted are in Box 7–6, "How Do You Educate Aristotle?"

Today more and more parents turn to home schooling because they feel their children's needs cannot be met by the public education available to them. Other parents may choose to move and change schools. Parents who recognize that a certain gifted program is not benefiting their child may simply withdraw them from the program and continue to

BOX 7-6   MAKING A DIFFERENCE

KEVIN KEARNEY

HOW DO YOU EDUCATE ARISTOTLE?

Prodigies like our son Michael are *hothouse* children. You never know when one of them will mature and make a significant contribution that will forever change our present understanding of life. These children succeed or fail depending on how well their parents and teachers prepare and control the environment around them. We have tried to ensure that the following factors are always present:

- Our children are always learning something new.
- Our children are enjoying the learning.
- Our children are with intelligent people.
- Our children are always under positive expectations.

Whenever Cassidy and I didn't know whether or not Michael could perform at the adult level, we shrugged our shoulders and said, "He's always succeeded before. Let's find out." When professors couldn't make the leap of faith that children are in fact more intelligent than they thought, the resulting negative expectations were almost a tangible force. In that environment, Michael, with an enormous track record of success in college, couldn't even recite his own name much less

logarithmic tables. He began to doubt himself and became disinterested in participating in the learning at hand. His grades declined. When we remove him from that type of environment with negative expectations, he reverts to his usual behavior. So, when needed, we drop courses and professors.

We now allow Michael at age twelve to attend the graduate school in chemistry at Middle Tennessee State University in order to help him become as normal an individual as he is likely to be. Those on the teaching staff who have gotten to know us realize that we don't consider Michael a genius. He is probably a prodigy, but on the other hand, he may in fact be this century's Aristotle, Plato, or Einstein. We still don't know.

In the Kearney family, we hold to an equation that reads B.A. + M.S. + Ph.D. = 0. Instead, we continually ask ourselves, "what does a successful person really need to know?" By success, we mean that Michael will be a happy, social, productive twenty-five-year-old. If anyone has proven ideas on how to successfully raise a possible genius, we are most ready to listen. Until then, we intend to continue with our own program of ensuring Michael is comfortable, happy, challenged, and emotionally secure by planning appropriate childhood activities for him. As a secondary issue, somewhere down the line he'll earn a master's degree or Ph.D. or two.

---

provide opportunities for growth at home or in the community. Even young Winston Churchill was moved from one private school to another until a fairly appropriate match was found (Churchill, 1930; Malkus, 1957).

Finding the best supportive and nurturing environment for children who are gifted is not always an easy process. Box 7–7 introduces Marie Friedel, who overcame many difficulties to help her son and eventually others like him. Because of her success and the strength of her convictions, she has become an advocate for many young people who are gifted.

Two additional issues affect the families of children who are gifted. The first problem arises from the consistent underrepresentation of certain populations of students with exceptional ability, such as females, cultural and ethnic minority populations, and lower socioeconomic groups. Present models and structures of gifted education do not typically address the special needs of minority students like Nadine who are gifted, although recent reform movements are seeking to incorporate their needs (Comer & Haynes, 1991; Ford & Feist, 1993; Ford & Webb, 1994; Gallagher, 1988; Maker et al., 1995). It is logical to assume that families of children in these groups are also not yet well understood.

Second, few studies have yet reported on families of students who have exceptional leadership ability or visual and performing arts ability. The current federal definition focuses on five domains in which a student can be considered gifted, but all domains have not yet been widely supported by public schools. IQ and achievement test scores continue to dominate the school evaluation programs and the population of students who are identified and consequently served. Because of this incomplete representation, we cannot draw conclusions about the characteristics of families of children with exceptional ability and the ways they can best nurture their children's gifts and talents.

Can you think of some important outcomes that will result from these key relationships? How are these connections crucial to the quality of life for students who are gifted?

BOX 7-7 — MAKING A DIFFERENCE

MARIE FRIEDEL

My interest in gifted children began when a pediatrician informed my husband and me that our adopted baby was profoundly gifted. This child, less than a year old, appeared to understand all that was said to him. He read at an early age and loved the study of astronomy and maps of the world long before the legal age for school entrance. He was eager to begin his schooling, and I was confident that school officials would be prepared for his special needs. Unfortunately, this was not the case. We struggled to find a suitable learning environment and also began the nightmare of finding how these sensitive, beautiful children were being treated both academically and emotionally.

Since those days, which started in 1966, I have continued to study and to fight for the rights of these deprived children. My son suffered very much, and I had to remain strong for him. He is so sensitive and wanted so much to be accepted. When he found that a teacher disliked him, he began to change. It was bad for a while—for a year he was very withdrawn. This is sad for a parent who understands the compassionate nature of students who are highly gifted. He is now grown and a successful, happy human being. But it has not been an easy path. It took our continual intervention and advocacy.

As I met more and more of these children, I also became involved in their lives. Because of all we learned from these children and through my son's experience, I eventually began the National Foundation for Gifted and Creative Children, a tax-exempt organization that functions at both the state and national levels. When I formed this foundation, I had to write about what my goals were. They were, and remain, that I will help any child or parent who seeks our intervention. As a result, I never have the time to do the writing that people have begged me to do.

At this time, though I am seventy-three years old, I am involved with a young lad from New York who wrote to me for information. He is fifteen years old and could become a very famous writer. I am working to prevent this boy from going to a detention center. When I become discouraged I think of those I have assisted and hope they may be able to change that which must be done if we are to stop the present loss of much-needed leadership in our nation. Not until we see these children in a new light and allow them to advance at their own pace and in their own way will we begin to overcome the severe problems plaguing our society today.

I hope that all teacher-training schools will have future teachers learn about our gifted and creative children—how to save them from a life of failure, crime, suicide, or mental illness. I want to close by telling you about one first-grade student with whom we worked. He was failing math, although his mother had told the teacher that her boy was able to calculate the right answers for math problems that involved real-life skills, such as figuring how much change is due to a buyer who tenders more than the sales price of an item. The teacher said, "If he is so gifted, why can't he do these simple math problems?" One day the head of the math department in our city came, and we told him about this boy. He took the boy into our study and when they returned, the boy was all smiles. The math expert was excited and said, "This boy who cannot do the easy math is doing high school math and loving it. He must learn from an exploratory level—what is easy for the average student is boring and difficult for him!"

Marie Friedel
Executive director, National Foundation
for Gifted and Creative Children

Peer and Community Collaboration. How today's communities respond to the needs of students who are gifted can affect our communities of tomorrow. Historically, these students have found a community outlet with extracurricular activities such as library reading programs, 4H, Scouts, sports activities, community centers and volunteer programs. Today many communities are in a transitional phase: Traditional programs continue to be important, yet some new programs are becoming available. More businesses and universities are now getting involved and demonstrating greater collaboration among schools, parents, and communities.

Mentorships are a good example of collaboration. Mentors are people who know more than students in a particular area and are willing to work with them on an individual basis. Typically, they are community experts who provide specialized knowledge and/or skills to expand students' talents in a particular area of study. They have the potential to develop students' interest in various trades and professions, interest that might otherwise be stunted (Ellingson, Haeger, & Feldhusen, 1986; Reilly, 1992; Timpson & Jones, 1989).

The interest Nadine shows in writing and publishing is promising. What difference could a mentor excited about writing (e.g., a local newspaper editor) make for her?

Mentorships of students who are gifted is becoming an increasingly popular model, especially for students who are highly gifted (Ambrose, Allen, & Huntley, 1994; Shaw, 1996). The positive effects upon metacognitive abilities and career development are many. Emotional and social support is an added benefit.

Mentorships are demonstrated in a variety of ways. Because they are individualized, they can be an excellent opportunity for peer collaboration and integration across grade levels. Older students who are gifted in a particular area can become mentors to younger students who show aptitude in that area. Within the business community, students who are gifted can learn problem-solving and critical thinking skills necessary in successful businesses before encountering the realities of the world of work. School projects can be built around developing business plans under the direction of community business leaders, thus preparing students to interact with the business world at a much earlier age.

Mentorships provide an excellent opportunity for community collaboration and allow students who are gifted to be apprenticed to community leaders in any area of giftedness. Because giftedness is usually domain-specific, and students with high ability are very different in their needs, it is important to provide individualized and high-quality resource people to enrich these students' special abilities. Mentorships seem to be an area where more schools and more individuals could be of great service to students who are gifted and talented.

Careers

Working with students who are gifted is an exciting challenge. Many professional career opportunities for working with these students are school-based. The most obvious professions are those of the general educator who has students who are gifted as a regular part of the class and the special educator who receives specialized training to work with these students in general and special education settings.

Both of these professions have their own set of challenges. For the general educator, learning how to work with and adequately challenge students who are gifted can be a time-consuming but rewarding job. For the educator of students who are gifted, identifying specific learning strategies and areas for development in different domains of giftedness can be a delightful challenge.

Becoming either a classroom teacher or gifted education specialist takes not only a college degree, but also ongoing reading, research and graduate education to learn more effective ways to teach students who are gifted. Other career options for individuals interested in working with students who are gifted include the school psychometrician, school psychologist, or professional counselor who works with students who are gifted (usually one part of the job). Local, county, and state coordinators of gifted education, researchers, and college professors are additional career options for working with individuals who are gifted. These careers also include many challenges and require graduate preparation and ongoing training. Each type of career professional makes a necessary and positive contribution to helping students who are gifted reach their full potential.

WHAT ARE PROGRAM OPTIONS?

Many exemplary models of programs that challenge students who are gifted exist at all levels of education, although early intervention and preschool models are only now developing. The following descriptions—admittedly only a small sample—demonstrate their diversity and the many possibilities for educating students who are gifted.

Early Intervention and Preschool Years

Ironically, at an age when children's giftedness is in its formative stage, gifted programs have been rare. A primary concern has been how to differentiate the program for very young gifted students (Gallagher & Gallagher, 1994). Today, however, with the educational focus moving toward early readiness, some new and innovative programs are coming forth. Children with diverse gifts are being offered new opportunities to develop their gifts.

One such program for early learners can be found at Montgomery Elementary School in Silver Spring, Maryland. This program is particularly interesting because it was originally begun with a grant to help identify and educate underserved children with gifts and talents, including children experiencing economic disadvantages, cultural diversity, language differences (primary language not English), and developmental delays indicating learning disabilities. The program is based on Gardner's model of different domains of intelligence and focuses on identifying and serving different types of giftedness.

The Montgomery Knolls Early Childhood Gifted Model Program trains all faculty to look for different types of giftedness, to plan activities specific to these areas, and then to provide options for each child. Twice a year, teachers fill out a checklist on each child, working to identify their areas of strength.

A strong focus for these young students is the theme approach, where children use their different gifts to express their own understanding of the topic as well as learn about others. This approach helps young students to make abstract concepts concrete and real. For instance, during a study of dinosaurs, one group of children with a spatial orientation wanted to know how big they really were. To do this, they blew up pictures with an overhead on the school wall to grasp the concept of size. Other children with a linguistic orientation developed seven questions and then e-mailed them to a paleontologist who answered their questions. More questions followed and were answered. Other children with an artistic leaning wanted to make life-size features of the dinosaurs and used papier-mâché to do so. Still others with a musical ability wrote and sang songs about dinosaurs. Many created stories and drew accompanying pictures.

Dr. Waveline Starnes, initiator of the program, reports that there has been enthusiastic support from parents, teachers, and children. Dr. Starnes says that "There have been great benefits for teachers. The 'verbal veil' that had hidden the children's varying potentials has been removed, and teachers are looking for and seeing giftedness in all areas."

  Because family and professional collaborators have great expectations of these students at Knolls Early Childhood Program, students have many opportunities to learn and discover new areas of giftedness.

Elementary Years

Programs that properly identify and challenge elementary school students who are gifted are important to these children's success in school as well as vital to the future of our nation. During these years, most districts initiate some sort of identification program and begin working with these students. For example, it was during her elementary years when Nadine was identified as gifted and placed in a special program.

As mentioned, pullout programs are the most common type of program used in the elementary years. Historically, there has been tension between gifted education and middle school education (Tomlinson, 1992), with few programs developed specifically for middle school students who are gifted. But new areas of shared belief now acknowledge strengths and contributions of both practices and seek to communicate, cooperate, and collaborate at every level of educational practice (Tomlinson, 1995).

One example of an effective pullout program at the elementary level that would be easy to incorporate at the middle school level is the "Kids Development Corporation" used in one Florida school system (Davison, 1993). During this program, a class of students from ages seven to nine participate in a mock demonstration of the structure of the economic life of a community. Students meet three times a week for eight weeks. The project can be adjusted to older students by changing the critical thinking levels.

The goal of the program is for students to build a functional community from the ground up. Each student selects and researches an occupational role in the community and then uses imagination to form a corporation. They begin the project with the equivalent of $100,000.00 and must provide a rationale for how they acquired their money. In the process they learn how to purchase land, plan for building construction, and use banking and investing strategies. Some of their activities include the following:

- Choosing their individual roles

- Writing a short story

- Researching their occupation

- Listening to five guest speakers

- Going on four field trips

- Making a picture collage of their occupation

- Going on a personal interview of an adult business person

- Writing a classroom script to present to city planning board

- Making individual scrapbooks

- Appearing before the city planning board

- Being hosts and hostesses at a tea following the board meeting

Evaluation covers such areas as key vocabulary, comparisons of the value of money, written evaluations of their role-playing occupations, a word search or crossword puzzle of their occupations, written interviews, and a scrapbook of collected materials.

Results have been impressive. Parent participation is high, and relationships are being forged among teachers, students, parents, and business community members. Not only did these young students enjoy the experience, but they also progressed from very little knowledge about a planned urban community to a rather extensive understanding of a community's economics. As Davison (1993) reported, "Students went from asking, 'What is that?' or 'What does that mean?' to 'Hey, I'm the banker. You have to consult me to do that!' . . . These statements proved our students had 'arrived'" (p. 6).

Middle and Secondary Years

In the past, many educators perceived middle- and secondary-level programs for students who are gifted and talented as unnecessary and therefore not to be included in course offerings (Clark, 1997). Rather, they assumed that the secondary structure had many classes and programs from which students could choose and that students who were gifted would choose programs that challenged and met their needs.

Today, however, many districts are providing additional course work or other activities for these students. Special honors or advanced placement courses, which are substitute courses for normally required course work, are available in many schools. Elective courses, taken in addition to the requirements for graduation, are available, although they may have to limit their electives due to scheduling constraints. Some districts now offer extra hours before and/or after school for additional electives.

In addition, program options such as Saturday programs, seminars, and summer institutes may also prove beneficial. Although these types of programs are successful in meeting the needs of students who are gifted, fees and transportation are most often the parents' responsibility; thus, those programs may be prohibitive for families with limited resources.

An exemplary secondary program model for students who are gifted involves the Purdue Three-Stage Model. This model is effective at the secondary level because of the hands-on real-life experience it provides for students. At the secondary level, the first and second stages require mastery of core content and increased critical thinking skills. During the third stage, students must apply the knowledge to real problems, function as a professional in their talent area, and develop real products to share with real audiences (Moon, Feldhusen, Powley, Nidiffer, & Whitman, 1993). The teacher moves from leading the class to acting as a resource person for the students.

Students accomplish the mastery and application process through studies in specific academic, artistic, and vocational areas and may include components such as seminars, honors classes, independent studies, and mentorships. A program will typically span two years of student research and work on projects, culminating in a written summary and a twenty- to thirty-minute presentation to peers, teachers, parents, mentors, and community leaders involved in the process. These experiences not only give students hands-on learning in their various areas of giftedness, but also provide a pool of youth ready for high-level creative careers (Moon, Feldhusen, & Dillon, 1994).

Programs of this type can easily be integrated with mentorships at the application level. Mentorships can help expand the curriculum and also provide opportunities for career exploration. One successful example, the Carnegie Unit, is a year-long course providing both cognitive and affective support (Milan & Schwartz, 1992). Students are actually placed on site with the mentor for thirty hours. During this time, the specialist makes at least one visit to the site to observe the training.

Even with these types of programs available, there remains an important need to more thoroughly include girls in gifted programs. Fortunately, some programs are recognizing the talents of girls. For instance, Charleston Southern University, with the aid of several grants, has developed an innovative summer enrichment program specifically aimed at girls and minority students (Karges-Bone, 1992). The focus for these grants, which represents collaboration among university faculty, public school personnel, and local industry, is to encourage these students to pursue careers in mathematics and science. The program provides role models successful in their field as well as individual tutoring from professors and teachers.

Transitional and Postsecondary Years

Programs beyond the high school years are harder to find, although there is an acknowledged need for career education for individuals who are gifted (Clark, 1997). Most colleges and universities offer many challenging courses for all students, and some provide special courses for students who are gifted. However, specific honors programs are more often found at an earlier level.

There is one well-known organization primarily for adults who are gifted: MENSA, which means *table* in Latin and signifies a round table of equals. It is an international organization with only one requirement for membership, a standardized IQ score higher than ninety-eight percent of the general population (MENSA, 1993). Members come from all occupations, including presidents of companies, movie stars, professional boxers, airplane pilots, teachers, pianists, mail carriers, and chimney sweeps. You can see the wide diversity representing all domains of giftedness.

Although MENSA is primarily a social organization, it also offers programs for individuals who are gifted, including resource programs for students. Every year MENSA also awards college scholarships to approximately sixty students. In addition, it sponsors the MENSA Education and Research Foundation (MERF) to conduct research projects in the social and psychological sciences. Officially, MENSA's stated goals are "to identify and foster human intelligence for the benefit of humanity; to encourage research in the nature, characteristics, and uses of intelligence; and to provide a stimulating intellectual and social environment for its members" (MENSA, 1993).

In the United States alone, nearly 5 million people are eligible for membership in MENSA (MENSA, 1993). Those who are members—from age four to ninety-four—also have access to special interest groups that study everything from philosophy to chocolate to scuba diving. MENSA also has its own research journal, *MENSA Research Journal,* which is devoted to the best research in the field of human intelligence and giftedness. This program appears to be meeting a social and educational need for individuals who are gifted, as well as providing needed research into areas of giftedness not yet fully investigated.

A VISION FOR THE FUTURE

Thinking about Nadine's future brings to mind endless possibilities. The hopes of Nadine's parents are not directed toward any particular career. Rather, Pat says, "What's important is that she does what she enjoys and that she does it well."

Nadine has lots of ideas but says,

> *Right now it's hard to see far in the future. But just imagining, I'd probably like to be an anthropologist. I'd go all over the world. I wouldn't study just one particular culture, but view all different cultures. That seems most interesting. I like geography and learning about people, and I think that would help me get along better with people. I could also figure out answers to world problems and share my findings to help people, offering options for the future.*
>
> *I'd also like to be an author of children's books. I'd write stories like those of my favorite authors, Laurence Yep and Ann Martin. Laurence Yep's books deal with kids in other cultures. Martin's books, sort of realistic adventures, are fun to read. I'd like to write about other cultures and adventures so other kids could enjoy more good books.*

Nadine also has some advice for teachers of the future. She says that

> *A good teacher prepares in advance and really knows the subject and can make it fun. Good teachers also give more projects rather than busy work and worksheets. A good teacher keeps kids from being unruly so you can learn.*
>
> *If a child is slow, but bright, give them more time and build on things they enjoy doing. Put yourselves in the children's shoes and don't expect kids to be on the same schedule as you are. Remember they have family and friends who want to see them and be with them too.*

So what are the potential pitfalls for a student like Nadine? Pat says, "I want her to do the best she can with what she has. Things don't always go as planned, and we can't always choose the people we work with. I want my daughter to be able to say, 'I will do my best in everything, regardless.' That takes a lot of maturity."

What Would You Recommend . . .

1. To help Nadine develop her present interests in anthropology and writing children's books?

2. To provide the best possible communication between Nadine's regular and gifted education teachers?

3. To encourage Nadine to do her "best in everything, regardless?"

SUMMARY

WHAT IS GIFTEDNESS?

- Students who are gifted and talented demonstrate unusual capabilities in intellectual, creative, academic, or leadership areas, as well as in the performing and visual arts. Although not covered by IDEA, these students require special services not ordinarily provided by the school.

- Recent changes in how educators define students who are gifted focus on the developmental nature of giftedness and stress that a definition of talent or giftedness must include multiple domains of potential ability and not be determined solely by IQ.

- A multicultural perspective of giftedness recognizes that different cultures value and encourage specific domains of giftedness that are important to the survival of that culture.

- Students who are gifted may demonstrate unexpected characteristics that look antisocial such as boredom, hyperactivity, or even insubordination. Educators who build on students' strengths help them to reach their potential.

- Many populations are vastly underrepresented in current gifted programs. Girls and minorities who are gifted often go undetected or have to work their way through successive levels of adverse circumstances.

- Most researchers today attribute giftedness to a combination of nature (genetic factors) and nurture (environmental factors), but they also disagree about the proportions between the two factors.

- Giftedness identified by an IQ of at least 130 includes the top 2 percent of the general population. Using a talent pool that includes students with an IQ of a minimum of 115 means that 16 percent of students will be served.

WHAT ARE EVALUATION PROCEDURES?

- To determine the presence of intellectual giftedness, students typically take IQ tests, achievement tests, and/or creativity tests such as the Torrance Tests of Creative Thinking (Torrance 1966a, 1966b).

- To ensure that assessments do not discriminate against students from minority populations, several types of measurement for determining the presence of giftedness should be used.

- Once educators identify a student as gifted, educational planning and regular evaluations based on IEP goals are implemented. Students who are gifted are often able to help design and take responsibility for the process of evaluation.

- Recent innovative evaluation procedures based upon multiple domains of giftedness, such as the Multiple Intelligences DISCOVER Assessment (Maker, 1996), offer an alternative form of assessment for identifying and serving students who are gifted.

WHAT AND HOW DO PROFESSIONALS TEACH?

- Three types of curricula that instill critical and creative thinking include curriculum that is modified according to the interests of the student, curriculum that modifies the pace of the learning, and curriculum that modifies the depth of content coverage.

- Many curricula for students who are gifted include strate-gies to increase critical and creative thinking such as Bloom's taxonomy (1956). A focus on higher level thinking skills rooted in the content areas continues to be popular today.

- A variety of methods are appropriate for teaching students who are gifted. Acceleration is a method that modifies the pace of the learning for students who are extremely gifted. Compacting curriculum is another way to modify the pace of learning.

- Content enrichment and pullout programs are common methods to work closely in a resource room with students who are gifted.

- Magnet schools that focus on particular domains of talent are becoming increasingly popular as a means for educating students who are gifted.

HOW IS PARTICIPATION ENCOURAGED?

- Although there are concerns over inclusion for gifted students in regular classrooms, difficulties can be overcome with a strong in-service program, a gifted education specialist, and curriculum materials based on differentiation.

- When general educators, gifted specialists, and parents all collaborate on short-term and long-term curricular goals, everyone benefits.

- Collaboration with the community is often demonstrated through the involvement of businesses and mentorship programs that seek to pair experts with students desiring expanding learning in a particular area of study.

- Career opportunities for working with students who are gifted are numerous. In addition to being a general educator or specialist in gifted education, you may want to consider being a school guidance counselor, psychometrician, psychologist, local/county/state coordinator, researcher, or professor.

WHAT ARE PROGRAM OPTIONS?

- Identifying preschool students with exceptional ability is confounded by many factors, but the current educational focus on early readiness is encouraging the development of new programs.

- Pullout programs are the most common programs used during the elementary years.

- The most common programs at the secondary level are special honors or advanced placement courses. Saturday programs, seminars, and summer institutes are also available.

- Program models beyond the high school years are harder to find. MENSA is an organization that offers programs for individuals who are gifted, including resource programs for students.

 **RESOURCES**

BOOKS

Curriculum Development and Teaching Strategies for Gifted Learners (2nd ed.). (1996). By C. J. Maker and A. Nielson. Austin, TX: Pro-Ed. A valuable guide for teachers, coordinators, and specialists as well as a resource for program development.

Gifted Children. (1996). By E. Winner. New York: HarperCollins. An in-depth look at the lives of unusually gifted children, exploring nine myths about giftedness.

Growing Up Gifted (5th ed.). (1997). By B. Clark. New York: Merrill/Macmillan. Offers a classic overview on what it means to be gifted in home, school, and society today.

Handbook of Gifted Education. (1997). Edited by N. Coangelo & G. A. Davis. Boston: Allyn & Bacon. A useful handbook with up to date information on a wide variety of topics in giftedness.

Multiple Intelligences in the Classroom. (1994). By T. Armstrong. Alexandria, VA: ASCD. An insightful description for how educators can bring Gardner's theory of multiple intelligences into the classroom every day.

Students may be interested in the following resource books:

Gifted Kids Speak Out. (1987). By J. R. Delisle. Minneapolis, MN: Free Spirit. Students who are gifted share ideas on their experiences and concerns.

The Gifted Kids Survival Guide. (1983). By J. Galbraith. Minneapolis, MN: Free Spirit. A wonderful compendium of advice for students who are gifted, exploring survival strategies for various life situations in educational settings.

JOURNALS, MAGAZINES, AND CATALOGS

Gifted Child Quarterly. National Association for Gifted Children, 1155 Fifteenth Street NW Suite 1002, Washington, DC 20005. Official publication of the National Association for Gifted Children (NAGC); NAGC membership includes the journal.

Gifted Child Today. Box 637, Holmes, PA 19043. Primarily for parents and teachers of children who are gifted.

Gifted Education Review. P.O. Box 2278, Evergreen CO 80439-2278. A quarterly publication that summarizes papers in 13 journals that specialize in gifted education.

Journal for the Education of the Gifted (JEG). TAG, 1920 Association Drive, Reston, VA 22091. This is the official publication of The Association for the Gifted (TAG), and is aimed at the experienced reader of the literature.

Journal of Creative Behavior. 1050 Union Road, Buffalo, NY 14224. Publishes research aimed at enhancing creative behavior.

The Prufrock Journal: The Journal of Secondary Gifted Education. 1617 North Valley Mills Dr., Suite 237, Waco, TX 76710. Published quarterly, focusing on secondary education.

Roeper Review. Roeper City and Country School, P.O. Box 329, Bloomfield Hills, MI 48303-0329. Quarterly refereed journal that focuses on current research and issues related to the lives and experiences of gifted children.

MULTIMEDIA

Being Gifted: The Gift. (1991). Council for Exceptional Children, 1920 Association Drive, Department K3092, Reston, VA 22091-1589. Phone (703) 620-3660. Package includes a training video, a guidebook, a list of resources, and twenty-five practice activities.

MI: Intelligence, Understanding, and the Mind. (1996). Into the Classroom Media, 10573 W. Pico Blvd. #162, Los Angeles, CA 90064. Package includes a seven-part training video and comprehensive instructor's package on Howard Gardner's multiple intelligences, featuring Howard Gardner.

Giftedness. Insight Media, 2162 Broadway, New York, NY. 10024-6620. Phone (800) 233-9910. This company offers many videos dealing with giftedness.

ON-LINE INFORMATION, USEFUL DATABASES, AND SOFTWARE

Critical Thinking Press & Software. P.O. Box 448, Pacific Grove, CA 93950. Phone (800) 458-4850. Offers software to develop higher-level thinking skills.

Programs and Practices in Gifted Education Funded by the Jacob K. Javits Gifted and Talented Students Education Act of 1988. Edited by Sandra L. Berger. Phone (703) 264-9474. Available only on Macintosh or DOS-formatted disk.

Prufrock Press. P.O. Box 8813, Waco, TX 76714-8813. Phone (800) 998-2208. Software and other materials for students who are gifted.

Gifted Resources Home Page.
http://www.eskimo.com/~user/kids.html. Lots of links to on-line gifted resources, enrichment programs, talent searches, summer programs, gifted mailing lists, and early acceptance programs.

Prufrock Press Gifted Education Home Page.
http://www.prufrock.com. Offers links to additional information, provides free samples for magazines, journals, and catalogs.

ORGANIZATIONS

American Association for Gifted Children. c/o Talent Identification Program, Duke University, 1121 West Main Street, Suite 100, Durham, NC 27701.

The Association for the Gifted (TAG). 2216 Main Street, Cedar Falls, IA 50613. (319) 266-0205. A division of the Council for Exceptional Children.

Gifted Children's Information Office. 12657 Fee Fee Road, St. Louis, MO 63146. Provides a hotline, library, referral service for testing, information about programs and activities, and a bureau of available speakers.

MENSA. American MENSA Ltd., 2626 E. 14th St., Brooklyn, NY 11235-3992. (718) 934-3700. FAX: (718) 332-1183.

National Association for Gifted Children. (NAGC). Suite 550, 1707 L. Street, NW, Washington, DC 20036. Phone (202) 785-4268. Membership includes the journal *Gifted Child Quarterly.*

CHAPTER 8

MENTAL RETARDATION

Educating
Ryan Banning

Now that their son has reached the age of twenty, Ryan Banning's parents, Martha and Bob, face the future with a wariness borne of years of intense advocating for him in the educational system. "We had to fight to get anything and everything," says Bob, reflecting on their now-successful efforts to have Ryan benefit from an inclusive education.

There is palpable, explicit, and justified tension between past and future, between the inclusion that occurred because so many people collectively and individually added value to Ryan's life and the inclusion that put Ryan at risk among some of his peers and school administrators.

Make no mistake about it, his parents' advocacy opened many opportunities for Ryan that were not available to other students with mental retardation. All three years he was a member of the percussion section in the Lawrence, Kansas, high school band. Martha vividly recalls the first home football game at which Ryan performed with the band:

The band members had to be at the high school by 6:00. Ryan began to don his band uniform around 4:00. It was quite an outfit, very

complicated to get on with lots of zippers and snaps. When he finished, he beamed. He was so proud of being a part of the band; band class was the best part of his school day. I dropped him off by the band door just before 6:00 and he said "Bye, Mom. See you later!" Without a backward glance, he shut the door and ran to the band room. After so many years of segregated education and stigma associated with his disability, I remember feeling that as he entered the band room, he was entering a place of belonging in his school for the very first time.

The selection of Ryan's general education courses was always a challenge because inclusive education was not a priority for his school and most of its staff. Ryan's class selection was guided primarily by finding those general educators who were willing to accept Ryan into their classes. Of these few classes, Ryan was most successful in greenhouse science and natural resources, displaying an intelligence in hands-on science that astonished his teachers.

During his school day, Ryan practiced those skills he would need to live independently in the community. He learned the county bus schedule to get from home to his two jobs: one as a clerical aide with the National Association of Golf Club Superintendents and the other at a fast-food restaurant.

Ryan now deposits his pay checks into his own checking account, having learned such simple banking skills as how to deposit and withdraw money with little assistance. He also learned more subtle skills, such as how long to talk with the cashier, what voice volume to use in the bank, and when it is appropriate to get a drink (before

getting in line or when exiting, but not in the middle of a transaction!).

Ryan now decides his lunch menus for the week, develops a shopping list, shops for needed groceries, and prepares such favorite meals as spaghetti, pizza, hamburgers, tacos, and fajitas. He pays for his groceries independently if he has one bill that is greater than the total (a $20 bill for $19 worth of groceries); however, he needs assistance to use multiple bills (one $20 and two $5 dollar bills).

Notwithstanding the successes, the past three years were fraught with

significant challenges. Ryan's propensity to seek the approval of some of his schoolmates has made him the victim of their taunting and mischievous goading. This past year, Ryan was taunted into a fight in the high school cafeteria. Solely because of his disability, Ryan was wrongly blamed by school administrators for the incident. Martha and Bob are acutely aware that, should Ryan ever become involved in a scuffle with anyone else, he and he alone may again be blamed for the incident. To have mental retardation, they understand, means that you can be victimized in many different ways.

Martha and Bob also realize that they may have to create a system of inclusive supports for his adult years, using their own resources at a time when they themselves are greatly depleted from years of intense advocacy. On the other hand, if they use adult service agencies in their community, they may reverse Ryan's inclusion because these agencies tend to be disability-only.

Martha and Bob face another concern. How can they continue to find the kind of people who have been so valuable to Ryan and them? Those were the ones who saw Ryan as a person and not as a disability. They had high expectations and a vision for him and translated it into action. They believed in his right to belong to an inclusive America. They had a sense of humor even at the hardest of times, were not afraid to be humble and ask questions, and were also not afraid to be part of a team.

"We don't have another year to waste, for the system to get its act together," says Martha. Bob agrees and adds, with not a small bit of frustration, "We've been in transition to an inclusive adulthood for ten years, and we're still on the front line."

In this chapter, you will learn how you can develop high expectations that will respond to the particular needs of students who have mental retardation.

What Do You Think?

1. How would you increase Ryan's own decision making (self-determination) about his future?

2. How would you teach Ryan and other students skills that will ensure their success in adult life?

3. How can teachers relieve parents of such overwhelming advocacy responsibilities?

WHAT IS MENTAL RETARDATION?

Defining Mental Retardation

Mental Retardation as a Social Construct.   Reflect on your own understanding of mental retardation. Were people with mental retardation in school with you? How did you, your teachers, and fellow students relate to them? Have you lived, worked, or played with people with mental retardation? What images have you acquired from movies or television? Whatever the source of your present understanding about mental retardation, you probably got it from society. That is, others socialized you to understand it in certain ways. This is a simple way of saying that mental retardation (like other disabilities) is, in part, a **social construct**—a concept that derives from society's views about people. In sociological terms, a social construct reflects how society collectively expects people like Ryan Banning to function intellectually in, interact with, and adapt to the world around them. Burton Blatt, an educator, poet, advocate, journalist, and one-time president of the American Association on Mental Retardation (AAMR), interpreted mental retardation as a social construct:

> *Mental retardation is not something that can be simply and scientifically defined, discussed, dissected, applied or studied. Mental retardation is related to our very understanding of humanity, of human potential, of educability, of equality, of rights and privileges, of everything we are and everything that relates to us. Asking someone to comprehend a concept of mental retardation is akin to asking him to comprehend a concept of spirituality or decadence, beauty or ugliness, strength or weakness, good people or bad people. Mental retardation can't be encapsulated and "pictured" by IQ parameters, or even etiological descriptions, or behavioral assessments. It must always be anchored to other people, a community, values, expectations, and hopes. (Blatt, 1981)*

The Evolving Definition.   The American Association on Mental Retardation (AAMR) first defined mental retardation in 1921, when it categorized the condition according to

ᏗᏍ Mental retardation is a social construct that reflects what society expects of individuals with intellectual limitations. Today we recognize that individuals with mental retardation can be fully included, contributing members of their community—*full citizens.*

Social construct is a concept that derives from society's views about people.

ᏗᏍ *Project TASSEL in Shelby, North Carolina, is profiled later in this chapter. This program involves students such as this one in community activities that help them to identify and pursue personal and career goals beyond high school.*

The AAMR is the nation's oldest and largest professional association concerned with individuals who have mental retardation.

EMR classroom refers to a classroom for students with mild mental retardation. "EMR" is an outdated term that stands for educable mentally retarded.

Educable students is an outdated term that refers to students with mild mental retardation.

Trainable students is an outdated term that refers to students with moderate mental retardation.

Referring to a student as *EMR* or *TMR* is outdated and dehumanizing. You should label jars, not people.

levels of severity of intellectual impairment (Luckasson et al., 1992). The AAMR has revised and republished its definition and classification system nine times since then (Reiss, 1994), most recently in 1983 and 1992. Each time it has focused on permanent intellectual impairment as the distinguishing characteristic, and each time until 1992 it retained a classification system—a categorization—based on severity (Luckasson et al., 1992). For example, the 1983 definition says "Mental retardation refers to significantly subaverage general intellectual functioning existing concurrently with deficits in adaptive behavior and manifested during the developmental period" (Grossman, 1983) (see Table 8-1).

IDEA (1997) relies on the 1983 AAMR definition but specifically defines mental retardation according to a student's educational performance: "Mental retardation means significantly subaverage general intellectual functioning existing concurrently with deficits in adaptive behavior and manifested during the developmental period that adversely affects a child's educational performance" (34 C.F.R., Sec. 300.7[b][5]).

The AAMR's 1983 classification system categorized "significantly subaverage general intellectual functioning" as existing at mild, moderate, severe, and profound levels. Table 8-1 shows the AAMR 1983 classification system in the first two columns and the resulting special education classification terminology in the third column (MacMillan, 1982). Many school systems set up special classes for students with mental retardation according to this classification system, and today you may still hear the term **EMR classroom.** As a general rule, educators based their expectations about students on the categories to which students had been assigned. They generally believed that **"educable" students,** those with mild mental retardation, would be able to develop functional academic skills at a third- or fourth-grade level and that **"trainable" students,** those with moderate mental retardation, would be able to learn self-care and some social skills but would not be able to learn to read (Kolstoe, 1970). This classification system and its resulting expectations may well limit students by creating a self-fulfilling prophesy: Teachers may think the students can do nothing beyond the old expectations for people in that category.

Although the 1983 definition seemed useful, it also had some very serious deficiencies (H. R. Turnbull, 1986). Primarily, it failed to emphasize sufficiently what had been well and long established—namely, that individuals with mental retardation have the potential to develop when they are provided with appropriate services (Baumeister & Muma, 1975).

The 1992 AAMR Definition. In 1992, the AAMR published a new definition and a classification manual (Luckasson et al., 1992) that is similar to but more skill-based than the 1983 version:

> *Mental retardation refers to substantial limitations in present functioning. It is characterized by significantly subaverage intellectual functioning, existing concurrently with related limitations in two or more of the following applicable adaptive skill areas: communication, self-care, home living, social skills, community use, self-direction, health and safety, functional academics, leisure, and work. Mental retardation manifests before age 18. (Luckasson et al., 1992, p. 5)*

But a significant change occurs in the definition's concepts and explanations. Proponents of the 1992 definition (Reiss, 1994; Schalock et al., 1994; Smith, 1994) and its opponents

TABLE 8–1 *AAMR 1983 classification system (Grossman, 1983)*

AAMR 1983 Classification	IQ Range	Educational Classification
Mild mental retardation	50–55 to 70	Educable mental retardation
Moderate mental retardation	35–40 to 50–55	Trainable mental retardation
Severe mental retardation	20–25 to 35–40	Severely/multiply handicapped
Profound mental retardation	Below 20 or 25	Severely multiply handicapped

(MacMillan, Gresham, & Siperstein, 1993, 1995; Vig & Jedrysek, 1996) have debated its merits and concerns. We take all perspectives into account as we describe for you this highly significant definitional change.

Figure 8-1 shows the following key elements: capabilities, environments, and functioning. According to the 1992 definition, mental retardation is a by-product of how a person's intellectual and adaptive behavior impairments interact with that person's environments. In the AAMR's words, it is a "particular state of impaired functioning within the community" (Luckasson et al., 1992).

Like previous definitions, the 1992 one recognizes both intellectual and adaptive behavior limitations and their effects on the person; but unlike the earlier ones, it also recognizes the importance of the individual's environments and their impact on the person's functioning. The definition asserts that when the person and the environments do not fit each other, the result is a need for services. Reiss (1994), one of the professionals who helped to develop the definition, explained: "An important goal of the new definition is to hold the environment responsible for providing needed supports for greater inclusion of individuals with disabilities."

For example, Ryan needs to learn and use effective communication at home, school, work, leisure, and recreation activities, and as a participant in his Group Action Planning activities (described later in this chapter). To increase Ryan's abilities across these environments, his communication partners—those people with whom he regularly communicates—have developed strategies that allow him to use more complex communication; they do this by changing the way they communicate with him. Because communication that directs a person to do or say something actually inhibits spontaneous communication (Mirenda & Don-

How could the AAMR define mental retardation, taking the strengths of individuals with mental retardation into account? There were, after all, increasing numbers of people who believed, like Blatt, that mental retardation is anchored to "other people, a community, values, expectations, and hopes."

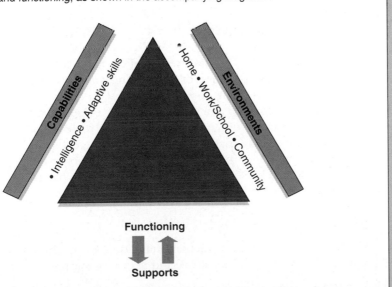

FIGURE 8–1 *General structure and three key elements of the 1992 AAMR definition of mental retardation*

General Structure of the Definition

Mental retardation refers to a particular state of impaired functioning within the community, first manifested in childhood, in which limitations in intelligence coexist with related limitations in adaptive skills. For any person with mental retardation, the description of this state of functioning requires knowledge of the individual's capabilities and an understanding of the structure and expectations of the individual's personal and social environment.

The key elements in the definition of mental retardation are *capabilities* (or competencies), *environments*, and *functioning*, as shown in the accompanying diagram.

Capabilities
• Intelligence • Adaptive skills

Environments
Home • Work/School • Community

Functioning

Supports

Note: From *Mental Retardation: Definition, Classification, and Systems of Supports*, by R. Luckasson, D. L. Coulter, E. A. Polloway, S. Reiss, R. L. Schalock, M. E. Snell, D. M. Spitalnik, & J. A. Stark, 1992, Washington, DC: American Association on Mental Retardation. Copyright 1992 by the American Association on Mental Retardation. Reprinted with permission.

BOX 8-1   MAKING A DIFFERENCE

COMMUNICATION PARTNERS ACROSS ENVIRONMENTS

1. Pause expectantly and give Ryan the opportunity to communicate.
2. Begin a new topic with a declarative statement and then pause and wait for Ryan to respond. "I had a good weekend, Ryan." (Pause for response.)
3. Use a declarative statement and pause followed by another declarative statement and pause. "I had a good weekend. (Pause) I went to the football game." (Pause)
4. Suggest a specific topic area. "I had a good weekend. Ryan, you could tell me what you did last weekend."

5. Use a declarative statement followed with a question. Try to avoid "wh" questions, such as what, who, when, where. At this level, you should try to be as subtle as possible, but a bit more obvious than the previous levels. "I had a good weekend. Ryan, could you tell me about your weekend?"
6. Use a conversational partner to prompt initiation from Ryan. "I had a good weekend. I wonder what _____ did last weekend. (Pause) Ryan, you could ask _____ what she/he did last weekend."

(Culp & Carlisle, 1988)

Note: From J.R. Wegner, Personal Communication, August 1997.

nellan, 1986), his partners are trying, instead, to be more facilitative, eliciting from Ryan the kind of communication he wants and needs. In facilitating his communication, they are shaping his environments to support him and his inclusion. That is consistent with the AAMR approach of holding others responsible for supporting the person with a disability. In Box 8-1, you will find examples of how they facilitate his communication.

To emphasize this new component of the definition, the AAMR revised the title of its manual. The previous manual was titled *Classification in Mental Retardation* (Grossman, 1983). The current manual is titled *Mental Retardation: Definition, Classification, and Systems of Support* (Luckasson, 1992). The new phrase, *systems of support,* means a coordinated set of services and accommodations matched to the person's needs. That phrase makes all the difference in how society defines and responds to mental retardation. Societal response to intellectual impairment is just another way of saying that mental retardation is a social construct. To its credit, the AAMR was explicit about that fact.

And to its further credit, the AAMR was explicit about the consequences of that fact. Because mental retardation is a state of functioning, something created in part by a person's extent of difficulty in being competent in certain environments, people who have impaired functioning abilities need certain systems of support to help them function more capably. These systems of support will be more or less intense, depending on the person's needs in one or more particular situations. The greater the person's impairments, the more intensive should be the supports to help the person function in society as successfully as possible (Luckasson et al., 1992). Figure 8-2 explains the 1992 AAMR definition and the four assumptions essential to its application.

The four assumptions on which the 1992 AAMR definition of mental retardation is based account for cultural and linguistic diversity, assess adaptive behavior within typical environments, recognize that people with mental retardation have strengths as well as needs, and express great expectations for people with mental retardation.

Describing the Characteristics

The three main characteristics of mental retardation are limitations in intellectual functioning, limitations in adaptive skill areas, and needs for supports.

Limitations in Intellectual Functioning. A diagnosis of mental retardation under both the 1983 and 1992 AAMR definitions requires an IQ score of 70 to 75. This score is two or more standard deviations below the mean of 100 on an individually administered intelligence test. (You read about IQ tests in Chapter 2.) The proponents of the 1992 definition argue that the new definition offers flexibility to multidisciplinary evaluation teams in upper IQ ranges (70 to 75) to help ensure that teams do not misdiagnose students from culturally different backgrounds as having mental retardation (Reiss, 1994). Students with

FIGURE 8–2 *Explanation of the 1992 AAMR definition of mental retardation*

Mental retardation refers to substantial limitations in present functioning.

Mental retardation is defined as a fundamental difficulty in learning and performing certain daily life skills. The personal capabilities in which there must be a substantial limitation are conceptual, practical, and social intelligence. These three areas are specifically affected in mental retardation, whereas other personal capabilities (e.g., health and temperament) may not be.

It is characterized by significantly subaverage intelligence functioning . . .

This is defined as an IQ standard score of approximately 70 to 75 or below, based on assessment that includes one or more individually administered general intelligence tests developed for the purpose of assessing intellectual functioning. These data should be reviewed by a multidisciplinary team and validated with additional test scores or evaluative information.

existing concurrently . . .

The intellectual limitations occur at the same time as the limitations in adaptive skills.

with related limitations . . .

The limitations in adaptive skills are more closely related to the intellectual limitation than to some other circumstances such as cultural or linguistic diversity or sensory limitation.

in two or more of the following applicable adaptive skill areas . . .

Evidence of adaptive skill limitations is necessary because intellectual functioning alone is insufficient for a diagnosis of mental retardation. The impact on functioning of these limitations must be sufficiently comprehensive to encompass at least two adaptive skill areas, thus showing a generalized limitation and reducing the probability of measurement error.

communication, self-care, home living, social skills, community use, self-direction, health and safety, functional academics, leisure, and work.

These skill areas are central to successful life functioning and are frequently related to the need for supports for persons with mental retardation. Because the relevant skills within each adaptive skill area may vary with chronological age, assessment of functioning must be referenced to the person's chronological age.

Mental retardation manifests before age 18.

The 18th birthday approximates the age when individuals in society typically assume adult roles. In other societies, a different age criterion might be determined to be more appropriate.

The following four assumptions are essential to the application of the definition:

1. Valid assessment considers cultural and linguistic diversity as well as differences in communication and behavioral factors.

2. The existence of limitations in adaptive skills occurs within the context of community environments typical of the individual's age peers and is indexed to the person's individualized needs for supports.

3. Specific adaptive limitations often coexist with strengths in other adaptive skills or other personal capabilities.

4. With appropriate supports over a sustained period, the life functioning of the person with mental retardation will generally improve.

Note: From *Mental Retardation: Definition, Classification, and Systems of Supports,* by R. Luckasson, D. L. Coulter, E. A. Polloway, S. Reiss, R. L. Schalock, M. E. Snell, D. M. Spitalnik, & J. A. Stark, 1992, Washington, DC: American Association on Mental Retardation. Copyright 1992 by the American Association on Mental Retardation. Reprinted with permission.

a label of mental retardation who function in the high IQ range often function in school more similarly to students with learning disabilities than students with substantially lower IQs. Some researchers have even suggested that these students might be more appropriately labeled as having "generalized learning disabilities," as contrasted to "specific learning disabilities" discussed in Chapter 4 (MacMillan, Siperstein, & Gresham, 1996). Regardless of the precise IQ score, students with mental retardation typically have impairments in the learning process, including attention, memory, and generalization. They also may have decreased motivation as a result of repeated failures attributable to their limitations in intellectual functioning.

Attention. Individuals with mental retardation have difficulty distinguishing and paying attention to relevant cues in a social situation and attending to several different cues simultaneously (Zeaman & House, 1963, 1979). For example, a student, trying to be "cool," will flip the bill of someone's baseball cap as a playful gesture. If the person wearing the cap expresses annoyance after, say, the student gives the cap a second flip, the student might not pick up on the person's facial or body cues but needs to be explicitly told to stop.

As you work with students with mental retardation, you will want to help them focus their attention immediately on relevant cues rather than leave it up to them to identify the cues without your help. For example, teachers can use physical proximity and cue words such as, "get ready," "stop," "look," and "listen" to maintain students' attention.

Memory. Individuals with mental retardation also have impairments in memory, especially short-term memory (Ellis, 1970). Short-term memory is the mental ability to recall information that has been stored for a few seconds to a few hours, such as the sequential instructions a job supervisor gives an employee. People with mental retardation have problems with short-term memory largely because they typically do not use active memory strategies when they first encounter new information. These strategies, also called rehearsal, include verbally practicing the sequence of a task or associating steps of a task with a mental picture (Butterfield, Wambold, & Belmont, 1977; Mercer & Snell, 1977). Students with mental retardation can be taught to use active memory strategies, such as learning to quietly repeat instructions to themselves (A. P. Turnbull, 1974). These covert verbal memory strategies can be difficult to learn and use, and students with mental retardation tend to benefit more from external memory strategies such as moving objects in a particular order as an aid to remembering a verbal item sequence (Fletcher & Bray, 1995).

Generalization. *Generalization* refers to the ability to transfer knowledge learned from one task to another task and to do so across different settings or environments (Horner, Dunlap, & Koegel, 1988; Stokes & Baer, 1977). Individuals with mental retardation typically have difficulty in generalizing the skills learned in one setting to other settings that involve different cues, expectations, people, and environmental arrangements (Langone, Clees, Oxford, Malone, & Ross, 1995). This is one reason educators emphasize instruction in typical environments rather than simulated ones and why IDEA prefers the general education program to a separate program. For students with mental retardation, this means having real work experiences during the school day rather than staying in their classroom and simulating a work station. This is why Ryan's transition program is based in the community rather than at the high school.

Motivation. Lack of motivation often results from experiencing frequent failure. Individuals with mental retardation who have experienced repeated failure tend to expect failure, so to minimize or prevent future failure, they set low goals (Balla & Zigler, 1979). In this way, some of them develop **learned helplessness** (Seligman, 1975). Some also have a problem-solving style that has been called **outer-directedness,** meaning they distrust their own solutions and seek cues from others (Zigler & Burack, 1989). Looking to others to guide them, they lack their own motivation to learn or act; they are not inner-directed. For example, J.T., a thirty-year-old, knows he must rise up every morning at a certain hour so he can catch the bus to work and keep his job. If, however, J. T. sometimes

---

✑ What rehearsal strategies do you use in trying to remember a telephone number or a social security number?

Learned helplessness refers to a condition in which individuals who have experienced repeated failure tend to expect failure. To minimize or prevent failure, these individuals often set low expectations.

Outer-directedness refers to a condition in which individuals distrust their own solutions and seek cues from others.

chooses to sleep in or is slow in dressing and eating, he will miss the bus and risk losing his job. How to motivate him to be prompt every morning is a problem. The problem is compounded because his housemates will drive him to work if he misses the bus, thereby reinforcing his bad choice but enabling him to keep his job. Again, this example illustrates the interaction between a person's choices and the environment.

In Chapter 5, you learned about applied behavior analysis, which can enhance motivation. A different approach relates to the expectations that people with retardation have for themselves and that others set for them. Students such as Ryan need and can learn to attribute their success to themselves and to their own hard work. Box 8–2, "Into Practice," describes how a teacher implemented an approach to decrease outer-directedness (learned helplessness) and enhance inner-directedness (learned capacity).

Limitations in Adaptive Skill Areas. In addition to significant subaverage intelligence, the definition of mental retardation requires that a person also must have limitations in two or more of the ten adaptive skill areas essential for daily functioning. These adaptive skill areas are communication, self-care, home living, social skills, community use, self-direction, health and safety, functional academics, leisure, and work (see Figure 8–3). The 1992 definition is a "conceptual improvement" (Smith, 1994, p. 181) over the 1983 AAMR definition because it specifies two or more adaptive skill areas rather than leaving adaptive behavior as a global skill. The 1992 definition now ties into IDEA's unified evaluation–program–placement approach. In this section, we briefly focus on three adaptive skill areas: self-direction, functional academics, and home living.

Self-direction. The term *self-direction* refers to the ability of individuals to live their lives the way that they choose to live them, consistent with their own values, preferences, and abilities (Powers, Singer, & Sowers, 1996; Sands & Wehmeyer, 1996; A. P. Turnbull & Turnbull, 1985). Although the AAMR term for this adaptive skill area is self-

〽 Which teachers helped you believe in your own ability to make good decisions? How did they differ from teachers who pre-empted your decision making? What impact did their different approaches have on you?

〽 *J.T.'s housemates encourage him to adopt an inner-directed approach to meeting his needs. He knows that he can choose to be on time for his morning bus and that by doing so he will be able to maintain his schedule at work.*

BOX 8-2   INTO PRACTICE

THE EFFICACY MODEL

All kids can learn. Sounds grand. Do you believe it? I once believed my students could learn some things, but not very much. After all, they had mild mental retardation. My "smartest" junior high students had late second-grade academic skills. They were born smarter, weren't they? Not so, according to Dr. Jeff Howard of the Massachusetts-based Efficacy Institute. The Efficacy model teaches that effective effort, rather than innate intelligence, will produce success.

Did this model apply to my students? The Efficacy framework assumes that everyone who can speak and understand the English language at an early age (three) is born with the potential to do the highest level of intellectual work. Because most of my students exhibited mild-to-moderate delays in language development, they did not fit into the framework.

As the seminar progressed, I learned about the model—a process of building identity, character, analytic and operational capability, and self-confidence. My students could be successful at many things. I stopped defining my students in terms of what they could not do and began to dream of the things they could accomplish when not limited by my expectations.

Having enthusiastically embraced the ideals of the Efficacy model, I decided to try out the program in my class. Beyond believing for myself that all children can learn, I had to communicate that to my students. They had to believe they could learn. It is amazing how young children believe whatever you tell them! It wasn't long before they had memorized the simple version of one Efficacy principle, "think you can, work hard, get smart." Catchy phrase, but did it mean anything? Did they understand that working hard involved using feedback (not referred to as failure) to set objectives that were moderately challenging for which they had a realistic probability of consistent success? Did they understand that with demonstrated success they would grow more confident (think you can) and incrementally take on more challenge (work hard) until they had moved further along their zone of development, accomplishing skills (getting smart) they had previously believed too hard? Would they push the red line, the line of challenge, beyond which stood goals and objectives that were unrealistic—for now? Or would they be content to sit on the green line, the line of realism, beyond which stood goals and objectives that presented no challenge, no chance to fail, where success was achieved with little or no effort?

I resolved to work hard at creating a positive, secure environment where children believed in themselves, demonstrated effective effort, and accomplished objectives previously dismissed as unrealistic. To my delight, I learned that the Efficacy model works. Looking up from her cutting, tears streaming down her face, eight-year-old Katie cried "I've tried and tried as hard as I can, but I still can't do it." Hands shaking from a neurological impairment, she could not hold the paper firmly and make good cuts near the line. "That's OK," Jackie offered, "you did the best you could, I'll help you." Eric encouraged Jeffrey to look at a practice chart while stuck on a math problem. Holding his head in his hands, Jeffrey told Eric, "you just have to think." Several weeks later, a frustrated Chris pushed away from his math assignment, "I give up, it's too hard." Jeffrey went over to his desk pleading, "you have to try, if you don't try, you'll never get smart."

Confidence and risk taking were contagious. When eight-year-old Christine said she wanted two Bingo cards instead of one, seven-year-old Jackie stated she wanted three so she could really push the red line. Soon everyone began with two cards while playing Bingo or Lotto. Successful experiences bred motivation as eight-year-old David frequently requested more difficult work and admonished his peers for making fun of other children. "Hey," he yelled, getting their attention, "you're letting your weak [negative] side take over, you have to use your strong [positive] side."

Successful, confident children unwittingly influence those around them, even their parents. Participation in Special Olympics rose from 17 percent the previous year to 67 percent. One year later it was up to 87 percent! Where attendance at parent–teacher conferences had averaged 20 to 25 percent, the spring following introduction of the Efficacy model, attendance was 92 percent! Believing, embracing, and incorporating the Efficacy principles caused the dramatic improvement in my students.

David's development was like watching a locomotive, gathering steam and taking off. Even his expressive face burned red with excitement as he proudly announced each new accomplishment to his classmates. One year later, from his second-grade class (where he was fully included), he continued to show us his perfect papers. Thrusting them at me, beaming from ear to ear he'd state, "It's like you said Miss Emery, if you work hard, you get smart." David believes!

Sandy Emery
Leavenworth, Kansas, Public Schools

1. Communication: Skills include the ability to comprehend and express information through symbolic behaviors (e.g., spoken word, written word . . ., graphic symbols, sign language . . .) or nonsymbolic behaviors (e.g., facial expression, body movement, touch, gesture). . . .

2. Self-Care: Skills involved in toileting, eating, dressing, hygiene, and grooming.

3. Home Living: Skills related to functioning within a home, which include clothing care, housekeeping, property maintenance, food preparation and cooking, planning and budgeting for shopping, home safety, and daily scheduling. . . .

4. Social: Skills related to exchanges with other individuals. . . .

5. Community Use: Skills related to the appropriate use of community resources, including traveling in the community. . . .

6. Self-Direction: Skills related to making choices. . . .

7. Health and Safety: Skills related to maintenance of one's health in terms of eating; illness identification, treatment, and prevention; basic first aid; sexuality; physical fitness; basic safety considerations . . . . .

8. Functional Academics: Cognitive abilities and skills related to learning at school that also have direct application to one's life. . . .

9. Leisure: The development of a variety of leisure and recreational interests (i.e., self-entertainment and interactional) that reflect personal preferences and choices and, if the activity will be conducted in public, age and cultural norms. . . .

10. Work: Skills related to holding a part- or full-time job or jobs in the community in terms of specific job skills, appropriate social behavior, and related work skills .

Note: From *Mental Retardation: Definition Classification, and Systems of Supports*, by R. Luckasson, D. L. Coulter, E. A. Polloway, S. Reiss, R. L. Schalock, M. E. Snell, D. M. Spitalnik, & J. A. Stark, 1992, Washington, DC: American Association on Mental Retardation. Copyright 1992 by the American Association on Mental Retardation. Reprinted with permission.

FIGURE 8–3 *Definitions of adaptive skill areas*

direction, it is also called self-determination. Wehmeyer (1996), a leading researcher, believes the following components should be included in a curriculum on self-determination:

- Choice making

- Decision making

- Problem solving

- Goal setting and attainment

- Self-observation, evaluation, and reinforcement

- Internal locus of control

- Positive attributions of efficacy and outcome expectancy

- Self-awareness

- Self-knowledge (Wehmeyer, 1996, p. 27)

For Ryan and others with mental retardation, this adaptive skill area is particularly important, given data from a comprehensive national survey indicating that adults with mental retardation express few choices (choosing a place to live, selecting roommates) and have minimal control over the few decisions in their lives (Wehmeyer & Metzler, 1995). You may recall from the opening vignette that Bob and Martha are taking Ryan's preferences into account in deciding where he will live after he graduates from high school.

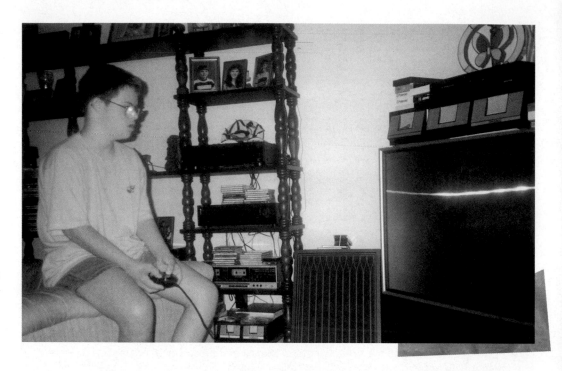

❧ *Ryan typically chooses his leisure activities. Playing video games is one of his favorites.*

Functional Academics.   Functional academics are the school subjects that directly apply to and teach the skills needed in one's everyday environment, especially those skills that students will need after they leave school, such as:

- Learning to complete a job application form
- Learning to use a city map or a telephone directory
- Learning survival words (men/women, entrance/exit, walk/don't walk, emergency, caution)
- Learning to carry on a reciprocal conversation
- Learning to identify denominations of money and to make change

You may remember that Ryan has already learned some similar skills, such as those related to transportation, banking, shopping, and cooking.

Home Living.   *Home living skills* refer to the requirements that individuals must meet to live successfully within a home setting. A home-living skill that is challenging for Ryan is learning how to take messages over the telephone. Ryan is learning to use his **augmentative communication device,** the MessageMate, to respond to callers who cannot understand his speech and to take messages over the phone. If a caller does not understand Ryan, Ryan can simply switch on his MessageMate. One of the recordings on it is, "He is not available right now. May I take a message?" Ryan then records the caller's response on his MessageMate and has the appropriate person return the call later. It is easy to see the relationship between functional academics and home-living skills. If you teach students to learn to read recipes, medicine labels, and rental contracts in school, they are far more likely to be able to use these skills at home.

An **augmentative communication device** is equipment that is used to increase an individual's ability to communicate effectively.

Need for Supports.   As IDEA acknowledges, special education itself is a system of supports. So, after determining a student's intellectual and adaptive skill capabilities and limitations, the evaluation team should (according to the 1992 AAMR definition and consistent with IDEA) determine what supports the student needs in the following four areas:

- Intellectual functioning and adaptive skills (including the ten specified skill areas)

- Psychological and emotional considerations

- Physical health and etiology considerations

- Environmental considerations

The distinguishing new feature of the 1992 approach is that it links strengths and limitations in these four dimensions to a student's need for systems of supports: "With appropriate supports over a sustained period, the life functioning of the person with mental retardation will generally improve" (Luckasson et al., 1992). That is also what IDEA requires and intends.

The traditional social view of people with mental retardation has been that the limitations reside within the person and that all efforts to ameliorate the limitations' effects should be directed primarily at the person, not also at the person's environments. Under the 1992 AAMR approach, however, a person should have "an array of services, individuals, and settings that match the person's needs" (Luckasson et al., 1992). The services may range from intermittent to pervasive. Figure 8–4 provides a brief definition and an example of the four levels of the intensities of support.

How can evaluation teams apply these definitions? Table 8–2 illustrates the Support Intensity Decision Grid, which evaluation teams can use to determine how much support an individual needs. The five factors influencing the intensity of support are listed vertically (time/duration, time/frequency, settings, resources, and intrusiveness) and the four levels of support intensity are identified horizontally (intermittent, limited, extensive, and pervasive). With appropriate supports, identified and provided vertically and horizontally, nearly everyone will improve in skills and life functioning (Luckasson et al., 1992).

AAMR's 1992 approach asserts that individuals with mental retardation need supports. IDEA presumes the support will be in regular education, to the maximum extent appropriate. That increases their opportunities for relationships.

FIGURE 8–4 *Definition and examples of intensities of support*

Intermittent

Supports on an "as-needed" basis. Characterized by episodic nature, person not always needing the support(s), or short-term supports needed during life-span transitions (e.g., job loss or an acute medical crisis). Intermittent supports may be high or low intensity when provided.

Limited

An intensity of supports characterized by consistency over time, time-limited but not of an intermittent nature, may require fewer staff members and less cost than more intense levels of support (e.g., time-limited employment training or transitional supports during the school to adult provided period).

Extensive

Supports characterized by regular involvement (e.g., daily) in at least some environments (such as work or home) and not time-limited (e.g., long-term support and long-term home living support).

Pervasive

Supports characterized by their constancy, high intensity; provided across environments; potential life-sustaining nature. Pervasive supports typically involve more staff members and intrusiveness than do extensive or time-limited supports.

Using the AAMR Approach in Schools. In Iowa, a statewide task force (including representatives from special and general educators and administrators, researchers and teacher-trainers in institutions of higher education, parents of students with mental retardation, related service providers, and the state department of education) has responded to the AAMR's new approach to mental retardation. Why did it do so? First, it knew that a number of students were being classified as having mental retardation (in the so-called mild range of IQ 75 to 85), yet many of them did not meet the other criterion for mental retardation; they did not have significant problems in adaptive behavior. Second, many were from diverse racial backgrounds. Last, the doctrine of the least restrictive alternative caused many students to be placed in the general curriculum, yet general educators were not fully prepared to teach them in that curriculum.

Accordingly, the task force created a six-part manual for schools, containing a brief historical perspective on definitions, guidelines for evaluation teams, general considerations regarding evaluation and multicultural issues, the 1992 AAMR approach, criteria for classifying a student as having mental retardation, and the AAMR adaptive behavior skill areas. The task force's essential message was that evaluation teams must consider how students function within various environments and then must evaluate the nature and demands of each environment. Mental retardation, the task force emphasized, is not a state of global incompetence defined by an IQ score (Iowa Department of Education, 1997). It is situational, as AAMR long ago recognized (H. R. Turnbull, 1978).

Identifying the Causes of Mental Retardation

Identifying specific causes of a student's mental retardation is not easy. Although more than one thousand causes of mental retardation are known, it is often not clear which causes apply to a particular individual (Baumeister, 1989; Coulter, 1992). In addition, mental retardation rarely results from a sole cause. It more often results from complex interactions among multiple causes (Batshaw & Shapiro, 1997; McLaren & Bryson, 1987; Scott, 1988).

TABLE 8–2 ❧ *Supports intensity decision grid: Applying the definitions of supports*

	Intermittent	**Limited**	**Extensive**	**Pervasive**
TIME duration	As needed	Time limited, occasionally ongoing	Usually ongoing	Possibly lifelong
TIME frequency	Infrequent, low occurrence	Regular, anticipated, could be high frequency		High rate, continuous, constant
SETTINGS Living, Work, Recreation, Leisure, Health, Community, etc.	Few settings, typically one or two settings	Across several settings, typically not all settings		All or nearly all settings
RESOURCES Professional/ Technological Assistance	Occasional consultation or discussion, ordinary appointment schedule, occasional monitoring	Occasional contact, or time limited but frequent regular contact	Regular, ongoing contact or monitoring by professionals, typically at least weekly	Constant contact and monitoring by professionals
INTRUSIVENESS	Predominantly all natural supports, high degree of choice and autonomy	Mixture of natural and service-based supports, lesser degree of choice and autonomy		Predominantly service-based supports, controlled by others

Note: From "The 1992 AAMR Definition and Preschool Children: Response From the Committee on Terminology and Classification," by R. Luckasson, R. L. Schalock, M. E. Snell, and D. M. Spitalnik, 1996, *Mental Retardation,* August, pp. 247–253. Copyright 1996 by the American Association on Mental Retardation. Reprinted with permission.

The AAMR categorizes causes in two ways: by timing and by type (Luckasson et al., 1992). Causes that are grouped by timing depend on the specific time of onset (see Table 8–3):

- Prenatal (before birth)

- Perinatal (during the birth process)

- Postnatal (after birth)

Causes that are categorized by type traditionally have been divided into two broad categories: biomedical (developing within the individual) and psychosocial disadvantage (developing from social and environmental influences).

Biomedical Causes.   **Biomedical causes** develop within the individual. Although biomedical causes are most frequently associated with severe mental retardation, a significant percentage of mild mental retardation also has a biomedical cause (McLaren & Bryson, 1987). You will learn about two biomedical causes in this chapter: chromosomal disorders and oxygen deprivation. In Chapter 9 you will learn about genetic abnormalities, and in Chapter 11 you will focus on environmental influences (such as drugs and toxins).

Chromosomal Disorders.   Chromosomal disorders are biomedical factors that occur at or soon after conception (in the prenatal period). When the egg and sperm unite during conception, they bring together genes from the mother and father. These genes determine the personal characteristics of the developing embryo and are found on thread-like structures called **chromosomes.** A chromosomal disorder occurs when a parent contributes either too much (an extra chromosome is added) or too little (all or part of a chromosome is missing) genetic material. Abnormal chromosomes may also develop soon after conception during the early cell division of the fertilized egg.

Down syndrome is one of the most common chromosomal disorders, occurring in approximately 1 in 700 live births (Kozma & Stock, 1993). Ryan was only six hours old when his parents learned that he had Down syndrome. How could the physician have known so quickly? Newborns with Down syndrome usually have certain unique physical characteristics that often make diagnosis possible soon after birth. At birth, Ryan exhibited two of these characteristics: short hands and feet and low muscle tone.

Researchers have identified three separate chromosomal aberrations resulting in Down syndrome (Roizen, 1997). All three types of Down syndrome are associated with abnormality of the twenty-first pair of chromosomes. The most common form of Down syndrome is trisomy 21, which occurs at conception when extra genetic material is attached to the twenty-first pair of chromosomes in every cell.

Chromosomal disorders are verified through a procedure called **karyotyping,** in which the chromosomes of a single cell are arranged and examined (Blackman & Thomson, 1983). In Figure 8–5, you will see a comparison of the karyotypes of an individual with a normal chromosome pattern and one with a Down syndrome pattern (trisomy 21).

Oxygen Deprivation.   Two types of oxygen deprivation exist: reduction **(hypoxia)** and termination **(anoxia)** of the flow of oxygen to the infant's brain. These can create mental retardation (McLaren & Bryson, 1987). Oxygen deprivation, however, does not necessarily result in mental retardation; its adverse effects depend on variables such as the area of the brain affected and the length of time the child is deprived of oxygen (Kozma & Stock, 1993).

Biomedical causes refer to disability-causing conditions that develop within the individual.

Chromosomes direct each cell's activity. Humans have twenty-three pairs of chromosomes in each cell, with one chromosome in each pair coming from the mother and one from the father.

Karyotyping involves arranging the chromosomes under a microscope so that they can be counted and grouped according to size, shape, and pattern.

Hypoxia is the reduction of oxygen content in body tissues.

Anoxia is the termination of the flow of oxygen reaching body tissues.

Prenatal	Perinatal	Postnatal
Down syndrome	Premature labor	Head injuries
Phenylketonuria (PKU)	Meningitis	Lead intoxication
Maternal malnutrition	Head trauma at birth	Child abuse and neglect

TABLE 8–3 ॐ *Causes of mental retardation from timing factors*

FIGURE 8–5 *Karyotype comparisons*

Illustration of the karyotype of a typical female (46, XX). To produce this karyotype, a teaspoon of blood was obtained, and a chemical was added to start mitosis of the white blood cells. Subsequently, another chemical was inserted to arrest the division in metaphase. The cell was then photographed under a microscope and a print was made. The chromosomes were cut out; matched in pairs; and numbered according to size, shape, position of the centromere, and banding pattern. (Courtesy of Dr. Beverly Emanuel, The Children's Hospital of Philadelphia.)

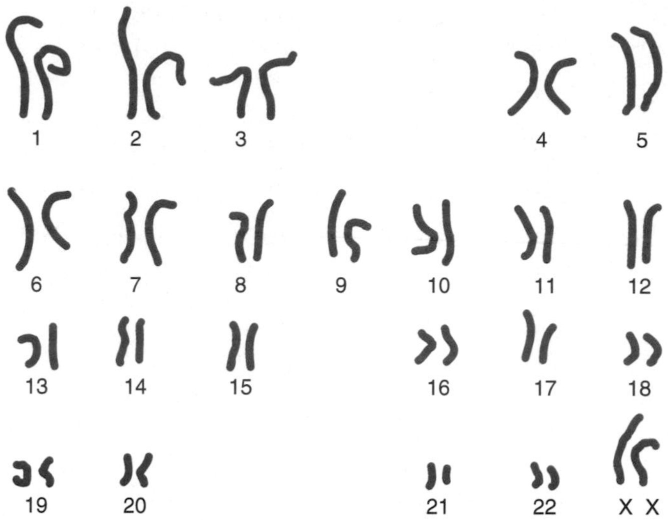

Karyotype of a boy with Down syndrome (47, XY). Note that the child has 47 chromosomes; the extra one is #21.

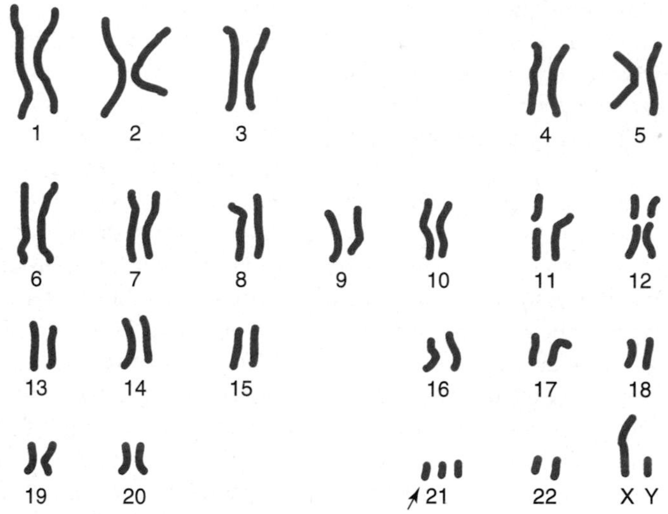

Note: From "Understanding Your Chromosomes," by M. L. Batshaw, in *Children With Disabilities* (4th ed., pp. 3–16), edited by M. L. Batshaw, 1997, Baltimore, Paul H. Brookes. Copyright 1997 by Paul H. Brookes. Reprinted with permission.

Psychosocial disadvantage refers to conditions of individuals that develop from social and environmental influences.

Psychosocial Disadvantage. Professionals traditionally have grouped a variety of other causes into one single category: **psychosocial disadvantage.** AAMR subdivides the psychosocial disadvantage category into three subcategories: social, behavioral, and educational (Luckasson et al., 1992). Their boundaries often overlap, making the distinction between them difficult.

The majority of cases of mental retardation are the result of adverse psychosocial influences (Batshaw & Shapiro, 1997; Coulter, 1988). The precise nature of the association between poverty and mental retardation is not clearly understood, but children with economic disadvantages clearly grow up in environments that can impair their physical, mental, and behavioral development (Baumeister, 1989). Such factors in an impoverished environment as poor nutrition, late or absent prenatal care, low birth weight, maternal mental retardation, and abuse or neglect can interact and, singly or jointly, threaten children's development (Baumeister, 1989; Feldman & Walton-Allen, 1997; Stark, Menolascino, & Goldsbury, 1988).

As Chapter 1 pointed out, special education programs contain a disproportionate representation of students from diverse racial and ethnic backgrounds, many of whom are identified as having mental retardation (Harry, 1992). One effect of a nondiscriminatory evaluation may be to keep a student from being classified as having mental retardation. Indeed, if the real reason for a student's school problems is the lack of effective instruction in math or English or limited English proficiency, IDEA prohibits schools from classifying the student into special education.

A study of the effects of poverty and race/ethnicity reveals that the disproportionate representation of African American students in special education is a function of low income: Disability is associated with poverty, especially in inner cities (U.S. Department of Education, 1996; Wagner, 1995). The insidious effects of poverty contribute most to the psychosocial influences that ultimately cause mental retardation. High numbers of students with psychosocial causes of mental retardation are particularly congregated in inner-city schools. In the inner cities, 30 percent of all students live in poverty, but outside of the inner cities, only 18 percent of students live in poverty (U.S. Department of Education, 1996).

Interaction of Biomedical and Psychosocial Causes. Although the AAMR distinguishes between biomedical and psychosocial causes, there is significant interaction between the two (Batshaw & Shapiro, 1997). A real-life example is perhaps the best way to better understand this interaction. Julie's story is described in Table 8–4. What causes of

> "Just as we instinctively associate things like sleep with bed, food with table, Spanish language with Mexico, AIDS with homosexuality, many individuals also link axiomatically cultural diversity with disability" (Artiles & Trent, 1994, p. 425).

TABLE 8–4 *Interaction of biomedical and psychosocial factors.*

Julie's Story

Julie was born prematurely, approximately two months early. Her mother was infected with HIV and had used cocaine through her pregnancy. Julie had difficulty breathing after birth and was on a ventilator for several weeks. On the third day of life, she had a severe intracranial hemorrhage with bleeding in several areas of her brain. After extended hospitalization, Julie was discharged to her mother's care. Tests revealed that she was not infected with HIV but that she did have brain damage. She developed seizures when she was about a year old and asthma shortly after that. Although she was referred for early intervention services, she never received these services consistently because of a long waiting list, disorganization in her mother's life, the lack of individualized supports to help her mother, and Julie's own frequent hospitalizations for seizures or asthma. An evaluation when she was three years old found that her intellectual functioning and adaptive behavior were at approximately the level of an eighteen-month-old child.

The causes for Julie's mental retardation include the following:

Factor	Biomedical	Social	Behavioral	Educational
Prematurity	X			
Intracranial hemorrhage	X			
Mother's HIV		X		
Lack of organization in the home		X		
Mother's drug use			X	
Lack of early intervention				X

Note: From "An Ecology of Prevention for the Future," by D. L. Coulter, 1992, *Mental Retardation*, December. Copyright 1992 by the American Association on Mental Retardation. Reprinted with permission.

Julie's mental retardation can you identify? In what way did these causes interact? Review Table 8–4 to see how thoroughly you identified and classified the causes.

Preventing Mental Retardation. Prevention efforts are classified into three types: primary, secondary, and tertiary (Baumeister, Kupstas, & Woodley-Zanthos, 1993). *Primary prevention* refers to intervention before the cause occurs. Examples of primary prevention include vaccines for the prevention of diseases such as rubella, educational programs that address the abuse of drugs by pregnant women, prenatal testing (such as **amniocentesis**), and programs to reduce infant mortality. With respect to infant mortality, Kozol (1991) points out these alarming statistics:

> *In Central Harlem, according to* The New York Times, *the infant death rate is the same as in Malaysia. Among black children in East Harlem, it is even higher: 42 per thousand, which would be considered high in many Third World nations. "A child's chance of surviving to age 5,"* noted New Jersey Senator Bill Bradley, *"are better in Bangladesh than in East Harlem." (pp. 115–116)*

The most effective interventions are initiated at the earliest point at which risk of disability is incurred. *The Guide to State Planning for the Prevention of Mental Retardation and Related Disabilities Associated with Socioeconomic Conditions* (Peterson & Cleveland, 1987) and Baumeister et al. (1993) describe the causes, their interactive and cumulative nature, and prevention strategies and identify the following critical areas for prevention:

- Lack of prenatal care
- Infant mortality
- Low birth weight
- Adolescent pregnancy and child bearing
- Poor nutrition
- Environmental or toxic exposures
- Sexually transmitted diseases including pediatric human immunodeficiency virus (HIV) and acquired immune deficiency syndrome (AIDS)

Amniocentesis is a technique for prenatal diagnosis that involves withdrawing and studying, between the fifteenth and seventeenth weeks of pregnancy, the amniotic fluid that surrounds the baby.

BUILDING BRAINS: THE SOONER, THE BETTER

"Is it ever too early to begin educating children?" Ted Koppel asks in "Building Brains: The Sooner, the Better." According to Judie Jerald of the Vermont Early Education Service, "We can't wait." A baby's brain grows a thousand times faster than a 15-year-old's brain. Severe abuse and neglect during infancy can significantly decrease brain size and mass, increasing the risk of mental retardation. Vermont's program is teaching parents to be teachers, especially those who are in high-risk categories such as teenage parents and those living in poverty. The program identifies six kinds of experiences in the early years that promote intelligence and morality: opportunities to learn to pay attention, fall in love, be logical, give and take, problem solve, and state opinions.

What do you think? How might you incorporate those six experiences in your classroom for students with mental retardation who might not have had these opportunities in infancy?

The Vermont program focuses extensively on providing support and education to the parents. Do you believe this approach is as effective for children, and as cost-efficient in the long-term, as providing nurturing early child-care programs? Why or why not?

How should early childhood programs in your community be accountable for providing experiences that promote intelligence and morality?

- Injuries

- Child abuse and neglect

- Lack of early intervention

- Other biomedical considerations

Secondary prevention refers to intervention soon after detection of a biomedical or psychosocial problem and includes early intervention programs, lead screening, phenylketonuria (PKU) screening (see Chapter 9), and medical control of seizure disorders. **Tertiary prevention** refers to special education and physical, occupational, or vocational training on a long-term basis for the purpose of reducing the effects of a present disability.

Experts in mental retardation have increasingly recognized the escalating negative effects of poverty, policy changes related to welfare reform, and the accelerated risk of disabilities. This phenomenon, described as the New Morbidity, refers to the interaction of biomedical and psychosocial disadvantages in creating developmental problems (Baumeister, Kupstas, & Woodley-Zanthos, 1996). The basic premise of the *New Morbidity* is that "Adversity begets adversity" (Baumeister, et al., 1996, p. 87).

> *Poverty is closely connected to adverse and costly developmental outcomes for children, regardless of why they are impoverished. Health and behavior disorders of poor children, only touched upon here, must be addressed within a comprehensive, flexible, and integrated program that has as its primary objective the prevention of conditions that place many at a competitive disadvantage— call it "Even Start." (Baumeister et al., 1996, p. 101)*

The cumulative effects of "adversity begetting adversity" can be devastating.

> *Four little boys are asleep on the green rug an hour later when I leave the room (of a preschool). I stand at the door and look at the children, most of whom are sitting at a table to have their milk. Nine years from now, most of these children will go to Manley High School, an enormous ugly building just a block away that has a graduation rate of only 38 percent. Twelve years from now, by junior year of high school, if the neighborhood statistics hold true for these children, 14 of these 23 boys and girls will have dropped out of school. Fourteen years from now, four of these kids, at most, will go to college. Eighteen years from now, one of these four may graduate from college, but three of these 12 boys in this kindergarten will already have spent time in prison. (Kozol, 1991, p. 45)*

Identifying the Prevalence of Mental Retardation

It is difficult to obtain an accurate prevalence rate for mental retardation. Reported rates are inconsistent (MacMillan, Siperstein, & Gresham, 1996), ranging from less than 1 to 3 percent of the general population (Grossman, 1983; MacMillan, Siperstein, Gresham, & Bocian, 1997). Perhaps most useful for educational purposes is the rate reported in the U.S. Department of Education's *Eighteenth Annual Report to Congress* (1996). During the 1994 to 1995 school year, 569,533 students with mental retardation, ages six to twenty-one, received special education services. This represents 12 percent of all children/youth receiving special education.

A noteworthy trend is the declining percentage of students identified as having mental retardation. The U.S. Department of Education (1993) reported a 39 percent decline during the 15 years between 1976 to 1977 and 1991 to 1992. During this same period, the number of children identified as having a learning disability increased 198 percent. This decline occurred before the 1990 to 1991 school year. Between 1990 to 1991 and 1994 to 1995, the number of students identified as having mental retardation increased 3.5 percent.

Tertiary prevention refers to special education and physical, occupational, or vocational training on a long-term basis for the purpose of reducing the effects of a present disability.

❧ *Failure to address the negative effects of poverty multiplies the risks children experience for mental retardation and other disabilities.*

Numerous factors seem to have contributed to the substantial shift in identification of students. According to the U.S. Department of Education (1993), states have used more stringent classification criteria, court rulings such as the ones you read about in Chapter 1 have limited classification of children from culturally diverse backgrounds who had been inappropriately identified as having mental retardation because of discriminatory practices, and professionals and families have preferred to identify children and youth with mild-to-moderate cognitive impairments as having specific learning disabilities rather than mental retardation, believing that the *learning disabilities* label is less stigmatizing than the *mental retardation* label (Gottlieb, Alter, Gottlieb, & Wishner, 1994; MacMillan, Siperstein, & Gresham, 1996).

Another factor contributing to the decline in the number of students identified as having mild mental retardation is an increase in the number of students identified as having limited English proficiency. The U.S. Department of Education (1991) estimates that almost 2 million students had limited English proficiency in 1990. The vast majority (approximately three-fourths) of these students speak Spanish, and the rest speak many different languages (U.S. Department of Education, 1993). Because there are such inadequate resources for bilingual special education, many students with limited English proficiency (including those with mental retardation) tend to be enrolled in bilingual general educational programs (Grossman, 1995). You may recall that IDEA now prohibits a student from being classified as having a disability solely because the student is not proficient in English. This provision probably will reduce still further the number of students classified as having mental retardation.

WHAT ARE EVALUATION PROCEDURES?

Determining the Presence of Mental Retardation

Consistent with IDEA's nondiscriminatory evaluation role, the AAMR proposes a comprehensive evaluation process (see Figure 8-6). The 1992 AAMR approach requires assessments of four dimensions:

- Intellectual functioning and adaptive skills
- Psychological and emotional considerations
- Physical and health considerations
- Environmental considerations

The assessment of intellectual functioning and adaptive skills determines whether the student has mental retardation, and the other three assessments focus on identifying what services and supports the student may need in various domains (Luckasson et al., 1992).

FIGURE 8-6 *AAMR evaluation guide*

Dimension I:
Intellectual Functioning
and Adaptive Skills

Step 1. *Diagnosis of mental retardation* determines eligibility for supports. Mental retardation is diagnosed if:
1. The individual's intellectual functioning is approximately 70 to 75 or below.
2. There are significant disabilities in two or more adaptive skill areas.
3. The age of onset is below 18.

Dimension II:
Psychological/
Emotional
Considerations

Dimension III:
Physical Health/
Etiology
Considerations

Dimension IV:
Environmental
Considerations

Step 2. *Classification and description* identifies strengths and weaknesses and the need for supports. Describe the individual's:
1. Strengths and weaknesses in reference to physical/emotional considerations.
2. Overall physical health and indicate the condition's etiology.
3. Current environmental placement and optimal environment that would facilitate continued growth and development.

Step 3: *Profile and intensities of needed supports* identifies needed supports. Identify the kind and intensity of supports needed for each of the four dimensions:
1. I—Intellectual Functioning and Adaptive Skills.
2. II—Psychological/Emotional Considerations
3. III—Physical Health/Etiology Considerations
4. IV—Environmental Considerations

The 1992 AAMR definition is based on a multidimensional approach that requires the complete assessment of an individual to include evaluation of four dimensions: (a) intellectual functioning and adaptive skills, (b) psychological/emotional considerations, (c) physical/health considerations, and (d) environmental considerations. The four dimensions included in AAMR's three-step procedure provide the basis for diagnosis as well as the basis for determining the support needs of the individual.

Note: From *Mental Retardation: Definition, Classification, and Systems of Supports*, by R. Luckasson, D. L. Coulter, E. A. Polloway, S. Reiss, R. L. Schalock, M. E. Snell, D. M. Spitalnik, & J. A. Stark, 1992, Washington, DC: American Association on Mental Retardation. Copyright 1992 by the American Association on Mental Retardation. Reprinted with permission.

FIGURE 8–7 *Evaluating whether a student has mental retardation*

Nondiscriminatory Evaluation

Observation

Medical personnel observe	The child does not attain appropriate developmental milestones or the child has characteristics of a particular syndrome associated with mental retardation.
Teacher and parents observe	If the student has not been identified as having mental retardation before entering school, the student, when placed in the general classroom, (1) does not learn as quickly as peers, (2) has difficulty retaining and generalizing learned skills, and (3) has more limitations in adaptive behaviors than peers.

Screening

Assessment measures	Findings that indicate need for further evaluation
Medical screening	A child may be identified through a physician's use of various tests as being at risk for mental retardation before starting school.
Classroom work products	A student who is not identified before starting school has difficulty in academic areas in the general classroom; reading comprehension and mathematical reasoning/application are limited.
Group intelligence tests	A group intelligence test is difficult because of the test's heavy reliance on reading skills. Intelligence score is below average.
Group achievement tests	The student performs significantly below peers.
Vision and hearing screening	Results do not explain academic difficulties.

Prereferral

Teacher implements suggestions from school-based team.	The student still performs poorly in academics or continues to manifest impairments in adaptive behavior despite interventions. (If the student's deficits in academics or adaptive behavior are obviously severe or if the child has been identified as having mental retardation before starting school, prereferral is omitted.)

Referral

If the child still performs poorly in academics or still manifests adaptive behavior challenges, the child is referred to a multidisciplinary team for a complete evaluation.

Nondiscriminatory evaluation procedures and standards

Assessment measures	Findings that suggest mental retardation
Individualized intelligence test	The student has significantly subaverage intellectual functioning (falls in bottom 2 to 3 percent of population) with IQ standard score of approximately 70 to 75 or below. The nondiscriminatory evaluation team makes sure the test is culturally fair for the student.
Adaptive behavior scales	The student scores significantly below average in two or more adaptive skill domains, indicating deficits in skill areas such as communication, home living, self-direction, and leisure.
Anecdotal records	The student's learning problems cannot be explained by cultural or linguistic difference.
Curriculum-based assessment	The student experiences difficulty in one or more areas of the curriculum used by the local school district.
Direct observation	The student experiences difficulty or frustration in the general classroom.

Nondiscriminatory Evaluation Team determines that student has mental retardation and needs special education and related services.

Appropriate Education

Interestingly, many people assume that a student's IQ score is the primary factor determining special education placement and that the adaptive behavior assessment is often overlooked. To the contrary, research indicates that teachers often disregard IQ tests as well, even when the students have an IQ that would put them in the mild mental retardation range (MacMillan, Gresham, Siperstein, & Bocian, 1996). Instead, they use clinical judgment in determining which students are classified as having learning disabilities and which are classified as having mental retardation. The students classified as having mental retardation typically had extremely low reading scores and extensive problem behaviors. Their combined academic and behavioral problems led evaluation teams to assign a label—mental retardation—that they perceived to be "very pessimistic" (MacMillan, Siperstein, Gresham, & Bocian, 1996, p. 172).

Because you learned about intelligence testing in Chapter 2, we focus in this chapter on assessing adaptive skill areas. It is important, however, for you to be familiar with the entire assessment process, which includes observation, screening, and nondiscriminatory evaluation (see Figure 8-7).

To meet the 1992 AAMR criteria, a student must experience limitations in two or more adaptive skill areas and those limitations must exist concurrently with limitations in the student's intellectual functioning. Adaptive skills enable an individual to meet the social demands of the environment. The adaptive skill areas must be age-relevant within the context of environments typical of the individual's community. To measure adaptive skills, professionals use adaptive behavior scales. Unlike intelligence tests, which are given to the individual being assessed, most adaptive behavior scales are completed by a parent, teacher, or other individual familiar with the student's daily activities.

A commonly used adaptive behavior scale is the *AAMR Adaptive Behavior Scale—School Edition* (2nd edition) (Lambert, Nihira, & Leland, 1993). As Figure 8-8 shows, the scale is divided into two parts. Part 1 assesses personal independence in daily living and includes nine behavior domains and eighteen subdomains, and part 2 concentrates on social behaviors in seven domains. The score for each domain is norm-referenced so that it is possible to compare an individual student's performance to others of the same age. The domains in the figure do not exactly match the ten adaptive skill areas in the 1992 AAMR definition (see Figure 8-3), but there is some overlap.

A supplement to the *AAMR Adaptive Behavior Scale—School Edition* enables evaluators to convert a student's scores into the ten adaptive skill areas specified by the 1992 definition. The supplement allows the evaluation team to assess both the broad range and specific areas of adaptive skills of a particular student, thereby identifying what supports the student needs, and thus how special education can benefit the student (Luckasson et al., 1992).

Determining the Nature and Extent of Special Education and Related Services

Many other procedures also help the evaluation team determine what kind of special education and related services will be appropriate to meet a student's needs. These include curriculum-based assessment (see Chapter 4) and behavioral observations using applied behavior analysis techniques (see Chapter 5).

A particularly useful assessment is The Arc's Self-Determination Scale (Adolescent Version) (Wehmeyer & Kelchner, 1995; Wehmeyer, 1995). This scale allows secondary school students to report the extent to which they think that they exercise self-determination. The scale has four domains, each measuring an essential characteristic of self-determination: autonomy, self-regulation, psychological empowerment, and self-realization. Figure 8-9 includes sample questions from the autonomy domain. The first two domains are further subdivided (Wehmeyer, 1995, 1996).

Students may complete the scale on their own, or teachers may read the items aloud so students can respond verbally. Students pick the most appropriate choice from a range

FIGURE 8–8 *Domains and subscales of AAMR Adaptive Behavior Scale— School Edition*

Part One	Part Two

I. Independent Functioning
   A. Eating
   B. Toilet Use
   C. Cleanliness
   D. Appearance
   E. Care of Clothing
   F. Dressing and Undressing
   G. Travel
   H. Other Independent Functioning
	X. Social Behavior
	XI. Conformity
	XII. Trustworthiness
	XIII. Stereotypical and Hyperactive Behavior
	XIV. Self-Abusive Behavior
	XV. Social Engagement
	XVI. Disturbing Interpersonal

II. Physical Development
   A. Sensory Development
   B. Motor Development	

III. Economic Activity
   A. Money Handling and Budgeting
   B. Shopping Skills	

IV. Language Development
   A. Expression
   B. Verbal Comprehension
   C. Social Language Development	

V. Numbers and Time	
VI. Prevocational/Vocational Activity	

VII. Self-Direction
   A. Initiative
   B. Perseverance
   C. Leisure Time	

VIII. Responsibility	
IX. Socialization	

Note: From *AAMR Adaptive Behavior Scale—School: Examiner's Manual* (2nd ed.), by N. Lambert, K. Nihira, and H. Leland, 1993, Austin, TX: PRO-ED. Copyright 1993 by PRO-ED. Reprinted with permission.

of four options. Items are written at approximately a fourth-grade reading level or lower. The scale is scored in a way that yields both a total self-determination score as well as scores for all domains and subdomains. Raw scores are converted into percentile scores and can be graphed to monitor individual progress. In Box 8–3, "My Voice," the scale's senior developer, Dr. Michael Wehmeyer, shares his vision of how the scale would be used both now and in the future.

WHAT AND HOW DO PROFESSIONALS TEACH?

Now that you have learned about the general approaches for evaluation, you are ready to learn about curriculum and methods for students with mild and moderate mental retardation. (In Chapter 9, you will learn about those same issues as they relate to students with severe mental retardation.)

Curriculum

Three major curriculum options are available for students with mild and moderate mental retardation: remedial, general classroom support, and adult outcomes (Cronin & Patton, 1993). The remedial emphasis usually occurs in separate resource rooms and programs. It

Subdomain
Area
Question

Independence
   Routine Personal Care and Family Oriented Functions
      I make my own meals or snacks.
      I care for my own clothes.
      I do simple first aid or medical care for myself.
   Interaction With the Environment
      I make friends with other kids my age.
      I use the post office.
      I deal with salespeople at stores and restaurants.
Acting on the Basis of Preferences, Beliefs, Interests and Abilities
   Recreational and Leisure Time
      I do free time activities based on my interests.
      I am involved in school-related activities.
      My friends and I choose activities that we want to do.
   Community Involvement and Interaction
      I volunteer in things that I am interested in.
      I go to movies, concerts, and dances.
      I take part in youth groups (like 4-H, scouting, church groups)
   Post-School Directions
      I work on school work that will improve my career chances.
      I work or have worked to earn money.
      I am in or have been in career or job classes or training.
   Personal Expressions
      I choose my clothes and the personal items I use every day.
      I choose my own hair style.
      I decorate my own room.

Note: From "Student Self-Report Measure of Self-Determination for Students With Cognitive Disabilities," by M. L. Wehmeyer, 1996, *Education and Training in Mental Retardation and Developmental Disabilities,* December, pp. 282–292. Copyright 1996 by the Council for Exceptional Children. Reprinted with permission.

FIGURE 8–9 *Sample questions from the autonomy domain of The Arc's Self-Determination Scale (Adolescent Version)*

teaches basic academic and social skills and provides intensive programming in reading, math, and language arts.

General classroom support organizes content for students to help them succeed with the general education curriculum. This emphasis includes tutorial assistance, arranging alternative ways of achieving goals, and developing learning strategies (see Chapter 4). As schools implement IDEA (and as they do so consistently with its stronger inclusion provisions), the general education curriculum, with support to accommodate a student's abilities and disabilities, should be used more often.

The third option is adult outcomes/life-skills preparation. Of these three options, professionals now typically emphasize the life-skills curriculum. As you learned in Chapter 1, the adult outcomes for students with disabilities, especially those with mental retardation, are discouraging. Three years after graduation, only 41 percent were competitively employed and 15 percent were living independently. For this reason and consistent with IDEA's emphasis on student results, there is an increasing emphasis on a life-skills orientation from the early years (Beck, Broers, Hogue, Shipstead, & Knowlton, 1994; Clark, 1994; Clark, Carlson, Fisher, Cook, & D'Alonzo, 1991).

A life-skills curriculum identifies the expectations of the environments where students will live, work, and play after they leave school. It teaches skills that prepare them to function successfully in those environments. Figure 8-10 illustrates a top–down process in which a teacher follows the sequence of identifying adult domains, subdomains, major life demands, specific life skills, and an appropriate curriculum.

The adult outcome/life-skills curriculum is sometimes referred to as a functional curriculum.

MY VOICE

MICHAEL WEHMEYER: USING THE ARC'S SELF-DETERMINATION SCALE

The most valuable use of the scale [The Arc's Self-Deter-mination Scale (Wehmeyer, 1995)] is to provide a vehicle for students to self-direct assessment in self-determination, generate some areas of instructional need, and work col-laboratively with teachers to set instructional goals and identify instructional strategies. . . . The barrier for many students, remains . . . the medium: . . . it is the paper/pen-cil scale and scoring is too difficult for most students to complete alone. . . . A CD-ROM based, multimedia ver-sion of the scale . . . would utilize multiple input/output options (e.g., audio, video, adapted keyboard, touch screen, switches) etc. that would enable students with

more significant disabilities to assume more control in the assessment process. The CD-ROM version could also be computer scored and based on the students' unique answers. My ideal scenario is that a student with mental retardation sits down, answers questions about him or her-self using the computer, selects one or two goals that he or she wants to work on, and takes these goals to the ITP [individualized transition plan] or IEP meeting and puts them on the table to be considered . . . without having to rely on anyone else . . . unless the student wants to have someone else help!

M. L. Wehmeyer,
Personal Communication,
March 17, 1997

Note: The Self-Determination Scale is available from The Arc, 500 East Border Street, Suite 300, Arlington, TX 76010; 1-800-433-5255.

Figure 8–11 identifies the six adult domains and the twenty-three subdomains associ-ated with these six domains. As IDEA's transition provisions require, it is essential for teachers to tie the content of the curriculum in each domain and subdomain to the cul-ture of each community. For example, the curriculum for Native American students who live on the Fort Apache Indian Reservation will need to be referenced to their participa-tion in the community's spiritual activities, family chores such as wood gathering and herding, and traditional crafts (Shafer & Rangasamy, 1995).

Increasingly, educators are trying to merge an adult-outcomes curriculum for stu-dents with mild and moderate mental retardation into the general education curricu-lum. That effort is just what IDEA commands. But it is not an easy task; as you learned in Chapter 3, the general education curriculum is moving toward a higher academic standard, so it is especially challenging to incorporate into it an adult-outcomes cur-

FIGURE 8–10 *Top-down approach to curriculum development*

Adult Domains	Areas of adult functioning that require minimal degrees of competence and independence
[Subdomains]	Subcategories of adult domains useful for understanding the complexities of adulthood
Major Life Demands	Events or activities typically encountered by most adults in everyday life
Specific Life Skills	Specific competencies of local relevance needed to perform major life demands
Organize for Instruction	Curricular considerations for teaching life skills; a function of educational setting

Note. From Life Skills Instruction for All Students With Special Needs: A Practical Guide for Integrating Real-Life Content Into the Classroom, by M. E. Cronin and J. R. Patton, 1993, Austin, TX: PRO-ED. Copyright 1993 by PRO-ED. Reprinted with permission.

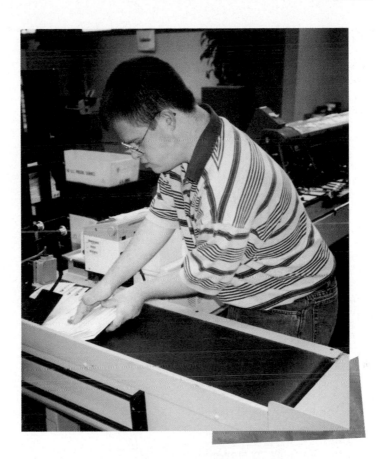

❤ *While in high school, Ryan has learned to meet the expectations of actual workplace environments. Here, he is sorting mail in an office setting.*

riculum for students with mild and moderate mental retardation. Nonetheless, this and a variety of successful models have been developed (Beck et al., 1994; Field, LeRoy, & Rivera, 1994; Helmke, Havekost, Patton, & Polloway, 1994). One of these models, implemented at a middle school, is described at the end of this chapter in the program models section.

Methods

Many instructional methods used for students with learning disabilities (see Chapter 4), emotional and behavioral disorders (see Chapter 5), and attention-deficit/hyperactivity disorder (see Chapter 6)—such as peer tutoring, cooperative learning, establishing clear goals and expectations, and praise/reinforcement of success—are also appropriate for students with mental retardation.

You have already learned the importance of self-determination as an adaptive skill area. Because individuals with mental retardation often experience difficulty with problem solving, especially in generating alternatives and having an adequate background knowledge to evaluate alternatives (Short & Evans, 1990; Wehmeyer & Kelchner, 1995), instruction in this area is particularly important and is a priority of the U.S. Department of Education (Ward, 1996). The central element is instruction in the following skills:

1. Self-assessment of skills

2. Recognition of the limits of personal decision making

3. Setting goals

4. Identifying options

5. Accepting responsibilities

FIGURE 8–11 *Life skills domains and subdomains*

Employment/Education

• General Job Skills

• General Education/Training Considerations

• Employment Setting

• Career Refinement and Reevaluation

Home and Family

• Home Management

• Financial Management

• Family Life

• Child Rearing

Leisure Pursuits

• Indoor Activities

• Outdoor Activities

• Community/Neighborhood Activities

• Travel

• Entertainment

Community Involvement

• Citizenship

• Community Awareness

• Services/Resources

Physical/Emotional Health

• Physical Health

• Emotional Health

Personal Responsibility and Relationships

• Personal Confidence/Understanding

• Goal Setting

• Self-Improvement

• Relationships

• Personal Expression

Note: From *Life Skills Instruction for All Students With Special Needs: A Practical Guide for Integrating Real-Life Content Into the Classroom,* by M. E. Cronin and J. R. Patton, 1993, Austin, TX: PRO-ED. Copyright 1993 by PRO-ED. Reprinted with permission.

6. Communicating preferences and needs

7. Self-monitoring and evaluating progress (Ward & Kohler, 1996)

Box 8–4, "Into Practice," describes the methods used in one of these projects.

It is critical to realize how rooted self-determination is in the Euro-American culture (A. P. Turnbull & Turnbull, 1997). In that culture, a transition goal for high school students usually is to choose the employment and living options that they would most prefer as adults; in that culture and consistent with IDEA, competitive employment and independent living are typical goals. Yet other cultures place far more emphasis on children con-

BOX 8-4   INTO PRACTICE

TEACHING SELF-DETERMINATION SKILLS

PURPOSE is an instructional model to teach students self-determination skills. Developed by Dr. Loretta Serna at the University of New Mexico, this model incorporates instructional methods that are especially effective in teaching students with mental retardation. The model name, PURPOSE, is a mnemonic strategy to assist educators in remembering the instructional steps.

DID THE INSTRUCTOR:

Prepare the student to learn the skill?
    Define the skill?
    Discuss the different situations where the skill could be used?
    Explain the different reasons for using the skill?

Have the student **U**nderstand and learn the skill steps?
    Read and define each skill step?
    Give rationales for each skill steps?
    Give examples of how each skill step should be performed?

Have the students **R**ehearse the skill correctly?
    Model the skill for the students?
    Engage the students in the memorization of the skill?
    Have the students rehearse the skill in partners?

Have the students **P**erform a self-check of the skill?
    Have each partner check to see if the skill user performed all the skill steps and rehearse the skill until each student reaches a 100 percent criteria?
    Have the students perform a self-check of their skill performance?

Help the student **O**vercome any skill performance problems?

Have the students **S**elect other situations where the skill can be used?

Have the students **E**valuate any skill performances outside the teaching setting?

The *Learning with Purpose* curriculum includes criterion-referenced assessment tools for teachers, students, and parents. These tools identify the skills that have already been mastered and the ones that are important to teach next. The program includes an instructor's manual to guide teachers in teaching each of the skills in the curriculum and a lesson plan manual with actual scripts of how teachers can conduct each instructional session and a manual containing rationales, role-play situations, and student worksheets.

In addition to this instructional component, PURPOSE also has a family component. The family component involves a two-day workshop of six hours each day. Meeting in separate rooms, students focus on skills of action planning (setting goals, making a plan to implement the goal, deciding on self-management approaches), and parents learn how they can best support their son or daughter in accomplishing the action plans (negotiating differences, providing positive feedbacks, providing rationales for requests, and networking). Throughout the two days, students and parents meet together to discuss their progress and share the goals and plans that the students are in the process of developing.

The program developers recommend that one approach is to arrange forty-five minute blocks of time for instruction. To progress through the entire curriculum, a sequence of four years is recommended (Serna, 1996; Serna & Lau-Smith, 1995).

Loretta Serna
University of New Mexico

Note: The PURPOSE strategy checklist is from "Learning With PURPOSE: A Lifelong Learning Approach Using Self-Determination Skills," by L. A. Serna in *Self-Determination Across the Life Span: Independence and Choice for People With Disabilities* (pp. 285–310), edited by D. J. Sands and M. L. Wehmeyer, 1996, Baltimore: Paul H. Brookes. Copyright 1996 by Paul H. Brookes P.O. Box 10624, Baltimore, MD 21285. Reprinted with permission.

tinuing to live with their parents as adults. For example, some Latin American parents expressed their cultural preferences as follows: "We never separate from our children. We never cut the cord." Another stated, "It is against the family for the children to live alone as adults" (A. P. Turnbull & Turnbull, 1996, p. 200).

Teachers should consider a family's and student's culture when developing instructional methods in self-determination. Like many other professional families in the Anglo cultural tradition, Bob and Martha (Ryan's parents) early on set independence as the goal for themselves, Ryan, and their other children. For Ryan, they envisioned independence, working without much support from a job coach, living on his own without much support from an independent-living support person, and being able to arrange transportation, recreation, shopping, and banking by himself. Increasingly, however, Bob and Martha have realized that interdependence is what they and Ryan should seek because Ryan needs support people in all he does and will do. For them, Ryan's Group Action Planning team (see the "Inclusion Tips" in the next section) is a form of interdependence; it helps them physically and emotionally. With interdependence comes yet another benefit, namely, less isolation and more friendship and emotional well-being. Independence is important, but so too is interdependence.

HOW IS PARTICIPATION ENCOURAGED?

Inclusion

To what extent are students with mental retardation included in general education classes? Figure 8–12 illustrates the percentage who were educated in the continuum of educational environments during the 1993 to 1994 school year. Trends indicate the following (U.S. Department of Education, 1995):

- Other than students with deaf-blindness, students with mental retardation are the least likely to be educated in the general education classroom.

- Students with specific learning disabilities are approximately five times more likely to be in a general education classroom, as compared to students with mental retardation.

- Students with serious emotional disorders are approximately three times as likely to be in a general education classroom.

- Students with mental retardation are approximately twice as likely to be educated in a separate special class, as compared to the aggregate of all other students with exceptionalities.

Now that IDEA has been amended (in 1997) and made more inclusive (as you learned in Chapter 3), these placement trends might change. That certainly is what Congress intended, emphasizing in IDEA that inclusion should occur in the student's academic, extracurricular, and other school activities. Largely as a result of their insistence on an

FIGURE 8–12 *Percentage distribution of students with mental retardation in educational placements*

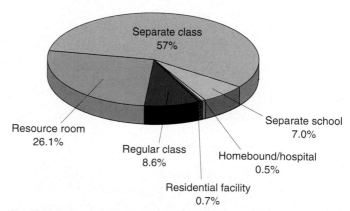

Note: From *To Assure the Free Appropriate Public Education of All Children with Disabilities: Eighteenth Annual Report to Congress on the Implementation of the Individuals with Disabilities Education Act*, Washington, DC: U.S. Department of Education.

Inclusion Tips

	What You Might See	What You Might Be Tempted to Do	Alternate Responses	Ways to Include Peers in the Process
Behavior	The student demonstrates potentially distracting behavior such as loud laughter.	Tell her to stop the behavior (laughter) and be quiet or leave the room.	Model your acceptance of her. Help her identify an alternative acceptable behavior, such as quiet laughter. Role play the new behavior.	Teach peers to show acceptance in spite of annoying behavior.
Social Interactions	The student tries to hug a peer who does not want a hug.	Tell her that hugging is not appropriate behavior at school.	Give her an alternative: "Give me five" instead of hugging.	Give peers responsibility for helping to select and practice the alternatives with her.
Educational Performance	The student shows an apparent lack of interest and boredom with class activities.	Discipline her for lack of cooperation.	Maintain high expectations but modify the curriculum: same topic, different focus.	Establish a peer tutoring system within the class: different students help with different subjects.
Classroom Attitudes	The student demonstrates learned helplessness with new activities.	Let her be excused from the activity.	Give her many opportunities to do well on parts that she can successfully accomplish. Provide her with appropriate leadership opportunities.	Pair her with a partner who needs help in an area of her strength (e.g., music).

inclusive education but also in part because they had the law on their side, Ryan's parents were able to secure some academic and much extracurricular inclusion for him. The "Inclusion Tips" box provides suggestions for successfully including students.

Many people strongly favor IDEA's policy of inclusion for students with mental retardation. Some find the placement data disappointing. For example, The Arc, a strong proponent of inclusion, conducted a state-by-state analysis of placement patterns and issued a "Report Card to the Nation on Inclusion and Education of Students with Mental Retardation" (The Arc, 1992), concluding that:

> *The grades are in and essentially the country has failed in meeting its obligations to educate children with mental retardation in regular classes alongside their non-disabled peers. . . . The Arc calls specifically on the federal government and all state governments as well as advocacy organizations, including all chapters of The Arc, to initiate or renew their efforts to achieve the full inclusion of children with mental retardation in the nation's schools by the year 2000.*

The Arc has 140,000 members, most of whom are parents of persons with mental retardation. It is the nation's largest voluntary organization committed to improving quality of life for people with mental retardation.

The Board of Directors of CEC's Division on Mental Retardation and Developmental Disabilities adopted a position statement that stresses the need for thorough preparation and training of educators in order to implement inclusion successfully:

> *Preparation and training are essential to ensure the creation of schools that effectively include students with developmental disabilities. Such preparation and training must focus not just on students with developmental disabilities in the area of academic, study and social skills but on all members of the education community. This preparation and training must include other students, parents, secretarial and custodial staff, bus drivers, professional support staff, teachers and administrators. (Smith & Hilton, 1997, p. 3)*

The article describing this position statement used the term *optimal inclusion* rather than *full inclusion,* to emphasize that inclusion means striving to find the most satisfactory educational environment for each student (Smith & Hilton, 1997, p. 5).

Collaboration

As you learned in Chapter 3, inclusion often occurs because of collaboration, one form of which is person-centered planning. This process calls for problem solving by and among families, friends, and professionals, each of whom pays close attention to a student's preferences, strengths, and great expectations. Person-centered planning approaches include Personal Futures Planning (Mount, 1987; Mount & Zwernik, 1988), MAPs (Falvey, Forest, Pearpoint, & Rosenberg, 1994), Essential Lifestyle Planning (Smull & Harrison, 1992), PATH (Falvey et al., 1994), Circle of Friends (Falvey et al., 1994), and Group Action Planning (A. P. Turnbull & Turnbull, 1996). In Box 8-5, "My Voice," Ryan's mother, Martha, describes Group Action Planning and its meaning for Ryan and his family.

Ryan's family, friends, teachers, and related service providers have been implementing Group Action Planning for the last five years. The members of Ryan's action group originally collaborated to plan and implement an inclusive educational program to enhance his current and future success.

Action group members have worked collaboratively with his IEP team to increase his communication competence. The collaborative process is highlighted in the "Collaboration Tips" box.

Professional Collaboration. Many professionals have participated in Ryan's action group over the last five years. These include his special education teachers, inclusion facilitator, assistant principal, speech and language pathologist, job coach, and vocational coordinator. Each and everyone has made valuable contributions as they have shared their expertise and resources with the group. These professionals have also commented about how beneficial it is for them to come together with Ryan, his family, friends, and people from the community to plan together. Group Action Planning enables professionals to get creative ideas from others and to enhance the quality of their own contributions.

Family Collaboration. Ryan's family have been indispensable members of the action group. Both of his parents regularly participate, and frequently his brother and sisters participate as well. As Ryan's mother comments in Box 8-5, his family has found it beneficial to have reliable allies with many other people.

Action group meetings are almost always held in the family's home. Martha and Bob have welcomed people with warm hospitality and plentiful snacks. All action group members have gotten to know Ryan and his family as friends and have developed very comfortable communication and trust.

Through Group Action Planning, Ryan has increased his ability to express his preferences, engage in group discussion, attend to a long agenda, and develop self-esteem from having so many people genuinely care about his preferences. Action groups can create a

---

What do you see as the difference between full inclusion and optimal inclusion? What position do you predict The Arc would take on the definition of optimal inclusion?

What contributions do you think you might make to an action group? What benefits might you personally derive from participating?

BOX 8-5   MY VOICE

Ryan's Mother, Martha, on Group Action Planning

During the first fifteen years of Ryan's life, Bob and I learned to actively advocate for Ryan's right to "a life." Our hopes and visions for Ryan have always been that he would live in his own home with supports, have a job, and one day get married if that is what he wanted. We truly believed that having opportunities with his same-age peers in general education classes and extracurricular activities was the type of education that would lead to the achievement of our visions for Ryan. Our efforts at advocating for him to have inclusive education and a true sense of belonging at his schools were met with much resistance from the educational system. Frequently, it seemed that educational personnel saw us as the "opponent" rather than true partners in Ryan's education. Bob and I both had a profound sense of isolation.

This all changed five years ago when we began an action group for Ryan. Our action group started as a result of our realization that Ryan's life was filled with family, professionals, and peer "helpers" but was bereft of friends. I was talking with a friend about our concerns, and she suggested that we use a planning process called Group Action Planning to increase Ryan's social network. We invited people to the first meeting who were really committed to Ryan's future. I vividly remember two things from that meeting. First, I remember thinking that we had accomplished more in one meeting toward increasing Ryan's social network than in years of meeting with school staff alone. Second, I experienced an incredible sense of relief that we weren't alone in our efforts to achieve our visions for Ryan's future. This immediate feeling of success was really motivating.

The connections that were started at that meeting five years ago are now stronger than ever. Many of our current action group members have been with us since the beginning. They have truly become our reliable allies, our cherished friends, members of our extended family. We have met each month to help create a lifestyle for Ryan that is consistent with his preferences and visions for the future. Ryan now has a job that he enjoys and where he is proud to be a good employee. He has co-workers who provide the natural supports he needs to be successful. Moving into his own apartment and getting married are a part of his future plans. We earnestly support these visions. And now we have a committed group of friends who also share this vision with us, who plan with Ryan rather than for him, and who support Ryan, the person, rather than Ryan, the disability.

The focus of our action group has broadened over the years from increasing Ryan's social network to his full inclusion at the high school. We've had our ups and downs over the years, but when the down times came, we always had our reliable allies to problem solve with us. Problems become more a challenge than a threat.

Our focus is now changing as we face Ryan's transition from high school to adulthood. Ryan has had a right to a free appropriate education. This right to supports and services will change soon because after high school there are no mandated services for young adults with disabilities. We are now faced with the next fifty years of Ryan's life in a community where many adult service agencies believe that sheltered workshops and congregate living comprise an acceptable way of life. If it were not for the members of our action group, we would feel more frightened and alone than ever before. They make all the difference in the world to us. We know that we aren't making this journey alone. I recognize that we have only taken first steps in a long journey that will involve a lot of risk and faith. It is frightening to let go of Ryan to live in his own home in a community where many others do not share our great expectations for individuals with disabilities. But, risks are a part of life, and being an active participant is what it's all about. And with our reliable allies I have no doubt that the journey will be a successful one.

Martha Banning
Lawrence, KS
Summer, 1997

responsive context in which students can practice self-determination skills and get encouragement from others in directing their own lives (Turnbull, Blue-Banning, Anderson, Turnbull, Seaton, & Dinas, 1996). Ryan's Group Action Planning facilitator commented,

> *When we first started having Group Action Planning meetings, Ryan would participate for a short while and then quickly would want one of his classmates to go with him to his bedroom to play Nintendo® games. It was more important to Ryan to have his friends over to his house than it was, at that point, to engage in his own self-determining problem-solving. As he has developed skills over the years, it is especially gratifying to have him share his preferences and concerns in the group, contribute to brainstorming, listen to the brainstorming of others, and quite emphatically state the alternatives he would like to pursue. He is now*

Collaboration Tips

INCREASING STUDENT COMPETENCE WITH AUGMENTATIVE COMMUNICATION DEVICES

COLLABORATION GOAL   To identify and develop communication skills with the MessageMate for the student with mental retardation.

Collaborators	Roles and Preparation	Possible Barriers	Solutions to Barriers	Modifications to Implementation	Ongoing Evaluation
Student	Choose vocabulary and phrases for MessageMate.	Reluctance to use MessageMate.	Make use of MessageMate more functional/ meaningful	Include jokes on MessageMate.	Increases willingness to use MessageMate.
Parents	Choose vocabulary and phrases for MessageMate. Identify pictures, activities for conversation book.	Too little time due to other responsibilities.	Schedule weekly time to review and update conversation book.	Offers son choices of pictures and preferred activities for conversation book.	Observe frequency son uses conversation book and MessageMate in the community.
Communication Specialist	Assess student's needs; develop and implement intervention plan.	Lack of time to collaborate across all environments.	Provide in-service training collectively to team members.	Model intervention strategies for collaborators across environments.	Observation and consultation with team members in all environments.
Job Coach	Model use of augmentative device at job site.	Focus strictly on job skills to the exclusion of communication needs.	Describe to co-workers the communication demands specific to work site.	Model aided input for co-workers (coach demonstrates use).	Observation and consultation with team members in all environments.
Co-workers and Shift Boss	Identify communication skills co-worker (student) needs on the job.	Lack of experience with people with disabilities.	On-site training and becoming members of student's action group.	Changing own communication style (e.g., use open-ended questions, declarative statements).	Evaluate own communication skills/style.

outspoken in describing the life that he wants to lead, and, through this process, his own self-determination has grown by leaps and bounds.

Although peers and friends are valuable sources of insights, particularly about how to make social and academic inclusion work, most individualized education programs (IEPs) do not regularly capitalize on peer contributions.

Student and Community Collaboration.   In the action group's beginning years, Ryan's classmates had many useful ideas about how to respond to his preferences. They orchestrated efforts to include him in more school activities and served as peer tutors in his computer class. Matt, one of Ryan's classmates and an action group member, commented that the group succeeded because of the combination of adult and peer perspectives: "Adults know what's best for us, and we know what we want." Matt explained further that the group can accomplish almost anything because Ryan has adults' support and peers' creativity, inventiveness, and grassroots knowledge about how to make things happen for each other.

Since his classmates graduated and because he is in his last school year, Ryan's peers in the action group are several college students with whom he hangs out several afternoons and

Ryan and his family have used Group Action Planning for several years to promote his inclusion at school and in the community. Action Group meetings such as this one often convene in a member's home and include family, friends, professionals, and peers.

evenings each week. Given that one of Ryan's major transition goals is to live in an apartment with roommates, Jon, a college student, has been helping Ryan list what skills he will need to live on his own, based on Jon's college dorm experiences. At action group meetings, Jon shares, based on his own experiences, the skills Ryan will need to live independently.

How is Group Action Planning different from other planning? Figure 8–13 compares a typical individualized education program (IEP) process and a typical Group Action Planning process. Interestingly, on most dimensions they vary significantly, and in one respect they differ fundamentally: Group Action Planning consists of a long-term network of support from family, friends, and professionals who concentrate on creative problem solving and on group social support.

Careers

Many careers are available for people interested in students with mental retardation. General and special education teachers and related-services providers are needed at all levels (early intervention through postsecondary education). At the secondary and postsecondary levels, challenging opportunities exist for professionals interested in vocational training to serve as job developers and coaches. Some of the administrative roles include director of special education, principal, and assistant principal. Each role has certification requirements combining expertise in curriculum, instruction, supervision, and administration. In Box 8–6, "Making a Difference," you learn how an effective administrator can get everyone involved and collaborating.

WHAT ARE PROGRAM OPTIONS?

Early Intervention and Preschool Years

As you learned when reading about causes of mental retardation, children living in poverty are at risk for mental retardation. Although the association between mental retardation and psychosocial disadvantage is complex and not perfectly understood (Pope & Tarlov, 1991), clearly, poor nutrition, late or absent prenatal care, low birth weight, premature birth, and

FIGURE 8–13 *Group Action Planning and IEP comparison*

IEP	Group Action Plan
Involves many professionals, one or two family members, and typically excludes individual with disability and friends	Individual with disability typically attends; family, friends, and professionals are in approximately equal proportions
Annual meeting	Meets frequently, often monthly
Based on test scores	Based on felt needs, great expectations
Develops written document of goals, objectives, and related services	Specifies action steps to make preferred options happen
Monitors implementation of goals and objectives annually	Accountable for action steps daily and weekly
Emphasizes completion of paperwork	Emphasizes action steps for each member to take
Professionals dominate discussion and typically review information with families	Families, friends, and professionals equally engage in creative problem solving
Structured/formal meeting	Balance of structure and informality, engaging in problem solving and having fun
Goals are on annual basis	Great expectations over the lifespan
Meeting held at school or agency; may set uncomfortable tone for parents coming into "professional zone"	Meeting held at place where everyone is at ease; no "turf" advantage

lack of early stimulation all create risk (Stark et al., 1988). To make matters worse, social services for families in poverty are often fragmented and consequently ineffective.

Recognizing these problems, Congress in 1988 funded research demonstration projects in child development to provide comprehensive services to young families at risk because of poverty. Project EAGLE (Early Guidance Leading to Empowerment), at the Kansas University Medical Center in Kansas City, became one of those centers (M. Staker, personal communication, August 1, 1997). When Congress in 1995 reauthorized the Head Start program, it created Early Head Start Programs, and Project EAGLE became one of those programs. As a Head Start program, Project EAGLE must comply with three standards: It must serve families who have incomes below the federal guidelines and have a child under the age of one living in the home; at least 10 percent of the families served in Head Start must have a child with a disability; and the entire project must have a Parent Policy Council that has significant responsibility and authority with respect to how Project EAGLE functions.

Project EAGLE operates on the theory that all families have strengths and needs, and parallel services must be offered to help them meet their basic needs while achieving their parenting, educational, and employment goals. Accordingly, Project EAGLE works with a host of other community-based programs to provide comprehensive services to the families. For example, it has linked up with Kansas University's Juniper Gardens Children's Project, a research center that has demonstrated how to improve the academic skills of inner-city children through more effective teaching and parental involvement.

Project EAGLE also connects with the Part C (infants/toddlers) program in the Kansas City public schools, with local offices of the state's health, mental health, welfare, and child protective services agency, and with transportation agencies, vocational and educational institutions, child care providers, and private foundations.

With Project EAGLE as their hub, these agencies pool their financial and personnel resources and in some situations even share space with each other. Each family in Project EAGLE's Early Head Start program can now have a unified service system, one that brings together such otherwise diverse and unconnected services as child care, early education,

BOX 8-6   MAKING A DIFFERENCE

DWIGHT FLEMING

Behind every good program in special and regular education is an excellent administrator, a professional like Dwight Fleming. Dwight was born, grew up, and now works in the northeast quadrant of Hartford, Connecticut, a deprived urban area where the greatest majority of the families are African-American, many from Jamaica. It's a place characterized by single parenthood, poverty, homelessness, housing development, incarceration, and hard work for low wages (when work is available). At the Martin Luther King, Jr., Elementary School, with approximately eight hundred students from preschool through the sixth grade, Dwight, an assistant principal with responsibilities for K–3 and special education services, performs special education administration functions for the families of the 25 percent of the students who have disabilities and are formally classified into special education programs.

The service he renders has nothing to do directly with classrooms but everything to do with students' education, their self-esteem, their families, the school, the neighborhood it serves, and the future.

Each parent is a potential service provider or connector. My job is to help them become part of the education team, a team that consists of the school, the student, and the parents. I want them to see school as a positive experience for their children and the children to see it as a safe place to learn to grow.

How does Dwight help parents or any caregiver become a part of the team?

I don't care who's taking care of the kid at home . . . a mother, aunt, grandparent, father, sister, whoever I find a way to get them to spend time at King School, and then to feel good about being here and then share their talents here. You know, everyone has talents.

So, does Dwight take advantage of all opportunities that come his way? Absolutely!

I'm a very positive person. I smile at parents, pay attention to what they say, invite them to come here, tell them we'd like to have them involved here, walk them around, show them what other parents have done, give them some ideas about what we need to have done, and let their imaginations go to work. I make them feel like somebody. Everybody is somebody special. I work one to one.

The good thing, Dwight points out, is that the students also feel good about the school and about learning. There is also a spillover effect, from school to neighborhood.

It does kids good to see neighborhood people in school and then after school. They know they're being supported and watched. And with neighbors looking in during school and after school, I can find out a lot about students that I couldn't learn just by the student being here and by talking with the family.

The King School has become the neighborhood, and the neighborhood has become the school.

I begin to draw a circle, starting with the student and then extending to family and friends and neighbors. In each of these contacts, I offer hope, not pity.

For the parents and families of students with disabilities, Dwight also offers assurances.

I tell them that my job, the King School's job, is to give the student the best education we can and to protect that child's development and future.

health, mental health, social services, adult education for parents who have not completed their high school programs, and job-find for parents who have to find work or lose their welfare benefits.

And in part because the Head Start law requires it and in part because Project EAGLE believes in family empowerment, families have a very large say in what the program does overall and for each of them. Just what does Project EAGLE do?

Project EAGLE works with families to help them meet their basic needs and supports them as they work toward parenting and self-sufficiency goals. Each Project EAGLE family has a family support advocate who works in partnership with the family on a weekly basis to identify needs, establish goals, and coordinate and link appropriate community resources on the family's behalf. This person also provides information on normal developmental milestones and helps adult family members acquire parenting skills and education to promote the optimum growth and development of their children.

Since the beginning of the project, the birth weights of babies born to Project EAGLE mothers have been excellent, cesarean-section rates have been low, and premature births have been rare. The number of families who have found jobs has increased dramatically, and many adults in these families have enrolled in formal education programs.

In addition, Project EAGLE programs have become more family sensitive because of the significant role that the Parent Policy Council plays. Members of that Council are liaisons between the Project and other families, explaining how the Project works and what it seeks to accomplish, why welfare reform (get a job or lose benefits) was enacted, how to respond to the challenge of finishing high school and finding and keeping work, and how to benefit from the Individualized Family Service Plan under Part C of IDEA.

What factors contribute to Project EAGLE's success? The families themselves play a large part, but so do practices that are an integral part of the Project:

- The Project is home based. Family support advocates go to families, and this approach helps overcome the traditional barriers to service such as transportation, child care, and safety concerns.

- The comprehensive services are individualized, intensive, and continuous. One program addresses all of the physical, emotional, social, and cognitive needs of the family for an extended time.

- Staff members combine their professional skills with their own life experiences to bring a personalized and caring professional approach to the families. Many of the staff members share similar backgrounds with the families.

- Staff members receive two hours of in-service education per week on parenting, early childhood development, and strategies for parent–professional partnerships.

⋈ *Working in partnership with families and using innovative practices, Project EAGLE enhances the development of children and their families.*

- The Project seeks professional staff who have a bachelor's degree in early childhood education and training and experience in working with the whole family across many domains of its life (Staker, 1993).

Elementary Years

At the Morristown Elementary School in Morristown, Vermont, six factors contribute to the school's accomplishments in educating students with mental retardation in general education classrooms:

- Underlying values and beliefs
- Responses to educational initiative regarding classroom organizations and instruction
- Schools and classroom climate
- Leadership
- Capacity building
- Connections to the community (Hasazi & Furney, 1996)

Values and Beliefs.   Morristown Elementary School is a school with a vision. Its vision is reflected in the school's mission statement, which was developed by teachers, administrators, parents, and community members and describes the school as a "community of learners with the courage to grow." The values and beliefs underlying this statement reveal a deep commitment to meeting the needs of all learners, including those with disabilities. Students' needs drive all decisions made at the school. One teacher noted, "We always put kids first and then figure out what we need to do to meet [their needs]."

> The courage to grow assumes that all students have strengths.

Both special and general education teachers at Morristown Elementary School recognize that collaborative teaching and planning are essential to students' success. Collaboration requires time and energy, but it results in people feeling "more like a community than like isolated beings," according to staff.

Responses to Educational Initiatives.   The values and beliefs at Morristown Elementary School are reflected in school reform and restructuring, such as establishing multiage classrooms, using team-teaching models to deliver special education services in the classroom, organizing grade-level planning and problem-solving teams, and establishing a team of teachers that participates in making school-wide decisions. The school has adopted a conflict-mediation program, which trains students and teachers in proactive discipline and conflict resolution strategies. It also has developed an interdisciplinary curriculum, measured student progress through portfolio assessment, installed computers in classrooms, and ensured that all students achieve maximum success in reading. Although change requires energy, risk taking, mutual support, stress, and even failure, one teacher summarized her colleagues' experiences noting, "If you're supporting one another and encouraging one another, then you know that sooner or later the water is going to flow smoothly."

School and Classroom Climate.   At Morristown Elementary School, the climate supports all children, including those with disabilities, and is consistent throughout the school: the hallways, the cafeteria, the playground, and each of its classrooms. Interactions between and among teachers, students, parents, and administrators are characterized by respect for others and their opinions. An instructional assistant commented, "The kids here accept all students as they are." Classrooms are structured in a way that is decidedly student-centered, with the goal of involving all students in their own learning. As one teacher described it, "Instead of being teacher-centered, there are cooperative groups, class meetings, and an attempt to begin collaborating decision making." Discipline policies and practices are

> Relationships through inclusion are intended outcomes of school reform.

proactive and involve students as well as teachers. A model of shared decision making is used throughout the school, from faculty meetings to IEP meetings, grade-level meetings, and classroom meetings. Students with disabilities and their parents participate as full team members in developing and following up on their IEPs. The walls at Morristown Elementary are covered with artwork and written messages that welcome newcomers and demonstrate the ways in which students and faculty appreciate and support one another.

Leadership.   The principal, classroom teachers, special education teachers and staff, the school superintendent, school board members, and students collectively use a model of shared leadership. Collaboratively, they developed the school's mission, its commitment to students with disabilities, its willingness to explore new organizational models, educational approaches and curriculum, and its movement toward collaborative decision making.

Capacity Building.   Teachers participate in a wide variety of courses, workshops, summer institutes, master's degree programs, and in-service training activities. They recognize the importance of connecting with new ideas and opportunities and are involved with model demonstration and research efforts sponsored by the state education agency and a number of universities.

Connections to the Community.   Finally, teachers and administrators at Morristown Elementary School value their connections to their local community. They have established strong partnerships with parents, involving them in IEP planning, training opportunities, school activities, and the development of the school mission statement. In addition, special and general educators have established links with community agencies and providers. Some of these have come through collaborative problem solving around the needs of individual students, while others have occurred as teachers and service providers have worked together on interagency committees and joint school and community initiatives. As a result, school and community partnerships have helped to ensure that students and families with significant needs receive the support that they require. These partnerships are working to increase the community's capacity to support the needs of all of its

Sixth-grade students at Morristown Elementary School take part in team building and activities through adventure-based learning activities at the Lotus Lake Discovery Center in Williamstown, Vermont.

families. Discussions of community ultimately lead back to discussions of the community values that support helping all students and community members succeed. As a school administrator described it, "There seems to me to be more of a sense of community here than there is in some other places, and a real willingness to help people. That's a shared community value."

Middle and Secondary Years

Some people believe that you have to choose between teaching functional outcomes to students with mental retardation in special classes or providing them with inclusive experiences in general education classes. The Birmingham Public Schools in Birmingham, Michigan, found that these two strategies are not mutually exclusive (Field, LeRoy, & Rivera, 1994). Three activities make this middle school program and the two strategies successful.

The first key is preparation of general and special education teachers. All middle school teachers participate in comprehensive staff development where they learned about functional skill instruction for all students. After all, students with and without mental retardation alike need to learn functional skills. During staff development, teachers focus on making teachers' suggestions and activities more concrete and practical for each student.

The second key involves comprehensive collaborative planning. The planning team for one of the students, Sarah, consisted of a general educator, a special educator, the school social worker, Sarah's parent, and Sarah herself. After identifying Sarah's individual learning style, the team used the Making Action Plans (MAPs) process (see Chapter 9) to learn about her history, her own and other team members' dreams and nightmares, Sarah's unique characteristics, her strengths, and her needs. To truly understand Sarah, the team focused on her academic needs and on her entire life across school, home, and community settings and developed a functional academic curriculum, such as leading educators approve (Clark, 1994).

The MAPs process, like the Group Action Planning process is a form of person-centered planning and action.

At the beginning of the school year, Sarah's team used a variety of instructional methods and social groupings to determine the best way to instruct her. They developed the matrix in Table 8-5 to cross-reference her IEP goals with her general education classes. Her IEP goals were drawn directly from what was learned during the MAPs process.

> *For example, a regularly scheduled activity in a social studies class was completing a report on a European country. For Sarah, this activity was used as an opportunity to teach transportation skills (to get to the library), money skills (for using public transportation and the copying machine at the library), initiating conversation (to access materials), and using the telephone (to obtain information on library hours).*

In addition to learning functional skills within the ongoing curriculum, Sarah also received intensive instruction in a special education resource room.

The third key is to put into place a system of comprehensive and continuous support. Sarah's general education teachers need daily support to adapt the general education curriculum and incorporate functional skills:

> *Using reading materials written at a lower grade level; using a report-writing assignment to develop keyboarding skills, rather than for mastering the academic content; using a social studies project on Greece to work on calendar and time management skills; and using lecture/discussion in academic classes to work on communication skills . . . rather than focusing on the content.*

Sarah's Circle of Friends, similar to the one that Danny Ramirez had (see Chapter 3) and like Ryan Banning's group action team, provided additional social support for her in making friends and solving social problems. Sarah's parents were regular members of the educational planning team and assisted her with homework on a routine basis.

TABLE 8–5   *Curriculum matrix for Sarah*

IEP Goals*	General Education Classes									Other Environments**			
	Homeroom	Language Arts	Social Studies	Physical Education	Lunch	Reading	Life Skills (3 days/wk.)	Music (2 days/wk.)	Science	Math	Library	Public Transport	Store
Speak in front of a group	X	X	X					X	X				
Initiate peer conversations	X	X	X	X	X		X		X		X	X	X
Improve money skills	X				X		X			X	X	X	X
Use public transportation												X	
Improve reading		X	X			X			X	X	X		
Research and write reports		X	X			X			X	X			
Improve math calcuation skills	X				X		X		X	X			X

*Sarah's content-specific goals for each class were not listed if they were the same as her classmates' goals.
**Community sites are identified to ensure functional skill application and generalization.

Note: From "Is a Functional Curriculum Approach Compatible With an Inclusive Education Model?" by G. M. Clark, 1994, *Teaching Exceptional Children*, Winter, pp. 36–39. Copyright 1994 by the Council for Exceptional Children. Reprinted with permission.

Transitional and Postsecondary Years

What makes it possible for a student with mental retardation to graduate from a high school as president of the student body, a four-sport participant in Special Olympics, a member of the honors chorus and a drumming group, and a recipient of three school-wide awards? And then to take a job in a large textile factory where he works for good pay and benefits and receives positive work evaluations? The answer, in a word, is *collaboration.*

The Shelby, North Carolina, city school system consists of 3,000 students, grades K–12, of whom 250 have disabilities. Shelby is the county seat of a largely rural county that is home to approximately twenty-five large manufacturing industries.

Project TASSEL is the system's transition program. It serves 120 students, ages 14 to 22 years old. Most of them are 14 to 18 years old, and more than half of them have mental retardation, as does Jerry Moss (not his real name). By creating school-level transition teams and a community-based interagency team, Project TASSEL makes it possible for school and community to collaborate, beginning when students reach the ninth grade and until they graduate. If there is a phrase that describes Project TASSEL, it must be "school with and school without walls," for what a student learns within the walls of the school system itself is mirrored by what the student learns in the community, in the school without walls.

Within the school system, Project TASSEL involves students and their families in identifying their future work and adult life goals through MAPs, self-advocacy, and training in job-hunting skills. Students and families also select either an academic or a vocational course of study to attain the goals. The school-level transition team (teachers, transition coordinators, transition assistants, and functional-academic teachers) provides the necessary support and services, on-campus and off-campus, to achieve the goals.

Students who, like Jerry, chose an occupational curriculum have classes and activities in career preparation, community services, family life, health, life skills science, job skills math, employment English, physical education, and vocational education. They are involved in community-based instruction, recreation, daily living skills, consumerism, and money management.

So that their functional academics will generalize to the world of work, students have school-without-walls experiences. They work in the community in restaurants, retail, and industrial sites and custodial positions; develop a portfolio of skills; work in the school's

 Jerry Moss and other students who choose Project TASSEL's occupational curriculum have schools-without-walls experiences. At this industrial site, Jerry receives on-the-job training that supplements his classroom instruction.

own factory; and work part-time elsewhere. With assistance from the local vocational rehabilitation agency, they get on-the-job training and follow-up services.

All students benefit from the cooperation of local businesses that provide contracts to the school's own factory, job-shadowing sites, paid community-based contracts, and individual job placements. This kind of school–industry collaboration means that, when a student graduates with a diploma in the occupational curriculum, local employers know that the student is well trained.

A VISION FOR THE FUTURE

For as long as they can remember, Martha and Bob Banning have had only one vision for the future: Ryan would live on his own, work in competitive employment for at least the minimum wage, have a wide range of friends (those of his same age or not, and those with disabilities or not—it doesn't matter, as long as they are friends), be able to get about his community pretty much by himself, and have the companionship, perhaps through marriage, of a person who is close and dear to him over a long time.

They candidly acknowledge that Ryan is a puzzling combination of endearing and challenging attributes. They recognize the same paradox in the school system and in professionals who have come into their lives: Some pose intractable barriers and some are barrier busters. What seems immeasurable is, in Bob's words, "the impact of those who don't get paid but who make all the difference." And what they seek, Martha is quick to say, is a collection of just those kind of people, professional or not, who make the difference because of who they are and what they value.

They are apprehensive about the future—a future in which Ryan has no right under the Individuals with Disabilities Education Act (IDEA) to education when he becomes twenty-two, only a right under the Americans with Disabilities Act and Section 504 of the Rehabilitation Act not to experience discrimination solely because of his disabilities. It will be a future, they know, in which Ryan will have to live without them, for they will predecease him. He may also have to live without the support of his sisters Jenni and Meg and his brother Josh, because they may live in different parts of the country.

And yet they also welcome the future. It will be a time when Ryan will continue to develop his work, communication, social, and reading skills. Now, they are in "seventh heaven" so far as Ryan's work is concerned: Excellent job coaches and natural support at jobs that Ryan likes to do give them confidence. And they know that Ryan's action group, though changing in membership, will itself remain permanent.

What Would You Recommend . . .

1. To enable Ryan to take more responsibility for himself and his own behavior?

2. To increase Ryan's work and independent living skills?

3. To create, for and with Martha and Bob and Ryan's action group, an opportunity for Ryan to have his own home?

4. To foster a school climate that welcomes the challenges of building inclusive communities?

SUMMARY

WHAT IS MENTAL RETARDATION?

• *Mental retardation* refers to substantial limitations in present functioning. It is characterized by significantly subaverage intellectual functioning existing concurrently with related limitations in two or more adaptive skill areas. Mental retardation manifests before age eighteen.

• The definition of mental retardation has been evolving over time and has substantially changed between the 1983 and 1992 definitions of the AAMR (Grossman 1983; Luckasson et al., 1992). The 1992 definition links a person's intellectual and adaptive skill limitation to his or her need for systems of support.

• The three main characteristics of mental retardation relate to intelligence, adaptive skills, and need for supports.

• The diagnosis of mental retardation requires an IQ score of 70 to 75 or below.

• Regarding intelligence, individuals with mental retardation have impairments in the learning process including attention, memory, and generalization. They also may have decreased motivation.

• The ten adaptive skill areas identified by the AAMR include communication, self-care, home living, social skills, community use, self-direction, health and safety, functional academics, leisure, and work.

• The four levels of support identified by the AAMR include intermittent, limited, extensive, and pervasive.

• Two ways to categorize causes of mental retardation include timing and type. Timing includes prenatal, perinatal, and postnatal. Type includes biomedical and psychosocial disadvantage.

• Mental retardation typically results from interactions among multiple causes.

• Prevention encompasses primary, secondary, and tertiary prevention.

• Prevalence rates vary; from less than 1 to 3 percent of the general population are people with mental retardation.

• A trend related to prevalence is the declining percentage of students identified as having mental retardation and the increase in the identification of children with learning disabilities.

WHAT ARE EVALUATION PROCEDURES?

• The AAMR proposes a comprehensive assessment that involves diagnosing mental retardation, classifying and describing the student's strengths and weaknesses and the need for supports, and developing a profile that includes intensities of needed supports.

• A measure frequently used to assess school-aged children's adaptive behavior is the *AAMR Adaptive Behavior Scale—School* (2nd edition) (Lambert et al., 1993).

• *The Arc's Self-Determination Scale* (Wehmeyer, 1995) is sometimes used for secondary students with mental retardation to self-report on the extent to which they think that they exercise self-determination.

WHAT AND HOW DO PROFESSIONALS TEACH?

• Three major curriculum options for students with mild and moderate mental retardation are remedial, general classroom support, and adult outcomes.

• Professionals typically emphasize a life-skills curriculum that identifies the expectations of the environments where students will live, work, and play after they leave school. It then teaches the skills the students need to succeed in those environments.

• A current emphasis for secondary students with mental retardation is instruction to enhance self-determination.

• Person-centered planning approaches, such as Group Action Planning, bring together family, professionals, and friends for problem solving and social support.

• Action groups can provide a context in which students can practice self-determination skills.

HOW IS PARTICIPATION ENCOURAGED?

- With the exception of students with deaf-blindness, students with mental retardation are more likely to receive their education in more restrictive placements than other students with disabilities.

- Career opportunities for people interested in supporting students with mental retardation exist at early intervention, elementary, secondary, and postsecondary levels.

WHAT ARE PROGRAM OPTIONS?

- Project EAGLE is designed to provide comprehensive services to families and to prevent psychosocial disadvantages.

- Morristown Elementary School attributes its students' success to the school's underlying values and beliefs, responses to educational initiatives, school and classroom climate, the model of shared leadership, capacity building, and community connections.

- Schools do not have to choose between teaching functional outcomes to students with mental retardation in special classes and providing inclusive experiences in general education classes; they can do both as the Birmingham Public Schools do.

- Collaboration between schools and industry is used by Project TASSEL to ensure that their students are prepared for competitive employment.

RESOURCES

BOOKS

Count Us In: Growing Up With Down Syndrome. (1994). By Jason Kingsley & Mitchell Levitz. San Diego, CA: Harcourt Brace. Written by two young adults with Down syndrome, this book provides a glimpse of disability issues from their own perspectives. Topics include school, careers, friendships, sex, marriage, and independence.

Couples With Intellectual Disabilities Talk About Living and Loving. (1994). By Karin Melberg-Schwier. Bethesda, MD: Woodbine House. This book profiles fifteen couples, many of whom have Down syndrome, who talk about how they have found companionship and love.

The Effectiveness of Early Intervention. (1997). Edited by Michael J. Guralnick. Baltimore: Brookes. The twenty-five chapters in this recently published book provide an up-to-date understanding of early intervention over the last ten years. Focus is given to children at risk as well as those with established disabilities.

Life Skills Instruction for All Students With Special Needs. (1993). By Mary E. Cronin & James R. Patton. Austin, TX: PRO-ED. This guide discusses attainment of life skills necessary to meet the major demands of adulthood. Topics include the identifica-

tion of major life demands and specific life skills, integration of life-skills content into the classroom, instructional and material considerations, and life-skills assessment and transition planning. An extensive materials and resource list is included.

Mental Retardation: Definition, Classification, and Systems of Support (9th ed.). (1992). By Ruth Luckasson, David L. Coulter, Edward A. Polloway, Steven Reiss, Robert L. Schalock, Martha E. Snell, Deborah M. Spitalnik, & Jack A. Stark. Washington, DC: American Association on Mental Retardation. Provides an in-depth overview of the 1992 AAMR definition and the diagnostic process of mental retardation. Major sections include definition, diagnosis and systems of supports, intellectual functioning and adaptive skills, psychological and emotional considerations, health and physical considerations, etiology considerations, environmental considerations, and practical applications of the definition.

New Voices: Self-Advocacy by Persons With Disabilities. (1996). Edited by Gunnar Dybwad & Hank Bersani. Cambridge, MA: Brookline Books. This collection of original papers by self-advocates and others explores past, present, and potential future directions of the three-decade-old self-advocacy movement.

JOURNALS, MAGAZINES, AND CATALOGS

American Journal on Mental Retardation. American Association on Mental Retardation, 444 North Capitol Street, NW, Washington, DC 20001-1512. Internet address: www.aamr.org. A bimonthly journal for professionals in mental retardation. Articles are primarily research related.

Education and Training in Mental Retardation and Developmental Disabilities. Council for Exceptional Children, Division on Mental Retardation and Developmental Disabilities, PO Box 79026, Baltimore, MD 21279 0026. Internet address: www.cec.sped.org. A quarterly journal that includes articles on research and reviews of the literature concerning mental retardation.

Mental Retardation. American Association on Mental Retardation, 444 North Capitol Street, NW, Washington, DC 20001-1512. Internet address: www.aamr.org. A bimonthly journal with an applied focus on policy, practice, and perspectives in mental retardation.

MULTIMEDIA

The following videos are available at local rental or retail stores:

Beautiful Dreamers. (1992, PG-13, Canada, 107 minutes). American poet Walt Whitman befriends Dr. Maurice Bucke, who progressively treats persons with mental retardation.

Being There. (1979, PG, U.S. 130 minutes). A man with a cognitive impairment experiences a drastic lifestyle change from gardener to political insider when an influential businessman perceives him as insightful.

Best Boy. (1980, not rated, U.S., color, 111 minutes). Oscar-winning documentary about filmmaker Ira Wohl's fifty-two-year-old cousin, who has mental retardation.

Forrest Gump. (1994, PG-13, U.S. 142 minutes). Life story of a southern man with cognitive impairment.

Light in the Piazza. (1962, not rated, U.S., color, 101 minutes). A mother wants her daughter with mental retardation to marry.

Of Mice and Men. (1992, PG-13, U.S., color, 110 minutes). John Steinbeck's novel adapted for film. Lennie, a quiet farm worker, teams up with his cousin who has mental retardation.

What's Eating Gilbert Grape? (1994, PG-13, U.S., color, 120 minutes). An adolescent provides support and encouragement for his younger brother with mental retardation.

ON-LINE INFORMATION AND USEFUL DATABASES

Best Buddies. Internet address: www.gate.net/~bestbud. Site includes information about programs, regional offices, and links to other sites related to mental retardation.

Mental Retardation Research Center. Internet address: www.mrrc.npi.ucla.edu. Includes information about research activities, training programs, federal agencies, and links to other mental retardation research centers.

The National Down Syndrome Society. Internet address: www.ndss.org. Home page for this national organization on Down syndrome. Includes information on inclusion.

Special Olympics International home page. Internet address: www.specialolympics.org. A comprehensive catalog of Special Olympics information.

ORGANIZATIONS

The American Association on Mental Retardation. 444 North Capital Street, NW, Washington, DC 20001-1512. Internet address: www.aamr.org.

National Down Syndrome Congress. 1605 Chantilly Drive, Suite 250, Atlanta, GA 30324. (800) 232-NDSC. Internet address: members.carol.net/~ndsc. E-mail: ndsc@charitiesusa.com.

The Arc. 500 East Border Street, Suite 300, Arlington, TX 76010. (817) 261-6003 Internet address: TheArc.org/welcome.html. E-mail: thearc@metronet.com.

Council for Exceptional Children, Division on Mental Retardation and Developmental Disabilities. PO Box 79026, Baltimore, MD 21279-0026. Internet address: www.cec.sped.org.

CHAPTER 9

SEVERE AND MULTIPLE DISABILITIES

Educating
Joshua Spoor

To use a familiar word in the lexicon of political correctness and say that Joshua Spoor is "challenged" is to put it mildly. Nearly every part of his body is affected by severe disabilities; that is why one way to describe him is to say that he has severe and multiple disabilities. Those alone, however, do not constitute the entire set of challenges facing this young boy. There is another, equally important and no less significant challenge: Joshua lives outside his family's home, a fact that requires the professionals who operate the residential center where he lives, his teachers in the school in the community where the center is based, and his father and new mother, who also live in the same community, to create a triangle of collaboration for Joshua's inclusion in the local school. The root of these dual challenges is the condition that was diagnosed the moment after his birth.

Joshua was born with **encephalocele,** a rare disorder in which a baby is born with an opening in the skull. The membranes that cover the brain and brain tissue come through this opening. The opening may be covered by skin and/or membrane

of varying thickness. As is usual in individuals with encephalocele, Joshua has developmental delays, mental retardation, seizures, and blindness.

Joshua's early years were difficult. He often had seizures; some were mild (absence seizures, formerly called *petit mal*) and others were more severe (tonic-clonic, formerly called *grand mal*). Sometimes he had to be rushed to the hospital after his severe seizures, and it was not unusual for Josh to spend a couple of days in the hospital after one of these episodes. When Joshua was three years old, he went into the hospital after a seizure but developed an infection and had a longer stay than usual. He quit eating, and his health rapidly deteriorated. The doctors guessed that the surgically implanted shunt in his head was infected. Joshua was too ill at this point, however, to handle the trauma of another medical procedure. Because there was nothing medically to be done, Joshua's parents took him home after being told that Joshua probably would die.

Under his parents' care and with the help of two shifts of nurses from a home health agency, Joshua surprised everyone. Little by little, he regained his strength. His period of recovery has lasted for nearly five years, and he has only recently reached his former level of wellness.

When his mother's health started failing because of terminal cancer, Joshua's parents were faced with a difficult decision. Joshua needed twenty-four-hour care, but neither Joshua's mother nor his father could care for him at home. A social worker recommended looking into what services might be available at the Broome Developmental Center, a nearby residential facility.

While Joshua's parents were reluctant to place him in any residential setting, they felt secure with the decision after meeting the staff. Until that time in his life, every health professional had emphasized what Joshua could not do. By contrast, Joshua's father, Alan, wanted professionals who were willing to take a chance on Joshua and to focus on the possibilities for Joshua's development. He found them at the center. There, the staff emphasize Joshua's strengths; they see the possibilities.

Joshua entered the center when he was four. At first, he attended the in-house school. But, when Joshua was nearing first grade, the staff approached Alan about moving Joshua from the center's school to a general education classroom in the Johnson City, New York, school district. Alan first thought it was a great idea. Then, after thinking about it a while, he was a bit apprehensive. He was concerned that the other children might be cruel to Joshua. He was happy to find that his fears were unwarranted. Instead of teasing Joshua, the other children took an interest in him and included him in their activities. According to Alan, Joshua was "definitely welcomed into the school system."

Today, Joshua's classmates take turns reading to Joshua, drawing pictures for him, writing notes to him, and helping him paint and color. With the assistance of an aide, Joshua participates in as many activities as possible in the general education classroom. He spends at least half of each day in the general education classroom, leaving it for services such as physical, occupational, and vision therapy. Joshua's teachers and related

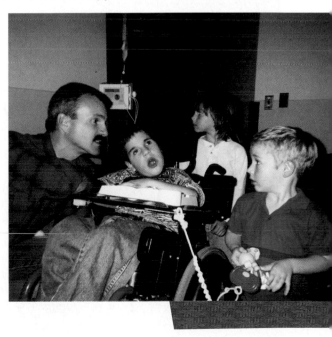

service providers are working with him on increasing muscle control and learning to use pressure switches. They are laying the groundwork for future use of an augmentative communication device.

The many people involved in Joshua's life keep a correspondence notebook in Joshua's book bag. Joshua's peers sometimes write notes to Joshua in the notebook. They also draw pictures for him and send them home in the notebook.

When Joshua passes through the hallways at school, staff and students recognize him and cheerfully greet him. Alan is not surprised that Joshua is liked by his peers and the staff. "He's a pretty happy and outgoing little guy," stated Alan. "He's pretty fun to be around."

As you read this chapter, consider what you as a professional can do to promote an educational environment that benefits students with severe and multiple disabilities.

What Do You Think?

1. How would you explain to parents from a strengths perspective what to expect from their child with severe and multiple disabilities?

2. How would you maintain collaboration among those involved in the life of a student with such disabilities?

3. How would you foster continued interactions between Joshua and his peers?

WHAT ARE SEVERE AND MULTIPLE DISABILITIES?

Defining Severe and Multiple Disabilities

No single definition covers all the conditions that special educators associate with severe and multiple disabilities. Schools operationalize the definition by linking the two areas (severe disabilities, multiple disabilities) into a single program. In such a program, the students typically have severe mental retardation and other accompanying disabilities, such as extensive physical impairments and language delays. Some of these students, however, may have normal intelligence, though their extensive physical and language disabilities may mask their intelligence.

One of the regulations of the Individuals with Disabilities Education Act (IDEA) defines multiple disabilities (but not severe disabilities) as follows:

> *Multiple disabilities means concomitant impairments (such as mental retardation–blindness, mental retardation–orthopedic impairment, etc.), the combination of which causes such severe educational problems that they cannot be accommodated in special education programs solely for one of the impairments. The term does not include deaf-blindness. (34 C.F.R., Sec. 300: [b] [6])*

Another IDEA regulation, related to programs and services for students with severe disabilities, defines severe disabilities as follows:

> *The term "children with severe disabilities" refers to children with disabilities who, because of the intensity of their physical, mental, or emotional problems, need highly specialized education, social, psychological, and medical services in order to maximize their full potential for useful and meaningful participation in society and for self-fulfillment. The term includes those children with disabilities with severe emotional disturbance (including schizophrenia), autism, severe and profound mental retardation, and those who have two or more serious disabilities such as deaf-blindness, mental retardation and blindness, and cerebral palsy and deafness. Children with severe disabilities may experience severe speech, language, and/or perceptual-cognitive deprivations, and evidence abnormal behaviors such as failure to respond to pronounced social stimuli, self-mutilation, self-stimulation, manifestation of intense and prolonged temper tantrums, and the absence of rudimentary forms of verbal control; and may also have intensely fragile physiological conditions. (34 C.F.R., 315.4[d])*

Two major characteristics pervade these different definitions: The extent of disability is beyond mild or moderate levels, and typically two or more disabilities occur simultaneously.

The vast majority of students who are served in programs for students with severe and multiple disabilities have severe mental retardation. As you learned in Chapter 8, pre-1992 definitions of mental retardation classified students at mild, moderate, severe, and profound levels. Under that definition, students with severe and multiple disabilities typically have severe or profound mental retardation and, under the 1992 definition, require more rather than less support than, say, Ryan Banning (Chapter 8). Figure 9–1 highlights

---

FIGURE 9–1 *Four intensity levels of support*

Intermittent

Supports on an "as-needed" basis. Characterized by episodic nature, person not always needing the support(s), or short-term supports needed during life-span transitions (e.g., job loss or an acute medical crisis). Intermittent supports may be high or low intensity when provided.

Limited

An intensity of supports characterized by consistency over time, time-limited but not of an intermittent nature, may require fewer staff members and less cost than more intense levels of support (e.g., time-limited employment training or transitional supports during the school to adult provided period).

Extensive

Supports characterized by regular involvement (e.g., daily) in at least some environments (such as work or home) and not time-limited (e.g., long-term support and long-term home living support).

Pervasive

Supports characterized by their constancy, high intensity; provided across environments; potential life-sustaining nature. Pervasive supports typically involve more staff members and intrusiveness than do extensive or time-limited supports.

Note: From Mental Retardation: Definition, Classification, and Systems of Supports, by R. Luckasson, D. L. Coulter, E. A. Polloway, S. Reiss, R. L. Schalock, M. E. Snell, D. M. Spitalnik, & J. A. Stark, 1992, Washington, DC: American Association on Mental Retardation. Copyright 1992 by the American Association on Mental Retardation. Reprinted with permission.

again the four intensity levels of support. As you consider Joshua's support needs, think about these dimensions of his life:

- Intellectual functioning and adaptive skills
- Psychological and emotional considerations
- Physical and health considerations
- Environmental considerations

For each one, now consider the intensity of support that he needs:

- Intermittent
- Limited
- Extensive
- Pervasive

Isn't it clear that Joshua's support needs are pervasive? That is why Joshua has an aide who assists him with all his physical needs at school.

Describing the Characteristics

Just as developing a single definition of severe and multiple disabilities is difficult, so is accurately describing all characteristics of all people with those disabilities. In fact, it may well be that "the differences among persons with [multiple] disabilities are greater than the similarities" (Guess & Siegel-Causey, 1992). Nevertheless, six categories of characteristics help describe these students: intellectual functioning, adaptive behavior, motor development, sensory functioning, health care needs, and communication.

Intellectual Functioning.   Most individuals with severe and multiple disabilities have severe impairments in intellectual functioning. As you learned in Chapter 2, intellectual functioning is traditionally measured by intelligence test scores. Yet for many persons with severe and multiple disabilities, traditional methods of intelligence testing arguably are inappropriate. Many of the commonly used tests are poorly designed for them, and many evaluators lack training or experience in testing these students. Nevertheless, two indicators of intellectual functioning in these students are their academic skills and levels of awareness.

Functional academic skills are skills that students need to function independently in the community.

Academic Skills.   Students with severe multiple disabilities vary widely in their academic skills. Some students develop **functional academic skills** such as how to count dollar bills, find items in a grocery store, and read a recipe (Browder & Snell, 1993). Other students' disabilities are so pervasive that the focus of their educational program may be on learning to make eye contact, track objects with their eyes, and expand their range of motion. As is true with many individuals with severe and multiple disabilities, Joshua does not read, write, or perform traditional academic tasks.

According to Piaget's stages of development, many students with severe disabilities function cognitively at the early childhood sensorimotor stage of development (Siegel-Causey, Guy, & Guess, 1992).

Level of Awareness.   Another characteristic of persons with extensive intellectual impairment is their limited level of awareness (Richards & Sternberg, 1994). Their limited levels of awareness can range from having a short attention span to being unresponsive to people, noise, movement, touch, odors, or other stimuli in their environment. Those with the most extensive intellectual disabilities may spend a large portion of their day sleeping, crying, or engaging in stereotypic behavior. Yet even for students with significantly limited levels of awareness, periods of time can occur throughout the day when they are alert and interested in what is going on around them (Guess, Roberts, Siegel-Causey, & Rues, 1995).

Adaptive Behaviors.   As you will remember from Chapter 8, adaptive behaviors are the skills needed to live and work in the community. Two of the ten categories of adap-

 Even though Joshua cannot communicate verbally, he does interact socially in other typical and appropriate ways.

tive behaviors, as defined by the American Association on Mental Retardation (AAMR) (Luckasson et al., 1992), are especially relevant for individuals with severe and multiple disabilities: self-care skills and social skills.

Self-care Skills. The majority of these individuals can attain some level of independence in caring for their own needs (Snell & Farlow, 1993). Their school and adult programs include instruction in such self-care skills as dressing, personal hygiene, toileting, feeding, and simple household chores. Joshua needs assistance with all of his self-care skills but is learning to feed himself.

For some students with pervasive support needs, the goal is not to perform self-care skills independently but to participate to the fullest extent possible when being assisted. This might mean staying alert while eating, not crying while having their teeth brushed, and making eye contact when being dressed.

Social Skills. Many individuals with severe and multiple disabilities do not have typical social interactions with others. Some are withdrawn; some with pervasive support needs can be unaware of people around them. Joshua is aware of the people around him, and although he is unable to verbally communicate with them, demonstrates his pleasure by smiling and seems to have an understanding of what is said to him. While his social interactions are generally not typical, some interactions, such as the exchange of school pictures, are.

A common misunderstanding is that individuals with severe and multiple disabilities always exhibit inappropriate social interactions. In fact, in successful heterogeneous schools, teachers, family, and friends often describe ways in which they have participated in **reciprocal friendships** with individuals with severe and multiple disabilities (Amado, 1993; Bishop, Jubala, Stainback, & Stainback, 1996; Falvey & Rosenberg, 1995). "Making a Difference," Box 9–1, describes a friendship between Meili, a twelve-year-old with severe cerebral palsy and mental retardation, and her friend Carolyn, who does not have a disability.

Social skills often determine the success or failure of students' interpersonal, employment, and independent living adjustment (Aveno, 1987; Chadsey-Rusch, 1990; Kennedy,

A reciprocal friendship is one in which both individuals **contribute** to and benefit from the exchanges of support.

Have you ever had a friend with a severe and multiple disability? How would you characterize the reciprocity in your relationship? Were there opportunities to experience such a friendship that you decided to not pursue? What stood in the way of your taking the initiative to be friends?

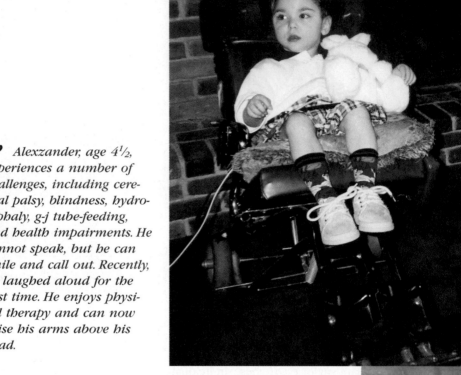

🐚 *Alexzander, age 4½, experiences a number of challenges, including cerebral palsy, blindness, hydrocephaly, g-j tube-feeding, and health impairments. He cannot speak, but he can smile and call out. Recently, he laughed aloud for the first time. He enjoys physical therapy and can now raise his arms above his head.*

Horner, & Newton, 1990). Having opportunities to participate in extracurricular and inclusive community activities increases the likelihood that these students will develop friendships such as the one that Meili and Carolyn have (Moon, 1994; Turnbull, Pereira, & Blue-Banning, 1997; Schleien, Green, & Heyne, 1993).

Motor Development.   Individuals with severe and multiple disabilities usually exhibit a significant delay in motor development. Their sensorimotor impairments often result in abnormal muscle tone. Some will have floppy and underdeveloped muscle tone, but others will have increased muscle tension and extremely tight muscles. Any abnormal muscle tone can interfere with the ability to perform functional tasks successfully (Campbell, 1993).

Despite their delayed motor development, many students with severe and multiple disabilities learn to walk with assistance. Joshua uses a wheelchair for mobility. He is able to hold up his head, and his range of motion is better on his left side than his right. Many students like him develop secondary physical disabilities and **muscle atrophy** (Heller, Alberto, Forney, & Schwartzman, 1996). Muscle atrophy is the wasting away and reduction of the muscle, usually from a disease, injury, or lack of use. Joshua has been working hard to build overall strength and muscle control.

Muscle atrophy is the wasting away and reduction of the muscle, usually from a disease, injury, or lack of use.

Sensory Impairments   Hearing and vision impairments are common among individuals with severe and multiple disabilities (Utley, 1994). Indeed, two of every five students with severe and multiple disabilities typically have sensory impairments (Sobsey & Wolf-Schein, 1991). (Chapters 15 and 16 give you more information about hearing and vision impairments.)

BOX 9-1 MAKING A DIFFERENCE

"GIVE ME MORE"

What do two preteen girls do together when they are best friends? To hear Carolyn tell it, they do pretty much what every other pair of close friends do. "We visit each other. We talk. We play around. Make stuff. Sing along with tapes. Sometimes I go over and read with my friend, Meili."

Carolyn has no disabilities, but Meili has both cerebral palsy and mental retardation. Carolyn learned early on that the disability is a distinction but it doesn't matter. That was a lesson she learned from her mother, who provides personal care assistance for Meili.

At her mother's suggestion, Carolyn introduced herself to Meili at school, "Hi, I'm Carolyn. My mother takes care of you." The two "just clicked." Big for her age and from a foreign country, Carolyn knew what it meant to feel "pushed aside" (as her mother puts it). "She knows," says Carolyn's mother, "Meili is against all odds, too." From that common experience grew a close friendship. "Now," says Carolyn, "it's like we are family."

Meili, whose speech is hard to understand, nevertheless wholeheartedly agrees. Asked how she feels about Carolyn, she struggles to get the words out, but succeeds: "Give me more." That's her way of expressing her happiness.

Note: From *Amistad: Stories of Hispanic Children with Disabilities and Their Friendships*, by the Beach Center on Families and Disability, The University of Kansas, Lawrence. Copyright 1997 by the Beach Center on Families and Disabilities. Reprinted with permission.

Students who are deaf-blind constitute a particularly challenging group. Individuals defined as deaf-blind

> *may experience diverse combinations of vision and hearing impairments with normal or gifted intelligence or they may have additional mental, physical, and behavioral disabilities. . . . Because these individuals do not receive clear and consistent information from either sensory modality, a tendency exists to turn inward to obtain the desired level of stimulation. The individual may appear passive, nonresponsive, and/or noncompliant. Students with dual sensory impairments may not respond to or initiate appropriate interactions with others and often exhibit behavior that is considered socially inappropriate. (Downing & Eichinger, 1990)*

> IDEA distinguishes students with severe and multiple disabilities from those who are deaf-blind.

Although the Helen Keller National Center estimates that approximately 40,000 persons are deaf-blind in the United States (Ingraham, Davis, Carey, Danek, & Watson, 1996; McNulty, 1990), the U.S. Department of Education (1996) reports that approximately 1,300 students with deaf blindness (ages six to twenty-one) were served under the IDEA during the 1994 to 1995 school year. Approximately half of these students were served in public or private day or residential facilities (U.S. Department of Education, 1996).

Health Care Needs. Individuals with severe and multiple disabilities frequently experience health care problems (Ault, Graff, & Rues, 1993). As students with health care needs increasingly attend neighborhood schools, teachers and other school staff are carrying out procedures that in the past were the responsibility of medical professionals, such as clean intermittent catheterization, gastrostomy tube feeding, respiratory ventilation, and the administration of medications for seizures, hyperactivity, and muscle relaxation (Graff, Ault, Guess, Taylor, & Thompson, 1990; Haslam & Valletulli, 1996; Levy & O'Rourke, 1997). **Clean intermittent catheterization** (CIC) involves inserting a catheter (tube) into the urethra to the bladder to drain off urine for collection in a basin (you will read about CIC and Jimmy Chipman in Chapter 12). **Gastrostomy** tube feeding, used with individuals who cannot ingest adequate nutrition through oral feeding, means feeding the individual through a tube that directly enters the stomach. **Respiratory ventilation,** which is necessary for individuals who accumulate large amounts of mucus in their respiratory tract, involves suctioning mucus by machine inserted into the student's lungs through a small

> **Clean intermittent catheterization** involves inserting a catheter into the urethra to the bladder to drain off urine for collection in a basin.

> **Gastrostomy tube feeding** involves feeding an individual through a tube that directly enters the intestine.

> **Respiratory ventilation** involves suctioning mucus from the respiratory tract through a small tube.

tube. Students who use these kinds of medical aids challenge school systems. IDEA entitles them to school health services (as a type of related services). These services, however, require schools to maintain a child's health so the child can attend school.

Communication Skills.
Students with severe and multiple disabilities frequently experience communication challenges (Reichle, 1997). Being unable to speak, however, does not mean that they cannot communicate. In fact, professionals, friends, and families alike have found that even those students with the most pervasive support needs can and do communicate with others through eye movements, touching, facial expressions, gesturing, or using **augmentative and alternative communication** such as communication boards or computers (Goetz & Hunt, 1994; Johnson, Baumgart, Helmstetter, & Curry, 1996). The critical factor is the communication partner's ability to identify and correctly interpret a student's particular method of communication.

Joshua does not possess a formal system of communication. To express himself, he uses a series of sounds and kicks his legs. Joshua is almost always happy. On those rare occasions when he appears to be unhappy, he will cry, challenging his teachers to try to figure out what he needs. Is he in pain? Is he hungry? Too hot or cold? Usually, this process is similar to the way a parent figures out, through trial and error, what their baby needs when it cries. Trial and error will not do for the future, so Joshua's teachers are helping to lay the groundwork for his future use of an augmentative communication device.

Identifying the Causes of Severe and Multiple Disabilities

Identifying an exact cause of severe and multiple disabilities can be difficult. In fact, there is no identifiable cause for these disabilities in an estimated 40 percent of all children born with them (McLaren & Bryson, 1987). The majority of known causes, however, relate to prenatal biomedical factors. They include chromosomal abnormalities (which you learned about in Chapter 8), genetic metabolic disorders, developmental disorders of brain formation, and prenatal environmental influences (which we discuss in Chapter 11). In addition, complications during birth (perinatal causes) and after birth (postnatal causes) account for many of these disabilities. In this chapter you will learn about the prenatal biomedical causes of genetic metabolic disorders and disorders of brain formation.

Genetic Metabolic Disorders.
Abnormalities in a parent's genes can cause a disorder in a child's metabolism (Batshaw, 1997a, 1997b; Coulter, 1994). **Metabolism** is important for body functions such as energy, growth, and waste disposal (Glanze, Anderson, & Anderson, 1985). A parent does not have to have a particular disorder to pass the problem gene on to the child if the abnormal gene is recessive. A dominant gene always produces the presence of the trait. A recessive gene, however, is masked, or hidden, and it requires the presence of another recessive gene to produce the trait.

If both parents carry the recessive gene for a disorder, then the child has a 25 percent chance of being affected by the disorder (Batshaw, 1997a). A recessive gene might be passed on for generations before anyone develops the disorder because it may take that long for two recessive genes to meet. Figure 9-2 illustrates the inheritance pattern for recessive genes. An example of a recessively inherited error of metabolism that can result in severe and multiple disabilities is phenylketonuria (PKU). PKU occurs when there is a build up of a group of chemicals—phenylketones. If one parent actually has a disease and is not just carrying a recessive gene, then the gene is dominant (see Figure 9-3). In this case, the child has a 50 percent chance of developing the disorder. If both parents have the dominant gene, the disease can be fatal for the child.

The genetic metabolic abnormalities most frequently associated with severe and multiple disabilities cause a dysfunction in the production of **enzymes** that the body needs (Batshaw, 1997a). Enzymes that have not been converted to a useful substance accumulate to toxic levels, thus damaging physical and mental development.

Augmentative and alternative communication are techniques and devices used by students to supplement whatever degree of naturally acquired speech they possess. (You will learn more about augmentative and alternative communication in Chapter 12.)

Metabolism refers to the body's chemical processes that help break down toxins (poisons) and move nutrients through the bloodstream.

Enzymes are proteins that cause or speed up chemical reactions.

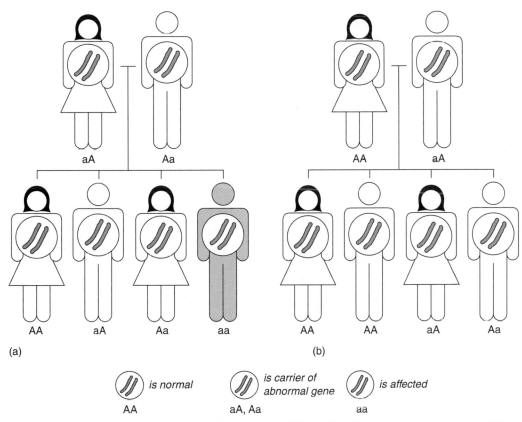

Note: From "Heredity: A Toss of the Dice," by M. L. Batshaw, in *Children With Disabilities* (4th ed.), edited by M. L. Batshaw, 1997, Baltimore: Paul H. Brookes Publishing Company, P.O. Box 10624, Baltimore, MD 21285-0624. Copyright 1997 by Mark L. Batshaw. Reprinted with permission.

FIGURE 9–2 *Inheritance of autosomal recessive disorders. Two copies of the abnormal gene (aa) must be present to produce the disease state. (A) Two carriers mating will result, on average, in 25% of the children being unaffected, 50% being carriers, and 25% being affected. (B) A carrier and a noncarrier mate, resulting in 50% normal children and 50% carriers. No children are affected.*

Disorders of Brain Formation.   The congenital defects that most commonly lead to severe and multiple disabilities result from disruptions in the development of the brain and spinal cord (Coulter, 1994). When disruptions occur, structural abnormalities result, with the brain being malformed, having missing elements, or being too small (Lynch & Batshaw, 1997). As you read in the opening vignette, Joshua's disability was caused by a disorder of brain formation called **encephalocele**. Joshua also was affected by **amniotic band syndrome.** This is a condition in which the fibrous bands on the outside of the placenta contract around the baby and restrict normal growth and development. Because of this, Joshua was born without a big toe on his left foot, two fingers on his right hand are misshapen, and one finger on his right hand is missing.

Encephalocele is a rare disorder in which one is born with an opening in the skull from which membranes that cover the brain and brain tissue protrude. The opening may be covered by skin and/or membrane of varying thickness.

Preventing Severe and Multiple Disabilities.   Many factors can cause severe and multiple disabilities. Given the current level of medical technology, some, but not all, are preventable. Advances in prenatal testing, such as amniocentesis, chorionic villi sampling, and ultrasound, can help to identify and possibly prevent multiple disabilities (Batshaw & Rose, 1997; Bowe, 1995). Figure 9–4 describes chorionic villi sampling and ultrasound.

The ultimate goal of prenatal diagnosis is to identify and treat the developing child before or immediately after birth. Prenatal fetal therapy, such as in-utero surgery, is rapidly expanding through medical research. A recent breakthrough involved transplanting bone marrow from a father into a sixteen-week-old fetus who was found through prenatal testing to have a severe immunodeficiency (referred to in the popular literature as the "Bubble Baby" syndrome). The bone marrow transplant was successful, and the baby, who was eleven months at the time of the report, was healthy and did not require ongoing therapy (Flake, Roncarolo, Puck, et al., 1996, reported in Batshaw & Rose, 1997).

Amniotic band syndrome is a condition in which fibrous bands on the outside of the placenta contract and restrict normal growth and development of the fetus.

FIGURE 9–3 *Inheritance of autosomal dominant disorders. Only one copy of the abnormal gene (A) must be present to produce the disease state. (A) An affected person marries an unaffected person. Statistically, 50% of the children will be affected and 50% will be unaffected. (B) If two affected people marry, 25% of the children will be unaffected, 50% will be affected, and 25% will have an often fatal double dose of the abnormal gene.*

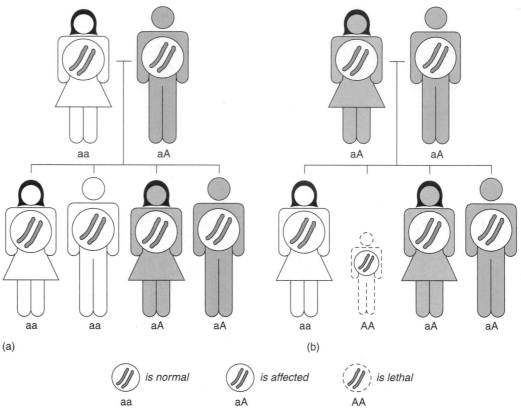

Note: From "Heredity: A Toss of the Dice," by M. L. Batshaw, in *Children With Disabilities* (4th ed.), edited by M. L. Batshaw, 1997, Baltimore: Paul H. Brookes Publishing Company, P.O. Box 10624, Baltimore, MD 21285-0624. Coypright 1997 by Mark L. Batshaw. Reprinted with permission.

Routine postnatal screenings can detect a variety of genetic, metabolic, and viral infections. For example, all children are screened for PKU, a metabolic disorder. If detected early, a child born with PKU can be placed on a special diet to reduce the risk of mental and physical disabilities. In Box 9–2, "Making a Difference," you will read about one physician's very significant contributions to PKU detection and prevention. Other medical advances such as routine immunization for rubella have all but eliminated some congenital infections that lead to severe and multiple disabilities. Medical research will no doubt continue to develop effective vaccines for other infectious diseases that can lead to these disabilities.

Maternal education is another important component of prevention, as you learned in Chapter 8. Early prenatal care includes teaching women of child-bearing age who suspect they might be pregnant to avoid certain environmental influences such as drugs, alcohol, and exposure to lead. Genetic counseling also is helpful for identifying and preventing genetic disorders. The purpose of genetic counseling is to identify the genetic cause of a disorder and to determine the risk of occurrence (Carey, 1997). When individuals at high risk for genetically caused disabilities are identified, methods are increasingly available to mitigate the effects of the disorder. For conditions whose treatment or prenatal genetic identification are not yet available, options for genetic prevention include contraception, adoption, or artificial insemination.

Identifying the Prevalence of Severe and Multiple Disabilities

How many people are classified as having severe and multiple disabilities? No one really knows for sure. The disparities in prevalence data arise out of the differences in the definitions of severe and multiple disabilities. Moreover, some states classify students as hav-

Recall that there are different definitions of multiple disabilities and severe disabilities, described earlier.

Real-time Ultrasound	• Noninvasive procedure in which sound waves are sent into the womb.
	• The sound waves bounce off the fetus and provide a picture-like image of the unborn baby.
	• Procedure is used to obtain assessment of baby's size and development, thereby enabling the physician to make a more accurate estimation of due date.
Chorionic villi sampling	• Certain structural abnormalities can be detected, such as spina bifida, hydrocephalus, and congenital heart disease.
	• A small sample of placenta is obtained for chromosomal, genetic, DNA analysis, and biochemical studies.
	• Advantages over amniocentesis: results from the chromosomal analysis are available within a few hours; can be performed much earlier in the pregnancy.
Percutaneous umbilical blood sampling	• Needle is inserted through abdominal and uterine walls and into the umbilical vein.
	• Fetal blood is sampled.
	• Used to detect infections, anemia, and blood type.

FIGURE 9–4 *Prenatal tests*

ing severe and multiple disabilities, and others classify them as having one of the primary disabilities (e.g., mental retardation or physical disability) (Brimer, 1990). When considering what proportion of the general population has severe and multiple disabilities, "any figure is open to debate and is at best an educated guess" (Brimer, 1990).

Nevertheless, the U.S. Department of Education (1996) reported that 89,144 students ages six to twenty-one were served in 1994 to 1995 under IDEA's programs for students with *multiple* disabilities. This number represents 1.6 percent of all students in this age group who were served in IDEA programs. What about the category of *severe* disabilities?

RACE FOR A MIRACLE

In "Race for a Miracle," Brad and Vicki Margus, parents of two sons with a rare genetic disease called ataxia telangiectasia, share their determination to help solve the genetic mysteries surrounding their sons' conditions. Dr. Francis Collins says of Brad and Vicki, ". . . . it's the nobility of the human spirit," in referring to their effort to seek the cause of the disease that causes a gradual neurological deterioration. Two other parents, Richard and Lori Riggins, try a new gene therapy procedure to reduce the risk of their child being born with another genetic condition: Severe Combined Immune Deficiency.

Vicki Margus explains why so many parents of children with disabilities are willing to make such risks and sacrifices: "Never in my wildest dreams could we know how much you could love someone until you have these children. And there's nothing that we wouldn't do for them. . . ."

What do you think? Parents are frequently the leaders in achieving new standards of medical and educational care for their children with disabilities. What does this suggest about how teachers should respond to parents' attempts to advocate for their children when those attempts go against the grain of current policy?

How might gene therapy affect the prevalence of severe and multiple disabilities?

Do you have ethical concerns about current genetic research? Why or why not?

BOX 9-2   **MAKING A DIFFERENCE**

BOB GUTHRIE, THE GREAT PREVENTER

Bob Guthrie was multitalented and multifaceted. As a professional, he held a doctorate in biology and chemistry; he also earned his medical degree. As a man, he was the father of a son, John, who had severe mental retardation; unable to find the cause of John's disability, he was particularly sensitive to the needs of families affected by disability and to society's needs to eradicate the biological causes of mental retardation. And, as a scientist-father, he was an indomitable proselytizer for prevention of mental retardation. In that role, he was particularly well qualified.

He demonstrated how safe and simple it was to obtain blood specimens from a pin-prick to the heel of a newborn baby and put those blood spots on filter paper—the now-famous "Guthrie cards" that made early diagnosis so easy.

He also developed the means for testing for phenylalanine in the blood spot. This test, called a bacterial inhibition assay for phenylketonuria (PKU), was a specific means for testing for a condition that, if not corrected by diet, usually resulted in severe mental retardation. Finally, he was a world-travelled evangelist who, through persistence coupled with scientific evidence, persuaded state after state, indeed, country after country, to adopt procedures for early detection of PKU and other disabling conditions.

By the time he died in 1995, just a few days shy of his seventy-ninth birthday, Bob Guthrie was universally acknowledged as a humble man but a giant in the history of medicine and disability. Making a difference means, among other things, having a cause to which to commit oneself wholly and the competence to carry out one's cause. Bob Guthrie had both.

Bob Guthrie developed a system to detect phenylketonuria (PKU) using a dropsize blood sample on the special filter paper shown here. Nearly all newborn babies in the United States now undergo this test.

PKU TESTING CENTER
for
INBORN ERRORS OF METABOLISM

PKU ☐ MSUD ☐ GAL ☐ OTHER: _____

FIRST SPECIMEN   No. **G   7394**

Hospital _____

Hosp. No. _____ Premature ☐ Full Term ☐

Infant's Name: (Male ☐ Female ☐)

Baby's Doctor _____

Birth Date _____ Time _____

Birth Weight _____ Lbs. _____ Oz.

Date of First Feeding _____ Time _____

Baby Feeding: Well ☐   Poorly ☐

                       Breast ☐   Bottle ☐   Both ☐

Present Weight _____ Lbs. _____ Oz.

Date of Specimen _____ Time _____

**COMPLETELY FILL ALL CIRCLES WITH BLOOD
SOAK THRU FROM REVERSE SIDE**

It is important to recognize that many students with *severe* disabilities also have *multiple* disabilities. So the prevalence of severe and multiple disabilities appears to be between 1 percent and 1.6 percent of students served under IDEA.

WHAT ARE EVALUATION PROCEDURES?

As you will recall from Chapter 2, IDEA's nondiscriminatory evaluation process determines whether the student has a disability and, if so, what the student's special education and related services needs are (see Figure 9-5).

Determining the Presence of a Disability

For the most part, infants with severe and multiple disabilities are detected at birth through the screening process that physicians are required to perform on all newborns. The physician checks for observable disabilities, genetic and metabolic disorders, and potential developmental problems. An example of a screening process for newborns is the Apgar test (Evans, 1997). The physician ranks the child on five physical traits (heart rate, respiratory effort, muscle tone, gag reflex, and skin color) at one minute and at five minutes after birth. The newborn receives a score of 0, 1, or 2 for each trait. Physicians assume that children with cumulative scores below 4 are more at risk to have disabilities (Evans, 1997). Table 9-1 shows examples of the Apgar score. In Table 9-1, David is substantially more at risk than Michael for having disabilities.

Once an Apgar screening is complete and assuming that the infant's Apgar score reveals potential complications, the next step is to conduct more precise and thorough testing to identify the nature of the disability, possible causes, and the extent of the disabling conditions. This kind of diagnostic testing involves medical and physical examinations that are usually done over a period of several years to determine the extent of neurological impairments, sensory deficits, concurrent medical needs, and motor involvement (Batshaw & Shapiro, 1997; Coulter, 1994; Heller et al., 1996).

TABLE 9–1 ⊗ *The Apgar scoring system*

	Points			Score			
				1 minute		5 minutes	
	0	**1**	**2**	**Michael**	**David**	**Michael**	**David**
Heart rate	Absent	Less than 100	More than 100	2	0	2	1
Respiratory effort	Absent	Slow, irregular	Normal respiration, crying	2	0	2	1
Muscle tone	Limp	Some flexion	Active motion	1	0	2	1
Gag reflex	No response	Grimace	Sneeze; cough	2	0	2	1
Color	Blue all over; pale	Blue extremities	Pink all over	1	0	2	1
			Totals	8	0	10	5

Note: From "The First Weeks of Life," by J. R. Evans, in *Children With Disabilities* (4th ed., pp 93–114), edited by M. L. Batshaw, 1997, Baltimore, Paul H. Brookes Publishing Company. Copyright 1997 by Paul H. Brookes Publishing Company, P.O. Box 10624, Baltimore, MD 21285-0624. Reprinted with permission.

FIGURE 9–5 *Evaluating whether a student has severe and multiple disabilities*

```
                        ⬭ Nondiscriminatory Evaluation ⬭
```

Observation

Physician/medical professional observes	The newborn may have noticeable disabilities associated with a syndrome or may have medical complications that are often associated with severe disabilities.
Parents observe	The child has difficulties with nursing, sleeping, or attaining developmental milestones.

Medical screening

Assessment measures	Findings that indicate need for further evaluation
Newborn screening measures such as the Apgar	Apgar scores are below 4, indicating possibility of severe disabilities.
Genetic evaluations	Evaluation leads to identification of genetic cause.
Physical examinations	Medical procedures including vision and hearing tests, blood work, metabolic tests, spinal tests, etc., reveal presence of disabling condition.

Prereferral

Prereferral is typically not used with this population, because the severity of the disability indicates need for special education and related services.

Referral

Children with severe and multiple disabilities should be referred by medical personnel or parents for early intervention during the infancy/preschool years. Many states have Child Find organizations to make sure these children receive services. The child is referred upon reaching school age.

Nondiscriminatory evaluation procedures and standards

Assessment measures	Findings that suggest severe and multiple disabilities
Individualized intelligence test	Student scores at least two standard deviations below the mean (70 to 75 or lower), indicating that mental retardation exists. Most students with severe and multiple disabilities have IQ scores that are significantly below 70, indicating severe cognitive impairment.
Adaptive behavior scales	The student scores significantly below average in two or more areas of adaptive behaviors, indicating severe deficits in skills such as communication, daily living, socialization, gross- and fine-motor coordination, and behavior.
Profiles of intensity of needed support	The student rates in the extensive to pervasive level of support in the majority of areas: communication, self-care, social skills, home living, community use, self-direction, health, and safety.

```
   Nondiscriminatory Evaluation Team determines that student has severe and multiple
        disabilities and needs special education and related services.

                          ⬭ Appropriate Education ⬭
```

Determining the Nature and Extent of Special Education and Related Services

It is important to identify those who have severe and multiple disabilities as soon after birth as possible. The evaluation team will probably rely heavily on the physicians' diagnoses and recommendations but will also perform its own evaluation. The teams typically administer a standardized intelligence test and adaptive behavior measures (see Chapters 2 and 8). As we pointed out earlier, standardized intelligence tests arguably are invalid for most individuals with severe and multiple disabilities (Linehan, Brady, & Hwang, 1991), primarily because the psychologist may be inexperienced in testing students with severe and multiple disabilities and will conclude that the student is untestable when, in fact, the test is not suitable for the student's physical or behavioral differences (Browder, 1991; F. Brown & Snell, 1993a). Indeed, some professionals have argued that "IQ tests, as currently constituted, have no place in the assessment of individuals with severe intellectual disabilities" (Evans, 1991). Nevertheless, standardized intelligence tests continue to carry significant weight during the nondiscriminatory evaluation process (Browder, 1991; Linehan et al., 1991).

Four approaches can be used to assess a student's skills for specific curriculum goals and program development: developmental, ecological, behavioral states, and Making Action Plans (see Table 9–2).

Developmental Model.   Traditionally, the evaluation of students with severe and multiple disabilities has borrowed heavily from a developmental approach. Under this approach, the teacher assesses a student by administering one or more norm-referenced tests or standardized developmental checklists (designed for children without disabilities). Most of the norm-referenced tests that are used for students with severe and multiple disabilities have been normed for students younger than the students for whom they are being used (Sigafoos, Cole, & McQuarter, 1987).

Developmental checklists require the teacher to indicate whether the student lacks specified developmental milestones and skills. The teacher targets the first skill item that a student cannot perform for instruction. Then the teacher instructs the student in skills that are arranged into specific developmental sequences from the targeted skill. This evaluation-and-teaching approach assumes that until students acquire a particular skill, they cannot learn a higher-level skill. Thus, developmentalists assume that a child must crawl before he or she can walk.

Several problems occur when using this approach for students with severe and multiple disabilities. First, these children may not develop in the same "normal" sequence as children without disabilities. In fact, many may never acquire certain developmental skills because their limitations are so extensive. Second, this approach assumes that the students have to possess certain skills before they can acquire "higher-level" ones. To teach these prerequisite skills, teachers might instruct and help the student develop skills that are neither age-appropriate nor functional. Third, this approach emphasizes the form of the skill rather than its function (White, 1985). Students who fail the eye–hand coordination test might be required to put pegs in pegboards to learn this skill. This precludes teaching them the same skill in a functional context, such as putting coins into a vending machine, putting silverware into the dishwasher, or turning on a tape recorder.

Ecological Model.   In response to problems associated with the developmental model, educators in the late 1970s began to focus their attention on a different approach to educational assessment (L. Brown et al., 1979). Professionals have now refined this method—**ecological assessment**—to reliably assess the needs of students with severe and multiple disabilities (F. Brown & Snell, 1993a; Fredericks & Brodsky, 1994).

There is a major difference between the developmental and ecological approaches. In a developmental approach, the teacher considers what particular skills the student needs in order to perform a particular behavior. In an ecological approach, the teacher examines

Ecological assessment involves examining environments within which a student is expected to function and identifying the specific activities and skills that the student needs to participate successfully there. Those activities and skills become the basis for assessment.

TABLE 9–2 ⚮ *Comparison of assessment methods*

	Developmental Model	Ecological Model	Behavior States	Making Action Plans
Overview of approach	• Uses a "bottom–up" approach • Compares students with severe disabilities with development of infants • Developmental skills checklists are used to target skill areas • Skills are arranged in sequence; students must acquire target skill prior to moving to next skill level • Curricular areas include language/cognitive, social/emotional, gross and fine motor skills, self-help skills	• Uses a "top–down" approach • Examines environments within which students are to function • Targets specific skills and activities within each environment for instruction • Takes into account issues of partial participation and use of adaptations	• Identifies levels of awareness and responsiveness of students with severe and multiple disabilities • Calculates amount of time throughout the day in behavior states of asleep, drowsy, dazed, awake inactive, awake active/alert, self-stimulatory, crying/agitated, seizure	• Uses a broad collaborative network for creative brainstorming • Customizes student's educational program by focusing on vision, strengths, preferences, and needs • Focuses on comprehensive lifestyle enhancement

Examples of approach	*Curricular area:* Motor
	   Skill: Eye–hand coordination
	   Activities:
	     • Put pegs in pegboard
	     • Put rings on dowel
	     • String beads
	     • Stack blocks
	Curricular area: Self-help
	   Skill: Identify body parts
	     • Point to body parts on dolls/in pictures
	     • Names body parts from pictures
		Curricular domain: Community
		   Environment: Grocery store
		   Subenvironment: Aisles
		   Activity: Locating grocery items on shelves
		   Skills:
		     • Move down aisles
		     • Locate section of aisle
		     • Locate item on shelf
		     • Remove item from shelf
		     • Place item in cart
		Adaptations:
		     • Picture grocery list
		     • Device to grasp items out of reach
		     • Use bag instead of cart
			Behavior state: Awake active/alert
			   Environment: playground
			   Goal: 10 minutes in awake active alert state
			   Target behaviors:
			     • Reach out for ball
			     • Look in direction of peers playing
			     • Do not drowse
			     • Vocalize when asked direct questions
				Ideal day: Spend time after school with friends
				   Setting: Neighborhood, community
				   Goal: To "hang out" at the community rec center two afternoons per week
				   Curricular area: Home economics, physical education, music
				   Activities: Dance to popular music, operate a CD, prepare microwave popcorn

the environments (ecologies) within which a student is expected to function and then identifies the specific activities and skills the student needs to participate successfully there. In turn, the student is assessed on those specific activities and skills.

The type of assessment can influence the nature of the curriculum and placement for students with severe and multiple disabilities. As contrasted to educators who use developmental assessment, educators who use ecological assessment to formulate the students' individualized education programs (IEPs) typically have higher expectations for students' capability of mastering functional skills (Linehan et al., 1991) and are more likely to recommend more typical educational and vocational placements (Linehan & Brady, 1995).

Behavior States.   A third assessment process for students with severe and multiple disabilities seeks to identify their levels of awareness and responsiveness—their behavior states (Ault, Guy, Guess, Bashinski, & Roberts, 1995; Guess et al., 1995). The assessment of behavior states focuses on five physiological and behavioral conditions:

- Dazed

- Drowsy

- Awake/alert

- Agitated/crying

- Stereotyped

Using this method, teachers can determine when students are most alert and responsive to instruction. Then they can develop intervention strategies to increase a student's ability to stay awake and alert and they also can schedule the interventions at the student's optimal learning times. This approach is geared toward the student's learning characteristics (Guess, Roberts, Halvoet, & Rues, 1997).

Making Action Plans.   Making Action Plans is a structured, problem-solving process for customizing students' educational programs to their specific visions, strengths, and needs (Falvey, Forest, Pearpoint, & Rosenberg, 1994; Forest & Lusthaus, 1989; Gage & Falvey, 1995). The MAPs process can involve the required members of evaluation teams, but it usually also includes the student, peers, parents and other family members, and friends. The facilitator of the process may be any one of these individuals and needs to ensure a positive brainstorming process to generate as many creative ideas as possible. The brainstorming generally follows eight key questions.

> *Question 1:* What is a MAPs? *At the beginning of the meeting the facilitator explains the purpose of the process, questions that will be asked and the general ground rules for open-ended and creative problem solving. The facilitator especially tries to create an upbeat, energized, and relational ambience.*
>
> *Question 2:* What is the student's history or story? *Typically, the student and family share background information, highlighting the triumphs and challenges that have been associated with the student's having a preference-based way to live his or her life.*
>
> *Question 3:* What are your dreams? *It is especially important for students to share their great expectations for the future. Families also should share their dreams and great expectations and supplement what the student is saying if the student cannot or chooses not to communicate with the group members. The key aspect of the MAPs process is to identify these dreams and great expectations as the basis for planning the customized school schedule and extracurricular activities.*

Question 4: What are your nightmares? *Because students with exceptionalities and their families often have major fears that serve as barriers to their working toward great expectations, identifying nightmares lets everyone know what those are so they can put adequate supports into place. Some nightmares cannot be prevented, such as the progressive course of a chronic illness, but sharing them can help everyone know issues around which the student will need support.*

Question 5: Who is this person? *The group will use as many adjectives as it takes to get behind the exceptionality label and describe the real or essential aspects of the student's personhood.*

Question 6: What are the person's strengths, gifts, and talents? *Many times teachers, friends, family members, and others can lose sight of the characteristics that the person can bring to bear to achieve the great expectations. So the MAPs meeting takes the time to identify them.*

Question 7: What does the person need? *What will it take to make the student's and family's dreams and great expectations come true? What barriers stand in the way of where the student is at the present time and having the dreams come true? Identifying these needs can serve as the basis for educational programming.*

Question 8: What would the student's ideal day look like, and what must be done to make it happen? *This question needs to generate some "next steps" that need to happen in order to accomplish the dream. The "next steps" might be of a more general nature and be used to guide specific planning of the IEP committee. Another alternative is for the "next steps" to be more specific and detailed— more like a plan of action. This plan of action can involve tasks, time lines, resources, and any other detailed information that will help lead to significant progress. (Turnbull & Turnbull, 1997, pp. 169-170)*

Figure 9-6 illustrates the MAPs process for Libby Bridge, to whom you will be introduced in the section on inclusion and collaboration.

WHAT AND HOW DO PROFESSIONALS TEACH?

Curriculum

The **ecological curriculum** approach is conceptually similar to the ecological assessment approach that you learned about earlier in the chapter. Ecological curriculum involves identifying the environment within which a student is expected to function and the specific activities and skills that the student will need to be successful there. Those activities and skills become the basis for instruction.

Until the late 1970s, only a few curricular materials had been specifically designed for students with severe and multiple disabilities. Most often, teachers borrowed from the developmental approach (which we described earlier in this chapter), targeting the following skill areas: language/cognitive development, social/emotional development, motor development, and self-help skill development.

Since the mid-1980s, however, new curriculum guides, differing sharply from the developmental approach, have been developed. Emphasizing the **ecological curriculum** approach, these guides focus on identifying the skills and activities the students need in order to participate successfully in the environments where they are expected to live and work (Ford et al., 1989; Neel & Billingsley, 1989; Wilcox & Bellamy, 1987). These curriculum guides adhere to a similar set of values and principles, first described by Brown and his colleagues in the 1970s (L. Brown et al., 1979).

An ecological curriculum approach is similar to the life-skills curriculum that you learned about in Chapter 8. As you may recall, the key to this kind of curriculum is to identify the adult domains, subdomains, and specific life skills as a basis for organizing instruction. These same steps are appropriate in planning an ecological curriculum.

In the literature about students with mild and moderate retardation, the terms *life-skills curriculum* or *functional curriculum* are often used. In the literature related to students with severe disabilities, the same general approach is referred to as an ecological curriculum.

An ecological curriculum is justified by research that reports that parents of students with moderate and severe/profound disabilities prefer them to spend the largest percentage of their school week learning functional life skills (Hamre-Nietupski, 1993) and, next, to acquire academic skills and then friendship/social relationships.

FIGURE 9–6 *Libby's MAPs meeting, March 11, 1996*

Libby's History

Eleven years old.

Has two sisters, Hilary and Hayley, ages 9 and 4.

Libby has always been in the right place at the right time—has never had a bad educational experience.

Good start at infant development center with physical therapy and speech therapy.

First attended KU Preschool and received physical therapy, occupational therapy, and speech therapy. At the same time, attended an inclusive program two mornings a week at a Montessori preschool close to home.

Started elementary school at Whittier Elementary School's "reverse integration" program; moved to White Church's inclusion program when it began.

Has always had good teachers and paraprofessionals.

Our Dreams for Libby

Learn more

Talk, communicate

Do things by herself, more independent

Aware of relationships

Know that kids care for her

Sing

Fine motor skills improved

Connect sounds with speech

Communicate with kids

Supportive, caring environment

Say Hilary's name

Consistency in learning progress

Live with friends when adult and have job

More independent in self-care needs

Our Nightmares for Libby

Will have to go to hospital (seriously hurt)

Falling down stairs

Won't get to go to school with her friends

Be frustrated by her limitations

Being unhappy

Not progressing with walking skills

Quit trying

Having worse seizures

Who will give continued support?

Being mistreated

Her education not funded

continued

FIGURE 9–6 *continued*

No continued progress

Institutionalized

Who Is Libby?

Giggle box, good eater, sometimes messy

Beautiful rosebud, nice friend, happy face

Cooperative, great gross motor skills

Joyful noise, steadiness, happy, strong-willed, aware of effect, persistent, good sense of humor, laughs a lot

Opportunity, smiles, spasms of delight, frustrating

Opinionated, victim, demanding, attitude, stubborn

Gifts, Strengths, and Abilities

Draws good, reading

Says a few words, listens well

Walks by herself, categorizes

Signing/signalling, body movements

Gestures what she wants and when finished

Makes sounds

Gives silverware to the cook

Strong-willed (inner strength)

Knows colors

Persistence

Walking stairs—almost on her own

Charisma

Gift of making others laugh

Challenge

Knows where she is

Pretty, nice smile

Libby Needs

Talk

Walk better

Pay more attention

Friend's attention and love

Friends	*Family*	*Educators*
Support	Communicate better	Opportunities
Physically	Open door to opportunities	Communication consistency
Emotionally	(middle and high school—full inclusion)	Academic opportunities
		Job skills
		Money skills
		Concepts

An Ideal Day for Libby

Elementary School	*Middle School*
Fun	Friends
Tell time	Walk up stairs independently
Write	Uses a watch
Read	Opens lockers
Do things by herself	Read, pays attention
Daily progress	Accepted in environment
Willingness to participate in all activities	In school
Enjoys setting and accepted by those in the setting	Job skill training provided
Bus to school and enjoy school	
Needs met and wishes met	

Next Steps

Continue with this collaborative process.

Hold onto Libby's current paraprofessional, if possible. If not, provide supportive paraprofessional who has been trained to work with Libby and to carry out responsibilities outlined by teachers and related service providers.

Continue education in inclusive settings.

Need support (philosophy, personnel, and equipment) for inclusion in middle school in order to maintain the same type of inclusive practices.

Students with severe and multiple disabilities who are included in general education classes often have a greater opportunity for an academic emphasis in their curriculum. There are two ways for adapting the general education curriculum so that students with severe and multiple disabilities can participate, namely, multilevel curriculum/instruction and curriculum overlapping (Giangreco, 1997b):

> *Multilevel curriculum/instruction occurs when a student with disabilities and nondisabled peers participate together in a shared activity (e.g., science lab experiment); students have individually appropriate learning outcomes at multiple levels, but all within the same curricular area (e.g., science). Curriculum overlapping occurs when a student with disabilities and nondisabled peers participate together in a shared activity (e.g., science lab experiment) and students have individually appropriate learning outcomes, but from different curricular areas. For example, nondisabled students could have science objectives while the student with disabilities has communication objectives within the science lab activity. These approaches allow each student to pursue individually appropriate curricular content and are successful when teachers use learning approaches rather than passive instruction (e.g. lecturing). (p. 57)*

In Chapter 8, the middle/secondary model program described a way to incorporate a functional curriculum within a general education classroom's academic curriculum. (As you have learned, the terminology for a functional curriculum in the area of severe and multiple disabilities is an ecological curriculum.) The program models that we feature in this chapter combine the potential benefits of an ecological and an academic curriculum for the benefit of students with severe and multiple disabilities (Jorgensen, 1996).

Methods

Deciding on what to teach is only the first step in developing a curriculum that meets a student's needs. Professionals then must determine how best to teach so that students will meet their educational goals. Two of the most effective ways to teach are through the methods known as systematic instruction and partial participation with adaptations.

Systematic Instruction. Professionals who use systematic instruction follow a series of specific procedures. Throughout the instruction, they collect data on their students' performance to evaluate and guide their instruction (Billingsley, Liberty, & White, 1994). Professionals who use systematic instructional procedures are more effective than those who do not (Horner & Carr, 1997; O'Reilly et al., 1992; Wolery & Schuster, 1997).

To ensure that the students learn the correct steps in a skill sequence, teachers often verbally or manually prompt students to demonstrate the behavior. Prompts help students make correct responses, which teachers can reinforce and students eventually learn. Once a student has learned the correct response, the teacher gradually removes the prompts so that the student is responding independently. Prompts range from those that are least intrusive (gesture or verbal cue) to the most intrusive (physical guidance) (Snell & Brown, 1993; Wolery, Ault, & Doyle, 1992). Figure 9–7 illustrates eight prompting strategies and how they are used to teach a student to sort silverware.

> Natural cues or prompts occurring within the environment help the student to perform a desired behavior.

FIGURE 9–7 *Eight prompting strategies to teach sorting silverware*

Environment: Vocational

Subenvironment: Dishroom

Activity: Sorting silverware from drying racks to correct bins

Level of Prompt	Teacher and Student Behaviors
Natural	Without prompting and given the presence of a drying rack with clean silverware in it, Kasey will begin to sort silverware into bins.
Gestural	Teacher points to correct bin to put the forks in. Kasey puts the forks in.
Indirect Verbal	Teacher says, "Kasey, where do the forks go?" Kasey puts the forks in correct bin.
Direct Verbal	Teacher says, "Kasey, put the forks in the bin." Kasey puts the forks in correct bin.
Model	Teacher shows Kasey how to put the forks in the bin correctly. Kasey puts forks in correct bin.
Minimal Physical	Teacher touches Kasey's hand and slightly pushes it in the direction of the correct bin. Kasey moves hand rest of way and places fork in bin.
Partial Physical	Teacher positions Kasey's hand directly over correct bin. Kasey places fork in bin.
Full Physical	Teacher places her hand over Kasey's (hand-over-hand guidance), moves Kasey's hand through all motions of placing fork in correct bin.

Note: From "Instructional Strategies," by M. Haney and M. A. Falvey, in *Community-Based Curriculum: Instructional Strategies for Students With Severe Handicaps* (2nd ed., pp. 63–90), edited by M. A. Falvey, 1989, Baltimore: Paul H. Brookes Publishing Company, P.O. Box 10624, Baltimore, MD 21285-0624. Copyright 1989 by Paul H. Brookes Publishing Company. Adapted with permission.

The student needs to move as quickly as possible from relying on prompts to relying on natural cues. When professionals develop their instructional programs, they must identify these natural cues that can trigger the performance of a particular behavior. These cues could involve the setting, materials, or interactions that are present in order for the behavior to start (Billingsley, Liberty, & White, 1994). If students are not taught to respond to natural cues, they may rely on the professional or others, or they may associate the wrong cues with a skill they should perform.

Rewarding correct performance is another important part of systematic instruction. Identifying natural reinforcers is the first step to ensuring successful skill attainment. Many students with severe and multiple disabilities, however, need more immediate forms of reinforcement. Teachers must identify specific reinforcers and consistently pair them with completion of the desired behavior (Wolery & Schuster, 1997). Because Joshua likes the sounds made by battery-operated toys, Joshua's teachers are taking advantage of this by using the types of toys that make noises when he presses buttons on them. In this way, they are helping him understand the connection between pressing the button and the resulting noise. Eventually, he will use this skill, acquiring the important ability to communicate through an alternative communication device.

Why are you reading this material and learning this information? Are you influenced to do so by natural or artificial reinforcers?

Partial Participation and Adaptations. The second issue related to effective instruction is the principle of partial participation and the use of adaptations. The partial participation principle holds that students with severe and multiple disabilities should not be categorically denied all access to daily activities solely because they lack the ability to function independently in these environments. It asserts that these students are able to participate and learn, even if only partially and, indeed, often can complete the task if it is adapted in some way. Six types of partial participation include the following:

- Sensory participation: Students use their ears and eyes within an instructional activity.

- Motor participation: Students use gross and fine motor skills to handle objects and interact with people within the instructional activity.

- Mobility participation: Students move from one location to another.

- Cognitive participation: Students learn relationships between their own movement and a response or between environmental objects.

- Communicative participation: Students learn that their motor or sensory participation can elicit responses from others.

- Social participation: Students learn interactions with another person. (Logan, Alberto, Kana, & Waylor-Bowen, 1994)

Instead of excluding students with severe and multiple disabilities from activities, instructional strategies can make individualized adaptations. Four types of adaptations are adapting skill sequences, adapting rules, using personal assistance, and using materials and devices (Kimm, Falvey, Bishop, & Rosenberg, 1995). Chapter 12 shows how assistive technology has significantly contributed to increased opportunities for community participation (Goetz & Hunt, 1994; Hutinger, 1996). Table 9–3 contains examples of different types of adaptations.

In this section, you learned important techniques for instructing students with severe and multiple disabilities. Sometimes, however, a carefully designed and implemented program is not enough. Samantha's story, in Box 9-3, "Into Practice," illustrates this point.

TABLE 9–3 ✿ *Examples of adaptations to facilitate independence*

Student	Task	Adaptation
Adapting Skill Sequences		
Needs pureed food	Eating with peers in cafeteria	Pick up lunch tray early; prepare in classroom; take to cafeteria
Five-year-old student has ataxic cerebral palsy; has no mobility; unable to crawl	Being independently mobile in all events	Student may pass over crawling stage and learn to be mobile by walking
Fatigues extremely easily	Cleaning classroom	Clean one part of a classroom instead of cleaning whole classroom in one day
Has short attention span	Playing table games	Provide reinforcement throughout the game instead of just at the end
Has difficulty with balance	Using toilet independently	Sit on toilet, then remove pants
Is unable to maintain balance while bending and reaching	Picking up puzzle pieces from the classroom floor	Sit down on the floor, then pick up pieces into a box
Adapting Rules		
Has difficulty eating quickly	Eating with peers in cafeteria	Allow a longer lunch period for this student by starting earlier
Is unable to locate bus-stop landmarks	Riding the bus independently	Student asks bus driver to tell him or her when they are at the right stop
Has difficulty bending and maintaining balance	Sweeping floors	Sweeps dirt out the door instead of using a dustpan
Is unable to write name	Writing names on personal belongings	Write name with assistance or have a rubber stamp made
Cannot discriminate between written numbers	Doing math problems	Uses objects to count and solve math problems
Uses a wheelchair	Going to gym where there are stairs	Student goes around the gym to use a ramp

HOW IS PARTICIPATION ENCOURAGED?

Inclusion

✿ Did you have opportunities to go to school with students who had severe and multiple disabilities? How did your experiences or lack of them influence your current attitudes and understanding of these students?

At the present time, students with severe and multiple disabilities are taught in a variety of settings, from totally segregated to fully inclusive. Over 60 percent of the students identified as having multiple disabilities, however, were taught in residential facilities, special schools, and separate classes within a regular school during the 1993 to 1994 school year (U.S. Department of Education, 1996). As we discussed in Chapter 3, the doctrine of the least restrictive environment, as applied to students with severe and multiple disabilities, has usually resulted in placement in a special education classroom within a regular school. Such a classroom is homogeneous: All of the students have severe and multiple disabilities. But their participation in general education classes often has been limited to nonacademic

Student	Task	Adaptation
Uses crutches	Using school cafeteria	Ask peer to carry tray of food
Has limited cooking skills	Eating a complete meal	Have a team meal where each person prepares one course in a home economics class
Has poor fine motor skills	Using shop class appliances	Ask a friend or a teacher to plug in appliance
Has low reading ability	Reading directions for a group assignment	Peer reads all questions while student and peer take turns answering
Utilizing Personal Assistance		
Has poor fine motor skills	Turning book pages	Ask a friend to assist with turning pages
Uses a wheelchair	Riding in an elevator	Ask someone to push button for correct floor if button is out of reach
Materials and Devices		
Is unable to add or subtract amounts	Doing math assignment	Use calculator to add and subtract
Has low reading ability	Identifying home phone number	Use color-coded numbers
Uses a wheelchair	Cleaning classroom	Use long-handled brushes/sponges
Has difficulty matching colors	Dressing independently	Tag clothes that match with coded labels
Has poor fine motor skills	Playing table games	Use enlarged pieces and adapting switches
Has difficulty with balance	Walking to the classroom	Use a cane, handrails, or wheelchair

Note. From "Motor and Personal Care Skills," by C. H. Kimm, M. A. Falvey, K. D. Bishop, and R. L. Rosenberg, in *Inclusive and Heterogeneous Schooling: Assessment, Curriculum, and Instruction* (pp. 203–204), edited by M. A. Falvey, 1995, Baltimore: Paul H. Brookes Publishing Company, P.O. Box 10624, Baltimore, MD 21285-0624. Copyright 1995 by Paul H. Brookes Publishing Company. Reprinted with permission.

courses such as art, music, and home economics; and in many cases, the students have not been attending their neighborhood school. The box on page 389 contains tips for including students in typical programs.

You have already read in Chapter 3 that leaders in the field of severe and multiple disabilities are advocating for inclusive education (Falvey, 1995; Stainback & Stainback, 1996; Thousand, Villa, & Nevin, 1994). Based on a comprehensive analysis and synthesis of nineteen research studies on the inclusion of students with severe disabilities, Hunt and Goetz (1997) identified six major themes related to successful inclusion with this group of students. These themes, included in Chapter 3, are repeated here:

1. *Active collaboration with parents is essential (Erwin & Soodak, 1995; Ryndak, Downing, Jacqueline, & Morrison, 1995).*

BOX 9–3 INTO PRACTICE

A BLUE HAIR RIBBON

Samantha's teachers were doing all the right things. At ten years old, she was in an inclusive program with nondisabled peers, her therapy program used a collaborative model, objectives were functional and age-appropriate, and instructional methods included systematic instruction and task analyses. Samantha's program was exemplary. However, she pouted, cried, and stiffened up when asked to participate. Her teachers concluded that their program was not exemplary for Samantha.

Samantha needed meaningful participation. Her teachers realized that they were interacting with her on tasks in an assistive rather than a social way. Her nondisabled peers had modeled this approach from their teachers. Thus, everyone was helping Samantha put a tape into a tape recorder, but they weren't taking time to listen and enjoy the music with her.

Instead of concentrating solely on motor or core skills, her teachers began to work on enrichment skills, which include choice, communication, and appropriateness. For example, in learning to brush her hair, Samantha can (1) communicate when she wants her hair brushed by pointing to her head, (2) demonstrate appropriateness by pointing to the bathroom to indicate that she wants her hair brushed there instead of in the classroom, and (3) make a choice by selecting a blue hair ribbon from those that are layed in front of her.

Brown and Lehr (1993) summarize how to make activities meaningful:

• First, for an outcome to be meaningful, it must result in participation in daily routines according to the individual's strengths as well as areas of need.

• Second, instruction should result in the student's having more meaningful control over personal routines and events in his or her environment.

---

2. *Students with severe disabilities successfully learn new skills in general education classrooms (Giangreco, Dennis, Cloninger, Edelman, & Schattman, 1993; Hunt, Staub, Alwell, & Goetz, 1994).*

3. *Students with severe disabilities have successful friendships in inclusive settings and often have more friendships in general education settings than they do in separate settings (Hunt, Farron-Davis, Beckstead, Curtis, & Goetz, 1994; Hunt, Alwell, Farron-Davis, & Goetz, 1996; Staub, Schwartz, Galluci, & Peck, 1994).*

4. *Classmates without disabilities experience positive outcomes when students with severe disabilities are included in their classes (Giangreco, Edelman, Cloninger, & Dennis, 1993; Hollowood, Salisbury, Rainforth, & Palombaro, 1994; Sharpe, York, & Knight, 1994).*

5. *Successful inclusion requires collaboration among professionals and parents at classroom, building, and system levels (Salisbury, Palombaro, & Hollowood, 1993; York-Barr, Schultz, Doyle, Kronberg, & Crossett, 1996).*

6. *Successful inclusion requires curriculum adaptation (Giangreco, Dennis, Cloninger, et al., 1993; Hunt et al., 1996).*

Community inclusion is equally important to individuals with severe and multiple disabilities. The Association for Persons with Severe Handicaps (TASH) advocates strongly for full inclusion and has developed guidelines for full inclusion (see Figure 9–8).

Inclusion Tips

	What You Might See	What You Might Be Tempted to Do	Alternate Responses	Ways to Include Peers in the Process
Behavior	The student may have temper tantrums and hit himself or others.	Discipline and isolate him from the rest of the class.	Learn to identify cues that trigger positive behaviors. Reward appropriate behaviors.	Support the peers closest to the student, and teach them to recognize and give cues that encourage positive behavior in a way that is respectful of the student.
Social Interactions	The student is unable to communicate needs or wants using words.	Allow him to remain a class "observer" rather than a participant.	Use communication boards and other assistive technology to allow him to make his needs and wants known.	Teach peers to use the same assistive technology he uses so they can effectively communicate.
Educational Performance	The student is not able to read or write and his functional skills may be poor.	Give up and let him color or do something quiet.	In collaboration with the special education specialist, provide direct instruction and task analyses in functional areas. (See "Into Practice: Developing a Task Analysis.")	Allow peers to assist him with follow through on task completion. Support them to be friends as well as learning how to peer tutor.
Classroom Attitudes	The student may appear bored or unresponsive and may sleep during class instruction.	Ignore him and focus on other more attentive students.	Use times of alertness to give him choices for ways to respond and interact during instruction.	Pair her with buddies who can interact during class instruction based on her preferences.

Collaboration

Successful collaboration is essential if students with severe and multiple disabilities are to be included in schools and communities. Because the students' support needs can be extensive, families, educators, physical and occupational therapists, speech and language pathologists, and medical personnel need to work closely with each other to ensure that students receive an appropriate and inclusive education. In addition, students without disabilities and community members need to understand their roles in the collaborative planning process.

Libby Bridge is typical of a student who receives a wide range of support services. Libby is eleven years old and is included in a fifth-grade general education classroom. She loves school (almost as much as she loves chocolate pudding) and is excited each day when the school bus slows to a stop outside her home in Kansas City, Kansas.

FIGURE 9–8 *TASH guidelines for full inclusion*

- Children and adults with disabilities have gifts that contribute to the diversity and strength of communities, and these should be at the heart of identifying and meeting people's needs.

- Children and adults with disabilities should have opportunities to be involved with ordinary people on an equal basis and to develop relationships with neighbors, classmates, coworkers, and community members.

- All children, regardless of disability, belong with families and need enduring relationships with adults.

- Adults, whether married or single, should have the opportunity to make choices about where and with whom they should live.

- Adults should have an opportunity to live in homes where they can exercise choice, preference, and control in their daily lives with companions, families, and friends.

- Supports shall enable children and adults with disabilities to participate in every aspect of social-cultural life.

- Support should be considered a human and civil right.

- Supports should be government entitlement, and people should not risk the loss of material support in order to obtain such supports.

- Adults and families of children with disabilities shall have maximum control over their personal assistance and other supports, with advocacy and support, independent of service agencies, in making these decisions.

- Adults or families of children with disabilities must have the right to choose the type of support needed and wanted and how that support will be provided.

- Individuals with disabilities and families must be entitled to decent and affordable housing, financial security to meet basic needs, and community transportation, recreation, and employment.

- People with disabilities should be involved and represented formally and decisively at all levels of policy-making and practice.

Note: From *TASH Resolutions and Policy Statements,* by The Association for Persons with Severe Handicaps, 1993, Seattle, Association for Persons with Severe Handicaps. Copyright 1993 by The Association for Persons with Severe Handicaps. Reprinted with permission.

Libby has cerebral palsy, mental retardation, epilepsy, and visual impairment. She has mild seizures five or six times each day, and more severe seizures about seven times each month. Through the collaborative efforts of Libby's parents, Mike and Molly Bridge, and the many general education and special education professionals involved with Libby, her school experiences have been very positive.

Professional Collaboration. Libby is in an inclusive program that was created through cooperation among the Kansas City, Kansas, School District and The University of Kansas. The professionals in Libby's life exemplify the way collaboration can make a difference in the life of a child.

Besides the standard IEP meetings, each week after school, Libby's general education teacher, special education teacher, and paraprofessional meet to discuss her progress. For a while, her teachers and the paraprofessional were holding team meetings once a month for the individuals involved with Libby, and they held an extensive MAPs meeting for the purpose of general planning. Libby's MAPs appears in Figure 9-6.

Mike and Molly describe the principal and the general education and special education teachers as Libby's "head cheerleaders." Libby's teachers work together to adapt the classroom activities for Libby. The special education teacher facilitates the MAPs process and coordinates the services that Libby receives. The general education teacher puts Libby's

 Libby, age 11, is shown here with her sisters Hilary, 9, and Hayley, 4. Libby, who receives a variety of support services, is included in a fifth-grade general education classroom.

goals into action in the classroom. The principal ensures that Libby has the support that she needs to stay in her classroom. This support is literal and figurative. Libby needs tangible supports, such as adaptive equipment and the presence of qualified professionals, and intangible supports, such as an atmosphere of acceptance and an example of support for inclusion.

Mike describes the paraprofessional as Libby's "arms, legs, and voice." She is an important person in Libby's life, as she is expected to carry out and follow through on activities designed by the teachers and related service providers. Beyond helping Libby with the adapted classroom activities, she helps exercise her arms and legs, puts her into the stander and leg braces recommended by the physical therapist, attends to her toileting needs, assists her with lunch, and tries to help her communicate her needs. A good relationship is important, as Libby is sometimes uncooperative. The paraprofessional knows Libby well enough to understand what Libby is trying to communicate and can work through the difficult times.

The related service providers work with Libby within their respective specializations. The physical therapist helps Libby to keep her muscles loose and to improve her mobility. The physical education teacher helps Libby to develop her strength and coordination. The occupational therapist works with her on her fine motor skills.

The speech teacher works with Libby to increase her ability to communicate by using a Macaw augmentative communication device. Libby also works on communication through music and art, and Libby especially loves music. The music teacher helps Libby to find alternate ways to communicate, in addition to providing a fun and relaxing time for Libby. Music class lifts Libby's spirits. The music teacher finds ways to include Libby in all of the school music programs. She has also found a way for Libby to play music on the computer by using a mouse. Libby's art teacher provides sensory stimulation for her and helps her to communicate in alternate ways.

As you see, the professionals working with Libby have overlapping goals, but each professional's expertise is needed. Effective collaboration is essential so that Libby's needs are addressed holistically, with each professional building on and complementing the work of the others.

Collaboration Tips

INCREASING SUPPORT AND RESOURCES AVAILABLE TO ENHANCE A STUDENT'S LEARNING POTENTIAL

COLLABORATION GOAL   To ensure that all of the people involved with the student with severe and multiple disabilities are working toward the same goals.

Collaborators	Roles	Possible Barriers	Solutions to Barriers	Modifications to Implementation	Ongoing Evaluation
Parents	Carry out plans at home to ensure continuity and uniformity.	Student's attitude—not wanting to cooperate.	Actively listen to find out what is causing the negative attitude and motivate student	Problem solve. Reward positive behaviors. Wait for time when student's more receptive.	Monitor own behavior.
Administrator	Make sure student has support she needs in the building. Work on problems brought up by teacher.	Being unaware of unmet needs; other responsibilities: and limited time and resources available.	Request general and special educator(s) and parents make needs known.	Request general and special educator(s) and parents take initiative/ responsibility to make needs known.	Self-evaluation; IEP process.
General Educator(s)	*"Head Cheerleader."* Put plan into motion; work with special educators to adapt curriculum.	Not enough support or proper equipment.	Maintain current level of support.	Make preferences and needs known to principal and special education teacher.	IEP review process.
Facilitator/ Special Educator(s)	Work with general educator(s) to adapt classroom activities.	Time limitations due to working with other students with exceptionalities; lack of proper equipment.	Maintain current level of support.	Good communication. Make preferences known to general education teacher, paraprofessional, and related service providers.	IEP review process.

Family Collaboration.   Mike and Molly work to provide continuity and uniformity between Libby's school and home. This can be difficult at times because Libby sometimes does not want to cooperate. Libby's two sisters, Hilary and Hayley, ages nine and four, are very helpful. Hilary, for example, acts as a "go-for," walks with her, plays with her, sometimes sleeps with her at night, and helps Libby when she is standing but unable to move her legs. Libby's grandparents and other extended family members live in town, and, among other things, provide periods of respite for Mike and Molly, join in problem solving and brainstorming to help meet Libby's needs, and are good sources of emotional support.

Student and Community Collaboration.   Through parent support groups, Molly and Mike have formed friendships with others who have children with disabilities. To know that they are not alone has been comforting to them. Some of Libby's peers and the

Collaborators	Roles	Possible Barriers	Solutions to Barriers	Modifications to Implementation	Ongoing Evaluation
Paraprofessional	Carry out activities designed by special education and general education teacher; motivate student.	Student's attitude—refusal to cooperate; lack of proper equipment and training.	Good communication. Find ways to distract student. Try to help student communicate needs. Give paraprofessional adequate training for what she is asked to do.	Work with school to keep current paraprofessional.	Collaborate with special educator(s) teacher and general educator(s) to assess student's needs periodically.
Related Service Provider	Work with student on communication, motor skills, and strength.	Support, training, knowledge, proper equipment insufficient.	Provide necessary training, supplies, equipment, and support.	Special education teacher makes needs known to administrator.	Special education teacher will monitor through IEP process and observation.
Peers and their parents	Interact with and encourage student. Verbal exchanges. "Cheerleaders." Parents and peers show support for inclusion.	Other students' conflicting goals; time restraints; lack of information about benefits of inclusion.	Classroom structure that is conducive to the type of interaction; good communication between school and parents.	Build interaction into lessons; informational meetings to foster communication.	Teachers and paraprofessional will observe interaction and seek feedback from

parent of one of her peers even participated in Libby's MAPs process. Mike and Molly appreciated the perspectives of these participants, especially because one parent of a peer was eager to show her support for inclusion, and Libby's classmates in the MAPs meeting expressed their desire for Libby to be able to walk and talk. Molly describes them as Libby's "cheerleaders." To help her meet her goals, the peers help Libby practice responding to verbal prompts. For example, throughout the day, they approach Libby and ask her for specific items.

The "Collaboration Tips" box shows some of the professionals involved in Libby's life and the role that they played at the MAPs session. Molly described the MAPs process as "one of the most wonderful experiences I've ever had." She continued, saying, "It showed me how many people are genuinely concerned about Libby and where she is going from this point on in her life."

Careers

If you want to work with individuals who have severe and multiple disabilities, you have many career options. If your interests are medical, you might consider becoming a pediatrician, a pediatric nurse, a speech-language pathologist, a physical therapist, or an occupational therapist. Or perhaps you would prefer psychology or rehabilitation counseling. If you plan to be a special educator, you can receive specialized training in working with students, or you can choose to be a general educator who is committed to including these individuals into your classroom. If you think these occupations require too much formal education, you might want to consider becoming a paraprofessional who serves as an aide in a classroom (Boomer, 1994; Jones & Bender, 1993).

WHAT ARE PROGRAM OPTIONS?

Early Intervention and Preschool Years

Some people have long believed that students with severe and multiple disabilities should be in separate, special programs only, those that have no typically developing peers. As you learned early in this chapter, that is the usual placement for those students, and some of those placements have been quite appropriate, given the extent of students' needs and schools' capacities to respond to those needs in more integrated settings. At the same time, many professionals have believed that any placement other than a highly separate one is not apt to benefit a student. In addition, in the face of the argument that IDEA favors placement in natural environments for infants, toddlers, and preschoolers, many professionals often asked for evidence that inclusion can work. That kind of evidence does exist.

Over the past ten years, researchers at The University of Kansas have developed and demonstrated a method for including infants, toddlers, and preschoolers with severe and multiple disabilities in typical programs (Thompson et al., 1993; Thompson et al., 1991; Thompson, Wickham, Wegner, & Ault, 1996). The Circle of Inclusion program has been implemented in twenty-three preschool classrooms within ten different early childhood programs (including two Head Start programs) and ten K–3 programs. Over 600 typically developing children and 35 with severe and multiple disabilities have participated in the program.

Among the thirty-five who participate are such youngsters as Dana (who has mental retardation, spastic quadriplegia with very limited head control, and no ability to walk, sit unsupported, or speak), Ashley (who has spinal cord injury, paralysis, a permanent tracheostomy, a respirator for assisted breathing, and a button gastrostomy), and Sheronda (who has autism and severe communication difficulties).

You may recall from Chapter 3 that the doctrine of inclusion has six components (repeated earlier in this chapter), some of which are reflected in the Circle of Inclusion.

What makes the Circle of Inclusion program effective? Not surprisingly, there are many factors: (1) a value-based commitment to including children with significant disabilities in programs available to typically developing children, not a "fix-up-the-child" approach that requires the child to meet certain developmental milestones before being "rewarded" by an inclusive placement; (2) relationships between infants/toddlers and young children with and without disabilities; (3) collaboration among all parents and professionals; (4) development of choice-making skills by the children; (5) classrooms that reflect the natural proportions of those with and without disabilities; (6) ongoing evaluation of how to make inclusion work; (7) commitment to child-initiated, child-centered education grounded in developmentally appropriate practice; and (8) the presence of child-care components.

In Circle of Inclusion programs, parents help children with and without disabilities learn about and accept each other, without regard to their inherent differences. For example, the mother or father of a child with a disability might explain the cause and effects of the disability to other students and to their parents, and a parent of a child

These students partici-pate in a Circle of Inclusion early education program. These programs include students who have severe and multiple disabilities in typical settings alongside students who do not have disabilities.

who does not have a disability might volunteer to work with one of the students who has a disability.

In addition, general and special early educators learn to sort out the confusion that can result from changing their traditional roles to new ones. A teacher who has been trained to work with typically developing students will learn how to feed, transport, provide special interventions to, and communicate with a student with a disability, relying on the expertise of a special educator. And the special educator will assume some of the regular educator's roles.

Finally, every parent and every staff member receives assurances from each other that all of them are bona fide members of a team, that they are valued rather than judged, and that they are supported but not intruded upon in contributing their unique talents. No suggestion is rejected out of hand; no hesitation about inclusion is dismissed as fanciful or prejudiced; and expertise based on training as well as on being a parent is respected, though the source of the expertise differs.

Do Circle of Inclusion programs really work? The resounding answer is "yes." Ten years of quantitative and qualitative data reveal that an inclusive program "offers a more desirable social and communicative environment for children with significant disabilities (than a special-education only preschool) . . . and can match a high-quality special education program on environmental adaptations" (Thompson et al., 1997, p. 38). In a word, the students with severe and multiple disabilities learn to be part the natural environment, just as IDEA's Part C requires.

Elementary Years

In the Johnson City Central District, New York, schools (where Joshua goes to school), twelve students with severe and multiple disabilities benefit from collaborative problem solving by their teachers and their peers. For example, Amy, a first-grader, needs to spend twenty minutes each day in a prone standing device. This holds her in an upright position but keeps her from doing her desk work. Similarly, Rich has a double shunt in his head, so his doctor has prohibited him from participating in contact sports and baseball. How can gym classes be modified to include him?

The solutions to these problems came from a collaborative problem-solving process that teachers and students alike used. The process is fairly simple: identify the problem, generate possible solutions, screen each to determine how feasible it is, chose a solution that maximizes inclusion, and evaluate the solution after it has been put into operation. Her classmates without disabilities suggested that Amy use the prone stander when all of the students are in the sharing-and-caring circle; they may be on a rug or sitting or standing in a circle, and Amy stands with them. Rich participates in gym as a helper, leads warm-up activities, and gives "start/stop" directions, suggestions that his physical therapist, gym teacher, and peers proposed and carried out.

Teachers were the first to learn to use collaborative problem solving; they then modeled it for their students. Typically, the students called attention to situations in which their peers were not participating with them; challenges of equity and inclusion then provoked collaborative problem solving by faculty and peers alike to devise solutions. The results were promising. Collaborative problem solving became a routine and then an integrated, normal process for the staff; it became intuitive. Increases of physical, social, and instructional integration occurred, in part because faculty and students themselves identified the problems and the solutions. The faculty came to value collaborative problem solving as a means to increase inclusion.

None of those results would have occurred, however, if it had not been that the school district mission statement valued diversity, district administrators intentionally shared decision making with faculty and students, the district was structured to promote connectedness at all levels, and all instruction was grounded in concepts of mastery and cooperative learning. When students are involved and allowed to be creative, when teachers are flexible and share the decision-making process with their peers and with students, and when an organization is committed to outcome-based education (where the outcomes are positive social, cognitive, and communication skills), then inclusion, based on collaborative problem solving, can occur (Salisbury, Evans, & Palombaro, 1997).

Middle and Secondary Years

You read earlier that fewer than three of ten students with severe and multiple disabilities are taught in inclusive settings. Some schools, however, are successfully integrating students with severe and multiple disabilities. Whittier High School, serving Southeast Los Angeles County and some surrounding communities, is one of them.

A few years ago, Whittier High School made some ambitious changes to improve the quality of education for all its students. One plan included designing an inclusive program that would implement appropriate strategies and modifications to the general curricula. Whittier staff hoped to improve the performance of students identified as having disabilities as well as those who were not performing at grade level academically but were not identified as having a disability.

In their restructuring efforts, the site plan committee made some significant changes that benefit all students. One included dividing the school into smaller units, essentially, three teams at each grade level. Students remain in their team during their ninth and tenth grade years. These teams are formed by a group of eight to ten core curriculum teachers, two support teachers, an administrator, and a school counselor. The special and general educators work together, drawing from one another's expertise. They work to meet the needs of all students: that is, students who have received special education labels, students who have not qualified for special education services but are at risk of school failure, and students who have succeeded in traditional school systems.

Another change was made to eliminate the negative special education labels placed on students. The staff adopted a noncategorical support system for all students, eliminated the term *special education teacher*, and discarded the idea that only specialists can work with those students. To carry out these strategies, the students within each team are divided into heterogeneous groups. These groups include students of all ability levels, including students who have been identified as having a disability. Each group then works on a curriculum of core courses that each student must take throughout their high school years.

The teachers also group themselves heterogeneously. Each team contains math, science, social studies, English, and support teachers who work together to develop and carry out curriculum goals. Each support teacher works with colleagues to serve students who were identified in their middle school setting (but are not labeled at Whittier High) as *severely handicapped, learning handicapped,* or *eligible for resource services.* The support staff provide whatever supports students need to succeed in their core curriculum courses. The school also uses block scheduling. Each teacher is responsible for two periods within the team and one period outside the team. Switching to block scheduling has decreased the teacher-to-student ratio from 1:180 to 1:80, allowing for more personalization, advisement, and support. Finally, Whittier staff meet the needs of students with severe and multiple disabilities by using **authentic assessment** rather than traditional standardized methods to measure the students' performance.

Whittier staff have made special efforts to foster positive interactions between students who have disabilities and those who do not. The school provides ability awareness in-services for all freshmen, peer tutoring arrangements, Circle of Friends, mapping activities, and other activities designed to encourage friendships. Many students enroll in a school service program for which they earn credit. Through this service program, they provide support to students who need assistance to fully participate in academic or elective classes.

Authentic assessment requires students to generate a response, often through developing a product or demonstrating a skill.

Transitional and Postsecondary Years

As you read in Chapter 3, proponents of inclusion advocate educating all students in age- and grade-appropriate placements. If students with disabilities should be educated with their age-appropriate peers, then where should students with disabilities who are ages eighteen through twenty-one be educated? This was the question Steve Snyder, a teacher in Washington, D.C., schools, asked and answered. Steve based his answer on his belief that people with disabilities belong with their same-age peers without disabilities, and that people with disabilities need to learn job skills through supervised work experiences. Because a university is a natural setting for eighteen- to twenty-two-year-olds, Steve saw it as a natural setting for educating students with significant disabilities as well. The university setting also provides many opportunities for work sites. There are plenty of generic services and resources on college campuses and the surrounding neighborhoods, and a similarity exists between college students and individuals with disabilities in their community needs. For example, they both need places to eat, shop, do laundry, access public transportation, and have leisure and recreation activities (Snyder, 1991).

While many universities offer services to students with disabilities, very few have programs for students with severe/multiple disabilities (Snyder, 1993). Steve worked to establish the University Connection, a partnership between the District of Columbia Public Schools and George Washington University. The purposes of the University Connection are to prepare students for supported employment and to foster inclusion of students ages eighteen to twenty-two. The University Connection helps students develop work skills, personal management skills, domestic and leisure skills, communication skills, and friendships.

Steve's students with severe disabilities attend the University Connection program on the campus of George Washington University. On a typical day, several students use the city's public transportation system—subway and buses—to arrive at the university. Three days each week, they spend the morning learning functional academics and community skills, social skills, and work-related skills. In the afternoon, they go to their various work sites, rotating through work sites each semester. After completing their afternoon work, they meet with Steve to review their day.

In the mornings of the other two days each week, the students participate in community instruction and campus service activities. Community instruction includes such activities as going to libraries, parks, museums or art galleries, shopping in stores or malls, or attending concerts. The students practice following verbal and written instructions, language and communication, leisure and behavioral skills, and interactions with individuals

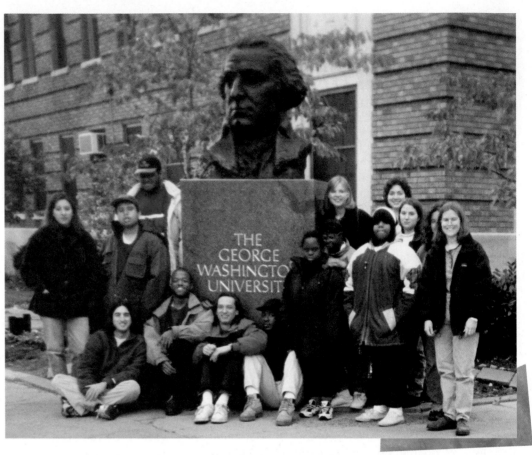

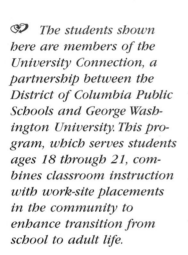 *The students shown here are members of the University Connection, a partnership between the District of Columbia Public Schools and George Washington University. This program, which serves students ages 18 through 21, combines classroom instruction with work-site placements in the community to enhance transition from school to adult life.*

who do not have disabilities. Campus service activities are coordinated with other student groups on campus. One of the students' service activities is "Flyer Posting." The students receive flyers pertaining to upcoming events from student groups, take them to the thirty-five bulletin boards on campus, read dates on old flyers and take them down, and put up the new flyers in the empty spaces. They eat lunch with staff and friends or at the Sigma Nu fraternity house.

In the afternoons, they work on domestic, leisure, and community instruction in and around the Sigma Nu house. They clean up from lunch, do some housekeeping activities, and practice calendar, time, numbers, money, and reading skills. Their leisure activities might include playing basketball, card games, board games, or working on a scrapbook. Before going home for the day, they prepare their lunches for the following day.

When Steve started this program, he thought that inclusion of his students on the university campus would naturally foster positive social interactions and friendships. Through observation and a qualitative study, however, Steve found that friendships between the university students and his students were not occurring naturally. He found that planned interventions were necessary to facilitate interactions between his students and students without disabilities on campus. The solution was found in the Best Buddies program, a one-on-one pairing of college students with high school students with disabilities. Programs like this are commonly used in high schools to create friendships between students with disabilities and their peers. Steve readily acknowledges that the Best Buddies program "did the trick" in helping his students to develop friendships with their peers without disabilities. More than that, the university students will undoubtedly be the future neighbors, teachers, doctors, nurses, employers, and co-workers of people with disabilities. This makes the university campus an ideal place to lay the groundwork for the continued support of people with severe/multiple disabilities.

A VISION FOR THE FUTURE

What does Joshua's future hold? It seems that the hardest times are over: Josh's health has improved, and he is surrounded by people who care about him: his father, Alan, and his stepmother, Linda, his little brother and sister, the professionals at the Broome Developmental Center, and the professionals and students in the Johnson City schools.

Joshua's supporters take pride in the gains he makes. "Anything he does (since fighting his way back from his illness) is remarkable," Alan explained, even learning to sit up without assistance. Alan believes that it is important for people to accept children with disabilities as they are and to allow them to work at their own pace, instead of ours. "You've got to find that pace" that is unique for each child and then help them to build on their strengths.

Alan's biggest wish for Joshua is that he will learn to use an augmentative communication device so he can communicate his needs to others. Joshua will continue to work toward that direction, at his own pace. He has proved to be a determined fighter before, and will surely continue to amaze those who teach and care for him.

What Would You Recommend . . .

1. To ensure that, as Joshua learns the important skill of communication at his own pace, his peers without disabilities can assist him while they receive their education at their own pace?

2. To coordinate his school-based team, developmental center team, and family for long-range planning and short-term, immediate communication?

3. To give Joshua an opportunity to participate in school leisure and recreation activities, using partial participation and adaptations?

SUMMARY

WHAT ARE SEVERE AND MULTIPLE DISABILITIES?

- The term *severe and multiple disabilities* defines a diverse group of people, and no one definition satisfies all occurrences of multiple disabilities.

- IDEA has two separate definitions, one for multiple disabilities and one for severe disabilities.

- Intellectual functions of students with severe and multiple disabilities include limited academic skills, limited levels of awareness, deficits in self-care skills, a lack of typical social interactions, and challenging behaviors.

- Other common characteristics include delayed motor development, sensory impairments, health care needs, and limited ability to communicate.

- The prevalence data vary, but there are very few students with severe and multiple disabilities (between 1 percent and 1.6 percent of all students in IDEA programs).

- Etiology is unknown in 40 percent of this population. The majority of known causes are due to prenatal biomedical factors, which include chromosomal abnormalities, genetic metabolic disorders, developmental disorders of brain formation, and environmental influences. In addition, complications during and after birth can account for multiple disabilities.

- Some severe and multiple disabilities are preventable through medical technology, maternal education, and genetic counseling.

WHAT ARE EVALUATION PROCEDURES?

• Screening tests such as the Apgar are used by physicians to determine the type and extent of the disability. The evaluation process is usually begun right after birth and may continue over several years.

• While controversial with this population, IQ tests and adaptive behavior scales are most often used to make classification decisions.

• Approaches to assessing skills for curriculum and program development include the developmental model, the ecological model, assessment of behavioral states, and Making Action Plans.

WHAT AND HOW DO PROFESSIONALS TEACH?

• In the early 1970s, curriculum guides borrowed heavily from the model in which developmental skills were identified and taught in a prerequisite manner.

• Since the mid-1980s, curriculum has focused on the ecological approach, which identifies the critical environments in which the student is expected to function as well as the skills and activities needed to participate successfully there.

• Multilevel instruction and curriculum overlapping are effective ways for students with severe and multiple disabilities to participate in shared activities with their nondisabled peers.

• Systematic instruction is necessary to teach skills effectively to students with severe and multiple disabilities. Components of systematic instruction include the procedures used to teach skills and the ways to reinforce correct responses.

• One way for students with severe and multiple disabilities to receive effective instruction is to provide opportunities to participate as fully as possible (partial participation) in activities. This can often be accomplished using adaptations.

HOW IS PARTICIPATION ENCOURAGED?

• Because of the intense medical and health care needs of this group of students, families, educators, physicians and occupational therapists, speech and language pathologists, and medical personnel need to work closely together.

• Students with severe and multiple disabilities are taught in a variety of settings, ranging from segregated institutions and special centers to general education classrooms. The majority of students are taught in separate facilities or programs.

• Many advocates for people with disabilities argue strongly for programs that involve integration or full inclusion into the general education classrooms.

• To work with individuals with severe and multiple disabilities, you might consider becoming a pediatrician, a nurse, a speech-language pathologist, a rehabilitation counselor, or a special education teacher.

WHAT ARE PROGRAM OPTIONS?

• Twenty-three preschool programs have successfully included infants, toddlers, and preschoolers with severe and multiple disabilities through the Circle of Inclusion program.

• The Johnson City schools provide an excellent model of inclusion and collaboration.

• Whittier High School made significant positive changes for people with disabilities as part of a school-wide improvement plan. Negative special education labels were removed, and all students are grouped heterogeneously.

• Students who are ages eighteen to twenty-two can be educated on a college campus, such as demonstrated by the University Connection in Washington, D.C.

RESOURCES

BOOKS

Children With Disabilities (4th ed.). (1997). Edited by Mark L. Batshaw. Baltimore, MD: Brookes. This comprehensive book provides detailed, yet easy-to-understand, information on the causes and medical characteristics of a wide range of disabilities including mental retardation. Background information is also provided on heredity, prenatal diagnosis, and early typical and atypical development.

Friendships and Community Connections Between People With and Without Developmental Disabilities. (1993). Edited by Angela Novak Amado. Baltimore, MD: Brookes. Twenty chapters written by leaders in the field focus on the dimensions of friendships, stories about reciprocal friendships, and strategies for building friendships.

Self-Determination Across the Lifespan: Independence and Choice for People With Disabilities. (1996). Edited by Deanna J. Sands & Michael L. Wehmeyer. Baltimore, MD: Brookes. The research and model program development that has occurred over the last five years is synthesized in this book. Many practical suggestions enable readers to make a difference in the lives of people with mental retardation in promoting self-determination.

Instruction of Students With Severe Disabilities (4th ed.). (1993). By Martha E. Snell. Upper Saddle River, NJ: Merrill/Prentice Hall. In-depth information about students with severe and multiple disabilities. Topics include inclusion, family involvement, assessment, instructional planning, special health care needs, physical management and handling procedures, augmentative communication, self care skills, functional academics, and daily living skills.

JOURNALS, MAGAZINES, AND CATALOGS

The Advance. Association for Persons in Supported Employment, 5001 West Broad Street, Suite 34, Richmond, VA 23230. Monthly newsletter about supported employment.

The Journal of the Association for Persons with Severe Handicaps. The Association for Persons with Severe Handicaps (TASH), 29 W. Susquehanna Avenue, Suite 210, Baltimore, MD 21204. Quarterly journal for professionals in the field of severe disabilities. The majority of the articles are research-related.

Supported Employment InfoLines. Training Resource Network, PO Box 439, Saint Augustine, FL 32085-0439. (904) 823-9800. Internet address: www.oldcity.com/trn. This newsletter is published ten times a year for professionals working in the field of supported employment.

MULTIMEDIA

The Miracle Worker. (1962.) Helen Keller, a child with dual sensory impairments, learns from her teacher, Annie Sullivan.

ON-LINE INFORMATION AND USEFUL DATABASES

Alternative Work Concepts. Internet address: www.teleport.com/~awc. E-mail: awc@teleport.com. A supported employment agency that assists persons with physical and multiple disabilities to obtain and maintain employment in their communities.

Association for Spina Bifida and Hydrocephalus. Internet address: www.asbah.demon.co.uk. E-mail: postmaster@asbah.demon.co.uk. A site with information, publications, and links to related sites.

ORGANIZATIONS

American Association on Mental Retardation. 444 North Capitol Street NW, Suite 846, Washington, DC 20001-1512. Internet address: www.aamr.org. E-mail: aamr@access.digex.net. International multidisciplinary association of professionals that focuses on promoting understanding of mental retardation.

The Association for Persons with Severe Handicaps (TASH). 29 West Susquehanna Avenue, Suite 210, Baltimore, MD 21204. (410) 828-8274. Internet address: www.tash.org. E-mail: info@tash.org. Advocacy and research organization composed of professionals, family members, and individuals with severe disabilities.

Association for Persons in Supported Employment. 1627 Monument Avenue, Richmond, VA 23220. (804) 278-9178. Internet address: www.apse.org. E-mail: apse@apse.org. Organization for professionals involved in supported employment for individuals with severe disabilities. Provides guidance and information, publishes a quarterly newsletter, and holds a national conference.

CHAPTER 1

AUTISM

Educating
A.J. Poston

There's an ancient Chinese saying, "Every crisis is an opportunity." This saying begins to capture the life of A.J. Poston, his mother, and his school: Every challenge can be met and can create an opportunity. The emphasis has to be on *can,* because A.J.'s autism, his mother's life, and his school's capacities are not yet developed enough to always create the opportunities that they all want.

A.J. is a fourth grader at Howard Wilson Elementary School, Leavenworth, Kansas. He spends most of the school day in the structured learning classroom with a few other students who have autism and other disabilities. Again, emphasis is important: *most of the day.* When the fourth graders meet for English, science, physical education, recess, and lunch, A.J. usually participates. For the rest of the school day, A.J. and a few of the other students with disabilities have their own classroom and their own curriculum. A.J.'s mother, Denise, his teachers Stephanie Mathew and Jim Wolfe, all agree: That's not an ideal situation.

At Howard Wilson, the staff, along with Denise, collaborate to build on A.J.'s strengths,

preferences, and needs. A.J. has a great sense of humor and a strong memory, and is especially creative in his art and play with video games.

But A.J. also has communication impairments. He exhibits unpredictable tantrums, sometimes aggressive or self-injurious behavior, and occasional destruction of property. He has his idiosyncratic allegiance to his own rules and routines, such as wearing only short pants with short-sleeve shirts. He responds in unusual ways to external stimuli, covering his ears with his hands when noises are at a certain pitch. And he likes to be surrounded by, but not always to interact with, peers who do not have disabilities.

Denise candidly admits to being afraid about the future. She worries that his behavior will cause him to be totally isolated from his schoolmates, and she longs for him to have friends. She also is concerned that his hidden competence as an intelligent problem solver will be undiscovered; it took her quite a while to realize that he can reason, at least to some extent. For example, if he wants to go out in the hallway at school, he can ask to go to the bathroom and probably get an affirmative answer. Although one could interpret this as manipulation, Denise and his teachers acknowledge that he can reason to solve problems. But how long will it take others to learn that, and will they give A.J. enough chances to demonstrate his capabilities?

Denise also acknowledges other challenges that she faces. She daily commutes for an hour to work each way, and A.J.'s father lives in Washington, D.C. And although A.J. has an IEP, Denise believes it's not nearly as important on a daily basis as the informal communication she has with his teacher. Finally, although A.J. has made tremendous improve-

ments, she has been unable—because of the lack of time, energy, and support staff—to develop comprehensive positive behavioral support for A.J.

Diane Cox, the school principal, and Karen Wilson, the school psychologist, understand all those challenges. Like Denise, however, they see the opportunities, not the barriers the challenges create. Using the school as a "cluster" for other students with autism underscores the faculty's commitment to "make the school OK for all children." Until the school became a cluster site, says Diane, "we didn't know enough, system-wide," how best to develop an alliance with the families of children with disabilities and to help all students, faculty, and fam-

ilies relate positively to each other. As Karen notes, "A.J. has come a long way in interacting with others. And so have we all."

A.J. is somewhat connected to life in the neighborhood. Some of his age peers attend a different school; but because they know A.J.'s brother Jim, they hang out with A.J., too. And, because Denise distributed a flyer about A.J. with his name, photograph, address, telephone, Denise's neighbors have been alerted that he may wander through their yards or even into their homes. So far, that's not been a problem, and Denise characterizes most of them as "subtly supportive."

Nowhere is the sense of an inclusive community better manifest than at Sally's Choices, a gift boutique in the heart of downtown Leavenworth. There, amid easily breakable crystal and pricey antiques, A.J. has found a place where he belongs. After all, the owners, Sally and John, sell wooden toy trains; they pay no heed when A.J. comes to the store to play with, rearrange, and rearrange again, the engines, cars, cabooses, tracks, and little towns that they display. And their best saleslady—Bernie—is also A.J.'s friend: "A.J. is always

welcome here. Where has he been lately? Why, I even bought extra circus tickets for him. It's good to see him again . . . he's my buddy."

To be always welcome, to be invited in, to be someone's buddy: The challenge is to overcome the autism that can impede those relationships. Many people are meeting that challenge. What's more, they're overcoming it.

As you read this chapter, consider how you as a professional would support students with autism in overcoming the barriers to learning that they face.

What Do You Think?

1. How would you support A.J. and his teachers to build on his problem-solving strengths and remediate some of his communication and behavior challenges?

2. How would you help the Howard Wilson school staff increase its capacities to be a more inclusive school?

3. How would you enable A.J. to be as welcome in his school and his neighborhood as he is at Sally's Choices?

What Is Autism?

Defining Autism

Leo Kanner, a psychiatrist at the Johns Hopkins Hospital in Baltimore, first identified autism in 1943. He described the background and behavior of eleven children with strikingly similar characteristics:

- Difficulty developing relationships with people
- Delayed speech acquisition and inability to use speech once it developed
- Repetitive and stereotypical behavior
- Lack of imagination
- Good rote memory
- Obsessive insistence on sameness of routine
- Normal physical appearance

Kanner called this new condition *early infantile autism,* deriving the term from the Greek word for self *(auto),* because these children seemed to be locked inside themselves.

For the next thirty years or so, professionals and families adhered to Kanner's definition and regarded autism as an emotional disturbance. Indeed, when first enacted in 1975, IDEA classified autism as a subcategory of serious emotional disturbance. The Autism Society of America lobbied to remove autism from this category, arguing that many people erroneously equated autism with different types of emotional disorders such as schizophrenia or various psychoses. In 1981 Congress responded by placing autism into the category in the Individuals with Disabilities Education Act (IDEA) of "other health impairments." Many parents and educators still believed, however, that this classification led to confusion and misunderstanding about the nature of autism. Finally, in 1991, Congress identified autism as a separate IDEA disability. The law now defines autism as follows:

> *Autism means a developmental disability significantly affecting verbal and nonverbal communication and social interaction, generally evident before age 3, that adversely affects educational performance. Other characteristics often associated with autism are engagement in repetitive activities and stereotyped movements, resistance to environmental change or changes in daily routines, and unusual responses to sensory experiences. The term does not apply if a child's educational performance is adversely affected primarily because the child has a serious emotional disturbance. (34 C.F.R., Part 300, § 300.7[b][1])*

Autism is a severe form of a broader group of disorders referred to as **pervasive developmental disorders** (Bauer, 1995; Mauk, Reber, & Batshaw, 1997). By contrast, people with **Asperger disorder** have some of the social and behavioral characteristics of those with autism; however, they do not have accompanying delays in language development or impairments in intellectual functioning (Szatmari, 1991).

Describing the Characteristics

The IDEA definition of autism specifies a broad range of characteristics. In this section, you will learn more about (a) language, (b) social interaction, (c) stereotypical behavior, (d) behavioral challenges, (e) need for environmental predictability, (f) sensory and movement disorders, and (g) intellectual functioning.

Language Development.   Students with autism have a broad range of language abilities ranging from no verbal communication to quite complex communication. They generally

There was a 21 percent increase in the number of students in schools nationwide identified as having autism from between the 1992 to 1993 and the 1993 to 1994 school years. Because autism is a new separate category, schools are just beginning to improve their capacity to accurately identify students with autism (U.S. Department of Education, 1995).

Pervasive developmental disorder includes impairments in communication, impairments in reciprocal social interactions, and stereotyped patterns of behavior, interests, and activities (Mauk et al., 1997).

Asperger disorder describes individuals with behavioral and social features associated with autism but without significant delays in language development or impairments in cognition (Mauk et al., 1997).

have a number of language impairments. Two common ones are (a) delayed language and (b) **echolalia.**

Delayed Language. A long-standing expectation within the field of autism is that approximately half of the children with autism do not develop communication enabling them to converse with others (Prizant, 1983; Schuler, 1995). Through the use of improved language intervention programs during the last decade, however, the majority of the children with autism who have been expected to remain nonverbal have been found to develop some expressive language capability (L. K. Koegel, 1995). Language intervention is most successful if it occurs in natural contexts and begins before the age of five.

Students with autism who do have some speech tend to speak in limited ways and often do not develop the ability to have a conversation with others (L. K. Koegel, Koegel, Hurley, & Frea, 1992). They use language frequently to request objects or to protest objectionable aspects of their environment (L. K. Koegel, 1995), not for reciprocal communication.

Educators use several procedures to help individuals overcome neuromotor difficulties and increase their ability to communicate (Biklen, 1992; Crossley & Remington-Gurney, 1992). A highly publicized and controversial form of communication is **facilitated communication.** Facilitated communication is a training method that involves supporting a person who does not speak or has highly repetitive speech to use a human facilitator and keyboard to communicate. The basic premise of facilitated communication is that people with autism have more unrecognized intact cognitive processes but these processes are blocked by a **neuromotor impairment.** A neuromotor impairment is caused by a breakdown in the brain's capacity to direct the body to engage in movement that produces speech, gestures, written formats, or other alternatives (Layton & Watson, 1995). Box 10-1, "Into Practice," highlights the six major elements of facilitated communication.

Rarely has any issue in the disability field created such divided opinion as facilitated communication (Cohen, 1998; Crossley, 1997; Twachtman-Cullen, 1997). The opponents of facilitated communication point to a large body of research studies using traditional research designs in which the facilitators have been found to be the source of message production in many of the investigations (Eberlin, McConnachie, Abel, & Volpe, 1993; Green & Shane, 1994; Smith & Belcher, 1993; Wheeler, Jacobson, Paglieri, & Schwartz, 1993). A factor escalating furor over facilitated communication is that facilitated communication messages have resulted in some accusations of sexual abuse, often directed toward the family of the individual with autism. Understandably, a major concern has evolved over the authorship of the message—the facilitator or the individual.

Just as there has been strong opposition, there is also support for facilitated communication. Research evidence suggests that some individuals with autism have been found to be the authors of their own messages in at least some circumstances (Cardinal, Hanson, & Wakeham, 1996; Sheehan & Matuozzi, 1996; Simon, Toll, & Whitehair, 1994; Vasquez, 1994; Weiss, Wagner, & Bauman, 1996). The proponents of facilitated communication emphasize that this approach encourages greater attention, more appropriate behavior, and even independent typing at a later time.

You may be wondering if there is any middle ground in this debate. The answer to that question is yes. Leaders in the field of language intervention for individuals with severe disabilities describe their position as follows:

> *We favor considering the use of FC [facilitated communication] on a case-by-case basis. This calls for careful assessment and full description of an individual's oral and augmentative . . . communication characteristics and capabilities when determining candidacy or validating the use of FC. (Koppenhaver, Pierce, & Yoder, 1995, pp. 5–6)*

These authors encourage the use of assistive technology, such as the communication devices that you will learn about in Chapter 12, for people who have been successful with facilitated communication.

A grandfather commented on his granddaughter's successful use of facilitated communication as follows: "It's disturbing to read these findings [that are critical of facilitated communication]. We see the difference with Shalyn before and after facilitation. It has changed her life and ours. . . . I wish the people doing this research had lived with Shalyn before and after facilitation." How do you reconcile the difference between a body of research findings and this grandfather's perspective?

BOX 10-1

ELEMENTS OF FACILITATED COMMUNICATION

- *Physical support.* The facilitator does not assist the student to make a selection of letters or other targets but may help the student to isolate the index finger and stabilize the student at the hand, wrist, or arm during typing while generally pulling the student's arm back after each selection.
- *Initial training/introduction.* Students are initially given activities with fairly predictable answers: for example, spelling their names and doing matching exercises. Then they are encouraged to progress to open-ended conversation.
- *Maintaining focus.* When necessary, the facilitator reminds the student to keep his or her eyes on the keyboard or other communication aid; to isolate the

index finger used for pointing; to reduce extraneous actions such as screeches, slapping of objects, or biting; and, if the student exhibits echoed or stereotyped spoken language, to type what he or she intends to communicate.
- *Avoiding competence testing.* A key element is emotional support or encouragement; it is important to treat the person as competent, with the knowledge that the person's thinking and literacy will reveal themselves over time.
- *Generalization.* Students will often develop a high level of communication ability with one or two facilitators and will need encouragement and repeated attempts to generalize to more facilitators.
- *Fading.* Students become more independent over time; thus, it is important to work on fading physical support.

Note. From "Typing to Talk: Facilitated Communication," by D. Biklen, 1992, *American Journal of Speech-Language Pathology, 1(?)*, pp. 15–17. Copyright 1992 by the American Journal of Speech-Language Pathology. Reprinted with permission.

Echolalia. People with autism often echo other people's language by constantly repeating a portion of what they hear. This type of communication—called *echolalia*—tends to happen with almost all young children who are beginning to talk, whether they have autism or not; but usually it begins to disappear around the age of three (Howlin, 1982). Some people with autism, however, may have echolalia throughout their lives.

Some specialists have described echolalia as speech that is repeated in an automatic manner without having communicative intent (Howlin, 1982). Some intervention procedures, based on this view, give children the command "Don't echo" in order to eliminate echolalia (Lovass, 1977). Others, however, believe that children and youth with autism may use echolalia to communicate a desire for the attention of their listener, to fill the silence in a communication exchange, to make a request, to indicate affirmation, to protest the actions of others, and/or to provide information (Prizant & Rydell, 1984; Rydell & Prizant, 1995).

The children who engage in immediate echolalia may repeat what they have just heard because they are unaware of an appropriate response. Teaching children to say, "I don't know" or "I need some help, please" is effective in reducing echolalia and providing a response that has the potential of leading to a meaningful communication opportunity (L. K. Koegel, 1995). Box 10-2, "Into Practice" includes suggestions for conversing with people who are nonverbal or have delayed language.

Social Interaction. A lack of social interaction is a hallmark of autism (Denkla, 1986; Rutter, 1978). People with autism often have a pattern of not making eye contact with others; forming weak attachments to people, including their parents; voluntarily spending a

BOX 10-2 INTO PRACTICE

CONVERSING

Here are some suggestions for conversing with people who have delayed language or use echolalia:

- Keep the same proximity and eye contact that you would with a person who has typical verbal skills.
- Choose topics that you think might interest your conversation partner. If you are unsure of your partner's interest, ask the person's family or other friends about favorite conversation topics.
- Longer-than-usual pauses are OK. Try not to be uncomfortable with silence.
- If your partner is using echolalia, try to intuit what is being communicated. Then verbalize to your partner what you believe is being communicated. Ask your partner if you are correct.
- Develop the capacity to be spontaneous and try not to feel awkward if the conversation does not go exactly as you expect it to.
- Animation in your voice can heighten communication connections.
- Use familiar phrases that your partner can anticipate (e.g., "What's happening, big guy?"). As opposed to a barrage of different conversation, familiar phrases can be quite enjoyable.
- Develop a special handshake that you use with your partner every time you meet.

Stereotypical behaviors are inappropriate, repetitive acts that an individual frequently displays. Examples include rocking back and forth, waving fingers in front of the face, and twirling objects.

Do you have any stereotypical behaviors? Do you wiggle your foot in class, curl your hair with your finger, or rock in your chair? Think about when and why you do these behaviors. Are your reasons similar to or different from a student with autism?

Challenging behaviors can impede relationships and full citizenship.

---

disproportionately large amount of time alone; developing a strong attachment to particular objects; and tending not to seek comfort from others when hurt or upset (Schreibman, 1988).

Students with autism face an enormous challenge in expressing their own feelings and needs in a socially acceptable way. They find it hard to connect with the feelings or needs of others and may not be not aware of their own and others' thought processes and moods (Baron-Cohen, 1991; Tager-Flusberg, 1992; Yirmira, Sigman, Kasari, & Mundy, 1992).

Stereotypical Behavior. **Stereotypical behaviors** are inappropriate, repetitive acts that individuals with autism frequently display. For examples, they may rock back and forth, waving their fingers in front of their faces, and twirling objects. Although many individuals with autism have stereotypical behavior, there is great variability among them. Indeed, A.J. does not engage in stereotypical behavior. For many years, professionals believed that these repetitive, rhythmic motor behaviors did not have any constructive purpose. Increasingly, however, researchers are discovering that stereotypical behaviors are attempts to communicate boredom and agitation or to regulate their own level of awareness (Carr et al., 1994).

Teachers should help students reduce stereotypical behaviors. These behaviors interfere with students' ability to learn, and they often inhibit students' successful inclusion in typical work, school, and community settings. Decreasing stereotypical behaviors, however, is not sufficient; teachers also should teach the student more appropriate communication methods and more enjoyable leisure activities (Carr et al., 1994; Quill, 1995a, 1995b).

Behavioral Challenges. Four categories of behavioral challenges include self-injurious behavior, aggression, tantrums, and property destruction. We will focus on the first two.

Self-Injurious Behavior. Some individuals with autism have self-injurious behaviors, such as head banging, biting, or scratching. These behaviors often persist into adulthood and create continuing demands for support from families and care providers (Ruble

& Dalrymple, 1996). Individuals with severe self-injurious behaviors may permanently injure themselves; and for a rare few, self-injurious behaviors are life-threatening. A.J. pulls his hair, scratches his face, and/or bites his hands usually about three or four times a week. Denise has noticed that most of his self-injurious behavior occurs when he does not get something he wants.

Aggression. Aggressive behaviors are similar to self-injurious behaviors, but the behavior is directed toward others. Aggressive behaviors can be problematic in all settings. One of Denise's worst experiences with A.J.'s aggression occurred at a soccer game. Because she had had to stop for several errands before they got to the game, A.J. felt particularly frustrated. He bolted from the car and pushed a little girl down on the ground before Denise could intervene. The girl had a seizure disorder, and her fright instigated a seizure. At times like this, Denise particularly wishes for support from teachers, related service providers, and friends in handling very awkward situations. The principles of positive behavioral support (discussed later in the chapter) enable students to express their frustration in more appropriate ways and even to eliminate sources of their frustration, to the extent possible.

All types of challenging behavior serve as a communicative function, enabling the student to seek attention, avoid an undesirable activity, or escape an unpleasant situation. Given the functions challenging behavior serves, your role becomes one of teaching the student other ways to communicate these same intentions (Carr et al., 1994; Hodgdon, 1995).

> The model programs described later in the chapter show you how to teach students other ways to communicate.

Need for Environmental Predictability.

Predictability and structure appear to be sources of security for many individuals with autism (Dalrymple, 1995). When their need for predictability and structure is interrupted by school vacations, overnight stays of friends or extended family, the celebration of holidays, a change in television schedules, or the move of students from one classroom to another, people with autism often experience a high degree of anxiety (Rutter, 1978). Most of us do not think much about whether the telephone is straight on a desk, the location of cosmetics on the bathroom counter, or whether a door is open or closed. These sorts of seemingly insignificant environmental patterns, however, can hold great significance for an individual with autism.

A variety of classroom supports can enable students with autism to experience more predictability. The supports include schedules, routines, and strategies for accepting some change (Dalrymple, 1995). For example, students who do not read might have picture schedules to outline the different activities or classroom periods through which they will be advancing during the day. Students who have higher cognitive abilities may find that a daily and weekly work schedule is helpful.

Routines also enable students to understand when things will occur. For example, some students with autism need to have activities that are almost always associated with the same time of day or the same day of the week. That kind of rigid routine can create a problem, however, when those times need to change, and many students require instruction and support in learning to accept time changes. It is often helpful to let students know in advance when there will be a time change and when the schedule and routines will return to the typical schedule. ("We will not have music this afternoon, because there is a special school program. You will get to go to music again next Tuesday afternoon, and you can look forward to the fun that you will have.")

Sensory and Movement Disorders.

Many children and youth with autism evidence sensory and movement disorders. Some have under- or overresponsiveness to sensory stimuli (Rosenblatt, Bloom, & Koegel, 1995; Sullivan, 1994). Temple Grandin (1992), who was identified as having autism as a child, is now one of the most successful designers of livestock equipment in the world. She provides examples of some typical problems with sensory stimuli as well as some practical solutions in "My Voice" (Box 10–3).

BOX 10-3

MY VOICE

TEMPLE GRANDIN: DIAGNOSED AS HAVING AUTISM AS A CHILD

- As an adult I find it difficult to determine exactly when I should break into a conversation. I cannot follow the rhythmic give and take of conversation. People have told me that I often interrupt, and I still have difficulty determining where the pauses are.
- Noise was a major problem for me. When I was confronted with loud or confusing noise, I could not modulate it. I either had to shut it all out and withdraw or let it all in like a freight train.
- I think a classroom should be quiet and free from distracting noises, such as a high-pitched vent fan. Some teachers have found that disturbing noises can be blocked out with headphones and music. When a child has to make a trip to a busy shopping center, a head set with a favorite tape can help make the trip more peaceful.
- I often misbehaved in church and screamed because my Sunday clothes felt different—scratchy petticoats drove me crazy; a feeling that would be insignificant to most people may feel like sand paper rubbing the skin raw to an autistic child. . . . Most people habituate to different types of clothes, but I keep feeling them for hours.
- Calming sensory activities immediately prior to school lessons or speech therapy may help to improve learning. These activities should be conducted as fun games.

- Abstract concepts such as getting along with people have to have a visual image. For example, my visual image for relationships with people was a sliding glass door. If you push it too hard it will break. To make the abstract concept more real, I would sometimes act it out—for example, by walking through a real sliding door.
- At puberty I was desperate for relief from the "nerves." . . . At my aunt's ranch, I observed that the cattle sometimes appeared to relax when they were held in the squeeze chute, a device for holding cattle for veterinary procedures. The animal is held tightly between two sides, which squeeze the body. After a horrible bout of the "nerves" I got in the squeeze chute. For about 45 minutes I was much calmer. I then built a squeeze-chute-like device which I could use to apply pressure (which I controlled). . . . I have made a successful career based on my fixation with cattle squeeze chutes. I have designed livestock handling systems for major ranches and meat companies all over the world. When I was in high school, many of my teachers and psychologists wanted to get rid of my fixation on cattle chutes. I am indebted to Mr. Carlock, my high school science teacher. He suggested that I read psychology journals and study so I could learn why the cattle chute had a relaxing effect. If my fixation had been taken away, I could have ended up in an institution. Do not confuse fixations with stereotyped behavior, such as hand flapping or rocking. A fixation is an interest in something external that should be diverted and used to motivate.

Note: From "Teaching Tips From a Recovered Autistic" by T. Grandin, 1988, *Focus on Autistic Behavior, 3*(1). Copyright 1988 by PRO-ED, Inc. Reprinted by permission

Another adult with autism, Donna Williams (1996), described that one of the biggest challenges with sensory input is the information overload that occurs when a person with autism is unable to filter irrelevant stimuli. She compared her sensory system to a sound track, by saying that she often works in a monotrack mode rather than a multitrack mode.

Can you think of times when your mind works on a multi-track and other times when it works on a monotrack? What are some of the complicating factors that occur when your mind mostly works on a monotrack?

> *Most people know what their body is doing while they are speaking or what their face is doing while they are using sign. Most people are able to consistently monitor all of these things because they are multi-tracked. People who work in monotrack are not so efficient at this. While speaking they may have no idea of their movement or facial expressions. While they are monitoring their facial expressions they may lose track of the volume of their speech or its intonation or its pace. While they are monitoring their volume, their pace, or their intonation, they may lose track of the word order or even lose track of the words they are using and whether they are saying what they meant to say. (Williams, 1996, p. 22)*

In addition to sensory disorders, movement disorders also are associated with autism. Examples of these disorders include abnormal posture; abnormal movements of the face, head, trunk, and limbs; abnormal eye movements; repeated gestures and mannerisms; and awkward gait (Leary & Hill, 1996). The Autism National Committee, a national organization comprised of families and professionals, applauds the growing emphasis on sensory and movement disorders:

> *The movement and sensory aspects of autism have long been noted and brushed aside, unstudied. Research evidence demonstrating the prevalence of serious movement disorders in people diagnosed with autism, . . . and their detection at an early age, suggests that these issues may be of central importance. The social impairments, stereotypies, preservation, and related behaviors found in autism may reflect . . . inability to establish movement-based patterns necessary for the development of relationship with caregivers. (National Institutes of Health Convene Autism, 1995, p. 4)*

Intellectual Functioning. Autism occurs in children with all levels of intelligence, ranging from those who are gifted to those who appear to have profound mental retardation (Rutter, 1978). The majority of people with autism, however, have been identified as having mental retardation. Although data from different studies vary, about 60 percent of people with autism have IQs below 50, 20 percent have IQs between 50 and 70, and 20 percent have IQs above 70 (Ritvo & Freeman, 1978).

It should be noted, however, that the administration of IQ tests is problematic for many children and youth with autism in terms of standardized administration (Sturmey & Sevin, 1995). For example, being in a strange environment with an unfamiliar examiner might be a catalyst for disruptive behavior. If the student refuses to participate and, instead, engages in self-injurious behavior, should the testing be stopped and postponed until a later time, or does the examiner fail the student on all the items? When interpreting IQ scores, the nondiscriminatory evaluation team needs to know about the conditions under which the test was administered.

Higher functioning autistic disorder refers to a condition in which individuals with autism have an intellectual quotient above 70 (Myles, Constant, Simpson, & Carlson, 1989; Tsai & Scott-Miller, 1988). As you learned earlier, higher functioning autism is often associated with Asperger disorder. Those people with higher cognitive abilities can pursue a fairly wide range of academic endeavors. Although they typically are able to develop spoken language, they often have patterns of less severe sensory and social challenges, such as those described by Temple Grandin in Box 10–3 (Bartak & Rutter, 1976; Tsai & Scott-Miller, 1988).

Another intellectual functioning variation is called the **savant syndrome.** These individuals typically display extraordinary abilities in areas such as calendar calculating, musical ability, mathematical skills, memorization, and mechanical abilities. But their unusual ability in these areas also occurs in conjunction with low ability in most other areas (Cheatham, Smith, Rucker, Polloway, & Lewis, 1995; Rimland, 1978; Treffert, 1989). For example, an individual with savant syndrome may be able to recite the baseball game scores and the batting averages of seemingly all games and players who have ever participated in the sport. A familiar example of savant ability is the betting calculations of Raymond in the movie *Rainman.*

What is the prevalence of savant syndrome? The estimations vary. On the conservative side, the prevalence of savants with truly extraordinary ability has been estimated to be fewer than 100 cases within the past 100 years (Treffert, 1989). A more liberal estimation is that there are hundreds and maybe even thousands of savants with extraordinary musical ability (Bergman & DePue, 1986). The theory of multiple intelligence (Gardner, 1987) has been applied to individuals with autism who have the savant syndrome.

One of the key implications for you as a teacher is to capitalize upon a student's strengths, provide meaningful and appropriate opportunities for skills to be applied, and simultaneously seek to broaden interests and strengths to related areas (Cheatham et al., 1995; Donnelly & Altman, 1994).

Higher functioning autistic disorder refers to a condition in which individuals with autism have an intellectual quotient above 70.

Savant syndrome is a condition in which individuals typically display extraordinary abilities in areas such as calendar calculating, musical ability, mathematical skills, memorization, and mechanical abilities. This unusual ability typically manifests itself in conjunction with low ability in most other skill areas.

The theory of multiple intelligence is discussed in Chapter 7.

❉ *A.J. is shown here with his classroom's calendar. Students who have autism find reassurance in structured, predictable schedules.*

Identifying the Causes of Autism

Historical Perspective on Causes.   There have been profound changes in our understanding of autism's causes. In his early work, Kanner (1943) suggested that parents of children with autism "were strongly preoccupied with abstractions of a scientific, literary, or artistic nature, and limited in genuine interest in people." From the beginning, then, parents were often seen as intelligent and achieving people of high socioeconomic status who were also "cold." Incredibly, mothers of children with autism became known as "refrigerator mothers."

A strong proponent of this view was Bruno Bettelheim (1950, 1967), who developed a theory called *psychogenesis*. In Box 10–4, Ruth Sullivan explains this theory and its impact on parents. As a parent of an adult with autism, Ruth has been a long-time advocate for appropriate services for individuals with autism and their families.

By the 1970s, research clearly established that autism is caused by brain or biochemical dysfunction before, during, or after birth, and that it is totally unwarranted to blame parents. In 1977 the National Society for Autistic Children (now known as the Autism Society of America) asserted, "No known factors in the psychological environment of a child have been shown to cause autism." The best way to understand the impact of the pervasive condemnation of parents is to hear their anger about being blamed by professionals. Frank Warren (1985), a leading advocate, service provider, and parent of a son with autism, expresses his anger about the Bettelheim theories in Box 10–5. Today, parents are not seen as the patients or as the cause of problems; they are seen as collaborators, as contributors to the solution of problems—a topic we will discuss later in this chapter.

❉ What are other areas within the disability field where you have heard parents blamed for their children's problems? From reading Ruth Sullivan's and Frank Warren's comments, what damage do you think blaming creates in family–professional partnerships?

Biomedical Causes.   There is broad agreement that autism is caused by an abnormality in brain development or by brain damage (I. C. Gillberg & Coleman, 1996).

> *As of 1997, the neurobiological underpinnings of autism have eluded our efforts at understanding (Bauman & Kemper, 1994; [I. C.] Gillberg & Coleman, 1996). Neuroimaging studies, electroencephalograms (EEGs), autopsy studies and neurochemical investigations have not revealed a consistent pattern of abnormalities. . . .*

BOX 10-4 MY VOICE

RUTH SULLIVAN: IMPACT OF THE PSYCHOGENESIS THEORY ON PARENTS

Parents who were not around in the 1950s, 60s, and even 70s trying to get a diagnosis for their (usually) beautiful young child with extremely difficult and inexplicable behavior might have a hard time understanding the oppressive and guilt-provoking dogma of most mental health professionals at that time. For some parents that I knew then, *each* time they took their child for an evaluation, they were told that they (especially the mother) had caused the autism. Families who could afford it went into psychotherapy or psychoanalysis. No assistance was given to the parents in handling the day-to-day worrisome behavior of their child. The theory, acted upon as fact, was that once the parents recognized and confronted their repressed and deep-seated anger (which caused their child to withdraw) they would then be fit to raise their otherwise normal child.

Bruno Bettelheim, the most articulate proponent of this mindset, was a skillful and much published writer as well as a popular and frequent guest on certain television talk shows, notably Dick Cavett's. In Bettelheim's book, *The Empty Fortress*, he compares the homes of autistic children to Nazi concentration camps (where, as an Austrian Jew, he was once a prisoner).

On 10 March 1967, a *New York Times* book review called the book "inspiring":

[Autism] is one of the severest forms of childhood schizophrenia . . . a suicide of the soul. . . . "Wherever we have penetrated," Bettelheim writes, "we have found hatred, extreme and explosive . . . eternally thwarted . . . so as to keep it from coming to awareness in unbearable pain." . . .

Dr. Bettelheim suggests that hatred and longing stem from extreme frustration in the mother–infant relationship. . . . "[Autism is a] phenomenon of dehumanization under extreme situations such as those imposed in the German concentration camps."

The professional and popular press unremittingly reported autism to be caused by parents, further isolating families of children with autism at a time when they desperately needed understanding and help.

The single most important event that laid that noxious psychogenic theory to its final rest (at least in the U.S.) was the founding in 1965 of the National Society for Autistic Children by Bernard Rimland, Ph.D. It took a generation (mine) of parents and a small group of brave professional colleagues who supported us. Psychogenesis in autism has been proven wrong.

That battle is won. Now we must continue the war for more and better services.

Ruth Sullivan
Huntington, West Virginia

> *The most interesting studies to date have focused on neurochemistry and neuroimaging . . . (Bailey, Phillips, & Rutter, 1996; Lotspeich & Ciaranello, 1993). The correction of these abnormalities underlies the approaches to drug therapy. Magnetic resonance imaging (MRI) and neuropathology studies have identified abnormalities in the . . . cortex (which controls emotions) and underdevelopment of the brainstem and cerebellum (Filipek, 1995; see also Bachevalier, 1994; Courchesne, Townsend, & Saitoh, 1994; Haas, Townsend, & Yeoung, 1996; Piven, Arndt, & Palmer, 1995). (Mauk et al., 1997, pp. 432–433)*

An exciting new development in the study of the cause of autism is a five-year, $27 million international network to conduct research for the purpose of pinpointing autism's cause and course of development. Headquartered at the National Institutes of Health, this international network will involve twenty-four universities throughout the United States and in four foreign countries working collaboratively with families to focus on autism diagnosis, brain development, social development, and communication.

Identifying the Prevalence of Autism

The prevalence rate for autism is approximately 1 of every 1,000 children (Costello, 1996). Several surveys reported three to four times as many males as females (C. Gillberg, 1984; Lotter, 1966; Steinhausen, Gobel, Breinlinger, & Wohleben, 1983). During the 1994 to 1995 school year, the U.S. Department of Education (1996) reported that 22,768 students with autism were served by the schools.

A.J. lives in a community of about 42,250 people, and there are approximately 4,500 students in the school district from kindergarten through twelfth grade. How many people with autism would you estimate attend the district's schools? How would you promote relationships among them?

BOX 10–5 | MY VOICE

FRANK WARREN: PERSPECTIVE ON PARENTAL BLAME

Do you hear that out there, Bruno Bettelheim? . . . Do you hear? Are we getting through to you? We said, *No known facts in the psychological environment of a child have been shown to cause autism.* Now do you hear? Do you understand?

   That means we didn't do it, Bruno. We've known that all along. It means that careful, objective, scientific people have carried out study after study, test after test, interview after interview, and have written paper after paper and journal after journal which showed that we, the parents of autistic children, are just ordinary people. Not any crazier than others. Not "refrigerator parents" any more than others. Not cold intellectuals any more than others. Not neurotic or psychopathic or sociopathic or any of those words that have been made up. It means, Dr. Bettelheim, that you, and all those others like you who have been laying this incredible guilt trip on us for over twenty years, you are wrong and ought to be ashamed of yourself. "Feral mothers" indeed! You are a feral mother, Bruno. Take that and live with it for a while. It doesn't feel very good, does it? And "parentectomy"? It is my considered professional opinion, after having carefully examined all the facts, that nothing short of Bruno-ectomy will improve conditions in this case. And a Freud-ectomy. And a psychiatrist-ectomy. And a jargon-ectomy, and a professional baloney-ectomy.

Note: From "A Society That Is Going to Kill Your Children," by F. Warren, in *Parents Speak Out: Then and Now,* edited by H. R. Turnbull and A. P. Turnbull, 1985, Upper Saddle River, NJ: Merrill/Prentice Hall. Copyright 1985 by Merrill/Prentice Hall. Reprinted with permission.

WHAT ARE EVALUATION PROCEDURES?

Determining the Presence of Autism

The diagnosis of autism is a complex process. Many children receive the initial diagnosis of autism from a physician or a nondiscriminatory evaluation team, typically during their early childhood years. Evaluators usually administer some of the same tests as they give to students with mental retardation (see Chapter 8) and students with severe and multiple disabilities (see Chapter 9). According to a national survey of assessment practices in 42 states, the areas most frequently assessed to determine eligibility for the diagnosis of autism include "speech and language (18 states), academic achievement (15 states), cognitive functioning (14 states), and medical physical status (14 states)" (Conderman & Katsiyannis, 1996, p. 32). Figure 10–1 highlights the types of assessments used for observations, screening, and nondiscriminatory evaluation and associated findings.

   One of the most frequently used diagnostic scales is the Childhood Autism Rating Scale (CARS), which requires behavioral observations in fifteen areas of a child's functioning. Examples include impairment in human relationships, inappropriate affect, resistance to environmental change, and verbal communication. Each of the fifteen areas is rated on a continuum from typical to severely atypical behavior. The ratings depend on the frequency and intensity of the student's behavior and on how age-appropriate it is.

   The CARS was compared to other diagnostic instruments used for students with autism and was found to be the most valid in distinguishing students with autism from those with mental retardation (Teal & Wiebe, 1986). The CARS can be used on a longitudinal basis to assess changes in behaviors over time (Mesibov, Schopler, Schaffer, & Michal, 1989). But even though the CARS has adequate reliability and validity, it should not be used as the sole measure in the diagnosis of autism. Like other diagnostic instruments, it does not yield the kind of information that is necessary for individualized educational programming (Morgan, 1988; Parks, 1988).

FIGURE 10–1 *Evaluating whether a student has autism*

Nondiscriminatory Evaluation

Observation

Medical or psychological professionals and parents observe	Child is challenged by social conversations, does not play with others, is frequently unresponsive to voices, may exhibit echolalia or other unusual speech patterns, usually has language development delays, is disrupted by changes in daily routine, has difficulty sleeping, or engages in stereotypical behaviors.

Screening

Assessment measures	Findings that indicate need for further evaluation
Physical examinations	Physician notes that child is not reaching developmental milestones, especially in areas of social and language development. The child's physical health is usually normal. The physician may refer the child to a psychiatrist or psychologist for further evaluation.
Psychological evaluations	The child meets the Diagnostic Standards Manual-IV criteria for autism, including (1) qualitative impairment in social interaction, (2) qualitative impairment in communication, and (3) restricted repetitive and stereotyped patterns of behavior.

Prereferral

The student is usually identified before starting school. In rare circumstances in which the student is not identified before starting school, the severity of the disability may preclude the use of prereferral.

Referral

Children with autism should be referred by medical personnel or parents for early intervention during the infancy/preschool years. The child is referred upon reaching school age.

Nondiscriminatory evaluation procedures and standards

Assessment measures	Findings that suggest autism
Individualized intelligence test	Seventy-five percent of students with autism perform two or more standard deviations below the mean, indicating mental retardation. Others have average or even gifted intelligence. Evaluating intelligence is generally difficult because of challenging social and language behaviors.
Individualized achievement tests	Students with autism who have average or above-average intelligence may perform at an average or above-average level in one or more areas of achievement. Some individuals with autism have unusual giftedness in one or more areas. Students with autism typically have below-average intelligence.
Adaptive behavior scales	The student usually scores significantly below average in areas of adaptive behavior, indicating severe deficits in skills such as communication, daily living, socialization, gross- and fine-motor coordination, and socially appropriate behavior.
Autism-specific scales	The student's scores meet the criteria for identifying the student as having autism.
Direct observation	The student's self-initiated interactions with teacher and peers are limited. The student exhibits language delays and may use unusual speech patterns such as echolalia. The observer may notice that the student has difficulty in changes of routine and manifests stereotypical behaviors.
Anecdotal records	Records suggest that performance varies according to moods, energy level, extent and pile-up of environmental changes, and whether or not individual preferences are incorporated.

Nondiscriminatory Evaluation Team determines that student has autism and needs special education and related services.

Appropriate Education

Determining the Nature and Extent of Special Education and Related Services

The previously mentioned survey of forty-two states revealed that few states use ecological procedures as part of their assessment approach for students with autism (Conderman & Katsiyannis, 1996). These authors lamented this fact and recommended a much wider usage of ecological assessment in order to determine the appropriateness of individualized programming for students with autism. One kind of useful ecological assessment is functional assessment. A functional assessment identifies specific relationships between challenging behaviors and the circumstances that trigger the incidences of challenging behavior. Although functional assessment is helpful for many students, regardless of the specific category of exceptionality, it is particularly apt for students with autism. Here are five steps for conducting a functional assessment (Demchak & Bossert, 1996; Foster-Johnson & Dunlap, 1993):

1. Specify and carefully define the target challenging behavior so it can be observed and measured.

FIGURE 10–2 *Circumstances that influence problem behaviors*

1. *Physiological Factors*

   Sickness/allergies

   Side effects of medication

   Fatigue

   Hunger or thirst

   Increased arousal due to a fight, missing the bus, a disruptive routine

2. *Classroom Environment*

   High noise level

   Uncomfortable temperature

   Over- or understimulation

   Poor seating arrangement

   Frequent disruptions

3. *Curriculum and Instruction*

   Few opportunities for making instructions

   Lack of predictability

   Inadequate level of assistance provided to the student

   Unclear directions provided for activity completion

   Few opportunities for the student to communicate

   Activities that are too difficult

   Activities that take a long time to complete

   Activities that the student dislikes

   Activities for which the completion criteria are unclear

   Activities that might not be perceived as being relevant or useful by the student

Note: From "Using Functional Assessment to Develop Effective, Individualized Interventions for Challenging Behaviors" by L. Foster-Johnson and G. Dunlap, *Teaching Exceptional Children, 25,* 1993, pp. 44–50. Copyright 1993 by The Council for Exceptional Children. Reprinted with permission.

2. Identify all circumstances that are regularly associated with the occurrence and nonoccurrence of the behavior. Determine what events occur before, during, and after the student's appropriate and inappropriate behavior (see Figure 10–2). Teachers, family members, teacher aides, and other students can all help pinpoint antecedents—factors that occur before challenging behavior. Figure 10–3 includes a sample data collection chart that illustrates a time-efficient way to record teacher observations.

> Antecedents are conditions that occur just before the challenging behavior.

3. Determine the student's reasons for the behavior. Often, behavior serves the function of either getting or escaping from something. If a student is trying to get something, find out what he or she is trying to get and why; perhaps it is attention from classmates, sensory stimulation, or access to some favorite activity. If a student is trying to escape something, determine the specific circumstances that the student is attempting to avoid, such as seat work, interaction with particular people, or the change of an activity.

> From analyzing the scatter plot in Figure 10–3, what do you learn about the timing of Jerry's head hitting?

4. Describe in very specific hypothesis statements the relationship between the behavior and the environmental events or circumstances, based on a careful analysis of the available information. Focus on factors and environments that can be changed so that the student's behavior also can change. Table 10–1 shows sample hypothesis statements.

FIGURE 10–3 *Scatter plot recording teacher observations of challenging behaviors*

Student: Jerry Mitchell

Date: 3/11 to 3/22

Behavior: Head hitting—any occurrence in which contact is made between Jerry's open hand (palm) and any part of his head or face

Respondent: Ms. McClean

■ = More than 3 hits   □ = Less than 3 hits

Activity	Time	1	2	3	4	5	6	7	8	9	10
Breakfast	8:30–9:00									□	
Personal hygiene	9:00–9:15									□	
Schedule/assignments	9:15–9:30				■					■	
Community-based instruction	9:30–10:45										
PE/music	10:45–11:15									■	
Domestic	11:15–12:00		■		□		■				
Lunch	12:00–12:30				□						
Personal hygiene	12:30–12:45								■	□	
Vocational activities	12:45–1:30	■		□	□		■	■			
Leisure	1:30–2:00					■					
Prepare for home	2:00–2:15					■			■		
Bus	2:20									□	

Note: From "Using Functional Assessment to Develop Effective, Individualized Interventions for Challenging Behaviors" by L. Foster-Johnson and G. Dunlap, *Teaching Exceptional Children, 25,* 1993, pp. 44–50. Copyright 1993 by The Council for Exceptional Children. Reprinted with permission.

TABLE 10–1 ❧ *Sample hypothesis statements and possible interventions for challenging behaviors*

	Intervention	
Hypothesis Statement	**Modify Antecedents**	**Teach Alternative Behavior**
Suzy starts pinching herself and others around 11:00 A.M. every day because she gets hungry.	Make sure Suzy gets breakfast. Provide a snack at about 9:30 A.M.	Teach Suzy to ask for something to eat.
Jack gets into arguments with the teacher every day during reading class when she asks him to correct his mistakes on the daily reading worksheet.	Get Jack to correct his own paper. Give Jack an easier assignment.	Teach Jack strategies to manage his frustration in a more appropriate manner. Teach Jack to ask for teacher assistance with the incorrect problems.
Tara starts pouting and refuses to work when she has to sort a box of washers because she doesn't want to do the activity.	Give Tara half the box of washers to sort. Give Tara clear instructions about how much she has to do or how long she must work.	Teach Tara to ask for a break from the activity.
Frank kicks other children in morning circle time and usually gets to sit right by the teacher.	Give each child a clearly designated section of the floor that is his or hers.	Teach Frank how to ask the children to move over. Teach Frank how to ask the teacher to intervene with his classmates.
Harry is off task for most of math class when he is supposed to be adding two-digit numbers.	Ask Harry to add the prices of actual food items. Intersperse an easy activity with the more difficult math addition so Harry can experience some success.	Teach Harry how to ask for help. Teach Harry how to monitor his rate of problem completion and provide reinforcement for a certain number of problems.

Note: From "Using Functional Assessment to Develop Effective, Individualized Interventions for Challenging Behaviors" by L. Foster-Johnson and G. Dunlap, *Teaching Exceptional Children, 25,* 1993, pp. 44–50. Copyright 1993 by The Council for Exceptional Children. Reprinted with permission.

5. Develop an intervention plan based on the hypothesis statements. The plan should change environmental events and circumstances so that problem behavior is less likely to occur and desirable behavior is more likely to occur. Emphasize teaching alternative behaviors so the student will be able to achieve the same function (e.g., getting attention from classmates) but in a socially acceptable manner (see Table 10-1).

Several researchers have particularly focused on strategies for supporting parents to carry out functional assessments (Fox, Dunlap, & Philbrick, in press; Lucyshyn & Albin, 1993; Mullen & Frea, 1995), as you will read about in the early childhood program model later in the chapter.

WHAT AND HOW DO PROFESSIONALS TEACH?

As with all students with exceptionalities, individualization in curriculum and methods is the key to appropriate, beneficial education for students with autism. It is essential to remember that, among the broad range of functioning of people with autism, most have mental retardation, but some have normal or above-average intelligence. Thus, the student's cognitive development is an important consideration in determining the appropriate curriculum and methods.

IDEA requires a functional assessment when students' behavior interferes with their or other students' learning. Since IDEA requires a student's parents to be part of the evaluation and individualized education program (IEP) teams, the basis for functional assessment and the positive behavioral support program based on it probably will generalize across the student's life in school and at home.

BOX 10-6

SELF-DETERMINATION

A self-determination curriculum for youth with autism who have a higher cognitive functioning level was field-tested by high [school] teachers in ten different high school classes with over 100 students. Each class included one or two students with autism. Classes were set up so that peer tutors who did not have disabilities were paired with the students with autism.

The curriculum entitled *Putting Feet on My Dreams* included the following seven units:

Unit 1: Introduction to Self-Determination and Program Overview
Unit 1 introduces the program to students and establishes ground rules so that students feel safe sharing their experiences and learning about themselves.

Unit 2: Life Knowledge for Self-Determination
Students explore what adults must know, do, and decide in order to be independent in specific life tasks.

Unit 3: Life Planning
Students first develop a Life Map which is then used to identify goals. Each student then explores the steps needed to reach their goals through a Goal-Planning Meeting and Action Plan (which students begin to implement).

Unit 4: Communication
Students learn the importance of being an effective communicator, verbal and nonverbal actions can promote and inhibit communication, ways to assess their own communication skills.

Unit 5: Learning
Students become aware of how one uses one's senses to learn and of learning strategies that can facilitate learning, thinking, and problem solving.

Unit 6: Organizing
Students develop organizational skills related to tasks, materials, and time. They become aware of how they use their time to accomplish one project and develop a weekly schedule.

Unit 7: Sharing Self-Folio With Others
Students organize self-folios and identify ways they can use their self-folio in the future. They share what they have learned with family members and friends or with other students.

Parents of students who completed the program reported significant improvement in their son or daughter's skills and attitudes related to self-determination. They also reported that the students initiated changes in their own behavior. Effective instructional strategies included providing information visually (e.g., diagrams were used to visually depict concepts, students drew a life map to illustrate long-term goals and more specific short-term goals) and social structuring of situations (e.g., videotaping, communication role-plays).

Note: Reprinted from *Journal of Vocational Rehabilitation, 5,* A. Fullerton, "Promoting Self-Determination for Adolescents and Young Adults With Autism," pp. 337–346, 1995, with kind permission from Elsevier Science Ireland Ltd., Bay 15K, Shannon Industrial Estate, Co. Clare, Ireland.

Curriculum

Students with autism who function at higher cognitive levels should have a thorough educational assessment of their academic achievement and potential (Myles et al., 1989). Just as self-determination is an important curriculum area for students with mental retardation (as discussed in Chapter 8), so it is also an emerging, new curriculum area for students with autism (Fullerton, 1995). Box 10-6, "Into Practice," describes a self-determination curriculum for adolescents and young adults with autism who function at a higher cognitive level.

The majority of students with autism also have mental retardation, and their curriculum is often similar to that for students with mental retardation (see Chapter 8) and severe and multiple disabilities (see Chapter 9). The curriculum domains for these students typically include the following (Berkell, 1992):

• Life skills for integrated community living

• Vocational preparation

• Functional academics

When you read the descriptions of program models at the end of this chapter, you will find examples of each of these curriculum domains. Each one can promote full citizenship.

The life skills curriculum begins early in a student's elementary career and includes an emphasis on social interaction, communication, safety, and daily living skills. Vocational preparation begins in elementary school by teaching the student to develop work habits and carry out classroom responsibilities. The emphasis in middle school is on exposure to a variety of different jobs, and the secondary school emphasis is on actual job training in inclusive community work sites. Functional academics concentrates on skills useful in everyday living (e.g., counting money, telling time, reading survival words, and understanding transportation schedules) and is carried out in all years of schooling.

Methods

Instructional methods vary for students with autism. Two frequently used methods are (a) positive behavioral support and (b) social stories.

Positive Behavioral Support.   Applied behavior analysis, which you read about in Chapter 5, is being expanded to a more comprehensive approach of **positive behavioral support** (Carr et al., 1994; Horner & Carr, 1997; L. K. Koegel, Koegel, & Dunlap, 1996; Weigle, 1997) (see Figure 10–4). Positive behavioral support recognizes that students' challenging behaviors often reside in someone else's failure to provide individualized and comprehensive support (Turnbull & Ruef, 1996, 1997). Thus, this approach seeks to create a responsive environment that is personally tailored to the preferences, strengths, and needs of individuals with challenging behavior. As you know from reading Chapter 1, IDEA requires educators to consider using functional assessment and to position behavioral support when behavior impedes a student's learning or other students' learning.

Positive behavioral support is an approach to decreasing or eliminating challenging behavior by creating a responsive environment that is personally tailored to the preferences, strengths, and needs of individuals with challenging behavior.

A peer buddy system matches each student who has autism with other students who may offer one-on-one tutoring and companionship.

1. Focus on the person's entire life-style and emphasize procedures for helping to build relationships and for including the person in preferred activities, places, and events.

2. Use functional assessment to pinpoint the reasons for the problem behavior and to ensure that the intervention program responds to those reasons.

3. Use multiple interventions and recognize that a single one is rarely adequate.

4. Build the plan around many different events such as exercise, noise levels, sleeping patterns, and eating schedules.

5. Change the events that seem to elicit problem behavior.

6. Teach adaptive behavior such as communication skills so the student can express frustrations rather than act out.

7. Help the student develop a wider range of interests so that effective reinforcing events can be arranged.

8. Minimize punishers.

9. Put emergency procedures into place so that families and educators know exactly how to respond in crisis situations.

10. Choose behavioral interventions that respond precisely to problems and that are the least intrusive possible.

11. Make sure that all behavioral interventions maintain and support the person's dignity.

12. Do not use procedures that typical members of the community would find offensive.

FIGURE 10–4 *Principles of positive behavioral support*

Note: From "Toward a Technology of 'Nonaversive' Behavioral Support," by R. N. Horner, G. Dunlap, R. L. Koegel, E. G. Carr, W. Sailor, J. Anderson, R. W. Albin, and R. E. O'Neill, 1990, *Journal of the Association for Persons with Severe Handicaps, 15*(3). Copyright 1990 by JASH. Reprinted with permission.

Figure 10-4 lists positive behavioral support principles. As you will note, the second principle addresses the importance of using functional assessment to pinpoint challenging behavior. The evaluation procedures that you have already learned in this chapter will prepare you in carrying out this principle.

The elementary program description in the program options section later in the chapter features a twelve-year-old student, Samantha, who receives positive behavioral support for challenges that she faces at school, as well as at home and within the community. When you read this description, you will see that through positive behavioral support, Samantha truly did "get a life." Getting a life is exactly the emphasis of positive behavioral support (Horner et al., 1990; Risley, 1996; Turnbull & Turnbull, 1996). Risley describes what it means to support a person to get a life as follows:

> The patterns of the person's weekly and monthly life, and of his or her interactions with the people, places, and things he or she prefers or despises, are the units of consideration. The programming . . . is to arrange for a life reduced in stress, deprivation, and fear; enriched in those things that attract and engage the person's interest and repertoire; and richly responsive to his or her activities— And I would add, a life that provides the varied and complex experiences over months and years that will produce development *in the person's reinforcers, repertoire, and fluency. For emphasis, let me label this level of intervention* life arrangement. *(Risley, 1996, p. 428)*

By applying the positive behavioral support principles outlined in Figure 10-4 with the students you teach, you will be able to provide relevant and comprehensive support that can enable them also to get a life.

A.J. would particularly like to have more friends and to have more activities, such as soccer, in which he could participate. As his teacher, what steps do you think you might take to help him get a life in these ways?

STEPHEN'S WORLD

Although still a teenager, Stephen Wiltshire's drawings of his travels are worth thousands of dollars. This "accidental tourist from an inner world of his own" has autism. "Stephen's World" profiles his inner life as well as his whimsical architectural renderings, which have garnered international acclaim. In addition, this video explores attempts to provide Stephen with a well-rounded education—one that results in opportunities for him to develop his talent while receiving social and functional skill training.

What do you think? Margaret Henson, Stephen's literary agent, commented, "I treated him the same way that I would probably treat any child in my family. Had I read what one could and could not do [with a person who has autism], I think I would have been so scared, really, that we would never have had a relationship at all." How has the information you have received through reading this textbook affected your comfort level with people with autism? Why?

Temple Grandin emphasizes that fixations should not be confused with stereotypical behavior. "A fixation is an interest in something external that should be diverted and used to motivate." How was that accomplished in Stephen's life? How would you use a student's fixation with weather broadcasts to help motivate him to learn new skills?

Social stories, usually written by parents or educators, describe social situations in terms of important social cues and appropriate responses to those cues.

Social Stories.   Social stories, written by parents or educators, describe social situations in terms of important social cues and appropriate responses to those cues (Gray, 1994). Social stories help students with autism to focus on relevant social cues, learn new routines and rules, and expand their social skills (Gray & Garand, 1993). Figure 10–5 includes a social story that A.J.'s teacher wrote to help address a particularly sensitive issue for A.J.—putting his hands in his pants.

A recent research study examined the use of social stories with three students with autism. One of these students was A.J. For this study, the researchers

- Identified a target behavior or problem situation for intervention.

- Defined the target behaviors and collected baseline data on each.

- Worked with the student in writing a social story using descriptive, directive, perspective, and controlling sentences.

- Placed one to three sentences per page and used accompanying photographs, pictures, or icons.

- Read the social story to the student and modeled the desirable behavior.

- Collected intervention data on the target behaviors.

FIGURE 10–5 *Private places—A social story*

> A private place is a part of your body that most other people do not see. It is OK for you and your mom and dad to see those places.
>
> Usually, a private place is covered by underwear. When you are a boy, your private places are your penis and your bottom.
>
> Everybody has private places on their bodies. Sometimes people want to look at or touch their private places. It is OK to want to know about your body.
>
> If you want to look at or touch your private places, you need to go to a bathroom by yourself. It is OK to look at or touch private places in a private bathroom when you are alone there.
>
> If you touch your private places in the bathroom, you need to wash your hands when you are done.
>
> It is OK to want to know about your body. Everybody wants to know about their own bodies.

Note: From Stephanie Mathew.

The social stories for all of the students focused on decreasing aggressive behavior, and the postintervention data showed decreases for all students (Swaggart et al., 1995).

HOW IS PARTICIPATION ENCOURAGED?

Inclusion

Approximately 80 percent of students with autism are educated in separate environments, as illustrated in Figure 10–6. Only about 9 percent received the majority of their education in a general education classroom.

Denise is thankful that A.J. does not need to leave his community, and she also appreciates the specially trained personnel and resources available at his school. A.J. has peer buddies who help him in his fourth-grade class. These peer buddies come to the structured learning class and work with A.J. in a quieter, more structured environment. They also accompany the students with autism on community-based instruction trips. On the down side, she believes a neighborhood school would enable A.J. to attend school closer to home and that there would be only one school for her to be involved in; now, she has to devote herself to the two different schools that her children attend.

When Denise begins to think about neighborhood schools for her community, she recognizes that there are eleven students with autism who attend the primary and intermediate class. These students are now clustered at two sites (one primary school and one elementary), but they would attend eight different schools if they all attended in their neighborhoods. Major school reform would be needed in Denise's community for this to occur.

Professionals and families alike have different opinions about the appropriateness of educating students with autism in inclusive settings (Berkell, 1992; Turnbull & Ruef, 1997). The following quotation expresses the nature of some of the debate:

> *The full inclusion debate has too often been reduced to superficial arguments over who is right, who is moral and ethical, and who is a true advocate for children. . . . We are of the opinion that full inclusion of children and youth with autism is the right thing to do only if it benefits students with disabilities and their normally developing peers, or (ideally) if it is beneficial to both groups. (Simpson & Sasso, 1992)*

Obviously, inclusion that does not benefit students is unwarranted. Educators, however, must ensure that the lack of benefit is not due to their own inabilities to individualize instruction. We encourage you to consider the "Inclusion Tips" box for students with autism.

Social stories written by children and adults with autism are compiled in a book entitled *The Original Social Story Book* (Broek et al., 1993).

IDEA funds state and local school improvements grants so that students such as A.J. and others with autism will be more included in their neighborhood schools in the general education curriculum, extracurricular activities, and other nonacademic activities.

FIGURE 10–6 *Educational environments of students with autism*

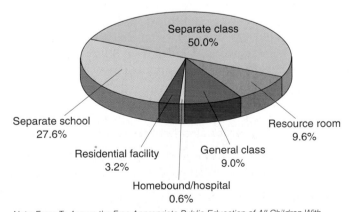

Separate class
50.0%

Separate school
27.6%

Resource room
9.6%

Residential facility
3.2%

General class
9.0%

Homebound/hospital
0.6%

Note: From *To Assure the Free Appropriate Public Education of All Children With Disabilities: Eighteenth Annual Report to Congress on the Implementation of the Individuals with Disabilities Education Act,* by the U.S. Department of Education, 1996, Washington, DC: U.S. Department of Education.

Inclusion Tips

	What You Might See	What You Might Be Tempted to Do	Alternate Responses	Ways to Include Peers in the Process
Behavior	The student often rocks back and forth over and over during class activities he's not interested in.	Ignore the behavior or tell him to stop.	Collaborate with the inclusion specialist. Suggest a preferred activity that builds on his strengths and interests.	Help peers to understand the behavior. Encourage and support their acceptance of him.
Social Interactions	He bites others who try to work with him and may repeat their language.	Isolate him from other students and discipline his behavior.	Collaborate with the inclusion specialist to establish a method of communication.	Pair him with students who understand his preferred communication method.
Educational Performance	The student learns very slowly and needs a great deal of extra help to learn simple concepts.	Expect less and make the requirements less structured.	Use visual images and music to teach abstract concepts.	Provide opportunities for peer tutoring with visual images and music.
Classroom Attitudes	The student has an inability to focus and may become antagonistic during activities in which there is much noise or confusion.	Remove him from class activities to work alone.	Use social stories to help him predict activities and plan attitudes and responses for difficult situations.	Teach peers to write social stories that include all students. Have small groups including the student revise and work out different scenarios.

Some inclusion models are producing benefits for students with autism and their classmates. One of those models has concentrated on including in general classroom settings eleven children with autism who also present severe challenging behaviors (Quill, 1990). These students were included from 50 to 80 percent of the school day. This inclusion program has the following components (Quill, 1990):

- Active parental involvement in the development and implementation of the program

- Technical support for all school faculty and family members

- An individually designed inclusion plan that matches children's learning styles and interests to their curriculum of daily activities with typical peers

- A peer buddy program

- An ecological approach to curriculum development

- Creative management of challenging behaviors

BOX 10-7

INTO PRACTICE

KATE'S INCLUSION

Upon entry to the program, "Kate" (not her real name) was a nonverbal six-year-old with high frequencies of screaming, tantrums, and destruction of materials. Kate did not have access to an alternative system of communication. She was a very active child who enjoyed movement activities, a variety of art activities such as coloring, cutting, and pasting, and "the color red." During the first weeks of school, Kate engaged in one or more of the three challenging behaviors 80 percent of her day. The two-week functional analysis revealed that these behaviors usually served as a specific communication request, typically when she was distracted by her desire to obtain a red item nearby, and/or occurred in situations when adult expectations were confusing to her, particularly during transitions. Kate's behaviors were cyclical in nature, beginning with screaming and accelerating into material destruction and tantrums.

The intervention plan for Kate's challenging behaviors consisted of:

1. Teaching the use of a pictographic *communication* board
2. Teaching the use of a pictorial schedule for her daily curriculum of highly *preferred activities,* including many gym and art experiences
3. Establishing *explicit routines* for adult–Kate interactions within each activity
4. Establishing *clear skill expectations* within each curricular activity
5. Providing Kate with the *option to choose* red materials during each activity
6. Teaching *relaxation* techniques
7. *Redirecting* Kate when she needed assistance, while ignoring her screaming

Within five months of the onset of the program, Kate's challenging behaviors had been virtually extinguished. Kate was using eighty pictographs to augment her gestural communication at that time, and had developed a special relationship with a third-grade boy who befriended her on the playground. She continues to expand her communication and social skills, at home and school.

Note: From "A Model for Integrating Children with Autism" by K. A. Quill, 1990, *Focus on Autistic Behavior, 5*(4). Copyright 1990 by PRO-ED, Inc. Reprinted by permission.

The children learned to engage in appropriate behavior in small and large group settings, developed play skills, expanded their communication with peers and adults, and made friends with their classmates. The classmates without disabilities were able to communicate socially, interact, and make friends with the children with autism. They also showed an increasing acceptance of individuals with differences (Quill, 1990).

"Into Practice" (see Box 10–7) describes how the program was designed for a six-year-old student.

Collaboration

A successful inclusion model relies heavily on collaboration among professionals, families, and peers. The one highlighted in the "Collaboration Tips" box later in this section, exemplifies collaboration in each of the following areas:

Professional Collaboration. A number of professionals have helped to make the program described in the "Collaboration Tips" box successful:

- *Parent–educator liaison:* A special educator with broad experience in teaching children with autism whose primary role was to increase communication and collaboration among educators and families

- *Program consultants:* Two special educators with graduate-level training provided assistance for teachers in conducting comprehensive evaluations, developing curriculum, and designing the inclusion model

- *Related-service personnel:* A physical therapist, occupational therapist, and a speech-language pathologist who consulted with teachers, families, and children

Family Collaboration.   The home–school partnership had four components:

- *School-based observations.* Parents were encouraged to observe their child at school in instructional activities. During the observations, the parent–educator liaison provided parents with an ecological inventory of the activity they were observing so that they could follow the instruction.

- *Home-based parent education.* Depending on their preferences, parents received either biweekly or monthly home visits. Particular attention focused on helping the child to be as successful at home as possible in areas such as interacting with family members, communication, play, and appropriate behavior. Priorities were identified that became part of the child's instructional program at school. Teachers and parents also communicated daily through written notes that the child took back and forth between home and school.

- *Parent support group.* A monthly parent support group discussed topics important to families, including problems at home, resources families need, and issues associated with feelings and needs. The parent–educator liaison shared a monthly newsletter with information for families on reading materials available in the project's library.

- *Crisis management.* The parent–educator liaison was always available to families by phone when a crisis arose. If families needed it, they were helped to locate child care so that they could take a break from their parenting responsibilities.

Compare and contrast the family collaboration described here with the earlier approach (advocated by Bruno Bettelheim) of blaming parents for their child's problems.

There were many ways in which families helped to promote the success of inclusion. Approximately half of them volunteered from two to six hours per week with children at school (not their own children), helping to implement specific instructional and positive behavioral support programs. Families also cooperated with the faculty and administration in helping to sensitize others to individual differences. Their approaches included a meeting at the beginning of the school year for all faculty, an open forum to discuss the inclusion model, and the use of puppets to help make other students aware of the needs of children with autism.

Although this inclusion model did an excellent job in involving families of students with autism and in providing information to families of all students in this school, all inclusion is not implemented in such a systemic way. In some situations, parents of children without disabilities, as well as those with autism, have major concerns about the extent to which their children's educational needs are appropriately being met. The "Collaboration Tips" box suggests collaborative roles and tasks that might be undertaken to address parental concerns.

Student and Community Collaboration.   Peers had important roles in helping this program to succeed. Every child with autism had two or more peers who were involved in a buddy program. These peer buddies served as tutors, companions, and playmates during various portions of the school day. Teachers provided specific guidance and support as needed to help enhance the social connection between the children with autism and their peer buddies.

At the end of the year, the peer buddies commented on the program. Their responses indicated more similarities than differences between themselves and their friends with autism. They learned to deal with the challenging behaviors of the students and regarded these behaviors simply as part of the way that their classmates interacted. One of the peer

BOX 10-8 MY VOICE

ANNE M. DONNELLAN: CLASSROOM TEACHING

According to my observations, outstanding teachers of students with autism have a very good sense of humor, are analytical, are bright, and demonstrate a fundamental intuitiveness. Intuitiveness allows excellent teachers to read the behavior of others and respond in a respectful way. I remember one summer observing students in a Quonset hut in New Mexico where a seventeen-year-old student with autism was seated in the corner being given lots of busywork. It was 110 degrees and everyone was oppressively hot. All of a sudden this student jumped up and ripped his shirt off. His teacher turned to me in frustration and asked, "What causes this inappropriate behavior?" I recall telling her that this student was so hot he absolutely couldn't stand it any longer and didn't know how to unbutton his shirt. If you are the kind of person who can intuit why people behave as they do, even when they do not have words to tell you, teaching individuals with autism is a field you might consider.

Anne M. Donnellan
Professor, University of Wisconsin, Madison

buddies noted that his friend with autism "only had tantrums when she is with her teacher, never me" (Quill, 1990).

It is obvious that successful inclusion requires the collaboration of all key stakeholders. Earlier, you learned about some of Denise's perspectives on the benefits and drawbacks of inclusion for her school and community.

Careers

As you read this chapter, did you picture yourself as a teacher of students with autism? In the "My Voice" box (Box 10–8), Anne M. Donnellan, a leading special educator in the field of autism, advises college students about some of the essential characteristics of outstanding teachers of students with autism.

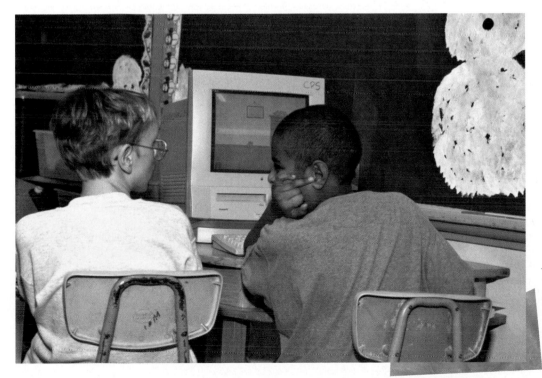

❤ *Peer buddies, with support and guidance from teachers, often form mutually beneficial connections with students who have autism.*

Collaboration Tips

RESPONDING TO CONCERNS OF PARENTS OF STUDENTS WITHOUT DISABILITIES

COLLABORATION GOALS   To listen to the concerns of parents of students without disabilities and develop an action plan to address their concerns about time and attention focused on needs of student with autism or other disability.

Collaborators	Roles and Preparation	Possible Barriers	Solutions to Barriers	Modifications to Implementation	Ongoing Evaluation
Parents of students without disabilities	Be prepared to discuss concerns about the time and attention required of general educator to meet needs of student with disability.	Fear sons/daughters are not getting appropriate time and attention of general educator; may not have complete or accurate information.	Invite parents to observe classes as a way to alleviate concerns.	Invite parents to share any ongoing concerns and to generate satisfactory alternatives to be included in action plan(s).	Monitor the implementation of action plan(s).
Peers of students with disabilities	Assess calssroom experiences with student(s) who has (have) disability; relate learning experiences.	May not be able to judge fair allocation of general educator's time.	Invite students to comment on any situations where they believe some students are receiving extra time and attention.	Have students keep a journal to dialogue about perceptions of general educator's time spent expressly to meet students with disabilities needs.	Encourage regular journal dialogue reviewing students' perspectives on an ongoing basis.
Parents of student(s) with disability	Prepare list of positive experiences son/daughter has had in general education classroom; generate list of effective alternatives to respond to concerns offered.	Fear that son or daughter will be penalized or ostracized.	Invite parents to observe classroom to explore and discuss concerns.	Participate in group problem solving to generate alternatives to respond to each concern and to help develop action plan(s).	Monitor the implementation of action plan(s).
General Educator(s)	Document the time and resources required by students with disability; listen to concerns, and help develop action plan to ensure that instructional time for all students is fairly appropriated.	Sensitivity to being criticized by parents.	Recognize all parental concerns, informing parents of federal requirements of IDEA. Ask parents to brainstorm ways to ensure class time is fairly allocated among students. Set up plan to use parent volunteers.	Seek to understand parents and solicit other professionals to help devise a "win-win" action plan.	Monitor the implementation of the action plan to ensure an appropriate education for all students.

Collaborators	Roles and Preparation	Possible Barriers	Solutions to Barriers	Modifications to Implementation	Ongoing Evaluation
Special Educator(s)	Review procedures for developing a group action plan; prepare to share information about IDEA.	Feel protective of students with disabilities and experience guarded feelings toward others who do not.	Stand in the parents' shoes, and look at the situation from their point of view.	Brainstorm alternatives to provide supplementary support to general educator(s).	Monitor the implementation of action plan, and continue to weigh benefits and drawbacks for all students.
Administrator	Observe the student's class to document that time and attention required by student with disability; ensure that people do not scapegoat inclusion as a whole but recognize that the process can be improved.	Worry that there will be a strong backlash against inclusion throughout the school district.	Shore up knowledge of IDEA and its principles; share concerns with group, and ask for their help in addressing them.	Ensure that the action plan represents the input of any group members.	Provide administrative leadership in ensuring equity for all students.
School Counselor	Review problem solving strategies and be prepared to share any steps for effective communication.	Worry that some group members will assume close-minded stance.	Seek to understand each member's perspectives and offer processes and procedures for conflict resolution.	Ensure that the action plan represents the input of all group members.	Assume responsibility for communicating with all groups for ongoing monitoring.

BOX 10–9

MY VOICE

ALICE ANN DARROW: MUSIC THERAPY

A career in music therapy offers many exciting opportunities for individuals who are musicians and wish to be in a helping profession. Music therapy practitioners use music as a medium to work with children and adults who require special services because of behavioral, learning, or physical disabilities. Their work primarily involves using music as a therapeutic agent to meet educational or treatment objectives; however, it may also involve musically educating persons with disabilities or assisting them in the development of appropriate leisure skills. Music therapists find employment in various settings such as hospitals, community mental health centers, nursing homes, correctional facilities, rehabilitation centers, substance abuse facilities, schools, hospice programs, and private practice.

The Joint Commission on the Accreditation of Healthcare Organizations recognizes music therapy as one of the creative arts therapies. IDEA identifies music therapy as a related service that enhances a student's ability to benefit from special education. The National Association for Music Therapy (NAMT), founded in 1950, offers a professional registration program for individuals who have met educational and clinical training requirements. Sixty-seven colleges and universities offer degree programs in music ther-

apy that prepare individuals for NAMT registration. A separate independent organization, the Certification Board for Music Therapists (CBMT), certifies music therapists who have passed a national certification examination recognized by the National Commission on Certifying Agencies.

Primary areas of academic study required for registration and certification in music therapy are music theory and history, musical performance, psychology, human science, exceptional children, psychology of music, and music therapy principles. A six-month internship in an NAMT-approved music therapy program under the supervision of a registered music therapist is required in addition to the academic degree program. Several publications can provide further information about the music therapy profession: *Journal of Music Therapy* a quarterly research-oriented journal; *Music Therapy Perspectives,* a semiannual practice-oriented journal; *NAMT Notes,* a bimonthly newsletter; and a variety of other monographs, bibliographies, and brochures. For more information, write or call the National Association for Music Therapy, 8455 Colesville Road, Suite 1000, Silver Spring, MD 20910, (301) 589-3300.

Alice Ann Darrow
Professor, University of Kansas, Lawrence

✿ *Lillie Cusick is a music therapist who works with Dustin Michel. She helps him communicate his feelings, practice his social skills, and articulate better—all through music.*

In addition to a career as a teacher, you might also consider a career as a music therapist. Alice Ann Darrow, a professor at the University of Kansas in the area of music therapy and special education, describes in Box 10–9 the career of music therapy—a career in which you might make a difference to students with autism and their families.

WHAT ARE PROGRAM OPTIONS?

Early Intervention and Preschool Years

One of the most consistent findings in the research literature is the importance of early intervention for young children with autism (Fenske, Zalenski, Krantz, & McClannahan, 1985). Different models have been developed for providing early intervention and preschool programs, including models that give particular emphasis to the following (Anderson, Avery, DiPietro, Edwards, & Christian, 1987; Greenspan, 1992; Lovaas, 1987; McGee, Jacobs, & Regnier, 1993; Strain, Hoyson, & Jamison, 1985):

- Providing programming in the home

- Using peers without disabilities to teach social skills to their classmates with autism

- Preparing families for incidental teaching and advocacy

- Increasing the social relationships of children with significant others in their environment

- Providing intensive one-on-one instruction for approximately forty hours each week

A well-known early childhood model consists of intensive, one-to-one teaching for forty hours per week (Lovaas, 1987; McEachlin, Smith, & Lovaas, 1993). Often referred to as the "Lovaas model," therapeutic treatment often starts at around two years of age, and children go through hundreds of individual lessons to teach language, academic, and social behaviors. The primary methods include prompting and reinforcing behavior. The research on this model is limited to a small sample of children who received treatment in Lovaas's own clinic. He reports that almost half of the children who were in his early childhood program did not need special supplementary aides and services in the general classrooms at the elementary level. He also reported that the experimental subjects had significantly higher functioning on intelligence, adaptive behavior, and personality tests. The children with the most favorable outcomes in the experimental group were reported to exhibit average intelligence and adaptive behavior (McEachlin et al., 1993).

The cost of this program is approximately $20,000 to $60,000 per child per year. Some parents who have heard the results have challenged their school systems to enroll their children in the program at the school's expense. Currently, there is a great deal of controversy about the credibility of findings. One critique of the research rigor of this program points out that the participants in the experimental and control groups were not randomly assigned (the experimental group participants had higher IQs to start with), the children who participated in the experimental group had more advanced skills than most children with autism, the treatment was not explicitly described, different instruments were used at pretest and post-test, and instruments were administered under nonstandardized conditions (Gresham & MacMillan, 1997).

A different early childhood model, one that incorporates the principles we have discussed in this chapter, has been developed by Drs. Lise Fox and Glen Dunlap at the Florida Mental Health Institute, University of South Florida, Tampa. Their program has three parts (Fox et al., in press):

- Help the child develop functional communication and other skills, so the child can have opportunities and be reinforced to interact with other people.

- Ensure that the child actively participates in inclusive child care, preschool, and community environments, also so the child can have nurturing social interactions with other children.

Doesn't it make sense that IDEA now requires a student's parents to be a member of the evaluation team and the individualized family services plan (IFSP) team? And for them to have a family-directed plan of service to the family, not just the young child? That's how parent–professional relationships can be fostered.

❧ *When children learn such skills as how to complete tasks, how to participate in play with others, and how to ask for what they want and need, they experience less problem behavior.*

Review the characteristics of autism at the beginning of the chapter. What approaches are being used in the Fox-Dunlap early childhood program that are associated with each of these characteristics?

• Provide family support through a family–professional partnership, so that the family can be supported, to the degree it wants support, in learning how to help the child acquire various skills and in having access to information and emotional support.

The Fox-Dunlap program teaches the children to complete tasks, participate in play, ask for and get what they want, and regulate and respond to their hunger or fatigue. If children have these skills, they can manage many environmental events. When children have some control over their life, their behaviors will be less problematic and more adaptive. Moreover, the program helps the children acquire, practice, and expand these skills in settings where other children, including those without disabilities, are present.

As a necessary prerequisite to this instruction in typical settings, the professionals, in partnership with the families, conduct a functional assessment of the challenging behaviors, determining what communication underlies them. They use the functional assessment procedures (discussed earlier in this chapter) to document how each child acts in various settings and with different individuals.

Even as they are doing a functional assessment and beginning to put the behavioral-communication instruction in place, the professionals and families are identifying the family's needs. What information and emotional support does the family need and want? The program staff recognize that some families will want long-term professional colleagues. Thus, the professionals commit to helping the family get information and emotional support, negotiate the service-delivery maze, and stay in touch with the program long after the child leaves it.

Elementary Years

The first comprehensive state-wide program serving students with autism was developed in North Carolina and is referred to as the TEACCH model (Mesibov, 1995). This program has over 100 self-contained classes for children and youth with autism in typical public school facilities. The major principles of the TEACCH program are as follows:

- *Autism is a neurologically based condition.* A key concept is to identify the *different* ways that people with autism perceive the world because of their neurologically based condition and to provide supports consistent with those differences. The TEACCH philosophy contrasts this principle with the view that people with autism simply need to be treated *normally.*

- *Parent–professional collaboration.* Collaborative relationships are recognized as the best way to develop effective instruction and to gain political clout.

- *Generalist model.* This approach adopts a holistic view of recognizing the broad needs of children and families rather than keying in on discrete deficiencies.

- *Comprehensive, coordinative, lifelong, community services.* Services are provided from preschool through adulthood, and efforts are made to provide consistency over time and across different settings.

- *Individualization.* Instruction is tailored to the specific needs, strengths, and interests of each student and family.

Over 100 classrooms in North Carolina and many throughout the United States use the TEACCH model. Usually, these classes have from five to nine students with autism, and the staff includes a teacher plus a sufficient number of paraprofessionals so that there is an adult-to-student ratio of 1:3.

In addition to the TEACCH model, there are a number of other approaches to instruction for students with autism at the elementary level. One of these approaches was implemented at the Tiffany Park Elementary School in Seattle, Washington (Family Connection Staff, DeVault, Krug, & Fake, 1996). The staff at Tiffany Park collaborated to design an inclusive program for a third-grader, Samantha ("Sam") Fake, who like many students with autism, had challenging behaviors. Unhappily, and seemingly inevitably, Sam was tumbling down the deep, dark hole that could easily lead—as it has for so many students with autism—to segregation in school and isolation from friends and community activities. Two years later, Sam has made remarkable academic progress. She is now an honor student, writes poetry, and uses a computer. Just as importantly, she has friends of her own age who do not have disabilities. She takes swimming lessons and attends day camp with peers who do not have disabilities, participates in Special Olympics, and regularly attends church. What happened to make this kind of difference? What kind of "life arrangement" occurred?

The bottom line is that Sam has benefitted from positive behavior support. As you have already learned, positive behavioral support emphasizes creating responsive environments, not just "fixing" the student through traditional applied behavior analysis interventions that focus on discrete behaviors and that is delivered in one environment. Moreover, this approach involves a team—in Sam's case, her mother and father, her teachers, and specialists from the University of Washington. Still, how did Sam's team accomplish such a remarkable turnaround?

Because the team knows that challenging or other inappropriate behaviors occur for a reason, they first tried to learn why Sam fled her third-grade class, fought with faculty who tried to prevent her exit or to return her to class, and broke school property during these episodes. To solve this puzzle, the team conducted a thorough functional assessment.

When doing a functional assessment, the team looked beyond behavior to find its purposes. To understand the communicative intent of Sam's behaviors, the team talked with

Sam's strengths and her ability to develop relationships with others were brought out by the positive behavioral support she received. IDEA now requires schools to consider this kind of support for students with challenging behaviors.

 Honor student Samantha Fake, second from right, shown here with three of her friends, has made remarkable academic and social progress through positive behavioral support.

people who know her well. They directly observed her behavior in a variety of settings and circumstances. They described her inappropriate behaviors and the circumstances that usually immediately preceded them. They predicted when and why her behaviors would occur, and they confirmed their hypothesis by putting Sam in situations that were likely to, and in fact, did cause her to act out. Finally, they determined that her challenging behavior was more apt to occur when too many setting events (those that seem to trigger challenging behaviors) mount up and snowball.

The functional assessment did more than show the team what triggers Sam's behavior. It also helped them identify what Sam likes, such as a consistent and predictable daily schedule; rewarding social interactions with others; and quiet, private spaces where she can calm down by herself.

Knowing that Sam could choose the environments that work for her, the team set about helping Sam acquire a sense of control over her life. With the team's support, Sam learned new, more appropriate ways to influence her environments, to interact with peers, and to use individually contracted goal sheets to show that she has completed her academic work. For example, when Sam wanted to avoid a stressful situation at school, she would leave class, go to her own relaxation room, calm herself down, and then return to class. No adult would try to keep her in class or make a big deal about her leaving temporarily. Not only did Sam have to change, but so, too, did her teachers.

Every time Sam displayed appropriate behaviors—and she displayed them more and more as she had greater control over her own life—the team would reinforce that behavior with "points" that she could redeem for a trip to a Dairy Queen store or a local video-rental place. Soon, Sam and the team realized that it was more important for Sam to have a choice than to have the rewards. In time, the tangible rewards were simply phased out, but Sam's opportunities to choose were kept in place.

The key in all of this was the team's consistent restructuring of Sam's environments. Her parents and teachers monitored her progress daily and sent a notebook back and forth every day, reporting on her behavior, moods, and any setting events that might cause her to have challenging behavior.

All of the adults involved with Sam—her parents, teachers, therapists, school choir director, physical education teacher, and even her bus driver—learned how to recognize and respond to the changes in her moods or behaviors that usually preceded a behavioral problem. Most of all, they learned what to do when Sam displayed those behaviors.

Sam's success is not so much a matter of fixing Sam as it is a result of helping her accommodate to the demands of an inclusive world and helping that world, and the people in it, accommodate to her. This dual accommodation is the essence of positive behavioral support: Assuming that behavior is a form of communication, assessing the function that the behavior serves, letting Sam know that she can have choices, structuring her environments so that all the people in them heed her choices, and ensuring communication between all the significant people in her environments.

Without positive behavioral support, Sam's challenging behaviors, which caused her exclusion from school and community activities with her peers, would have been the typical course of events. With positive behavioral support, however, Sam's challenging behaviors receded and her opportunities for inclusion increased.

Middle and Secondary Years

Equity and Excellence is more than the name of a newsletter published by the University of New Hampshire Institute on Disability's School Restructuring and Inclusive Education Project. It's also the challenge that faced students with disabilities, their teachers, and their classmates at a recently formed New England high school that was committed from the start to accommodating student diversity (Jorgensen, 1996).

How can there be equity in the sense that the students with autism, just like their peers who do not have disabilities, will have access to the benefits of a new school, a progressive philosophy, and a new curriculum? And how can there be excellence, in the sense that all students there can demonstrate, when they graduate, that they

- Can achieve high test scores and get into competitive colleges?

- Have the basic skills their future employers need?

- Can apply new technologies, solve problems, and work in teams?

- Can show respect for learning and for others?

Did equity and excellence really apply to one of this school's students, Joel (a pseudonym), who has a label of autism? The answer, achieved after hard work by the faculty, the community, the student body, and Joel, was a resounding, "Yes" (Jorgensen, 1996).

The community and newly hired faculty worked hard at articulating the school's philosophy: The student is a worker, the teacher is a coach, and inclusion means that all students with disabilities will participate in the full range of academic and extracurricular offerings throughout the school. To put that philosophy into operation, the faculty redefined its roles. With the support of the special education staff, the general educators adapted their curricula and taught it to Joel during general education class periods. For all students, the curriculum design included the following steps:

1. Identify an overarching theme or topic.

2. Link that theme to other subjects and classes.

3. List the outcomes (proficiencies and skills) that the students should demonstrate.

4. Specify the essential questions to stimulate students' interest.

5. Put on performance-based exhibitions of what the students learned.

6. Use appropriate activities, materials, and resources.

7. Plan for the students with extraordinary learning challenges.

8. Plan daily lessons.

9. Evaluate students.

For Joel, modifications in outcomes, exhibitions, and evaluation were put into place on an individualized basis, and Joel benefited from the process of curriculum design and delivery. Special educators became case managers for Joel, supporting the general educators, facilitating inclusion, and helping him prepare for tests or other evaluation procedures. They also took the major role in special education paperwork—evaluating the students' communication, academic, and social skills and writing the IEP.

More than faculty-role reform was necessary. Students, too, were essential. They helped to brainstorm and be allies in solving challenges that Joel faced:

- His need to have material read to him or greatly enlarged due to his visual impairment

- His own and others' frustration on the days when he could not communicate easily through facilitated communication

- His tendency to scratch other students or his facilitator, and

- Extra time that it took for his peers to get to know him, including his particular blend of humor and playfulness

At the beginning of ninth grade, students regarded Joel with distant curiosity. After getting to know him and being supported to learn how he communicated, they started talking to them like a "regular kid." Students modeled the faculty's reaction, which is one of respectful interaction. Bit by bit, the distance between Joel and his classmates grew shorter.

Joel and his teachers and fellow students developed several creative adaptations to lessen the challenges he faced. For example, Joel learned to answer multiple-choice questions using a portable board, on which were written the letters *a, b, c,* and *d.* He also learned to use an adapted answer sheet. When Joel joined the rest of his class for a biology field trip to make observational drawings in a river's wooded edge, he was not able to use his hands to draw. But another student let him use copies of that student's drawings so that Joel could participate in the follow-up learning activities back in the classroom. Teachers implemented adaptations for Joel within the school's overall context of working to meet each and every student's instructional needs.

Transitional and Postsecondary Years

There is now abundant evidence that adults with autism can lead lives characterized by independence, productivity, and inclusion, especially if they are involved with Community Services for Autistic Adults and Children (CSAAC), a Rockville, Maryland, nonprofit agency. With CSAAC's support, they have worked in thirty-four different jobs, in both companies and government agencies. The employing companies and agencies ranged in size from very small (a few workers) to very large (more than 1,000 workers).

Significantly, most of the adults served by CSAAC work with co-workers without disabilities (Smith, Belcher, Juhrs, & Nabors, 1994). Indeed, the longer they are employed, the more they associate with co-workers. What stands in the way of their inclusion is not their aggression, self-injury, or a history of institutionalization. Instead, the barriers are their low levels of cognitive functioning, poor language skills, and unusual verbalizations.

CSAAC's success rests on several factors. Its philosophy guides its activities:

- All people, regardless of the severity of their disability, can live and work in their community.

- People with disabilities have a right to specialized services that facilitate living and working among people without disabilities.

- People with autism and other disabilities have the right to programs and services available to other members of the community and should not be denied access to those services on the basis of their disability.

Relationships can produce benefits for everyone, not just the student with autism.

Despite the fact that many of the workers at CSAAC had been institutionalized or inadequately educated, they have averaged 23.8 hours of work each week, held jobs for as long as 12 years or as short as a month, and earned a mean of at least the federal minimum hourly wage. They proved their ability to make positive contributions.

 Adults with autism have benefitted from the community-based training they receive from CSAAC in Montgomery County, MD, and have demonstrated that, as shown here, they can engage in regular jobs, with support, for regular wages.

• The least restrictive, most positive methods should be used in instruction, behavior management, and programs.

• The principles of normalization should be implemented in all facets of the lives of the people receiving services from CSAAC.

• Consumer choice and satisfaction should play an integral role in all of CSAAC's work.

To put its philosophy into practice, CSAAC provides intensive support. The workers have thoroughly trained job coaches to be responsible for the following:

• Teach the workers how to travel from home to work, or transport the workers to their jobs.

• Teach specific tasks, work skills, social skills, and money management.

• Oversee the employee's productivity, accuracy, and behavior.

• When necessary to prevent self-injury, aggression, or property destruction, implement a positive behavioral support.

CSAAC also provides comprehensive residential support so that adults with autism can live in condominiums, garden apartments, or town houses, where, as at work, they share the facilities (swimming pools, recreation areas, and laundry facilities) with their neighbors who do not have disabilities.

In every activity, CSAAC uses state-of-the-art positive behavioral support principles. To ensure quality, it trains all of its employees in these principles and then has a large staff of supported-employment or residential-service coordinators who closely monitor the direct-service staff's implementation of instructional programs.

Finally, all CSAAC staff facilitate interaction between the adults with autism and co-workers or neighbors who do not have disabilities. In this way, CSAAC promotes inclusion and friendships, proving that interdependence—between adults with autism, paid staff, and friends—is entirely possible.

CSAAC has great expectations for people with autism.

By combining philosophy with technology, ideals with practice, CSAAC demonstrates that people with autism can look forward to an enviable life after high school. To those who might be inclined to dismiss the outcomes of interdependence, contribution, and inclusion as pipe dreams for adults with autism, CSAAC has but a single retort: "You're mistaken." And to those who regard the education of a student with autism as a prelude to an enviable life, CSAAC has but a single affirmation: "You're right on target." These days, there's no excuse for not knowing how to get an enviable life; it's now just a matter of will and work, of philosophy and instructional support programs.

A Vision for the Future

When asked to paint a picture of A.J.'s future, Denise Poston pauses, gazes into space for a moment, and then, thoughtfully but hesitantly, answers.

"A.J. *will* have a meaningful life. He will work in a regular job, a supported-employment situation. He will not be in a workshop. He could stock shelves in any store, given his preference for an orderly world. He might have a chance to work in an art studio or an artists' supply shop, because he loves to create figurines from clay. He loves animals, so perhaps he could work with them on a farm or in a vet's office. He might even know how to operate a computer, so he could express himself better."

Then, pausing, Denise seems to admit the challenges that lie ahead. "We have to be creative about adapting our environment to meet A.J.'s needs. We have to concentrate on his social skills."

Asked to be specific, Denise readily identifies the missing elements of A.J.'s future. Positive behavior support has to be present, all the time, especially as A.J. grows bigger and older. But to put such comprehensive support into place requires so much from the school and home, and neither school nor home is yet able to launch such a comprehensive, labor-intensive system.

Two other assurances of an enviable life—enviable for A.J. and for Denise as well—are underdeveloped. One is shared lives. Denise still needs something like Group Action Planning (see Chapter 8)—a way to spread more of the responsibilities around, to have home, school, and community join in providing more support for A.J. and for her. The other is celebration. So much time and effort are spent by everyone in A.J.'s life working to meet the challenges of his autism, that so few of those people celebrate what they and A.J. have been able to do. To share, to celebrate successes, those are simply human instincts. So, why are they not yet a larger part of life for A.J. and Denise?

What Would You Recommend . . .

1. To restructure A.J.'s neighborhood school, as well as the cluster school, so that all students' strengths, preferences, and needs can be supported in inclusive settings and relationships?

2. To develop a system of positive behavioral support for A.J., in all of the environments in which he lives?

3. To remind Denise, A.J.'s teachers, and his neighbors that, despite the challenges of autism, everyone has much to celebrate?

4. To develop an action group to support A.J., Denise, and their other family members?

SUMMARY

WHAT IS AUTISM?

- Autism is a developmental disability significantly affecting verbal and nonverbal communication and social interaction. It is generally evident before age three and adversely affects educational performance. Other characteristics include behavioral challenges, need for environmental predictability, unusual responsiveness to sensory stimulation, and below-average intellectual functioning.

- Two language impairments associated with autism are delayed language and echolalia.

- Facilitative communication is a training method that involves supporting a person who does not speak or has highly repetitive speech to use a facilitator and keyboard to communicate. There has been a strong debate in the field about its efficacy, and research studies have typically failed to document the use of facilitative communication when the facilitator was not informed in advance about the answer.

- People with autism often have fewer and weaker social interactions with others than do people without disabilities.

- Stereotypical behaviors are inappropriate, repetitive acts that an individual frequently displays.

- Behavioral challenges faced by people with autism include self-injurious behavior, aggression, tantrums, property destruction, and aggression.

- Predictability and structure are important sources of security for many individuals with autism.

- Sensory disorders often result in under- or overresponsiveness to sensory stimuli; movement disorders include abnormal posture; abnormal movements of various body parts; abnormal ocular movements; repeated gestures; and awkwardness of gait.

- The majority of people with autism function intellectually in the IQ range of mental retardation.

- Although parents have historically been seen as the cause of their child's autism, this viewpoint is totally unwarranted.

- Autism is biologically caused, but the specific biological trigger is unknown at this time.

- The prevalence of autism is approximately one person per 1,000.

WHAT ARE EVALUATION PROCEDURES?

- The Childhood Autism Rating Scale (CARS) is an assessment tool that is frequently used as part of the multidisciplinary process for identifying students as having autism.

- A functional assessment identifies specific relationships between environmental events and a student's problem behavior. It leads to an individually tailored intervention plan aimed at helping students to function as successfully as possible.

WHAT AND HOW DO PROFESSIONALS TEACH?

- The typical curriculum domains for students with autism include life skills for integrated community living, vocational preparation, and functional academics.

- Positive behavioral support seeks to create a responsive environment that is personally tailored to the preferences, strengths, and needs of individuals with problem behavior.

- Social stories, written by parents or educators, describe social situations in terms of important social cues and appropriate responses to those cues.

HOW IS PARTICIPATION ENCOURAGED?

- There are many different viewpoints on the appropriateness of inclusion for students with autism. Inclusive models have been implemented in which students have been successful.

- Collaboration with professionals, families, students, and communities can significantly increase successful inclusion for individuals with autism.

WHAT ARE PROGRAM OPTIONS?

- A model early intervention program emphasizes family support, communication, and community and preschool inclusion.

- Positive behavioral support can be used to promote model elementary school practices and to aid students with autism to get a life within and outside of school.

- Music therapy is a promising career option offering opportunities to work with students with autism.

- Systematic school reform at the secondary level can result in successful inclusion for students with autism.

- Community Services for Autistic Adults and Children (CSAAC) has demonstrated that adults with autism can live in typical homes and work in typical jobs when state-of-the-art training and supports are provided.

RESOURCES

BOOKS

Autism: An Inside-Out Approach. (1996). By Donna Williams. London: Kingsley. Donna Williams describes her own personal experiences, especially about sensory and perceptual challenges that keep people with autism from experiencing control of their lives.

Higher Functioning Adolescents and Young Adults With Autism. (1996). By Ann Fullerton, Joyce Stratton, Phyllis Coyne, & Carol Gray. Austin, TX: Pro-Ed. This book centers on the high school years, but its strategies can apply to elementary and college settings as well.

Positive Behavioral Support: Including People with Difficult Behavior in the Community. (1996). By Lynn Kern Koegel, Robert L. Koegel, & Glen Dunlap. Baltimore: Brookes. The four major topics include family issues/support, educational issues, social inclusion, and community inclusion. Leaders in the field provide practical information on interventions.

Teaching Children With Autism: Strategies for Initiating Positive Interactions and Improving Learning Opportunities. (1995). Edited by Robert L. Koegel & Lynn Kern Koegel. Baltimore: Brookes. This book provides a comprehensive research review on topics such as language, social communication, self-management, friendships, and family–professional partnerships.

Teaching Children With Autism: Strategies to Enhance Communication and Socialization. (1995). By Kathleen Ann Quill. New York: Delmar Publishers Inc. Twelve chapters describe research and give practical information on curriculum and methods. One of the chapters is by Temple Grandin, featured in Box 10-3.

Thinking in Pictures: And Other Reports of My Life With Autism. (1995). By Temple Grandin. New York: Doubleday. Temple Grandin explains autism by citing examples from her own life. She also discusses the education and treatment of individuals with autism.

JOURNALS, MAGAZINES, AND CATALOGS

The Communicator. The Autism National Committee, Inc., 635 Ardmore Avenue, Ardmore, PA 19003. The Autism National Committee endorses inclusive approaches and positive procedures for dealing with challenging behavior. This newsletter carries articles on those and other topics.

Focus on Autism and Other Developmental Disabilities. Pro-Ed Journals, 8700 Shoal Creek Boulevard, Austin, TX 78757-6897. This quarterly journal includes articles summarizing research and best practice.

MUTLIMEDIA

The following videos are available at local rental or retail stores:

House of Cards. (1993, PG-13, U.S., color, 109 minutes). A fictionalized account of a girl who develops autistic symptoms and her mother's and psychologist's conflict over treatment.

Rainman. (1988, R, U.S., color, 140 minutes). After his father's death, Charlie Babbitt gets to know and value his brother, Raymond, who has autism.

ON-LINE INFORMATION AND USEFUL DATABASES

Autism Resources. Internet address: http://www.syr.edu/~jmwobus/autism/#libraries. This extensive online resource links to other sites with information about autism, bibliographies, interventions, research, and discussion groups.

Center for the Study of Autism. Internet address: http://www.autism.org/contents.html/#subgroup. The Center provides information and conducts research, in collaboration with the Autism Research Institute in San Diego, into the efficacy of interventions. Offers some information in Chinese, Korean, and Spanish. Contents include information on siblings, the autism spectrum disorder, interventions, sensory integration, and self-injurious behavior.

O.A.S.I.S.—On-line Asperger Syndrome Information and Support. Internet address: http://www.udel.edu/bkirby/asperger/index.html. This site provides information on Asperger syndrome, including current research, evaluation centers, and articles by persons with Asperger syndrome.

Recovery Zone. Internet address: http://pages.prodigy.com/damianporcari/recovery.htm. A resource designed to help people interested in establishing, running, and paying for an in-home program. Designed to supplement books, tapes, and articles by Lovaas and others. Information on finding and training therapists, law, school issues, conferences, and parent groups.

Positive Behavioral Support. Under construction, see link from Beach Center on Families and Disabilities. Internet address: http://www.lsi.ukans.edu/beach/beachhp.htm. A web site devoted to positive behavioral support, including articles, upcoming conferences, state training team contact list, and ongoing research.

ORGANIZATIONS

The Autism National Committee. 635 Ardmore Ave., Ardmore, PA 19003. Internet address: http://www.enginnet.com/autcom/. An organization of families and professionals committed to community inclusion and positive behavioral support.

Autism Society of America. 7910 Woodmont Avenue, Suite 650, Bethesda, MD 20814. Internet address: http://www.telepath.com/canance/society/autism2.html. This family and professional organization is dedicated to the education and welfare of those with severe disorders of communication and behavior. Provides information and referral service and has affiliated local chapters.

CHAPTER 11

OTHER HEALTH IMPAIRMENTS

Educating
Jacob Empey

Eleven-year-old Jacob, a.k.a. Jake, is a fifth grader who lives in Texas and likes to crack jokes. Here are two of his favorites:

How do you keep an elephant from charging? Take away his credit cards.

The teacher said, "Give me a sentence with the word gruesome *in it." The student said, "The man stopped shaving and* gruesome *whiskers."*

Jacob, who has had epileptic seizures since he was six years old, uses humor "to put others at ease with his disability," according to his parents Tom and Geri Empey. Deb Williamson, one of his health impairments teachers, concurs, "His weird, witty, off-the-wall sense of humor helps him connect with kids."

Jacob also has a "very deep soul and a very strong personality," Geri says. "He is thoughtful about things and handles whatever gets thrown in his way."

Tom adds, "He has a lot of inner strength—fighting the good fight."

"Because they make me," Jacob quips.

The battle Jacob fights is a challenging one. He averages one or two generalized tonic-clonic (grand mal) seizures a day, with one usually occurring at school. Tom says, "Sometimes he pops back from them; sometimes he needs to sleep." Jacob describes the procedures he has endured to try to control his seizures:

I tried medication. That didn't work. I tried a ketogenic diet. That didn't work. We went to a herbalist. That didn't work for me either. I had surgery to put an implant in my chest. There's a magnet that stops my seizures. As time goes on, a doctor will be turning it up. Someday I hope I won't have to use that magnet so much. My brain will start working by itself.

Although Jacob did not experience his first seizure until he was six-and-a-half, he received early intervention services beginning at age three-and-a-half. His parents say he was slow in developing social, motor, and language skills. He had surgery for a lazy eye when he was six. Soon after, "we noticed some unusual eye movements and slouching in his chair," Geri says. Jacob said, "My eyes are stuck! My eyes are stuck!" The Empeys thought something had gone wrong with the surgery. When they returned to the ophthalmologist, he said he thought Jacob had experienced a seizure.

It wasn't long before Jacob experienced his first major seizure. Tom remembers:

The first tonic-clonic seizure was very frightening. It stayed isolated to one half of his body that shut down after his seizure, even though he was alert and awake. He asked me if he was going to die. I didn't know myself.

When the neurologist performed an MRI, he found exten-sive brain damage on the right side of Jacob's brain. We are very fortunate he has done as well as he has.

Geri explains, "Something affected the migration of the nerve cells that form the brain. It happened at gestation—about ten weeks. Nobody knows why. He does almost everything with his left brain."

Jacob sustained two concussions when he fell during seizures. Tom and Geri resisted for a while but finally decided that Jacob needed a helmet. At first, he wore a bicycle helmet with a hat over it. Even with the bicycle helmet, Jacob broke his teeth when he fell while walking in the hallway at school. Now he

wears a hockey helmet that protects both his head and chin when he's playing or moving around. "With the school helping with that transition, it worked," Geri says. "The teacher asked if he wanted to talk to the class about it. Jake said, 'I think they can figure it out.'"

One positive event related to Jacob's epilepsy is the partnership he shares with his service dog, Hunter. Jacob says the black lab's job "is to tell me I'm going to have a seizure before I have it. He's just kind of started, but it's going pretty good. If I know I might have a seizure, my parents might have me sit down for a while."

Micheal Goehring, who trained Hunter, believes that the successful partnership Jacob and Hunter experience is due, in large part, to the attitude Jacob and his parents exhibit:

> *Jake is a phenomenal kid who is very adaptive. If I ask him to do something and he knows he can't do it, he takes a minute, thinks about it, and finds a way to make something work for himself. His parents are also wonderful. They have a great attitude that is reflected in Jake's attitude. His parents neither pretend that Jake's epilepsy does not exist, nor do they let it become a barrier for him. They have a very realistic view of it all, which I think is a big factor in Jake's survivability. Jake is a responsible young man. His parents surround him with a network of people who will work with him and not in opposition to him.*

One person who is an important part of that network is Jacob's younger sister, Molly. Although, like typical siblings, they tease each other, Molly provides a dependable relationship for Jacob. "I'm not sure he would admit how important his sister is," Linda Dickson, the special education team leader at Jacob's current school, comments.

Jacob's epilepsy has interfered with his ability to keep up with his peers academically. During second and third grade, he took medication that kept him from functioning at the same academic level as his peers. His parents took him off the medication in third grade. "Quality of life has been a critical issue," Tom says. Jacob could concentrate better, but he had seizures frequently. At the end of third grade, he told his parents, "I'm not ready for fourth grade. Is there anything we can do?" His parents asked to have him retained.

"I was apprehensive," Deb Williamson says. "We don't retain kids anymore, because we know the research says it usually doesn't benefit them. But the team had faith in Jacob's knowing what he needed. And, for him, it was a success."

Although Jacob's epilepsy causes him to process information more slowly, he reveals many inherent strengths to his teachers, along with his sense of humor. "Jacob is a child who has the most creative ideas," his fourth-grade teacher Jeanine says. "He is very articulate. Jacob also has strong interpersonal skills. In my class, I had him tutor math to students with learning disabilities. He can empathize."

"Jacob's strength? Perseverance—and what a strength! He is always willing to try and keep at a task," Deb Williamson says. "He also has insight and maturity that other kids his age don't have. I was surprised someone so young would understand about life as he did. Maybe his epilepsy contributes to that understanding. He's been through a lot more than most kids."

Jacob views himself as more like than unlike others: "I can do most everything. I'm just a normal kid, but I have seizures."

What Do You Think?

1. We referred to Jacob's tonic-clonic seizures. Are there other types of seizures? How can they be recognized?

2. How can a service dog like Hunter become part of a classroom?

3. How would the individualized education program of a student like Jacob with health impairments differ from those of other students with disabilities?

WHAT ARE OTHER HEALTH IMPAIRMENTS?

If Only

. . . *If only my mother and I didn't have HIV, then my whole family wouldn't have to go through what they have to go through.*

. . . *If only my dad would be able to talk to us about us being sick.*

. . . *If only we didn't have to worry so much about money.*

. . . *If only my mom would stop being so stubborn and start taking some medicine so that she would not get sick.*

. . . *If only the world would be a more understanding place.*

Dawn, age eleven (Wiener, Best, & Pizzo, 1994. p. 40)*

Dawn's poem illustrates the overwhelming sense of powerlessness students with health impairments sometimes experience. In this chapter, you will learn methods for empowering these students and including them in your classroom.

Students who receive services under the health impairments category of the Individuals with Disabilities Education Act (IDEA) vary greatly in their educational, social, medical, and emotional needs. Some are born with the condition; others develop the health impairment during childhood or adolescence. Some are incapacitated; others are rarely inconvenienced by their condition. Some experience pain; others are free from any symptoms of illness. For some, the condition is life-threatening. For others, a long and productive life lies ahead, and death will come from some other cause. A particular health impairment may affect more students from one race or gender, or the condition may be distributed evenly across the general population.

*The essays by Dawn, age 11, and Tanya, age 6, were developed during therapeutic sessions with Lori S. Wiener of the National Cancer Institute, and excerpted from BE A FRIEND: CHILDREN WHO LIVE WITH HIV SPEAK compiled by Lori S. Wiener, Ph.D., Aprille Best, and Philip A. Pizzo, M.D. Copyright © 1994 by Albert Whitman & Company. Used by permission of the publisher.

Students with health impairments also vary in cognitive and social skills. For example, one person with asthma might be gifted; another could have mental retardation. One student with cancer receives support and comfort from loving family members and friends; another spends lonely days and nights at home or in a hospital. In other words, a health impairment can strike anyone at any time under any circumstances. The impairment may cause some temporary, minor lifestyle changes or dramatically and forever change the lives of the student and those who are close to the student.

Defining Health Impairments

What do these individuals have in common? The IDEA definition unifies their characteristics under the term **other health impairments.** You will note that we drop the word *other* throughout this chapter. The IDEA definition uses the word *other* to distinguish these conditions from health impairments such as physical disabilities (conditions that affect muscles, joints, and bones), severe and multiple disabilities, brain injuries, and so forth. These impairments are served under separate categories that we discuss specifically in other chapters.

The IDEA definition describes a wide range of conditions affecting students' health and causing them to need special education and/or related services. Describing the characteristics of these individuals using three major criteria, IDEA (1997) defines other health impairments as follows:

> *Having limited strength, vitality, or alertness due to chronic or acute health problems such as a heart condition, tuberculosis, rheumatic fever, nephritis, asthma, sickle cell anemia, hemophilia, epilepsy, lead poisoning, leukemia, or diabetes that adversely affect a child's educational performance. (20 U.S.C., §§ 1400 et seq.)*

The three major criteria of the other health impairments category are limitations in *strength, vitality,* or *alertness* that affect a student's educational needs. Epilepsy affects Jacob's strength and vitality after he has a seizure. The seizures also affect his alertness to his environment. Moreover, unless researchers find a cure for human immunodeficiency virus (HIV), Dawn, who wrote "If Only," will eventually experience limitations in all three areas. By contrast, students like Taylor, who you met in Chapter 6, on attention-deficit/hyperactivity disorder—a condition that is also served under health impairments—experience difficulty only with alertness.

The IDEA definition also emphasizes that the conditions can be chronic or acute. A **chronic condition** develops slowly, and the symptoms are long-lasting. An **acute condition,** on the other hand, develops quickly, and the symptoms are intense but last for a relatively short period of time. Dawn's HIV is a chronic condition that eventually will become acquired immune deficiency syndrome (AIDS); her symptoms progress over a period of years and are ongoing. Although Jacob's epilepsy is chronic, the seizures themselves are acute because they develop quickly and subside suddenly.

Describing the Characteristics of Other Health Impairments

Besides having limitations in strength, vitality, or alertness, individuals with health impairments have few common characteristics. For that reason, we decided to select a few conditions to highlight in this chapter. As you become familiar with the needs of students with these conditions, you will find that students with many other types of health impairments have similar needs. We will describe the characteristics of students with HIV, prenatal substance exposure, cancer, asthma, epilepsy, and diabetes in separate sections.

As you read, you will discover that students with health impairments are more like their peers than different. For some, modifications in curricula, methods, and classroom

Other health impairments include chronic and acute health problems that limit strength, vitality, or alertness and adversely affect educational performance.

A **chronic condition** develops slowly and results in long-lasting symptoms. A person can have a chronic condition such as juvenile diabetes all or most of his or her lifetime.

An **acute condition** develops quickly; the symptoms are intense and often end quickly. Pneumonia is an example.

BOX 11-1 **MY VOICE**

RYAN WHITE

There were so many TV lights in my eyes I couldn't see the crowd. But I could hear them. Thousands and thousands of people were clapping and cheering for me. And I hadn't even opened my mouth yet!

I'd had a pretty good year even before this. I had fought for the right to go back to school in my hometown—Kokomo, Indiana—and I'd won. People there had tried to keep me out because I have AIDS. . . . Plenty of people in Kokomo thought I could give other kids AIDS if I kissed them or sneezed on them in school, or if I dripped sweat or tears on them. Fat chance! I mean, that's disgusting! I'd *never* do that. Even if I did, nothing would happen—except that I wouldn't be too popular.

Well, panic spread all over town anyway. Lots of times kids flattened themselves against walls when I walked by. I heard kids telling Ryan White jokes. And grown people passed along lies about how they had seen me biting people, or spitting on vegetables at the grocery store. I never did and I never would.

When I finally did get back into class, after a judge said the school was wrong, an awful lot of people still wanted me gone. To make the point, someone even put a bullet through our front window. So my mom, my sister, and I moved to a new town—Cicero, Indiana. People here were much friendlier, especially at my new school. . . .

So here I was in New Orleans, giving a speech at this national convention of 10,000 teachers about having AIDS. I wondered if . . . my math teacher back at my old school was out there somewhere. I remembered how I couldn't believe it when I'd heard him say on TV that *he* didn't want me in school—my favorite teacher.

Note: From *Ryan White: My Own Story* by Ryan White and Ann Marie Cunningham. Copyright © 1991 by Jeanne White and Ann Marie Cunningham. Used by permission of Dial Books for Young Readers, a division of Penguin Books (Putnam, Inc.)

routine are essential, and those students will need to be served under IDEA with an individualized education program (IEP). For the majority of students with even the most severe conditions, however, the general classroom setting is usually the appropriate educational placement.

In fact, many students with the conditions covered by IDEA never need to be identified as health impaired for special education purposes. Despite their health impairment, they participate fully in general education successfully without specially designed instruction and related services. They may even choose not to reveal their conditions to school officials, or they may require a 504 plan (see Chapter 6) that provides them with accommodations in the general classroom.

Unfortunately, fear, stigmatization, and ignorance can create additional challenges for some students, families, and educators who are seeking typical educational experiences for those with atypical health needs. Throughout this chapter, we discuss strategies for overcoming that stigma.

Human Immunodeficiency Virus. Imagine what it would be like if you had to take pills four times a day every day, have your blood drawn and tested each month, and had so much trouble breathing that you had to be hospitalized for pneumonia several times a year. You might resent all these intrusions on your life. You might be angry about the pain of the procedures. You might be afraid.

Now imagine that your parents have told you not to talk to anyone about why you are sick. Not even your rabbi, your piano teacher, your little sister, or your best friend must know that you have **HIV**. "When I told the kids at school I had AIDS," Tanya, age six, says, "they made fun of me. I told them by accident. Now I want to run away from school" (quoted in Wiener, Best, & Pizzo, 1994, p. 15).

This was what many students with HIV experienced in the late 1980s and what some continue to experience today. Not only do they have to deal with their medical needs, but they frequently do so under a veil of secrecy, without the full support of their friends, family, or community. In Box 11-1, Ryan White, a teenager with hemophilia who contracted

Human immunodeficiency virus (HIV) is spread through contact with blood or sperm from another person. The virus attacks the immune system, ultimately resulting in AIDs.

❧ *Ryan White, an adolescent who died from AIDS, captured the heart of America as he fought for the right to attend public school.*

HIV from a blood transfusion, describes what it is like to have the condition and to be ostracized by his teachers and peers.

The results of Ryan White's pioneering advocacy for people with HIV continue today. In 1996, President Bill Clinton signed the *Ryan White CARE Act Amendments,* expanding services provided in the *Ryan White CARE Act* of 1990. In a speech from the White House, Clinton said, "There is a long way to go toward finding a cure or a vaccine for HIV and AIDS. Until then, the Ryan White CARE Act programs will continue to help people with HIV disease get the care-related services they need" (Clinton, 1996).

What Is HIV? HIV is a condition that gradually infects and eventually destroys important cells in the immune system, which protects the body from disease. If you know someone with HIV, you might have heard her or him talk about having blood tests to determine T4 cell count. T4 immune cells are a major target of HIV. When HIV destroys T4 and other immune cells, the body becomes increasingly unable to fight infections.

As the virus progresses and the immune system becomes weaker, a person with HIV is more susceptible to **opportunistic infections.** The germs or viruses from opportunistic infections are usually harmless for the general population. Instead, they most often infect individuals who have another condition that has affected their ability to fight off disease. Opportunistic infections associated with HIV include some cancers, recurrent fungus infections (such as thrush, athlete's foot, or yeast infections), pneumonia, and tuberculosis.

Opportunistic infections usually do not affect the general population but only those who have immune deficiency because of another illness. People with HIV are among those who are susceptible to opportunistic infections.

Stages of HIV. HIV progresses through distinct stages. Increased levels of illness and severity of symptoms mark the progression from one stage to another. People in the earliest stage of HIV, called the **asymptomatic, or latency, stage,** have the virus in their bloodstream but do not have any outward symptoms of illness. One woman describes her reaction to learning that she was HIV positive during the latency stage. "I couldn't believe it when [the doctor] told me. I wasn't sick!"

Two-thirds of children born with HIV do not have any symptoms initially. It is not until they are older, usually between two and five years of age, that they begin to experience symptoms (Grubman, 1991). Several children born with the HIV virus have actually been able to rid themselves of the virus ("Babies Who Beat AIDS," 1996). In adolescents and adults who contract HIV through contaminated body fluids, symptoms may not develop for eight to twelve years (Prater & Serna, 1995). The use of three medications in a drug cocktail (approximately twenty pills a day taken at precise times) can ward off AIDS even longer if taken as prescribed (The Times Mirror Company, 1997). Furthermore, women with HIV who take the drugs ZDV or AZT during pregnancy, labor, and delivery and give their babies AZT for six weeks after birth reduce the likelihood of their child being HIV positive by two-thirds (Centers for Disease Control, 1997).

When HIV progresses to the middle, **symptomatic, stage,** the virus reproduces more actively, the immune system begins losing its effectiveness, and people begin to experience minor symptoms. Fatigue is a common symptom of HIV at this stage. Other middle-stage symptoms include persistent fevers, night sweats, chronic diarrhea, recurring vaginal yeast infections, and swollen glands. As their immune system weakens, people in the middle stages begin to experience more frequent illnesses and opportunistic infections.

In the final stage of the condition, which is known as **acquired immune deficiency syndrome (AIDS),** the opportunistic infections increase in frequency and severity. Symptoms often include seizures, memory lapses, impaired vision, blindness, and, in children, loss of cognitive abilities. Eating usually is difficult, and the body's ability to obtain nutrients from food is affected. This contributes to the wasting symptoms (severe weight loss) often seen in people with late-stage infection. Cancerous lesions and respiratory infections are common. Antibiotic and antiviral therapies have only minimal effect because of the low number of T4 cells. Pain is generally severe, and death is imminent.

The Centers for Disease Control (CDC) specify that HIV has progressed to the AIDS stage if a person's T4 cell count is less than 200 and if he or she has developed one or more specified opportunistic infections. Physicians are not required to report HIV cases until the condition progresses to AIDS, but in 1993, the CDC estimated that one million individuals were infected with the virus in the United States. This life-threatening illness has reached epidemic proportions.

HIV and the Classroom. Teachers deal with two major issues related to HIV in the classroom. First, they are concerned about preventing the spread of HIV in schools. Second, to better meet the educational needs of students with HIV, they need to know how the condition can affect learning and behavior.

Transmission of HIV. As a professional, you can help prevent the spread of HIV in two ways. First, you need to use precautions to help prevent the spread of HIV in your school. Carefully examine Figure 11-1, which presents universal precautions that can help prevent the accidental contraction of HIV by students and personnel. It is not necessary to wear latex gloves for typical school contact. Furthermore, the CDC states that universal precautions do not apply to saliva, feces, nasal secretions, sweat, tears, urine, and vomit unless blood is visible (see Beverly, 1995, for a complete list of appropriate hygienic procedures for the classroom).

We want to emphasize that HIV does not appear to spread through casual contact such as "living in the same household with the infected person, caring for an AIDS patient, being sneezed on by an infected person, casual kissing, or swimming with an infected person" (Wishom, Swaim, & Huang, 1989). As of early 1994, the CDC had reported no cases of viral transmission in a school setting.

During the **asymptomatic, or latency, stage,** a person has the HIV virus in his or her bloodstream but does not have outward symptoms of illness.

During the **symptomatic stage,** HIV reproduces more actively, and the infected person begins to experience illnesses, including opportunistic infections.

Acquired immune deficiency syndrome (AIDS) is the final stage in the progression of HIV. The infected person has a T4 cell count less than 200 and one or more opportunistic infections.

FIGURE 11-1 *By teaching universal precautions, teachers can decrease the risk of spreading infectious diseases, including HIV.*

UNIVERSAL PRECAUTIONS

GLOVE	WASH	GOWN/APRON	MASK/EYEWEAR
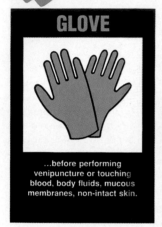	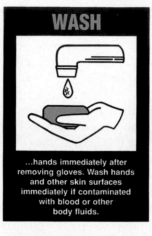	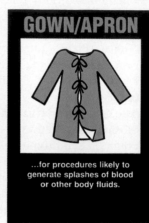	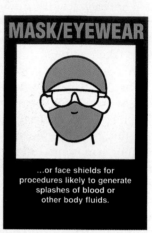
...before performing venipuncture or touching blood, body fluids, mucous membranes, non-intact skin.	...hands immediately after removing gloves. Wash hands and other skin surfaces immediately if contaminated with blood or other body fluids.	...for procedures likely to generate splashes of blood or other body fluids.	...or face shields for procedures likely to generate splashes of blood or other body fluids.

This hospital uses Universal Precautions for <u>ALL</u> patients to protect patients, family and hospital personnel.

Thus, the general classroom is the most appropriate placement for the majority of students with HIV (Prater & Serna, 1995). Sometimes, however, a student will need to receive educational services at home or in a school setting that allows for individualized instruction, perhaps because the student's behavior or medical condition (biting, open sores, lack of control over body secretions) creates risks for other students (Wishom et al., 1989). Such an educational approach is also appropriate if the student's risk of contracting infections from other students is high due to immune deficiency, or if the condition has caused academic limitations.

A second way you can help prevent the spread of HIV is by honestly informing your students about the disease. But remember that your students also need to be taught interpersonal skills to help them resist peer pressure (Popham, 1993). Colson and Carlson (1993) emphasize that the following information should be included in such a curriculum: "general knowledge (AIDS 101), affective development, sexuality and physical growth, positive self-esteem, personal relationships, sexual abuse, drug abuse, and sexual responsibility/safer sex practices."

Students With HIV. Professionals once thought that cognitive impairments were common and severe in children with HIV. However, the results a study by Cohen et al. (1991) comparing the intelligence scores and school achievement scores of students infected by neonatal blood transfusions soon after birth are encouraging. In that study, the children with HIV infection did not differ from the HIV-1 seronegative (uninfected) group in overall intellectual functioning four-and-one-half to eight-and-one-half years after infection. For the group of HIV-1 infected children who were tested in this study, the mean score was in the average range of intelligence, and some children scored within the high average range (Cohen et al., 1991).

These findings from Cohen et al. (1991), along with studies of children infected with HIV through vertical transmission (mother to child), offer good evidence that "average over-all intellectual functioning can be maintained for many years even in symptomatic children."

The Cohen et al. (1991) study did reveal some significant differences between children and youth with and without HIV in terms of tasks requiring motor speed, visual scanning, or cognitive flexibility. In general, even children with HIV who have no impairments in their immune system experience some "slowing in motor speed, impaired attention and concentration, and problems in academic skills." Thus, special education services might be necessary for some children as the condition progresses. However, it is important to keep in mind that these differences are subtle and not seen in every child who has HIV.

Prenatal Substance Exposure. Prenatal substance exposure affects children in a variety of ways:

> One of the infants in the sterile hospital room wailed disconsolately, frantically flailing its tiny arms and legs as children born to crack-using mothers often do. Next to her, at the Bellevue Hospital center in Manhattan, another child slept peacefully, her face sculpted in an angelic expression.

The contrast seemed to confirm what everyone knows about cocaine exposed babies. But contrary to assumptions, hospital officials said it was the peaceful child, not the cranky one, whose mother had been using the potent drug.

Eight years after crack hit New York and other cities around the country, and concern about a generation of "crack babies" began spreading, medical experts say their worst fears are not being realized: While up to a third appear to have been seriously damaged, 20 to 40 percent seem unscathed. (Treaster, 1993)

What Is Prenatal Substance Exposure? We have already discussed how a mother can transmit HIV to her child. The mother's use of drugs or alcohol can also affect her unborn child's well-being. Such children have a higher risk of developing learning or behavior problems than the general population. The drugs can be prescription or illegal, and nicotine is included. The period of time during the pregnancy when the mother ingests the substance and the frequency of ingestion can affect the child's risk of having symptoms.

In the early 1990s, widespread panic and misinformation occurred among educators, social-service workers, and the general public about children whose mothers used cocaine during pregnancy (Schutter & Brinker, 1992). This phenomenon closely followed the rapid increase in cocaine use in the United States during the 1980s. Caught up in the near hysteria, both popular and professional writers defined crack kids as a new kind of child, one with inevitable and permanent developmental damage, the inability to know and return love, and no conscience (Zuckerman & Frank, 1992).

But according to Vincent, Paulsen, Cole, Woodruff, and Griffith (1991), that view is not necessarily accurate:

> The media have painted a dire picture of infants who were exposed to alcohol and other drugs in utero. This picture is not fully supported by research or clinical experience with these children: We do not know the incidence of prenatal exposure to alcohol and other drugs, nor do we know the long-term effects of such exposure.

The future for many of these children is bright, even for those who have symptoms as a result of their prenatal exposure.

Characteristics of Prenatal Substance Exposure. Definitive characteristics can be observed in some but not all of the children who have been prenatally exposed to alcohol. These characteristics are evidenced at birth, during the neonate/infancy stage, and in later years. However, not all the conditions can necessarily be attributed to prenatal substance exposure. Psychosocial factors such as "poverty, multigenerational substance abuse,

Prenatal substance exposure, the use of drugs or alcohol by the mother during pregnancy, may cause learning or behavior problems

and the impact of growing up in a drug-seeking environment" might have additive or interactive effects (Chasnoff, Griffith, Freier, & Murray, 1992).

At or Before Birth. The risks created to mother and child during pregnancy when the mother uses drugs or alcohol can cause health problems for the developing fetus. Complications during birth can also result. These problems begin before the child is born and can continue to cause health, behavioral, and learning problems in later life. Despite the risks, however, most children of mothers who engage in substance abuse have a normal birth with no complications and no physical abnormalities.

Children exposed to alcohol sometimes have characteristics associated with **fetal alcohol syndrome.** A syndrome is a group of symptoms associated with a particular condition. According to Conlon (1992), "when the mother drinks, so does the fetus." Children with fetal alcohol syndrome tend to be small for their gestational age, remain small after birth, and have facial deformities including droopy eyelids, a wide nose, and a flattened midface. Microcephaly (small head circumference) is also common. These children often have congenital heart defects and mild or moderate mental retardation.

Fetal alcohol syndrome and fetal alcohol exposure cause approximately 5 percent of congenital abnormalities and 10 to 20 percent of cases of mild mental retardation (Conlon, 1992). Even among chronic alcohol users, however, 50 to 70 percent of children will be born without these symptoms (Conlon, 1992). On the other hand, even mothers who use alcohol moderately during pregnancy may give birth to babies with fetal alcohol syndrome (Glanze, Anderson, & Anderson, 1985). Thus, it is important for mothers and physicians to discuss any alcohol consumption during pregnancy.

During Infancy. Most infants with prenatal substance exposure do not differ significantly from other infants on standardized developmental tests (Chasnoff et al., 1992). Nevertheless, of greater concern, according to researchers, are the neurobehavioral characteristics of some of these infants (Vincent et al., 1991). These characteristics include irritability; being difficult to handle for bathing, feeding, and diapering; high pitched and piercing crying; and unresponsiveness to attempts at comforting.

Children who are unresponsive and difficult to manage are generally more at risk for abuse or neglect from caregivers (Vincent et al., 1991). Even in the most stable families, parents will frequently find caring for a child with these symptoms extremely challenging (Vincent et al., 1991). As you will recall, however, many children with prenatal substance exposure do not have these characteristics, and others who have the characteristics did not have prenatal substance exposure.

Later Years. Subtle cognitive and behavioral effects may not begin to manifest until the child is three years or older. Environmental differences may be more of a factor than prenatal drug exposure in these cases (Carta et al., 1994).

Children with prenatal substance exposure can be divided into three groups (Vincent et al., 1991): (1) those with developmental disabilities including seizures, physical abnormalities, cerebral palsy, or mental retardation; (2) those with normal development; and (3) those at risk for learning and behavior problems. The majority will have normal development, but one researcher has found that 30 to 40 percent of children with substance exposure have language delays or attention deficits (Griffith, 1991).

Prenatal Substance Exposure and the Classroom. Students with substance exposure who are at risk for learning and behavior problems may develop any or all of the following (Vincent et al., 1991):

- Behavioral extremes

- Being easily overstimulated

- Testing limits

- Inability to read social cues

- Low tolerance for change

Fetal alcohol syndrome results from the mother's alcohol use during pregnancy. The children often are small for gestational age, have facial deformities, and have congenital heart defects. Mild-to-moderate mental retardation is common.

- Poor peer relationships

- Language delays

- Sporadic skill mastery

- Difficulty initiating and organizing play

- Poor attention and concentration

- Difficulty with auditory processing and word retrieval

- Poor problem-solving skills

Therefore, this group may need special education services. Early intervention is especially important to minimize the effects of substance exposure. If you have a student whose learning is affected by prenatal substance exposure, you might find that some of the interventions for students with attention-deficit/hyperactivity disorder are also applicable (see Chapter 6).

Professionals can help students who have these learning and behavioral problems, as teacher Nichelle Timoll and her colleagues at the Odyssey House, a preschool for children with prenatal substance exposure, are proving:

> One girl, just under three years old, arrived [at Odyssey House] balky and whiny. Anything she came across on the floor—a button, a coin, a crayon—she jammed into her mouth. She wet her pants and refused to lie on a cot at nap time. Instead of trying to fit together a jigsaw puzzle, she would throw the pieces across the room and walk away. If she spoke at all, it would be to blurt out a single word: "car," perhaps, or "water" or "door."
>
> After four months in the nursery, in a classroom with ten children and four special education teachers as well as regular sessions with a speech therapist and a psychologist, the girl still has difficulty focusing on a particular task. But she may work at a puzzle now for five minutes before giving up, and she is speaking in five-word sentences.
>
> "She can follow along with others in the group now," said Nichelle Timoll, one of the teachers, "and she understands when something ends and something else begins." (Treaster, 1993; Copyright 1993 by The New York Times Company. Reprinted by Permission.)

Asthma. Asthma, the most prevalent chronic illness of children, is a condition that affects the lungs and causes breathing difficulties (Simeonsson, 1995). Some people have only occasional symptoms. Others experience breathing difficulties almost daily. Symptoms may be mild, as when a student experiences occasional shortness of breath after a challenging football game, or they may be life-threatening, requiring emergency hospitalization.

What Is Asthma? The most common lung disease among children, asthma begins in about half the childhood cases before age three. About twice as many boys have asthma than girls, and boys are more likely to have severe asthma. The general tendency is for asthma symptoms in boys to decrease with age but for girls to experience more problems as they go into adolescence (Paul & Fafoglia, 1988).

Asthma has three primary features (National Heart, Lung, and Blood Institute, 1992):

- Airway linings are swollen.

- Airways narrow and breathing becomes difficult. This narrowing may reverse (but not completely in some people) by itself or with treatment.

- Airways are hypersensitive or are supersensitive. They react to a variety of stimuli, or triggers, including physical changes (cold air or exercise), allergens (cat dander,

In one study, 90 percent of children with recurrent wheezing tested positive for allergies (National Environmental Health Association, 1995).

dust mites, and molds), and irritants (smoke, strong odors, and sprays). Coughing, wheezing, or difficult breathing—also known as asthma attacks, or episodes—may result.

The symptoms and severity of asthma vary widely from person to person. The National Asthma Education Program (1991) classifies individuals as having mild, moderate, or severe asthma. Although most students you encounter with asthma will probably only have mild or moderate symptoms, asthma can cause a medical emergency and, in rare cases (about five thousand per year), lead to death. It is important that students with severe asthma use medication as soon as they experience symptoms. If a student has the following symptoms, you should seek emergency treatment immediately (Paul & Fafoglia, 1988):

- Over a period of three to four days, asthma symptoms cannot be controlled with usual medications.

- The individual experiences more asthma symptoms than usual over a period of several hours.

- To feel relief, the person needs to take medication more often than prescribed.

- Mucous secretions cannot be cleared by coughing.

Asthma and the Classroom.   When you have a student with asthma in your class, it is important to know some basic preventions and treatments. For students with asthma, these include taking medications, monitoring lung functioning, managing stress and exercise, and controlling triggers.

"Kids who don't have asthma will understand about it if they just breathe through a straw with their noses pinched," Brian, who has asthma, recommends. "Another thing they could do is hold their breath when their friends are having attacks" (Fleitas, 1997).

🐟 *Students with asthma have a positive role model in Jackie Joyner-Kersee, who didn't let asthma stop her from becoming an Olympic gold-medal winner.*

Taking Medications.   Physicians commonly prescribe anti-inflammatory drugs and bronchial dilators. Students with mild asthma only need medication when an asthma episode occurs. For others whose asthma interferes with routine activities, sleep, or exercise, daily medications are useful.

Monitoring Lung Functioning.   Your student might also monitor lung functioning through the use of a peak flow meter. To operate the device, a person with asthma simply exhales as hard as possible into the mouthpiece. The higher the reading, the better the lungs are working. Lower readings indicate that the airways are obstructed and the use of medications or avoiding allergens is warranted to prevent an asthma episode.

Managing Stress and Exercise.   Much misunderstanding exists regarding the role of emotions in asthma. It is important to remember that no amount of stress causes an asthmatic episode unless the person already has hyperactive airways: "Asthma begins in the lungs, not in the head" (National Jewish Center for Immunology and Respiratory Medicine, 1992). Characterizing asthma as a stress-related condition perpetuates this misunderstanding, and professionals should avoid doing so. An overemphasis on the role of emotions may divert attention from preventing the inflammation of the airways, which is a critical need for these individuals.

Relaxation techniques do not prevent episodes of impaired breathing, but they are useful for responding to episodes once they have begun. Deliberate self-calming activities help avoid the additional constriction of airways that often accompany fear and panic and are especially useful in the ten- to-fifteen-minute interval before the medications take full effect.

Tremendous advances in treating and preventing asthma episodes now make it possible for people with asthma to lead active lives. Vigorous exercise (especially in cold air) is a frequent trigger of asthma episodes; but moderate exercise is an excellent way to improve breathing efficiency and overall health. Medications are now available that can be taken before exercising to prevent asthma episodes. Other medications, such as bronchial muscle relaxers, are effective in treating symptoms that may arise during or after exercising.

Avoiding and Controlling Triggers.   Triggers, which we described earlier in this section, do not cause asthma. The underlying condition, the asthma itself, enables these agents to interfere with normal breathing. These triggers are common features of our environment, and it is important that you do what you can to help the individual with asthma avoid them. An air purifier in your classroom, for example, might make a significant improvement in a student's health.

The National Heart, Lung, and Blood Institute (1992) recommends that teachers develop an action plan for their students with asthma. With your support, most of these students will be able to be included in the typical routine of your classroom.

During the 1950s, children with asthma were treated in hospital-run facilities in the mistaken belief that they needed a "parentectomy." In 1966, physicians recognized asthma as an immune system dysfunction (Dowling, 1997).

Cancer.   What would be your reaction to hearing a diagnosis of cancer? In the following passage, Melissa Price, who had cancer as an adolescent, shares her feelings:

> *It started in 1989. I didn't think anything was seriously wrong. I just didn't feel very well, but I was sure it was the flu or something. I was scared to death of all the tests they were running on me, not because I believed something was wrong, but because I hate needles and hospitals.*
>
> *Mom knew what the tests were checking for, so she was much more scared than me. She told me the night before the doctor told me. She said they were checking for one of two things: Hodgkin's disease or hepatitis. I just lay there and cried. When I went to have the biopsy, I was more scared than I have ever been. When I went to the hospital, I was so scared of everything that I couldn't stop crying. I thought the doctor would be mad, but he was so nice to me.*

The next doctor I saw was my oncologist. He said I had Hodgkin's disease, and he explained what he wanted to do to fight it. He said chemotherapy right away. I was listening, but none of it was sinking in until he said that I had a 60 percent chance of living and only a 40 percent chance that I would ever have children. I cried for the children I might never have.

I started chemo. I just tried not to think about it. When I got in the bed, I was given a tranquilizer and sedative, so I slept. I was not scared of dying, but of what they might do to me before I died.

What Is Cancer?   Cancer, a condition that causes unrestrained growth of cells in body organs or tissues, unfortunately does affect students like Melissa. In 1993, approximately 1,500 children and adolescents died from cancer, one-third of those from leukemia (American Cancer Society, 1993). Although rare in children, cancer is the primary cause of death by disease in young people between ages one to fourteen.

The good news about childhood cancer is that improved treatment using a combination of therapies has dramatically improved the survival rate. For instance, in the early 1960s, the five-year survival rate for childhood leukemia was only 4 percent. Now the survival rate is 72 percent. The survival rate for childhood cancers at all sites is 68 percent, and 88 percent of those with Hodgkin's disease survive beyond five years. Currently, the number of children who are long-term childhood cancer survivors is estimated at 45,000 (Peckham, 1993). Therefore, young people like Melissa and their families have every reason to hope.

Unfortunately, the treatments for cancer generally cause side effects. Chemotherapy, for example, works indiscriminately on all rapidly dividing cells and can adversely affect the bone marrow, intestinal lining, hair follicles (resulting in baldness in many people), and mouth (Clayman, 1989). In addition, the treatments often lower the student's white cell count, which increases vulnerability to infections from others.

Cancer in the Classroom.   If you are responsible for teaching a student who has been treated for cancer, it is important to know that students who have had cranial radiation or brain tumors often develop learning disabilities (American Cancer Society, 1988). Thus, when the student reenters school, teachers should make arrangements for a comprehensive evaluation to determine educational needs.

The American Cancer Society (1988) recommends that all students with cancer have an IEP completed before school reentry. Even if the student is not experiencing any difficulties at the time, the IEP provides an opportunity for teachers and caregivers to watch and consult. The IEP can also include a provision for home tutoring and individual instruction if the medical condition changes. Furthermore, the IEP committee should list general classroom modifications on the IEP, such as allowing the student to go to the nurse's station for a nap, if needed.

The condition itself, as well as the treatment side effects, may contribute to frequent school absences. However, attending school as much as possible allows the student to have structure, contact with peers, a chance to keep up with developmental skills, a sense of independence, and hope for the future. Therefore, you will want to do everything you can to help the student be (and also feel) included at school as much as possible. Box 11–2, "Into Practice," describes what parents find helpful from teachers.

Current practice is to inform even young children that they have cancer and have them actively participate in their treatment. Fear of the unknown is usually worse than reality, and a lack of honesty from adults can cause students to feel guilty and isolated (Peckham, 1993). This honesty should extend to the student's classmates. To generate a discussion with students, you might want to ask questions such as the following: "How many of you know someone who has cancer? Does anyone know what cancer is? Do you know how kids get cancer? Can you get cancer by sitting next to or playing with someone with cancer?" (Peckham, 1993).

Many students with cancer will live to adulthood and realize their dreams. In 1993, Melissa Price gave birth to a healthy baby girl. She shares her thoughts about her life today:

BOX 11-2   INTO PRACTICE

HOW TEACHERS CAN HELP A CHILD WITH CANCER

THE BEST TEACHERS (A PARENT'S VIEW)

1. Call or visit my child during times of absence.
2. Know that parents need a little TLC, too. Cards, phone calls, visits—all are appreciated.
3. Listen to my concerns and fears.
4. Take time to become familiar with treatments given [to] my child and [understand] their effect on school performance.
5. Visit with my child before re-entry to talk about any fears she/he may have.
6. Adjust regular lesson plans to account for change in my child's ability to complete lengthy tasks or assignments.
7. Gently encourage my child to reach his/her current potential.
8. Follow my and the doctor's instructions regarding bathroom visits, snacks, wearing a hat, etc.
9. Accept the sometimes hard-to-accept side effects of cancer or its treatment (slurring words, falling asleep in class, diminished temper control or ability to accept discipline, etc.).
10. Are supportive of us during setbacks in the illness.
11. Encourage classmates to call or write my child during periods of extended absence.
12. Prepare the class for physical and emotional changes in my child as a consequence of treatment; suggest ways to be helpful.
13. Treat my child as normally as possible, given the restrictions imposed by disease and its treatment; don't impose their own limits.
14. Are supportive and encouraging, but not phony in their praise.
15. Know when a situation is over their heads and call the parents, doctor, or administrators for help.
16. Include my child in as many class functions as possible. She/he may not have the stamina for a full day of school, but may be able to come to the holiday party or class outing.

THE WORST TEACHERS (A PARENT'S VIEW)

. . . Not only don't do the above, but:

1. Show fear about having my child in their class.
2. Allow pity for him or her within the classroom.
3. Fail to share information about my child's appearance, special needs, etc., with colleagues, substitutes, and aides.
4. Convey an attitude that assumes my child won't be able to do things.
5. Fail to educate themselves about the disease, its treatment, and possible changes in a child's appearance, mannerisms, etc.
6. Make an issue of my child's differences in front of the whole class.
7. Ignore problems classmates have in adjusting to their friend's disease, which may manifest as teasing, mimicking, etc.
8. Do not give my child an opportunity to at least try whatever the others are doing.
9. Do not give my child the benefit of the doubt whenever possible on assignments and homework.

Now it's been seven years since my last treatment, and I still get scared sometimes. But mostly, I forget about it, and I don't feel like I was ever sick. I do still get extremely nervous about seeing my doctor for checkups because he could find something wrong. But I believe I lived for a special reason. God has a plan for my life. Maybe it was to be Rachel's mother. I don't know for sure what it is. But I feel thankful to have had the past three years, and to have my daughter.

 Melissa Price realized her dream of having a healthy baby, despite her battle with cancer as a teenager. She is shown here with her husband and Rachel, the baby her doctors say is a miracle.

Juvenile Diabetes.   One young girl exhibits confidence in dealing with her diabetes:

> *[She] used her artistic talents to share her diabetes with her class. She told her mother that she'd easily recognize which drawing of the body was hers at the next open house. Her mother was surprised to find an out-of-order sign where the pancreas should have been. (Loring, 1991)*

This girl's story demonstrates that students with diabetes can confront their condition with humor, courage, and openness. However, the condition requires many adaptations from affected children and youth. Students with juvenile diabetes need your understanding and support.

What Is Juvenile Diabetes?   Juvenile diabetes results when the pancreas stops producing or produces too little of the hormone insulin. This condition occurs in some people who are genetically predisposed and sometimes develops after a viral infection. When this happens, the cells do not absorb glucose, and unused sugar builds up in the blood. The kidneys try to filter out the excess sugar; therefore, people with diabetes test their urine to see if sugar is present (National Institute of Diabetes and Digestive and Kidney Diseases, 1997). A sign of poorly controlled diabetes is increased thirst, increased urination, and weight loss. Little (1991) describes the potential results:

> *Cellular starvation results in weakness, weight loss, and the inability to lead a normal life, but the excess blood sugar itself can also cause immediate and long-term illnesses. It can produce a diabetic coma, or period of unconsciousness, and over time it can damage nerves, weaken the circulatory system, impair healing, and endanger pregnancies.*

Type I, or juvenile-onset diabetes, usually develops before the age of thirty-five and is most common in young people between the ages of ten and sixteen. The condition generally results in a complete or near-complete halt in the production of insulin. The onset is rapid; and without injections of insulin, the individual will become comatose and die (National Institute of Diabetes and Digestive and Kidney Disease, 1997). Type II diabetes usually occurs in individuals over forty and is associated with obesity and genetic factors.

Juvenile Diabetes and the Classroom.   The need to give themselves insulin shots, monitor their blood glucose levels, and watch their diet sets these students apart from their peers. According to Little (1991), "perhaps no other disease requires so much personal involvement." Feelings of denial, anger, isolation, fear, and rebellion are not uncommon, even among the most well-adjusted individuals (Loring, 1991).

Having diabetes, on the other hand, can also lead to increased self-esteem. Parents and teachers can help by focusing on the positive and praising young people for taking responsibility for monitoring their condition; by encouraging them to feel confident about their ability to handle the diabetes; by not blaming them when they have high blood-sugar readings but enlisting their help in figuring out how to lower them; and by reminding them of their ability to make wise decisions, comprehend technical information, and understand the importance of a healthy diet (Loring, 1991). The following example illustrates the sense of competence that can accompany the condition:

> *[When one preschooler] feels hungry, which may be a sign of low blood sugar, she knows her mom will test her blood. She merely tells her mom "Let's do a blood sugar" and climbs up on the kitchen counter to get the blood testing machine. She then does her own finger prick and puts the test strip in the machine. (Loring, 1991)*

Our discussion will not explain how to help individuals control their diabetes. If you have a student in your class with diabetes (and the same goes for all other serious health impairments), you need to work closely with the parents, school nurse, and physician to help meet the student's medical needs. Each student will have a particular regimen that he or she must follow for controlling diabetes. Figure 11–2 is a list of items that parents can provide to help you respond in case of an emergency. Often, the student's diet will include a morning and afternoon snack. One thing you can do to help reduce the stigma associated with this requirement is to include the entire class in snack time.

People with diabetes can live an active life. One student says, "I love soccer and gymnastics, but people are always worrying that I'm doing too much. Really, they shouldn't make such a big deal out of it" (Fleitas, 1997).

---

1. Shot and test kit containing
   (a) Insulin (if needed during school hours)
   (b) Syringes (if needed)
   (c) Blood testing equipment (a good idea whether or not your child regularly takes a test before lunch; can be used in emergencies)
   (d) Brochures designed for school personnel describing signs of low and high blood sugar and treatment
   (e) An index card with your child's allotted food exchanges for snacks and meals, with examples and doctors' phone numbers

2. Insulin reaction kit
   (a) Quick sugar source: liquid glucose, cake frosting in a tube, cans of orange juice
   (b) Snacks to stabilize the blood sugar: prepackaged cheese or peanut butter and crackers
   (c) Blood testing equipment

FIGURE 11–2 *Information and supplies for a child with diabetes*

Note: From Loring, G. (1991). *Parenting a Diabetic Child.* Chicago: Contemporary Books. Reprinted by the permission of RGA Publishing Group, Inc. Copyright © 1991 RGA Publishing Group, Inc. and Gloria Loring.

Two serious medical conditions can occur in the classroom if the student's diabetes is not under good control. If the individual does not have enough insulin, he or she can develop **hyperglycemia** (too much sugar), which can cause **ketoacidosis.** If insulin is not administered, the individual will fall into a diabetic coma. Symptoms that suggest ketoacidosis include hunger, fatigue, excessive urination, thirst, and blurred vision. Sometimes the person can appear to be drunk. The treatment, of course, is insulin. Stress, eating too many carbohydrates, illness, and forgetting to take insulin can all cause hyperglycemia.

At the opposite end of the spectrum is **hypoglycemia,** or not enough sugar. Increased physical activity, taking too much insulin, or not eating enough can cause a person to have too much insulin. Insulin shock or insulin reaction may occur before mealtimes, especially if the meal is delayed. Common symptoms include feeling dizzy, sweaty, shaky, or nervous, and having headaches or blurred vision.

If you have a student who is diabetic, you will probably be able to tell that he or she is hypoglycemic before the student even notices. You can generally notice a change in behavior. For example, the student might usually be outgoing; but when hypoglycemic, she becomes withdrawn or apathetic. Hypoglycemia often causes confused thinking, so you will need to be alert to how an individual behaves when she becomes hypoglycemic. The treatment is to give them a sugar source such as some fruit juice, milk, or a soda (not sugar free); check with parents to find out what the student should have for low blood glucose. If, however, the person begins to have convulsions or loses consciousness, it is important *not* to give any food or fluids. Instead, seek immediate medical attention from someone who can administer a shot of glucagon. It is important to remember that the only way to tell if the student's blood sugar is too high or too low is by testing blood sugar. You will want to help the student find a way to check blood sugar that is comfortable and unobtrusive. One student may prefer to check her blood sugar quietly at her seat, but another might prefer to go outside the classroom or to the nurse's office. Let the child be in charge as much as possible.

Fortunately, new methods of treating and monitoring diabetes are resulting in better control and improved quality of life for individuals with the condition. For some students in your classes, this can mean that they will not to be identified as health-impaired. Others, however, especially those with brittle diabetes (a condition in which stabilizing blood sugar is extremely difficult), may need some modifications in classroom routine and close supervision for symptoms.

There is hope that one day soon more effective treatments and possibly a cure will be found for diabetes. Some scientists are attempting to genetically engineer cells to produce insulin (Steeves, 1997). One scientist is testing the hypothesis that a fish islet transplant may one day replace the damaged islets of a person with diabetes, eliminating a need for insulin injection (Bannister, 1997). Also, pancreas transplantation is becoming more common for people with Type 1 diabetes (Midwest Diabetes Care Center, Inc., 1997).

Epilepsy. Jacob Empey's fourth-grade teacher, Jeanine, describes her first experience with Jacob having a seizure in her class:

> *I was so scared. I had never seen a seizure before in my life. As a mother, I had an intuitive sense to stop what I was doing and meet the immediate physical or safety needs. Then my emotional feelings came into play. Being scared or upset came sliding in afterwards. When Jacob left with the nurse, I talked to the other kids about their feelings. I asked them, "Were you feeling scared? I was, too." I was honest and straightforward with them. We talked a lot about Jacob's feelings. How would you feel if this happened to you? What would you want people to do? Jacob also answered the students' questions later. It was especially important for them to hear from him that it didn't hurt. Each time he had a seizure, it became easier because I became more adept at handling the situation.*

Hyperglycemia occurs when a person has too much sugar in his or her bloodstream as a result of lack of insulin.

Ketoacidosis results when lack of insulin prevents the use of glucose as a source of energy. The body uses fats instead, leading to the release into the bloodstream of fatty acids called ketones. If untreated, the condition can result in confusion, unconsciousness, or death.

Hypoglycemia occurs when blood sugar is too low because of having too much insulin.

Some students with difficult-to-control diabetes may require the use of an *insulin pump,* which injects insulin at programmed levels and times through a needle inserted in the stomach.

The Epilepsy Foundation of America prefers the term *epilepsy* to *seizure disorder,* although the terms can be used interchangeably. Spokesperson Peter Van Haverbeke believes that educating people about the term *epilepsy* to overcome their misunderstandings is more important than changing the term.

If you have never seen a seizure, having reactions like Jeanine's are normal. However, like Jeanine, you will also find that you can learn to respond to a student's seizures quickly and efficiently, without any major limitations in classroom routine.

What Is Epilepsy? The more you know about seizures, the easier it will be to respond in a positive way. Epilepsy is a condition characterized by seizures: temporary neurological abnormalities that result from unregulated electrical discharges in the brain. If a person has seizures only once or temporarily, perhaps from a high fever or brain injury, they do not have epilepsy (The Epilepsy Foundation of America, 1997). Although you may be familiar with convulsive seizures, you may not know that an individual can also have a seizure that manifests as a brief period of unconsciousness or altered behavior that is sometimes misinterpreted as daydreaming (The Cleveland Clinic Foundation, 1997).

There are two types of seizures: generalized or partial. **Generalized seizures** cause a loss of consciousness; the whole body is affected when the electrical discharge crosses the entire brain. **Tonic-clonic** seizures (once known as **grand mal**) and **absence seizures** are generalized seizures. When an individual has a tonic-clonic seizure, she or he falls, loses consciousness, and has a *convulsion,* which is a sudden involuntary contraction of a group of muscles. During an absence seizure, the person also loses consciousness, but only for a brief period lasting from a few seconds to a half minute or so (Spiegel, Cutler, & Yetter, 1996). The individual and others around them might not realize that a seizure has taken place. Absence seizures can occur up to 140 times a day and severely affect learning. Jacob experiences absence as well as tonic-clonic seizures. Many times during the day, he momentarily misses what others are doing or saying.

During **partial seizures,** the electrical discharge is limited to one area of the brain. A **temporal lobe, or psychomotor, seizure** causes an individual to appear to be in a dreamlike state (Epilepsy Foundation of America, 1997). The person, who usually has no memory of what happened afterward, makes random movements called *automatisms,* such as picking at clothes, repeating a sentence several times, or even running. A focal motor seizure causes the person to have sudden, jerky movements of one part of the body. The individual who is having a **focal sensory seizure,** however, will see things and hear sounds that are not really occurring. **Myolonic seizures** mostly affect infants and young children and cause them to look startled or in pain during the seizure. Sometimes these children suddenly drop their heads forward and jerk their arms upward. Table 11–1 lists some appropriate first-aid measures for seizures.

Epilepsy and the Classroom. When you work with students who have epilepsy, you will want to help them identify any environmental factors that seem to trigger their seizures. Extreme stress or fatigue, as well as infectious diseases (especially if accompanied by fever), trigger a seizure in individuals. Bright lights and certain sounds or odors also can trigger seizures in some cases. By avoiding triggers and taking prescribed medications regularly, a person can usually reduce the number of seizures.

Some people also experience an *aura,* an unusual sensation that always occurs right before a seizure (Epilepsy Foundation of America, 1985). Occasionally, people with epilepsy can learn how to distract themselves when they experience the aura, thus aborting the seizure (Clayman, 1989).

Having students share about epilepsy if they are comfortable doing so, as Jacob did with students at both his schools, can help them learn to handle their condition with confidence instead of embarrassment. It is also important that peers know first aid for seizures. Being able to respond to a seizure and to help the student can help decrease the other students' fears and a possible response of teasing or avoidance.

Identifying the Causes of Other Health Impairments

The causes, or etiology, of health impairments vary. Most are caused by infections, genetic factors, and environmental influences. Sometimes the etiology is unknown or is trauma related, as when a child is severely burned.

Generalized seizures cause a loss of consciousness. There are two types of generalized seizures: (1) a **tonic-clonic,** or **grand-mal,** seizure causes someone to fall and have a convulsion; (2) an **absence seizure** causes the person to lose consciousness only briefly.

In **partial seizures,** electrical activity is limited to one area of the brain. There are three types of partial seizures. (1) **Temporal lobe, or psychomotor, seizures** cause a dreamlike state in which the person makes random movements called *automatisms.* (2) **Focal sensory seizures** cause the person to see or hear things that are not there. (3) **Myolonic seizures** cause an infant or young child to look startled or in pain.

Video or computer games may trigger seizures in some students. The British Epilepsy Foundation (quoted in National Council for Educational Technology, 1993) recommends that (a) students sit at least two feet away from the screen, (b) the room should be well lit, (c) the screen should never be set at maximum brightness, and (d) students never play these games when tired. The larger the screen, the greater the risk.

TABLE 11–1 ♃ *First aid for seizures*

Seizure Type	Characteristics	First Aid	Possibility of Injury
General Seizures			
Tonic-clonic	Uncontrolled jerking Loss of consciousness Disorientation Violent reactions Cessation of breathing Vomiting Loss of continence	Lay person on side Move potentially dangerous or fragile objects Place pillow under head Never attempt to restrain or place anything in mouth	Fairly high, due to bumping into objects during seizure
Tonic	Sudden stiffening of muscles Rigidity Falling to ground	Reassure individual Provide place to lie down afterward Stay calm	Quite high, due to possibility of striking an object while falling
Atonic	Sudden loss of muscle tone resulting in a collapse on ground	Reassure individual Provide a place to rest	High, due to possibility of falling into object
Absence	Very brief interruption in consciousness Appearance of momentary déjà vu	Reassure individual following the event	Fairly low
Partial Seizures			
Simple partial	Twitching movements Sensation of déjà vu	Reassure student	Fairly low
Complex partial	Altered state of consciousness Psychomotor movements	Provide verbal reassurance during occurrence	Fairly low unless there is increased physical activity

Seek medical attention immediately if . . .

There is no previous history of seizures, especially if the student is experiencing a tonic-clonic seizure
Several tonic-clonic seizures follow one another in rapid succession
A tonic-clonic seizure lasts for more than 2 to 3 minutes
An injury occurs during the seizure

Note: From "What Every Teacher Should Know About Epilepsy," by G. L. Spiegel, S. K. Cutler, and C. E. Yetter, 1996, *Intervention in School and Clinic, 32*(1), pp. 35, 36, and 37. Copyright 1996 by PRO-ED, Inc. Adapted and reprinted with permission.

Infections.　Numerous diseases are caused by infections from some type of microorganism. Certainly, the colds and flus you have experienced over your lifetime do not mean that as a child you should have been identified as having a particular health impairment. However, some infections cause long-lasting consequences and can even lead to death. Even a common infection such as strep throat can result in rheumatic fever, a condition associated with heart problems if not treated. Other infection-caused conditions include HIV, tuberculosis, and some cancers. In addition, epilepsy can result from brain infections such as encephalitis and meningitis.

One primary concern about infections is that they are communicable: in other words, they are contagious or transmittable from one person to another. Some are more easily transmitted than others; however, precautions must be taken when a student has any communicable disease to prevent other people from becoming infected. Following the universal precautions we mentioned earlier in the chapter should help prevent the spread of all infections.

Genetic Factors. You have already learned about the role of genetics in the development of mental retardation and severe and multiple disabilities (see Chapters 7 and 8). Medical research is also uncovering a genetic component in the development of diabetes, asthma, epilepsy, and specific cancers as well as some of the conditions more readily identified as genetic, such as cystic fibrosis, hemophilia, or sickle cell anemia.

A child born with the abnormal gene that indicates cystic fibrosis, hemophilia, or sickle cell anemia will inherit the disease. But in the other conditions we've mentioned, the abnormal gene apparently causes the individual to be predisposed to getting the condition, but the condition is not inevitable. Other currently unknown factors (e.g., environmental factors or infections) seem to work in conjunction with the genetic predisposition to cause the condition. Loring (1991) summarized the role of genetics in the development of diabetes:

> *Diabetes is a disease born of genetic susceptibility. That means [a child can be] born with a genetic background that makes him prone to diabetes. This genetic defect is linked to the body's ability to recognize its own tissue as friend or foe. Not everyone with this background gets diabetes, but you will not get it if the genetic susceptibility is not present.*

Environmental Influences. The environment can play a substantial role in a person's health. For example, a treatment regimen that includes avoiding triggers can prevent death due to severe asthma. Doctors debate whether poor access to health care or air pollution might be contributing to the deaths of students with asthma in inner cities (Podolsky, 1997). Environmental factors can not only worsen but actually cause some conditions.

Pre- and Perinatal Influences. As you know, a mother's substance use during pregnancy can affect her unborn child. The substance or substances she uses are known as *teratogens*—environmental influences that prohibit normal growth development in the fetus. Teratogens include exposure of the mother to infections; trauma, x-rays, or other radiation; and drugs, tobacco, or alcohol. We have already mentioned that a mother's alcohol abuse increases the risk of the child's development of fetal alcohol syndrome. But prenatal substance exposure also increases the child's risk for developing other conditions, such as seizure disorder and HIV (Conlon, 1992; Vincent et al., 1991). In particular, maternal smoking has been linked to asthma in children (DiFranza & Lew, 1996).

Postnatal Influences. Exposure to environmental agents after birth can also cause health impairments, such as lead poisoning and some types of cancer. Lead poisoning is the most common environmental disease of childhood and can cause "learning disabilities, decreased growth, hyperactivity, impaired hearing, and even brain damage" (Environmental Protection Agency, 1992). One of six children has a high level of lead in his or her blood (Environmental Protection Agency, 1992), and even low levels of lead can affect learning and behavior (Childhood Lead Poisoning Prevention Program, 1996). Lead poisoning is especially a hazard for young children under age nine who live in buildings built before 1978 that used lead paint. The most common method for a child to be poisoned is by lead dust (Childhood Lead Poisoning Prevention Program, 1996). Chipping or peeling paint, opening and closing lead-painted windows, and repairing or renovating lead-painted surfaces creates this dust. Children touch surfaces with the dust and then put their hands in their mouths. Children may also be poisoned by eating paint chips or by contaminated water or soil.

Chemical and physical agents in the environment can be carcinogens, or cancer-causing agents. For example, you have probably read and heard numerous warnings about the link between cigarette smoking and lung cancer. More recently, researchers have emphasized the dangers of secondhand smoke on children and other nonsmokers (DiFranza & Lew, 1996). Currently, the Food and Drug Administration screens food additives,

In 1996, researchers identified a gene that leads to myoclonus epilepsy when both parents carry a defective copy. Myers, one of the researchers, comments, "Any time a person can find a genetic cause for a disease, even if it has multiple causes, you have the potential for understanding the biochemical pathway that gives rise to the disease" (P/S/L Consulting Group, Inc., 1997).

cosmetics, and chemicals used in drugs for possible carcinogens. Researchers have also linked high-energy radiation to cancer, including high doses of x-rays, asbestos fibers, radon, and ultraviolet radiation from sunlight.

Dietary factors may also contribute to the development of health impairments. Food allergies can trigger asthma in some individuals, and a high-fat, low-fiber diet seems to increase a person's risk of developing some cancers. Diet can also stabilize or worsen conditions such as diabetes.

Identifying the Prevalence of Other Health Impairments

In the 1994–1995 school year, schools served 106,000 students (1.9 percent of the school-age population) under IDEA as "other health impaired" (U.S. Department of Education, 1997). In Figure 11–3 you will find the prevalence data for specific conditions that have

FIGURE 11–3 *Prevalence of health impairments and specific conditions*

Other Health Impairments

106,000 (1.9%) of schoolchildren were served as having other health impairments in 1995.

Asthma

Twelve million Americans total (four million children, or 6.1 percent of children under the age of eighteen) have asthma.

Cancer

One in 330 children will develop cancer. Cancer is the primary cause of death in children ages one through adolescence.

Diabetes

123,000 school-age children, or 0.16 percent, have juvenile or Type I diabetes.

HIV

In 1997, an estimated 23 million people worldwide and one million children under 15 worldwide were infected with HIV; nationwide, 2,953 adolescents ages 13 to 19 and 7,902 children under 13 had a reported case of AIDS in 1997 (because HIV often does not become AIDS for 8 to 10 years, these figures are low); more female than male adolescents are currently being infected with HIV.

Prenatal Substance Exposure

The following are estimated in women of childbearing age:

- 3 percent are problem drinkers.
- 10–15 percent from low socioeconomic status use cocaine.
- Fetal alcohol syndrome estimated at 2 of 1,000.
- Drug-exposed babies estimated at 100,000 born per year in the United States.

Epilepsy

About 1 percent of the general population, or 2,500,000 Americans, has epilepsy; 30 percent are under age 18.

been addressed in this chapter. Approximately 3 percent (2,984 out of 100,000 children) have a health impairment (Newacheck, 1991). As you can see, many more students have health impairments than the number served under the category of "other health impaired," most likely because IDEA's definition of other health impaired requires a student's condition to have an adverse educational effect. The statistics in Figure 11–3 suggest that the health impairments affecting many students may not require special educational intervention.

On the other hand, many students may not be receiving the special education services they need. Surveys of eighty school districts revealed that only eight school districts had IEPs for all students with chronic illnesses, and thirteen districts did not have IEPs for any of their students with chronic illnesses (Lynch, Lewis, & Murphy, 1993). Overall, 31 percent of the students with chronic conditions had IEPs, and general educators served 87 percent of the students. Lack of funding was the major reason that most districts gave for not serving these students.

WHAT ARE EVALUATION PROCEDURES?

The evaluation to determine if a student has a particular health impairment generally rests with the physician. The evaluation team will conduct an educational assessment if the student's condition appears to adversely affect educational progress.

Determining the Presence of Other Health Impairments

The first step that physicians use when making a diagnosis is to take a medical history, "perhaps the most important part of the diagnostic procedure" (Clayman, 1989). Any information about symptoms that you have noticed in the classroom should be documented in writing and given to the parents. They will want to share that information with the physician during the medical history.

After a physician makes a diagnosis, school personnel have to decide if the student qualifies for special education services such as those provided under the IDEA's other health impairments category. In most cases, the teacher or parents will have noticed that the student needs classroom modifications because of his or her health impairment. If the student has been hospitalized or is homebound, the school district needs to make arrangements to provide educational services in those settings. For students whose conditions might affect their cognitive skills or behavior, the multidisciplinary team needs to administer individualized intelligence tests, achievement batteries, and behavior rating scales to decide if the student qualifies for special educational services or modifications in the general classroom. Figure 11–4 explains the evaluation process for these students in more detail.

Jacob moved from Minnesota to Texas last summer. The diagnostician at his new school, Linda Dickson, explains what happens when a student with disabilities transfers:

> We requested a copy of his assessment and IEP from his previous district. Because of the medical issues he faced, he was served by homebound when he first moved to Texas, which gave us time to prepare for his arrival. His doctor here supported his need to receive special education services for his severe seizure activity. We served him with a temporary IEP initially. We added two more assessments that he didn't have at his previous school: occupational therapy and assistive technology. We held meetings for the faculty and his fifth-grade class. Jake brought Hunter and spoke. During the IEP meetings, collaboration was essential. The meetings included the parents, an assistive technology representative, the speech therapist, a diagnostician, representatives from general and special education, the school nurse, and his aides.

Nondiscriminatory Evaluation

Observation	
Parent or teacher observe	Student may seem sluggish or have other symptoms that suggest illness. Parent takes student for medical exam.
Physician observes	During routine physical or a physical resulting from symptoms, the physician determines reasons why the student needs further medical assessment. Some health impairments are determined before or shortly after birth.

Medical screening	
Assessment measures	**Findings**
Battery of medical tests prescribed by physician and/or specialists	Results reveal that student has a health impairment. A physician makes the diagnosis.

Prereferral

Prereferral may or may not be indicated, depending on the severity of the health impairment. Some students function well in the general classroom. A decision may be made at this point to serve the student with a 504 plan if accommodations are needed solely to monitor medications and/or to make sure that faculty know what to do if the student has a medical emergency (e.g., hyperglycemia or hypoglycemia if the student is diabetic).

Referral

Students with health impairments that adversely affect their learning or behavior need to be referred for educational assessment.

Protection in evaluation procedures	
Assessment measures	**Findings**
Medical history	Completed conjointly by parents, medical and school personnel, the history yields information needed to develop a health care plan.
Individualized intelligence test	The student's condition or treatment may contribute to a decrease in IQ from previous assessments.
Individualized achievement test	The student's medical condition and/or treatment regimen may affect achievement.
Behavior rating scales	Student may exhibit internalizing or externalizing behavior disorders resulting from the condition or the stress of treatment or environmental factors.
Curriculum-based assessment	The student is not mastering the curriculum in one or more areas as a result of the condition, treatment, and/or resulting absences.
Direct observation	The student may experience fatigue or other symptoms resulting from the condition or treatment, detrimentally affecting classroom progress.

Nondiscriminatory Evaluation Team determines that special education and related services are needed for other health impairments.

Appropriate Education

Determining the Nature and Extent of Special Education and Related Services

The student should receive an IEP if the condition limits his or her strength, vitality, or alertness and adversely affects educational performance. Furthermore, when the student has a medical condition that is likely to worsen or improve in a short period of time, the committee should review the IEP often.

Appropriate education decisions for students with health impairments will often be made through the use of informal evaluation tools such as curriculum-based evaluation, interviewing, and behavioral observations, as well as formal testing results. Once the student is assessed, has been identified as having a health impairment, and receives an IEP, the committee needs to maintain the watch-and-consult attitude we mentioned earlier to decide on the student's educational needs (American Cancer Society, 1988). Thus, when a student has to be absent for an extensive period, curricular modifications may need to be made to help the student catch up. While undergoing treatments, the student's educational performance may also be adversely or beneficially affected.

When you develop an IEP for a student with a health impairment, you will want to stay in close contact with parents, medical professionals, and other support personnel as well as watch the student closely for any academic or behavioral changes to determine educational needs. It will be useful to develop a **health care plan** that is attached to the IEP (Bruder, 1995). This plan will allow coordination and dissemination of essential medical information among the family and medical and school staffs, who complete the form conjointly. The plan, which is written in understandable language, makes sure that everyone is working together to enhance student care. Along with health information, the plan can include information on support services for the family, including respite care.

A **health care plan** coordinates a student's medical information and needs among family and medical and school staff. All participants receive a copy, and one copy is attached to the IEP.

WHAT AND HOW DO PROFESSIONALS TEACH?

The curricular needs for most students with health impairments are similar to those for students without disabilities. Even for the student who has a terminal illness, the teacher wants to provide as normal a school environment as possible when the child is able to attend. However, professionals need to collaborate extensively with parents and other professionals to make sure the medical, social, and emotional as well as educational needs of the student with health impairments are being met.

Effective teaching practices for working with students without disabilities are useful for teaching most students with health impairments who do not have cognitive impairments as a result of their condition. The special curricular and methodological strategies you have learned throughout this book will be helpful when you work with students who have cognitive or behavioral limitations caused by their condition.

Curriculum

When planning a curriculum for students with health impairments, you will want to "set goals that reflect the child's cognitive level or potential, not goals based on physical condition or energy level" (Wadsworth, Knight, & Balser, 1993). Thus, many students will have the same curriculum as their peers. For the student whose absences are frequent, we suggest that you ask yourself three questions:

- What are the most important academic objectives that this student needs to meet this year?

- How can I ensure that the student attains these objectives in the most efficient way possible?

- How can I motivate the student to attain these objectives?

By asking yourself the first question, you might find that a student in your American history class does not need to memorize the dates of Civil War battles. Instead, you determine that it is more important for the student to understand why the Civil War happened, when it took place, who some of the major players were on both sides, the outcome of some of the most significant battles, and how the war ended. Your second step is to decide how to make sure the student masters that information. Can you videotape some of your lectures? Will the student profit from having a peer tutor who is willing to work with the student after school? Can you cut reading or other work requirements that provide supplemental information but do not relate to the most important objectives you have for the student?

When you ask yourself how you can motivate the student, you might consider some of the movies about the Civil War that are available in video rental stores. The student can watch these at home during school absences. Instead of written assignments, you might contract with the student to do an art project that demonstrates knowledge of a particular facet of the Civil War. Allowing the student to research an area of interest can also give him or her a purpose for developing skills. Additionally, if the student's condition is terminal, you can provide opportunities to do written or art projects that will leave a legacy. One junior high English teacher describes how she used journaling with one of her students who had leukemia:

> *I told Bill that I would give him English credit for keeping a journal in a spiral notebook that I brought for him. I would go to visit him in the hospital, and we would talk about what he had written. Some days, Bill wrote stories about riding his motorbike or going hunting with his father. On other days, he wrote about his cancer treatments and hospital experiences. The journal gave him opportunities to escape the hospital through fantasy and to deal honestly with his condition. He was also creating a treasure for his family: a gift of himself.*

In Figure 11–5, Deb Williamson, Jacob's health impairments teacher during first through fourth grades, describes the accommodations her school provided for Jacob to allow him full participation in the general classroom curriculum. Making accommodations does not mean lowering expectations, however. "Expectations are key to what the child perceives he or she can do," Jeanine Salisbury, Jacob's general fourth-grade teacher says. "I don't treat children equally; I treat them fairly and give them what they need. Instead of cutting Jacob's assignments, I told him, 'I want you to do as many as you can.' I find that children often surprise you when you tell them that. This was the first year Jacob worked on grade level."

❤️ Despite their limitations, students with health impairments need their teachers to have great expectations for them.

Methods

In this section, we highlight three important topics related to students with health impairments that you might face in your classroom. We explain strategies for including a service dog and helping students handle insensitive comments. We also believe it is important for future teachers to understand the grief process and how to support peers and the family if a student dies.

Including Service Dogs. "There have been some major steps in integrating people with disabilities in our society; dogs help," Micheal Goehring, whose program trained Hunter for Jacob, says. "We just need to think of the dogs as being adaptive, auxiliary aids that come with four legs, a warm body, and a smile." Mike's organization, Great Plains Assistance Dogs Foundation, which is a member of Assistance Dogs International, is one of many that provide service dogs for people with a variety of disabilities. Mike stresses that "both Great Plains and Assistance Dogs International are legitimate organizations with a legitimate job to do: aiding people with disabilities." "Into Practice" Box 11–3 lists approaches that Mike believes will improve a service dog's inclusion in the classroom.

FIGURE 11–5   *Accommodations for Jacob*

1. *Difficulty with sequencing and completing tasks*   Used task analysis (breaking tasks down into subtasks and teaching the subtasks one at a time).

2. *Following verbal instructions*   Presented oral and written directions one at a time.

3. *Written work limitations*   Greater issue as progressed through grades; modified assignments as needed.

4. *Seizures required that an adult be with him at all times*   Assigned a paraprofessional to work only with Jacob.

5. *Missing class time*   Resulted from inability to attend school at times as well as loss of time in class due to seizures, including time needed to sleep; teacher and/or paraprofessional modified and re-explained tasks from a day-to-day and hour-to-hour basis.

6. *Difficulty with memory, especially short-term memory*   Incorporated visual and mnemonic cues, taught memory strategies, and used repetition.

7. *Organizational difficulties*   Paraprofessional helped him stay organized; provided external tools such as a wire basket with color-coded folders for each class; limited contents of his desk to a pencil box and books; made sure he cleaned out his desk every couple of weeks.

8. *Handwriting limitations*   Difficulty with far-point copying and legibility; completed assignments with a small word processor that he could use at his desk and then plug into a printer (provided a boost to his self-esteem when he taught others how to use the classroom computer); taught him keyboarding skills.

9. *Written language*   Had excellent skills with verbal language and creative expression but problems getting these stories on paper; used a tape recorder to allow him to share the stories and someone else copied them for him; he helped edit them and shared them with the other students.

10. *Behavioral issues*   Difficulty controlling impulses at times; seated him close to the teacher; gave cues to encourage positive behavior; worked on problems with identifying nonverbal body language and not taking everything others said literally.

11. *Difficulty focusing*   Hard to know if caused by an absence seizure or daydreaming; cued him to bring his attention back to the classroom; used timer for completing work assignments (paraprofessional set the timer and verbally reinforced Jacob for working independently for that period of time).

12. *Need for individualized curriculum*   Needed support for math, language arts, and speech and language; worked as a team; health impairments teacher collaborated with learning disabilities teacher and provided direct services to Jacob in the general classroom; health impairments teacher and general educator planned together.

13. *Needs related to seizure activities*   Provided in-service training about epilepsy for all teachers and students; Jacob actively participated; nurse monitored medications and seizure activity.

14. *Need for parental involvement*   Teachers and parents participated together as a team; parents helped select which teacher Jacob would have and were able to help match his needs and style with the teacher's strengths; maintained close communication about academics, behavior, and seizure activity.

You may be wondering how Hunter recognizes when Jacob is going to have a seizure. Mike explains:

> *Dogs have an olfactory system that is far beyond what humans can understand. There are no scientific data, yet, although research is ongoing, the theory is that the chemical electrical change that occurs before and during seizure*

BOX 11–3   INTO PRACTICE

SERVICE DOGS

The following procedures encourage effective integration of service dogs in schools, according to Micheal D. Goehring of Great Plains Assistance Dogs Foundation, an Assistance Dogs International member:

1. School administrators familiarize themselves with the Americans with Disabilities Act and their state laws regarding service dog access. Each state has a law that specifies the right of a student with a disability to be accompanied by a service dog. After reviewing these laws, the school board or governing board establishes a policy that follows these laws. "This is the number one problem we have," Mike says. "People don't know the law."

2. Any staff—whether full-time or part-time—also become familiar with the laws and information about service dogs through training and literature provided by various service dog programs around the country. This information prepares them for what their involvement can or should be.

3. When encountering a situation in which a student has a service dog, administrators and teachers offer their assistance. "In my program," Mike says, "we welcome schools to send a representative to learn about the dog's training. Children are only so reliable

with animals. They leave the training center with a high degree of function with the dog. There can be a tendency to get sloppy with commands as time goes on, and they are not under the watchful eye of their trainer." Therefore, the representative must know what is expected and can determine if deterioration in obedience skills or trained tasks is occurring. The representative can contact the training center if a pattern develops of the student having to repeat commands. "In this case, the educational representative not only takes a role that is tolerant and accepting, but is an integral part of making sure the student–dog partnership continues to be effective—a plus for the student, training center, and, ultimately, the school."

4. The school incorporates the dog into the student's curriculum. "The school is missing great potential for learning otherwise," Mike emphasizes. For example, a speech therapist works on the student's commands for the dog to improve speech formation.

5. The school develops a flyer or pamphlet to pass out to every student who might have contact with the dog as well as their parents. The students should receive the literature before the dog arrives at school. They need to know that they should not have any interaction with the dog unless they are authorized to do so. It can be very distracting if they try to pet the dog.

activity causes a change in the person's body odor that only a dog can sense. We select dogs that are very aware of their surroundings but are not distracted by them. We train them toward identifying seizures and then eventually alerting at the earliest onset, before the person and others become aware. We allow the dogs to pick the behavior they will exhibit. In Hunter's case, the behavior is nudging. He nudges someone he perceives as alpha who could let Jacob know.

Hunter not only benefits Jacob by letting others know when he is going to have a seizure. "The first time we met," Jacob says, "Hunter's tail just wagged. He's my best friend."

"Finding a way to help Jake gain independence has been critical," his father Tom comments. "He understands his disability, and he doesn't feel very safe when he goes out on his own. He's never without an adult. He's going to start going through puberty soon, and he's not going to want to hang around Mom and Dad. That's why Hunter is so important. He can help give Jake that independence. Hunter helps in another way, too. Jake is always around other adults who take care of him. Jake takes care of Hunter. That responsibility has helped his self-esteem a lot."

They need to know, of course, that they are still welcome to approach the child.

6. The school invites the student and parent to share about the disability and the dog in an assembly or in individual classrooms, if they are comfortable doing so. This opportunity can increase the student's self-esteem and self-advocacy skills as well as helping to prepare the other students for the service dog.

7. The school prepares for special challenges. Some students fear dogs. For most of these students, slow and methodical introduction of the dog can help them overcome this fear. "Talk to the child and come up with a concession," Mike suggests. "Ask the child, 'would you be comfortable sitting on this side of the room and the dog on the other side of the room?' Give the student some sense of control." The one thing that should not be done is to try to force the child to come close or pet the dog. If the student has a mental or emotional disability, it will be important to talk to the student's counselor to determine the best way to proceed. "Some of these children actually become animal lovers." Another challenge occurs when a student is allergic to dogs. Consulting with the student's physician is helpful to determine the severity of the allergy and specific recommendations. The use of skin products that are readily available at veterinary clinics and pet stores can reduce allergens. Air purifiers may also help. In some cases, either the student with the phobia or allergy or the student with the service dog may need to move to another classroom.

8. The school plans a toilet area for the dog of about 40 to 50 square feet. "Some people seem to have canine urine phobia," Mike says. "They need to understand that part of the dog's training is toileting—when and where. The dog is leashed or tied to a wheelchair at all times. In many cases, the student can maintain the area; in others, another adult or student will need to scoop. It's not that big of a problem."

9. Personnel feel confident in the dog's behavior and ability. "These dogs are thoroughly tested and screened. They are with us for two years. If we have any indication that a dog might have the slightest aggressive tendency, it does not move on through the program."

10. Each person involved "views the dog as a plus instead of a problem and helps to make the experience a network trying to provide independence for the student. This is a perfect experience to teach other students about disabilities. The administrator or teacher can say, 'This is what this student needs. It doesn't mean he has to be excluded. We can find a way to involve him.'"

"The school's willingness to work with Hunter has been wonderful. Hunter's just like the other kids," Tom says.

His wife Geri laughs, "Actually, he's better," she says.

"The most successful situations occur when the school not only allows us to participate, but participates with us," Mike comments. Jacob is fortunate that both his schools have participated actively. His fourth-grade teacher, Jeanine Salisbury, sums up what everyone seems to think, "Hunter is so cool!"

Handling Insensitivity.   In her web site *Band-Aides and Blackboards* (see Web Sites in the Resource section), Joan Fleitas, an Assistant Professor of Nursing, provides a forum for students with health impairments to share information. She asked some students to share their thoughts about insensitive comments:

"This kid called me the human bowling ball when I came back to school without hair."

"When I can't play basketball because of my heart problem, there's one mean boy in my class who makes fun of me and calls me lazy. I hate it when he does that."

❧ *Hunter helps Jacob function more independently in the general classroom.*

"My brother has cystic fibrosis. I hate it when he coughs and people tell my mom she should take him to the doctor for his cold. They act like she isn't taking good care of him. They even say, 'he shouldn't be out in stores when he is sick like that.' It really bugs me, cause my mom works hard to take care of my brother." (Fleitas, 1997)

Sometimes people can be insensitive when they think they are being sensitive:

"How about when people's kids ask, 'Why's he in that wheelchair?' and the parents say, 'Shh . . . Don't you ever ask questions like that!!!' and drag their kid away like Owen is gonna give them some disease or like the kid is in big trouble or something? I hate that!!! I wish that people would ask more questions, instead of acting like Owen is some sort of freak."

"The thing that I hate the worst, even worse than IVs in the hospital, is when kids whisper behind my back and when they tell me how brave I am. Like I had a choice about all of this!"

"The teacher was probably trying to be nice, but when she saw somebody teasing me, she told the whole class that I had a disease, and that they should be nice to me. I could feel my face get real hot, and I know that I blushed. It was horrible!" (Fleitas, 1997)

❧ Do you remember being teased or teasing others when you were in school? How did you feel? What strategies did you try to handle teasing? How effective were they?

One little girl with a disability was so distraught by the insensitive remarks she experienced that she asked Santa Claus for a day without teasing (National Public Radio, 1994). Helping students with exceptionalities handle teasing is an important, albeit challenging task.

Students need to know the difference between playful and hurtful teasing. For example, a grandfather says to his young granddaughter who brings home straight A's, "They stand for 'Awful,' don't they?" The little girl laughs because she already understands the ritual of affectionate teasing (Meisner, 1996).

Playful teasing reduces tension and helps people enjoy their relationships with others, especially when they can laugh at themselves. Dave Bensen, Jacob's paraprofessional, taught Jacob the value of humor in dealing with a disability, which has become a strength in Jacob's life. Dave has physical disabilities; he was born without extremities below the knees and elbows. Jacob recalls with fondness the time Dave said to him, "Give me five! Well, in this case, give me one!" Certainly, this comment would not have been funny if anyone else had said it, but when Dave said it about himself, he exemplified to Jacob self-acceptance and enjoyment of life. (Dave is in the first photo of this chapter with Jacob and Hunter.) Figure 11–6 lists rules for teasing.

Students list teasing as the number-one type of bullying (peer abuse) (Lister, 1995). There are appropriate times to intervene when students are being teased, but it is usually more effective to help students problem solve options and decide which approach(es)

1. Teasing plays off the truth. If teasing comments are actual truth, it's not teasing. It's insulting.
2. Save your teasing for people you know well so there is some way to predict their responses. Avoid teasing strangers and casual acquaintances. Also avoid teasing people from other cultures who may not understand your own teasing culture.
3. Try not to poke fun at any serious problems that the person may have.
4. Don't tease about things that a person cannot or would not want to change. Don't tease someone about their name or their height. Those are very old jokes.
5. Never tease people about their weight or any speech impediments they may have. This is cruel.
6. The safest thing to tease about is behavior. You can poke fun at a person's hobbies or traits.
7. Remember that the teasee sets the rules. If he or she doesn't like the teasing, stop.
8. Unwanted sexual remarks are not teasing. These remarks are sexual harassment and illegal.
9. People who are obsessive about being in control usually don't like to be teased.
10. Never tease anyone at work about his professional capacities. This is very demeaning and threatening to the livelihood of the individual.
11. Try to think about your objective, what you are trying to do with your teasing. Perhaps what you need is a serious discussion with the teasee.
12. If teasing is the only way you know to express yourself, try to develop a new style. To figure out a new style of relating to others, do a lot of listening to others while trying to understand them and their needs.
13. If you must tease, give nonverbal hints that your verbal sting is meant in a playful fashion. A wink, a smile, or a shoulder poke can soften the blow.
14. Remember, it's fun to kick someone off his high horse, but not if the person is going to break his neck.
15. If you dish it out, people will expect you to take it when your turn comes.
16. If you can't take it, don't dish it out.

FIGURE 11–6 *Basic rules of teasing*

Note: From "Basic Rules of Teasing," in *Teasing: Innocent Fun or Sadistic Malice?* by L. S. Feinberg, 1996, Far Hills, NJ: New Horizon Press. Copyright 1996 by New Horizon Press. Reprinted with permission.

they want to try to handle the situation. You may want to discuss the following possibilities with students:

1. Keeping silent about the abuse is doing exactly what the bully wants. There is a difference between tattling and telling. Telling is reporting that you or someone else is in danger.

2. Ignoring bullying does not make it stop. Tell the bully to leave you alone or answer with a comeback.

3. Take advantage of peer mediation (see Chapter 5) to stop the abuse.

4. Students with friends who stand up for each other are less of a target. Work on developing some close friendships.

5. Consider taking an assertiveness training or self-defense course. Gaining confidence in yourself will help make you less likely to be bullied. (adapted from Lister, 1995)

In *The Meanest Thing to Say*, Bill Cosby (1997) addresses the issue of teasing for children. The protagonist learns to address teasing with one word: "So?" We recommend sharing this book with your students.

Jacob does not have to deal with teasing much anymore. The education provided to the whole school about epilepsy has helped. Sometimes he experiences teasing about the helmet he must wear. "He carries himself so well," his father Tom says. "If somebody does say something, he turns around and confronts them, 'I don't understand what you are saying. Why would you say that about me?' Then he explains about his disability. He has shut a lot of that down. One student in particular bullied him. But once, the bully was the one who picked Jake up off the bathroom floor after he had a seizure. The teacher made a big deal out of it. Jake and the bully became friends after that."

As a teacher, your attitude about the student will influence how peers respond. If you demonstrate that you value students with health impairments, peers are more likely to do the same. Jacob's fourth-grade teacher, Jeanine, emphasizes:

> *The acceptance and respect of everyone in my room is paramount. I ask my students, "How are we going to learn about each other if we don't jump in with both feet?" Once Jacob interviewed me for a local TV station. He asked me, "Mrs. Salisbury, do you think I'm different?" And I said, "Yes, because you never give up. In fact, you are one of my heroes." I know that there were times Jacob felt different, but in my classroom he felt safe. He could be Jacob, and that was cool.*

In a classroom like Jeanine's, all students feel safe. When they feel safe, they are less likely to hurtfully tease others and are more likely to have the confidence needed to cope with insensitive comments.

Grief in the Classroom.   Ryan White died from AIDS in 1990. His death caused people throughout the world to grieve.

The sad reality is that some students with health impairments do not live to adulthood. When a student in your classroom dies, you will need to face your own grief as well as support the family and your students through their grief process.

Your Need to Grieve.   It's a common response when you hear that someone you know is critically ill or has died to ask theological questions, be irritable with those around you, suffer from depression, or deny that the person has died. You may also feel that it is better not to talk about what you or those around you are experiencing. You may find yourself wanting to pull away emotionally from the one who is dying. Dr. David Bearison, a psychologist who works with young cancer patients, describes his experience:

> *When I first began working with children who had cancer, it was always on a Thursday. I thought that I was handling my emotions fairly well until I began to*

realize that friends or family would always find excuses to avoid being with me on Thursday evenings. When I recognized this pattern and asked some of them about it, even those who had not been aware of how I was spending those particular days told me that I appeared different to them on Thursday evenings. I was more impatient, edgy, and irritable, often intolerant of others, and more prone than usual to being provoked. I then realized that it was important to get help in dealing with this behavior, so I began meeting with one of my former therapy supervisors. During our meetings, I began to discern how much I was identifying with these children who had cancer and how much I was experiencing and acting out in an empathic, yet inappropriate, way to their anger, frustration, and need to assign blame. I had to work through these reactions emotionally in therapy supervision; simply being intellectually aware of their source and the symptomatic processes that led to their expression was not adequate. (Bearison, 1991)

Give yourself permission to grieve and feel angry when a student in your class is dying. As David Bearison discovered, it is important to find supportive friends, family members, your religious leader, or a mental health professional to talk to about your feelings. When you are dealing with the potential loss of a child or an adolescent, addressing your issues will give you the strength to help the student who is dying and his or her family and peers address their own issues.

Supporting the Student Who Is Dying. Children and adolescents who are dying often fear that they will be abandoned and forgotten as they approach death. Many times they feel guilty for the pain they are causing their family and friends. The silence from others about what is happening only increases their isolation and guilt. Children are generally perceptive enough to know they are dying, and well-meaning adults who try to protect them from the truth are doing them no favors. Geralyn Gaes shared what happened when she told her son Jason that his friend Jill, whom he had met in the hospital, had died:

Jason's reaction stunned me. "Where did she die?" he asked breathlessly.
"What do you mean, honey?"
"Where? Was she in the hospital, or did she die at home?"
"Well, she died at home."
"Oh, good," he replied, appearing almost relieved.
"Good?"
"Because," Jason explained, "the last time I saw her, she told me, 'I sure hope I can die at home and don't have to go to the hospital.'"
I thought back to that day, a few months before. While Jason had kept his friend company in one of the outpatient chemotherapy rooms, her mother and I stepped out into the hallway.
"Things just aren't working," she confided tearfully.
"Does Jill know?"
"Oh, my God no! We don't know how to tell her or what to say."
But the little girl knew. Of course she knew. (Gaes & Gaes, 1992)

What can you do to provide support? Relieve the student's fears by staying close, being honest, and reassuring the child that he or she is not and will not be forgotten. Box 11-4 describes how one school provided support for a dying child.

Supporting the Family. According to Cassini and Rogers (1990), the entire family is off balance when faced with a terminal illness that confronts them daily with new and painful challenges. The family also knows, no matter how hard they try, that they cannot return to the way life was before the illness.

How can you help? The family members, like the dying student, need to know that you will not abandon them. By staying in close contact, visiting their sick child or

BOX 11-4   **MAKING A DIFFERENCE**

SUPPORTING ELYSE FANDON

It was doubtful that Elyse would ever return to the classroom, but she still considered herself a part of the fourth grade. Pictures of Elyse, sent by the parents, were shared by the teacher with her classmates, so they gradually saw the progression of her illness. Weekly snapshots of her classroom assured Elyse that her friends had not forgotten her.

Mr. and Mrs. Fandon gave permission for the school to contact Elyse's physician for a clinical explanation of the illness. It was suggested that a representative from the Education Department at the Children's Medical Center visit the fourth grade to supply students with an accurate description of Elyse's illness, and field any questions the children might have. (Children of all ages need to be told in so many words that an illness, like nephritis or leukemia or heart disease, is not contagious.)

A bulletin board was set aside in the classroom for Elyse's work, assuring the other students that she was still a contributing member of their class. A math computer was sent home for her use.

The principal made a point of visiting Elyse once a week. The following suggestion was included each Monday in all school announcements: "If anyone has a card, message, or drawing to send Elyse Fardon, please bring it to the office tomorrow morning. I will be visiting her after school."

The teacher realizes that when the time span before the death is handled openly and respectfully, the mourning period following the death takes on the same disposition. When the death does occur, the teacher will be dealing with a deeply saddened group of classmates and faculty, rather than a frenetic, anxious crowd of teachers and fellow students.

Note: From *Death and the Classroom,* by K. K. Cassini and J. L. Rogers, 1990, Cincinnati, OH: Griefwork. Copyright 1990 by Griefwork. Reprinted with permission.

teenager, listening, and continuing to reach out to them after the student has died, you provide invaluable support. You might feel inadequate and not know what to say at such a difficult time. Sharing your feelings of inadequacy with the family is appropriate. Your openness can help them to be more open. You do not need to give advice; in fact, you should not give advice unless you are asked specific questions related to your expertise.

Siblings also need to be remembered. Sometimes their needs take second priority to the care of the sick child. Therefore, they often feel relief and guilt mixed with their intense grief at losing a brother or sister. If you have a sibling in your class, you might find that a simple touch or look can communicate that you care. Here's what one sibling wrote:

> *I was thirteen years old, in the eighth grade, when my brother, Joshua, died. He was the youngest in the family and everyone at school knew him. I don't recall what any of the teachers said when my brother died, but I do remember the actions of one teacher; simple as the action was, it showed she was grieving with me. She reached out as I walked by and touched my shoulder. She didn't try to use words to make it all better. Not until years later did I realize how I had needed that small sign of affection and how much that touch (her gesture) meant when I was so painfully missing Joshua. (Cassini & Rogers, 1990)*

Supporting the Dying Student's Peers. As you read about Elyse in Box 11-4, you learned that keeping classmates honestly informed about the student's condition helps them to cope when a peer dies. Your students know that they can trust what you tell them, and they will feel free to ask questions.

Peers deserve an honest explanation. Cassini and Rogers (1990) recommend that a prepared statement from the principal be read in all classes in the school. This statement should tell students about the circumstances of the death. After reading the statement, it is important to field questions. Your answers need to be honest and not contain euphemisms for *died* such as "passed away" or "went to sleep forever." Such euphemisms

CHILDREN'S LEGACY

In our looks-oriented society, most people style their children's hair and dress them in their finest clothes to be photographed. For some parents, however, photographs of a child who has lost her hair and become emaciated because of illness become especially precious. Denver photographer Katy Tartakoff, founder of Children's Legacy, encourages children to keep a journal and take photographs chronicling their battle with disease. Katy even shaved her head to share the experience many of her young clients face. Katy remarks, "I think that being around death in the capacity that I am is teaching me how to live."

What do you think? Correspondent Jay Schadler asks one child what it means to be brave. As you consider the experiences of a child with a life-threatening illness must undergo, what meaning does the word brave have for you? For parents? For a child's teacher?

Children's Legacy attempts to break the silence between children and their parents about a life-threatening illness. Under these conditions, do you believe there are times when feelings and fears should be kept secret from a child, family members, peers, teachers, and/or medical personnel? Why or why not?

can create confusing images for young children and also suggest that the topic of death is not to be dealt with directly. You should relate facts and not draw conclusions or make judgments. For example, if the student died from HIV, this is not the appropriate time to lecture about sexual practices. Students will also need to be reassured that young people rarely die.

Students' coping behaviors will vary widely and may range from direct confrontation about the student's death to complete avoidance and detachment (Schnieders & Ludy, 1996). Some students may be able to express their grief more effectively through art or drama rather than by talking. The questions and concerns they have may be related to their developmental stage, and examples of those developmental responses are listed in Figure 11–7.

You do not need to fear expressing your own grief in front of the students. Sharing your emotions, including crying, can give your students permission to do the same. Be sure to allow opportunities for students to be together and provide support for each other. One student explained his need to be with his peers when his friend died:

> *We spent that first day as a unit. Some classes were held, but if you couldn't sit still or if you started to cry, it was okay. Nobody made fun of anybody. I remember we asked the adults a lot of questions. We needed all those answers. By the end of the school day, I was still very sad about William, but I wasn't scared anymore.*

Dealing with the death of a young person will be painful and difficult for all involved. However, by breaking the silence and facing death openly, you will help yourself and others to heal as well as to honor the memory of the one who has died.

HOW IS PARTICIPATION ENCOURAGED?

Inclusion

We have emphasized throughout this chapter that students with health impairments need to have age-appropriate experiences with their peers. They should be included in the routine of the general classroom as much as possible. As Fauvre (1988) noted, "a sick child is first and foremost a child"; and for most of these children, the general classroom is the least restrictive environment. Figure 11–8 gives you some information about the educational placement of students with health impairments.

FIGURE 11–7 *Developmental responses to death*

Newborn to Age Three

- Senses that the family routine has been disrupted and that a significant person is missing.
- May show marked behavioral changes in eating or sleeping habits, crankiness, altered nursing habits in infants.
- Cannot comprehend death but can understand sadness.
- Need to have routine maintained as much as possible and be given extra affection and attention.

Ages Three to Six

- Think death is reversible and that the dead person will come back.
- May not seem to be affected by the death because they expect the dead person to return.
- Connect events that should not be connected such as thinking that, because Grandpa died with a headache, Mommy might die when she has a headache.
- Because they are at the stage of magical thinking, they might think that they are responsible for the death.
- Need to be reassured that it is okay to express any emotions they are feeling and that crying and feeling bad or mad are normal.

Ages Six to Nine

- Most understand that death is final, but some may still expect the dead person to come back.
- Need a more detailed explanation of how the person died.
- May fear losing others close to them.
- May think that death "comes and gets you" or that it is contagious; therefore, they may not want to go to the house or funeral home.
- Need an explanation of the feelings they are experiencing and observing.
- May be helped if adults share what they are feeling.
- Often associate death with violence so may ask, "Who killed him?"
- Need to be reassured that they are not in any way responsible for the death.

Ages Nine to Twelve

- More aware of the finality of death.
- Concerned about how the death affects them personally.
- Experience many of the same feelings and concerns as adults, so they are helped when an adult shares their thoughts and feelings.
- May show more anger, guilt, and grief than adults.

Teenagers

- Dangerous to assume that they can handle themselves and their problems.
- Will need help from adults to understand their feelings.

Note: From *How Do We Tell the Children? A Step-by-Step Guide for Helping Children Two to Teen Cope When Someone Dies,* by Dan Schaefer and Christine Lyons. Copyright © 1986, 1988, 1993 Daniel J. Schaefer. Reprinted by permission of Newmarket Press, 18 E. 48th St., New York, NY 10017.

Inclusion Tips

	What You Might See	What You Might Be Tempted to Do	Alternate Responses	Ways to Include Peers in the Process
Behavior	Student may be absent a great deal with major health impairments.	Treat the student as though he is not able to do the work.	Call or visit him during times of absence. Provide extra supports and help to complete needed work.	Set up a support system for when he is absent. Encourage peers to help him at home.
Social Interactions	He may be self-conscious or embarrassed about his illness so that he withdraws from others.	Allow him to work alone, assuming he is merely low on energy or needs to be by himself.	Structure situations that encourage him to share his ideas and thoughts and allow others to recognize his strengths.	Building on his areas of academic strength, have him tutor peers as well as younger students.
Educational Performance	With some illnesses, lack of strength and alertness hinder the student's capacity for full participation.	Call him down for not paying attention or excuse him from completing assignments.	Encourage him and offer extra help. Adjust assignments to create meaningful tasks.	Ask students who are capable or interested in similar areas to locate information and literature to share.
Classroom Attitudes	May appear bored, confused, or overwhelmed with class activities when not feeling well.	Ignore the behavior or make an issue in front of the class.	Give him the benefit of the doubt. Check how he is feeling, then clarify, repeat instructions, or get needed help.	Have peers work with the student to develop a cueing system that encourages him to signal when he is not feeling well.

FIGURE 11–8 *Educational placement of students with other health impairments*

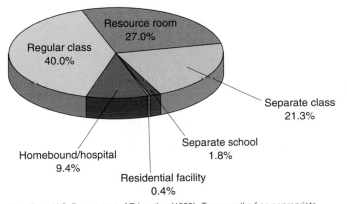

Note: From U.S. Department of Education (1995). *To assure the free appropriate public education of all children with disabilities: Seventeenth annual Report to Congress on the implementation of the Individuals with Disabilities Education Act.* Washington, DC: Author.

In Jacob's current school in Texas, he has a bean bag in each classroom. That way, when he has a seizure and needs to sleep, he can remain with his peers in the classroom.

Inclusion and collaboration are inseparable issues for these students. Because of each student's different medical needs, inclusion in the general classroom necessitates ongoing communication and problem solving among parents, teachers, medical personnel, peers, and the student. When such collaboration exists, even students who are medically fragile or technology-dependent (e.g., requiring a device such as a ventilator) can be successfully integrated into the mainstream (Wadsworth et al., 1993).

Jeanine Salisbury, Jacob's fourth-grade general educator, believes strongly in inclusion. She explains, "With a class of twenty-seven, it's not always easy, but these students can be welcomed and included. I wanted to make sure that Jacob didn't feel singled out or uncomfortable. I remember one time I held Jacob in my arms while he had a seizure and kept on teaching. His seizures usually only lasted for a minute. If one interrupted class for a moment, so what? The students all understood, and when Jacob would come back from the seizure, he would ask, 'Okay, what did I miss?'"

"How my students grew by having Jacob in their classroom!" Jeanine adds. "He was such a positive role model. I miss him terribly. I feel sad for teachers who hesitate to take these children in their classrooms. They are missing so much."

We provide recommendations for including students with health impairments in the accompanying box.

Collaboration

Collaboration with Parents and Professionals.   Parents and professionals need to have "a high level of trust and understanding" to meet the needs of the student with a health impairment successfully (Fauvre, 1988). For example, we have mentioned the importance of service dogs for some students with health impairments. Incorporating a service dog requires extensive collaboration. In the accompanying box (pp. 482–483), we describe collaboration tips for including service dogs at school.

Close communication with the student's physician will be essential to make sure the student receives appropriate services. We want to emphasize, however, that a teacher's primary contact will be with the parents instead of the physician. Nevertheless, hospitals sometimes provide liaisons between teachers and parents to make sure that communication is effective.

If you want to make direct contact with the physician to receive more clarification about a student's condition than the parents can supply, you should do so only after receiving parental consent (Fauvre, 1988). Furthermore, you can encourage good communication by having regular phone or face-to-face conferences with the parents and by providing documentation of any changes in a student's behavior or academic performance in the classroom. This documentation will be especially valuable when the physician wants to know the effects of a particular treatment on a student. It is also important to make sure that you have developed a contingency plan with the parents in the event of emergency (Wadsworth et al., 1993). It can also be helpful to develop a medical management form that the physician can complete. This form asks questions such as "Will medication or treatment be administered at school? What considerations affect this child's ability to participate in the classroom? What aspects of the child's condition might require preparing other children in the classroom? What side effects of medications might affect the child's behavior? When would you like the teacher to contact you?" (Fauvre, 1988).

Collaboration with Peers.   The need for peers to understand their classmate's condition is essential. It is important to encourage questions from peers and not make them feel that either the subject or the student is off limits. (Of course, you should respect the student's preferences about whether to conduct an open discussion with the class.) Peers can also be involved in brainstorming ideas for including the student in the mainstream.

BOX 11-5 **MAKING A DIFFERENCE**

HAMILTON HEIGHTS HIGH WELCOMES RYAN WHITE

"Hi, Ryan, . . . I'm Jill Stewart. I live two doors down from you."

A new neighbor dropping in! It seemed like years and years since that had happened. I'd spent so much time by myself, watching other people talk on TV, I was rusty when it came to conversations with anyone who wasn't family. My mouth almost creaked when I spoke, and I squeaked, as usual.

"Hi," I managed to say.

"I'm president of the student body at Hamilton Heights High," Jill added. That meant she must be one of the most popular kids there. Jill was a senior, but she was only a year older than I was. She explained, "I wanted to invite you to our school. Now you'll know someone when you come your first day."

Jill said that Hamilton Heights had already stepped up their AIDS education program in case I enrolled. "No one is planning on treating you badly," she told me. "We just want to be normal. . . ."

Hamilton Heights had called the State Board of Health . . . and asked them to send some experts on AIDS who could talk to teachers and students about how you can and can't catch it. In the beginning everyone was at least a little bit afraid, deep down inside. So there were lectures, tapes, and films for teachers first, and then for students. And in any class, students and teachers could have spontaneous discussions. Someone might mention that I was coming, and pretty soon everyone would jump in and bring in whatever they weren't sure about. A student might ask something like, "Well, what is AIDS, anyway?" There was no such thing as a stupid question. Nobody ever replied, "I can't believe you don't know! How dumb can you get?" Instead, people who did know passed it on.

After all this, students who were still confused or frightened could ask for a private appointment with Mr. Cook or a guidance counselor to get the straight scoop. If they were too sheepish to sit down and talk face to face, they could still ask questions by stuffing anonymous notes in a special locker. The experts posted the answers on a separate bulletin board. Jill told me that by the second week, many of the unsigned questions read, "How can we help Ryan?"

Once the kids and teachers were in gear, the school took its AIDS education campaign out into the community. They told the press what they were doing and they sent speakers to church meetings. The school board held a meeting that was open to the public, and one of the state's AIDS experts answered parents' questions.

A few parents told the school board, "I don't know whether I want my children in this school now. I may not let them go." But the school's idea of starting with the students worked. Kids told their parents they understood AIDS wasn't contagious, they weren't scared of me, and they wanted to be in school. One family asked their kid to stay home, and the kid said no!

My first day of school finally rolled around, and I rose to the challenge. . . . Wendy and Jill and some other student government officers met me right at the door, and helped me find all of my classes. I'd kept to myself so long, it was like being on another planet. When I walked into classrooms or the cafeteria, several kids called out at once, "Hey, Ryan! Sit with me!" .

As I left after my first day, a reporter asked me, "How do you like this school?"

"Oh, I think I'm going to like it here," I said. He must have noticed I was beaming. I'd been welcomed with open arms. I felt like I had hundreds of friends. It seemed like everyone said to themselves, "What if you were standing in his shoes? How would you feel?"

Note: From *Ryan White: My Own Story* by Ryan White and Ann Marie Cunningham. Copyright © 1991 by Jeanne White and Ann Marie Cunningham. Used with permission of Dial Books for Young Readers, a division of Penguin Books Putnam Inc.

In Box 11-1, you read about Ryan White's frustration in school when his teachers and peers shunned him because of misconceptions about HIV. However, when Ryan transferred to Hamilton Heights High School, he received a warm reception. As you read Box 11-5, consider how preparing peers for Ryan's enrollment helped students feel comfortable enough to include him as one of their own.

Jacob benefitted from sharing about epilepsy with his classes. Sometimes, however, the attention students with disabilities receive can cause more difficulty fitting in with peers. For example, Linda Dickson, Jacob's diagnostician, says, "We had to ask ourselves how to make having a full-time aide as normal as possible. A little boy needs to be a little boy. We didn't want to make it too intrusive."

Collaboration Tips

INCLUDING A SERVICE DOG AT SCHOOL

COLLABORATION GOAL To prepare for the arrival of a service dog and inform all students and school personnel about rules for adapting to the inclusion of a service dog to meet the needs of a student with a disability or health impairment.

Collaborators	Roles and Preparation	Possible Barriers	Solutions to Barriers	Modifications to Implementation	Ongoing Evaluation
Student	Student tells the school as soon as the decision to get a service dog is made; the student participates actively in preparing peers for the dog.	The student may be shy about presenting this information to peers.	Have the student role play what will be said in front of trusted adults and/or a few close friends.	Make sure the student clearly understands what peers need to know. The special educator, the speech teacher, and/or the school counselor may need to work with the student in preparation.	Provide the student with positive feedback on the presentation; ask the student to reflect on the experience and invite him to participate in other opportunities to share.
Parents	Prepare school personnel by formally letting them know of the dog's arrival, sharing information about training and the needs of the student and dog.	May assume the school will welcome the dog and project the needs of the student and dog.	Request special educators send information home to all parents of students with and without disabilities to let them know (a) what service dogs do, (b) places they can contact to find out more about service dogs, and (c) what the school's needs will be if they obtain one for their child.	Encourage someone from a service dog organization to speak at a parent–teacher meeting.	Maintain close contact with parents or guardians to determine if they perceive that the needs of the student and the dog are being met.
The dog's trainer	Keeps in close contact with the student, parents, and school personnel to monitor successful inclusion of dog and provide suggestions as needed.	Thes training facility might be a long distance call from the student's school.	Because of the limited funding of some of these organizations, the school may want to initiate phone calls.	Correspond with the trainer through e-mail or letters.	Decide on a specific time frame for communicating with the trainer, and ask the trainer under what circumstances it would be important to contact the program other than scheduled times.

Collaborators	Roles and Preparation	Possible Barriers	Solutions to Barriers	Modifications to Implementation	Ongoing Evaluation
Administrator	Become familiar with federal and state laws about service dogs; help determine the school's policies.	May fear that the dog will endanger other students.	Have the trainer talk to the administrator directly and address concerns.	Ask the trainer to provide names of other administrators who have successfully included dogs and would be willing to share their successes with your administrator.	Communicate often with administrator to determine any ongoing concerns; encourage administrator for efforts.
General Educator(s)	Review literature on service dogs; help prepare student's peers for the dog's arrival; plan for the dog's basic needs.	May feel uncomfortable about having a dog in the classroom.	All collaborators could answer the general educator's questions openly, honestly, and nonjudgmentally.	Plan for the general educator to visit a training facility; encourage problem solving; if general educator remains adamant, move student to another classroom.	Support personnel collaborate with the general educator often to address any concerns that may arise and to encourage positive responses.
Special Educator(s)	Review literature on service dogs; attend training program as an educational facilitator if possible; address concerns of faculty and student's peers.	May feel unequipped to handle this responsibility.	Admit lack of knowledge; ask questions of the parents, the student, the dog's trainer, and local dog handlers as needed.	Attend local obedience class if cannot attend the training program to learn how commands are used with dogs and to gain a better understanding of handler–dog partnership.	Closely monitor how faculty and peers respond to the student–dog team; watch for any decrease in the dog's willingness to follow the student's commands.
Peers	Recognize responsibility not to pet or distract dog; continue to approach the student.	May find not approaching the dog difficult, especially if students are young.	Prepare the students in advance for the dog's arrival; share books about children with service dogs; acknowledge that it is tempting for them to play with the dog; address questions openly; role play how they will approach the student without distracting the dog.	Have another classroom pet that the students can pet and for which they take responsibility.	Praise peers for approaching the student and not approaching the dog.

BOX 11-6 — MAKING A DIFFERENCE

CAROL OPPERMAN ON HOMEBOUND INSTRUCTION

When I first met Amy, who had leukemia, I agreed to take her case only until my supervisor could find someone who could emotionally handle a terminally ill child. After all, I was a teacher, not a miracle worker. How could I ever bear working with a child who was not going to live?

My initial encounter with Amy was the moment that I fell in love with her. She was one of those rare children who smiles at you as she wraps herself around your heart and never lets go. Every person whom Amy met felt the same way: we all loved her. The doctor, nurses, teachers, friends, and family alike knew that she was very special. I meant to stay only long enough for my supervisor to find someone else to teach this child, but I did not let go for three years.

During the hours I spent with Amy, we primarily studied reading and math; often she would crawl into my lap to read to me and fall asleep trying her best to do a good job. At other times we would discuss her condition as well as her treatment. She would laugh about her hairless scalp and always find humor in the worst of circumstances.

Even after I stopped teaching her, she called me often. She struggled with her condition for eight years. Just after Christmas in 1992, I called to check on her, and for the first time I heard Amy say that she was not able to go any further. She had fought a good fight. Not long after that phone call, Amy died.

I shall never forget how hard I fought to give away Amy's case. Little did I know that this child would change my life; she gave far more than she ever received. The brief encounter that I had with her has been my reward for taking the chance of teaching and knowing her.

Carol Opperman

Although Amy Priestly's life was brief, she made a lasting impression on her homebound teacher Carol Opperman.

"Jacob also sort of had celebrity status when he came," his special education team leader Janice Loncoria adds. "This can make it difficult for a student to fit in. He had to act out some to try to become a kid who belongs. We had to remember that he was a normal child with needs for friendship and privacy."

"We tend to handle children with disabilities with kid gloves when they first come and go through a honeymoon period with them," Linda says. "We need to hurry up and get over it to let them become a normal part of the group. Accept the disability and move beyond it."

Janice agrees, "Jacob tests limits, as all children do. He needs to know clearly where those limits are. He's corrected just like any other child."

Careers

If you are interested in working with individuals with health impairments, you have many career options. Occupational therapy, physical therapy, pediatrics, nutrition, and nursing are a few of the medically oriented careers you might choose. As a mental health professional, you could specialize in the care of individuals with health impairments. Many social workers provide invaluable services to families, either through hospitals or community agencies. Hospice workers and counselors who specialize in grief therapy can provide support and comfort when an individual with health impairments is terminally ill. You will recall from reading in Box 11-5 about Ryan White's high school that school counselors play an important role in making sure that the emotional needs of individuals with health impairments and their peers are being met in an inclusive setting. We mentioned the important role Dave Bensen, a paraprofessional, had in Jacob's life. His example of how to cope with a disability with grace and humor impacted Jacob's ability to cope with epilepsy.

If you decide to be a general educator, you can be committed to welcoming students with health impairments in your classroom. Administrators will play an important role in coordinating collaboration among school personnel, family, and community agencies. As a special educator, you might provide homebound services for students who are too ill to come to school or provide classroom support for those who have learning or behavioral problems as a result of their condition. In Box 11-6, you can read about Carol Opperman's experience as a homebound instructor for students with health impairments.

WHAT ARE PROGRAM OPTIONS?

The personal, social, and medical needs of people with health impairments change as they progress through various life-span stages. Those with chronic conditions such as infection with HIV will probably need more intensive support services as they mature and as the disease progresses. Other people, including many with life-threatening conditions such as childhood leukemia, will be fortunate enough to leave the illness behind them and live full and productive lives. In this section, we discuss how those needs can change, and we share examples of programs that appear to be meeting the needs of people with health impairments at each of the life-span stages.

Early Intervention and Preschool Years

Intervention for infants and toddlers with special health needs begins as soon as their needs are identified—often at birth. During this period, professionals inform parents of the diagnosis in a supportive, timely, and accurate manner; include parents on the health care team as fully as they desire; enlist the assistance of a knowledgeable service coordinator in the development of an individualized family service plan (IFSP); and provide services in community-based settings.

The Smiths' story will give you a glimpse of these practices in action. Angie Smith weighed only four and a half pounds when she was born five weeks prematurely. Dr. Ruth Ray, Angie's neonatologist (a physician who specializes in the care of newborns), discovered that Angie had a serious heart defect. Shortly after Bill and Sarah Smith, Angie's parents, returned to Sarah's room after Angie's birth, the neonatologist came in, sat down, and told them about Angie's prospects for survival. Dr. Ray described Angie's strengths: her strong grasping reflex and her perfect features. Then she described Angie's heart abnormalities and the symptoms that caused doctors to suspect the condition.

Angie had her first heart surgery when she was only ten days old. The surgery was successful, but Angie needed five more surgeries over the next three years before her heart was fully able to meet the needs of her growing body. During this first surgery, the doctors inserted a gastrostomy tube in Angie's abdomen to bypass her immature digestive system so that they could keep her well nourished if she lacked the energy to bottle-feed.

By the time Angie was ten weeks old, she was growing so well that her parents and the other members of her health care team began to plan for her discharge. Ellen took on the role of service coordinator and helped Bill, Sarah, and others on Angie's health care team develop Angie's IFSP. The IFSP included a plan for the neonatal intensive care unit staff to share information about Angie's needs with the pediatrician in Angie's community. The team also developed a plan to help Bill and Sarah find a family day-care home that could care for Angie when Sarah returned to work.

Angie's health care team agreed that a family day-care home, with fewer caregivers and fewer children than a day-care center, would be the setting most likely to give Angie the special care she needed while minimizing her exposure to infectious diseases. Bill and Sarah chose Mrs. Foster from the list they received of family day-care centers that accepted children with health impairments. They especially liked the fact that Mrs. Foster seemed eager to learn exactly how Bill and Sarah wanted her to manage Angie's feedings and medications. The Smiths also appreciated that Mrs. Foster was interested in providing appropriate developmental experiences for little Angie.

Mrs. Foster made several trips to the hospital with Angie's parents to meet Angie and learn about her special needs. She discussed with Bill, Sarah, and Ellen how she planned to include Angie in typical routines of the other children. She hammered a nail into the window frame near the rocking chair to hang Angie's gastrostomy bag so Angie could be held during feedings just like the other infants. In addition, Mrs. Foster suspended a beach ball so it would be just above Angie's feet. That way Angie could make the ball move with a light kick. Mrs. Foster recognized how important cause-and-effect experiences are for all babies. You can imagine Bill and Sarah's joy as they started shifting their thinking from meeting Angie's atypical needs and began, instead, to envisioning Angie as a typical, busy toddler.

Mrs. Foster enjoyed including Angie in her family day-care home. She appreciated being able to continue her professional growth as she gained skills and knowledge about Angie's special health care needs. As a member of Angie's IFSP team, Mrs. Foster contributed valuable suggestions when she interacted with Angie's parents, the neonatal intensive care unit staff, the pediatrician, and an early childhood consultant from the local school district.

Elementary Years

For children with health impairments, the condition that affects their body can make them feel different and alone. During elementary school, children become more concerned about their relationships with peers. As a miniature version of society at large, school gives children an opportunity to see themselves through the eyes of others besides their families. Thus, peers and teachers play an important role in the child's developing self-esteem. Beth Stewart has developed a program to help students with cancer feel better about themselves and their reentry to school.

The good news for sixth-grader Cindy Watson was that her cancer treatments were over and successful. The bad news was that she would have to face the kids in her class. It was bad enough that her face was so puffy that she hardly recognized herself in the mirror. But her wig was even worse. Would the other kids notice it? Would it fall off during gym class? She knew how lucky she was to be going home, and she felt guilty about having these worries.

Enter Beth Stewart, R.N., family coordinator of Duke University Medical Center's pediatric brain tumor family support program. This program recognizes the importance of school for a child with a brain tumor. School is often a safe haven from concerned family members and the intensity and pain associated with the hospital. School also means being normal again and sends a positive message to the child with cancer that he or she can have hope and plan for a future.

To ensure that a child's return to school is as stress-free as possible, Beth is available to visit her patient's school district in North Carolina. So with permission from Cindy and her parents, Beth talked to Cindy's principal and teachers, sent some excellent reading materials to the school, and offered to come to Cindy's classroom to educate her classmates and teachers about Cindy's diagnosis and treatment plan.

Cindy's principal, Mrs. Black, and the teachers were enthusiastic and readily accepted Beth's offer to visit. Mrs. Black scheduled an extra faculty meeting so that all teachers could meet with Beth, and she endorsed their willingness to alter their lesson plans for Beth's visits to their classes. She also requested that the school librarian order some new books for children about cancer.

Cindy and Beth talked openly about common myths and fears and emphasized that brain tumors are not contagious. The session was informal, and several classmates asked questions. They asked how Cindy got the tumor and whether she would die. Beth answered all questions with honesty and reassurance. She also talked about how the other children could support Cindy and help her as she returned to school. She pointed out the importance of friendship and consideration.

Next, Beth, Mrs. Watson, and Cindy visited her seven-year-old brother Sam's second-grade class. They were bombarded with questions; Sam's classmates were as interested in learning about Cindy's tumor as the sixth graders were. Sam answered many of their questions and enjoyed being in the spotlight. After having to stay with his grandparents while Cindy and his parents went to Duke University for her treatments, he welcomed this chance to be the center of attention with his family and peers.

After school, Beth joined the faculty at a teacher meeting. She spent part of the time describing some of Cindy's increased health risks, which resulted from the tumor and the treatments. Beth described the importance of seeking immediate attention if Cindy had an accident and was bleeding. She also addressed the teacher's concerns about Cindy's educational needs and how the cancer treatments had affected her cognitive skills. They discussed the IEP that Cindy's multidisciplinary team had already written after providing her with a nondiscriminatory evaluation.

Beth ended the session by encouraging the teachers to call Cindy's mother or father whenever they had any questions or concerns. Although she realized that sometimes professionals worry that asking parents questions about the child's symptoms may alarm them unnecessarily, she talked about how much Mr. and Mrs. Watson had learned about Cindy's care during her hospitalization. They had definitely become experts!

In this example, the teachers, principal, nurses, doctors, family, and peers shared responsibility for meeting Cindy's educational, emotional, and medical needs. They made talking together and sharing information and concerns a priority. Each knew whom to call when they had questions. The multidisciplinary team members learned to trust each other, respond honestly, and respect each others' expertise.

Middle and Secondary Years

The adolescent years are difficult for most students with or without disabilities. At a time when having a sense of belonging and fitting in with the crowd are paramount, students with a chronic disability can become sensitive about the way their disability makes them different from their peers. Some students, in fact, feel that "the cause of their social problems is their . . . chronic illness, and if the disability were eliminated, their social relationships would be fine" (Kapp-Simon & Simon, 1991).

The Maternal and Child Health Improvement Project (Kapp-Simon & Simon, 1991) developed Meeting the Challenge to improve the social skills of adolescents with health impairments. Schools can offer the program for course credit or to meet IEP objectives. Meeting the Challenge teaches five categories of interpersonal skills: self-awareness, social imitation and conversational skills, assertion or direct communication, empathy or active listening, and conflict resolution and problem solving.

The program helps students identify maladaptive and adaptive reactions to specific situations. For example, students might be given a simulation experience of not being invited to a party that *everyone* is going to. The facilitator asks students to think about what might be common reactions to such an experience. Common maladaptive reactions that students typically identify include "I look terrible" or "if I could just walk normally, I would have been invited." Other possible responses include bodily reactions such as getting a headache or a stomachache. Students can also experience such resentment and anger that they avoid talking to students who are going to the party. Or they might stay home from school on the day of the party.

The students then brainstorm adaptive reactions. They can tell themselves, "I'm not the only one who wasn't invited. Carl and Jamie weren't invited either, and they don't have anything wrong with them" or "maybe I need to be friendlier." Students learn that they can minimize bodily reactions by relaxation techniques. They can also attempt to be friendlier and more outgoing at school.

From Meeting the Challenge, students gain insight about how their thoughts and feelings affect their behavior. By learning coping strategies, students with health impairments develop a sense of control over their life and their condition.

Transitional and Postsecondary Years

The needs of individuals with health impairments during the postsecondary years include finding meaningful employment and leisure activities, knowing their legal rights to full citizenship and how they can advocate to protect those rights, and managing their condition to function as independently as possible.

Accomplishing these tasks can be especially challenging when a young adult is HIV-positive. "One of the hardest parts of living with HIV or AIDS is dealing with the anger and frustration of a disease that makes most of us feel powerless," a group of women with HIV write (HIV University, 1995). They decided to take back that power by starting their own AIDS education school.

HIV University started with a question asked by women with HIV who wanted to live as fully as possible: "How can I channel my sadness, anger, and frustration in a positive direction so that it doesn't destroy me?" The women agreed on the foundational philosophy: The students own it. "It took a while for some people to get used to this idea," the women say. "Each time someone would ask a question (will we study "X"?), whoever was facilitating the meeting would say, 'That's up to you to decide. It's your school'" (HIV University, 1995).

As the women became acquainted, they started viewing themselves more as a family than a class. They had no models for their university, which freed them from concerns about what others would think about how their school should be organized. The school developed programs that (a) provided emotional support; (b) eliminated barriers to participation (e.g., through on-site child care, transportation, and Spanish translation); (c) emphasized group problem solving to help women find solutions to particular challenges they faced; and (d) provided classes on relevant topics, such as anatomy and physiology, gynecology and sexually transmitted diseases, nutrition, treatment programs, monetary issues, self-advocacy, coping with grief and loss, and addiction.

The students elected a Dean of Students and a Dean of Instruction who were both HIV-positive. One of the jobs of the Dean of Students is to check on absent students. "Sick members got cards; depressed members got support." The Dean of Instruction coordinated classes and contacted volunteer experts to teach the classes. The students brainstormed about which professionals should be contacted. They provided a list of guidelines for the instructors, encouraging them to define terms, make classes interactive and relevant, consider diversity and address specific student needs in their content, use visuals, and tell people how to access services.

The first graduation from HIV University took place in April 1995. As each student received a diploma, she shared her experiences. One lady who is HIV-negative shared that she had found support at HIV University that she had never known before. A short time later, "this woman was diagnosed with breast cancer. Though she doesn't have HIV," the women write, "she does have us, and we will be there to support her with cancer, just like she supported us with HIV."

The women summarize what they have learned through their university:

We hear a lot about empowerment *in the AIDS movement, but you can't empower other people. Each of us can, however, offer the people we care about tools to empower themselves, and we can choose to claim responsibility for our own lives. (HIV University, 1995)*

A VISION FOR THE FUTURE

What does the future hold for people with health impairments? Perhaps cures will follow as research uncovers the genetic mysteries of many of these conditions. Already, geneticists have discovered the responsible gene for some conditions and hope that they will eventually be able to alter genetic codes to prevent them. As the role of environmental influences in the development of health impairments is better understood, people will be able to avoid exposure to agents that can cause disease. Perhaps one day, through brain research, Jacob will be seizure free.

Jacob's parents share their philosophy about his future. "Why not let him succeed in what he can do rather than worry about what he can't do?" Tom asks. What do his parents want most for him? "We want him to be happy and healthy. Quality of life is critical. Right now he's falling solidly in the middle of his class. We're taking it one day at a time. Our aim is for him to graduate with a diploma. We're working for Jacob to have a normal education and be mainstreamed as much as possible. Currently, he's doing well. Our expectations are for him to stay the course."

The Empeys know that middle school will present new challenges. "The atmosphere is different," Tom says. One of Jacob's teachers comments that she is concerned about him having a seizure as he moves through the hallway between classes. The middle school will need to work closely with the Empeys to make sure that Jacob's academic, social, emotional, and physical needs continue to be met.

Jacob's teachers are already recognizing vocational possibilities for Jacob. According to Deb Williamson, his former health impairments teacher, "Jacob has an innate ability to use AV equipment. He loves camcorders and running the projector or videotape equipment at school. He enjoyed conducting interviews here at school about his epilepsy for a local TV station. His ability is a source of pride for him and his family. His father has mentioned that he and Jacob might start a photojournalism business someday."

Jacob has his own dream right now. "I want to be an actor because I'm funny," he says. Others agree that he has a remarkable gift for making people laugh.

Jacob has many choices. No matter what path he chooses, his father Tom believes he will compete successfully with his peers: "I don't think he is going to accept less than what everybody else is going to do. Jacob is bright, cheerful, and has a good outlook on life. As long as he is nurtured and treated respectfully, he'll do fine." With Jacob's attitude, he has all he needs to make surprising and wonderful things happen.

What Would You Recommend . . .

1. To encourage Jacob's success in middle school?

2. To help Jacob use his talent for humor in productive ways at school?

3. To develop Jacob's ability to work with technology?

Part of our vision for the future is that, by the time we start writing the next edition of this textbook, a vaccine and a cure for HIV will be found.

SUMMARY

WHAT ARE OTHER HEALTH IMPAIRMENTS?

• The conditions in this category vary widely in symptoms and prognosis.

• Students with health impairments have limitations in strength, vitality, or alertness. The condition can be chronic or acute.

• To be served in the IDEA category of other health impaired, an individual's educational needs must be affected by the condition. The characteristics vary widely and are condition-specific, but their unifying criteria are strength, vitality, and alertness.

• Health impairments include, among many others, infection with HIV, prenatal substance exposure, cancer, asthma, juvenile diabetes, and epilepsy.

WHAT ARE EVALUATION PROCEDURES?

• Although a physician usually makes a diagnosis, school personnel have to decide if the student can be served under the IDEA as other health impaired. Teachers should have a watch-and-consult attitude with regard to monitoring the IEP.

WHAT AND HOW DO PROFESSIONALS TEACH?

• The curricular needs for most students with health impairments are similar to those for students without disabilities. The teacher, however, should be willing to make accommodations as necessary.

HOW IS PARTICIPATION ENCOURAGED?

• The general classroom is the least restrictive environment for most students with health impairments.

• Close collaboration with medical personnel is essential when a student has a health impairment. Use of a medical management form is advised.

WHAT ARE PROGRAM OPTIONS?

• The needs of an individual with health impairments vary depending on the condition and the student's age. Professionals have developed successful programs and treatment models from birth through adulthood for these individuals.

• Health impairments can be caused by infections, genetic factors, and environmental factors, including prenatal teratogens and postnatal influences.

• Schools served 1.9 percent of students as IDEA-eligible in the category of other health impaired in 1995, but approximately 3 percent of all students have some type of health impairment that does not qualify them for IDEA special education. Most IDEA-eligible students are served in the general classroom.

• When a student is dying, teachers should give themselves and other students permission to grieve and should provide honesty and support to the student, family, and peers.

• Many career options are available for working with students who have health impairments, including homebound teaching.

RESOURCES

BOOKS

Alex: The Life of a Child. (1984). By Frank Deford. New York: Signet. Deford shares his daughter's courageous battle with cystic fibrosis.

Death and the Classroom. (1990). By Kathleen Cassini and Jacqueline Rogers. Griefwork of Cincinnati, Inc., 1445 Colonial Drive, Suite B, Cincinnati, OH 45238. (513) 922-1202. Suggestions teachers and counselors can use to help students cope with death.

How It Feels to Fight for Your Life. (1989). By Jill Krementz. Boston: Little, Brown. Children and teenagers with a variety of health impairments share their stories.

I Want to Grow Hair, I Want to Grow Up, I Want to Go to Boise. By Erma Bombeck. (1989). New York: Harper & Row. Heartwarming stories of children surviving cancer.

I Will Sing Life: Voices from the Hole in the Wall Gang Camp. (1992). By Larry Berger, Dahlia Lithwick, and Seven Campers. Boston: Little, Brown. Children and adolescents with serious illnesses share their celebration of life.

On Children and Death. (1983). By Elisabeth Kubler-Ross. New York: Macmillan. Sensitive and compassionate look at death.

Special Children, Special Care. (1993). Edited by Karen Moffitt, John Nackahsi, and John Reiss. USF Bookstores, 4202 East Fowler Avenue, Tampa, FL 33620-6550. (813) 974-2631. A comprehensive, practical guide for collaboration among professionals and families caring for children who have medically complex health impairments.

JOURNALS, MAGAZINES, AND CATALOGS

Death and Grief Bibliography. Good Morning, Juanita Johnson, 12 Locust Street, Norwich, NY 13815. (607) 336-8457. Extensive book list for children, teens, parents, and professionals.

Straight Talk: A Magazine for Teens. The Learning Partnership. P.O. Box 199, Pleasantville, NY 10570. (914) 769-0055. Motivational activities and articles help students with disabilities build self-esteem, resist peer pressure, and avoid sexually transmitted diseases.

MULTIMEDIA

Fetal Alcohol Syndrome and Other Drug Use During Pregnancy. Films for the Humanities and Sciences. P.O. Box 2053. Princeton, NJ 08543-2053. (800) 257-5126. Profiles a young boy with fetal alcohol syndrome.

HANC (Home Assisted Nurturing Care). HealthTech Service Corporation. A computer with a male human voice dispenses medications and monitors bodily functions.

Mayo Clinic Family Health Book CD-ROM. IVI Publishing, 1380 Corporate Center Curve, Suite 305, Eagan, MN 55121. (800) 937-6463. Comprehensive information about health and illness.

Play It Straight. Curriculum Associates, 5 Esquire Rd., North Billerica, MA 01862-2589. (800) 225-0248. Board game helps intermediate and secondary students resist peer pressure to use alcohol and drugs.

Tutorial for Health Care Providers to Control Blood-Borne Disease Infections. Learner Managed Designs, 2201-K West Twenty-fifth Street, Lawrence, KS 66047. (913) 842-9088. Software teaches professionals about HIV and hepatitis, including precautions that prevent their spread.

The following videos are available at local rental or retail stores:

Awakenings. (1990, PG-13, U.S., color, 121 minutes). Neurologist Dr. Malcolm Sayer temporarily awakens people who have developed catatonia as a result of an encephalitis epidemic.

Common Threads: Stories From the Quilt. (1989, not rated, U.S., color, 75 minutes). Documents five diverse individuals, including a child with AIDS.

Echoes of a Summer. (1976, PG, U.S., color, 99 minutes). A twelve-year-old girl confronts death with courage.

The Elephant Man. (1980, PG, U.S., B&W, 125 minutes). John Merrick copes with a condition that disfigures him while struggling with prejudice during the Victorian era.

Go Toward the Light. Cabin Fever Entertainment. An emotional story of a family with a child who has AIDs and how they learn to live, love, and let go.

Lorenzo's Oil. (1992, PG-13, U.S., color, 135 minutes). Parents of a son with a rare fatal nerve disease seek to discover a cure.

Mask. (1985, PG-13, U.S., color, 120 minutes). Teenager Rocky Dennis shows humor and courage as he copes with craniodiaphyseal dysplasia, which causes calcium deposits to form on his skull and leaves him disfigured.

Philadelphia. (1994, PG-13, U.S., Color 125 minutes). A man who is HIV-positive fights to regain his job under the Americans with Disabilities Act.

Promises in the Dark. (1979, PG, U.S., color, 115 minutes). A young girl dying of cancer finds support from a caring doctor.

Six Weeks. (1982, PG, U.S., color, 107 minutes). A girl dying from leukemia wants to dance in the *Nutcracker* ballet.

Steel Magnolias. (1989, PG, U.S., color, 118 minutes). A young woman with juvenile diabetes copes with humor and courage and the support of family and friends.

The Teacher and the Miracle. (1961, not rated, B&W, 88 minutes). A man copes after the loss of his son.

ON-LINE INFORMATION AND USEFUL DATABASES

Band-Aides and Blackboards: When Chronic Illness or Some Other Medical Problem Goes to School. Internet address: http://funrsc.fairfield.edu/~jfleitas/kidsintro.html. Entertaining site navigates children through dealing with teasing and going through medical procedures. Children share their stories. Suggestions are provided for peers and teachers as well.

Bearable Times. Internet address: http://www.tiac.net/users/bearkids/. Maintained by a young teenager, this site lists links and contributions by students with health impairments.

Cancer Kids. Internet address: http://www.cancerkids.org/ Stories of children with cancer. Of special interest is the journal kept by one father in Ashley's Story, illustrating the ongoing impact of cancer on the family.

Convomania. Internet address: http://www.mania.apple.com. Apple Computers, Inc., provides an opportunity for children with health impairments to interact with others around the world.

Countdown for Kids. Internet address: http://www.jdfcure.com/cdk_001.htm. The Juvenile Diabetes Foundation provides a web site for children with diabetes.

Twelve Common Myths and Misconceptions About Epilepsy. Internet address: http://www.efa.org/what/education/myths.html. Epilepsy Foundation of America clears up misconceptions about epilepsy. They also provide "A Child's Guide to Seizure Disorders."

EpiNet. Internet address: http://www.epinet.org.au/. Provides suggestions for talking to children about epilepsy, as well as other helpful resources.

ORGANIZATIONS

See *Exceptional Parent, 24*(1) (January 1994) for a complete listing of national organizations, associations, products, and services for individuals with specific health impairments. Several of the following organizations also publish newsletters. Many of these organizations have web sites.

Asthma and Allergy Foundation of America. 1125 Fifteenth Street NW, Suite 502, Washington, DC 20005. (800) 727-8462.

Candlelighters Childhood Cancer Foundation. American Cancer Society, 1599 Clifton Road NE, Atlanta, GA 30329-4251. (800) 366-2223.

Center for Children With Chronic Illness and Disability. Box 721-UMHC, Harvard St. at East River Rd., Minneapolis, MN 55455.

Centers for Disease Control. 1600 Clifton Rd. NE, Atlanta, GA 30333. Information about specific diseases.

Children's Hospice International. 901 North Washington Street, Alexandria, VA 22314. (800) 2-4-CHILD.

Epilepsy Foundation of America. 4351 Garden City Drive, Landover, MD 20785. (800) EFA-1000. http://www.efa.org/

Foundation for Children with AIDS. 55 Dimock, Roxbury, MA. (617) 442-7442.

Juvenile Diabetes Foundation International. 432 Park Avenue South, Sixteenth Floor, New York, NY 10016. (800) 533-2873.

National AIDS Hotline. (800) 342-AIDS. Operates twenty-four hours a day.

National AIDS Information Clearinghouse. P.O. Box 6003, Rockville, MD 20850. (800) 458-5231.

National Easter Seal Society. 70 East Lake Street, Chicago, IL 60601. (800) 221-6827.

National Organization on Fetal Alcohol Syndrome. 1815 H Street NW, Suite 710, Washington, DC 20006. (800) 666-6327.

National Pediatric HIV Resource Center. Children's Hospital of New Jersey, 15 South Ninth Street, Newark, NJ 07107. (201) 268-8251.

National STD Hotline. (800) 227-8922. Operates from 8 A.M. to 11 P.M. Monday through Friday, eastern standard time.

CHAPTER 12

PHYSICAL DISABILITIES

Educating
Rommel Nanasca

When Rommel Nanasca leaves home for school each morning, he has already benefitted from extraordinary care. His mother, Lorna, and his father, Romy, have lifted him from his bed and bathed him; he lacks the strength to do that for himself. Using a machine, one of them has administered intermittent positive-pressure breathing because Rommel seems congested. The machine applies positive pressure to Rommel's chest, causing his lungs to exhale; he then inhales without help. As one parent administers this treatment, the other checks out the respirator from which he may have to receive oxygen.

They have begun his day-long feeding process, using a J-tube (jejunum tube) fed into his intestines to drip nutrition into his system. Before they did this, however, they made sure that the pump that pushes the liquid nutrition through the tube and into their son was working. They also have slipped a T-shirt onto Rommel and then strapped him into an armless vest of flexible plastic that supports Rommel's weakened upper body. The vest holds him erect and prevents further curvature of his spine (he has 90 percent

scoliosis). Finally, they have lifted him from his bed and into a wheelchair whose back and seat have been specially shaped to fit exactly and comfortably with his jacketed torso. It is rather extraordinary that Rommel, unlike so many other students who have the same kind of disability as his, does not have any communication problems. He speaks clearly and independently. It undoubtedly helps that Lorna is a nurse, that Romy is strong, and that Rommel is up for whatever comes his way . . . and a plethora of challenges have already been his lot in his short thirteen years of life.

Rommel (pronounced roh-MELL, as he quickly points out to everyone he meets) has spinal muscular atrophy. The intermittent positive-pressure breathing machine helps his weakened chest muscles perform normal breathing functions. Respiratory distress is the primary complication of persons with that kind of atrophy. Despite precautions and the good climate in the San Diego, California, area, Rommel has been hospitalized for pneumonia at least twice a year since he was a year old.

When pneumonia struck Rommel in December of 1996, he had just survived a life-threatening episode at Twin Peaks Middle School, Poway, California. His breathing had become so labored that he was "coded," given immediate cardiopulmonary resuscitation, and rushed by ambulance to a local hospital.

The coding, emergency hospitalization, subsequent hospitalization for pneumonia a few weeks later, and Rommel's dramatic loss of 10 pounds (to a weight of 44 pounds, 9 ounces) led his physicians, his parents, and Rommel himself to agree to the surgery to implant a tube so he can get his nutrition. Feeding himself and chewing regular food was too tiring for Rommel. Those events also led them and his school team to develop a regimen to maintain his health and prevent crises while enabling him to still be included in regular academic courses.

Lorna and Romy face the challenges presented by spinal muscular atrophy in not just Rommel but also his younger brother, Ariel, who has the same condition but not to such an extensive degree. And they have to help Rom-

mel's sister, sixteen-year-old Melanie, lead her very typical life. But they also have help from Lorna's three sisters and one brother, who live nearby, and from her mother and father, who live with them.

Ask them how they live in the face of these disabilities and with so many responsibilities but without much help, Lorna and Romy reply, "Day by day,

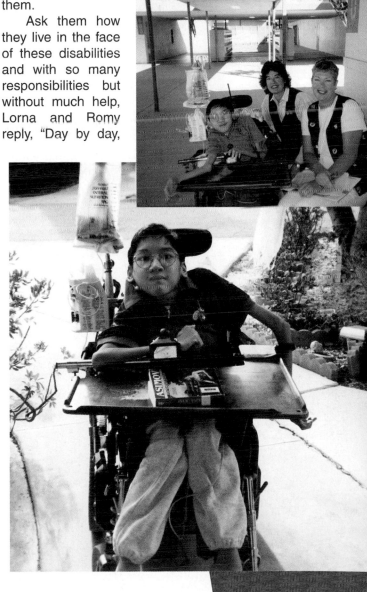

we do our best." Asked about the family, Rommel's occupational therapist agrees: "The Nanascas are unique. Theirs is a joyful home. They are upbeat despite their concerns. They go on with their lives. They make the best of everything."

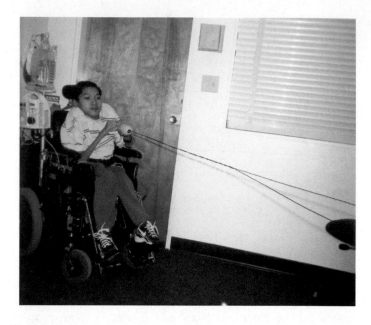

What Do You Think?

1. How would you ensure collaboration among all of the many people on Rommel's team?

2. How would you help Rommel and students like him continue to receive academic work in the general curriculum with help from peers there?

3. How would you provide an appropriate education to Rommel and other students with physical disabilities if he has to stay home or is in the hospital?

4. How would you ensure that Rommel has access to his school using his wheelchair and its apparatus?

WHAT ARE PHYSICAL DISABILITIES?

Defining Physical Disabilities

The Individuals with Disabilities Education Act (IDEA) refers to physical disabilities as orthopedic impairments:

> *"Orthopedic impairment" means a severe orthopedic impairment that adversely affects a child's educational performance. The term includes impairments caused by congenital anomaly (e.g., clubfoot, absence of some member, etc.), impairments caused by disease (e.g., poliomyelitis, bone tuberculosis, etc.), and impairments from other causes (e.g., cerebral palsy, amputations, and fractures or burns that cause contractures). (C.F.R. Sec. 300.7 (b)(7))*

Although IDEA uses the term *orthopedic impairments*, educators typically use the term *physical disabilities* when referring to these same students. For example, within the Council for Exceptional Children, there is a Division of Physical and Health Disabilities. So there are two terms in use: the IDEA term and the practitioner's term. But special educators and special education agencies also refer to students with severe and multiple disabilities (see Chapter 9), other health impairments (see Chapter 11), or traumatic brain injury (see Chapter 13) as having physical disabilities. So there is also a lumping-together usage—the tendency of some educators or agencies to use the term *physical disabilities*

〜 Many individuals with physical disabilities can participate in a full range of typical experiences, including independent living.

〜 *Wilderness Inquiry was formed to allow people of all abilities to share the adventure of wilderness travel. Adventures are open to people of all ages and abilities, including people with sensory, cognitive, or mobility impairments. Photo courtesy of Wilderness Inquiry, 1313 Fifth Street, S.E., Box 84, Minneapolis, MN 55414, (612) 379-3858.*

to refer to a very broad group of students. It is impossible for one chapter to cover all types of physical disabilities. We focus on three of the most usual: cerebral palsy, spina bifida, and spinal muscular atrophy (a form of muscular dystrophy).

Describing the Characteristics

Cerebral Palsy. When Camille Durfee was still in high school, she gave a presentation at a special education conference. Using a custom-made communication device, Camille titled her presentation, "Consumers Speak Out: Everything I Always Wanted to Tell a Professional but *They* Were Afraid to Ask." Here is how she described herself:

> *Hi, my name is Camille Durfee. . . . I am using a Liberator® to communicate. . . . Give disabled people time to talk to you. I would like to be treated like a normal person. Look at me when you talk to me. Don't treat me like a baby. I like to listen to music and watch television. I also enjoy going to games and meeting new people. The hardest thing about being disabled is when my equipment breaks at the same time. I don't care if someone comes up and says, "Why are you in a wheelchair?" I have cerebral palsy.*

What Is Cerebral Palsy? *Cerebral* refers to brain injury. This injury does not damage the child's muscles or the nerves connecting them to the spinal cord, but it does affect the brain's ability to control the muscles. *Palsy* describes the resulting lack of muscle control that affects a person's ability to move and to maintain balance and posture. Thus, cerebral palsy is "a disorder of voluntary movement or posture" (Heller, Alberto, Forney, & Schwartzman, 1996, p. 92).

Two characteristics distinguish cerebral palsy: the brain damage is nonprogressive and nonhereditary, and it occurs before the brain fully matures (which happens at about age sixteen) (Overeynder, Turk, Dalton, & Janicki, 1992). Therefore, neither Rommel, who has spinal muscular atrophy (a progressive, inherited disease), nor a twenty-year-old who received a brain injury in an automobile accident can be diagnosed as having cerebral palsy (Pellegrino, 1997; Alexander & Bauer, 1988).

One of the most common ways to characterize cerebral palsy is by movement. The terms *spastic, athetoid, ataxic,* and *mixed* all reflect various movement patterns. Spastic cerebral palsy is the most prevalent pattern (about half of the half-million people with cerebral palsy in the United States have this form), while the other types account evenly for the other individuals with cerebral palsy (Pellegrino, 1997). A second way to characterize cerebral palsy's different forms is to indicate the different areas of the brain affected (see Figure 12–1). The central nervous system consists of three motor systems:

1. The pyramidal system comprises a motor strip and pathways and exerts control over voluntary motor movement.

2. The extrapyramidal system comprises the basal ganglia and functions to connect the pathways running to and from the motor strip paths of the pyramidal system. When impulses must take different circuits through the basal ganglia, involuntary movements are produced in an atypical way.

3. The cerebellum, when functioning properly, enhances balance and muscle tone. Brain damage in this area results in problems associated with equilibrium (Heller et al., 1996).

These clinical descriptions are, of course, necessary and valid, but they do not capture the essence of a person, explaining the person's journey through life, her inner self, and her future, nearly as well as a family member can. In Box 12–1, Will Morse, Camille's grandfather, describes her more powerfully but just as accurately as any evaluation might.

Spastic, or hypertonic, form. Spastic cerebral palsy involves tightness, or **hypertonia,** in one or more of the muscle groups, which causes limited movement. The muscles of a

---

Margin notes:

❤ Although Camille has physical challenges, she has many strengths, too, namely, her wit, self-determination, and intelligence.

Hypertonia means tightness in a muscle or muscle group.

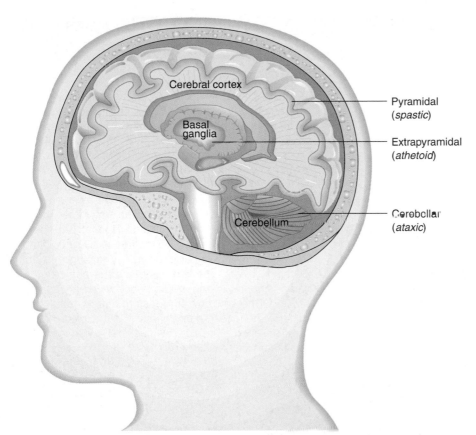

Note: From E. E. Bleck and D. A. Nagel. *Physically Handicapped Children.* 1982, Boston. Allyn & Bacon. Copyright © 1982 by Allyn & Bacon. Reprinted with permission.

FIGURE 12–1 *Area of brain affected by cerebral palsy*

person with spastic cerebral palsy are often like a pocketknife. When a limb is first moved, it becomes initially rigid and resists. However, this rigidity and resistance give way quickly, almost suddenly, just like the blade of a pocketknife when it is closed.

When Camille is transferred from her bed into her wheelchair, her body straightens out and becomes extremely rigid, making placement in her wheelchair difficult. She is like a stiff new pocketknife. Her parents have found that placing Camille on the seat of the wheelchair and then tipping the chair backward allows her body to bend gradually into a sitting position. She becomes more like an old, well-oiled pocket knife.

Athetoid, or low-tone, form. Athetoid cerebral palsy means that a person has abrupt, involuntary movements of the head, neck, face, and extremities, particularly the upper ones. In addition, changes in muscle tone vary from one period of time to another. Whereas those with the spastic form have trouble initiating movement, students with athetoid cerebral palsy experience difficulty controlling movement and maintaining posture.

Ataxic form. Students with ataxic cerebral palsy experience unsteadiness, lack of coordination and balance, and varying degrees of difficulty with standing and walking. Ataxia often accompanies the spastic (high tone) and athetoid (low tone) forms of cerebral palsy.

Mixed form. Mixed cerebral palsy (which Camille has) combines spastic (high) muscle tone and the involuntary movements of athetoid (low-tone) cerebral palsy. Mixed cerebral palsy occurs when there is injury to more than one area of the brain. Students with the mixed form usually have **quadriplegia** (Bleck & Nagel, 1982).

In addition to characterizing cerebral palsy by the nature of movement, professionals frequently classify it by referring to the part of the body that is affected. This is referred to

Camille's neck and head are affected by spastic, or hypertonic, cerebral palsy, making it sometimes difficult for her to hold up her head. At other times, she has difficulty controlling her head movements.

Quadriplegia refers to a weakness or paralysis of all four extremities—both arms and both legs.

BOX 12-1   MY VOICE

WILL MORSE TALKS ABOUT HIS GRANDDAUGHTER CAMILLE

I have six grandchildren. Like all grandchildren, mine are perfect. The five older ones are scattered on three continents, each doing his or her own thing and happy doing it. Camille is the youngest. She is my favorite.

After a suitable trial period, my daughter and her husband became the adoptive parents of Camille when she was three years old. My son-in-law, Michael Durfee, M.D., had seen her at a public institution in a ward for children with massive retardation. She was there because, like the other inmates, she required around-the-clock care and there was no other place for her, even though she was not mentally retarded. She had massive physical disabilities caused by birth injuries to the head: cerebral palsy.

Camille could not effectively move on command any part of her body except her eyes and her smile. Both eyes and smile were beautiful. I suspect they were the reason Dr. Durfee was certain that the many tests performed by experts in their fields were right in advising that she possessed a reasonably good mind, although experientially deprived by her isolation during her first three years—something that probably could largely be overcome in time. She had 20/20 eyesight and sharp hearing but poor tactile feedback. She had difficulty swallowing due to lack of full control over her tongue and throat. Food had to be pushed to the back of her mouth, and liquids poured down her throat. Worst of all, she could not vocalize. In effect, she was mute and too paralyzed to sign.

The entire family, including the two Durfee children, set about making the most of Camille's limited physical faculties to enhance her knowledge of a world previously sealed away from her. She had never been in a family situation or exposed to children other than those in her ward. She received new clothes, a pair of Mary Jane shoes, a lot of loving attention, and much talking to. She learned to communicate, answering yes–no questions by movements of her eyes or the flash of a smile. She was forced to use her limited tongue control and accept food at her lips rather than back in her mouth. She learned to allow fluids to flow down her throat without choking. By seeing and actually touching objects, she was introduced to numerous adjectives: *smooth/rough, heavy/light, wet/dry, coarse/fine, hot/cold.* She saw, felt, and tasted various fruits and vegetables. She rode in a buggy and a car, explored the malls, and developed a passion for music. She was introduced to animals by pictures or in the flesh. She learned that everybody and everything had a name that should be remembered. "Catch up" was the game. Catch up for three largely lost crucial years. Her cognitive skills and memory proved outstanding. She heard and saw all about her and was alert in reacting.

My part in Camille's early education was to design and produce devices so we could test her limited physical control in an effort to find muscles that could be harnessed to allow her to operate a mechanical or electronic communication tool. There were series of switches and toys and also electronic boards covered with icons that could be lighted up to make a need known. But she could not use

---

A **topographical classification system** ascribes a disability to the part of the brain that is affected.

as a **topographical classification system.** The specific body location of the movement impairment is correlated with the location of the brain damage. Figure 12–2 describes the topographical classification system evaluation teams often use.

What Causes Cerebral Palsy?   Cerebral palsy is caused by **prenatal** (e.g., infection, brain malformation), **perinatal** (e.g., lack of oxygen, infection), or **postnatal** (e.g., brain injury, meningitis) factors.

The severity of a person's cerebral palsy generally depends on the type and timing of the injury. For example, in very premature babies, bleeding in the brain can cause extensive damage. Camille, however, experienced a normal birth and seemed physically sound. Only after she reached the age of one and had not developed normally did a brain scan show damage caused by a cyst. Although the brain damage left her without the capacity to speak or move anything but her head, little damage was done to the part of her brain that affects her intelligence.

Prenatal means before birth; **perinatal** means at birth; and **postnatal** means after birth. They refer to the time when a disability or impairment occurs.

What Other Conditions Are Associated with Cerebral Palsy?   There is much uncertainty regarding the type and extent of the conditions that accompany cerebral palsy (Parette, Hourcade, & Brimer, 1996). Because cerebral palsy results from brain damage, there is a significant relationship between cerebral palsy and mental retardation. Almost 3 percent of all children born in the United States have mental retardation, but 50 to 70 per-

her limbs, head, or body; she could not blow out or suck in; nor could she use a bite switch or one operated by her tongue. Ultimately, we had to fall back on learning to detect which icon she was looking at on her board or by a twenty-question procedure in which she turned her eyes or flashed a smile when questions revealed what she intended to say.

Then a few years ago, there came onto the market a rather crude electronic device called the Light Talker. What a wonder! It consisted of a keyboard displaying rows of tiny receptors that reacted to a beam of light from a small electronic device attached to Camille's head. Each receptor activated a computer to print out a word, letter, or figure on a monitor. A later generation of the Light Talker—the one now used by Camille—contains a better monitor, a printer, a calculator, a data bank, and a synthetic voice. (She can "speak" in any one of five female voice options.)

Camille is presently in a Wake County, North Carolina, public high school that provides specially trained teachers and attendants for students with disabilities. She has all the body chemistry, desires, and reactions of other teenagers; enjoys football and basketball; and follows the careers of her teen heroes. In short, she is a person in her own right. Until recently, before she got the Light Talker with a calculator, she did her math entirely in her head. However, she still has difficulty reading: she cannot turn pages or use phonetics because she has no voice of her own.

An operation to place two stainless steel rods along her spine improved Camille's posture and has helped her hold her head up, thereby permitting better head motions. As a consequence, she has recently obtained an electric wheelchair. She is learning to operate it by means of four switches, some of which serve dual functions. The switches are activated by slight head movements that Camille has developed after years of operating the Light Talker. She is looking forward to living someday with an attendant in her own apartment. She is a determined person and may well do so.

What is Camille's future? Who knows? With the loving support she has received thus far, and no doubt will continue to receive in the future, there is no reason to believe that she will not live a happy adult life. Her patience and resilience in the face of frustrations and her ability to accept her disability will assure it. A year or so ago, I asked her what she saw herself doing as an adult. Her answer was "I like to think that one disabled person can help other disabled persons." I do too. Just how is not a pressing problem at this time. She has been active in workshops and expositions of hardware available for people with disabilities, where she has demonstrated her Light Talker. Her picture has appeared in various publications pertaining to special education in the public schools. She has recently agreed to try her hand at writing a series of vignettes on subjects she is interested in. If and when her production reaches proper quality, it may be published in book form, with royalties going for her support. Maybe it won't work out, but then again, who knows? Every person with a disability needs and has a right to seek a future.

Will Morse

A. *Monoplegia:* one limb

B. *Paraplegia:* legs only

C. *Hemiplegia:* one-half of body

D. *Triplegia:* three limbs (usually two legs and one arm)

E. *Quadriplegia:* all four limbs

F. *Diplegia:* more affected in the legs than the arms

G. *Double Hemiplegia:* arms more involved than the legs

FIGURE 12–2 *Topographical classification system*

 Camille uses a Liberator® to help her communicate. Using a light sensor attached to her head, she activates this device, which displays her messages and also speaks them aloud.

cent of those with cerebral palsy also have mental retardation (Alexander & Bauer, 1988; Pellegrino, 1997).

One of the biggest challenges that some people with cerebral palsy face is an expressive language impairment and/or articulation problems because of uncoordinated muscle movement around the mouth and throat. This is why Camille communicates with her teachers and peers using her eyes, facial gestures, and her Liberator®. The Liberator® is an example of **assistive technology.**

Assistive technology refers to devices or services that restore, maintain, or replace lost bodily functions through the use of technology. The principles of engineering and ergonomics are applied to create devices that also are known as adaptive equipment.

The Liberator® is a rectangular box, similar in size to a laptop computer, that sits at Camille's eye level and attaches to her motorized wheelchair by a tubular mounting device. The surface facing Camille is divided into a grid programmed with messages that she often uses. A symbol in each grid cell cues Camille as to which word or phrase it contains. Cells also contain the letters, numbers, and many of the functions found on a standard computer keyboard. Once Camille has activated a particular cell by a light sensor attached to her head, the Liberator® then displays the letter, number, word, or message and speaks it in a feminine voice. Without a doubt, Camille's Liberator® makes a big difference in her life. Assistive technology is a means that collaborators use to secure desired results. You will learn about assistive technology later in the chapter.

Spina Bifida. High in the Appalachian mountains, Jimmy Chipman, his mother Cindy, and his teacher Edith Lopes diligently apply themselves to the task of overcoming the daily challenges of spina bifida. As a sixth grader in the Cullasaja Elementary School in Franklin, North Carolina, Jimmy moves around school with the help of braces on his legs. When he is too tired to walk or when he and his peers have recess on the hilltop playground at school, he relies on his wheelchair to get to the playground; unfortunately, its sandy or gravel-chipped play areas are simply inaccessible to him. With the assistance of a physical therapist and an occupational therapist, he, Cindy, and Edith work to improve or maintain his strength. Being strong enables him to participate in some general education classes. Because he has missed so much time in school while hospitalized for five surgeries, however, he takes some of his academic work outside of the general curriculum. One aspect of his disability is especially problematic: spina bifida, though it has affected him only from his knees down, has left him incontinent.

All that aside, Jimmy uses a computer easily and looks forward to attending the local community college when he earns his certificate of attendance at school. The word "certificate" is important in Jimmy's life. He won't earn a diploma because he has been excused from state and district assessment tests on account of his disability; state law prohibits him from receiving a diploma unless he passes those tests in the third-, sixth-, ninth-, and eleventh-grade years. The ripple effects of spina bifida, Jimmy is learning, can be vast.

What Is Spina Bifida? *Spina bifida* refers to a divided or split spine (Sandler, 1997). Spina bifida is a malformation of the spinal cord that occurs for unknown reasons during the very early days of pregnancy. The spine is made up of separate bones called vertebrae, which normally cover and protect the spinal cord. In a person with spina bifida, the spinal column does not completely close and cover the spinal cord, usually resulting in a protrusion of the spinal cord, its coverings, or both. A saclike bulge may occur in any part of the spine from neck to buttocks. The higher the spinal defect, the more severe the loss of function. Typically, the defect occurs in the lower region and causes complete or partial paralysis of only the lower extremities and loss of skin sensation (Blackman, 1984; Bleck & Nagel, 1982; Rowley-Kelley & Reigel, 1993).

Spina bifida is not a progressive condition; but the three most common forms—spina bifida occulta, meningocele, and myelomeningocele—have varying degrees of severity (see Figure 12–3). Jimmy's condition affects only his lower legs; his friend, Ross, who also

FIGURE 12–3 *Types of spina bifida*

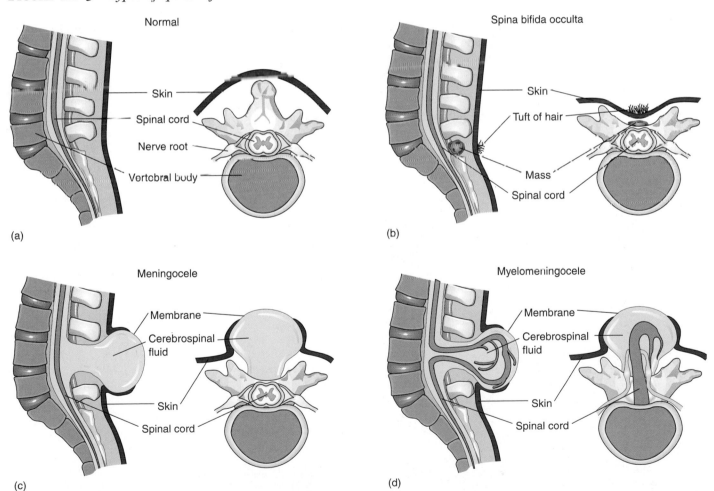

Note: From *Physical Disabilities and Health Impairments: An Introduction* (p. 118), edited by J. Umbreit, 1983, Upper Saddle River, NJ: Prentice Hall. Copyright 1983 by Prentice Hall. Reprinted with permission.

has spina bifida, is paralyzed from the waist down. Jimmy's disability is called *meningocele;* Ross's is called *myelomeningocele.* When Jimmy was born, his disability was obvious and required immediate surgery. His first surgery closed the opening in his back. Several years later, another surgery removed a vertebra from his lower spine, easing the pressure and pain that he had been feeling. Despite the surgeries, Jimmy has limited use of his legs.

Spina bifida occulta. Spina bifida occulta is the mildest and most common form of spina bifida. In this form, the spinal cord or its covering do not protrude; and only a small portion of the vertebrae, usually in the low spine, is missing. Spina bifida occulta usually is not detectable by physical examination and is not disabling. It is typically discovered on a routine x-ray (Rowley-Kelley & Reigel, 1993).

Meningocele. Meningocele is a more serious form of spina bifida. The covering of the spinal cord, but not the cord itself, actually protrudes through the opening created by the defect in the spine. The skin-covered mass may be surgically removed. This condition usually does not cause the child to lose any abilities (Bleck & Nagel, 1982; Rowley-Kelley & Reigel, 1993).

Myelomeningocele. When the protrusion or sac contains not only the spinal cord's covering but also a portion of the spinal cord or nerve roots, myelomeningocele occurs. This severe form of spina bifida results in varying degrees of physical disability. More than 90 percent of people with this type of spina bifida have some degree of weakness in their legs, an inability to control their bowels or bladder, and a variety of physical problems such as dislocated hips or club feet (Rowley-Kelley & Reigel, 1993). In addition, approximately four of five children born with this kind of spina bifida also develop hydrocephalus, an excessive accumulation of cerebrospinal fluid in the brain. Figure 12–4 shows a normal brain, a brain affected by hydrocephalus, and a brain with a shunt inserted.

FIGURE 12–4   *(a) Normal brain, (b) brain with hydrocephalus, and (c) brain with shunt inserted*

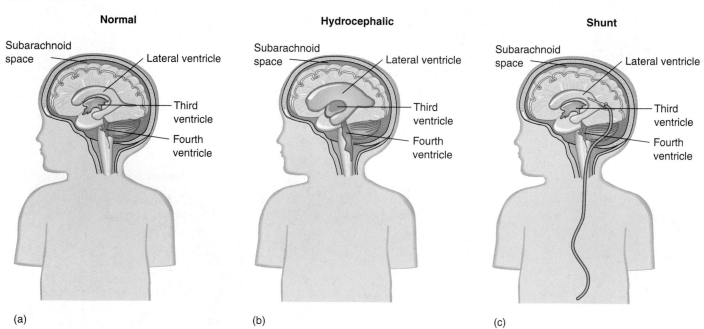

Note: (a), (b) from Illinois Spina Bifida Association. Reprinted by permission; (c) From *Physical Disabilities and Health Impairments: An Introduction.* (p. 123), edited by J. Umbreit, 1983, Upper Saddle River, NJ: Prentice Hall. Copyright© 1983 by Prentice-Hall, Inc. Reprinted with permission.

When a child has hydrocephalus, a blockage prevents the cerebrospinal fluid from circulating in the brain and spinal column. Fluid accumulates in the brain and causes pressure. If the excess fluid is not redirected by means of a surgically implanted shunt (a system of valves and flexible tubing) to a part of the body able to dispose of excess fluids, the resulting pressure can result in mental retardation and death (Blackman, 1984; Heller et al., 1996). Jimmy has had three shunt operations, one just after he was born and two later ones to replace or repair the previous shunts. His hospitalizations, not his native cognitive abilities, are the reasons his academic work is two years behind grade level in the core subjects of math and reading. His individualized education program (IEP) calls for him to have those subjects taught in a pull-out, entirely special education class with his teacher, Edith Lopes. His other classes—science, health, library, and physical education—are in the general curriculum, and he is in an accelerated computer class.

Persons with myelomeningocele may walk with braces and crutches, require wheelchairs at all times, or, like Jimmy, use a combination of these devices (Sandler, 1997). Figure 12-5 shows that the spinal defect's location determines the degree to which mobility is affected. If the defect occurs at thoracic vertebra T-12 or above, total paralysis of the legs results. The lumbar nerves move the leg muscles, and the sacral nerves control the foot muscles. The lower the defect in the lumbar or sacral regions, the greater the ability to walk without braces and crutches.

FIGURE 12–5 *Location affects degree of mobility (T = thoracic, L = lumbar, S = sacral)*

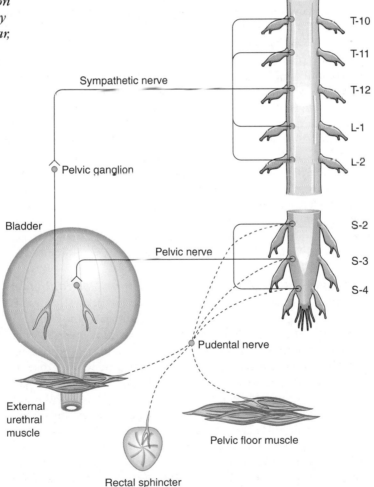

Note: From Bleck, E. E., & Nagel, D. A., *Physically Handicapped Children.* Copyright © 1982 by Allyn & Bacon. Reprinted by permission.

What Causes Spina Bifida?   To date, spina bifida's exact cause is unknown, although it is known that it occurs during the very early days of pregnancy. Parents do not carry any particular gene that specifically causes spina bifida, although their genes may interact with environmental factors (e.g., nutrition, medication, and exposure to high temperatures) to trigger the malformation in the developing embryo (Blackman, 1984; Heller et al., 1996; Umbreit, 1983).

In addition, factors such as race and ethnicity may be involved. Spina bifida occurs in four to five births per thousand in Northern Ireland but in fewer than 0.1 births per thousand in Colombia. It occurs only rarely in African Americans and Asians (Rowley-Kelley & Reigel, 1993). There seems to be a family tendency or predisposition. "If one child in a family has spina bifida, the risk increases to five percent for subsequent children and to twelve to fifteen percent if two children in the family have it" (Rowley-Kelley & Reigel, 1993).

A substantial reduction of neural tube defects (including spina bifida) has occurred among women who used daily vitamin supplements containing folic acid (Centers for Disease Control, 1992; Daly, Kirke, Malloy, Weir, & Scott, 1995; Werler, Shapiro, & Mitchell, 1993). An advisory panel to the Food and Drug Administration also has recommended that food should be fortified with folic acid in order to prevent birth defects such as spina bifida (Kurtzweil, 1996). Researchers have called for studies in effectiveness of folic acid in preventing spina bifida (Yen et al., 1992).

What Are Other Conditions Associated with Spina Bifida?   Approximately 75 percent of children and youth with spina bifida have intelligence in the normal range (Liptak, 1997); however, some of these students experience learning difficulties (Heller et al., 1996).

Bowel and bladder control are major concerns associated with myelomeningocele (Liptak, 1997). The extent of the paralysis in students with spina bifida depends on the level at which the protrusion on the spinal cord occurs: the higher the protrusion, the more the body is affected by paralysis and by loss of sensation (Bigge, 1991). Myelomeningocele almost always occurs above the part of the spinal cord that controls the bladder. Therefore, bladder paralysis, urinary tract infections, and resulting **incontinence** are common. Constipation and bowel accidents may occur. Kidney failure can also result.

Many students can be taught the technique of clean intermittent catheterization and effective bowel management (Lutkenhoff & Oppenheimer, 1997). Working with a school nurse trained in these techniques, teachers can reinforce learning and monitor students' self-management abilities (Rowley-Kelley & Reigel, 1993). Jimmy has learned to catheterize himself. Given that there is no school nurse at his school (despite the fact that it is the magnet school for students with disabilities and has students with a variety of health needs, including spina bifida and diabetes) and that his teacher and her two aides are women, it is understandable why Jimmy wants to perform that procedure alone.

Muscular Dystrophy.   *What Is Muscular Dystrophy?*   You will recall that Rommel has spinal muscular atrophy—a form of muscular dystrophy. Although you may be familiar with the term *muscular dystrophy,* you may not know that there is no single disease of that name. The term designates a group of nine hereditary muscle-destroying disorders that vary in inheritance pattern, age of onset, initial muscles attacked, and rate of progression. The type of muscular dystrophy called Duchenne's disease affects one in every 3,500 males and is the most common form. Rommel has spinal muscular atrophy, which itself is a term for a group of neuromuscular diseases. The spinal muscular atrophies are disorders of motor nerve cell bodies in the brain stem and in the spinal cord.

Spinal muscular atrophy is an inherited disease characterized by muscle atrophy and weakness (Heller, Alberto, Forney, & Schwartzman, 1996). Instead of attacking the muscles themselves, as do many muscular dystrophies, all forms of spinal muscular atrophy attack specialized nerve cells called *motor neurons,* which control the movement of voluntary muscles. Figure 12–6 shows the location of the motor neurons involved in spinal muscular atrophy and the locations of other neuromuscular diseases related to spinal muscular atrophy and muscular dystrophy.

Incontinence means the inability to control one's bladder or bowels. Clean intermittent catheterization is a process whereby a tube is inserted into the urinary tract to allow elimination through the tube.

In its second special education decision, the U.S. Supreme Court held that clean intermittent catheterization is a related service that schools must provide to students who need it, reasoning that, without it, students would not be placed in inclusive settings (*Irving Independent School District* v. *Tatro,* 1984).

Locations of Neuromuscular Injury

FIGURE 12–6 *Location of neurons*

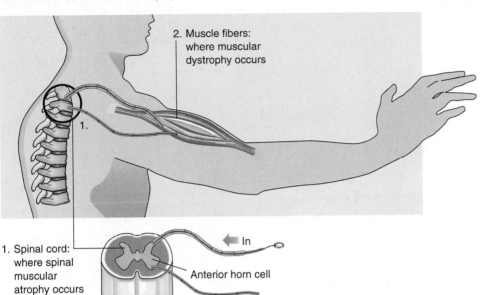

1. Spinal cord: where spinal muscular atrophy occurs

2. Muscle fibers: where muscular dystrophy occurs

Anterior horn cell

In

Out

Note. From *Neuromuscular Disorders: A Guide for Patient and Family* (p. 9), by S. P. Ringel, 1987, New York: Raven Press. Copyright 1987 by Raven Press. Reprinted with permission.

Spinal muscular atrophy causes lower motor neurons (those in the base of the brain and the spinal cord) to disintegrate gradually, preventing them from delivering the electrical and chemical signals that muscles depend on for normal function. "As a result, muscles concerned with facial expression, speaking, swallowing, and movement, potentially including all voluntary muscles of the trunk and extremities, may be partially or completely paralyzed" (Ringel, 1987).

As is true of neuromuscular diseases in general, persons of all ages can develop spinal muscular atrophy. Rommel showed signs of developmental delay almost immediately after birth, while his brother Ariel didn't develop juvenile spinal muscular atrophy until early childhood. The age of onset for the adult form of spinal muscular atrophy can vary from age eighteen to fifty. Persons with spinal muscular atrophy do not, however, experience sensory loss, seizures, or muscle spasticity (Ringel, 1987).

There are three types of spinal muscular atrophy. Type I, acute infantile spinal muscular atrophy, is the most severe form with symptoms present at birth. These symptoms include extreme weakness, inability to sit up or maintain head control, and rapid symptom progression (Heller et al., 1996).

Type II, intermediate spinal muscular atrophy, is what Rommel experiences. His mother, Lorna, is a nurse who noticed by the time he was four months old that he could not bear his own weight and had trouble sitting, even when supported. He was tested at six months and diagnosed at nine months as having spinal muscular atrophy. Because he has no use of his legs, he has **paraplegia.**

Rommel's condition has progressed at a slower rate. This is typical of persons with Type II spinal muscular atrophy. After initial periods of worsening, the condition may stabilize for a long time. Estimating the life expectancy of anyone with spinal muscular atrophy is difficult, but, as one neurology professor points out, "Perhaps the wisest course is not to try and predict the time at which death may occur but to plan for possible survival into adult life" (Brooke, 1986).

Rommel's younger brother Ariel has Type III, juvenile spinal muscular atrophy. Appearing any time after age two through childhood and even into adulthood, this form typically causes weakness in the leg and hip muscles and sometimes in the facial and respiratory

❧ When asked whether he wanted to be featured in this book, Rommel answered, "I'm up for it!" Beneath his infectious positive attitude is his positive contribution to your education.

Paraplegia refers to the impairment and limited use or no use of the arms.

 Romel's parents take precautions against colds and pneumonia by giving him regular treatments on an intermittent positive-pressure breathing machine whenever he starts to show signs of a cold.

It is unwise and nonproductive to blame parents for their children's disability. When, however, there is a clear genetic link, the issue is not one of "blame" but one of causation and intervention (Turnbull & Turnbull, 1997).

Scoliosis is a lateral curve of the spine.

An **intermittent positive-pressure breathing** (IPPB) machine is used outside a person's body and forces the lungs into an exhale function, facilitating breathing.

muscles. Shoulders and arms become weak in the later stages of the illness. The disease began gradually for Ariel. Life span is not affected, and people with this form can walk (although with difficulty) for at least ten and up to thirty years after symptoms first become apparent (Brooke, 1986).

What Causes Spinal Muscular Atrophy? Spinal muscular atrophy is always inherited. Parents who have been identified as carriers of the disease run a one-in-four risk of having children who have the disease and a one-in-two risk of children who will carry the disease (Brooke, 1986). Although some neuromuscular diseases (such as Duchenne's muscular dystrophy) affect only boys, both males and females can develop spinal muscular atrophy.

What Other Conditions Are Associated with Spinal Muscular Atrophy? Children and youth with spinal muscular atrophy usually have normal intelligence. Accompanying conditions are typically associated with skeletal problems such as **scoliosis** (a lateral curve of the spine). Rommel wears a body jacket during the day that supports his weakened upper torso and helps prevent scoliosis. Children and youth with spinal muscular atrophy also can have respiratory problems similar to those experienced by Rommel. Paradoxically, one factor contributing to Rommel's illnesses is his own desire to do so much on his own; his fatigue makes him susceptible to colds. Also, he has had trouble in getting enough nutrition, another cause of his illness; with the new J-tube, Rommel should not face that problem again. He has frequent colds and pneumonia, conditions that have kept him hospitalized once or twice a year for one or two weeks at a time. Because these infections pose the greatest danger for Rommel, his parents and his teacher take the greatest precautions in this area. His parents give him regular treatments on his **intermittent positive-pressure breathing (IPPB)** machine at the slightest sign of a cold, and he rarely goes outside the school building for physical education.

❧ *Rommel attends only general education classes, except for physical education, for which he receives special one-on-one instruction. His adaptive physical educator works with him on such activities as range-of-motion exercises and games to strengthen his respiratory capacity.*

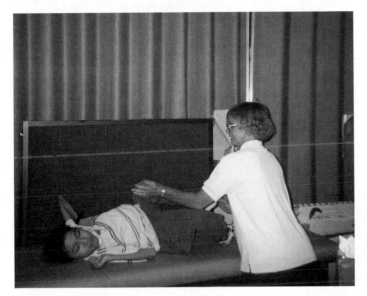 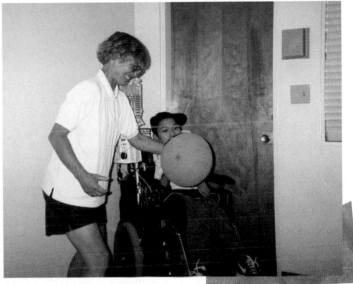

Because he has coded at school when his breathing was interrupted so much that he needed CPR, a basket attached to the back of Rommel's wheelchair contains everything Rommel needs to maintain daily and regular health care and to meet that kind of crisis. There is a suction machine that his one-on-one nurse, Rebecca Draper, can use to suction mucus from his throat, a **pulseoximeter** that she can use to read his pulse and check blood oxygen saturation simply by clamping the device to his index finger, an oxygen tank, and a notebook that describes in detail all his daily procedures, including what should be done if Rommel needs emergency help. In brief, Rommel has with him at all times the technology he needs to meet his breathing challenges.

A **pulseoximeter** is a clamp attached to a person's finger that reads the person's pulse and tells how much oxygen is in his blood system.

Identifying the Prevalence of Physical Disabilities

How many students have physical disabilities? Because physical disabilities are conditions that often occur in combination with others, accurately determining their prevalence is difficult. Nevertheless, the U.S. Department of Education (1996) reported that schools served 60,552 students ages six to twenty-one in this area of exceptionality during the 1994–1995 school year. This figure represents 1.2 percent of all students receiving special education services.

As distinguished from those categories of exceptionality that have a high incidence rate (such as learning disabilities), physical disabilities are considered to be a low incidence disability.

Preventing Physical Disabilities

There are several approaches to preventing physical disabilities. Some prevention programs educate pregnant women about the risks involved from exposure to x-rays, drugs, alcohol, prescription or over-the-counter medications, and viruses and other infections.

Some prevention programs are secondary or tertiary measures; they try to reduce the effect of a disability or prevent a related disability from occurring. For example, a **neonatal intensive care unit (NICU)** in a hospital treats very high-risk babies: those who are born very prematurely or have mothers who used alcohol or drugs during pregnancy.

Some of these babies may already have some type of permanent disability, and the NICU treatment may reduce the effect of that disability. In that sense it is a form of prevention. Other babies may be at great risk for a disability but not yet have an identifiable one. In these cases, the NICU does not ameliorate the effect of a present disability but actually prevents a disability from occurring.

A **neonatal intensive care unit (NICU)** is a hospital facility for treating newborns with serious birth defects. It contains feeding, oxygen, and other life-support services.

Indeed, one consequence of prevention measures is that many babies who are born with severe disabilities are now surviving their first days and weeks of life and are living healthier lives. For example, although much more needs to be discovered about preventing spina bifida itself, a great deal is known about diagnosing infants who have the condition during pregnancy and about closing their back lesions as early as possible after birth to decrease the severity of meningomyelocele side effects (Liptak, 1997). Modern medicine cannot yet prevent spina bifida, but it certainly can treat some of its related complications and improve the lives of those who have it. That is a form of prevention—reducing the effects of a disability.

WHAT ARE EVALUATION PROCEDURES?

Determining the Presence of Physical Disabilities

The evaluation team typically consists of the parents, the teachers, and professionals who represent different specialty areas. These professionals frequently include physicians, nurses, physical and occupational therapists, speech pathologists, psychologists, rehabilitation counselors, transition specialists, and social workers. The exact makeup of the team depends on the student's age and known or assumed needs. For example, while a transition specialist or rehabilitation counselor is important to a team considering competitive employment or community living options for an older student such as Camille, an early childhood specialist is important to the team of an infant or toddler. Because mobility evaluation and intervention are typical needs for persons with physical disabilities, occupational and physical therapists usually play pivotal roles. Other team members may be physicians, general and regular educators, nurses, and adaptive physical education specialists.

Screening may take place before or directly after birth or at a later date when infants fail to meet developmental milestones (such as rolling over, sitting, or reaching for an object). In spina bifida, for example, amniocentesis (see Chapter 9) is a maternal blood test taken early in a pregnancy that can alert physicians to the possibility of a spinal defect and the need for additional testing, such as ultrasonographic imaging of the fetus (Batshaw & Rose, 1997; Liptak, 1997). In Box 12–2, "My Voice: My Son Sam," you will read about early detection, its benefits, the challenges it poses to parents, the stigma that can arise even before the birth of a child who has been detected to have a disability, and the effects of early intervention.

For many infants, an Apgar screening after birth may yield first indication of a problem. Physicians become particularly alert if high-risk factors are involved during the pregnancy or delivery (Schleichkorn, 1983). An infant's poor response to the sucking reflex, convulsions, stiffness, or an unusual amount of irritability might indicate cerebral palsy. Initial screenings may also detect respiratory problems that are frequently associated with spinal muscular atrophy.

For many children with physical disabilities, there may be no indication of problems at birth or in the newborn period. The initial identification of children who appear normal at birth and later fail to develop normally varies according to the age at which the developmental delay is noticed or to the type of disability. Time may elapse between the point when a child's symptoms are first noticed and when a diagnosis can be made. For example, when a child presents symptoms associated with spinal muscular atrophy, doctors may recommend electromyography and muscle biopsies to establish a diagnosis (Heller et al., 1996). Electromyography testing allows doctors to detect abnormal electrical activity within the muscle. A muscle biopsy involves removing a small cylinder of muscle, approximately the size of a pencil eraser, for direct examination. This safe technique, performed with minimal discomfort using a local anesthetic, allows doctors to make an absolute diagnosis (Ringel, 1987). This was how Rommel was diagnosed with spinal muscular atrophy.

BOX 12-2   MY VOICE

MY SON SAM

My name is Kim. I am twenty-seven years old. My son Sam was born in May 1992 with spina bifida.

I first found out there was possibly a problem with my pregnancy at fifteen weeks when I had the AFP (alphafetoprotein) test done. . . . [One] day, my obstetrician called me at work and told my AFP had come back slightly elevated. "My what? Is what? What does that mean? Is my baby going to be all right?" My heart jumped to my throat, I could feel my pulse racing, I felt nauseous, and the tears started pouring. I had so many questions, and I was scared to death. I immediately made an appointment to have an ultrasound done in Chapel Hill. I then left work. I just had to!

Now came time for the ultrasound. Almost immediately, the technician saw "something suspicious." Then the tears started flowing again. She went to get the doctor. Dr. Cheschier came in, looked at the ultrasound, and began explaining what she saw. I can't remember all that was said. I still couldn't believe this was happening to me.

After the ultrasound, Dr. Cheschier, Michael (my husband), and I went into her office and began discussing Sam's condition. The one good thing that came out of this day was that we found out that we were going to have a boy. From that day on the baby wasn't a fetus or an "it"; he was Sam.

For the next five months, my life revolved around doctor's appointments, gathering every bit of information I could find about spina bifida, working full-time, spending every moment I could with our daughter, buying a house, keeping my sanity, being optimistic, and keeping a smile on my face. I had meetings with all the specialists. I remember meeting with Dr. Sandler, asking him a thousand questions, and wishing he had a crystal ball so he could answer them. Will Sam be able to walk, to play sports, to go to the bathroom, to have girlfriends, to go to college, to get married, to have a family? No one knew the answers.

Then Sam was born May 6, 1992, at 10:00 A.M., in Chapel Hill. Sam weighed eight pounds, thirteen ounces, and was twenty inches long. He was beautiful!

Yes, he did have an opening in his spine, and he had to have surgery within the first few hours of his life. The operation went well. Sam was out of surgery in about three hours and went to the neonatal intensive care unit. I asked the doctors if Sam would be able to go home with me. Dr. Sandler said it was highly unlikely that a baby born with spina bifida would go home at the same time as the mother. Well, not only did Sam go home with me, he was in the NICU for only two days before he was moved to the regular nursery (although I kept him rooming in with me most of the time)!

Sam is now eighteen months old. He is walking, running, climbing, dancing, just like any other eighteen-month-old child. He did not develop hydrocephalus, and so he never had to have a shunt. Sam is unquestionably a miracle baby, and I know the chances of a child with spina bifida turning out to be this healthy are slim, but it happened.

Note: From *Living With Spina Bifida: A Guide for Families and Professionals* (pp. 6-8), by A. Sandler, 1997, Chapel Hill: University of North Carolina Press. Copyright 1997 by University of North Carolina Press. Reprinted with permission.

As you have learned, a battery of assessment procedures are used for all students with exceptionalities. Figure 12-7 summarizes assessment procedures and findings for students with physical disabilities.

Determining the Nature and Extent of Special Education and Related Services

In Chapter 9 you learned that some children with physical disabilities may also have mental retardation. Students such as Camille may need augmentative communication devices. Students such as Rommel may have above-average intelligence. Still other students such as Jimmy may have concurrent academic needs and academic strengths. Clearly, determining the nature and extent of a student's special education needs is not a simple process.

Having read in other chapters about various types of educational assessments and evaluations, you may be asking yourself, What about assessment and evaluation of students with physical disabilities? What is special about that process? The answer relates primarily to the importance of mobility in everyone's life. To assess mobility, educators and other professionals follow fundamental assessment principles very much like the ones they use

FIGURE 12–7 *Assessment process for determining the presence of physical disabilities*

Nondiscriminatory Evaluation

Observation

Teacher and parents observe	The student has difficulty with moving in an organized and efficient way, with fine motor activities, with activities of daily living such as dressing, with postural control, and with speaking, comprehending, or organizing.
Physician observes	The child is not passing developmental milestones. Movement is better on one side of the body than the other. Muscle tone is too floppy or stiff. The child has problems with balance or coordination or has neurological signs that suggest a physical disability.

Medical screening

Assessment measures	Findings that indicate need for further evaluation
Developmental assessment	The child is not meeting developmental milestones or shows poor quality of movement on measures administered by physicians, physical therapists, occupational therapists, and psychologists.
Functional assessment	Activities of daily living are affected.

Prereferral

Prereferral is typically not used with these students, because of the need to quickly identify physical disabilities. Also, most children with physical disabilities will be identified by a physician before starting school.

Referral

Students with physical disabilities who are identified before starting school should receive early intervention services and a nondiscriminatory evaluation upon entering school. Because some physical disabilities may develop after a student enters school, teachers should refer any student who seems to have significant difficulty with motor-related activities.

Nondiscriminatory evaluation procedures and standards

Assessment measures	Findings that suggest physical disabilities
Individualized intelligence test	Standardization may be violated because the student's physical disabilities interfere with the ability to perform some tasks. Therefore, results may not be an accurate reflection of ability. The student may be average, above average, or below average in intelligence.
Individualized achievement test	The student may be average, above average, or below average in specific areas of achievement. Standardization may need to be violated to accommodate the student's response style. Thus, results may not accurately reflect achievement.
Motor functioning tests	The student's differences in range of motion, motor patterns, gaits, and postures may present learning problems. Also, length and circumference of limbs, degree of muscle tone, or muscle strength may affect ability to learn specific skills.
Tests of perceptual functioning	The student is unable to or has difficulty in integrating visual/auditory input and motor output in skills such as cutting and carrying out verbal instructions in an organized manner.
Adaptive behavior scales	The student may have difficulty in self-care, household, community, and communication skills because of the physical disability.
Anecdotal records	Reports suggest that the student has functional deficits and requires extra time or assistance in mobility, self-help, positioning, and use of adaptive equipment.
Curriculum-based assessment	The student's physical disabilities may limit accuracy of any timed curriculum-based assessments.
Direct observation	The student is unable or has difficulty in organizing and completing work.

Nondiscriminatory Evaluation Team determines that special education and related services are needed for a physical disability.

Appropriate Education

in determining the special education needs of other students. What is different in the assessment of students with physical disabilities are the roles of two professionals: the physical therapist and occupational therapist.

Physical therapists are primarily concerned with movement. They intervene through exercise, heat, light, and massage treatments. Occupational therapists are more concerned with upper-body movement, fine-motor activities, and the activities of daily living such as bathing and dressing. They intervene primarily by adapting the student's skills and environment to the student's tasks. Rommel's physical therapist, Robin Haupt, is responsible for devising a system that helps him with his positioning in his wheelchair. Without proper positioning, Rommel's scoliosis (curvature of the spine) can become much more severe, his comfort level can deteriorate, and his mobility can be curtailed. Robin's goal for Rommel is to maintain his positioning status and comfort levels.

Upon noticing that his wheelchair was no longer adequate for positioning and comfort and upon learning that Rommel uses a J-tube for feeding and needs a lap tray to hold the computer he uses to write his assignments, Robin contacted Rommel's orthopedist, Scott Mubarek. She requested a prescription for a new chair, one that would accommodate all the new devices without sacrificing positioning and comfort.

With the prescription, Robin then called Freedom Designs, Inc., to order a special insert for the chair, having already determined that Rommel's insurance company will work with that company as an approved vendor. Using technology designed by the National Aeronautics and Space Administration for astronauts, Freedom Designs created a "foam in place" seat and back for Rommel. When a combination of various chemicals is poured into a bag that constitutes Rommel's back and seat in his chair, the bag expands to fit precisely to Rommel and to provide him with a soft back and seat.

  Rommel's younger brother Ariel, shown here boarding the family van, has less extensive spinal muscular atrophy than Rommel.

You may want to review the discussion of ecological inventories in Chapter 9.

Because their roles overlap and complement each other, occupational and physical therapists often work together. Occupational therapists help general and special educators overcome the physical inaccessibility of some of the classrooms. Their skills in making environmental adaptations seem to be even more important in general education settings (Barnes, Schoenfeld, & Pierson, 1997). Karen Boyd, Rommel's occupational therapist, completes an ecological inventory (Rainforth & York-Barr, 1997), talking with Rommel's teacher and visiting Rommel in all of his different environments (home, classroom, lunch room, playground, library). Karen also observes his hand and finger use, head control, arm extension, mobility, muscle tone, and strength.

Observing Rommel's movement patterns is also important. Karen looks for postures that Rommel likes to use but that hamper or prevent him from using the joy stick to drive and steer his motorized wheelchair. She is also concerned how to place a lap tray across the arms of his chair in such a way that he can place his computer on the tray, have access to his joy stick, and still be able to be fed by the external pump for his J-tube and any oxygen that he may need. At school, he wants to be able to use his computer easily, and he doesn't want it to fall off the lap desk that crisscrosses his wheelchair. Taking a standard, off-the-shelf table, cutting it to fit him and his chair, and putting a nonskid rubber pad under the computer, Karen makes it possible for Rommel to use his computer easily and safely.

Karen also observes how Rommel sits in his wheelchair because incorrect positioning hampers a student's ability to perform activities well. In addition, she observes how able Rommel is to use both sides of his body in a coordinated manner. For students who use computers, bilateral skills may not be as important as they are for students who still use pencil/pens and paper or scissors (holding the writing or cutting tool with one hand and the paper with another). Many such tasks are involved in school activities, and it is important to determine a student's ability to perform them successfully.

An occupational therapist also evaluates a student's self-help skills and activities of daily living. Karen now is concerned about other skills of daily living, especially bathing. Rommel weighs between forty-four and forty-five pounds. Because he has such limited mobility, he cannot bathe himself. That task falls to Lorna and Romy, his mother and father. To help them, Karen has devised a flat bed, made of mesh, that fits into the tub in their home. Lorna or Romy place Rommel on that bed every day and use a hand-held shower to clean him. That is a good alternative to lifting him up and down into a tub, a practice that can injure Rommel if he were dropped and one that could cause back injury to his parents. At school, Rommel has access to the bathroom used only for students with disabilities. There, he also has a cot that is heated with an electric-blanket-like device. Now he can rest during the winter without being chilled and risking the pneumonia that can lead to hospitalization. Like many other boys his age, Rommel regularly wants to watch television and adjust the lights and temperature in his room. By following Karen's suggestion to use an adapted TV remote-control device, Rommel can do just that.

Without taking an ecological inventory of Rommel's life at school and home, Karen would not have been so skilled in prescribing assistive technology that enhances his independence and inclusion. With that inventory and especially by observing Rommel, listening carefully to what he says he wants, and consulting with his parents and his teachers, Karen links technology to his many environments and his many caregivers.

Ideally, two or three team members participate in conducting the ecological inventory, switching between the roles of facilitator, observer, and recorder. The facilitator's job is to engage a student in routine daily activities while the observer watches and suggests alternative strategies. The recorder takes notes not only on what a student does and does not do but also on how he performs the activities. Ideally, an assessment takes a number of sessions to complete (Rainforth & York-Barr, 1997).

Team members complete a discrepancy analysis to identify gaps between a student's performance and that of his peers without disabilities. After identifying discrepancies, the

❧ Although Rommel may seem to be a high-tech student, his occupational therapist, Karen, is quick to file this caution: At the core of all the interventions is a "real kid"—one whose choices must be taken into account.

team discusses possible factors that might contribute to a student's difficulties. The team then uses both formal and informal diagnostic assessment techniques to test the influence of various factors on the student's performance.

Based on the results of these tests and on informal observations made at home and in the student's other environments, the team writes an assessment report and uses its results to develop educational objectives for the IEP.

WHAT AND HOW DO PROFESSIONALS TEACH?

Curriculum

Because IDEA requires an individualized education, the curriculum for students with physical disabilities varies, just as the students themselves vary. Some will need augmentative communication (such as Camille uses); others will need a substantial amount of health-related services but still be in the general curriculum full-time or part-time (as Rommel and Jimmy are). And some may be especially talented in some areas of learning (Rommel is classified into California's gifted and talented programs). In light of their specific mobility and communication impairments, they might receive modifications in the academic curriculum to accommodate for the time and methods they use to meet the standards of students without disabilities. In every other way, their curriculum is comparable to the curriculum for students without disabilities, including students who have special gifts and talents (see Chapter 7), and many students with physical disabilities achieve at or above grade level.

Mobility impairments are, however, sources of significant intervention. These impairments often restrict Camille, Jimmy, and Rommel from exploring their environments and learning from them, hinder opportunities for social relationships, and curtail their typical quest for physical and other kinds of independence. For them and for other students and their teachers, a curriculum on mobility is not simply an end in itself but a way to secure independence and greater inclusion in their schools and communities.

Mobility Opportunities via Education (Project M.O.V.E.) is a curriculum that specifically focuses on mobility and is designed to teach students the age-appropriate motor skills needed for adult life (Bidabe & Lollar, 1990). Some of the activities include eating with the family or peers, bathing or showering, getting in and out of bed, dressing and grooming, toileting, communicating, shopping, going to appointments, eating in restaurants, attending social activities, using public restrooms, and riding on public transportation or in regular cars. These activities are categorized into identifying sixteen mobility skills (e.g., maintains a sitting position, stands, walks forward, walks up steps, walks down slopes).

Each of the sixteen skills is divided into four levels of success. For example, in "Walking Forward," the level of success at one end of the continuum requires a person to walk forward a minimum of 20 feet without assistance. At the other end, success occurs if a person can tolerate being placed in a vertical position (Bidabe & Lollar, 1990). Figure 12–8 illustrates the M.O.V.E. continuum of skills for walking forward.

The M.O.V.E. curriculum uses many of the same concepts that you have previously learned, including an ecological approach (see Chapter 9), partial prompts for partial participation (see Chapter 9), and applied behavior analysis (see Chapter 5). Students and parents are encouraged to choose their priority activities, and then teachers and therapists integrate the mobility skill instruction into learning to accomplish these activities.

By integrating functional mobility training throughout the student's day, educators can improve the functional skills and physical health of 99 percent of the participating students, regardless of their age or the severity of their disabilities (Bidabe & Lollar, 1990). M.O.V.E. equipment, manufactured by the Rifton Company, is designed so that students can practice their motor skills independently and so that assistance can be reduced as students' skills increase (Bidabe & Lollar, 1990).

A student who is mobile (because of occupational therapy) can participate in many school activities, as IDEA requires, and thereby develop relationships with peers who do not have disabilities.

The role of choice in a curriculum is consistent with the values you are learning in this book.

FIGURE 12–8   *Project M.O.V.E.*

Walking Forward	Grad Level	Level I	Level II	Level III
G.1. Can walk forward a minimum of 20 feet without assistance.	☐ DATE			
G.2. Can walk a minimum of 1,000 feet with one hand held.	☐ DATE			
G.3. Can walk a minimum of 300 feet with one or both hands held or with a walker.		☐ DATE		
G.4. Can move legs reciprocally for a minimum of 10 feet while bearing own weight when another person assists with shifting weight and maintaining balance.			☐ DATE	
G.5. Can move legs reciprocally for a minimum of 20 feet while being supported by a front leaning walker.			☐ DATE	
G.6. Can tolerate fully prompted reciprocal leg movements while being supported in a front leaning walker or by another person.				☐ DATE
Can tolerate fully prompted extension of hips and knees. See C.5.				☐ DATE
Can tolerate being placed in a vertical position. See C.6.				☐ DATE

Note: From *M.O.V.E.: Mobility Opportunities via Education* (p. A–9), by L. Bidabe and J. M. Lollar, 1990, Bakersfield, CA: Kern County Superintendent of Schools. Copyright 1990 by Kern County Superintendent of Schools. Reprinted by permission.

Methods

A variety of important instructional methods are available for students with physical disabilities. In this section, you will learn about assistive technology. Although assistive technologies are not instructional methods in the traditional sense, they are valuable instructional resources for students with a range of exceptionalities, including those with physical disabilities.

The Technology-Related Assistance to Individuals with Disabilities Act of 1988 (the "tech act" that you read about in Chapter 1) authorizes funds to the states so they can create or improve statewide systems for delivering assistive technology devices and services. Senator Tom Harkin, from Iowa, was the major sponsor of this important legislation. Box 12–3 highlights how and why he has made such a difference in creating assistive technology opportunities for students with disabilities.

Assistive technology includes such off-the-shelf but adaptive equipment as Rommel's computer (provided by his school), wheelchair (paid by insurance coverage), and lapboards and baskets (created by his team at school). Assistive technology also includes the communication aids described later in this chapter. "The technology involved may be as simple as Velcro or as complex as the computer chip" (Pellegrino, 1997, p. 520). All adaptive equipment has the purpose of increasing or maintaining a student's mobility, communication, social relationships, and overall classroom performance (Hedman, 1997; Light, 1997). In this section you will learn about adaptive equipment, computers, augmentative and alternative communication, and medical technology assistance.

BOX 12-3   MAKING A DIFFERENCE

U.S. SENATOR TOM HARKIN

You may remember from Chapter 1 that Tom Harkin is a U.S. Senator from Iowa and that he was the principal sponsor of the Americans with Disabilities Act (ADA). Even before he shepherded ADA through Congress in 1990, Tom sponsored the "tech act," Technology-Related Assistance for Individuals with Disabilities Act of 1988. That law provides federal funds to states so they can create statewide systems for delivering assistive technology to people with disabilities. (Tom also was the co-sponsor, with Senator Bill Frist of Tennessee, of the 1997 reauthorization of the Individuals with Disabilities Education Act.)

Tom Harkin is more than an exceedingly able legislator; he is also a keen listener to people with disabilities. He heard about high-tech innovations that were custom-made for people with disabilities and based on NASA space technology. He wondered how technology could be translated into the lives of those with complex physical needs. He heard that people who are deaf couldn't tune into television shows because there was no closed-captioning in the TV sets or on the shows. He also knew that people who have visual or physical disabilities couldn't have access to worldwide cyberspace because keyboards or monitors on standard computers were not adapted for their use.

Tom often wondered: How can people with disabilities have the same access that people without disabilities take for granted? To such an experienced legislator, the answer was clear: through a law, specifically, the "tech act." The what and how of Tom Harkin's life as a disability advocate are straightforward.

But the why is indirect and ironical. Being a keen listener has great irony for Tom Harkin. Because his older brother is profoundly deaf, Tom learned how to sign when he was a very young boy. A keen listener is one thing Tom's brother couldn't be—certainly not without technology. And that's why Tom Harkin was committed to making assistive technology more accessible through federal law. Tom's making a difference simply builds on his brother's positive contributions to Tom and, through him, to all Americans with disabilities.

Adaptive Equipment. Figure 12-9 highlights a broad range of equipment used in classrooms to increase mobility. Using that equipment requires training and practice for students. For example, students need driving lessons in learning to use scooters or wheelchairs, especially power chairs. Camille learned to operate her power wheelchair by means of four switches, some of which serve dual functions. She activates the switches through slight head movements, a skill that required special instruction and built on her long-term use of a more primitive communication device that also required slight head movements.

Adaptive equipment includes playground equipment and instructional aids for the classroom. Box 12-4 describes how a playground for all children was brought about through community efforts.

Adaptive equipment accommodates a student while at school and elsewhere, too. Just as Rommel's home has ramps, so too is the family's car large enough to transport him and his chair. Increasingly, students and their families use adaptive aids for transportation, both as a passenger as well as a driver (Plank, 1996). Accordingly, secondary schools should provide instruction in using adaptive equipment for adult living: home living, transportation, parenting, and employment (Behrmann & Schepis, 1994; DeMoss, Rogers, Tuleja, & Kirshbaum, 1995; Kirshbaum, 1997; Powers, Sowers, & Stevens, 1995; Scherer, 1993). Even adolescents with physical disabilities need to learn to use equipment that can enable them to care for their children in the most convenient and nurturing way. One example of adaptive parenting equipment is a play center that a family keeps in its home:

> *The size of the play center is large enough to encourage the child's gross motor skills. The height of the center is just right for a wheelchair-using parent to be close enough to the child while playing with a toy or performing baby care activities such as changing a diaper, feeding, or putting the baby down for a nap. (DeMoss et al., 1995, p. 4)*

FIGURE 12–9 *Common equipment to facilitate various motor skills*

Positioning	
Bolsters/sand bags	Pillow-like objects used to support desired positions
Triangle/corner chairs	Provide three-sided support in upright position; can also be used with table
Bean bags	Allow comfortable positioning; adjust to individual
Wedges	Wedge-shaped foam pads used in prone position; allow work on head control, use of hands/arms
Car seats	Provide safety and appropriate positioning
Wheelchairs/inserts	Upright positioning and mobility inserts, individually designed and fitted
Prone boards	Standing positioning, allowing use of hands/arms
Mobility	
Scooters	Used by young children from many positions
Walkers	Style varies with need
Crutches	Style varies with need
Bicycles (two or three wheels)	Can have adapted seats, handlebars, or pedals, as necessary
Wheelchairs (power and regular)	Standard: with specific equipment such as footrests, neckrests, headrests, side supports, and inserts
	Travel chairs: serve as both therapeutic chairs and car seats (rear wheels are collapsible)
Isolated Support	
Braces	Plastic, fiberglass, or cloth; are removable support for scoliosis or joint strengthening; metal braces are being used less frequently
Splints	Used on hands, wrists, arms, knees, and ankles, for support or to help inhibit contractures
Activity-Oriented	
Mercury switches	Devices worn on part of student's body where movement is desired; attached to radio or device that switches on when body part moves; other switches controlled by hands, feet, cheeks, voice, breath
Battery-operated devices	Toys, wheelchairs, communication systems adapted with special switches
Computer aids	Communication, leisure/recreation, calculators for shopping, and so forth
Toy modifications	Larger handles, switches, controls, adapted to be operated by different modalities (e.g., by voice)
Radio-controlled devices	Door openers, telephone answering machines, toys
Mobility devices	Battery-operated riding toys, power wheelchairs, scooters

Note: From "Motor and Personal Care Skills," by C. H. Kimm, M. A. Falvey, K. D. Bishop, and R. L. Rosenberg, in *Inclusive and Heterogeneous Schooling: Assessment, Curriculum, and Instruction* (p. 208), edited by M. A. Falvey, 1995, Baltimore, MD: Paul H. Brookes. Copyright 1995 by Paul H. Brookes Publishing Company, P. O. Box 10624, Baltimore, MD 21284-0624. Reprinted with permission.

BOX 12-4

MAKING A DIFFERENCE

RYAN GRAY'S LEGACY

Before he died in 1990 at the age of seventeen, Ryan Gray was one of many avid fans of the Kansas University men's basketball team, the Jayhawks. But unlike those thousands, he was the talisman who, coach Larry Brown used to say, brought the team its good luck. So uplifting to the team and the coach was Ryan—all smiles, all sweetness, all confined to a wheelchair, so dependent for daily care on his mother, Kitty, and his father, Cap—that, in the Jayhawks' national championship season of 1987–1988, Ryan sat at courtside at each game, all the way through the team's run at and capture of the NCAA trophy.

Ryan's legacy is not, however, being known as the team's good-luck kid. It is something far more enduring: the Ryan Gray Playground at the Hillcrest School in Lawrence, Kansas. Built as a memorial to Ryan to accommodate chil-

dren who, like him, could not get around or play without their wheelchairs, the playground is open year-round to all kids, but especially to those who have disabilities.

Along its pathways, wheelchairs roll easily; onto its low-set climbing bars, children can hoist themselves from their chairs and ascend a height in the jungle gym that they could not otherwise attain; and amid the swings, there is an accessible one, readily mounted from a wheelchair, on which the sense of flying can be known to those who cannot walk.

At the entrance to the playground, etched into bronze and set within Kansas limestone, is the likeness of Ryan Gray—his smile welcoming all. A person who makes a difference is one whose contribution endures beyond his own lifetime . . . a person like Ryan Gray.

The Ryan Gray Playground at Hillcrest School in Lawrence, Kansas, is open year-round to all kids, but especially to those with disabilities. It features climbing bars, a jungle gym, and a swing that are all readily accessible for kids who use wheelchairs.

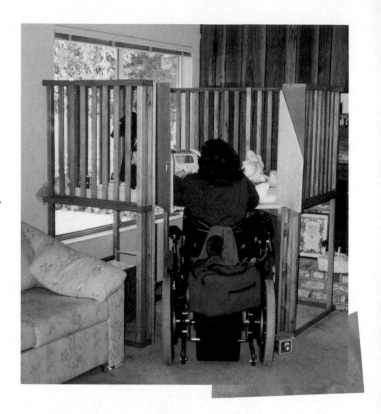

✑ *Secondary schools should instruct students with physical disabilities in using adaptive equipment for adult living. Shown here is an adaptive play/care center, one of many adaptive parenting innovations developed by Through the Looking Glass in Berkeley, California. Photo courtesy of "Through the Looking Glass," 2198 Sixth Street, Suite 100, Berkeley, CA 94710.*

Computers. Computers are another form of assistive technology. In Rommel's case, the school district has provided him with a computer and has adjusted its keys to the most sensitive setting. He has also enjoyed using a computer graphic software program in a computer class. Because Rommel is so bright and relies on a computer for so much of his written work, he has been admitted to an upper-level computer course; that also makes him feel especially good about himself. Computer applications assist children with physical disabilities, as well as with other types of disabilities, to learn a wide variety of skills within a highly motivating context, such as the following:

- For students unable to use their hands, drawing with a switch and graphics software (Hickman, 1994)

- For students unable to hold a pencil, using switch, voice, and/or eye gaze input for a word processing program

- For students who experience mobility challenges, making simulated visits to art galleries using real-time video, speech, music, text, and graphics

- For many students using open-ended software, encouraging problem-solving and emergent literacy skills (see Chapter 7) while minimizing fine motor requirements (Hutinger, 1996).

Computer technology for providing instruction and controlling the environment can be highly sophisticated. In addition, extensive hardware advances ensure computer accessibility—switches, touch tablets, voice synthesizers, timers, and multimedia. Some of the switch-operated keyboards enable students to type with almost any part of their body, and keys can be custom-designed in terms of size, function, and position.

Students with physical disabilities can have access to computers through **speech recognition technology.** Students speak into a microphone, and the computer converts the speech into a print display on the computer screen. This kind of technology "holds the promise of increased environmental control, freedom of movement, and access to a wider

Speech recognition technology gives students with physical disabilities access to computers by converting their speech into a print display on the computer screen.

range of personal choices in all settings (Cavalier & Ferretti, 1996, p. 82). For example, *Multimedia Macs,* an IBM-compatible multimedia computer, enables individuals with physical disabilities to use voice activation to turn on/off over 200 appliances, including speaker phones, answering machines, fax machines, computer modems, and television sets (Hosmer, 1996, p. 1).

Students with disabilities increasingly acquire and provide information via the Internet (Wong, 1997). Just as self-determination is important to people with mental retardation (see Chapter 8), so it is equally important for individuals with physical disabilities and can be enhanced through Internet linkages (Fullmer & Majaumder, 1991; Fullmer & Walls, 1994). The Internet contains a significant amount of disability-related information about advocacy, equipment resources, electronic bulletin boards, news groups, databases, and funding resources.

Medical Technology Assistance.

Medical technology assistance involves a mechanical device to replace or augment vital body functions (Office of Technology Assessment, 1987). These devices include

- Respiratory technology assistance (e.g., **tracheostomy** to provide medical ventilation and suctioning of secretions)

- Surveillance devices (e.g., cardiorespiratory monitor to record heart and respiratory rate)

- Nutritional assistive devices (e.g., a **jejunum** tube, or J-tube, to provide for feeding through a tube directly to the intestine)

- Ostomy care (e.g., a **colostomy** which is an opening through the abdominal wall)

- Intravenous therapy (e.g., a provision of nutrition or medication through a central venous line)

- Kidney dialysis (e.g., a procedure to eliminate toxins from the kidneys through inserting a dialysis solution through a catheter surgically implemented through the abdominal wall) (Levy & O'Rourke, 1997; Porter, Haynie, Bierle, Caldwell, & Palfrey, 1997).

A **tracheostomy** is the surgical creation of an opening into a person's trachea (wind pipe). Into the opening is placed a tube that allows the person to breathe, almost always with the help of mechanical ventilation. The **jejunum** is the second portion of a person's small intestine; a tube placed in it allows the person to receive nutrition through the tube. A **colostomy** is a surgical procedure that involves creating an opening into a person's abdomen so that bowel contents can be drained into a bag attached to the person's body.

You have already learned that Rommel uses a J-tube (jejunum tube) for nutrition, because he finds it too tiring to feed himself and to chew regular food. Figure 12–10 illustrates the insertion of the J-tube directly into the small intestines.

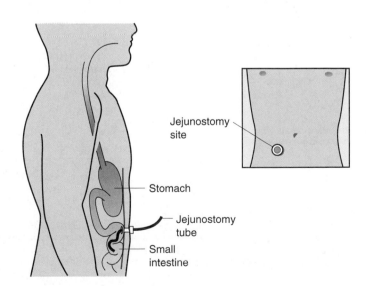

FIGURE 12–10 *A jejunostomy tube in position*

Jejunostomy site

Stomach

Jejunostomy tube

Small intestine

The use of medical technology assistance raises some complicated issues for educators, families, and students. Parents of students who are ventilator assisted, almost half of whom have physical disabilities, want their children to have more physical therapy but otherwise seem satisfied that schools are meeting their children's academic, health care, and socialization needs. They also are generally satisfied with the fact that their children are, by and large, nearly fully included in schools' academic programs. The barriers to inclusion were, at first, attitudinal (educators did not believe that inclusion was possible and health care providers did not believe that it was desirable) and, later, logistical (planning is necessary but once plans have been put into place, inclusion is not difficult) (Jones, Clatterbuck, Marquis, Turnbull, & Moberly, 1996).

In the literature, you will frequently see augmentative and alternative communication referred to as AAC.

Augmentative and Alternative Communication. Augmentative and alternative communication (AAC) refers to techniques and devices used by students to supplement whatever degree of naturally acquired speech they possess. It includes the aids such as Camille's Liberator®, the system of symbols programmed into it, and the techniques and

FIGURE 12–11 *A set of decision rules for consideration in selecting an AAC system*

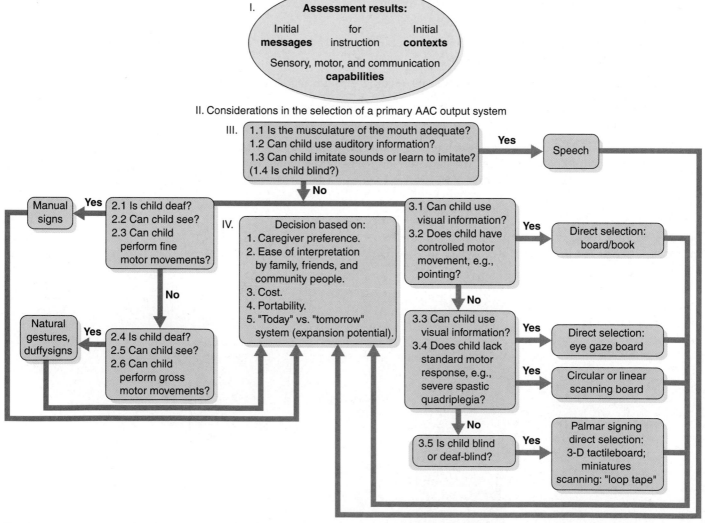

Note: From L. Goetz and P. Hunt, "Augmentative and Alternative Communication," in E. C. Cipani and F. Spooner, (eds.), *Curricular and Instructional Approaches for Persons With Severe Disabilities* (p. 270), 1994, Boston: Allyn & Bacon. Copyright © 1994 by Allyn & Bacon. Reprinted with permission.

strategies that speech pathologists and teachers use to enable their students to acquire language skills. AAC provides options for students with communication challenges to overcome those challenges in having an effective communication system for "expressing needs and wants, developing social closeness, exchanging information, and fulfilling social etiquette routines (Light, 1988)" (Light, 1997, p. 61).

AAC assumes that all students are capable of communication, so educators and therapists have to evaluate students and then customize the appropriate AAC system (Johnson, Baumgart, Helmstetter, & Curry, 1996; Mirenda & Iacono, 1990). Decision rules to guide the evaluation are illustrated in Figure 12-11. Any system must be feasible and accessible to the student (Sax, Pumpian, & Fisher, 1997; Scherer, 1993) and supported by family members (Angelo, Kokoska & Jones, 1996; Brotherson, Cook, & Parette, 1996; Parette & Angelo, 1996), educators (Cottier, Doyle, & Gilworth, 1997; Goetz & Hunt, 1994), and peers (Beck & Dennis, 1996).

AAC devices can use low-tech or high-tech approaches (Silverman, 1995). An example of a low-tech approach is a communication board such as the one depicted in Figure 12-12. Communication boards typically are not expensive, do not require special training to operate, and do not need to be repaired (Bruno, 1996).

Alternatively, high-tech AAC approaches provide extensive communication symbols and even remote control for consumer appliances. Figure 12-13 provides an example of DynaMyte, a highly sophisticated AAC device developed by Sentient Systems Technology, Inc.

Camille is an example of a nonverbal student who needed specialized language and computer instruction on AAC devices to enable her to succeed in her general education classes. Although it would have been theoretically possible for her to receive this instruction in a general education classroom, her teachers found that it was more time efficient

🫰 The principle of choice comes to play in a student's choice of methods for using communication devices.

FIGURE 12–12 *A communication board allows students with physical and/or severe and multiple disabilities the ability to interact and communicate with others.*

FIGURE 12–13 *The DynaMyte augmentative and alternative communication device*

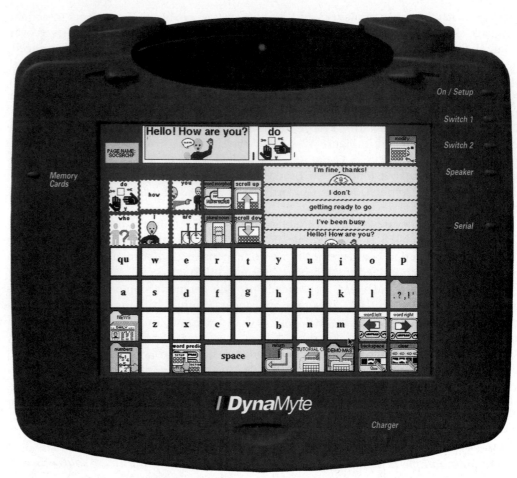

Note: Courtesy of Sentient Systems Technology, Inc., Pittsburgh.

and less distracting for her to receive it from a trained professional in a resource room. Remembering how Camille communicated through her Liberator® to a special education conference, you can begin to appreciate how using ACC empowered her to be a self-determining young woman. Box 12-5, "Into Practice," suggests how you can communicate comfortably with a person who uses AAC.

HOW IS PARTICIPATION ENCOURAGED?

Inclusion

❧ IDEA asks educators to have high expectations for students with disabilities; that's the same as asking everyone to have great expectations for them.

In the 1960s, parents and teachers who had secured separate and usually segregated programs for students with physical disabilities began to abandon their typical goals of maintaining the students' health. Having recognized what students with physical disabilities could accomplish, they began to focus on securing students' total development. Early assistive technology, such as motorized wheelchairs and augmentative communication devices, allowed students more control, choice, and independence in their lives. As students were able independently to initiate both movement and speech, educational expectations for them began to rise dramatically.

In 1963 Dr. June Bigge, professor of special education at San Francisco State University, started one of the nation's first programs aimed at integrating students with physical disabilities and their peers without disabilities. From that point on, there has been a slow

INTO PRACTICE

BOX 12–5

TIPS FOR COMMUNICATING WITH STUDENTS WHO USE ALTERNATIVE AND AUGMENTATIVE COMMUNICATION

- Introduce yourself.
- Ask the user to show you how the communication system works.
- Pause and wait for the user to construct message. Be patient. It might take a while.
- Don't feel you have to keep talking all the time. Relax and get into this slower rhythm of exchanging information.

- Give the user an opportunity to ask you questions or make comments.
- Don't finish the user's sentences/words for him/her unless you get permission.
- Interact at eye level if at all possible. Grab a chair if the user is in a wheelchair.
- Pay attention to facial expressions and gestures.
- Be honest. If you don't understand, admit it. Ask the user to try again.
- Talk directly to the user, not to his/her friend.

but systematic inclusion effort involving students with physical disabilities. Figure 12-14 shows the school placement of students with physical disabilities during the 1994–1995 school year (U.S. Department of Education, 1996).

Box 12-6 shows you what stands in the way of including students with physical disabilities in general education classrooms and what one determined parent and educator did to secure inclusion.

The accompanying "Inclusion Tips" box will help you include students with physical disabilities in general classrooms.

FIGURE 12–14 *Percentage of students with physical disabilities in educational placements during the 1994–1995 school year*

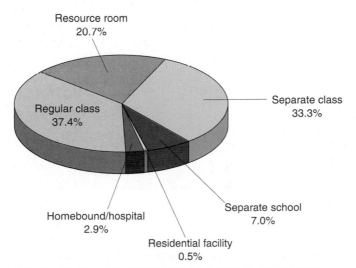

Resource room
20.7%

Separate class
33.3%

Regular class
37.4%

Separate school
7.0%

Homebound/hospital
2.9%

Residential facility
0.5%

Note: From U.S. Department of Education (1996). *To assure the free appropriate public education of all children with disabilities: Seventeenth annual Report to Congress on the implementation of the Individuals with Disabilities Education Act.* Washington, DC: Author.

BOX 12-6   **MY VOICE**

PAT HACKETT-WATERS TALKS ABOUT ACHIEVING INCLUSION

"You're an idealist. Your expectations are too high. Your son is unique. You are an exceptional teacher. This would never work with other kids." That's what the experts told me fifteen years ago. Some experts!

I never set out to be a leader in special education. It just happened because I didn't think educators' ideas were fair. The school district said, "If your son Glen needs an aide for mechanical support [handwriting] and for bathrooming, he has to go to the special school for students with physical disabilities."

What I envisioned for my son's educational needs was quite different, and it seemed reasonable to me. It just needed a little accommodation and an open mind.

In 1978 I took a look at the "crip" school. It was located in a creaking old dinosaur of a building with uneven gymnasium floors and an atmosphere of despair. Although another school for regular education students was located next door, the students in the "crip" school never had the opportunity to attend mainstream classes, play with those other students at recess, or even have lunch with them. It was unfair. It was inferior. No, my son wouldn't be attending that school.

That's how it all started. I wouldn't accept less for my son. I registered him as a regular education student at our neighborhood school. The first year was difficult, but Glen's new kindergarten buddies showed the adults how easy accommodation and modification was. Over the years, Glen's friends took notes for him, modified his work load, adapted physical education activities to include him, learned wheelchair repair, and did respiratory therapy so he wouldn't miss school.

When we later moved to a new home in a new state, Florida, the district was shocked when Glen wheeled in and enrolled himself as a regular education student. He didn't think he needed special education, especially adapted instruction—just some help. The school district got over it. Still, they raised eyebrows when he joined the baseball team as statistician. During out-of-state games, you should have seen these guys hook up a G-tube at night and do bowel and bladder management. These macho, very popular guys were just helping their buddy. It wasn't special. They just did it because it had to be done.

But could this approach work for other kids? For many years I had jokingly said, "Give me ten kids I did not give birth to, and I'll show you this can work." I got my chance in 1991. I was offered a position to start a class at a new middle school for students who had physical disabilities or health impairments. At a home visit before school started, I met my first student, Faye. She had a dynamite smile and gorgeous curly black hair. She traveled by fancy red motorized wheelchair and used a headstick on her augmentative device to communicate. She had fire in her eyes and a loving supportive family. After I left her house, I panicked. I didn't know anything about this kind of device, and she used a computer for her written work. The only thing I knew about a computer was how to plug it into the wall.

Then it dawned on me. What I was feeling was probably what other people had felt about my son. *Never* would I want a child or a family to receive those feelings. I shifted gears and declared that I would learn to do whatever it took to integrate Faye and my other new students.

I learned quickly about computers. But the new school's equipment hadn't arrived yet and school was about to start. So my husband and I took out a second mortgage and bought several used computers to get the class started. Many times, my staff and I were just one chapter ahead of the kids.

Here's an interesting note: all my students, while physically stronger than Glen, were less independent. Of the fourteen students, only three had been in inclusive programs. In one year, however, I had every one of them mainstreamed in homeroom, an elective course, and an academic class. Some were fully integrated with adult aide support, and we later trained peers. Two years later, Faye was fully integrated, earned a 4.0 GPA, and was inducted into the National Junior Honor Society. She now has a boyfriend and a wide circle of friends: Faye has a life.

What's the bottom line? *Urgency.* Kids can't wait for the system. If they need it now, get it now. They also need *vision.* Your actions today produce results tomorrow. Teachers, ask your families what their plan is for their child in four years; then teach and prepare this kid to meet and be ready for this plan. Empower, skill-build, retool. Create a parent network so they can find mentors. You can make a difference!

Pat Hackett-Waters

Most educators do not question the benefits of inclusion for students with physical disabilities. Some, however, believe that the key to inclusion is technology and that specialized instruction is necessary to teach students to use technology properly. They question the appropriateness of including students with physical disabilities in general classrooms while simultaneously trying to teach them such specialized and necessary technical

Inclusion Tips

	What You Might See	What You Might Be Tempted to Do	Alternate Responses	Ways to Include Peers in the Process
Behavior	The student may have restricted movements, need special physical care, or use a wheelchair.	Allow her to be excused from many class activities or treat student as "invisible."	Collaborate closely with the nurse, the aide, the inclusion specialist, and physical therapist to strive for her full potential.	Encourage friends who can socialize as well as provide classroom support.
Social Interactions	She may not be able to speak except with her eyes and gestures.	Avoid bringing her into situations with other students.	Use direct eye contact and AAC devices. Socialize with her, and treat her as other students.	Teach peers to use AAC devices. Provide many opportunities to use these in natural social interactions.
Educational Performance	The student may take more time to complete class assignments because of physical limitations.	Grade her down for work not completed on time.	Provide her extra time and help to complete work. Take advantage of available computer technology.	Provide a computer partner.
Classroom Attitudes	Her attitude may be poor or resistant because she is not treated in a typical way	Instruct and reinstruct her on appropriate ways to participate.	Get to know her and spend time with her discussing her interests and what she is daily experiencing.	Provide opportunities for cooperative learning activities consistent with strengths and preferences.

skills as computer use and life management. They argue that some amount of individual instruction time with a trained resource teacher is often necessary (J. L. Bigge, personal communication, June 12, 1993; M. Polancih, personal communication, May 29, 1993).

Collaboration

Professional Collaboration. Rommel's school-based team includes a school district resource nurse, Cathy Schmitz, who oversees all of the many services he receives. She is the majordomo of his school-based team. More than any other person, she has the overall picture of Rommel's health needs and how those needs can be met within the academic environment. Accordingly, her duties involve her with a host of people. They include staying in regular touch with his parents and getting their consent for various interventions and modifications at school. She is the liaison to his physicians, making sure that their prescriptions and orders are faithfully recorded in Rommel's records and carried out. She trains Rommel's one-on-one nurse how to meet his daily needs, the school staff who are responsible for responding to health emergencies in all children, and all other school personnel who work with Rommel regarding his nonemergency needs and accommodations. In particular, she works with his teachers so they can change some of what they require of him (without lowering the standards he has to meet in the gifted and talented program). Finally, she works closely and frequently with the nurse who provides one-on-one support for him.

A registered nurse, Rebecca Draper, works one-on-one with Rommel and accompanies him throughout the school day, performing a wide range of activities with and for him. Her most important duty is to help Rommel expel secretions that build up in his respiratory tract by applying pressure to his chest so that mucus is moved up to his mouth and can be suctioned out easily. She also monitors his pulse and oxygen saturation, makes sure that his nutrition pump and tube are working (Rommel takes his nutrition over a sixteen-hour period), and, if necessary, administers the oxygen from the portable tank that accompanies him at all times. When he takes his regular rest periods of fifteen to thirty minutes every two hours, she lifts him from his chair, removes his plastic jacket, changes his T-shirt, and helps him in toileting.

Because Rommel tires so easily and has very limited use of his hands and arms when he is fatigued, Rebecca also plays an important role in his academic program. She takes notes for him in class, writes his papers as he dictates what he wants them to contain, and keeps in touch with the classroom teachers if he is home ill or in the hospital. Rommel prefers to take his tests independently, but her assistance is available as necessary for essay questions. Rommel may use a separate room when he takes his tests, speaking his answers while someone else records them. As Cathy puts it, Rebecca is Rommel's "hands and arms."

You have already learned that Robin, his physical therapist, and Karen, his occupational therapist, suggested the specially molded wheelchair and designed an adaptation to his motorized wheelchair so he can easily reach the joy stick that steers his chair. Both evaluate Rommel and consult with his school-based team. In addition, Linda McMoran, an adaptive physical educator, works with him one-on-one; and his general education teachers and "JJ" Barlow, his special education teacher, make it possible for Rommel to be fully included in the general academic curriculum. Cathy gives credit to her own staff of other resource nurses and secretarial staff, the academic members of Rommel's IEP team, and the bus transportation department for their significant contributions. "We are so integrated as a team that, if each player did not work with all the others, all would be lost. Everyone who knows Rommel thinks he is a great kid and would do whatever they could to help."

Indeed, with the exception of his physical education class (where he works one-on-one in stretching and strengthening his body and on any exercise that increases his respiratory capacity) and with time-out for rest periods, Rommel attends only general education classes, including English, history, social studies, and sciences. In those classes, he uses a computer (placed on a lap-board over the arms of his wheelchair) or has help from Rebecca to do his work. Should the time come when he cannot stroke the keyboard, he will use a microcassette dictating machine to record his homework and Rebecca will write his in-school assignments and tests.

Rommel also benefits from other modifications. He is allowed to come to school one hour later than other students and to leave it one hour earlier. That kind of flexibility accommodates his need for rest but does not interfere with his schedule of core academic classes. He has been excused from doing art projects because he has limited use of his hands and arms, and from regular physical education so he can take adaptive physical education. If he misses school, his teachers change their homework demands, asking him to complete only those assignments that are absolutely necessary or giving him an extension on deadlines. Although she is not required to do this, Rebecca will take Rommel's assignments to him at home; like Rommel and his parents, school staff don't want him to miss out on learning. Finally, his entire team keeps a sharp eye out for how Rommel feels, physically, on a daily basis and how he interacts with his peers. Rebecca and Cathy inform the school staff of the ever-changing needs related to his disability and, with them, are ever watchful to anticipate new needs and modifications.

Although Rommel can and does communicate very effectively, he is a quiet, noncomplaining young man, so sometimes he does not admit a need until he is extremely fatigued.

Rommel's team illustrates the value of having and being reliable allies—those who, through collaboration, make it possible for students with physical disabilities to be included in school and the general curriculum.

As Cathy has observed, "We have found that occasionally we subtly alter things to make it easier on him without bringing attention to his 'differentness' from his peers." For example, when Rebecca notices that Rommel is "holding back" from interacting with his peers, she and his teachers can maneuver situations so as to include him as fully as possible in his peers' activities.

Four physicians complete Rommel's team. A pediatrician oversees his general health. An orthopedic specialist prescribed the fitted jacket and then arranged for it to be further customized to accommodate the feeding tube. A pulmonary specialist prescribed the ventilator and a regimen for regularly monitoring Rommel's congestion, pulse, and breathing. A surgeon performed the operation that made it possible for Rommel to receive his nutrition through the J-tube.

In the accompanying "Collaboration Tips" box, you will learn how Rommel, his family, and the many professionals in his life collaborate around his health-related needs.

Family Collaboration. Family members perform valuable functions not only in the evaluation and educational decision-making process, but also in the cognitive, emotional, and physical development of their children. Adolescents with spina bifida and cerebral palsy report harmonious relationships with their parents, and the majority characterize their parents' treatment of them as being age-appropriate (Blum, Resnick, Nelson, & St. Germaine, 1991). Although classroom teachers traditionally have been responsible for educating students with physical disabilities, families and other professionals collaborate with teachers and each other. Besides being skilled in diagnosing their son's physical and psychological condition and in how to use the IPPB, J-tube, respirator, and body jacket, Lorna and Romy also have learned how to negotiate the maze of school, health, and insurance systems that surround Rommel. Finally, Lorna and Romy provide care at home and backup for Rommel's school. Whenever the school believes that he is close to being in respiratory distress, its staff call Lorna so she can bring him home. Likewise, whenever Lorna or Romy believe that Rommel is not strong enough to go to school, they call the school to explain his absence and get his assignments for him to do at home.

Although Lorna and Romy are limited by their work schedules and cannot easily visit Rommel's class, they, in collaboration with Rommel's teachers, have worked out a method of contributing on a regular basis. Every day the family communicates by notebook or telephone with the school nurse, teachers, and other staff as necessary. For example, when Rommel is overly congested, the family rearranges schedules to be sure at least one family member (including grandparents) can be reached during Rommel's school day. The Nanasca family supports Rommel's educational program by encouraging and assisting him in daily living activities and by listening to him read. When reading books that Rommel has selected, Lorna reinforces and extends this important skill within the family's natural routine. By including reading as part of an established bedtime routine, Lorna is able to support Rommel's academic program on a consistent basis.

Student and Community Collaboration. Rommel himself is a crucial member of the collaboration team. An academically bright youngster, he also is one whose disposition glues people to him, making them reliable allies. He participates in all of the key decisions involving his medical treatment and educational program. His attitude is positive: "I'm up for it" has become his slogan. Rommel's peers help him to be recognized by his teachers. Because he cannot always raise his arms to signal that he wants to speak, his buddies do that for him, on his request.

Careers

The field of physical disabilities has many career options. **Dually certified** teachers are critically needed, especially in rural areas (Ammer, Best, & Kulik, 1994), and experts in rehabilitative engineering and computer technology are needed everywhere. Rehabilita-

IDEA requires schools to provide health-related services but not medical services except for diagnosis, as you read in Chapter 2.

Dual certification means being certified in the categorical area of physical disabilities as well as another area such as elementary education or other health impairments.

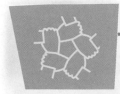

Collaboration Tips

PLANNING FOR THE USE OF SPECIALIZED EQUIPMENT

COLLABORATION GOAL To make sure that everyone involved with the student with physical disabilities knows about his new J-tube and chair and how to accommodate them in nonemergency and emergency situations.

Collaborators	Roles and Preparation	Possible Barriers	Solutions to Barriers	Modifications to Implementation	Ongoing Evaluation
Student	Express student's needs and preferences about comfort and driveability of new chair.	May not know all personal needs until school is under way for awhile.	Try out chair in school before school begins, do role play with general and special educators and aides.	Use chair in real school . . . an "actual" school test drive.	Report regularly to nurse and occupational therapist on how well or poorly student's chair fits and how useful it is.
Parents	Learn all about how new J-tube and chair works.	Short time for learning before student goes to school.	Collaborate with occupational therapist in designing tube and joy-stick attachments.	Attend school with student, see him and chair in action.	Ask student, school staff how they can help son use chair more effectively.
General Educator(s)	Learn all they can about how J-tube and chair work; learn emergency protocols.	Time and expertise may be absent.	Have short in-service on student's needs, know to call on school's emergency response team.	Practice "drill" (like fire drill) once a semester.	Review any action taken, get technical assistance from student's nurse as needed.
Student's nurse	Be primary provider of services to student.	Time off for lunch, sickness, emergencies.	Train teachers who work with student and school-based emergency team.	Get pager or cell phone for quick contact with emergency team, resource nurse, parents, hospital.	Keep in regular contact with emergency team and occupational therapist.

tion engineers and computer software specialists devise individual adaptations and computer programs that help students with physical disabilities participate more fully in every aspect of life. As you have read, occupational and physical therapists play especially important roles in the lives of students with physical disabilities. And, for Rommel and other students with complex physical disabilities, a nurse becomes the key person. In Box 12–7, "Making a Difference," you will read about Cathy Schmitz, the resource nurse in Rommel's school district.

Collaborators	Roles and Preparation	Possible Barriers	Solutions to Barriers	Modifications to Implementation	Ongoing Evaluation
Parapro-fessional	Carry out activities designed by spe-cial and general educators. Moti-vate student.	Student's atti-tude—refused to cooperate. Lack of proper training on equipment.	Develop good communication; find ways to dis-tract student. Try to help student com-municate needs. Give paraprofes sional adequate training for what she is asked to do.	Work with school to maintain same paraprofessional who has devel-oped rapport with student and skills with equipment.	Evaluate services being shared by special and gen-eral educators and paraprofessional(s) to assess student's needs.
Special Edu-cator/Related-service Provider	Work with student on communication, motor skills, and strengths	Not having enough support, training, knowledge, proper equipment avail-able.	Provide necessary training, supplies, equipment, and support.	Special educator makes needs known to adminis-trator.	Special educator will monitor through IEP process and observation.
Administrator	Make sure student has support he needs in building. Work on problems brought up by teacher.	Being unaware of unmet needs; other responsibili-ties and limited time and resources available.	General and spe-cial educators make needs known.	General and spe-cial educators take initiative/responsi-bility to make needs known.	Self-evaluation; IEP process.
Peers and their parents	Seek some knowl-edge from special educator/parapro-fessional about physical equipment purposes; Interact with and encour-age student.	Other students' conflicting goals. Time restraints. Lack of information about benefits of inclusion, function of social interac-tions.	Classroom struc-ture that is con-ducive to social interaction. Good communication between school and parents and family of student with disability.	Build interaction into lessons; infor-mational meetings to foster communi-cation.	General and spe-cial educators and paraprofessional observe interaction and seek feedback from parents and peers.

WHAT ARE PROGRAM OPTIONS?

Early Intervention and Preschool Years

Sevick School in El Cajon, California, is a good example of best practices at work for preschool students with physical disabilities. The five major components of the Sevick pro-gram are inclusion, parent participation, implementation of the M.O.V.E. curriculum, inter-agency collaboration, and technical assistance.

BOX 12–7   MAKING A DIFFERENCE

Cathy Schmitz is both a registered nurse and a credentialed health teacher. Although employed by Rommel's school district to oversee a wide variety of health-related services for a fairly large number of students, she keys in on Rommel. The reasons she does so are not hard to understand.

Rommel is bright—so bright that he is in the gifted and talented program. That alone does not mean he necessarily will get Cathy's special attention. It does mean, however, that Rommel tells people what he needs and wants and how they can assist him. Rommel is an expert on himself. Cathy knows that and honors it.

Rommel is complex—and not just because he faces emergencies that require CPR techniques and the hurried administration of oxygen. On a daily basis, Rommel needs assistance to maintain his health and accommodations so he can be included in the academic program.

Rommel is at risk. The sudden interruption of his breathing is life-threatening. So Cathy has to make sure that all staff involved with him knows exactly what to do if he needs emergency help.

And Rommel and his family are endearing. They respond in kind, says Cathy, to each and every effort made by anyone who tries to help Rommel and them. That kind of reciprocity, coupled with her deep dedication to Rommel and her commitment to do her best day by day, make it easy for Cathy to become very loyal to them.

"When you work closely with a family over many years and get to know them well, it is only natural to get attached to them. That's just basic human nature . . . to care so much for those who are working well to achieve a common goal and who care so much about what you do for them."

And, Cathy adds, when you care for daily intimate needs that Rommel has, breathing, feeding, resting, and toileting, as well as his academic needs, it is nearly impossible to not go the extra mile for Rommel.

Thus, although school policy requires a student to be hospitalized or ill at home for two consecutive weeks before becoming entitled to tutoring from the school district, school staff do not feel restrained by that policy. Whenever Rommel is hospitalized or kept home because of health reasons, most often his one-on-one nurse will bring his assignments to him, making the daily trip from school to home just so Rommel can stay abreast of his work . . . and undoubtedly making it so that each has the psychic rewards of working with such a fine young man.

"Everyone works more hours and more effectively when Rommel has a special need," Cathy explains. "We double our focus. We think we are focused on each student all the time, but the fact is that, when it is absolutely necessary to rise to a challenge, we do more and become much more effective in doing it."

The real challenge, Cathy adds, is not the emergency situation, although she does not minimize it. The real challenge is putting into place, and maintaining, a regular program to accommodate and maintain Rommel's health, keep him included in school, and respond to his well-articulated sense of who he is.

Hand-picking his teachers, discussing the appropriateness of his modifications, making sure that his homework is brought to him if he misses school, and checking in regularly with him and his parents—those are the kind of actions that make a difference. And, of course, being the careful, thoughtful, professional, and caring majordomo—Rommel's reliable ally and conductor of so many different players.

Inclusion.   Sevick School began by creating an inclusive environment for preschoolers with disabilities in a unique way: it opened its special education preschool classes to the entire community, practicing reverse mainstreaming. It then connected those programs with the existing preschool classes and encouraged teachers to team-teach (J. Gwinnup, personal communication, June 27, 1993).

Parent Participation.   Parents volunteer in the preschool classroom and attend parent discussion groups, bringing together families of students with and without disabilities.

The M.O.V.E. Curriculum.   A resource specialist for students with physical disabilities conducts staff development sessions for teachers (using the M.O.V.E. curriculum described in the "Curriculum" section), demonstrates the equipment that the Rifton Company designed for the school, and provides teachers with direct assistance.

Interagency Collaboration. A Sevick resource teacher for students with physical disabilities gives presentations to parent groups at the Exceptional Family Resource Center on how parents can improve their children's mobility. The Exceptional Family Resource Center, in turn, offers support groups for parents, for fathers only, and for families who speak only Spanish. Many of these groups meet at Sevick. In addition, Sevick School and the California Children's Services provide health clinics for families of students with physical disabilities. Approximately twice a year, each student's multidisciplinary team of doctors, therapists, resource teacher, teacher, and parents meets to discuss topics such as future surgeries, adaptive equipment needs, and other medical and educational concerns.

Technical Assistance. The itinerant resource specialist for children with physical disabilities provides technical assistance for students, their families, and teachers. With the students, she assesses and increases their mobility skills. In the classroom, she assists teachers in positioning children correctly so that they are in a position to participate in all activities. She also provides supplies, such as light pressure switches, which can activate battery or electrically operated toys and appliances, adaptive crayons, and nonslip surfaces; and she gives teachers tips on where to find inexpensive adaptations and on how parents and teachers can inexpensively adapt supplies for their children's use (J. Gwinnup, personal communication, June 27, 1993).

Elementary Years

The metropolitan school district in Madison, Wisconsin, recognizes that very young students with physical disabilities generally are not ready to handle all of their physical needs and do not yet have the skills that will enable them to succeed in general education classes. The district therefore has designed a system that offers varying support levels for students with physical disabilities using both itinerant teachers and resource centers.

Itinerant Teachers. Students who have relatively slight physical needs or who have learned skills that enable them to attend the regular elementary schools in their own neighborhoods receive help from itinerant resource teachers. These teachers support students directly and consult with their general education teachers up to three hours per week.

The Resource Center Concept. Resource centers serve students who have academic needs that are greater than an itinerant teacher can support. Resource centers are located in two regular elementary schools, so they are not necessarily the home schools for all students who have physical disabilities.

Each school is staffed like other elementary schools but also has one full-time resource teacher for students with physical disabilities, an on-site nurse, on-site therapists, and more paraprofessional assistance than any of the other elementary schools. At each school, students with physical disabilities generally are included in classes with their peers without disabilities but also receive some instruction apart from their classmates. Because the resource teacher is always present, she is able to support the general education staff more effectively.

Although the resource center approach is not fully inclusive, its goal is inclusion. It seeks to provide students at the elementary level with the skills they need to be more responsible for themselves—and consequently to be more independent and need a lower level of special education. Typically, students receive more intensive service in kindergarten and first grade. As they get older, they become better able to manage for themselves physically and intellectually, and their peers become more able to assist them with tasks such as managing their books and handling school materials. When the students leave for middle school, they may still need an assistant; but usually by this time they are intellectually more independent and can take some responsibility for directing the assistant. If a child at the middle or high school level needs more resources than the itinerant teacher can provide, the special education team at that school provides the extra support (D. Medearis, personal communication, June 2, 1993; M. Polancih, personal communication, June 12, 1993).

Middle and Secondary Years

Is it possible for adults with a disability to make a difference in the lives of students with disabilities? To increase their self-determination, confidence, independent living skills, and community participation? To help them become more self-efficacious, where "self-efficacy" refers not to a person's skills but to one's own judgment of what one can do with the skills one has. The answer to each is "absolutely." Adults with disabilities are experts in disability because they themselves face roughly the same kinds of challenges as the students (Powers, Sowers, & Stevens, 1995).

In a community of 100,000 in the Pacific Northwest, four students with cerebral palsy and one with spina bifida were paired with five adult mentors who have cerebral palsy, multiple sclerosis, muscular dystrophy, or rheumatoid arthritis. One student was 12 years old, another 15, another 18, and two were 19. Only one of the students had any cognitive limitation (mild mental retardation). Their mentors were professionals in fields other than education (mental health counselor, attorney), executives (office manager), and creative artists (dancer/musician, writer/college advisor). They ranged in age from 27 to 51. Each lived independently.

The students and their mentors engaged in two one-on-one activities over a total of six months (for a total of twelve activities) and attended three two-hour conferences on disability issues (for a total of six conferences). In the individual activities, the mentors helped the students learn how to handle a challenging situation in the community. The situations involved accessibility, housing adaptations, managing personal care assistance, engaging in recreation and leisure activities, eating and drinking in public, riding the bus, finding jobs, and using public bathrooms.

The mentors also suggested how to solve the challenge, encouraged the student to ask questions about the challenge and even questions not related to the activity. The men-

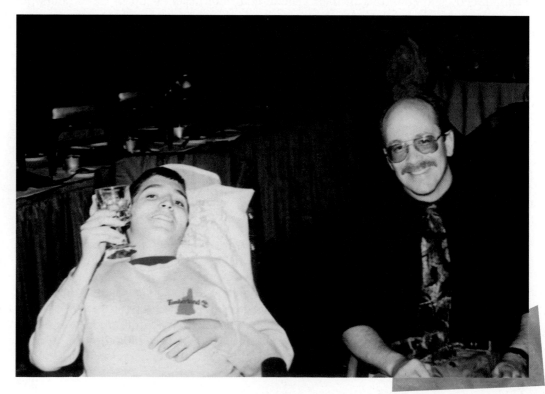

℘ *Students with physical disabilities can get information and inspiration from having an adult mentor who also has a physical disability. Photo courtesy of Laurie E. Powers, Oregon Health Sciences University.*

tors shared information about past disability challenges and emphasized the importance of making one's own decisions, being responsible about taking risks, and never giving up.

When students who had mentors were compared with students (of the same age and with the same disability) who did not have mentors, the results of the mentoring program were remarkable. Those who had mentors showed marked improvement in their disability-related self-efficacy, they demonstrated more knowledge of strategies to meet challenges, and their parents regarded their children as more informed and self-confident. In addition, they began to participate in the community to a much greater degree and in more activities than before they had mentors. They also initiated independent-living skills that they had not tried before (such as getting a telephone with a speaker system, riding a bicycle, advocating in school for greater disability accessibility). And they regarded their disabilities more positively and set higher postschool goals for themselves (such as going to college and living on their own).

The mentors were sources of information and, more importantly, inspiration. It's as though they were telling and showing the students: "I've been there, I've been like you, and now you can be like me."

❧ A successful mentor can say and demonstrate some key lessons: Play from your strengths, have great expectations, you are a full citizen.

Transitional and Postsecondary Years

At the postsecondary level, universities now provide the academic and other support services necessary to equalize educational opportunities for students with physical and other types of disabilities. One such pioneering program is located at the University of California at Berkeley (J. Baliff & C. Jay, personal communication, September 1, 1993) and is described in the following sections.

Promoting Personal Independence.   Preadmission advising is available on housing options, mobility systems, academic support services, sources of financial aid, state and federal benefits, and resources for personal care assistance.

The Residence Program.   The Disabled Students' Program offers assistance in finding accessible housing in residence halls, co-ops, or the community. In addition, for students who have quadriplegia and have lived at home or in nursing homes but are eager to live more independently, the Residence Program provides most students with the skills they need to use campus and community resources.

❧ The Disabled Students' Program at the University of California at Berkeley grew out of the self-advocacy of a group of students led by the late Ed Roberts. Ironically, Ed, who once was denied vocational rehabilitation services because he was regarded as too disabled to benefit from them, later became California's commissioner of vocational rehabilitation, an appointment that testified to his abilities and allowed him to demonstrate that he, like others with disabilities, can be full citizens.

VIDEO REFLECTIONS

MY CHILD

"Many of the 43 million Americans with physical disabilities have jobs, live on their own, even get married," ABC anchor Sam Donaldson says. "Which is all fine and good, it seems, until they decide to have children. . . ."

In this video several parents share their joy in parenting. "I am not a handicapped mom," one parent emphasizes. "I am a mom." Despite the love they feel, some of these parents struggle to maintain custody because they have trouble with the routine care of their child. If the child were born with a disability, programs and money would be available to help with the child's care. Because the child is born without a disability, no funds are available to support par-

ents who have disabilities. In fact, just the opposite happens. These parents must prove that they have the ability to care for their children physically and financially.

What do you think?   Do you think the parents in this video should be allowed to keep their children? Why or why not?

What would you think about people with disabilities becoming parents when their condition could be inherited by their children? What does your response say about your view of disability?

Do you believe society should provide assistance with childcare for parents with disabilities? Why or why not?

Attendant Referral Service.   The program offers a comprehensive and extensive attendant referral service, including a crosslisting of attendants and students so that both are able to obtain names and numbers and arrange for interviews. An attendant (usually a person of the same sex as the person with the disability) assists in such self-care matters as feeding, dressing, grooming, toileting, communicating, transportation, and operating assistive technology. The attendant service screens initial applicants and provides students with a list of qualified persons. Students are responsible, however, for interviewing, training, and discharging attendants as well as for negotiating hourly wage rates and payment procedures.

Special Training and Recreation Program.   The program arranges for students to work individually with recreation instructors to set up tailor-made recreational programs. Students choose from more than a hundred different classes, ranging from intramural basketball to recreational adventures such as rafting and bungee jumping.

Promoting Academic Independence.   The program assists students with registration, fee authorizations, class scheduling, and priority enrollment. It offers advocacy services to help students obtain services and benefits available from various local, state, and federal agencies. An accommodation letter explains the nature of a student's disability, how it affects learning, and what specific accommodations can be made related to the effects of the disability. Students meet early in the semester with professors to discuss those accommodations. Finally, the program tutors students on the strategies necessary for studying, test taking, paper writing, and disability management (J. Baliff & C. Jay, September 1, 1993).

Auxiliary Aides.   Note takers, test-taking assistants, readers, lab assistants, and mobility assistants provide help as appropriate for classes, research, field trips, reports, and homework required by academic courses. Students are allowed to choose which aide will assist them, but the aides' wages are paid by the program.

Career Planning.   The placement program helps students develop job experience while in school and find jobs after they graduate, including part-time, summer, and volunteer work as well as paid and unpaid internships. It also offers specialized consultation for employers and students in areas such as job accommodation, job restructuring, and assistive technology or rehabilitation (J. Baliff & C. Jay, September 1, 1993).

A VISION FOR THE FUTURE

Rommel Nanasca and his family have to adjust their vision as his physical disabilities change over time. There is practically nothing constant about his disabilities. Inexorably, they compel new visions and elicit new responses.

There are, however, constants in their life: Rommel's indominatable spirit; his razor-sharp mind; Lorna and Romy's unending and loving commitment to Rommel, Ariel, and Melanie; the support of Rommel's grandparents and uncles and aunts; and the loyalty and competence of an extraordinary team of professionals.

Who would have thought that a boy with so many and such extensive physical challenges would have been able to attend school with students who do not have disabilities?

What Would You Recommend . . .

1. To ensure, through specific action steps, that Rommel's family and the school-based team continue to have positive collaboration?

2. To provide Rommel with interaction with his classmates should he have to receive a good deal of his education at home?

3. To enable Rommel to increasingly use the assistance of the school nurse or other aides as he attends classes and takes tests?

SUMMARY

WHAT ARE PHYSICAL DISABILITIES?

- A physical disability, often referred to as an orthopedic impairment, is caused by congenital anomaly, disease, or other causes and adversely affects a student's mobility and educational performance.

- Cerebral palsy describes a group of disabling conditions that occur before the brain fully matures and that are characterized by nonprogressive and nonhereditary brain damage.

- Cerebral palsy is commonly characterized by spastic, athetoid, ataxic, or mixed movement patterns.

- Spina bifida is a malformation of the spinal cord. Its severity is dependent on both the extent of the malformation and its position on the spinal cord. It is often accompanied by hydrocephalus.

- Recent studies show that taking folic acid early in pregnancy can greatly reduce the incidence of spina bifida.

- Muscular dystrophy designates a group of nine hereditary muscle-destroying disorders.

- Spinal muscular atrophy, a member of the muscular dystrophy family, is an inherited progressive disease that attacks the motor nerve cells.

- Approximately 1.2 percent of all students receiving special education services have physical disabilities.

- Primary prevention of physical disabilities includes efforts to educate pregnant women about the risks involved from exposure to x-rays, drugs, alcohol, prescription and over-the-counter medications, and viruses and other infections.

- Other types of prevention include trying to reduce the effect of a disability or trying to prevent a related disability from occurring.

WHAT ARE EVALUATION PROCEDURES?

- Screening may take place before or directly after birth or at a later date when an infant fails to meet developmental milestones.

- A functional assessment is conducted in a student's natural environments and leads to a plan designed to overcome or compensate for discrepancies found between a student's actual performance and the performance expected from peers without disabilities.

- Occupational and physical therapists play pivotal roles in the assessment of motoric abilities.

WHAT AND HOW DO PROFESSIONALS TEACH?

- The curriculum for students with physical disabilities varies according to the students' individual strengths and needs.

- Mobility should be fostered as early as possible to ensure richness of experience. Advances in technology as well as curricular programs (such as M.O.V.E.) and programs that foster responsibility and mobility enable students to interact with people and objects that they naturally encounter.

- Some students rely on assistive technology, adaptive equipment, or medical technology assistance.

- Augmentative and alternative communication techniques and devices supplement whatever degree of naturally acquired speech students might have.

HOW IS PARTICIPATION ENCOURAGED?

- Inclusion challenges professionals to provide a balance between fully including students and providing them with the fundamental enabling skills they need to succeed.

- Collaboration involves the concerted, orchestrated effort of professionals, family, the student with a disability, peers, and community, who work together as a team to deliver services.

- Professionals in the field of physical disabilities include dually certified teachers, rehabilitation engineers, computer software specialists, occupational therapists, physical therapists, physicians, and nurses.

WHAT ARE PROGRAM OPTIONS?

- A model early intervention program such as Sevick School combines inclusion, parent participation, a curriculum to foster mobility, interagency collaboration, and technical assistance.

- One model used at the elementary level includes the use of itinerant teachers for students without a disability and the use of resource centers and resource teachers for students who have not yet learned the enabling skills necessary for a lower level of service.

- A program that facilitates a mentor relationship between adults with physical disabilities and students with physical disabilities can help increase students' self-determination, confidence, independent living skills, and community participation.

- A program for university students, such as the Disabled Students' Program at Berkeley, philosophically grounded in self-determination and self-advocacy, offers programs that assist students in gaining both personal and academic independence.

RESOURCES

BOOKS

Augmenting Basic Communication in Natural Contexts. (1996). By Jeane M. Johnson, Diane Baumgart, Edwin Helmstetter, & Chris Curry. Baltimore: Paul H. Brookes. This book offers practical techniques to establish a basic communication system for people with cognitive, motor, or sensory impairments regardless of age.

Caring for Children With Cerebral Palsy: A Team Approach. (1997). By John Paul Dormans & Louis Pellegrino. Baltimore: Brookes. Written by a team of interdisciplinary authors, this guide provides detailed information from a broad range of issues including diagnosis, etiology, feeding and nutrition, health management, assistive technology, and medical treatment.

Children and Youth Assisted by Medical Technology in Educational Settings: Guidelines for Care. (2nd ed.). (1997). Edited by Stephanie Porter, Marilynn Haynie, Timaree Birele, Terri H. Caldwell, & Judith Palfrey. Baltimore: Brookes. This extremely detailed guide provides practical guidelines and emergency techniques for working with students who use assistive medical technology. In addition to information on specific medical procedures, topics such as transportation, legal requirements, inclusion, and transition are also addressed.

Living With Spina Bifida: A Guide for Families and Professionals. (1997). By Adrian Sandler. Chapel Hill, NC: The University of North Carolina Press. This is an extremely thorough and readable reference book providing a comprehensive overview of spina bifida. Helpful illustrations and a thorough list of suggested readings are included.

Spinabilities: A Young Person's Guide to Spina Bifida. (1997). Edited by Marlene Lutkenhoff & Sonya Oppenheimer. Bethesda, MD: Woodbine House. This book advises teenagers and young adults on four broad topics: health and personal care, relationships, responsibilities of growing up, and wellness.

Coping with Being Physically Challenged (1991) and *Coping with a Physically Challenged Brother or Sister* (1992), by Linda Lee Ratto. New York: Rosen. Young adults describe their situations, followed by practical coping techniques and suggestions.

JOURNALS, MAGAZINES, AND CATALOGS

Closing The Gap. P.O. Box 68, Henderson, MN 56044. (507) 248-3294. Internet address: www.closingthegap.com. E-mail: info@closingthegap.com. Bimonthly newsletter about assistive computer technology for persons with disabilities. Includes section on new product reviews.

Exceptional Parent: Annual Technology and Products-Services Issue: Resource Guide. (January issue). P.O. Box 3000, Denville, NJ 07834. To order resource guide: (800) 535-1910. For subscription information: (800) 562-1973. Once-a-year issue provides straightforward information on assistive technology, products, and services.

The Networker. United Cerebral Palsy Associations, 330 W. 34th St., New York, NY 10001. (212) 947-5770. Published quarterly to provide affiliate staff, volunteers, and others with a way of exchanging information on best practices and resources.

New Mobility. Mirimar Communications, Inc., 23815 Stuart Ranch Road, Malibu, CA 90265. (800) 543-4116. Internet address: www.newmobility.com. E-mail: miriam@mirimar.com. Monthly magazine with a variety of informational articles relating to mobility.

MULTIMEDIA

The following videos are available at rental and retail stores:
My Left Foot. (1989, R, Ireland, color, 103 minutes). Excellent portrayal of Christy Brown, whose cerebral palsy leaves him with movement only in his left foot.

Passion Fish. (1992, R, U.S., color, 134 minutes). With the help of a young nurse, a TV soap opera actress learns to accept a disability after an accident.

The Waterdance. (1992, R, U.S., color, 106 minutes). A young novelist becomes paraplegic after an accident and restructures his life in a rehabilitation center.

ON-LINE INFORMATION AND OTHER USEFUL DATABASES

ABLE.NET. Internet address: ablenet.sdsu.edu/alblenet.html. E-mail: webmaster@interwork.sdsu.edu. Provides networking among interested students, people with disabilities, and professionals.

Assistive Technology Resource Alliance. Internet address: www2.atra.com/atra. E-mail: kweaver@atra.com. Links assistive technology product developers and entrepreneurs with technologists, investors, policy makers, and consumers.

Discover Technology. Internet address: discovertechnology.com. Provides a list of links, art, information, and adaptive software information.

National Spinal Cord Injury Hotline, Inc. Internet address: members.aol.com/SCIHOTLINE. E-mail: SCIHOTLINE@aol.com. (800) 526-3456. A nonprofit information and referral service for people who have sustained a traumatic spinal cord injury resulting in paralysis, members of their families, and health care providers.

ORGANIZATIONS

Muscular Dystrophy Association. 3300 East Sunrise Drive, Tucson, AZ 85718. (520) 529-2000. Internet address: mdausa.org. E-mail: mda@mdausa.org. A voluntary health agency, composed of scientists and concerned citizens, aimed at conquering neuromuscular diseases.

National Multiple Sclerosis Society. 733 Third Avenue, New York, NY 10017. (800) FIGHT-MS. Internet address: www.nmss.org. E-mail: info@nmss.org. A voluntary multiple sclerosis organization dedicated to ending the devastating effects of multiple sclerosis.

Spina Bifida Association of America. 4590 MacArthur Boulevard NW, Suite 250, Washington, DC 20007. (202) 944-3285. Internet address: www.sbaa.org. E-mail: sbaa@sbaa.org. A national association working on behalf of persons with spina bifida, their families, and medical professionals to address education, prevention, research, and social issues.

United Cerebral Palsy Associations. 330 W. 34th Street, New York, NY 10001. (212) 947-5770. A nationwide network of approximately 180 state and local voluntary agencies that provide services, conduct public and professional education programs, and support research in cerebral palsy.

CHAPTER 13

TRAUMATIC BRAIN INJURY

Educating
Jimmie Eagle McVay

Twelve-year-old Jimmie explains what happened on a day that changed his life forever:

"My brain got hurt. Now I have to think harder to learn things. Sometimes I still get scared when I remember getting hit in the accident."

Jimmie, then eight years old, was walking from school to his home on the Mohawk reservation. A drunk driver hit Jimmie at high speed and threw his body more than fifty feet in the air onto a stone wall. Another motorist, who notified the local ambulance service, found Jimmie approximately one hour later.

After a two-hour ambulance transport to the nearest community medical center, an emergency team airlifted Jimmie to a level 1 trauma center. This delay in available emergency medical treatment detrimentally affected Jimmie's recovery, causing massive brain swelling and blood loss. After more than three hours of intensive surgery to stop the bleeding in his brain, Jimmie entered the pediatric intensive care unit. He had sustained a serious traumatic brain injury, and his prognosis was guarded at best.

But Jimmie fought to live. Over the next five weeks, a medical team stabilized him, monitored him for intracranial pressure, and operated two additional times to remove blood from his swollen and badly bruised brain. Then a medical team moved Jimmie from pediatric intensive care to a rehabilitation facility.

At that facility, Jimmie received therapy and specialized nursing care for his brain injury. A team of therapists, nurses, and physicians worked with him on his cognitive functioning, motor responses, and continued wellness. Within two weeks, Jimmie began to communicate, and by week six, he stood independently. He had progressed well.

Jimmie's mother, brother, and sister already faced many challenges as a result of unemployment. But none of those challenges were as great as those they now faced resulting from Jimmie's injury. Agnes Eagle, his mother, felt unprepared for Jimmie's long rehabilitation:

"At the hospital, we thought once he woke up from the coma, he would be okay. He wasn't."

Agnes arranged for her other two children to stay with their aunt so she could remain at the hospital and rehabilitation facility with Jimmie. She quietly observed her son's care, standing in the background. However, she thanked medical personnel for their care of her son. When she was alone with Jimmie, she encouraged him and helped him exercise. Agnes did voice her concerns about medications to medical personnel, though. She was careful to ask questions about what the medications were for, possible side effects, and how long Jimmie would need them.

Agnes remarked to medical personnel during Jimmie's rehabilitation:

When he was first brought to the emergency room, I prayed that he would live, even though the doctors said he might die. Then I was told that he might never wake up, but he did—slowly—but he did. We did not know if he would ever walk or talk again, but now he can walk and he seems to be understanding more every week. I just hope and pray that someday he will be okay. For now I am just happy that I have my Jimmie. But I am afraid that when we go home, who will help us?

In this chapter, you will read about some of the people who helped Jimmie and his family when he left the rehabilitation facility. His transition from rehab to school would require extensive collaboration between personnel at both facilities. Jimmie had changed dramatically from the "B" student he was before the accident. Ongoing monitoring of his cognitive, academic, physical, and social/behavioral functioning continues to be essential.

As you will see, extended family, especially Jimmie's grandfather and aunts, as well as the Mohawk tribe would provide invaluable support for Jimmie, his siblings, and mother. Furthermore, cultural differences obliged all the important people in Jimmie's life to collaborate extensively. Most importantly, Jimmie and his family would learn to advocate for themselves.

What Do You Think?

1. How do the location and seriousness of Jimmie's brain injury affect his prognosis?

2. How can Jimmie, his family, school, and community be encouraged to accept the academic, social/emotional, physical, and behavioral changes resulting from his brain injury?

3. How can Jimmie's school provide appropriate services for him after he leaves the rehabilitation facility?

4. What can professionals do to demonstrate respect for Jimmie's Native American culture in his treatment and education?

5. What future issues are likely to be faced by Jimmie's mother, brother and sister, extended family, and tribe?

What Is Traumatic Brain Injury?

Once I Was

A boy, tall, slender,
Talented and diligent.
Notes to music
Rippled my mind,
Touched my fingers.
J.S. Bach could be heard on my lips
Like a bee hums
Or the wind whispers.
J.P. Rampal was there
In my imagination,
Leaving me the sounds
Of somebody going to France.
I was fourteen, then.
I played hockey, too:
Tough, I thought.
Now all I do is sleep
And write poetry
About yesterdays,
And when . . .

Peterson (1994)

"Brain injury can change your life forever."—Slogan of the Brain Injury Association

"To look into our hearts is not enough . . .," T. S. Eliot wrote, "One must look into the cerebral cortex." Eliot's quote emphasizes the brain's importance in determining who we are. A traumatic brain injury often shatters "the sense of 'I'" (Shobris, 1994). Because of the changes experienced by Jimmie, Hugh Peterson—the author of "Once I Was"—and others who have a traumatic brain injury, they must reestablish a sense of self.

A traumatic brain injury can cause dramatic changes in a person's intellectual, emotional, linguistic, social, and/or physical functioning. The extent of the disability may not be known for some time after the injury. Nevertheless, rehabilitation efforts frequently succeed in helping students with brain injuries dramatically improve quality of life. In some cases, they may even overcome the effects of the injury. Jimmie, for example, has regained many of his pre-accident skills, and his family, teachers, and friends have learned to accept and value the new person he has become.

Defining Traumatic Brain Injury

Students with **traumatic brain injury,** a brain injury caused by an *external physical force*, are served under a separate category by the Individuals with Disabilities Education Act (IDEA). The regulations define traumatic brain injury as:

> *an acquired injury to the brain caused by an external physical force, resulting in total or partial functional disability or psychosocial impairment, or both, that adversely affects a child's educational performance. The term applies to open or closed head injuries resulting in impairments in one or more areas, such as cognition; language; memory; attention; reasoning; abstract thinking; judgment; problem-solving; sensory, perceptual, and motor abilities; psychosocial behavior; physical functions; information processing; and speech. The term does not apply to brain injuries that are congenital or degenerative, or brain injuries induced by birth trauma. (34 C.F.R., Sec. 300.7[6][12])*

Currently, two types of brain injury are not served under the IDEA definition. One of those, *anoxia*, results when a person loses oxygen to the brain from an illness or an accident such as stroke, choking, or drowning. Students can also suffer brain damage from diseases such as meningitis or tumors. Because neither anoxia nor disease is considered an external physical force as specified by the IDEA definition, students with these causes of brain injuries are served under the category of *other health impairments* (see Chapter 11).

The rehabilitation needs of students with brain injury from anoxia or disease are similar to those with brain injuries caused by external physical forces. Therefore, many professionals believe that these students should also be served under the IDEA category of traumatic brain injury. Savage (1994) comments, "The brain is still the brain after all. Whether it is injured by an 'explosion' from the outside or an 'implosion' from the inside is irrelevant when it comes to identifying the needs of the child."

The National Head Injury Foundation (now the Brain Injury Association) Pediatric Task Force (Savage, 1994) recommended that the federal definition be amended to rename the category **acquired brain injury** and include injuries caused by internal occurrences such as anoxia (see Chapter 8) and disease as well as by external physical forces. However, the term would still not include brain injuries that are **congenital** or those induced by birth trauma. These latter two causes do not disrupt the person's identity as acquired injuries do; therefore, service needs differ. At the time this chapter was written, the change in the federal definition was still forthcoming (see Figure 13–1).

Because IDEA refers to the condition as traumatic brain injury, we use that term as the title of this chapter. However, most of what you read in this chapter applies to any type of brain injury.

Types of Traumatic Brain Injury.

Under IDEA, a student can receive services for a traumatic brain injury for one of two types of head injuries: a closed head injury or an open head injury. Unfortunately, students with closed head injuries are sometimes undiagnosed or misdiagnosed.

Closed Head Injury. You probably remember from your science classes that "For every action, there is an opposite and equal reaction." An example of that principle occurs

---

A **traumatic brain injury** is caused by an external physical force, resulting in impaired functioning in one or more areas. Educational performance is adversely affected. The injury may be open or closed.

An **acquired brain injury** includes injuries caused by internal as well as external forces.

A **congenital condition** is present at birth but is not inherited.

FIGURE 13–1 *Types of brain injury: Continuum of possible brain injuries*

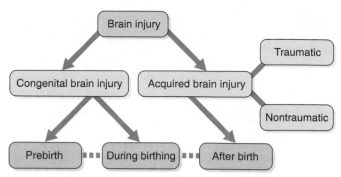

Note: From *Pediatric Traumatic Brain Injury: Proactive Interventions,* by J. L. Blosser and R. DePompei, 1994, San Diego, CA: Singular Press. Copyright 1994 by Singular Press. Reprinted with permission from Singular Publishing Group, Inc.

A **closed head injury** results when the brain whips back and forth during an accident, causing it to bounce off the inside of the skull.

A **postconcussional syndrome** refers to a mild closed head injury that may not show damage on medical tests but results in changes in personality or cognitive functioning.

when a person is jolted from behind, causing the brain to undulate. A **closed head injury** results from the brain's being whipped back and forth rapidly, gelatin-like, causing it to rub against and bounce off the rough, jagged skull interior. Bleeding and swelling frequently result (Neurotrauma Law Center, 1996).

This type of injury, often caused by a motor vehicle accident (see Figure 13–2), damages the neurofibers that are responsible for sending messages to all parts of the body. A closed head injury also places enormous stress on the *brain stem,* a relay station for sensations going to the brain and signals going from the brain to the rest of the body. The brain stem connects the brain to the spinal cord and is the center of "consciousness, alertness, and basic bodily functions" (Neurotrauma Law Center, 1996). Thus, a closed head injury can affect a person physically, emotionally, and cognitively.

Researchers have discovered that even a mild closed head injury, sometimes called **postconcussional syndrome** or *mild traumatic brain injury* (MTBI), can cause "serious and far-reaching impact on a person's ability to enjoy life and work and to earn a living" (Brain Injury Association of Connecticut, 1996). A whiplash, for example, with no striking of the head against an object or unconsciousness, may result in a mild head injury (Holliday, Lent, & Selden, 1996).

FIGURE 13–2 *Closed head injury accident: When the head smashes into a car windshield, momentum throws the brain against the inside of the skull. Brain damage often occurs in the frontal lobes (A) at the point of impact, the temporal lobes (B) as they jam against the skull: and at the junction of the frontal and temporal lobes (C). Large veins above the ear (D) may also tear, causing a subdural hematoma.*

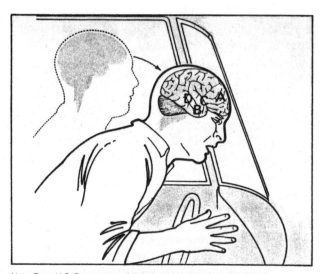

Note: From U.S. Department of Health and Human Services, (1984), *Head injury: Hope through research* Bethesda, MD: Author.

BOX 13-1 **MY VOICE**

LINDA MCLAUGHLIN

Before the accident, most academic skills came easily to my nine-year-old son Seth. But after his head injury, Seth's successful school performance changed dramatically. Following directions, being motivated to accomplish anything, and behaving appropriately in the classroom and with his peers were no longer second nature to him. His subsequent loss of self-esteem and his grief over what he could no longer do easily were extremely difficult for me to handle.

Seth's head injury was the result of his hitting a tree head on while sledding. Although Seth had been unconscious for five to six minutes, normal EEG readings and x-rays did not prepare us to look for any residual brain damage. A few weeks after the accident, however, I ran into Seth's teacher at the grocery store. She asked me if I had noticed any changes in Seth's behavior at home. I told her that I thought Seth was beginning to show signs that he was entering puberty. It was several weeks later that Seth's teacher made a formal call to me to describe behavior changes at school that were totally unlike the Seth that either of us had known. But most important, the results of an Iowa Basic Skills Test shouted the alarm.

The achievement test had been given to all fourth graders in early March, six weeks after the accident. When compared with his second-grade results, Seth's achievement scores dropped from the 99th percentile with a verbal IQ at the 87th percentile to barely 50th percentiles in all achievement areas with a verbal IQ percentile of 13.

On the basis of many different kinds of physical exams, a neurologist confirmed that Seth indeed took a blow to his head that apparently caused some damage. The result is that Seth has difficulty using certain cognitive thinking abilities and often lacks motivation. His ability to read on a twelfth-grade level was not affected. Thus, he had some holding skills that he acquired before the accident and could continue to use. The neurologist did tell us that during the next fifteen years Seth might reacquire many of his other previous abilities. Unfortunately, he will be finished with his formal schooling when that happens.

During Seth's fifth-grade year he became very disruptive at school. His teacher reported that many mornings he lay in front of the classroom door at school as classmates entered the room. And on other occasions he refused to participate in any classroom activities or discussions. He went from being one of the most popular students in the room to being jeered at by classmates. He often came home crying because old friends told him he was stupid. His grades fell from all As to Cs.

Seth's interpretation of the neurologist's exam was that his "brain was half dead." And for several months he was convinced that he could no longer do anything well. Actually, he did find things difficult. He no longer wrote using complex sentences; and to understand any mathematical concept, he had to have it presented with very concrete materials.

It has been several years now since the accident. Seth's wonderful ability to understand very subtle humor has returned. He practices much more appropriate behavior in school, and he is beginning to like himself again. He still doesn't do much unless he is told what, when, and how, but we love him just the same. And although I want people to be aware that Seth has a disability to overcome, I am quite protective in making sure that teachers and others relate their great expectations to Seth, affirming to him that he is whole and bright and has every reason to expect great things for himself.

Linda McLaughlin
Seth's mother

Seth's story is an example. He was nine when he sledded into a tree. Although he was unconscious for a few minutes after his accident, Seth's electroencephalogram (EEG), which graphs electrical activity of the brain, did not reveal any brain damage. In Box 13-1, Linda McLaughlin, Seth's mother, talks about his postaccident changes in intellectual, social, and behavioral functioning and how he finally received a diagnosis of mild traumatic brain injury.

Like Seth, many individuals who feel dazed, have seemingly minor injuries, or have no medically detected symptoms immediately after an accident experience long-lasting symptoms. For as many as 10 percent of those who sustain mild traumatic brain injury, symptoms can last a lifetime (Blosser & DePompei, 1994). Students with mild traumatic brain injury may have problems with (a) memory; (b) learning new information (although preinjury learning is often unaffected); (c) attention and concentration; (d) information

Physicians often use two other procedures in addition to EEGs to diagnose brain injury. Computerized tomography scans provide a computerized series of x-rays of the brain, and positron emission therapy reveals chemical activity in the brain.

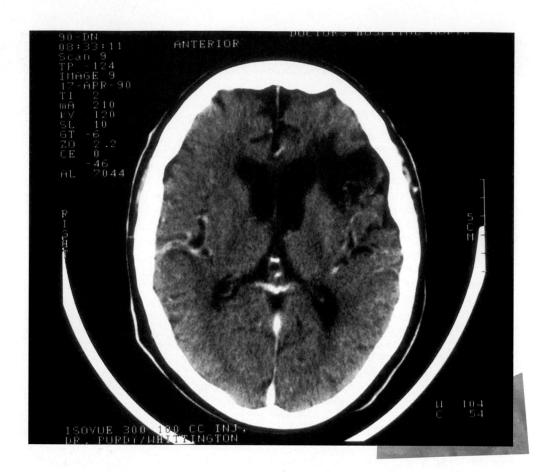

❧ *Computerized tomography helps physicians to locate which areas of the brain have been affected by a traumatic brain injury.*

FIGURE 13–3 *Symptoms of mild head injury*

- Becomes restless or fussy
- Doesn't pay attention
- Forgets things
- Gets mixed up about time and places
- Takes longer to get things done
- Doesn't act the same
- Acts without thinking
- Becomes easily upset
- Loses his or her temper a lot
- Tires easily or needs extra sleep
- Doesn't see or hear as well
- Drops things or trips a lot
- Develops problems with words or sentences
- Has a harder time learning

Note: From *When Your Child Goes Home After Being Examined for Head Injury in an Emergency Department,* by May Institute Center for Education and Neurorehabilitation, n.d., Randolph, MA: May Institute Center for Education and Neurorehabilitation. Copyright by May Institute Center for Education and Neurorehabilitation. Reprinted with permission.

FIGURE 13–4 *Areas of the brain and related general functions*

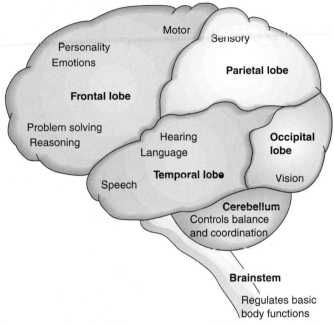

Note: From *Missouri Head Injury Guide for Survivors, Families, and Caregivers*, by Missouri Head Injury Foundation, 1991, Jefferson City, State of Missouri. Copyright 1991 by State of Missouri. Reprinted with permission.

processing speed and capacity; (e) executive functions such as planning and establishing priorities; and (f) disruptions to emotional centers of the brain (Levin & Eisenberg, 1990). Yet, currently available medical technology often discloses no evidence of brain damage.

A teacher was the first person to alert Linda McLaughlin that Seth's behavior and cognitive changes were more than the normal changes that often occur at puberty. If you have a student with a recent head injury, even if the injury did not appear to be serious, watch for any changes in behavior or academic functioning. Conversely, if you note changes in any student like those described in Figure 13-3, inquire whether the student has recently injured her head.

Open Head Injury.   An **open head injury** results from an insult to a specific area or focal point of the brain, such as might be caused by a gunshot wound or a blow to the head. Because different lobes or areas of the brain are responsible for specific functions (see Figure 13-4), an open head injury generally affects only those functions controlled by the injured part of the brain.

For example, if a student's open head injury has affected the part of the brain responsible for speech, the student may have a difficult time speaking. However, he might not have any problems writing what he wants to say on a piece of paper.

In some cases, a student can receive both an open and a closed head injury. Jimmie, for example, received a closed head injury when the car hit him and an open head injury when he struck the wall.

Relationship of Brain Injury to Other Disabilities

Because students with brain injury differ in onset, complexity, and recovery (Savage, 1991) from students with other disabilities, their planning and service needs are unique. The difference in onset occurs because a student with a brain injury generally has a normal developmental period until the injury. Furthermore, in most cases, not all skills are affected; the student has holding (intact) skills. This factor can cause even greater discrepancies among skills than those experienced by students with learning disabilities.

Do you remember sustaining a mild or more severe head injury as a child? What were the results?

An **open head injury** results when a specific area or focal point of the brain is injured. A gunshot wound would cause an open head injury. The types of changes in personality or cognitive functioning depend on the area of the brain affected.

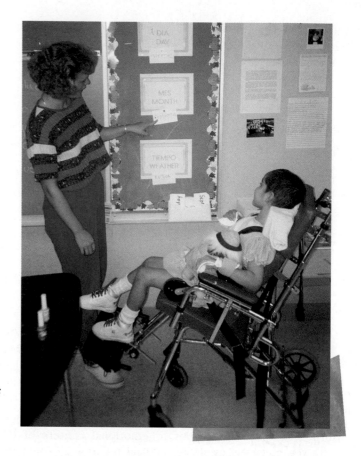

⚬ *Regaining language skills that have been lost after a traumatic brain injury is even more challenging when the student is bilingual.*

Students with traumatic brain injury also differ in the complexity of their disability. Because their condition may affect them in so many areas, they can share characteristics with students from categories such as speech and language impairments, physical disabilities, and health impairments as well as learning disabilities, mental retardation, or emotional and behavioral disorders. You can see why their rehabilitation programs must address each of their diverse needs.

The prognosis for students with traumatic brain injury also differs from students with other disabilities. Students with traumatic brain injury often experience significant improvement in skills as the injury heals or the brain learns to bypass the damaged area. Improvements are often particularly rapid during the early stages following the injury (UW Rehabilitation Medicine, 1995).

Describing the Characteristics

Students with brain injuries vary widely in their characteristics, but some physical, cognitive, linguistic, and behavioral changes among those with acquired injuries from disease or accident are common. As you read about these changes, keep in mind that a student in your class will probably not exhibit all and may exhibit only a few of these changes. The number and magnitude of changes will vary according to the site and extent of injury, the length of time the student was in a coma, and the student's maturational stage at the time of the injury (Allison, 1992a; Urbanczyk & Savage, 1995; UW Rehabilitation Medicine, 1996; Walker, 1993). Some key points to remember about these changes are listed in Figure 13-5.

Physical Changes. The extent of physical changes can range from nonexistent (Seth) to moderate (Jimmie) to severe. In 20 percent of traumatic brain injuries, the student experiences seizures, which often decrease or disappear with the passage of time

FIGURE 13–5 *Key points about brain injury characteristics*

- Each student with [brain injury] has a unique pattern of abilities and deficits.

- Initial physical effects of injury often resolve quickly. Long-term cognitive, behavioral, and sensorimotor difficulties are often present.

- Memory, attention, and executive function difficulties are common.

- Slowed processing of information is common.

- Pre-injury skills may be preserved but are not predictive of new learning abilities.

- Psychosocial problems are complex and often the most debilitating.

- The relationships among cognitive, communication, social, behavioral, and physical difficulties have significant and complicating effects on the student's school success.

Note: From *Traumatic Brain Injury: A Guidebook for Educators,* by James DeLorenzo and Patricia Geary, State University of New York, 1995, Albany: New York State Department of Education, Office of Special Education Services. Copyright 1995 by New York State. Reprinted with permission.

(Forness & Kavale, 1993). Sometimes the injury causes a temporary or permanent physical disability such as spasticity or paralysis (The Perspectives Network, 1997) (see Chapter 12 for more information about physical disabilities). The student may also experience growth-related problems, depending on the site of the injury (Allison, 1992a). The brain injury may also cause sleep disorders or photosensitivity (The Perspectives Network, 1995).

More common than spasticity or paralysis are coordination problems, physical weakness, and fatigue (State University of New York, 1995). For students who were previously athletic, these changes can be especially frustrating. Fortunately, however, coordination and physical strength usually improve as the brain heals and the student undergoes rehabilitation. Fatigue often lingers, though. Agnes reports that Jimmie still has trouble getting up in the morning, and Jimmie says that he gets tired in the afternoon.

Jimmie, a skilled athlete, played baseball and soccer before he was hit by a drunk driver. The accident damaged the area of the brain that is associated with hand–eye coordination. Jimmie will probably never be able to hit a ball with a bat. However, because his coordination from the waist down is unaffected, he continues to play soccer for his school team.

Another common physical change is headaches (State University of New York, 1995). Almost one-third of students with traumatic brain injury report headaches during the first year after the injury (Tyler, 1990). The student with brain injury who has frequent headaches will need schedule and work adjustments as well as opportunities to rest and take medications. Jimmie's individualized education program (IEP) calls for him to take a nap during the school day.

Some students with brain injury also have vision or hearing impairments. They may experience adverse changes in their senses of taste, touch, and smell (State University of New York, 1995). Others may have perceptual impairments, which means that their vision and hearing are within normal limits with correction but that they have difficulty interpreting the information they receive through their senses. Jimmie, a case in point, does not have trouble seeing, but he does have trouble with visual perception as a result of damage to his occipital lobe. This sometimes causes problems for him on the soccer field because he has difficulty orienting himself visually in relation to the other players and the soccer ball.

For most students with traumatic brain injury, physical changes are temporary or compensated for through rehabilitation. Jimmie is active physically. Besides playing soccer, his favorite activities include hiking in the woods, mastering Nintendo, riding bikes, and building forts.

However, one problem sometimes occurs as the physical evidence of a brain injury heals. Others also expect that the student has healed in all other areas. Novack and

"I wish I had a glass head," Jimmie remarked recently. "Then people could see how my brain is hurt."

Caldwell (n.d.) remind professionals that once the initial medical and physical challenges are overcome, "over the long run traumatic brain injury becomes a psychological, sociological, and *educational* problem."

Cognitive Changes.   The cognitive changes associated with a traumatic brain injury can be obvious or subtle. Some common changes include attention and concentration deficits, long- or short-term memory limitations, difficulty with reasoning and problem solving, slowed processing, and problems with academic skills that were satisfactory before the injury (Forness & Kavale, 1993; State University of New York, 1995; Tyler, 1990; Wood, 1988). The student might also exhibit poor judgment and lack of foresight (Tyler, 1989) and find planning and sequencing difficult (State University of New York, 1995). Teachers need to be especially aware of how these cognitive changes affect educational performance. Jimmie, for example, was a "B" student pretrauma. Now he says, "I wish I could read better and remember my spelling words better."

Seth experienced a similar skill divergence but in different areas than Jimmie. You will recall that Seth's mother, Linda, described how his achievement scores and academic grades dropped considerably. Over time, many of Seth's abilities have returned. However, test taking and, in particular, essay tests, still challenge him. In a test-taking situation, organizing information to identify salient points, it is difficult for him to write. To overcome this, while studying for a test, Seth dictates his responses into a tape recorder. Then he "replays" in his head the thoughts he remembers from listening to his tape, bypassing the process of thinking, then mentally organizing, then writing.

Seth's story points out another dilemma for students with traumatic brain injury. Although it took several years for Seth's cognitive skills to return, Seth experienced a period of time when he fell behind in basic academic skills. Thus, not only did he have to keep up with new information presented to him in general classrooms, but he also needed to catch up on skills he missed when he had cognitive processing limitations. His IEP had to reflect these needs.

Linguistic Changes.   Many students with brain injuries regain most of their speech and language facility, especially expressive language (Ylvisaker, Szekeres, Haarbauer-Krupa, Urbanczyk, & Feeney, 1994). Thus, they give the appearance of being able to communicate well. However, their problems with receptive and written language communication are often long-term impairments (Tyler, 1990). Learning new concepts and vocabulary may also prove challenging (Ylvisaker, Szekeres, Haarbauer-Krupa, et al., 1994).

Sometimes students with traumatic brain injury experience **aphasia,** an inability to use language appropriately, for a period of time after the injury (Marquardt et al., 1988). More commonly, the students may have difficulty finding the words they want to say, or their speech may be slow (State University of New York, 1995). Imagine the frustration these children can experience when called on in class. Other students have problems understanding language. Students with this type of problem may find following instructions difficult (Ylvisaker, Szekeres, Haarbauer-Krupa, et al., 1994).

Because of problems with understanding or using language, the student "may revert to communicating in a more immature fashion, using phrases and gestures which might have been more appropriate for a younger age" (Novack & Caldwell, n.d.). Along with problems caused by immature language, the student may find socialization difficult because of an inability to perceive voice inflections and nonverbal cues to interpret another person's communication signals (Ylvisaker, Szekeres, Haarbauer-Krupa, et al., 1994).

Social, Behavioral, and Personality Changes.   Personality and behavioral changes are common in students with traumatic brain injury. They are struggling with a new identity that often differs dramatically from the one they previously had (Pollack, 1994; Tucker

---

Another cognitive processing change that can occur is *anosognosia.* Students who have this condition are unable to recognize strengths and deficits. Thus, they overestimate or underestimate their abilities and/or deny they have changed as a result of the injury (Altman, 1996).

Despite Seth's difficulty in catching up to grade level in some areas, his teachers did not retain him in the same grade. Why do you think retention is generally not advised for these students?

Aphasia describes an injury to certain areas of the brain that results in problems with speaking or total loss of speech. Possible causes are traumatic brain injury, lack of oxygen, stroke, or an illness that causes brain swelling.

A student with brain injury may comprehend less of what you say with increases in (a) rate of your speech, (b) the amount of information to be processed, (c) abstract language, (d) environmental interference (noise) (State University of New York, 1995).

& Colson, 1992). Their identity struggle can result in nonproductive self-concept (Ylvisaker, Szekeres, & Hartwick, 1994), which contributes to more social and behavioral challenges. In addition, they may become egocentric (self-centered) or try to deny the existence of the new identity created by the injury (Lezak & O'Brien, 1988).

Students may begin to respond emotionally in ways that differ from or are more extreme than their preinjury responses. These responses can include temper outbursts, euphoria, restlessness, irritability, anxiety, and fatigue (Forness & Kavale, 1993; Lezak & O'Brien, 1988; Tyler, 1990).

Agnes says that Jimmie "sometimes gets very sad." From 15 to 25 percent of brain injury survivors struggle with depression (Gardner, 1993). Along with low mood, students may manifest depression through agitation and be high risk for suicide. You will want to be aware of the symptoms of depression (see Chapter 5) and ensure that depressed students with brain injury receive therapy.

Behaviorally, students with brain injury often experience an inability to initiate tasks, which is sometimes inappropriately perceived as a lack of motivation or laziness (State University of New York, 1995). Students may also exhibit disinhibition (an inability to inhibit inappropriate behavioral responses) and poor self-monitoring skills (Tyler, 1990).

Students with brain injuries may also have poor coping and social skills (State University of New York, 1995). Mrs. Anderson, Jimmie's special education teacher, says he "is very social most of the time, but he is fearful of new situations. We practice and role play any new social situation/community activity."

Peers frequently find adapting to the student's behavioral changes difficult and may shun or tease the student, increasing the sense of social difference and isolation. You will recall that Seth's teacher said "he laid down in front of the classroom door first thing every morning." Seth did not seem to realize this was inappropriate behavior. He struggled to maintain friendships during this time.

As the brain heals, personality and behavioral changes often become less noticeable or disappear. Unfortunately, for some, the pain and frustration they experience while their brain is healing can result in long-term emotional and behavioral issues. Later in this chapter, you will learn about programs to help students overcome adverse personality and behavioral changes.

Prognosis. In the 1970s, 90 percent of people with brain injuries died; today at least 50 percent survive (Russo, 1991). Most of those who survive will have to cope with changes in their lives. As you have learned, some of those changes will be temporary, others long-lasting or permanent. Research (Jaffe cited in UW Rehabilitation Medicine, 1995) suggests that those with mild head injuries may have negligible effects and little change over a three-year period. Those with the most severe injuries show the highest initial deficits and highest improvement at one year. Generally, students with moderate and severe brain injury are "at risk for chronic intellectual, psychological, and academic deficits" (UW Rehabilitation Medicine, 1995). For full recovery, students must not only relearn pretrauma skills but must accelerate their acquisition of posttraumatic skills to catch up with peers, a feat that "requires extraordinary measures" (UW Rehabilitation Medicine, 1995).

Despite these trends, no generalizations can be made about outcomes for specific students with mild, moderate, and severe head injuries. As expected, sometimes students with severe injuries have adverse and long-lasting academic, social, and behavioral changes (Fletcher, Ewing-Cobbs, Miner, Levin, & Eisenberg, 1990). In other cases, these students do as well as many with mild or moderate injuries. In fact, some students with mild injuries have more detrimental and long-lasting changes than do students whose injuries are more severe (Savage, 1991).

Lifetime effects are present for 10 percent of those with mild injuries, 33 to 50 percent of those with moderate injuries (coma less than 24 hours), and 80 percent of those with severe injuries (coma more than 24 hours) (Blosser & DePompei, 1994b). Almost 10

"It must be like listening to the door of your past shut before the door to your future opens," commented one college student learning about brain injury (Pollack, 1994).

🐾 Seth has come a long way from this difficult period several years ago. He was recently elected president of his student council.

"A brain injury for a child is a lifetime experience, not merely a moment in time. . . . The injury that occurred when [a student] was seven years old . . . has everything to do with the challenges she now faces with thinking, feeling, and interacting at the age of 16" (Urbanczyk & Savage, 1995).

ABCNEWS

VIDEO
REFLECTIONS

BILLY GOLFUS

"I define who I am," Billy Golfus says. "I don't want someone who is a do-gooder to say, 'You are a handicapable person.' I don't want to be Mr. Disability. I want to make movies."

Billy Golfus sustained a traumatic brain injury that caused memory loss and partial paralysis. Since then, he has struggled to gain acceptance for his work as a filmmaker. His documentary "How Billy Broke His Head and Other Tales of Wonder" reveals the barriers society creates, limiting people with disabilities from living their lives fully. Billy Golfus emphasizes that people with disabilities "don't want pity, they just want to belong."

For more information about Billy Golfus's documentary, see the following web sites:

http://www.itvs.org/programs/WBBHH/ and http://www.daily.umn.edu/ae/Print/ISSUE21/afterhours.htlm.

What do you think? Have you ever felt that people with disabilities were "abusing the system"? Why or why not?

Why do you think Billy Golfus resents being called "handicapable"?

Do you know any people with disabilities who have suffered from society's misconceptions? What would have to happen for those misconceptions to change?

Do you feel sorry for people with disabilities? Why or why not? How do your feelings affect the way you treat them?

percent of those who survive a traumatic brain injury require long-term care; for some, life-support technology is required (Missouri Head Injury Foundation, 1991). Others such as Seth have minimal, if any, permanent loss of function. However, they may continue to experience subtle changes that affect them academically and personally (Missouri Head Injury Foundation, 1991).

What does it feel like to cope with these changes? Frederick Linge, a clinical psychologist, describes how his traumatic brain injury changed his life (see Box 13–2).

For many individuals with brain injury, even for those with permanent changes, the future can still be filled with hope and productivity. A sibling explains:

The Brain—is wider than the Sky—.
—Emily Dickinson

> *It's been six years since Fran's accident. The waiting was worth it. Fran continues to improve, but mentally and physically she will never be the same. My sister is becoming a new person, a strong young woman whom I am growing to respect. It does no good to look for the Fran of yesterday—she is no more. There is only the Fran of today. I've learned to understand that [individuals with brain injuries] are new people with their own unique needs and desires. It is our responsibility to understand and accept. (U.S. Department of Health and Human Services, 1984)*

Identifying the Causes of Traumatic Brain Injury

The term *brain injury* includes both congenital and acquired brain injuries. Figure 13–6 shows the causes of brain injuries. Congenital factors are discussed in Chapter 9. Nontraumatic brain injuries can be the result of anoxic injury, infections, stroke, tumor, metabolic disorder, or a toxic substance that is ingested or inhaled by the student (Blosser & DePompei, 1994b).

There are three major causes of the traumatic brain injuries that are currently included under the definition used in the Individuals with Disabilities Education Act (IDEA) (Russo, 1991) (see Figure 13–7). The first is accidents; 28 percent of all accidents result in head injuries (Medical Research and Training Center in Rehabilitation and Childhood Trauma, 1993). Half of all traumatic brain injuries are caused by motor vehicle accidents, and falls cause another 21 percent (Russo, 1991).

BOX 13-2 **MY VOICE**

FREDERICK LINGE

I have no memory of the automobile collision that took place one spring evening. . . . The diagnosis, after extensive testing, was damage to the left temporal lobe of the brain, several cranial nerves, and lesser damage to the right parietal area. The results of this damage were: lack of taste and smell, impaired short-term auditory and visual memory, lessened emotional control, and a greater tendency toward depression. . . .

I initially denied that I had any deficits at all, and it was only after the process of physical and psychological healing was well under way that I could accept that I had damage in some areas and begin to cope with it. For example, for weeks I denied that I had any loss of taste or smell, yet these senses were, in fact, totally absent for over a year and have only partially returned even two years later. . . . I never mentioned this loss to anyone while I was in the hospital, and it was only on the "safe ground" of home that I took the first steps toward admission of this deficit. This was to complain to my wife that food "tasted funny." I accused her of having added something strange to it; then I theorized that she had bought food that wasn't fresh or that had gone bad. Finally, when I was able to accompany her to the store, buy the food myself and be assured of its quality, and do the actual cooking myself, I had to admit that the fault was not in the food itself but in my own senses. The same process had to be gone through in other areas of deficiency, mental and physical, as I denied the deficits, came up against the hard edge of reality, and finally accepted them.

My short-term visual and auditory memory was severely impaired for a long time. Here again, I initially denied this and it was quite frustrating for my family to tell me things, which I would forget immediately, later on insisting vehemently that I had not been told anything in the first place. Again, I would meet a person for the first time and, seeing them an hour later, fail to recognize them. Or I would read a simple paragraph in the newspaper and by the time I got to the last sentence, have no recollection what the first one was.

Having been a highly self-controlled person all my life, I found myself with a hair-trigger temper and labile emotions. . . . A corollary of this deficit is the perseveration. . . . I realize that I have much more of a "one track mind" than I used to, and my thinking tends to proceed along linear lines. . . . When once embarked on a train of thought, I find it very hard to stop, deal with a side issue, and then return quickly to the original theme. Distractions, either external or internal, are hard to handle, and I find myself most comfortable in dealing with clearcut issues, where I can reason in a straightforward fashion. . . .

[The problems I faced] were greatly alleviated by my taking on gradually increasing responsibilities. . . . I had made a decision to resign from my job. . . . My director, backed by the rest of the staff. . . . refused to accept my resignation. . . . I found that I could handle the work, and thanks to her, retained my job. . . .

No matter how hard it is for family members, teachers, and others to let the . . . person "do it on his own" . . . no matter how much easier it would be to take pity on him and do it yourself . . . no matter how long it takes or how messy the job when done, . . . the [person with traumatic brain injury] must keep moving towards the fullest development of his potential.

No one really knows just how great an individual's potential is. In my case, I was given a slender chance of survival and it was thought that I would be a human vegetable if I did live. Instead, I am living a full and productive life and, in fact, can quite honestly say that I enjoy it more than I did before.

People close to me tell me that I am easier to live and work with, now that I am not the highly controlled person that I used to be. My emotions are more openly displayed and more accessible. . . . I have come through the crisis in my life with more respect for myself and more trust in others. My new openness of feeling makes it easier for me to communicate with others and for others to understand me. People know "where they stand" with me at all times and trust me more.

Furthermore, my blood pressure is amazingly low! My one-track mind seems to help me take each day as it comes without excessive worry and to enjoy the simple things of life in a way that I never did before. As well, I seem to be a more effective therapist, since I stick to the basic issues at hand and have more empathy with others than I did previously.

I do not bewail what I have lost because I am at peace with myself. I have fought a hard battle, given it my best, and won far more battles than I or anyone else ever thought I would.

Note: From *What does it feel like to be brain damaged?* Linge, F. R., *Canada's Mental Health, 28*(3) 1980. Reproduced with permission of the Minister of Public Works and Government Services Canada 1997.

Figure 13–6 *Causes of brain injury*

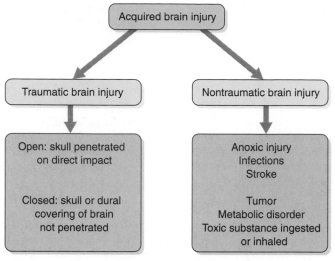

Note: From *Pediatric Traumatic Brain Injury: Proactive Interventions,* by J. L. Blosser and R. DePompei, 1994, San Diego, CA: Singular Press. Copyright 1994 by Singular Press. Reprinted with permission by Singular Publishing Group, Inc.

Statistics from the National Pediatric Trauma Registry suggest that taking safety precautions may significantly reduce the number of injuries and their severity (Medical Research and Training Center in Rehabilitation and Childhood Trauma, 1993):

- Sixty-three percent of all children involved in motor vehicle accidents were not wearing restraints.

- Ninety-nine percent of those injured in bicycle accidents were not wearing helmets.

- Seventy percent of those injured in motorcycle accidents did not wear helmets.

- Fifty-four percent of those injured while riding on all-terrain and recreational vehicles did not use restraints.

Sports and recreational injuries are the fourth major cause of traumatic brain injury (Russo, 1991). Activities such as diving, playing contact sports, or being hit by a ball cause 10 percent of traumatic brain injuries. Gambard, a sports physician, warns:

> *These injuries involving the head are definitely not benign and should never be dismissed as "Johnny just made a good hit, got his bell rung, and got right back into the action." Head trauma in football, especially if there is a rotation of the head upon impact, can lead to long-term degenerative neurologic consequences, including Parkinson's disease. (quoted in Tucker & Colson, 1992)*

Figure 13–7 *Causes of traumatic brain injury*

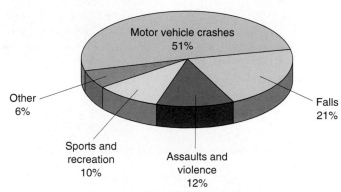

Note: From National Institute of Neurological Disorders and Stroke. (1995). *Interagency Head Injury Task Force Reports.* Bethesda, MD: National Institutes of Health.

🐦 *Safety measures such as wearing a bicycle helmet reduce the risk of traumatic brain injury.*

The third major cause of traumatic brain injury is violence. Gunshot wounds, assault, and child abuse (see Chapter 5 for a discussion of child abuse) cause 12 percent of these injuries (Russo, 1991). Child abuse accounts for the majority of infant head injuries (Russo, 1991), and more than 80 percent of deaths from head trauma in children under age two are the result of nonaccidental trauma (Savage, 1993). Furthermore, more than three-fourths of children under age three who are physically abused suffer a traumatic brain injury (Savage, 1993). One type of traumatic brain injury caused by child abuse is often difficult to diagnose:

> *It is a tragic oversight, but one that is not difficult to make. The infant simply appears to be sick, listless, and unresponsive. There is no external trauma, no evidence that the child has suffered a blow to the head or elsewhere. After meningitis and other infections are ruled out, the baby is sent home; the child's lethargy and irritability are attributed to [a cause] that will resolve on its own. But days or weeks later, the baby is brought to the emergency department with a more severe brain injury. And, sometimes, the child is dead. (Schroeder, 1993)*

A child who has *shaken-impact syndrome* is injured when the caretaker becomes frustrated and loses control. The caretaker shakes the child violently to try to make the child stop crying; and in 10 to 25 percent of the cases, the child dies (Schroeder, 1993). Children who do not die can suffer mild to severe brain damage. This type of closed head injury is often overlooked by physicians and is "a particularly insidious form of child abuse."

Identifying the Prevalence of Traumatic Brain Injury

Someone in the United States receives a head injury every fifteen seconds; every five minutes, one dies and one becomes permanently disabled (Brain Injury Association of Connecticut, 1996). Called the *silent epidemic* because it is so widespread and unrecognized, traumatic brain injury is the most common cause of death and disability in children and young adults (Missouri Head Injury Foundation, 1991). An estimated one million young people under the age of fifteen (220 of every 100,000) receive head injuries each year. Of those, approximately 165,000 have injuries severe enough to warrant hospitalization (Brain Injury Association of Connecticut, 1996). This suggests that approximately one of every five hundred children and adolescents will survive a head injury that requires hospitalization this year (Tyler, 1990).

Approximately 0.5 to 1 percent of the school-age population has sustained a recognized traumatic brain injury (Forness & Kavale, 1993). As many as 3 percent of adolescents may have sustained a brain injury that is serious enough to cause school problems (Forness & Kavale, 1993). A metropolitan school district will probably have about seventy-five students who sustain a traumatic brain injury each year, while a small community may have three or four students with this disability annually (Tucker & Colson, 1992).

Until IDEA passed into law, students with traumatic brain injury were not served under a separate category. Even now, many students are being served under some other category. Also, many students with mild traumatic brain injuries may be misidentified as having learning disabilities or behavior disorders. Thus, it is difficult to identify how many of these students are actually being served in the schools.

In the 1991–1992 school year, only 330 students were reportedly served as having a traumatic brain injury. Many of these students have been misclassified as having learning disabilities, emotional or behavioral disorders, or other health impairments. However, by the 1992–1993 school year (as more states began to classify students under the new category), 3,887 students received services (Bryan, 1993). This dramatic increase will probably continue as states develop and reevaluate their criteria for classifying these students. Identifying the prevalence of students with nontraumatic brain injuries is even more challenging because most are served under other health impairments or severe and multiple disabilities.

WHAT ARE EVALUATION PROCEDURES?

Recovery from a brain injury can be inconsistent. A student might take one step forward, two back, do nothing for a while, and then unexpectedly make a series of gains. A "plateau" is not evidence that functional improvement has ended. (Disability Services at the University of Minnesota, 1996)

This inconsistency makes assessing students with brain injuries challenging. Evaluation needs to be comprehensive and ongoing (Telzrow, 1991). You can see why multidisciplinary teams and IEP teams need to have strong collaborative relationships to increase the likelihood of positive long-term outcome for the student (Farmer, Clippard, Luehr-Wiemann, Wright, & Owings, 1996).

Determining the Presence of Traumatic Brain Injury

The multidisciplinary team first evaluated Jimmie in the hospital when he was stabilized and able to concentrate for a thirty-minute period. This information provided a baseline for interpreting other results. The team studied medical records to determine the injured areas of his brain and his prognosis for recovery. Before he left the rehabilitation facility, the team assessed him more extensively to prepare for his school reentry.

Although the team administered standardized intelligence and achievement tests to Jimmie, they interpreted the results cautiously. Intelligence tests are useful for identifying the student's recall of previously learned material, especially if records are available about the student's preinjury scores on intelligence tests. These tests do not, however, provide a global picture of the cognitive skills that are often affected by a brain injury. In some cases, the intelligence score lessens after the injury but will improve rapidly as the brain heals. In other cases, the student may have average or higher intelligence but still have problems processing information (Disability Services at the University of Minnesota, 1996; Farmer et al., 1996; Tyler & Myles, 1990).

Achievement test scores can be misleading as well (Telzrow, 1991). They indicate only what information the student has been able to recover since the injury but not the student's ability to learn new information (Tyler, 1990). Deficits in achievement may not be obvious until later, at a time when the student is unable to learn new information and begins to lag behind peers.

Jimmie also received neuropsychological assessment of his cognitive processing skills and continues to do so yearly. Mrs. Anderson, his special education teacher, said these scores were helpful for her, and she asked for assistance in interpreting them. The tests measured Jimmie's ability to attend, memorize and learn, perceive through his senses, use motor skills and language, problem solve, and apply abstract reasoning. An example of a neuropsychological test is the *Test of Problem Solving* (TOPS), by LinguiSystems. Available at both the elementary and secondary levels, the test determines how students like Jimmie can explain inferences, determine causes of events, answer negative why questions, determine solutions, and avoid problems. Neuropsychological testing is also used for planning cognitive retraining for students with brain injuries, which we discuss in more detail in the curriculum section of this chapter.

Additionally, the team asked people who knew Jimmie well to complete adaptive behavior (see Chapter 8) and behavior rating scales (see Chapter 5). A speech pathologist evaluated Jimmie's speech and language skills, and an occupational therapist and physical therapist assessed fine and gross motor skills. A psychologist determined his social, emotional, and behavioral strengths and needs. Functional assessment, including direct observation and curriculum-based assessment, helped the team determine Jimmie's least restrictive environment. Because Jimmie is Native American, interviews with his family were important to make sure the assessment process was nondiscriminatory.

The team then collaborated to determine Jimmie's need for special education and related services. Figure 13-8 lists the nondiscriminatory assessment process for students with brain injuries.

Because Jimmie is now in middle school, he also receives prevocational assessment during reevaluations.

Determining the Nature and Extent of Special Education and Related Services

The primary goal of programming for students with traumatic brain injury should always be "to ensure academic and social success" (Ylvisaker, Hartwick, & Stevens, 1991). However, this task is not always easy, as Larkin (1992) notes: "Children with brain injury are a difficult population for school systems. Their recovery is on a completely different rhythm and doesn't fit well with the set schedules and staffing of other special education programs." Thus, "this means that flexibility in programming is essential and that the IEP is an evolving program" (Clark, 1996).

The team needs to make sure that the IEP meets the student's needs, not the school's. The following example demonstrates how a student's needs can be overlooked (Savage, 1991): In Jamaica's case, "the IEP was written initially by the school's special educator to cover all the makeup work she had missed while she was in coma for six weeks and out of school for two months." Jamaica's needs could not have been met by such a plan. As she was making up the paperwork she missed, she would be losing time that would be better spent retraining the cognitive and academic skills she had lost.

The IEP team, which should include parents and the student when appropriate, should make at least five decisions for students with brain injuries (Savage, 1991):

1. What can the student do now?

2. What does the student need to do next?

3. What environmental or program changes does the student need in school?

4. Who will be responsible for the student's educational program?

5. How will the team determine if the educational program is working for the student?

FIGURE 13–8 *Nondiscriminatory assessment process for determining the presence of traumatic brain injury*

Nondiscriminatory Evaluation

Observation

Parents observe	Student receives a head injury from an accident, fall, sports injury, or act of violence.
Physician observes	The student has an open or closed head injury caused by an external physical force. The student may be in a coma.
Teacher observes	In the case of a mild head injury that might not have been treated by a physician, the teacher observes changes in behavior, personality, social functioning, cognitive skills, language, or motor skills.

Medical screening

Assessment measures	Findings that indicate need for further evaluation
Coma scale	In instances of moderate-to-severe head injury that induce comas, these scales provide some information about probable outcome.
Neurological exam	Neurologist examines student for indications of brain injury.
Scanning instruments	EEGs, CAT scans, MRIs and other technology determine extent of injury.

Prereferral

Prereferral typically is not used with these students, because the severity of the disability indicates a need for special education or related services.

Referral

Student with moderate-to-severe traumatic brain injuries should be referred while still in rehabilitation. Teachers should refer students with mild head injuries if they notice any changes in behavior, motor, cognitive, or language skills.

Nondiscriminatory evaluation procedures and standards

Assessment measures	Findings that suggest traumatic brain injury
Individualized intelligence test	Student often shows extreme peaks and valleys on subtests and retains some skills but not others. Scores often look very different than scores received on tests taken before the injury.
Individualized achievement tests	Student usually has peaks and valley in scores. The student often has holding skills in some areas while other skills are affected adversely by the injury.
Adaptive behavior scales	Student may have difficulty in social, self-care, household, and community skills as a result of the injury.
Cognitive processing tests	Student may have difficulty in areas of attention, memory, concentration, motivation, and perceptual integration.
Behavior, social skills, and personality measures	Student may demonstrate difficulty relating to others and behaving in socially appropriate ways. Personality may have changed from before the injury.
Anecdotal records	Student's cognitive, language, motor, and behavior skills appear to have changed from what was indicated in records before the accident.
Curriculum-based assessment	Student may have difficulty in areas of curriculum that were not problematic before the injury.
Direct observation	Student appears frustrated, has limited attention span, fatigues easily, or lacks motivation to perform academic tasks. Student may have difficulty relating appropriately to others. Skills often improve rapidly, especially during early post-injury stage.

The Evaluation Team determines that special education and related services are needed.

Appropriate Education

In the early stages of his recovery, Jimmie received a new IEP every two to three months (essential for students with brain injury due to dramatic changes in functioning during this time). At his first IEP meeting in the rehabilitation facility, the director, occupational therapist, physical therapist, and speech language pathologist from the facility as well as the school special education and general classroom teachers and Jimmie's mother and grandfather attended. Gradually, the rehabilitation facility served only in a consultation role as the school assumed more responsibility.

To answer the five questions just listed, each time Jimmie receives a new IEP, his team members review the information gathered during nondiscriminatory evaluation. They also look closely at his work products, anecdotal reports, and functional assessment that has been taking place in Jimmie's current setting.

Jimmie's goals and objectives take into consideration his current health, social, emotional, and behavioral needs in addition to academic needs, which include cognitive processing and thinking skills. The team writes in accommodations such as restructuring classroom areas and providing extra time, study guides, color aids, outlines, and books on tapes to help Jimmie function with students without disabilities in general classrooms. His IEP considers his needs as a whole person and includes out-of-school activities such as babysitting and taking care of his dog Buster.

Furthermore, the team concentrates on transitional issues in their IEP planning. "Change is hard for Jimmie," his mother, Agnes, says. "I wish he could have the same teacher every year." Change, however, is inevitable albeit challenging for people with brain injuries. The team plans carefully for grade transitions and other changes that will occur in Jimmie's life. Although he is only in the seventh grade, they must plan now toward his move to high school and ultimate need for vocational and independent living skills.

WHAT AND HOW DO PROFESSIONALS TEACH?

The multifaceted needs and skills of students with brain injury require that professionals from diverse fields work together closely to ensure their inclusion in the least restrictive environment. Considering the needs and preferences of the student and family during this collaboration is essential.

The key word as you are thinking about curriculum and methods for students with brain injury is *creativity*. Strategies you learn for working with students with other disabilities are often useful for this population as well. "Good insights," according to Blosser and DePompei (1994b), "can also be gained through experimentation, practice, and observation."

Curriculum

Effective teachers have several goals for their students with brain injury: helping them to (a) recover lost abilities, skills, and knowledge, (b) compensate for nonrecoverable skills, and (c) accept and adjust to the new person they are becoming (Ylvisaker, Szekeres, Hartwick, & Tworek, 1994). For many students with brain injury, cognitive retraining assists in accomplishing these goals. **Cognitive retraining** is the "treatment of cognitively-based communicative, behavioral, and psychosocial deficits" (Tyler, 1990). Actually, the word *retraining* can be misleading: The curriculum may not involve retraining lost functions so much as helping the student use residual cognitive and perceptual skills more efficiently (Prigatano, 1987).

There are three forms of cognitive retraining (Tyler, 1990). **Component training** provides intensive and systematic training of specific cognitive skills such as memory, attention, organization, and perceptual motor skills. For example, Jimmie's coach might have him practice walking on a balance beam to improve his spatial orientation skills.

What life changes were difficult for you? How could the important people in your life have helped to make them easier? In *Signs and Strategies for Educating Students With Brain Injuries*, Wolcott, Lash, and Pearson (1995) provide charts to plan for changes that students with brain injuries must face.

Cognitive retraining helps students regain perceptual processing, communication, behavioral, and social skills that were lost as a result of traumatic brain injury.

Component training is a form of cognitive retraining that provides students who have traumatic brain injury with intensive and systematic training of specific cognitive skills such as memory, attention, organization, and perceptual processing.

BOX 13-3

INTO PRACTICE

GUIDELINES FOR USING COGNITIVE RETRAINING

1. Avoid underestimating the severity of a cognitive deficit. Test scores can be misleading.
2. Take for granted that the student does not recognize the severity of the cognitive deficit.
3. Determine the nature of the deficits with the student and brainstorm together how to compensate for them.
4. After recording personal performance on a cognitive task, allow the student to observe your strengths and weaknesses in performing the task.
5. Instead of lecturing the student about the need for cognitive retraining, show the student that compensa- tion improves performance by carrying out the activity with the student.
6. Meticulously record training activities and their results. This provides tangible information about progress for the student.
7. The student needs cognitive retraining activities in everyday interpersonal activities rather than always in one-on-one tasks. The student must generalize the skills.
8. Cognitive retraining stimulates an affective response— boredom or interest are two possibilities. Therefore, the pace and difficulty level of the activities should be closely monitored.
9. Provide the student with an abundance of repetition and practice.

Note: From "Recovery and Cognitive Retraining After Craniocerebral Trauma" by G. P. Prigatano, 1987, *Journal of Learning Disabilities, 20,* 603–613. Copyright 1987 by PRO-ED, Inc. Reprinted by permission.

Compensatory strategy training is a form of cognitive retraining that helps students who have traumatic brain injury to clarify, remember, organize, and express information.

Functional retraining is a form of cognitive retraining that uses everyday curriculum and activities of a student with traumatic brain injury to teach cognitive skills.

"My dog Buster is a great dog," Jimmie comments. "He sleeps with me. He cries when I go to school. He and my brother are my best friends."

Compensatory strategy training helps the student clarify, remember, organize, and express information. One of the compensatory techniques that Jimmie's teachers used was to have him check in and out with a special educator every day at school to make sure he was organized, had all his materials, and knew what was expected of him.

Functional retraining makes use of a student's everyday curriculum and activities to teach cognitive skills. Jimmie's IEP team decided that having a dog would motivate him to develop cognitive skills. Before they got the dog for him, they worked with him on planning how to care for Buster. Jimmie read books and memorized how often Buster would need to be fed and watered. Training the dog taught him important sequencing and structure skills. He also had to learn to organize his activities to make sure the dog would receive enough attention. The team members encouraged judgment and problem-solving skills by asking him questions: "What would you do if Buster started to limp?" "What would you do if he acted like he wasn't hungry?" Because Jimmie takes such good care of Buster, the team decided he could also begin to baby-sit. Jimmie enjoys working with young children on the reservation, and he has had many opportunities to put his retrained cognitive skills into practice.

Box 13–3, "Into Practice," provides guidelines that may help you use cognitive retraining effectively with your students.

The use of computers (a form of assistive technology that is a related service) is popular for cognitive retraining, and software programs have been specifically designed for this purpose. Effective ones are age appropriate, provide motivation, furnish as much drill and practice as the student needs, and adapt easily to a student's ability level. Simulation software, such as the *Where Is Carmen Sandiego?* series (Bróderbund) or *The Oregon Trail II* (MECC), asks students to make choices based on a scenario and is readily available in local retail stores. The software, which can be enjoyed with students without disabilities, enhances problem solving, judgment, organizing, and sequencing skills. Even using a

🦋 *Seth took drum lessons for over two years. Performing the repetitive rhythmic patterns retrains cognitive abilities.*

joy stick retrains cognitive abilities because it develops perceptual motor skills (see the resources section later in the chapter for a list of other useful technology).

Cognitive retraining is not a panacea (Ylvisaker, Szekeres, & Hartwick, 1994). Students may or may not be able to regain the skills they had previously, depending on the extent of their injury. However, for many individuals, cognitive retraining, especially when taught functionally and with opportunities for generalization in a variety of settings, can improve their ability to perform in both academics and other daily activities.

Methods

It is important to keep your expectations for students with brain injuries high but also to realize that they may need extra time or extra practice opportunities without penalty to master skills (Hux & Hacksley, 1996). L. L. Ratto (personal correspondence, 1993) emphasizes that "goal accomplishment, however small, should be recognized and rewarded, for within achievement the seed of wellness is nurtured."

Instructional Methods.   Because students with brain injury often have limited attention spans and memory problems, teachers should keep instructional times short and use frequent repetition. Research suggests that you can increase students' productivity by teaching them to use a memory notebook (an electronic or paper organizer) (Mateer, Kerns, & Eso, 1996). You will want to monitor the student's use of the system periodically.

Errorless learning is also a valuable tool for teaching skills that involve memorization (Mateer et al., 1996). Instead of allowing the student to guess, give students the correct answer; then tell them to say it and write the answer on paper. Permitting the student with brain injury to practice an incorrect answer can reinforce the error.

Emphasizing major points and using a variety of modalities (auditory, visual, and kinesthetic) will help the students learn important academic content. Seth's teacher, for example, used concrete, hands-on materials to help him learn new math concepts. In Box 13–4, you will find a list of suggestions for improving instruction.

"Everyone who works with brain injury survivors will tell you that cognitive rehabilitation is not a cure," comments Ina Jaffe, a reporter for National Public Radio, "but that even a small improvement can make a dramatic difference in someone's life. And sometimes there is a chance for true independence" (Jaffe, 1996).

Seth struggled with computerized scoring sheets for tests. For a few years after his injury, he became so frustrated trying to go back and forth between test and scoring sheet, to find the right bubble, that he simply filled in answers at random.

BOX 13-4 — INTO PRACTICE

IMPROVING INSTRUCTION

1. Organize small groups.
2. Provide verbal and written instructions.
3. Give ample time.
4. Use examples (pictures, written, verbal).
5. Allow time for processing.
6. Repeat instructions.
7. Redefine words and terms.
8. Accompany homework assignments with written instructions.
9. Select a classroom buddy.
10. Permit tape recorders, calculators, typewriters, and computers.
11. Develop a system for maintaining organization.
12. Modify and individualize assignments and tests.
13. Structure the classroom environment.
14. Question the student to be sure the information is clear.
15. Plan fun learning activities.
16. Encourage discussion of problems.

Note: From "Facilitating School Return for the Head Injured," by J. L. Blosser and R. DePompei, 1987. Paper presented at the American Speech and Hearing Association convention, New Orleans. Reprinted with permission.

Methods to Improve Behavior. It is important to remember that students with brain injury may exhibit challenging behaviors as a direct result of their injury. They must relearn appropriate behaviors just as they must relearn academic skills. Proactive rather than aversive treatment is preferred. In fact, "customary aversive treatments may not only be unnecessary, but sometimes may contribute to the problem" (McMorrow, 1994).

Prevention strategies can help avoid challenging behaviors from your students with brain injury. Garey and Wambold (1994) recommend "(a) minimizing common distractors such as background noise, movement, clutter, and harsh colors, (b) increasing predictability in daily routines, (c) decreasing demands that stress the student's current coping skills, and (d) matching educational expectations to the student's cognitive functioning skills." Moreover, gradually and systematically exposing the student to potentially difficult life situations helps them manage their responses (McMorrow, 1994).

Once a challenging behavior occurs from one of your students, you can remove the source of the problem, redirect the student's attention, or help the student deescalate through modeling a calm, quiet response. Encouraging relaxation strategies may also stop the behavior (Garey & Wambold, 1994).

Self-control techniques involving personal goal setting can work well for these students (McMorrow, 1994). Dunn (1992) describes this approach:

> *Although children are assisted in program setup, they have control over selecting the behaviors they want to change, collecting information about their behavioral patterns, choosing techniques they feel comfortable with, and providing their own reinforcement.*

A **Personal Intervention Plan** includes information on what triggers inappropriate behavior, the typical behaviors displayed by the student, the desired behaviors, goals for achieving the behaviors, and supports the student needs to achieve the goals.

McMorrow (1994) emphasizes the need for a **Personal Intervention Plan** that a therapist helps develop. The plan includes (a) information on triggering events, (b) the types of emotional and behavioral responses the student tends to demonstrate in the sequence they generally occur, (c) the desired behaviors, (d) goals for achieving those behaviors, and (e) supports that will be needed to help the student achieve those goals.

Teaching the student through the use of models can be valuable, but self-modeling may be even more beneficial (Kehle, Clark, & Jenson, 1996). In self-modeling, the teacher videotapes the student exhibiting appropriate or exemplary behaviors. Inappropriate behaviors are edited out. This approach helps with self-confidence and self-esteem and requires fewer of the attention and problem-solving demands of some other self-monitoring approaches.

Kehle et al. (1996) also recommend several strategies you can use for encouraging compliance. Sit the student near compliant students; describe the desired behavior specifically; preplan negative consequences for noncompliance with the student; and follow compliance with immediate praise. In addition, have the student choose and practice a compliant response such as "Sure I will" or "Okey dokey." Randomly reinforce the student's use of the phrase.

A type of positive reinforcement called **differential reinforcement of other behavior** encourages appropriate behavior. When using this approach, you reinforce a positive behavior that is incompatible with the undesired behavior. In other words, praise the student for being good instead of punishing the student for doing something inappropriate. As one professional says, "When a child is doing the right thing, we are prompt in reinforcing that behavior with our praise, a tangible reward, or one of the child's preferred activities" (Dunn, 1992).

Praise should specify the appropriate behavior and be delivered immediately after the behavior (Kehle et al., 1996). It is important for you to deliver praise privately to those students for whom public praise is embarrassing. Your use of praise should exceed reprimands by at least a four-to-one margin. "Mystery motivators" such as snacks or privileges that are delivered on surprise days add to motivation for appropriate behavior by creating high anticipation.

> **Differential reinforcement of other behavior** encourages appropriate behavior by reinforcing a positive behavior that is incompatible with the undesired behavior. The focus is on praising good behavior rather than punishing inappropriate behavior.

Methods to Improve Self-Esteem. According to Branden (1984), "of all the judgments we pass, none is as important as the one we pass on ourselves." For students with brain injury, a change in who they once were frequently causes them to struggle with their new identity and to judge that identity harshly. An effective teacher wants to help these students develop the four components of a productive self-concept identified by Coopersmith (1967): significance, power, competence, and virtue.

As a teacher, you can incorporate these components into everyday activities. For example, taking care of Buster helped Jimmie's self-esteem. Buster made Jimmie feel significant, and learning that he could care for his dog without help renewed his sense of competence. Jimmie exhibited virtue by meeting Buster's basic needs for food, water, shelter, and affection. He also felt a sense of power from knowing that he was responsible for Buster's care.

> Teachers in elementary and middle school deliver a reprimand on an average of every two minutes. High school teachers deliver one every four minutes. Students with disabilities are likely to receive substantially higher rates, even though research indicates reprimands have a negative effect on mood, initiative, and self-esteem (Kehle et al., 1996).

HOW IS PARTICIPATION ENCOURAGED?

Inclusion

Data on placement are limited because many students with traumatic brain injury are still served under other categories such as learning disabilities or health impairments. However, information about placements of students who are leaving rehabilitation facilities might provide some clues about their initial least restrictive environment. The May Institute has identified the following placements for students who are leaving such facilities: general education (10 percent), full-time special education (38 percent), part-time special education (11 percent), institution (14 percent), adult education (8 percent), and postsecondary education (3 percent) (Russo, 1991). Many students enter inclusive settings immediately upon leaving a rehabilitation facility. Seth and Jimmie currently participate in the general classroom all day.

Two priorities require attention for inclusion of students with brain injury: "(a) establishing an organizational structure for the reintegration program and (b) exploring, implementing, and evaluating potential strategies for minimizing a student's persistent challenges" (Hux & Hacksley, 1996). Students recently discharged from rehabilitation facilities

> Declaration of Empowerment by the National Survivors Council of the Brain Injury Association, Inc: We persons with head injuries are reassuming a new role in our lives and in our communities. In this capacity we empower ourselves to assume control over our lives, accept responsibility for our decisions, and pursue opportunities to attain independence as is our right as equal participants in society (quoted in Ohio Valley Center for Brain Injury Prevention and Rehabilitation, n.d.).

need to have a gradual transition back to school (Savage, 1991). For example, Jimmie visited school before his first day back. Then he came to school in the morning but rested and had homebound education in the afternoon. As he regained energy, he began to stay at school for lunch and gradually added afternoon attendance along with rest periods in the school clinic.

Students with brain injury should attend general education classes as much as possible (Carter & Savage, 1984). For a majority, full-time placement in the general classroom is appropriate and desirable. In fact, Carter and Savage have warned:

> *Self-contained classrooms frequently are designed to meet the needs of [other] special school populations such as [those with mental retardation or emotional and behavioral disorders]. Placement [of students with brain injury] in such inappropriate environments will only inhibit cognitive remediation and the redevelopment of psycho-social skills. . . . Students [with brain injury] need to be placed in the least restrictive environment and be reassessed often in order to return them to higher levels of educational placement as they increase their cognitive awareness.*

A student with brain injury should be placed in the "least restrictive, most challenging environment you can imagine the child would be successful in" (Larkin, 1992). The placement should allow for both academic and social success (Ylvisaker et al., 1991). Furthermore, many students need related services such as counseling, speech and language, occupational or physical therapy, or an aide. See the accompanying "Inclusion Tips" box to help you work with students with brain injury in their general classrooms.

The May Center for Education and Neurorehabilitation in Randolph, Massachusetts, is one example of a special program that strongly emphasizes preparing its students who have a brain injury for transition back to general education. The center offers a continuum of services. These include a residential program, a day school, and consultation with students in transition back to general education or who do not ever need a full-time special placement. The center also provides training for public school teachers and various supports for families.

Collaboration

Adults are often told not to return to work after they have been in rehabilitation for a head injury, due to the difficulty of trying to produce at the same level as before the injury. Children, by contrast, usually return to school shortly after discharge (Lehr & Savage, 1992). Close collaboration can make this transition successful.

The success of a student's reentry to school after a traumatic brain injury depends upon collaboration among school, hospital, family, community, and the student. Box 13–5 describes the way professionals, Jimmie's mother, and his peers collaborated to meet Jimmie's needs when he reentered school after being struck by a drunk driver.

Collaboration Among Professionals. Collaboration among professionals at the school and the rehabilitation facility helped Jimmie to overcome the academic, behavioral, and social changes he experienced as a result of his injury. Unfortunately, the emphases of hospital and school can sometimes differ and create conflict. As Pearson says, "School people are concerned with academic issues; hospital people are geared toward saving lives" (Larkin, 1992). Nevertheless, a common perspective can be achieved. The school must remember that the rehabilitation center can provide insight into the student's brain functioning and prognosis. The rehabilitation center should realize the important role the school plays in the student's lifelong well-being.

Many facilities employ a hospital–school liaison (sometimes referred to as a school reentry specialist) to improve collaboration. Grandinette-Miller explains the importance of her role as a school reentry specialist:

Inclusion Tips

	What You Might See	What You Might Be Tempted to Do	Alternate Responses	Ways to Include Peers in the Process
Behavior	The student may show behavior and personality changes, such as temper outbursts, anxiety, fatigue, or depression.	Respond with strong disapproval and discipline the student's new behavior.	Reward the student's positive behaviors. Provide predictable routines that encourage normal behavior patterns while teaching new ways to respond within the school environment.	Give the student time to work in natural settings with peers who will encourage appropriate behavior yet show acceptance during the relearning stage.
Social Interactions	The student may have forgotten social skills and experience social misunderstandings because of his new identity struggles.	Ignore the student's social difficulties and hope they go away.	Work with both the speech-language pathologist and the school counselor to plan the best ways to use language and social skills in successful situations.	Allow friends with whom he feels secure to role play social activities. Structure many opportunities for successful interactions. Use videotapes for self-evaluation.
Educational Performance	Learning new information may be difficult for her, or it may take her much longer to process information.	Require extra work in areas of difficulty rather than focus on holding skills and what she can accomplish.	Capitalize on what is familiar to retrieve and develop memory, organization, and cognitive processes. Prioritize the academic skills she needs to learn.	Have the student brainstorm and work with her peers/friends to practice skills as well as to plan future projects and educational aspirations.
Classroom Attitudes	She may appear easily distracted, have headaches, or show a lack of motivation during instruction.	Reprimand her apparent lack of participation. Discipline her or excuse her from class activities.	Allow rest periods. Modify the amount and intensity of assignments.	Pair her with a partner and friend who can help her focus and participate meaningfully during instruction.

I remember when children with brain injury were simply dropped into my classroom without my having any information about them. The situation was extremely frustrating. Now, I do everything in my power to make sure teachers have all the information they need. (Larkin, 1992)

Beth Urbanczyk talks about her role as a school-reentry specialist in Box 13–6, "My Voice."

This collaboration needs to begin when the student is in rehabilitation. Jimmie's teachers and principal visited him soon after the accident. The hospital and the school remained in close contact throughout the rehabilitation process, and a team consisting of rehabilitation and school personnel jointly developed an IEP before Jimmie was discharged. The

BOX 13-5   MAKING A DIFFERENCE

JIMMIE'S TEAM

"I am afraid. When we go home, who will help us?" Jimmie's mother asked while he was still in rehabilitation. She didn't need to be concerned. Jimmie's school team cared about him, and the family would not be alone on its recovery journey. Jimmie's school principal, a special educator, and his fifth-grade teacher showed their support, first of all, by visiting Jimmie in the rehabilitation center on three occasions.

After being discharged from the rehabilitation facility, Jimmie gradually returned to school over a three-week period. He still fatigued easily and could not concentrate for longer than fifteen minutes. He began each day by checking in with his special educator, who sat with him to go over his day. At the end of the school day, Jimmie would check out with her and review the school day. He also had an aide assigned to him daily to provide support in his classroom and to help him get to his physical therapy and speech-language sessions.

A physical therapist traveled to Jimmie's isolated school only once every two weeks. Therefore, the physical education teacher and his mother reinforced his therapy at school and home.

Despite these support measures, Jimmie's initial school adjustment was not easy. His teacher noted that he had difficulty staying on task, shifting from one subject to another (for example, from math to reading), finding the main idea, and following multiple directions. Some days he could complete his in-class work; however, on other days he could not give correct answers even though he had learned the information the day before. Friends began to shy away from him as his outbursts and temper flareups became more frequent. After three months, his teachers reevaluated his IEP because of his erratic performance in school and his psychosocial problems.

The school contacted the rehabilitation center, which sent a neuropsychologist and a cognitive therapist to attend the meeting with Jimmie's teachers and his mother. After an extensive interdisciplinary discussion, the team felt that Jimmie's continued fatigue factors and the damage to his frontal lobes significantly contributed to his declining school performance and behavioral episodes. They decided to build two rest periods into Jimmie's schedule to help alleviate the fatigue. Moreover, the speech-language pathologist and the school psychologist received training in the language-based behavioral program that was successful with Jimmie when he was at the rehabilitation facility. The team felt that this behavioral model would help Jimmie recognize and monitor his behavior by using his language strengths. Likewise, his mother learned to use the behavioral strategies at home. The team also decided to continue his program with the speech-language pathologist and the special educator through the summer months.

After an uneventful summer, Jimmie returned to school in September of that year. His sixth-grade teacher learned about his needs and spent some time with him before school began. When school started, she organized his work space so that he would be less distracted by classroom activity. Together, Jimmie and his teacher developed a hand signal that would cue him to refocus his behavior. In addition, she gave him color-coded worksheets to help him sequence his independent work.

Jimmie still took a twenty-minute rest period following lunch, which helped him to maintain concentration in the afternoon. He continued to meet with his special educator in the morning and at the end of school to keep organized and focused. By the end of sixth grade, Jimmie experienced success in school and enjoyed close friendships. His mother reported that he also seemed much happier at home.

relationship, which was solidified by frequent contacts during rehabilitation, continued after the discharge. When Jimmie began to experience difficulties, the team met again and brainstormed solutions. Because of this problem-solving, collaborative approach, Jimmie became successful in the general classroom. His mother says that the collaboration between Jimmie's school teachers and the rehabilitation staff helped relieve many of her greatest fears about Jimmie's future.

Jimmie will always need this kind of collaboration. Life for him will be a series of transitions; issues of independence, sexuality, work, and adulthood will present new challenges. Continued collaboration among professionals, Jimmie, and his family will make those transitions easier.

Collaboration With Family.   A child with a brain injury is "only one member of an injured family system" (Conoley & Sheridan, 1996). Lash (1991) comments:

BOX 13-6 **MY VOICE**

BETH URBANCZYK

As a school entry and reentry specialist, I have the unique opportunity of working in the world of rehabilitation, early intervention, and education simultaneously. Infants, toddlers, and preschoolers present a unique challenge to rehabilitation and educational professionals. At issue is not only what the results of the injury will be for these children, but when they will manifest themselves. The child's developing brain is injured, and as the brain continues to mature and develop, the eventual outcome is uncertain. The professionals involved, therefore, need to understand the functioning of the developing brain as well as the effects of a traumatic brain injury on a child.

These children have many transitions ahead of them. They need school reentry specialists to share information with the current program; this includes the injury and recovery process, functioning in previous settings, and plans for the future. If the initial entry into educational services is not carefully and thoughtfully planned, the future may be significantly compromised for these children.

What else do school entry and reentry specialists need to know? It is especially important to understand the systems that provide child services and the laws that guarantee children's rights to those services. Furthermore, I work with a variety of professionals across New York. Good communication skills (spoken and written) are essential in my occupation as I talk to these people and produce written documents that summarize our findings and plans.

These communication skills are also important when I work with families. Often families are unfamiliar with early intervention and special education. I teach them how to advocate effectively for their children within those systems.

There is nothing more exciting than seeing a child you have worked with enter an early intervention program or preschool and succeed. I feel that the work I have done has made a difference in the lives of a number of children.

Beth Urbanczyk
Early intervention school reentry specialist
Midwest Rehabilitation Center, Waterford, Wisconsin

Many parents describe events in terms of "before" and "after" the accident. Although their child is alive, a normal reaction of parents is to mourn the loss of certain characteristics or abilities. Many parents describe this as a "partial death" of their child. This is particularly true when a child's ability to walk, talk, breathe, or remember has been seriously affected.

Being sensitive to the issues facing these families is crucial. This "partial death" can lead to an extended and necessary grief process by all members of the family. L. L. Ratto (personal communication, 1993) states:

Their loss is real and magnified. This is not for the professional to deny. . . . Anger is frequently a difficult, often lingering stage, and is the most common stage of grief the practitioner will have to work through with the family.

Listening without judgment, avoiding defensiveness, and continuing to offer support are important ways that you can help families work through anger and other grief stages.

Professionals also need to recognize the important role of family for the general "well-functioning" of students with brain injury (Conoley & Sheridan, 1996). Jimmie's family provides him with strong support. When Jimmie speaks of his family, he says "I love everybody." Aunts and uncles assisted in Jimmie's care, and his mother, Agnes, says, "All our family helps each other. We get together and talk and tell stories. My father always finds a way to make us laugh." Jimmie's grandfather is an important role model and mentor. Also, the Mohawk tribe is both community and family. The tribe raised money for his care through their casinos.

Jimmie shares that his brother is his best friend and "helps me a lot." When asked what he wishes for, Jimmie does not wish for himself. He wants "my mom to be happy and my brother to get a new bike." The cultural richness of the Mohawk tribe has contributed to Jimmie being "a kind and gentle person who always wants to help."

Expenses can be devastating for families. A student with severe brain injury generally faces 5 to 10 years of intensive services at an estimated cost of $4 million (Brain Injury Association of Connecticut, 1996).

Collaboration Tips

Collaborators	Roles and Preparation	Possible Barriers	Solutions to Barriers	Modifications to Implementation	Ongoing Evaluation
Student	Needs to understand how a student's culture differs from that of her classmates.	Without this knowledge, student may misinterpret the responses of others.	Talk openly with family and student about their culture. Ask about previous difficulties in dealing with reactions of others at school. Clarify which difficulties result from cultural difference and which result from the student's disability.	Share literature, music, art, stories, etc. from the student's culture in class, and ask the student to participate.	Watch the student's interactions with peers to determine level of acceptance and involvement.
Parents and/or guardians	Needs to be willing to communicate openly with school personnel about cultural differences.	May hesitate to share this information for cultural reasons.	Read and talk to others who are familiar with the culture.	Express your desire to parents to understand the culture to meet the student's needs more effectively; ask questions based on information learned from research.	Periodically ask family if student is experiencing difficulty with peers or at school. Determine if the cause is cultural misunderstanding. Ask the family for suggestions.
Administrator	Needs to make sure that academic, social, and discipline policies respect cultural differences.	May believe *fair* is treating everybody the same rather than giving each student what he or she needs.	Research the cultural differences of students in the school.	Encourage acceptance of diversity by bringing in guest speakers from various cultures and organizing a Diversity Day at the school (food, costumes, activities, etc.).	Observe the behavior of students in the school to determine cultural barriers and stressful interrelationships.

Collaborators	Roles and Preparation	Possible Barriers	Solutions to Barriers	Modifications to Implementation	Ongoing Evaluation
General Educator(s)	Needs to help the student become an active participant in the general classroom and maintain effective collaboration with the family.	May know little about the student's culture and feel that too many cultures are represented in the classroom to warrant special consideration.	Special educator can share information gleaned from research; general educator may need information about how accommodations can be made that enhance classroom atmosphere rather than disrupting it.	Special educator and general educator can meet together for initial parent conference and discuss cultural needs afterward.	Periodically, ask parents for comments about the student's comfort level in the classroom and for their suggestions.
Special Educator(s)	Needs to make sure that the family, teachers, administrators, and peers are recognizing and respecting the student's culture with respect to disability.	May not understand how the student's culture differs or how cultural perceptions of disability affects family's regard of special education services.	Should meet with parents and ask for guidelines, be willing to talk to others from the same culture, and conduct other research.	Special educators in the school may want to coordinate their efforts in collecting information about various cultures. A centrally located file with articles, information gathered from people from specific cultures, Internet web sites, etc., could be a time-saver in the long term.	Talk to parents, student, teachers, and administrators periodically to determine if the student's culture is being respected.
Peers	Needs to seek ways to understand and respect student's cultural diversity and differentiate cultural values and traditions from special education needs.	May not understand the student's culture and make fun of or avoid the student.	Plan activities to help peers become tolerant of cultural differences; to incorporate opportunities for open discussion of culture into the classroom can be helpful; to include special speakers, art, literature, music, etc., from the student's culture into the classroom.	Ask students to choose a culture other than their own and research it. Have them share something they learned about that culture with the class. Encourage them to interview someone from that culture as part of the research.	Monitor student interactions in the hallway, at lunch, on the playground, etc., to determine their level of tolerance.

569

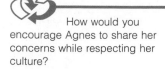

How would you encourage Agnes to share her concerns while respecting her culture?

Agnes explains the importance of professionals respecting her family's culture and their ability to make wise decisions about Jimmie's needs:

> *My family is Mohawk. We believe things in certain ways. Sometimes my father thinks the school should help Jimmie do more work with his hands. Jimmie loves to carve and draw. But we are quiet people. We do not have much education. But I know my Jimmie.*

Professionals need to be open to learning as much about a student's culture as possible. Initially, professionals at the rehabilitation facility misinterpreted the way Agnes stayed in the background as disinterest. Then they saw her exercising and encouraging Jimmie when she was alone with him and realized their erroneous thinking. They made sure she could see what they were doing during therapy and offered explanations for their procedures. Jimmie's rehabilitation director explains:

> *Jimmie's mother is very compliant. The school and myself have had to work hard to gain her trust. She also respects professionals so much for helping her son that she rarely speaks up when she's concerned or upset.*

Respect for Jimmie's culture has created a positive relationship between family and school. "The school has good people," Agnes says. "They all care about Jimmie." See the accompanying box for collaboration tips for working with families from diverse cultures.

Collaboration With Peers.   Many of the strategies discussed in Chapter 11 for encouraging peer involvement in understanding and supporting a student with a health impairment also apply to students with brain injury. While the student is in the hospital and rehabilitation facility, interested peers need to be kept honestly informed of their classmate's condition.

As Jimmie's medical condition stabilized, a few of his closest friends began to visit and participate in his rehabilitation. His class created and sent a videotape to let Jimmie know that he was not forgotten. The rehabilitation center also sent videotapes of Jimmie to the class. This helped the class prepare for how the injury had changed him.

Jimmie's school reentry specialist gave his classmates information about brain injury before he returned to the classroom. It was important for classmates to know that his behavior as well as cognitive functioning had changed and why. Mrs. Benson, Jimmie's general classroom teacher, enlisted their help in planning for his reentry. Peers can be a valuable part of a student's group action plan (see Chapter 8).

Seth, who was already frustrated as a result of the changes caused by his injury, also had to cope with teasing from peers who did not understand his injury. If you have a student like Seth who has suffered a mild head injury and has never been hospitalized, you might want to have a classroom presentation on brain injury. If the student feels comfortable, talking about the accident with the help of a counselor or nurse to classmates can be beneficial. First, however, you must determine whether the student and family want to have the condition discussed publicly—and honor that preference. Seth chose not to discuss his brain injury.

Strategies such as "circle of friends," a structured network that promotes positive peer responses, can be valuable. However, Farmer and Peterson (1995) warn that this approach "must avoid interfering with naturally occurring friendships and to truly develop reciprocal, rather than one-sided relationships."

Careers

Numerous career options are available to you if you want to work with students who have received head injuries. Physicians, nurses, mental health professionals, speech-language pathologists, administrators, teachers, and therapists (including occupational, recreational, and physical) all play important roles in students' recovery. If you are working in the school system, you can commit to making sure these students' unique needs are recognized and that they are appropriately served as having a traumatic brain injury. The school reentry specialist also plays an important role in facilitating collaboration between the rehabilitation facility and the school. You might want to choose this career if you want to work directly with students who have brain injury and their families.

WHAT ARE PROGRAM OPTIONS?

"We never watered down an adult program," Dr. Ron Savage, Jimmie's rehabilitation director, comments. "Instead, we took a developmental model based on what we know about normal growth and development of kids and applied that to providing rehabilitation for children and adults with traumatic brain injury." Whether the facility is a rehabilitation center or a school, it is essential that students with brain injury be provided services that are appropriate for their developmental level.

Close collaboration between the rehabilitation center and the school will help make sure that students transition as smoothly as possible to their everyday lives. Most rehabilitation centers have the same two purposes as Jimmie's program: to look like the student's world and to connect with the family and school. In the program options that follow, you will see how these purposes can be accomplished. You will also read some of the innovative strategies schools and postsecondary programs are using to help students with brain injury realize their potential.

Early Intervention and Preschool Years

The preschool years are the age of the "supercharged brain" because cells are rapidly expanding and becoming more numerous (Savage & Mishldn, 1991). Although an injured brain may recover faster during this period, the ability to develop compensatory strategies may be hampered.

At one large pediatric brain injury rehabilitation facility in the United States, all students, regardless of age, are served by a team that includes the family, a social worker, a physician, a primary care nurse, an occupational and a physical therapist, a speech-language pathologist, a psychologist, a special educator, and a therapeutic recreation specialist. A team serves ten to twelve children, adolescents, or young adults. Each staff member also serves as an advocate for two students, attends team meetings, and follows the student's progress to make sure her needs are being met.

The cause of traumatic brain injury in 90 percent of children under the age of three is abuse. Certainly, having a team with many different experts involved in the care of these young children is important. However, for an infant, being held and prodded by so many people can prevent bonding, an important part of development. This lack of bonding is of special concern if the child has been abused and the parents are not participating as team members.

"If a child bonds once, a child will bond twice," the rehabilitation director comments. With that philosophy in mind, a nanny is assigned to each child who has been abused. The nanny stays with the infant during most of the day and participates in all therapies with her. After leaving rehabilitation, the child will most likely be able to bond more readily with her new caretaker because of the affection and care given by the nanny.

For young children beyond infancy, the facility provides a preschool environment. The child's therapy revolves around the particular theme the preschool has for that period of time. Four-year-old Sara, for example, received rehabilitation because of a head injury she sustained when she fell down some steps. On the day of the preschool's Valentine theme, she frosted cupcakes for physical therapy, cut out hearts for her occupational therapy, and answered questions for cognitive therapy after hearing a story about Valentine's Day. The preschool is also language centered. Because this is a crucial age for language development, all types of therapy and activities encourage Sara's understanding and use of language.

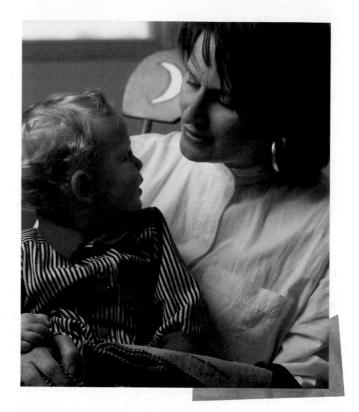

≈ *All babies need an opportunity to bond with a nurturing adult. A "nanny" cuddles an infant with a traumatic brain injury.*

To ease the transition from rehabilitation, Sara's parents were given training about their legal rights and a list of preschools in their area. They were also given a checklist of things to look for in a good preschool program. With that information, staff encouraged her parents to choose the preschool program that they think would best meet Sara's and their needs. The staff trained Sara's future teachers at her new preschool, These Our Treasures (TOTs), and continued to work with them after Sara left the facility.

One of the facets of TOTs that appealed to Sara's parents was the support they knew their family would get from the program. TOTs requires active participation by parents. In fact, the parents rotate spending time in the classroom. Activities and training programs are available for parents, grandparents, and siblings. Sara loved seeing her grandparents come to visit her at school, and they enjoyed feeling like they were a valued component of her recovery. The teachers worked closely with the facility to make sure that Sara's needs continued to be met.

During Sara's last year at TOTs, she and her family received graduation training. TOTs provided seminars that her parents attended to help them with the transition to advocating for Sara at the elementary school. TOTs' faculty, the rehabilitation staff, and Sara's parents met with the elementary special education teacher to make sure that the school knew about Sara's needs and would have a plan to serve her on her first day. The staff at TOTs knew they would miss Sara when she left them, but they also knew that she was well prepared for her next step.

Elementary Years

During the elementary years, connections in the brain, both between and within hemispheres, become more efficient (Savage & Mishkin, 1994). Children build basic academic, prosocial, and self-confidence skills during this period. Brain injury can severely disrupt this process.

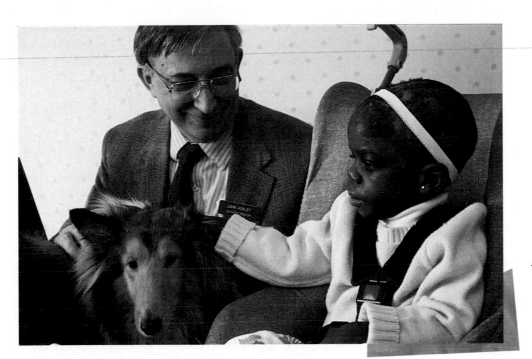

❧ *Being surrounded by familiar people and objects helps students to regain memories of the past. Here a little girl's collie helps her remember.*

Even while Jimmie was in a coma, he received exposure to stimulating and familiar activities. Ron Savage, his rehabilitation director, comments:

> You don't wait for the baby to be able to respond before you pick it up, rock it, talk to it, and provide other stimulation. We don't wait for the child to come out of a coma to begin stimulation. We want them to emerge from a coma faster and healthier for rehabilitation.

Jimmie's family visited him any time they wanted; no limits were placed on visiting hours or age. Even pets were welcome. A nurse dressed Jimmie in school clothes every day, and his room was decorated with items from home.

After Jimmie woke from his coma, his rehabilitation facility provided an environment that was as much like his elementary school as possible. When Jimmie first entered his classroom each morning, he had orientation: After the pledge to the flag, Jimmie and his classmates were oriented to time, place, and person by identifying the day of the week and the date, who they were, where they were, and what time it was, all before attending class.

The purpose of such a program is to provide elementary students like Jimmie with a holistic environment that makes sense and that will ease their transition from rehabilitation. Thus, Jimmie referred to Dr. Savage as the principal rather than the program director. He went to gym class for physical therapy, and cognitive rehabilitation was called study hall. In general, the therapists (whom Jimmie referred to as teachers) integrated their therapies into the classroom rather than working with Jimmie alone in an office.

Jimmie used the textbooks from the school he attended before his injury. His teacher and therapists capitalized on what was familiar to develop the important skills of memory, organization, sequencing, planning, attention, and concentration through the use of classroom materials and activities. On a particular day, Jimmie's occupational therapist had him develop fine-motor skills by copying and answering a problem from his math book, using a computer keyboard to write a sentence for English, and turning pages as he read from his language arts book. His cognitive therapist had him memorize the first two lines of a favorite song to develop attention, concentration, memory, and sequencing.

Being in a school-like setting helped Jimmie to retrieve information and skills that he had mastered before his injury. He was also prepared to participate in a classroom routine when he left rehabilitation.

Jimmie's teachers were ready when he arrived. A multidisciplinary team evaluated Jimmie several times while he was still in rehabilitation, so preliminary information was available. His teachers had already met with the staff and Jimmie at the rehabilitation facility, and they carefully reviewed his evaluation and medical information. The principal and special and general education teachers participated in in-service training on brain injury. They and his family brainstormed ideas for educating Jimmie in the general classroom as much as was appropriate.

What is the philosophy of the faculty about working with Jimmie? "We are looking down the road," commented one teacher. "We want to help him get where he's going, socially as well as academically. We are committed to Jimmie and his integration."

Middle and Secondary Years

The stabilized, efficient adult brain emerges during this period. The student becomes capable of logical thought. Brain injury often interferes with skills such as abstract reasoning, problem solving, and social interaction. Additionally, brain injury can inhibit the emergence of self-identity and intimacy skills, crucial tasks of adolescence (Savage & Mishkin, 1994).

"We ensured her success," Tony Persico, Project Director of the Western New York Traumatic Brain Injury Project says of Susan's team. A middle school student, Susan attended a suburban school, was popular, and had parents who had high expectations for her. After her car accident, she received inpatient pediatric rehabilitation. The rehabilitation facility and her school worked to help her regain lost social skills and acceptance of her new identity. She received counseling and participated in an adolescent support group. Susan struggled with depression and needed the important people in her life to bolster her.

That is why the Traumatic Brain Injury Project focuses on a team approach and gradual inclusion of a student. Susan's team consisted of an occupational therapist, physical therapist, speech pathologist, guidance counselor, school psychologist, nurse, principal, general educator, tutor, mother, Susan herself, and her best friend. "I insist that parents come," Persico says. "If the student is in middle or high school, I always insist that the child comes, too."

For the team to function effectively, they required collaboration skills. Persico taught them the team process and modeled problem solving approaches. However, he comments, "I was not running the team; I was a member of the team. I became a faithful observer."

Each person had a role to play that increased their effectiveness, and the roles rotated. By the fourth meeting, Susan's mother led the team. A potentially adversarial situation proved to be cooperative and supportive. The meetings, initially scheduled every three weeks and gradually reduced, "were faithfully attended," comments Persico, "because people owned the problems."

Susan received tutoring during the summer after the accident, and by September she returned to school. Her team decided that her tutor and therapist should come to her school. Initially, Susan's tutor taught her in a separate room in the school. Susan attended one class after she adjusted to being back with the students. Her psychologist and tutor continued to work with her on social skills. Gradually, Susan added more classes with her peers. Now, two years after the accident, she is a cheerleader, has a 96 percent average, and her prognosis is excellent.

Persico credits Susan's drive and her team. "There were lots of bumps. So many people were knowledgeable and they helped."

Transitional and Postsecondary Years

Nordlund (1994) lists four important assessment considerations as students with brain injury transition to postsecondary education or employment: academic strengths and weaknesses, acceptance of disability, level of independence, and stage of rehabilitation.

After assessment, students need to establish personal and professional goals, keeping in mind that those goals may need to be altered as skills improve and they have new experiences.

Finding a way to support students whose goals include college can prove challenging. Many colleges do not have specialized programs for students with traumatic brain injury. For that reason, close collaboration between the transition team at the secondary school and the college is essential to make a successful student–college match (Bergland and Hoffbauer, 1996).

The special educator needs to identify postsecondary settings that are consistent with the student's abilities and needs (Bergland & Hoffbauer, 1996). Other tasks include determining how services will be coordinated at the college and how staff training will be provided. A meeting between the special educator and the campus disability support specialist provides an opportunity to gather information and develop a plan for accommodation. The student will need instruction in self-advocacy skills from the special educator, along with help in identifying college and community advocates.

Families vary in their cultural values about when or even if it is appropriate for young people to move away from the family's home. For some families, especially those from the majority culture, locating an alternative living environment is an important step toward independence (Bergland & Hoffbauer, 1996). However, barriers such as the noise and distractions of dorm life or the difficulty of finding reliable public transportation may prove prohibitive. The student may choose to stay with family while getting used to the routine of college life before changing living environments.

Completing the following checklist (Bergland & Hoffbauer, 1996, p. 55) will help with planning:

Physical Accessibility

- To what degree are building, dorms, and activities accessible?

- Are transportation alternatives and mobility assistance available?

- Are health and medical care available, and are personnel knowledgeable about traumatic brain injury?

- Are living arrangements accessible, safe, and modifiable to needs?

- Are fatigue, endurance, stress, and energy parameters known?

Academic Programs and Support Services

- Have campus support services/informed resources been identified?

- Have student information processing skills/deficits been identified?

- What accommodations are made for admissions/registration/changes?

- Are faculty/advisors/staff trained or knowledgeable about traumatic brain injury?

- Are syllabuses, texts, and instructional formats available before class?

- Are alternative assignments/testing formats/compensatory aids allowed?

Social and Personal Support Systems

- Have social functioning and at-risk situations been assessed?

- How well are student disability-related needs and concerns articulated?

- How well does the student accept/manage assistance?

- Are accessible social networks and leisure/recreation activities present?

Vocational Training and Job Placement

- Are career counselors experienced in working with students with disabilities?

- Are Division of Rehabilitation Services or other agencies involved?

- Are apprentice/intern/supported employment opportunities known?

This careful planning can result in academic success for the student with traumatic brain injury. In addition, the student will have opportunities for social interactions in an inclusionary setting.

A Vision for the Future

I Live

I live
and I always hope
that tomorrow will be
better than today;
that my future will look
completely different than now.

I live in my way but I live.
I live and I always have hope.
I live!

> *Bertolodo (1995)*

The above poem was written by Mirta Bertolodo, who has a brain injury, and reflects the vision and hope that is possible for students with brain injury. Improved diagnostic procedures, including advances in scanning technology, might allow students with mild head injuries, such as Seth, to have the extent of their injuries readily identified so that intervention can begin immediately (Allison, 1992b). Jimmie and others who have sustained more serious injuries will benefit from new medical research and innovative rehabilitation programs that emphasize collaboration and inclusion.

Four years have passed since Jimmie's injury. Jimmie has regained many of the skills he lost because of the accident and continues to make good progress in learning new skills. Jimmie once asked, "How long will I be head injured? Will I be head injured forever?" The answer, of course, is yes.

Jimmie continues to face challenges as a result of his brain injury. The twelve-year-old is now entering adolescence and feels his differences from his peers more profoundly. The transition from elementary school to middle school has produced new difficulties. Every day he struggles to remember his locker combination and find his way to his classes. Other kids don't understand why these tasks are difficult for him because he looks okay. And, although he tries to fit in as much as possible, social and academic difficulties sometimes make him an easy target for teasing.

His ability to use language has been affected, and Jimmie faces major challenges in learning the Mohawk language. The stories his grandfather tells of the Mohawk tribe are difficult to remember. His sister, who is three years younger, has begun to pass Jimmie socially and academically. The rivalry between the siblings grows stronger.

And yet, with problems are the potential for solutions. Jimmie's team continues to work together to help Jimmie find those answers. Jimmie is maturing into a compassionate young man with the potential to be a valuable member of society.

Agnes voices her vision for Jimmie's future: "when he grows up, that he will be able to work and get married and that he will feel good about himself and be happy."

Jimmie remains positive about his present and his future. Science class is his favorite school subject, especially when the topic is animals. He says that when he grows up, "I would like to work with animals and have a big farm."

With the support of his tribe, family, and team, we envision Jimmie and his mother's dreams coming true. We see his team making sure he develops the vocational skills he needs to be a farmer. He will participate in 4-H, Future Farmers of America, and learn first-hand about farming by spending his summers working on a farm. Perhaps his team will arrange for him to learn more about caring for animals by participating in a work–study program in high school with a local veterinarian or humane society.

Jimmie shares his vision for your future: "Be good to all your kids. Be 'special' good to the kids like me who don't learn easy."

What Would You Recommend . . .

1. To help Jimmie find more acceptance in middle school?

2. To enable Jimmie to pass on the traditions of his tribe?

3. To improve Jimmie's relationship with his sister?

4. To provide other transition services for Jimmie to help him become the farmer he hopes to be?

SUMMARY

WHAT IS TRAUMATIC BRAIN INJURY?

• The IDEA definition of traumatic brain injury includes acquired injuries to the brain caused by an external force but does not include brain injuries caused by anoxia or disease or congenital brain injuries.

• Closed head injuries and open head injuries are the two types of brain injuries included under the IDEA definition.

• Mild head injuries, called postconcussional syndrome, can adversely affect personal, academic, and social performance.

• Traumatic brain injury differs from other disabilities in onset, complexity, and prognosis.

• Students with traumatic brain injury often experience physical, cognitive, linguistic, and social, behavioral, or personality changes.

• No generalizations can be made about prognosis based on the injury's mildness or severity.

• The three major causes of closed and open head injuries are accidents, sports and recreational injuries, and violence.

• Shaken impact syndrome is a dangerous form of child abuse that can cause traumatic brain injuries or even death.

• Called the *silent epidemic*, the effects of brain injury are widespread but often unrecognized.

• Approximately 0.5 to 1 percent of school-age students have sustained a traumatic brain injury.

• About 3 percent of adolescents have sustained head injuries that are severe enough to cause school problems.

WHAT ARE EVALUATION PROCEDURES?

• Because the needs of students with traumatic brain injury are diverse and rapidly changing, evaluation needs to be comprehensive and ongoing.

• The multidisciplinary team should evaluate the student in all areas of functioning, including cognitive processes such as problem solving and memory.

• The IEP team should update the student's document frequently, probably every six to eight weeks initially.

WHAT AND HOW DO PROFESSIONALS TEACH?

- Students receive three forms of cognitive retraining: component retraining, compensatory strategy training, and functional training.

- Computer-assisted instruction helps students develop cognitive skills.

HOW IS PARTICIPATION ENCOURAGED?

- The general classroom is the least restrictive environment in most cases.

- Close collaboration among rehabilitation staff, school personnel, family, peers, and the student is essential to meet the diverse, ever-changing needs of individuals with traumatic brain injury.

WHAT ARE PROGRAM OPTIONS?

- The emphases of programs differ according to students' maturational stage: language for early intervention, social skills and self-acceptance for older children and adolescents, and vocational training for secondary and postsecondary students.

- Methods for improving behavioral and social skills include differential reinforcement of other behaviors, stimulus control, environmental control, and self-control techniques.

- Professionals can improve self-esteem by fostering a sense of significance, competence, power, and virtue.

- An important career for this field is the school reentry specialist.

RESOURCES

BOOKS

Developing Minds. (1991). By Arthur Costa. Alexandria, VA: Association for Supervision and Curriculum Development. Two-volume set assists teachers in planning a thinking-skills curriculum.

An Educator's Manual: What Educators Need to Know about Students with Traumatic Brain Injury. (1988). By Ronald C. Savage & Gary F. Wolcott. Washington, DC: National Head Injury Foundation. (202) 296-6443. Manual contains practical advice for educators.

Making Connections: Teaching and the Human Brain. (1991). By Renate Nummela Caine & Geoffrey Caine. Alexandria, VA: Association for Supervision and Curriculum Development. Emphasizes brain-based learning strategies for all students. Teachers will be able to apply these methods to students with traumatic brain injury.

Traumatic Head Injury: Cause, Consequence, and Challenge. (1987). By Dennis Swiercinsky, Terrie Price, & Leif Eric Leif. Shawnee Mission, KS: Kansas Head Injury Association. (913) 648-4772. Booklet discusses how traumatic brain injuries occur, the resulting changes, and the rehabilitation process.

Traumatic Head Injury in School-Aged Children: A Training Manual for Educational Personnel. (1990). By Janet Siantz Tyler. Children's Rehabilitation Unit, University of Kansas Medical Center, Thirty-ninth and Rainbow Boulevard, Kansas City, KS 66103. (913) 588-5900. Guidelines and information for educators.

When Your Child Goes to School After a Head Injury. (1992). By Marilyn Lash. Washington, DC: National Head Injury Foundation. (202) 296-6443. Booklet provides suggestions for parent, teacher, and administrator collaboration to facilitate school reentry.

JOURNALS, MAGAZINES, AND CATALOGS

Catalog of Educational Materials. National Head Injury Foundation, 1140 Connecticut Avenue NW, Suite 912, Washington, DC 20036. (202) 296-6443. Lists books and materials helpful for professionals and families.

Health Care: Pediatric through Geriatric. LinquiSystems. 3100 Fourth Avenue, P.O. Box 747, Department HC, East Moline, IL 61244-0747. (800) 776-4332. Catalog lists a variety of resources for cognitive rehabilitation and daily living.

Journal of Head Trauma Rehabilitation. Aspen Publishers, 200 Orchard Ridge Drive, Gaithersburg, MD 20878. (301) 417-7500. Peer-reviewed journal contains research-based and practical articles about individuals with head injuries.

NeuroRehabilitation: An Interdisciplinary Journal. Andover Medical Publishers, 125 Main Street, Reading, MA 01867. Peer-reviewed journal provides practical information on acquired and congenital neurological disabilities.

NHIF 1994 National Directory of Head Injury Rehabilitation Services. National Head Injury Foundation, Washington, DC. (202) 296-6443. Lists thousands of services with detailed descriptions.

Rehabilitation: Traumatic Brain Injury Update. University of Washington, Rehabilitation Medicine RJ-30 (Attention: TBI Newsletter), Seattle, WA 98195. Newsletter about traumatic brain injury rehabilitation.

MULTIMEDIA

Brain Train. (1992). By Janna Spark. Des Moines, IA: Prentice Hall. (800) 288-4745. Teacher's manual, reproducible worksheets, and audiocassettes provide a multisensory, cognitive approach that combines music, imagery, humor, and relaxation techniques to help students gain confidence in their ability to learn.

HeadSmart. National Head Injury Foundation, 1140 Connecticut Avenue NW, Suite 912, Washington, DC 20036. (202) 296-6443. A variety of posters, booklets, and activities teach students how to prevent traumatic brain injuries.

Life Skills Series. (1993). San Antonio, TX: PCI Educational Publishing. Call (800) 594-4263 for a catalog. Eight programs teach ninety-three basic life skills in a board-game format.

The following video is available at local rental or retail stores:

Regarding Henry. (1991, PG-13, U.S., color, 107 minutes). Henry (Harrison Ford) is a lawyer, who, after a head injury, becomes a more caring and sensitive person.

The following companies produce useful software:

Critical Thinking Press & Software. P.O. Box 448, Pacific Grove, CA 93950. (800) 458-4850. Offers software to develop cognitive processes.

Life Care Planning Support System. Publications Department, National Head Injury Foundation, 1776 Massachusetts Avenue NW, Suite 100, Washington, DC 20036-1904. (202) 296-8850. Software helps case managers keep records of needs and expenditures.

Marblesoft. 21805 Zumbrota NE, Cedar, MN 55011. Offers software that can be used to develop cognitive skills in young children with head injuries.

Speech Viewer and THINKable Software. IBM Independence Series, IBM Educational Systems, 1 Culver Road, Dayton, NJ 08810. (800) 426-4832. Software enhances speech and cognitive skills of individuals with head injuries.

ON-LINE INFORMATION AND USEFUL DATABASES

The Perspectives Network. Internet address: http://www.tbi.org. Primary focus is collaboration. Numerous articles, frequently asked questions, and resources are provided.

Brain Injury Association, Inc. Internet address: http://www.biausa.org. Provides information on national and state offices, resources, prevention and treatment, as well as a community forum and bulletin board.

Centre for Neuro Skills. Internet address: http://biggulp.callamer.com/~cns/. An extensive resource guide on traumatic brain injury.

The Brain Injury Connection. Internet address: http://www.tbihelp.com/BIC/. Includes articles for and about people with traumatic brain injury.

Brainindex.com. Internet address: http://www.brainindex.com/tbi.html. A starting point for links to brain injury information on the web.

Glossary of TBI terms. Internet address: http://www.neuroskills.com/~cns/tbi/hdi/glb.html.

ORGANIZATIONS

Andrew Blake Foundation. Box 866, Winona, MN 55987. (507) 452-5734.

Children's Brain Diseases Foundation. 350 Parnassus Avenue, Suite 900, San Francisco, CA 94117. (415) 565-6259.

Brain Injury Foundation, Inc. (formerly National Head Injury Foundation). 105 N. Alfred Street, Alexandria, VA 22314. (703) 236-6000.

National Rehabilitation Information Center. 8455 Colesville Road, Silver Spring, MD 20910. (800) 227-0216.

COMMUNICATION DISORDERS

Contributing writer
Joyce McNeill, Ph.D.
Educational Consultant
Spanish Fort, AL

Educating
Martin Krecker

When Martin Krecker's mother Marina describes the many wonderful characteristics of her four-year-old son, she first summarizes his inherent strengths: "He's smart, he doesn't have a mean bone in his body, and he'll try anything, if you give him a few minutes to warm up."

Then, she adds, as an elaboration on Martin's strengths, that he did not talk at all until he was two and a half, and that, for several months after, he used only one- or two-word sentences like "Milk," or "Cookie gone." His sister Amy, just turned two, says, "I want milk to drink, right now." "It shows me we had reasons to be concerned about Martin's language," says Marina. Now four, Martin is speaking in full sentences.

Marina continues, "I was first concerned about his speech—he never imitated by saying 'Bye, bye.' We were pretty ignorant, thinking he just had a speech delay, especially because he communicated to us by pointing or gesturing or making noises. No red lights went on for us, but he wouldn't talk then, ever. We asked our pediatrician why Martin wasn't speaking, and the pediatrician

told us to wait until he was two to see any specialists. When Martin turned two, we continued to be stumped as to why his speech and language were delayed. He communicated by his actions, but didn't say a word. So, we took him to a speech-language pathologist in private practice who started working with him. She gave us good ideas, like paying attention to things that were obviously of interest to Martin and using an exciting tone with him. We learned a lot by watching her, and we then would do the same activities with Martin that she did with him. We found that, when we followed her model in sessions and at home, Martin paid more attention to our talk to him, but still, he wouldn't talk."

Smiling, Marina comments, "When I remember where we were two years ago, I know that Martin is really coming along. His class at a local Jewish preschool has only five students, and a wonderful teacher who is loving, warm, and makes learning fun for Martin. He is doing so well. Still, we want to know where he will be placed in kindergarten in two years, and what kind of teacher he will have, and if she'll be patient with him."

How has Martin progressed from being a withdrawn two-and-a-half-year-old who didn't speak to becoming a quiet, capable four-year-old? Marina says, "The journey has been long, and continues to be hard." When Marina contacted the local early intervention office, the only times during the following week in which its staff indicated that they could assess Martin, then not yet two and a half, were early afternoons, ". . . his nap time. That wasn't fair to Martin, if they wanted to get a picture of what he was able to do." So, Marina continued taking Martin to the private pathologist twice a week for one-hour speech and language sessions for the next several months, at the fam-

ily's expense. As time passed, Martin became more responsive, laughing with and at his speech-language pathologist and his parents, yet did not speak.

A few months before Martin turned three, he and his family moved to Florida. When Marina contacted the local school system to determine whether Martin qualified to receive special services when he turned three, she was told Martin needed to be evaluated before he could be admitted. The evaluation results were devastating to Marina and Martin's father, Martin Sr. Young Martin was labeled as having "delays across all developmental areas" with an IQ nearing that of mild mental retardation.

Martin's father reacted predictably. "I was angry. We'd had a pediatric neurolo-

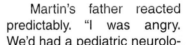

gist in Mobile suggest that Martin might have 'Einstein's syndrome,' meaning he'd start speaking in full sentences and show that he was brilliant. Then, the other end of the spectrum shows up within six months, possible mild mental retardation, and they say that after spending less than two hours with Martin!"

Amid their many tears, discussions, and arguments, Martin's parents sought help, appropriate help. What they found was "a lifeline." But they did not find it easily. "We saw just a small chance that someone could help, so we contacted a highly recommended play therapist in our area."

Pat, the play therapist, turned out to be more than a small chance for help. "She continues to be our beacon of hope. Pat got Martin to talk. Specifically, she helped him overcome his fears of simple things—playing pretend, wearing a fireman hat, and laughing freely—by challenging him to interact with these things. Before Pat, all he ever wanted to do was play dinosaur."

After six months of play therapy and their continued use of strategies learned from Pat and Martin's former speech-language pathologist, the Kreckers returned to Mobile in 1996, confident that he was not "nearly at the range of intelligence for mental retardation, and certainly not developmentally delayed in all major areas." In Mobile, the Kreckers enrolled Martin at the Jewish preschool

"because it was recommended to us by our early childhood special educator friend as being child-centered."

Martin's teacher, Kathy Getto, says, "I treat Martin no differently than the other children. Yesterday on the playground, he told me and some of his friends about going to the moon. He pretended that the climbing gym was a rocket, saying, 'I'm blasting off, I'm closing the door. . . .' The story was clear and vivid. He fits right in."

In this chapter, you will learn more about Martin and his family, his pathologist, his teacher, and others involved in his development. You will discover that his development requires the participation of his parents, teacher, and speech-language pathologist.

What Do You Think?

1. What needs to happen so that Martin's speech and language development will continue to improve? So that his social skills will continue to flourish?

2. When Martin enrolls in kindergarten in the local public schools, what services, if any, will he need?

3. How will his therapists, teachers, and parents collaborate when he is in public schools?

What Are Communication Disorders?

Defining Communication Disorders

Communication, the exchange of information and ideas, involves receiving, understanding, and expressing ideas. It is such a natural part of our daily occurrences that most of us take for granted our ability to communicate. Most of us take part in a multitude of communicative interactions each day. For example, we communicate verbally with others face-to-face or on the phone; we demonstrate social awareness by quieting our voices when seeing a raised eyebrow combined with a frown; and we wink at friends over privately shared jokes.

Although spoken language is the primary means by which we communicate, it is far from the only means used to communicate. We communicate in many ways. Some people communicate manually, using sign language and/or gestures. While speaking, others add nonlinguistic cues such as body posture, facial and vocal expression, gestures, eye contact, and head and body movements. Many speakers vary their voices by changing their pitch or rate of speaking. All of these skills make our communication more effective.

Nonlinguistic communication clues greatly influence the meaning of the spoken word. For example if Susan, speaking to Mike says, "Mike, Mary received flowers from Joe today," and if Susan says this with an exasperated sigh at the beginning of her statement and then looks at a calendar, she is telling Mike that he needs to determine why Joe sent flowers to Mary on this particular day. Mike hears Susan's tone and slow-paced speech, sees her frown, and follows her gaze to the calendar. He sees that the date is February 14, Valentine's Day. Mike now understands Susan's meaning. He has forgotten to purchase flowers for her, his girlfriend! However, if Susan had spoken with an excited, higher tone and direct eye contact coupled with a broad smile, she might have registered her anticipation that she, like Mary, knew she would be receiving flowers.

Examples such as this demonstrate that effective communication is a complicated process. It requires knowledge of spoken and unspoken rules and nuances of communicative interaction. When an individual does not understand and follow these rules,

Because communication is crucial to our daily existence, a communication disorder would cause most of us difficulties, sometimes dramatic difficulties, in our social interactions. Our inability to communicate effectively can alter the course of our lives.

Communication involves speaking as well as a multitude of nonverbal behaviors such as facial expression, gestures, and head and body movements.

disordered communication may occur (Hedge, 1991). For example, if an individual's social interactions or emotional growth are delayed because of communication problems, a communication disorder may be present (Emerick & Haynes, 1986). Likewise, if an individual's spoken statement is incorrect, a communication disorder may exist. A communication disorder may result in ineffective interactions.

The Distinction Between Communication Disorders: Speech and Language.

The American Speech-Language-Hearing Association (ASHA) defines a communication impairment as either a speech disorder or a language disorder (ASHA, 1993). A **speech disorder** reflects problems in delivering messages orally, such as when repeating words, mispronouncing sounds, or speaking with inadequate breath. A **language disorder** is a problem in receiving, understanding, and formulating ideas and information. Both types of communication disorders are addressed in the Individuals with Disabilities Education Act (IDEA) as being disorders that adversely affect a student's educational performance (C.F.R., Part 300, Section 300.7, 1992). Martin has a speech impairment, as demonstrated when he says, "Nyes," for "Yes." Two years ago, he also exhibited a serious language delay, because, although he communicated nonverbally by pointing, gesturing, and looking toward desired objects, he did not speak. The order of the words in his sentences still is sometimes incorrect, a less serious language disability than he manifested two years ago, as when he said, "I want now to do that."

Martin used to manifest further language delays when he had difficulties processing what others said to him or asked him. For example, a year ago, his early childhood educator asked him what his pet dog might do after it slid down the fire chute. Martin repeated a portion of what he had heard ("Dog do after slide?"), demonstrating echolalia (see Chapter 10). Echolalia gave Martin time to process what he had been asked, yet he did not respond. A year later, in response to the same question, Martin replied immediately, not requiring time to process before answering, "He could climb in truck with firemen."

Although Martin's communication continues to improve, his sentence structure, social responses, and speech are still somewhat different from that of others his age; indeed, they are different enough to be considered communication delays, or possibly, disorders.

Speech disorders and language disorders are often associated with other disorders. Specifically, speech disorders are sometimes associated with cerebral palsy, unrepaired **cleft lip and/or palate,** or hearing loss. Likewise, language disorders are sometimes the primary feature by which other disorders (e.g., mental retardation, autism, and **central auditory processing disorders**) are identified. Auditory processing requires several skills, such as attending to input, discriminating between important and unimportant input, blending sounds that are heard, and remembering input (Nicolosi, Harryman, & Kresheck, 1996). The inability to use language skills such as these results in language disorders.

Speech and language disorders are often associated with other disabling conditions, so speech-language therapy is one of the most frequently provided related services for children with these additional disabilities. One-fifth of all children identified for special education services (one million total) receive services for language and/or speech disorders (U.S. Department of Education, 1996).

Cultural Differences in Communication.

Although many individuals have a speech or language difference, they do not necessarily have a language or speech disorder. Difference does not always mean disorder. Every language contains a variety of forms, called **dialects.** Dialects are language variations used by a group of individuals that reflect their shared regional, social, or cultural/ethnic factors (ASHA, 1983). For example, individuals in the midwestern United States might say that they are going *tooling,* driving around town, while many others in the United States might wonder if *tooling* means working in a tool shop. Families with roots in Appalachia may *tote* rather than *carry* materials, a word derived by mountaineers from the African language. Deaf individuals in California have a

---

Speech disorders are a group of communication disorders or impairments that affect an individual's production of sounds, rhythm of speech, or voice quality.

Language disorders are a group of communication disorders or impairments that reflect the individual's inability to use the rules of the language system to produce or understand a message.

Cleft palate/lip is a condition in which there is a split in the upper part of the oral cavity or the upper lip.

Central auditory processing disorders are manifested by difficulty with auditory skills such as attending to input, discriminating between important and unimportant input, blending sounds that are heard, and remembering input.

Dialect is a regional variety of a language, such as when someone speaks English using terms or pronunciations used only in that region.

distinct technological sign for *computer,* because Silicon Valley in California is the nation's center for computer technology. Similarly, individuals in the South may say that they are *fixin' to* do something, rather than that they are going to do something.

To consider the impact of historic, geographic, and societal factors on students' language, some researchers and educators advise teachers to encourage students to study how their language differs from the traditional language of the larger community. For example, the topic of having African American students study the differences and similarities in the grammatical makeup of black English in order that they be able to understand and use standard English has been suggested. This idea has been fraught with contention since becoming known to the majority of the American population as the **ebonics** controversy in late 1996.

In a move that sparked national debate, the Oakland, California, Unified School District applied for federal funding to provide teachers with the knowledge necessary to identify black English grammar so that they can help African American students who use black English to use standard English grammar. Some African Americans applauded the study of ebonics, saying that its study ensured the continuation of the African American historical influence in America and the acculturation of many black Americans to the social norms of a predominant culture. Others reacted negatively, believing that ebonics would doom many African Americans to social or economic failure. This controversy has no simple solution.

> **Ebonics** is the study of the differences and similarities in the grammatical makeup of black English and standard English.

Like language differences, speech differences occur across the United States. In the South, many individuals say *fahv* and *nahn* for *five* and *nine,* and midwesterners may say that they want to *mayzure* something, rather than *mehzure* (measure). Many Bostonians delete the "r" in the middle and at the ends of words, as do many Southerners (*car* sounds like *kah* and *hurt* like *hu-t.*) These speech differences result from geographic factors. Specifically, many speech differences of those living in the South are attributable to the heritage of many of their ancestors, who came from the United Kingdom to the Northeast United States, then to the South.

While differences in dialects do not necessarily indicate communication disorders, a student with a dialectical difference may exhibit a communication disorder. The ASHA requires that a specialist be able to distinguish characteristics that are based on dialects from communication errors (ASHA, 1983).

Describing the Characteristics

To become an effective communicator, a student must (a) master the many systems and rules that produce correct speech and language and (b) know and follow the language and speech rules of the different settings. For most children, the development of speech and language follows a predictable pattern and timetable. For others, it does not; these children may have a communication disorder. In this section, you will learn about the characteristics of normal speech and language development, so that you may better understand atypical speech and language development.

Typical Speech Development. Speech is the expression of language in sounds (McCormick, 1990b). The sounds are formed by varying the position of the lips, the tongue, and the lower jaw as the air passes through the larynx (voice box), pharynx (a space extending from the nasal cavities to the esophagus), mouth, and nose. The larynx sits on top of the trachea and contains the vocal folds (ligaments of the larynx); voice is produced here. As air is pushed from the lungs, the vocal folds are moved by the muscle of the larynx, producing sounds. Figure 14–1 illustrates the physical mechanisms used for speech.

Children quickly learn to produce speech sounds during their early years. By the age of eight, they have learned to produce nearly all the consonants and vowels that make up the words of the family's native language. Learning these sounds usually proceeds in a fairly consistent sequence, but there may be as much as a three-year variance between

FIGURE 14–1 *Speech mechanism*

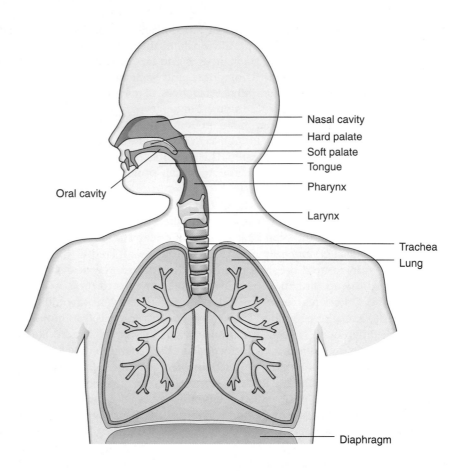

Nasal cavity
Hard palate
Soft palate
Tongue
Pharynx
Larynx
Trachea
Lung
Oral cavity
Diaphragm

Articulation is the speaker's production of individual or sequenced speech sounds.

Like other students with speech impairments, Martin's great expectations are within his reach, especially as he receives more therapy and makes more progress.

the time that some children learn a particular sound and the time when others learn the same sound (McCormick, 1990a). Figure 14–2 illustrates the times at which 90 percent of English-speaking children have mastered the consonant sounds needed for speech.

Because 90 percent of children have mastered "r" by the time they are six, it is understandable why a three-year-old might continue to say "wabbit" for "rabbit." Similarly, a three-year-old may say "lellow" for "yellow," but a seven-year-old who still says "lellow" may demonstrate an **articulation** (pronunciation) problem that is severe enough for a speech-language pathologist to identify the problem as an articulation disorder.

Characteristics of Speech Impairments. Speech impairments can include disorders of articulation, voice, and fluency (rate of speech). These disorders can occur alone, in combination with each other, or in conjunction with other disorders. For example, students who have hearing losses (see Chapter 15) or cerebral palsy (see Chapter 12) often

FIGURE 14–2 *Typical ages for mastery of consonant sounds*

By age 3:	/p/, /m/, /h/, /n/, /w/
By age 4	/b/, /k/, /g/, /d/, /f/, /y/
By age 6:	/t/, /ng/, /r/, /l/, /s/
By age 7:	/ch/, /sh/, /j/, /th/ as in "think"
By age 8:	/s/, /z/, /v/, /th/ as in "that"
Even later:	/zh/ as in "measure"

Note: From "When Are Speech Sounds Learned?' by B. Sander, 1972, *Journal of Speech and Hearing Disorders, 37,* pp. 55–63. Copyright 1972 by the American Speech-Language-Hearing Association. Adapted with permission.

have articulation or voice disorders, as well as language disorders. Similarly, some students with mental retardation may demonstrate no communication delays, while others demonstrate speech delays, language delays, or both speech and language delays.

Articulation Disorders.   Articulation disorders are by far the largest group of speech impairments. An articulation disorder occurs when the student is unable to produce correctly the various sounds and sound combinations of speech (Hulit & Howard, 1993). When skills are atypical for a child's age, the child may have an articulation disorder (Weiss, Gordon, & Lillywhite, 1987).

Articulation errors may consist of substitutions, omissions, additions, and distortions. Substitutions are common, such as when a child replaces the appropriate speech sound, called a *phoneme,* with one that is more easily produced. Common substitutions are "d" for the voiced "th," as in *doze* for *those,* "t" for "k", as in *tat* for *cat,* or "w" for "r", as in *wabbit* for *rabbit.*

Omissions are also very common. Omissions occur when a child leaves a phoneme out of a word. Children often omit sounds from consonant pairs (*boo* for *blue*) and from the ends of words (*kah* for *car*). When Martin began speaking, he omitted many final consonant sounds, so that words such as *cup* and *hat* were produced as *kuh* and *hah.*

Additions typically occur when a vowel is placed between two consonants, such as when "tree" becomes "tahree."

Distortions are modifications of the production of a phoneme in a word; a listener gets the sense that the sound is being produced, but it sounds distorted. Martin's *nyes* is not truly an addition of the sound "n" to *yes.* It is a distortion of the production of the sound "y" which begins *yes,* caused by weak muscle tone in his tongue. Common distortions, called lisps, occur when the "s," "z," "sh," and "ch" are mispronounced.

Articulation problems, like all communication disorders, vary; many children have mild or moderate articulation disorders; their speech is understood by others yet contains mispronunciations. Other children have serious articulation disorders, making them nearly impossible for others to understand.

There are many reasons for you to refer a student with articulation problems to a speech-language pathologist. If an articulation problem has a negative effect on the child's interactions in your class or negatively affects the child's educational performance, referral is needed. Likewise, if a child's mispronunciation makes his speech difficult or impossible to understand, referral is needed. Furthermore, articulation problems resulting from neurological damage (e.g., cerebral palsy and stroke) require therapy. Therapy is also needed to assist students with clefts of the palate or lip if they are unable to produce speech sounds or sound combinations correctly. Additionally, therapy may be needed to help a student with a hearing loss who is experiencing difficulty in correctly producing speech sounds.

Voice Disorders.   Each person has a unique voice. This voice reflects the interactive relationship of pitch, duration, intensity, resonance, and vocal quality.

Pitch is determined by the rate of vibration in the vocal folds; men tend to have lower pitched voices than do women. Pitch is affected by the tension and size of the vocal folds, the health of the larynx, and the location of the larynx. Duration is the length of time any speech sound requires; voice disorders associated with duration may manifest as lengthened or shortened vowels or consonants.

Intensity (loudness or softness) is based on the perception of the listener and is determined by the air pressure coming from the lungs through the vocal folds. Rarely do individuals believe that their voices are too loud. Rather, they may seek professional voice therapy because their voices are too soft. If you have a student who speaks too loudly, you may refer the student to the speech-language pathologist.

Resonance is determined by the way in which the tone coming from the vocal folds is modified by the cavities of the throat, mouth, and nose. Individuals with unrepaired cleft palate may experience resonance problems because the opening from their mouth to their nasal cavity may be too large or inappropriately shaped.

Among children with other disabilities, the prevalence of articulation disorders is higher than in the general population.

All too often, a student's voice disorders can stand in the way of relationships with others.

Resonance (of the voice) is the perceived quality of the voice. Perceptions of harshness or breathiness are included in the judgments of the resonance of the voice. Resonance is determined by the characteristics of the mouth and throat.

Hyponasality is a speech problem in which air cannot pass through a speaker's nose as it is supposed to and comes through the speaker's mouth instead. The speaker may sound as if the nose is being held.

Sometimes, students without a cleft palate have resonance problems; they may sound as if they are holding their noses when speaking. This is called **hyponasality,** because air cannot pass through their nose and comes through their mouth instead. Other of these students have a different trait, **hypernasality,** in which air is allowed to pass through their nasal cavity on sounds other than "m," "n," and "ng," those that are supposed to be produced by allowing air to pass through their nasal passages. Speech therapy may be needed to teach them the appropriate ways to produce nonnasal sounds.

The quality of the voice is affected by problems of breath support or vocal-fold functioning. Students' most common voice disorders are **vocal nodules** caused by yelling. You might have experienced short-term vocal quality problems after a football game. The abuse of the vocal folds causes vocal nodules, callous-like growths that result from the rubbing together of the vocal fold edges. When the folds cannot vibrate properly or come together completely, the sound of your voice will change temporarily, until the vocal nodules heal. This short-term vocal quality problem usually heals because the vocal-fold abuse is not constant. However, if vocal nodules develop and persist, therapy may be needed to help a student learn to talk in a way that is less abusive to the vocal mechanisms. In most cases, nodules disappear following vocal rest and/or voice therapy. If vocal nodules are the result of an organic problem, therapy alone may not resolve the vocal nodules, and surgery may be required to remove them.

Hypernasality is a speech problem in which air is allowed to pass through a speaker's nasal cavity on sounds other than those for which air is supposed to pass through the nasal passage.

Fluency Disorders.   Normal speech requires correct articulation, vocal quality, as well as fluency (rate of speaking). **Fluency problems** are characterized as interruptions in the flow of speaking, such as atypical rate, rhythm, and repetitions of sounds, syllables, words, and phrases (ASHA, 1983).

All children and adults have difficulties with fluency on occasion (Palmer & Yantis, 1990). Occasional misfluency is not considered stuttering. **Stuttering,** repeating words or sounds, is suspected when the disruptions in speech are frequent and are accompanied by the speaker's anxiety or compensatory behaviors like grimacing (Cantwell & Baker, 1987). Approximately 1 percent of the population—two to three million Americans—stutter. More males than females stutter, and the cause of stuttering is not definitely known.

When people experience allergy problems or have a cold with a sore throat, their resonance is usually affected, because the air going through their nose and/or throat cavity is restricted.

Because stuttering can be emotional and socially stigmatizing, researchers continue to search for a "cure" for stuttering. A variety of treatments have been attempted, with varying levels of success. These include encouraging the child who stutters to (a) prolong certain sounds, (b) stop other activities while communicating, (c) speak more slowly, (d) practice speaking to a rhythmic beat, and (e) read aloud while listening to audiotaped

Vocal nodules are small knots or lumps on the speech mechanism.

Fluency problems are difficulties with the accuracy and the rate with which speech is produced. Fluent speech is smooth, flows well, and is effortless.

Stuttering is interruption in the fluency of speech. It is characterized by the frequent occurrence of speech disfluency, tension, and struggle, and may include other related behaviors.

James Earl Jones reports that he experienced severe stuttering problems as a child. Now, he is well-known for his fluent speech and deep voice.

books. When you talk to students who stutter, you will want to speak more slowly, pause, and listen attentively (LaBlance, Steckol, & Smith, 1994; Pierangelo, 1995).

Typical Language Development.

Children's language development, the development of their abilities to receive, understand, and formulate language, is complex. By three weeks of age, infants provide messages; specifically, the newborns with normal development engage their caregivers in jointly referring to objects (e.g., infants look, and caregivers reply with, "Oh, do you see that?" or "You are looking at mommy's face!"). They also engage caregivers with their deliberate, social smiles (Hedge, 1991) in the first weeks of life. By two to three months of age, infants coo. By four to six months, they produce universal speech sounds. Later that first year, babbling turns to vocal play, where babies string English sounds together, as in "ba, la, ba, la, ba." By their first birthdays, babies make sounds when spoken to, change vocal pitch and intensity, and experiment with rhythm; they may even say their first words. Within the next year, their spoken vocabularies increase to 200 to 300 words. By the age of three, toddlers understand simple questions and prepositions such as *in, on, under,* and *up,* and they are able to follow two-step directions. The rapid development continues, and by age four, preschoolers ask questions using *who, what, when, where, why,* and *how,* and have vocabularies of 1,000 to 1,500 words. By six, they use irregular verbs such as *be, go, run,* and *swim,* and can verbally share their feelings and thoughts. Figure 14–3 provides further information regarding normal language development for children ages birth through six.

Some children do not demonstrate normal language development. Some may have serious difficulties in receiving and then understanding language; this is a **receptive language disorder.** For example, a child may not understand a series of commands, such as, "After you hang up your paint smock, go close the paint buckets and wash your hands." A student might not comprehend what is said, because he or she may have language limitations resulting from central auditory processing difficulties, mental retardation, hearing loss, or **multilingualism** (use of more than one language for communication).

Children who have difficulties organizing their ideas to express them through spoken language have an **expressive language disorder.** Students with expressive language problems may lack appropriate vocabulary (a five-year-old saying, "I have two shoes" for all pairs of foot coverings); may use verb tenses incorrectly (a seven-year-old stating, "I goed to that store"); and/or may use plurals incorrectly ("I got three truck and one car"). Expressive language problems result from a variety of causes, including hearing loss, deafness, recurring middle ear infections, mental retardation, multilingualism, and **early expressive language delay,** a significant delay in the development of expressive language that is apparent by age two.

Receptive language disorders are difficulties with receiving and understanding language.

Multilingualism is the ability to use more than one language for communication.

Expressive language disorders are difficulties with expressing ideas verbally, manually, or in other ways.

Early expressive language delay is a significant delay in the development of expressive language that is apparent by age two.

A child with early expressive language delay demonstrates a significant delay in expressive language that he or she does not outgrow. Nonetheless, a student with that kind of delay can be included in school if early and sustained therapy is available.

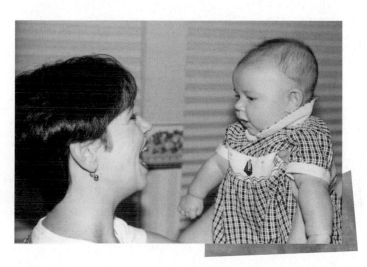

 Babies' social smiles make communicating more rewarding for mothers, as the babies respond positively to mothers. Because of this, mothers communicate more often with babies, making communication more rewarding for the babies, too.

FIGURE 14–3 *Typical language development*

Age	Developmental Milestones
Birth to 6 Months	Differentiated cry for emotions and needs such as hunger and pain Coos in response to familiar situations Laughs Responds to voices and other sounds differentially
6 to 12 Months	Listens to new words Understands own name and "No" Uses many sounds differentially and with inflection; babbles Imitates sound patterns and motor acts such as waving good-bye Responds to simple commands such as "come here," "give me _____" Recognizes the names of familiar people and objects
12 to 18 Months	Names familiar objects with single words Mixes jargon (speech sounds with inflection) with single words Uses speech socially to interact with others Recognizes more words and commands Five- to fifty-word vocabulary Identifies one to three body parts (at eighteen months), such as "Where's your nose?" Points to pictures named in a book.
18 to 24 Months	Strings two or more words together 200–300 word vocabulary by twenty-four months Understands possessives Uses plurals No longer uses jargon by twenty-four months Uses simple adverbs and adjectives (big, nice, good) Uses some verbs Understands (but may ignore) simple directives Listens to caregiver's speech and imitates important parts

Age	Developmental Milestones
24 to 36 months	Understands objects by use, such as "what do we eat with?" Understands simple questions and pronouns Understands the prepositions *in, on, under, up,* and *down* Follows two-step directions Listens to stories Uses turn-taking in communicating with others Uses two-word and longer phrases Vocabulary of 900–1,000 words Recounts events Asks simple questions
36 to 48 months	Asks questions using *who, what, when, where,* and *how* Tells stories, both real and imaginary Understands most compound and complex sentences and uses some Can explain and describe events Vocabulary of 1,000–1,500 words Asks *why* questions Uses communication to engage playmates Uses verb contractions Some articulation difficulties with /l/, /r/, /s/, /z/, /ch/, /sh/, /j/, /th/ Can complete verbal analogies, such as "Joe is a boy, Mary is a _____ "
4 to 5 Years	Uses the prepositions *in, on,* and *under* Understands *if, because, when,* and *why* Uses conjunctions and longer, more complex sentences Still makes some grammatical errors Can give first and last name, gender, and telephone number Uses past tense
5 to 6 Years	Vocabulary of 2,500–2,800 words Responds to most complex sentences though sometimes confused Uses comparative adjectives (big, bigger, biggest) Uses irregular verbs (be, go, swim) Correctly uses articles *a* and *the* Tells familiar stories and imaginative tales Shares personal feelings and thoughts verbally Talks things out rather than always acts them out Can use the telephone Recognizes and tells jokes

Note: From *Early Language Intervention: An Introduction* (2nd ed.), edited by L. McCormick and R. L. Schiefelbusch, 1990, Upper Saddle River, NJ: Merrill/Prentice Hall. Copyright 1990 by Merrill/Prentice Hall. Reprinted with permission.

According to ASHA (1993), the five dimensions that work together to produce language are phonology (sounds), morphology (word forms), syntax (word order and sentence structure), semantics (word and sentence meanings), and pragmatics (social use of language). Each dimension works together with the others, usually resulting in effective communication.

Phonology. The use of sounds to make meaningful syllables and words and the function of these sounds to signal a change of meaning is called **phonology.** Phonology is a much broader concept than articulation. Phonology encompasses the wide repertoire of individual phonemes and how they are produced, depending on their placement in a syllable or word. For example, consonants at the beginning of syllables or words (e.g., *t*ap) are produced slightly differently from those in the middle (e.g., ca*tt*le) or end of syllables or words (e.g., pa*t*). Phonological use requires correct pronunciation as well as awareness of sound differences as they signal change in meaning (Fey, 1992). In English, for instance, the word *bill* is different from *pill* by only one phoneme: "b." The other phonemes in each word, short vowel "i" and "l," are the same. By changing one phoneme, a speaker can produce a totally different word.

Morphology. **Morphology** is the system that governs the structure of words and the construction of word forms (ASHA, 1993). Phonemes have little meaning on their own, but some can be grouped into syllables or words that have meaning. The smallest meaningful unit of speech is called a *morpheme.* For instance, when "s" is added to *bill,* the word becomes plural. Formerly, having one morpheme, the word now has two—*bill* (a mouth structure, or a written document), and *-s* (denoting plurality). Morphological rules allow speakers to add plurals, past-tense markers to verbs, inflection, and affixes. For example, correct use of morphological rules allows a child to change "swim" to "swimmed," then, as the child matures, to "swam," an irregular past-tense verb.

Syntax. **Syntax** provides rules for putting together a series of words to form sentences and provides rules necessary to form relationships among the elements within the sentences (ASHA, 1993). The ability to use syntax is both a receptive and an expressive skill. Receptively, a child must be able to note the significance in the order of others' words (e.g., "I want that cookie," means that a cookie is desired by the speaker, whereas "Do I want that cookie?" indicates a question in which the speaker is determining if he or she wants a cookie). Expressively, a child must be able to use word order appropriately (e.g., "I want a cookie" to indicate that a cookie is desired, rather than "Cookie, I want"). Just as morphology provides the rules for putting together strings of phonemes, syntax provides rules for putting together series of morphemes.

The first three dimensions of language—phonology, morphology, and syntax—all combine to determine the form of language, that is, what the language looks like. The next two dimensions of language—semantics and pragmatics—are more advanced dimensions of language, determining the content and social use of language (Bloom & Lahey, 1978).

Semantics. **Semantics** refers to the content of what is expressed, the meaning as well as the relationship between words that determines meaning. Semantic development has both receptive and expressive components. Children first learn to understand the meaning of words and then to verbally or manually use the words and sentences meaningfully. Children start out with a small number of words that represent a large number of objects in their environments. For example, Martin first labeled all animals as "doggie." As he developed more precise semantic rules, he differentiated various categories of animals (e.g., "dog," "cat"), and then refined their definition from categories of animals to specifics within the category (e.g., he referred to types of dogs as poodles, Pomeranians, or Dalmatians).

Pragmatics. The term **pragmatics** refers to the use of communication in social contexts. Caregivers and infants use the rules of pragmatics in their interactions (Rossetti, 1991), and children learn to use social communication very early. After using social smiles and simple verbalizations, children request objects, actions, or information; protest actions; comment on objects or actions; greet; and acknowledge comments (Roberts & Crais,

---

Phonology is one of the five sets of rules in our language system. This set of rules defines the way sounds are combined to form words and how those sounds are changed to alter word meanings.

English uses forty-five different speech sounds.

Morphology is one of the five sets of rules governing our language system. Morphological rules dictate how the smallest meaningful units of our language, called *morphemes,* will be combined to form words. A word may be one morpheme, as in *duck.* Adding another single morpheme, /s/, changes the meaning. Morphological rules allow us to make this change in meaning consistently and to understand the change when we hear it.

Syntax is one of the five sets of rules governing our language system. Syntactic rules determine how word order will be used and interpreted in communication.

A student who chooses to use the correct grammar rules may have a better chance at being included in school and community than a student who does not make that choice.

Semantics is one of the five sets of rules governing our language system. Semantic rules prescribe how words will be used meaningfully in communication.

Caregivers and children interact pragmatically through their spoken and unspoken communication.

1989). These skills allow children to use language to socially interact within their environments more efficiently.

No one knows for sure just how the five dimensions of language come to work together so that children acquire useful language. However, theories explaining how children acquire language abound. In the 1950s, Chomsky (1957) proposed that children are born ready to develop language skills because of an inborn language acquisition device. Later, behaviorists proposed that the ability to learn and use language is not inborn but that it results as children imitate and practice. Today, researchers investigate the effects of child imitation, practice, and other social interactions on language development, and the compilation of their research is referred to as the social interaction theories.

Social interaction theories emphasize that communication skills are learned through social interactions. These theories hold that language development is the outcome of a child's drive for attachment with his or her world; in other words, communication develops in order that the child may convey information about his or her environment to others. The means that the child uses to communicate is determined by the child's assessment of the listener's knowledge about the social context of the communication (Duchan, Hewitt, & Sonnenmeier, 1994; Hulit & Howard, 1993).

The belief that social context and interaction within that context influence communicative choice is supported by the philosopher Lev Vygotsky. In his book *Thought and Language* (1978), Vygotsky suggests that children's development is determined by supplementing their independent problem-solving abilities with adult guidance or peer collaboration. In other words, children learn by doing, from interacting with their more experienced partners. Social interactionists agree with Vygotsky's premise that children learn language by interacting with adults, who naturally have more experience, or peers, who may have more or different experience (Berk, 1994; Dixon-Krauss, 1995; Ninio & Bruner, 1978; Wells, 1992).

The social interactional theories highlight that the desire to communicate is the impetus for children to learn the rules and symbols of language. Some children, however, do not

Most children interact pragmatically with their parents through speech, physical actions, facial expressions, and body language. Most parents respond in pragmatic ways as well. These kinds of interactions can be the keys to relationships outside families, too.

Social interaction theories are the theories proposed by researchers like Lev Vygotsky (1978) that support the belief that language is learned through encounters with others.

appear motivated to communicate. For example, three-year-old Martin rarely spoke or gestured, and when he did, it was only to one of his parents. His expressive language delays negatively impacted others' perceptions of him, including the psychologist who found him to be globally delayed. The heavy emphasis on expressive and receptive language skills used in the tests designed for preschoolers depressed his scores in the areas of cognition and language. Today, however, his more age-appropriate, interactive communication skills cause his peers to treat him "like one of the gang," according to his teacher.

Characteristics of Language Impairments.   Recently, speech-language pathologists have shifted their focus from correction of speech disorders to correction of language disorders, in large part because they have been actively involved in providing services to students with special needs. The pathologists work with children who have problems with one or more of the dimensions of language to help them receive, understand, formulate, and express a message. Most children with language disorders experience impairments in more than one dimension of language. In this section, you will learn about the characteristics of disorders in language.

Phonology.   Students with phonological disorders may be unable to discriminate differences in sounds or sound segments that signify differences in words. For example, the word *pen* may sound no different from *pin,* or *whale* from *well* or *wail* to students with phonological disorders. Their inability to differentiate sounds may cause them to experience reading and/or spelling difficulties (Aaron & Joshi, 1992; Kamhi & Catts, 1991; Stanovich, 1988).

Morphology.   Children with morphological disorders have difficulty using the structure of words to get or give information. They may make a variety of errors. For example, they may match subjects and verbs incorrectly (e.g., "the ducks swims") or use the incorrect verb tense ("I done did it"). When a child is unable to use morphological rules appropriately, the average length of the child's utterances is sometimes shorter than that expected for the child's age, as plurals, verb markers, and affixes may be missing from their statements.

Incorrect morphology is associated with differences in dialects as well as with a variety of disabling conditions, including autism, hearing loss or deafness, mental retardation, and expressive language delay. Incorrect use of morphology is also associated with **specific language impairment,** those language impairments with no directly known cause and apparent normal development in all other developmental areas.

Syntax.   According to Peterson (1989), **syntax errors** are errors in word order, such as ordering words in a manner that does not convey meaning to the listeners ("Where one them park at?"); using immature structures for a given age or developmental level (e.g., a three-year-old child using two-word utterances, such as "him sick"); misusing negatives (a four-year-old child saying "Him no go"); or omitting structures (e.g., "He go now").

Again, as with phonology and morphology, differences in syntax sometimes are associated with dialects and difficulties caused by bi- or multilingualism. Syntactical disorders may result from specific language impairment, mental retardation, hearing loss, or a combination of these or other factors.

Semantics.   Children who have difficulty with semantic rules often do not have difficulty with single word meanings; rather, their problems involve using words together in sentences. Students with semantic disorders may have difficulty with words with double meanings (e.g., *break,* as a verb meaning "to rupture, or ruin," or as a noun meaning "time off from"); abstract terms (e.g., *cooperate*); synonyms (e.g., *warm* and *tepid*); and idioms (e.g., "slip your coat on") (Owens, 1995). Some students with semantic disorders may have problems with words that express time and space *(night, dark);* cause and effect (e.g., *push button, ball goes*); and inclusion versus exclusion (e.g., *all, none*).

Sometimes, students with semantic language disorders rely on words with fairly non-specific meanings (e.g., *thing, one, that*) because of their limited knowledge of vocabu-

Specific language impairment is a language disorder with no identifiable cause and with apparent normal development in all other developmental areas.

Syntax errors are mistakes in using the rules that govern the arrangement of words in a language.

lary. Specifically, these students find it much easier to say, "Give me that thing, please," than to try to remember a vocabulary word that is not part of their automatic language repertoires (e.g., *protractor, scissors*).

Pragmatics. **Pragmatics** focus on the social use of language—the communication between a speaker and listener within a shared social environment. Pragmatic skills include using appropriate manners in varied situations, obtaining and maintaining eye contact, using appropriate body language, maintaining topic, and turn-taking in conversations.

A student who talks for long periods of time and does not allow anyone else an opportunity to converse may be displaying signs of a pragmatic disorder. Students whose comments are not related to the conversational topic may also be displaying signs of a pragmatic disorder. A student who asks questions but does not acknowledge the answers by responding to them may be exhibiting a pragmatic disorder.

One group of students who have difficulty with classroom language is students with traumatic brain injury (see Chapter 13). The social use of language can be especially frustrating for them, because they have acquired a language disorder after a period of normal development or have acquired one that is more severe than the developmental language disorder that they had before their injury. The acquisition of a language disorder after normal language development can be devastating to these students. Whereas the student most likely did not suffer from problems in formulating, retrieving, decoding, or expressing language before the injury, he or she now experiences receptive and expressive language problems (Szekeres & Meserve, 1994). Acquired aphasia (see Chapter 13) is particularly difficult for the individual with traumatic brain injury, who typically retains his or her preinjury intelligence yet may be unable to understand relatively simple comments and questions or to respond appropriately (Szekeres & Meserve, 1994).

Effects of Communication Disorders. The impact of a communication impairment is evident in many aspects of a person's life. Students with articulation disorders that cause them to be difficult or impossible to comprehend are not as likely to be selected as social partners by others (Rice, Hadley, & Alexander, 1993). Those with mild-to-moderate articulation problems are sometimes ridiculed or ignored by their peers (LaBlance et al., 1994). Students with fluency disorders may have difficulty developing positive feelings about themselves (Bobrick, 1995; Culatta & Goldberg, 1995).

Similarly, language disorders can result in social and academic difficulties. Students with language impairments are more likely than other students to experience academic problems. They are more likely to have problems with reading and writing than their peers, because they may not be able to recognize rhyming words or words that differ in only one phoneme (e.g., *bit* and *pit*) (Fey, Catts, & Larrivee, 1995; Hodson, Nonmura, & Zappia, 1989; Wallach & Butler, 1994). They are also more likely to experience difficulties in social interactions (Bashir, 1989). As Goldstein and Kaczmarek (1992) attest, communication skills provide a means for controlling the social environment. Without appropriate communication skills, social interactions may be severely limited, less satisfying, and frustrating. In Box 14–1, see how Bob Martel has dealt with the frustration caused by the setback in his expressive vocabulary and memory that occurred when he experienced a loss of oxygen to his brain.

Identifying the Causes of Communication Disorders

Researchers have divided the types of speech and language disorders into two classifications relating to their cause: (a) functional disorders, those with no identifiable organic or neurological cause, and (b) organic disorders, those caused by an identifiable problem in the neuromuscular mechanism of the person. Most children have functional disorders. The causes of organic disorders are numerous; they may originate in the nervous system, the muscular system, or in the formation of the speech mechanism. They may include hereditary malformations, prenatal injuries, toxic disturbances, tumors, traumas, seizures, infectious diseases, muscular diseases, and vascular impairments (Wang & Baron, 1997).

Pragmatics is one of the five sets of rules governing our language system. Pragmatic rules are those that dictate how we use language in interactions and in context. Pragmatic rules recognize that language usage occurs between at least two people and takes place in a setting.

A student who is ignorant of pragmatics may find it difficult to have relationships with others.

Speech disorders can result in serious social and/or academic difficulties.

BOX 14-1   MY VOICE

BOB MARTEL

Bob Martel was an honor student, a skilled golfer, and a very popular person in his high school. He also had a heart condition and knew he shouldn't run a race. Nevertheless, he made the decision to do it anyway. "When I fell everyone thought I was just joking." Bob had a heart attack, suffered a loss of oxygen to his brain, and became comatose.

He recalls waking up from his coma and being able to say three words: "mom," "dad," and "bullets." Thinking about why he was able to use those three words, Bob says, "My dad and I went to all the Washington Bullets ball games." When he found he was unable to use his expressive language, Bob says, "It was like the words would form in my head but not in my mouth."

After leaving the hospital, Bob initially went to the Children's Rehabilitation Center in Charlottesville, Virginia. There he learned to walk and talk all over again. Some of his language and physical skills returned as a part of the natural recovery process. Speech and language therapy to facilitate and maximize his recovery focused on helping him recall words that were in his head but not in his mouth. He was asked to name things, to recall their function, and to make sentences to express himself. This work continued when he returned home and was enrolled in a program in Springfield, Virginia, which provided individualized language therapy and educational services. Some of the activities included recalling items or stories, making sentences from scrambled words, and describing likenesses and differences in objects.

Through special instruction and speech and language therapy, Bob's skills have greatly improved. He finished high school and was awarded the Outstanding Student Award in special education along with his diploma.

Today Bob is a handsome young man of thirty with a terrific sense of humor. When asked to describe how he is doing, he says his memory is the biggest problem. He has a great deal of difficulty with details and must write everything down to remember it.

"I used to take hard subjects like advanced calculus and American history, but now I don't remember anything. I don't remember any French either, but that's a godsend."

Organic language problems are difficulties in understanding or using language that are caused by a known problem in a person's neuromuscular mechanism.

Functional language problems are those difficulties associated with using language in everyday, real-life activities that have no known biological basis.

Speech disorders may be functional or organic. **Organic language problems** causing a fluency or an articulation disorder sometimes occur for children with cerebral palsy as they substitute or repeat sounds because of neuromuscular disabilities. Organic problems related to voice sometimes occur when students have cleft palate; the cleft causes oral malformations resulting in the voice disorder.

Language disorders also may be functional or organic. A **functional language problem** causing a fluency disorder is stuttering, where the cause is unknown. Likewise, a functional problem related to a voice disorder may be a temporary loss of voice resulting from temporary emotional distress.

Sometimes, communication disorders are both functional and organic. For example, a student with cerebral palsy may have poor speech, caused by an organic neuromuscular problem. Additionally, he may have language problems with no known cause. For instance, he may have difficulty using plurals (a morphological problem) and putting words in sentences in the correct order (syntax). Because no apparent cause for his language delays exists, the cause of the language delay is functional, whereas the cause of the speech disorder is organic. As you can see in Box 14-2, "My Voice," Fred Smith appears to have functional language disorders; he exhibits articulation disorders and difficulty using plurals that are not definitely related to his seizures or attention-deficit/hyperactivity disorder.

Communication disorders can be classified further according to when the problem began. Children can be born with a problem causing a disorder, such as a child who is born with cleft palate, cerebral palsy, autism, brain damage, mental retardation, hearing loss, or deafness. When the disorder is present at birth, it is called a *congenital impairment*. A disorder that is acquired occurs after a period of normal communication. For example, if a student's speech and language develop normally, but something happens that affects the development, the disorder is acquired. The acquired disorder can be caused by an accident (e.g., traumatic brain injury) or by illnesses or infections (e.g., high fever, meningitis, and recurring middle ear infection). The illness, fever, or infection can nega-

BOX 14.2 **MY VOICE**

ELIZABETH JOHNSTON

Fred Smith "amazes everybody," according to his mother, Elizabeth. "He's learning to read, and likes being read to. Fred reading—that is a big step."

Why is learning to read a big step for Fred?

Fred, age eight, has both expressive and receptive language delays, attention-deficit/hyperactivity disorder, and a seizure disorder. He takes medication for his seizures and attention-deficit/hyperactivity disorder. Elizabeth explains: "He has trouble expressing his thoughts and his feelings. This year, for the first time since he was three, he is not receiving speech therapy. He comprehends what others say more quickly than before. We also agreed at his IEP meeting that he learns useful language when talking with his friends in his classes."

Her positive tone fades: "Still, though, Fred doesn't talk a lot. I have to ask him questions like 'Did you color at school today?' or 'Did you go to music?' to get him to start talking, and then he will usually tell me more about that particular activity. Also, I ask him what he is feeling or thinking, and usually give him a word to use, like, 'Fred, are you feeling angry or are you tired?' Then, he can usually tell me, using one of those words, how he is feeling."

At school, Fred receives his education in a special education classroom half of the day, and in a general education second-grade classroom the other half of the day. Mary (Bo) McElmurray, his special education teacher, maintains close contact with his general education teacher, Marilyn Ammons, so that they can both be actively involved in making sure that Fred does his best.

Bo notes, "His general education classroom teacher has worked very hard to provide modifications for him. For instance, she went over information from a social studies unit on symbols with Fred. However, even with the practice,

Fred Smith and his special education teacher enjoy his successes as he discusses a positive day of social interactions with his friends in his general education classroom.

he had a great deal of difficulty comprehending the information, so he couldn't tell me and his classmates in special education much about it. Even with repeated review, he repeated words or phrases his teacher had said, rather than sharing about it."

Although he is performing better than "even six months ago," Elizabeth continues to have concerns about Fred's social development. Fred does not have neighbors to play with "out in the country. But, he has several kids he gets in trouble with at school," she adds, laughing.

Elizabeth concludes, "All of us have worked together to help Fred, and we all have benefited. That's what is special about special education—taking care to meet the needs of individual children."

tively affect the student's hearing and/or cognitive abilities and, in turn, his or her communicative abilities.

Environmental factors can cause poor language development. Some young children have insufficient stimulation from peers or adults, providing them with less time to learn through interaction. Others have few appropriate adult models from whom to learn, delaying their mental and language development. Without intervention, children with delayed language development are at risk for developing and maintaining language disorders.

Identifying the Prevalence of Communication Disorders

Approximately 5 percent of all children and youth have a speech or language impairment serious enough to warrant special services (U.S. Department of Education, 1996). Roughly 3 percent of school-aged children have articulation disorders, 4 percent have fluency disorders, 6 percent have voice disorders, and 6.5 percent have language disorders serious

FIGURE 14–4 *Educational placement of students with communication impairments in the 1994–1995 school year*

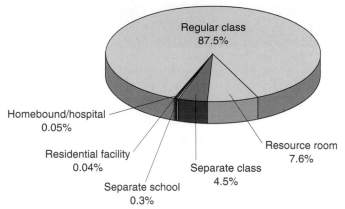

Regular class
87.5%

Homebound/hospital
0.05%

Residential facility
0.04%

Separate school
0.3%

Separate class
4.5%

Resource room
7.6%

Note: From U.S. Department of Education (1996). *To assure the free appropriate public education of all children with disabilities: Eighteenth annual Report to Congress on the implementation of the Individuals with Disabilities Education Act.* Washington, DC: Author.

Between two and three million children in the United States have a communication disorder.

enough that the disorders negatively affect their academic performance, qualifying them for speech-language therapy as a related service under IDEA (U.S. Department of Education, 1996). Twenty-one percent of all students receiving special education services receive speech and language services (U.S. Department of Education, 1996). Of the students with communication disorders served in the early 1990s, 49 percent had learning disabilities as their primary disability, with the communication disorder a secondary disability (Haynes, Moran, & Pindzola, 1994).

As Figure 14-4 illustrates, nearly 90 percent of students with communication disorders are in general education classrooms for the entire school day. Another 7.6 percent are removed from the general education classroom only when receiving speech/language therapy. Less than 5 percent of students with communication disorders spend their academic days in segregated placements, including separate classes in public schools, separate schools, residential facilities, and homes and hospitals.

WHAT ARE EVALUATION PROCEDURES?

Determining the Presence of Communication Disorders

Identifying the presence of communication disorders is not an easy task. To determine whether a speech impairment, a language impairment, or both impairments are suspected, a speech-language pathologist must have information on the student's hearing, motor functioning, oral and respiratory systems, cognitive functioning, and developmental history before actually assessing the student's communicative abilities. The pathologist gathers this information from school records, parental interviews, informal interviews with the student's teacher, and hearing and vision screenings to determine the possible presence of other disabilities and/or causes for possible communication disorders. Knowing if other disabilities exist provides information necessary for determining the presence of a communication disorder. Then, the student's communication skills can be assessed through formal and informal methods.

A speech assessment determines the presence of articulation, voice, or fluency problems. An articulation test is a formal diagnostic tool used to pinpoint articulation problems. This test allows a pathologist to evaluate a student's abilities to produce speech sounds in single words and in sentences. The test presents pictures for the student to name, allowing the evaluator to assess the student's production of consonants in pictured items. Test items include use of consonants in the initial, middle, and final positions (e.g., for "p," students might name a *pig, zipper,* and *cup*).

Some research suggests that articulation, voice, and fluency should be assessed informally through natural conversation (Morrison & Shriberg, 1992), rather than through formal diagnosis, because conversation is the natural way people use speech everyday. Furthermore, speech problems such as articulation, voice, and fluency problems occur and are noted by others as students converse with them. If conversational sampling indicates that delay or disorder is probable, the speech-language pathologist may conduct a diagnostic assessment to determine the presence and extent of speech problems (Haynes, Moran, & Pindzola, 1994).

A conversational sample can also provide a sample of a child's language that can be analyzed, after transcription, for a child's ability to use language appropriately. Specifically, a pathologist or teacher can examine the transcription of a child's words to see if the child has language problems. For example, if an eight-year-old child stated several sentences similar to, "I goed to store and candy buyed me," a speech-language pathologist or teacher might suspect problems with the child's use of morphological rules (past tense), syntax (word order for sentences and phrases similiar to "I buyed candy"), and semantics (if the listener was informed that the child bought a popsicle rather than candy). Morrison and Shriberg (1992) suggest that conversational speech sampling provides richer, more useful information for language assessment than do formal tests, and encourage speech-language pathologists to increase their use of informal diagnostic techniques such as language sampling.

Assessment of Students Who Are Bilingual or Multilingual.

Sometimes specialized speech or language assessment is needed. One involves bilingual or multilingual students. The speech-language pathologist must be particularly skilled when assessing the communicative capabilities of students for whom English is not the primary language. Fair, unbiased evaluation is difficult for a student who is bilingual (one who uses two languages equally well), **bidialectal** (one who uses two variations of a language), or for whom language dominance (the primary language of the student) is not easily determined. The instruments used to determine a student's communicative disorder must be nondiscriminatory, meaning that testing is not simply a matter of translating test items into the child's primary language. The pathologist must determine whether a bilingual student should be tested in his or her first language or in English. Then, the student is tested in the dominant language with appropriate diagnostic tools to determine whether a language disorder or disability exists. When a student's language strengths and preferences are determined and an appropriate assessment tool used, the student's communicative abilities and needs can be appropriately determined, and therapy planned for. It is important to note that IDEA (1997) prohibits schools from classifying into special education those children who are not English-language proficient unless they also have an identifiable disability (over and above English nonproficiency).

Assessment of Communication Skills in Infants and Toddlers.

If a child's language is delayed or different enough that problems are apparent before a child turns three, informal assessment of spoken language sometimes cannot occur, because the child is not speaking (MacDonald & Carroll, 1992). In this case, the speech-language pathologist will analyze the child's prelinguistic communicative behaviors. These behaviors include pointing and grunting for attention, gesturing, taking an adult's hand and leading the adult to a desired object, and making a noise as a greeting (Roberts & Crais, 1989; Yoder, Warren, Kim, & Gazdag, 1994). For example, Martin's pathologist determined the types of prelinguistic communicative behaviors he used, their frequency, and his parents' responses to these behaviors. Then, the pathologist helped Martin's parents plan activities to use to increase his communicative behaviors.

The development of a young child like Martin is best determined when the pathologist joins a team of individuals who work together to observe and assess the child's development. All team members seat themselves in a circle around the child or the child and the caregiver, where they can all see the same behaviors and write down information

Because Martin was not speaking in words when his speech-language pathologist first assessed his communicative abilities, she assessed his prelinguistic skills like eye focus, use of gestures, finger pointing, and grunts and other verbalizations.

Bidialectal people have the ability to use two variations of a language, such as being equally fluent in black English and standard English.

**EBONICS AND THE TEACHING
OF STANDARD ENGLISH**

A teacher comments, "We value the language
[students who are African-American] bring from
home, and we add a new language some of
them have never had before: Standard English."

The teacher describes a program referred to
as Ebonics, being taught in an Oakland, California school district. The program teaches Black
English as a second language. This video highlights viewpoints from both sides of this controversial issue and demonstrates how Ebonics is
used in classrooms.

What do you think?   Do you believe
bilingual education funds should be used to
teach Ebonics? Why or why not?

What do you think about teaching students
with regional dialects, such as those from
Appalachia, to use Standard English as a second language?

What is your opinion about a teacher who is
not African-American teaching Ebonics? What
considerations would teachers need to make if
the class is multicultural?

about their observations for later discussion. The team discusses findings and reaches a
consensus regarding the child's developmental level and possible interventions to
enhance development. This team approach to assessment is called *arena assessment* and
is recommended for many reasons, including that the child is able to be observed doing a
wider variety of activities across many domains (Bailey & Wolery, 1992).

Assessment of Communication Skills During the School Years.   Communication disorders are commonly identified when a child is enrolled in school. The earlier the
disorder is identified, the better the chance for planning and implementing effective intervention. If a child reaches school age before the communication problem has been noted
and a speech-language pathologist consulted, you may spot a problem (using a checklist
such as in Figure 14–5) and bring concerns to the pathologist, who then determines if an
assessment of the student's speech and language skills is needed. By observing the student
and speaking with the student, the speech-language pathologist usually can determine if
further assessment is needed. Figure 14–6 displays the referral and assessment processes,
should a formal assessment of communication skills be needed.

Determining the Nature and Extent
of Special Education and Related Services

To determine the extent of services needed and to ensure appropriate services, speech
and language assessments are needed. When conducting an assessment, the speech-language pathologist seeks to describe the problem (is it a speech problem, e.g., articulation,
or a language problem, e.g., pragmatics?) and its severity, as the basis for anticipating the
time needed for improving or remediating the problem and to plan intervention. An intervention plan, developed in cooperation with the child's parents and teachers, addresses
communication objectives as well as the methods used to ensure that the objectives are
met. The frequency of therapy as well as the duration of services also are determined.
Speech-language therapy is a related, rather than direct, service under IDEA, and, if a student's individualized education program (IEP) requires it, the student will have speech-
language therapy in order to benefit from special education.

WHAT AND HOW DO PROFESSIONALS TEACH?

When determining the appropriate curriculum and methods to use to improve a student's
communicative functioning, the student's needs are of utmost importance. A curriculum,
per se, is not used. Rather, depending on the student's communicative abilities and any

The following behaviors may indicate that a child in your classroom has a language impairment and may need clinical intervention.

____ Child omits word endings, such as plural **s** and past tense **ed.**

____ Child omits small unemphasized words, such as auxiliary verbs or prepositions.

____ Child uses an immature vocabulary, overuses empty words such as **one** and **thing,** or seems to have difficulty recalling or finding the right word.

____ Child has difficulty comprehending new words and concepts.

____ Child's sentence structure seems immature or overreliant on forms such as subject-verb-object. It's unoriginal, dull.

____ Child's questions or negative sentence style are immature.

____ Child has difficulty with one of the following:

____ Verb tensing	____ Articles	____ Auxiliary verbs
____ Pronouns	____ Irregular verbs	____ Prepositions
____ Word order	____ Irregular plurals	

____ Child has difficulty relating sequential events.

____ Child has difficulty following directions.

____ Child's questions are often inaccurate or vague.

____ Child's questions are often poorly formed.

____ Child has difficulty answering questions.

____ Child's comments are often off topic or inappropriate for the conversation.

____ There are long pauses between a remark and the child's reply or between successive remarks by the child.

____ Child appears to be attending to communication but remembers little of what is said.

____ Child has difficulty using language socially for the following purposes:

____ Request needs	____ Pretend/imagine	____ Protest
____ Greet	____ Request information	____ Gain attention
____ Respond/reply	____ Share ideas/feelings	____ Clarify
____ Relates events	____ Entertain	____ Reason

____ Child has difficulty interpreting the following:

____ Figurative language	____ Humor	____ Gestures
____ Emotions	____ Body language	

____ Child does not alter production for different audiences and locations.

____ Child does not seem to consider the effect of language on the listener.

____ Child often has verbal misunderstandings with others.

____ Child has difficulty with reading and writing.

____ Child's language skills seem to be much lower than other skill areas, such as mechanical, artistic, or social skills.

Note: From *Language Disorders: A Functional Approach to Assessment and Intervention,* by R. E. Owens, Jr., 1991, Upper Saddle River, NJ: Merrill/Prentice Hall. Copyright 1991 by Merrill/Prentice Hall. Reprinted with permission.

FIGURE 14–6 *Assessment process for determining the presence of speech and language disorders*

Nondiscriminatory Evaluation

Observation

| Teacher and parents observe | The student has difficulty understanding and/or using language. |
| Physician observes | The student is not achieving developmental milestones related to communication skills. |

Screening

Assessment measures	Findings that indicate need for further evaluation
Classroom work projects	The student may be hesitant to participate in verbal classroom work. Written classroom projects may reflect errors of verbal communication or, in some instances, be a preferred avenue of expression for the student.
Group intelligence tests	Tests do not differentiate the student from other students in many cases. Verbal portions of the tests may be affected by language deficits.
Group achievement tests	The student may perform below expectations from intelligence tests because of language (reading) requirements.
Vision and hearing screening	The student may have history of otitis media (middle-ear infections); hearing may be normal or the student may have hearing loss. Limited vision may impact language skills.

Prereferral

Prereferral is typically not used with these students.

Referral

Students with significant language delays may be identified prior to starting school. These students should receive early intervention services and protection in evaluation procedures upon entering school. Because many speech and language disorders are not identified until a student enters school, teachers should refer any student who seems to have difficulty with speech or language.

Protection in evaluation procedures

Assessment measures	Findings that suggest speech and language disorders
Individualized intelligence test	The student may be average, above average, or below average in intelligence. However, this student, like some others, often scores lower on sections of the test requiring language skills.
Individualized achievement test	A strong connection exists between language skills and performance on achievement tests. Therefore, language-related subtest scores may be lower than scores on subtests such as mathematics that do not require language skills.
Speech and language tests (articulation/phonology, language sample, receptive language, expressive language)	The student performs significantly below average in one or more areas. Performance may vary according to mood, energy level, extent and pile-up of environmental changes, and whether individual preferences are incorporated.
Oral-muscular functioning	In most instances, no problems are present.
Adaptive behavior scales	Tests may reveal that the student has significant difficulty in communication skills.
Anecdotal records, including medical history	The student may have genetic or medical factors that contribute to difficulties with speech or language. Moreover, students with other disabilities, including mental retardation, physical disabilities, hard of hearing or deafness, and learning disabilities are at risk for having speech and language disorders.
Curriculum-based assessment	A language disorder may cause the student to perform below average in reading or written language.
Direct observation	The student may avoid oral tasks and/or appears confused during conversations. Others may have difficulty understanding the student's speech.

Evaluation Team determines that special education and related services are needed for a speech or language disorder.

Appropriate Education

additional disabling conditions, the speech-language pathologist and others determine how the student's communicative functioning is best enhanced, and the methods used to enhance the functioning are determined. In this section, the means for deciding the approach (curriculum) and methods by which to enhance communication are explained.

Curriculum

The speech-language pathologist and others involved in the child's education must determine how best to facilitate the child's communicative development and use. Basically, assessment and experience with the student indicate whether the pathologist and other adults working with the student should try to remediate the speech or language disorder or to compensate for it. Remediation, the most common intervention option, helps students change inappropriate patterns or develop appropriate patterns. Speech remediation mainly focuses on correcting inappropriate pronunciation patterns and developing appropriate ones. Language remediation primarily focuses on enhancing pragmatic use of language, rather than on modifying language forms (Bloom & Lahey, 1978).

Compensation, as the name suggests, helps students offset deficits that are not possible to remediate. Alternative or augmentative communication systems allow students to learn a compensatory skill and to substitute that new skill for such uncorrectable impairments as unintelligible speech or inability to communicate manually. These communication devices are related services provided under IDEA (see Chapter 1). Professionals and parents can use resources such as those discussed in Chapter 12 to determine the best means for helping students compensate for their communication difficulties.

> Curriculum and methods, especially if they focus on pragmatics, can increase the chance that the student will be included in the general curriculum and have relationships with peers who do not have disabilities.

Methods

Helping students overcome communication difficulties is a primary area of emphasis for speech-language pathologists. For classroom teachers, the primary emphasis is enhancing students' pragmatic abilities. Bloom and Lahey (1978) suggest that students best learn correct pragmatics by participating in conversations. Following are several means you can use to enhance students' pragmatic skills during conversations.

You may want to repeat students' comments and questions in a more semantically or grammatically correct way. This is called *expansion.* For example, the child says, "Tree big," and you respond, "The tree is big" (Nelson, 1977). You can also provide extra information. When a student says, "Tree big," you respond, "That tree is so big that I could not climb it."

You also can provide statements or ask questions that explain a student's nonverbal behaviors. For example, if a student points to a cookie, you can respond by asking, "Oh, you want that cookie, don't you?" These statements or questions provide students models of what they might have said or would like to have said if they could explain their wants and needs verbally. Always, you will want to respond positively to students' comments and utterances, as it shows them that their participation is valued and appreciated (McNeill & Fowler, 1998; Ninio & Bruner, 1978).

Structuring the social environment facilitates teacher-to-student and student-to-student communication (Alpert & Kaiser, 1992; Hemmeter & Kaiser, 1994; Kaiser, Hemmeter, Ostrosky, Alpert, & Hancock, 1995). Naturalistic **milieu** (environmental) language interventions occur in real or simulated activities. Procedures involve following the child's interest, arranging the natural environment, establishing a positive interaction, and incorporating natural consequences. Thus, when a prelinguistic child wants a cookie at snack time, as indicated by her glance at the box, you might say, "Oh, you want a cookie. Here you are," giving the child the cookie. Here, the child's interest is the focus, the interaction is brief, ends positively, and occurs in a natural school interaction.

Figure 14–7 includes explanations of many ways you can encourage children's communicative efforts and development, while Box 14–3 explains how teachers, parents, and siblings can arrange a preschool classroom (or interactions at home) to facilitate linguistic interaction.

> Techniques useful for facilitating language learning and use include expansion, open-ended questioning, praise, and statements that explain a child's action or continue a topic of conversation.

> **Milieu teaching** is an approach to language intervention in which the goal is to teach functional language in a natural environment.

SEVEN STRATEGIES FOR ARRANGING THE ENVIRONMENT TO STIMULATE LANGUAGE USE

1. **Interesting Materials**
Materials and activities that children enjoy should be available in the environment. Young children are most likely to initiate communication about the things that interest them. Thus, increasing the likelihood of children's interest in the environment increases the opportunities for language use and teaching. . . .

2. **Out of Reach**
Placing *some* desirable materials within view but out of reach will prompt children to make requests in order to secure the materials. Materials may be placed on the shelves, in clear plastic bins, or simply across the table during a group activity to increase the likelihood that the children will request access to them either verbally or nonverbally. . . .

3. **Inadequate Portions**
Providing small or inadequate portions of preferred materials such as blocks, crayons, or crackers is another way to arrange the environment to promote communication. . . . When the children use the materials initially provided, they are likely to request more. . . .

4. **Choice Making**
There are many occasions when two or more options for activities or materials can be presented to chil-

dren. In order to encourage the children to initiate language, the choice should be presented nonverbally. Children may be most encouraged to make a choice when one of the items is preferred and the other is disliked. . . .

5. **Assistance**
Creating a situation in which children are likely to need assistance increases the likelihood that they will communicate about that need. The presence of attractive materials that require assistance to operate may encourage children to request help from adults or peers. . . .

6. **Sabotage**
Setting up a "sabotage" by not providing all of the materials the children will need to complete a task (e.g., paints and water but no paintbrush following an instruction to paint), or by otherwise preventing them from carrying out an instruction, will also encourage them to make requests. . . .

7. **Silly Situations**
The final environmental strategy is to create a need for children to communicate by setting up silly or absurd situations that violate their expectations. For example, an adult who playfully attempts to put a child's shoes on the adult's feet may encourage the child to comment on the absurd situation. . . .

Note: From "Preschool Environments That Promote Communication" by Michaelene M. Ostrosky and Ann P. Kaiser, *Teaching Exceptional Children,* vol. *23*, no. 4, 1991, pp. 8–9. Copyright 1991 by The Council for Exceptional Children. Reprinted with permission.

HOW IS PARTICIPATION ENCOURAGED?

Most students with speech or language impairments spend most of their school day in general education classrooms. Therefore, speech-language services are often provided within the general education classroom. For these students' communicative development to be ensured, classroom teachers and speech-language pathologists must collaborate regarding the students' communicative objectives and means for achieving them.

Inclusion

It is apparent, as students with language delays are included in general education classrooms, that effective intervention to facilitate communication can occur in those classrooms. Specifically, teachers can utilize ideas such as those mentioned in this chapter to facilitate communicative learning for students with communication disorders who are

- Talk about things that interest the child at least once a day.

- Follow the child's lead. Reply to the child's initiations and comments. Get excited with the child.

- Don't ask too many questions. If you must, use such questions as **how did/do, why,** and **what happened** that result in longer explanatory answers.

- Encourage the child to ask questions. Respond openly and honestly. If you don't want to answer a question, say so and explain why. ("I don't think I want to answer that question; it's very personal.")

- Use a pleasant tone of voice. You need not be a comedian, but you can be light and humorous.

- Don't be judgmental or make fun of the child's language. If you are overly critical of the child's language or try to correct all errors, the child will stop talking to you.

- Allow enough time for the child to respond.

- Treat the child with courtesy by not interrupting when the child is talking.

- Include the child in family discussions. Encourage participation and listen to the child's ideas.

- Be accepting of the child and the child's language. Hugs, acceptance, and compliments go a long way.

- Provide opportunities for the child to use language and to have that language help the child accomplish some goal.

Note: From Language Disorders: A Functional Approach to Assessment and Intervention, by R. E. Owens, Jr., 1991, Upper Saddle River, NJ: Merrill/Prentice Hall. Copyright 1991 by Merrill/Prentice Hall. Reprinted with permission.

FIGURE 14–7 *Teacher and family interaction styles*

included in general education classrooms. With the collaborative efforts of the school's speech-language pathologist, you can arrange opportunities for interaction that encourage the students' linguistic growth. You can serve as the facilitators of communicative interactions, ensuring that effective interactions occur.

In the inclusive classroom-based therapy model (Miller, 1989), the speech-language pathologist comes into the general education classrooms to provide therapy. This model allows students with communication delays to remain in their general education classes with peers who serve as communication models. Sometimes, the pathologist may teach a lesson to the student(s) with communication disorders within the context of teaching the entire class (e.g., focus on use of plurals in the context of playing a game). Other times, he or she may work with a small group of students in the back of the room on a language or speech activity that will benefit all students in the group while meeting the special needs of the students within the group who have communication delays (e.g., assist students in a game of concentration in which cards depicting words of opposite meanings, a problem area for the students with communication delays, are used). The speech-language pathologist works with the classroom teacher to determine how they can collaborate to ensure that the needs of the students with communication difficulties are met.

Sometimes, the pathologist may consult with a general education classroom teacher, serving as an outside collaborator. In this situation, the student participates in communicative-enhancing opportunities in the general education classroom, rather than being pulled from the general education classroom for therapy. Regularly, the pathologist meets with the teacher and, if appropriate, with the student with communication delays and/or parents, to develop strategies that can be used by the general education teacher in the classroom and at home to improve the student's communication skills.

In the more traditional pull out model, the speech-language pathologist is removed from the general education classroom for therapy. In this case, the pathologist works with the student one-on-one or in a small group to meet the communicative objectives. In this

When pathologists provide therapy in general education classrooms, students have increased opportunities to learn the social dynamics of group settings. Specifically, students practice using skills such as getting, keeping, and relinquishing turns and saying something appropriate and relevant.

Inclusion Tips

	What You Might See	What You Might Be Tempted to Do	Alternate Responses	Ways to Include Peers in the Process
Behavior	The student may have difficulty expressing his ideas in a large group.	Tell him to hurry up; the class is waiting. Do not allow him time to complete his idea, and move on to another student. Never call on him.	Ask for information in ways that do not emphasize his disability—for example, single-word responses or rehearsed responses.	Have small groups of students work with him so that each one can contribute. Model recognition of all students' talents.
Social Interactions	The student may play alone.	Assume she is happy alone and let her be.	Give her responsibility in the classroom and other areas. Demonstrate that you value her contributions.	Pair students in the classroom with her for tasks. Plan these pairings to match interests and encourage friendships.
Educational Performance	The student may not verbally use comparative forms such as *big, bigger, biggest* and may have these same difficulties with written language.	Constantly correct him with red pen or ignore his written difficulties. Assume the speech-language pathologist will remediate this problem.	Structure activities in which the correct forms are predictable and he has the opportunity to use the patterns successfully in different contexts.	Provide a peer with opportunities to play card or board games with him in which a win depends on the players' ability to use comparatives.
Classroom Attitudes	The student may rely on the teacher as her sole support, expecting him to intercede with other students.	Tell her to go play with others. Be flattered by the student's friendship.	Give specific suggestions on how to initiate interaction with others. For example, if she asks for something, suggest she ask another student instead.	Construct group situations in which she can be the leader of a small group and practice sharing her expertise.

case, the student is excluded from the general education classroom for the time he or she is receiving speech-language therapy.

Tips that you can use in your own classrooms to facilitate inclusion of students with communication disorders are included in the accompanying box.

Collaboration

Professional Collaboration. General education teachers, special education teachers, and speech-language pathologists have a responsibility to facilitate students' language development and interaction. Collaboration with the pathologist can help general and special education classroom teachers embed students' language objectives within the context of their regular routines. In this way, general education teachers are empowered to use their strengths to enhance the learning of the students in their general education classrooms who have communication disorders.

Martin's preschool teacher, Kathy Getto, gives an example, based on a collaborative meeting she requested with Martin's pathologist and special education consultant: "When I ask a question, I usually look away, maybe at another student, to give Martin a second or two to process what I said. Then, I look back at him to show him I am waiting for his answer, and he answers." Kathy also tried a strategy the pathologist suggested as a way to help him initiate or comment. She may stop talking or ask the entire class a question and then discreetly hold up a finger, showing Martin that he can take his time to respond and that she would like him to respond (she explained this strategy to him beforehand). He usually responds, and Kathy has found that Martin is proud of his participation and now comments and initiates more frequently than before. Kathy says, "It's great to collaborate to get some suggestions that work. Whatever it takes to help Martin—that's what we do."

Sometimes, speech-language pathologists and teachers communicate without face-to-face interactions. For example, general education teachers may fill out a checklist on a daily basis to inform the pathologist of a particular student's success at using targeted behaviors while included in the classroom. Other times, pathologists and teachers may collaborate by writing to each other in a communication notebook. Or, the tradition of leaving messages for each other in the mailroom may serve as a means for teachers and pathologists to collaborate on a regular basis. Whatever means used, communication is essential for effective collaboration necessary for appropriate inclusion. The accompanying box lists many collaboration tips.

Family Collaboration.   Families are usually the first to identify speech or language differences in their children. If their concerns are ignored by doctors, preschool teachers, or friends, parents' responses to the formal diagnosis of a language or speech delay can range from extreme upset to calm acceptance (Turnbull & Turnbull, 1996). Sometimes, parents are relieved to find that their concerns were warranted, yet later they become upset that time was spent waiting for the child to speak or to have intelligible speech when that time could have been better spent actively intervening to enhance the child's communicative development. Other times, they are upset immediately upon diagnosis, as they were subconsciously hoping that their speculations were incorrect. Other parents react in yet different ways and with differing levels of emotion. Certainly, speech-language pathologists and teachers need to realize that parents will vary in the time they require to accept the diagnosis and that understanding the parents at their own stages of acceptance is prerequisite to partnership with them (Turnbull & Turnbull, 1996).

Today, knowing that they may see a student only once or twice a week for a brief period, pathologists collaborate with parents when identifying remediation strategies (Hart & Risley, 1995). For example, Martin's pathologist watched his parents interact with Martin. Then, she and his parents jointly decided on several strategies to help him become more involved in his world and in his interactions with his parents. They decided that they all would talk to Martin about everything in his environment; they would talk about things that were of obvious interest to him (e.g., dump trucks), and they would use an "isn't life exciting?" tone with Martin. His play therapist and early childhood special educator later corroborated and emphasized this and many other activities to help Martin develop the desire to communicate verbally.

Because they are empowered by collaborating with pathologists, families like Martin's are more likely to use the modeled strategies in their daily lives with their children than are parents who are not encouraged to participate in therapy sessions (Bailey & Wolery, 1992). The result of collaboration usually is that the child's communication improves. As Marina said, "It was more natural for Martin, when he started talking, to say, 'Dump truck' after I had said it as we were following one down the road than it was for him to label a pretend dump truck at his therapist's house. I appreciate how she educated us."

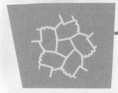

Collaboration Tips

DEVELOPING OPPORTUNITIES IN THE GENERAL EDUCATION CLASSROOM TO ENHANCE COMMUNICATION

COLLABORATION GOALS To identify and plan means to verbally and physically engage the preschool student with a language impairment in classroom activities and interactions.

Collaborators	Roles and Preparation	Possible Barriers	Solutions to Barriers	Modifications to Implementation	Ongoing Evaluation
Student	Share what student likes to do and wants to do.	May only state what student does in isolation.	Use photos of different settings to help student share other preferences.	Invite student to draw his preferences.	Create a tracking system with rewards to monitor people student has interacted with.
Parents	Share what student likes to do at home.	Parents unaware of student's preferences.	Ask parents to write down for a week what son likes to do at home.	Ask parents to track and write down what son likes to do in other settings.	Expand number of settings for preferences.
General Educator(s)	Note times student is not playing cooperatively or is playing alone.	Frustration that student is a "loner" and general educator feels inadequate.	Focus on difficulties as a team effort with solutions offered by all.	Look at student's positive interactions first to see progress and accomplishments.	Keep running record of each accomplishment.
Early Childhood Special Educator(s)	Prepare data collection sheets of student's participation and nonparticipation.	Seeing student only at school.	Develop a communication notebook with parents.	Collect data from many sources such as extracurricular activities.	Share student's strengths and contributions with his peers and family.
Speech-Language Pathologist	Provide information on facilitating communication and interaction.	Seeing student for only short periods.	Adding observation periods at home and/or school.	Gathering information from other sources and collaboration team members.	Documenting increases in eye contact, physical and verbal interactions.
Peers	Make a list of student's preferred activities.	Not aware of student's preferences.	Provide more time to relate to/communicate with student in different settings.	Provide unusual activities that encourage student interaction with different peers.	Create simple charts where peers indicate with whom student interacts.

Community Collaboration. The Americans with Disabilities Act (ADA) and IDEA have brought about many changes in the way people with communicative impairments are included in the community. Hence, several means of enabling individuals with communication disorders to more fully participate in their communities now exist. Specifically, the ADA requires that programs and businesses make reasonable accommodations, including providing auxiliary aids or services to ensure effective communication. For example, interpreters for deaf and hard-of-hearing individuals who attend public performances provide them equal access to information. Similarly, McDonald's restaurants offer picture menus (see Figure 14–8) for individuals who are unable to speak so that they may point to their selections (Diggs, 1992).

FIGURE 14–8 *To ensure effective communication with all of their customers, McDonald's Restaurants have created picture menus.*(Used with permission from McDonald's Corporation.)

Breakfast Menu

THIS PROGRAM IS ENDORSED BY THE AMERICAN SPEECH-LANGUAGE AND HEARING ASSOCIATION, ROCKVILLE, MD.

EGG McMUFFIN

SAUSAGE McMUFFIN WITH EGG

SAUSAGE BISCUIT

SAUSAGE BISCUIT WITH EGG

BACON, EGG AND CHEESE BISCUIT

HOTCAKES AND SAUSAGE

BIG BREAKFAST

HASH BROWNS

LOWFAT APPLE BRAN MUFFIN

BREAKFAST DANISH

COFFEE: REGULAR AND DECAF
Large   Medium   Small

1% LOWFAT MILK

ORANGE JUICE

The following trademarks are owned by McDonald's Corporation: Egg McMuffin, Sausage McMuffin, Big Breakfast. © 1991 McDonald's Corporation. Printed on recycled paper. **Revised 1/98. PRODUCT ITEM AVAILABILITY MAY VARY BY LOCATION. ALSO, PRODUCTS MAY VARY FROM THE PICTURES SHOWN ON THIS MENU.**

BOX 14-4   MAKING A DIFFERENCE

MILDRED TEMPLIN

When I entered the field in the mid-1930s, the speech-language discipline was still relatively new. Only a small number of professionals existed, but each was motivated by a desire to help people by means of therapy and by the intellectual curiosity that underlies all research and scientific inquiry. Although the Speech Correction Association (the forerunner of ASHA) had only some 250 members when I joined, it helped focus, define, and organize the field. The areas within the discipline then, as now, covered a wide range: articulation, stuttering, voice, hearing, and speech and language problems both in themselves and as they may be associated with physical and sensory impairments.

The prevailing concepts at that time focused on helping each person achieve his or her maximum potential of good communication skills. Our means were therapy and research. The basic concepts have remained the same over time, but the approaches have been more deeply explored, defined, and refined. The major catalysts for change included the following:

- The establishment of the field as an accepted discipline, which probably resulted from the increased number of established and accepted programs throughout the United States, the licensing of professionals in many states, and the certification of workers by ASHA and state associations
- The development of psycholinguistics and its impact upon the whole area of communication disorders

- Technological developments that permit research and therapeutic approaches that were previously impossible
- Cooperative relationships with other fields such as psychology, otology, and special education

Nowadays, professionals are expanding and improving techniques of research and therapy, the relationships of various disciplines, and the cooperation among them without sacrificing their traditional concern for the well-being of individuals. It is exciting to see the field incorporate a diversity of interests and knowledge while establishing a clearer identity. I expect that in the future this process will continue and strengthen the field.

The growth of a professional field is, however, a continuing process. The speech-language-hearing field has developed over a relatively short time. It continues to provide room for innovation, curiosity, and contributions by any person who is sufficiently committed to sustain interest, increase knowledge, and develop competencies.

I believe that a newcomer to the field who identifies an area of interest, develops knowledge and skills, and stays with the interest despite environmental, personal or professional interferences is likely to find personal fulfillment. This kind of task orientation, concentrating on doing the best possible job rather than on personal and professional advancement, frequently leads to satisfying recognition by professional peers.

Dr. Mildred Templin
Minneapolis

Another means to assist community collaboration is by having technological devices that assist communication available for use. One technological advancement is the text telephone (TT) (formerly known as the telephone device for the deaf, or TDD). Another is close-captioned television programming. (More information is available in Chapter 15.) Still other advancements are alternative and augmentative communication devices. (More information is available in Chapter 12.)

Careers

Professional careers include the field of speech-language pathology, audiology, and/or education of students who are deaf or hard of hearing. Professionals in these fields must have extensive training before they are qualified to practice. If they are working as teachers, professionals must hold certification in education for students who are deaf or hard of hearing. Speech-language pathologists and audiologists must earn a certificate of clinical competence to practice their respective professions to the fullest extent possible. To qualify for the certificates, individuals must have earned a master's degree from an academic training program accredited by the American Speech-Language-Hearing Association, completed 375 supervised practicum hours with individuals with a variety of impairments, completed a year of supervised practicum, and passed a national examination. Many speech-language pathologists work in school settings, while others work in clinics, nurs-

BOX 14-5   MAKING A DIFFERENCE

RHONDA FRIEDLANDER

Rhonda Friedlander, who is a member of the Confederated Salish and Kootenai Tribes of the Flathead Nation, is a speech-language pathologist on the tribal reservation in northwestern Montana. Her caseload is drawn from the 6,700 tribal members who reside on the 1.2 million-acre reservation. A home visit for Rhonda often requires a 120-mile round trip. But that's not the least of it. She also has to take care not to let any of the family's livestock escape at the gate, and she usually has to meet the whole family—not only the nuclear family but also the aunts, uncles, grandfathers, and, most important of all, the grandmothers.

Talking about her work for her tribe's future, Rhonda notes that rates of communication disorders among American Indians are much higher than the national average. Because of many therapists' lack of cultural sensitivity, the remoteness of the reservations, low professional salaries, and high client caseloads, maintaining speech and language services for the tribal population is difficult.

Rhonda grew up on the reservation, so she understands the vocabulary variations of both Indian and non-Indian words and is able to respect a child's use of either vocabulary. She knows the cultural expectations of the children's language and experience. For example, tribal culture values listening and observing more than speaking and questioning. She can also relate to families' poverty and encourage children to take advantage of educational opportunities

to make changes for themselves, their tribes, and all American Indians.

The family is a critical part of Rhonda's program to improve children's speech and language skills. Traditionally, all learning is transmitted through the family members. Children learn survival skills and daily living skills from aunts, uncles, and grandparents. They also have the support of their community. So this is how Rhonda's speech and language program operates.

Other traditions also influence the way in which Rhonda provides speech and language services. The tribal tradition of community support brings strong community backing for her efforts with the children. Although this support exists, she herself rarely gets any praise or recognition. Individual contributions of one particular person are not valued above the contributions of another. Traditionally, all human beings are equal, regardless of accomplishment.

Rhonda believes that her program's success results from tribal support of her efforts and the support of individual families. The tribes support her program because they regard it as an effort to increase employment opportunities for tribal members. Families support Rhonda's efforts because they recognize her concern and respect for them and their children. When asked how she can provide such an exemplary program, Rhonda responds that it takes persistence, self-direction, and intrinsic motivation. But she adds that the full support of her tribe has been her greatest motivator.

ing homes, hospitals, rehabilitation agencies, or private practices. In Box 14-4, Mildred Templin, a pioneer in the profession of speech-language pathology, describes some of the changes in the field and her own beliefs about how to remain satisfied with the profession. In Box 14-5, Rhonda Friedlander shares how she works with families of children with communication disorders in the Salish and Kootenai Tribes of the Flathead Nation, tribes of which she is a member.

WHAT ARE PROGRAM OPTIONS?

Early Intervention and Preschool Years

Services for children under the age of three who qualify for speech-language therapy usually take place in the privately owned homes or offices of speech-language pathologists, the children's homes, day-care centers, in the home of child-care providers, or in centers where various types of therapy are provided. The model of service provision is determined after a child is evaluated and found to qualify for therapy when the private therapist makes recommendations, or when the individualized family services plan (IFSP) is developed by the parents, service coordinator, pathologist, and other early intervention professionals at the local service agency. For families with infants and toddlers with communication delays, the pathologist typically works with the family to help the family members implement suggested strategies to ensure that the child's linguistic objectives are met.

The largest national program that integrates preschoolers with disabilities into preschool classes is Head Start. Head Start, a federally funded preschool program based on the proposition that the negative effects of poverty can be reduced through intervention, provides free or low-cost services to young children, including those with communication disorders. The Billings, Montana, Head Start program staff have been collaborating with staff from the local school district for over ten years. In Billings, Teri Hammerquist, the speech-language pathologist employed by the local school district, has been working with staff to allow the preschoolers with special needs to receive therapy in their preschool classrooms. To facilitate inclusion, Teri and the two Head Start teachers often divide the group into thirds, with each adult working with a group. However, if the approach gets noisy, any group—not necessarily Teri's group—may go to the speech room to work. Teri uses natural occurrences to facilitate speech and language development: for example, eating lunch with a group of children may provide her an opportunity for helping children take turns, whereas joining a group of children during social play may allow her to model other types of conversational skills to them. She comments, "Speech and language intervention is happening all the time—not just when you're sitting across the table from the child."

Elementary Years

The largest portion of language learning occurs for most elementary-aged students with communication impairments as they informally interact with peers in their general education classrooms. Sometimes, however, the speech-language pathologist may provide therapy to remediate students' communicative errors, helping these interactions to be more appropriate and beneficial to the students with communication disorders and their peers.

Melanie Waters, a speech-language pathologist employed in the Baldwin County, Alabama, schools, believes that therapy is most effective and interesting when nontraditional and traditional approaches are combined. Melanie elaborates:

> *I incorporate **whole language techniques** as well as arts and crafts into speech and language activities so that students learn to communicate more pragmatically. The students enjoy the art activities while their communication skills improve. For instance, if we were weaving, we could use verb forms like 'weaving,' 'shaping,' 'twisting,' 'bending,' 'holding,' 'molding,' and many, many others. Then, they expand their semantic knowledge and use of verbs while truly experiencing the verbs.*
>
> *Another alternative way I teach is that I use the general education classroom curriculum; I incorporate what is going on in the classroom into the students' speech and language goals. For instance, we work on their classroom skills, like spelling words, academic vocabulary, and rehearsing lines for plays. This requires that I collaborate with teachers. It's been a positive change for me to incorporate innovative teaching strategies, as my training included more traditional methods, i.e., 'repeat after me' or 'say it five times.' I like to involve parents in therapy, because I want parents to see what's happening during therapy, so they can see what's happening during the sessions and follow-up with everyday activities at home to see how their children are progressing. My responsibility is to find alternative means—whatever means necessary, including augmentative communication—to ensure that the students meet their communicative goals.*

Middle and Secondary Years

For a variety of reasons, students attending middle school or high school may no longer participate in therapy. Some have acquired age-appropriate skills. Others choose to discontinue therapy because of busy schedules or as a response to negative peer pressure regarding their participation. Others, however, continue to participate in therapy. Those students who continue to receive services for communication disorders throughout mid-

Whole language techniques are strategies and activities used for teaching language in its spoken and written forms that incorporate naturally occurring behaviors, such as speaking, writing, and reading in helping students to use language more effectively, correctly, and appropriately.

Traditionally, professionals gave families lists of words or sentences to have their children practice at home. However, these words or sentences often were not tied to children's true-to-life interests and experiences; hence, children were not as apt to display progress.

An innovative speech-language pathologist meets with students' general education classroom teachers so that he or she may effectively incorporate students' day-to-day language objectives in therapy sessions.

dle school and into high school usually have other disabling conditions that cause their language or speech problems. These students receive therapy geared to help them learn and maintain the pragmatic skills that they will need in order to function as independently as possible upon completion of school.

For her middle school- and high school-aged students with communication disorders who have mild mental retardation, Kimberly Peters, a speech-language pathologist, works on improving students' skills in auditory processing. Kimberly says that her students

> *have severe to profound auditory processing disorders that are documented, and they probably have visual processing problems, too. For instance, visually, they mix letters or process text information poorly. I have noticed that their visual problems occur with two-dimensional objects (e.g., print). They are much better at anything three-dimensional. Every student I have is an artist or can take apart a machine, or can sculpt beautifully—all require three-dimensional skills.*
>
> *How do I help them learn? I have two major methods for remediation: I provide them with my self-made memory sheets, and with mind mapping activities, both visual activities. My memory sheets help the students because the sheets provide visual, semantic, spatial, and auditory cues for learning the rules that dictate the way in which sounds are sequenced (phonology) and rules that dictate the way words are sequenced (syntax). The sheets help students with spelling and reading. When students work on spelling, reading comes naturally.*

An example of a student's annual speech-language goal and five related objectives is included in Figure 14–9.

Kimberly elaborates on her teaching methods:

> *To compensate for students' auditory processing disorders and comprehension difficulties, I help them learn to mind map. That is, first we listen, looking for main details from a brief amount of auditory information. I participate, too, and tell them which main ideas I pick out, so that they can understand using my model. After the students listen, we draw out the main idea (and later, several related ideas) on a piece of paper. We use the map information to list facts about the main ideas identified. Then, we write short paragraphs. Later, we practice mind mapping by listening to short lectures. Then, the students can use the mind map to write. They also use their memory sheets to help them write. Because the students practice their new skills in therapy sessions and then use them in their general education classrooms, they are more likely to use the communicative skills in real-life situations after they have completed school. That's the major purpose of education—owning and using skills.*

FIGURE 14–9 *Using a phonics program to teach reading and spelling*

A phonics program can provide opportunity for all populations to learn reading and spelling.

Population with central auditory processing disorder (CAPD)

Population with right brain dominant function

Population with left brain dominant function

Population with CAPD and associated language disorder

An IEP goal might be:

A client's ability for making associations to memorize select curriculum-based information (phonics) will improve.

Objectives might be:

1. Given visual (oral placement) cues, the student will make sound–symbol associations for 15 vowels and 24 consonants with 100% accuracy across 3 trials.

2. Given multisyllabic words, the student will divide the word into individual syllables with 100% accuracy across 3 trials.

3. Given individual syllables, the student will identify each sound or set of symbols representing a sound within a syllable as: consonant short vowel, long vowel, diphthong ("weird" vowel), or "word part" with 100% accuracy across 3 trials.

4. Given individual syllables, the student will sound blend the syllables into whole multisyllabic words with 90% accuracy across 3 trials.

5. The student will complete sentence dictation tasks and spell target words correctly with 90% accuracy across 3 trials.

Transitional and Postsecondary Years

Once students leave school, the speech-language services available to them as young adults must be located and paid for by the individuals themselves or be provided at little or no cost through local services agencies such as those supported by The Arc (Association for Retarded Citizens) and United Cerebral Palsy. In these cases, the speech-language pathologist's goal for the individuals usually is maintenance of communication skills, rather than remediation of or compensation for inappropriate or incorrect skills.

Sometimes therapy is initiated or continued when young adults attend college. At the University of Illinois Urbana-Champaign's Speech and Hearing Clinic, full-time students may receive a complete speech and language evaluation, conducted by a supervised master's-level trainee for a fraction of the cost of such an evaluation conducted outside of the university. Therapy sessions for communication disorders also are provided for students at a low cost. Students can receive therapy for traditional speech (e.g., articulation, voice, duration) and language (e.g., syntax, pragmatics) problems, or they might access less-common therapy such as accent reduction therapy, requested by many foreign-born students. Unfortunately, as is the case at many university clinics, more students request therapy than are able to be served. Regardless, adults seeking intervention for communication disorders need to seek the interventions appropriate to meet their communicative needs.

A VISION FOR THE FUTURE

Marina envisions that "Martin should be whatever he wants to be" when he is an adult. She is sure that Martin's future will not be limited by his communication skills. "I see him happy, working, having a family. I see him involved with other people. I want exactly for

Martin what any mother wants for her child." She looks forward to the future with confidence, believing that, with therapy, a positive classroom situation, and continued family support, Martin easily will be able to "verbally express what he wants to say."

Marina is pleased that, at age four, Martin imagines choices for what he wants to be when he's "growed up" (as he puts it): a pilot of a space shuttle or a construction worker. She adds, "Martin has many strengths that he can use to make positive contributions to society. He says he wants to be a space shuttle pilot or a construction worker, which is perfect—he loves to work with his hands, do artsy things, and take charge."

Martin Sr. concurs, stating that he wants Martin "to be what he wants to be, to be successful at whatever he wants to do, and to interact with others and 'connect' with them."

What will help Martin reach his potential? Marina answers,

> I know Martin is very smart. I want his teachers to foster that. He should be around people whose behavior he can copy and whose language he can listen to and learn from. I just want him to be the best that he can be, and I want everyone involved with him to do the most and best for him, too. We have to make sure that he has every opportunity that he needs and deserves, and the opportunity to make choices about his future, rather than having them made for him. He has come so far, and I am so hopeful for his future.

Space shuttle pilot, construction worker, or other professional, Martin will do well.

What Would You Recommend . . .

1. To make sure that Martin's social and communicative needs are best met?

2. To help Martin's family, teachers, and friends to create and maintain an environment that will facilitate Martin's development and help him "to be the best that he can be"?

3. To ensure Martin's continued academic success?

SUMMARY

WHAT ARE COMMUNICATION DISORDERS?

- Communication disorders include both speech and language impairments.

- A speech disorder is an impairment of one's articulation of speech sounds, fluency, or voice. A speech disorder reflects a problem in sending a message.

- A language disorder reflects problems in receiving information, understanding it, and formulating a spoken, written, or symbolic response.

- Communication differences that are related to the culture of the individual are not considered impairments.

- Most speech disorders are articulation disorders. When mispronouncing, an individual may add, omit, substitute, or distort sounds.

- Voice impairments affect the quality of one's voice. Voice impairments may be noted in pitch, intensity, resonance, and vocal quality.

- Language is a shared system of rules and symbols for the exchange of information. It includes rules of phonology, morphology, syntax, semantics, and pragmatics.

- *Phonology* is the use of sounds to make meaningful words.

- *Morphology* governs the structure of words and the construction of word forms.

- *Syntax* provides rules for putting together a series of words to form sentences.

- *Semantics* refers to word meaning.

- *Pragmatics* refers to the social use of language.

- Five to ten percent of the population has a communication disorder.

- Communication impairments can impact a student's academic, social, and emotional development.

WHAT ARE EVALUATION PROCEDURES?

- The speech-language pathologist is the professional most likely to determine the presence and extent of a speech and/or language impairment.

- Assessments include the use of formal and informal measures. They should occur in settings comfortable and natural to the student.

- Formal assessments are used to determine language problems. Analyses of an individual's conversation can also provide information to use to assess language development and use.

WHAT AND HOW DO PROFESSIONALS TEACH?

- A speech-language pathologist uses approaches to remediate or to compensate for communication impairments.

- The speech-language pathologist may use a variety of service delivery models, from one-on-one, small group, or large group intervention occurring within the general education classroom to one-on-one or small group intervention provided away from the student's general education classroom or in the child's home.

- Persons with communication disabilities are protected by the IDEA.

HOW IS PARTICIPATION ENCOURAGED?

- Many students receive their speech-language therapy while included in their general education classrooms, rather than in classrooms used only for speech and language therapy.

- The collaborative participation of students, their teachers, speech-language pathologists, and parents to enhance communicative development results in students' language objectives being targeted by these collaborators in many settings.

- Careers include the field of speech-language pathology, audiology, and/or education of students who are deaf or hard of hearing.

WHAT ARE PROGRAM OPTIONS?

- The primary emphasis for infants, toddlers, and preschoolers with communication disorders is the development of language and its use. Therapy can occur in the home, day-care setting, school, or other placement, preferably in a natural environment.

- Programs for elementary-aged students focus on helping the students develop social, interactive language and comprehensible speech. Therapy occurs in the general education classroom or in a classroom other than the general education classroom.

- Some middle school- and high school-aged students either no longer require therapy or choose to discontinue therapy. Therapy is often provided in general education classrooms.

- Collaboration between the speech-language pathologist, general education classroom teacher, special education teacher, family, and individual with communication disorders is required in order that the individual, no matter what age, will have opportunities to practice new skills with a variety of people in a variety of settings and situations.

- Postsecondary job-training programs for individuals with disabilities sometimes include therapy.

- Universities with a training program in speech-language pathology and audiology may offer these services to full-time students at low cost.

RESOURCES

BOOKS

Born To Talk. (1993). By L. M. Hulit & M. R. Howard. New York: Macmillan. Fully covers language development from birth through preschool years.

Children's Language and Learning. (1986). By J. W. Lindfors, Upper Saddle River, NJ: Prentice Hall. Introduces language and strategies for use by the classroom teacher in working with children who have language impairments.

Family-Centered Early Intervention for Communication Disorders. (1993). By G. Donahue-Kilburg. Gaithersburg, MD: Aspen. Describes assessment and intervention planning for infants and young children through collaboration with the family.

Introduction to Communication Disorders. (1991). By M. N. Hedge. Austin, TX: Pro-Ed. Introductory text about communication disorders.

Language Intervention: Preschool Through Elementary Years. (1995). Edited by M. E. Fey, J. Windsor, & S. F. Warren. Baltimore, MD: Brookes. Explains language development and language facilitation strategies for use by parents and teachers.

JOURNALS, MAGAZINES, AND CATALOGS

Augmentative Communication News. 1 Surf Way, Suite 215, Monterey, CA 93940. Monthly newsletter covering intervention, equipment, research, and governmental issues in augmentative communication.

Journal of Childhood Communication Disorders. Division for Children with Communication Disorders, Council for Exceptional Children, 1920 Association Drive, Reston, VA 22091. Twice-a-year publication includes articles for special educators addressing the nature, assessment, and treatment of communication disorders.

American Journal of Speech-Language Pathology. American Speech-Language-Hearing Association (ASHA), 10801 Rockville Pike, Rockville, MD 20852. Quarterly publication includes articles dealing with nature, assessment, and treatment of communication disorders.

Language, Speech and Hearing Services in Schools. American Speech-Language-Hearing Association (ASHA), 10801 Rockville Pike, Rockville, MD 20852. Quarterly publication addresses issues of providing speech-language-hearing services to school-age children.

MULTIMEDIA

Adaptive Communication Systems. 1400 Lee Drive, Coraopolis, PA 15108. (800) 247-3433. Offers a variety of communication boards.

Alliance for Technology Access. 1307 Solano Avenue, Albany CA 94706-1888. (415) 528-0747. Offers assistance on technology for communication.

Apple's Worldwide Disability Solutions Group. Apple Computer, 20525 Mariani Avenue, Cupertino CA 95014. (800) 732-3131, ext. 950; (408) 974-7911 (TT). Offers assistance on communication aids.

IBM Special Needs and Referral Center. 4111 Northside Parkway, Internal Code H06R1, Atlanta GA 30327. (800) IBM-2133. A database to help identify available products.

Learn to Sign. Reasonable Solutions, 1221 Disk Drive, Medford, OR 97501-6639. (800) 876-3475. American Sign Language software.

Phonic Ear. 3880 Cypress Drive, Petaluma, CA 94954. (800) 227-0735. Offers electronic communication aids with speech synthesis.

U.S. Society for Augmentative and Alternative Communication. 202 Barkley Memorial Center, University of Nebraska, Lincoln, NE 68583-0732. (402) 472-5463. Offers information and materials on alternative communication devices.

ON-LINE INFORMATION AND USEFUL DATABASES

American Speech, Language, and Hearing Association. Internet address: http://www.asha.org. Information on the national association for speech-language pathologists, audiologists, and teachers of students who are deaf or hard of hearing.

Boys Town Center on Deafness. Internet address: http://www.boystown.org. Information on disorders of hearing, speech, language, and learning.

Hanen Language Program. Internet address: http://www.hanen.org/educomm.html. Information for families and their young children with language delays.

Hyperlexia and other disorders. Internet address: http://www.hyperlexia.org. Information on Asperger's syndrome, hyperlexia, semantic pragmatic disorder, and other topics.

Learning Disabilities. Internet address: http://www-ld.ucsf.edu. Information on language-based learning disabilities and dyslexia.

Yale New Haven Medical Center. Internet address: http://info.med.yale.edu. Links with information on Asperger's syndrome and on social learning disabilities.

ORGANIZATIONS

American Speech-Language-Hearing Association (ASHA). 10801 Rockville Pike, Rockville MD 20852. (800) 638-8255 or (301) 897-5700 (ex. 157 for TT). Organization primarily for professionals in the field of speech, language, and hearing. Anyone interested in the field is invited to join. An annual national conference is held the weekend before Thanksgiving.

Division for Children with Communication Disorders. Council for Exceptional Children. 1920 Association Drive, Reston VA 22091. Organization focuses on teachers and communication disorder specialists. It also sponsors sessions at state, provincial, and national conferences of the Council for Exceptional Children.

CHAPTER 15

HEARING LOSS

Contributing writer
Barbara R. Schirmer
Kent State University

Educating
Amala Brown

Amala turned fourteen years old on February 5, or at least that's the date she and her family celebrate as her birthday. They don't know the actual date, or even the actual year, because Amala was born in India and was found living on the streets when she was a toddler. The caretakers in the orphanage realized that she was deaf and unable to communicate in any identifiable language. Amala was four years old and had lived in the orphanage less than a year when Robyn Brown adopted her and brought her home to live in Salem, Oregon.

Robyn was a teacher of children who are deaf and a sign language interpreter for many years before adopting Amala. That doesn't mean that life with Amala was without challenges. When she first brought Amala home, Amala would babble in what sounded like an Indian language and used just two gestures.

Amala started preschool at Salem Heights Elementary School, where Robyn teaches. Her colleague, Eleni Boston, was Amala's first teacher and many days she could hear Amala in the room above. It took incredible self-control,

and vast confidence in Eleni, for Robyn not to run upstairs and fix things.

Throughout elementary school, some years Amala attended Salem Heights full-time and some years she attended Oregon School for the Deaf for part of each day. Amala is currently in the seventh grade at Crossler Middle School, and she spends full days in general education classes with hearing students. She takes two of her elective courses in the Resource Room with Tina Harrison, a teacher of the deaf. In the reading course, Tina teaches reading skills and study strategies, and in the support course, Tina helps the students with assignments from their classes.

Robyn is very satisfied with Amala's education in the Salem Public Schools, but she worries about Amala's social development. Every year, she and Amala talk about the possibility of Amala attending the school for the deaf, because Robyn feels that it would offer Amala more peers that she could communicate easily with, increased opportunity to play a leadership role in school activities, and greater ease in participating in sports. On the other hand, Robyn believes that the public school program continues to maintain high academic standards for Amala and to provide her with a quality education.

Amala's teachers also feel that developing social relationships with hearing peers is a challenge for Amala. She interacts relatively little with the hearing children during lunch or break times, preferring her friends who are deaf and hard of hearing. One reason for Amala's reserve with hearing students is her personality, because she is naturally a quiet and studious person. The other reason is the communication barrier. The other students in

her classes respect her because they know she's a good student and they enjoy working in groups with her. But it's difficult to carry on a conversation with Amala unless you know at least some sign language, which few of the students have learned.

Another challenge for Amala is keeping up with the curriculum as she moves through middle school and into high school. For Amala, like other individuals who are deaf, not much incidental information is available, because they do not *overhear* the news on television, other people's conversations, and so on. Yet inci-

dental information has a strong influence on vocabulary development. Amala often misunderstands information presented in class or in her textbooks because she doesn't understand the terminology. For example, recently she had to write a report about Cuba. Robyn explained the concept of *infant mortality* and when she finished, Amala asked her if the United States has a rule about infant mortality, too. She had misunderstood the concept of incidence and thought that it was Cuba's rule that 11 of 1,000 babies died. Robyn worries that at some point, Amala may become so frustrated in school that she gives up because she has to expend so much more concentration and effort than hearing students do.

Independence is also a challenge for Amala. At home, she has a TT (text telephone), a light hookup, and a flashing alarm clock, and she frequently uses the telephone relay service to talk with individuals who don't have TTs. But Robyn hasn't figured out how to have an answering machine for Amala without having to pay for two separate phone lines and she hasn't hooked up the doorbell flasher because she doesn't want Amala's younger brother, Juan, who is also deaf, answering the door. Amala goes to the dentist on her own, but hasn't yet gone to the doctor without Robyn.

Accessibility has been another tremendous challenge for Amala. A major obstacle is not having interpreters for community activities such as Little League. As Amala has gotten older, she is less inclined to want her mother at her side interpreting for her. She is developing skills for dealing with these types of situations, such as bringing a pad of paper so that others can communicate with her through writing, but it's cumbersome, and so she tends to center her activities at school, where she has interpreters.

Amala's strengths have enabled her to deal successfully with many of the challenges she has faced. Her mom calls her a real self-starter. She is also incredibly responsible, independent, and very interested in other

people. Tina, her Resource Room teacher, notes that the qualities that help Amala the most are her work habits, organizational skills, and motivation to do her best.

Robyn often thinks about the future for Amala. She is confident that Amala will go to college and pursue whatever field she wants. Right now, Amala is thinking about becoming a veterinarian. But when asked, she says that there are a lot of choices and she can become many things when she grows up.

For the present, Amala enjoys playing sports, having sleepovers with her friends, and watching Friday night videos with Juan and Robyn. When asked what being deaf means to her, she replied that it's normal, natural. Sometimes she feels jealous of her hearing friends, particularly during volleyball games, because she can't respond to her name being called. And sometimes she's a little resentful at school because she has to take two electives in the Resource Room. But she prefers being deaf.

What Do You Think?

1. What could Amala's teachers and parent do to understand how her hearing loss impacts her educational, psychological, and social development?

2. How could Amala's teachers and parent determine the type of educational program and curriculum she needs?

3. How could Amala's teachers and interpreters develop collaborative relationships?

What Is Hearing Loss?

Defining Hearing Loss

Hearing loss has been surprisingly difficult to define because it has been impossible to state with assurance the point at which hearing stops being normal and starts being a disability. The Individuals with Disabilities Act (IDEA) sets forth two categories: **deafness** and hearing impairment. IDEA's definition of deafness is:

> *Hearing impairment that is so severe that the child is impaired in processing linguistic information through hearing, with or without amplification, that adversely affects a child's educational performance. IDEA's definition of hearing impairment is: An impairment in hearing, whether permanent or fluctuating, that adversely affects a child's educational performance but which is not included under the definition of deafness in this section.*

The IDEA *hearing impairment* definition is confusing because for many years it was used to describe all individuals with hearing losses, mild to profound. Most educators today use two categories of hearing loss: deaf and hard of hearing. But the problem with any categorization is that (a) hearing losses exist on a continuum, (b) many factors beyond the results of an audiological examination influence auditory behavior, and (c) substantial differences exist between aided and unaided hearing (Moores, 1996).

Audiologists are health care professionals who identify and evaluate hearing loss, select and evaluate hearing aids and other amplification devices, and habilitate/rehabilitate individuals with hearing loss (Bess & Humes, 1995). They evaluate hearing in terms of pitch and loudness. They then chart the results on an **audiogram.** As you can see in Figure 15-1, pitch is charted on the horizontal axis and is measured in terms of frequency in cycles per second; loudness is charted on the vertical axis and is measured in terms of hearing level in decibels.

You can also see in Figure 15-1 that the most commonly used terms to identify degree of hearing loss are slight, mild, moderate, severe, and profound. The banana-like shape in the top center is often called the *speech banana* because it is the range of frequencies and decibel levels found in speech sounds.

Figure 15-2 shows where everyday sounds occur for you and for individuals like Amala. For example, you need to be able to hear at the 10- to 20-decibel level to distin-

Deafness is hearing impairment that is so severe that the child is impaired in processing linguistic information through hearing with or without amplification, and educational performance is adversely affected.

An **audiologist** is a specialist who is trained to identify and evaluate hearing disorders, select and evaluate hearing aids, and recommend habilitation or rehabilitation.

An **audiogram** is a graph used to display the results of a hearing test. The intensity is plotted on the ordinate and frequency on the abscissa.

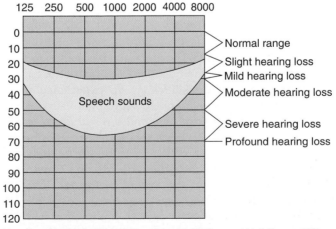

Figure 15–1 *Degrees of hearing loss*

Note: From *Hearing in Children* (4th ed.), by J. L. Northern and M. P. Downs, 1991, Baltimore, Williams & Wilkins. Copyright 1991 by Williams and Wilkins. And from *Deafness* (5th ed.), p. 53, by B. W. Lawton and J. C. Ballantyne, 1993, London: Whurr Publishers. Copyright 1993 by Whurr Publishers. Adapted with permission.

FIGURE 15–2 *Frequency spectrum of familiar sounds*

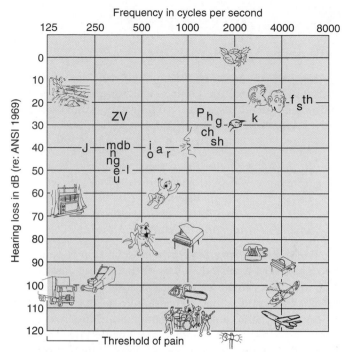

Note: From *Hearing in Children* (4th ed.), by J. L. Northern and M. P. Downs, 1991, Baltimore, Williams & Wilkins. Copyright 1991 by Williams & Wilkins. Reprinted with permission.

Even students with a hearing loss of just 15 decibels may miss speech sounds important for learning to read.

guish the sounds of a waterfall. If you can hear at the 60-decibel level, you can hear a baby crying. But if your hearing level is at the 80-decibel level, you won't hear the baby but you will hear a dog barking, the phone ringing, and a helicopter flying overhead.

The language that distinguishes between medical, educational, and cultural definitions also can be confusing. Medical definitions focus on the loss of hearing, educational definitions focus on the relationship between hearing and the need for special education services, and cultural definitions focus on the ways that deaf individuals share a cultural identity. There is no consensus about how to refer to people who are deaf or hard of hearing. Some prefer the disability-first approach *(deaf person);* others prefer the people-first approach *(person who is deaf).* It is common practice for the term *deaf* with a lower-case *d* to refer to medical and educational definitions and contexts, and the term *Deaf* with an upper-case *D* to refer to culturally deaf people. Padden and Humphries (1988) used the disability-first approach when they noted, "Deaf people are both Deaf and deaf" (p. 3).

In this book we have adopted a people-first approach, and we will continue that approach in this chapter. The approach basically says that people with disabilities are, first and foremost, people; their disabilities are part, but by no means all, of who and what they are. If people with disabilities are to experience the opportunities of inclusion, they should be seen as people first. In short, people-first language is inclusive.

We also use the terms *deaf* and *hard of hearing* as they are used by the Council for Exceptional Children (1995). We do not use the term *hearing impaired* because *impaired* implies a deficiency or pathology and carries a strong negative connotation although some authors we quote use the term *hearing impaired.* You will also notice that we use the terms *teacher of the deaf, school for the deaf, deaf education, Deaf culture,* and *Deaf community* because these are considered acceptable and are widely used among educators and individuals who are deaf. As you interact with students with hearing loss, remember that individual preferences vary. Try to find out what terms they use and be consistent with their choices.

Describing the Characteristics

Language and Communication. Learning language is the single greatest challenge for children who are deaf or hard of hearing. For children who are deaf, language must be acquired largely through the visual modality. For children who are hard of hearing, auditory information is incomplete and often distorted.

Individuals who are deaf or hard of hearing typically communicate in one of three ways (as you will learn more about later in this chapter):

- Oral/aural: speech, speechreading, residual hearing, and amplification of sound

- **American Sign Language (ASL):** sign language of the Deaf community in the United States

- Simultaneous communication: sign language (usually a manually coded English or signs from ASL used in English word order), fingerspelling, speech, speechreading, residual hearing and amplification of sound

Psychosocial Dimensions. Until quite recently, research and anecdotal information supported the belief that children and adolescents who are deaf and hard of hearing are more likely to have delayed or disordered social and emotional development than those who are hearing. Recently, many professionals have questioned the assumptions upon which a psychology of deafness are based. Instead of focusing on deafness as a pathological condition that views the individual as deficient, they now focus on how deafness impacts the child's interactions and, in turn, the child's social, emotional, cognitive, and language development.

Parent–child interaction plays a fundamental role in psychosocial development. For hearing parents with a child who is deaf or hard of hearing, communication is the first obstacle to positive interaction and parent–child bonding. Ultimately, easy communication enables parents to share their values and beliefs, socialize their child into the family and the community, and nurture a positive self-concept. But if communication is never easy or clear, their child's social and emotional development can suffer.

Peers and teachers also play significant roles in a child's psychosocial development. Again, communication is the key. When peers and teachers can communicate easily and effectively, the child can learn social norms, rules of conversation, appropriate ways of responding to different situations, and how to develop close relationships. If, however,

American Sign Language (ASL) is the sign language of the Deaf community in the United States; it possesses all of the grammatical complexity of spoken languages.

Parents look to professionals to help them figure out which communication method is right for their child.

〰 More than 90 percent of children who are deaf have hearing parents. Research has shown that mothers play a key role in family adjustment and that having a child who is deaf can result in personal growth and enhanced family relationships (Feher-Prout, 1996).

〰 *How would you communicate differently if your baby had a hearing loss?*

BOX 15-1   INTO PRACTICE

ENHANCING THE ACCESSIBILITY OF SPORTS AND EXTRACURRICULARS

Schools should consider incorporating into their extracurricular activities opportunities to promote greater awareness of social options available in the Deaf community. This can occur in a number of ways.

- Emphasize opportunities for participating in Deaf sports. Deaf sports are perhaps the best organized social institution in the Deaf community. Various sports are sponsored by Deaf associations at the local, regional, national and international levels. For example, a deaf volleyball player could play for the Greater Vancouver Association of the Deaf, participate in a tournament sponsored by the British Columbia Deaf Sports Federation, compete in the Canada Deaf Summer Games, and ultimately represent Canada in the World Games for the Deaf. Knowledge of these opportunities could be a strong motivational force for deaf youngsters to compete in high school sports.

- Relate adult Deaf activities to extracurricular activities. School clubs such as drama, photography, yearbook and computer all offer a chance to hone skills that could be useful in the Deaf community or elsewhere. Drama is a popular event in talent shows; a good photographer can contribute photos to newsletters, magazines or books about deaf people; yearbook experience can be used in the layout of newsletters and magazines; and computer skills can help a person bal-

ance the books as the treasurer of a Deaf association, keep statistics at sports events, or correspond through electronic mail. As in sports, a rationale for involvement in an extracurricular activity that highlights future social possibilities may be the deciding factor in convincing a deaf or hard of hearing student to participate.

- Extracurriculars designed specifically for Deaf students. Just as many schools sponsor choirs and bands, those with sufficient numbers of deaf students should consider having clubs that are either primarily for deaf students or for both hearing and deaf students. In one instance, a school might endorse a deaf Club that will allow students to dictate their own line of activities. Deaf awareness week, Deaf culture explorations, or camping trips are examples of some of the activities that students might pursue. Schools might also endorse a club that mainstreams hearing students into the communication world of deaf students. A sign language club would be an excellent opportunity for deaf students to assume responsibility for planning and teaching signs. In this situation, their rank among hearing peers is elevated because their language (e.g., American Sign Language) and their mode of communication become the status quo. Teaching peers to sign is a good means for expanding the social group with whom deaf students may communicate. As a result, more meaningful social interactions are likely to ensue throughout the school day.

Note: Reprinted by permission of the publisher from Kluwin, T.N., Moores, D. F., & Gaustad, M. G. (Eds.), TOWARD EFFECTIVE PUBLIC SCHOOL PROGRAMS FOR DEAF STUDENTS, (New York: Teachers College Press, © 1992 by Teachers College, Columbia University. All rights reserved), pp. 144–145.

communication is incomplete or so difficult that little time is spent interacting with the child, the child's ability to understand, be a part of the social environment, and positive self-concept are likely to be hampered.

A third important influence on psychosocial development is incidental information—that is, social cues that we overhear. Although children who are deaf and hard of hearing may notice visual cues quite readily, they miss spoken ones. "Not being able to overhear, rather than not being able to hear, is the real turn of the screw" (Wright, 1993, p. 130).

Finally, language competence is a key component in the social and emotional development of children who are deaf and hard of hearing (Weisel & Bar-Lev, 1992). We interact with the world, and learn about it, largely through language.

Recent research has indicated that individuals who are deaf or hard of hearing do not differ from hearing individuals in self-esteem; academic success is correlated with positive

BOX 15-2

MY VOICE

I NEED SOMEONE

I need someone to take the time to understand my world:
A world where silent trains go by,
A world where soundless jets can fly.
A world where car horns beep, beep, beep, yet never once
  disturb my sleep.
A world where sirens blaring loud make no more noise
  than a cirrus cloud.

I need someone to take the time to understand my world:
A world of signing I love you's.
A world of wondering what's the news.
A world where speech is hard to learn and often causes
  heads to turn.

A world of thoughts that fill my head, but you don't know
  what I've just said.

I need someone to take the time to understand my world:
A world of being an upstream rower.
A world where it helps if you talk slower.
A world where if you bend your knee, what you are saying
  I might see.
A world of loving without end, the ones with time to be my
  friend.

Donna Borchardt
1977

self-concept; and children who identify with others who are deaf or hard of hearing have higher self-esteem than children who associate solely with hearing individuals who do not sign (Bat-Chava, 1993; Cartledge, Paul, Jackson, & Cochran, 1991; Cates, 1991; Chovan & Roberts, 1993; Cole & Edelmann, 1991; Foster, 1989).

For adolescents like Amala, social interaction with peers is extremely important. Into Practice (Box 15-1) provides suggestions for ways that public school programs can offer extracurricular activities for students who are deaf, hard of hearing, and hearing.

The poem in Box 15-2, written by a mother of two sons who are deaf, presents a poignant picture of her children's social needs and their desire for friendships.

Education. Educators and even national commissions are greatly concerned about the academic achievement of students who are deaf or hard of hearing. In 1988, the Commission on Education of the Deaf issued a report to the Congress and the President of the United States that included fifty-two recommendations in seven categories: prevention and early identification, elementary and secondary education, postsecondary education, research, professional standards, technology and other. In 1994, the Deaf Education Initiative Project of the National Association of State Directors of Special Education issued guidelines in five areas of programs: foundations for educating students who are deaf or hard of hearing, supportive structures and administration, assessment, placement and program options, and personnel.

Despite these concerns, relatively little research has been conducted to determine the factors that most influence student achievement. Research exists on the effects of student placement and student background, but almost none exists on school-level variables (such as facilities, organization, and administrative support and attitudes), teacher characteristics, or students' attitudes toward one another (Mertens, 1990).

Two issues have recently come to the forefront. The first is the effects of inclusive educational settings versus segregated ones. Much of the research on placement has shown that students who are deaf and hard of hearing in general education classrooms demonstrate higher academic achievement than students in self-contained classrooms (Holt, 1994; Kluwin, 1993). However, no one has satisfactorily taken into account the confounding effect of how students are chosen for inclusion. Are students like Amala more successful than their peers who are in self-contained public school classrooms or schools for the deaf because the general education setting incorporates qualities that the other settings do not? Or are

What kinds of school facilities, organization, administrative support, teacher attitudes, and student attitudes do you think are helpful for students who are deaf and hard of hearing?

As you think about students from diverse ethnic, racial, and linguistic backgrounds, contemplate the issues that confront them in school where most of their teachers do not share their cultures.

students like Amala placed in inclusive settings because they embody the qualities that will enable them to be successful?

The second issue is the achievement levels of children from diverse racial, ethnic, and linguistic backgrounds. Educators of children who are deaf and hard of hearing seem to be less likely to acknowledge the differential educational experiences of children from minority backgrounds. And yet recent studies have shown that African American and Hispanic students perform significantly lower on measures of achievement than white students who are deaf or hard of hearing (Cohen, Fischgrund, & Redding, 1990; Kluwin, 1993). Kluwin noted, "Race is a pernicious factor in the school achievement of deaf students" (p. 79).

Academic achievement is strongly related to reading ability. Learning the English language is a challenge for children who are deaf or hard of hearing. Regardless of whether spoken English, simultaneous communication, or ASL are used for communication, the child must learn English for reading and writing. The average high school graduate who is deaf reads at the fourth/fifth grade level. Students who are deaf and hard of hearing average one-third of a grade equivalent change for each year they are in school and their reading achievement levels off at a point equivalent to the average fourth grade hearing student (Wolk & Allen, 1984).

A student's achievement levels reveal nothing about the student's potential. Children who are deaf or hard of hearing have the same intellectual abilities as children who are hearing (Braden, 1992; Schirmer, 1994). They also have the same cognitive abilities to process written language. When they read, they use the same types of knowledge and skills as hearing readers.

But some of their knowledge and skills are less well-developed. Because of diminished exposure to incidental information, they often have incomplete background knowledge, yet comprehension depends on how much the reader already knows about the author's topic. Because English is hard for them, they may have difficulty figuring out the meaning of particular English sentence structures. However, they have no more trouble learning to recognize individual words than any other reader. And when teachers spend instructional time on reading comprehension strategies that encourage them to think deeply about what they read, rather than on deciphering the meaning of individual sentences, they can be proficient and enthusiastic readers (Schirmer, 1993, 1995; Schirmer & Winter, 1993; Schirmer & Woolsey, 1997).

ʘ *Reading is an important classroom activity for children who are deaf or hard of hearing.*

Identifying the Causes of Hearing Loss

To understand the causes of hearing loss, it will help you to understand how hearing works. As you can see from Figure 15–3, the ear consists of three parts: the outer, middle, and inner ear. The middle ear links the air-filled outer ear with the fluid-filled inner ear. The ear is like a radio system: The inner ear is the radio receiver, the middle ear the radio-station transmitter, and the outer ear the microphone in the studio. To be effective, all must work. Hearing loss occurs when some part of the outer, middle, or inner ear is not functioning as it should. When this happens, it is either a conductive hearing loss or a sensorineural hearing loss.

Any problem of the outer or middle ear when the inner ear is unaffected is called a **conductive hearing loss.** The hearing loss is caused not by sound perception, but by sound conduction. For example, when fluid collects behind the eardrum in the middle ear and becomes infected, the result is an ear infection and a conductive hearing loss. If you think of the ear as a radio system, with a conductive loss, the microphone (outer ear) or the transmitter (middle ear) is not working perfectly. Generally, conductive hearing losses result in less severe hearing loss than sensorineural hearing losses, are often improved through surgery, and are likely to be improved by amplification.

Sensorineural hearing loss is caused by problems in the inner ear or along the nerve pathway from the inner ear to the brain stem. Using the analogy of the radio system, with sensorineural hearing loss, the receiver is not working perfectly. The microphone may be picking up the sound and the transmitter may be conducting the sound, but the inner ear is not receiving the sound, or all aspects of the sound, and therefore little, no, or distorted sound is heard.

A **hearing aid** will make sounds louder but cannot correct the hearing loss. There are many types of hearing aids, and you will see individuals with hearing aids on the body, behind the ear, in the ear, built into glasses or built onto a headband. There is always some distortion with hearing aids; unlike corrective lenses in eye glasses or contacts, hearing aids do not restore normal hearing to the person. In addition to hearing aids, many individuals use assistive listening devices such as telephone amplifiers and personal FM

Conductive hearing loss refers to any problem of the outer or middle ear when the inner ear is not affected.

Sensorineural hearing loss is caused by problems in the inner ear or along the nerve pathway from the inner ear to the brain stem.

A **hearing aid** is an electro-acoustic device designed to make sounds louder. The microphone and receiver can be worn on the body, near or in the ear; the amplifier is attached to an ear mold and worn inside the ear.

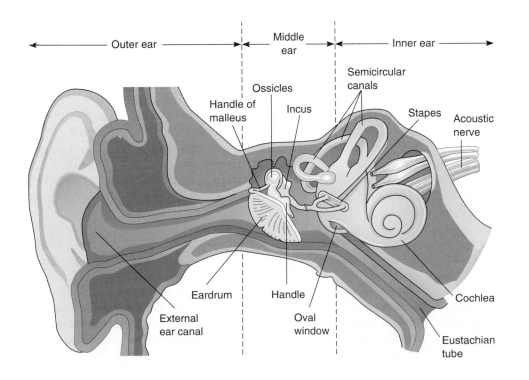

FIGURE 15–3 *Diagram of ear*

A **cochlear implant** is a device that converts sound into electrical current to stimulate the auditory nerve fibers; the part with electrodes is surgically implanted, and the part with a microphone and processor is worn externally.

Prelingual hearing loss is hearing loss at birth or before the child has learned language.

Postlingual hearing loss is hearing loss that occurs after the child has developed language.

systems. Others opt for surgery called cochlear implant. A **cochlear implant** is a device that converts sound into electrical current to stimulate an individual's auditory nerve fibers. A cochlear implant consists of two components: One part is a device with electrodes that is surgically implanted near the auditory nerves, and the other part is a microphone and processor that is worn externally. Not every person with a hearing loss is a candidate for a cochlear implant, and the surgery carries risks, but many individuals have benefited greatly. The cochlear implant has been particularly controversial for children because of the surgical risks, the potential discomfort, and the belief by many individuals in the Deaf community that deafness is not a disorder or disease that should be cured.

Prelingual Causes. A hearing loss at birth or before the child has learned language is called **prelingual hearing loss** (*pre* for before and *lingual* for language). The majority of all students who are deaf or hard of hearing, approximately 95 percent, are prelingual. A hearing loss that occurs after the child has developed language is called **postlingual.** Only 5 percent of students who are deaf or hard of hearing have postlingual hearing losses (Commission on Education of the Deaf, 1988). The distinction is important educationally because the child with a postlingual hearing loss has a language base for learning and communicating.

Prelingual causes include premature birth, heredity, maternal rubella, congenital cytomegalovirus, and unknown causes.

Premature Birth. Hearing loss is one of many disabilities exhibited by some infants who are born very prematurely, with a resulting low birth weight, possible hemorrhage in the brain, or reduced oxygen to the inner ear.

Heredity. Hereditary childhood deafness is a primary feature of between 150 and 175 different genetic syndromes, and there are an additional 16 types of genetic deafness that are not associated with other anomalies (Bess & Humes, 1995). Since most hereditary deafness is the result of a recessive genetic trait rather than a dominant genetic trait, "the marriage of two deaf persons gives only a slightly increased risk of deafness in their children because there is small chance that two such persons would be affected by the same exact genetic deafness" (Northern & Downs, 1991, p. 90). Genetic counseling is available for families with relatives who are deaf or hard of hearing.

Maternal Rubella. The fetus is especially vulnerable to certain viruses. For example, as a result of the 1964–1965 rubella epidemic, incidence of hearing loss in children increased dramatically. Although rubella (often referred to as German measles) in children and adults is generally benign, in pregnant women, particularly during the first trimester, the virus attacks the developing fetus, often causing hearing loss as well as other conditions. In 1969, the rubella vaccine was introduced in the United States, and since that time rubella has declined, although it still is a cause of hearing loss (Moores, 1996).

Congenital Cytomegalovirus and Unknown Causes. The cytomegalovirus (CMV) is a common virus that can remain in an inactive state in the body, possibly for the remainder of the person's lifetime. Pregnancy can reactivate the virus and can be contracted within the uterus, through passage down the birth canal, or through breast milk. Based on a 1988 survey, it has been estimated that almost 50 percent of children may be deaf or hard of hearing as a result of CMV (Schildroth, Rawlings, & Allen, 1989). In addition to hearing loss, children may develop other central nervous system disabilities including developmental delay (Northern & Downs, 1991).

Postlingual Causes. The most common examples of postlingual hearing losses are those resulting from meningitis, recurring middle-ear infections, side effects from medications, and unknown causes.

Meningitis. Meningitis is a disease of the central nervous system that may extend to other organs, including the brain and the ear. Despite the use of antibiotics that have reduced infant mortality, almost 50 percent of children with bacterial meningitis still experience serious complications, the most common of them being sensorineural hearing loss (Northern & Downs, 1991).

Otitis Media.   Otitis media, or inflammation of the middle ear, is common in young children, whether or not they have a hearing loss. This is of particular importance for early childhood educators, because some children are prone to contracting otitis media frequently. Between 76 and 95 percent of children experience otitis media at least once by the time they are six years old, and approximately one-third of all children will experience three episodes. The condition is the most common reason for a doctor visit for children below the age of six (Bess & Humes, 1995). When a child has frequent ear infections, it is important to have a speech and language evaluation to serve as a baseline for future reference. Delays in speech or language development may be caused by the lack of auditory input when the child is unable to hear fully because of the ear infections and fluid in the middle ear. Medical treatment, including both antibiotics or surgical placement of tubes in the ear, is an important line of defense.

Unknown Causes.   Figure 15-4 shows the statistics for all causes of hearing loss for the 1996–1997 school year (Gallaudet University, 1998). It reveals that most causes, both prelingual and postlingual, are unknown. Robyn Brown, for example, does not know what caused Amala's hearing loss. She suspects that Amala may have had some hearing when she was born, and perhaps had no hearing loss initially, but then suffered illness or injury when she was an infant.

Identifying the Prevalence of Hearing Loss

Prevalence of hearing loss in children is estimated to be 1.6 percent, based on interviews conducted through the National Health Interview Survey (Bess & Humes, 1995). You will find additional prevalence information in Figure 15-5.

Prevalence figures refer to the number of people in a defined group with a particular characteristic at a certain point in time. Children who are deaf and hard of hearing do not

FIGURE 15–4   *Causes of hearing loss: Percentage of total number of students reporting a cause for their hearing loss, 1996–1997 (cause was not reported for 54.4% of students who reported a hearing loss; some students reported more than one cause)*

At birth	
Maternal rubella	2.9
Trauma at birth	4.8
Other complications of pregnancy	4.6
Heredity	27.8
Prematurity	9.9
Cytomegalovirus	3.5
RH incompatibility	0.7
Other cause at birth	13.5
s	
Meningitis	14.4
High fever	4.3
Mumps	0.1
Infection	4.3
Measles	0.3
Otitis media	8.8
Trauma after birth	1.3
Other cause after birth	7.2

Note: From *1996–1997 Annual Survey of Deaf and Hard-of-Hearing Children and Youth*, by Gallaudet University, Center for Assessment and Demographic Studies, 1998, Washington, DC. Copyright 1998 by Gallaudet University. Reprinted with permission.

FIGURE 15–5 *Useful facts about prevalence of hearing loss*

- One child in 1,000 is born with profound deafness.

- An additional two children in 1,000 will become deaf in early childhood.

- Newborn infants requiring intensive medical care are at risk, resulting in one child in fifty becoming deaf or hard of hearing from intensive care nurseries.

- Ear infection, the most common infectious childhood disease, is associated with hearing loss.

- Nearly all children from birth to eleven years of age will develop some period of hearing loss related to ear infections.

- Ten to fifteen percent of children who receive school hearing screenings fail because they do not hear within normal limits.

Note: From Hearing in Children (4th ed.), by J. L. Northern and M. P. Downs, 1991, Baltimore: Williams & Wilkins. Copyright 1991 by Williams & Wilkins. Reprinted with permission.

necessarily distribute themselves evenly throughout the United States or within a state, county, or city. Some communities of equal size will have larger numbers of children and some will have smaller numbers, and from year to year the numbers will change. For example, sometimes parents will move to a community because it has a good reputation for providing educational services to children who are deaf and hard of hearing. This has often been true of communities where there are schools for the deaf.

WHAT ARE EVALUATION PROCEDURES?

Determining the Presence of Hearing Loss

Hearing difficulties need to be identified as early as possible in order to plan an appropriate educational program. But as Hans Furth (1973) wrote (see Box 15-3) more than two decades ago, determining the presence of hearing loss is not simple.

What happens when a screening indicates a possible hearing problem? Figure 15-6 shows you that a diagnostic evaluation is then needed. For an infant, this means a diagnostic auditory brain stem response test. Sensors are placed on the baby's head and in the ear, computer clicks are sounded, and the baby's responses are measured by a computer and an audiometer. In another approach, acoustic immittance, a microphone is placed in the baby's ear canal, and it measures the sounds that the hair cells in the inner ear make when they vibrate in response to external sound (Clarkson, Vohr, Blackwell, & White, 1994).

For older children, a behavioral audiological evaluation is appropriate. These evaluations are called *behavioral* because the audiologist is drawing conclusions based on the child's behaviors during the testing situation. You have undoubtedly had one of these hearing tests at some time in your life, probably at school. You put on earphones and heard tones ranging from very low to very high, very soft to loud. When you heard the tones, you pushed a button or raised your hand. When these tests are conducted at school, they are used to screen those children who should receive further evaluation.

During the evaluation, the audiologist uses a sound system with speakers in a soundproof booth. The child enters the booth, listens to sounds heard through the ear phones, and indicates if he or she hears the sound. With young children, the mother or father may place the child on the lap, or they both may sit inside the booth with the child.

In Figure 15-7, you can see an example of Amala's completed audiogram. The audiogram, which shows hearing test results, includes responses for frequency and intensity. Frequency means the number of vibrations that occur in one second. A high sound has more vibrations. For example, if a vibration makes one hundred up–down movements in one second, its frequency is one hundred cycles per second. We commonly think of the highness or lowness of a sound as its pitch.

BOX 15-3 **MAKING A DIFFERENCE**

By far, most deaf children are born to hearing parents. In addition, the sense organ for hearing is not accessible to the casual observer—indeed, it is difficult for the specialist to reach—and deafness does not betray its presence until you speak to the person and wait for a linguistic response. But because we do not expect speech behavior in the new-born infant and because our speech directed to him is usually accompanied by looking and appropriate gestures, the deaf infant may respond quite normally by smiling, struggling, and cooing. This situation results in a unique characteristic of deafness: if the baby is otherwise healthy, deafness cannot be observed in his behavior. It is difficult to obtain a reliable measurement for hearing at a very early age. Pediatricians do not routinely test for it, and often even specialists can only make an educated guess.

Thus, the deaf baby is born into a hearing world that does not suspect him of being deaf. He is nursed, he cries and smiles, he is curious and fascinated by moving things and faces, and he responds affectionately to the care and love given him. He begins to crawl and sit up, he handles things and attempts to put them in his mouth, his teeth grow in, he becomes accustomed to eating solid food and to drinking from a cup, he is first unwilling and then quite fussy and insistent about holding the spoon himself. He recognizes persons and things and has his favorite toys and blanket. He toddles and holds on and finally walks around the home and soon outside too. By now he may be eighteen months old and he is a beautiful lovable little boy. The parents dream and talk of his future and their future with him. In retrospect they recall remarks like the following, but at the time they did not feel disturbed about them: "Has he not started to talk yet?" "He must be a late talker, but so was cousin Jean." "Are you sure he can hear well?" "Of course he can hear. See how he runs to me when I clap my hands."

Note: From *Deafness and Learning,* by H. G. Furth, 1973, Belmont, CA: Wadsworth. Copyright 1973 by Wadsworth. Reprinted with permission.

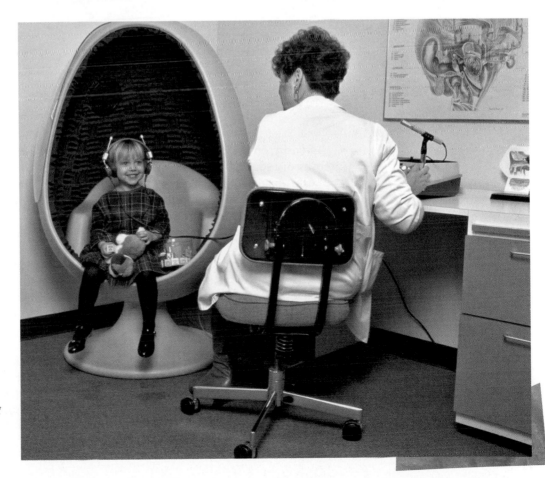

🕭 *Audiologists can obtain an accurate hearing assessment when the child is relaxed and attentive.*

FIGURE 15–6 *Infant
hearing screening*

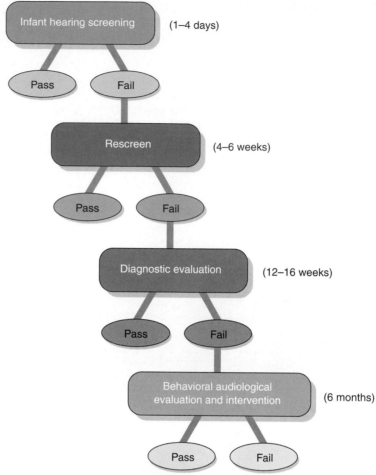

Note: From "Universal Newborn Hearing Screening Using Transient Evoked Otoacoustic
Emissions: Results of the Rhode Island Hearing Assessment Project," by K. R. White, B. R. Vohr,
and T. R. Behrens, 1993, *Seminars in Hearing, 14*(1), pp. 18–29. Copyright 1993 by Thieme
Medical Publishers. Reprinted with permission.

Intensity, on the other hand, refers to the pressure of a sound, not its movements. The
intensity of a sound is measured in decibels (dB), named in honor of Alexander Graham Bell.
The scale on an audiogram shows a range in intensity from silent to very loud. The decibel
scale is also based on ratios. Each 10-dB increment represents a tenfold increase in intensity.
Therefore, a 20-dB sound is one hundred times more intense than a sound at 10 dB, and so on.

In summary, intensity refers to the loudness of a sound and frequency to the pitch of
a sound. Figure 15-2 will help you understand the hearing levels of different sounds. For
example, a rock band registers at 120 dB, but a whisper is only 20 dB.

The frequencies that audiologists test range from 125 to 8,000 cycles per second, and
hearing levels range from 0 to 110 dB. The audiologist tests both ears and marks responses
on the audiogram for the right ear with an *O* and for the left ear with an *X*. A child who
has a hearing aid is also tested with the aid on, and those responses are recorded with an
A or an asterisk.

When you look at Amala's audiogram (Figure 15-7), you see that she has more hearing
in the lower frequencies and very little or no hearing in the middle and higher frequencies.
These results caused Amala's audiologist to classify her hearing as severe to profound. Amala
benefits from amplification in her right ear, and so her audiogram also provides information
regarding how her hearing measures with hearing aids. There is a notable difference
between aided and unaided hearing.

FIGURE 15–7 *Amala's audiogram*

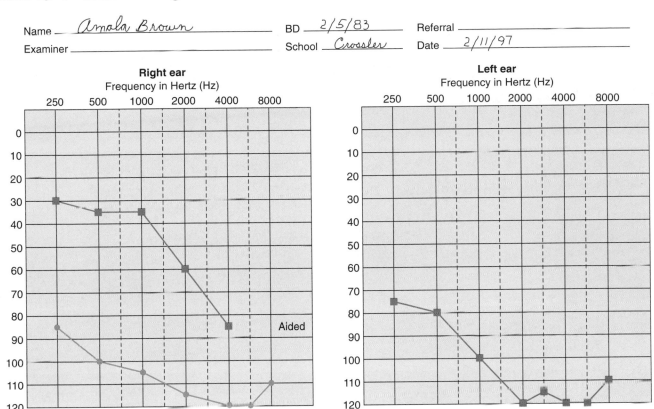

Name _Amala Brown_   BD _2/5/83_   Referral _____

Examiner _____   School _Crossler_   Date _2/11/97_

Note: Used with courtesy of Robyn Brown.

When you look at an audiogram, the *Xs* and *Os* are marked at the child's hearing threshold; it is "the lowest (softest) sound level needed for a person to detect the presence of a signal approximately 50 percent of the time" (Bess & Humes, 1995, p. 106). A sound at a particular pitch and frequency outside of the testing booth may be difficult for the child to both recognize and understand. Look back at Figure 15-1, and compare the range of the speech banana with the child's hearing level, because the most important sounds in the classroom are speech sounds.

If you saw an audiogram in a student file, you could tell if the student were more hard of hearing or deaf by where the *Xs* and *Os* were on the audiogram. If there were significant improvements with the hearing aids, you would know that the student should wear the hearing aids at all times and that you should make sure the batteries have power. You would also know if the student would benefit from preferential seating in your classroom so that he or she is near the person who does the most speaking or close to the interpreter. If the child had significantly more hearing in one ear, you would know that he or she should sit on a particular side of the room.

After completing the hearing evaluation, the audiologist usually recommends hearing aids. For babies, audiologists retest hearing four times a year until age three, twice a year until age six, and annually after six years of age.

About 25 percent of students who are deaf and hard of hearing have one additional disability, and 9 percent have two or more other disabilities (Schildroth & Hotto, 1994). Of particular importance is vision, which is so crucial for language development, communication, and learning for children with hearing loss. In addition, program decisions may be different if motor difficulties or cognitive delays are present. The range of assessment procedures and the general pattern of findings for students who are deaf and hard of hearing is included in Figure 15-8.

FIGURE 15–8 *Assessment process for determining the presence of a hearing loss*

Nondiscriminatory Evaluation

Observation

Parents observe	In the early months, the behavior of deaf and hearing babies is similar. Parents may notice if there is no startle reflex to loud noises.
Physician observes	The baby does not show startle reflex to loud noises. As the child matures, speech and language are delayed.
Teacher observes	If child has not been identified before starting school, the teacher may observe communication misunderstandings, speech difficulties, and inattention.

Medical screening

Assessment measures	Findings that indicate need for further evaluation
Early screening surveys	Newborns may undergo routine hearing screening. Some states use a high-risk survey to determine which infants need a hearing evaluation.
Auditory brainstem response	Results may show inadequate or slow response in the brain to sounds.
Transient evoked otoacoustic emissions	Using a microphone, the evaluator finds that measurement of sound in the ear is lower than normal.
Behavioral audiological evaluation	Students who can only hear tones at or above 70 decibels are deaf; those who can hear tones from 35 to 69 decibels are hard of hearing.

Prereferral

Prereferral is typically not used with these students because of the need to quickly identify hearing loss.

Referral

Students who are deaf and hard of hearing should receive early intervention as soon as they are diagnosed. Children receive protection in evaluation procedures as soon as they enter school. Some students with mild hearing loss may be referred by teachers for evaluation.

Protection in evaluation procedures

Assessment measures	Findings that suggest hearing loss
Audiological reassessment	Recent scores with audiograms may indicate that the student's hearing loss is stabilized or worsening. Testing for hearing aid function is a regular need.
Individualized intelligence test	Normally this is not done unless another disability is suspected.
Individualized achievement test	The student may score significantly lower than peers if hearing loss has not been corrected before starting school or if academic program has not used alternative or augmentative communication.
Speech and language evaluation	The student may have significant problems with receptive and expressive language. The student's speech is usually affected.
Adaptive behavior scales	Because of hearing problems, the student may score below average in communication and socialization skills, and possibly in other areas of adaptive behavior.
Anecdotal records	The student's records may indicate difficulty with alertness or speaking in class. Increased hearing loss may be indicated by the student asking the interpreter to speak for her more frequently.
Curriculum-based assessment	The student may be performing below peers in one or more areas of the curriculum because of reading and/or language difficulties.
Direct observation	The student's speech may be difficult to understand and the student misunderstands others. Observer may notice the student turning head to one side to try to hear, asking for information to be repeated, and looking at other students to determine instructions.

Evaluation Team determines that special education and related services are needed for hard of hearing or deafness.

Appropriate Education

Determining the Nature and Extent of Special Education and Related Services

During the preschool and school years, the individualized family services plan (IFSP) and individualized education program (IEP) teams must consider a number of factors as they determine the nature and extent of special education and related services. Each of the following factors is critical in determining an appropriate educational setting and the related services and supplementary aids that the child will need:

I. Communication
   A. Hearing Loss
      1. Unaided
      2. Aided
      3. Aural functioning/speech perception
   B. Language
      1. Spoken English/manually coded English/American Sign Language
      2. Language ability
   C. Speech intelligibility
   D. Speechreading ability
   E. Sign proficiency

II. Achievement
   A. Academic achievement as indicated by standardized tests
   B. Academic achievement as indicated by classroom performance

III. Socialization

IV. Motivation

V. Parent expectation and preference

VI. Presence of additional disability

Some information will come from testing the child and other information from observing the child. When Amala has her annual IEP meeting, her mother, Robyn, shares her observations of how Amala interacts at home with family members and friends; she also provides information about Amala's ability to carry out school homework assignments. Tina Harrison, the teacher of the deaf at Amala's school, contributes information about how well Amala is progressing in the curriculum at school and also provides recent testing information, the most important being Amala's written language development and reading ability. Ginny Chinn, Amala's seventh-grade teacher, shares information about Amala's academic performance, her study skills, and her social interactions with the other seventh graders. The sign language **interpreters** provide input about Amala's ability to access information in the classroom through the interpreter.

At some IEP meetings, other professionals might provide additional valuable information. The speech-language pathologist might provide information about the child's ability to make him- or herself intelligible to others, and also explain what can enhance or hinder the child's ability to speechread. For example, female teachers who wear lipstick are easier to speechread, but male teachers with mustaches and beards are more difficult to understand. The audiologist may relate recent testing information indicating whether hearing levels are stable or worsening, if hearing aids are functioning well and are appropriate or need to be changed, and may provide information about the frequencies of sounds that are more difficult or impossible for the child to hear. For example, if the child has more hearing at the lower frequencies, the audiologist can explain why male teachers are more understandable than female teachers. The school psychologist may provide the team with the most recent achievement test results.

Interpreters are professionals who translate from one language to another; sign language interpreters translate from spoken language to sign language and from sign language to spoken language.

FIGURE 15–9 *Questions to guide the observations of classroom teachers*

1. When the student participates in class discussions:
   • Does the student prefer small group or full class discussions?
   • Does the student volunteer or prefer to be called upon?
   • Are some topics more likely to evoke interest than others?

2. When the student talks to others before or after class:
   • Is it common or unusual?
   • Does the student always talk to the same one or two individuals or to many different peers?

3. When the student asks the teacher questions:
   • Is it common or unusual?
   • Do the questions require you to repeat information you have already explained or to expand on what you presented in class or what is presented in the book?

4. When you call on the student in class:
   • Does it seem as if the student has been following the presentation or discussion?
   • Is the student comfortable responding?

5. When the student participates in class activities:
   • Are there individuals that the student would prefer to be grouped with?
   • Does the student prefer to work independently, with a peer, or in a small group?

Amala herself is an important source of information about her strengths and needs. Robyn has been trying to get Amala to participate in her IEP meetings but has so far been unsuccessful. Robyn recognizes that it must be difficult for Amala to sit at a meeting while everyone talks about what she does and doesn't need to do. But Amala has been part of parent–teacher conferences where she has been able to respond to questions and concerns raised by her teachers. Also, Tina and Amala have gone through the IEP together, discussing the educational goals, and Tina has encouraged Amala to become involved in the IEP meetings by telling her that they are discussing Amala's educational future and they do not want to do that without her.

Figure 15-9 will guide your observations if you have students who are deaf or hard of hearing.

WHAT AND HOW DO PROFESSIONALS TEACH?

Three questions have been a constant source of related controversy throughout the history of deaf education in the United States, and indeed the world:

   • Where should students who are deaf and hard of hearing be taught?

   • What should they be taught?

   • How should they be taught?

As Moores (1991) noted, the issues underlying these questions are complex and interrelated. Simply stated, the question of *where* has recently focused on inclusion and how to determine the least restrictive environment for students who are deaf and hard of hearing. The question of *what* focuses on the similarities and differences between curriculum for all students and special curriculum for students who are deaf and hard of hearing. The question of *how* focuses on communication mode—oral/aural, simultaneous communication in spoken English and a manually coded English, or ASL.

We will address the first question later, in the section entitled "Inclusion." We will address the questions of *what* and *how* next, in the sections entitled "Curriculum" and "Methods," respectively.

Curriculum

There are two schools of thought about curriculum for students who are deaf and hard of hearing. According to one, these students need special curriculum in all subject areas. Several schools for the deaf, such as the Kendall Demonstration Elementary School in Washington, DC, have developed curriculum guides in language arts, science, social studies, and math.

According to the other, these students do not need specialized curriculum for content subjects, because they have no special learning needs in these areas; they are able to learn as much material and at the same level of complexity as hearing children. Instead of a specialized content curriculum, they need teaching models and strategies that capitalize on their learning strengths and build on their current abilities and knowledge.

Both schools of thought recognize the importance of specialized curriculum in the areas of Deaf culture, speech, and aural habilitation. Both also acknowledge that language is at the heart of any curriculum.

Language, Reading, and Writing. Historically, a curriculum in language, reading, and writing was analytical in nature. Students were taught the rules, or grammar, of spoken and written language, and they were given practice in applying the rules. A curriculum in language often consisted of teaching the students English sentence patterns, starting with basic patterns and moving to increasingly complex structures. A curriculum in reading regularly involved using books with relatively simple grammatical structures, or basal reading materials that were designed so that sentence patterns increased in difficulty from book to book. A typical writing curriculum required students to learn the rules for different types of discourse, such as writing essays and paragraphing, and the rules of grammar because this was the most obvious area with which the students had difficulty.

Language and literacy curriculum today can best be described as holistic in nature. Teachers of the deaf recognize that students who are deaf and hard of hearing have the same cognitive abilities to make sense of language, face-to-face language, and written language as hearing students. They employ curriculum that emphasizes context over structure. In the language curriculum, spoken and sign language are most often in the context of conversation and discussions; grammatical rules are presented but only after the child has demonstrated understanding of the grammatical form when used by others or after it has appeared in the child's expressive language. In the reading curriculum, literature is used, and the teacher emphasizes the student's comprehension of the material, recognizing that all readers miss some story details and textbook facts. And in the writing curriculum, emphasis is placed on helping students see that writing involves many qualities, and English grammar is just one of these qualities.

Deaf Culture. Culture is a pattern of beliefs, values, behaviors, arts, customs, institutions, social forms, and knowledge that are characteristic of a community. Culture is transmitted to succeeding generations through material products, physical interaction with members of the community, and language. A curriculum in Deaf culture is important regardless of the educational setting, though many educators and members of the Deaf community argue that it is even more important in public school programs because children in these settings typically have relatively little contact with deaf adults.

The following components form the nucleus of a Deaf culture curriculum:

- American Sign Language: the linguistic differences between ASL and English; how ASL developed as a visual-gestural language of the Deaf community in the United States; interaction norms and conversational rules in ASL

- Political activism: activist movements such as the Deaf President Now protest at Gallaudet University (Christiansen & Barnartt, 1995); advocacy activities that have led to the passage of laws and regulations designed to improve education and accessibility for individuals with hearing loss

• History and biography: Deaf individuals who have made important contributions to society, such as the persons portrayed in Lang and Meath-Lang's, *Deaf Persons in the Arts and Sciences: A Biographical Dictionary* (1995); contributions from the Deaf community such as the football huddle, originally developed at Gallaudet University by all-deaf football teams

• Theater and art: Groups such as the National Theater of the Deaf; visual art of Deaf artists

• Clubs and organizations: Information about and participation in the activities of local Deaf clubs and organizations; competitions such as the Deaf Olympics and Miss Deaf America

• Folklore: legends and traditions of the Deaf community; jokes and humorous stories; games and sign play; naming practices

Speech. A speech curriculum involves teaching the skills involved in producing spoken language, and then in improving speech. Often, speechreading is integrated with speech instruction because the visual cues the student receives through speechreading are integral for both understanding and producing speech. Not all students benefit from speech instruction, and as students become older, their motivation for speech intervention often declines.

Aural Habilitation. It is useful for most students to use even their minimal residual hearing effectively. For many students, instruction that focuses on hearing for speech use is an important part of their curriculum, especially in the younger years. An aural habilitation curriculum involves teaching students how to use their residual hearing, through amplification or cochlear implant, and to respond to sound along a continuum from awareness, to localization, to discrimination of sound differences, to recognizing the sound (e.g., meowing is the sound of a cat), to comprehending the sound (e.g., the sounds of c-a-t refer to a cat). As with speech, not all students benefit from aural habilitation.

Methods

Communication. As you learned earlier in this chapter, individuals who are deaf and hard of hearing typically communicate in one of three ways: oral/aural, ASL, and simultaneous communication. These three communication modes are directly related to the three methods of communication used in educational programs: oral/aural, bilingual-bicultural, and total communication.

Oral/Aural. Oral/aural methods are characterized by instruction in spoken English, curriculum in speech and aural habilitation, and the expectation that the students will use speech, speechreading, and auditory skills for communication.

Bilingual-Bicultural. Bilingual-bicultural methods are characterized by instruction in ASL, the expectation that the students will use ASL for communication, and the teaching of English through the written form with no or little use of spoken English. Most bilingual–bicultural programs in deaf education are based on English-as-a-second-language models. American Sign Language is taught as the child's first language, and English is introduced as the second language.

American Sign Language is a visual-gestural language because it involves the use of gestures with specific placement and movement, facial expression, and body movement. American Sign Language has distinct grammatical rules that are quite different from English. For instance, word order in standard English specifies that nouns go before verbs. In ASL, verbs go before nouns. Because of the different rules for each language, it is not possible to speak English and sign ASL at the same time.

How do you think hearing teachers can provide students who are deaf and hard of hearing with meaningful information and experiences about Deaf culture?

When ASL is taught as the child's first language, it means that the parents must also learn ASL so that they can communicate with their child.

Total Communication. Total communication methods are characterized by instruction in simultaneous communication, which is the use of speech and a manually coded English. The expectation is that the students will use simultaneous communication. Total communication methods also incorporate curriculum in speech and aural habilitation, and sometimes include curriculum in ASL. Total communication is an approach that has gone out of favor. One reason is that the idea of using every communication technique and mode available seems unrealistic. Teachers typically emphasize speech and audition at the expense of sign language, or vice versa. And students attend more to one mode than the other. A second reason total communication as a method has become controversial is because it was predicated on having the teacher use speech and sign language simultaneously, and as you previous learned, it is not possible to speak and use ASL at the same time. Therefore, teachers use either a manually coded English sign system or pidgin sign language. Many educators and members of the Deaf community are vociferous opponents of manually coded English systems because they believe that these are not languages at all but rather distortions of features of American Sign Language. Researchers have found that most teachers using total communication methods actually use pidgin sign language, which is an idiosyncratic mix of English and ASL incorporating simplified grammatical features and vocabulary from both languages (Luetke-Stahlman, 1988; Wood, Wood, & Kingsmill, 1991).

Recently, programs that use total communication methods have modified the approach to incorporate language switching. In this approach, the teacher individualizes so that information is presented to some students orally/aurally, and to others in simultaneous communication or ASL.

In both ASL and manually coded English systems, **fingerspelling** is used to represent words for which there are no signs. With fingerspelling, a person uses the manual alphabet to spell words letter by letter. A chart of the manual alphabet is presented in Figure 15–10.

"Into Practice" Box 15–4 provides illustrations of what it would be like for you if you used these communication modes.

Instructional Strategies.

Instructional strategies for students with hearing loss are particularly effective when they emphasize experiential learning, build on the students' current knowledge and skills, require them to interact with peers, capitalize on the visual medium, and reduce environmental distraction.

Experiential Learning. Engaging students in activities that enable them to experience a concept is much more effective than telling them about the concept. Examples include the following:

- Use drama or role play to illustrate an historical event, the actions of characters in a novel, and other such episodes.

- Have students conduct experiments to test out scientific principles.

- Take students on field trips to see actual artifacts, art, events, and individuals.

- Act out the actions of physical phenomena such as how the heart works or the eruption of Mount St. Helens.

Scaffolding. Scaffolding involves two major steps. The first step is developing a sequence of instruction that starts with what the student knows and connects new information to previously learned information. The second step is providing the student support at each step in the learning process, and gradually reducing the support until the student is independent. These guidelines should be followed:

- Before teaching new concepts, assess the students' knowledge about the topic.

- Develop a sequence of instruction so that each new piece of information or new skill is the logical next step based upon what the students already know or are able to do.

Researchers are currently working on developing techniques that can enable teachers to become proficient in conveying English in sign language (Stewart, Akamatsu, & Becker, 1995).

Fingerspelling is the hand configurations that represent the letters of the alphabet; fingerspelling is generally used to spell words that have no known sign.

FIGURE 15–10 *Chart of manual alphabet*

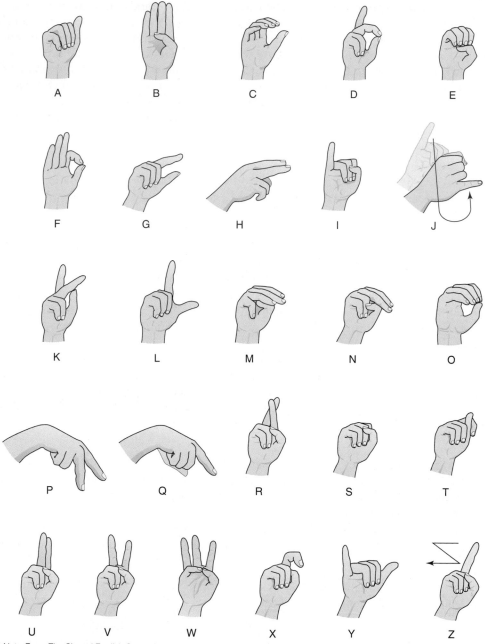

Note: From *The Signed English Starter,* by H. Bornstein and K. Saulnier, 1984, Washington, DC: Gallaudet University Press. Copyright 1984 by Gallaudet University Press. Reprinted with permission.

• Provide opportunity for the students to use the information or practice the skill and gradually reduce the amount of support you provide.

Collaborative Learning and Peer Tutoring. Collaborative learning and peer tutoring require students to depend on one another during learning activities. Students in collaborative learning teams each play an integral role needed by the group. Students in peer tutoring can take turns so that one individual can be the teacher some of the time. Both of these strategies provide students who are deaf and hard of hearing the opportunity to be equal participants with peers. The following are recommended when planning collaborative learning and peer tutoring activities:

• Set up collaborative learning teams that are heterogeneous so that students with varying ability levels comprise each group.

BOX 15-4   INTO PRACTICE

DIFFERENT COMMUNICATION MODES

- If you were using the oral/aural mode, you would be solely relying on whatever hearing you have and your speechreading abilities. Try turning down the volume during a newscast or a favorite comedy show to a sound that is a bit difficult to hear, now lower it so that it is barely audible. What do you understand? What do the speakers do that is helpful? What makes it impossible for you to comprehend the speaker?

- If you were using American Sign Language to communicate to a friend that you were going out to eat, you would sign the location ("restaurant") first, then sign who is going ("me"), and finally sign the verb ("going"). Much of your meaning would be expressed by your hands but you would also use body movement, facial expression and other gestural devices that are part of the grammatical structure of American Sign Language to express modulations of meaning. What would happen when you gave your order to the waitperson in the restaurant? If he or she didn't know American Sign Language, how would you make yourself understood?

- If you were using simultaneous communication to convey the same idea to your friend, you would speak, "I am going to a restaurant" and at the same time use a sign for each word and inflection, "I am go-ing to a restaurant." There are seven signs involved, even though there are only six words in the sentence, because you would add the sign for *ing* to the sign *go*. Would it be hard to sign every English word and inflection? How tedious would it be to sign complex sentences such as the following: "I want-ed Mary to come but she is un-reach-able because she was teach-ing this morning and so I was think-ing that we could bring back some taco-s for her."

- Make sure that each student has an assignment to carry out that the other members of the team need.

- Develop an assessment that enables each student to succeed at a level of mastery appropriate to the individual.

- Use peer tutoring activities that allow students to take turns at being tutor and tutee.

Visual Aids. Illustrations, semantic maps, graphic organizers, flow charts, videos, slides, television, and computer technology are very valuable adjuncts during classroom instruction for students with hearing loss. When planning a lesson, think about the following ideas:

- Visually represent information presented orally whenever possible.

- Instead of a chalkboard, use an overhead projector. Your face is in view for students, and the light on your face is helpful for speechreading. However, pay attention to the noise level of the cooling fan, because it can be very distracting for students with hearing aids.

- If videos or slides are not captioned, be sure your students who are deaf and hard of hearing have the text, preferably before the presentation in class. If an interpreter is present, make sure there is light on the individual.

Classroom Design Modifications. Classroom design and acoustics can enhance or hinder learning for students who are deaf and hard of hearing. The following modifications to your classroom can be highly beneficial:

- Seat students who are able to speechread where they are closest to the individuals who will do the most talking during the school day, and encourage students to feel

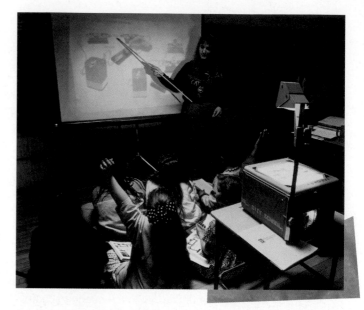

Instruction that emphasizes the visual medium helps children with hearing loss to understand and remember information.

free to move their seats depending on the activity so that they can speechread the other students. Possibly arrange for the student to have a swivel chair for ease in following group discussions.

- Make sure that the classroom is well lighted and without shadows or glare from sunlight. Always have the light on your face, not behind you.

- Consider assigning a peer to be a *buddy* who can signal changes in speakers, help the student with hearing loss to follow along, and alert the student to the intercom and fire alarm.

- Move potential sources of noise, such as electric pencil sharpeners, to a location that is distant from the student.

- If the classroom is not carpeted, obtain a rug to cover as much area as possible because rugs and carpeting absorb extraneous noises.

- Add pieces of carpeting or bulletin boards to bare walls to serve as sound absorbers.

Based on what you have already learned about students with hearing loss, what other instructional strategies would be effective?

How Is Participation Encouraged?

Inclusion

A highly charged issue in deaf education today involves the question, Where should students who are deaf and hard of hearing be taught? What is the most appropriate educational placement? Which is the more enabling and less restrictive setting: general education classrooms, special education classrooms in public schools, or schools for the deaf? Virtually all professional and parent organizations involved in the field of deafness recently have issued position statements regarding the importance of maintaining a spectrum of educational options for children who are deaf and hard of hearing. Moores (1993, p. 251) reflected the opinions of many educators and parents when he wrote the following:

> *I do not have the expertise to speak for other areas of special education, but it seems to me that for many deaf children the concept of total inclusion, as currently promulgated, could in reality be exclusionary in practice. Placing a deaf child in a classroom in physical contiguity to hearing children does not automatically provide equal access to information. In fact, it can be isolating, both academically and socially. We should be past the point where we advocate any*

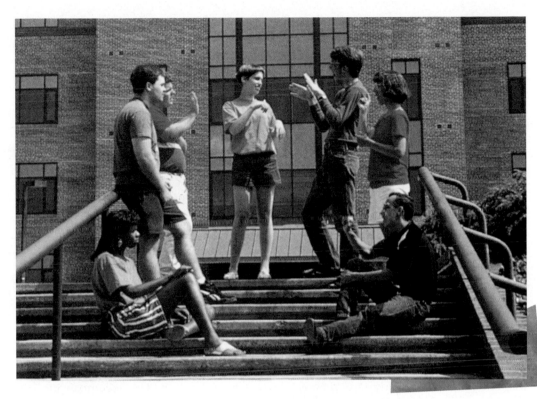

 Gallaudet University is a federally funded liberal arts university where all undergraduate students are deaf or hard of hearing.

one approach—in terms of placement, mode of instruction, or curricular content—for all children in a particular category. In this pluralistic society, we will have to be particularly sensitive to the need to open up educational opportunities to all children while addressing individual differences,

Under IDEA, meeting students' needs is the most important criteria for determining program placement. These two issues—appropriate program and less restriction—can conflict. What is more typical (less restrictive because less separate) is not always more appropriate. That is why the Commission on Education of the Deaf (1988) asked the Department of Education to emphasize appropriateness over least restrictive environment:

> *Regular educational settings are appropriate and adaptable to meet the unique needs of only some children who are deaf. There are cases when the nature of the handicap dictates a specialized setting that provides structured curriculum and/or special methods of teaching and that focuses on visual presentation of information.*

The 1997 amendments to IDEA now require the IEP team to pay particular attention to special factors involving the educational placement of deaf and hard of hearing students.

Educational Placement.   Educational placement generally follows the least restrictive guideline. Figure 15–11 displays the percentage of students with hearing loss in six categories of educational placements. As you can see, more than 80 percent of students are being served in the public schools, and of those, more than one-third are fully included in regular classrooms.

Public Schools.   Placement has evolved from primarily day and residential schools to classrooms in public schools. Today most children are educated in their home school district. Public schools, sometimes local and sometimes a consortium of school districts or educational service districts, provide general education classrooms, resource rooms for

Teachers in one public school program reported that inclusion had positive effects on academic achievement, social adjustment, and self-confidence/esteem if the students who are deaf and hard of hearing received social encouragement, if teachers and parents supported the program, and if a range of educational options were available so that students did not feel forced into general education classrooms (Afzali-Nomani, 1995).

FIGURE 15–11 *Educational placement of students with hearing loss in the 1993–1994 school year*

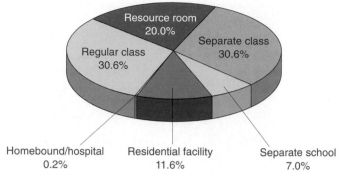

Resource room 20.0%

Separate class 30.6%

Regular class 30.6%

Homebound/hospital 0.2%

Residential facility 11.6%

Separate school 7.0%

Note: From U.S. Department of Education (1995). *To assure the free appropriate public education of all children with disabilities: Seventeenth annual Report to Congress on the implementation of the Individuals with Disabilities Education Act.* Washington, DC: Author.

A study of adolescents who are deaf suggested that education placement with both hearing students and students who are deaf contributes positively to social adjustment (Musselman, Mootilal, & MacKay, 1996).

supplemental help, and separate classes for students with hearing loss. The degree of inclusion depends on each student's capabilities, needs, and preferences, and on the school's philosophies and resources. When included in general classes, students may need support from notetakers, tutors, and interpreters.

Amala attends general education classes at her local public middle school but has two classes in the resource room with Tina, a teacher of the deaf. Amala also receives the services of sign language interpreters for all of her general classes. Indeed, her IEP stipulates that she must receive interpreting for 6.5 hours each school day. The accompanying box provides you with inclusion tips for when you have students in your class who are deaf or hard of hearing.

Day Schools. Day schools are generally located in large metropolitan areas. The students live close enough to commute daily by bus, van, or car. No hearing students are enrolled, the teachers and administrators have professional preparation in deaf education, and full-time staff often includes a school psychologist, audiologist, speech-language pathologist, and teacher aides.

Residential Schools. Institutional instruction has a long history in the United States. Most states still have a residential school for students who are deaf or hard of hearing. Students living too far to commute daily stay there overnight and go home for weekends and school vacations. Students living near the school may also elect to live in the school residence. Others may be commuter students like Amala who attended the Oregon

◈ *Interpreters are the communication link between the student and others in the school who do not know sign language.*

Inclusion Tips

	What You Might See	What You Might Be Tempted to Do	Alternate Responses	Ways to Include Peers in the Process
Behavior	The student might not play games with others at recess.	Tell the student in front of the rest of the class to get in the game.	Using an interpreter or written rules, be sure the student understands the game.	A buddy system at recess may foster more social interactions.
Social interactions	The student's speech may be difficult to understand, and this may limit social interactions.	Force the student to be part of a chosen group; assume the student is content with current social interaction.	Discuss the situation with the interpreter, deaf educator, or parents. Small group work is often more comfortable for students.	Structure natural opportunities for social interaction. Arrange instruction for peers to learn more sign language.
Educational performance	The student may miss some things you say and appear not to understand.	Tell the student to read it in the textbook.	Be sure you are facing the student so that your lips are easily seen and that the light falling on your face is good. For students using an interpreter, talk to the interpreter about the apparent communication problem.	Check the notes taken by the student note-taker to be sure they are adequate.
Classroom attitudes	The student may appear bored or inattentive because of not hearing all that is said.	Discipline the student for inattentiveness.	Be sure the student's hearing aids are working and that interpreting needs are being met in class activities.	Have the student sit with friends who will help stay keyed in to changes in class activities.

School for the Deaf when she was in third and fourth grades. The percentage of students attending residential schools has declined dramatically in the past two decades. Some schools, such as the Boston School for the Deaf, have closed, and most others have experienced increasingly lower enrollments.

The Deaf community has expressed grave concern over the declining role that residential schools are playing in the lives of children and youth who are deaf. Traditionally, residential schools passed on **Deaf culture** and ASL to succeeding generations. The weakening of residential schools for the deaf may, some fear, result in cultural disintegration because these schools, often referred to as Deaf schools, were vehicles for cultural transmission to generations of children who are deaf, thus enabling them to become Deaf children.

Deaf culture is the pattern of beliefs, values, behaviors, arts, customs, institutions, social forms, and knowledge that are characteristic of the Deaf community.

MAGGIE LEE SAYRE

"A sheltered life can be a very daring life," author Eudora Welty wrote, "for all serious daring starts from within." This video explores the daring life of Maggie Lee Sayre. Deaf from birth, Maggie lived on a houseboat with her family. When her deaf sister died at age 16, no one else in Maggie's family knew American Sign Language. She turned to photography as a way to communicate. This video relates Maggie's story. For information on the book *Deaf Maggie Lee Sayre: Photographs of a River* Life see http://imp.cssc.olemiss.edu/register/95/summer/09maggie.html and http://www.amazon.com/exec/obidos/ISBN=0878057889/001-6624107-2143868.

What do you think? Put yourself in Maggie's place. What do you think it would be like to live in a world in which no one understood your language?

You do not know sign language. You are alone in a room with someone who is deaf. Would you attempt to communicate with that person? (If you are deaf, would you attempt to communicate with the hearing person who does not know sign language?) Why or why not? If you would attempt to communicate, how would you do so?

Kluwin and Stinson (1993) conducted a longitudinal study of adolescents who are deaf attending local public schools, and their conclusions are worth noting:

> Local public school education for deaf children is here and will no doubt continue in some form into the future. Sometimes it works miracles and sometimes it doesn't work at all. When the issue of the very existence of these kinds of programs is put aside, the problems of this system and the solutions to those problems become apparent. First, we saw children and teachers do better in programs where the political and governance integration of adult professionals was formalized. Second, regardless of the traits of the children, when goals were clearly defined and standards upheld, the children achieved higher than the average. Third, programs with "happy" individuals were programs where the students had more positive attitudes toward hearing peers and achieved at higher levels. Fourth, programs with more structured and supportive extracurricular opportunities produced graduates who were more interested in other people, regardless of their hearing status. (p. 152)

Although the trend in placements is definitely toward inclusion, controversy over placement continues with no definite resolution. What is important to remember is that educational plans are made individually and must consider what is an appropriate education in the least restrictive environment for each particular student.

Collaboration

You can see that many people are involved in Amala's life, and each person's contribution makes an important difference. Family members, friends, professionals, and community members have all contributed to Amala's growth.

Professional Collaboration.   Ideally, special and general educators, speech-language pathologists, audiologists, interpreters, and other professionals together encourage academic, social, and language development. It is especially crucial for general educators to be supported in their efforts to serve students who are deaf and hard of hearing. Ginny Chinn, Amala's seventh-grade teacher, feels that she is a much better teacher for Amala because of continuous collaboration with Tina, the resource room teacher; Amala's interpreters; and Robyn, Amala's mother. Box 15-5 shares Ginny Chinn's perspective.

BOX 15-5 — MAKING A DIFFERENCE

COLLABORATION IS THE KEY

Working with Tina, the resource room teacher, has helped a lot, because then I know how strict I should be, how far I should push. The written materials help, but talking with a teacher who has been through a teacher of the deaf program, who specializes in working with deaf students and knows the language—that I think is very beneficial. Without that contact, it would be extremely hard. If Amala were a deaf girl put into my classroom without the support of the regional program for the deaf, it would be a lot harder. I don't think I'd be servicing her quite as well. I don't think she'd be making as much progress in the classroom. That's a real key piece. The resource room and the classroom are working together. The kids know that we're working together as a unit. This also includes home and school. When the students know that all sides are working together, you can always get better results.

When I was asked to take a deaf student in my class, my first thought was fear of the unknown, thinking that the interpreters will be listening to everything I say and perhaps judging my teaching, and I questioned whether I would be good enough. I was also a little nervous about how much I was going to have to modify what I was doing. But this was an ideal situation for me because I was at a point where I was ready for something new. I was very enthusiastic about having the kids integrated into my classroom and working with the resource room teacher.

Working as a team member, I've learned to think more about how I give information out to the students. I've always tried not to have too much lecture, but I'm even more par-ticular about that now. I try to have a variety of activities so that the kids aren't inundated with a ton of information. I have things written out so that not all information is presented orally, and I'm careful to avoid including information on an oral exam that might give away the answer when the interpreter signs or fingerspells it. I also try to use more visuals so that all of the information isn't just spoken. I'm even more careful than before about checking for understanding. Reminding myself to be concerned about how the interpreters are getting the information out to the students is important, because then they are able to do their job the best they can without being completely worn out.

I talk a lot with the interpreters, going over what we're doing and determining the best methods. I even tend to go over seating charts with them first. That's what makes the team seem more like a team. It's not just the resource room teacher and myself, but it's the interpreters, myself, the resource room teachers, and then, of course, the parents.

If I were to give advice to other teachers, I would tell them to make sure that you use all the resources available to you, find out what each other's roles are, respect what each person is doing as a professional, and use that. Take advantage of each other. Use others as a resource, respecting their expertise and their knowledge. I think that's one thing that's made the program here successful and the kids in my classroom successful.

Ginny Chinn
Teacher, Crossler Middle School, Salem, Oregon

Family Collaboration. Robyn has been a strong and persistent advocate for Amala. When she has felt that the school should offer services that it wasn't offering, she worked tenaciously with administrators and other professionals. During the summer between sixth and seventh grade, Robyn spent two weeks in Seattle so that Amala and Juan could participate in a theater camp for deaf students. Robyn has also found that friends and colleagues are a wonderful source of support and collaboration, as she notes in Box 15-6.

The accompanying box, "Collaboration Tips," shows how one collaborative group that includes the student, peers, parents, general education teacher, teacher of the deaf, and interpreter can work together to identify reading strategies that enable the student to read and study subject area textbook material written at several grade levels above the student's reading ability level.

Community Collaboration. Communities today have come a long way toward offering services and programs for people with disabilities, including those with hearing loss. Dr. Robert Davila, former assistant secretary in the U.S. Department of Education, Office of Special Education and Rehabilitative Services, describes these changes in Box 15-7.

BOX 15-6   **MY VOICE**

ROBYN BROWN: SUPPORTIVE AND COLLABORATIVE FRIENDS

Two of my friends, Greg and Eileen, were incredibly supportive when the kids were young. They gave me a lot of perspective on raising kids. And they gave me a break. They would take the kids, spend time with them. And we have a couple of other friends now. We trade off: Their kids come here and my kids go there. It's been difficult sometimes to build a community of friends, because some of the people I know, the teachers who sign, their kids don't sign. Or the kids who do sign, the parents don't sign. And it's not like how it was growing up for me, and that's been hard. When I was growing up, our house was the neighborhood house where all the baseball games were played. I'm sure I just kind of assumed that's how it was going to be when I was a mom, and it hasn't been that way because of the communication difficulties between the kids and the par-

ents. But we do have a couple of families with hearing impaired kids we spend time with. A couple of years ago, we went to Disneyland with a deaf woman and her kids. That was wonderful because everyone signed really well. We just had a great time. The kids could be with me, they could be with her, they could be with the other kids, all without any interpreting. That was good. But those experiences don't happen very frequently.

When I talk with my friends who have hearing kids, I ask, "Is this a thirteen-year-old thing or is this a deafness thing?" That's one of my challenges, to realize what is normal behavior. My teacher aide has a deaf daughter at Gallaudet right now. And that has been really helpful. I go in and say, "Amala is making me crazy." And she'll say, "You know, when Libby was thirteen. . . ." It's just so helpful for me to hear from other parents, "Well that's thirteen."

Robyn Brown, Amala's mother

Community services that provide accommodations include sign language interpreters, special telephones, captioned television and real-time graphic display, and the Internet.

Interpreters. Interpreters generally specialize in either community-based interpreting or educational interpreting. The Registry of Interpreters for the Deaf certifies sign language and oral interpreters and has developed a professional code of ethics (Hunt & Marshall, 1994). The registry has created categories and levels of certification so that the individuals who hire and use the services of interpreters are aware at the outset the skill level of any given interpreter.

At the community level, interpreter services are sometimes coordinated through a state or local service center. Many states have a commission for citizens who are deaf and hard of hearing. The commission may maintain a list of qualified interpreters for schools, hospitals, courts, police departments, and other organizations. The commission may also be responsible for determining quality assurance of interpreters.

Special Telephones. With the implementation of the Americans with Disabilities Act (ADA), all states have relay services to connect callers who use telecommunication devices for the deaf to people who do not, and vice versa. Telecommunication devices for the deaf were originally referred to as TTYs; the name was then changed to TTDs and recently has been renamed **TTs,** for **text telephones.** An 800 number allows anyone to make a business appointment, order merchandise, call for a pizza, or carry out any other type of business over the phone; and anyone without a TT can contact a friend, relative, employee, student, or patient who uses one. For example, Amala recently used the relay service to call a travel agent because she was doing research for a school report. She called the 800 number of the relay and gave the operator the name and phone number of the travel agent; the operator called the travel agent, and the operator acted as the interpreter between Amala and the travel agent during the conversation, voicing for Amala to the travel agent and keyboarding the travel agent's responses into the TT so that Amala could read the responses on her home TT. Many businesses have purchased their own TTs and advertise their availability so that customers can call directly without using the relay service. State relay services are usually listed in the front of the telephone directory's white pages.

A **TT (text telephone)** is a telecommunications device that enables individuals to carry on a phone conversation in written form.

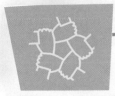

Collaboration Tips

ADAPTING THE CURRICULUM FOR STUDENTS HAVING DIFFICULTY WITH CONTENT AREA SUBJECTS

COLLABORATION GOAL   To adapt the classroom environment for the student who is deaf or hard of hearing and is having difficulty reading content area textbooks.

Collaborators	Roles and Preparation	Possible Barriers	Solutions to Barriers	Modifications to Implementation	Ongoing Evaluation
Student	Write out reading strengths, interests, difficulties, and goals.	Expected failure at understanding the material and negative attitude.	Relate strengths and interests to subject area topics.	Try out new reading strategies and practice with peers.	Keep a dialogue journal with general and special educator(s) to note successes and difficulties.
Parents	Make a list of observations of daughter's homework and reading habits at home.	Fear that there may not be any useful strategies to meet daughter's needs.	Set aside time daily to discuss material daughter is reading.	Make sure discussions are open-ended rather than question–answer; praise daughter for successes.	Regularly evaluate and reward daughter's positive changes.
General educator(s)	Bring a record of student's strengths and difficulties with subject area text material.	Insufficient information about how English language ability relates to ability to read.	Meet with teacher of the deaf to share assessment information and discuss impact of deafness on reading.	Discuss specific reading strategies effective for students having reading difficulties or for whom English is a second language.	Keep a portfolio of projects and tests and conference with other collaborators; participate in dialogue journal.
Special Educator(s) for the deaf and hard of hearing	Bring language and reading assessment data and information about reading expository material.	Lack of time to work with student and other educators to discuss strategies.	Periodically meet with student and peers to model reading strategies and peer tutoring.	Include general educator in meetings to discuss strategies.	Develop pre- and post-assessments of text that both student and peers can use; participate in dialogue journal.
Interpreter	Prepare observations of student's contributions during class discussions.	Concern that the interpreter will be expected to be a tutor.	Encourage student to make class contributions.	Participate in the sign language club to teach hearing peers signs and fingerspelling.	Conference with other collaborators.
Peers	Talk with the general educators about the role of a peer tutor.	Fears about communicating well with the student.	Learn some basic sign language in sign language club.	Schedule peer tutoring during the school day; let student tutor peers in sign language.	Periodically meet with collaborators to share problems and successes.

MY VOICE

ROBERT DAVILA

When I was a high school student at the California School for the Deaf, at least 80 percent of this country's students who are deaf were being educated in special schools for the deaf. This pattern has completely reversed, with only 18 percent of students who are deaf receiving services in special schools in 1992. More and more public schools are better able to offer the specialized services that students who are deaf require, but quality is still an issue, especially for students with the most severe hearing needs. There is a continuing need for a full spectrum of services to meet the individual needs of *all* students who are deaf.

As a youth, I hoped for admission to Gallaudet University, then a very small college just for deaf people. There were literally no other options for postsecondary study, so I had to wonder how I would prepare myself for independence if I were not admitted to Gallaudet. Fortunately, I was admitted. Today, postsecondary opportunities proliferate for deaf men and women, ranging from vocational-training programs to community colleges to advanced-degree programs. Students who are deaf participate in postsecondary programs at higher rates than students with any other disability. The task is to continue to develop and maintain appropriate services so that these students can achieve their full potential.

Major milestones in attaining community inclusion include the following:

- The 1960s rubella epidemic that doubled the deaf student population
- The 1965 report to the president and Congress from the National Advisory Committee on the Deaf, reporting on the poor quality of educational programming; passage of federal special-education laws that opened the doors of all schools to all students who are deaf
- The positive impact of advances in communication technology; the empowerment movement that has promoted disability rights

- The 1988 report of the Commission on Education of the Deaf, which reported progress since 1965 but also reported continuing serious needs
- Recognition of sign language as an educational tool
- Passage of the Americans with Disabilities Act in 1990

These catalysts for change have generally heralded progress in the education and rehabilitation of deaf persons. Yet as noted in the 1988 report to the president and Congress, there has been little real improvement in achievement and employment levels. The average deaf eighteen-year-old still reads at the third- or fourth-grade level, the same as twenty-five years ago. That is simply not good enough. Surveys continue to highlight the unemployment and underemployment levels of persons who are deaf.

Deaf education in America has a rich heritage. It is the oldest continuous public system of special education. Those entering this field should work to continue the heritage's tradition of using new knowledge and practices to expand and enrich opportunities for deaf children and adults. Most important, professionals should listen to and learn from people who are deaf or hard of hearing and actively support their individual and collective empowerment.

For the future, I am excited about the challenges posed by the disability civil rights movement and the trend toward community inclusion of people with disabilities, including people who are deaf. As professionals, we need to be held accountable for the quality of the services we provide. As we move toward empowerment and increased community inclusion of deaf people, we will also increase our own burden of accountability. We all should welcome this challenge. The result can only improve services and better the quality of life for deaf people.

Dr. Robert R. Davila
Assistant secretary (1990–1992); U.S. Department of
Education, Office of Special Education and
Rehabilitative Services

Telecommunication companies have also expanded their options to include a vibrating beeper that can hold up to sixty messages. Instead of using an auditory signal, the beeper vibrates to let the user know there is a message. Customers may respond to the message at their convenience.

Captioned Television and Real-Time Graphic Display. Captioned television is another avenue of accessibility. Most programs on commercial, public, and cable networks are closed captioned. Viewers with a decoder (either built into the television or functioning from a separate box about the size of a VCR) can receive captions that show what is being said across the bottom of the screen. Many shows such as sports, news, and awards are captioned as they occur. This is referred to as real-time captioning.

Captioning is also beneficial for individuals learning English as a second language and persons with reading challenges.

🐬 *Using a TT, a person who is deaf or hard of hearing can call a friend, make an appointment, or order a pizza.*

Individuals who attend lecture-type events will more and more frequently see presentations captured on real-time graphic display. An individual trained as a stenotypist or court reporter types into a device with phonetic shorthand symbols, the device is connected to a computer that translates these codes into English, and the English is displayed on a screen that the audience can view.

Internet. The Internet has opened up exciting communication possibilities for everyone, and it is a perfect medium for individuals with hearing loss. Through e-mail, individuals who are deaf and hard of hearing can communicate rapidly and clearly to anyone in the world who also has e-mail. And the World Wide Web offers entertainment and information to anyone with a computer, modem, and an Internet software package.

Careers

You have read in this chapter about teachers, interpreters, speech-language pathologists, audiologists, school psychologists, and other related-services personnel such as school counselors, residence life personnel, and social workers. Each one plays a significant role in helping students who are deaf and hard of hearing to have the same access to opportunities and choices in life that other students have.

Teachers of the Deaf. At present, more than seventy colleges or universities in the United States and Canada offer teacher preparation programs for individuals who want to become teachers of students who are deaf and hard of hearing. Some of these programs are at the baccalaureate level and some at the master's level. Teachers of the deaf are certified by the department of education or state certification department of the state in which they teach. National certification is offered through the Council on Education of the Deaf.

Teachers of the deaf can work in self-contained classes with small groups (usually six to eight) of students who are deaf or hard of hearing and in resource rooms with students from a range of grade levels who spend portions of each school day in general education classes. They can also be itinerant or consulting teachers who have a case load of students from several schools. Some of these students spend one or a few periods of time each week with the itinerant teacher, and some are fully included in general classes, and the consulting teacher works strictly with the classroom teachers. In Box 15–8, you will read about how one teacher decided to become a teacher of the deaf.

BOX 15-8   MY VOICE

BARBARA SCHIRMER

In 1899 my grandmother became deaf. She had just come home from her first day of school. Feeling sick, angry at her mother for working in the dry goods store, wanting to stay away from the housekeeper she disliked, she hid in a barrel. She could hear the rain pouring down. How long she was in the barrel, she doesn't know. Someone finally found her there, but by then she was burning up with fever. From what illness, no one ever diagnosed. Perhaps scarlet fever. When she recovered, her ability to hear was gone. Everyone said that the fever had burned out her hearing. Frieda Steckler was just six years old. Her grandfather was a rabbi. There were no schools in Galicia, Poland, for a little deaf girl. He patiently taught her to read other people's lips when they talked Polish or Yiddish, the two languages Frieda knew before she became deaf. He taught her to read and write Yiddish and to do arithmetic. When Frieda was fourteen, her family moved to the United States. Her mother and father, Rose and Abraham, knew that the challenge would be getting Frieda through Ellis Island. If the U.S. officials knew that Frieda was deaf, her parents were sure that she would be sent back to Poland. They made arrangements with one of her aunts to take her in if the worst happened. But the official who interviewed Frieda at Ellis Island never knew she was deaf. He asked her a few questions in Polish, she watched his lips intently, and she responded appropriately. She was in America, but her family worried that someone would report her. Not someone in the Jewish community of New York where they lived. But if they sent her to school, someone might report her to the government. So Frieda never went to school. Her father taught her to sew and got her a job in a shirt factory making Gibson blouses. A few years later, she married Morris Schiller, and they had three sons and one daughter, Bella, my mother.

I spent a lot of time with my grandmother. Sometimes she babysat for me. And for several years, my family lived with her and my grandfather. Even as a child, I knew that she was often angry at the world. I didn't know why but later realized that it wasn't her deafness that was her disability, it was her lack of education. And she knew it. She was so intelligent and yet so limited. She never learned to read and write English, never became a citizen of the United States. In the early years in New York, everyone in her community spoke Yiddish. But gradually, hardly anyone outside of her family did. It was isolating and lonely.

In the summer of 1970, I began my studies in deaf education at the University of Pittsburgh. That fall, my grandmother died. Surprisingly, I am the only one in my extended family who became a teacher of the deaf. It's surprising because many professionals in the field have deaf family members. A few years ago, I was at a family gathering, and one of my cousins and I started talking about our grandmother. Robert told me that even though he didn't speak Yiddish, he and Grandma had some kind of special language that he's never been able to explain to anyone else. I did, too, I told him. And I had thought it was unique to my relationship with her. So although she had told my mother how sad it was for her that none of her grandchildren had learned Yiddish, we had each developed a special way to communicate with her. My own teaching of deaf children, and teaching of future teachers, has been guided by the conviction that all children who are deaf are entitled to an education that enables them to communicate with the broader community, to integrate within society to whatever extent they wish, and to compete successfully in the work place.

Interpreters. Interpreter training programs are currently offered at more than seventy colleges or universities in the United States, with many of the programs at community colleges. While the need for educational interpreters has grown dramatically due to IDEA and ADA, interpreter training programs have tended to continue focusing on community-based interpreting. The Registry of Interpreters of the Deaf, in collaboration with the Council on Education of the Deaf, have established certification standards specifically for educational interpreters.

An interpreter's purpose is to facilitate communication and equalize learning opportunities, not to be a tutor. For students such as Amala who are in general classes, interpreters are the communication bridge between the teacher and classmates to Amala, and from her to them. Amala's interpreters sign everything the teacher and students say during classroom instruction, and she voices for Amala when she signs. Into Practice (Box 15-9) lists strategies for teachers to use to increase their effectiveness with interpreters (Luetke-Stahlman & Luckner, 1991).

TEACHER–INTERPRETER TIPS

- Take time before class to orient the interpreter to the topic being discussed, the general lesson plan, and key vocabulary or concepts.
- Minimize movement so that the student can view the teacher, the interpreter, and any visual aids simultaneously.
- Be sensitive to lag time between speaking and the student's receiving the message; make sure that the student has time to respond to questions that are posed. (When you use slides or overhead projectors, be sure that the student has time to receive both the media and the interpreted information concurrently.)
- Provide comprehensive checks periodically to make sure the student is understanding the information presented.
- Expect students to repeat information or actively participate in class discussions.

WHAT ARE PROGRAM OPTIONS?

As you read examples of best practices in educational programs, keep in mind that no *best practice* is best for every child in every program. We have learned a great deal about effective educational practices, but we also have a great deal to learn. Given this perspective, the examples will be discussed in light of the recommendations made by the Commission on Education of the Deaf (1988) a decade ago and the report on progress made in implementing the recommendations that was published three years later (Bowe, 1991).

Early Intervention and Preschool Years

The Commission was particularly interested in identification programs having a direct connection to early intervention programs.

At the Tucker-Maxon Oral School in Portland, Oregon, preschool children are in a self-contained classroom with Brigitte Frank, a teacher of the deaf, three mornings each week. The other two mornings they attend classes in the general preschool, Childswork, that is located on the Tucker-Maxon campus. Every day, they have *lunch bunch* with the children at Childswork and then spend another hour with Brigitte in the self-contained classroom. During the mornings when Brigitte doesn't teach in the self-contained classroom, she goes into the Childswork classrooms to facilitate the children's conversations with hearing peers, troubleshoot equipment, consult with the early childhood teachers, and see what progress the children are making on their goals for the mainstream setting, which are largely socialization goals. When Brigitte is in the Childswork classrooms, her major goal is to develop relationships with all of the children so that it's comfortable and natural for them and they think of her as one of the teachers, not just the teacher of the deaf. Brigitte is able to focus self-contained instructional time on developing the language and speech of the children with hearing loss and encourage the development of social interaction skills during general preschool activities.

What was it like for parents before early intervention programs were available?

Elementary Years

The Commission on Education of the Deaf recommended that for students to acquire the English language, top priority should be placed on program models, research, curricula, materials, assessment instruments, and training of parents and professionals that focus on language development.

Lynda Ross is a teacher of students who are deaf and hard of hearing within a self-contained classroom at David Lubin Elementary School in the Sacramento Public Schools. Her class participates with Bonnie Townzen's general education class of first graders for a teaching model called *Writer's Workshop.* Three class periods each week, the students with hearing loss go into the first-grade classroom. The objectives of the model are to help the students become increasingly skilled writers by encouraging them to experience the writing process that authors use. Each Writer's Workshop class period begins with a brief minilesson, taught by either Lynda or Bonnie, on writing strategies and skills. The students then spend twenty to thirty minutes working on writing projects at tables with their writing group; each group is a heterogeneous combination of students who are deaf, hard of hearing, and hearing. Students move through the stages in the writing process (prewriting, drafting, revising, editing, and publishing) at their own pace. The teachers circulate throughout the room, conferencing briefly with individual students. When the student has completed between four and six stories, the teacher asks the student to choose one to be published.

Lynda works with the students with hearing loss in editing these to-be-published stories. Completed books are placed in the classroom library, where the students can choose to read them during sustained silent reading class periods.

For the last ten minutes of each Writer's Workshop class period, the whole class gathers together to share their works in progress or their new publications. The students who sign are interpreted by the sign language interpreter.

Middle and Secondary Years

The Commission on Education of the Deaf wanted to see standards set for curriculum and professional training and for quality to be defined and reflected in educational programs.

The Utah School for the Deaf Extension Consultant Division serves students with hearing loss throughout the state of Utah who are not served by the state residential school for the deaf or the Salt Lake City program. According to Judy Parmelee, Program Specialist, the quality of education the students receive is judged largely by the extent to which they are able to succeed competitively within general education classrooms in the student's neighborhood school. "Our goal is to provide students with the skills to access all areas of life with a lifelong family support system, and to do this, the student must be part of the family and community on his or her own merits."

To this end, most of the standardized tests used as diagnostic tools are normed on hearing students. Because the goal is for the students to compete successfully in school and work, the program needs to know whether they are competing successfully with hearing individuals, not just individuals with hearing loss.

The program offers students two tracks (oral/aural and total communication), three levels of consultation service for students in general education classes part- or full-time, and self-contained classrooms. The first level of consultation service involves the least intervention. Consultants at this level provide assistance to teachers and other professional staff who work with the students, and they also often provide assessment services. Consultants at the second level use a consultation/collaboration model in which they provide more intensive intervention with staff, carrying out all the activities of consultants at the first level plus providing periodic direct intervention with the students, modeling teaching strategies in the classroom, and sharing materials with the teachers. The third level is the most intense intervention. At this level, consultants use a consultation/tutorial model in which they carry out the activities of the first two levels but work with the students on a set schedule and ongoing basis, sometimes one-on-one and sometimes within the context of the general education classrooms. While the Extension Consultant Division also provides services within self-contained classrooms, by the time students are in high school, most are in general education classrooms for at least parts of each day.

Transitional and Postsecondary Years

The Commission on Education of the Deaf recommended that postsecondary educational programs be increased and strengthened. Currently, the U.S. Congress funds six postsecondary programs for students who are deaf and hard of hearing: Gallaudet University, National Technical Institute for the Deaf at Rochester Institute of Technology, and four Regional Postsecondary Education Programs for the Deaf at California State University at Northridge, St. Paul Technical College, Seattle Community College, and University of Tennessee Consortium. With the passage of ADA, all colleges and universities offer support services to students who request them. During the four-year period between the 1989–1990 and 1992–1993 academic years, 47 percent of the 5,000 two-year and four-year postsecondary educational institutions in the United States enrolled one or more students who identified themselves as deaf or hard of hearing (Lewis & Greene, 1994). The most typical support services offered are interpreters, notetakers, tutors, and assistive listening devices. Institutions also frequently offer testing accommodations, counseling or advising, assistance with registration, classroom seating arrangements, recording of class sessions, and advocacy or consultation with instructors.

A Vision for the Future

Amala will have many choices about her future when she graduates from high school. She can choose to pursue virtually any career. She can apply to any college or vocational school, knowing that she will be judged on the merits of her past academic performance and not on the basis of her hearing abilities. She will be able to choose her social and recreational activities because they are the ones she enjoys and not because they're the only ones open to her. She can travel, and she can live wherever she would like. She will always be a big sister to Juan and she will have the same mother–daughter joys and struggles with Robyn that all mothers and daughters have. And she can choose her own friends from among individuals who are hearing and individuals who are deaf or hard of hearing.

What Would You Recommend. . .

1. To encourage Amala to socialize with diverse peers?

2. To help guide Amala's decisions about education and work after high school?

3. To provide a learning environment that nurtures and motivates Amala?

SUMMARY

What Is Hearing Loss?

• Hearing loss exists on a continuum, but educationally, individuals with hearing loss are categorized as deaf and hard of hearing.

• Degrees of hearing loss are identified as slight, mild, moderate, severe, and profound.

• Communication modes used by people who are deaf and hard of hearing include oral/aural, American Sign Language, and simultaneous communication in sign language and spoken English.

- Communication with parents, peers, and teachers plays a major role in the psychological, social, and emotional development of children with hearing loss.

- Achievement levels continue to be a primary concern, particularly among children from diverse racial, ethnic, and linguistic backgrounds.

- A conductive loss is caused by a problem in the outer or middle ear, and a sensorineural loss is caused by a problem in the inner ear or along the nerve pathway to the brainstem.

- Hearing aids make sounds louder, but they do not restore normal hearing to the person, and they always involve some distortion of sounds.

What Are Evaluation Procedures?

- Infants who fail screenings have their hearing tested using an auditory brain stem response (ABR) test or acoustic emissions procedures.

- With older students, a behavioral audiological evaluation for measuring hearing levels is used, and hearing levels of pitch and loudness are graphed on an audiogram.

What and How Do Professionals Teach?

- Language, reading, and writing form the central curriculum focus for students who are deaf or hard of hearing. Students with hearing loss also receive specialized curriculum in Deaf culture, speech, and aural habilitation.

- Communication methods used in educational programs include oral/aural, bilingual-bicultural, and total communication.

- Oral/aural methods are characterized by instruction in spoken English and the expectation that students will use speech, speechreading, and auditory skills for communication.

- Bilingual-bicultural methods are characterized by classroom communication in American Sign Language, and the teaching of English through the written form with no or little use of spoken English.

How Is Participation Encouraged?

- There is no agreement about the importance of inclusion, with most educators favoring appropriateness as the most significant consideration but many members of the Deaf community advocating for placement in schools for the deaf.

- Educational placement generally follows the least restrictive guideline, and, currently, more than 80 percent of students with hearing loss are being served in the public schools.

- Prevalence of hearing loss in children is estimated at 1.6 percent.

- Cochlear implants are devices in which one part is surgically implanted near the individual's auditory nerves to stimulate the nerve fibers and the other part is worn externally to receive and process sound.

- Prelingual hearing loss (at birth or before learning language) accounts for 95 percent of students who are deaf and hard of hearing; postlingual hearing loss (after learning language) accounts for 5 percent.

- More than one-third of students with hearing loss have other disabilities.

- Regular reassessments of language, hearing, speech and/or sign, speechreading, academic achievement, and socialization are essential to provide an appropriate education for students who are deaf or hard of hearing.

- Total communication methods are characterized by classroom communication in a manually coded English or pidgin sign language along with the simultaneous use of spoken English.

- Instructional strategies for students with hearing loss are particularly effective when they emphasize experiential learning, build on the students' current knowledge and skills, require them to interact with peers, capitalize on the visual medium, and reduce environmental distraction.

- Many professionals contribute to the welfare of students who are deaf and hard of hearing. Teaching the deaf and interpreting are two important careers in deaf education.

- Communities accommodate the needs of individuals with hearing loss through sign language interpreters, special text telephones (TTs), telephone relay services, captioned television and real-time graphic display, and the Internet.

WHAT ARE PROGRAM OPTIONS?

- It is important for early identification programs to have a direct connection to early intervention programs.

- A top priority in elementary and middle school programs is English language acquisition.

- During the secondary school years, the priority in educational programs is to maintain high academic standards and expectations for students who are deaf and hard of hearing.

- The U.S. Congress funds six postsecondary programs for students who are deaf and hard of hearing. All colleges and universities offer support services for students who request them; the most typical services are interpreters, notetakers, tutors, and assistive listening devices.

- Transition programs recognize that difficulties with English-based communication is the most significant obstacle to successful transition.

RESOURCES

BOOKS

Educating the Deaf: Psychology, Principles, and Practices (4th ed.) (1996). By D. F. Moores. Boston: Houghton Mifflin.

Language and Literacy Development in Children Who are Deaf. (1994) By B. R. Schirmer. Needham Heights, MA: Allyn & Bacon.

No Walls of Stone: An Anthology of Literature by Deaf and Hard of Hearing Writers. (1993). By J. Jepson. Washington, DC: Gallaudet University Press.

The following books of fiction are suitable for adolescents and adults:

In This Sign. (1970). By J. Greenberg. New York: Holt, Rinehart, and Winston.

The Heart is a Lonely Hunter. (1940). By C. McCullers. Boston: Houghton Mifflin.

The following books of fiction are suitable for children:

Buffer's Orange Leash. (1989). By S. Golder. Washington, DC: Gallaudet University Press.

Claire and Emma. (1977). By D. Peter. New York: Day.

The Day We Met Cindy. (1989). By A. Marie. Washington, DC: Gallaudet University Press.

JOURNALS, MAGAZINES, AND CATALOGS

American Annals of the Deaf. Convention of American Instructors of the Deaf, PO Box 377, Bedford, TX 76095-0377. Focuses on research and practice in the education of deaf and hard of hearing individuals.

Dawn Sign Press. 6130 Nancy Ridge Drive, San Diego, CA 92121-3223. Publishes books and videos about American Sign Language, deaf individuals, and deaf culture.

Gallaudet University Press. 800 Florida Avenue NE, Washington, DC 20002. Internet address: http://www.gallaudet.edu. Focuses on books and other resources related to individuals with hearing loss.

HiP Magazine. 1563 Solano Avenue #137, Berkeley, CA 94707. Internet address: http://www.hipmag.org. Magazine for deaf and hard of hearing children ages eight to fourteen.

Journal of Deaf Studies and Deaf Education. Oxford University Press, Great Clarendon Street, Oxford, OX2 6DP England. Internet address: http://www.oup.co.uk/deafed. Focuses on research related to individuals who are deaf, including cultural, cognitive, developmental, linguistic, and educational topics.

Modern Signs Press. PO Box 1181, Los Alamitos, CA 90720. Publishes materials to teach Signing Exact English, a sign language system designed to replicate spoken and written English.

Sign Language Studies. 9306 Mintwood Street, Silver Spring, MD 20910. Focuses on research related to sign language.

The Volta Review. Alexander Graham Bell Association for the Deaf, 3417 Volta Place NW, Washington, DC 20007. Focuses on research and practice in deaf education, speech and language development of deaf and hard of hearing children, and aural habilitation.

Volta Voices. Alexander Graham Bell Association for the Deaf, 3417 Volta Place NW, Washington, DC 20007. Focuses on providing up-to-date information for teachers and parents about issues and events related to deafness.

MULTIMEDIA

Captioned Films/Videos for the Deaf. Modern Talking Picture Service, 5000 Park Street North, St. Petersburg, FL 33709. Lends for only the cost of return postage captioned films and videos to organizations that have deaf or hard-of-hearing participants.

ON-LINE INFORMATION AND USEFUL DATABASES

Council on Education of the Deaf. Internet address: http://www.educ.kent.edu/deafed. Internet site that provides comprehensive information about the education of deaf and hard-of-hearing individuals.

Deaf World Web. Internet address: http://deafworldweb.org. Internet site that provides information on all subjects related to deafness.

EDUDEAF Electronic Forum. E-mail address: listserv@ukcc.uky.edu. Internet forum for the discussion of curriculum, teaching strategies, IEPs, and other concerns of teachers of children who are deaf or hard of hearing. To subscribe, send the following message to the e-mail address above: sub EDUDEAF firstname lastname.

ORGANIZATIONS

Alexander Graham Bell Association for the Deaf. 3417 Volta Place NW, Washington, DC 20007. Internet address: http://www.agbell.org. Organization for teachers and parents; promotes oral/aural communication; publishes books, periodicals and newsletters, and sponsors conferences and workshops.

American Society for Deaf Children. 2848 Arden Way, Suite 210, Sacramento, CA 95825-1373. Internet address: http://www.deafchildren.org/. Organization for families with deaf and hard of hearing children; provides information about deafness.

Convention of American Instructors of the Deaf. PO Box 377, Bedford, TX 76095-0377. Organization for teachers; publishes a periodical and newsletter, and sponsors conferences.

National Association of the Deaf. 814 Thayer Avenue, Silver Spring, MD 20910. Internet address: http://www.nad.org. Organization for individuals with hearing loss; advocates for deaf individuals; sponsors conferences and activities for deaf individuals and their families.

Self-Help for Hard of Hearing People (SHHH). 7910 Woodmont Avenue, Suite 1200, Bethesda, MD 20814. Internet address: http://www.shhh.org. Organization for hard of hearing individuals; offers advocacy and support activities for individuals who are hard of hearing.

National Information Center on Deafness. Gallaudet University, 800 Florida Avenue NE, Washington, DC 20002. Internet address: http://www.gallaudet.edu:80/~nicd. Distributes information about hearing loss and provides resource assistance.

CHAPTER 16

BLINDNESS AND LOW VISION

Contributing Writer
Sandra Lewis
Florida State University

Educating
Tracy Kiel

One day last week, Tracy asked her itinerant teacher of the visually impaired, "Why can I go to college for free? Do you think that is fair?" On another day she asked, "Why do I need an IEP? I don't think I should have to have one."

Tracy, a high school sophomore who is blind, has grown up in rural Minnesota and has attended her local public school since she was four years old. When asked about having a disability, she says, "I'm visually impaired and even though I wish I could see, I don't dwell on it and I do the best with what I have. With a few modifications, I can do anything I set my mind to."

She sees herself as an equal, which is why she is struggling with certain questions. If she is truly equal, why should she be given privileges that others are not? She has been raised and educated to live, play, and work in a society where all citizens are equal and she anticipates a future environment that is similar to growing up in her local community. This attitude is apparent in her advice to future teachers: "I think it's important to treat students as individuals. Just because someone has

a disability doesn't make them any more special than anyone else, but it doesn't make them more ignorant either. Try to give them the respect that you would want if you were in their places."

Tracy's experience growing up is no different from that of her seventeen-year-old sighted sister. At sixteen, Tracy spends a lot of time on the phone and loves to go shopping, attend school games, and spend evenings at the movies or a friend's home. She has many friends who call out their greetings to her when she walks down the hallways at school. Living in the country and being a nondriver, Tracy calls friends to make transportation arrangements and knows to offer money to assist with gas expenses. When she goes shopping in a mall, Tracy knows what stores have the items she wants to buy; she directs a sighted guide to the store to find certain items, but it is Tracy who very carefully compares quality and cost and looks at each item before making the final buying decision.

Tracy also has received the same access to educational opportunities as her sister and is as independent. She chooses her classes and is learning to order her own books in braille. Tracy prefers her reading materials in braille but is flexible and has many strategies to complete her work if braille is unavailable. She manages and problem solves issues related to print access on a daily basis. She knows how to use the variety of access technology at school and at home that allows her to complete assignments independently. If she needs additional assistance, information, or ideas, she initiates communication with service providers, such as the itinerant teacher of the visually impaired. She does not wait for people to ask her about what she needs.

Tracy realizes that organization is very important to managing her daily schedule and understands the time required to plan a successful school day and semester. She decides what books and equipment she wants in different classrooms and keeps track of both print and braille materials, using a system she developed and that works well for her. Tracy does not question responsibility for all the extras that need to be done to ensure success. She accepts the need for modifications and does not struggle with the whys.

A very important part of her school life is involvement in extracurricular activities. Tracy participates in drama productions, speech team, and the

symphonic, marching, pep, and jazz bands. Participating in marching band presents certain challenges, especially when the band director adds marching movements that require changes in line patterns and directions. Tracy and her director problem solve strategies together. Judges at competitions are not aware a blind student is marching, thus applying the same criteria to this band as all others.

Tracy does not expect or want attention or rewards based on her disability. She has struggled through this issue and has asked when receiving an award, *Is it because I am blind?* She only wants recognition for a job well done and based on the merits of her performance. She knows when it is otherwise and resents the implication that different standards might apply to her.

Tracy also knows how to show her appreciation for others. She frequently demonstrates a caring spirit and understands the sharing necessary for reciprocal relationships. She realizes that she has been fortunate to have parents who believe in the power of positive attitudes and humor—and who have encouraged her to be well-rounded through participation in church activities, babysitting, working in the family store, and community

classes. She hopes that after college she will create the same positive atmosphere and opportunities for the family she will be raising.

What Do You Think?

1. What obstacles to learning the skills needed for participation in society did Tracy's blindness create?

2. Who have been the professionals who have facilitated Tracy's success in school, and what has their role been?

3. How is Tracy different from other students who have significant visual impairments?

4. What can professionals do to ensure positive outcomes for all students who are visually impaired?

What Is Visual Impairment?

Defining Visual Impairment

When you think about blindness, you might imagine someone like Tracy, who sees nothing at all and must use adaptive techniques for tasks that typically require vision, such as braille for reading or a cane to detect objects when traveling. It may surprise you to learn that most individuals with **legal blindness** have some usable vision, and the majority of students who have visual impairments are print readers.

Two different definitions describe visual impairment. The legal definition of blindness, based on a clinical measurement of visual acuity, was established through federal law in 1935 (Koestler, 1976). Acuity is determined by having the individual look at the Snellen chart from a distance of twenty feet. The ability to read the 20/20 line is considered typical. Individuals who can only read the first *E* when using both eyes and wearing their glasses have 20/200 vision; these people are considered legally blind. Individuals are also legally blind if their **field of vision** (the area around them that they can visually detect when looking straight ahead) is less than 20 degrees (normal is 160 degrees), even if their visual acuity is normal. These individuals have **tunnel vision**. Figure 16-1 illustrates what people with tunnel vision and other types of visual impairment might see.

The legal definition of blindness is an arbitrary clinical measure that the federal government uses to determine who is entitled to special government allowances, including an extra income tax deduction, specialized job training, and eligibility for certain support services such as the Talking Book Program. State, local, and private agencies also use the federal definition of legal blindness as their eligibility requirement. A person who is legally blind may have a great deal of useful vision; the legal definition of blindness is simply a standard for eligibility for some services but does not provide meaningful information about the way a person experiences and learns about the world.

How a person experiences and learns about the world is at the core of the definition of visual impairment in the Individuals with Disabilities Education Act (IDEA). IDEA

Legal blindness is a term that refers to individuals whose central visual acuity, when measured in both eyes and when wearing corrective lenses, is 20/200 or who has a visual field of no more than 20 degrees.

Field of vision, or **visual field,** is the entire area of which an individual is visually aware when that individual is directing his or her gaze straight ahead.

Tunnel vision occurs when an individual's visual field is reduced significantly so that only a small area of central visual acuity remains. The affected individual has the impression of looking through a tunnel or tube and is unaware of objects to the left, right, top, or bottom. A person with tunnel vision may be able to read small print but is considered severely visually impaired because of the difficulties associated with safe travel and locating objects in the environment.

FIGURE 16-1 *Tunnel vision and other visual impairments*

Note: Photo courtesy of Jewish Guild for the Blind, New York.

The Talking Book Program is a federal project funded through the Library of Congress that produces and distributes recorded books for legally blind adults and children as well as for individuals with physical disabilities.

Visual disability, including blindness, is defined by IDEA as an impairment in vision that, even with correction, adversely affects a child's educational performance.

Low vision is experienced by individuals with a visual impairment who can use their vision as a primary channel for learning. Generally, people with low vision can increase their visual abilities through the use of adaptive devices (such as magnifiers) or materials (such as large print).

Functionally blind is a term used to describe those individuals who can use their available vision to some limited degree (to sort color or to determine the presence of a light source), but who primarily acquire information about the environment through their auditory and tactual senses.

Totally blind individuals use their tactual and auditory senses to acquire information about their environment. These individuals do not receive meaningful input through the visual sense.

defines **visual disability including blindness** as "an impairment in vision that, even with correction, adversely affects a child's educational performance." Key to this definition is that the student has some kind of disorder of the visual system that interferes with learning.

Students with visual impairments represent a wide range of visual abilities. Consistent with IDEA, educators classify students with visual impairments by their ability to use their vision or their tendency or need to use tactile means for learning (Bishop, 1996; Corn, 1983; Hazekamp & Huebner, 1989):

- **Low vision** describes individuals who can generally read print, although they may depend on optical aids, such as magnifying lenses, or other means to enlarge the size of the print. A few read both braille and print. Individuals with low vision may or may not be legally blind but are able to use their visual sense for learning.

- **Functionally blind** describes individuals who typically use braille for efficient reading and writing. They may rely on their ability to use functional vision for other tasks, such as moving through the environment or sorting clothes by color before washing them. Thus, they use their limited vision to supplement the combination of tactual and auditory learning methods.

- **Totally blind** describes those individuals who do not receive meaningful input through the visual sense. These individuals use tactual and auditory means to learn about their environment.

Like an eye specialist's visual acuity measurement, these broad categories are only minimally useful. Every individual with visual impairment uses vision differently and in a way that is difficult to predict. When you teach these students, try to avoid the common errors of assuming that a student who is functionally blind cannot see anything and that a student with low vision is actually efficiently using that vision to learn. Carefully observe how a student functions, and present instructional activities in such a way as to maximize that student's learning for a particular task.

People who are visually impaired vary in their preferences for the labels used to describe them. Unless their degree of vision is significant, we refer to all students who qualify under the IDEA category of visual impairment including blindness as *visually impaired.* Usually, we prefer people-first language (e.g., "person with visual impairments" rather than "visually impaired person"), but you will see many references that do not use this terminology.

Labeling serves as a unifying sense of identity for some people who share this disability. Read the resolution passed by the National Federation of the Blind (see Box 16–1, "Into Practice") and try to appreciate the perspective held by this organization of people working to improve the image and inclusion of its members.

When you have a student with a visual impairment in your class, ask for the student's preference. You'll probably be told that using the pupil's first name is all that's important!

Describing the Characteristics

The population of students with visual impairments is very heterogeneous. This heterogeneity relates to the many areas that affect their learning, including visual functioning, socioeconomic status, parenting style, cultural background, age of onset of visual impairment, the presence of concomitant disabilities, and innate cognitive abilities. Some of these students are gifted or have special talents. A large number also have severe and multiple disabilities (Erin, 1996; Harrell & Curry, 1987; Scholl, 1986a; Silberman, 1986). Yet each possesses an important common characteristic, one that you have to consider when planning appropriate educational interventions: the limited ability to learn incidentally from the environment (Hatlen & Curry, 1987).

BOX 16-1

INTO PRACTICE

THE NATIONAL FEDERATION OF THE BLIND'S POSITION ON LABELING

WHEREAS, the word *blind* accurately and clearly describes the condition of being unable to see, as well as the condition of having such limited eyesight that alternative techniques are required to do efficiently the ordinary tasks of daily living that are performed visually by those having good eyesight; and

WHEREAS, there is increasing pressure in certain circles to use a variety of euphemisms in referring to blindness or blind persons—euphemisms such as *hard of seeing, visually challenged, sightless, visually impaired, people with blindness, people who are blind,* and the like; and

WHEREAS, a differentiation must be made among these euphemisms: some (such as *hard of seeing, visually challenged,* and *people with blindness*) being totally unacceptable and deserving only ridicule because of their strained and ludicrous attempt to avoid such straightforward, respectable words as *blindness, blind, the blind, blind person,* or *blind persons;* others (such as *visually impaired* and *visually limited*) being undesirable when used to avoid the word blind, and acceptable only to the extent that they are reasonably employed to distinguish between those having a certain amount of eyesight and those having none; still others (such as *sightless*) being awkward and serving no useful purpose; and still others (such as *people who are blind or persons who are blind*) being harmless and not objectionable when used in occasional and ordinary speech but being totally unacceptable and pernicious when used as a form of political correctness to imply that the word *persons* must invariably precede the word *blind* to emphasize the fact that a blind person is first and foremost a *person;* and

WHEREAS, this euphemism concerning people or persons who are blind—when used in its recent trendy, politically correct form—does the exact opposite of what it purports to do since it is overly defensive, implies shame instead of true equality, and portrays the blind as touchy and belligerent; and

WHEREAS, just as an intelligent person is willing to be so designated and does not insist upon being called a person who is intelligent and a group of bankers are happy to be *called* bankers and have no concern that they be referred to as persons who are in the banking business, so it is with the blind—the only difference being that some people (blind and sighted alike) continue to cling to the outmoded notion that blindness (along with everything associated with it) connotes inferiority and lack of status: Now, therefore,

BE IT RESOLVED by the National Federation of the Blind in Convention assembled this ninth day of July, 1993, in the City of Dallas, Texas, that the following statement of policy be adopted:

We believe that it is respectable to be blind, and although we have no particular pride in the fact of our blindness, neither do we have any shame in it. To the extent that euphemisms are used to convey any other concept or image, we deplore such use. We can make our own way in the world on equal terms with others, and we intend to do it.

Almost from the moment they are born, children with good vision learn spontaneously and seemingly effortlessly through their visual sense. Their vision helps them organize, synthesize, and give meaning to their perceptions of the environment (Alonzo, 1987; Ferrell, 1996; Harrell, 1992; Lowenfeld, 1973). For example, a sighted baby spends hours looking at his or her hand before that hand becomes an efficient tool. A young child will drop a toy over and over again, watching its path to the floor until he or she learns to understand *down.*

Think about the way a young child learns the concept of a *table.* Even before she has a name for that particular object, she has observed a variety of tables in her environment in the kitchen, living room, family room, at the homes of relatives and friends, at preschool. Tables are everywhere, and the sighted child begins to recognize that the things people

 Young children develop a "scheme" about tables through their experience with them. This incidental learning is different for a child who has always been visually impaired.

call tables ("Put your cup on the table." or "Leave the magazine on the table." or "Go get Daddy's glasses off the table.") have certain characteristics in common: a flat surface raised above the ground with some kind of support touching the ground. Soon she begins to perceive a relationship between that particular object and the word *table*. Later, after more visual experiences, she will be able to distinguish between desks, tables, sideboards, counters, and other flat surfaces on which objects are placed. No one ever really needs to teach this kind of information; it's learned incidentally with little or no direct instruction.

Incidental learning is at risk in all visually impaired children (Ferrell, 1985; Ferrell, 1996; Hatlen & Curry, 1987; Scott, Jan, & Freeman, 1995). For the child with limited visual access to the environment, it may be necessary for her family and teachers to give her opportunities to explore carefully and completely, either visually at a close distance or through tactual means, every part of a variety of tables before she can acquire, organize, and synthesize this same information about *tableness*.

Tracy's sister got out of bed one morning and made toast for the first time. At age six, she had no difficulty with any of the steps involved in this rather complex task because she had observed adults in her environment complete those steps hundreds of times during her six years. It is unlikely that Tracy had experienced this same rich background of incidental visual learning. She needed more direct instruction and more opportunities for practicing the skill before she could make toast independently. Even youngsters with low vision, who may not see clearly at a distance of two or three feet, probably would have needed special instruction and practice time to perform this task.

Because of the significant role played by incidental learning for most individuals, the presence of a visual impairment has the potential to influence the development of motor, language, cognitive, and social skills. Generally, however, these influences are not long-lasting when appropriate interventions are implemented. These interventions must be designed to reduce the following limitations imposed on an individual by a significant visual impairment:

Limitations in the range and variety of experiences

Limitations in the ability to get around

Limitations in interactions with the environment

Limitations in the Range and Variety of Experiences.   Vision allows a person to experience the world meaningfully and safely from a distance. Touch is an ineffective substitute for vision: some objects are too big (skyscrapers, mountains), too small (ants, molecules), too fragile (snowflakes, moths), too dangerous (fire, boiling water), or too distant (the sun, the horizon) for their characteristics to be learned tactually (Lowenfeld, 1973). The other senses do not fully compensate for what can be learned visually: the song of a bird or the smell of baking bread may provide evidence that those objects are nearby but does not provide one with useful information about their properties. Individuals with visual impairment often have not shared the experiences of their peers with typical vision, so their knowledge of the world may be different.

As you have already learned, early concept development is particularly influenced by the limitations in a child's range and variety of experiences. Language development can also be affected. Some students with visual impairments learn the names for objects in their environment but acquire very few words to describe those objects' characteristics. Other pupils can give extremely detailed explanations about objects or events but have limited understanding of them (Andersen, Dunlea, & Kekelis, 1984; Tuttle & Tuttle, 1996). Both of these circumstances impact a person's ability to socialize because conversational language may lack a common basis among conversational partners.

Social interactions also are influenced by a lack of common experiences. The student who has not seen the latest dinosaur movie, played the newest video game, or taken driver's training may be at a disadvantage within the school culture. The potential for inadequate development of appropriate social skills and the related negative impact on self-esteem are serious concerns that may have a lifelong impact (Hazekamp & Huebner, 1989).

Career development is another area that is affected. While many individuals with visual impairments are employed in a wide variety of occupations, many more young adults struggle with the determination of an appropriate vocation because they are unaware of the jobs that people (with or without vision) perform (Vander Kolk, 1981; Wolffe, 1996).

❧ A good teacher will recognize a student's strengths and, taking them into account, increase the student's choices for employment and other postschool opportunities.

Limitations in the Ability to Get Around. Individuals who are visually impaired are limited in their spontaneous ability to move safely in and through their environment. This restriction influences a child's early motor development and early exploration of the world, which in turn affects knowledge base and social development. For an adult with a visual impairment, the limited ability to move spontaneously through the environment probably is the one area of functioning over which only moderate control can be exercised and is therefore a continuing source of frustration (Corn & Sacks, 1994; Tuttle & Tuttle, 1996; Welsh, 1980).

For individuals who have significant visual impairment, the limitation in movement through space directly affects their opportunities for experiences (Lowenfeld, 1973). Vision directs the gross- and fine-motor involvement of even very young infants. The child with impaired vision may not know what in the environment is interesting. Even if that child is aware of something to explore, he or she may not know how to negotiate the environment to get to the desired object. Passivity frequently results, leading to reduced opportunities for intellectual stimulation.

A strong relationship exists between independent travel and self-esteem (Hill & Snook-Hill, 1996; Welsh, 1980). Many leisure and recreation activities, especially those activities in which young children typically engage, depend on free movement through the environment. The necessity to carefully prearrange travel plans creates the need to prearrange most social activities as well, potentially limiting the range of those experiences (Kirchner, McBroom, Nelson, & Graves, 1992).

Limitations in Interactions with the Environment. Knowledge about and control over the environment often are areas of concern for individuals with visual impairments. In some cases, their limited vision reduces their level of readily acquired information about their environment and their ability to act on that information. For instance, they cannot determine at a glance the source of a loud crash or a burning smell, and thus they cannot quickly determine an appropriate reaction. Similarly, they cannot adequately inform themselves about the effects of their actions on the people and things around them.

 Young children with impaired vision need opportunities to explore a variety of environments to develop a healthy sense of competency.

For young children, reduced vision correlates with poor motivation to move through the environment, manipulate toys, and initiate interactions with peers (Fazzi, Kirk, Pearce, Pogrund, & Wolfe, 1992). This tendency toward physical and social detachment (Harrell, 1992; Lowenfeld, 1973; Tuttle & Tuttle, 1996) and low motivation can have long-lasting consequences, affecting the development of a healthy sense of competence and mastery. Individuals who have a poor sense of their ability to effect change on their environment are at risk for the development of poor self-esteem, poor academic achievement, and reduced language and social skills (Harrell, 1992; Harrell & Akeson, 1987).

Another consequence of not being able to monitor the environment is a sense of anxiety related to not knowing if someone is watching or to whom someone is directing verbal or physical anger. If a teacher is reprimanding one student *(you stop that right now!),* a child with a visual impairment often has no way to determine who is the object of the teacher's wrath or what is supposed to be stopped. Individuals often report being apprehensive that their every action is watched and judged. Consequently, they feel they must remain controlled and may be less able to relax or less willing to take risks.

In short, the limitations in the range and variety of experiences, in the ability to get around, and in interactions with the environment influence how a student with a visual impairment experiences the world. Visual impairment can result in experiential and environmental deprivation. Students with visual impairments, even those who have severe intellectual disabilities, can learn; but because they receive unclear, incomplete, or no visual input, they require directed interventions to develop an understanding of the relationships between people and objects in their environment (Freeman, Goetz, Richards, & Groenveld, 1991). In short, visual impairment and blindness affect how students learn a skill but do not prevent them from acquiring that skill (Bishop, 1996; Ferrell, 1986).

FIGURE 16–2 *Cross-section of the eye*

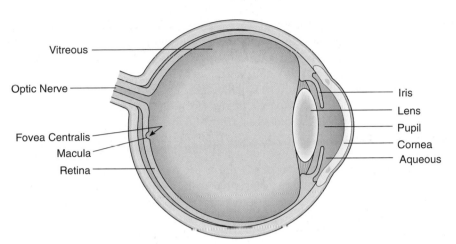

Vitreous

Optic Nerve

Fovea Centralis

Macula

Retina

Iris

Lens

Pupil

Cornea

Aqueous

Note: From *The Eye and How We See,* by Prevent Blindness America (formerly National Society to Prevent Blindness), 1992, Schaumburg, IL: Prevent Blindness America. Copyright 1992 by Prevent Blindness America. Reprinted with permission.

Identifying the Causes of Visual Impairment

There are many structures within the eye and its visual pathway (see Figures 16-2 and 16-3), all of which play important roles in the process of what we refer to as seeing. Seeing involves (a) the transmission of light energy through the eye, (b) the conversion of light energy to electrical energy, (c) the transmission of electrical impulses to the brain, and (d) the interpretation of what is viewed by the brain. Damage to or malfunction of any part of the visual system can lead to a significant loss of visual functioning.

Transmission of Light Energy. Transmission of light energy involves the cornea, iris, pupil, lens, aqueous, and vitreous. The purpose of these structures is to collect and bend the light rays that have reflected off objects in the environment. If any of these structures is not working correctly, then either too much or not enough light enters the eye, or the light rays are not brought together so as to be of maximum use to the individual. **Albinism, cataracts,** and **myopia** are types of visual disorders that affect the transmission of light through the eye.

Albinism is a hereditary condition that often results in lack of pigmentation of the skin and parts of the eye, resulting in reduced visual acuity (low vision) and, usually, legal blindness.

A **cataract** is a disorder of the eye that occurs when the lens of the eye becomes cloudy or opaque, usually resulting in low vision.

Myopia is the medical term for near-sightedness, which results when light rays entering the eye focus in front of the retina.

FIGURE 16–3 *Visual pathway, including brain*

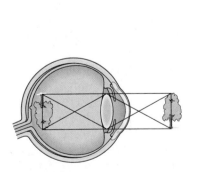 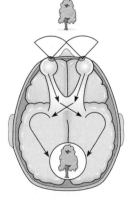 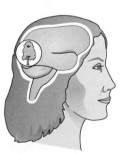

1. Eye sights tree

2. Optic nerves carry messages to brain

3. Messages arrive at vision center

Note: From *The Eye and How We See,* by Prevent Blindness America (formerly National Society to Prevent Blindness), 1992, Schaumburg, IL: Prevent Blindness America. Copyright 1992 by Prevent Blindness America. Reprinted with permission.

The **anterior visual pathway** comprises the parts of the eye that are located in front of the lens (i.e., pupil, iris, cornea, etc.).

The **fovea** is the point on the retina of the eye where light rays are supposed to focus and that is responsible for the clearest visual acuity.

The **retina** is the innermost layer of nerve cells located at the back of the interior eyeball whose purpose is to convert light energy into electrical energy, which is then transmitted to the brain.

The **macula** is the thinnest area of the retina. Most of the nerve cells of the macula are responsible for vision in good light and provide a sense of detail and color.

Macular degeneration is a type of visual disorder that results in the loss of function of the macula, the part of the eye responsible for detail and color vision.

Retinopathy of prematurity is a type of visual disorder that is associated with premature exposure of the developing retina of the eye to oxygen, resulting in various levels of visual impairment.

A student who has difficulty visually processing messages that are sent intact by the visual cortex to the associative parts of the brain does not have a visual impairment but might be eligible for other special education and related services, generally as a student with a learning disability.

Conversion of Light to Electrical Impulse.   In an eye that works well, light rays passing through the **anterior visual pathway** are brought together (focused) on the posterior of the eye at a spot on the retina called the **fovea.** The **retina** is a layer of nerve cells whose purpose is to convert light energy into nerve, or electrical, energy. Different parts of the retina respond to different kinds of light energy. The fovea and the area immediately surrounding it, the **macula,** are primarily responsible for vision in adequate lighting, for color, and for viewing detail. Any kind of impairment of the macula, such as in **macular degeneration** or **retinopathy of prematurity,** will result in poor central vision and reduced color perception.

The nerves in the outer portion of the retina are particularly sensitive to light and the presence of motion. These nerves are essential to a person's ability to see at night or in poor lighting conditions. They also are the primary visual cells involved when a person moves through the environment or views moving objects. Damage to the periphery of the retina can result in tunnel vision and the inability to see in dark environments (e.g., when a person has retinitis pigmentosa or glaucoma).

Brain Connection.   After the retina converts light energy to electrical nerve impulses, these impulses are transmitted along the optic nerve to the visual cortex at the base of the brain. In the visual cortex, the nerve impulses are sorted and transmitted further to the association areas of the brain, where interpretation takes place. Damage to the optic nerve or the visual cortex can result in having incomplete or inaccurate messages sent to these interpretive centers. This kind of visual impairment is often very difficult to understand because the eye itself is working well and the individual appears to be seeing. Nevertheless, the visual message sent by the eye is impaired in some way by the messenger, and the brain has difficulty interpreting the message. **Cortical visual impairment, optic nerve atrophy,** and **optic nerve hypoplasia** are types of disorders that affect these parts of the visual system.

Timing.   Damage to the structures involved in the visual process can be the result of an event that happens during the development of the embryo, can occur at or immediately after birth, or can result from an injury or disease that occurs at any time during the child's development. Congenital visual impairment has the potential to affect the child's earliest access to information and experiences and thus the child's early development of motor, social, and language skills. These effects can be significant for children with low vision, as well as those who are totally or functionally blind.

Students who acquire a vision loss after having normal vision have an adventitious visual impairment. That is, their impairment results from an advent (e.g., loss of sight caused by a hereditary condition that has just manifested itself) or an event (e.g., loss of sight caused by trauma). While the educational needs of students with adventitious and congenital visual impairments may be similar, even a short period of good vision and concomitant typical development can enrich the student's understanding of self, others, and the relationships between people and things in their environment.

Table 16–1 lists the leading causes of childhood visual impairment and the distribution of visual impairment.

Identifying the Prevalence of Visual Impairment

Because state and local educational agencies vary so much in measuring and reporting visual impairment, it is extremely difficult to count accurately the number of students with visual impairments served in schools (Kirchner, 1988; Nelson & Dimitrova, 1990; Scholl, 1986b). Nonetheless, the best estimates are that approximately one student in a thousand has a visual disorder that interferes with learning; that child is eligible to receive special education services. Visual impairment accounts for less than 1 percent of the total special education population (U.S. Department of Education, 1995).

TABLE 16–1 〽 *Leading causes and percentage distribution of visual impairment among young children (Born between 1990 and 1996)*

Cause	Percentage
Albinism	5
Anophthalmia	2
Cataract	5
Coloboma	6
Cortical visual impairment	22
Glaucoma	2
Leber's congenital amaurosis	2
Microophthalmia	4
Myopia/hyperopia	3
Optic nerve atrophy	2
Optic nerve hypoplasia	10
Retinopathy of prematurity	13
Retinoschisis/persistent hyperplastic primary vitreous	6
Other categories	18

Note: (Personal communication, Kay Ferrell, March 1997.)

Cortical visual impairment is the diagnosis given to a visual impairment that results from damage to the part of the brain responsible for reception of visual information from the eye and initial transmission of this information to the associative parts of the brain.

Visual impairment is more or less evenly divided among males (55 percent) and females (45 percent) of school age. No reliable trends have been reported pertaining to relationships between school-age visual impairment and ethnicity (Scholl, 1986b).

In the United States, most of the preventable causes of visual impairment in children and youth have been eradicated. There is some indication, however, that the rate of visual impairment among the school-age population is increasing, partly because of the growing number of people of child-bearing age living in poverty who do not receive adequate pre- and postnatal care. (Sound prenatal care is inversely related to the number of premature births, which often result in significant visual impairment.) In addition, many more medically fragile infants survive today than they did in previous times, and some of these infants have disorders of the visual system (Kirchner, 1990; Kirchner & Stephen, 1987; Pogrund, Fazzi, & Lampert, 1992).

Optic nerve atrophy is a disorder of the optic nerve, the nerve that transmits visual information from the eye to the brain, which often results in reduced visual acuity, or low vision.

WHAT ARE EVALUATION PROCEDURES?

Determining the Presence of a Visual Impairment

Like students with other disabilities, a student with visual impairment receives a nondiscriminatory evaluation (see Figure 16–4). Of course, evaluations of students with visual impairments do have several highly idiosyncratic aspects.

Medical specialists usually determine the presence of a disorder of the visual system. Often, medical examinations detect a serious visual disorder when the child is very young or has just experienced a trauma. Diagnosis generally is followed by a search for a medical solution. This time is especially difficult for parents, who often must meet their child's immediate medical and physical needs, spend hours waiting for appointments with eye specialists, and watch their child endure uncomfortable or even painful medical procedures. Even more difficult is the need for parents to confront their own feelings about blindness and disability. Few parents have positive memories of this phase of the diagnostic process.

Tracy's parents never learned the cause of her complete blindness, which was identified when she was about six months old. Whenever possible, however, it is essential to

Optic nerve hypoplasia is a disorder of the optic nerve that often is associated with midline or other brain abnormalities that may result in varying degrees of visual impairment, including total blindness.

You may recall that, in Chapter 1, we pointed out the correlation between poverty and disability. Here, you learn how it relates to blindness and visual impairment.

FIGURE 16—4 *Assessment process for determining the presence of a visual impairment.*

Nondiscriminatory Evaluation

Observation

Parents observe	The child may not have any eye turn or may not respond to visual stimuli as expected.
Physician observes	The newborn or infant may have an identifiable visual disorder.
Teacher observes	The student squints or seems to be bothered by light, the student's eyes water or are red, the student holds books too close, or the student bumps into objects.

Medical screening

Assessment measures	Findings that indicate need for further evaluation
Ophthalmological	Medical procedures indicate the presence of a visual disorder or reduced visual functioning that cannot be improved to typical levels through surgery or medical intervention.
Functional vision evaluation	Visual disorder interferes with the student's ability to incidentally learn from the environment and identifies the student's use of vision for performance of tasks.
Low vision specialist	Specialist evaluation indicates that visual functioning cannot be improved to typical levels through the use of lenses.
Vision screening in schools	For students with low vision who have not been identified before entering school, screening indicates the need for further evaluation.

Prereferral

Prereferral is typically not used with these students because the severity of the disability indicates a need for special education or related services.

Referral

Students with visual impairments should be referred by medical personnel or parents for early intervention during the infancy/preschool years. Many states have child-find organizations to make sure these students receive services. Children are referred for protection in evaluation procedures upon entering school. Teachers should refer any students with possible vision impairments for immediate evaluation.

Protection in evaluation procedures

Assessment measures	Findings that suggest need for special education services
Individualized intelligence test	Standardization may need to be violated because the student's visual impairment interferes with the ability to perform some tasks. Therefore, results may not be an accurate reflection of ability. Student may be average, above average, or below average in intelligence.
Individualized achievement tests	The student may not achieve in concept development and academic areas at levels of peers. Also, standardization of these tests, unless developed for students with visual impairments, may have to be violated because of the visual impairment. Results may not accurately reflect achievement.
Adaptive behavior scales	The student may have difficulty in self-care, household, and community skills because of vision and mobility problems.
Orientation and mobility evaluation	The student's ability to orient to the environment and to travel to desired locations may be limited.
Anecdotal records	The student may not participate in age-appropriate self-help, social, and recreational activities in home, community, or school.
Curriculum-based assessment	The student may not possess age-appropriate knowledge or skills in areas of communication, daily living, career awareness, sensory and fine motor, social, and self-advocacy.
Direct observation—learning media assessment	The student is unable or has difficulty in responding to print media without use of magnification or alternative strategies, or the student cannot sustain reading in these texts for long periods of time.

Evaluation Team determines that special education and related services are needed for a vision impairment or blindness.

Appropriate Education

know the cause of a student's visual impairment. While a diagnosis of the underlying cause may not provide accurate information about how much the student sees, this information is invaluable for educational program planning. An accurate diagnosis provides an indication of characteristics that may be typical of students with a particular eye condition, including their probable lighting needs, the genetic/hereditary nature of the condition, a potential prognosis, and possible related medical disorders or learning problems.

Determining How a Student Uses Vision.   After a medical specialist (usually an ophthalmologist or an optometrist) determines that a student has a disorder of the visual system, educational specialists need to work with the student and the family to determine the effects of this disorder on the student's visual functioning. Even given an accurate diagnosis and standard visual acuity measurements, it is impossible to predict how a student with usable vision puts that vision to work to learn incidentally from the environment and perform age-appropriate tasks. As might be expected, this kind of evaluation must be repeated frequently as the student grows, matures, and acquires new skills.

A trained teacher with expertise in visual impairment conducts a functional vision evaluation—a critical component of any educational evaluation—in conjunction with the orientation and mobility specialist, the student's parents, and others familiar with the student. While the results of an examination by an ophthalmologist, optometrist, or low vision specialist may be reported in clinical terms (such as 20/120), the results of a functional vision examination are reported in language that informs educators and others in more concrete ways: For example, the student can see three-inch-high commercially printed letters on a reading chart at a distance of no more than five feet or can imitate facial expressions at a distance of three feet. Figure 16-5 gives you an example of part of a functional vision evaluation for children under kindergarten age.

Functional vision evaluations describe a student's use of vision in a variety of natural environments, such as under the fluorescent lights in a grocery store, on the playground in the glare of the midday sun, or walking down a dimly lit corridor to the school library. Appropriate functional vision evaluations also take into consideration different activities that occur in these environments. For example, a student at a grocery store may be able to see the products on the shelves but may not be able to read the aisle labels that hang directly below the bright lights or the value of paper money at the checkout counter. Obviously, this kind of information is extremely valuable to the educators who work with the student because it helps them to understand and appreciate the student's particular needs and to design relevant instructional strategies (Bishop, 1996; Langley, 1980; Levack, 1991).

Most youngsters with usable vision need and benefit from periodic evaluations by a low vision specialist, an optometrist or ophthalmologist with special training in the visual evaluation of people with severe visual impairment, and the prescription of appropriate optical and nonoptical aids (Jose, 1983; Stiles & Knox, 1996). Ideally, a functional vision evaluation should occur before an examination by a low vision specialist so that the teacher can share comprehensive information about the student's functioning. Of course, if the low vision specialist recommends optical aids or other devices, a follow-up functional vision evaluation may be necessary to describe the student's functioning while using these devices and to prescribe and make any necessary adjustments.

Determining the Appropriate Reading Medium.   For students like Tracy, it is easy for teachers to determine how educational materials should be presented to her. Since she cannot see, braille clearly is the appropriate **reading medium** for her. You will remember, however, that most students who are visually impaired have low vision; for them, the determination of the appropriate reading medium is more complex. Many children who

Functional vision evaluations provide teachers with valuable information about how students function in a variety of environments. As stated in IDEA, these evaluations should be repeated whenever conditions warrant. For students like Tracy, who have no vision, functional vision evaluations are never warranted.

Reading medium is a term used to describe the format(s) preferred by people who have visual impairments to access written materials and generally refers to print, large print, or braille.

FIGURE 16–5 *Functional vision evaluation, pre-kindergarten level*

Distant Vision:

- Mimics teacher facial expressions at _____ feet.

- Locates the drinking fountain at _____ feet.

- Recognizes our name, shapes, numbers at _____ feet.

- Interprets major forms in a picture at _____ feet but needs to be at _____ feet to identify details of 3 inches in height.

- Identifies classmates at _____ feet.

- Locates personal possessions (lunchbox, jacket, backpack) in closet at _____ feet.

- Locates own cubby at _____ feet.

- Locates _____ of four dropped coins on a _____ (color) floor: quarter at _____ feet; nickel at _____ feet; dime at _____ feet; penny at _____ feet.

- Tracks and locates a _____ (size) moving ball at _____ feet.

- Avoids obstacles when moving round P.E. apparatus. Yes _____ No _____

- Visually detects and smoothly navigates contour changes in surfaces such as ramps and steps. Yes _____ No _____

Near Vision:

- Completes _____ (number of pieces) puzzle with head _____ inches from the board (describe how student performs task—e.g., trial and error, quickly, visually, tactually, etc.).

- Places pegs in a pegboard at _____ inches with head _____ inches from pegs (describe how student performs task).

Note: From *Functional Visual Evaluation,* by the Los Angeles Unified School District, 1990. Copyright 1990 by the Los Angeles Unified School District. Adapted with permission.

can read print do so at such slow speeds or with such inefficiency that they also benefit from using braille. Teachers determine the appropriate reading media for students by conducting a Learning Media Assessment (Koenig & Holbrook, 1993). The Learning Media Assessment begins with a functional vision evaluation but also includes additional considerations, such as students' approaches (tactual or visual) to new situations or environments, the nature and stability of the eye condition, and students' visual stamina and motivation.

Like a functional vision evaluation, the Learning Media Assessment needs to be repeated at regular intervals throughout a student's life to determine whether circumstances and skills have changed and whether additional instruction in a different reading medium is necessary. Students who learn both braille and print have the advantage of being able to choose the reading medium that works best for them under different conditions, such as in a dimly lit restaurant or when reading assignments are long and eye fatigue is a problem.

The Amendments to IDEA, passed in 1997, require for the first time that members of the individualized education program (IEP) team consider the use of braille or other appropriate reading and writing media for a student who is blind or visually impaired. The results of the Learning Media Assessment will provide important information as team members consider the most effective literacy tools for students.

❧ Never say to students that they *have to* learn braille. Instead, emphasize that they *get to* learn to read more efficiently and that one of the tools they will be using is braille. This approach emphasizes students' choices.

To use braille is to use a tactile code of a printed alphabet.

Determining the Nature and Extent of Special Education and Related Services

The provision of special education services must be based on a student's specific needs as identified through a comprehensive evaluation of the student's current level of functioning and knowledge in the following areas:

- Academic skills

- Communication skills

- Sensorimotor skills

- Social/emotional skills

- Orientation and mobility skills

- Daily living skills

- Career/vocational skills

Evaluation is best accomplished by a team of individuals with previous and continuing experience with students with visual disabilities. In addition to those people who, under the new IDEA, must be members of the team (see Figure 2-6), the team also should consist of an orientation and mobility specialist and a teacher of students with visual impairments. Specific student characteristics dictate additional specialists who also should be included on the team—perhaps occupational therapists, behavior specialists, audiologists, low vision specialists, physical therapists, or teachers with special knowledge of the needs of students with physical or intellectual disabilities. Of course, the parents must be on the team, and other family members or caretakers and the student usually are essential team members.

Parent involvement is the focus of a model assessment program for students with visual impairments developed by the California School for the Blind. In this program, parents and students reside on the residential school campus for a week while a multidisciplinary team

IDEA provides that orientation and mobility is a related service, so an orientation and mobility specialist should be a member of the evaluation team.

conducts a thorough evaluation of the student. Parents establish the emphasis of the assessment, provide information about their child's past and present levels of functioning, and share their hopes and expectations. They watch each component of the assessment, including the administration of standardized tests, and are asked to confirm the results. If they believe their child's performance was not typical, they are encouraged to elicit the desired behavior or information. Finally, throughout the week, parents demonstrate the techniques they use to work with or teach their child new skills.

Given their level of involvement, parents gain trust in the findings of the assessment, in large part because the professionals actively elicit and value their opinions and observations. Because they have seen and been a part of the testing, parents tend to consider the results valid, even when the findings are contrary to their original estimation of their child's functioning. Parent involvement during testing also allows for the immediate explanation of why a particular skill is being evaluated, the effects of a visual impairment on the child's ability to acquire the skill easily, and possible teaching techniques that will facilitate skill acquisition.

Although based at a state residential school, this model could be replicated in local school districts. The following considerations are essential for any replication to be successful (Curry, 1993):

- Assign specific individuals to the team. It is particularly important for school psychologists, speech-language pathologists, and other specialists who have had limited opportunities to develop the experiential base necessary to interpret test results to remain consistently involved on the team. Consistency helps them to develop expertise in their specific area as it applies to students with visual impairments and as team members.

- Provide assigned personnel with adequate release time to conduct their evaluation in a variety of environments, to confer with other team members, and to write their report.

- Involve the child's parents by asking them to observe and participate in testing; by observing the child in their home; by asking to view home videotapes; and by carefully listening to parental hopes, expectations, and requests for assistance.

Generally speaking, while extended time may be necessary for tests, teachers who have high expectations for their students will encourage them to finish classroom and homework assignments within the same time frame as is allowed for sighted peers.

The outcome of any comprehensive evaluation should be a description of the student's current level of functioning in all areas of potential need and the identification of skills that need to be addressed for that child to function optimally in current and future home, school, and community environments (Curry, 1993; Hall, Scholl, & Swallow, 1986; Hazekamp & Huebner, 1989). Comprehensive evaluations include standardized and norm-referenced tests (which are often timed) and informal assessment techniques. An issue to consider about timed tests is the additional time needed by students, which can be directly related to their visual impairment. Taking tests often requires complex use of vision, such as frequent eye movements between the test booklet and the answer sheet or scanning of multiple-choice answers and stimulus paragraphs. Similarly, readers who use braille, who tend to have reading rates significantly below their peers with sight and whose system of reading is not conducive to efficient scanning, have difficulty with tests. Generally, students with visual impairments are allowed at least time and a half to complete standardized tests (Olmstead, 1991; Packer, 1989; Torres & Corn, 1990).

Informal assessment techniques, including family and student interviews, the use of checklists, observation in natural environments, and authentic and performance assessments, are the most valuable methods for determining the level of unique functioning of students with visual impairments. Few teachers would consider it important to evaluate a straight-A high school student's ability to order a meal at a fast-food restaurant or to launder clothes, yet a student with a visual impairment who achieves at grade level may not be learning to function appropriately outside of the classroom. Many students lack these skills, a fact revealed by a comprehensive assessment in each area of potential unique need.

When selecting material for informal assessments, educators should evaluate the age appropriateness of a task from two perspectives. First, what are the student's peers doing? If Tracy's friends are at the stage of social development where shopping at the mall is common, an assessment of Tracy's social skills should investigate this aspect of her functioning. Second, because sighted students are incidentally learning to perform some skills long before it is age-appropriate to expect mastery of these tasks, educators should evaluate a student's involvement in these tasks earlier than they would for sighted students. For example, while many students are not expected to launder clothes independently until late adolescence, educators should assess this task's component parts as students with visual impairments mature—that is, before late adolescence.

Teachers should avoid making assumptions about a student's previously learned information. For example, an eighteen-year-old woman with low vision, when tested to determine her knowledge of contraceptive devices, revealed that she was unaware that men's sexual organs differ from her own. Unfortunately, the teacher did not learn this fact until after the class had been discussing contraception for several days. Unaware of the learning styles of students with visual impairments, she had assumed that all eighteen-year-olds were knowledgeable about gender differences.

WHAT AND HOW DO PROFESSIONALS TEACH?

Curriculum

A common problem faced by IEP teams is how to meet as many of the educational needs as possible of students with visual impairments. Students who do not also have cognitive disabilities should be expected to master the general education curriculum. In addition, they must master the skills necessary to access that curriculum: reading braille, using adapted equipment and assistive technology, and developing specialized study skills. Finally, because of the impact of their visual impairment on learning and development, they need to learn and practice a separate set of disability-specific skills (Alonzo, 1987; California Leadership Action Team for the Visually Impaired, 1985; Curry & Hatlen, 1988; Hatlen & Curry, 1987; Spungin, 1984). Thus, in addition to the general academic curriculum, students with visual impairments must develop skills in three major areas:

- Skills needed to access the academic curriculum

- Skills learned incidentally by seeing students

- Skills specific to students with visual impairments

As you read about these activities, you will note some overlap among these three divisions. For example, learning to read braille is a skill specific to blind students, but it also supports their academic curriculum: learning to read is a skill expected to be mastered by most students, including those who are blind.

Accessing the Academic Curriculum.
As you have already read, blindness and visual impairment do not affect what a student can learn as much as they affect how a student learns. Many students who learn efficiently through their visual sense are supported in their academic curriculum through methodological adaptations such as large-print materials, instruction in the use of magnification devices, and cooperative efforts among their special and general education teachers to determine effective ways to involve the student fully in all instructional activities. You will learn more about these approaches later in the chapter.

Students who do not learn as efficiently through their visual sense may need to access the academic curriculum through braille, a tactile method of reading. Like the print alphabet, it is a code—a way of presenting spoken language in written form. As you can see in Figure 16-6, there is one braille symbol for each of the twenty-six symbols (letters) of the

Math in braille is produced in Nemeth code, which uses some of the same symbols as the literary code but assigns them different meanings. For every symbol in a math or science textbook, there is a corresponding symbol in the Nemeth code.

FIGURE 16–6 *English braille symbols*

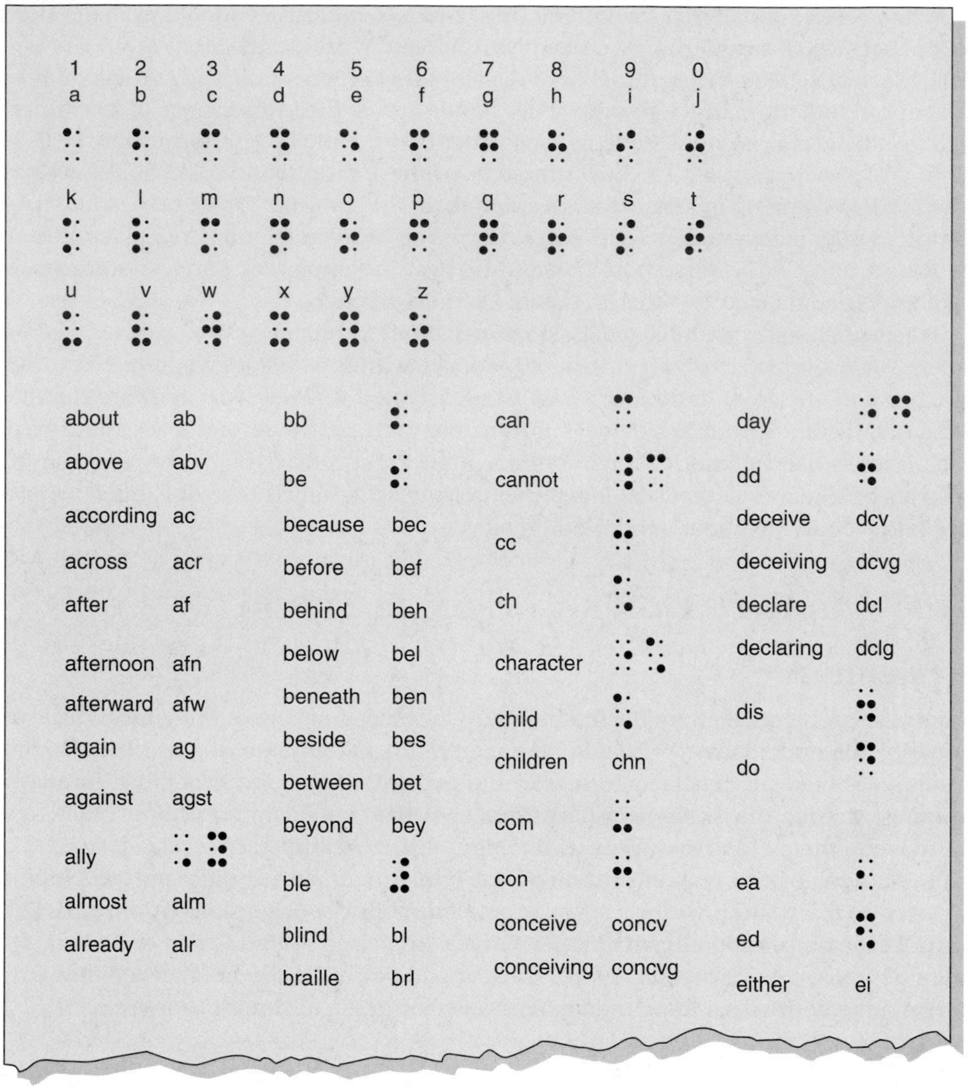

Note: Courtesy of Victor H. Hemphill.

English alphabet. However, because braille requires more space and is bulkier and more expensive than print to produce, the early publishers of braille developed numerous shortcuts for writing common words or letter combinations, which are called *braille contractions.*

Because of the contractions, there is no one-to-one correspondence between print and braille. Therefore, the level of difficulty in early reading books for print and braille readers is not the same. In Figure 16–7, compare the print passage, taken from a popular first-grade primer, with its braille translation. As you can tell, the number of braille contractions in this passage requires the braille reader to learn more difficult material much earlier—sometimes before all the print letters of the alphabet have been introduced to the sighted students. A special programmed reading series called *Patterns* (Caton, Pester, & Bradley, 1980) introduces the symbols of the braille alphabet in a logical manner, presenting the easiest symbols and contractions before the more difficult ones that are used less frequently. Many new readers who are blind learn to read using *Patterns.* Often they also participate with their peers in the reading curriculum selected for that school, as Tracy did.

There are two other ways that special teachers support their students' access to the academic curriculum. They provide direct instruction in difficult or highly visual academic

Do you think you could learn to read or write braille? Most sighted teachers of students with visual impairments read braille with their eyes, and it takes more than three months to learn all the rules for the contractions. Learning to write the twenty-six letters of the alphabet, however, typically takes less than a week for someone who is familiar with printed writing.

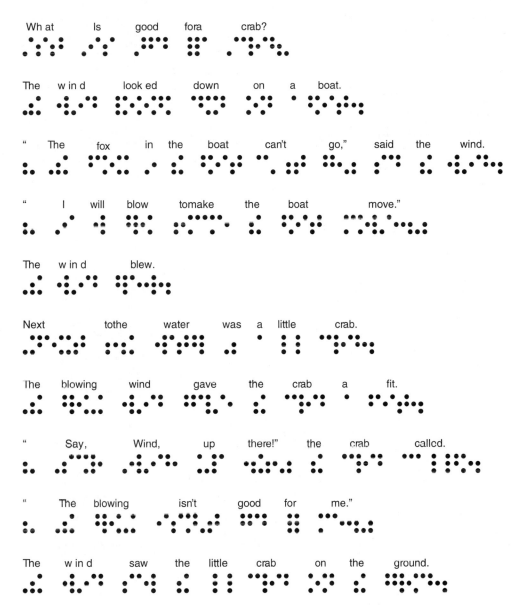

Figure 16–7 *Comparison of a passage in braille and print*

Note: From "What Is Good for a Crab" STORY CLOUDS, SCOTT, FORESMAN READING: AN AMERICAN TRADITION by Richard Allington et al. Copyright © 1987 by Scott, Foresman and Company. Reprinted by permission of Addison Wesley Educational Publishers Inc.

areas such as geometry and in specialized skills related to work in the classroom such as braille writer and slate-writing skills, computer use and word processing, use of recording devices, listening skills, study and organization skills, and use of other specialized communication equipment. They also collaborate with other educators to ensure that the students use these newly learned skills in a variety of academic environments.

Teaching Skills Learned Incidentally by Students with Vision. As mentioned earlier, students with visual impairments are at risk for having difficulty acquiring many of the life and social skills that students with adequate vision learn simply by watching their parents, siblings, other adults, and peers. As you can tell from Figure 16-8, even the simplest task may require direct instruction before students with visual impairments are able to perform the activity independently.

Effective teachers recognize how a visual impairment impedes skill acquisition such as sensorimotor development, orientation and mobility, recreation, social/emotional

FIGURE 16–8 *Potential unique needs of students with visual impairments*

Concept Development and Academic Skills

- Development of concepts
- Determination of learning mode
- Academic support
- Listening skills
- Organization and study skills
- Reading charts, maps, graphs
- Use of reference materials

Social/Emotional Skills

- Knowledge of self
- Knowledge of human sexuality
- Knowledge of visual impairment
- Knowledge of others
- Development of interaction skills
- Development of social skills
- Lifelong recreation and leisure skills
- Self-advocacy skills

Orientation and Mobility Skills

- Development of body image
- Development of concrete environmental concepts
- Development of spatial concepts
- Development of directional concepts
- Understanding traffic and traffic control
- Trailing techniques
- Sighted guide techniques
- Use of vision for travel and orientation
- Development of orientation skills
- Use of long cane
- Independent travel in a variety of environments
- Public interaction skills

Communication Skills

- Handwriting
- Development of legal signature
- Use of braille writer
- Use of slate and stylus
- Use of word processors
- Use of adaptive equipment
- Note-taking skills

Sensory/Motor Skills

- Development of maximum use of vision
- Development of gross-motor skills

---

development, activities of daily living, and career education. Several descriptions of general curricula and specific teaching methods have been published to help teachers and parents learn how to facilitate a student's development in some of these areas (Heydt, Clark, Cushman, Edwards, & Allon, 1992; Los Angeles Unified School District, 1990; Loumiet & Levack, 1991; Pogrund et al., 1993; Santa Clara County, 1993; Tapp, Wilhelm, & Loveless, 1991).

Orientation and mobility, now an IDEA related service, is a curriculum area that requires very specific instructional techniques. Orientation and mobility skills are those skills that people with visual impairment use to know where they are in their environment and how to move around that environment safely. Imagine crossing a street in your city when you cannot clearly see the traffic lights, cars, or other obstacles in your path. How would you know where you were if you could not read street signs or see the house numbers or the names of the businesses along your route? Orientation and mobility specialists teach students with visual impairments to learn to listen to the flow of traffic; react to changes of street and road surfaces; and use their vision, other senses, and perhaps a cane or other mobility device to detect objects in the environment and to help them know where they are along their route.

Close your eyes, and visualize yourself at the bus stop of an elementary school. Think of the challenges involved in getting to a specific classroom, the front office, the library, or the cafeteria and in walking across the playground. With proper instruction, students with visual impairments manage these tasks every day.

- Development of fine-motor skills
- Development of auditory skills
- Development of strength, stamina and endurance in legs, arms, hands
- Identification of textures tactually and under foot
- Identification of kinesthetic sources
- Identification of olfactory sources

Daily Living Skills

- Personal hygiene
- Eating
- Dressing
- Clothing care
- Food preparation
- Housekeeping
- Basic home repair
- Money identification and management
- Use of telephone and information
- Use of desk tools
- Time and calendar
- Shopping skills
- Restaurant skills

- Community skills
- Knowledge and use of community services

Career and Vocational Skills

- Knowledge of relationship between work and play
- Understanding of value of work
- Knowledge of characteristics of valued workers
- Awareness of the variety of jobs people hold
- Awareness of jobs people with visual impairments often hold
- Awareness of jobs teenagers hold
- Job acquisition skills (want ads, resumes, applications, interviews)
- Typical job adaptations made by workers with visual impairments
- In-depth knowledge of a variety of jobs of interest
- Work experience
- Laws related to employment
- Management of readers, drivers

The development of orientation and mobility skills begins at birth and continues until the individual is able to reach desired destinations safely using a variety of techniques. Young children concentrate on developing strong body image, mastering spatial and positional concepts, learning the layout of their homes and schools, and developing their environmental awareness. Older students focus on crossing streets safely and negotiating travel in increasingly complex situations, such as a town's business district or a shopping mall. Even after a student acquires certain skills, it is sometimes necessary to use the services of an orientation and mobility specialist. For example, visually impaired adults who must orient themselves to new homes, neighborhoods, or work sites often contract with an orientation and mobility specialist to help them learn the layout of an area, useful landmarks, and the direct and alternate travel routes that they will use for orientation and travel.

Teaching Skills Specific to Students with Visual Impairments.   Individuals with visual impairments must learn unique skills that typically are not taught to other students but are critical to their inclusion in a school and a community. Among these skills are the ability to advocate for individual needs; to access and use the health care system as it

On one October orientation and mobility lesson, Tracy's teacher helped her explore the Halloween decorations that neighbors had hung in their front yards. In this way, Tracy learned neighborhood concepts and important social concepts related to the holiday.

❧   When students learn self-advocacy skills, they take a big step toward full citizenship.

MARLA RUNYON

"There's no sense listening to what someone else tells you," ABC anchor Forrest Sawyer comments. "What's more important is what you believe possible." That is what developing inherent strengths and having great expectations is all about.

Marla Runyon proves this point. A world class athlete, Marla is legally blind. Yet, she won the bronze medal in the heptathlon competition at a US Olympic festival. "For Marla," Forrest Sawyer says, "track is a game of numbers, not vision." She shares her story in this video.

What do you think? Marla teaches students who are blind or deaf. What do you think about a person who is blind teaching in a general classroom? What challenges would the teacher need to overcome? How could that happen?

"I don't like to be stereotyped as disabled," Marla Runyon says. In this textbook, you've read about providing accommodations to students with disabilities. How can accommodations be provided (a) without stereotyping, (b) without making the student feel singled out, and (c) while maintaining great expectations?

Marla's doctor and teachers told her she might not even finish high school. She surprised them all. Suppose you are engaged in transitional planning with a student, and the student's goals seem unrealistic based on his test scores and disability. How would you handle this situation?

relates to eye care; and to hire, fire, and effectively use readers, drivers, personal shoppers, and other support providers.

As adults, most people with visual impairments are required to explain their abilities and special needs to other people they meet: bus drivers, prospective employers, landlords, restaurant and hotel workers, and flight attendants. Sometimes these explanations are simple, such as asking a bus driver to call out the name of every bus stop, but some-

This young student who is blind first works with an orientation and mobility specialist to learn how to move safely within his neighborhood before tackling the challenge of a busy city street.

times they require detailed and deliberate descriptions. For example, when Tracy goes to college, she will need to approach each of her teachers and ask permission to tape-record their lectures, request personal copies of any overhead transparencies they use, explain that it will be necessary for them to say aloud what they write on the blackboard, and describe the special accommodations that she requires (e.g., a reader and additional time during testing). Very likely, she will need to convince each of her professors that she is capable of doing the work for the class. In brief, she will have to advocate for herself.

Tracy has been involved in this kind of activity with each of her teachers since entering the seventh grade, so she is confident that she will be able to explain her abilities and needs effectively—that she will be assertive but not offensive. At first, she simply listened as her itinerant teacher explained her needs to her elementary and middle school teachers, but gradually she has become fully responsible for this task.

Tracy is less confident about her abilities in other new situations she will face as a young adult, such as advocating for her rights with landlords and, if she should get a dog guide, advocating for access to public buildings, including movie theaters, stadiums, and restaurants. Her teachers are helping her to learn the laws (especially the Americans with Disabilities Act, or ADA, which you read about in Chapter 1) and the communication techniques she can use to avoid confrontations (if possible) and to assert herself (if necessary). As part of Tracy's lessons in self-advocacy, her teacher is introducing her to adults who are blind. She was particularly impressed when she attended the local meeting of the American Council of the Blind and learned of the power of group action.

Medical advocacy is another area in which many youngsters with visual impairments must learn information that is unique to their disability. Most likely, continuing contact with eye care and related service professionals is necessary throughout one's life. Learning to deal effectively with these professionals is a long, complex process that involves understanding how the eye works, gaining information about one's specific visual disability and the techniques and equipment used by eye care specialists, overcoming a reluctance to question medical experts, and developing a thorough knowledge of one's visual functioning and the ability to evaluate the usefulness of suggested optical and electronic adaptations.

Another set of skills is associated with employing sighted individuals to read mail or act as drivers. Skills for hiring, directing, evaluating, and firing such employees can be learned in school.

As you see, there is a great deal for students with visual impairments to learn. Determining the nature and extent of special education services for these youngsters frequently becomes a balancing act that demands the same kind of finesse and dexterity required of the individuals involved in a human pyramid. Members of the IEP team, including the student, must work together to prioritize goals in each of the potential areas of unique educational need. They need to be creative about the way these goals are met and be vigilant in assuring that each area of unique need is addressed thoroughly.

Even within the academic area, achieving a balance becomes tricky. When Tracy was younger, she required at least twice as much time as her peers to complete a typical math assignment, in part because the braille math code was so unfamiliar to her. Her teachers wanted to reduce the length of her assignments, but it was also obvious that because of her lack of experiences with numbers, she needed additional experiences to achieve the level of her classmates. The IEP team had to deal with her competing needs for more time to complete the assigned work and more experiences to understand it thoroughly.

Now at the high school level, Tracy still requires additional time to understand and complete her school assignments. She often spends more time each night doing homework than her classmates do. Her IEP team struggles each year to work with her to determine when she is going to receive instruction in orientation and mobility, career education alternatives, and skills needed to manage an apartment of her own—skills that they each agree she needs to master and that Tracy believes are essential to her success.

Box 16–2, "Into Practice," suggests some creative ways to make time for teaching unique skills.

Developing relationships with other people who will do tasks such as reading mail or driving out of friendship is also an important aspect of a student's curriculum, as is understanding the impact on relationships of an overreliance on free assistance. Students need to be aware that friendships involve both taking and giving.

BOX 16-2   INTO PRACTICE

CREATIVE WAYS TO MAKE TIME FOR TEACHING UNIQUE SKILLS

- Teach thematically and experientially, providing opportunities for all students to read and hear about the subject and to touch and appreciate how the parts of an activity connect to make the whole.
- Provide regular and frequent opportunities for parents of students with visual impairments to meet together with the specialist teacher to discuss concerns about their children's development and to share how they have tried, with or without success, to help their children develop skills.
- Rearrange the school day so that the specialist begins and ends later. This way, the specialist can work with students after school.
- Rearrange the school week so that the specialist works from Tuesday through Saturday, with Saturday instruction taking place individually in students' homes or in groups in community environments.

- Arrange for adults with visual impairments to teach unique skills related to career education and social and living skills. These classes may take place in their homes or businesses or in students' homes.
- Collaborate with community agencies serving adults with visual impairments to teach living, career, social, and orientation and mobility skills to students after school and on Saturdays.
- Collaborate with community agencies serving adults with visual impairments and with residential schools for the blind to provide intensive educational opportunities focusing on unique needs. Instruction may take place during school vacations, on weekends, or as short-term out-of-school placements to improve skills needed for school success.

Creativity is the answer to many questions: creativity in scheduling, in instruction, in use of free time, and in collaboration among the many adults involved in each pupil's program. Critical to the success of this endeavor is that members of the team assume responsibility for the instruction and practice of newly learned skills whenever the natural opportunity to do so occurs. Each IEP team member also must believe that ultimate successful adult functioning depends on the student's acquisition of skills in all of the curriculum areas—that no one area is more or less important than the others. It's a delicate balance.

Methods

Review the learning characteristics of blind and visually impaired children, presented earlier in the chapter.

A commonsense approach to involving the student in an activity and having (as IDEA emphasizes) high expectations that the skill can be acquired are critical factors in the acquisition of skills in the key curriculum areas. Effective instructional methods include acquiring and adapting materials, using a tactual/kinesthetic approach, and providing additional learning experiences.

Commonsense Approach. Choosing a commonsense approach depends to a large degree on the characteristics of the individual student. Generally, effective teaching strategies involve repeated visual or hand-over-hand kinesthetic demonstrations (or both), systematic instruction, gradual fading of assistance and prompts, and significant periods of practice. They also involve assisting the student to understand how a particular part of the task relates to the whole. More important than a specific technique is the teacher's appreciation of how the student experiences and mentally creates a view of the world, a conception that may be very different from the teacher's.

Unlike sighted students who can view the whole of an object or activity and then explore its parts, most students with visual impairments must develop their understanding of a whole object or activity from its related parts. For example, Tracy's sister, Trisha, has experienced through visual observations the entire activity of cleaning up the kitchen after a meal. She knows there are dishes to put in the dishwasher, pans to soak in the sink, counters to wipe, and food to return to the cupboards and refrigerator. One glance at the kitchen tells her if it is clean or not. When Tracy was younger, the only part of this activity that she was aware of was her assigned role: taking her plate from the dinner table to the counter next to the sink. Only over time has she been gradually introduced to more parts of this activity. Even now, when she is asked if the kitchen is clean, she must feel each of the counter tops and other kitchen surfaces, one at a time, before replying.

Keeping Expectations High.   Because many adults think of people who are blind as helpless, they have low expectations for students with visual impairments to acquire typical skills. In addition, because adults may assume that students with low vision see more clearly than they do, they do not show these youngsters how to perform some of the activities that sighted children perform naturally, such as buttoning a shirt or holding a spoon correctly. When these students do not spontaneously develop these skills, teachers may mistakenly think that the students also have additional cognitive disabilities, and their expectations for achievement become even more diminished.

Low and inaccurate expectations of their abilities are students' worst enemies. Skilled teachers know to be constantly alert to what students are not doing for themselves and are prepared for the subtle ways in which adults who are unfamiliar with the capabilities of people who are visually impaired lower expectations, promote a sense of inferiority, and decrease self-motivation.

Adapted Materials.   Acquisition or preparation of adapted materials, either in braille or large print or on recorded tape, is an important and time-consuming activity. An enlarging machine is one way to prepare large-print material for some students and some activities; but for some assignments, adaptations must be made that take the layout of the page into consideration.

Consider, for example, the arithmetic page shown on the left of Figure 16–9. The information on this page may be too crowded and visually confusing for some students with low vision. Teachers can adapt the page so that it appears as on the right of Figure 16–9. With this modification, a student with low vision could spend math time working on the problems, not concentrating on trying to find them on the page.

Adapting print materials for use by blind students sometimes is an art. Look at the page from a children's workbook (Figure 16–10). It was found at a grocery store by the mother of three-year-old Alexandria March, who sees well, and four-year-old Jonathan, who is functionally blind.

Alexandria had no difficulty with the activity. Her mother wanted to provide Jonathan with the same early learning experiences and asked his special teacher for help. The teacher knew that braille would not help, because he could not read yet. She also knew that models of real objects are not easily interpreted by young children who are blind. In addition, she understood the limited value of raised line illustrations for Jonathan, who still experienced the world in three dimensions. So the teacher collected five real objects with which Jonathan was familiar because of his exposure to them at preschool: a braille writer, a stick of gum, a braille book, a lunch box, and a spatula. She said, "There are five real objects on the table top in front of you. When you have identified all five, I want you to hand me the three objects that belong in school." Jonathan's mother caught on to the guidelines for this kind of project easily and worked with Jonathan on other pages in the workbook. She was surprised at the amount of time and work that adapting each page required, but she was pleased with Jonathan's progress

FIGURE 16–9 *Adaptation of a math assignment*

Name _____

P15

Rounding to tens and hundreds

Sharpen your skills

What sea animals also go by the name of "sea-cows"?

Round each number to the nearest ten. Match each letter to its answer in the blanks below.

1. 654   **2.** 896   **3.** 122   **4.** 980

_____ N   _____ S   _____ E   _____ E

5. 582   **6.** 607   **7.** 345   **8.** 989

_____ A   _____ M   _____ T   _____ A

Round each number to the nearest hundred.

9. 399   **10.** 454   **11.** 790

_____ H   _____ T   _____ E

_____ _____ _____
350 400 120

_____ _____ _____ _____ _____ _____ _____ _____
610 580 650 990 500 980 800 900

Round each number to the nearest ten and then to the nearest hundred.

12. 603   **13.** 356   **14.** 298   **15.** 465

_____   _____   _____   _____

_____   _____   _____   _____

16. 476   **17.** 302   **18.** 873   **19.** 776

_____   _____   _____   _____

_____   _____   _____   _____

Practice/EXPLORING MATHEMATICS © Scott, Foresman and Company   Use after pages 48–49.

Note: From *Exploring Mathematics* (Practice Workbook) by Scott, Foresman and Company, 1991, Glenview, IL: Scott, Foresman and Company. Copyright © 1991 by Scott, Foresman and Company. Reprinted with permission.

and delighted to be able to be involved with Jonathan in the same way she was with Alexandria's early learning experiences.

A variety of adapted materials are available for use by students with visual impairments, including braille and large-print maps, rulers, measuring devices, graph paper, writing paper, calendars, flash cards, and geometric forms. A good source of adapted materials is the American Printing House for the Blind in Louisville, Kentucky. (Contact information is included in the "Resources" section, later in the chapter.)

Tactual/Kinesthetic Approach.   Some academic subject areas require adaptation of the materials that have been designed for sighted learners and of the methodology used

What sea animals also go by the name of "sea cows?"

Round each number to the nearest ten.
Match each letter to its answer in the blanks below.

1. 654 _____ N   5. 582 _____ A

2. 896 _____ S   6. 607 _____ M

3. 122 _____ E   7. 345 _____ T

4. 980 _____ E   8. 989 _____ A

Round each number to the nearest hundred.

9. 399 _____ H   11. 790 _____ E

10. 454 _____ T

___   ___   ___
350   400   120

___   ___   ___   ___   ___   ___   ___   ___
610   580   650   990   500   980   800   900

to teach the subject matter. Many of the concepts related to science, social studies, mathematics, art, and other subjects need to be introduced to a student with a severe visual impairment by using a tactual/kinesthetic approach.

For example, when Tracy's science class studied seed germination, her teachers arranged for her to sprout a different kind of seed, one that she could feel easily. Instead of having her plant her seed in the dirt in a yogurt container, as her classmates did, Tracy planted her seed in water and checked daily for changes in the way the seed felt and smelled. By using this method, she learned about root growth (which had been presented through pictures in her science book) as well as the purpose of the lesson: seed germination and the growth of the leafy part of the plant.

FIGURE 16–10   *Preschool workbook page*

Circle **3** things that **belong** in the school.

Note: From *Does It Belong?* (1983). Grand Haven, MI: School Zone Publishing.

To teach a student to read often requires important methodological changes. Children's books designed for sighted children rely heavily on pictures to convey the meaning of the story. In addition, the pictures reveal to the young reader information about the world that he or she may not have experienced. Not all new readers have been for a walk in a forest or have gone for a ride in a rowboat, but from a picture they can discern what the words in the story are trying to convey. For children who are blind or have low vision, difficulty seeing and interpreting pictures may necessitate engaging in the pictured activity before they can achieve full understanding of the meaning conveyed by the words (Koenig & Farrenkopf, 1997).

Additional Experiences.   Often, blind and visually impaired students need many additional experiences to make up for their lack of incidental learning. Box 16–3, "Into Practice," suggests ways to provide these experiences.

Think of all of the opportunities that three-year-old children with typical vision have to see letters in the environment, long before they are expected to read. Letters appear on cereal boxes, on toys, on the newspaper or envelopes delivered daily to the house, on billboards, on street signs, on television, in books. They are everywhere. Even if these children are not learning the names of the letters, they are being exposed to them, incidentally comparing their outlines and shapes, and establishing a background from which further learning will occur.

Teachers of students with low vision need to make certain that students have opportunities to be exposed to letters and words that can be seen clearly. An essential component of a prereading program for blind children is systematically introducing the braille symbols as well as flooding their environment with incidental opportunities to encounter braille: braille labels, storybooks, notes, and magazines.

BOX 16–3

GUIDELINES FOR WORKING WITH STUDENTS WITH VISUAL IMPAIRMENTS

- Lack of incidental learning often results in gaps in basic knowledge. When approaching a new task with unfamiliar students, it is best to assume that no prior learning has occurred. Then move on to more advanced levels as students demonstrate mastery of prerequisite steps.
- Learning occurs when students are actively involved in the task. Allow the students' hands to be involved in whatever you want them to learn. If they use vision, allow them to get as close as possible to the action. Especially with younger students, it is a good idea to work from behind them, so that they can feel and not resist the appropriate motor actions required to complete a task.
- Lack of visual experiences results in the need for increased opportunities to practice new skills. The learning rate of many of these students is relatively slow when compared to the learning rate of students with sight, who unconsciously practice new skills through visual experiences.
- Students with visual impairments learn best when real objects are used. A toy street sweeper is a poor substitute for learning about the real thing. Toys and miniatures of objects are best introduced after the students have had experience with the real object so that comparisons between the abstract and the concrete can be made.
- Students with visual impairments learn functional tasks more easily in natural environments and at naturally occurring times of the day.

A trip to a sculpture garden at the zoo provides a natural opportunity to encourage peer interactions.

HOW IS PARTICIPATION ENCOURAGED?

Inclusion

In 1900, the first public school program for blind students was established in Chicago. Using the resource room model, these students attended class with their peers without disabilities for most of the school day while receiving specialized instruction from a

BOX 16-4   MAKING A DIFFERENCE

STATEMENT BY THE JOINT ORGANIZATIONAL EFFORT

"Full inclusion," a philosophical concept currently advanced by a number of educators, is not a federal requirement of special education law. Proponents of "full inclusion" nevertheless take the position that all students with disabilities must receive their total instruction in the regular public school classroom regardless of individual needs. Unfortunately, "full inclusion" would eliminate all special placements, including "pull out" services, resource rooms and specialized schools. Such an arrangement would be seriously detrimental to the educational development of many students with disabilities.

We, the national organizations of and for the blind listed below, are firmly committed to appropriate educational opportunities designed to provide students with the competencies necessary to ensure full participation in society. It is significant to recognize that our field was the first to develop a broad range of special education options beginning with specialized schools as early as 1829, and extending to public school programs since 1900. These options have provided critically important educational preparation for several generations of highly successful and independent blind people. Based on this long and impressive record of success in making optimal use of both special and public school programs to meet the diverse needs of blind students, we strongly agree upon the following:

- If provided with timely and adequate specialized services by appropriately certified teachers, students who are blind or visually impaired can develop skills that will enable them to achieve success and independence as responsible citizens in a fully integrated society. If these students do not receive appropriate instruction designed to develop competencies that meet the sensory deficits of blindness and low vision, critical learning opportunities will be lost, thus diminishing the potential for future accomplishments. In this context, ample opportunities for instruction in such areas as braille, abacus, orientation and mobility, and use of prescribed optical devices must be made available to students, as needed.
- Educational decisions must be made on a case by case basis consistent with the Individuals with Disabilities Education Act (IDEA) which guarantees a Free Appropriate Public Education in the "Least Restrictive Environment" (LRE) from among a "Full Continuum of Alternative Placements," based on the Individual Education Plan for each student. Educational decisions should not be made simply on the basis of philosophy, limited school budgets, administrative convenience, or concerns about socialization.
- Full inclusion in regular education classrooms for all students with disabilities irrespective of individual needs is in sharp conflict with procedural guarantees of IDEA.
- Least Restrictive Environment and Full Continuum of Alternative Placements are critically important IDEA

A standardized form of braille was not established until 1932; and a fast and easy method of writing braille, using the Perkins brailler, was not invented until 1951. Educational inclusion for blind students was particularly challenging without these critical tools of literacy.

Retrolental fibroplasia is an older term for the condition now described as *retinopathy of prematurity.*

teacher provided by the state's residential school program. Other large cities adopted the Chicago model during the next several years, but most blind students during the first half of the twentieth century received their education at residential schools. These programs graduated educated individuals, many of whom married, worked, and interacted in their communities as full participants.

In 1941, an alarming increase was noted in the incidence of blindness in premature infants due to a condition then called **retrolental fibroplasia** (now labeled retinopathy of prematurity). By 1950, school systems around the country were inundated by the families of children with visual impairments who wanted their children to be educated. The residential schools did not have the capacity to meet the high demand, so local school districts, which for the first time had a large enough base of students with visual impairments to justify hiring special teachers, established their own resource or itinerant programs (Lowenfeld, 1975).

Accounts by individuals involved in this exciting and innovative time of local program development are filled with hopefulness and optimism for the future (American Foundation for the Blind, 1954, 1957; Hatlen, 1980–1981). Satisfied that the drawbacks associated with residential schools (removal from family and community) had been eliminated, families and educators were convinced that they had found the answer to educating all students with visual impairments through inclusion. Many residential schools for the blind

provisions. LRE is not one sole physical location. It is, rather, a principle, which if properly applied, matches the need of the student with an appropriate school setting which provides meaningful challenges, realistic expectations, and maximum opportunities for achievement and development of healthy self-esteem.

- The regular education classroom may be considered the LRE if the student possesses sufficient readiness and survival skills and can be provided adequate supports, specialized services (from personnel trained in education of the visually impaired), and opportunities to develop skills commensurate with his or her potential. Extreme caution must be exercised so that full inclusion does not result in "full submersion," social isolation, "lowered" self-esteem, poor performance, or a setting in which services are unavailable.

- In cases where the needs of the student cannot be met in the regular classrooms, an alternative education must be provided and be recognized as the LRE for that particular student. Such alternative placements should not be negatively viewed as discriminatory or as "segregated" settings when legitimately warranted to develop the needed skills for future integration in school and society.

- Since it has been clearly demonstrated that blind children benefit from interacting with disabled and non-disabled children, both interaction opportunities should be fully encouraged in whatever setting that is considered appropriate. We believe that the mandate in IDEA

which states that "to the maximum extent appropriate, children with disabilities [should be] educated with children who are non-disabled," does not intend that blind children avoid interaction with each other.

We strongly urge that decision makers carefully consider and be sensitive to the impact of reform initiatives on the education of students with visual disabilities. Caution must be exercised to ensure that educational philosophy and trends such as full inclusion do not seriously endanger appropriate and specialized services for students who are blind or visually impaired. If properly implemented, IDEA can provide legal safeguards to ensure that all individual children can realize their full potential for independence and success.

AMERICAN COUNCIL OF THE BLIND

AMERICAN FOUNDATION FOR THE BLIND

ASSOCIATION FOR EDUCATION AND REHABILITATION OF THE BLIND AND VISUALLY IMPAIRED

BLINDED VETERANS ASSOCIATION

CANADIAN COUNCIL OF THE BLIND

CANADIAN NATIONAL INSTITUTE FOR THE BLIND

NATIONAL FEDERATION OF THE BLIND

NATIONAL LIBRARY SERVICE FOR THE BLIND AND PHYSICALLY HANDICAPPED

began closing their doors or accepting a population of students with multiple disabilities, including blindness.

By the time the first wave of this new generation was graduating from high school, however, people began to express quiet doubts about the efficacy of these models for all students. Although many pupils had achieved well and were prepared to go to college or find adult employment, too many other graduates had very limited social and daily living skills (Hatlen, LeDuc, & Canter, 1975; Hoben & Lindstrom, 1980). Educators began to evaluate the needs of these graduates and the ways in which their school programs had failed them. They also evaluated their more successful graduates. The result of this self-review was a resounding declaration of support for individualized services designed to meet individualized needs, taking place in the environment that best facilitates learning for each particular student (California Leadership Action Team for the Visually Impaired, 1985; Curry & Hatlen, 1988; Huebner & Koenig, 1991; Tuttle, 1986). Although IDEA has strengthened the presumption of placement in favor of inclusion, it remains, first and foremost, a law that calls for individualization that leads to specified outcomes. Box 16–4 presents a position statement on this issue signed by several organizations of and for blind persons in the United States and Canada, each of which makes a difference for people with visual impairments.

Currently less than 15 percent of blind and visually impaired students are served outside of the regular school (U.S. Department of Education, 1995). As you can see in Figure

FIGURE 16–11 *Educational placement of students with visual impairments in the 1993–1994 school year*

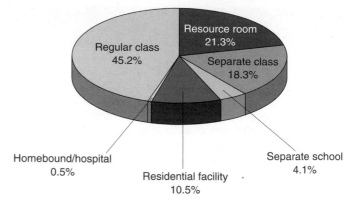

Note: From U.S. Department of Education (1995). *To assure the free appropriate public education of all children with disabilities: Seventeenth annual Report to Congress on the implementation of the Individuals with Disabilities Education Act.* Washington, DC: Author.

16-11, in the 1993–1994 school year, 45 percent of of students were served primarily in the general education class, with another 21 percent receiving services for more than 60 percent of the school day in a general education class. Residential schools across the nation educate little more than 10 percent of the total number of students with visual impairments.

Inclusion is valued and practiced by educators of students with visual impairments, as you can see from the suggestions provided in the accompanying box, "Inclusion Tips."

Most educators of students with visual impairments consider each of these options equally; they do not perceive one type of placement as better than the others or feel that students assigned to a particular option have more potential than others. They reject the notion that a residential placement, for example, is by definition more restrictive than a resource room. Instead, they believe that a student is in a restrictive environment when the pupil's access to learning needed skills is restricted. These teachers generally are flexible, recognizing that as individuals' needs change, so might the appropriate placement. Their focus is on ensuring that the student has the skills necessary to be fully included as an adult. Some students, like Tracy, blossom throughout their time in school under the itinerant model, where time away from the general education classroom is carefully limited to ensure her inclusion in all activities. For other students who receive educational services in general education classes, but who need more intensive direct instruction to understand academic material and master functional skills, learning can be restricted even though opportunities for inclusion with students without disabilities are great. These youngsters are more appropriately served for a period of time in resource rooms or other pullout programs, or special classes or special schools, where more of their teachers understand the impact of visual impairment on learning and development and are skilled at meeting their many needs. They benefit from the flexibility of a system that recognizes that their needs are constantly changing and that it is reasonable that the place where their needs are met also may change.

As you know, the 1997 Amendments to IDEA require that special educators provide supplementary aids and services to support a student's access to and participation in the general curriculum. When you think about Tracy and students like her, you might guess that providing books and materials in braille or on computer disk might be an important job of her special education teacher. Of equal importance, however, is the special educator's job of teaching Tracy what she is not learning incidentally—what clothing brands are *in,* how to get an after-school job, and what to expect at a prom. Access to this kind of knowledge and acquisition of related skills are essential to Tracy's full participation in the general curriculum.

Inclusion Tips

	What You Might See	What You Might Be Tempted to Do	Alternate Responses	Ways to Include Peers in the Process
Behavior	The student is a loner on the playground, choosing to play or walk alone.	Allow the student to stay in class and read or do homework.	Teach the student board or card games.	Once the student has mastered the game, set up a game table during recess where anyone who wants to play can.
Social interactions	The student doesn't say hello to peers in hallways or acknowledge peers' presence when entering room.	Assume the student is stuck up and unfriendly.	Have entire class prepare autobiographies including life history, special interests, and photo or object identifiers for the student and others to study.	Teach peers to say both the student's name and their own in greeting, as student may not be able to recognize them from their voices alone.
Educational performance	The student is not learning new concepts or ideas as quickly as peers and needs experiences with concrete materials.	Expect less from the student or require the student to practice difficult skills over and over.	Create meaningful situations where use of a concept or idea is required by the student in a variety of novel environments.	Have the student act as cross-age tutor to other students who benefit from use of concrete materials in learning.
Classroom attitudes	The student might seem bored or uninterested during class demonstrations or teacher-directed activities.	Assume it is too difficult or simply ignore the inattention.	Make sure that the student can "see" teacher's materials by having copies of printed/brailled materials at the student's desk during lesson.	Have the student and peer help teacher prepare lesson by getting out materials and preparing overheads and hands-on materials for class use.

Collaboration

Professional Collaboration.   Professional collaboration begins in the office of the physician or optometrist who explains to the parents of a newly diagnosed child that there is hope for their child through appropriate and early educational services. Many teachers with specialization in visual impairments try to develop close relationships with the eye specialists in their geographic area so that referrals are made immediately. These affiliations also prove beneficial later when the teacher and the eye specialist share information about the medical and visual functioning of particular students, thereby improving ophthalmological, optometric, and educational services.

A major role of the teacher who specializes in visual impairments is to help other professionals understand and appreciate the impact of blindness and low vision on a student's learning and development. Ideally, these professionals work with the student together or jointly review videotapes of the student to explore creative options for assessing the student and combining intervention goals into rich, meaningful activities. This kind of professional collaboration should continue throughout the student's involvement in school.

For most students with visual impairments to achieve success in itinerant and resource room placements, close collaboration with general educators is essential. Itinerant and resource teachers are responsible for getting assignments far enough in advance to make them accessible for their students. Most general education teachers need some initial coaching on how to adapt their teaching style to benefit students enrolled in their classes. They also need a basic understanding of how students with visual impairments in their classes experience the world and learn new material and what level of expectations are appropriate.

The accompanying box, "Collaboration Tips," describes how Tracy, her family, and the school collaborated to create the opportunity for her to be a member of the school's marching band.

As older students prepare to leave school, collaborative relationships between educators and the service agencies assigned to work with adults become essential for successful transition. When she attends college, Tracy will need to contract with a local orientation and mobility specialist to receive training in her new environment and probably with the college's disability resource center to arrange for needed accommodations. She may need resources to which she can turn if she experiences discrimination based on her disability. Establishing these linkages while still in high school will ease the transition to adult functioning.

Family Collaboration.

Few parents are prepared to raise a child with a visual impairment. Often parents have never met a blind person, have no idea of the capabilities of people with visual impairments, and are unaware of the special needs of infants with visual impairments and how parents can enhance their child's motor, language, and social development.

An early role of the teacher who has specialized in visual impairment (preferably one who has had additional preparation in early childhood intervention strategies) is to be a listener. Parents need to talk about their experiences, their emotions, and their conflicting feelings of ignorance, fear, despair, and hope. By listening, the teacher learns much about the strengths of the family and over time promotes the development of trust that will be essential for effective collaboration and intervention.

Throughout this early period, effective teachers of students with visual impairments encourage positive thinking and high expectations. When parents hear of the accomplishments of other blind children—of the possibilities for their children—they often begin to change their own attitudes about blindness and are eager to become involved in their child's early development.

Having developed trust and hopefulness, special teachers can begin to make suggestions for families to try to enhance the learning opportunities of their infants, using trial and error to discover what works for one family or child but not for another. Close and frequent collaboration with parents can be extremely constructive and has powerful rewards. Parents can identify problems, ask questions, make suggestions for intervention, and become confident about their positive role in the development of their sons and daughters (see "My Voice," Box 16–5).

In best practice, the collaborative efforts between families and teachers continue throughout a student's school career. Every new development in the child's life can present a baffling situation for the parent: how to teach a youngster to cut meat, how to assist a young woman to handle her menstrual period, or how to counsel a sixteen-year-old with low vision about driving. If the parent and teacher have a well-established relationship, it becomes natural to discuss these issues and problem solve them together.

Imagine the effect if someone visiting your home held your baby with a visual impairment high in the air and said aloud, "I wonder what you'll be when you grow up. You look like a lawyer to me!" Great expectations are key to the success of all children.

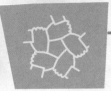

Collaboration Tips

MODIFYING THE ENVIRONMENT FOR INCLUSION IN EXTRACURRICULAR SCHOOL ACTIVITIES

COLLABORATION GOAL To identify adaptations and provide support to include a student who is totally blind in the marching band.

Collaborators	Roles and Preparation	Possible Barriers	Solutions to Barriers	Modifications to Implementation	Ongoing Evaluation
Student	Plan how to explain proposed adaptations to band coordinator.	Fear of failure.	Role-play explanation with teacher of visually impaired.	Create braille list of potential modifications to use in explanation to band coordinator.	Journal of band experiences with successes and difficulties.
Parents	Make a list of student's inherent musical strengths and successes.	May be concerned that student will be hurt if unsuccessful.	Keep other musical options open; plan ways to support and encourage.	Accept student's choices that may be mistakes and allow her to learn from them.	Regularly dialogue with her about progress to share successes and concerns.
Marching band coordinator	Bring music and marching routines for discussion.	Lack of knowledge of potential adaptations.	Willingness to make adaptations for student's success.	May need to make minor changes to routines to accommodate student needs.	Keep records of routines that work and why.
Orientation and mobility specialist	Network with other orientation and mobility specialists to find ways to help student.	Lack of time to meet with orientation and mobility specialists.	Use the Internet to find ideas others have used.	Meet intensively with student and peers to implement new routines being learned.	Help student to evaluate the successful solutions.
Special educator for students with visual impairments	Meet with marching band coordinator and then prepare musical scores in braille.	May not know braille music code.	Identify resource personnel throughout country to assist in locating scores.	Have student order materials or determine if different technique is needed.	Reward student for successes in new skills developed.
Administrator	Bring regulations about legal requirements for inclusion.	Concern with possible accidents and insurance liability.	Inform all collaborators that students are entitled to full participation in all school activities.	Contact advocacy groups for legal support if necessary.	Sponsor event to recognize efforts of team to create inclusion for student.
Peers	Make a list of ways students can be supportive: e.g., offering ride assistance.	May not be familiar with student's needs.	Get together with student to discuss needs.	Plan ways to help: student offers to pay gas for ride assistance.	Have meeting with teacher of visually impaired to review how it's going.

BOX 16-5 **MY VOICE**

TOM AND KRIS KIEL

As parents, we feel the responsibility of raising a healthy, happy, and productive child. When a visual disability affects your child, the pressures and responsibilities become even greater. We have found that the major resources available to us are our attitude and our sense of humor. We must not let ourselves focus on Tracy's blindness but rather on the whole child in which her blindness is just one small part of her whole being.

She is a sophomore who is being included in our local school, and we realize how important it is to her to fit in with her peers. We have tried to challenge her in every aspect of her life, allowing her to explore and experience as much as possible. For example, when she wanted to know how high her house was, we put up the extension ladder and took her onto the roof. She now has a perception of how high it is. We feel that in order for her to fit in she must have the ability to understand what is happening around her, even when she cannot see it. She must be able to perceive or sense by what she hears and what she knows. Her life's experiences are the foundations that equip her to build bridges among her peers.

We as parents must use our own common sense and take command of our child's education. Each child is unique, and his or her learning style must be individualized to meet personal special needs. Tracy has attended our local public school since she was four years old. Our expectations for Tracy in school are that she will always be challenged. We have seen in her early school years how learning braille opened up her world and have watched the enjoyment she has found in her leisure reading. Assistive technology has also played an important role in Tracy's education. It has helped her to work more independently, thus becoming more self-sufficient.

Perhaps most important to us as parents has been the way attitude, life's experiences, and education can be woven together as the foundation for a happy and productive life. To laugh at life's experiences gives you the wisdom to build a brighter tomorrow.

Tom and Kris Kiel
Tracy's parents

❧ If you were at a party and could not see well, how would you locate a group of people to talk to? How would you break into their conversation? Once you talked with members of the group, how would you recognize them the next time you met?

Peer Collaboration. For many youngsters with visual impairments, the social benefits of inclusion do not occur unless teachers and parents specifically direct their efforts toward this end (Hoben & Lindstrom, 1980; Sacks, 1992). Visual impairment has the ability to interfere with relationships in a variety of ways. Interactions in informal group situations are particularly difficult. Natural opportunities for socializing provided at school (physical education, lunch, and recess) often are visually and auditorially confusing and tend to emphasize the student's weaknesses (e.g., mobility or ball-handling skills) and differences. Even group work in classrooms does not always have the desired social result: for example, a blind ten-year-old who had just worked with some classmates in a cooperative lesson reported that he was not sure of their names.

These kinds of problems can be reduced by having students work in pairs and by allowing social as well as work-related conversation. Students with visual impairments who have adequate conversation skills generally can connect with a sighted peer in a one-on-one situation, which sometimes leads to planned contacts for after-school interactions. Many orientation and mobility instructors include a sighted peer on a mobility lesson that ends at a bakery or ice cream store, thereby providing the opportunity for socializing.

❧ How do teenagers who are blind or have low vision handle dating? For the best answers, ask other teens and young adults who experience this disability.

When planning peer interactions, teachers should not imply that the sighted student is always more capable than the visually impaired student. If they use peer tutoring, teachers should allow the student with visual impairment an equal opportunity to provide assistance to another pupil. These students need to know that they have something of value to offer other students, just as they have something to learn.

For students who are served in itinerant programs, and frequently for those served in the resource room model, there are few opportunities to interact with peers with similar disabilities. This situation often is cited as a major disadvantage of these two service-delivery models. Students are able to learn about and accept their disability from other students who are blind or visually impaired. In these interactions, the tricks of living successfully can be shared by the experts: people who are living the same experience. Many blind adults report that it was at camp or in other situations where sighted children were not involved that they felt most at ease and comfortable with themselves. This phenomenon is natural; you probably would feel more comfortable with a group of your peers than with a group of octogenarians. Successful educational programs provide frequent and continuing opportunities for sharing among peers with visual impairments.

Community Collaboration. Adults with visual impairments can provide a positive force of hope and inspiration. Educators can rely on these individuals to assist them as they prepare students for careers, independent living, mobility, self-advocacy, and adjustment.

Educators also should develop other collaborative links to the community. Service organizations, such as the Lions Club, have been invaluable over the years in providing financial assistance to students with visual impairments who need expensive eye care, glasses, or electronic equipment, thus making a significant difference in the lives of many students with visual impairments. Local business owners and employees provide critical opportunities to practice emerging social, career, and independent living skills. Store and restaurant owners near one residential school learned to avoid being overly helpful to students who came by to shop, thereby allowing the students to practice their communication and assertiveness skills. When one student expressed an interest in working at the pet store that she had often visited during orientation and mobility lessons, her teachers and the manager of the business worked together to help her better understand the kinds of jobs she might be able to do in the store. After a period of successful volunteering, the young woman eventually was hired to work part time after school and on weekends.

Careers

You have already been introduced to two of the primary service providers for students with blindness or low vision: teachers with specialization in visual impairments and orientation and mobility specialists. Special certification to work with students with visual impairments (birth to age twenty-one) is required in most states. Preparation for these careers involves obtaining either a bachelor's or master's degree with course work that emphasizes the needs of children and youth who are visually impaired.

Because the work encompasses so many areas of instruction, offers so much flexibility, and results in observable student success, it is not unusual for professionals to remain in these careers for many years. In Box 16–6, "My Voice," Donna McNear, Tracy's itinerant teacher, describes the satisfaction she receives from her job.

The braille transcriber is another professional critical to students' academic success. A transcriber, who spends hours learning the hundreds of rules needed to transcribe print into braille accurately, must be adept at adapting materials to meet students' needs. This expertise includes adapting articles, chapters, and entire books as well as pictures, maps, charts, and graphs. Special training is required to transcribe textbooks, and foreign language, mathematics, computer, and music books. Many braillists volunteer their time, although in larger districts some are paid.

WHAT ARE PROGRAM OPTIONS?

Early Intervention and Preschool Years

When Megan Smith was born, her parents, Beth and Kevin Smith of Sacramento, California, had two surprises awaiting them. For starters and contrary to all their expectations, Megan was totally blind in one eye and had only the barest of sight in her other eye. But their second surprise was how much Megan could learn and how much they could learn to help her with the assistance of an early intervention program.

BOX 16–6

MY VOICE

DONNA MCNEAR

"To teach is to learn twice" is a quotation I've placed in my home, my notebook, and my office (J. Joubert, 1754–1824). As a teacher of children with visual impairments, I am continually traveling a path of learning. My work day is immersed in learning to create caring school communities and learning opportunities where children can be successful.

As an itinerant teacher in seven rural school districts in east central Minnesota, I begin my day in my car, traveling to see children in their home school districts. At the first school, I observe Chad, a preschool student with low vision, and assist the school staff in providing materials and arranging the classroom so he can easily see and participate in all activities.

I also stop at the high school to teach Tracy, who reads and writes in braille. I bring the worksheets the teachers have given me to put into braille and quickly visit with teachers between classes to answer questions and problem-solve. Mr. Johnson, the science teacher, and I discuss the possibilities of providing tactual materials in a genetics unit. He comes up with a great idea and benefits from my support, approval, and encouragement. I meet with Tracy who wants help learning new Nemeth code braille signs in the beginning algebra math unit and wants to review the route to the new girls' locker room for gym.

After an hour reviewing the information with Tracy, I travel to the next town and have lunch with the adapted physical education teacher. This gives us the opportunity to plan the physical education activities for Shannon, an eighth-grade student who is blind and who is now working on swimming goals. After lunch I go to my office to make phone calls and have a meeting with the braillist, Connie. She wants to discuss the format for braille music.

On my way to the next town, I make a brief stop at Cory's house. He is fourteen months old and has low vision. He just received glasses, and I spend a few minutes observing and assessing the difference his glasses make in how he uses his vision in daily activities at home. His parents also want to share new information from his ophthalmologist and ask a few questions.

My day ends with a mobility lesson with Annie, a high school student who is blind. I am also dually certified as an orientation and mobility specialist, which allows children in rural areas to receive needed training. We review the route to the post office so Annie can pick up a package.

Sharing a description of my day with my family at dinner, I remember a statement attributed to Lewis Mumford: "It is not what one does, but in a manifold sense what one realizes, that keeps existence from being vain and trivial." I do many things in a day for children, but what I realize about teaching and my students is what my work life is all about. I realize I am a mirror, a window, and a doorway for my students: a mirror to reflect positively who they are and their capabilities, talents, and dreams; a window to show them their opportunities, possibilities, choices, and other ways of being; and, finally, a doorway for their future.

I have also realized my own mission in my work life: I see the meaning in my labor (beyond the reward of a check); I see my abilities recognized and valued; I view myself as a craftsperson, creating something of beauty and value; I have a job that is large enough for my spirit; and I feel I am leaving the world better than when I found it. Through my day-to-day teaching I have learned love, fortitude, respectfulness, and humbleness. I have also learned to be delicate and to have passion for my time with children.

Donna McNear
Itinerant teacher; Minnesota

Donna McNear uses a variety of ways to help students who are visually impaired learn more about their world.

Within months after her birth, Megan and her family began to receive once-a-week visits from Lois Harrell, a specialist in the area of visual impairment. Lois helped Beth *think like a blind person,* like her daughter Megan, to comprehend what the lack of sight meant for Megan's development. In that way, Beth could stimulate Megan and thereby compensate for that lack without delaying Megan's development. For example, many babies have brightly colored mobiles hanging above their cribs that they can respond to. Megan had mobiles made of bells, rattles, and tactually interesting objects that she could reach. Similarly, many babies naturally learn to crawl and explore their environments. Megan, however, had to learn through systematic instruction from Lois and Beth how to rock and move her arms and legs, all preliminary to learning to crawl.

Lois also helped Beth, Kevin, and Anna, who is Megan's older sister, move beyond grief to determination and optimism. By being positive about Megan's development and obvious intellectual precociousness, by showing them how much Megan had progressed from one month to the next, and by giving them examples of other blind children who had been expected to live rewarding lives, Lois encouraged great expectations in all of them. Finally, Lois spent a lot of time with Anna, who is two years and a few months older than Megan, talking with her about her sister's blindness, assuring her that her sister would be just fine as soon as she learned how to "see" by other means, and making certain that any publicity that came to Megan also reflected Anna's own commitment to her sister.

What happened to Megan and her family is not unusual in early intervention programs. These programs generally are home based, although many successful programs also offer a center-based component where parents of infants go to observe preschool children with visual impairments and to meet the families of other youngsters who are blind or who have low vision. The focus of early intervention and preschool education is to help parents understand the effects of visual impairment on learning and to present effective methods that reduce the impact of these effects on development. These programs emphasize strategies that enhance the child's acquisition of body image, language, early self-help skills, sensorimotor skills, development of concepts, gross- and fine-motor abilities, orientation, and early social interactions in the home, school, and community environments where young children spend their time.

Megan entered an early education program when she turned three. Now at age five in her public school class, which is only for students with visual impairments, Megan is learning to read and write braille, use a cane as part of her orientation and mobility training in school and the school's neighborhood, and do calisthenics as part of physical education. Her intellectual gifts are increasingly evident in the questions she asks her teacher, Andrea Slavin: *What are stoplights and why are they? How do car motors work?* Her accelerated training in braille reading, coupled with her mother's and older sister's braille training, make it possible for her to read independently and to have brailled books read to her at night. Her social life consists of friendships within her own family (she now has two younger siblings, twins Kevin and Audrey), with her cousins, and with classmates in her child-care program and at preschool.

Megan is now aware of her differentness. Considering her one prosthetic eye, she asks family and friends, "Do you have a hard eye and a squishy eye?" Concerning her blindness she asks, "Why am I blind? Do you have long eyes so you can see things far away? Why don't I have long eyes?" Her family and her teacher, Andrea Slavin, reassure her: "You were born that way, and it's nothing to be ashamed of. It's not your fault or anyone else's."

Beth and Kevin are in no hurry to enter Megan into kindergarten or a more inclusive program. "We never rushed Anna, and we aren't rushing the twins." When Megan is ready for a general education class, with its hourly bells and many activities, she will go there, probably a year later than is typical. There is another reason for that slight delay: Megan was born with a septal wall defect and has had open heart surgery. The surgery was successful, and now Megan, who has been very short and light for her age, is beginning to gain height and weight.

Is a cut watermelon the same as a watermelon that is whole? How can they both be watermelons? Which should a student with a visual impairment recognize? How did it get cut? Preschool programs are designed to stress the importance of being involved in every part of an activity so that the pupil understands the relationships among objects in the environment.

Meanwhile, her transition options include part-time participation in a local preschool (with help from a consultant in the area of visual impairment) and recreation and play-time activities with peers without disabilities in the kindergarten program. Beth expects Megan to use both options during the year she delays starting kindergarten.

Again, Megan's preschool program is fairly typical. These programs for children with visual impairments, which in highly populated areas are organized specifically for this population, continue early intervention goals and provide the multiplicity of experiences that are the foundation for learning. Most of the activities are hands on, meaningful, and related to real-life experiences. Students make their own snacks, wash their dishes, and find opportunities to change their clothes often, thereby practicing needed daily living skills. They collect tangible memories of their day and include them in braille or large-print experience stories that they dictate to their teachers. Teachers facilitate and encourage their students' movement, meaningful language, exploration, and the ability to control the environment to reduce the impact of the visual impairment on development.

Many students with visual impairments are in heterogeneously grouped preschools and in preschools for children without disabilities. With the proper supports, these programs can be valuable learning environments for some children. It is easy to forget, however, that sighted children are acquiring many of the benefits of these programs through incidental learning, which is often unavailable to those with visual impairments. Although the students with visual impairments participate, there is potential that they will fall behind the others in the class unless they get supplemental help.

Elementary Years

Imagine that you have absolutely no sight at all and are at the top of the beginners' ski slope in Aspen, Colorado. You have been given your first pair of skis and told, "You are about to ski for the first but not the last time. It takes something extreme to get you to believe in yourself, and nothing is more extreme than what you are about to master. Get ready, get set, go!"

That's what Mary Gordon of Lawrence, Kansas, has been doing for eighteen years with students who have visual impairments throughout Kansas and Missouri. That and more.

When her students are in music class, she presents sheet music in the braille music code. When they are in art class, she creates papier-mâché models of the Venus de Milo, Michelangelo's *David,* and the Parthenon so that her students can handle and "see" the art. When they study geography, she provides maps with raised continents and tactually different countries. When they are in science class, she reaches into the formaldehyde jar, extracts the specimens, and describes them as students handle them. And when students seem exhausted, she is always ready with an encouraging word for the student and a teaching strategy for the general educators. Mary says,

> *When you can't see the chalkboard and you can't see exactly where the rooms are and you can't see this and you can't see that, it takes twice as much energy to get through the day as it does for someone with sight. So I provide instruction, materials, and support for students who may require many hours to master what a sighted child can learn through casual observation.*
>
> *My philosophy . . . has been to assure my students the opportunity to learn everything their sighted peers do. Turning the philosophy into reality requires that every handout, map, graph, or other instructional device used in the regular classroom be transformed into large print, braille, or a tactual display so that my students have access to everything their sighted classmates use.*

Mary does one other thing: She teaches inclusion.

> *While providing tactual experience is essential, I don't believe that it is enough. . . . Each blind and visually impaired student should also become a real and integral part of his or her classroom rather than a passive receptor of information. Since so much of our social interaction is visual, blind children*

must learn behaviors of sighted persons in order to obtain acceptance from their peers. To accomplish this, my students and I spend many hours practicing social skills that other students learn by observing. Learning to face the person to whom they are speaking, standing or sitting with appropriate postures, and eliminating mannerisms which might detract from their appearance are all imperative. Imagine how you might "learn" a language which you cannot hear, and you have some idea of the challenge of students who must present themselves in a fashion which they have never seen in order to be accepted in a sighted society.

As Mary Gordon has told you, elementary school is the time for sighted children to develop a positive self-image, lay a solid foundation in academic and communication skills, and safely explore the world. For pupils with visual impairments, the focus of the educational program is the same as that for students with vision; however, the techniques for accomplishing these goals may be different, requiring specialists to teach or reinforce concepts presented in class. In addition, and depending on the student's needs, the teacher emphasizes the development of career-awareness skills, additional self-help skills, social skills, knowledge of human sexuality, knowledge of one's visual impairment, and early advocacy skills. At the same time, the orientation and mobility instructor may be increasing the environments in which the youngster can travel knowledgeably and safely.

Middle and Secondary Years

Martin Martinez groans as the alarm clock rings at 5:15. He wills himself to get out of bed, knowing that if he doesn't start moving right away he will miss his 6:30 bus. He turns on the light and looks through his clothes as he decides what to wear. Since it is cold outside, he chooses the heavy blue sweater to go with his white jeans. After quickly blow-drying his hair and moving closer to check it in the mirror, he tiptoes to the kitchen at the end of the trailer where he lives with his mother and little sister, Angela. As he prepares and eats his breakfast of hot cereal, orange juice, and toast, he thinks about the busy day ahead. Next, his lunch: he slices cheese for a sandwich, looks through the bags of chips for the familiar gold Fritos package, wraps two chocolate cookies, and throws a green apple in for good measure. Hearing the bus down the street, he runs into his mother's room, tells her it's time to get up for work, zips up his winter coat, and slides on the heavy backpack. As usual, there was no extra time this January morning.

As a senior in high school, Martin often thinks about graduation and his future. He wonders if he will be ready to make the move to living by himself in an apartment. Why, only five years ago he still couldn't make a sandwich or fix anything but cold cereal for breakfast. Living on his own, he will not be able to rely on his mother to shop, cook meals, or do laundry. Martin occasionally thinks that it might be better to live at home longer.

Martin's life has changed dramatically since entering middle school and being assigned first two periods, then only one hour, each day to the resource room of Sandi Serventi, the teacher of students with visual impairments. Until that time, most of his teachers had had low expectations for him, and his mother, not knowing how to deal with a child with a serious visual impairment, had tended to limit the demands placed on her son. Many of the adults in his life had assumed that his ability to see detail was better than it was; they considered him to be lazy and not motivated to learn, when in fact, his visual impairment was limiting his ability to learn without direct instruction.

Sandi, a teacher with many years of experience, recognized Martin's talents and the efforts he was making to *get by*. She immediately focused on increasing the types of literacy tools that Martin used to access the general education curriculum. Sandi taught him how to use tape recordings efficiently and introduced him to the use of a closed circuit television to enlarge printed assignments. She also convinced Martin of the value of using braille for reading and writing. Over the past four years, Martin has made remarkable progress in learning to read tactually and now reads approximately fifty words per minute. Although slower than the print reading of his peers, this rate is twice as fast as his own print reading speed! Sandi also spent some of the time that Martin was assigned to her resource room teaching Martin some basic skills of daily living, like learning to style his hair and prepare meals.

These days, Martin and Sandi usually work on transition skills. Today they are making a list of the utilities services that he will need to contact when he moves into an apartment. Martin practices his telephone and note-taking skills as he contacts directory assistance to request the telephone numbers of the different utility companies and writes them down on index cards inserted in his slate and stylus. Later, he will call to request additional information on having the utilities started.

On some days, Martin also works with Nancye Rubin, his orientation and mobility instructor. Recently, they have been exploring apartment complexes close to the vocational school where Martin will enroll next year. Although Martin never needs to use his cane in the familiar environment of Leon High, in new areas it is critical to have the cane to detect unfamiliar stairs, curbs, cracks in the sidewalk, and other unexpected hazards. He and Nancye will need to spend many long hours learning to negotiate safely the routes to use around the school's campus and to the grocery store, to the mall, and other community areas he will be using.

For some students, like Martin, the middle and high school years are a time to catch up, to learn skills that students with good vision have been learning incidentally but that are not used until the teen years. Special teachers of these visually impaired students generally have to spend more time with them to meet their academic and disability-specific needs, while at the same time students are enrolled in general education classes to meet the school's academic graduation requirements. Sometimes, graduation has to be delayed in order to master all the skills needed for successful independent adult living.

Tracy's situation is different than Martin's. She has received excellent ongoing intervention by teachers of the visually impaired and orientation and mobility specialists. She has few difficulties with access to the general education curriculum and needs very little direct academic assistance from her special education teacher. Like Martin and Sandi, though, Tracy and her special education teacher, Donna, focus on the more complex skills necessary for competent adult living. Tracy and Donna now meet only once a week to address these goals. Both Tracy and Martin, like many other young adults with visual impairments, will need to work with their orientation and mobility specialists to master difficult travel situations (e.g., use of buses, trains, or subways) or travel in complex environments (e.g., downtown business areas, snow-covered dirt roads, and wide, noisy intersections).

ℓ As with other disabilities, education for students with visual impairments needs to include the learning of skills that will help them seek and find gainful employment.

Transitional and Postsecondary Years

Not all students with visual impairments go to college any more than all sighted students do. But many of those who have been effectively educated can go to college. At the University of Kansas, and at many other institutions of higher education throughout the United States, students with visual impairments are taking advantage of their public school education. For example, Mindy Knepp, one of Mary Gordon's students during her twelve years in Lawrence, is studying music therapy. She gets around the large, hilly campus with help from her dog guide, Vanessa; by using the university's paratransit system for students with disabilities; and simply by asking students and faculty for assistance. She requires orientation and mobility training almost every semester because her classes move from building to building.

Her social network consists of fellow music therapy students, and accommodations in her academics are basically no different at the university level than they were in high school. They are still individualized but hard to secure. For example, Mindy advertises for readers and pays them with funds she gets from the state vocational rehabilitation agency. She prefers readers who take the same classes as she does. She rarely uses braille books, because they frequently are not available. Most of her professors accommodate her readily, although she has had difficulties with some teaching assistants. Mindy already plays the piano and guitar but will have to take classes in them, like every other music therapy student.

Another of Mary Gordon's students, Lisa Thompson, wanted to attend college but was apprehensive about her grades, filling out college applications, and taking the SATs. She reports that Mary helped her get excellent grades by staying after school several hours every evening. Mary also helped Lisa fill out applications to twelve different universities and read and filled in the answer sheet for the SATs. When Lisa graduated from Rice University in Houston, she won a National Scholastic Achievement Award administered by Recordings for the Blind and presented by President George Bush. At the White House ceremony Lisa was allowed only two guests. She had no problem selecting them: her mother, "the woman who brought me into the world," and Mary Gordon, "the woman who made me what I am today."

A VISION FOR THE FUTURE

Tracy finished high school about the same time she became eligible to vote. Having registered, she also became eligible for jury service; and sure enough, a year after registering to vote she was called to serve on the county's grand jury.

She was fascinated by the legal process: the presentation of testimony to the grand jury, which was investigating white-collar crime; the state's attorney general pleading for a criminal indictment; and the witnesses' use of the Fifth Amendment privilege against self-incrimination. Indeed, her interest was so piqued that she decided to study law. She graduated from college with a degree in political science. Her grades and law-school aptitude scores were so good that she was then admitted to the University of Minnesota's law school. There, she utilized appropriate accommodations, including special techniques for taking examinations, access technology to complete class assignments, and the employment of a person to serve as a reader of the vast amounts of material required to complete this degree. These accommodations allowed her to compete on an even plane with other law students; they did not provide her with differential standards of performance. She graduated from law school in the top fifth of her class based on her own well-developed skills.

Tracy is now an assistant state's attorney in the white-collar crime division. As a lawyer, she uses an accessible computer to retrieve cases. She knows her way around the courthouse because she has contracted with an orientation and mobility specialist, and she knows how to practice law effectively using the social, critical thinking, organizational, and life skills she developed as a result of the hard work of her parents, teachers, specialists, and herself.

What Would You Recommend . . .

1. To Tracy's teacher of the visually impaired as a response to Tracy's questions about the need for IEPs and the availability for specialized treatment as an adult who is blind?

2. For transition services for Tracy as she plans to move from her local community to college?

3. To parents of young children with visual impairments who want their children to grow up with attitudes and skills similar to Tracy's?

SUMMARY

WHAT IS VISUAL IMPAIRMENT?

- Legal blindness is defined as a central visual acuity of 20/200 or less in the better eye (with corrective lenses) or central visual acuity of greater than 20/200 if the field of vision is less than 20 degrees. Legal blindness is a measurement that is used primarily to entitle people for government or private-assistance programs.

- Within education, visual impairment, including blindness, is defined as an impairment in vision that adversely affects a student's educational performance. This definition emphasizes how a student uses vision.

- Students with visual impairments and blindness have a limited ability to model visually and learn incidentally from the environment. They are at risk of being experientially deprived because they are not able to learn about the world from a distance.

WHAT ARE EVALUATION PROCEDURES?

- Ophthalmologists determine the presence of a visual disorder.

- Optometrists and low vision specialists determine if the visual disorder can be corrected through lenses or other optical devices.

- A functional low vision evaluation determines how the student uses his or her vision in a variety of situations or circumstances.

- A Learning Media Assessment assists educators to determine the most efficient mode of reading and learning: braille, magnification, large print, and so on.

- Educators determine the effects of the visual impairment on the student's development of academic, communication, social/emotional, sensorimotor, orientation and mobility, daily living, and career/vocational skills. They use observations, parent and student interviews, and other informal testing procedures.

- Students learn through meaningful involvement in activities from beginning to end. Often they take a hands-on approach that maximizes the use of all senses, including vision. Through practice, they have increased opportunities to develop new skills.

- They are also exposed to real objects and meaningful experiences in natural environments at naturally occurring times of the day.

WHAT AND HOW DO PROFESSIONALS TEACH?

- Professionals meet the academic and communication needs of students through direct instruction, modification of methodology, and adaptation of materials.

- They meet the functional and life-skill needs of students to facilitate their eventual integration and full participation in adult society. Instruction must focus on those skills acquired incidentally by sighted students through vision and those skills that are specific to students who are blind or have visual impairments.

HOW IS PARTICIPATION ENCOURAGED?

- Most students with visual impairments who do not have other disabilities are educated for most of the school day in general education classrooms. Special education services for these students are provided by a teacher of the visually impaired who is assigned to that school either on a part-time or full-time basis.

- Professionals providing educational services to students with visual impairments support the full continuum of placement options and do not perceive any option as being more or less restrictive than others.

- Collaboration among professionals involves eye care specialists, general and special education teachers, related services personnel, and rehabilitation professionals. The role of the teacher of the visually impaired is to help other professionals understand and appreciate the impact of visual impairment on students' learning and development.

WHAT ARE PROGRAM OPTIONS?

- In early intervention and preschool programs, desirable strategies include home visits, parent and sibling support and information, parent training, teaching the infant to develop a sense of space and his or her body within space, teaching fundamental skills such as how to crawl, stimulating the infant's other skills (such as touch), and providing opportunities for experiential learning.

- In elementary school programs, the student learns to read and write with braille, magnification, or large print; participate in orientation and mobility training; do physical education; and develop friendships with sighted and blind peers.

- Professionals provide opportunities for students to develop competence, experience success, and acquire confidence in a variety of situations and circumstances.

- Collaboration with parents must continue throughout the time that their child is enrolled in school in order to maximize the child's potential.

- Students who have visual impairments must be provided opportunities to contribute equally—to help and be helped—during interactions with peers at school.

- In middle and secondary school programs, students' self-confidence, self-esteem, and social skills are especially important issues. Students with visual impairments are expected to learn everything their sighted peers learn but use methods that take blindness or low vision into account.

- In postsecondary education, students continue to receive orientation and mobility training. They adapt the way they learn but not necessarily what they learn: skills that prepare them for work or graduate school.

RESOURCES

BOOKS

Foundations of Education for Blind and Visually Handicapped Children and Youth: Theory and Practice. (1986). Edited by Geraldine T. Scholl. New York: American Foundation for the Blind. A comprehensive textbook for teachers of students with visual impairments. Includes information on definitions, development, and theory; components of a quality educational program; and special curriculum considerations.

Itinerant Teaching: Tricks of the Trade for Teachers of Blind and Visually Impaired Students. (1991). By Jean E. Olmstead. New York: American Foundation for the Blind. A practical book on meeting the needs of students with visual impairments who are placed in general education classes and receive services from an itinerant teacher of the visually impaired.

Low Vision: A Resource Guide With Adaptations for Students With Visual Impairments. (1991). By Nancy Levack. Austin, TX: Texas School for the Blind. A useful guide for teachers, parents, and others who work with students with low vision. Includes information on medical conditions, adaptations, teaching, and the impact of other physical impairments on visual performance.

Program Planning and Evaluation for Blind and Visually Impaired Students: National Guidelines for Excellence. (1989). By Jack Hazekamp and Kathleen M. Huebner. New York: American Foundation for the Blind. Guidelines for developing appropriate educational programs for students with visual impairments. Includes explanations of the unique educational needs related to visual impairment, methods for identifying and assessing those needs, planning and providing instruction and services, and organizing and supporting programs.

JOURNALS, MAGAZINES, AND CATALOGS

Journal of Visual Impairment and Blindness. The American Foundation for the Blind, 11 Penn Plaza, Suite 300, New York, NY 10001. Bimonthly journal for professionals in the field of visual impairment. The majority of the articles published are research related.

RE: view. Heldref Publications, 1319 Eighteenth Street NW, Washington, DC 20036-1802. Published quarterly by the Association for Education and Rehabilitation of the Blind and Visually Impaired. Includes both research-based and practical information for individuals who work with people who are visually impaired.

MULTIMEDIA

Blind and Visually Impaired Children . . . Can Do! Visually Impaired Preschool Services, 1215 South Third Street, Louisville, KY 40203. A series of videos on the development of children who are visually impaired. Includes "Seeing Things in a New Way: What Happens When You Have a Blind Baby," "Learning about the World: Concept Development," "Becoming a Can-do Kid: Self-help Skills," "Making Friends: Social Skills and Play," and "Going Places: Orientation and Mobility." New titles released in 1997 include: "Through their Eyes: An Introduction to Low Vision," "Moving Through the World: Gross Motor Skills and Play," "Hands-On Experience: Tactual Learning and Skills," and "Successfully Adapting the Preschool Environment."

Building Blocks: Foundations for Learning for Young Blind and Visually Impaired Children. (In English and Spanish) American Foundation for the Blind, 11 Penn Plaza, Suite 300, New York, NY 10001. Video presents the essential components of a successful preschool program for students with visual impairments.

Oh, I See! American Foundation for the Blind, 11 Penn Plaza, Suite 300, New York, NY 10001. Video suggests ways to help students who are blind and visually impaired adapt to the general education classroom.

Personal Touch: Braille for Lifelong Enrichment. The Hadley School for the Blind, 700 Elm Street, Winnetka, Illinois 60093-0299. Moving video that depicts the various ways that adults and children who are blind use braille for literacy.

Understanding Braille Literacy. American Foundation for the Blind, 11 Penn Plaza, Suite 300, New York, NY 10001. Video covers all critical components of a successful braille education program, including a positive attitude, fostering independence, teaching techniques, and use of braille in the home, school, and community.

The following videos are available at local rental and retail stores:

Eighty Steps to Jonah. (1969, G, U.S., color, 107 minutes). Fictional account of a loner charged with a crime who changes his outlook on life after stumbling on a camp for children who are blind.

Ice Castles. (1979, PG, U.S., color, 109 minutes). Ice skating champion becomes blind after an accident.

If You Could See What I Hear. (1982, PG, Canada, color, 103 minutes). Writer, composer, athlete, and TV personality Tom Sullivan is blind and tells his life story.

Mask. (1985, PG-13, U.S., color, 120 minutes). A teenager who is blind falls in love with a teenager who is disfigured with craniodiaphyseal dysplasia.

The Miracle Worker. (1962, not rated, U.S., B&W, 107 minutes). Oscar-winning biography of Helen Keller, who is deaf and blind, and her teacher Annie Sullivan.

A Patch of Blue. (1965, not rated, U.S., B&W, 105 minutes). A young white woman who is blind falls in love with an African American man.

Scent of a Woman. (1992, R, U.S., color, 137 minutes). The Colonel, who has recently become blind and is alcoholic and self-pitying, teams with Charlie, a student at a local prep school, for a weekend adventure.

Wild Hearts Can't Be Broken. (1991, G, U.S., color, 88 minutes). Sonora Webster is a 1930s "diving girl" who continues her career after losing her sight.

The following companies produce or distribute adaptive media:

Achrontech Intl., Inc., The Williamsville Executive Center, 5500 Main Street, Williamsville, NY 14221. (800) 245-2020. Distributes closed circuit televisions, speech synthesizers, optical character readers, and checkbook management programs adapted for use by users with visual impairments.

Arkenstone, 555 Oakmead Parkway, Sunnyvale, CA 94086-4023. (800) 444-4443. Distributes electronic reading systems and optical character readers modified for people with visual impairments.

Blazie Engineering, 105 East Jarrettsville Road, Forest Hill, MD 21050. (410) 893-9333. Distributes electronic note takers, braille embossers, screen reader software, speech synthesizers, and specialized software.

Duxbury Systems, 435 King Street, P.O. Box 1504, Littleton, MA 01460. (508) 486-9766. Develops and markets software for braille in English and other languages on MS-DOS, Windows, Macintosh, and other systems.

Enabling Technologies Company, 3102 SE Jay Street, Stuart, FL 34997. (800) 777-3687. Distributes braille embossers.

Humanware, Inc., 6245 King Road, Loomis, CA 95650. (800) 722-3393. Distributes electronic note takers, braille printers, mobility devices, electronic braillers, speech synthesizers, optical character readers, and closed circuit televisions.

Raised Dot Computing. 408 South Baldwin, Madison, WI 53703. (800) 347-9594. Offers braille-generating software.

TeleSensory, Inc., 455 North Bernardo Avenue, Mountain View, CA 94043. (415) 960-0920. Distributes electronic note takers, braille printers and embossers, screen reader software, speech synthesizers, audio signage, closed circuit televisions, and specialized software.

ON-LINE INFORMATION AND USEFUL DATABASES

Some websites focusing on visual impairment and blindness:

American Foundation for the Blind. Internet address: http://www.afb.org/afb/. This site presents a history of services to individuals with visual impairments, describes the services and projects sponsored by the American Foundation for the Blind, and provides information about the technology used by people with visual impairment.

American Printing House for the Blind. Internet address: http://www.aph.org/. This site provides an overview of policies for eligibility and a catalog of books and educational materials available from the American Printing House for the Blind.

Blind Links. Internet address: http://seidata.com/~marriage/rblind.html. Provides links to organizations, vendors, and listservers in the field of visual impairment.

DB-Link. Internet address: http://tr.wosc.osshe.edu/dblink/index2.htm. Provides information on issues related to deaf-blindness, such as communication, travel, and family concerns.

Resources for Parents and Teachers of Blind Kids. Internet address: http://www.az.com/~dday/blindkids.html. Provides information about services, equipment, and fun home-based activities for parents of children with visual impairment.

Texas School for the Blind and Visually Impaired. Internet address: http://www.tsbvi.edu/index.htm. Describes services at the Texas School for the Blind and Visually Impaired and provides links to educational resources, organizations, and more.

ORGANIZATIONS

American Council of the Blind (ACB). 1155 Fifteenth Street NW, Suite 720, Washington, DC 20005. A membership organization of people who are visually impaired. Provides referrals, scholarships, leadership and legislative training, and consumer advocacy. ACB-Parents is a special-interest affiliate for parents of children who are visually impaired.

American Foundation for the Blind (AFB). 11 Penn Plaza, Suite 300, New York, NY 10001. Provides information and referral; promotes leadership in the field; monitors legislation affecting blind persons; and facilitates collaboration among medical, educational, orientation and mobility, rehabilitation professionals, and parents and families.

American Printing House for the Blind (APH). 1839 Frankfort Avenue, P.O. Box 6085, Louisville, KY 40206-0085. A national organization for the production of literature and the manufacture of educational aids for persons with visual impairment, primarily individuals of school age.

Association for Education and Rehabilitation of the Blind and Visually Impaired (AER). P.O. Box 22397, Alexandria, VA 22304. This professional organization promotes all phases of education and work for persons of any age who are blind or have low vision. Holds national and regional conferences as well as workshops on topics of interest to educators, rehabilitation professionals, orientation and mobility specialists, and family members.

National Association for Parents of the Visually Impaired (NAPVI). P.O. Box 317, Watertown, MA 02272-0317. Provides support for parents and families of visually impaired children and serves as a national clearinghouse for information. Holds annual national conferences, and many local chapters also meet regularly. Publishes a parent newsletter, *Awareness.*

National Federation of the Blind (NFB). 1800 Johnson Street, Baltimore, MD 21230. A membership organization of blind persons with affiliates in all states. Monitors legislation affecting blind people, assists in promoting needed services, provides scholarships, maintains an assistive technology center, and conducts public education programs.

A

Absence seizure   Causes the person to lose consciousness only briefly.

Acquired brain injury   Includes injuries caused by internal as well as external forces.

Acquired immune deficiency syndrome (AIDS)   The final stage in the progression of human immunodeficiency virus. The infected person has a T4 cell count less than 200 and one or more opportunistic infections.

Acute condition   Develops quickly; the symptoms are intense and often end quickly. Pneumonia is an example.

Adaptive behavior   Skill areas that are central to successful life functioning, such as communication, self-care, home living, and social skills.

Albinism   A hereditary condition that often results in lack of pigmentation of the skin and parts of the eye, resulting in reduced visual acuity (low vision) and usually, legal blindness.

American Sign Language (ASL)   The sign language of the Deaf community in the United States; it possesses all of the grammatical complexity of spoken languages.

Amniocentesis   A technique for prenatal diagnosis that involves withdrawing and studying, between the fifteenth and seventeenth weeks of pregnancy, the amniotic fluid that surrounds the baby.

Amniotic band syndrome   A condition in which fibrous bands on the outside of the placenta contract and restrict normal growth and development of the fetus.

Anoxia   The termination of the flow of oxygen reaching body tissues.

Anterior visual pathway   The parts of the eye that are located in front of the lens (i.e., pupil, iris, cornea, etc.).

Anxiety disorder   Characterized by overwhelming fear, worry, and/or uneasiness. The condition includes phobia, generalized anxiety disorder, panic disorder, obsessive-compulsive disorder, and post-traumatic stress disorder.

Aphasia   An injury to certain areas of the brain that results in problems with speaking or total loss of speech. Possible causes are traumatic brain injury, lack of oxygen, stroke, or an illness that causes brain swelling.

Applied behavior analysis   The systematic collection and graphing of data to ascertain a student's progress toward a specific objective.

Articulation   The speaker's production of individual or sequenced speech sounds.

Asperger disorder   Characterized by behavioral and social features associated with autism but without significant delays in language development or impairments in cognition.

Assessment   The specific instruments used to gather information and usually includes standardized and nonstandardized tests; the student's cumulative records and work products; and teacher and other observations of the student in the classroom, other school environments, and even outside the school.

Assistive technology   Devices or services that restore, maintain, or replace lost bodily functions through the use of technology.

Asymptomatic, or latency, stage   During this stage, a person has the human immunodeficiency virus in his or her bloodstream but does not have outward symptoms of illness.

Attachment disorder   Behavior disorders and difficulty empathizing with others caused by a lack of bonding to a primary caregiver during early childhood.

Attention-deficit/hyperactivity disorder (AD/HD)   Characterized by symptoms of inattention, hyperactivity, and/or impulsivity that are developmentally inappropriate and are not the result of other conditions. Symptoms must have occurred before age seven and exist in two or more settings. Students may be classified with one of three types: predominantly inattentive, predominantly hyperactive-impulsive, or combined.

Audiogram   A graph used to display the results of a hearing test; intensity is plotted on the ordinate and frequency on the abscissa.

Audiologist   A specialist who is trained to identify and evaluate hearing disorders, select and evaluate hearing aids, and recommend rehabilitation.

Augmentative and alternative communication   Techniques and devices used by students to supplement whatever degree of naturally acquired speech they possess.

Augmentative communication device   Equipment that is used to increase an individual's ability to communicate effectively.

Authentic assessment   Requires students to generate a response, often through developing a product or demonstrating a skill.

B

Basic psychological processes   The ability to interpret information received through auditory (oral), visual (sight), kinesthetic (motor), and tactile (touch) channels, and to communicate information through those channels.

Behavioral earthquakes   High-intensity, low-frequency behaviors that can be externalizing or internalizing.

Bell-shaped curve   Depicts the normal distribution of a characteristic (e.g., intelligence) in the general population.

Benefit standard   A U.S. Supreme Court interpretation of "appropriate education" requiring the education to benefit the student.

Bidialectal   The ability to use two variations of a language, such as being equally fluent in black English and standard English.

Biomedical causes   Disability-causing conditions that develop within the individual.

Bipolar disorder   Characterized by extreme mood swings from depressive to manic phases.

C

Cataracts   A disorder of the eye that occurs when the lens of the eye becomes cloudy or opaque, usually resulting in low vision.

Central auditory processing disorders   Manifested by difficulty with auditory skill such as attending to input,

G1

discriminating between important and unimportant input, blending sounds that are heard, and remembering input.

Central nervous system dysfunction　A disorder in the messaging system of the brain and/or spinal cord.

Chromosomes　Direct each cell's activity. Humans have twenty-three pairs of chromosomes in each cell, with one chromosome in each pair coming from the mother and one from the father.

Chronic condition　Develops slowly and results in long-lasting symptoms. A person can have a chronic condition such as juvenile diabetes all or most of his or her lifetime.

Clean intermittent catheterization　Involves inserting a catheter into the urethra to the bladder to drain off urine for collection in a basin.

Cleft palate/lip　A condition in which there is a split in the upper part of the oral cavity or the upper lip.

Closed head injury　Results when the brain whips back and forth during an accident, causing it to bounce off the inside of the skull.

Cochlear implant　A device that converts sound into electrical current to stimulate the auditory nerve fibers; the part with electrodes is surgically implanted, and the part with a microphone and processor is worn externally.

Cognitive retraining　Helps students regain perceptual processing, communication, behavioral, and social skills that were lost as a result of traumatic brain injury.

Collaboration　"An interactive process" that "enables people with diverse expertise to generate creative solutions to mutually defined problems" (Idol, L., Paolucci-Whitcomb, P., & Nevin, A., 1986. *Collaborative consultation*. Austin, TX: Pro-Ed).

Colostomy　A surgical procedure that involves creating an opening into a person's abdomen so that bowel contents can be drained and into a bag attached to the person's body.

Conductive hearing loss　Any problem of the outer or middle ear when the inner ear is not affected.

Combined type of attention-deficit/hyperactivity disorder　Manifesting characteristics of both the inattentive type and hyperactive-impulsive type of attention-deficit/hyperactivity disorder.

Compensatory strategy training　A form of cognitive retraining that helps students who have traumatic brain injury to clarify, remember, organize, and express information.

Component training　A form of cognitive retraining that provides students who have traumatic brain injury with intensive and systematic training of specific cognitive skills such as memory, attention, organization, and perceptual processing.

Concomitance　Occurring at the same time without causal relationship.

Conduct disorder　Characterized by acting out destructive feelings or impulses, which results in serious and repeated violations of society's rules and the rights of others.

Congenital condition　Present at birth but not inherited.

Contingency contract　A signed agreement between student and teacher that if the student performs in a certain way, the teacher will provide the student with a desired reinforcer.

Continuous performance tests　Machines or computer software that measure sustained attention or vigilance, reaction time, distractibility, and impulsivity.

Continuum　The concept that services for students with disabilities begin with the most typical and extend to the least typical, most segregated, as the students' disabilities become more and more severe.

Cooperative learning　Provides a structure for students to work together toward mutual goals and emphasizes the importance of having all members in the group work together to achieve their individual and collective goals.

Cortical visual impairment　The diagnosis given to a visual impairment that results from damage to the part of the brain responsible for reception of visual information from the eye and initial transmission of this information to the associative parts of the brain.

Creativity　Unusual or unique expressions within a domain. Students who are creative may be more adventurous, independent, curious, spontaneous, flexible, sensitive, intuitive, and insightful than their peers. They also have more original ideas and may have a zany sense of humor.

Criterion-referenced tests　Determine whether a student has mastered a particular skill; thus, these tests compare a student to a standard of mastery.

Cross-categorical classes　Special education classes in which students with various kinds of disabilities are educated together.

Curriculum-based assessment　A test whose items reflect the content of the student's curriculum; the test may be norm-referenced or criterion-referenced.

D

Deaf culture　The pattern of beliefs, values, behaviors, arts, customs, institutions, social forms, and knowledge that are characteristic of the Deaf community.

Deafness　Hearing impairment that is so severe the child is impaired in processing linguistic information through hearing, with or without amplification, and educational performance is adversely affected.

Developmental delay of inhibition　A feature of attention-deficit/hyperactivity disorder that results in immature responses to separating facts from feelings, having a sense of past and future, using self-directed speech, and breaking apart and recombining information.

Developmental first grade　Provides a transition year between kindergarten and first grade for children who are not ready for first grade.

Dialect　A regional variety of a language, such as when someone speaks English using terms or pronunciations used only in that region.

Differential reinforcement of other behavior　Encourages appropriate behavior by reinforcing a positive behavior that is incompatible with the undesired behavior. The focus is on praising good behavior rather than punishing inappropriate behavior.

Direct observation　Obtaining specific information on a student's behavior through watching and recording to what degree, how often, or for what length of time a behavior does or does not occur.

Documentation　Types of measurement used to determine giftedness.

Domain-specific giftedness　Giftedness that occurs in a specific area such as math, art, leadership, or athletics. This does not imply that giftedness operates in isolation but rather that some children have specific abilities that are not revealed by test scores alone. Researchers agree that within each domain or category, there are varying degrees of giftedness, ranging from gifted and talented to the rare genius.

Dual certification   Being certified in a categorical area such as physical disabilities as well as another area such as elementary education or other health impairments.

Due process hearing   A structured and formal opportunity to present conflicting positions and to have a decision by an impartial person called a hearing officer.

Due process hearing officer   The impartial person who presides over a due process hearing and ensures that both parties have a fair opportunity to present their case.

Dyslexia   A disorder in recognizing and comprehending written words as a result of a developmental language impairment.

E

Early expressive language delay   A significant delay in the development of expressive language that is apparent by age two.

Eating disorders   Inappropriate eating behaviors resulting in eating too little (anorexia nervosa) or too much at one time and purging (bulimia nervosa).

Ebonics   The study of the differences and similarities in the grammatical makeup of black English and standard English.

Echolalia   A form of communication in which people with autism echo other people's language by constantly repeating a portion of what they hear.

Ecological assessment   Involves examining environments within which a student is expected to function and identifying the specific activities and skills that the student needs in order to participate successfully there. Those activities and skills become the basis for assessment.

Ecological curriculum   Involves identifying the environment within which a student is expected to function and the specific activities and skills that the student will need in order to be successful there. Those activities and skills become the basis for instruction.

Educable students   An outdated term that refers to students with mild mental retardation.

Emotional or behavioral disorder   A chronic condition that is characterized by behavioral or emotional responses that differ from age, cultural, or ethnic norms to such a degree that educational performance is adversely affected.

EMR classroom   A classroom for students with mild mental retardation. *EMR* is an outdated term that stands for "educable mentally retarded."

Encephalocele   A rare disorder in which one is born with an opening in the skull from which membranes that cover the brain and brain tissue protrude. The opening may be covered by skin and/or membrane of varying thickness.

Enzymes   Proteins that cause or speed up chemical reactions.

Evaluation   The interpretation of information secured through assessment.

Evaluation team   The term used in the Individuals with Disabilities Education Act to refer to the team responsible for administering a nondiscriminatory evaluation to determine if the student qualifies for special education.

Expertise   The technical mastery of skills and lore within a domain.

Expressive language disorders   Difficulties with expressing ideas verbally, manually, or in other ways.

Externalizing behaviors   Behavior disorders comprising aggressive, acting-out, and noncompliant behaviors.

F

Facilitated communication   A training method that involves supporting a person who does not speak or has highly repetitive speech to use a human facilitator and keyboard to communicate.

Facilitative role   Helping your colleagues develop a capacity to solve problems, engage in tasks, or deal independently with professional challenges.

Fetal alcohol syndrome   Results from the mother's alcohol use during pregnancy. The children often are small for gestational age, have facial deformities, and have congenital heart defects. Mild-to-moderate mental retardation is common.

Field of vision, or **visual field**   The entire area of which an individual is visually aware when that individual is directing his or her gaze straight ahead.

Fingerspelling   The hand configurations that represent the letters of the alphabet; fingerspelling is generally used to spell words that have no known sign.

Fluency problems   Difficulties with the accuracy and the rate with which speech is produced. Fluent speech is smooth, flows well, and is effortless.

Focal sensory seizures   Cause the person to see or hear things that are not there.

Fovea   The point on the retina of the eye where light rays are supposed to focus and that is responsible for the clearest visual acuity.

Functional academic skills   Skills that students need to function independently in the community.

Functional language problems   Those difficulties associated with using language in everyday, real-life activities that have no known biological basis.

Functional retraining   A form of cognitive retraining that uses everyday curriculum and activities of a student with traumatic brain injury to teach cognitive skills.

Functionally blind   Those individuals who can use their available vision to some limited degree (to sort color or to determine the presence of a light source), but who primarily acquire information about the environment through their auditory and tactual senses.

G

Gastrostomy tube feeding   Feeding an individual through a tube that directly enters the intestine.

Generalization   The ability to apply what is learned in one setting to another.

Generalized seizures   Cause a loss of consciousness. There are two types: (1) tonic-clonic, or grand mal seizure, (2) absence seizure.

Genius   Persons or works that are not only expert and creative but also assume a universal, or quasiuniversal, significance.

Gifted   People who have high performance capability in areas such as intellectual, creative, artistic, leadership, physical, or intuitive/intrapersonal ability, or in specific academic fields.

H

Health care plan   Coordinates a student's medical information and needs among family and medical and school staff. All participants receive a copy, and one copy is attached to the individualized education program.

Hearing aid   An electroacoustic device designed to make sounds louder. The microphone and receiver can be worn on the body, near or in the ear; the amplifier is attached to an ear mold and worn inside the ear.

Higher functioning autistic disorder   A condition in which individuals with autism have an intellectual quotient above 70.

Human immunodeficiency virus (HIV)   Spread through contact with blood or sperm from another person. The virus attacks the immune system, ultimately resulting in acquired immune deficiency syndrome.

Hyperglycemia   Too much sugar in the bloodstream as a result of lack of insulin.

Hypernasality   A speech problem in which air is allowed to pass through a speaker's nasal cavity on sounds other than those for which air is supposed to pass through the nasal passage.

Hypertonia   Tightness in a muscle or muscle group.

Hypoglycemia   Blood sugar is too low because of too much insulin.

Hyponasality   A speech problem in which air cannot pass through a speaker's nose as it is supposed to and comes through the speaker's mouth instead. The speaker may sound as if the nose is being held.

Hypoxia   The reduction of oxygen content in body tissues.

I

Inclusion   The term educators use to describe the goal of integrating students with disabilities into the same classrooms, community activities and resources, and home settings as students who do not have disabilities. Inclusion means no longer segregating students with disabilities into separate classrooms, schools, transportation, and living arrangements.

Incontinence   The inability to control one's bladder, or bowels, or both.

Individualized education program (IEP)   A written plan for serving students with disabilities, ages three to twenty-one.

Individualized family services plan (IFSP)   A written plan for serving infants and toddlers, ages zero to three, and their families.

Information-giving role   Providing direct assistance to your colleagues so they are better equipped to deal with problems on an ongoing basis.

Intermittent positive pressure breathing machine (IPPB)   Used outside a person's body and forces the lungs into an exhale function, facilitating breathing.

Internalizing behaviors   Behavior disorders comprising social withdrawal, depression, anxiety, obsessions, and compulsions.

Interpreters   Professionals who translate from one language to another. Sign language interpreters translate from spoken language to sign language and from sign language to spoken language.

J

Jejunum   The second portion of a person's small intestine. A tube placed in it (J-tube) allows the person to receive nutrition through the tube.

Job coach   A person who supports an individual with a severe disability to be successful in supported employment by teaching the individual job skills and helping him or her perform the job.

K

Karyotyping   Involves arranging the chromosomes under a microscope so that they can be counted and grouped according to size, shape, and pattern.

Ketoacidosis   Results when lack of insulin prevents the use of glucose as a source of energy. The body uses fats instead, leading to the release into the bloodstream of fatty acids called ketones. If untreated, the condition can result in confusion, unconsciousness, or death.

L

Language disorders   A group of communication disorders or impairments that reflect the individual's inability to use the rules of the language system to produce or understand a message.

Learned helplessness   A condition in which individuals who have experienced repeated failure tend to expect failure. To minimize or prevent failure, these individuals often set low expectations.

Learning disabilities   Include disorders involved in understanding or in using spoken or written language that result in substantial difficulties in listening, speaking, reading, written expression, or mathematics. Other conditions such as emotional disturbance or sensory impairments may occur along with a learning disability but are not the cause of the learning disability.

Legal blindness   A term that refers to an individual whose central visual acuity, when measured in both eyes and when wearing corrective lenses, is 20/200 or who has a visual field of no more than 20 degrees.

Low vision   Experienced by individuals with a visual impairment who can use their vision as a primary channel for learning. Generally, people with low vision can increase their visual abilities through the use of adaptive devices (such as magnifiers) or materials (such as large print).

M

Macula   The thinnest area of the retina. Most of the nerve cells of the macula are responsible for vision in good light and provide a sense of detail and color.

Macular degeneration   A type of visual disorder that results in the loss of function of the macula, the part of the eye responsible for detail and color vision.

Magnet school   A school that educates gifted and talented students by placing a strong instructional emphasis on one or two specific domains of talent.

Major depression   Excessive perceptions of sadness and worthlessness characterized by changes in emotion, motivation, physical well-being, and thoughts.

Mediation   The process whereby both parties to a dispute agree to try to resolve their differences with the help of an independent third party.

Metabolism   The body's chemical processes that help break down toxins and move nutrients through the bloodstream.

Metacognition   The ability to think about one's thinking or organize one's thoughts in a meaningful way.

Milieu teaching   An approach to language intervention in which the goal is to teach functional language in a natural environment.

Mnemonic   A device—for example, a rhyme, formula, or acronym—used to aid memory.

Morphology   One of the five sets of rules governing our language system. Morphological rules dictate how the smallest meaningful units of our language, called *morphemes,* will be combined to form words. A word may be one morpheme, as in *duck.* Adding another single morpheme, /s/, changes the meaning. Morphological rules allow us to make this change in meaning consistently and to understand the change when we hear it.

Multilingualism   The ability to use more than one language for communication.

Multimodal treatment   The use of concurrent treatment approaches. For those with attention-deficit/hyperactivity disorder, treatment may include as many as six components: medical management, education, coaching, counseling, organizational training, and behavior modification.

Multiple intelligences   Different kinds of giftedness that are found across cultures and societies.

Muscle atrophy   The wasting away and reduction of the muscle, usually from a disease, injury, or lack of use.

Myoclonic seizures   Cause an infant or young child to look startled or in pain.

Myopia   The medical term for near-sightedness, which results when light rays entering the eye focus in front of the retina.

N

National Council on Disability   An independent federal agency responsible for making recommendations on policy matters to Congress and the President.

Natural or logical consequence   A consequence for behavior that relates directly to the offense.

Neonatal intensive care unit (NICU)   A hospital facility for treating newborns with serious birth defects.

Neuromotor impairment   Involves a breakdown in the brain resulting in the brain's inability to direct the body in movement that produces speech, gestures, written formats, or other alternatives.

Norm-referenced tests   These tests compare a student with his or her age- or grade-level peers and have two purposes: to help to determine whether a student has an exceptionality and to assess various skills.

O

Open head injury   Results when a specific area or focal point of the brain is injured. A gunshot wound would cause an open head injury. The types of changes in personality or cognitive functioning depend on the area of the brain affected.

Opportunistic infections   Usually do not affect the general population but only those who have immune deficiency because of another illness. People with human immunodeficiency virus are among those who are susceptible to opportunistic infections.

Oppositional-defiant disorder   Characterized by negativistic, disobedient, hostile, and defiant behaviors without serious violations of the rights of others.

Optic nerve atrophy   A disorder of the optic nerve, the nerve that transmits visual information from the eye to the brain, which often results in reduced visual acuity, or low vision.

Optic nerve hypoplasia   A disorder of the optic nerve that often is associated with midline or other brain abnormalities that may result in varying degrees of visual impairment, including total blindness.

Organic language problems   Difficulties in understanding or using language that are caused by a known problem in a person's neuromuscular mechanism.

Other health impairments   Include chronic and acute health problems that limit strength, vitality, or alertness and adversely affect educational performance.

Outer-directedness   A condition in which individuals distrust their own solutions and seek cues from others.

P

Paraplegia   The impairment and limited use or no use of the arms.

Paraprofessional   A person who may have as much training as a teacher and usually has less but who functions essentially like a teacher and works under a teacher's supervision.

Partial seizures   Electrical activity is limited to one area of the brain. There are three types: (1) temporal lobe, or psychomotor seizures, (2) focal sensory seizures, and (3) myoclonic seizures.

Peer tutoring   Instruction of one student by another for the purposes of instructional and social support.

Perinatal   At birth.

Personal Intervention Plan   Includes information on what triggers inappropriate behavior, the typical behaviors displayed by the student, the desired behaviors, goals for achieving the behaviors, and supports the student needs to achieve the goals.

Pervasive developmental disorder   Includes impairments in communication, impairments in reciprocal social interactions, and stereotyped patterns of behavior, interests, and activities.

Phonological awareness   A foundational reading skill in which a student recognizes sound segments in words presented orally.

Phonology   One of the five sets of rules in our language system. This set of rules defines the way sounds are combined to form words and how those sounds are changed to alter word meanings.

Portfolio assessment   A technique for assembling exemplars of a student's work, such as homework, in-class tests, artwork, journal, and other evidence of the student's strengths and needs.

Positive behavioral support   An approach to decreasing or eliminating challenging behavior by creating a responsive environment that is personally tailored to the preferences, strengths, and needs of individuals with challenging behavior.

Postconcussional syndrome   A mild closed head injury that may not show damage on medical tests but results in changes in personality or cognitive functioning.

Postlingual hearing loss   Hearing loss that occurs after the child has developed language.

Postnatal   After birth.

Pragmatics   One of the five sets of rules governing our language system. Pragmatic rules are those that dictate how we use language in interactions and in context. Pragmatic rules recognize that language usage occurs between at least two people and takes place in a setting.

Predominantly hyperactive-impulsive type of attention-deficit/hyperactivity disorder Characterized by fidgeting, restlessness, difficulty engaging in quiet activities, excessive talking, driven personality, blurting out inappropriate comments, and/or tendency to interrupt or intrude.

Predominantly inattentive type of attention-deficit/hyperactivity disorder Characterized by daydreaming, careless work, inability to follow through, organizational difficulties, losing things, distractibility, hypoactivity, lethargy, and/or forgetfulness.

Prelingual hearing loss Hearing loss at birth or before the child has learned language.

Prenatal Before birth.

Prenatal substance exposure The use of drugs or alcohol by the mother during pregnancy. May cause learning or behavior problems.

Prereferral Occurs when a student's general education teacher asks others (educators and families) to help problem solve in order to identify instructional strategies to adequately address learning and behavioral challenges.

Prescriptive role Prescribing a path of action to your colleagues.

Process definition A U.S. Supreme Court interpretation of "appropriate education" as one that effectively implements the six principles of the Individuals with Disabilities Education Act.

Prodigy A gifted individual who shows extraordinary promise in a specific task or domain.

Projective test A psychological test in which a student's responses to unstructured stimuli, such as pictures or incomplete sentences, are analyzed for underlying personality traits, feelings, or attitudes.

Pseudo-ADD Characteristics of attention-deficit/hyperactivity disorder resulting from living in a fast-paced society that emphasizes self-gratification.

Psychosocial disadvantage Conditions of individuals that develop from social and environmental influences.

Psychotropic medication Medication that alters perception, feelings, and/or behavior.

Pulseoximeter A clamp attached to a person's finger that reads the person's pulse and tells how much oxygen is in his or her bloodstream.

Q

Quadriplegia A weakness or paralysis of all four extremities—both arms and both legs.

R

Reading medium The format(s) preferred by people who have visual impairments to access written materials, generally, print, large print, or braille.

Receptive language disorders Difficulties with receiving and understanding language.

Reciprocal friendship Both members of the friendship contribute to and benefit from the exchanges of support.

Referral Occurs when an educator or a parent submits a formal request for the student to be considered for a full and formal nondiscriminatory evaluation.

Reliability How consistently a test yields similar results across time and among raters.

Resonance (of the voice) The perceived quality of the voice. Perceptions of harshness or breathiness are included in the judgments of the resonance of the voice. Resonance is determined by the characteristics of the mouth and throat.

Respiratory ventilation Involves suctioning mucus from the respiratory tract through a small tube.

Retina The innermost layer of nerve cells located at the back of the interior eyeball whose purpose is to convert light energy into electrical energy, which is then transmitted to the brain.

Retinopathy of prematurity A type of visual disorder that is associated with premature exposure of the developing retina of the eye to oxygen, resulting in various levels of visual impairment.

Retrolental fibroplasia An older term for the condition now described as retinopathy of prematurity.

S

Savant syndrome A condition in which individuals typically display extraordinary abilities in areas such as calendar calculating, musical ability, mathematical skills, memorization, and mechanical abilities. This unusual ability typically manifests itself in conjunction with low ability in most other skill areas.

Schizophrenia Characterized by psychotic periods resulting in hallucinations, delusions, inability to experience pleasure, and loss of contact with reality.

Scoliosis A lateral curve of the spine.

Scope and sequence chart A list of objectives in grade-level sequence used in a particular curriculum.

Screening A routine test that helps school staff identify which students might need further testing to determine whether they qualify for special education.

Self-advocates Individuals who are skilled in standing up for themselves and protecting their own interests.

Self-determination The ability of individuals to live their lives the way that they choose to live them, consistent with their own values, preferences, and abilities.

Semantics One of the five sets of rules governing our language system. Semantic rules prescribe how words will be used meaningfully in communication.

Sensorineural hearing loss Caused by problems in the inner ear or along the nerve pathway from the inner ear to the brain stem.

Severe discrepancy A statistically significant difference between ability and achievement as measured by standardized tests.

Social construct A concept that derives from society's views about people.

Social interaction theories The theories proposed by researchers like Lev Vygotsky that support the belief that language is learned through encounters with others.

Social maladjustment An adaptive response to environmental conditions resulting in socialized aggression (e.g., gang-related behavior or juvenile delinquency).

Social stories Usually written by parents or educators, describe social situations in terms of important social cues and appropriate responses to those cues.

Specific language impairment A language disorder with no identifiable cause and with apparent normal development in all other developmental areas.

Speech disorders A group of communication disorders or impairments that affect an individual's production of sounds, rhythm of speech, or voice quality.

Speech recognition technology Gives students with physical disabilities access to computers by converting their speech into a print display on the computer screen.

Stereotypical behaviors Inappropriate, repetitive acts that an individual frequently displays. Examples include rocking back and forth, waving fingers in front of the face, and twirling objects.

Stress-induced agitation syndrome Characteristics of attention-deficit/hyperactivity disorder resulting from the stress of living in poverty and potentially violent situations.

Stuttering Interruption in the fluency of speech. It is characterized by the frequent occurrence of speech disfluency, tension, and struggle, and may include other related behaviors.

Subtyping Dividing students into smaller groups based on common characteristics.

Supplementary aids and support services Provided in general education classes or other education settings so that students with disabilities will be educated with students who do not have disabilities to the maximum extent appropriate for the students with disabilities.

Supported employment The employment of a person with a disability for at least the minimum wage, working alongside of other employees who do not have disabilities.

Symptomatic stage The stage when human immunodeficiency virus reproduces more actively, and the infected person begins to experience illnesses, including opportunistic infections.

Syntax One of the five sets of rules governing our language system. Syntactic rules determine how word order will be used and interpreted in communication.

Syntax errors Those mistakes in using the rules that govern the arrangement of words in a language.

T

Temporal lobe, or psychomotor, seizures Causes a dreamlike state in which the person makes random movements called *automatisms.*

Teratogens Substances that can interfere with normal fetal development.

Tertiary prevention Special education and physical, occupational, or vocational training on a long-term basis for the purpose of reducing the effects of a present disability.

Text telephone *See TT.*

Tonic-clonic, or grand mal, seizure Causes someone to fall and have a convulsion.

Topographical classification system A classification system that ascribes a disability to the part of the brain that is affected.

Totally blind Individuals who are totally blind use their tactual and auditory senses to acquire information about their environment. These individuals do not receive meaningful input through the visual sense.

Tracheostomy The surgical creation of an opening into a person's trachea (wind pipe). Into the opening is placed a tube that allows the person to breathe, almost always with the help of mechanical ventilation.

Trainable students An outdated term that refers to students with moderate mental retardation.

Traumatic brain injury Caused by an external physical force, resulting in impaired functioning in one or more areas. Educational performance is adversely affected. The injury may be open or closed.

TT (text telephone) A telecommunications device that enables individuals to carry on a phone conversation in written form.

Tunnel vision Occurs when an individual's visual field is reduced significantly so that only a small area of central visual acuity remains. The affected individual has the impression of looking through a tunnel or tube and is unaware of objects to the left, right, top, or bottom. A person with tunnel vision may be able to read small print but is considered severely visually impaired because of the difficulties associated with safe travel and locating objects in the environment.

V

Validity How well a test measures what it says it measures.

Visual disability, including blindness Defined by IDEA as an impairment in vision that, even with correction, adversely affects a child's educational performance.

Vocal nodules Small knots or lumps on the speech mechanism.

W

Whole language techniques Strategies and activities used for teaching language in its spoken and written forms that incorporate natural-occurring behaviors, such as speaking, writing, and reading in learning to use language more effectively, correctly, and appropriately.

CHAPTER 1

Adelman, H. S. (1992). LD: The next 25 years. *Journal of Learning Disabilities, 25,* 17–21.

Adelman, H. S. (1996). Appreciating the classification dilemma. In W. Stainback & S. Stainback (Eds.), *Controversial issues confronting special education: Divergent perspectives* (2nd ed., pp. 96–111). Boston: Allyn & Bacon.

Adelman, H. S., & Taylor, L. (1984). Ethical concerns and identification of psychoeducational problems. *Journal of Clinical Child Psychology, 13,* 16–23.

Americans with Disabilities Act, 42 U.S.C. §§ 12101–12213 (1990).

Blackorby, J., & Wagner, M. (1996). Longitudinal postschool outcomes of youth with disabilities: Findings from the national longitudinal transition study. *Exceptional Children, 62,* 399–413.

Board v. Cooperman, 105 N. J. 587, 523 A 2d 655 (S. Ct. N.J. 1987).

Board of Education, Sacramento City Unified School District v. Holland, 786 F. Supp. 874, 73 Ed. Law Rep. 969 (E.D. Cal. 1992), *affirmed sub nom.* Sacramento City Unified School District, Board of Education v. Rachel H., 14 F. 3d 1398, 89 Ed. Law Rep. 57 (9th Cir. 1994).

Braddock, D., Hemp, R., Fujiura, G., Bachelder, L., & Mitchell, D. (1990). *The state of the states in developmental disabilities.* Baltimore: Brookes.

Brendtro, L. K., Brokenleg, M., & Van Bockern, S. (1990). *Reclaiming youth at risk: Our hope for the future.* Bloomington, IN: National Educational Services.

Brown v. Board of Education. 347 U.S. 483 (1954).

Coleman, M. R., Gallagher, J., & Foster, A. (1994). *Updated report on state policies related to the identification of gifted students* [Report]. Chapel Hill: University of North Carolina, Gifted Education Policy Studies Program.

Daniel R. R. v. State Board of Education. 874 F. 2d 1036 (5th Cir. 1989).

Deno, E. (1970). Special education as developmental capital. *Exceptional Children, 37,* 229–237.

Deno, E. (1994). Special education as developmental capital revisited: A quarter century appraisal of means versus ends. *The Journal of Special Education, 27,* 375–392.

Dunn, L. M. (1968). Special education for the mildly retarded—Is much of it justifiable? *Exceptional Children, 35,* 5–22.

Gallagher, J. J. (1972, March). The special education contract for mildly handicapped children. *Exceptional Children,* pp. 527–535.

Goffman, E. (1963). *Behavior in public places: Notes on the social organization of gatherings.* Glencoe, NY: Free Press.

Gottlieb, J., Alter, M., Gottlieb, B. W., & Wishner, J. (1994). Special education in urban America: It's not justifiable for many. *Journal of Special Education, 27(4),* 453–465.

Hobbs, N. (1975). *The futures of children: Categories, labels, and their consequences.* Nashville, TN: Vanderbilt Institute for Public Policy Studies.

Honig v. Doe. 484 U.S. 305, 108 S. Ct. 592, 98 L. Ed. 2d 686 (1988).

House Committee Report on the Education of All Handicapped Children Act, H.R. Rep. No. 94-332, 94th Cong., 1st Sess. (June 1975).

Individuals with Disabilities Education Act, 20 U.S.C. §§ 1400 *et seq.* (1997).

Kirp, D. (1973). Schools as sorters: The constitutional and policy implications of student classifications. *University of Pennsylvania Law Review, 121(4),* 705–797.

Kliewer, C., & Biklin, D. (1996). Labeling: Who wants to be called retarded? In W. Stainback & S. Stainback (Eds.), *Controversial issues confronting special education: Divergent perspectives* (2nd ed., pp. 83–95). Boston: Allyn & Bacon.

Larry P. v. Riles. 343 F. Supp. 1306, *aff'd.,* 502 F. 2d 963, *further proceedings,* 495 F. Supp. 926, *aff'd.,* 502 F. 2d 693 (9th Cir. 1984).

Lippman, S., & Goldberg, I. (1973). *Right to education.* New York: Teachers College Press.

Lipsky, D. K., & Gartner, A. (1989). *Beyond special education: Quality education for all.* Baltimore: Brookes.

Locust, C. (1988). Wounding the spirit: Discrimination and traditional American Indian belief systems. *Harvard Educational Review, 58(3),* 315–330.

MacMillan, D. L., & Meyers, C. E. (1979). Educational labeling of handicapped learners. In D. Berliner (Ed.), *Review of research in education* (Vol. 7). Washington, DC: American Educational Research Association.

Martin, R. (1991). *Extraordinary children, ordinary lives: Stories behind special education case law.* Champaign, IL: Research Press.

Mills v. Washington, DC, Board of Education. 348 F. Supp. 866 (D.DC 1972); *contempt proceedings,* EHLR 551: 643 (D.DC 1980).

National Council on Disability (Ed.). (1995). *Improving the implementation of the Individuals with Disabilities Education Act: Making schools work for all of America's children.* Washington, DC: National Council on Disability.

Parents in Action in Special Education [PASE] v. Hannon. 506 F. Supp. 831 (N. D. Ill. 1980).

Parrish, T. B., O'Reilly, F., Dueñas, I. E., & Wolman, J. (1997). *State analysis series: State special education finance systems, 1994–95.* Palo Alto, CA: Center for Special Education Finance.

Pennsylvania Association for Retarded Citizens [PARC] v. Commonwealth of Pennsylvania. 334 F. Supp. 1257, 343 F. Supp. 279 (E.D. Pa. 1971, 1972).

President's Committee on Employment of People with Disabilities. (1992). *Words with dignity: Guidance on how to write and speak about people with disabilities.* Washington, DC: Author.

Rehabilitation Act, 29 U.S.C., §16 (1996 Supp.).

Reschly, D. J. (1988). Minority MMR overrepresentation: Legal issues, research findings, and reform trends. In M. C. Wang, M. C. Reynolds, & H. J. Walberg (Eds.), *Handbook of special education, research and practice. Volume 2: Mildly handicapping conditions* (pp. 23–42). New York: Pergamon.

Reschly, D. J. (1996). Identification and assessment of students with disabilities. *Future of Children, 6(1),* 40–53.

Reynolds, M. C. (1991). Classification and labeling. In J. W. Lloyd, N. N. Singh, & A. C. Repp (Eds.), *The regular education initiative: Alternative perspectives on concepts, issues, and models* (pp. 29–42). Sycamore, IL: Sycamore.

Reynolds, M. C., Wang, M. C., & Walberg, H. J. (1987). The necessary restructuring of special and regular education. *Exceptional Children, 53,* 391–398.

Sarason, S. B., & Doris, J. (1979). *Educational handicap, public policy, and social history.* New York: Free Press.

Senate Committee Report on the Education of All Handicapped Children Act, Sen. Rep. No. 94-168, 94th Cong, 1st Sess., June 1975.

Sorgen, M. (1976). The classification process and its consequences. In M. Kindred, J. Cohen, D. Penrod, & T. Shaffer (Eds.), *The mentally retarded citizen and the law* (pp. 214–243). New York: Free Press.

Technology-Related Assistance to Individuals with Disabilities Act of 1988, P.L. 100-407, 29 U.S.C. § 2201 *et seq.* (1997).

Timothy W. v. Rochester School District. EHLR 559: 480 (D.N.H. 1988).

Turnbull, H. R., Bateman, D. F., & Turnbull, A. P. (1993). Families and empowerment. In P. Wehman (Ed.), *The ADA mandate for social change* (pp. 157–174). Baltimore: Brookes.

Turnbull, H. R., & Turnbull, A. P. (1996). The synchrony of stakeholders: Lessons from the disability rights movement. In S. L. Kagan & N. E. Cohen (Eds.), *Early care and educa-*

tion: A vision for a quality system (pp. 290–308). San Francisco: Jossey-Bass.

U.S. Department of Education. (1992). To assure the free appropriate public education of all children with disabilities: Fourteenth annual report to Congress on the implementation of the Individuals with Disabilities Education Act. Washington, DC: Author.

U.S. Department of Education. (1996). To assure the free appropriate public education of all children with disabilities: Eighteenth annual report to Congress on the implementation of the Individuals with Disabilities Education Act. Washington, DC: Author.

U.S. Department of Education, Office of Civil Rights. (1993). Annual report to Congress. Washington, DC: Author.

Valdés, K. A., Williamson, C. L., & Wagner, M. (1990). The national longitudinal transition study of special education students, Statistical almanac, Vol. 1: Overview. Menlo Park, CA: SRI International.

Vergason, G. A., & Anderegg, M. L. (1997). The ins and outs of special education terminology. Teaching Exceptional Children, 29(5), 35–39.

Wagner, M. (1995). The contributions of poverty and ethnic background to the participation of secondary school students in special education. Washington, DC: U.S. Department of Education.

Ward, N. (1989, January). Self-determination. Paper presented at the National Conference on Self-Determination, Arlington, VA.

Weintraub, F., Abeson, A., & Braddock, D. (1971). State law and education of handicapped children. Reston, VA: Council for Exceptional Children.

CHAPTER 2

Artiles, A. J., & Trent, S. C. (1994). Overrepresentation of minority students in special education: A continuing debate. Journal of Special Education, 27, 410–437.

Baca, L., & Almanza, E. (1991). Language minority students and disabilities. Reston, VA: Council for Exceptional Children.

Bartoli, J. S. (1989). An ecological response to Cole's interactivity alternative. Journal of Learning Disabilities, 22(5), 292–297.

Bursuck, W. D., Epstein, M. H., Jayanthi, M., McConeghy, J., Plante, L., & Polloway, E. A. (1996). Report card grading and adaptations: A national survey of classroom practices. Exceptional Children, 62, 301–319.

Cummins, J. (1984). Bilingualism and special education: Issues in assessment and pedagogy. Clevedon, Avon, UK: Multilingual Matters.

Day, J. D., & Borkowski, J. G. (Eds.). (1987). Intelligence and exceptionality: New directions for theory, assessment, and instructional practices. Norwood, NJ: Ablex.

Day, J. D., & Hall, L. K. (1987). Cognitive assessment, intelligence, and instruction. In J. D. Day & J. G. Borkowski (Eds.), Intelligence and exceptionality: New directions for theory, assessment, and instructional practices (pp. 57–80). Norwood, NJ: Ablex.

Donahue, K., & Zigmond, N. (1990). Academic grades of ninth-grade urban learning disabled students and low-achieving peers. Exceptionality, 19, 505–517.

Evans, I. M. (1991). Testing and diagnosis: A review and evaluation. In L. Meyer, C. Peck, & L. Brown (Eds.), Critical issues in the lives of people with severe disabilities (pp. 25–44). Baltimore: Brookes.

Fuchs, D., Fuchs, L., & Bahr, M. W. (1990). Mainstream assistance teams: A scientific basis for the art of consultation. Exceptional Children, 56, 128–138.

Fuchs, D., Fuchs, L., Bahr, M. W., Ferstrom, P., & Strecker, P. M. (1990). Prereferral intervention: A prescriptive approach. Exceptional Children, 56, 493–513.

Galagan, J. E. (1985). Psychoeducational testing: Turn out the lights, the party's over. Exceptional Children, 53, 288–299.

Garcia, S., & Ortiz, A. (1988). Preventing inappropriate referrals of language minority students to special education. New Focus, 5, pp. 1–12.

Harry, B. (1992). Cultural diversity, families, and the special education system: Communication and empowerment. New York: Teachers College Press.

Harry, B., Allen, N., & McLaughlin, M. (1995). Communication versus compliance: African-American parents' involvement in special education. Exceptional Children, 61, 364–377.

Harry, B., Grenot-Scheyer, M., Smith-Lewis, M., Park, H. S., Xin, F., & Schwartz, I. (1995). Developing culturally inclusive services for individuals with severe disabilities. Journal of the Association for Persons with Severe Handicaps, 20, 99–109.

Heath, S. B. (1986). Sociocultural contexts of language development. In California State Department of Education, Beyond language: Social and cultural factors in schooling language minority students (pp. 143–186). Los Angeles: California State University; Evaluation, Dissemination, and Assessment Center.

Johnson, D. W., & Johnson, R. (1989). Cooperation and competition: Theory and research. Edina, MN: Interaction.

Johnson, D. W., & Johnson, R. (1991). Learning together and alone: Cooperation, competition, and individualization. Upper Saddle River, NJ: Prentice Hall.

Johnson, R. T., & Johnson, D. W. (1994). An overview of cooperative learning. In J. S. Thousand, R. A. Villa, & A. I. Nevin (Eds.), Creativity and collaborative learning: A practical guide to empowering students and teachers (pp. 31–44). Baltimore: Brookes.

Kubiszyn, T., & Borich, G. (1996). Educational testing and measurement: Classroom application and practice (5th ed.). New York: HarperCollins.

Larry P. v. Riles. 343 F. Supp. 1306, aff'd., 502 F. 2d 963, further proceedings, 495 F. Supp. 926, aff'd., 502 F. 2d 693 (9th Cir. 1984).

Mattes, L., & Omark, D. (1984). Speech and language assessment for the bilingual handicapped. San Diego, CA: College-Hill Press.

Matthews, M. (1992, October). Gifted students talk about cooperative learning. Educational Leadership, pp. 48–50.

Overton, T. (1992). Assessment in special education. New York: Macmillan.

Parents in Action in Special Education [PASE] v. Hannon. 506 F. Supp. 831 (N. D. Ill. 1980).

Polloway, E. A., Epstein, M. H., Bursuck, W. D., Roderique, T. W., McConeghy, J. L., & Jayanthi, M. (1994). Classroom grading: A national survey of policies. Remedial and Special Education, 15(3), 162–170.

Ramírez, M., & Castañeda, A. (1974). Cultural democracy, bicognitive development and education. New York: Academic Press.

Roach, V., Ascroft, J., & Stamp, A. (1995). Winning ways: Creating inclusive schools, classrooms, and communities. Alexandria, VA: National Association of State Boards of Education.

Salisbury, C. L., Palombaro, M. M., & Hollowood, P. M. (1993). On the nature and change of an inclusive elementary school. Journal of the Association for Persons with Severe Handicaps, 18(2), 75–84.

Salvia, J., & Ysseldyke, J. E. (1985). Assessment in remedial and special education (3rd ed.). Boston: Houghton Mifflin.

Santelli, B., Turnbull, A. P., Marquis, J. G., & Lerner, E. P. (1993). Parent to Parent programs: On-going support for parents of young adults with special needs. Journal of Vocational Rehabilitation, 3(2), 25–37.

Saville-Troike, M. (1978). A guide to culture in the classroom. Wheaton, MD: National Clearinghouse for Bilingual Education.

Sigafoos, J., Cole, D., & McQuarter, R. (1987). Current practices in the assessment of students with severe handicaps. Journal of the Association for Persons with Severe Handicaps, 12, 264–273.

Smith, S. W. (1990, September). Individualized education programs (IEPs) in special education—From intent to acquiescence. Exceptional Children, pp. 6–14.

Stainback, W., & Stainback, S. (Eds.). (1996). Controversial issues confronting special education: Divergent perspectives (2nd ed.). Boston: Allyn & Bacon.

Strickland, B., & Turnbull, A. P. (1990). Developing and implementing individualized education programs (3rd ed.). New York: Merrill/Macmillan.

Thousand, J. S., Villa, R. A., & Nevin, A. I. (1994). *Creativity and collaborative learning: A practical guide for empowering students and teachers.* Baltimore: Brookes.

Truch, S. (1993). *The WISC-III companion.* Austin, TX: Pro-Ed.

Turnbull, A. P., & Turnbull, H. R. (1997). *Families, professionals, and exceptionality: A special partnership* (3rd ed.). Upper Saddle River, NJ: Merrill/Prentice Hall.

Valdés, K. A., Williamson, C. L., & Wagner, M. (1990). *The national longitudinal transition study of special education students, Statistical almanac, Vol. 1: Overview.* Menlo Park, CA: SRI International.

Vandercook, T., Fleetham, D., Sinclair, S., & Tetlie, R. R. (1988). Cass, Jess, Jules, and Ames . . . A story of friendship. *Minnesota University Affiliated Program Impact, 1*(2), 4.

Villa, R., & Thousand, J. S. (1992). Student collaboration: An essential for curriculum delivery in the 21st century. In S. Stainback & W. Stainback (Eds.), *Curriculum considerations in inclusive classrooms: Facilitated learning for all students* (pp. 117–142). Baltimore: Brookes.

Wechsler, D. (1991). *Manual for the Wechsler Intelligence Scale for Children—III.* Cleveland, OH: Psychological Corporation.

Ysseldyke, J. E., Reynolds, M. C., & Weinburg, R. A. (1984). *School psychology: A blueprint for the future of training and practice.* Minneapolis, MN: National School Psychology Inservice Training Network.

CHAPTER 3

American Federation of Teachers, AFL-CIO. (1996). *Full Inclusion for special needs students* [Position statement]. Washington, DC: Author.

American Occupational Therapy Association, School System/Early Intervention Guidelines Revision Task Force. (1997). *Occupational therapy services for children and youth under the Individuals with Disabilities Education Act.* Bethesda, MD: Author.

American Physical Therapy Association. (1990). *Physical therapy practice in educational environments.* Alexandria, VA: Author.

American Speech-Language-Hearing Association (ASHA). (1996). Inclusive practices for children and youths with communication disorders. *ASHA, 38,* 35–44.

Baker, J. M., & Zigmond, N. (1990). Are regular education classes equipped to accommodate students with learning disabilities? *Exceptional Children, 56,* 515–526.

Baker, J. M., & Zigmond, N. (1995). The meaning and practice of inclusion for students with learning disabilities: Themes and implications from the five cases. *Journal of Special Education, 29*(2), 163–180.

Bauwens, J., & Hourcade, J. J. (1995). *Cooperative teaching: Rebuilding the schoolhouse for all students.* Austin, TX: Pro-Ed.

Bell, T. H. (1993). Reflections one decade after "A nation at risk." *Phi Delta Kappan, 74*(8), 592–597.

Biklen, D. (1985). *Achieving the complete school: Strategies for effective mainstreaming.* New York: Columbia University Press.

Biklen, D., & Zollers, N. (1986). The focus of advocacy in the LD field. *Journal of Learning Disabilities, 19,* 579–586.

Blalock, G. (1991). Paraprofessionals: Critical team members in our special education programs. *Intervention in School and Clinic, 26,* 200–214.

Boomer, L. W. (1994). The utilization of paraprofessionals in programs for students with autism. *Focus on Autistic Behavior, 9*(2), 1–9.

Brown, L., Schwarz, P., Udvari-Solner, A., Kampschroer, E. F., Johnson, F., Jorgansen, J., & Geuenewald, L. (1991). How much time should students with severe intellectual disabilities spend in regular education classrooms and elsewhere? *Journal of the Association for Persons With Severe Handicaps, 16*(1), 39–47.

Bryan, J., & Bryan, T. (1988). Where's the beef? A review of published research on the adaptive learning environments model. *Learning Disabilities Focus, 4*(1), 15–23.

Bryan, T., Bay, M., & Donahue, M. (1988). Implications of the learning disabilities definition for the regular education intiative. *Journal of Learning Disabilities, 21*(1), 23–28.

Buswell, B. (1993). *Discussions about school reform: Strategies for families of students with disabilities.* Washington, DC: U.S. Department of Education.

Carlberg, C., & Kavale, K. (1980). The efficacy of special class versus regular class placement for exceptional children: A meta-analysis. *Journal of Special Education, 14,* 295–309.

Chapple, J. (1994, October). *Data demonstrate inclusion works in Ohio.* Paper presented at the Fourth International Conference on Mental Retardation and Developmental Disabilities, Arlington Heights, IL.

Cook, L., Weintraub, F., & Morse, W. (1995). Ethical dilemmas in the restructuring of special education. In J. L. Paul, H. Rosselli, & D. Evans (Eds.), *Integrating school restructuring and special education reform* (pp. 119–139). Fort Worth, TX: Harcourt Brace.

Cooley, E., & Yovanoff, P. (1996). Supporting professionals-at-risk: Evaluating interventions to reduce burnout and improve retention of special educators. *Exceptional Children, 62,* 336–355.

Council for Children with Behavior Disorders (CCBD). (1993, June). Position statement: Inclusion. *CCBD Newsletter,* p. 1.

Council for Exceptional Children (CEC). (1993). CEC policy on inclusive schools and community settings. *Teaching Exceptional Children, 25*(4), supplement.

Council for Exceptional Children. (1997). Eighteenth annual report affirms CEC's policy on inclusive settings: Full continuum of services a must. *CEC Today, 3*(7), 1, 4.

Council for Learning Disabilities. (1993). Concerns about the full inclusion of students with learning disabilities in regular education classrooms. *Learning Disability Quarterly, 16*(2), 126.

Council of Administrators of Special Education (CASE). (1994). *CASE position paper on delivery of services to students with disabilities.* Albuquerque, NM: Author.

Cross, G., & Villa, R. A. (1992). The Winooski School System: An evolutionary perspective of a school restructuring for diversity. In R. A. Villa, J. S. Thousand, W. Stainback, & S. Stainback (Eds.), *Restructuring for caring and effective education* (pp. 219–240). Baltimore: Brookes.

Cuban, L. (1989). The "at-risk" label and the problem of urban school reform. *Phi Delta Kappan, 70,* 780–801.

Daniel R. R. v. State Board of Education. 874 F. 2d 1036 (5th Cir. 1989).

DeGangi, G. A., Wietlisbach, S., Poisson, S., Stein, F., & Royeen, C. (1994). The impact of culture and socioeconomic status on family–professional collaboration: Challenges and solutions. *Topics in Early Childhood Special Education, 14,* 503–520.

Division for Early Childhood (DEC), Council for Exceptional Children. (1993, December). DEC position statement on inclusion. *DEC Newsletter,* p. 1.

Doktor, J. E., & Poertner, J. (1996). Kentucky's family resource centers: A community-based, school-linked model. *Remedial and Special Education, 17,* 293–302.

Erwin, E. J., & Soodak, L. C. (1995). I never knew I could stand up to the system: Families' perspectives on pursuing inclusive education. *Journal of the Association for Persons with Severe Handicaps, 20*(2), 136–146.

Falvey, M. A. (Ed.). (1995). *Inclusive and heterogeneous schooling: Assessment, curriculum, and instruction.* Baltimore: Brookes.

Ferguson, D. L. (1995). The real challenge of inclusion: Confessions of a "rabid inclusionist." *Phi Delta Kappan, 77,* 281–287.

Ferguson, P. M., Ferguson, D. K., & Jones, D. (1988). Generations of hope: Parental perspectives on the transitions of their children with severe retardation from school to adult life. *Journal of the Association for Persons with Severe Handicaps, 13,* 177–187.

Frith, G. H., & Lindsey, J. D. (1982). Certification, training, and other programming variables affecting special education and the paraprofessinal concept. *Journal of Special Education, 16,* 229–236.

Frith, G. H., & Mims, A. (1985). Burnout among special education paraprofessionals. *Teaching Exceptional Children, 17,* 225–227.

Fuchs, D., & Fuchs, L. S. (1988). Evaluation of the adaptive learning environments model. *Exceptional Children, 55,* 115–127.

Fuchs, D., & Fuchs, L. (1992). Framing the REI debate: Abolitionists versus conservationists. In J. W. Lloyd, N. N. Singh, & A. C. Repp (Eds.), *The regular education initiative: Alternative perspectives on concepts, issues, and models* (pp. 241–255). Sycamore, IL: Sycamore.

Fuchs, D., & Fuchs, L. S. (1994). Inclusive schools movement and the radicalization of special education reform. *Exceptional Children, 60,* 294–309.

Fuchs, D., & Fuchs, L. S. (1995, March). What's "special" about special education? *Phi Delta Kappan,* pp. 522–530.

Full inclusion of students who are blind or visually impaired: A position paper. (1993). *The Braille Forum, 32*(1), 44–45.

Gartner, A., & Lipsky, D. K. (1987). Beyond special education: Toward a quality system for all students. *Harvard Educational Review, 57*(4), 367–395.

Giangreco, M. F., Cloninger, C. J., & Iverson, V. S. (1993). *Choosing options and accommodations for children: A guide to planning inclusive education.* Baltimore: Brookes.

Giangreco, M. F., Dennis, R., Cloninger, C., Edelman, S., & Schattman, R. (1993). "I've counted Jon": Transformational experiences of teachers educating students with disabilities. *Exceptional Children, 59,* 359–372.

Giangreco, M., Edelman, S., Dennis, R., & Cloninger, C. (1993). My child has a classmate with severe disabilities: What parents of nondisabled children think about full inclusion. *Developmental Disabilities Bulletin, 21*(1), 77–91.

Givens-Ogle, L., Christ, B., & Idol, L. (1991). Collaborative consultation: The San Juan Unified School District Project. *Journal of Educational and Psychological Consultation, 2*(3), 267–284.

Goals 2000: Educate America Act, Sen. Rep. 103-85, 103d Cong., 1st Sess. (1993).

Gottlieb, J., Alter, M., Gottlieb, B. W., & Wishner, J. (1994). Special education in urban America: It's not justifiable for many. *Journal of Special Education, 27*(4), 453–465.

Green, S. K., & Shinn, M. R. (1994). Parent attitudes about special education and reintegration: What is the role of student outcomes? *Exceptional Children, 61,* 269–281.

Grosenick, J. K., & Reynolds, M. C. (1978). *Teacher education: Renegotiating roles for mainstreaming.* Minneapolis, MN: National Support Systems Project.

Hallahan, D. P., & Kauffman, J. M. (Eds.). (1994). Theory and practice of special education: Tak-

ing stock a quarter century after Deno and Dunn [Special issue]. *The Journal of Special Education, 27*(4).

Hallahan, D. P., Keller, C. E., McKinney, J. D., Lloyd, J. W., & Bryan, T. (1988). Examining the research base of the Regular Education Initiative: Efficacy studies and the adaptive learning environments model. *Journal of Learning Disabilities, 21,* 29–35.

Harry, B., Allen, N., & McLaughlin, M. (1995). Communication versus compliance: African-American parents' involvement in special education. *Exceptional Children, 61,* 364–377.

Hocutt, A., & McKinney, D. (1995). Moving beyond the Regular Education Initiative: National reform in special education. In J. L. Paul, H. Rosselli, & D. Evans (Eds.), *Integrating school restructuring and special education reform* (pp. 43–62). Fort Worth, TX: Harcourt Brace.

Hoerr, T. R. (1996). Collegiality: A new way to define instructional leadership. *Phi Delta Kappan, 77,* 380–381.

Hollowood, T. M., Salisbury, C. L., Rainforth, B., & Palombaro, M. M. (1994). Use of instructional time in classrooms serving students with and without severe disabilities. *Exceptional Children, 61,* 242–253.

Houck, C. K., & Rogers, C. J. (1994). The special/general education integration initiative for students with specific learning disabilities: A "snapshot" of program change. *Journal of Learning Disabilities, 27,* 435–453.

Hunt, P., Alwell, M., Farron-Davis, F., & Goetz, L. (1996). Creating socially supportive environments for fully included students who experience multiple disabilities. *Journal of the Association for Persons with Severe Handicaps, 21*(2), 53–71.

Hunt, P., Farron-Davis, F., Beckstead, S., Curtis, D., & Goetz, L. (1994). Evaluating the effects of placement of students with severe disabilities in general education versus special classes. *Journal of the Association for Persons with Severe Handicaps, 19,* 200–214.

Hunt, P., & Goetz, L. (1997). Research on inclusive educational programs, practices, and outcomes for students with severe disabilities. *Journal of Special Education, 31,* 3–29.

Hunt, P., Staub, D., Alwell, M., & Goetz, L. (1994). Achievement by all students within the context of cooperative learning groups. *Journal of the Association for Persons with Severe Handicaps, 19,* 290–301.

Idol, L., Paolucci-Whitcomb, P., & Nevin, A. (1986). *Collaborative consultation.* Austin, TX: Pro-Ed.

Individuals with Disabilities Education Act, 20 U.S.C. §§ 1400 *et seq.* (1997).

Jakupcak, J. (1993). Innovative classroom programs for full inclusion. In J. W. Putnam (Ed.), *Cooperative learning and strategies*

for inclusion: Celebrating diversity in the classroom (pp. 163–179). Baltimore: Brookes.

Jenkins, J. R., Jewell, M., Leicester, N., O'Connor, R. E., Jenkins, L. M., & Troutner, N. M. (1994). Accommodations for individual differences without classroom ability groups: An experiment in school restructuring. *Exceptional Children, 60,* 344–358.

Jones, K. H., & Bender, W. N. (1993). Utilization of paraprofessionals in special education: A review of the literature. *Remedial and Special Education, 14*(1), 7–14.

Kagan, S. L., & Neville, P. R. (1993). *Integrating services for children and families: Understanding the past to shape the future.* New Haven, CT: Yale University Press.

Kauffman, J. M., Gerber, M. M., & Semmel, M. I. (1988). Arguable assumptions underlying the Regular Education Initiative. *Journal of Learning Disabilities, 21,* 6–11.

Keogh, B. K. (1988a). Improving services for problem learners: Rethinking and restructuring. *Journal of Learning Disabilities, 21*(1), 19–22.

Keogh, B. K. (1988b). Perspectives on the Regular Education Initiative. *Learning Disabilities Focus, 4*(1), 3–5.

Kohler, P. D. (1993). Best practices in transition: Substantiated or implied. In P. Kohler et al. (Eds.), *Transition from school to adult life: Foundations, best practices, and research directions.* Champaign-Urbana, IL: University of Illinois. (ERIC Document Reproduction Service No. ED 358 607)

Lewis, A. (1989). *Restructuring America's schools.* Arlington, VA: American Association of School Administrators.

Lieberman, L. M. (1985). Special education and regular education: A merger made in heaven? *Exceptional Children, 51,* 513–516.

Lipsky, D. K., & Gartner, A. (1989). *Beyond special education: Quality education for all.* Baltimore: Brookes.

Lutkemier, D. (1991). Attitudes and practices regarding the implementation of collaborative educational services. *The Consulting Edge: A Publication of the Association for Educational and Psychological Consultants, 3*(2), 1–3.

Madden, N. A., & Slavin, R. E. (1983). Mainstreaming students with mild handicaps: Academic and social outcomes. *Review of Educational Research, 53,* 519–569.

Madden, N. A., Slavin, R. E., Karweit, N. L., Dolan, L. J., & Wasik, B. A. (1993). Success for all: Longitudinal effects of a restructuring program for inner-city elementary schools. *American Educational Research Journal, 30,* 123–148.

Manset, G., & Semmel, M. I. (1997). Are inclusive programs for students with mild disabilities effective? A comparative review of model programs. *The Journal of Special Education, 31,* 155–180.

Marston, D. (1996). A comparison of inclusion only, pull-out only, and combined service models for students with mild disabilities. *Journal of Special Education, 30,* 121–132.

Martin, J. E., & Marshall, L. H. (1996). Choice-Maker: Infusing self-determination instruction into the IEP and transition process. In D. J. Sands & M. L. Wehmeyer (Eds.), *Self-determination across the life span: Independence and choice for people with disabilities* (pp. 215–236). Baltimore: Brookes.

McDonnell, L. M., McLaughlin, M. J., & Morison, P. (Eds.). (1997). *Educating one and all: Students with disabilities and standards-based reform.* Washington, DC: National Academy Press.

McIntosh, R., Vaughn, R. S., Schumm, J. S., Haager, D., & Lee, O. (1993). Observations of students with learning disabilities in general education classrooms. *Exceptional Children, 60*(3), 249–261.

McKinney, J. D., & Hocutt, A. M. (1988). The need for policy analysis in evaluating the Regular Education Initiative. *Journal of Learning Disabilities, 21,* 12–18.

Michael, M. G., Arnold, K., Magliocca, L. A., & Miller, S. (1992). Influences on teachers' attitudes of the parents' role as collaborator. *Remedial and Special Education, 13*(2), 24–30.

Minke, K. M., Bear, G. G., Deemer, S. A., & Griffin, S. M. (1996). Teachers' experiences with inclusive classrooms: Implications for special education reform. *Journal of Special Education, 30,* 152–186.

Odom, S. L., & McEvoy, M. A. (1990). Mainstreaming at the preschool level: Potential barriers and tasks for the field. *Topics in Early Childhood Special Education, 10*(2), 48–61.

Paul, J. L., & Rosselli, H. (1995). Integrating the parallel reforms in general and special education. In J. L. Paul, H. Rosselli, & D. Evans, (Eds.), *Integrating school restructuring and special education reform* (pp. 188–213). Fort Worth, TX: Harcourt Brace.

Pearman, E. L., Huang, A., & Mellblom, C. I. (1997). The inclusion of all students: Concerns and incentives of educators. *Education and Training in Mental Retardation and Developmental Disabilities, 32,* 11–20.

Peck, C. A., Odom, S. L., & Bricker, D. D. (Eds.). (1993). *Integrating young children with disabilities into community programs: Ecological perspectives on research and implementation.* Baltimore: Brookes.

Pickett, A. L. (1986). Certified partners: Four good reasons for certification of paraprofessionals. *American Educator, 10*(3), 31–47.

Pugach, M. C. (1995). On the failure of the imagination in inclusive schools. *Journal of Special Education, 29,* 212–223.

Pugach, M. C., & Johnson, L. J. (1995). A new framework for thinking about collaboration. In *Collaborative practitioners, collaborative schools* (pp. 27–44). Denver, CO: Love.

Pugach, M. C., & Warger, C. L. (1996). *Curriculum trends, special education, and reform: Refocusing the conversation.* New York: Teachers College Press.

Pugach, M. C., & Wesson, C. L. (1995). Teachers' and students' views of team teaching of general education and learning-disabled students in two fifth-grade classes. *Elementary School Journal, 95*(3), 279–295.

Putnam, J. W. (Ed.). (1993). *Cooperative learning and strategies for inclusion: Celebrating diversity in the classroom.* Baltimore: Brookes.

Reynolds, M. C. (1991). Classification and labeling. In J. W. Lloyd, N. N. Singh, & A. C. Repp (Eds.), *The Regular Education Initiative: Alternative perspectives on concepts, issues, and models* (pp. 29–42). Sycamore, IL: Sycamore.

Reynolds, M., & Wang, M. C. (1983). Restructuring "special" school programs: A position paper. *Policy Studies Review, 2,* 189–212.

The road to inclusion can be smooth or hellish. (1995, April 2). *School Board News/Conference Edition,* p. 5.

Ryndak, D. L., Downing, J. E., Jacqueline, L. R., & Morrison, A. P. (1995). Parents' perceptions after inclusion of their children with moderate or severe disabilities. *Journal of the Association for Persons with Severe Handicaps, 20*(2), 147–157.

Sailor, W. (1991). Special education in the restructured school. *Remedial and Special Education, 12*(6), 8–22.

Sailor, W., Gerry, M., & Wilson, W. C. (1987). Policy implications of emergent full inclusion models for the education of students with severe disabilities. In M. C. Wang, H. J. Walberg, & M. C. Reynolds (Eds.), *The handbook of special education* (Vol. 4, pp. 175–196). Oxford, UK: Pergamon.

Sailor, W., & Skrtic, T. (1995). Modern and postmodern agendas in special education: Implications for teacher education, research, and policy development. In J. L. Paul, H. Rosselli, & D. Evans, (Eds.), *Integrating school restructuring and special education reform* (pp. 418–432). Fort Worth, TX: Harcourt Brace.

Salisbury, C. L. (1991). Mainstreaming during the early childhood years. *Exceptional Children, 58,* 146–155.

Salisbury, C. L., Palombaro, M. M., & Hollowood, P. M. (1993). On the nature and change of an inclusive elementary school. *Journal of the Association for Persons with Severe Handicaps, 18*(2), 75–84.

Salzberg, C. L., & Morgan, J. (1995). Preparing teachers to work with paraeducators. *Teacher Education and Special Education, 18*(1), 49–55.

Sands, D. J., & Wehmeyer, M. L. (Eds.). (1996). *Self-determination across the life span: Theory and practice.* Baltimore: Brookes.

Saver, K., & Downes, B. (1991). PTI crew: A model for teacher collaboration in the elementary school. *Intervention in School and Clinic, 27*(2), 116–122.

Schulte, A. C., Osborne, S. S., & McKinney, J. D. (1990). Academic outcomes for students with learning disabilities in consultation and resource programs. *Exceptional Children, 57,* 162–172.

Schumaker, J. D., & Deshler, D. D. (1988). Implementing the Regular Education Initiative in secondary schools: A different ballgame. *Journal of Learning Disabilities, 21,* 36–42.

Schumm, J. S., & Vaughn, S. (1991). Making adaptations for mainstreamed students: General classroom teachers' perspectives. *Remedial and Special Education, 12,* 18–27.

Scruggs, T. E., & Mastropieri, M. A. (1996). Teacher perceptions of mainstreaming/inclusion, 1958–1995: A research synthesis. *Exceptional Children, 63,* 59–74.

Semmel, M. I., Abernathy, T. V., Butera, G., & Lesar, S. (1991). Teacher perceptions of the regular education initiative. *Exceptional Children, 58,* 9–24.

Sharpe, M. N., York, J. L., & Knight, J. (1994). Effects of inclusion on the academic performance of classmates without disabilities: A preliminary study. *Remedial and Special Education, 15,* 281–287.

Skrtic, T. M. (1987). An organizational analysis of special education reform. *Counterpoint, 8*(2), 15–19.

Skrtic, T. M. (1991). *Behind special education: A critical analysis of professional culture and school organization.* Denver, CO: Love.

Smart, J. F., & Smart, D. W. (1992). Cultural issues in the rehabilitation of Hispanics. *Journal of Rehabilitation, 58*(2), 29–37.

Smith, M. J., & Ryan, A. S. (1987). Chinese-American families of children with developmental disabilities: An exploratory study of reactions to service providers. *Mental Retardation, 25,* 345–350.

Snell, M. E. (1988). Gartner and Lipsky's "Beyond special education. Toward a quality system for all students." *Journal of the Association for Persons with Severe Handicaps, 13,* 137–140.

Snell, M. E. (1991). Schools are for all kids: The importance of integration for students with severe disabilities and their peers. In J. W. Lloyd, A. C. Repp, & N. N. Singh (Eds.), *The Regular Education Initiative: Alternative perspectives on concepts, issues, and models* (pp. 133–148). Sycamore, IL: Sycamore.

Stainback, S., & Stainback, W. (1984). A rationale for the merger of regular and special education. *Exceptional Children, 51,* 102–111.

Stainback, S., & Stainback, W. (Eds.). (1992). *Curriculum considerations in inclusive classrooms: Facilitating learning for all students.* Baltimore: Brookes.

Stainback, S., Stainback, W., & Ayres, B. (1996). Schools as inclusive communities. In

W. Stainback & S. Stainback (Eds.), *Controversial issues confronting special education: Divergent perspectives* (2nd ed., pp. 31–43). Boston: Allyn & Bacon.

Stainback, W., & Stainback, S. (1990). *Support networks for inclusive schooling: Interdependent integrated education.* Baltimore: Brookes.

Stainback, W., & Stainback, S. (Eds.). (1996). *Controversial issues confronting special education: Divergent perspectives* (2nd ed). Boston: Allyn & Bacon.

Staub, D., Schwartz, I. S., Galluci, C., & Peck, C. (1994). Four portraits of friendship at an inclusive school. *Journal of the Association for Persons with Severe Handicaps, 19,* 314–325.

TASH (The Association for Persons with Severe Handicaps). (1993). *Resolution on inclusive education.* Baltimore: Author.

Taylor, S. (1988). Caught in the continuum: A critical analysis of the principle of least restrictive environment. *Journal of the Association for Persons with Severe Handicaps, 13*(1), 41–53.

Thousand, J. S., Fox, T., Reid, R., Godek, J., Williams, W., & Fox, W. (1986). *The homecoming model: Educating students who present intensive challenges within regular education environments.* Burlington: University of Vermont, Center for Developmental Disabilities.

Thousand, J. S., Villa, R. A., & Nevin, A. I. (1994). *Creativity and collaborative learning: A practical guide for empowering students and teachers.* Baltimore: Brookes.

Thousand, J., Villa, R. A., & Nevin, A. (1996). Collaboration. In National Council on Disability (Ed.), *Improving the implementation of the Individuals with Disabilities Education Act: Making schools work for all of America's children* (pp. 565–602). Washington, DC: National Council on Disability.

Turnbull, A. P., & Schulz, J. B. (1979). *Mainstreaming handicapped students: A guide for the classroom teacher.* Boston: Allyn & Bacon.

Turnbull, A. P., & Turnbull, H. R. (1997). *Families, professionals, and exceptionality: A special partnership* (3rd ed.). Upper Saddle River, NJ: Merrill/Prentice Hall.

U.S. Department of Education. (1993). *To assure the free appropriate public education of all children with disabilities: Fifteenth annual report to Congress on the implementation of the Individuals with Disabilities Education Act.* Washington, DC: Author.

U.S. Department of Education. (1996). *To assure the free appropriate public education of all children with disabilities: Eighteenth annual report to Congress on the implementation of the Individuals with Disabilities Education Act.* Washington, DC: Author.

U.S. Department of Education and American Educational Research Association. (1995). *School-linked comprehensive services for children and families: What we know and what we need to know.* Washington, DC: Authors.

Van Reusen, A. K., & Bos, C. S. (1994). Facilitating student participation in individualized education programs through motivation strategy instruction. *Exceptional Children, 60,* 466–475.

Vaughn, S., & Schumm, J. S. (1995). Responsible inclusion for students with learning disabilities. *Journal of Learning Disabilities, 28,* 264–270.

Villa, R. A., & Thousand, J. S. (Eds.). (1995). *Creating an inclusive school.* Alexandria, VA: Association for Supervision and Curriculum Development.

Villa, R. A., Thousand, J. S., Meyers, H., & Nevin, A. I. (1996). Teacher and administrator perceptions of heterogeneous education. *Exceptional Children, 63,* 29–45.

Villa, R. A., Thousand, J. S., Stainback, W., & Stainback, S. (1992). *Restructuring for caring and effective education: An administrative guide to creating heterogeneous schools.* Baltimore: Brookes.

Walker, H. M., & Bullis, M. (1991). Behavior disorders and the social context of regular class integration: A conceptual dilemma? In J. W. Lloyd, N. W. Singh, & A. C. Repp (Eds.), *The regular education initiative: Alternative perspectives on concepts, issues, and models* (pp. 75–93). Sycamore, IL: Sycamore.

Wang, M., & Birch, J. (1984). Comparison of a full-time mainstreaming program and a resource room approach. *Exceptional Children, 51,* 497–502.

Wang, M. C., Peverly, S., & Randolph, R. (1984). An investigation of the implementation and effects of a full-time mainstreaming program. *Remedial and Special Education, 5*(6), 21–32.

Warger, C. L., & Pugach, M. C. (1993). Collaboration: A curriculum focus for collaboration. *Learning Disabilities Forum, 18*(4), 26–30.

Werts, M. G., Wolery, M., Snyder, E. D. & Caldwell, N. K. (1996). Teachers' perceptions of the supports critical to the success of inclusion programs. *Journal of the Association for Persons with Severe Handicaps, 21*(1), 9–21.

Will, M. C. (1986). Educating children with learning problems: A shared responsibility. *Exceptional Children, 52,* 411–415.

Will, M. C. (1993). The question of personal autonomy. *Journal of Vocational Rehabilitation, 3*(2), 9–10.

Wolery, M., Venn, M. L., Holcombe, A., Brookfield, J., Martin, C. G., Huffman, K., Schroder, C., & Fleming, L. A. (1994). Employment of related service personnel in preschool programs: A survey of general early educators. *Exceptional Children, 61,* 25–39.

York-Barr, J., Schultz, T., Doyle, M. B., Kronberg, R., & Crosset, S. (1996). Inclusive schooling in St. Cloud: Perspectives on the process and people. *Remedial and Special Education, 17,* 92–103.

Ysseldyke, J. E., & Algozzine, B. (1990). *Introduction to special education* (2nd ed.). Boston: Houghton Mifflin.

Ysseldyke, J. E., Algozzine, B., & Epps, S. (1983). A logical and empirical analysis of current practices in classifying students as handicapped. *Exceptional Children, 50,* 160–166.

Ysseldyke, J. E., Thurlow, M. L., Algozzine, B., & Nathan, J. (1993). Open enrollment and students with disabilities: Issues, concerns, fears, and anticipated benefits. *Exceptional Children, 59,* 390–401.

Ysseldyke, J. E., Thurlow, M. L., Wotruba, J. W., & Nania, P. A. (1990). Instructional arrangements: Perceptions from general education. *Teaching Exceptional Children, 22*(4), 4–8.

Zigmond, N., & Baker, J. M. (1995). Concluding comments: Current and future practices in inclusive schooling. *The Journal of Special Education, 29,* 245–250.

Zigmond, N., Jenkins, J., Fuchs, L. S., Deno, S., Fuchs, D., Baker, J. N., Jenkins, L., & Couthino, M. (1995, March). Special education in restructured schools: Findings from three multi-year studies. *Phi Delta Kappan,* pp. 531–540.

Zionts, P. (Ed.). (1997). *Inclusion strategies for students with learning and behavior problems: Perspectives, experiences, and best practices.* Austin, TX: Pro-Ed.

CHAPTER 4

Abeel, S. (1994). *What once was white: Reach for the moon.* Duluth, MN: Pfeifer-Hamilton.

Albinger, P. (1995). Stories for the resource room: Piano lessons, imaginary illness, and broken-down cars. *Journal of Learning Disabilities, 28*(10), 615–621.

Anderson-Inman, L., Knox-Quinn, C., & Horney, M. A. (1996). Computer-based study strategies for students with learning disabilities: Individual differences associated with adoption level. *Journal of Learning Disabilities, 29,* 461–485.

Artiles, A. J., & Trent, S. C. (1994). Overrepresentation of minority students in special education: A continuing debate. *Journal of Special Education, 27,* 410–437.

Barga, N. K. (1996). Students with learning disabilities in education: Managing a disability. *Journal of Learning Disabilities, 29,* 413–421.

Behrmann, M. M. (1994). Assistive technology for students with mild disabilities. *Intervention in School and Clinic, 30*(2), 70–83.

Bracker, P. O. (1994). The advantages of inclusion for students with learning disabilities. *Journal of Learning Disabilities, 27,* 581–582.

Brigham, F. J., & Scruggs, T. E. (1995). Elaborative maps for enhanced learning of historical information: Uniting spatial, verbal, and imaginal information. *Journal of Special Education, 28,* 440.

Bunce, B. H. (1995). *Building a language-focused curriculum for the preschool classroom: Volume II, a planning guide.* Baltimore: Brookes.

Castro, P. (1997, February 3). Goodbye, friend. *People Magazine,* 68–75.

Coopersmith, S. (1967). *The antecedents of self-esteem.* San Francisco: Freeman.

Cosby, E. W. (1993). [Personal papers]. Unpublished manuscript, Hello Friend Ennis William Cosby Foundation, Los Angeles.

Cosby, E. W. (1996). [Personal papers]. Unpublished manuscript Hello Friend Ennis William Cosby Foundation, Los Angeles.

Council for Learning Disabilities. (1986a). Measurement and training of perceptual and perceptual-motor functions. *Learning Disability Quarterly, 9,* 247.

Council for Learning Disabilities. (1986b). Use of discrepancy formulas in the identification of learning disabled individuals. *Learning Disability Quarterly, 9,* 245.

Council for Learning Disabilities. (1997). *Infosheet: What do we know about the characteristics of learning disabilities?* [On-line]. Available: http://www.winthrop.edu./cld/Info sheet%20Character istics html

Coutinho, M. J. (1995). Who will be learning disabled after the reauthorization of IDEA? Two very distinct perspectives. *Journal of Learning Disabilities, 29,* 664–668.

Dawes, C. (1996). Learning disabilities research encompasses education and biology. *CHDD Outlook, 9*(2), 1–3.

Deci, E. L., Hodges, R., Pierson, L., & Tomassone, J. (1992). Autonomy and competence as motivational factors in students with learning disabilities and emotional handicaps. *Journal of Learning Disabilities, 25*(7), 457–471.

Deshler, D. D., Schumaker, J. B., Alley, G. R., Warner, M. M., & Clark, F. (1982). Learning disabilities in adolescents and young adult populations: Research implications (part 1). *Focus on Exceptional Children, 15,* 1–12.

Driver, B. L. (1996). Where do we go from here? Sustaining and maintaining co-teaching relationships. *Learning Disabilities Forum, 21*(4), 29–32.

Duffy, F. H., & McAnulty, G. B. (1985). Brain electrical activity mapping (BEAM): The search for a physiological signature of dyslexia. In F. H. Duffy & N. Geschwind (Eds.), *Dyslexia: A neuroscientific approach to clinical evaluation* (pp. 105–122). Boston: Little, Brown.

Dyson, L. L. (1996). The experiences of families of children with learning disabilities: Parental stress, family functioning, and sibling self-concept. *Journal of Learning Disabilities, 29,* 280–286.

Eden, G. F., Stein, J. F., & Wood, F. B. (1995). Verbal and visual problems in reading disability. *Journal of Learning Disabilities, 28,* 272–290.

Edyburn, D. L. (1992). Aligning technology tools with powerful instructional interventions. *Learning Disabilities Forum, 18*(1), 31–35.

ERIC (Educational Resources Information Center) Clearinghouse on Disabilities and Gifted Education. (1995, December). Beginning reading and phonological awareness for students with learning disabilities. *ERIC Digest,* No. E540 [Online]. Available:http://www.ed. gov/databases/ERIC_Digests/ed392197.html

Fisher, G., & Cummings, R. (1990). *The survival guide for kids with LD.* Minneapolis, MN: Free Spirit.

Fitzgerald, G. E., & Koury, K. A. (1996). Empirical advances in technology-assisted instruction for students with learning disabilities. *Journal of Research on Computing in Education, 28,* 526–553.

Forness, S. (1996). Social and emotional dimensions of learning disabilities. In B. J. Cratty & R. L. Goldman (Eds.), *Learning disabilities: Contemporary viewpoints* (pp. 61–86). Amsterdam: Harwood Academic.

Frankenberger, W., & Fronzaglio, K. (1991). A review of states' criteria and procedures for identifying children with learning disabilities. *Journal of Learning Disabilities, 24,* 495–500.

Good, T. L., & Brophy, J. E. (1990). *Educational psychology: A realistic approach* (4th ed.). Reading, MA: Addison Wesley.

Greene, J. F. (1995–1996). *Language! A curriculum for at-risk and ESL students at grades 2–12.* Longmont, CO: Sopris West.

Greenwood, C. R. (1991). Classwide peer tutoring: Longitudinal effects on the reading, language, and mathematics achievement of at-risk students. *Journal of Reading, Writing, and Learning Disabilities International, 7*(2), 105–123.

Greenwood, C. R., & Delquadri, J. (1995). Classwide peer tutoring and the prevention of school failure. *Preventing School Failure, 39,* 21–25.

Gresham, F. M., MacMillan, D. L., & Bocian, K. M. (1996). Learning disabilities, low achievement, and mild mental retardation: More alike than different? *Journal of Learning Disabilities, 29,* 570–581.

Hallahan, D. P. (1992). Some thoughts on why the prevalence of learning disabilities has increased. *Journal of Learning Disabilities, 25,* 523–538.

Hallenbeck, M. J. (1996). The cognitive strategy in writing: Welcome relief for adolescents with learning disabilities. *Learning Disabilities Research and Practice, 11,* 107–119.

Hammill, D. D. (1993). A brief look at the learning disabilities movement in the United States. *Journal of Learning Disabilities, 26,* 295–310.

Hammill, D. D., & Larsen, S. (1974). The effectiveness of psycholinguistic training. *Exceptional Children, 41,* 5–15.

Howard-Rose, D., & Rose, C. (1994). Students' adaptation to task environments in resource room and regular class settings. *Journal of Special Education, 28*(1), 3–26.

IEPs made in Heaven. (1996, March/ April). *LDA (Learning Disabilities Association) News Briefs,* p. 13.

Individuals with Disabilities Education Act (IDEA). 20 U.S.C. § 1400 *et seq.* (1997).

Kavale, K. A., Forness, S. R., & Lorsbach, T. C. (1991). Definition for definitions of learning disabilities. *Learning Disability Quarterly, 14,* 257–265.

Kavale, K. A., Fuchs, D., & Scruggs, T. E. (1994). Setting the record straight on learning disability and low achievement: Implications for policymaking. *Journal of Learning Disabilities, 9,* 70–77.

King-Sears, M. E., & Bradley, D. F. (1995). Classwide peer tutoring. *Preventing School Failure, 40*(1), 29–36.

Kolstad, R., Wilkinson, M. M., & Briggs, L. D. (1997). Inclusion programs for learning disabled students in middle grades. *Education, 117,* 419–426.

Kotaoka, J. C., & Patton, J. R. (1996). Integrated programming and mathematics: An attractive way to plan for generalization. *LD Forum, 21*(3), 16–20.

Landmark College. (1997). *Landmark College* [On-line], Available: http://www.landmarkcollege.org

Learning Disabilities Association. (1993). *Fact sheet: Transition services* [On-line]. Available: http://www.ldanatl.org/factsheets/transition.html

Lee, C., & Jackson, R. (1992). *Faking it: A look into the mind of a creative learner.* Portsmouth, NH: Boynton/Cook.

Lenz, B. K., Marrs, R. W., Schumaker, J. B., & Deshler, D. D. (1993). *The lesson organizer routine.* Lawrence, KS: Edge Enterprises.

Levy, N. R. (1996). Teaching analytical writing: Help for general education middle school teachers. *Intervention in School and Clinic, 32*(2), 95–103.

Light, J. G., & DeFries, J. C. (1995). Comorbidity of reading and mathematics disabilities: Genetic and environmental etiologies. *Journal of Learning Disabilities, 28,* 96–106.

Lovitt, T. C., & Horton, S. V. (1994). Strategies for adapting science textbooks for youth with learning disabilities. *Remedial and Special Education, 15*(2), 105–116.

Maag, J. W., & Webber, J. (1995). Promoting children's social development in general education classrooms. *Preventing School Failure, 39,* 13.

Madge, S., Affleck, J., & Lowenbraun, S. (1990). Social effects of integrated classrooms and resource room/regular class placements on elementary students with learning disabilities. *Journal of Learning Disabilities, 23*(7), 439–445.

Manis, F. R. (1996). Current trends in dyslexia research. In B. J. Cratty & R. L. Goldman (Eds.), *Learning disabilities: Contemporary viewpoints* (pp. 27–42). Amsterdam: Harwood Academic.

Marks, J. W., Van Laeys, J., Bender, W. N., & Scott, K. S. (1996). Teachers create learning strategies: Guidelines for classroom creation. *Teaching Exceptional Children, 28,* 34–38.

McCarthy, J. J., & Kirk, S. A. (1961). *The Illinois Test of Psycholinguistic Abilities: Experimental edition.* Urbana, IL: University of Illinois Press.

McCarthy, J. M., Harris, M. J., & Reeves, K. K. (1997). Specific learning disabilities in preschool children: Shifting paradigms in the middle of the stream. *Learning Disabilities Research and Practice, 12,* 146–150.

McLeskey, J., & Waldron, N. L. (1991). Identifying students with learning disabilities: The effect of implementing statewide guidelines. *Journal of Learning Disabilities, 24,* 501–506.

Meltzer, L., & Reid, D. K. (1994). New directions in the assessment of students with special needs. *Journal of Special Education, 28,* 338–355.

Mercer, C. D. (1997). *Students with learning disabilities* (5th ed.). Upper Saddle River, NJ: Merrill/Prentice Hall.

Mercer, C. D., Jordan, L., Allsopp, D. H., & Mercer, A. R. (1996). Learning disabilities definitions and criteria used by state education departments. *Learning Disabilities Quarterly, 19,* 217–231.

Mercer, C. D., & Lane, H. (1994). Principles of responsible inclusion. *LDA (Learning Disabilities Association) Newsbriefs, 29*(4), 1, 7.

National Joint Committee on Learning Disabilities. (1994). Learning Disabilities: Issues on definition, a position paper of the National Joint Committee on Learning Disabilities. In *Collective perspectives on issues affecting learning disabilities: Position papers and statements* (pp. 3–8). Austin, TX: Pro-Ed.

Ochoa, S. H., Rivera, B. D., & Powell, M. P. (1997). Factors used to comply with the exclusionary clause with bilingual and limited-English-proficient pupils: Initial guidelines. *Learning Disabilities Research and Practice, 12,* 161–167.

Oliver, J. M., Cole, N. H., & Hollingsworth, H. (1991). Learning disabilities as functions of familial learning problems and developmental problems. *Exceptional Children, 57,* 427–440.

Olivier, C., & Bowler, R. F. (1996). *Learning to learn.* New York: Fireside/Simon & Schuster.

Pechura, C. M., & Martin, J. B. (Eds.). (1991). *Mapping the brain and its functions: Integrating enabling technologies into neuroscience research.* Washington, DC: National Academy Press.

Phillips, N. B., Fuchs, L. S., & Fuchs, D. (1994). Effects of classwide curriculum-based measurement and peer tutoring: A collaborative researcher–practitioner interview study. *Journal of Learning Disabilities, 27,* 420–434.

Polloway, E. A., Epstein, M. H., Bursuck, W. D., Hayanthi, M., & Cumblad, C. (1994). Homework practices of general education teachers. *Journal of Learning Disabilities, 27,* 500–510.

The Psychological Corporation. (1992). *Wechsler Individual Achievement Test.* San Antonio, TX: Author.

Reiff, H. B., Gerber, P. J., & Ginsberg, R. (1997). *Exceeding expectations: Successful adults with learning disabilities.* Austin, TX: Pro-Ed.

Rice, M. L. (1995). The rationale and operating principles for a language-focused curriculum for preschool children. In M. L. Rice & K. A. Wilcox (Eds.), *Building a language-focused curriculum for the preschool classroom: Vol. 1. A foundation for lifelong communication.* (pp. 181–198). Baltimore: Brookes.

Rice, M. L., & Wilcox, K. A. (Eds.). (1995). *Building a language-focused curriculum for the preschool classroom: Vol. 1. A foundation for lifelong communication.* Baltimore: Brookes.

Rice, M. L., Sell, M., & Hadley, P. (1990). The Social Interactive Coding System (SICS): An on-line, clinically relevant descriptive tool. *Language, Speech, and Hearing Services in Schools, 21*(1), 2–14.

Roeper, A. (1996). Reflections from Annamarie. *Roeper Review, 18,* 224–225.

Salend, S. J., & Hofstetter, E. (1996). Adapting a problem-solving approach to teaching mathematics to students with mild disabilities. *Intervention in School and Clinic, 31*(4), 209–217.

Schumaker, J. B., & Deshler, D. D. (1992). Validation of learning strategy interventions for students with LD: Results of a programmatic research effort. In B. Y. L. Wong (Ed.), *Contemporary intervention research in learning disabilities: An international perspective* (pp. 22–46). New York: Springer.

Scott, C. M. (1991). Problem writers: Nature, assessment, and intervention. In A. G. Kamhi & H. W. Catts (Eds.), *Reading disabilities: A developmental language perspective* (pp. 303–344). Boston: Allyn & Bacon.

Seligman, M. E. P. (1990a). *Learned optimism.* New York: Pocketbooks.

Seligman, M. E. P. (1990b). *The optimistic child* [Audiotape].

Sergeant, J. (1995). Life after LAP. In M. L. Rice & K. A. Wilcox (Eds.), *Building a language-focused curriculum for the preschool classroom: Vol. 1. A foundation for lifelong communication* (pp. 181–198). Baltimore: Brookes.

Shank, M. S. (1997). *Making homework family friendly.* Manuscript in preparation, University of South Alabama, Mobile.

Shaw, S. F., Cullen, J. P., & Brinckerhoff, L. C. (1995). Operationalizing a definition of learning disabilities. *Journal of Learning Disabilities, 28,* 586–601.

Sherman, G. F. (1995). Dyslexia: Is it all in your mind? *Perspectives, 21*(4), 1.

Silver, A. A., & Hagin, R. A. (1990). *Disorders of learning in childhood.* New York: Wiley.

Smith, S. (1991). *Succeeding against the odds: Strategies and insights from the learning disabled.* Los Angeles: J. P. Tarcher.

Smith, S. L. (1995). *No easy answers: The learning disabled child at home and at school* (rev. ed.). New York: Bantam Books.

Spear-Swerling, L., & Sternberg, R. (1994). The road not taken: An integrative theoretical model of reading disability. *Journal of Learning Disabilities, 27,* 91–103.

Stoddard, K., Valcante, G., Roemer, F., & O'Shea, D. J. (1994). Preparing teachers for family support roles. *LD (Learning Disabilities) Forum, 19*(2), 33–35.

Tallent-Runnels, M. K., & Sigler, E. A. (1995). The status of the selection of gifted students with learning disabilities for gifted programs. *Roeper Review, 17,* 246–247.

Taylor, B. R. (1994). Inclusion: Time for a change—A response to Margaret N. Carr. *Journal of Learning Disabilities, 27,* 579–580.

Tuttle, C. G., & Tuttle, G. A. (Eds.) (1995). *Challenging voices.* Los Angeles: Lowell House.

U.S. Department of Education. (1995). *To assure the free appropriate education of all children with disabilities: Fifteenth annual report to Congress on the implementation of the Individuals with Disabilities Education Act.* Washington, DC: Author.

U.S. Department of Education. (1997). *The condition of education 1997, indicator 46* [Online]. Available: http://nces01.ed.gov/pubs/ce/c9746a01.html

Vaughn, S., Elbaum, B. E., & Schumm, J. S. (1996). The effects of inclusion on the social function of students with learning disabilities. *Journal of Learning Disabilities, 29,* 598–608.

Vaughn, S., & Schumm, J. S. (1995). Responsible inclusion for students with learning disabilities. *Journal of Learning Disabilities, 28,* 264–270, 290.

Voltz, D. L., Elliott, R. N., & Harris, W. B. (1995). Promising practices in facilitating collaboration between resource room teachers and general education teachers. *Learning Disabilities Research and Practice, 10,* 129–136.

Watkins, R. V., & Bunce, B. H. (1996). Natural literacy: Theory and practice for preschool intervention programs. *Topics in Early Childhood Special Education, 16,* 191–212.

Wiederholt, J. L. (1974). Historical perspectives on the education of the learning disabled. In L. Mann & D. Sabatino (Eds.), *The second review of special education* (pp. 103–152). Philadelphia: Journal of Special Education Press.

Woodcock, R. W. (1990). Theoretical foundations of the WJ-R measures of cognitive ability. *Journal of Psychoeducational Assessment, 8,* 231–258.

Yoder, D. I., Retish, E., & Wade, R. (1996). Service Learning: Meeting student and community needs. *Teaching Exceptional Children, 28*(4), 14–21.

Ysseldyke, J. E., Algozzine, B., & Thurlow, M. L. (1994). *Critical issues in special education* (2nd ed.). Boston: Houghton Mifflin.

CHAPTER 5

Achenbach, T. M., & Edelbrock, C. S. (1981). Behavioral problems and competencies reported by parents of normal and disturbed children aged four through sixteen. *Monographs of the Society for Research in Child Development, 46*(1), serial no. 188.

American Academy of Child and Adolescent Psychiatry. (1996a). *Child abuse: The hidden bruises* [On-line]. Available: http://www.psych.med.umich.edu/web/aacap/factsFam/chldabus.htm

American Academy of Child and Adolescent Psychiatry. (1996b). *Psychiatric medication for children* [On-line]. Available: http://www.psych.med.umich.edu/web/aacap/factsFam/psychmed.htm

American Academy of Child and Adolescent Psychiatry. (1996c). *Responding to sexual abuse* [On-line]. Available: http://www.psych.med.umich.edu/web/aacap/factsFam/rspdabus.htm

American Psychiatric Association. (1994). *Diagnostic and statistical manual of mental disorders: DSM-IV* (4th ed.). Washington, DC: Author.

Arllen, N. L., Gable, R. A., & Hendrickson, J. M. (1996). Accommodating students with special needs in general education classrooms. *Preventing School Failure, 41*(1), 7–13.

Barbetta, P. M. (1990). GOALS: Group-oriented adapted levels system for children with behavior disorders. *Academic Therapy, 25,* 645–656.

Baskervill, B. (1996, January 22). The turtle and the dragon: A story of childhood depression. Associated Press. *Mobile Press Register,* pp. 1D, 5D.

Bennett, N. (1996). Something to say. *Reaching Today's Youth, 1*(1), 11.

Berndt, T. J. (1989). Contributions of peer relationships to child development. In T. J. Berndt & G. W. Ladd (Eds.), *Peer relationships in child development* (pp. 407–416). New York: Wiley.

Braaten, S., Kauffman, J. M., Braaten, B., Polsgrove, L., & Nelson, C. M. (1988). The Regular Education Initiative: Patent medicine for behavioral disorders. *Exceptional Children, 55,* 21–27.

Brendtro, L. K., Brokenleg, M., & Van Bockern, S. (1990). *Reclaiming youth at risk: Our hope for the future.* Bloomington, IN: National Educational Service.

Bullis, M., & Paris, K. (1996). Competitive employment and service management for adolescents and young adults with emotional and behavioral disorders. *Special Services in the Schools, 10*(2), 77–96.

Burchard, J. D., & Clarke, R. T. (1990). The role of individualized care in a service delivery system for children and adolescents with severely maladjusted behavior. *The Journal of Mental Health Administration, 17*(1), 48–60.

Burns, B. J., & Friedman, R. M. (1990). Examining the research base for child mental health services and policy. *Journal of Mental Health Administration, 17*(1), 87–98.

Caseau, D., Luckasson, R., & Kroth, R. L. (1994). Special education services for girls with serious emotional disturbance: A case of gender bias? *Behavioral Disorders, 20*(1), 51–60.

Clarke, S., Dunlap, G., Foster-Johnson, L., Childs, K. E., Wilson, D., White, R., & Vera, A. (1995). Improving the conduct of students with behavioral disorders by incorporating student interests into curricular areas. *Behavioral Disorders, 20*(4), 221–237.

Colucci, S. (1993, May). Peer mediation: Creating opportunities for conflict resolution. *Communiqué,* pp. 25–27.

Colvin, G., Greenberg, S., & Sherman, R. (1993). The forgotten variable: Improving academic skills for students with serious emotional disturbance. *Effective School Practices, 12*(1), 20–25.

Coopersmith, S. (1967). *The antecedents of self-esteem.* San Francisco: Freeman.

Council for Children with Behavioral Disorders. (1993, June). Staff position statement: Inclusion. *CCBD Newsletter,* p. 1.

Curwin, R. L. (1992). *Rediscovering hope: Our greatest teaching strategy.* Bloomington, IN: National Educational Service.

DePaepe, P. A., Shores, R. E., Jack, S. L., & Denny, R. K. (1996). Effects of task difficulty on the disruptive and on-task behavior of students with severe behavior disorders. *Behavioral Disorders, 21*(3), 216–225.

Dreikurs, R. (1998). *Maintaining sanity in the classroom: Classroom management techniques* (2nd ed.). Bristol, PA: Hemisphere.

Duchnowski, A. J., & Friedman, R. M. (1990). Children's mental health: Challenges for the 1990s. *Journal of Mental Health Administration, 17,* 3–12.

Eber, L. (1996). Reconstructing schools through the wraparound approach: The LADSE experience. In R. J. Illback & C. M. Nelson (Eds.), *School-based services for students with emotional and behavioral disorders* (pp. 139–154). Binghampton, NY: Haworth.

Eber, L., Nelson, C. M., & Miles, P. (1997). School-based wraparound for students with emotional and behavioral challenges. *Exceptional Children, 63,* 539–555.

Engelmann, S., & Carnine, D. (1982). *Theory of instruction: Principles and applications.* New York: Irvington.

Epstein, M. H., Foley, R. M., & Polloway, E. A. (1995). Homework problems: A comparison of students identified as behaviorally disordered with nonhandicapped students. *Preventing School Failure, 40*(1), 14–19.

Epstein, M. H., Kinder, D., & Bursuck, B. (1989). The academic status of adolescents with behavioral disorders. *Behavioral Disorders, 14*(3), 157–165.

Faber, A., & Mazlish, E. (1980). *How to talk so kids will listen and listen so kids will talk.* New York: Rawson, Wade.

Faber, A., & Mazlish, E. (1996). *How to talk so kids can learn.* New York: Fireside.

Fact sheet: Oppositional defiant disorder. *Ask NOAH about: Mental health* [On-line]. http:///www.noah.cuny.edu:8080/illness/mentalhealth/cornell/conditions/odd.html

Fessler, M. A., Rosenberg, M. S., & Rosenberg, L. A. (1991). Concomitant learning disabilities and learning problems among students with behavioral/emotional disorders. *Behavioral Disorders, 16*(2), 97–106.

Foley, R. M., & Epstein, M. H. (1992). Correlates of the academic achievement of adolescents with behavioral disorders. *Behavioral Disorders, 18*(1), 9–17.

Forness, S., & Knitzer, J. (1992). A new proposed definition and terminology to replace "serious emotional disturbance." *School Psychology Review, 21,* 12–20.

Friend, T. (1994, December 14). Violence-prone men may be both born and made. *USA Today,* p. D5.

Friesen, B. J. (1989). Parents as advocates for children and adolescents with serious emotional handicaps: Issues and directions. In R. M. Friedman, A. J. Duchnowski, & E. L. Henderson (Eds.), *Advocacy on behalf of children with serious emotional problems* (pp. 28–44). Springfield, IL: Charles C. Thomas.

Friesen, B. J., & Huff, B. (1990). Parents and professionals as advocacy partners. *Preventing School Failure, 34*(3), 31–35.

Friesen, B. J., & Koroloff, N. M. (1990). Family centered services: Implications for mental health administration and research. *The Journal of Mental Health Administration, 17*(1), 13–25.

Furr, D. L. (1996). Now I understand the rage. *Reaching Today's Youth, 1*(1), 9–12.

Greenberg, M. (1997). Promoting social and emotional competence: The PATHS Curriculum and the CASEL Network. *Reaching Today's Youth, 4*(1), 49–52.

Gresham, F. M., MacMillan, D. L., & Bocian, K. (1996). "Behavioral Earthquakes:" Low frequency, salient behavioral events that differentiate students at-risk for behavioral disorders. *Behavioral Disorders, 21*(4), 277–292.

Guetzloe, E. C. (1991). *Depression and suicide.* Reston, VA: Council for Exceptional Children.

Hadley, S. (1995, March 27). Parents of disturbed children unite to seek understanding. *Los Angeles Times, Ventura East Edition,* p. B-1.

Hallowell, E. (1996). *When you worry about the child you love.* New York: Simon & Schuster.

Hayden, T. L. (1980). *One child.* New York: Avon.

Hayden, T. L. (1995). *The tiger's child.* New York: Scribners.

Henley, M. (1997). *Teaching self-control: A curriculum for responsible behavior.* Bloomington, IN: National Educational Service.

Heron, T. E., & Harris, K. C. (1993). *The educational consultant: Helping professionals, parents, and mainstreamed students.* Austin, TX: Pro-Ed.

Hetfield, P. (1994). Using a student newspaper to motivate students with behavior disorders. *Teaching Exceptional Children, 26*(2), 6–9.

Hobbs, N. (1982). *The troubled and troubling child.* San Francisco: Jossey-Bass.

Individuals with Disabilities Education Act, 20 U.S.C., secs. 1400 *et seq.* (1997).

Jablow, M. M. (1992). *A parent's guide to eating disorders and obesity.* New York: Delta.

Johnson, D., Johnson, R., Dudley, B., & Burnett, R. (1992). Teaching students to be peer mediators. *Educational Leadership, 50*(1), 10–13.

Johnson, H. (Ed.). (1993). *Child mental health in the 1990s: Curricula for graduate and undergraduate.* Washington, DC: U.S. Department of Health and Human Services.

Johnson, H. C., & Friesen, B. (1993). Etiologies of mental and emotional disorders in children. In H. Johnson (Ed.), *Child mental health in the 1990s: Curricula for graduate and undergraduate* (pp. 27–46). Washington, DC: U.S. Department of Health and Human Services.

Kaleidoscope. (1992, December). *Fact sheet.* Chicago: Author.

Karp, N. (1991). Family empowerment and family support: Commentary. In A. Algarin & R. M. Friedman (Eds.) *Fourth annual research conference proceedings. A system of care for children's mental health: Expanding the research base* (pp. 17–23). Tampa: Research and Training Center for Children's Mental Health, Florida Mental Health Institute, University of Florida.

Kauffman, J. M. (1993). *Characteristics of emotional or behavioral disorders of children and youth* (5th ed.). New York: Macmillan.

Kaufmann, M. (1997). Creature comforts: Animal-assisted activities in education and therapy. *Reaching Today's Youth, 1*(2), 27–31.

Kerns, L. L., & Lieberman, A. B. (1993). *Helping your depressed child.* Rocklin, CA: Prima.

Kerr, M. M., & Nelson, C. M. (1989). *Strategies for managing behavior problems in the classroom* (2nd ed.). Upper Saddle River, NJ: Merrill/Prentice Hall.

Knitzer, J., Steinberg, Z., & Fleisch, B. (1990). *At the schoolhouse door: An examination of programs and policies for children with behavioral and emotional problems.* New York: Bank Street College of Education.

Knoff, H. M. (1990, December). Summarizing the important elements of early childhood primary prevention programs for emotional or behavioral problems. *Communiqué,* pp. 8–10.

Knowlton, D. (1995). Managing children with oppositional behavior. *Beyond Behavior, 6*(3), 5–10.

Koplewicz, H. S. (1996). *It's nobody's fault: New hope and help for difficult children and their parents.* New York: Times Books.

Koyanagi, C., & Gaines, S. (1993). *All systems failure: An examination of the results of neglecting the needs of children with serious emotional disturbance.* Alexandria, VA: National Mental Health Association.

La Grange Area Department of Special Education. (1993). Making a difference with Project WRAP. *Making a Difference,* pp. 4–5.

Lahey, B. B., & Carlson, C. L. (1991). Validity of the diagnostic category of attention deficit disorder without hyperactivity: A review of the literature. *Journal of Learning Disabilities, 24,* 110–120.

Lantieri, L., & Patti, J. (1996). Waging peace in our schools. *Reaching Today's Youth, 1*(1), 43–47.

Long, N. J. (1994). Inclusion: Formula for failure? *The Journal of Emotional and Behavioral Problems, 3*(3), 19–23.

Lowenthal, B. (1996). Educational implications of child abuse. *Intervention in School and Clinic, 32*(1), 21–25.

Mansfield, L. G., & Waldmann, C. H. (1994). *Don't touch my heart: Healing the pain of the unattached child.* Colorado Springs, CO; Piñon Press.

Marston, S. (1990). *The magic of encouragement: Nurturing your child's self-esteem.* New York: Morrow.

Mathews, F. (1996). Being prepared to help. *Reaching Today's Youth, 1*(1), 52–54.

McCoy, K. (1994). *Understanding your teenager's depression.* New York: Perigee.

McDonald, S., & Moriarty, A. (1990). The Rich East High School mediation project. *School Social Work Journal, 14,* 25–32.

McGeady, M. R. (1997). Delivering respect, developing responsibility. *Reaching Today's Youth, 1*(4), 6–13.

McIntyre, T., & Forness, S. R. (1996). Is there a new definition yet or are our kids still seriously emotionally disturbed? *Beyond Behavior, 7*(3), 4–9.

McWhiter, C. C., & Bloom, L. A. (1994). The effects of a student-operated business curriculum on the on-task behavior of students with behavioral disorders. *Behavioral Disorders, 19*(2), 136–141.

Meek, M. (1992). The peacekeepers. *Teaching Tolerance, 1,* 46–52.

Mendler, A. N. (1992). *How to achieve discipline with dignity in the classroom.* Bloomington, IN: National Educational Service.

Milby, J. B., & Weber, A. (1991). Obsessive compulsive disorders. In T. R. Kratochwill & R. J. Morris (Eds.), *The practice of child therapy* (2nd ed., pp. 9–42). New York: Pergamon.

Miller, D. (1994). Suicidal behavior of adolescents with behavior disorders and their peers without disabilities. *Behavioral Disorders, 20*(1), 61–68.

Millhause, M. (1989). Gladiators and conciliators. *The Legal Reformer, 9*(2), 17–20.

Morgan, D. P., & Jenson, W. R. (1988). *Teaching behaviorally disordered students.* Upper Saddle River, NJ: Merrill/ Prentice Hall.

Murry, F. R. (1996). You think you have animals in your class? *Beyond Behavior, 7*(3), 10–13.

National Center for Injury Prevention and Control. (1997). *Violence* [On-line]. Available: http://www.cdc.gov.ncipc/ dvp/suifacts.htm

National Mental Health Services Knowledge Exchange Network. (1996). *Factsheet: Mental, emotional, and behavioral disorders in children and adolescents* [On-line]. Available: http://www.mentalhealth.org/child/ CONDUCT.HTM

Oster, G. D., & Montgomery, S. S. (1995). *Helping your depressed teenager.* New York: Wiley.

Perlman, S. E. (1996). The right stuff for our kids? [Special issue]. *Newsday,* p. A05.

Pipher, M. (1994). *Reviving Ophelia: Saving the lives of adolescent girls.* New York: Ballantine Books.

Rapaport, J. L. (1989). *The boy who couldn't stop washing.* New York: Dutton.

Rappaport, J. (1981). In praise of a paradox: A social policy of empowerment over prevention. *Journal of Community Psychology, 9,* 1–25.

Raser, J. (1997). Control the interaction, not the child! *Reaching Today's Youth, 1*(3), 44–49.

Reid, J. B., & Patterson, G. R. (1991). Early prevention and intervention with conduct problems: A social interactional model for the integration of research and practice. In G. Stoner, M. R. Shinn, & H. M. Walker (Eds.), *Interventions for achievement and behavior problems* (pp. 715–740). Silver Spring, MD: National Association of School Psychologists.

Research and Training Center on Family Support and Children's Mental Health. (1990). *Depression in childhood.* Portland, OR: Author.

Richards, C. M., Symons, D. K., Greene, C. A., & Szuszkiewicz, T. A. (1995). The bidirectional relationship between achievement and externalizing behavior disorders. *Journal of Learning Disabilities, 28,* 8–17.

Sadalla, G., Holmberg, M., & Halligan, J. (1990). *Conflict resolution: An elementary school curriculum.* San Francisco: Community Boards.

Schonert-Reichl, K. A. (1993). Empathy and social relationships in adolescents with behavior disorders. *Behavioral Disorders, 18*(3), 189–204.

Schrumpf, F. (1994). The role of students in resolving conflicts in schools. In J. Thousand, R. Villa, & A. Nevin (Eds.), *Creativity and collaborative learning: A practical guide to empowering students and teachers* (pp. 275–292). Baltimore: Brookes.

Schrumpf, F., Crawford, D., & Usadel, C. (1991). *Peer mediation: Conflict resolution in schools.* Champaign, IL: Research Press.

Scruggs, T. E., & Osguthrope, R. T. (1986). Tutoring interventions within special education settings: A comparison of cross-age and peer tutoring. *Psychology in the Schools, 23,* 187–193.

Siegel, W. L., Murdock, J. Y., & Colley, A. D. (1997). *START: Students training animals: Role therapy* [On line]. Available: http://picce.uno.edu/Faculty/Wendy/Page1.html

Smith, C. R., Wood, F. H., & Grimes, J. (1988). Issues in the identification and placement of behaviorally disordered students. In M. C. Wang, M. C. Reynolds, & H. J. Walberg (Eds.), *Handbook of special education: Research and practice* (Vol. 2, pp. 95–124). New York: Pergamon.

Soulsman, G. (1994, April 4). *Anti-depressants: Happy pills.* Gannett News Service.

Steinberg, Z., & Knitzer, J. (1992). Classrooms for emotionally and behaviorally disturbed students: Facing the chal-lenge. *Behavioral Disorders, 17,* 145–156.

Stuart, C. (1994). Resilient adolescents and peer counseling: Issues and opportunities. *The Journal of Emotional and Behavioral Problems, 3*(2), 48–49.

Talan, J. (1996, May 21). A link to strep: The infection may trigger obsessive-compulsive symptoms [Special issue]. *Newsday,* p. B-31.

U.S. Department of Education. (1990). *To assure a free appropriate public education: Twelfth annual report to Congress on the implementation of the Education of the Handicapped Act.* Washington, DC: Author.

U.S. Department of Education. (1992). *To assure a free appropriate public education: Fourteenth annual report to Congress on the implementation of the Individuals with Disabilities Education Act.* Washington, DC: Author.

U.S. Department of Health and Human Services. (1995). *National data show drop in homicide and increase in youth suicide* [On-line]. Available: http://www.cdc.gov/nchswww/releases/95news/95news/nr43_13.htm

University of Kentucky, Department of Special Education and Rehabilitation Counseling. (1997). *Behavior home page* [On-line]. Available: http://www.state.ky.us/agencies/behave/beexaman.html

Vachss, A. (1994, August 28). Emotional abuse: A plea for the wounded. *Parade,* pp. 4–6.

Walker, D. W., & Leister, C. (1994). Recognition of facial affect cues by adolescents with emotional and behavioral disorders. *Behavioral Disorders, 19*(4), 269–276.

Walker, H. M., & Bullis, M. (1991). Behavior disorders and the social context of regular class integration: A conceptual dilemma? In J. W. Lloyd, N. N. Singh, & A. C. Repp (Eds.), *The Regular Education Initiative: alternative perspectives on concepts, issues, and models* (pp. 75–93). Sycamore, IL: Sycamore.

Walker, H. M., & Severson, H. (1990). *Systematic screening for behavior disorders.* Longmont, CO: Sopris West.

Warr-Leeper, G., Wright, N. A., & Mack, A. (1994). Language disabilities of antisocial boys in residential treatment. *Behavioral Disorders, 19*(3), 159–169.

Wright-Strawderman, C., Lindsey, P., Bavarette, L., & Flippo, J. R. (1996). Depression in students with disabilities: Recognition and intervention strategies. *Intervention in School and Clinic, 31*(5), 261–275.

Zins, J. E., Conyne, R. K., & Ponti, C. R. (1988). Primary prevention: Expanding the impact of psychological services in schools. *School Psychology Review, 17,* 542–549.

CHAPTER 6

Ajibola, O., & Clement, P. (1995). Differential effects of methyphenidate and self-reinforcement on attention-deficit/ hyperactivity disorder. *Behavior Modification, 19,* 211–233.

American Psychiatric Association. (1994). *Diagnostic and statistical manual of mental disorders* (4th ed.). Washington, DC: Author.

Anastapoulos, A. D., Spisto, M. A., & Maher, M. C. (1994). The WISC-III freedom from distractibility factor: Its utility in identifying children with attention deficit hyperactivity disorder. *Psychological Assessment, 6,* 368–371.

Armstrong, T. (1996). ADD: Does it really exist? *Phi Delta Kappan, 77,* 424–428.

Auchenbach, T. M. (1986). *Child behavior checklist—Direct observation form* (rev. ed.). Burlington, VT: Center for Children, Youth, and Families.

Aust, P. (1994). When the problem is not the problem: Understanding attention deficit disorder with and without hyperactivity. *Child Welfare, 73,* 215–227.

Barabasz, M., & Barabasz, A. (1996). Attention deficit disorder: Diagnosis, etiology, and treatment. *Child Study Journal, 26,* 1–38.

Barbarin, O. A., & Soler, R. E. (1993). Behavioral, emotional, and academic adjustment in a national probability sample of African American children. *Journal of Black Psychology, 19,* 423–446.

Baren, M. (1994). *Hyperactivity and attention disorders in children.* San Ramon, CA: The Health Information Network.

Barkley, R. A. (1990). *Attention deficit hyperactivity disorder.* New York: Guilford Press.

Barkley, R. A. (1994). It's not just an attention disorder. *Attention!, 1*(2), 22–27.

Barkley, R. A. (1995a). ADHD and IQ. *ADHD Report, 3*(2), 1.

Barkley, R. A. (1995b). *Taking charge of ADHD: The complete, authoritative guide for parents.* New York: Guilford Press.

Barkley, R. A. (1996). *Research developments and their implications for clinical care of the ADHD child* [On-line]. Available: http://www.mhsource.com/edu/psytimes/p960738.html

Bauermeister, J. J. (1995). ADD and Hispanic (Puerto-Rican) children: Some thoughts and research findings. *Attention!, 2*(1), 16–19.

Beach, M. J., Landenberger, J., & Beach, J. (1997). *Take charge and succeed! Coaching* (2nd ed.). Hyannis, MA: Bridges Associates.

Brown, T. E. (1994). The many faces of ADD: Comorbidity. *Attention!, 1*(2), 29–36.

Burcham, B. G., & DeMers, S. (1995). Comprehensive assessment of children and youth with AD/HD. *Intervention in School and Clinic, 30,* 211–220.

Ch.A.D.D. (1995a). *The disability named ADD* [On-line]. Available: http://www.chadd.org/fact1.htm

Ch.A.D.D. (1995b). *Legal rights and services for children with AD/HD* [On-line]. Available: http://www.chadd.org/fact5.htm

Ch.A.D.D. (1996a). ADD research: A look at today and tomorrow: An interview with Richard D. Todd, Ph.D., M.D. *Attention!, 3*(2), 46–47.

Ch.A.D.D. (1996b). ADD research: A look at today and tomorrow: An interview with Russell A. Barkley. *Attention!, 3*(1), 8–14.

Ch.A.D.D. (1996c). *Parenting a child with attention deficit disorder* [On-line]. Available: http://www.chadd.org/fact2.htm

Ch.A.D.D. (1996d). Q&A: An interview with Judith Rappaport, M.D. *Attention!, 2*(3), 7–10.

Comings, D. E. (1992). Role of mutant dopamine receptor gene in ADHD: Implications for treatment and relationship to Tourette syndrome. *Ch.A.D.D.er Box, 6*(1), 12–15.

Conderman, G., & Katsiyannis, A. (1995). Section 504 accommodation plans. *Intervention in School and Clinic, 31,* 42–69.

Copps, S. M. (n.d.). *Stimulant medications.* Reprinted by the National Professional Consortium in Attention Deficit Disorders, the Medical Center of Central Georgia, Atlanta, GA.

Council for Exceptional Children's Task Force on Children with AD/HD. (1992). *Children with AD/HD: A shared responsibility.* Reston, VA: Author.

Council for Learning Disabilities. (n.d.). *Attention deficit disorder: Infosheet.* Overland Park, KS: Author.

Cowley, G., & Ramo, J. C. (1993, July 26). The not-young and the restless. *Newsweek,* pp. 48–49.

Crawford, H. J., & Barabasz, M. (1996). Quantitative EEG magnitudes in children with and without attention deficit disorder. *Child Study Journal, 26,* 71–86.

Curtiss, S. (Ed.). (1996). *You know you're ADD when . . .* [Brochure]. Tulsa, OK: Author.

Curtiss, S., Whitman, L., Rea, C., & Smith-Ruetz, J. (1996). *The Whitman-Curtiss unabridged dictionary for ADDers* [On-line]. Available: http://www.busprod.com/scurtiss/homepg.html

Dendy, C. A. Z. (1995). *Teenagers with ADD: A parent's guide.* Bethesda, MD: Woodbine House.

Donald, L. R. (in preparation). *Growing up organized at school.*

Edwards, G. (1995, April). Use of negative consequences in parent training. *The ADHD Report,* p. 13.

Epstein, M. A., Shaywitz, S. E., Shaywitz, B. A., & Woolston, J. L. (1991). The boundaries of attention deficit disorder. *Journal of Learning Disabilities, 24*(2), 78–86.

Flick, G. (1996). *Power parenting for children with ADD/ADHD.* West Nyack, NY: The Center for Applied Research in Education.

Fossey, R., Hosie, T., & Zirkel, P. (1995). Section 504 and "front-line" educators: An expanded obligation to serve students with disabilities. *Preventing School Failure, 39,* 10–14.

Ginsberg, M., & Sartain, J. (1996). Making it all ADD up! *Attention!, 2*(3), 14–19.

Goldstein, S. (1996, January/February). Sibling rivalry. *Ch.A.D.D.er Box,* pp. 11–13.

Goldstein, S. (1991, January). Young children at risk: The early signs of attention-deficit hyperactivity disorder. *CHADDer Box,* pp. 3–4.

Gordon, M. (1995). Certainly not a fad, but it can be overdiagnosed. *Attention!, 2*(2), 20–22.

Hallowell, E. (1996). *When you worry about the child you love: Emotional and learning problems in children.* New York: Simon & Schuster.

Hallowell, E. M., & Ratey, J. J. (1995). *Driven to distraction.* New York: Simon & Schuster.

Hendrick, B. (1995, November 16). Study suggests attention deficit disorder is biological, not psychiatric. *The Atlanta Constitution,* p. B/01.

Hoover, D. W., & Milich, R. (1994). Effects of sugar ingestion expectancies on mother–child interactions. *Journal of Abnormal Child Psychology, 22,* 501–515.

Hynd, G. (1995). *AD/HD and brain activity.* Paper presented at the meeting of the International Council for Exceptional Children, Indianapolis, IN.

Hynd, G., Voeller, K., Hern, K. L., & Marshall, R. M. (1991). Neurobiological basis of attention-deficit hyperactivity disorder (ADHD). *School Psychology Review, 20,* 174–186.

Ingersoll, B. (1995). ADD: Not just another fad. *Attention!, 2*(2), 17–19.

Klein, R. G. (1992). An update on the stimulant treatment of ADHD. *Ch.A.D.D.er Box, 6*(1), 19–22.

Koplewicz, H. S. (1996). *It's nobody's fault: New hope and help for difficult children and their parents.* New York: Times Books.

Lahey, B. B., & Carlson, C. L. (1991). Validity of the diagnostic category of attention deficit disorder without hyperactivity: A review of the literature. *Journal of Learning Disabilities, 24*(2), 110–120.

Landau, S., & McAnich, C. (1993, May). Young children with attention deficits. *Young Children,* pp. 49–57.

Lang, J. (1996). The ADHD puzzle. *The Hartford Courant* [On-line]. Available: http://www.courant.com/news/adhd main.htm

Leutwyter, K. (1996, August). Paying attention. *Scientific American* [On-line]. Available: http://www.sciam.com/0896issue/0896 infocus.html

Maag, J. W., & Reid, R. (1994). Attention-deficit hyperactivity disorder: A functional approach to assessment and treatment. *Behavioral Disorders, 20*(1), 5–23.

Machan, D. (1996, August 12). An agreeable affliction. *Forbes,* 148–151.

McBurnett, K. (1995). The new subtype of ADHD: Predominantly hyperactive-impulsive type. *Attention!, 1*(3), 10–15.

McCarney, S. B. (1989). *Attention deficit disorders evaluation scale.* Columbia, MO: Hawthorne Educational Services.

Murphy, K. R. (1992, Fall/Winter). Coping strategies for AD/HD adults. *CH.A.D.D. Special Edition: The Adult with AD/HD,* pp. 5–6.

Neuville, M. B. (1991). *Sometimes I get all scribbly.* La Crosse, WI: Crystal Press.

Nussbaum, N., & Bigler, E. (1990). *Identification and treatment of attention deficit disorder.* Austin, TX: Pro-Ed.

Parker, H. C. (1996). *Adapt: Accommodations help students with attention deficit disorders. ADD Warehouse Articles on ADD* [On-line]. Available: http:// www.addwarehouse.com

Ratey, J. J. (1992, Fall/Winter). The adult with AD/HD. *CH.A.D.D. Special Edition: The Adult with AD/HD,* pp. 3–4.

Reeve, R. E. (1990). ADHD: Facts and fallacies. *Intervention in School and Clinic, 26*(2), 70–78.

Reid, R. (1995). Assessment of ADHD with culturally different groups: The use of behavioral scales. *School Psychology Review, 24,* 537–560.

Riccio, C. A., Hynd, G. W., Cohen, M. J., & Gonzalez, J. J. (1993). Neurological basis of attention deficit hyperactivity disorder. *Exceptional Children, 60*(2), 118–124.

Roan, S. (1994, September 28). Square pegs? Being rejected by peers is not only hurtful, it can cause emotional problems and bad behavior. *Los Angeles Times Home Edition,* p. E–1.

Roberts, R., & Mather, N. (1995). Legal protections for individuals with learning disabilities: The IDEA, Section 504, and the ADA. *Learning Disabilities Research and Practice, 10*(3), 160–168.

Sandford, J. A., & Turner, A. (n.d.). *Intermediate Visual and Auditory Continuous Performance Test.* Richmond, VA: BrainTrain.

Seay, B. (1996). *The story of D* [On-line]. Available: http://add.miningco.com/

Shank, M. (1997). *Making curriculum sparkle for students with AD/HD.* Manuscript in preparation.

Shapiro, E. S., DuPaul, G. J., Bradley, K. L., & Bailey, L. T. (1996). A school-based consultation program for service delivery to middle school students with attention-deficit/hyperactivity disorder. *Journal of Emotional and Behavioral Disorders, 4*(2), 73–81.

Shekim, W. O. (1992, Fall/Winter). Adult attention deficit hyperactivity disorder, residual state (ADHD, RS). *CH.A.D.D. Special Edition: The Adult with AD/HD,* 7–8.

Stanford, L. D., & Hynd, G. W. (1994). Congruence of behavioral symptomatology in children with ADD/H, ADD/WO, and learning disabilities. *Journal of Learning Disabilities, 27*(4), 243–253.

Stein, M. A., Szumowski, E., & Halperin, J. M. (1994). Continuous performance tests: Using the computer to aid diagnosis. *Attention!, 1*(2), 18–20.

Sweeney, D. P., Forness, S. R., Kavale, K. A., & Levitt, J. G. (1997). An update on psychopharmacologic medication: What teachers, clinicians, and parents need to know. *Intervention, 23*(1), 4–21.

Szumowski, E. K. (1996). Help! My child is swinging from the chandelier! *Attention!, 3*(1), 40–45.

Tuminello, M. J. (1996, February). A life of ADD. *CHADDer Box,* p. 7.

Wallis, C., Bloch, H., Cole, W., & Willwerth, J. (1994, July 18). Life in overdrive. *Internet Mental Health* [On-line]. Available: http://www.mentalhealth.com/mag1/p5l-adhd.html

Wilens, T. E., & Lineham, C. E. (1995). ADD and substance abuse: An intoxicating combination. *Attention!, 1*(3), 24–31.

Williams, L., Lerner, M., Wigal, T., & Swanson, J. (1995). Minority assessment of ADD: Issues in the development of new assessment techniques. *Attention!, 2*(1), 9–15.

Zgonc, Y. (1996). The diagnostic evaluation for ADD/ADHD. *The Society for Developmental Education,* p. 981.

CHAPTER 7

Allen, D. (1995). Encouraging success in female students: Helping girls develop math and science skills. *Gifted Child Today Magazine, 18*(2), 44–45.

Ambrose, D., Allen, J., & Huntley, S. B. (1994). Mentorship of the highly creative. *Roeper Review, 17*(2), 131–133.

Baldwin, A. Y. (1987). I'm Black but look at me, I am also gifted. *Gifted Child Quarterly, 31,* 180–185.

Barkley, R. A. (1990). *Attention deficit hyperactivity disorder: A handbook for diagnosis and treatment.* Guilford Press: New York.

Begley, S. (1996, February 19). Your child's brain. *Newsweek,* pp. 55–62.

Benbow, C. P. (1991). Meeting the needs of gifted students through use of acceleration. In M. C. Whang, M. C. Reynolds, & H. J. Walberg (Eds.), *Emerging Programs* (Vol. 4, pp. 23–36). New York: Pergamon Press.

Bloom, B. S. (Ed.). (1956). *Handbook 1: Cognitive domain.* New York: David McKay.

Blythe, T., & Gardner, H. (1990). A school for all intelligences. *Educational Leadership, 47*(7), 33–37.

Borland, J. H. (1989). *Planning and implementing programs for the gifted.* New York: Teachers College Press.

Callahan, C. M., Cornell, D. G., & Loyd, B. H. (1992). The academic development and personal adjustment of high ability young women. In N. Coangelo, S. G. Assouline, & D. L. Ambroson (Eds.), *Talent development: proceedings from the 1991 Henry B. and Jocelyn Wallace national research symposium on talent development* (pp. 248–260). New York: Trillium Press.

Churchill, W. S. (1930). *My early life: A roving commission.* New York: Charles Scribner's Sons.

Clark, B. (1997). *Growing up gifted* (5th ed.). Upper Saddle River, NJ: Merrill/Prentice Hall.

Coady, J. (1989). Cultural ethos and the development of excellence. *Gifted Education International, 6*(1), 45–50.

Coleman, M. R. (1996). Recognizing social and emotional needs of gifted students. *Gifted Child Today, 19*(3), 36–37.

Comer, J., & Haynes, N. M. (1991). Meeting the needs of Black children in public schools: A school reform challenge. In C. V. Willie, A. M. Garibaldi, & W. L. Reed (Eds.), *The education of African-Americans* (pp. 66–71). New York: Auburn House.

Council for Exceptional Children. (1989). *Standards for programs involving the gifted and talented.* Reston, VA: Keirouz.

Council for Exceptional Children. (1995). *Toward a common agenda: Linking gifted education and school reform.* Reston, VA: Author.

Council of States Directors of Programs for the Gifted. (1994). *The 1994 State of the States Gifted and Talented Education Report.* Longmont, CO: Author.

Csikszentmihalyi, M., & Robinson, R. E. (1986). Culture, time, and the development of talent. In R. Sternberg & J. Davidson (Eds.), *Conceptions of giftedness* (pp. 264–285). Cambridge: Cambridge University.

Davis, G. A., & Rimm, S. B. (1994). *Education of the gifted and talented* (3rd ed.). Boston: Allyn & Bacon.

Davis, G. A., & Rimm, S. B. (1998). *Education of the gifted and talented* (4th ed.). Boston: Allyn & Bacon.

Davison, B. (1993). Kids development corporation. *Gifted Child Today, 16*(2), 2–6.

Del Prete, T. (1996). Asset or albatross? The education and socialization of gifted students. *Gifted Child Today, 19*(2), 24–25, 44–50.

Delisle, J. (1994). The inclusion movement is here: Good . . . it's about time. *Gifted Child Today, 17*(4), 30–31.

Doman, G. (1984). *How to multiply your baby's intelligence.* New York: Doubleday.

Dooley, C. (1993). The challenge: Meeting the needs of gifted readers. *The Reading Teacher, 46*(7), 546–551.

Dorry, G. (1994). The perplexed perfectionist. *Understanding Our Gifted, 6*(5), 1, 10–12.

Elkind, D. (1981). *The hurried child: Growing up too fast, too soon.* Reading, MA: Addison-Wesley.

Elkind, D. (1987). Superbaby syndrome can lead to elementary school burnout. *Young Children, 42*(3), 14.

Elkind, D. (1988). Mental acceleration. *Journal for the Education of the Gifted, 11*(4), 19–31.

Ellingson, M. K., Haeger, W. H., & Feldhusen, J. F. (1986). The Purdue mentor plan. *The Gifted Child Today, 9*(2), 2–5.

Feldhusen, J., & Robinson, A. (1986). The Purdue secondary model for gifted and talented youth. In J. S. Renzulli (Ed.), *Systems and models for developing programs for the gifted and talented* (pp. 153–179). Mansfield Center, CT: Creative Learning Press.

Feldhusen, J., Van Winkle, L., & Ehle, D. A. (1996). Is it acceleration or simply appropriate instruction for precocious youth? *Teaching Exceptional Children, 28*(3), 48–51.

Feldman, D. H. (1992). Has there been a paradigm shift in gifted education? In N. Coangelo, S. G. Assouline, & D. L. Ambroson (Eds.), *Talent development: Proceedings from the 1991 Henry B. and Jocelyn Wallace national research symposium on talent development* (pp. 89–94). New York: Trillium.

Ford, D. Y., & Feist, S. M. (1993). Educational reform and gifted African-American students. *Gifted Child Today, 16*(2), 40–43.

Ford, D. Y., & Webb, K. S. (1994). Desegregation of gifted educational programs. The impact of Brown on underachieving children of color. *Journal of Negro Education, 63*(3), 358–375.

Friedman, R. (1990). *Education of exceptional children: Gifted, talented, and creative.* Lawrence: University of Kansas.

Gallagher, J. (1988). National agenda for educating gifted students: Statement of priorities. *Exceptional Children, 55*(2), 107–114.

Gallagher, J. J., & Gallagher, S. A. (1994). *Teaching the gifted child* (4th ed.). Boston: Allyn & Bacon.

Gardner, H. (1983). *Frames of mind: The theory of multiple intelligences.* New York: Basic Books.

Gardner, H. (1993a). *Creating minds.* New York: Basic Books.

Gardner, H. (1993b). *Multiple intelligences: The theory in practice.* New York: Basic Books.

Gardner, H. (in press). Are there additional intelligences: The case for naturalist, spiritual and existential intelligences. In J. Kane (Ed.), *Education, information and transformation.* Englewood Cliffs, NJ: Prentice Hall.

Goldsmith, L. (1987). Girl prodigies: Some evidence and some speculations. *Roeper Review, 10*(2), 74–75.

Goleman, D. (1995). *Emotional intelligence.* New York: Bantam.

Goree, K. (1996). Making the most out of inclusive setting. *Gifted Child Today, 19*(2), 22–29.

Hansen, J. (1987). *When writers read.* Portsmouth, NH: Heinemann.

Hansen, J., & Feldhusen, J. F. (1994). Comparison of trained and untrained teacher of gifted students. *Gifted Child Quarterly, 38*(3), 115–121.

Hunsaker, S. L. (1994). Adjustments to traditional procedures for identifying underserved students: Successes and failures. *Exceptional Children, 61*(1), 72–76.

Idol, L., Paolucci-Whitcomb, P., & Nevin, A. (1986). *Collaborative consultation.* Austin, TX: Pro-Ed.

Jenkins-Friedman, R., & Nielsen, M. E. (1990). Gifted and talented students. In E. L. Meyen (Ed.), *Exceptional children in today's schools* (2nd ed., pp. 451–490). Denver, CO: Love Publishing.

Johnston, P. (1990). *Reevaluating the assumptions of current literacy tests: Some alternative assumptions.* Paper presented at the National Council on Measurement in Education, San Francisco.

Karges-Bone, L. (1992). Southern girls go for science and mathematics in the summertime. *Gifted Child Today, 15,* 10–12.

Kerr, B. (1991). Educating gifted girls. In N. Coangelo & G. A. Davis (Eds.), *Handbook of gifted education* (pp. 402–413). Boston: Allyn & Bacon.

Kerr, B. (1992). A twenty-year follow-up of gifted women. In N. Colangelo, S. G. Assouline, & D. L. Ambroson (Eds.), *Talent development: proceedings from the 1991 Henry B. and Jocelyn Wallace national research symposium on talent development* (pp. 240–247). New York: Trillium Press.

Kirschenbaum, R. J. (1995). An interview with Dr. Joseph Renzulli and Dr. Sally Reis. *Gifted Child Today, 18*(3), 26–29, 42.

Leal, D. J. (1990). *The power of reflective assessment.* Unpublished manuscript, Ohio University, Athens.

Leal, D., Kearney, K., & Kearney, C. (1995). The world's youngest university graduate: Examining the unusual characteristics of profoundly gifted children. *Gifted Child Today, 18*(5), 26–31, 41.

Lovecky, D. V. (1990). Warts and rainbows: Issues in the psychotherapy of the gifted. *Advanced Development, 2,* 65–83.

Lovecky, D. V. (1992). The exceptionally gifted child. *Understanding Our Gifted, 3*(3), 7–9.

Lovecky, D. V. (1994). Gifted children with attention deficit disorder. *Understanding Our Gifted, 6*(5), 1–10.

Lovecky, D. V. (1994/1995). Ramifications of giftedness for girls. *Journal of Secondary Gifted Education, 6*(2), 157–164.

Maker, C. J. (1993). Creativity, intelligence and problem solving: A definition and design for cross-cultural research and measurement related to giftedness. *Gifted Education International, 9,* 68–77.

Maker, C. J. (1995). Lessons learned from the children. *Understanding our Gifted, 8*(1), 1, 8–12.

Maker, C. J. (1996). Identification of gifted minority students: A national problem, needed changes, and a promising solution. *Gifted Child Quarterly, 40,* 41–50.

Maker, C. J., & Nielson, A. B. (1996). *Curriculum development and teaching strategies for gifted learners.* Austin, TX: Pro-Ed.

Maker, C. J., Nielson, A. B., & Rogers, J. A. (1994). Giftedness, diversity, and problems solving: Multiple intelligences and diversity in educational settings. *Teaching Exceptional Children, 27*(1), 4–19.

Malkus, A. S. (1957). *The story of Winston Churchill.* New York: Grosset & Dunlap.

McCarney, S. B. (1987). *Gifted Evaluation Scale.* Hawthorne Educational Services.

McKay, M. D. (1993). No one wants to be a bad teacher. *Gifted Child Today, 16*(3), 40–41.

MENSA. (1993). *MENSA—fact sheet.* Brooklyn, NY: American MENSA.

Milan, C. P., & Schwartz, B. (1992). The mentorship connection. *Gifted Child Today, 15*(3), 9–13.

Moon, S. M., Feldhusen, J. F., & Dillon, D. R. (1994). Long term effects of enrichment program based on the Purdue three-stage model. *Gifted Child Quarterly, 38*(1), 38–47.

Moon, S. M., Feldhusen, J. F., Powley, S., Nidiffer, L., & Whitman, M. W. (1993). Secondary applications of the Purdue three stage model. *Gifted Child Today,* 2–9.

Naidu, S. R., & Presley, P. H. (1995). An analysis of selected descriptive and experimental studies on program model designs for gifted students for potential use in rural school districts of developing countries. *Gifted Education International, 10*(2), 76–84.

Nichols, M. L., & Ganschow, L. (1992). Has there been a paradigm shift in gifted education? In N. Colangelo, S. G. Assouline, & D. L. Ambroson (Eds.), *Talent development: Proceedings from the 1991 Henry B. and Jocelyn Wallace national research symposium on talent development.* New York: Trillium Press.

Noble, I. (1972). *Israel's Golda Meir: Pioneer to prime minister.* New York: Julian Messner.

Ogle, D. M. (1986). K-W-L. A teaching model that develops active reading of expository text. *The Reading Teacher, 39,* 564–570.

Pappas, C., Kiefer, B., & Levstik, L. (1995). *An integrated language arts perspective* (2nd ed.). New York: Longmans.

Parke, B. (1989). *Gifted students in regular classrooms.* Boston: Allyn & Bacon.

Peterson, J. (1993). Peeling off the elitist label: Smart politics. *Gifted Child Today, 16*(2), 31–33.

Piirto, J. (1994). *Talented children and adults: Their development and education.* New York: Macmillan/Merrill.

Public Law 103-382—Title XIV. (1988). Jacob K. Javits Gifted and Talented Students Education Act.

Reid, N. (1989). Contemporary Polynesian conceptions of giftedness. *Gifted Education International, 6*(1), 30–38.

Reilly, J. (1992). When does a student really need a professional mentor? *Gifted Child Today, 15*(3), 2–8.

Reis, S. M. (1989). Reflections on policy affecting the education of gifted and talented students: Past and future perspectives. *American Psychologist, 44,* 399–408.

Reis, S. M., & Westburg, K. L. (1994). The impact of staff development on teacher's ability to modify curriculum for gifted and talented students. *Gifted Child Quarterly, 38*(3), 127–135.

Renzulli, J. S. (1977). *The enrichment triad model: A guide for developing defensible programs for the gifted.* Mansfield, CT: Creative Learning Press.

Renzulli, J. S. (1978). What makes giftedness? Reexamining a definition. *Phi Delta Kappan, 60,* 180–184.

Renzulli, J. S. (Ed.). (1986). *Systems and models for developing programs for the gifted and talented.* Mansfield Center, CT: Creative Learning Press.

Renzulli, J. S. (1996). Schools for talent development: A practical plan for total school improvement. *The School Administrator, 53*(1), 20–22.

Renzulli, J. S., & Reis, S. M. (1986). The enrichment triad/revolving door model: A school wide plan for the development of creative productivity. In J. Renzulli (Ed.), *Systems and models for developing programs for the gifted and talented* (pp. 16–66). Mansfield Center, CT: Creative Learning Press.

Renzulli, J. S., & Smith, L. H. (1978). *The compactor.* Mansfield Center, CT: Creative Learning Press.

Reyes, E. I., Fletcher, R., & Paez, D. (1996). Developing local multidimensional screening procedures for identifying giftedness among Mexican American border population. *Roeper Review, 18*(3), 208–211.

Richert, E. S. (1987). Rampant problems and promising practices in the identification of disadvantaged gifted students. *Gifted Child Quarterly, 31,* 149– 154.

Roeper, A. (1992). How the gifted cope with their emotions. *Roeper Review, 5*(2), 21–24.

Runnels, M. K., & Sigler, E. (1994). The states of the selection of gifted students with learning disabilities for gifted programs. *Roeper Review, 17*(4), 246–247.

Sapon-Shevin, M. (1994/1995). Why gifted students belong in inclusive schools. *Educational Leadership, 52*(2), 64–69.

Schack, G. B. (1996). All aboard or staying ashore? Gifted educators and the education reform movement. *Roeper Review, 18*(3), 190–197.

Scott, M. S., Peron, R., Urbano, R., Hogan, A., & Gold, S. (1992). The identification of giftedness: A comparison of White, Hispanic, and Black families. *Gifted Child Quarterly, 36*(3), 131–139.

Seraphim, C. K. M. (1997). *Observation of problem solving in multiple intelligences: Internal assessment of a DISCOVER assessment checklist.* Unpublished dissertation, University of Arizona.

Shaw, R. (1996, Spring). Enter the mentor. *Sky,* 95–99.

Shore, B. M., Dewey, G. C., Robinson, A., & Ward, V. S. (1991). *Recommended practices in gifted education: A critical analysis.* New York: Teachers College Press.

Silverman, L. K. (1993). *Counseling the gifted and talented.* Denver, CO: Love Publishing Company.

Silverman, L. K. (1994/1995). To be gifted or feminine: The forced choice of adolescence. *Journal of Secondary Gifted Education, 6*(2), 141–156.

Smutney, J., & Blockson, R. (1990). *Education of the gifted: Programs and perspectives.* Bloomington, IN: Phi Delta Kappa Educational Foundation.

Sternberg, R., & Davidson, J. (Eds.). (1986). *Conceptions of giftedness.* Cambridge: Cambridge University Press.

Sternberg, R. J., & Zhang, L. (1995). What do we mean by giftedness? A pentagonal implicit theory. *Gifted Child Quarterly, 39*(2), 88–94.

Tannenbaum, A. J. (1983). *Gifted children: Psychological and educational perspectives.* New York: Macmillan.

Tannenbaum, A. J. (1986). The enrichment matrix model. In J. S. Renzulli (Ed.), *Systems and models for developing programs for the gifted and talented* (pp. 391–428). Mansfield, CT: Creative Learning Press.

Terman, L. (1926). *Mental and physical traits of a thousand gifted children* (2nd ed., Vol. I). Palo Alta, CA: Stanford University Press.

Terman, L., & Oden, M. (1959). *The gifted group at midlife* (Vol. V). Palo Alto, CA: Stanford University Press.

Timpson, W. M., & Jones, C. (1989). The naive expert and the gifted child. *Gifted Child Today, 12*(1), 22–23.

Tomlinson, C. A. (1992). Gifted education and the middle school movement: Two voices on teaching the academically talented. *Journal for the Education of the Gifted, 15*(3), 206–238.

Tomlinson, C. A. (1994/1995). Gifted learners too: A possible dream? *Educational Leadership, 52*(4), 68–69.

Tomlinson, C. A. (1995). Gifted learners and the middle school: Problem or promise. *ERIC Digest,* E535.

Torrance, E. P. (1966a). *Thinking creatively with pictures.* Bensenville, IL: Scholastic Testing Service.

Torrance, E. P. (1966b). *Thinking creatively with words.* Bensenville, IL: Scholastic Testing Service.

U.S. Department of Education. (1993). *National excellence: A case for developing America's talent.* Washington, DC: Author.

U.S. Department of Education, Office of Civil Rights. (1993). *Annual report to Congress.* Washington, DC: Author.

VanTassel-Baska, J. (1989). *Comprehensive curriculum for gifted learners.* Boston: Allyn & Bacon.

Vaughn, V. L., Feldhusen, J. F., & Asher, J. W. (1991). Meta-analyses and review of research on pull-out programs in gifted education. *Gifted Child Quarterly, 35*(2), 92–98.

Ward, S. B., & Landrum, M. S. (1994). Resource consultation. An alternative service delivery model for gifted education. *Roeper Review, 16*(4), 276–279.

Webb, J. T. (1993). Nurturing social-emotional development of gifted children. In K. A. Keller, F. J. Monks, and A. H. Passow (Eds.), *International Handbook for Research on Giftedness and Talent* (pp. 525–538. Oxford, UK: Pergamon Press.

Webb, J. T., & Latimer, D. (1993). ADHD and children who are gifted. *Exceptional Children, 60,* 183–184.

Webb, J. T., Meckstroth, E. A., & Tolan, S. S. (1982). *Guiding the gifted child: A practical source for parents and teachers.* Dayton, OH: Ohio Psychology Press.

Winebrenner, S. (1992). *Teaching gifted kids in the regular classroom: Strategies and techniques every teacher can use to meet the academic needs of the gifted and talented.* Minneapolis: Free Spirit Publications.

Winebrenner, S. (1994, Winter). Interview with Susan Winebrenner. *Teaching Exceptional Children,* 54–55.

Winner, E. (1996). *Gifted children: Myths and realities.* New York: Basic Books.

Winograd, P., & Niquette, G. (1988). Assessing learned helplessness in poor readers. *Topics in Language Disorders, 8*(3), 38–55.

Witty, P. (1940). Some considerations in the education of gifted children. *Educational Administration and Supervision, 26,* 512–521.

CHAPTER 8

The Arc. (1992). *Report card to the nation on inclusion and education of students with mental retardation.* Arlington, TX: Author.

Artiles, A. J., & Trent, S. C. (1994). Overrepresentation of minority students in special education: A continuing debate. *Journal of Special Education, 27,* 410–437.

Balla, D. A., & Zigler, E. (1979). Personality development in retarded persons. In N. R. Ellis (Ed.), *Handbook of mental deficiency: Psychological theory and research* (2nd ed., pp. 154–168). Hillsdale, NJ: Erlbaum.

Batshaw, M. L. (1997). Understanding your chromosomes. In M. L. Batshaw (Ed.), *Children with disabilities* (4th ed., pp. 3–16). Baltimore: Brookes.

Batshaw, M. L., & Shapiro, B. K. (1997). Mental retardation. In M. L. Batshaw (Ed.), *Children with disabilities* (4th ed., pp. 335–360). Baltimore: Brookes.

Baumeister, A. A. (1989). Mental retardation. In C. G. Lask & M. Hersen (Eds.), *Handbook of child psychiatric diagnosis* (pp. 61–94). New York: Wiley.

Baumeister, A. A., Kupstas, F. D., & Woodley-Zanthos, P. (1993). *The new morbidity: Recommendations for actions and an updated guide to state planning for the prevention of mental retardation and related disabilities associated with socioeconomic conditions.* Washington, DC: U.S. Department of Health and Human Services.

Baumeister, A. A., Kupstas, F. D., & Woodley-Zanthos, P. (1996). Poverty, politics, and policy. In C. S. Stout (Ed.), *The integration of psychological principles in policy development* (pp. 81–101). Westport, CT: Prager.

Baumeister, A. A., & Muma, J. R. (1975). On defining mental retardation. *The Journal of Special Education, 9*(3), 293–306

Beck, J., Broers, J., Hogue, E., Shipstead, J., & Knowlton, E. (1994, Winter). Strategies for functional community-based instruction and inclusion for children with mental retardation. *Teaching Exceptional Children,* pp. 44–48.

Blackman, J. A., & Thomson, E. (1983). Genetics. In J. A. Blackman (Ed.), *Medical aspects of developmental disabilities in children birth to three* (pp. 115–120). Iowa City: University of Iowa.

Blatt, B. (1981). *In and out of mental retardation: Essays on educability, disability, and human policy.* Baltimore: University Park Press.

Butterfield, E. C., Wambold, C., & Belmont, J. M. (1977). On the theory and practice of improving short-term memory. *American Journal of Mental Deficiency, 77,* 654–669.

Clark, G. M. (1994, Winter). Is a functional curriculum approach compatible with an inclusive education model? *Teaching Exceptional Children,* pp. 36–39.

Clark, G. M., Carlson, B. C., Fisher, S., Cook, I. D., & D'Alonzo, B. J. (1991). Career development for students with disabilities in elementary schools: A position statement of the Division on Career Development, *CDEI, 14*(2), 109–120.

Coulter, D. L. (1988). The neurology of mental retardation. In F. J. Menolascino & J. A. Stark (Eds.), *Preventative and curative intervention in mental retardation* (pp. 113–154). Baltimore: Brookes.

Coulter, D. L. (1992). Reaction paper: An ecology of prevention for the future. *Mental Retardation, 30,* 363–369.

Cronin, M. E., & Patton, J. R. (1993). *Life skills instruction for all students with special needs: A practical guide for integrating real-life content into the curriculum.* Austin, TX: Pro-Ed.

Culp, D., & Carlisle, M. (1988). *P.A.C.T.: Partners in augmentative communication training.* Tucson, AZ: Communication Skill Builders.

Ellis, N. R. (1970). Memory processes in retardates and normals. In N. R. Ellis (Ed.), *International review of research in mental retardation* (Vol. 4, pp. 1–32). New York: Academic Press.

Falvey, M. A., Forest, M., Pearpoint, J., & Rosenberg, R. L. (1994). Building connections. In J. S. Thousand, R. A. Villa, & A. I. Nevin (Eds.), *Creativity and collaborative learning: A practical guide to empowering students and teachers* (pp. 347–368). Baltimore: Brookes.

Feldman, M. A., & Walton-Allen, N. (1997). Effects of maternal mental retardation and poverty on intellectual, academic, and behavioral status of school-age children. *American Journal on Mental Retardation, 101,* 352–364.

Field, S., LeRoy, B., & Rivera, S. (1994, Winter). Meeting functional curriculum needs in middle school general education classrooms. *Teaching Exceptional Children,* pp. 40–43.

Figueroa, R. A. (1989). Psychological testing of linguistic-minority students: Knowledge gaps and regulations. *Exceptional Children, 56,* 145–152.

Fletcher, K. L., & Bray, N. W. (1995). External and verbal strategies in children with and without mild mental retardation. *American Journal on Mental Retardation, 99,* 363–475.

Flugum, K. R., & Reschly, D. J. (1994). Prereferral interventions: Quality indices and outcomes. *Journal of School Psychology, 32,* 1–14.

Gottlieb, J., Alter, M., Gottlieb, B. W., & Wishner, J. (1994). Special education in urban America: It's not justifiable for many. *Journal of Special Education, 27,* 453–465.

Grossman, H. J. (Ed.). (1983). *Classification in mental retardation.* Washington, DC: American Association on Mental Deficiency.

Grossman, H. J. (1995). *Special education in a diverse society.* Boston: Allyn & Bacon.

Harry, B. (1992). *Cultural diversity, families, and the special education system.* New York: Teachers College Press.

Hasazi, S. B., & Furney, K. (1996). Least restrictive environment: Overview and upper school. In National Council on Disability (Ed.), *Improving the implementation of the Individuals with Disabilities Education Act: Making schools work for all of America's children. Supplement* (pp. 341–372). Washington, DC: National Council on Disability.

Helmke, L. M., Havekost, D. M., Patton, J. R., & Polloway, E. A. (1994, Winter). Life skills programming: Development of a high school science course. *Teaching Exceptional Children,* 49–53.

Horner, R. H., Dunlap, G., & Koegel, R. L. (Eds.). (1988). *Generalization and maintenance: Life-style changes in applied settings.* Baltimore: Brookes.

Individuals with Disabilities Education Act, 20 U.S.C. §§ 1400 et seq. (1997).

Iowa Department of Education. (1997). *Rules of special education.* Des Moines, IA: Author.

Kolstoe, O. P. (1970). *Teaching educable mentally retarded children.* New York: Holt, Rinehart, & Winston.

Kozma, C., & Stock, J. S. (1993). What is mental retardation? In R. Smith (Ed.), *Children with mental retardation* (pp. 1–49). Rockville, MD: Woodbine House.

Kozol, J. (1991). *Savage inequalities: Children in America's schools.* New York: Harper-Perennial.

Lambert, N., Nihira, K., & Leland, H. (1993). *AAMR Adaptive behavior scale—school* (2nd ed.). Austin, TX: Pro-Ed.

Langone, J., Clees, T. J., Oxford, M., Malone, M., & Ross, G. (1995). Acquisition and generalization of social skills by high school students with mild retardation. *Mental Retardation, 33,* 186–196.

Luckasson, R., Coulter, D. L., Polloway, E. A., Reiss, S., Schalock, R. L., Snell, M. E., Spitalnik, D. M., & Stark, J. A. (1992). *Mental retardation: Definition, classification, and systems of supports.* Washington, DC: American Association on Mental Retardation.

Luckasson, R., Schalock, R. L., Snell, M. E., & Spitalnik, D. M. (1996, August). The 1992 AAMR definition and preschool children: Response from the Committee on Terminology and Classification. *Mental Retardation,* pp. 247–253.

MacMillan, D. L. (1982). *Mental retardation in school and society* (2nd ed.). Glenview, IL: Scott, Foresman.

MacMillan, D. L., Gresham, F. M., & Siperstein, G. N. (1993). Conceptual and psychometric concerns about the 1992 AAMR definition of mental retardation. *American Journal on Mental Retardation, 98,* 325–335.

MacMillan, D. L., Gresham, F. M., & Siperstein, G. N. (1995). Heightened concerns over the 1992 AAMR definition: Advocacy versus precision. *American Journal on Mental Retardation, 100,* 87–97.

MacMillan, D. L., Siperstein, G. N., & Gresham, F. M. (1996). The labyrinth of IDEA: School decisions on referred students with subaverage general intelligence. *American Journal on Mental Retardation, 101,* 161–174.

MacMillan, D. L., Siperstein, G. N., Gresham, F. M., & Bocian, K. M. (1997). Mild retardation: A concept that may have outlived its usefulness. *Psychology in Mental Retardation and Developmental Disabilities, 23*(1), 5–12.

McLaren, J., & Bryson, S. E. (1987). Review of recent epidemiological studies of mental retardation: Prevalence, associated disorders, and etiology. *American Journal of Mental Retardation, 92,* 243–254.

Mercer, C. D., & Snell, M. E. (1977). *Learning theory research in mental retardation: Implications for teaching.* New York: Merrill/Macmillan.

Mirenda, P. L., & Donnellan, A. M. (1986). Effects of adult interactional style on conversational behavior in students with severe communication problems. *Language, Speech, and Hearing Services in Schools, 17,* 126–141.

Mount, B. (1987). *Personal futures planning: Finding directions for change.* Unpublished doctoral dissertation, University of Georgia, Athens.

Mount B., & Zwernik, K. (1988). *It's never too early, it's never too late: A booklet about personal planning for persons with developmental disabilities, their families and friends, case managers, service providers, and advocates.* St. Paul, MN: Metropolitan Council.

Peterson, R. M., & Cleveland, J. O. (1987). *A guide for state planning for the prevention of mental retardation and related disabilities.* Washington, DC: U.S. Department of Health and Human Services, Office of Human Development Services, President's Committee on Mental Retardation.

Pope, A. M., & Tarlov, A. R. (Eds.). (1991). *Disability in America: Toward a national agenda for prevention.* Washington, DC: National Academy Press.

Powers, L. E., Singer, G. H. S., & Sowers, J. A. (Eds.). (1996). *On the road to autonomy: Promoting self-competence among children and youth with disabilities.* Baltimore: Brookes.

Reiss, S. (1994). Issues in defining mental retardation. *American Journal on Mental Retardation, 99,* 1–7.

Roizen, N. J. (1997). Down syndrome. In M. L. Batshaw (Ed.), *Children with disabilities* (4th ed., pp. 361–376). Baltimore: Brookes.

Sands, D. J., & Wehmeyer, M. L. (Eds.). (1996). *Self-determination across the life span: Theory and practice.* Baltimore: Brookes.

Schalock, R. L., Stark, J. A., Snell, M. E., Coulter, D. L., Polloway, E. A., Luckasson, R., Reiss, S., & Spitalnik, D. M. (1994). The changing conception of mental retardation: Implications for the field. *Mental Retardation, 32,* 181–193.

Scott, G. G. (1988). Theoretical epidemiology: Environment and life-style. In J. F. Kavanagh (Ed.), *Understanding mental retardation* (pp. 23–33). Baltimore: Brookes.

Seligman, M. E. P. (1975). *Helplessness: On depression, development, and death.* San Francisco: Freeman.

Serna, L. A. (1996). Learning with PURPOSE: A lifelong learning approach using self-determination skills. In D. J. Sands & M. L. Wehmeyer (Eds.), *Self-determination across the life span: Independence and choice for people with disabilities* (pp. 285–310). Baltimore: Brookes.

Serna, L. A., & Lau-Smith, J. (1995). Learning with purpose: Self-determination skills for students who are at risk for school and community failure. *Intervention in School and Clinic, 30*(3), 142–146.

Shafer, M. S., & Rangasamy, R. (1995). Transition and Native American youth: A follow-up study of school leavers on the Fort Apache Indian Reservation. *Journal of Rehabilitation, 61*(1), 60–65.

Short, E. J., & Evans, S. W. (1990). Individual differences in cognitive and social problem-solving skills as a function of intelligence. In N. W. Bray (Ed.), *International Review of Research in Mental Retardation* (Vol. 16, pp. 89–123). San Diego, CA: Academic Press.

Smith, J. D. (1994, September). The revised AAMR definition of mental retardation: The MRDD position. *Education and Training in Mental Retardation and Developmental Disabilities,* pp. 179–228.

Smith, J. D., & Hilton, A. (1997). The preparation and training of the educational community for the inclusion of students with developmental disabilities: The MRDD position. *Education and Training in Mental Retardation and Developmental Disabilities, 32*(1), 3–10.

Smull, M., & Harrison, S. B. (1992). *Supporting people with severe reputations in the community.* Alexandria, VA: National Association of State Mental Retardation Directors.

Staker, M. D. (1993). Project EAGLE: A comprehensive child development program. *Proceedings from the 13th Annual National Rural Families Conference,* Manhattan, Kansas.

Stark, J. A., Menolascino, F. J., & Goldsbury, T. L. (1988). An updated search for the prevention of mental retardation. In F. J. Menolascino & J. A. Stark (Eds.), *Preventive and curative intervention in mental retardation* (pp. 3–25). Baltimore: Brookes.

Stokes, T. F., & Baer, D. M. (1977). An implicit technology of generalization. *Journal of Applied Behavior Analysis, 10,* 349–367.

Turnbull, A. P. (1974). Teaching retarded persons to rehearse through cumulative overt labeling. *American Journal of Mental Deficiency, 79,* 331–337.

Turnbull, A. P., Blue-Banning, M. J., Anderson, E. L., Turnbull, H. R., Seaton, K. A., & Dinas, P. A. (1996). Enhancing self-determination through Group Action Planning: A holistic emphasis. In D. J. Sands & M. L. Wehmeyer (Eds.), *Self-determination across the life span: Theory and practice* (pp. 237–256). Baltimore: Brookes.

Turnbull, A. P., & Turnbull, H. R. (1985). *Parents speak out: Then and now*. Upper Saddle River, NJ: Merrill/Prentice Hall.

Turnbull, A. P., & Turnbull, H. R. (1996). Group action planning as a strategy for providing comprehensive family support. In L. K. Koegel, R. L. Koegel, & G. Dunlap (Eds.), *Positive behavioral support: Including people with difficult behavior in the community* (pp. 99–114). Baltimore: Brookes.

Turnbull, A. P., & Turnbull, H. R. (1997). *Families, professionals, and exceptionality: A special partnership* (3rd ed.). Upper Saddle River, NJ: Merrill/Prentice Hall.

Turnbull, H. R. (1978). *Consent handbook*. Washington, DC: American Association on Mental Retardation.

Turnbull, H. R. (1986). Presidential address. *Mental Retardation, 24*(5), 265–276.

U.S. Department of Education. (1993). *To assure the free appropriate public education of all children with disabilities: Fifteenth annual report to Congress on the implementation of the Individuals with Disabilities Education Act*. Washington, DC: Office of Special Education and Rehabilitative Services, Division of Innovation and Development.

U.S. Department of Education. (1995). *To assure the free appropriate public education of all children with disabilities: Seventeenth annual report to Congress on the implementation of the Individuals with Disabilities Education Act*. Washington, DC: Office of Special Education and Rehabilitative Services, Division of Innovation and Development.

U.S. Department of Education. (1996). *To assure the free appropriate public education of all children with disabilities: Eighteenth annual report to Congress on the implementation of the Individuals with Disabilities Education Act*. Washington, DC: Office of Special Education and Rehabilitative Services, Division of Innovation and Development.

Vig, S., & Jedrysek, E. (1996, August). Application of the 1992 AAMR definition: Issues for preschool children. *Mental Retardation, pp.* 244–246.

Wagner, M. (1995). *The contributions of poverty and ethnic background to the participation of secondary school students in special education*. Washington, DC: U.S. Department of Education.

Ward, M. J. (1996). Coming of age in the age of self-determination: A historical and personal perspective. In D. J. Sands & M. L. Wehmeyer (Eds.), *Self-determination across the life span: Independence and choice for people with disabilities* (pp. 3–16). Baltimore: Brookes.

Ward, M. J., & Kohler, P. D. (1996). Promoting self-determination for individuals with disabilities: Content and process. In L. E. Powers, G. H. S. Singer, & J. Sowers (Eds.), *On the road to autonomy: Promoting self-competence among children and youth with disabilities* (pp. 275–290). Baltimore: Brookes.

Wehmeyer, M. L. (1995). *The Arc's self-determination scale: Procedural guidelines*. Arlington, TX: The Arc of the United States.

Wehmeyer, M. L. (1996, December). Student self-report measure of self-determination for students with cognitive disabilities. *Education and Training in Mental Retardation and developmental disabilities, pp.* 282–292.

Wehmeyer, M. L., & Kelchner, K. (1995). *The Arc's self-determination scale: Adolescent version*. Arlington, TX: The Arc of the United States.

Wehmeyer, M. L., & Metzler, C. A. (1995). How self-determined are people with mental retardation? The national consumer survey. *Mental Retardation, 33,* 111–119.

Zeaman, D., & House, B. J. (1963). The role of attention in retardate discrimination learning. In N. R. Ellis (Ed.), *Handbook of mental deficiency* (pp. 159–223). New York: McGraw-Hill.

Zeaman, D., & House, B. J. (1979). A review of attention theory. In N. R. Ellis (Ed.), *Handbook of mental deficiency: Psychological theory and research* (2nd ed.). Hillsdale, NJ: Erlbaum.

Zigler, E., & Burack, J. A. (1989). Personality development and the dually diagnosed person. *Research in Developmental Disabilities, 10,* 225–240.

CHAPTER 9

Amado, A. N (Ed.). (1993). *Friendships and community connections between people with and without developmental disabilities*. Baltimore: Brookes.

Association for Persons With Severe Handicaps. (1993). *TASH resolutions and policy statements*. Seattle: Author.

Ault, M. M., Graff, C., & Rues, J. P. (1993). Special health care procedures. In M. E. Snell (Ed.), *Instruction of students with severe disabilities* (4th ed., pp. 215–247). Upper Saddle River, NJ: Merrill/Prentice Hall.

Ault, M. M., Guy, B., Guess, D., Bashinski, S., & Roberts, S. (1995). Analyzing behavior state and learning environments: Application in instructional settings. *Mental Retardation, 33,* 304–316.

Aveno, A. (1987). A survey of activities engaged in and skills needed by adults in community residences. *Journal of the Association for Persons with Severe Handicaps, 12,* 125–130.

Batshaw, M. L. (1997a). Heredity: A toss of the dice. In M. L. Batshaw (Ed.), *Children with disabilities: A medical primer* (4th ed., pp. 17–34). Baltimore: Brookes.

Batshaw, M. L. (1997b). PKU and other inborn errors of metabolism. In M. L. Batshaw (Ed.), *Children with disabilities: A medical primer* (4th ed., pp. 389–404). Baltimore: Brookes.

Batshaw, M. L., & Rose, N. C. (1997). Birth defects, prenatal diagnosis, and fetal therapy. In M. L. Batshaw (Ed.), *Children with disabilities* (4th ed., pp. 35–52). Baltimore: Brookes.

Batshaw, M. L., & Shapiro, B. K. (1997). Mental retardation. In M. L. Batshaw (Ed.), *Children with disabilities: A medical primer* (4th ed., pp. 335–360). Baltimore: Brookes.

Billingsley, F. F., Liberty, K. A., & White, O. R. (1994). The technology of instruction. In E. C. Cipani & F. Spooner (Eds.), *Curricular and instructional approaches for persons with severe handicaps* (pp. 81–116). Boston: Allyn & Bacon.

Bishop, K. D., Jubala, K. A., Stainback, W., & Stainback, S. (1996). Facilitating friendships. In S. Stainback & W. Stainback (Eds.), *Inclusion: A guide for educators* (pp. 155–170). Baltimore: Paul H. Brookes.

Boomer, L. W. (1994). The utilization of paraprofessionals in programs for students with autism. *Focus on Autistic Behavior, 9*(2), 1–9.

Bowe, F. G. (1995). Ethics in early childhood special education. *Infants and Young Children, 7*(3), 28–37.

Brimer, R. W. (1990). *Students with severe disabilities. Current perspectives and practices* Mountain View, CA: Mayfield.

Browder, D. (1991). *Assessment of individuals with severe handicaps: An applied behavior approach to life skills assessment* (2nd ed.). Baltimore: Brookes

Browder, D. M., & Snell, M. E. (1993). Functional academics. In M. E. Snell (Ed.), *Instruction of students with severe disabilities* (4th ed., pp. 442–479). Upper Saddle River, NJ: Merrill/Prentice Hall.

Brown, F., & Lehr, D. H. (1993, Summer). Making activities meaningful for students with severe multiple disabilities. *Teaching Exceptional Children, 25*(4), 12–17.

Brown, F., & Snell, M. E. (1993a). Meaningful assessment. In M. E. Snell (Ed.), *Instruction of students with severe disabilities* (4th ed., pp. 61–98). Upper Saddle River, NJ: Merrill/Prentice Hall.

Brown, F., & Snell, M. E. (1993b). Measurement, analysis, and evaluation. In M. E. Snell (Ed.), *Instruction of students with severe disabilities* (4th ed., pp. 152–183). Upper Saddle River, NJ: Merrill/Prentice Hall.

Brown, L., Branston, M. B., Hamre-Nietupski, S., Pumpian, I., Certo, N., & Gruenewald, L. (1979). A strategy for developing chronological, age-appropriate and functional curricular content for severely handicapped adolescents and young adults. *The Journal of Special Education, 13,* 81–90.

Campbell, P. H. (1993). Physical management and handling procedures. In M. E. Snell (Ed.),

Instruction of students with severe disabilities (4th ed., pp. 248–263). Upper Saddle River, NJ: Merrill/Prentice Hall.

Carey, J. C. (1997). Genetic services in the care of children with disabilities. In H. M. Wallace, R. F. Biehl, J. C. MacQueen, & J. A. Blackman (Eds.), *Mosby's resource guide to children with disabilities and chronic illness* (pp. 318–328). St. Louis, MO: Mosby.

Chadsey-Rusch, J. (1990). Social interactions of secondary-aged students with severe handicaps: Implication for facilitating the transition from school to work. *The Journal of the Association for Persons with Severe Handicaps, 15,* 69–78.

Coulter, D. L. (1994). Biomedical conditions: Types, causes, and results. In L. Sternberg (Ed.), *Individuals with profound disabilities: Instructional and assistive strategies* (pp. 41–58). Austin, TX: Pro-Ed.

Downing, J., & Eichinger, J. (1990). Instructional strategies for learners with dual sensory impairments in integrated settings. *The Journal of the Association for Persons with Severe Handicaps, 15,* 98–105.

Erwin, E. J., & Soodak, L. C. (1995). I never knew I could stand up to the system: Families' perspectives on pursuing inclusive education. *Journal of the Association for Persons with Severe Handicaps, 17,* 205–212.

Evans, I. M. (1991). Testing and diagnosis: A review and evaluation. In L. Meyer, C. Peck, & L. Brown (Eds.), *Critical issues in the lives of people with severe disabilities* (pp. 25–44). Baltimore: Brookes.

Evans, J. R. (1997). The first weeks of life. In M. L. Batshaw (Ed.), *Children with disabilities: A medical primer* (4th ed., pp. 93–114). Baltimore: Brookes.

Falvey, M. A. (Ed.). (1995). *Inclusive and heterogeneous schooling: Assessment, curriculum, and instruction.* Baltimore: Brookes.

Falvey, M. A., Forest, M., Pearpoint, J., & Rosenberg, R. L. (1994). Building connections. In J. S. Thousand, R. A. Villa, & A. I. Nevin (Eds.), *Creativity and collaborative learning: A practical guide for empowering students and teachers* (pp. 347–368). Baltimore: Brookes.

Falvey, M. A., & Rosenberg, R. L. (1995). Developing and fostering friendships. In M. A. Falvey (Ed.), *Inclusive and heterogeneous schooling: Assessment, curriculum, and instruction* (pp. 267–284). Baltimore: Brookes.

Ford, A., Schnoor, R., Meyer, L., Davern, L., Black, J., & Dempsey, P. (1989). *The Syracuse community-referenced curriculum guide for students with moderate and severe disabilities.* Baltimore: Brookes.

Forest, M., & Lusthaus, E. (1989). Promoting educational equity for all students: Circles and maps. In S. Stainback, W. Stainback, & M. Forest (Eds.), *Educating all students in the mainstream of regular education* (pp. 443–457). Baltimore: Brookes.

Fredericks, B., & Brodsky, M. (1994). Assessment for a functional curriculum. In E. Cipani & F. Spooner (Eds.). *Curricular and instructional approaches for persons with severe disabilities* (pp. 31–49). Boston: Allyn & Bacon.

Gage, S. T., & Falvey, M. A. (1995). Assessment strategies to develop appropriate curricula and educational programs. In M. A. Falvey (Ed.), *Inclusive and heterogeneous schooling: Assessment, curriculum, and instruction* (pp. 59–110). Baltimore: Brookes.

Giangreco, M. F. (1997a). Persistent questions about curriculum for students with severe disabilities. *Physical Disabilities: Education and Related Services, 15*(2), 53–56.

Giangreco, M. F. (1997b). Responses to Nietupski et al. *The Journal of Special Education, 31,* 56–57.

Giangreco, M. F., Dennis, R., Cloninger, C., Edelman, S., & Schattman, R. (1993). "I've counted Jon": Transformational experiences of teachers educating students with disabilities. *Exceptional Children, 59,* 359–372.

Giangreco, M. F., Edelman, S., Cloninger, C., & Dennis, R. (1993). My child has a classmate with severe disabilities: What parents of nondisabled children think about full inclusion. *Developmental Disabilities Bulletin, 21*(1), 77–91.

Glanze, W. D., Anderson, K. N., & Anderson, L. E. (1985). *The Mosby medical encyclopedia.* New York: New American Library.

Goetz, L., & Hunt, P. (1994). Augmentative and alternative communication. In E. C. Cipani & F. Spooner (Eds.), *Curricular and instructional approaches for persons with severe disabilities* (pp. 263–288). Boston: Allyn & Bacon.

Graff, J. C., Ault, M. M., Guess, D., Taylor, M., & Thompson, B. (1990). *Health care for students with disabilities.* Baltimore: Brookes.

Guess, D., Roberts, S., Halvoet, J., & Rues, J. (1997, May). Observing alertness and responsiveness among infants with multiple and severe disabilities: Some interesting observations for parents of young children and early intervention specialists. *The Association for Persons with Severe Handicaps (TASH) Newsletter,* pp. 24–25.

Guess, D., Roberts, S., Siegel-Causey, E., & Rues, J. (1995). Replication and extended analysis of behavior state, environmental events, and related variables among individuals with profound disabilities. *American Journal on Mental Retardation, 100,* 36–51.

Guess, D., & Siegel-Causey, E. (1992). Students with severe and multiple disabilities. In E. L. Meyen & T. M. Skrtic (Eds.), *Exceptional children and youth: An introduction* (4th ed., pp. 293–320). Denver: Love.

Hamre-Nietupski, S. (1993, September). How much time should be spent on skill instruction and friendship development? Preferences of parents of students with moderate and severe/profound disabilities. *Education*

and Training in Mental Retardation, pp. 220–231.

Haney, M., & Falvey, M. A. (1989). Instructional strategies. In Falvey, M. A. (Ed.), *Community-based curriculum: Instructional strategies for students with severe handicaps* (2nd ed., pp. 63–90). Baltimore: Brookes.

Haslam, R. H. A., & Valletulli, P. J. (Eds.). (1996). *Medical problems in the classroom: The teacher's role in diagnosis and management* (3rd ed.). Austin, TX: Pro-Ed.

Heller, K. W., Alberto, P. A., Forney, P. E., & Schwartzman, M. N. (1996). *Understanding physical, sensory, and health impairments: Characteristics and educational implications.* Pacific Grove, CA: Brooks/Cole.

Hollowood, T. M., Salisbury, C. L., Rainforth, B., & Palombaro, M. M. (1994). Use of instructional time in classrooms serving students with and without severe disabilities. *Exceptional Children, 61,* 242–253.

Horner, R. H., & Carr, E. G. (1997). Behavioral support for students with severe disabilities: Functional assessment and comprehensive intervention. *Journal of Special Education, 31,* 84–104.

Hunt, P., Alwell, M., Farron-Davis, F., & Goetz, L. (1996). Creating socially supportive environments for fully included students who experience multiple disabilities. *Journal of the Association for Persons with Severe Handicaps, 21*(2), 53–71.

Hunt, P., Farron-Davis, F., Beckstead, S., Curtis, D., & Goetz, L. (1994). Evaluating the effects of placement of students with severe disabilities in general education versus special classes. *Journal of the Association for Persons with Severe Handicaps, 19,* 200–214.

Hunt, P., & Goetz, L. (1997). Research on inclusive educational programs, practices, and outcomes for students with severe disabilities. *Journal of Special Education, 31,* 3–29.

Hunt, P., Staub, D., Alwell, M., & Goetz, L. (1994). Achievement by all students within the context of cooperative learning groups. *Journal of the Association for Persons with Severe Handicaps, 19,* 290–301.

Hutinger, P. L. (1996). Computer applications in programs for young children with disabilities: Recurrent themes. *Focus on Autism and Other Developmental Disabilities, 11*(2), 105–114.

Individuals with Disabilities Education Act, 20 U.S.C., §§ 1400 *et seq.* (1997).

Ingraham, C. L., Davis, C. C., Carey, A., Danek, M., & Watson, D. (1996). Deaf-blind services in the 21st century: Changing faces and changing service delivery systems. *Journal of Vocational Rehabilitation, 6,* 125–132.

Johnson, J. M., Baumgart, D., Helmstetter, E., & Curry, C. (1996). *Augmenting basic communication in natural contexts.* Baltimore, MD: Paul H. Brookes.

Jones, K. H., & Bender, W. N. (1993). Utilization of paraprofessionals in special education: A review of the literature. *Remedial and Special Education, 14*(1), 7–14.

Jorgensen, C. M. (1996). Designing inclusive curricula right from the start: Practical strategies and examples for the high school classroom. In S. Stainback & W. Stainback (Eds.), *Inclusion: A guide for educators* (pp. 221–236). Baltimore: Paul H. Brookes.

Kennedy, C. H., Horner, R. H., & Newton, J. S. (1990). The social networks and activity patterns of adults with severe disabilities: A correlational analysis. *The Journal of the Association for Persons with Severe Handicaps, 15,* 86–90.

Kimm, C. H., Falvey, M. A., Bishop, K. D., & Rosenberg, R. L. (1995). Motor and personal care skills. In M. A. Falvey (Ed.), *Inclusive and heterogeneous schooling: Assessment, curriculum, and instruction* (pp. 187–228). Baltimore: Brookes.

Levy, S. E., & O'Rourke, M. (1997). Technological assistance: Innovations for independence. In M. L. Batshaw (Ed.), *Children with Disabilities* (4th ed., pp. 687–708). Baltimore: Brookes.

Linehan, S. L., & Brady, M. P. (1995). Functional versus developmental assessment: Influences on instructional planning decisions. *Journal of Special Education, 29,* 295–309.

Linehan, S. L., Brady, M. P., & Hwang, C. (1991). Ecological versus developmental assessment: Influences on instructional expectations. *Journal of the Association for Persons with Severe Handicaps, 16,* 146–153.

Logan, K. R., Alberto, P. A., Kana, T. G., & Waylor-Bowen, T. (1994). Curriculum development and instructional design for students with profound disabilities. In L. Sternberg (Ed.), *Individuals with profound disabilities: Instructional and assistive strategies* (3rd ed., pp. 333–384). Austin, TX: Pro-Ed.

Luckasson, R., Coulter, D. L., Polloway, E. A., Reiss, S., Schalock, R. L., Snell, M. E., Spitalnik, D. M., & Stark, J. A. (1992). *Mental retardation: Definition, classification, and systems of supports.* Washington, DC: American Association on Mental Retardation.

Lynch, D. R., & Batshaw, M. L. (1997). The brain and nervous system: Our computer. In M. L. Batshaw (Ed.), *Children with disabilities* (4th ed., pp. 293–314). Baltimore: Brookes.

McLaren, J., & Bryson, S. E. (1987). Review of recent epidemiological studies of mental retardation: Prevalence, associated disorders, and etiology. *American Journal of Mental Retardation, 92,* 243–254.

McNulty, J. (1990). *Helen Keller National Center annual report.* Sands Point, NY: Helen Keller National Center.

Moon, M. S. (1994). *Making school and community recreation fun for everyone: Places and ways to integrate.* Baltimore: Paul H. Brookes.

Neel, R. S., & Billingsley, F. F. (1989). *Impact: A functional curriculum handbook for stu-

dents with moderate to severe disabilities.* Baltimore: Paul H. Brookes.

O'Reilly, M. F., Renzaglia, A., Hutchins, M., Koterba-Bass, L., Clayton, M., Halle, J. W., & Izen, C. (1992). Teaching systematic instruction competencies to special education student teachers: An applied behavioral supervision model. *The Journal of the Association for Persons with Severe Handicaps, 17,* 104–111.

Reichle, J. (1997). Communication intervention with persons who have severe disabilities. *Journal of Special Education, 31,* 110–124.

Richards, S., & Sternberg, L. (1994). Assessing levels of state and arousal. In L. Sternberg (Ed.), *Individuals with profound disabilities: Instructional and assistive strategies* (3rd ed., pp. 61–88). Austin, TX: Pro-Ed.

Ryndak, D. L., Downing, J. E., Jacqueline, L. R., & Morrison, A. P. (1995). Parents' perceptions after inclusion of their children with moderate or severe disabilities. *Journal of the Association for Persons with Severe Handicaps, 20,* 147–157.

Salisbury, C. L., Evans, I. M., & Palombaro, M. M. (1997). Collaborative problem solving to promote the inclusion of young children with significant disabilities in primary grades. *Exceptional Children, 63,* 195–210.

Salisbury, C. L., Palombaro, M. M., & Hollowood, T. M. (1993). On the nature and change of an inclusive elementary school. *Journal of the Association for Persons with Severe Handicaps, 18,* 75–84.

Schleien, S. J., Green, F. P., & Heyne, L. A. (1993). Integrated community recreation. In M. E. Snell (Ed.), *Instruction of students with severe disabilities* (4th ed., pp. 526–555). Upper Saddle River, NJ: Merrill/Prentice Hall.

Sharpe, M. N., York, J. L., & Knight, J. (1994). Effects of inclusion on the academic performance of classmates without disabilities: A preliminary study. *Remedial and Special Education, 15,* 281–287.

Siegel-Causey, E., Guy, B., & Guess, D. (1992). Students with severe and multiple disabilities. In E. L. Meyen & T. Skrtic (Eds.), *Exceptional children and youth* (4th ed., pp. 415–450). Denver: Love.

Sigafoos, J., Cole, D., & McQuarter, R. (1987). Current practices in the assessment of students with severe handicaps. *Journal of the Association for Persons with Severe Handicaps, 12,* 264–273.

Snell, M. E., & Brown, F. (1993). Instructional planning and implementation. In M. E. Snell (Ed.), *Instruction of students with severe disabilities* (4th ed., pp. 99–151). Upper Saddle River, NJ: Merrill/Prentice Hall.

Snell, M. E., & Farlow, L. J. (1993). Self-care skills. In M. E. Snell (Ed.), *Instruction of students with severe disabilities* (4th ed., pp. 380–441). Upper Saddle River, NJ: Merrill/Prentice Hall.

Snyder, S. L. (1991). *Age-appropriate placement of young adult students with severe disabilities: The college campus alternative.* Unpublished manuscript.

Snyder, S. L. (1993). *The social inclusion of six public school students with significant disabilities receiving instruction on a university campus: A qualitative study.* Unpublished manuscript.

Sobsey, D., & Wolf-Schein, E. G. (1991). Sensory impairments. In F. P. Orelove & D. Sobsey (Eds.), *Educating children with multiple disabilities: A transdisciplinary approach* (2nd ed., pp. 119–154). Baltimore: Brookes.

Stainback, W., & Stainback, S. (Eds.). (1996). *Controversial issues confronting special education: Divergent perspectives* (2nd ed.). Boston: Allyn & Bacon.

Staub, D., Schwartz, I. S., Galluci, C., & Peck, C. (1994). Four portraits of friendship at an inclusive school. *Journal of the Association for Persons with Severe Handicaps, 19,* 314–325.

Thompson, B., Wegner, J. R., Wickham, D., & Ault, M. M. (1993). *Handbook for the inclusion of young children with severe disabilities: Strategies for implementing exemplary full inclusion programs.* Lawrence, KS: Learner Managed Designs.

Thompson, B., Wickham, D., Shanks, P., Wegner, J. R., Ault, M. M., Reinertson, B., & Guess, D. (1991, Winter). Expanding the circle of inclusion: Integrating young children with severe and profound disabilities into Montessori programs. *Montessori Life,* pp. 11–15.

Thompson, B., Wickham, P., Wegner, J. R., & Ault, M. M. (1996). All children should know joy: Inclusive, family-centered services for young children with significant disabilities. In D. H. Lehr & F. Brown (Eds.), *People with disabilities who challenge the system* (pp. 23–56). Baltimore: Paul H. Brookes.

Thousand, J. S., Villa, R. A., & Nevin, A. I. (Eds.). (1994). *Creativity and collaborative learning: A practical guide to empowering students and teachers.* Baltimore: Brookes.

Turnbull, A. P., Pereira, L., & Blue-Banning, M. J. (1997). *Successful friendships of Hispanic children and youth with disabilities.* Manuscript submitted for publication.

Turnbull, A. P., & Turnbull, H. R. (1997). *Families, professionals, and exceptionality: A special partnership* (3rd ed.). Upper Saddle River, NJ: Merrill/Prentice Hall.

U.S. Department of Education. (1996). *To assure the free appropriate public education of all children with disabilities: Eighteenth annual report to Congress on the implementation of the Individuals with Disabilities Education Act.* Washington, DC: Author.

Utley, B. L. (1994). Providing support for sensory, postural, and movement needs. In L. Sternberg (Ed.), *Individuals with profound disabilities: Instructional and assistive strategies* (3rd ed., pp. 123–192). Austin, TX: Pro-Ed.

White, O. R. (1985). The evaluation of severely mentally retarded individuals. In B. Bricker & J. Filler (Eds.), *Severe mental retardation: From theory to practice* (pp. 161–184). Reston, VA: Council for Exceptional Children.

Wilcox, B., & Bellamy, G. T. (1987). *The activities catalog: An alternative curriculum for youth and adults with severe disabilities.* Baltimore: Brookes.

Wolery, M., Ault, M. J., & Doyle, P. M. (1992). *Teaching students with moderate and severe disabilities: Use of response prompting strategies.* White Plains, NY: Longman.

Wolery, M., & Schuster, J. W. (1997). Instructional methods with students who have significant disabilities. *Journal of Special Education, 31,* 61–79.

York-Barr, J., Schultz, T., Doyle, M. B., Kronberg, R., & Crosset, S. (1996). Inclusive schooling in St. Cloud: Perspectives on the process and people. *Remedial and Special Education, 17,* 92–103.

CHAPTER 10

Anderson, S. R., Avery, D. L., DiPietro, E. K., Edwards, G. L., & Christian, W. P. (1987). Intensive home-based early intervention with autistic children. *Education and Treatment of Children, 10,* 352–366.

Bachevalier, J. (1994). Medial temporal lobe structures and autism: A review of clinical and experimental findings. *Neuropsychologia, 32,* 627–648.

Bailey, A., Phillips, W., & Rutter, M. (1996). Autism: Towards an integration of clinical, genetic, neurophysiological, and neurobiological perspectives. *Journal of Child Psychology and Psychiatry and Allied Disciplines, 37,* 89–126.

Baron-Cohen, S. (1991). Do people with autism understand what causes emotion? *Child Development, 62,* 385–395.

Bartak, L., & Rutter, M. (1976). Differences between mentally retarded and normally intelligent autistic children. *Journal of Higher-Functioning Autistic Disorder and Childhood Schizophrenia, 6,* 109–120.

Bauer, S. (1995). Autism and the pervasive developmental disorders. *Pediatrics in Review, 16,* 130–136.

Bauman, M. L., & Kemper, T. L. (Eds.). (1994). *The neurobiology of autism.* Baltimore: Johns Hopkins University Press.

Bergman, J., & DePue, W. (1986). Musical idiot savants. *Music Educators Journal, 72*(5), 37–40.

Berkell, D. E. (1992). *Autism: Identification, education, and treatment.* Hillsdale, NJ: Erlbaum.

Bettelheim, B. (1950). *Love is not enough.* Glencoe, NY: Free Press.

Bettelheim, B. (1967). *The empty fortress: Infantile autism and the birth of the self.* London: Collier-Macmillan.

Biklen, D. (1992). Typing to talk: Facilitated communication. *American Journal of Speech-Language Pathology, 1*(2), 15–17.

Broek, E., Cain, S. L., Dutkiewicz, M., Fleck, C., Gray, B., Gray, C., Gray, J., Jonker, S., Lindrup, A., & Moore, L. (Eds.). (1993). *The original social story book.* Arlington, TX: Future Education.

Cardinal, D. N., Hanson, D., & Wakeham, J. (1996). An investigation of authorship in facilitated communication. *Mental Retardation, 34,* 231–242.

Carr, E. G., Levin, L., McConnachie, G., Carlson, J. I., Kemp, D. C., & Smith, C. E. (1994). *Communication-based intervention for problem behavior: A user's guide for producing positive change.* Baltimore: Brookes.

Cheatham, S. K., Smith, J. D., Rucker, H. N., Polloway, E. A., & Lewis, G. W. (1995, September). Savant syndrome: case studies, hypotheses, and implications for special education. *Education and Training in Mental Retardation,* pp. 243–253.

Cohen, S. (1998). *Targeting autism: What we know, don't know, and can do to help young children with autism and related disorders.* Berkeley: University of California Press.

Conderman, G., & Katsiyannis, A. (1996). State practices in serving individuals with autism. *Focus on Autism and Other Developmental Disabilities, 11*(1), 29–36.

Costello, E. J. (1996). State of the science in autism: Report to the National Institutes of Health: Epidemiology. *Journal of Autism and Developmental Disorders, 26,* 126–129.

Courchesne, E., Townsend, J., & Saitoh, O. (1994). The brain in infantile autism: Posterior fossa structures are abnormal. *Neurology, 44,* 214–223.

Crossley, R. (1997). *Speechless: Facilitating communication for people without voices.* New York: Dutton.

Crossley, R., & Remington-Gurney, J. (1992). Getting the words out: Facilitated communicative training. *Topics in Language Disorders, 12*(3), 29–45.

Dalrymple, N. J. (1995). Environmental supports to develop flexibility and independence. In K. A. Quill (Ed.), *Teaching children with autism: Strategies to enhance communication and socialization* (pp. 243–264). New York: Delmar.

Demchak, M. A., & Bossert, K. W. (1996). Assessing problem behaviors. In D. Browder (Ed.), *Innovations: American Association on Mental Retardation Research to Practice Series, 4* [Special issue].

Denkla, M. B. (1986). New diagnostic criteria for autism and related behavioral disorders—Guidelines for research protocols. *Journal of the American Academy of Child Psychiatry, 25,* 221–224.

Donnelly, J. A., & Altman, R. (1994). The autistic savant: Recognizing and serving the gifted student with autism. *Roeper Review, 16*(4), 252–256.

Eberlin, M., McConnachie, G., Abel, S., & Volpe, L. (1993). Facilitated communication: A failure to replicate the phenomenon. *Journal of Autism and Developmental Disorders, 23,* 507–530.

Family Connection Staff, DeVault, G., Krug, C., & Fake, S. (1996). Why does Samantha act that way?: Positive behavioral support leads to successful inclusion. *Exceptional Parent, 26*(9), 43–53.

Fenske, E. C., Zalenski, S., Krantz, P. J., & McClannahan, L. E. (1985). Age at intervention and treatment outcome for autistic children in a comprehensive intervention program. *Analysis and Intervention in Developmental Disabilities, 5,* 49–58.

Filipek, P. A. (1995). Quantitative magnetic resonance imaging in autism: The cerebullar vermis. *Current Opinion in Neurology, 8,* 134–138.

Foster-Johnson, L., & Dunlap, G. (1993). Using functional assessment to develop effective, individualized interventions for challenging behaviors. *Teaching Exceptional Children, 25*(3), 44–50.

Fox, L., Dunlap, G., & Philbrick. (in press). Providing individual supports to young children with autism and their families. *Journal of Early Intervention.*

Fullerton, A. (1995). Promoting self-determination for adolescents and young adults with autism. *Journal of Vocational Rehabilitation, 5,* 337–346.

Gardner, H. (1987). *Frames of mind: The theory of multiple intelligences.* New York: Basic Books.

Gillberg, C. (1984). Infantile autism and other childhood psychoses in a Swedish region: Epidemiological aspects. *Journal of Child Psychology and Psychiatry, 25,* 35–43.

Gillberg, I. C., & Coleman, M. (1996). Autism and medical disorders: A review of the literature. *Developmental Medicine and Child Neurology, 38,* 191–202.

Grandin, T. (1988). Teaching tips from a recovered autistic. *Focus on Autistic Behavior, 3*(1), 1–8.

Grandin, T. (1992). An inside view of autism. In E. Schopler & G. B. Mesibov (Eds.), *High-functioning individuals with autism* (pp. 105–126). New York: Plenum Press.

Gray, C. (1994, October). *Making sense out of the world: Social stories, comic strip conversations, and related instructional techniques.* Paper presented at the Midwest Educational Leadership Conference on Autism, Kansas City, MO.

Gray, C., & Garand, J. D. (1993). Social stories: Improving responses of students with autism with accurate social information. *Focus on Autistic Behavior, 8*(1), 1–10.

Green, G., & Shane, H. C. (1994). Science, reason, and facilitated communication. *Journal of the Association for Persons With Severe Handicaps, 19,* 151–172.

Greenspan, S. I. (1992). Reconsidering the diagnosis and treatment of very young children with autistic spectrum or pervasive developmental disorder. *Zero to Three, 13*(2), 1–9.

Gresham, F. L., & MacMillan, D. L. (1997). Autistic Recovery? An analysis and critique of the empirical evidence on the early intervention project. *Behavioral Disorders, 22,* 185–201.

Haas, R. H., Townsend, J., & Yeoung, C. (1996). Neurological abnormalities in infantile autism. *Journal of Child Neurology, 11,* 84–92.

Hodgdon, L. Q. (1995). Solving social-behavioral problems through the use of visually supported communication. In K. A. Quill (Ed.), *Teaching children with autism: Strategies to enhance communication and socialization* (pp. 265–286). New York: Delmar.

Horner, R. H., & Carr, E. G. (1997). Behavioral support for students with severe disabilities: Functional assessment and comprehensive intervention. *The Journal of Special Education, 31,* 84–109.

Horner, R. H., Dunlap, G., Koegel, R. L., Carr, E. G., Sailor, W., Anderson, J., Albin, R. W., & O'Neill, R. E. (1990). Toward a technology of "nonaversive" behavioral support. *Journal of the Association for Persons with Severe Handicaps, 15*(3), 125–132.

Howlin, P. (1982). Echolalic and spontaneous phrase speech in autistic children. *Journal of Child Psychology and Psychiatry, 23,* 281–293.

Individuals with Disabilities Education Act. 34 C.F.R., Part 300, § 300.7 (b)(1)(1991).

Jorgensen, C. M. (1996). Designing inclusive curricula right from the start: Practical strategies and examples for the high school classroom. In S. Stainback & W. Stainback (Eds.), *Inclusion: A guide for educators* (pp. 221–236). Baltimore: Brookes.

Kanner, L. (1943). Autistic disturbances of affective contract. *Nervous Child, 2,* 217–250.

Koegel, L. K. (1995). Communication and language intervention. In R. L. Koegel & L. K. Koegel (Eds.), *Strategies for initiating positive interactions and improving learning opportunities* (pp. 17–32). Baltimore: Brookes.

Koegel, L. K., Koegel, R. L., & Dunlap, G. (Eds.). (1996). *Positive behavioral support: Including people with difficult behavior in the community.* Baltimore: Brookes.

Koegel, L. K., Koegel, R. L., Hurley, C., & Frea, W. D. (1992). Improving social skills and disruptive behavior in children with autism through self-management. *Journal of Applied Behavior Analysis, 19,* 425–430.

Koppenhaver, D. A., Pierce, P. L., & Yoder, D. E. (1995). AAC, FC and the ABCs: Issues and relationships. *American Journal of Speech-Language Pathology, 4*(4), 5–14.

Layton, T. L., & Watson, L. R. (1995). Enhancing communication in nonverbal children with autism. In K. A. Quill (Ed.), *Teaching children with autism: Strategies to enhance communication and socialization* (pp. 73–104). Boston: Allyn & Bacon.

Leary, M. R., & Hill, D. A. (1996). Moving on: Autism and movement disturbance. *Mental Retardation, 34,* 39–53.

Lotspeich, L. J., & Ciaranello, R. D. (1993). The neurobiology and genetics of infantile autism. *International Review of Neurobiology, 35,* 87–129.

Lotter, V. (1966). Epidemiology of autistic conditions in young children. I: Prevalence. *School Psychiatry, 1,* 124–137.

Lovass, O. I. (1977). *The autistic child: Language development through behavior modification.* New York: Irvington Press.

Lovaas, O. I. (1987). Behavioral treatment and normal education and intellectual functioning in young autistic children. *Journal of Consulting and Clinical Psychology, 55,* 3–9.

Lucyshyn, J. M., & Albin, R. W. (1993). Comprehensive support to families of children with disabilities and behavior problems: Keeping it "friendly." In G. H. S. Singer & L. E. Powers (Eds.), *Families, disability, and empowerment: Active coping skills and strategies for family interventions* (pp. 365–408). Baltimore: Brookes.

Mauk, J. E., Reber, M., & Batshaw, M. L. (1997). Autism. In M. L. Batshaw (Ed.), *Children with disabilities* (4th ed., pp. 425–448). Baltimore: Brookes.

McEachin, J. J., Smith, T., & Lovaas, O. I. (1993). Long-term outcome for children with autism who received early intensive behavioral treatment. *American Journal on Mental Retardation, 97,* 359–372.

McGee, G. G., Jacobs, H. A., & Regnier, M. C. (1993). Preparation of families for incidental teaching and advocacy for their children with autism. *OSERS News in Print, 5*(3), 9–13.

Mesibov, G. B. (1995). A comprehensive program for serving people with autism and their families: The TEACCH model. In J. L. Matson (Ed.), *Autism in children and adults* (pp. 85–98). Pacific Grove, CA: Brooks/Cole.

Mesibov, G. B., Schopler, E., Schaffer, B., & Michal, N. (1989). Use of the childhood rating scale with autistic adolescents and adults. *Journal of the American Academy of Child and Adolescent Psychiatry, 28,* 538–541.

Morgan, S. (1988). Diagnostic assessment of autism: A review of objective scales. *Journal of Psychoeducational Assessment, 6,* 139–151.

Mullen, K. B., & Frea, W. D. (1995). A parent–professional consultation model for functional analysis. In R. L. Koegel & L. K. Koegel (Eds.), *Strategies for initiating positive interactions and improving learning opportunities* (pp. 175–188). Baltimore: Brookes.

Myles, B. S., Constant, J. A., Simpson, R. L., & Carlson, J. K. (1989). Educational assessment of students with higher-functioning autistic disorder. *Focus on Autistic Behavior, 4*(1), 1–15.

National Institutes of Health convene "Autism 1995: The-state-of-the-science," (1995). *The Communicator, 6*(?), 4–5. (Available from the Autism National Committee, 635 Ardmore Avenue, Ardmore, PA 19003)

National Society for Autistic Children, Board of Directors and Professional Advisory Board. (1977). *A short definition of autism.* Albany, NY: Author.

Parks, S. L. (1988). Psychometric instruments available for the assessment of autistic children. In E. Schopler & G. B. Mesibov (Eds.), *Diagnosis assessment in autism.* New York: Plenum.

Piven, J., Arndt, S., & Palmer, P. (1995). An MRI study of brain size in autism. *American Journal of Psychiatry, 152*(8), 1145–1149.

Prizant, B. M. (1983). Language and communication in autism: Toward an understanding of the "whole" of it. *Journal of Speech and Hearing Disorders, 48,* 296–307.

Prizant, B. M., & Rydell, P. J. (1984). Analysis of functions of delayed echolalia in autistic children. *Journal of Speech and Hearing Research, 27,* 183–192.

Quill, K. A. (1990). A model for integrating children with autism. *Focus on Autistic Behavior, 5*(4), 1–19.

Quill, K. A. (1995a). Enhancing children's social-communicative interactions. In K. A. Quill (Ed.), *Teaching children with autism: Strategies for enhancing communication and socialization* (pp. 163–192). New York: Delmar.

Quill, K. A. (Ed.). (1995b). *Teaching children with autism: Strategies to enhance communication and socialization.* New York: Delmar.

Rimland, B. (1978). Inside the mind of the autistic savant. *Psychology Today, 12*(3), 68–80.

Risley, T. (1996). Get a life! Positive behavioral intervention for challenging behavior through life arrangement and life coaching. In L. K. Koegel, R. L. Koegel, & G. Dunlap (Eds.), *Positive behavioral support: Including people with difficult behavior in the community* (pp. 425–438). Baltimore: Brookes.

Ritvo, E. R., & Freeman, B. J. (1978). National Society for Autistic Children definition of the syndrome of autism. *Journal of Autism and Childhood Schizophrenia, 8,* 162–167.

Rosenblatt, J., Bloom, P., & Koegel, R. L. (1995). Overselective responding: Description, implications, and intervention. In R. L. Koegel & L. K. Koegel (Eds.), *Teaching children with autism: Strategies for initiating positive interactions and improving learning opportunities* (pp. 33–42). Baltimore: Brookes.

Ruble, L. A., & Dalrymple, N. J. (1996). An alternative view of outcome in autism. *Focus on Autism and Other Developmental Disabilities, 11*(1), 3–14.

Rutter, M. (1978). Diagnosis and definition of childhood autism. *Journal of Autism and Childhood Schizophrenia, 8,* 139–161.

Rydell, P. J., & Prizant, B. M. (1995). Assessment and intervention strategies for children who use echolalia. In K. A. Quill (Ed.), *Teaching children with autism: Strategies to enhance communication and socialization* (pp. 105–132). New York: Delmar.

Schreibman, L. (1988). *Autism.* Newbury Park, CA: Sage.

Schuler, A. L. (1995). Thinking in autism: Differences in learning and development. In K. A. Quill (Ed.), *Teaching children with autism: Strategies to enhance communication and socialization* (pp. 11–32). New York: Delmar.

Sheehan, C. M., & Matuozzi, R. T. (1996). Investigation of the validity of facilitated communication through the disclosure of unknown information. *Mental Retardation, 34,* 94–107.

Simon, W. S., Toll, D. M., & Whitehair, P. M. (1994). A naturalistic approach to the validation of facilitated communication. *Journal of Autism and Developmental Disorders, 24,* 647–657.

Simpson, R. L., & Sasso, G. M. (1992). Full inclusion of students with autism in general education settings: Values versus science. *Focus on Autistic Behavior, 7*(3), 1–13.

Smith, M. D., & Belcher, R. G. (1993). Facilitated communication with adults with autism. *Journal of Autism and Development Disorders, 1,* 175–183.

Smith, M. D., Belcher, R. G., Juhrs, P. P., & Nabors, K. (1994). Where people with autism work. *Journal of Vocational Rehabilitation, 4*(1), 10–17.

Steinhausen, H. C., Gobel, D., Breinlinger, M., & Wohleben, B. (1983, October). *A community survey of infantile autism.* Paper presented at the thirtieth annual meeting of the American Academy of Child Psychiatry, San Francisco.

Strain, P., Hoyson, M., & Jamison, B. (1985). Normally developing preschoolers as intervention agents for autistic-like children: Effects on class deportment and social interaction. *Journal of the Division for Early Childhood, 9,* 105–115.

Sturmey, P., & Sevin, J. A. (1995). Defining and assessing autism. In J. L. Matson (Ed.), *Autism in children and adults* (pp. 13–35). Pacific Grove, CA: Brooks/ Cole.

Sullivan, R. C. (1994). Autism: Definitions past and present. *Journal of Vocational Rehabilitation, 4,* 4–9.

Swaggart, B. L., Gagnon, E., Bock, S. J., Earles, T. L., Quinn, C., Myles, B. S., & Simpson, R. L. (1995). Using social stories to teach social and behavioral skills to children with autism. *Focus on Autistic Behavior, 10*(1), 1–15.

Szatmari, P. (1991). Asperger's syndrome: Diagnosis, treatment, and outcome. *Psychiatric Clinics of North America, 14,* 81–93.

Tager-Flusberg, H. (1992). Autistic children's talk about psychological states: Deficits in the early acquisition of a theory of mind. *Child Development, 63,* 161–172.

Teal, M. B., & Wiebe, M. J. (1986). A validity analysis of selected instruments used to assess autism. *Journal of Autism and Developmental Disorders, 16,* 485–494.

Treffert, D. A. (1989). *Extraordinary people: Understanding "idiot savants."* New York: Harper & Row.

Tsai, L., & Scott-Miller, D. (1988). Higher-functioning autistic disorder. *Focus on Autistic Behavior, 2*(6), 1–8.

Turnbull, A. P., & Ruef, M. (1996). Family perspectives on problem behavior. *Mental Retardation, 34,* 280–293.

Turnbull, A. P., & Ruef, M. (1997). Family perspectives on inclusive lifestyle issues for individuals with problem behavior. *Exceptional Children, 63,* 211–227.

Turnbull, A. P., & Turnbull, H. R. (1996). Group Action Planning as a strategy for providing comprehensive family support. In L. K. Koegel, R. L. Koegel, & G. Dunlap (Eds.), *Positive behavioral support: Including people with difficult behavior in the community* (pp. 99– 114). Baltimore: Brookes.

Twachtman-Cullen, D. (1997). *A passion to believe: Autism and the facilitated communication phenomenon.* Boulder, CO: Westview Press.

U.S. Department of Education. (1995). *To assure the free appropriate public education of all children with disabilities: Seventeenth annual report to Congress on the implementation of the Individuals with Disabilities Education Act.* Washington, DC: Author.

Vasquez, C. A. (1994). Brief report: A multitask controlled evaluation of facilitated communication. *Journal of Autism and Developmental Disorders, 24,* 369–379.

Warren, F. (1985). A society that is going to kill your children. In H. R. Turnbull & A. P. Turnbull (Eds.), *Parents speak out: Then and now* (2nd ed., pp. 201–221). Upper Saddle River, NJ: Merrill/Prentice Hall.

Weigle, K. L. (1997). Positive behavioral support as a model for promoting educational inclusion. *Journal of the Association for Persons with Severe Handicaps, 22,* 36–48.

Weiss, M. J. S., Wagner, S. H., & Bauman, M. L. (1996). A validated case study of facilitated

communication. *Mental Retardation, 34,* 220–230.

Wheeler, D. L., Jacobson, J. W., Paglieri, R. A., & Schwartz, A. A. (1993). An experimental assessment of facilitated communication. *Mental Retardation, 31,* 49–60.

Williams, D. (1996). *Autism: An inside– outside approach.* London: Kingsley.

Yirmira, N., Sigman, M. D., Kasari, C., & Mundy, P. (1992). Empathy and cognition in high-functioning children with autism. *Child Development, 63,* 150–160.

CHAPTER 11

American Cancer Society. (1988). *Back to school: A handbook for teachers of children with cancer.* Atlanta: Author.

American Cancer Society. (1993). *Cancer facts and figures—1993.* Atlanta: Author.

Babies who beat AIDS. (1996, June). *Discover Magazine,* p. 30.

Bannister, A. (1997). Fishing for a cure for diabetes. *DMRF* [On-line]. Available: http://www.mcms.dal.ca/rdmrf/dmrf diab.html

Bearison, D. J. (1991). *"They never want to tell you": Children talk about cancer.* Cambridge: Harvard University Press.

Beverly, C. L. (1995). Providing a safe environment for children infected with the human immunodeficiency virus. *Topics in Early Childhood Special Education, 15*(1), 100–110.

Bruder, M. B. (1995). The challenge of pediatric AIDS: A framework for early childhood special education. *Topics in Early Childhood Special Education, 15*(1), 83–89.

Carta, J. J., Sideridis, G., Rinkel, P., Guimaraes, S., Greenwood, G., Baggett, K., Peterson, P., Atwater, J., McEvoy, M., & McConnell, S. (1994). Behavioral outcomes of young children prenatally exposed to illicit drugs: Review and analysis of experimental literature. *Topics in Early Childhood Special Education, 14*(2), 184–216.

Cassini, K. K., & Rogers, J. L. (1990). *Death in the classroom.* Cincinnati, OH: Griefwork.

Centers for Disease Control. (1997, November 27). *Morbidity and Mortality Weekly Report, 46*(46), 1086.

Chasnoff, I. J., Griffith, D. R., Freier, C., & Murray, J. (1992). Cocaine/polydrug use in pregnancy: Two-year follow-up. *Pediatrics, 89*(2), 284–289.

Childhood Lead Poisoning Prevention Program. (1996). *10 frequently asked questions about lead poisoning and the lead law* [On-line]. Available: http://www.magnet.state.ma.us/dph/ques.htm

Clayman, C. B. (Ed.). (1989). *The American Medical Association encyclopedia of medicine.* New York: Random House.

Cleveland Clinic Foundation. (1997). *Frequently asked questions about neurological prob-*

lems [On-line]. Available: http://www. neus. ccf.org/patients/faq. html

Clinton, W. J. (1996, May 27). Statement on signing the Ryan White CARE Act Amendments of 1996 (Transcript). *Weekly Compilation of Presidential Documents,* pp. 899–900.

Cohen, C. B., Mundy, T., Karassik, B., Lieb, L., Ludwig, D. D., & Ward, J. (1991). Neuropsychological functioning in human immunodeficiency virus type 1 seropositive children affected through neonatal blood transfusion. *Pediatrics, 88,* 58–68.

Colson, S. E., & Carlson, J. K. (1993). HIV/AIDS education for students with special needs. *Intervention in School and Clinic, 28*(5), 262–274.

Conlon, C. J. (1992). New threats to development: Alcohol, cocaine, and AIDS. In M. L. Batshaw & Y. M. Perret, *Children with disabilities: A medical primer* (3rd ed., pp. 111–136). Baltimore: Brooks.

Cosby, B. (1997). *The meanest thing to say.* New York: Scholastic.

DiFranza, J. R., & Lew, R. A. (1996). Morbidity and mortality in children associated with the use of tobacco products by other people. *Pediatrics, 97*(4), 560–568.

Dowling, C. G. (1997, May). Discovery: An epidemic of sneezing and wheezing. *Life,* pp. 76–93.

Environmental Protection Agency. (1992, September). *Lead poisoning and your children.* Publication Number 800-B-92-0002. Cincinnati, OH: Author.

Epilepsy Foundation of America. (1997). *Frequently asked questions* [On-line]. Available: http://www.efa.org/FAQ/faq. htm

Fauvre, M. (1988). Including children with "new" chronic illnesses in an early childhood setting. *Young Children, 46*(6), 71–77.

Fleitas, J. (1997). *Band-aides and blackboards: When chronic illness or some other medical problem goes to school* [On-line]. Available: http://funrsc.fairfield.edu/~jfleitas/kidsitro. html

Gaes, G., & Gaes, C. (1992). *You don't have to die: One family's guide to surviving childhood cancer.* New York: Villard Books.

Glanze, W. D., Anderson, K. N., & Anderson, L. E. (Eds.). (1985). *The Mosby medical encyclopedia.* New York: New American Library.

Griffith, D. R. (1991). Intervention needs of children prenatally exposed to drugs. *DD Network News, 4*(1), 4–6.

Grubman, S. (1991). HIV infection in infants and children: Progress notes/pediatric HIV infection. *AmFAR, 5*(1), 4–7.

HIV University. (1995, December 1). *WORLD,* pp. 2+.

Kapp-Simon, K., & Simon, D. J. (1991). Meeting the challenge: Social skills training for teens with special needs. *Connections: The Newsletter of the National Center for Youth and Disabilities, 2*(2), 1–5.

Lister, P. (1995, November). Bullies: The big new problem you must know about. *Redbook, 186,* 116–119.

Little, M. (1991). *Diabetes.* New York: Chelsea House.

Loring, G. (1991). *Parenting a diabetic child.* Chicago: Contemporary Books.

Lynch, E. W., Lewis, R. B., & Murphy, D. S. (1993). Educational services for children with chronic illnesses: Perspectives of educators and families. *Exceptional Children, 59*(3), 210–220.

Meisner, J. S. (1996, June 7). There is often a fine line between playful and hurtful teasing. *Gannett News Service.*

Midwest Diabetes Care Center. (1997). Pancreas transplantation. *Diabetes Monitor* [On-line]. Available: http://www.mdcc.com/transplt. htm

National Asthma Education Program. (1991). *Managing asthma: A guide for schools.* Bethesda, MD: National Institutes of Health.

National Council for Educational Technology (NCET). (1993). Video games: Health hazards [On-line].Available: http://ncet.csv.warwick. ac.uk/WWW/fliers/videogames/health.html

National Environmental Health Association. (1995). Study shows reducing dust, other allergens, could cut kids' asthma. *Journal of Environmental Health, 58,* 38.

National Heart, Lung, and Blood Institute. (1992). *Data fact sheet.* Bethesda, MD: U.S. Department of Health and Human Services.

National Institute of Diabetes and Digestive and Kidney Diseases (NIDDK). (1997). Diabetes statistics. *NIDDK Home page* [On-line]. Available: http://www.niddk.nih.gov/Diabetes Statistics/DiabetesSta tistics.html

National Jewish Center for Immunology and Respiratory Medicine. (1992). *Understanding asthma.* Denver, CO: Author.

National Public Radio. (1994, December 20). Disabled girl asks Santa for a day without teasing. *All Things Considered* [Radio broadcast].

Newacheck, P. W. (1991). *State estimates of the prevalence of chronic conditions among children and youth.* San Francisco: Maternal & Child Health Policy Research Center.

Paul, G. H., & Fafoglia, B. A. (1988). *All about asthma and how to live with it.* New York: Sterling.

Peckham, V. C. (1993). Children with cancer in the classroom. *Teaching Exceptional Children, 26*(1), 27–32.

Podolsky, D. (1997, January 13). Gasping for life. *U.S. News and World Report,* 61–65.

Popham, W. J. (1993, March). Wanted: AIDS education that works. *Phi Delta Kappan,* pp. 559–562.

Prater, M. A., & Serna, L. A. (1995). HIV disease. *Remedial and Special Education, 16,* 68–78.

P/S/L Consulting Group, Inc. (1997). Epilepsy gene found. *Doctor's guide to medical and other news* [On-line]. Available: http://www. pslgroup.com/dg/6ec6.htm

Schaefer, D., & Lyons, C. (1988). *How do we tell the children?: Helping children understand and cope when someone dies.* New York: Newmarket Press.

Schnieders, C. A., & Ludy, R. J. (1996). Grief and death in the classroom. *Physical Disabilities: Education and Related Services, 14*(2), 61–69.

Schutter, L. S., & Brinker, R. P. (1992). Conjuring a new category of disability from prenatal cocaine exposure: Are the infants unique biological or caretaking casualties? *Topics in Early Childhood Special Education, 11*(4), 84–111.

Simeonsson, N. (1995). Asthma: New information for the early interventionist. *Topics in Early Childhood Special Education, 15*(1), 32–43.

Spiegel, G. L., Cutler, S. K., & Yetter, C. E. (1996). What every teacher should know about epilepsy. *Intervention in School and Clinic, 32*(1), 34–38.

Steeves, S. A. (1997). Scientists genetically engineer cells to produce insulin. *Southwestern* [On-line]. Available: http://www.swmed. edu/news/nonislet.htm

Times Mirror Company. (1997, October 6). Medicine: Encouraging news from the AIDS front. *Los Angeles Times,* p. S–8.

Treaster, J. B. (1993, February 16). For children of cocaine, fresh reasons for hope. *New York Times,* pp. A1, B12.

U.S. Department of Education. (1997). *The condition of education, 1997/Supplemental Table 46-1* [On-line]. Available: http:// nces01.ed.gov/nces/pubs/ce/c9746d01.html

Vincent, L. J., Paulsen, M. K., Cole, C. K., Woodruff, G., & Griffith, D. R. (1991). *Born substance exposed, educationally vulnerable.* Reston, VA: Council for Exceptional Children.

Wadsworth, D. E., Knight, D., & Balser, V. (1993). Children who are medically fragile or technology dependent: Guidelines. *Intervention in School and Clinic, 29*(2), 102–104.

White, R., & Cunningham, A. M. (1992). *Ryan White: My own story.* New York: Signet.

Wiener, L. S., Best, A., & Pizzo, P. A. (1994). *Be a friend: Children with HIV speak.* Morton Grove, IL: Albert Whitman.

Wishom, P. M., Swaim, J. H., & Huang, A. (1989). AIDS. *Middle School Journal, 20*(3), 3–7.

Zuckerman, B., & Frank, O. A. (1992). Crack kids: Not broken. *Pediatrics, 89,* 284–289.

CHAPTER 12

Alexander, M. A., & Bauer, R. E. (1988). Cerebral palsy. In V. B. Van Hasselt, P. S. Strain, & M. Hersen (Eds.), *Handbook of developmental and physical disabilities* (pp. 215–226). New York: Pergamon Press.

Ammer, J. J., Best, S. J., & Kulik, B. J. (1994). Meeting the needs of students with physical handicaps: A survey of administrators and teachers in California. *Physical Disabilities: Education and Related Services, 13*(1), 25–39.

Angelo, D. H., Kokoska, S. M., & Jones, S. D. (1996). Family perspectives on augmentative and alternative communication: Families of adolescents and young adults. *Augmentative and Alternative Communication, 12,* 13–20.

Barnes, K. J., Schoenfeld, H. B., & Pierson, W. P. (1997). Inclusive schools: Implications for public school occupational therapy. *Physical Disabilities: Education and Related Services, 15*(2), 37–52.

Batshaw, M. L., & Rose, N. C. (1997). Birth defects, prenatal diagnosis, and fetal therapy. In M. L. Batshaw (Ed.), *Children with disabilities* (4th ed., pp. 35–52). Baltimore: Brookes.

Beck, A. R., & Dennis, M. (1996). Attitudes of children toward a similar-aged child who uses augmentative communication. *AAC Augmentative and Alternative Communication, 12,* 78–87.

Behrmann, M. M., & Schepis, M. M. (1994). Assistive technology assessment: A multiple case study review of three approaches with students with physical disabilities during the transition from school to work. *Journal of Vocational Rehabilitation, 4*(3), 202–210.

Bidabe, L., & Lollar, J. M. (1990). *M.O.V.E.: Mobility opportunities via education*. Bakersfield, CA: Kern County Superintendent of Schools.

Bigge, J. L. (1991). *Teaching individuals with physical and multiple disabilities* (3rd ed.). New York: Macmillan.

Blackman, J. A. (1984). *Medical aspects of developmental disabilities in children birth to three*. Rockville, MD: Aspen.

Bleck, E. E., & Nagel, M. D. (1982). *Physically handicapped children: A medical atlas for teachers*. New York: Allyn & Bacon.

Blum, R. W., Resnick, M. D., Nelson, R., & St. Germaine, A. (1991). Family and peer issues among adolescents with spina bifida and cerebral palsy. *Pediatrics, 88,* 280–285.

Brooke, M. H. (1986). *A clinician's view of neuromuscular diseases* (2nd ed.). Baltimore: Williams & Wilkins.

Brotherson, M. J., Cook, C. C., & Parette, H. P. (1996). A home-centered approach to assistive technology provision for young children with disabilities. *Focus on Autism and Other Developmental Disabilities, 11*(2), 86–95.

Bruno, J. (1996). Communication devices. *Directions: Technology in Special Education* [On-line], *3*(2), Available: http://www.dreamms.org/sep96.htm

Cavalier, A. R., & Ferretti, R. P. (1996). Talking instead of typing: Alternate access to computers via speech recognition technology. *Focus on Autism and Other Developmental Disabilities, 11*(2), 79–85.

Centers for Disease Control. (1992). Recommendations for the use of folic acid to reduce the number of cases of spina bifida and other neural tube defects. *Morbidity and Mortality Weekly Reports, 41*(RR-14). 1–7.

Cottier, C., Doyle, M., & Gilworth, K. (1997). *Functional AAC intervention: A team approach*. Bisbee, AZ: Imaginart.

Daly, L. E., Kirke, P. N., Malloy, A., Weir, D. G., & Scott, J. M. (1995). Folate levels and neural tube defects: Implications for prevention. *Journal of the American Medical Association, 274,* 1698–1702.

DeMoss, A., Rogers, J., Tuleja, C., & Kirshbaum, M. (1995). *Adaptive parenting equipment: Idea book I*. Berkeley, CA: Through the Looking Glass.

Fullmer, S., & Majumder, R. (1991). Increased access and use of disability related information for consumers. *Journal of Rehabilitation, 57*(3), 17–22.

Fullmer, S., & Walls, R. (1994). Interests and participation on disability-related computer bulletin boards. *Journal of Rehabilitation, 60*(1), 24–30.

Goetz, L., & Hunt, P. (1994). Augmentative and alternative communication. In E. C. Cipani & F. Spooner (Eds.), *Curricular and instructional approaches for persons with severe disabilities* (pp. 263–288). Needham Heights, MA: Allyn & Bacon.

Hedman, G. E. (1997). Assistive technology. In H. M. Wallace, R. F. Niehl, J. C. MacQueen, & J. A. Blackman (Eds.), *Mosby's guide to children with disabilities and chronic illnesses* (pp. 393– 401). St. Louis, MO: Mosby.

Heller, K. W., Alberto, P. A., Forney, P. E., & Schwartzman, M. N. (1996). *Understanding physical, sensory, and health impairments: Characteristics and educational implications*. Pacific Grove, CA: Brooks/Cole.

Hickman, C. (1994). *Kid Pix 2* [Computer software]. Novato, CA: Brøderbund Software.

Hosmer, J. P. (1996). Controlling the environment. *Directions: Technology in Special Education* [On-line], *3*(5), Available: http://www.dreamms.org/dec96.htm

Hutinger, P. L. (1996). Computer applications in programs for young children with disabilities: Recurrent themes. *Focus on Autism and Other Developmental Disabilities, 11*(2), 105–114.

Individuals with Disabilities Education Act, P.L. 105-17, 20 U.S.C. §1401 *et seq.* (Supp. 1997).

Irving Independent School District v. Tatro, 468 U.S. 883, 104 S. Ct. 3371, 82 L. Ed. 2d 644 (1984).

Johnson, J. M., Baumgart, D., Helmstetter, E., & Curry, C. A. (1996). *Augmenting basic com-*

munication in natural contexts. Baltimore: Brookes.

Jones, D. E., Clatterbuck, C. C., Marquis, J. G., Turnbull, H. R., & Moberly, R. L. (1996). Educational placements for children who are ventilator assisted. *Exceptional Children, 63,* 47–58.

Kirshbaum, M. (1997). Baby care assistive technology for parents with physical disabilities: Relational, systems, and cultural perspectives. *American Family Therapy Academy Newsletter, 67,* 20–26.

Kurtzweil, P. (1996). *How folate can help prevent birth defects*. Rockville, MD: U.S. Department of Health and Human Services, Food and Drug Administration.

Levy, S. E., & O'Rourke, M. (1997). Technological assistance: Innovations for independence. In M. L. Batshaw (Ed.), *Children with disabilities* (4th ed., pp. 687–708). Baltimore: Brookes.

Light, J. (1988). Interaction involving individuals using augmentative and alternative communication: State of the art and future research directions. *Augmentative and Alternative Communication, 4,* 66–82.

Light, J. (1997). "Communication is the essence of human life": Reflections on communicative competence. *Augmentative and Alternative Communication, 13,* 61–70.

Liptak, G. S. (1997). Neural tube defects. In M. L. Batshaw (Ed.), *Children with disabilities* (4th ed., pp. 529–552). Baltimore: Brookes.

Lutkenhoff, M., & Oppenheimer, S. G. (Eds.). (1997). *Spinabilities: A young person's guide to spina bifida*. Bethesda, MD: Woodbine House.

Mirenda, P., & Iacono, T. (1990). Communication options for persons with severe and profound disabilities: State of the art and future directions. *The Journal of the Association for Persons with Severe Handicaps, 15,* 3–21.

Office of Technology Assessment. (1987). *Technology-dependent children: Hospital versus home care: A technical memorandum* (DHHS Publication No. TM-H-38). Washington, DC: U.S. Government Printing Office.

Overeynder, J., Turk, M., Dalton, A., & Janicki, M. P. (1992). *"I'm worried about the future . . .": The aging of adults with cerebral palsy*. Albany: New York State Developmental Disabilities Planning Council.

Parette, H. P., & Angelo, D. H. (1996). Augmentative and alternative communication impact on families: Trends and future directions. *The Journal of Special Education, 30,* 77–98.

Parette, H. P., Hourcade, J. J., & Brimer, R. W. (1996). Degree of involvement and young children with cerebral palsy. *Physical Disabilities: Education and Related Services, 14*(2), 33–59.

Pellegrino, L. (1997). Cerebral palsy. In M. L. Batshaw (Ed.), *Children with disabilities* (4th ed., pp. 499–528). Baltimore: Brookes.

Plank, B. (1996). *Disabled doesn't mean immobile: Adaptive aids for transportation, matching disability, vehicle, and equipment.* Tampa, FL: National Mobility Equipment Dealers Association.

Porter, S., Haynie, M., Bierle, T., Caldwell, T. H., & Palfrey, J. S. (Eds.). (1997). *Children and youth assisted by medical technology in educational settings: Guidelines for care.* Baltimore: Brookes.

Powers, L. E., Sowers, J. A., & Stevens, T. (1995). An exploratory, randomized study of the impact of mentoring on the self-efficacy and community-based knowledge of adolescents with severe physical challenges. *Journal of Rehabilitation, 61*(1), 33–41.

Rainforth, B., & York-Barr, J. (1997). *Collaborative teams for students with severe disabilities: Integrating therapy and educational services* (2nd ed.). Baltimore: Brookes.

Ringel, S. P. (1987). *Neuromuscular disorders: A guide for patient and family.* New York: Raven.

Rowley-Kelley, F. L., & Reigel, D. H. (1993). *Teaching the student with spina bifida.* Baltimore: Brookes.

Sandler, A. (1997). *Living with spina bifida: A guide for families and professionals.* Chapel Hill. University of North Carolina Press.

Sax, C., Pumpian, I., & Fisher, D. (1997, March). Assistive technology and inclusion. *Consortium on Inclusive Schooling Practices (CISP) Issue Brief*, pp. 1–5.

Scherer, M. J. (1993). *Living in the state of stuck: How technology impacts the lives of people with disabilities.* Cambridge, MA: Brookline Books.

Schleichkorn, J. (1983). *Coping with cerebral palsy: Answers to questions parents often ask.* Austin, TX: Pro-Ed.

Silverman, F. H. (1995). *Communication for the speechless* (3rd ed.). Boston: Allyn & Bacon.

Technology-Related Assistance to Individuals with Disabilities Act of 1988, P.L. 100-407, 29 U.S.C. § 2201 *et seq.* (1997).

Turnbull, A. P., & Turnbull, H. R. (1997). *Families, professionals, and exceptionality: A special partnership* (3rd ed.). Upper Saddle River, NJ: Merrill/Prentice Hall.

Umbreit, J. (Ed.). (1983). *Physical disabilities and health impairments: An introduction.* Upper Saddle River, NJ: Merrill/ Prentice Hall.

U.S. Department of Education. (1996). *To assure a free appropriate public education for all students with disabilities: Eighteenth annual report to Congress on the implementation of the Individuals with Disabilities Education Act.* Washington, DC: Author.

Werler, M. M., Shapiro, S., & Mitchell, A. A. (1993). Periconceptional folic acid and risk of occurrent neural tube defects. *Journal of the American Medical Association, 269*(10), 1257–1261.

Wong, M. A. (1997). Disability and the internet: Access and use as means toward greater self-advocacy. *Physical Disabilities: Education and Related Services, 15*(2), 23–36.

Yen, I. H., Khoury, M. J., Erickson, J. D., James, L. M., Waters, G. D., & Berry, R. J. (1992). The changing epidemiology of neural tube defects: United States, 1968–1989. *American Journal of Diseases of Children, 146*, 857–861.

CHAPTER 13

Allison, M. (1992a). The effects of neurologic injury on the maturing brain. *Headlines, 3*(5), 2–10.

Allison, M. (1992b). SQUID: Latest innovation in neuroimaging. *Headlines, 3*(5), 23.

Altman, I. M. (1996). Awareness: Do I know what I can do? *I.E. Magazine, 4*(2), 8, 11.

Bergland, M., & Hoffbauer, D. (1996). New opportunities for students with traumatic brain injuries. *Teaching Exceptional Children, 28*(2), 54–57.

Bertolodo, M. (1995, Summer). I live. *The Perspectives Network Magazine, 5*(3).

Blosser, J. L., & DePompei, R. (1987). *Facilitating school return for the head injured: Strategies and resources.* Paper presented at the American Speech and Hearing Association convention, New Orleans, LA.

Blosser, J. L., & DePompei, R. (1994a). Creating an effective classroom environment. In R. C. Savage & G. F. Wolcott (Eds.), *Educational dimensions of acquired brain injury* (pp. 413–452). Austin, TX: Pro Ed.

Blosser, J. L., & DePompei, R. (1994b). *Pediatric traumatic brain injury: Proactive interventions.* San Diego, CA: Singular Press.

Brain Injury Association of Connecticut. (1996). *Brain injury statistics* [On-line]. Available: http://www.connix.com/~dpyers/bia/tbisats .html

Branden, N. (1984, November/December). Honoring the self. *New Realities*, pp. 30–35.

Bryan, M. R. (1993, November). *Summary of progress on addressing needs of students with traumatic brain injury.* Paper prepared for Office of Special Education Programs, Office of Special Education and Rehabilitative Services, U.S. Department of Education.

Carter, R. R., & Savage, R. C. (1984). Re-entry: The head injured student returns to school. *Cognitive Rehabilitation, 2*(6), 28–33.

Centre for Neuro Skills. (1995). *Traumatic brain injury resource guide* [On-line]. Available: http://www.neuroskills.com/~cns/ injury.html

Clark, E. (1996). Children and adolescents with traumatic brain injury: Reintegration challenges in educational settings. *Journal of Learning Disabilities, 29*(5), 549–560.

Conoley, J. C., & Sheridan, S. M. (1996). Pediatric traumatic brain injury: Challenges and interventions for families. *Journal of Learning Disabilities, 29*(6), 662–669.

Coopersmith, S. (1967). *The antecedents of self-esteem.* San Francisco: Freeman.

Disability Services at the University of Minnesota. (1996). *Traumatic brain injury* [Online]. Available: http://disserv.stu. umn.edu

Dunn, C. (1992). Reaching challenging kids. *Headlines, 3*(5), 18.

Farmer, J., & Peterson, L. (1995). Pediatric traumatic brain injury: Promoting successful school reentry. *School Psychology Review, 24*, 230–243.

Farmer, J. E., Clippard, D. S., Luehr-Wiemann, Y., Wright, E., & Owings, S. (1996). Assessing children with traumatic brain injury during rehabilitation: Promoting school and community reentry. *Journal of Learning Disabilities, 29*(5), 532–548.

Fletcher, J. M., Ewing-Cobbs, L., Miner, M. E., Levin, H. S., & Eisenberg, H. M. (1990). Behavioral changes after closed head injury in children. *Journal of Consulting and Clinical Psychology, 58*(1), 93–98.

Forness, S. R., & Kavale, K. A. (1993). The Balkanization of special education: Proliferation of categories and sub-categories for "new" disorders. *The Oregon Conference Monograph, 5*, ix–xii.

Gardner, D. (1993). *Depression in brain injury.* San Diego, CA: Head Injury Foundation Press.

Garey, M. E., & Wambold, C. (1994). Behavior management strategies for students with traumatic brain injury. *Beyond Behavior, 6*(1), 26–29.

Holliday, A., Lent, B. C., & Selden, M. (1996). Rehabilitation following a mild traumatic brain injury: A team approach. *I.E. Magazine, 3*(3), 24, 26–28.

Hux, K., & Hacksley, C. (1996). Mild traumatic brain injury: Facilitating school success. *Intervention in School and Clinic, 31*, 158–165.

Individuals with Disabilities Education Act, 20 U.S.C., §§ 1400 *et seq.* (1997).

Jacobs, H. E., & DeMello, C. (1996). The Clubhouse model and employment following brain injury. *Journal of Vocational Rehabilitation, 7*, 169–179.

Jaffe, I. (1996, February 26). Recovering from brain injury—Part II [Radio broadcast]. *All Things Considered.*

Kehle, T. J., Clark, E., & Jenson, W. R. (1996). Interventions for students with traumatic brain injury: Managing behavioral disturbances. *Journal of Learning Disabilities, 29*(6), 633–642.

Larkin, M. (1992). New hospital–school liaisons: Ensuring success for the student with neurologic impairments. *Headlines, 3*(5), 12–17.

Lash, M. (1991). *When your child is seriously injured: The emotional impact on families.*

Boston: Tufts University/New England Medical Center.

Lehr, E., & Savage, R. C. (1992). Community and school integration from a developmental perspective. In E. Keutzer (Ed.), *Community integration* (pp. 301–310). Baltimore: Brookes.

Levin, H. S., & Eisenberg, H. M. (1990). Postconcussional syndrome. *KHIA Resource Journal*. University of Texas Medical Branch, Division of Neurosurgery.

Lezak, M. D., & O'Brien, K. P. (1988). Longitudinal study of emotional, social, and physical changes after traumatic brain injury. *Journal of Learning Disabilities, 21*(8), 456–462.

Linge, F. R. (1984). What does it feel like to be brain damaged? *Canada's Mental Health Letter, 28*(3), 4–7.

Marquardt, T. P., Stoll, J., & Sussman, H. (1988). Disorders of communication in acquired cerebral trauma. *Journal of Learning Disabilities, 21*(6), 340–351.

Mateer, C. A., Kerns, K., & Eso, K. L. (1996). Management of attention and memory disorders following traumatic brain injury. *Journal of Learning Disabilities, 29*, 618–632.

May Institute Center for Education and Neurorehabilitation. (n.d.). *When your child goes home after being examined for head injury in an emergency department*. (Available from May Institute Center for Education and Neurorehabilitation, 35 Pacella Park Dr., Randolph, MA 02369)

McMorrow, M. J. (1994, Spring). Toward proactive treatment of unwanted behavior following brain injury. *I.E. Magazine, 2*(2), 14–21.

Medical Research and Training Center in Rehabilitation and Childhood Trauma. (1993). *Facts from the National Pediatric Trauma Registry: Fact sheet 2*. Washington, DC: U.S. Department of Education.

Missouri Head Injury Foundation. (1991). *Missouri head injury guide for survivors, families, and caregivers*. Jefferson City: State of Missouri.

Neurotrauma Law Center. (1996). *Understanding brain injury* [On-line]. Available: http://www.neurolaw.com/brain.html

Nordlund, M. R. (1994). Transition to postsecondary education. In R. C. Savage & G. F. Wolcott (Eds.), *Educational dimensions of acquired brain injury* (pp. 507–518). Austin, TX: Pro-Ed.

Novack, T., & Caldwell, S. (n.d.). *Educating the traumatically brain-injured student*. Unpublished manuscript. Spain Rehabilitation Center, University of Alabama, Birmingham.

Ohio Valley Center for Brain Injury Prevention and Rehabilitation. (n.d.). *Project 3.3: Empowering survivors* [On-line]. Available: http://205.182.14.25/about/projects/3.3/index.html

Perspectives Network. (1997). TPN list of ABI effects [On-line]. Available: http://www.tbi.org/html/signs_symptoms_.html

Peterson, H. (1994). Once I was. *I.E. Magazine, 2*(3), 3.

Pollack, I. W. (1994). Reestablishing an acceptable sense of self. In R. C. Savage & G. F. Wolcott (Eds.), *Educational dimensions of acquired brain injury* (pp. 185–235). Austin, TX: Pro-Ed.

Prigatano, G. P. (1987). Recovery and cognitive retraining after craniocerebral trauma. *Journal of Learning Disabilities, 20*(10), 603–613.

Russo, D. C. (1991, November). *Behavioral treatment of pediatric head injury: Issues and outcomes*. Paper presented at conference on neurogenic developmental disorders, Niskayuna, NY.

Savage, R. C. (1991). Identification, classification, and placement issues for students with traumatic brain injuries. *Journal of Head Trauma Rehabilitation, 6*(1), 1–9.

Savage, R. C. (1993). Children with traumatic brain injury. *TBI Challenge! 1*(3), 4–5.

Savage, R. C. (1994, January 3). Letter to J. Heumann, Assistant Director of Special Education and Rehabilitative Services, U.S. Department of Education.

Savage, R., & Mishkin, L. (1994). A neurological model for teaching students with acquired brain injuries. In R. C. Savage & G. F. Wolcott (Eds.), *Educational dimensions of acquired brain injury* (pp. 393–412). Austin, TX: Pro-Ed.

Schroeder, H. (1993). Cerebral trauma: Accidental injury or shaken impact syndrome? *Headlines, 4*(5), 18–21.

Shobris, J. (1994). The dualism of psychology. *Genetic, Social, and General Psychology Monographs, 120*, 373.

State University of New York. (1995). *Traumatic brain injury: A guidebook for educators*. Albany: New York State Department of Education, Office for Special Education Services.

Telzrow, C. F. (1991). The school psychologist's perspective on testing students with traumatic brain injury. *Journal of Head Trauma Rehabilitation, 6*(1), 23–34.

Tucker, B. F., & Colson, S. E. (1992). Traumatic brain injury: An overview of school reentry. *Intervention in School and Clinic, 27*(4), 196–206.

Tyler, J. (1989). Serving students with traumatic brain injuries in the learning disabilities classroom. *LD Forum, 15*(4), 28–29.

Tyler, J. S. (1990). *Traumatic head injury in school-aged children: A training manual for educational personnel*. Unpublished manuscript, Children's Rehabilitation Unit, University of Kansas, Kansas City.

Tyler, J. S., & Myles, B. S. (1990). Serving students with traumatic brain injury: A new challenge for teachers of students with learning disabilities. *LD Forum, 16*(1), 69–74.

Urbanczyk, B., & Savage, R. C. (1995). Understanding TBI: Growing up with a brain injury. *The Perspectives Network Magazine, 5*(3), n.p.

U.S. Department of Health and Human Services. (1984). *Head injury: Hope through research*. Bethesda, MD: Author.

UW Rehabilitation Medicine. (1995). Study examines recovery rates in children. *Traumatic Brain Injury Update* [On-line]. Available: www.weber.u.washington.edu/~rehab/tbi/6-2/pediatric.html

UW Rehabilitation Medicine. (1996). Predicting functional outcome after TBI. *Traumatic brain injury update* [On-line]. Available: www.weber.u.washington.edu/~rehab/tbi/6-2/pediatric.html

Walker, C. (1993). The young pediatric patient: Predicting outcome after cerebral insult. *Headlines, 4*(5), 4–11.

Wolcott, G., Lash, M., & Pearson, S. (1995). *Signs and strategies for educating students with brain injuries: A practical guide for teachers and schools*. Houston, TX: HDI.

Wood, R. L. (1988). Attention disorders in brain injury rehabilitation. *Journal of Learning Disabilities, 21*(6), 327–332, 351.

Ylvisaker, M., Hartwick, P., & Stevens, M. (1991). School reentry following head injury: Managing the transition from hospital to school. *Journal of Head Trauma Rehabilitation, 6*(1), 10–21.

Ylvisaker, M., Szekeres, S. F., Haarbauer-Krupa, J., Urbanczyk, B., & Feeney, T. J. (1994). Speech and language intervention. In R. C. Savage & G. F. Wolcott (Eds.), *Educational dimensions of acquired brain injury* (pp. 185–235). Austin, TX: Pro-Ed.

Ylvisaker, M., Szekeres, S. F., & Hartwick, P. (1994). A framework for cognitive intervention. In R. C. Savage & G. F. Wolcott (Eds.), *Educational dimensions of acquired brain injury* (pp. 35–68). Austin, TX: Pro-Ed.

Ylvisaker, M., Szekeres, S. F., Hartwick, P., & Tworek, P. (1994). Cognitive intervention. In R. C. Savage & G. F. Wolcott (Eds.), *Educational dimensions of acquired brain injury* (pp. 121–184). Austin, TX: Pro-Ed.

CHAPTER 14

Aaron, P. G., & Joshi, R. M. (1992). *Reading problems: Consultation and remediation*. New York: Guilford.

Alpert, C. L., & Kaiser, A. P. (1992). Training parents as milieu language teachers. *Journal of Early Intervention, 16*, 31–52.

American Speech-Language-Hearing Association. (1983). Position paper on social dialects. *ASHA, 25*(9), 23–24.

American Speech-Language-Hearing Association. (1993). Definitions of communication disorders and variations. *ASHA, 35*(Suppl. 10), 40–41.

Bailey, D. B., & Wolery, M. (1992). *Teaching infants and preschoolers with disabilities.* Upper Saddle River, NJ: Merrill/ Prentice Hall.

Bashir, A. S. (1989). Language intervention and the curriculum. *Seminars in Speech and Language, 10*(3), 181–190.

Berk, L. E. (1994). Vygotsky's theory: The importance of make-believe play. *Young Children, 50*(1), 30–39.

Bloom, L., & Lahey, M. (1978). *Language development and language disorders.* New York: John Wiley & Sons.

Bobrick, B. (1995). *Knotted tongues: Stuttering in history and the quest for a cure.* New York: Simon & Schuster.

Cantwell, D. P., & Baker, L. (1987). *Developmental speech and language disorders.* New York: Guilford.

Chomsky, N. (1957). *Syntactic structures.* The Hague, The Netherlands: Mouton.

Culatta, R., & Goldberg, S. A. (1995). *Stuttering therapy: An integrated approach to theory and practice.* Boston: Allyn & Bacon.

Diggs, C. (1992). McMilestone-mcmenu. *ASHA, 34,* 40–41.

Dixon-Krauss, L. A. (1995). Partner reading and writing: Peer social dialogue and the zone of proximal development. *Journal of Reading Behavior, 27*(1), 45–63.

Duchan, J. F., Hewitt, L. E., & Sonnenmeier, R. M. (1994). *Pragmatics: From theory to practice.* Upper Saddle River, NJ: Merrill/ Prentice Hall.

Dunn, L., & Dunn, L. (1997). *Peabody picture vocabulary test—III.* Circle Pines, MN: American Guidance Service.

Emerick, L. L., & Haynes, W. O. (1986). *Diagnosis and evaluation in speech pathology* (3rd ed.). Upper Saddle River, NJ: Merrill/ Prentice Hall.

Fey, M. (1992). Clinical forum. Phonological assessment and treatment. Articulation and phonology: Inextricable constructs in speech pathology. *Language, Speech, and Hearing Services in Schools, 23,* 225–232.

Fey, M. E., Catts, H., & Larrivee, L. (1995). Preparing preschoolers for the academic and social challenges of school. In M. E. Fey, J. Windsor, & S. F. Warren (Eds.), *Language intervention: Preschool through elementary years* (pp. 3–38). Baltimore: Brookes.

Goldstein, H., & Kaczmarek, L. (1992). Promoting communicative interaction among children in integrated intervention settings. In S. F. Warren & J. Reichle (Eds.), *Causes and effects in communication and language intervention* (pp. 81–112). Baltimore: Brookes.

Hart, B., & Risley, T. R. (1995). *Meaningful differences in the everyday experience of young American children.* Baltimore, MD: Brookes.

Haynes, W. O., Moran, M. J., & Pindzola, R. H. (1994). *Communication disorders in the classroom* (2nd ed.). Dubuque, IA: Kendall/Hunt.

Hedge, M. N. (1991). *Introduction to communicative disorders.* Austin, TX: Pro-Ed.

Hemmeter, M. L., & Kaiser, A. P. (1994). Enhanced milieu teaching: Effects of parent-implemented language intervention. *Journal of Early Intervention, 18,* 269–289.

Hodson, B. W., Nonmura, C. W., & Zappia, M. J. (1989). Phonological disorders: Impact on academic performance? *Seminars in Speech and Language, 10*(3), 252–259.

Hulit, L. M., & Howard, M. R. (1993). *Born to talk.* New York: Macmillan.

Kaiser, A. P., Hemmeter, M. L., Ostrosky, M. M., Alpert, C. L., & Hancock, T. B. (1995). The effects of group training and individual feedback on parent use of milieu teaching. *Journal of Childhood Communication Disorders, 16,* 39–48.

Kamhi, A. G., & Catts, H. W. (1991). Reading disabilities: Terminology, definitions, and subtyping issues. In A. G. Kamhi & H. W. Catts (Eds.), *Reading disabilities: A developmental language perspective* (pp. 35–66). Boston: Allyn & Bacon.

LaBlance, G. R., Steckol, K. F., & Smith, V. L. (1994). Stuttering: The role of the classroom teacher. *Teaching Exceptional Children, 26*(2), 10–12.

MacDonald, J. D., & Carroll, J. Y. (1992). A social partnership model for assessing early communication development: An intervention model for preconversational children. *Language, Speech and Hearing Services in Schools, 23,* 113–124.

McCormick, L. (1990a). Sequence of language and communication development. In L. McCormick & R. Schiefelbusch (Eds.), *Early language intervention: An introduction* (2nd ed.). Upper Saddle River, NJ: Merrill/ Prentice Hall.

McCormick, L. (1990b). Terms, concepts, and perspectives. In L. McCormick & R. Schiefelbusch (Eds.) *Early language intervention: An introduction* (2nd ed.). Upper Saddle River, NJ: Merrill/Prentice Hall.

McCormick, L., & Schiefelbusch, R. L. (Eds.) (1990). *Early language intervention: An introduction* (2nd ed.). Upper Saddle River, NJ: Merrill/Prentice Hall.

McNeill, J. H., & Fowler, S. A. (1998). Let's talk: Encouraging mother–child conversations during story reading. *Journal of Early Intervention.*

Miller, L. (1989). Classroom-based language intervention. *Language, Speech, and Hearing Services in Schools, 20,* 153–169.

Morrison, J., & Shriberg, L. (1992). Articulation testing versus conversational speech sampling. *Journal of Speech and Hearing Research, 35*(2), 259–273.

Nelson, K. (1977). Facilitating children's syntax acquisition. *Developmental Psychology, 13,* 101–107.

Newcomer, P. L., & Hammill, D. D. (1996). *Tests of language development* (3rd ed.). Austin, TX: Pro-Ed.

Nicolosi, L., Harryman, E., & Krescheck, J. (1996). *Terminology of communication disorders: Speech-language-hearing* (4th ed.). Baltimore: Williams & Wilkins.

Ninio, A., & Bruner, J. (1978). The achievement and antecedents of labelling. *Journal of Child Language, 5,* 1–15.

Ostrosky, M. M., & Kaiser, A. P. (1991). Preschool environments that promote communication. *Teaching Exceptional Children, 23,* 6–10.

Owens, R. E. (1991). *Language disorders: A functional approach to assessment and intervention.* Upper Saddle River, NJ: Merrill/Prentice Hall.

Owens, R. E. (1995). *Language disorders: A functional approach to assessment and intervention* (2nd ed.). Boston: Allyn & Bacon.

Palmer, J. M., & & Yantis, P. A. (1990). *Survey of communication disorders.* Baltimore: Williams & Wilkins.

Peterson, N. (1989). *Early intervention for handicapped and at-risk children.* Denver: Love.

Pierangelo, R. (1995). *The special education teacher's book of lists.* New York: The Center for Applied Research in Education.

Rice, M., Hadley, P. A., & Alexander, A. L. (1993). Social biases toward children with speech and language impairments: A correlative causal model of language limitations. *Applied Psycholinguistics, 14,* 445–471.

Roberts, J., & Crais, E. (1989). Assessing communication skills. In D. Bailey & M. Wolery (Eds). *Assessing infants and preschoolers with handicaps* (pp. 337– 389). Upper Saddle River, NJ: Merrill/ Prentice Hall.

Rossetti, L. M. (1991). Infant-toddler assessment: A clinical perspective. *Infant-Toddler Intervention, 1*(1), 11–26.

Sander, E. K. (1972). When are speech sounds learned? *Journal of Speech and Hearing Disorders, 37,* 55–63.

Stanovich, K. E. (1988). The right and wrong places to look for the cognitive locus of reading disability. *Annals of Dyslexia, 38,* 154–177.

Szekeres, S. F., & Meserve, N. F. (1994). Collaborative intervention in schools after traumatic brain injury. *Topics in Language Disorders, 15*(1), 21–36.

Turnbull, A. P., & Turnbull, H. R. (1997). *Families, professionals, and exceptionality: A special partnership.* Upper Saddle River, NJ: Merrill/Prentice Hall.

U.S. Department of Education. (1996). *Eighteenth annual report to Congress on the implementation of the Individuals with*

Disabilities Education Act. Washington, DC: Author.

Vygotsky, L. (1978). *Thought and language*. Cambridge: Harvard University Press.

Wang, P. P., & Baron, M. A. (1997). Language and communication: Development and disorders. In M. L. Batshaw (Ed.), *Children with disabilities* (4th ed., pp. 275–292). Baltimore: Brookes.

Wallach, G. P., & Butler, K. G. (1994). *Language learning disabilities in school-aged children and adolescents: Some principles and applications*. Upper Saddle River, NJ: Merrill/ Prentice Hall.

Weiss, C., Gordon, M., & Lillywhite, H. (1987). *Clinical management of articulation and phonologic disorders*. Baltimore: Williams & Wilkins.

Wells, G. (1992, November). *Language and the inquiry-oriented curriculum*. Paper presented at the Annual Meeting of the National Council of Teachers of English, Louisville, KY.

Yoder, P. M., Warren, S. F., Kim, K., & Gazdag, G. E. (1994). Facilitating prelinguistic communication skills in young children with development delay II: Systematic replication and extension. *Journal of Speech and Hearing Research, 37,* 841–851.

CHAPTER 15

Afzali-Nomani, E. (1995). Education conditions related to successful full inclusion programs involving deaf/hard of hearing children. *American Annals of the Deaf, 140,* 396–401.

Bat-Chava, Y. (1993). Antecedents of self-esteem in deaf people: A meta-analytic review. *Rehabilitation Psychology, 38,* 221–234.

Bess, F. H., & Humes, L. E. (1995). *Audiology: The fundamentals* (2nd ed.). Baltimore: Williams & Wilkins.

Bornstein, H., & Saulnier, K. (1984). *The signed English starter*. Washington, DC: Gallaudet University Press.

Bowe, F. (1991). *Approaching equality: Education of the deaf*. Silver Spring, MD: T. J. Publishers.

Braden, J. P. (1992). Intellectual assessment of deaf and hard-of-hearing people: A quantitative and qualitative research synthesis. *School Psychology Review, 21,* 82–94.

Bull, B., & Bullis, M. (1991). A national profile of school-based transition programs for deaf adolescents. *American Annals of the Deaf, 136,* 339–348.

Cartledge, G., Paul, P. V., Jackson, D., & Cochran, L. L. (1991). Teachers' perceptions of the social skills of adolescents with hearing impairment in residential and public school settings. *Remedial and Special Education, 12*(2), 34–39, 47.

Cates, J. A. (1991). Self-concept in hearing and prelingual, profoundly deaf students: A comparison of teachers' perceptions. *American Annals of the Deaf, 136,* 354–359.

Chovan, W. L., & Roberts, K. (1993). Deaf students' self-appraisals, achievement outcomes, and teachers' inferences about social-emotional adjustment in academic settings. *Perceptual and Motor Skills, 77,* 1021–1022.

Christiansen, J. B., & Barnartt, S. N. (1995). *Deaf President Now!: The 1988 revolution at Gallaudet University*. Washington, DC: Gallaudet University.

Clarkson, R. I., Vohr, B. R., Blackwell, P. M., & White, K. R. (1994). Universal hearing screening and intervention: The Rhode Island program. *Infants and Young Children, 6*(3), 65–74.

Cohen, O. P., Fischgrund, J. E., & Redding, R. (1990). Deaf children from ethnic, linguistic and racial minority backgrounds: An overview. *American Annals of the Deaf, 135,* 67–73.

Cole, S. H., & Edelmann, R. J. (1991). Identity patterns and self- and teacher-perceptions of problems for deaf adolescents: A research note. *Journal of Child Psychology and Psychiatry and Allied Disciplines, 32,* 1159–1165.

Commission on Education of the Deaf. (1988). *Toward equality: Education of the deaf*. Washington, DC: U.S. Government Printing Office.

The Council for Exceptional Children. (1995). *What every special educator must know: The International Standards for the Preparation and Certification of Special Education Teachers*. Reston, VA: Author.

Feher-Prout, T. (1996). Stress and coping in families with deaf children. *Journal of Deaf Studies and Deaf Education, 1,* 155–166.

Foster, S. (1989). Social alienation and peer identification: A study of the social construction of deafness. *Human Organization, 48,* 226–235.

Furth, H. G. (1973). *Deafness and learning: A psychosocial approach*. Belmont, CA: Wadsworth.

Holt, J. (1994). Classroom attributes and achievement test scores for deaf and hard of hearing students. *American Annals of the Deaf, 139,* 430–437.

Hunt, J., & Marshall, W. (1994). *Code of ethics for interpreters of the deaf*. Silver Spring, MD: Registry of Interpreters of the Deaf.

Josephson, J. A., & Moore, W. G. (1993). Lowering the age of identification: Oregon's design and preliminary results. *The Volta Review, 95*(5), 33–40.

Kluwin, T. N. (1993). Cumulative effects of mainstreaming on the achievement of deaf adolescents. *Exceptional Children, 60,* 73–81.

Kluwin, T. N., & Stinson, M. S. (1993). *Deaf students in local public high schools: Backgrounds, experiences, and outcomes*. Springfield, IL: Charles C. Thomas.

Lang, H. G., & Meath-Lang, B. (1995). *Deaf persons in the arts and sciences: A biographical dictionary*. Westport, CT: Greenwood.

Lewis, L., & Greene, B. (1994). *Deaf and hard of hearing students in postsecondary education*. (Publication No. NCES 94-394). Washington, DC: Government Printing Office.

Ling, D. (1988). *Foundations of spoken language for hearing-impaired children*. Washington, DC: Alexander Graham Bell Association for the Deaf.

Luetke-Stahlman, B. (1988). Documenting syntactically and semantically incomplete bimodal input to hearing-impaired subjects. *American Annals of the Deaf, 133,* 230–234.

Luetke-Stahlman, B., & Luckner, J. (1991). *Effectively educating students with hearing impairments*. New York: Longman.

Mertens, D. M. (1990). A conceptual model for academic achievement: Deaf student outcomes. In D. F. Moores & K. P. Meadow-Orlans (Eds.), *Educational and developmental aspects of deafness* (pp. 11–72). Washington, DC: Gallaudet University.

Moores, D. F. (1991). The great debate: Where, how, and what to teach deaf children. *American Annals of the Deaf, 136,* 35–37.

Moores, D. F. (1993). Total inclusion/zero rejection models in general education: Implications for deaf children. *American Annals of the Deaf, 138,* 251.

Moores, D. F. (1996). *Educating the deaf: Psychology, principles, and practices* (4th ed.). Boston: Houghton Mifflin.

Musselman, C., Mootilal, A., & MacKay, S. (1996). The social adjustment of deaf adolescents in segregated, partially integrated, and mainstreamed settings. *Journal of Deaf Studies and Deaf Education, 1,* 52–63.

National Association of State Directors of Special Education. (1994). *Deaf and hard of hearing students: Educational service guidelines*. Alexandria, VA: Author.

Northern, J. L., & Downs, M. P. (1991). *Hearing in children* (4th ed.). Baltimore: Williams & Wilkins.

Padden, C., & Humphries, T. (1988). *Deaf in America: Voices from a culture*. Cambridge, MA: Harvard University.

Schildroth, A. N. (1994). Annual survey of hearing-impaired children and youth: 1992–93 school year. Center for Assessment and Demographic Studies, Gallaudet University, Washington, DC.

Schildroth, A. N., & Hotto, S. A. (1994). Inclusion or exclusion? Deaf students and the inclusion movement. *American Annals of the Deaf, 139,* 239–243.

Schildroth, A. N., Rawlings, B. W., & Allen, R. E. (1989). Hearing-impaired children under age 6: A demographic analysis. *American Annals of the Deaf, 134,* 63–69.

Schirmer, B. R. (1993). Constructing meaning from narrative text: Cognitive processes of deaf children. *American Annals of the Deaf, 138,* 397–403.

Schirmer, B. R. (1994). *Language and literacy development in children who are deaf.* Needham Heights, MA: Allyn & Bacon.

Schirmer, B. R. (1995). Mental imagery and the reading comprehension of deaf children. *Reading Research and Instruction, 34,* 177–188.

Schirmer, B. R., & Winter, C. R. (1993). Use of cognitive schema by children who are deaf for comprehending narrative text. *Reading Improvement, 30,* 26–34.

Schirmer, B. R., & Woolsey, M. L. (1997). Effect of teacher questions on the reading comprehension of deaf children. *Journal of Deaf Studies and Deaf Education, 2,* 47–56.

Stewart, D. A., Akamatsu, C. T., & Becker, B. (1995). Aiming for consistency in the way teachers sign. *American Annals of the Deaf, 140,* 314–323.

Stewart, D. A., & Stinson, M. S. (1992). The role of sport and extracurricular activities in shaping socialization patterns. In T. N. Kluwin, D. F. Moores, & M. G. Gaustad (Eds.), *Toward effective public school programs for deaf students: Context, process, and outcomes* (pp. 144–145). New York: Teachers College Press.

U.S. Department of Education. (1995). *To assure the free appropriate public education of all children with disabilities: Seventeenth annual Report to Congress on the implementation of the Individuals with Disabilities Education Act.* Washington, DC: Author.

Vernon, M., & Andrews, J. A. (1990). *The psychology of deafness: Understanding deaf and hard-of-hearing people.* New York: Longman.

Weisel, A., & Bar-Lev, H. (1992). Role taking ability, nonverbal sensitivity, language and social adjustment of deaf adolescents. *Educational Psychology, 12,* 3–13.

Wolk, S., & Allen, T. E. (1984). A 5-year follow-up of reading comprehension achievement of hearing-impaired students in special education programs. *The Journal of Special Education, 18,* 161–176.

Wood, H., Wood, D., & Kingsmill, M. (1991). Signed English in the classroom, II: Structural and pragmatic aspects of teachers' speech and sign. *First Language, 11,* 301–325.

Wright, D. (1993). *Deafness: An autobiography.* New York: HarperCollins.

CHAPTER 16

Alonzo, L. (1987). *Unique educational needs of learners with visual impairments.* East Lansing, MI: Hannah Technology and Research Center. American Foundation for the Blind.

American Foundation for the Blind. (1954). *The Pine Brook Report: National work session on the education of the blind with the sighted.* New York: Author.

American Foundation for the Blind. (1957). *Itinerant teaching service for blind children: Proceedings of a national work session held at Bear Mountain, New York, August 20–24, 1956.* New York: Author.

Andersen, E. S., Dunlea, A., & Kekelis, L. S. (1984). Blind children's language: Resolving some differences. *Journal of Child Language, 11,* 645–664.

Bishop, V. E. (1996). *Teaching visually impaired children* (2nd ed.). Springfield, IL: Charles C. Thomas.

California Leadership Action Team for the Visually Impaired. (1985). *Statement of educational needs of visually impaired students.* New York: American Foundation for the Blind.

Caton, H., Pester, E., & Bradley, E. J. (1980). *Patterns: The primary braille reading program.* Louisville, KY: American Printing House for the Blind.

Corn, A. L. (1983). Visual function: A theoretical model for individuals with low vision. *Journal of Visual Impairment and Blindness, 77*(8), 373–377.

Corn, A. L., & Sacks, S. Z. (1994). The impact of non-driving on adults with visual impairments. *Journal of Visual Impairment and Blindness, 88*(1), 53–68.

Curry, S. A. (1993). A model assessment program. *Journal of Visual Impairment and Blindness, 87*(6), 190–193.

Curry, S. A., & Hatlen, P. H. (1988). In support of specialized programs for blind and visually impaired children: The impact of vision loss on learning. *Journal of Visual Impairment and Blindness, 82*(10), 417–424.

Erin, J. (1996). Children with multiple and visual disabilities. In *Children with visual impairments: A parents' guide* (pp. 287–316). Bethesda, MD: Woodbine House.

Fazzi, D. L., Kirk, S. A., Pearce, R. S., Pogrund, R. L., & Wolfe, S. (1992). Social focus: Developing socioemotional, play, and self-help skills in young blind and visually impaired children. In Pogrund, R. L., Fazzi, D. L., & Lampert, J. S. (Eds.), *Early focus: Working with young blind and visually impaired children and their families* (pp. 50–69). New York: American Foundation for the Blind.

Ferrell, K. A. (1986). Infancy and early childhood. In G. T. Scholl, (Ed.), *Foundations of education for blind and visually handicapped children and youth* (pp. 119–135). New York: American Foundation for the Blind.

Ferrell, K. A. (1985). *Reach out and teach: Meeting the training needs of parents of visually and multiply handicapped young children.* New York: American Foundation for the Blind.

Ferrell, K. A. (1996). Your child's development. In M. C. Holbrook (Ed.), *Children with visual impairments: A parent's guide* (pp. 73–96). Bethesda, MD: Woodbine House.

Freeman, R. D., Goetz, E., Richards, D. P., & Groenveld, M. (1991). Defiers of negative prediction: A 14-year follow-up study of legally blind children. *Journal of Visual Impairment and Blindness, 85*(9), 365–370.

Hall, A., Scholl, G. T., & Swallow, R. M. (1986). Psychoeducational assessment. In G. T. Scholl, (Ed.), *Foundations of education for blind and visually handicapped children and youth* (pp. 187–214). New York: American Foundation for the Blind.

Harrell, L. (1992). *Children's vision concerns: Looks beyond the eyes!* Placerville, CA: L. Harrell Productions.

Harrell, L., & Akeson, N. (1987). *Preschool vision stimulation: It's more than a flashlight.* New York: American Foundation for the Blind.

Harrell, R. L., & Curry, S. A. (1987). Services to blind and visually impaired children and adults: Who is responsible? *Journal of Visual Impairment and Blindness, 81*(8), 368–376.

Hatlen, P. H. (1980–1981). Mainstreaming, origin of a concept. *Blindness Annual,* pp. 1–9.

Hatlen, P. H., & Curry, S. A. (1987). In support of specialized programs for blind and visually impaired children: The impact of vision loss on learning. *Journal of Visual Impairment and Blindness, 81*(1), 7–13.

Hatlen, P. H., LeDuc, P., & Canter, P. (1975). The blind adolescent life skills center. *The New Outlook for the Blind,* pp. 109–115.

Hazekamp, J., & Huebner, K. M. (1989). *Program planning and evaluation for blind and visually impaired students: National guidelines for excellence.* New York: American Foundation for the Blind.

Heydt, K., Clark, M. J., Cushman, C., Edwards, S., & Allon, M. (1992). *Perkins activity and resource guide* (vols. 1 & 2). Watertown, MA: Perkins School for the Blind.

Hill, E. W., & Snook-Hill, M. (1996). Orientation and mobility. In M. C. Holbrook (Ed.), *Children with visual impairments: A parents' guide* (pp. 259–286). Bethesda, MD: Woodbine House.

Hoben, M., & Lindstrom, V. (1980). Evidence of isolation in the mainstream. *Journal of Visual Impairment and Blindness, 74*(8), 289–292.

Huebner, K. M., & Koenig, A. J. (1991). *Student-centered educational placement decisions: The meaning, interpretation, and application of least restrictive environment.* Reston, VA: CEC Division for the Visually Handicapped.

Jose, R. T. (1983). *Understanding low vision.* New York: American Foundation for the Blind.

Kirchner, C. (1988). *Data on blindness and visual impairment in the U.S.* New York: American Foundation for the Blind.

Kirchner, C. (1990). Trends in the prevalence rates and numbers of blind and visually impaired schoolchildren. *Journal of Visual Impairment and Blindness, 84*(9), 478–479.

Kirchner, C., McBroom, L. W., Nelson, K. A., & Graves, W. H. (1992). *Lifestyles of employed legally blind people: A study of expenditures and time use* (Technical Report). Mississippi State, MS: Rehabilitation Research and Training Center on Blindness and Low Vision.

Kirchner, C., & Stephen, G. (1987). Statistics on users of services related to blindness and visual impairment. *Yearbook of the Association for Education and Rehabilitation of the Blind and Visually Impaired—1986 edition.* Alexandria, VA: Association for Education and Rehabilitation of the Blind and Visually Impaired.

Koenig, A. J., & Farrenkopf, C. (1997). Essential experiences to undergird the early development of literacy. *Journal of Visual Impairment and Blindness, 91*(1), 14–24.

Koenig, A. J., & Holbrook, M. C. (1993). *Learning media assessment of students with visual impairments: A resource guide for teachers.* Austin, TX: Texas School for the Blind and Visually Impaired.

Koestler, F. A. (1976). *The unseen minority: A social history of blindness in the United States.* New York: David McKay.

Langley, M. B. (1980). *Functional vision inventory for the multiply and severely handicapped.* Chicago: Stoelting.

Levack, N. (1991). *Low vision: A resource guide with adaptations for students with visual impairments.* Austin, TX: Texas School for the Blind.

Los Angeles Unified School District. (1990). *Specialized skills for the visually handicapped: An instructional manual.* Los Angeles: Author.

Loumiet, R., & Levack, N. (1991) *Independent living: A curriculum with adaptations for students with visual impairments* (3 vols.). Austin, TX: Texas School for the Blind and Visually Impaired.

Lowenfeld, B. (1973). Psychological considerations. In B. Lowenfeld (Ed.), *The visually handicapped child in school.* New York: John Day Co.

Lowenfeld, B. (1975). *The changing status of the blind: From separation to integration.* Springfield, IL: Charles C. Thomas.

Nelson, K. A., & Dimitrova, E. (1990). Severe visual impairment in the United States and in each state. *Journal of Visual Impairment and Blindness, 87*(3), 80–85.

Olmstead, J. E. (1991). *Itinerant teaching: Tricks of the trade for teachers of blind and visually impaired students.* New York: American Foundation for the Blind.

Packer, J. (1989). How much extra time do visually impaired people need to take examinations: The case of the SAT. *Journal of Visual Impairment and Blindness, 87*(3), 358–360.

Pogrund, R. L., Fazzi, D. L., & Lampert, J. S. (Eds.). (1992). *Early focus: Working with young blind and visually impaired children and their families.* New York: American Foundation for the Blind.

Pogrund, R., Healy, G., Jones, K., Levack, N., Martin-Curr, S., Martinez, C., Marz, J., Roberson-Smith, B., & Vrba, A. (1993). *TAPS: Teaching age-appropriate purposeful skills— An orientation and mobility curriculum for students with visual impairments.* Austin, TX: Texas School for the Blind and Visually Impaired.

Prevent Blindness America. (1992). *The eye and how we see.* Schaumburg, IL: Author.

Sacks, S. (Ed.). (1992). *The development of social skills by blind and visually impaired students: Exploratory studies and strategies.* New York: American Foundation for the Blind.

Santa Clara County. (1993). *Social skills curriculum for children with visual impairments.* San Jose, CA: Author.

Scholl, G. T. (1986a). Visual impairments and other exceptionalities. In G. T. Scholl, (Ed.), *Foundations of education for blind and visually handicapped children and youth* (pp. 135–144). New York: American Foundation for the Blind.

Scholl, G. T. (1986b). What does it mean to be blind? Definitions, terminology, and prevalence. In G. T. Scholl, (Ed.), *Foundations of education for blind and visually handicapped children and youth* (pp. 145–164). New York: American Foundation for the Blind.

Scott, E. P., Jan, J. E., & Freeman, R. D. (1995). *Can't your child see? A guide for parents of visually impaired children* (3rd ed.). Austin, TX: Pro-Ed.

Silberman, R. K. (1986). Severe multiple handicaps. In G. T. Scholl, (Ed.), *Foundations of education for blind and visually handicapped children and youth* (pp. 145–164). New York: American Foundation for the Blind.

Spungin, S. J. (1984). The role and function of the teacher of the visually handicapped. In G. T. Scholl, *Quality services for blind and visually handicapped learners: Statements of Position* (pp. 30–34). Reston, VA: Council for Exceptional Children.

Stiles, S., & Knox, R. (1996). Medical issues, treatments and professionals. In M. C. Holbrook (Ed.), *Children with visual impairments: A parent's guide* (pp. 21–48). Bethesda, MD: Woodbine House.

Tapp, K. L, Wilhelm, J. G., & Loveless, L. J. (1991). *A guide to curriculum planning for visually impaired students.* Madison, WI: Wisconsin Department of Public Instruction.

Torres, I., & Corn, A. L. (1990). *When you have a visually handicapped child in your classroom: Suggestions for teachers.* New York: American Foundation for the Blind.

Tuttle, D. W. (1986). Educational programming. In G. T. Scholl, (Ed.), *Foundations of education for blind and visually handicapped children and youth* (pp. 239–253). New York: American Foundation for the Blind.

Tuttle, D. W., & Tuttle, N. R. (1996). *Self-esteem and adjusting with blindness: The process of responding to life's demands* (2nd ed.). Springfield, IL: Charles C. Thomas.

U.S. Department of Education. (1995). *Seventeenth annual report to Congress on the implementation of the Individuals with Disabilities Education Act.* Washington, DC: Author.

Vander Kolk, C. J. (1981). *Assessment and planning with the visually impaired.* Baltimore, MD: University Park Press.

Walhof, R. (1993, September–October). Resolutions adopted by the annual convention of the National Federation of the Blind, July 1993. *Braille Monitor,* pp. 984–997.

Welsh, R. L. (1980). Psychosocial dimensions. In R. L. Welsh, & B. Blasch, *Foundations of orientation and mobility* (pp. 225–264). New York: American Foundation for the Blind.

Wolffe, K. (1996). Career education for students with visual impairments. *RE:view 28*(2), 89–93.

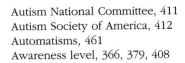

Chapter 1

Courtesy of the Ramirez family, pp. xx, 1; Scott Cunningham/Merrill, pp. 5, 9, 21; James L. Shaffer, p. 13; Reuters/Corbis-Bettmann, p. 19; Courtesy of N. Shelby School, Shelby, NC, p. 33; UPI Corbis-Bettmann, p. 35.

Chapter 2

Courtesy of the Ramirez Family, pp. 40, 41; Custom Medical Stock, p. 45; James L. Shaffer, p. 63; Anthony Magnacca/Merrill, p. 67; Tony Freeman/Photo Edit, p. 73.

Chapter 3

Courtesy of the Ramirez Family, pp. 78, 79; Robin L. Sacks/Photo Edit, p. 83; Courtesy of Madeline Will, p. 84; Amy B. Cart, p. 87; James L. Shaffer, p. 90; Paul Conklin/Photo Edit, p. 92; Scott Cunningham/Merrill, p. 96; David Young-Wolff/Photo Edit, p. 106; Michael Newman/Photo Edit, p. 114.

Chapter 4

Courtesy of the Osorto Family, pp. 120, 121, 149; Courtesy of Debbie Navarro, p. 128; Scott Cunningham/Merrill, p. 132; Anthony Magnacca/Merrill, pp. 140, 158; Todd Yarrington/Merrill, p. 144; People Weekly, 1994 George Kalinsky, p. 159.

Chapter 5

Anthony Magnacca/Merrill, pp. 170. 171; Barbara Schwartz/Merrill, p. 176; Bill Viernum, p. 184; Todd Yarrington/Merrill, p. 193; Scott Cunningham/Merrill, pp. 195, 197, 208; Courtesy of Alan Amtzis, p. 215; Tony Freeman/Photo Edit, p. 215.

Chapter 6

Courtesy of the Wiggand Family, pp. 222, 223, 243; Corbis-Bettmann, p. 225; James L. Shaffer, pp. 230, 247; Anthony Magnacca/Merrill, p. 236; Scott Cunningham/Merrill, 259.

Chapter 7

Courtesy of the Cambridge Family, pp. 266, 267, 284; AP/Wide World Photos, p. 272; Courtesy of Michael Kearney, p. 275; The Athens Messenger News, p. 277; Lorrie Lowe, p. 278; Todd Yarrington/Merrill, p. 284; Scott Cunningham/Merrill, p. 295; Karen Bulman/Knolls Early Childhood Program, p. 305.

Chapter 8

Courtesy of the Banning Family, pp. 314, 315, 316, 326, 341, 349; Courtesy of Project TASSEL, Shelby, NC, pp. 317, 357; Courtesy of the authors, p. 323; UPI/Corbis-Bettmann, p. 334; Courtesy of Project Eagle, p. 352; Courtesy of Morristown Elementary School, p. 354.

Chapter 9

Courtesy of the Spoor Family, pp. 362, 363, 367; Courtesy of the Wiggand family, p. 368; Courtesy of the Bridge family, p. 391; Dave Lutz/Lifespan Institute, p. 395; Courtesy of University Connection—George Washington University, p. 398.

Chapter 10

Courtesy of the Poston Family, pp. 402, 403, 404, 412; James L. Shaffer, p. 420; Anthony Magnacca/Merrill, p. 427; Courtesy of Lillie Cusick, p. 430; Courtesy of the authors, p. 432; Courtesy of the Fake family, p. 434; Todd Yarrington/Merrill, p. 437.

Chapter 11

Courtesy of C. Thomas Empey, pp. 442, 443, 444, 472; UPI/Bettmann, p. 448; UPI/Bettmann News Photos, p. 454; Courtesy of the Price Family, p. 458.

Chapter 12

Courtesy of the Nanasca Family, pp. 494, 495, 496, 508, 509, 513; Wilderness Inquiry, p. 497; Courtesy of the Durfee family, p. 502; Courtesy of the authors, p. 519.

Chapter 13

Courtesy of Ron Savage/The May Institute, p. 540; 1994 Doctors Hospital, Columbus, Ohio, p. 546; Courtesy of Hilltop Manor, p. 548; Todd Yarrington/Merrill, pp. 555, 561, 572; Tim Lynch/Hilltop Manor, p. 573.

Chapter 14

Courtesy of the Krecker Family, pp. 580, 581, 582; PH College, p. 583; Corbis-Bettmann, p. 588; Courtesy of Joyce McNeill, p. 589; Scott Cunningham/Merrill, p. 590; Susan Burger/Lasting Impressions, p. 593; Courtesy of Elizabeth Johnston, p. 597; Courtesy of Melanie Waters, p. 613.

Chapter 15

Courtesy of the Brown Family, pp. 620, 621, 622; Anthony Magnacca/Merrill, p. 625; James L. Shaffer, pp. 628, 646; Scott Cunningham/Merrill, p. 633; Todd Yarrington/Merrill, pp. 644, 653; Courtesy of Gallaudet University, p. 645.

Chapter 16

Courtesy of the Kiel Family, pp. 662, 663, 664; Todd Yarrington/Merrill, p. 668; Scott Cunningham/Merrill, pp. 670, 677, 684, 691, 704; Courtesy of Jewish Guild for the Blind, p. 665; Courtesy of Donna McNear, p. 700.